# COLLECTED
# ANCIENT GREEK
# NOVELS

# COLLECTED
# ANCIENT
# GREEK
# NOVELS

EDITED BY

## B. P. REARDON

UNIVERSITY OF CALIFORNIA PRESS

BERKELEY · LOS ANGELES · LONDON

UNIVERSITY OF CALIFORNIA PRESS
BERKELEY AND LOS ANGELES, CALIFORNIA

UNIVERSITY OF CALIFORNIA PRESS, LTD.
LONDON, ENGLAND

**LIBRARY OF CONGRESS**
**Library of Congress Cataloging-in-Publication Data**

Collected ancient Greek novels / edited by B.P. Reardon.
    p.    cm.
    Translations of what is extant of nineteen works.
    Bibliography: p.
    ISBN 0-520-04306-5 (alk. paper)
    1. Greek fiction—Translations into English.
    2. English fiction—Translations from Greek.
    I. Reardon, Bryan P.
    PA3632.C65 1989
    883'.01'08—dc19                  88-21093
                                            CIP

Printed in the United States of America

5  6  7  8  9

*To my wife,*
*who has lived with these*
*stories for many years*

# CONTENTS

# GENERAL INTRODUCTION

## BY B. P. REARDON

Stories abound in Greek literature. Many of them constitute what we call myth—for example, the myth of Prometheus, who stole fire from the gods and gave it to mankind. These stories express a community's perception of the forces that govern its existence, and their basic form is narrative. For others we use the term *legend*. Legends are often about shadowy Bronze Age figures, such as Achilles; they may form the basis of epic narrative, or they can appear in other forms of poetry, such as lyric or drama. In such cases the writer is not using them primarily for their narrative interest, but the story is there and is the basic material of the artistic product. Two features, however, mark such stories. First, in principle they are not fictitious. They are always in some sense based on real things, historical events or figures, and offered as in some sense true accounts. What Homer wrote about is the Trojan War, and whatever the truth about that obscure conflict, *some* kind of historical event assuredly lies behind his epics. Second, these stories are told in verse; in early antiquity verse is always the medium for what we call creative literature. Prose is used for other purposes, such as the collection and analysis of information in the field of history or philosophy, not for imaginative purposes.

The present volume offers a number of extended stories that are conceived and executed in a fundamentally different way. They are narrative fiction in prose—imaginative, creative literature, sufficiently similar to what we call novels to justify the use of the term here. They belong to a period several centuries later than the literature just evoked; their heyday is the second century A.D., and the latest of them were written a thou-

I

sand years after the earliest extant epic. Most of them offer a mixture of love and adventure; it would seem that as the form increased in sophistication, the proportion of adventure declined, and the theme of love was treated less simplistically than in the earliest stages. Hero and heroine are always young, wellborn, and handsome; their marriage is disrupted or temporarily prevented by separation, travel in distant parts, and a series of misfortunes, usually spectacular. Virginity or chastity, at least in the female, is of crucial importance, and fidelity to one's partner, together often with trust in the gods, will ultimately guarantee a happy ending. Such is the most common form of this fiction; as in later ages, the theme of love usually forms the kernel of the story's development. Sometimes, however, love is given little space, or none at all, and the excitement lies entirely in the adventure; or it may be treated ironically, resulting in some form of comic story.

We know of over twenty texts that fit the above description. Some are fully extant, but the majority exist only in incomplete form, in fragments or as mere references; other fragments, more uncertain of interpretation, may probably be added to their number. The core of this corpus is the five love-and-adventure romances that have come to be regarded as constituting the canon in this form: those of Chariton, Xenophon of Ephesus, Achilles Tatius, Longus, and Heliodorus. These, along with some other romances, have survived as complete manuscripts, in libraries (some think Xenophon's story is an epitome of the original). In some cases (e.g., the Alexander-romance, the *Story of Apollonius King of Tyre*) the manuscript tradition is bewilderingly complex; in others (e.g., Heliodorus) it is reasonably full; in two (Chariton and Xenophon) it is represented by a single, erratic manuscript. Two stories (Iamblichus's *Babylonian Story* and Antonius Diogenes' *The Wonders Beyond Thule*) survive in the summaries of a ninth-century Byzantine bibliophile, the patriarch Photius. These texts all survived in a manner similar to that of other Greek literature: preserved in Byzantium, they were diffused in Europe from the Renaissance onward. But in their case this resulted in a seriously inaccurate view of the genre, since practically nothing was known of their chronology or of any literary-historical picture into which they could be fitted.

Many novels, however, are known only from fragments, some of only a few lines. These have been the subject of one of the most dramatic developments in the history of classical scholarship. From the last decade of the nineteenth century onward a series of papyrological discoveries has been made—and continues to this day—that has radically changed our view of the ancient novel; no other form of ancient literature has known so major a change in its fortunes. Fragments of many new works have been brought to light, as well as passages from known works; and this has added considerably to the range of fiction we know to have existed. But even more importantly, since papyri can usually be dated at least approximately, it has become possible for the first time to establish a serviceable chronology for the form; this has overturned our whole assessment of it, and has enabled scholars to see it as forming a coherent pattern. It is scarcely an exaggeration to say that a whole literary genre has sprung from the sands of Egypt. Not surprisingly, it seems on the whole (there are exceptions) to be the best texts that survived best. But these are topics we shall return to; here we should say a word about the contents of the present volume and complete our survey of what exists in antiquity in the area of fiction.

The canonical texts here take pride of place, in their probable chronological order. They are followed by two comic novels from the second century, *The Ass,* once attributed to Lucian, and *A True Story,* certainly by him. Then come two works of somewhat different formation and descent, the *Alexander Romance* and the Latin *Story of Apollonius King of Tyre;* their inclusion is discussed below. Finally come the incomplete texts, the two summaries and the most extensive and important of the papyrus fragments; for practical purposes they are presented as a group. They are included in the volume because they constitute the literary-historical context of the fully extant texts. The volume thus contains what is available of nineteen novels; it is virtually certain that more, perhaps many more, once existed.

To return to the general literary history of the form, in addition to the works just described there is a penumbra of texts of a semifictional nature; narrative fiction is not a clearly defined category of literature. One important marginal case is fictional history. Some Greek historians and biographers readily embroider their themes, for purposes as close to the novelist's as to the historian's. At what point does history become fiction? The *Cyropaedia,* or *Education of Cyrus,* of Xenophon of Athens might well be regarded as a novel. An important variant of this question is, At what point does hagiography—which is ideologically directed biography—become fiction? In the genre "acts of apostles" much is invented, often, and there are related forms that are very similar in structure and content to the ideal romance: for instance, the Pseudo-Clementine *Recognitions,* which purports to recount the fortunes of the family of Clement of Rome, and *Joseph and Asenath,* a novelistic version of the Genesis story, with a Jewish slant. Yet other kinds of "fringe novel" are the travel tale and utopian literature, both of which are to be found in Greek, as far back indeed as the *Odyssey.* And these forms flow into one another in the *Life of Apollonius of Tyana,* an account of an itinerant wonder-worker, written in the third century A.D. by Philostratus.

It is worth while touching on such topics here to suggest the dimensions of "fiction" in Greek literature. It would be a formidable volume that would include everything the term might be held to embrace at its most generous—if one could get scholars to agree on the list. At the other extreme the purist, excluding all marginal cases and all incomplete texts, might end up with only the novels of Chariton, Achilles Tatius, Longus, and Heliodorus, along with *The Ass;* and that would be a pity. For the purposes of this volume a degree of comprehensiveness was desirable, but a choice had to be made; I have tried to make the book as complete as may be, in as reasonable a way as I know how, and am aware that others could choose differently. The texts mentioned in the previous paragraph are not included because they seem to me in one way or another to fall a little short of being prose fiction in the full sense; the reader may be referred for discussion of them to Tomas Hägg's *The Novel in Antiquity.* The historical fiction known as the *Alexander Romance* is included, however, partly on the grounds of the proportion of generally novelistic content in it. The *Story of Apollonius King of Tyre* is included too, on different grounds. Although the earliest surviving version of it is in Latin, it seems very likely that the original was in Greek, and the story is very closely bound to the whole indubitably Greek ideal tradition and to known Greek texts (see the introduction to the story). In the case of the latter works the balance has been tipped in favor of their inclusion by the great importance they have in the medieval tradition of fiction; it seemed desirable in such a collection as this to include what for several centuries were two of Europe's most popular secular stories, both of which are firmly based in the Greek romance tradition.

Finally, there are also two Latin novels, Petronius's *Satyricon* (or *Satyrica*) and Apuleius's *Metamorphoses* (*The Golden Ass*). Ideally I should have liked to see them included, in a *Collected Ancient Novels,* but they are more readily available than the Greek texts. They have generally been much better known than the Greek works and have often been thought of as a separate chapter, so to speak, in ancient literature. They do indeed differ considerably from the Greek novels, but increasingly in recent years they have been studied in relation to the Greek corpus. The *Satyricon,* long thought unique as a raffish tale of dissolute antiheroes, may well after all be closely connected to a Greek comic tradition, represented by the recently deciphered *Iolaus* (see the Fragments in this volume). But if it is, we cannot tell whether it was inspired by that tradition or was itself the model for it (which would constitute a rare case of Latin influence upon Greek literature). The *Metamorphoses* is certainly based on a Greek tale of a man transformed into an ass, but Apuleius has himself demonstrably brought about an almost equally striking transformation in the story (much greater, for instance, than has occurred in *The Story of Apollonius King of Tyre*), to the point where it is *sui generis,* a complex and major work of art—playfully serious, realistic, and comic, but at the same time edifying. The relationship between the two versions of the story is discussed in J. P. Sullivan's introduction to *The Ass* in the present volume.

Precise dating of the novels is impossible—the margin of doubt varies from a couple of decades to a century or more—and there is not complete agreement about when the genre first appeared or how long it lasted. It is commonly thought, though it cannot be demonstrated, that the first, shadowy "proto-novels" appeared in late Hellenistic times, and that the genre grew in confidence during the first century of our era. It certainly reached its peak in the second century, in the conditions of relative prosperity and renewed literary activity that mark the period of Hadrian and the Antonines—that is, the high *pax Romana*. Novels continued to be written and read in the third century, but the genre seems to have faded out in the great crises and disorder of that period. It is quite possible, however, that Heliodorus's *Ethiopica,* the "novel to end all novels," belongs to the late fourth century; if so, it is exceptional, and probably a throwback. The texts in this collection would be disposed roughly as follows.

| | |
|---|---|
| *Ninus* | first century B.C.? |
| Chariton, *Chaereas and Callirhoe* | mid–first century A.D.? |
| Xenophon, *An Ephesian Story* | ⎤ |
| Antonius Diogenes, *The Wonders Beyond Thule* | mid–second century? |
| Lucian, *A True Story* | ⎤ third quarter of |
| Pseudo-Lucian, *The Ass* | second century |
| Iamblichus, *A Babylonian Story* | 165–180 |
| Achilles Tatius, *Leucippe and Clitophon* | late second century |
| Longus, *Daphnis and Chloe* | 200? |
| Heliodorus, *An Ethiopian Story* | third century (or late fourth century) |
| *Alexander Romance* | third century (source: third century B.C.) |
| *Apollonius King of Tyre* | original: third century (Latin text: fifth or sixth century) |
| Fragments | variously, first–third century A.D. |

Although this list is probably not too far away from the truth, it is not easy to draw from the evidence any very detailed picture of the genre's development. We have no idea how many texts, or what kind, have disappeared completely, and there are reasons for thinking that from near the beginning of the genre polished texts existed contemporaneously with crude ones—as is the case with the modern novel, after all.

We may turn now to some general matters relating to the genre. How did such stories come into existence? What is the relationship between the Greek novel and earlier literature? Why is it such a late-blooming form? And how is it that these stories are so little known in the modern world? For today they *are* relatively little known, even among classicists, and *a fortiori* among scholars and readers of other literatures, although this was not always so. These questions merit comment.

In one sense every genre, indeed each individual work of literature, involves a deliberate act of original creation. B. E. Perry's dictum has become famous: "The first romance was deliberately planned and written by an individual author, its inventor. He conceived it on a Tuesday afternoon in July."[1] This conscious element should never be forgotten. For all that, even though literary works do not "develop" spontaneously as plants do, they do have predecessors that help to shape the writer's thoughts, and one can see embryonic narrative fiction from the beginnings of Greek literature. The *Odyssey* itself is a prime example. In the classical period there are short stories embedded in Herodotus's history, and Ctesias, the author of a fanciful history of Persia and a contemporary of Xenophon of Athens, is another candidate for the title of father of historical romance. Subsequently, emotionally colored historiography and travel tales, already mentioned, were a feature of the Hellenistic period. It would appear that these forms began to merge in writers' minds as the concept of fiction became clearer and clearer. But it may be noted that that concept had already more or less appeared in the fourth century, in the shape of the ideologically based stories conceived by Plato as one form of social engineering that could be used by authority in his ideal state; Plato himself, indeed, constructed several such fictions at the end of major dialogues (the myth of Er in *Republic* 10, for instance).

But why should the novel have taken the shape it did take? In particular, why should the love theme insert itself into a structure apparently based on exciting historiography? In one of the best-known analyses of the genre Rohde, over a century ago, put his finger on Hellenistic love poetry as the source of the erotic element in the novel. And perhaps that is not very far from the truth, although there may not have been direct literary filiation in the first place. The impulse that led Alexandrian poets

1. B. E. Perry, *The Ancient Romances: A Literary-Historical Account of Their Origins* (Berkeley, 1967), 175.

to treat romantic love as a worthy topic of literature—which it seldom had been in classical drama or other forms (lyric is an exception)—itself indicates that a new spirit was abroad, that the emotions of the individual, without regard to their social implications, were claiming attention more and more. This is certainly one of the features of postclassical society, visible for instance in sculpture, where the expression of the subject's personal psychology is of dominant importance. A late Hellenistic writer, however, would hardly need to know Apollonius of Rhodes' picture of Medea to be aware of the contemporary importance of the theme of love. He could assuredly see for himself that private emotions mattered, and that increasingly in the postclassical world they had become what mattered most. For in a world of large empires, essentially controlled from Alexandria or Antioch, there could not be the same intense interest in political matters as had characterized the classical city-state. The world had become bigger, and the individual, in consequence, smaller in it—smaller, and more absorbed in himself, his private life. And there is hardly any need to explain why romantic sentiment, love, should occupy his thoughts. The basic story was new in kind; the love story with a happy ending had never occupied center stage before. It is surely here that one must look for the most important impulse stimulating the new genre; this was the kind of experience people wanted to write and read about. The novel is a reflection of their personal experience, as the older forms of tragedy and Old Comedy had been a reflection of their civic experience.

By the early Christian era, then, there was a substantial core of love-romance, and around it a fringe of nonerotic forms. There was ample room for influences from a wide range of earlier literature: epic, tragedy, comedy, love poetry are the forms that most noticeably color the novel. In the early Hellenistic period there had already arisen a form of drama that focused on this personal theme: New Comedy shows us the small world of the family group, with a fictitious love-intrigue as the structural basis of the action. The novel extends this action, beyond the *polis* and into a Mediterranean world. The obstacles standing between hero and heroine become bigger and more dangerous; the protagonists are separated not only from each other but from their own familiar surroundings, as Fortune—a veritable deity in the Hellenistic world—drives them back and forth, from Syracuse to Babylon, from Delphi to Ethiopia. Each is essentially alone in the world, although the man may find a companion here and there (the woman seldom does). In this isolation they may benefit from the unpredictable providence of a deity, Isis or Artemis or Aphrodite, just as in the Hellenistic age people turned more and more to mystery religions for comfort. Their progress through the story seems, indeed, a figure of human progress through life; this is another form of myth, myth for postclassical times.

But along with a love theme, some apparently early texts (*Ninus* and *Chaereas and Callirhoe,* perhaps *Sesonchosis* and *Metiochus and Parthenope*) also contain an element of history. It is history with a difference though, history that is not afraid of anachronisms, that will readily displace its characters by a couple of generations or more; clearly it is not seriously concerned with representing an earlier epoch, as modern historical novels usually are. Some later novels also have a historical aura about them, but even less historical conscience: those of Xenophon of Ephesus, Achilles Tatius, certainly Heliodorus. No Greek novel, in fact, purports to represent its own times (although both Latin novels do). This may, as has been suggested, be a bow in the direction of academic tradition: romantic prose fiction was not intellectually respectable, but historiography, being information, was, and perhaps a veneer of history might be thought to render such fiction respectable. But there is in any case an inherent attraction in making a story seem to represent a recognizable society; realistic modern fiction operates on that principle. There is something that readers can hang on to, something that will authenticate the story they are consuming. And when kings and queens are involved, as in the Ninus-romance, there is also comfort to be derived from seeing that a known great personage (the fabulous king of Assyria, no less!) could have his own feelings, be governed by readily recognizable emotions, just like the reader's. It is the attitude that guarantees a sale for revelations from a royal household.

The mature ancient novel, then, is an imperial genre which reflects a late stage of the development of Hellenistic society and absorbs into itself several forms of antecedent literature. As the large empires of Alexander's successors became established in the eastern Mediterranean, and as thereafter the empire of Rome encroached progressively on them, there was an accelerating transformation to the values of a cosmopolitan world. Evidently this acceleration occurred in prose fiction too, for by the second century of our era the form shows much sophistication. It has become the predominant mode of creative literature, the major form portraying human beings.

Mention has already been made of the literary renaissance of the period. One important aspect of it was the rhetorical movement known as the Second Sophistic. Its principal manifestation was concert performances by itinerant orators who spoke on a multitude of topics, usually taken from classical Greek tradition—this was one expression of the contemporary classicizing fashion. The movement in itself need not concern us very closely here, but it constitutes a formative background to the writing of novels. Most of the writers whose works appear in this volume were trained in its schools (Chariton, for example, was the secretary of a *rhetor,* and Achilles Tatius is said to have been himself a sophist). The developed novel is thus heavily influenced by a broader literary movement; indeed, at one time it was thought to have been born of it. In the second century there was ample encouragement for writers to write, and great interest in the technical aspects of at least one form of literary expression, namely rhetoric. It is thus no suprise at all to find literary ambition and literary skill in at least some of the novels, with a liberal element of emotional rhetoric as a standard feature. We may here return to the individual texts, to consider briefly where they might fit in the above analysis.

The five canonical writers have commonly been seen as falling into two groups, the presophistic (Chariton and Xenophon) and the sophistic (Achilles Tatius, Longus, and Heliodorus). The labels are somewhat misleading, but they will serve for the purposes of preliminary assessment, since the latter group is certainly more adventurous in exploiting the possibilities of the basic pattern. Some of the fragments would no doubt fit into this classification—*Ninus,* notably, is clearly presophistic in every sense, and others may well be of the sophistic period and manner but are too brief to categorize with confidence. It may be, however, that we should think of an additional category, subsophistic. Iamblichus's *Babylonian Story,* for instance, can be dated to the later second century, the period of Lucian and Achilles Tatius, but with its ghosts, corpses, pursuits, and mistaken identities it clearly relies for its effect more on Grand Guignol than on other qualities; and as much can be said for the bloodthirsty, lurid *Phoenicica.* The higher level of the sophistic texts derives in large part from the way in which they adapt the structural basis of the form, the recital of the adventures that happen to the principals. Whereas Chariton and Xenophon straightforwardly (although in different ways) direct the reader's attention alternately to hero and heroine, their successors employ various devices to avoid the clumsiness to which this technique is vulnerable. Achilles employs ego-narrative, thus altering the reader's perspective on one of the two lines of action; Longus virtually does away with travel and physical adventure, thus avoiding the separation of his lovers, and turns our attention rather to psychological developments in them; and Heliodorus borrows from the *Odyssey* the technique of the flashback, thus building narrative tension into the structure of his story and (as J. R. Morgan's introduction points out) enlisting the reader's own hermeneutic effort. At this level, it could be argued, the genre has transcended whatever original sociocultural function it had and has become another literary game, as in our own day. Indeed, much in the Hellenistic and imperial world, and much in this product of that world, reminds us of our own condition; in Perry's formulation, the novel is the open form for the open society.[2]

2. See Perry, *The Ancient Romances,* 47; the idea is developed in his chapter 2, "The Form Romance in Historical Perspective."

Many tastes are catered for in this body of work. The *Ephesian Story,* the *Alexander Romance,* and *Apollonius of Tyre* represent a quite different kind of fiction. These works are made of folktale and folkhero; their authors are concerned less with literary refinement than with putting the reader in exciting situations, involving him in the search for happiness or the pursuit of the unattainable; they operate through identification and do not expect readers to employ their critical intellect. But there are also stories that rely on precisely this critical judgment, and operate through irony: Lucian's *jeu d'esprit, A True Story,* a satire on tall tales ("my story is all lies, and this is the only true statement in it"); the Greek *Ass*-story with its worm's-eye view of the world; and the tantalizing, cynical Iolaus-fragment. Each reader will pick his own favorite. The Renaissance liked Heliodorus for his epic and dramatic qualities; Longus's story, often taken as a rustic pipe dream, seems to our eyes a more subtle work of art. Achilles Tatius has his admirers too, as can be seen from the remarks of his present translator, John J. Winkler; he has seemed to some to mark the point at which naive sentimental romance turns into self-conscious novel. For myself, I confess to an unregenerate penchant for the naive sentimental romance *par excellence* in this collection, that of Chariton; he is still more interested in his story than in his presentation of it, while in fact he does present it with unobtrusive skill (it has, of course, its conventions).

To return to generalities: the obverse of the question why writers wrote novels is the question of why readers read them. Who read these stories? It is a fashionable question. No simple answer is possible, although a number have been offered: the poor-in-spirit; the young; women; the cultivated in their off-duty moments. But even in the restricted sample of texts that we have the range is too great for one answer, as the preceding paragraphs will have suggested. Could we answer the question Who reads novels today? We should have to ask, What novels? One cannot see Longus and Heliodorus being devoured by the uncultivated, and even among the melodramatic texts there are differences of purpose—Xenophon's story, for example, has been thought to have a proselytizing aim (and so have others, as we shall see). Different qualities imply different audiences. Besides the plain sentimentality of Chariton there is genuinely thoughtful analysis of emotion, not only in Longus but in *Metiochus and Parthenope,* little as we have of it, where a character describes love as a "movement of the intellect born of beauty and deepened by familiarity." Achilles Tatius combines refinement with melodrama; he offers us elaborate psychological theory, intrigue almost fit for Restoration comedy, and a heroine who after being disemboweled and (on a different occasion) decapitated, both before the eyes of her lover, survives to pass a virginity test for which, had she had her way, she would have disqualified herself before the story had properly begun. There is in these texts both barren and spectacular, penny plain and tuppence colored; in all probability their readers were as various. We can say that most, if not all, of the writers are careful about the way they write, but that is true of most writers at most times, for the very act of literary composition usually breeds care. If some are more ambitious than others, there is no simple progression in ambition; the earliest and the latest of the canonical authors, Chariton and Heliodorus, are both patently proud of the construction and writing of their stories. The form clearly existed on several levels simultaneously, perhaps even in its early days, as today it exists on several levels on drugstore book racks. No doubt the destination of many texts would be covered by a rubric like "the relaxation of the literate," but no simple formula could categorize the novel's whole audience.

It may well be that the most important influence in the writing and reading of these texts is simply the appetite for entertainment; perhaps it is overstating the case to see the novel as a myth for the times. Yet the two views are not incompatible. All myths are first and foremost entertaining stories. That does not mean that they do not figure various aspects of the human situation. Sophocles made a thrilling drama out of the legend of Oedipus, but matters do not stop there; others have seen much more in it than that. Stories can seep through the cracks in our consciousness. Even the writer who simply feels the itch to write has to write about something; it is not possible to write about nothing.

Closely related to the questions of the intentions of the writers and the perception of the stories by their readers is the interpretation of the stories as unreservedly religious texts—mystery texts, to be precise. The first such exposition was that of Kerényi in 1927 he saw the plots of all the novels as based on the Egyptian myth of Isis.[3] Her consort, Osiris, was killed by the evil Set, and his members were dispersed over the earth; Isis wandered the world in search of them and reconstituted and resuscitated the body; and Osiris was reborn to eternal life. This sequence formed the basis of Isiac mystery ritual, and the ritual, Kerényi maintained, in turn suggested the basis of the novels, which are likewise concerned with tribulation and apparent death, wandering, salvation, and ultimate happiness. Subsequently a stricter version of this theory, promulgated by Merkelbach in 1962, saw several of the novels as actually literary elaborations of the ritual of other mystery cults (Dionysus, Mithras, Helius) as well as that of Isis; the texts, Merkelbach claimed, are full of mystery symbols, and could thus be fully understood only by initiates.[4] By the common consent of scholars this goes too far in the direction of symbolic interpretation, but as we have seen, the novels do re-

3. K. Kerényi, *Die griechisch-orientalische Romanliteratur in religionsgeschichtlicher Beleuchtung* (Tübingen, 1927; reprint, Darmstadt, 1962).
4. R. Merkelbach, *Roman und Mysterium* (Munich and Berlin, 1962).

semble mystery cult in being modeled on life itself. But the purpose of this introduction is to present and situate such questions rather than try to settle them. To summarize, my own view is that these stories do have an underlying spiritual aspect to them, although their authors—most of them at any rate—were not consciously symbolizing; on the other hand, the literary elaboration of the genre is fully deliberate, and at its best very careful.

We may here turn to some associated questions. First, is the term *novel* justified? It does beg a question. We are accustomed to employ it of something more realistic than these works, with their improbable incident and stereotyped figures. Perhaps *romance* would be a better word? It has often been employed for this fiction, and is used in these remarks for variety. But it misses the essence of the form by as much on one side as *novel* does on the other, and tends to sell short writers who in some cases are capable of genuine psychological realism as well as considerable narrative skill. We tend to associate the term *romance* with princesses, castles, and dragons—or else with nurses who fall in love with doctors. But we could certainly fitly use the term as rehabilitated by Northrop Frye to cover that form of narrative which constitutes, in his words, a "secular scripture," embodying and authorizing the aspirations of man-centered society.[5]

Next, the fortunes of the genre and of these texts. In its own time the Greek novel was disregarded by literary historians and is not mentioned by other literary practitioners. Very little information about it has survived at all. There are a couple of uncomplimentary references in the works of figures of the literary establishment: the writer Philostratus, in the early third century, refers to one Chariton as a "nothing," whose writings are totally forgettable; and the highly literate emperor Julian, in the middle of the fourth century, talks of the love story as a genre of the past that is not worth serious attention.[6] Beyond that there are only a few references to the genre in later encyclopedias and similar works. On the whole, the novel made little lasting impression on educated antiquity. It is a commonplace that the form disappeared with Heliodorus, or thereabouts. But that is only half true; so basic a thing as fiction does not disappear; it adapts. In the early Byzantine period fiction is represented by hagiography, for in the writing of inspirational lives fact comes a very poor third to edification and excitement. The taste for narrative fiction never has died; it is simply conditioned by the circumstances of its times, by the shape of society, people's assumptions, and the literary vehicles that lie to hand. In the twelfth-century Comnenian renaissance in Byzantium there was a revival of the form in a group of four stories (modeled

5. Northrop Frye, *The Secular Scripture: A Study of the Structure of Romance* (Cambridge, Mass., 1976).
6. Philostratus, Letter 66; Julian, Letter 89B.

on the ancient texts), all but one in verse, and in the fourteenth century a further group appears, but these contain strong elements of folktale and Western medieval tradition.

To return to the ancient texts, Heliodorus, Longus, and Achilles Tatius were much appreciated in Western Europe at the time of the Renaissance, and were translated into several modern languages; some of these translations (e.g., Amyot's Longus) became classics in their own right. From the seventeenth century there is the story of how the young Racine, having twice had his copy of Heliodorus (probably in Amyot's translation) confiscated at Port-Royal as unsuitable reading, acquired yet another copy, which he took the precaution of learning by heart, according to his son. Chariton and Xenophon have always been the poor relations: after barely surviving the Middle Ages neither reappeared until the eighteenth century. The tone of modern study of the genre was set in 1876 by one of the magisterial works of a golden age of German scholarship, Rohde's *Der griechische Roman*. Without papyrology to guide him and with very little evidence of any kind available, Rohde deduced a history for the genre which, as we have seen, has since been exploded. He saw these texts as isolated outcrops of more or less subliterary material, certainly not as manifestations of an explicable genre. For him, they stretched from the first or second to the fifth or sixth century and were the products of Greek decadence, either fatally impoverished in content and expression or else contemptible examples of the frivolous and insincere art of the sophist. Although one or two voices were raised in protest, his authority carried the day. Less than twenty years after the publication of Rohde's massive book, the crucial papyrological discoveries had begun and had overthrown his chronological scheme, establishing essentially the picture set out earlier in this introduction. From the 1920s important work was done in the field by Lavagnini, Perry, Rattenbury, and others. But it was not until after the Second World War that the tide really began to turn; the first comprehensive, accurate, and measured account of the new state of things appeared in Lesky's *History of Greek Literature* in 1957, and the first collections of translations appeared, in French and Italian, in 1958.

But it was not only lack of information that determined the reception of the Greek novel. In the nineteenth and early twentieth centuries the imperial nations of the West—and one should remember that the study of the classics was the pursuit of an elite, an establishment—took it for granted that what was important about the early centuries of our era was the immensely impressive political fact of the Roman Empire; it naturally had the sympathy of people who themselves ruled empires, or aspired to do so, and the Greek world of the imperial period attracted less attention. But things have changed since the days of the gunboat. Wars and revolutions, the rise and fall of dictators, the swelling movement of democracy, the rise of a Third World all have changed the rules of the game; *imperialism* is now a dirty word. We are inclined today to look behind the Roman Empire, to analyze it more critically. In this perspective, the Greek East of the imperial period has seemed less negligible and has more and more attracted study.

Among the objects of that study has been the copious literature of that world. We can point to a veritable galaxy of early imperial writers: along with Longus and the other novelists, along with Plutarch and Lucian, there are Dio Chrysostom, Aelius Aristides, Marcus Aurelius, Galen, Arrian, Pausanias, and a score of lesser names. No one would claim that they shine as brightly as Homer, Pindar, and Sophocles, Thucydides, Aristophanes, and Plato, but the period is nonetheless well worth attention. The novel has profited particularly from recent scholarship. Texts have been edited afresh in the last generation and studies have multiplied, some of them of major importance. In 1976—the year was chosen as being the centenary of the appearance of Rohde's book—the first international conference on the ancient novel attracted several dozen scholars from Europe and North America, and since then several similar meetings have been held. The growing realization that there is a body of ancient fiction available for study comes at a time when the fiction of other periods is being analyzed with great energy. Such a collection as this may render service to others besides classicists.

Finally, the translations. They are new and were made for this volume (with the exception of my translation of Lucian's *True Story,* which first appeared in 1965); this is the first such collection ever to appear in English. For most of the works presented here good or adequate texts exist and have been followed in the translations with only occasional changes, minor departures generally not being noted. In the case of Chariton the current state of scholarship called for rather more modification of the text: the fluid traditions of the *Alexander Romance* and *Apollonius King of Tyre* invite some conjecture in the interests of clarity; and the papyrus fragments obviously constitute a special case. Since the problems vary from work to work it has not been practicable to follow an entirely systematic procedure, but in any case it is not the function of such a volume to enter into textual questions in detail. The translations are intended to be readable; they are also intended to be accurate, but accurate does not mean literal. Their manner varies with the originals: from the often extremely elaborate prose of the sophistic novels, where on occasion translators have deliberately resorted to minor reorganization of the matter in order to suggest its original flavor (see the introductions to Achilles Tatius and Heliodorus), through the undistinguished style of the popular stories, to the cribs that are all it is possible to give for some of the incomplete texts. The introductions and notes are by the translators; for the most part annotation is limited to what is necessary for understanding.

Some differences of convention will be found from work to work, for instance in the spelling of Greek names: should one write Heraclitus or Herakleitos? That is a perennial problem, and a matter of personal preference; complete consistency is in any case not practicable, in any convention. This volume is an anthology of individual contributions, rather than a homogeneous set; I have conceived it as the editor's function to elicit quality, not to impose uniformity. For the titles: these stories have various kinds of title in the ancient tradition, and hence in modern usage. Often they are called after their main characters, usually the pair of lovers (or sometimes the heroine alone); but some are also known by another name indicating, for instance, their geographical setting. Thus, the story by Heliodorus is called variously *Ethiopica (An Ethiopian Story), Theagenes and Chariclea,* or *Chariclea.* In this volume the stories are in general called by their most convenient modern English titles, but some variations occur. Variant titles are indicated in the individual introductions. For the fragments, the titles used here are mostly titles of convenience; we do not know for sure what these works were called in antiquity, except in the case of the *Phoenician Story.*

I should like to thank the contributors for their unfailing good nature in accepting an editor's sometimes extensive interventions, and particularly for the effort and skill that have gone into their versions; some of the translations, I venture to think, will become standard for our time. I am grateful also to August Frugé for the benevolent interest and help he has accorded this enterprise from its inception, in his not-quite-retirement from the University of California Press; the volume owes much to his experience and judgment. I thank the present staff, particularly Doris Kretschmer and Mary Lamprech, for patient assistance. Lastly, my own work on the book was completed in 1987–88 at the Institute for Advanced Study in Princeton, where I held a Visiting Professorship awarded by the Andrew W. Mellon Foundation; I wish to record my gratitude to both bodies.

—B. P. R.

## General Bibliography

### LITERARY HISTORIES

Bowie, E. L. "The Greek Novel." In *Cambridge History of Classical Literature,* edited by P. E. Easterling and B. M. W. Knox, vol. 1, 683–99. Cambridge, 1985.

Lesky, A. "Prose Romance and Epistolography." In *A History of Greek Literature,* translated by J. Willis and C. de Heer, 857–70. London, 1966. German edition: Bern 1957.

## GENERAL STUDIES

Hägg, Tomas. *The Novel in Antiquity*. Oxford and Berkeley, 1983. Best general account in English.

Heiserman, A. *The Novel Before the Novel*. Chicago, 1977. Literary study of the principal texts.

Holzberg, N. *Der antike Roman*. Munich and Zurich, 1986. General account.

Perry, B. E. *The Ancient Romances: A Literary-Historical Account of Their Origins*. Berkeley, 1967 (Sather Classical Lectures for 1951). Early stages of the form.

Reardon, B. P. "The Greek Novel." *Phoenix* 23(1969): 291–309. General interpretation of the form.

———."Le roman." In *Courants littéraires grecs des II<sup>e</sup> et III<sup>e</sup> siècles après J.-C,* 309–403. Paris, 1971. General account in the context of contemporary literature.

Rohde, E. *Der griechische Roman und seine Vorläufer*. Leipzig, 1876. Reprint. 4th. ed. Hildesheim, 1960. Now seriously out-of-date, but still a basic work because of its erudition.

Weinreich, O. *Der griechische Liebesroman*. Zurich, 1962. General account.

## SPECIAL STUDIES

Gärtner, H., ed. *Beiträge zum griechischen Liebesroman*. Hildesheim, 1984. Reprint of twenty major articles on individual authors and topics.

CHARITON

# CHÆREAS AND CALLIRHOE

## TRANSLATED BY
## B. P. REARDON

## Introduction

*Chaereas and Callirhoe* is probably the earliest extant work of Greek prose fiction. It is thus the first European novel, and as such is interesting on literary-historical grounds as well as for itself. Its author, Chariton, tells us at the outset that he is from Aphrodisias and is the secretary of the *rhetor* Athenagoras. The name Chariton means "man of graces," and was once thought too good to be true for an inhabitant of the city of Aphrodite; but it can be shown to be authentic. Aphrodisias lay inland in southwestern Turkey, just south of the fertile valley of the Maeander; it has been called the Florence of antiquity, from the flowering of sculpture and other arts there in late Hellenistic and early imperial times.[1] *Rhetor* in this context means "lawyer," and the story shows detailed knowledge of legal processes, as in the "sale" of Callirhoe in Book 1. Chariton's employer may possibly have been a known figure of the early second century A.D.,[2] but Chariton's style suggests a rather earlier date for his work: he does not "atticize," that is write in the archaizing Greek fashionable from the late first century A.D. onward, and was an ambitious enough writer to have done so had he lived in that period. But style is an unreliable criterion, and Chariton has been placed as early as the first century B.C.[3] My own guess at his date is about the middle of the first century A.D. The geographical and social background of one of the story's

1. The city is described by its excavator, Kenan T. Erim, in *Aphrodisias: City of Venus Aphrodite* (New York and London, 1986).

2. See C. Ruiz Montero, "Una observación para la cronologia de Caritón de Afrodisias," *Estudios Clásicos* 24(1980): 63–69; the article gives a useful summary of attempts to date Chariton.

3. See A. D. Papanikolaou, *Chariton-Studien* (Göttingen, 1973), on Chariton's language and (hence) date.

main locations, the region of Miletus, certainly seems to fit that area of Asia Minor in the early Roman Empire.

Chariton's own title for his story may well have been simply *Callirhoe*—as his last sentence would suggest—but we cannot be sure of that, and I have preferred to keep the traditional title.[4] Although the background of the work reflects the contemporary world, it is a historical novel, set in the fourth century B.C.; the historical setting is vague, however, and displays a number of anachronisms. Hermocrates, the father of the heroine Callirhoe, was a Syracusan statesman and leader in the successful resistance to the Athenian expedition against Sicily in 415–413. He died in 407, but the story reflects a number of historical events and people distributed over most of the fourth century, including the siege of Tyre by Alexander the Great in 332. Callirhoe herself shares this historical aura to some extent, for Hermocrates did have a daughter who died accidentally. Chaereas is not based on any known Syracusan figure, but his adventures recall, as well as those of Alexander, the exploits of an Athenian professional soldier of the early fourth century, Chabrias; and his father, Ariston, has the same name as the prominent member of the victorious Syracusan navy. Furthermore, the form of Chariton's opening sentence is modeled on those of Herodotus and Thucydides, and there are other echoes of historiographical and biographical writing throughout the work. The Persian king Artaxerxes clearly represents the historical Artaxerxes II Mnemon (reigned 404–358), whose wife, like Chariton's Persian queen, was called Statira; he may also recall Artaxerxes III Ochus (reigned 358–338), for he too successfully withstood a revolt by Egypt, as does Chariton's king. Dionysius, the noble seigneur in Chariton's story, has the same name as two fourth-century tyrants of Syracuse. His domain, Miletus, is in the Persian Empire, but historically Miletus was not under Persian control in the fourth century until 368.

It is not clear how this historical content should be interpreted. A number of early novels (*Ninus, Sesonchosis, Metiochus and Parthenope*—see the Fragments in this volume) share this historiographical character with the present work, as does the later *Ethiopica* of Heliodorus. If the whole genre of romance was a development of the rather melodramatic historical writing that characterized the Hellenistic period—which is entirely possible—then perhaps we need look no farther for an explanation. But it is perhaps just as likely that Chariton deliberately used a historical setting, and familiar episodes and names from Greek tradition, to titillate the interest of his audience, much as modern novelists sometimes do; such a setting carries with it a certain degree of superficial credibility, which in the early stages of the form would render the fictitious content the more palatable. In a somewhat similar vein, Chariton, who while not

---

4. The title appears in the manuscript as *The Love Story of Chaereas and Callirhoe* and in a papyrus as *Callirhoe*.

obviously erudite has clearly read his "classics," is always ready with a quotation from Homer or a reminiscence of Xenophon of Athens (*Anabasis, Cyropaedia*), and can produce echoes of Demosthenes and other writers to please the more cultivated of his readers. Certainly he is thoroughly devoted to the Greek tradition, and makes much play with the standard theme of the superiority of Greeks over all other races, notably Persians. The term *barbaros* comes readily to his pen; basically it means simply "non-Greek," but it often implies "consequently uncivilized."

Only one manuscript of the story survives, and it is late (thirteenth century) and unreliable. Some papyrus fragments strongly suggest that the story was popular and widely distributed in Egypt in the second century A.D. Thus Chariton (together with Xenophon of Ephesus, whose *Ephesian Story* also survived only in the manuscript just mentioned) represents the stage between the fragments (which have surfaced only in the last hundred years) and the fuller tradition of more sophisticated texts like that of Heliodorus. He survived by the skin of his teeth, and this fact is as good evidence as any for the reputation of the genre, especially the earliest specimens of it, in antiquity. There is also a snide, dismissive reference to one Chariton, a writer of "stories" (*logoi*), in a work by Philostratus from the early third century (it is quite possible that Chariton wrote other novels—see Fragments, *Chione* and *Metiochus and Parthenope*). In modern times Chariton, with Xenophon, had to wait until the eighteenth century to become known, no doubt largely because of the slender earlier tradition; the first edition of *Chaereas and Callirhoe* appeared in 1750. This tardy appearance has in turn contributed to modern neglect of his work, which was not edited scientifically until 1938, by W. E. Blake. It was also at one time considered (by the influential Rohde) to be a very late example of the genre, particularly simple in style and therefore particularly decadent. As a result of widespread disregard of Greek literature of the imperial period this opinion persisted, even though by the very beginning of this century papyri had already established a much earlier date for the story. The process of rehabilitation of Chariton began in the 1920s, but has only recently gathered momentum; Northrop Frye, for instance, in *The Secular Scripture,* a wide-ranging study of the romance form published in 1976, is apparently unaware of his existence, although he mentions other ancient novelists often.

In general the translation is based on Blake's text, which needs systematic attention but cannot receive it here. To reduce annotation I have refrained from mentioning my not infrequent departures from it where they can be followed from Blake's full critical apparatus. I have, however, indicated emendations based on more recent work, with brief references which I hope will be sufficient and convenient for those interested. Blake's edition, however, although it is indispensable for detailed study, is not always readily accessible; those who wish to consult a Greek text will find in the Budé series one which will serve for general purposes. As for the translation, Chariton's language is straightforward literary *koine,* and should be represented by unaffected though not cheap English; that is what I have aimed at. For extensive and scholarly discussion of several literary-historical topics that can only be adumbrated here, the reader is referred especially to the excellent introduction by K. Plepelits to his German translation; full and useful running commentary will also be found there and in another recent translation by C. Lucke and K.-H. Schäfer. I should like to acknowledge here my debt to the work of these scholars.

Other novels are elaborate in structure; *Chaereas and Callirhoe* is simple and linear, with an uncomplicated narrative manner. The amount of pure narration involved, in fact, is relatively small. The greater part of the text is occupied by *dramatic* presentation of the story, and much of that is actually in direct speech.[5] Drama is indeed the main quality of the story; Chariton is ever alert for dramatic possibilities and revels in their exploitation. He is also fond of rhetorical devices, especially paradox and antithesis. The modern reader may tire of it, but this is the style of such works, and as a style it is no more artificial than, say, that of opera. The work has indeed a certain affinity with opera: time and again a crisis in her life sees Callirhoe launch on an "aria," like a prima donna, and Chariton does not spare the melodrama as his heroine finds herself in ever more poignant situations. The most striking, no doubt, is that in which she is compelled to decide between loyalty to a husband whom she loves, but believes lost forever, and duty to and maternal affection for his unborn child: should she or should she not, in the child's interest, marry the rich and noble seigneur Dionysius? Chariton makes this heartrending choice the emotional center of his story, and builds his narrative around it; structurally the novel is for most of its length an account of the ever-mounting tension created by the claims to Callirhoe's hand of a series of increasingly highly placed suitors. The author gives the impression that Tyche—Fortune—is dominating the action, but again he does so for the emotional value of the idea, since in reality he is usually unobtrusively clever in motivating his action, as in distributing it among his cast of characters. Similarly, his rhetoric often cloaks acute psychological observation of his characters; this is especially true in the case of the minor actors, for hero and heroine attitudinize at every opportunity. One way or another, the reader's attention is constantly directed towards the emotion generated by his heroes' situation.

B. E. Perry called *Chaereas and Callirhoe* "Greek romance as it should be written." Certainly it makes the most of one set of possibilities that the form of prose fiction has developed in various periods—its potential

5. See Tomas Hägg, *Narrative Technique in Ancient Greek Romances: Studies of Chariton, Xenophon Ephesius and Achilles Tatius* (Stockholm, 1971).

for "romantic" content, in fact. In such a story, convention rules: Beauty will lead inevitably to Love, Love to Marriage, and Marriage—after vicissitudes—to Felicity. In this respect the story is far removed from the altogether sterner world of older Greek literature, tragedy and epic. *Chaereas and Callirhoe* is unmistakably postclassical. It cannot be said to transcend its times, but it may be thought to represent its Hellenistic-imperial world as well as any other specimen of that world's creative literature.

## Bibliography

TEXT

*Chariton: Le roman de Chairéas et Callirhoé.* Edited by G. Molinié. Paris, 1979 (Budé).

*Charitonis Aphrodisiensis de Chaerea et Callirhoe Amatoriarum Narrationum Libri Octo.* Edited by W. E. Blake. Oxford, 1938.

Jackson, J. "The Greek Novelists." *Classical Quarterly* 29(1935): 52–57 and 96–112.

See also Plepelits and Lucke-Schäfer below.

GENERAL

Lucke, C., and K.-H. Schäfer. *Chariton: Kallirhoe.* Leipzig, 1985. German translation with notes; postscript by H. Kuch.

Perry, B. E. "Chariton and His Romance from a Literary-Historical Point of View." *American Journal of Philology* 51(1930): 93–134.

————. *The Ancient Romances: A Literary-Historical Account of Their Origins.* Berkeley, 1967. See chapter 3

Plepelits, K. *Chariton von Aphrodisias: Kallirhoe.* Stuttgart, 1976. German translation with introduction and notes.

Reardon, B. P. "Theme, Structure and Narrative in Chariton." *Yale Classical Studies* 27(1982): 1–27.

Schmeling, Gareth L. *Chariton.* New York, 1974.

# CHÆREAS AND CALLIRHOE

## Book One

MY NAME IS CHARITON, of Aphrodisias, and I am clerk to the attorney Athenagoras. I am going to tell you the story of a love affair that took place in Syracuse.[1]

1. See the Introduction for Chariton himself and the historical setting of this story.

The Syracusan general Hermocrates, the man who defeated the Athenians, had a daughter called Callirhoe. She was a wonderful girl, the pride of all Sicily; her beauty was more than human, it was divine, and it was not the beauty of a Nereid or mountain nymph at that, but of the maiden Aphrodite herself.[2] Report of the astonishing vision spread everywhere, and suitors flocked to Syracuse, rulers and tyrants' sons, not just from Sicily but from southern Italy too and farther north, and from foreigners in those parts.[3] But Eros intended to make a match of his own devising. There was a young man called Chaereas, surpassingly handsome, like Achilles and Nireus and Hippolytus and Alcibiades as sculptors and painters portray them.[4] His father, Ariston, was second only to Hermocrates in Syracuse, and the two were political rivals, so that they would have made a marriage alliance with anyone rather than with each other. But Eros likes to win and enjoys succeeding against the odds. He looked for his opportunity and found it as follows.

A public festival of Aphrodite took place, and almost all the women went to her temple. Callirhoe had never been out in public before, but her father wanted her to do reverence to the goddess, and her mother took her. Just at that time Chaereas was walking home from the gymnasium; he was radiant as a star, the flush of exercise blooming on his bright countenance like gold on silver. Now, chance would have it that at the corner of a narrow street the two walked straight into each other; the god had contrived the meeting so that each should see the other. At once they were both smitten with love ...[5] beauty had met nobility.

Chaereas, so stricken, could barely make his way home; he was like a hero mortally wounded in battle, too proud to fall but too weak to stand. The girl, for her part, fell at Aphrodite's feet and kissed them. "Mistress," she cried, "give me the man you showed me for my husband!" When night came, it brought suffering to both, for the fire was raging in them. The girl suffered more, because she could not bear to give herself away and so said nothing to anyone. But when Chaereas began to waste away bodily, he found courage, as befitted a youth of noble

2. "Maiden" is not, of course, the usual attribute of Aphrodite, but is attested for her at her birth; in any event, the title can apply to others as little qualified for it, such as Hera and Cybele.

3. Literally "from Italy and the tribes on the continent." Here, Chariton appears to be carrying his historicizing approach to the point of using the term Italy in its classical Greek sense of "Southern Italy"—i.e., the toe of Italy, or modern Calabria, which was heavily hellenized and indeed known then as "Greater Greece." North of that, "on the continent," there were other Greek settlements, such as Neapolis (Naples). The "foreigners" are simply non-Greeks. See K. Plepelits, *Chariton von Aphrodisias: Kallirhoe* (Stuttgart, 1976), 159–60.

4. Achilles and Nireus are described in *Iliad* 2.673–74 as the handsomest men in the Greek army at Troy; Hippolytus's beauty notoriously attracted his stepmother, Phaedra. Alcibiades, the only historical figure in this list, was a notably handsome Athenian aristocrat and public figure of the late fifth century (see, for example, Plato's *Symposium*).

5. The text is incomplete and uncertain here.

and generous disposition, to tell his parents that he was in love and would die if he did not marry Callirhoe. At this his father groaned and said: "Then I have lost you, my boy! Hermocrates would certainly never give you his daughter when he has so many rich and royal suitors for her. You must not even try to win her, or we shall be publicly insulted." Then the father tried to comfort his son, but his illness grew so serious that he did not even go out and follow his usual pursuits. The gymnasium missed Chaereas; it was almost deserted, for he was the idol of the young folk. They asked after him, and when they found out what had made him ill, they all felt pity for a handsome youth who looked as if he would die because his noble heart was broken.

A regular assembly took place at this time. When the people had taken their seats, their first and only cry was: "Noble Hermocrates, great general, save Chaereas! That will be your finest monument! The city pleads for the marriage, today, of a pair worthy of each other!" Who could describe that assembly? It was dominated by Eros. Hermocrates loved his country and could not refuse what it asked. When he gave his consent, the whole meeting rushed from the theater; the young men went off to find Chaereas, the council and archons escorted Hermocrates, and the Syracusans' wives too went to his house, to attend the bride. The sound of the marriage hymn pervaded the city, the streets were filled with garlands and torches, porches were wet with wine and perfume. The Syracusans celebrated this day even more joyously than the day of their victory.

The girl knew nothing of all this; she lay on her bed, her face covered, crying and uttering not a word. Her nurse came to her as she lay there. "Get up, my child," she said. "The day we have all been praying so hard for has come: the city is here to see you married!"

And then her limbs gave way, her heart felt faint,[6]

for she did not know whom she was going to marry. She fainted there and then; darkness veiled her eyes, and she almost expired; the spectators thought it maidenly modesty. As soon as her maids had dressed her, the crowd at the door went away, and his parents brought the bridegroom in to the girl. Well, Chaereas ran to her and kissed her; and when she saw it was the man she loved, Callirhoe, like the flame in a lamp that is on the point of going out and has oil poured into it, at once grew bright again and bigger and stronger. When she appeared in public the whole crowd was struck with wonder, as when Artemis appears to hunters in lonely places; many of those present actually went down on their knees in wor-

6. A formulaic verse that occurs several times in Homer (e.g., *Iliad* 21.114) and is quoted by Chariton several times.

ship. They all thought Callirhoe beautiful and Chaereas lucky. It was like the wedding of Thetis on Pelion as poets describe it. But just as Strife turned up there, according to the story, so did a malicious spirit here.[7]

2     The suitors were distressed and angry at their failure to win Callirhoe's hand. So whereas they had so far been rivals, they now fell into accord; in that accord, and considering themselves insulted, they joined counsel; and their marshal in the campaign against Chaereas was Envy. A young Italian, the son of the tyrant of Rhegium,[8] rose to speak first. "If one of us had married her," he said, "I should not have been angry; as in athletic competitions, only one contestant can win. But we have been passed over for a man who made no effort to win the bride, and I am not putting up with that insult. We have lain waking at the door of her house, we have curried favor with her nurses and maids, we have sent presents to the servants who brought her up. How long have we been her slaves? What is worst of all, we have come to hate each other, as rivals. And with kings competing for the prize, this nancy-boy, this worthless pauper carries it off without lifting a finger. Well, he must get no good of it; let us make his marriage fatal to the bridegroom."

They all showed their approval except the tyrant of Acragas,[9] who opposed the suggestion. "It is not any goodwill towards Chaereas," he said, "that makes me object to this design against him; it is prudence. Hermocrates, remember, is not a man to be casually disregarded. An open fight with him is out of the question; an intelligent approach is better—after all, that is how we become tyrants, by cunning, not by force.  Elect me leader of the campaign against Chaereas, and I promise you I shall break up this marriage. I shall set Jealousy in arms against him, and with Love as ally he will bring about a catastrophe. Callirhoe, I know, is sensible, and she doesn't know what malice and suspicion are. But Chaereas has been brought up in the gymnasium, and he does know how young people misbehave; it will be easy to arouse his suspicions and make him jealous, as young men are liable to be. Besides, we can approach him more easily and talk to him."

They all acclaimed his proposal before the words were out of his mouth, and thinking him capable of anything, entrusted its execution to him. So he embarked on the following scheme.

---

7. When the Nereid Thetis, the future mother of Achilles, married the mortal Peleus on Mount Pelion, all the gods and goddesses were invited except Eris (Strife). Eris threw into the assembly an apple destined "for the fairest"; when Athena, Hera, and Aphrodite all claimed it, Zeus ordained that judgment be made by Paris, the son of Priam of Troy. This ultimately led to the abduction of Helen and to the Trojan War. The wedding of Peleus and Thetis is a favorite theme in art and literature.

8. Reggio, in Calabria.

9. Agrigento, in Sicily.

It was evening, and a man came with the news[10] that Chaereas's fa- 3
ther, Ariston, had fallen from a ladder on his farm and was very unlikely
to live. When Chaereas heard this, much as he loved his father, he was
even more distressed at having to go off by himself—because he could
not yet take his bride out.[11] During that night, although no one went so
far as to pay an obvious riotous visit to the house, they did come secretly *1st attempt*
and unseen, and left evidence of a party about: they hung wreaths about
the porch and sprinkled it with scent, they soaked the ground with wine,
they scattered half-burnt torches around.

Dawn broke. People are generally inquisitive, and everybody who
passed that way stopped. Chaereas, whose father was feeling better, was
hurrying to his wife. His first reaction when he saw the crowd at his
door was one of surprise, but when he found out why they were there he
ran in like a man possessed. He found the bedroom door still locked and
banged violently on it. When the maid opened it he burst in on Callirhoe; his anger gave way to grief, and he tore his clothes and began to
cry. She asked him what had happened; he stood dumb, unable either to
disbelieve what he had seen or to believe what he did not want to believe. He did not know what to think, and as he stood trembling, his
wife, who had no idea what had happened, begged him to tell her why
he was angry. His eyes bloodshot, he said in a voice hoarse with passion,
"It is what has happened to me that I am crying about; you have forgotten me straightaway!" and he reproached her with the riotous party. But
she was a general's daughter and a very proud girl; she flared up at this
unjust accusation and cried: "There has been no riotous party at my father's house! Perhaps *your* house is used to parties, and your lovers are
upset at your marriage!" With these words she turned away, covered her
face, and burst into tears. But lovers are easily reconciled; they gladly accept any justification from each other; and so Chaereas changed his tone
and began to talk winningly to her, and his wife quickly welcomed his
change of heart. This increased the ardor of their love, and the parents of
both thought themselves lucky when they saw how well their children
got on.

Faced with the failure of his first plot, the man from Acragas now em- 4
barked on a more effective plan, thinking up the following trick. He had

10. The opening words of this sentence are an exact quotation from a dramatic passage
of Demosthenes' famous speech *On the Crown* (169), where the orator is recalling how
news came to Athens of Philip's capture of Elatea in his advance into Greece in 339 B.C.
Chariton also uses the phrase later (8.1) in even briefer, but still recognizable, form, again
to foreshadow a rise in tension.

11. It was customary for a woman on marrying not to appear in public for a time.
When she had proved her loyalty by producing a child, she was entrusted with domestic
responsibilities (cf. 3.7) and with greater freedom.

a follower who was glib of tongue and fully endowed with social graces of every kind. He told him off to play the part of a lover; his job was to fall at the feet of Callirhoe's personal maid, the most prized of her servants, and gain her love. She was reluctant, but he was insistent and managed to win her over by giving her handsome presents and saying he would hang himself if he did not get what he wanted—a woman is easy prey when she thinks she is loved.[12] Well, when he had laid the groundwork, the director of this drama found another actor, not as ingratiating as the first, but a cunning, plausible fellow; he rehearsed him in what he was to do and say and quietly got him to approach Chaereas, who did not know him. The man did so as Chaereas was strolling idly around the palaestra. "Chaereas," he said, "I once had a son myself, of your age—he was a great admirer of yours and very fond of you, when he was alive. Now he is dead, I count you as my son—indeed, 'your happiness is a blessing shared'[13] by all Sicily. So let me talk to you when you have a moment to spare; I have something important to tell you, which affects your whole life."

By talking like that this wretch set the young man's mind agog and filled him with hope and fear and curiosity. When Chaereas begged him to speak, he held back, saying that the present moment was not suitable and that they should put things off until they had more time to spare. Chaereas began to suspect something serious and insisted all the more. The other grasped his arm and took him off to a quiet spot. Then he frowned, assumed a sad expression, and even let a tear drop from his eye. "Chaereas," he said, "it distresses me to have bad news to give you; I have been wanting to tell you for some time but could not bring myself to do so. But now that things have reached the point where you are being openly abused and the scandal is public gossip I cannot keep quiet; I detest wickedness anyway, that's my nature, but above all I am well disposed towards you. Know then that your wife is unfaithful to you. To convince you I will let you watch her lover compromise himself."

At these words a black cloud of grief covered him;
with both hands he took dark dust and poured it over his head,
defiling his lovely countenance.[14]

For a long time he lay dumb, unable to speak or raise his eyes from the ground. When he managed to find his voice—a small voice, not like his

12. Chariton is fond of sententious utterances of this kind; sometimes they echo extant phrases from New Comedy, especially Menander (here, frag. 290, "Any man in love is naturally easily led"), but sometimes we can only suspect an echo of a line now lost (as in 1.3, "Lovers are easily reconciled").

13. Another echo of Menander, frag. 542.

14. *Iliad* 18.22–24 (Achilles on hearing of the death of Patroclus); the passage is used again at 5.2.

normal one—he said: "It is a wretched favor to ask of you, to let me see my misfortune with my own eyes. Show it to me, though, so that I have better reason for killing myself; for I will not harm Callirhoe even though she is doing me wrong." "Say you are going off to the country," said the other, "and when it gets dark, watch your house; you will see her lover go in."

They agreed on this. Chaereas sent a message—he could not bear even to go into the house himself—to say he was going off to the country; and the villainous author of the slander set the scene. So, when night fell, Chaereas went to keep watch, and the man who had seduced Callirhoe's maid darted into the lane. He adopted the manner of a man who wants to keep his business secret, but in fact did everything he could to be noticed: his hair was gleaming and heavily scented; his eyes were made up; he had a soft cloak and fine shoes; heavy rings gleamed on his fingers. Then, after much looking about him, he went to the door, knocked softly on it, and gave the usual signal. The maid, who was very frightened herself, quietly opened the door a few inches, took his hand, and drew him in. When he saw this, Chaereas could restrain himself no longer and rushed in to catch the lover red-handed and kill him.[15]

Now the lover had hidden by the outer door, and he slipped out at once. Callirhoe, however, was sitting on her bed longing for Chaereas, so sad that she had not even lit a lamp. Footsteps sounded; she recognized her husband before anyone else did, by the sound of his breathing, and ran joyfully to him. He could not find his voice to revile her; overcome by his anger, he kicked her as she ran to him. Now his foot found its mark in the girl's diaphragm and stopped her breath. She fell down, and her maids picked her up and laid her on her bed.

So Callirhoe lay there unconscious, not breathing; she looked to everyone as if she were dead, and Rumor ran all over the town, spreading the news of the catastrophe and arousing cries of grief throughout the narrow streets right down to the sea; wailing was to be heard on all sides—it was like the fall of a city. Chaereas, whose heart was still seething, shut himself up all night, trying to extort information from the maids, especially Callirhoe's own maid. It was while they were undergoing fire and torture that he learned the truth.[16] At that, in an access of pity for his dead wife, he desperately wanted to kill himself; but Polycharmus would not let him (Polycharmus was a special friend of his, as Patroclus was of Achilles in Homer).

---

15. This was legal in Greece; this is the basis of Lysias's speech *On the Murder of Eratosthenes,* our principal source in the matter.

16. Slaves were tortured as a matter of course in trials or similar circumstances, on the assumption that they would not tell the truth otherwise

When day came, the council empaneled a jury to try the murderer and hurried the trial on out of respect for Hermocrates; and the whole body politic as well quickly gathered in the town square, with various excited cries. The unsuccessful suitors incited the crowd to anger—especially the man from Acragas, radiant and proud at having brought off a feat beyond everyone's expectations. And something strange happened, that had never happened before in a trial: after the speech for the prosecution, the murderer, when his time was allotted him,[17] instead of defending himself, launched into an even more bitter self-condemnation and took the lead in finding himself guilty. He used none of the arguments he could reasonably have used in his defense—that he was a victim of malicious slander, that he was moved by jealousy, that his action was involuntary; instead, he begged them all: "Stone me to death in public; I have robbed our community of its crowning glory! It would be charitable to hand me over to the executioner; that would have been my proper punishment if it had been merely Hermocrates' servant girl I had killed; try to find some unspeakable way to punish me. I have done something worse than any temple robber or parricide. Do not give me burial; do not pollute the earth—plunge my criminal body to the bottom of the sea!"

At these words a cry of grief burst forth; everybody abandoned the dead girl in sorrow for the living man. Hermocrates was the first to come to Chaereas's defense. "I know very well that what happened was unintended," he said. "I have my eye on those who are conspiring against us. They shall not have two deaths to gloat over; I am not going to give my daughter's spirit cause for sorrow—I often heard her say she would rather Chaereas should live than herself. So let us close this trial, which is futile, and move on to the funeral, which is necessary; we should not give her corpse into the hands of time; we should not let her body decay and lose its loveliness; let us bury Callirhoe while she is still beautiful."

6   So the jury acquitted Chaereas. But Chaereas could not acquit himself; rather, he desired passionately to die and sought every means to end his days. When Polycharmus saw that he had no other means of saving him, he said: "Traitor to your dead wife! Are you not even staying to bury Callirhoe? Are you entrusting her body to others' hands? Now is the time for you to make sure that she is buried with costly offerings and see to it that her funeral is fit for a queen." This argument convinced him; it inspired in him proper pride and serious concern. What description could do justice to that funeral? Callirhoe, as she lay there dressed in her bridal clothes, on a bier decorated with gold, bigger and lovelier than in life,

---

17. Speakers in trials were allotted a fixed period of time, which was measured by a water clock (*clepsydra*) in the manner of a domestic egg timer; the text here says, literally, "when his water was measured."

made everyone think how like the sleeping Ariadne[18] she looked. In front of the bier went, first, the Syracusan cavalry with their horses, in ceremonial dress; after them, infantry carrying reminders of Hermocrates' victories; then the council, and among the citizens, the archons,[19] all escorting Hermocrates. Ariston too, not yet recovered, was being carried; he kept calling Callirhoe his daughter and his lady. After this came the citizens' wives, dressed in black. Then there was a royal profusion of funeral offerings: first, the gold and silver from the dowry; beautiful clothing and jewelry—Hermocrates added to it a lot of the booty he had taken; and gifts from relatives and friends. Last of all followed Chaereas's wealth; he passionately wanted, if it had been possible, to consign all his property to flames along with his wife's corpse.[20] The bier was carried by the young men of Syracuse,[21] and the rest of the population followed it. Amid the lamentations of the mourners, Chaereas's voice was loudest. Hermocrates owned a magnificent vault near the sea—on a ship you could see it from far out. This was filled with the costly offerings, like a votive building.[22] And what was done in the intention of paying honor to the dead girl started a train of greater events.

This was what happened. There was a man called Theron, a scoundrel 7 whose criminal trade it was to sail the seas and have thugs handily stationed with boats in harbors under cover of being ferrymen; from them he made up pirate crews. Theron had been about at the funeral; his gaze had fastened on the gold, and when he went to bed that night he could not sleep for thinking: "Why should I risk my life battling with the sea and killing living people and not getting much out of it, when I can get rich from one dead body? Let the die be cast; I won't miss a chance like that of making money. Now, whom shall I recruit for the job? Think,

18. After Ariadne helped Theseus in his fight with the Minotaur (by giving him a ball of thread with which to retrace his steps in the labyrinth), Theseus took her away with him. On the way back to Athens, however, he abandoned her, leaving her sleeping on the shore of the island of Naxos; Dionysus found her there and lay with her. The theme of "Ariadne asleep" was popular in literature and art.

19. I have here adopted the emendation of Lucke-Schater, ἐν μέσῳ τῷ δήμῳ ⟨οἱ ἄρχοντες⟩.

20. This is what the text appears to say (unless in Chariton's non-Attic Greek the expression has a less precise meaning, such as "burn…over his wife's corpse"). Since there was no intention of burning Callirhoe's body, explanation has been thought necessary, and several explanations have been offered: that "burn" is a loose term for "bury"; that offerings to the dead were useless to them if not burnt (as in Herodotus 5.92); that the text needs emending. But perhaps there is more emotion than sense in Chaereas's mind at this juncture. We have already seen his suicidal impulse; it is being extended to embrace all that belongs to him.

21. These are the "ephebes," young men of an age for military service, such as was statutorily required in Athens from the fourth century; the institution later developed into a social organization, a club for the sons of the well-to-do, especially in the Greek diaspora.

22. Such buildings, known as *thesauri,* "treasuries," were erected near temples and shrines, as at Delphi.

Theron; who would be suitable, of the men you know? Zenophanes of Thurii? Intelligent, but a coward. Menon of Messana?[23] Brave, but untrustworthy." And he assessed each one in turn, like a man testing coins; many he rejected, but he did think some suitable. So at dawn he hurried to the harbor and began looking them out one by one; some of them he found in brothels, others in taverns—an army fit for such a commander. Saying that he had something important to talk to them about, he took them behind the harbor and began as follows. "I have made a rich find, and I have picked you out from everybody else to share it with me; there's enough in this for more than one. And it doesn't need much effort either; one night can make us all rich. We aren't novices at this kind of business. Fools condemn it, but sensible men find it pays." They saw at once that it was robbery with violence he was proposing, or breaking into a tomb or robbing a temple. "Never mind preaching to the converted," they cried. "Just tell us what the job is, and let's not miss our chance." Theron went on. "You've seen the gold and silver with the body," he said. "We ought to have it by rights—we're alive. My idea, then, is to open the vault at night, load our ship, sail wherever the wind takes us, and sell the cargo abroad as we can." They agreed. "Well then," he said, "go about your ordinary business for the time being; when it's dark, each of you make his way to the ship, and bring a builder's tool."

8      This, then, was what the robbers did. As for Callirhoe—she came back to life! Her respiration had stopped, but lack of food started it again; with difficulty, and gradually, she began to breathe. Then she began to move her body, limb by limb. Then she opened her eyes and came to her senses like someone waking up from sleep; and thinking Chaereas was sleeping beside her, she called to him. But since neither husband nor maids paid any attention, and everything was lonely and dark, the girl began to shiver and tremble with fear; she could not work out what had really happened. As she stirred into consciousness, she touched wreaths and ribbons and made gold and silver objects rattle; and there was a strong smell of spices. So then she remembered the kick and how it had made her fall; and she eventually realized that she had been buried as a result of losing consciousness.[24] She cried out at the top of her voice, "I have been buried alive! Help!" She shouted many times, but nothing happened; and then she abandoned all further hope of being rescued. Sinking her head into her lap, she fell to bewailing her lot. "Oh, what a terrible fate," she sobbed. "Buried alive! I haven't done anything wrong! Dying a lingering death! They're mourning for me, and there's nothing wrong with me! Who will send a messenger? Who will be the messenger? Wicked Chaereas, I blame you—not for killing me, but for being so

23. Thurii, Messana—local Greek coastal colonies (Messana = Messina).
24. I have adopted Jackson's emendations here and in the next sentence.

quick to remove me from the house. You should not have buried Callirhoe quickly, even if she had really been dead. But perhaps you already have plans for marriage!"

While she was pouring forth all her sorrows, Theron, who had waited till the dead of night, was silently drawing near the vault, his oars touching the water lightly. First ashore, he assigned jobs as follows. Four men he sent to keep a lookout, with instructions to kill anyone who came near the place if possible, and if not, to give warning of their arrival by an agreed signal. He himself went to the vault with four others. The rest—they were sixteen in all—he told to stay on board with oars poised, so that in an emergency they could quickly pick up the men on shore and row off.

When they began to use crowbars and hammer heavily to open the vault, Callirhoe was gripped by a variety of emotions—fear, joy, grief, surprise, hope, disbelief. "Where is this noise coming from? Is some divinity coming for me—poor creature!—as always happens when people are dying? Or is it not a noise but a voice—the voice of the gods below calling me to them? It is more likely that it is tomb robbers; there, there is an additional misfortune; wealth is of no use to a corpse." While these thoughts were still passing through her mind, a robber put his head through and came a little way into the vault. Callirhoe, intending to implore his help, threw herself at his knees; he was terrified and jumped back. Shaking with fear, he cried to his fellows: "Let's get out of here! There's some sort of spirit on guard in there who won't let us come in!" Theron laughed scornfully at him and called him a coward and deader than the dead girl. Then he told another man to go in; and when nobody had the courage to do so, he went in himself, holding his sword ready before him. At the gleam of the metal Callirhoe was afraid she was going to be murdered; she shrank back into the corner of the vault and from there begged him in a small voice: "Have pity on me, whoever you are— I have had no pity from husband or parents. Do not kill me now you have saved me." Theron took courage, and being an intelligent man, realized the truth of the matter. He stood there thinking. His first idea was to kill the woman—he thought she would get in the way of the whole enterprise. But he very soon thought of the profit he could make, and changed his mind. "She too," he said to himself, "can be part of the funeral treasure. There's a lot of silver here, and a lot of gold, but the woman's beauty is more valuable than anything here." So he took her by the hand and led her out; then, calling his colleague, he said: "There you are—there's the spirit you were afraid of. A fine brigand you are—scared of a mere woman! Well now, you look after the girl—I want to give her back to her parents; we'll get on with taking out what's inside, now that there isn't even the corpse to guard it."

10     When they had filled the ship with the loot, Theron told the man who was guarding the woman to stand a little way away with her; then he brought forward for discussion the question of what to do with her. They had different and opposing views. The first speaker said: "Comrades, we came for a different purpose, but what Chance has sent us has turned out better. Let's take advantage of it; we can have a successful operation without any risk. My proposal is that we leave the funeral offerings where they were and give Callirhoe back to her husband and father. We can say that we anchored near the tomb as we always do when fishing, and that when we heard someone calling out we opened the vault out of humanity, to rescue the woman who was shut up in it. Let's make her swear to support everything we say; she'll be glad to, out of gratitude to the benefactors who rescued her. Can you imagine how happy we'll make all Sicily? What rewards we'll get? And at the same time what we'll be doing will be right in men's eyes and a holy action in the eyes of the gods."

       While he was still speaking, another raised his voice in opposition. "You've chosen the wrong moment, you fool. Are you telling us now to act the philosophers? Has breaking into a tomb made us virtuous, then? Shall we take pity on her when her own husband didn't, but killed her? She's done us no harm, I suppose you'll say. No, but she will do—a great deal of harm. Look: first of all, if we give her back to her family, there's no knowing what they will think about the business, and people are bound to guess why we went to the tomb. And even if the woman's parents are prepared to let us off our punishment, the archons and the assembly itself will not let off tomb robbers who convict themselves by bringing them their booty. Someone may say that it is more profitable to sell the woman, since she will fetch a high price because of her beauty. But this is dangerous too. Gold can't talk, silver won't say where we got it; we can make up some story about them. But goods that have eyes and ears and a tongue—who can hide that? And, you know, her beauty isn't human, for us to get away with it. Shall we say she's a slave? Who's going to believe that once he sees her? So let's kill her here and not carry around the means of our own conviction."

       Many of them agreed with this. But Theron favored neither proposal. "*You,*" he said, "are inviting danger, and *you* are losing us our profit. I'll sell the girl rather than kill her. When she's on sale, she'll be too frightened to say anything, and once she's sold she can accuse us if she likes, we shan't be there; and after all, it's a risky life we lead. Come on, get on board and let's sail; it's nearly day already."

11     The ship put to sea and ran splendidly, since they were not struggling against sea and wind—they had no special course to follow; to their mind any wind was favorable, was a stern wind. As for Callirhoe, Theron

talked soothingly to her and thought up all sorts of things to try to fool her. She realized her situation and saw that she had gained nothing by being rescued, but she pretended not to be aware of this and to trust him—she was afraid they might really kill her after all if they thought she was angry. Saying she could not stand the sea, she covered her head and wept. "Father," she said, "in this very sea you defeated three hundred Athenian warships; a tiny boat has carried off your daughter, and you do nothing to help me. I am being taken off to a foreign land; I must be a slave—I, who was born noble. Perhaps it will be an Athenian master who will buy Hermocrates' daughter! How much better it would be for me to lie dead in a tomb! Chaereas would certainly have been buried with me; as it is, we are parted both in life and in death!"

While she was bewailing her lot in this fashion, the brigands were sailing past small islands and towns, because their cargo was not for poor men; they were looking for rich men. Well, they anchored across from Attica, in the shelter of a headland, at a spot where there was a spring with plenty of pure water, and a lovely meadow. There they took Callirhoe ashore and told her to refresh her countenance and get some rest from the sea journey, because they wanted to preserve her beauty. When they were alone they debated where to sail to. One of them said: "Athens is nearby—it's a big, prosperous city. We'll find any number of merchants and rich men there; you can see whole populations in Athens, the way you see men in a marketplace." And they all liked the idea of making for Athens. But Theron did not like the inquisitive ways of the town. "Look, are you the only people who don't know what busybodies they are in Athens? They're a nation of gossips, and they love lawsuits. There'll be hundreds of nosey parkers in the harbor wanting to know who we are and where we got this cargo we're carrying. Nasty suspicions will seize hold of their malicious minds—and it's the Areopagus[25] straightaway, in Athens, and magistrates who are more severe than tyrants. We should be more afraid of Athenians than of Syracusans. The place that suits us is Ionia. Why, there are princely fortunes there, pouring down from the Asian continent, and people who love luxury and don't look for trouble.[26] And I expect I'll find a few people I actually know in those parts." They took on water, got provisions from the merchantmen who were in the area, and sailed straight for Miletus. On the

25. The Areopagus (where Paul preached) was a hill on which met the highest court of Athens, whose influence was powerful both in early classical times and in the Roman period, but (ironically) less so in the period in which the story is set. The picture of Athenians as being inquisitive and litigious (cf. Aristophanes' *Birds* and *Wasps*) was standard in antiquity.

26. Ionia (roughly speaking, the west coast of Turkey) was throughout antiquity an area of prosperous and advanced Greek cities, such as Miletus, Ephesus, and Smyrna (Izmir).

third day they moored in an anchorage, a natural harbor ten miles from town.

12     There Theron told his crew to ship their oars, make a shelter for Callirhoe, and provide her with every comfort. He did this out of rapacity, not humanity, as businessman rather than as brigand. He himself hurried to town with two of his men. Then, since he did not judge it prudent to look for a buyer openly and have everyone talking about his business, he tried to make a quick sale privately, without intermediaries. But his property turned out to be hard to dispose of, because it was not within the reach of many people, or of just anyone; it needed somebody wealthy, some great man: and he was afraid to approach that kind of person. So rather a long time passed, until he could stand the delay no longer; and when night came, unable to sleep, he said to himself: "You're a fool, Theron. Look, you've left gold and silver behind in a lonely place for all those days now, as if you were the only brigand there was. Don't you know that there are other pirates sailing the sea as well? I'm afraid of our own band as well—they might desert us and sail off. Obviously it wasn't paragons of virtue you picked, who could be expected to be loyal to you—it was the wickedest rogues you knew. Oh, well," he said, "get some sleep now, since you must; but when day breaks, get to the ship quickly and throw the woman into the sea, she's no business being there and she's just an embarrassment to you. And don't ever again take on a cargo you can't get rid of."

When he fell asleep he had a dream in which he saw a closed door,[27] so he decided to wait for that day. In his random wanderings he sat down in a workshop, his thoughts in utter turmoil. Just then a crowd of people was passing, free men and slaves; and among them was a man in the prime of life, wearing mourning and looking sad. Theron got up—man is naturally inquisitive—and asked one of the people attending him, "Who is that?" "I think you must be a stranger," the man replied, "or come from a long way off if you don't recognize Dionysius. He is the wealthiest, noblest, and most cultured man in Ionia, and a friend of the Great King."[28] "Why is he wearing mourning, then?" "His wife has died; he loved her." Theron was all the more eager to continue the conversation now that he had found a rich man of romantic disposition, so he did not yet let the man go but asked him, "What position do you hold with him?" The other replied, "I am comptroller of his household, and I also look after his infant daughter, who has lost her poor mother early in

27. Dreams and their interpretation much interested antiquity, certainly late antiquity, and are a standard feature of novels. The *Dream Book* of Artemidorus, which dates to the second century A.D., offers an elaborate system of interpretation; a closed door, for instance, signified, as here, exclusion from an intended journey.

28. I.e., the King of Persia; the term Great King is standard in antiquity and was often reduced to simply the King.

life." "What is your name?" "Leonas." "I've met you at just the right moment, Leonas," he said. "I am a merchant, and I have just sailed in from Italy—that is why I know nothing about Ionia. A woman in Sybaris,[29] the richest woman in the town, who had a very beautiful maid, was jealous of her and sold her; I bought her. Now you can have the benefit—whether you want to get yourself a nurse for the child—she's quite well educated—or whether you think it worthwhile doing your master a good turn. It is to your advantage for him to have a slave concubine, so that he won't bring in a stepmother for the girl in your charge, over your head." Leonas was glad to hear Theron's proposal and said: "Some god has delivered you to me to be my benefactor. Why, you are setting out before me in reality what I dreamed about! You must come to the house and be my friend and my guest from this very minute. As for deciding about the woman, a look at her will tell me whether she is fit for my master to possess or just suitable for people like us."

When they reached the house, Theron was surprised at its size and luxuriousness—it was in fact equipped to receive the King of Persia—and Leonas told him to wait while he attended his master first. Then he collected him and took him to his own quarters, which were very much those of a free man, and gave instructions to lay the table. Theron, a clever rogue, good at adapting himself to any situation, set about eating and made a bid for Leonas's goodwill by drinking to him repeatedly—partly to demonstrate an open nature, but mainly to confirm their partnership. Meanwhile, they talked about the girl a great deal. Theron kept lauding her character rather than her beauty; he knew that whereas what cannot be seen needs recommendation, seeing is its own advocate. "Let's be going, then," said Leonas, "and you can show her to me." "She isn't here," said Theron. "We stayed outside the city because of the customs men;[30] the ship is moored ten miles away," and he told him where. "You're moored on our land," said Leonas. "All the better—Fortune is already leading you to Dionysius. Let's go down to the estate, then, and you can rest after your voyage—our country house is near you, and it's luxuriously equipped." Theron was still more pleased; it would be easier to make the sale, he thought, if it was not in the marketplace, but somewhere quiet. "Let's leave at dawn," he suggested. "You go to your country house and I'll go to our ship, and from there I'll bring the woman to you." They agreed on this; then they shook hands and parted. Both of them found the night long: the one in his hurry to buy, the other in his hurry to sell.

13

29. A Greek colony in Southern Italy, notorious for its luxury. It no longer existed by the dramatic date of this story, so this mention constitutes another anachronism; but Chariton wants to use the associations of the name.

30. Customs duties were a regular and important element in the income of Greek states.

The next day Leonas sailed along the coast to the country house, and took money with him as well, in order to take out an option with the seller. Theron appeared at the beach, where his band was waiting for him anxiously, and explained the business to them. Then he began to talk smoothly to Callirhoe. "My dear," he said, "at first I too wanted to take you back to your family. But an adverse wind sprang up, and I was prevented from doing so by the sea. You know how carefully I have looked after you; and most important of all, we have respected your honor. Chaereas will get you back untouched; you will have escaped from your tomb as safe and sound as if it were your bedroom, thanks to us. Well, now we must make a quick trip to Lycia;[31] but there's no need for you too to be put to hardship; there's no point in that, especially as you're a bad sailor. So what I'm going to do is leave you here in the care of reliable friends; on the return journey I shall pick you up and subsequently take you back very carefully to Syracuse. Take any of your things you want—we'll look after the rest for you."

At this Callirhoe, distressed as she was, laughed to herself, thinking him an absolute fool. She already knew she was being sold; but in her desire to get away from the pirates she considered being sold a happier condition than her previous noble rank. "Thank you, sir," she said, "for your kindness to me. And," she added, "may the gods grant all of you the rewards you deserve. But I think it would bring bad luck if I made use of the funeral offerings. Take good care of everything for me. I am content with a little ring I wore even as a corpse." Then she veiled her head and said: "Take me anywhere you like, Theron. Anywhere is better than the sea or the tomb."

14    As he approached the country house, Theron thought up the following move: he uncovered Callirhoe's head, shook her hair loose, and then opened the door and told her to go in first. Leonas and all the people in the room were awestruck at the sudden apparition—some of them thought they had seen a goddess, for people did say that Aphrodite manifested herself in the fields. There they were awestruck when Theron came in behind, went up to Leonas, and said, "Get up and see to receiving the woman; she is the one you want to buy." General joy and amazement followed. Well, they let Callirhoe lie down quietly in the most beautiful room they had—and distressed and tired and frightened as she was, she really did need a lot of rest—and Theron took Leonas by the hand and said: "There you are, my part of the bargain has been carried out faithfully. As for your part, you can take the woman now—you're a friend of mine from now on, after all; go into town, get the legal documents made out, and then you can pay me whatever price you want."

31. A region on the southern coast of Asia Minor, not very far from Miletus.

Leonas wanted to counter this. "Indeed not," he said. "I'll trust *you* with the money, here and now, and not wait for the contract." At the same time he also wanted to secure an option on the purchase, since he was afraid Theron might change his mind after all—there were many men in the town who would want to buy her. So he pressed on him a talent of silver[32] he had brought as a deposit. Theron made a show of refusing, but took it. When Leonas wanted him to stay for supper—it was in fact getting late—he said, "I want to sail to town this evening; we'll meet tomorrow at the harbor."

With this they parted. When he reached the ship, Theron gave orders to weigh anchor and put to sea immediately, before they were found out. So they left hurriedly, where the wind took them; Callirhoe, left to herself, was free now to lament her own lot. "There!" she said. "Another tomb, in which Theron has shut me up! It is more lonely than the first! My father would have come to me there, and my mother; and Chaereas would have poured out his offering of tears over me; and even dead I should have known. But whom can I call on here? Fortune, your curse is on me! You are pursuing me[33] on land and sea. You have not had your fill of my misfortunes. First you made my lover my murderer—Chaereas, who had never even struck a slave, kicked me and killed me, me who loved him; then you gave me into the hands of tomb robbers and brought me out from the tomb onto the sea, and set over me the pirates, who were more frightening than the waves. My celebrated beauty I was given to this end, that the brigand Theron should get a high price for me. I have been sold in a deserted spot and not even taken to a city like any other bought slave—Fortune, you were afraid people might see me and think me nobly born! That is why I have been handed over like a mere chattel to I know not whom, Greeks or barbarians or brigands once more." And as she beat her breast with her hand, she saw Chaereas's portrait on her ring. She kissed it and said: "Truly I am lost to you, Chaereas, separated from you by so vast an ocean! You are mourning for me and repenting and sitting by an empty tomb, proclaiming my chastity now that I am dead; and I, Hermocrates' daughter, your wife, have been sold this day to a master!" As she uttered this lament, sleep finally came to her.

---

32. A talent of silver (= six thousand drachmas) would be an enormous price to pay for a slave, perhaps twenty or thirty times the going rate at the novel's dramatic date; but the price had changed by Chariton's own time, of course, and in any case Chariton wants to emphasize both Callirhoe's beauty and Dionysius's wealth. The transaction here sketched is based on legal realities governing the sale of slaves; a contract, established by officials, was required to guarantee the legal status of the slave and the validity of the sale. See Plepelits, *Chariton*, 169 n.53.

33. The text here poses a serious problem; I have translated D'Orville's emendation as giving a suitable sense but doubt whether it is right.

## Book Two

1  Leonas told his steward Phocas to take great care of Callirhoe, and himself set out for Miletus before dawn. He was eager to bring his master the good news about the gift he had just bought; that would help a great deal, he thought, in consoling his grief. He found Dionysius still in bed. He was out of his mind with grief and for the most part even refused to go out, although he was sorely missed by Miletus; he kept to his room as if he still had his wife with him. When he saw Leonas, he said to him: "This is the first good night's sleep I have had since my poor wife died. I dreamed about her, in fact; she was taller and more beautiful—I saw her there beside me as clearly as if I were awake. In my dream it was the first day of our married life; I was bringing her home after our wedding, from my estate by the sea, and you were singing the wedding song." Leonas cried out before his master had even finished: "You're a lucky man, sir, asleep and awake! You're just going to hear the very thing you've dreamed about!" And he began his report. "I was approached by a trader who had a very beautiful woman for sale; he had anchored outside the town, to avoid the customs officers, and near your country house. I made an arrangement with him and went out to the estate. There we agreed on terms and concluded the sale, for practical purposes—I've given him a talent, and he has handed the woman over to me;[34] but the sale has to be legally registered here in town." Dionysius was glad to learn that the woman was beautiful—he was deeply attached to women—but not glad to learn she was a slave, for he was a true aristocrat, preeminent in rank and in culture throughout Ionia, and would not contemplate taking a slave as concubine. "Leonas," he said, "a person not freeborn cannot be beautiful. Don't you know that the poets say beautiful people are the children of gods? All the more reason for their human parents to be nobly born. You are struck by her because there was nobody else there; you compared her with peasant women. But you've bought her, so go to the marketplace, and Adrastus will see to the registration—he's a very experienced lawyer." Leonas was glad to be disbelieved; the surprise would have all the greater effect on his master. But when he went round all the harbors of Miletus,[35] and all the bankers' tables and the whole town, he could not find Theron anywhere. He asked shopkeepers and ferrymen, but no one knew him. Well, he had no idea what to do. He got a boat and rowed along the shore to the beach, and then to the country house; but he was not likely to find a man who was out at sea by then. So he went back to his master, reluctantly and slowly. When Dionysius saw him looking gloomy, he asked what was wrong.

---

34. I accept Cobet's supplement as improved by Jackson.
35. Multiple harbors were a common feature of Greek ports; Miletus had four.

"Sir, I've lost you a talent," he replied. "That will make you more careful in future. But what has happened? The woman you've just bought hasn't run away, has she?" "She hasn't, but the man who sold her to me has," said Leonas. "Then he must have stolen her. It's somebody else's slave he's sold you—that's why he did it in a lonely spot. Where did he say the girl was from?" "Sybaris, in Italy—he said her mistress sold her because she was jealous of her." "Find out if there are any Sybarites living here, and leave the woman where she is for the moment." So Leonas then went off very unhappy; his business deal had turned out unsuccessfully. He began to watch for a chance to persuade his master to visit his estate—the only hope Leonas had left was for him to see the woman.

As for Callirhoe, the countrywomen came to see her, and at once they 2 began to make up to her as if she were their mistress. The steward's wife, <u>Plangon,</u> quite an experienced creature, said to her: "My child, you're bound to miss your own people, of course; but you should think of people here as yours as well. Our master Dionysius, you know, is a good man, and kind. You're lucky the god has brought you to a good home; it will be like living in your own land. Come on, then, you've had a long journey. Wash off the dirt; you have servants." Callirhoe was reluctant, but Plangon finally managed to get her to the bath. They went in, rubbed her with oil, and wiped it off carefully; when she undressed, they were even more awestruck—indeed, although when she was clothed they admired her face as divinely beautiful, when they saw what her clothes covered, her face went quite out of their thoughts.[36] Her skin gleamed white, sparkling just like some shining substance; her flesh was so soft that you were afraid even the touch of a finger would cause a bad wound. The women murmured to one another, "Our mistress was beautiful, and celebrated for it; but she would have looked like this woman's servant." Callirhoe was distressed by their praise; it was ominous. When she had had her bath and they were arranging her hair, they brought her clean clothes. But Callirhoe said they were not suitable for a woman who had just been bought as a slave. "Give me a slave's tunic; why, *you* are superior to me!" So she put on ordinary clothes; but even they suited her well and looked expensive with her beauty shining on them. When the women had eaten, Plangon said: "Go to Aphrodite's shrine and pray. She appears in these parts, and not only the people round here but folk from town come and make sacrifice to her. She listens particularly to Dionysius's prayers; he never passes her shrine without stopping." Then they told her about the goddess's appearances. One of the countrywomen said, "Lady, when you look at Aphrodite, you'll think you're looking at a picture of yourself." When Callirhoe heard this, she burst into tears and

36. The received text is unacceptable; I hesitantly adopt Jackson's conjecture. The general sense is not in doubt.

said to herself, "This is disastrous! Even here it is the goddess Aphrodite who is the cause of all my troubles! But I will go; I have a lot I want to reproach her for."

The shrine was near Dionysius's house, just by the main road. Callirhoe kneeled in front of Aphrodite and embraced her feet. "You were the first to show Chaereas to me," she said. "You made a handsome couple of us, but you have not watched over us—and yet we paid you honor! But since that was your will, I ask one thing of you: grant that I attract no man after Chaereas." Aphrodite refused her prayer. After all, she is the mother of Eros, and she was now planning another marriage—which she did not intend to preserve either. Callirhoe, delivered from pirates and the sea, was regaining the beauty that was really hers; the peasants were awestruck to see her looking lovelier every day.

3 Leonas found a suitable opportunity to say to Dionysius: "Sir, you haven't been on your estate by the sea for a long time now. You're needed there. You have the herds and the crops to inspect, and it will soon be harvesttime. And we've built luxurious buildings as you told us to; you ought to enjoy them. Besides, you'll find your grief easier to bear in the country; you'll be distracted by having your estate to enjoy and run. And if you're pleased with some herdsman or shepherd, you can give him the woman I've just bought." Dionysius liked the suggestion and set a date for going. The order was passed along the line; coachmen got their coaches ready; grooms prepared their horses; boatmen their boats. Dionysius's friends were invited to join him on the journey, and so were a large number of freedmen—he was given to lavishness. When everything was ready, he gave instructions for the baggage and most of the people to go by sea and the vehicles to follow when he had gone ahead, because it was not proper for a man who was in mourning to have an elaborate escort. He mounted his horse at the crack of dawn, before most people realized he was leaving; he had four men with him, including Leonas.

Dionysius, then, was on his way to the country. That night Callirhoe had dreamed about Aphrodite, and decided to pay homage to her again. She was standing there praying when Dionysius dismounted and entered the shrine ahead of his companions. Callirhoe heard footsteps and turned to face him. So Dionysius saw her. "Aphrodite," he cried, "be gracious to me! May your appearance be propitious to me!" He was in the act of prostrating himself when Leonas caught him up and said: "Sir, this is the woman I bought—don't be alarmed. Woman, come to your master!" Well, when Callirhoe heard the word "master," she bowed her head and let loose a flood of tears—she was slow to forget her liberty. Dionysius struck Leonas. "Impious man!" he cried. "Do you speak to gods as if they were humans? Are you calling her a bought slave? No wonder you couldn't find the man who offered her for sale! Have you not heard what Homer tells us?

> And the gods,
> taking the shape of strangers from other lands,
> observe the insolence and the orderly behavior of mankind."[37]

At that Callirhoe replied: "Stop making fun of me! Stop calling me a goddess—I'm not even a happy mortal!" As she spoke, her voice seemed the voice of a god to Dionysius; it had a musical sound, with the effect of a lyre's note. He did not know what to do; he was too embarrassed to continue talking to her; so he went off to his house, already aflame with love. Soon the baggage arrived from town, and the rumor of the incident spread quickly, so they were all eager to see the woman—though they all pretended to be worshiping Aphrodite. Callirhoe was embarrassed by the crowd of people and did not know what to do; everything was strange to her; she could not see even the familiar Plangon, who was busy receiving her master. The hour grew late, and no one came to the house—they were all standing at the shrine as if bewitched. Leonas realized what had happened; he went to the sanctuary and brought Callirhoe out. Then you could see that royalty is born in people, as it is in a queen bee, because everybody followed Callirhoe spontaneously, as though she had been elected queen for her beauty.

So Callirhoe went off to her regular quarters. As for Dionysius, he was wounded; but he tried to cover up the wound, like the well-brought up man he was, who prided himself on behaving properly. Not wanting his servants to look down on him, or his friends to think him immature, he stuck it out the whole evening; he thought no one would notice, but in fact his silence made him all the more conspicuous. He took a portion of the meal and said, "Take this to the foreign woman; don't say it's from her master; say it's from Dionysius."

He prolonged the drinking after dinner as long as he could; he knew he would not be able to sleep, so he wanted his friends' company in his sleeplessness. The night was far advanced when he dismissed the company. He was too preoccupied to sleep. In thought he was in Aphrodite's shrine, recalling every detail: her face, her hair, the way she turned, the way she looked at him, her voice, her appearance, her words; her very tears inflamed him. There was a visible conflict in him now, between reason and passion; desire was flooding over him, but his noble soul tried to bear up against it; as if rising above the waves, he said to himself: "Dionysius, you ought to be ashamed of yourself! The most virtuous, the most distinguished man in Ionia, the admiration of satraps, kings,

4

37. Modified from *Odyssey* 17.485–87.

whole populations—and you behave like an adolescent! You fall in love at first sight—and while you're in mourning at that, before you've even paid proper respect to your poor wife's departed spirit! Is that what you've come into the country for—to marry in your mourning clothes? And to marry a *slave?* She may not even belong to you—you haven't even got the registration deed for her." This was good sense; but Eros, who took his restraint as an insult, set himself against Dionysius and fanned to greater heat the blaze in a heart that was trying to be rational about love. Unable to stand this solitary discussion any longer, Dionysius sent for Leonas. Leonas knew why he had been summoned, but pretended not to, and feigned alarm. "What's stopping you from sleeping, sir?" he asked. "It isn't fresh grief come over you at the death of your lady, is it?" "It is a lady, yes," said Dionysius, "but not the one who is dead. I have no secrets from you; you are well disposed and loyal to me. Leonas, I am finished, I tell you. You are the cause of my troubles. You brought fire into my house—or rather, into my own heart. And I am worried by the very mystery that surrounds the woman. You tell me a story about some trader you know nothing about[38]—who he is, where he came from, where he's gone off to. Would anyone who owned such a beautiful woman sell her in a deserted spot? And would he sell her for a talent? She's worth a king's fortune. Did some god mislead you?[39] Think, now—try to recall what happened. What men did you see? Whom did you talk to? Tell me the truth. You didn't see the boat." "I didn't see it, sir, but I heard about it." "There you are, you see! It is a nymph or Nereid who has come up from the sea. Even divine beings are at certain times caught in the grip of destiny and compelled to associate with human beings—poets and historians tell us that." Dionysius was only too ready to let himself build the woman up, to a stature too august for human associations. Leonas wanted to oblige his master. "Let's not insist on knowing who she is, sir," he said. "I'll bring her to you, if you like. Don't distress yourself about not getting what you want—you can satisfy your love." "I cannot do that," said Dionysius. "First, I must know who the woman is and where she comes from. So let us find out the truth from her tomorrow morning. I won't have her come here; I don't want to be suspected of violent intentions. No, our conversation shall take place where I first saw her—at Aphrodite's shrine."

5     That was what Dionysius decided, and the next day he arrived at the sanctuary with friends and freedmen and the most reliable of his servants, so as to have witnesses. He had dressed with some care, and even modestly adorned his person, seeing that he was going to meet the woman he loved; besides, he was naturally handsome and tall, and,

38. Adopting the reading ἔμπορόν τιν' ὄν, suggested by *POxy.* 2948.
39. Adopting the reading σέ τις of *POxy.* 2948.

above all, dignified in appearance. Leonas, accompanied by Plangon and Callirhoe's regular maids, went to Callirhoe. "Lady," he said, "Dionysius is a very just and law-abiding man; so go into the shrine and tell him truthfully who you really are; you can be sure of getting all the help you deserve. Just speak to him simply, and don't hide any of the truth; that will evoke his kindness to you all the more." Callirhoe was reluctant to go, but she felt safe because they were to meet in a shrine. When she got there, everybody admired her even more. Dionysius was struck dumb with wonder. He was silent for a long time, but finally found his voice. "Lady," he said, "you know all about me. I am Dionysius; I am the first man in Miletus, in fact practically in all Ionia; I am celebrated for my respect for the gods and my humanity. It is right and proper that you too should tell us the truth about yourself. The men who sold you said that you were from Sybaris and that your mistress was jealous of you and sold you away from there." Callirhoe blushed and bowed her head. "This is the first time," she said in a low voice, "that I have ever been sold. I have never seen Sybaris." Dionysius looked at Leonas. "I told you she wasn't a slave," he said, "and in fact I predict that she will turn out to be of noble birth. Tell me everything, lady; first, your name." "Callirhoe," she said—Dionysius liked her very name—and then she fell silent. Dionysius persisted in questioning her. "Sir," she said, "please do not make me talk about what has happened to me. What happened before is a dream, a fable. Now I am what I have come to be—a slave, and a foreigner." As she spoke, tears ran down her cheeks, though she tried to avoid attention. Dionysius too was moved to tears, and so were all those present; Aphrodite herself, you would have said, looked sadder. Dionysius continued questioning her even more insistently. "The first favor I ask of you, Callirhoe," he said, "is to tell me about yourself. You will not be talking to a stranger; people can be related by character as well. Don't be afraid, even if you have done something dreadful." This made Callirhoe angry. "Don't insult me!" she cried. "I have nothing to be ashamed of. But I am of higher rank than my present condition suggests, and I do not want people to think I am making unjustified claims; I do not want to tell a story that people who do not know the situation will not believe; my previous life says nothing about my present condition." Dionysius admired her spirit. "I understand already," he said, "even if you do not tell me. But tell us all the same; you can say nothing about yourself to compare to what we see. Impressive though your story be, nothing you can tell us will measure up to you." So, reluctantly, Callirhoe began to tell her story. "I am the daughter of Hermocrates, the Syracusan general. I had a sudden fall, and lost consciousness; and my parents gave me a costly funeral. Tomb robbers opened my tomb; they found me conscious again and brought me to this place, and Theron gave me to Leonas here in a deserted spot." She told them everything else but said nothing about Chaereas. "Dionysius, you are Greek, you live in a humane community, you are a civilized man—please don't be like the tomb robbers; don't take my country and my family away from me. You are a rich man; it is a trivial matter to you to let a human being go; you will not lose what you paid for me if you give me back to my father—Hermocrates is not an ungrateful man. You know how we admire Alcinous;[40] we all love him for sending his suppliant back home; well, I am your suppliant. I am a prisoner; I have lost my parents; rescue me! And if I cannot live as a woman of birth, I prefer to die free!" As he listened to her words, Dionysius began to weep, ostensibly for Callirhoe, but in fact for himself; he realized that he was not getting what he wanted. "Have courage, Callirhoe," he said. "Be of good heart. You shall not fail to get what you ask for—I take Aphrodite here to witness. Meanwhile, in my house you shall be attended like a mistress, not a slave."

6    Callirhoe went away, convinced that nothing could happen to her that she did not want to happen. Dionysius went sadly to his own house and sent for Leonas privately. "Nothing goes right for me," he said. "Eros hates me. I have buried my wife, and our new slave shuns me. I was hoping she was Aphrodite's gift to me and was painting for myself a life happier than that of Menelaus, Spartan Helen's husband—even Helen, I imagine, was not as beautiful as she is. And she is persuasive, too. My life is finished! The day Callirhoe leaves here, I shall die!" At that Leonas cried out: "Sir, don't *you* curse yourself! You're her master, you can make her do what you want whether she likes it or not—I bought her; I paid a talent for her!" "You bought her! A girl of noble birth! You miserable villain! Have you never heard of Hermocrates? He is the leader of the whole of Sicily, a man with a most distinguished record; why, the King of Persia admires him, loves him, sends him presents every year for destroying the fleet of Persia's enemy, Athens! Am I to lord it over a freeborn person? Am I, Dionysius, celebrated for my moderation, to force myself on an unwilling woman? Even the pirate Theron would not have forced himself on her!"

That was how he spoke to Leonas, but for all that he did not give up hope of winning Callirhoe over; Love is naturally optimistic, and he was confident that by attention to her he could achieve his desires. So he sent for Plangon. "You have already demonstrated your concern for me," he said. "Now I am entrusting to you the greatest and most precious of my possessions, the foreign woman. I want her to lack for nothing, I want her to have luxury. Consider her your mistress; serve her, treat her with

40. The king of Phaeacia who offered hospitality to the shipwrecked Odysseus in *Odyssey* 6–9.

respect, and make her well disposed to me. Praise me often to her; tell her about me as you know me—and be careful not to call me her 'master.'" Plangon was a quick-witted creature and understood what he was asking her to do. Unobtrusively she turned her mind to the job and set about it rapidly. She sought out Callirhoe's company but did not tell her that she had been told to serve her. Rather, she made it seem as if she felt personal sympathy for her; she wanted to be credible as an adviser.

Here is what happened. Dionysius continued to stay on his estate. He found various excuses, but the truth was that he was neither able to separate himself from Callirhoe nor willing to take her back with him, because when people saw her, they would all talk about her, her beauty would enslave the whole of Ionia, and report of her would reach the Great King himself. While living there he examined the affairs of the estate in detail; and he had occasion to criticize the work of his steward Phocas. His criticism did not go beyond words, but Plangon saw her chance. She ran to Callirhoe with an air of panic, tearing her hair, and grasped her knees. "My lady," she cried, "please save us! Dionysius is angry with my husband, and he's just as severe a man, when he's angry, as he is kind. You're the only person who can save us—Dionysius will gladly grant you the first favor you've asked for." Now Callirhoe was reluctant to go to him, but when Plangon begged and pleaded with her, she could not refuse, because she was under obligation to her for her services. So as not to appear ungrateful, then, she said, "I am a slave too, you know, and have no right to speak; but if you think *my* voice will carry any weight, I will add my appeal to yours—I hope we succeed!" When they arrived, Plangon told the doorkeeper to tell his master that Callirhoe was there. At that moment Dionysius was prostrate with grief; his very body had wasted. When he heard that Callirhoe was there, he felt faint, and a mist came over him at the unexpected news. He managed to recover. "Tell her to come in," he said. Callirhoe came and stood by him, her head bowed. At first she blushed deeply; then she managed to find her voice. "I am grateful to Plangon here," she said. "She loves me like a daughter. Master, I ask you not to be angry with her husband; let him off as a favor to me." She tried to say more but was unable to. Dionysius saw what Plangon's scheme was. "Yes, I am angry," he said, "and no one would have saved Phocas and Plangon from death for what they have done. But I gladly spare them as a favor to you. You two must realize that it is to Callirhoe you owe your lives." Plangon fell at his feet. "It is Callirhoe's feet you should fall at," said Dionysius. "She is the one who has saved you." Plangon saw that Callirhoe was pleased and delighted by the favor. "You must thank Dionysius for us, then," she said, and pushed her forward. Callirhoe stumbled a little and clutched at Dionysius's right hand. As if declining to give her his hand, he drew her to him, and he kissed her; then he let go of her immediately so that she would not suspect he had done it deliberately.

8    Well, the women went off, but the kiss penetrated Dionysius's heart like poison. He could not see; he could not hear. He had been taken by storm, heart and soul. He could find no remedy for his passion: gifts would not serve, for he could see that she was proud, nor threats of force, for he was convinced she would prefer death to violence. His one resource was Plangon, he thought, so he sent for her. "You have begun the campaign," he said, "and I thank you for the kiss. But it has either saved me or ruined me. So try to overcome her, as woman with woman; you have me on your side. I will tell you that the prize awaiting you is your freedom—and something much sweeter to you than freedom, I am sure: Dionysius's life." With this instruction before her, Plangon brought all her experience and skill to bear. But on all sides Callirhoe proved invincible; she stayed true to Chaereas alone. Fortune outwitted her, though; Fortune, against whom alone human calculation has no power. For Fortune relishes victory, and anything may be expected of her. So now she brought about an unexpected, indeed incredible, state of things. How she did it is worth hearing.

Fortune laid her plot against Callirhoe's loyalty to her husband. After Chaereas and Callirhoe were married, their first contact was passionate; they had an equal impulse to enjoy each other, and matching desire had made their union fruitful. So just before her fall Callirhoe became pregnant; but thanks to the subsequent dangers and hardships she did not realize her condition straightaway. But at the beginning of the third month her belly began to grow big. Plangon, with her woman's experience, noticed it in the bath. At the time she said nothing, since there were a lot of servant women there. But in the evening, when she got the chance, she sat beside Callirhoe on the couch and said, "You should know you are pregnant, my child." Callirhoe cried aloud, groaned, and tore her hair: "Fortune, you have added this as well to my misfortunes, that I should become a mother too—mother of a slave!" She struck her belly. "Poor creature!" she cried. "Even before birth you have been buried and handed over to pirates! What sort of life are you coming to? With what hopes shall I give birth to you—without father or country, a slave! Taste death—before you are born!" Plangon restrained her hands, with a promise that the next day she would find her an easier way to procure a miscarriage.

9    Left alone, each of the women followed her own line of reasoning. Plangon thought, "Here is the chance to satisfy your master's passion. Callirhoe's condition will help your cause. You have found a sure way of convincing her: her maternal instincts will be stronger than her loyalty to her husband." And she planned a convincing course of action. Callirhoe,

however, planned to destroy the child. "Am I," she said to herself, "to bring Hermocrates' descendant into the world to serve a master? Am I to bear a child whose father no one knows? Perhaps some envious person will say, 'Callirhoe became pregnant among the pirates!' It is enough for me alone to suffer misfortune. It is not in your interest to come into a life of misery, my child—a life you should escape from even if you are born. Depart in freedom, while no harm has befallen you, without hearing what they say about your mother!" And then again she changed her mind, and pity came over her for her unborn child. "Are you planning to kill your child? Was ever woman so wicked! Are you mad?[41] Are you reasoning like Medea? Why, people will think you yet more savage than that Scythian woman! She at any rate did hate her husband—but you want to kill Chaereas's child and not even leave behind any memorial of that celebrated marriage! What if it is a son? What if he is like his father? What if he is luckier than me? He has escaped from the tomb, from pirates—shall his mother kill him? How many stories are there of sons of gods and kings born in slavery, then coming into their rightful ancestral rank—Zethus, Amphion, Cyrus?[42] You too, my child—you will sail to Sicily, I am sure! You will go and find your father and your grandfather and tell them your mother's story! A fleet will sail from Sicily to rescue me! O my child, you will restore your parents to each other!" All night long she pursued these thoughts; and as she did so, sleep stole over her momentarily, and a vision of Chaereas stood over her, like him in every way,

> like to him in stature and fair looks and voice, and wearing just
> such clothes.[43]

As he stood there, he said, "I entrust our son to you, my wife." He wanted to say yet more, but Callirhoe jumped up and tried to embrace him. So on her husband's advice, as she thought, she decided to rear her child.

---

41. I adopt Jackson's conjecture. In the following lines the reference is to Euripides' famous play *Medea*, in which the heroine, who had become Jason's wife after helping him get the Golden Fleece, is abandoned by him for another woman; Medea kills not only her rival but also her own two children by Jason, to get her revenge on him. She is described here as Scythian—inaccurately, since she was from Colchis, on the east coast of the Black Sea. This is done to emphasize her savagery, since Scythia (southern Russia) was a byword for a land of savage barbarians; it was geographically close enough to Colchis for Chariton's rhetorical purpose here.

42. Zethus and Amphion, twin sons by Zeus of Antiope of Thebes, are a mythological instance of the point Callirhoe is making; exposed at birth by Antiope's family, they were saved from death and later came into their own rights as rulers of Thebes. Cyrus the Great of Persia is a historical example of a similar sequence of events.

43. *Iliad* 23.66–67.

10    The next day, when Plangon came, Callirhoe told her what she intended to do. Plangon did not fail to point out how ill judged her proposal was. "My lady," she said, "you cannot bring up a child in our house. Our master loves you; now, he will not force himself on you—he has more self-respect and self-control than that—but he will be too jealous to let you bring up a child. He will take it as an insult that you should think so much of a man who is not here and disregard himself, when he *is* here. So I think it would be better for the child to die before it is born, rather than after; that will save you pointless labor pains and a futile pregnancy. I am giving you honest advice because I love you." Callirhoe was distressed at what she said; she fell at Plangon's feet and begged her to help her think of some way she could bring up her child. But Plangon refused repeatedly and put off answering her for two or three days. When she had inflamed Callirhoe to more impassioned entreaties, and so acquired more authority over her, first she made her swear not to reveal her stratagem to anyone; then, knitting her brow and wringing her hands, she said: "My lady, big enterprises can only be brought off by big ideas. Out of sympathy for you I am going to betray my master. Now one of two things must happen: either your child dies one way or another, or he is born the wealthiest person in Ionia, the heir of its most illustrious family—and he will make you, his mother, happy. Which is it to be? Choose!" "Who would be foolish enough," said Callirhoe, "to choose death for her child rather than good fortune for herself? I cannot believe that what you are suggesting is possible—tell me more clearly what you mean." Plangon responded with a question. "How long do you think you have been pregnant?" "Two months," said Callirhoe. "Time is on our side, then. You can make it look as if it were Dionysius's child, born at seven months." Callirhoe cried out in protest, "Better for it to die!" Plangon pretended to agree with her. "You are quite right, my dear," she said "to prefer an abortion. Let's do that—it's less dangerous than trying to deceive the master. Remove all trace of your noble birth; give up hope of returning home. Adapt yourself to the condition you are in—really become a slave." Plangon's advice aroused no suspicion in Callirhoe; she was a young lady of quality and knew nothing of slaves' tricks. But the more Plangon urged abortion on her, the more pity Callirhoe felt for her unborn child. "Give me time to think," she said. "The choice is capital—my chastity or my child!" And this too Plangon approved—not deciding hastily, one way or the other. "There are good reasons for coming down either way: a wife's loyalty on one side, a mother's love on the other. All the same, there isn't time to put off the decision long. You absolutely must choose tomorrow, before it becomes known that you are pregnant." They agreed on this and separated.

Callirhoe went up to her room and shut the door. She held Chaereas's 11
picture to her womb. "Here are the three of us," she said, "husband,
wife, and child; let us decide what is best for us all. I shall give my view
first: I want to die Chaereas's wife and his alone. To know no other husband—that is dearer to me than parents or country or child. And you,
my child—what is your choice for yourself? To die by poison before seeing the light of day? To be cast out with your mother, and perhaps not
even thought worthy of burial? Or to live, and have two fathers—one
the first man in Sicily, the other in Ionia? When you grow up, you will
easily be recognized by your family—I am sure I shall bring you into the
world in the likeness of your father; and you will sail home in triumph,
in a Milesian warship, and Hermocrates will welcome a grandson already
fit for command. Your vote is cast against mine, my child; you will not
sanction our death. Let us ask your father too. No, he has spoken; he
came to me in person in my dreams and said, 'I entrust our son to you.'
I call you to witness, Chaereas—it is you who are giving me to Dionysius as his bride." And so she spent that day and night reasoning to herself like this; and she let herself be persuaded to live, not for herself, but
for her child. The next day, when Plangon came, at first she sat there
looking sad, with sympathy in her countenance; and neither spoke. After
a long time Plangon asked: "What have you decided? What are we going
to do? We cannot put off decision." Callirhoe, weeping in her distress,
could not answer immediately; but at last she managed to say: "The child
is betraying me; it is not what I want. You do what is best. But I am
afraid that even if I put up with his lust, Dionysius will treat me con-
temptuously, in my misfortune; he may treat me as a concubine rather
than as his wife and refuse to bring up another man's child; and I shall
lose my honor for nothing." Plangon replied even before she had
finished. "I have thought about this, before you did," she said, "because
by now I love you better than my master. Now, I have confidence in
Dionysius's character—he is a good man. All the same, I shall make him
swear an oath, master though he is; we must act with complete security.
And when he has sworn, you must trust him, my child. I am going, to
carry out my mission."

## Book Three

Dionysius could no longer suffer his failure to win Callirhoe's love. He 1
had determined to starve to death and was writing his last will and testament, with instructions for his burial; in it he begged Callirhoe to come
to him at least in death. Plangon wanted to go in to her master but was
prevented from doing so by his attendant, who had orders to let no one
in. Dionysius heard them squabbling at the door and asked who was

causing the trouble. The attendant said it was Plangon. "It is the wrong moment for her to come," he said (by now he did not even want to see anything that would remind him of his passion). "Still, tell her to come in." Plangon opened the door. "Why are you wearing yourself out with grief, sir," she said, "as though your cause were lost? Callirhoe invites you to marry her! Put on fine clothes, offer sacrifice, welcome the bride you love!" At this unexpected news Dionysius was thunderstruck. Mist covered his eyes; he went limp all over and presented a deathlike figure. Plangon began to wail; this brought everyone running to the spot, and the master was mourned as dead throughout the whole house. Even Callirhoe could not hold back her tears when she heard this; so great was the grief that even she wept for Dionysius as for her husband.[44] At last, and with difficulty, Dionysius regained consciousness. In a weak voice he said: "What spirit is deceiving me and trying to turn me back from the path that lies before me? Was I waking or dreaming when I heard those words? Is Callirhoe willing to marry me? Callirhoe, who is unwilling even to show herself?" Plangon, standing beside him, said: "Stop causing yourself unnecessary pain and disbelieving your own good fortune. I am not deceiving my master; Callirhoe sent me to talk to you about marriage." "Talk about it then," said Dionysius, "and tell me her actual words; do not omit or add anything; report exactly what she said." "She said, 'I belong to the first family in Sicily; I have suffered misfortune, but I still have my pride. I have been deprived of my country and my parents; the only thing I have not lost is my nobility. So if Dionysius wants to have me as his concubine, if he wants to enjoy the satisfaction of his own desires, I will hang myself rather than give my body up to outrage fit for a slave. But if he wants me as his legal wife, then I too want to be a mother, so that Hermocrates' line will be continued. Dionysius should reflect on this; not by himself and in haste, but together with his friends and family, so that no one will say to him afterwards "Are you going to bring up children born of that bought slave woman? Are you going to bring shame on your house?" If he does not want to be a father, he shall not be my husband either!'" These words inflamed Dionysius all the more, and he conceived some faint hope that suggested to him his love was returned. He raised his arms to heaven and said: "Zeus and Helius![45] Only let me see a child born to Callirhoe! Then I shall think myself happier than the Great King! Let us go to her—take me, my loyal Plangon!"

2    He ran upstairs. His first impulse was to fall at Callirhoe's feet, but he restrained himself and sat down in a dignified manner. "My lady," he said, "I have come to thank you for saving me; I would not have forced myself on you, and I had made up my mind to die if you refused me.

44. The text and sense of this sentence are uncertain.
45. The sun-god, to whom one prayed for children and personal prosperity in general.

Thanks to you I have been restored to life. But although I am deeply grateful to you, I do have a reproach to make: you did not believe that I would take you as my lawful wife, 'for the procreation of children, according to Greek law.'[46] If I did not love you, I should not have begged you to marry me on those terms. You seem to think I am out of my mind—to imagine that a woman of noble birth is a slave, that a descendant of Hermocrates would not be fit to be my son! 'Reflect,' you say. I have reflected. Are you afraid of my friends—you, who are the dearest friend of all? Who will dare to call a son of mine unworthy—with a grandfather greater than his father?" As he spoke, he approached her, with tears in his eyes. Callirhoe blushed, and kissed him gently. "I trust you, Dionysius," she said. "It is my own fortune I do not trust. It has brought me low before now, from greater fortune; I am afraid it has not yet settled its quarrel with me. So although you are a good and just man, invoke the gods as witnesses; not because of yourself, but because of your fellow citizens and family, so that people will know you have taken your oath, and so be prevented from mounting some yet more malicious plot against me. A woman, all alone and a foreigner, is easy prey for contemptuous treatment." "What sort of oaths do you want me to swear before the gods?" he said. "I am prepared to climb up to heaven, if it can be done, and lay my hand on Zeus himself." "Swear," she said, "by the sea that brought me to you and by Aphrodite who showed me to you and by Eros who is making me your bride." He agreed, and it was done at once.

Dionysius's passion raged fiercely and would not suffer the wedding to be delayed; self-control is painful when desire can be satisfied. He was a civilized man; he had been overwhelmed by a storm—his heart was submerged, but still he forced himself to hold his head above the towering waves of his passion. And so, at that time, he entered on the following line of reasoning. "Am I to marry her in a deserted spot, as though she were really a bought slave? I am not so ungracious as to fail to celebrate my marriage to Callirhoe. This is the first thing in which I must show respect for my wife. Besides, it provides security for the future. Rumor is the swiftest thing there is; Rumor travels through the air, and nothing bars its path; it uncovers any hidden surprise. Even now, Rumor is rushing to carry to Sicily the strange news that Callirhoe is alive—tomb robbers opened her tomb and carried her off, and she has been sold in Miletus! Syracusan warships will soon be descending on us with Hermocrates in command, demanding his daughter's restoration. What am I to say? 'Theron has sold her to me.' 'Theron? Where is he?' Even if they believe me, am I to tell them the truth—that I receive stolen goods from

46. A standard formula (similar to those in Christian wedding ceremonies); in its form here the phrase appears to be a quotation from a comedy.

a pirate? Practice your defense, Dionysius; you may have to plead it before the Great King. If you do, it would be best to say, 'I heard somehow that a freeborn woman was living here; she was willing to marry, and I married her in town, publicly, according to the laws.' That is the best way to convince people—even my wife's father—that I am not unworthy of my marriage. Endure a brief delay, my heart, to enjoy a secure pleasure for a longer time. In the trial my case will be stronger if I have a husband's position, not a master's."

That is what he decided to do. He called Leonas and said: "Go off to town and prepare things for the wedding in style. Have herds of cattle driven in, and grain and wine brought by land and sea. I have decided to give a public feast for the town." He gave careful instructions, and the next day he himself left, traveling in a carriage. As for Callirhoe, he did not want her to appear in public yet, and he had her taken by boat in the evening right to his house, which was by the harbor called Docimus; he put her in the care of Plangon. When she was on the point of leaving the estate, Callirhoe first offered a prayer to Aphrodite. She went into her temple, got everyone to leave, and said to her: "Lady Aphrodite, ought I to reproach you or be grateful to you? You joined me to Chaereas when I was a maiden; now you are marrying me to another man after him. I should never have agreed to swear by you and your son, if this child"—she pointed to her womb—"had not betrayed me. For his sake," she said, "not for mine, I implore you to keep my deceit a secret. Since my child does not have his real father, let him pass as Dionysius's son. When he has grown up, he will find his real father as well." As they saw her going from the temple precinct to the sea, the boatmen were awestruck, as though Aphrodite herself were coming to embark, and as one man they made to worship her.

The rowers rowed with such enthusiasm that the ship reached harbor more quickly than words can tell. At daybreak the whole town was already decorated with garlands of flowers. Every man offered sacrifice in front of his own house, and not just in the temples. People were talking about who the bride was. Because she was so beautiful and unknown, the common crowd were convinced that a Nereid had come up out of the sea or that a goddess had appeared from Dionysius's estate; those were the rumors spread by the sailors. All had but one desire—to see Callirhoe; and the crowd gathered round the temple of Concord,[47] where by tradition bridegrooms received their brides. Now, for the first time since she had been in her tomb, Callirhoe dressed up to look her best; for once she had decided to marry, she considered that her beauty consti-

---

47. Concord—*homonoia*, "social harmony"—was personified as an institution, in an attempt to allay the social discord endemic in Hellenistic cities.

tuted her country and lineage. She put on a Milesian dress[48] and bridal wreath and faced the crowd; they all cried, "The bride is Aphrodite!" They spread purple cloth and scattered roses and violets in her path; they sprinkled her with perfume as she passed; not a child nor an old man remained in the houses, or even at the harbors;[49] the crowd packed tight, and people even climbed on the roofs of houses. But once more, even on that day, the evil spirit vented his spite. How he did so I shall tell you shortly; first, I want to relate what happened in Syracuse during the same time.

That was as follows. The tomb robbers had been careless in closing the tomb—it was at night, and they were in a hurry. At the crack of dawn Chaereas turned up at the tomb, ostensibly to offer wreaths and libations, but in fact with the intention of doing away with himself; he could not bear being separated from Callirhoe and thought that death was the only thing that would cure his grief. When he reached the tomb, he found that the stones had been moved and the entrance was open. He was astonished at the sight and overcome by fearful perplexity at what had happened. Rumor—a swift messenger—told the Syracusans this amazing news. They all quickly crowded round the tomb, but no one dared go inside until Hermocrates gave an order to do so. The man who was sent in reported the whole situation accurately. It seemed incredible that even the corpse was not lying there. Then Chaereas himself determined to go in, in his desire to see Callirhoe again even dead; but though he hunted through the tomb, he could find nothing. Many people could not believe it and went in after him. They were all seized by helplessness. One of those standing there said, "The funeral offerings have been carried off—it is tomb robbers who have done that; but what about the corpse—where is it?" Many different suggestions circulated in the crowd. Chaereas looked towards the heavens, stretched up his arms, and cried: "Which of the gods is it, then, who has become my rival in love and carried off Callirhoe and is now keeping her with him—against her will, constrained by a more powerful destiny? That is why she died suddenly—so that she would not realize what was happening.[50] That is how Dionysus took Ariadne from Theseus, how Zeus took Semele.[51] It looks as if I had a goddess for a wife without knowing it, someone above my

3

---

48. Miletus was famous for its wool; Milesian clothes were of high quality and a symbol of wealth and luxury.

49. Harbors would normally be under constant guard.

50. The text is doubtful here.

51. Ariadne: a somewhat different version of the myth from that set out in note 18 above. Semele: again, apparently not the standard legend, according to which Zeus, Semele's lover, manifested himself to her in the form of a thunderbolt, thus killing her. Both Ariadne and Semele were transformed into divinities, which is the point of Chaereas's next remark.

station. But she should not have left the world so quickly, even for such a reason. Thetis was a goddess, but she stayed with Peleus, and he had a son by her; I have been abandoned at the very height of my love. What is to happen to me? What is to become of me, poor wretch? Should I do away with myself? And who would share my grave? I did have this much to look forward to, in my misfortune—that if I could not continue to share Callirhoe's bed, I should come to share her grave. My lady! I offer my justification for living—you force me to live, because I shall look for you on land and sea, and in the very sky if I can reach there! This I beg of you, my dear—do not flee from me!" At this the crowd broke out in lamentation; everyone began to lament for Callirhoe as though she had just died.

Triremes were launched at once, and many men shared the search. For Sicily, Hermocrates himself conducted the investigation; Chaereas took North Africa. Some were sent to Italy; others were instructed to cross the Ionian Sea.[52] Well, human efforts were altogether ineffectual; it was Fortune who brought the truth to light—Fortune, without whom nothing ever comes to completion, as one can see from what happened. The tomb robbers left Miletus when they had sold the woman—a hard cargo to dispose of—and headed for Crete; they were told that it was a prosperous and large island and hoped they would be able to find buyers for their cargo without difficulty. But a strong wind caught them and drove them into the Ionian Sea, where they then wandered in unfrequented waters. The villains were caught in thunder and lightning and lasting darkness—Providence was demonstrating that it was Callirhoe who had brought them fair sailing before. Each time they came close to death the god would not accord them quick release from their fear, but made their shipwreck drag out. Dry land would not accept the villains, and as they rode at sea for a long time, they came to lack the necessities of life, especially water. Their ill-gotten wealth availed them nothing; amid gold, they were dying of thirst. Slowly they came to repent of their reckless behavior and reproach one another, saying that it had brought them no profit. Now, the rest were all dying of thirst, but Theron proved a rogue even in that crisis: he contrived to steal some of the water, thieving from his fellow thieves. He thought he had done something clever, of course; but the fact was that it was Providence's doing—she was keeping him for torture and crucifixion. What happened was that Chaereas's ship came

52. It was the usual practice not to sail across open seas in winter. The fact that the Syracusans do just that here is shown to be exceptional by their having to *launch* their ships from their winter storage. It is an indication of the emotions of this moment in the story; Chariton is striving for effect. Later (3.5) he milks the same theme for the same purpose. (Cf. 8.6.) The Ionian Sea is the open stretch between Sicily and the Peloponnese (it has no connection with the region of Asia Minor known as Ionia); the normal route followed the coast of Southern Italy and crossed the Adriatic from Brindisi.

upon the pirates' cutter as it was wandering about erratically, and at first steered away, thinking it was a pirate craft. But when it became clear that it had no pilot and was drifting aimlessly, as the waves drove against it, one of the trireme's crew cried, "There isn't anyone on board! No need to be frightened—let's pull alongside and find out what the mystery is!" The helmsman agreed (Chaereas was in the body of the ship weeping, his head covered up). When they drew alongside, at first they hailed the crew. When no one answered, a man from the trireme boarded the ship; but all he saw was gold and dead bodies. He told his fellows, who were delighted; they thought themselves lucky, finding a fortune at sea. This caused a commotion, and Chaereas asked what the matter was; when he was told, he wanted to see this strange sight for himself. When he recognized the funeral offerings, he tore his clothes and uttered a loud, piercing cry: "Ah, Callirhoe! These are yours! This is the wreath I put on your head! Your father gave you this, your mother this; this is your bridal dress! The ship has turned into your tomb! But—I can see your things, but where are you? The tomb's contents are all there—except the body!" Theron heard this and lay there like the dead—in fact he was half-dead. He fully intended not to utter a sound or move a muscle, since he was well aware what would happen. But human beings are born with a love of life; not even in the worst disaster do we despair of a change for the better—the god who made the world has implanted this specious notion in all of us, so that we will not run away from a life of misery. So Theron, in the grip of thirst, first uttered, "Drink!" When he had been given something to drink and had received every attention, Chaereas sat down beside him and asked him: "Who are you men? Where are you sailing to? Where did you get these things? What have you done with the woman they belong to?" Theron summoned all his unscrupulous cunning. "I am a Cretan," he said, "and I am sailing to Ionia to look for my brother, who is a soldier. I was left behind by the ship's crew in Cephallenia, when they left there in a hurry, and joined this ship, which called in there, conveniently for me. But we were driven out into these waters by violent winds. Then we were becalmed for a long time, and everyone died of thirst except me—I survived because of my piety." When Chaereas heard this, he gave orders for the trireme to take the cutter in tow, until they reached harbor in Syracuse.

Rumor reached home before them; she is naturally swift, and on that occasion she was all the more eager to report these many strange marvels. So everyone hurried to collect by the shore, and the crowd, thunderstruck by the strange tale, displayed various emotions all at once—tears, astonishment, inquiring interest, disbelief. When Callirhoe's mother saw her daughter's funeral offerings, she cried out in distress: "I recognize everything—only you are missing, my child! Strange tomb robbers—they have preserved the clothing and gold, and stolen only my daughter!" Shores and harbors resounded as the women beat their breasts and filled land and sea with lamentation. But Hermocrates, a man of experience and used to authority, said: "This is not the place to examine the situation; we should pursue our inquiry more in accordance with law. Let us go to the assembly—who knows, we might actually need a jury."

"Before he had finished speaking,"[53] the theater was already packed. This assembly included women as well.[54] The people were sitting there, greatly agitated, when Chaereas came in first, dressed in black, pale, unwashed, looking as he did when he followed his wife to her tomb. He refused to go up onto the platform, but stood below it. At first he wept for a long time; he tried to speak but could not. The crowd shouted, "Take heart! Speak!" With a struggle he raised his head. "This is a moment for grief, not for an oration," he said. "I am compelled to speak by the same need that makes me live until I find out why Callirhoe has disappeared. That is why I sailed from here; I do not know whether to call my voyage successful or not. I saw a ship drifting in fair weather, weighed down with its own private storm, sinking in calm seas. We were surprised at this and approached it. I thought I was looking at my poor wife's tomb, with everything that belonged to her in it except herself. Dead bodies there were, many of them; but all were other people's bodies. This fellow, whoever he is, we found among them, half-dead. I gave him every care, restored him to life, and kept him for you."

Meanwhile public slaves brought Theron into the theater in chains. He had an escort that befitted him: that is, he was followed by the wheel, the rack,[55] fire, and whips—Providence was according him the proper prize for his efforts. When he had taken his position in the middle of the assembly, one of the magistrates asked him, "Who are you?" "Demetrius," he replied. "Where are you from?" "I am a Cretan." "Tell us what you know." "I was sailing to my brother in Ionia when I was left behind by my ship. I joined a cutter that was passing that way. At the time I thought they were merchants, but now I realize they were tomb robbers. We were at sea for a long time, and all the others died for lack of water; I have just managed to survive, because I have never done anything wicked in my life. Syracusans, you are a people celebrated for your humanity—do not be more cruel to me than thirst and the sea!"

53. A Homeric formula (e.g., *Iliad* 10.540) also used elsewhere by Chariton.
54. A gross anachronism; at the dramatic date of this story women took no part in politics, although they appear to have done so in Chariton's own times. But here as elsewhere the author is aiming at emotional effect—this was an exceptional meeting!
55. The word here translated "rack" is strictly "catapult," a term normally used of a military engine; this use has not been explained, but presumably the machine was used to stretch a victim.

When he said this, in pathetic tones, the crowd were touched with pity; and perhaps he would have convinced them, even to the point of being given money to take him home, had not some divinity, to avenge Callirhoe, felt indignant that he should be believed so unjustly. For it would have been the most outrageous thing possible for the Syracusans to believe that he alone had been saved because of his piety, when it was his impiety that saved him alone—but it saved him for worse punishment. Thus, a fisherman in the crowd recognized him and said quietly to the people sitting by him, "I've seen this man before, wandering about our harbor." His words were quickly passed on to more people, and someone cried out, "He's lying!" So the whole crowd turned towards him, and the magistrates ordered the man who had spoken first to come down. When Theron denied the accusation, the fisherman was more readily believed. At once they called for the torturers, and the impious rogue was whipped. He had fire applied to him; his flesh was torn; but he held out for a long time and almost overcame the torture. But conscience is a strong force in every one of us, and truth is all-powerful; with reluctance, and slowly, Theron confessed. He began his story. "I saw riches being enclosed in the tomb and assembled a gang of robbers. We opened the tomb and found the corpse alive. We carried everything away and put it in our cutter. We sailed to Miletus, sold the woman alone, and then started to take everything else to Crete; but we were driven out into the Ionian Sea by winds, and you have seen what happened to us." He told the whole story but failed to mention one thing—the name of the man who had bought Callirhoe.

At these words joy and grief came over everyone—joy that Callirhoe was alive, grief that she had been sold. Theron was condemned to death, but Chaereas begged that he should not be executed yet, "so that he can come and show me who bought her," he said. "Consider what I am compelled to do—plead for the man who sold my wife." Hermocrates would not allow this. "It is better," he said, "to make our search more laborious than allow the law to be broken. Syracusans, I ask you to recall my service as your general and my victories, and pay me back by saving my daughter. Send an embassy for her; she is a freeborn woman—let us recover her." While he was still speaking, the assembly cried out, "Let us all sail!" and most of the members of the council rose to volunteer their help. "I thank you all," said Hermocrates, "for the honor you have shown me; but two ambassadors from the assembly and two from the council are enough; and Chaereas will sail with the group as leader."

This was agreed and ratified, and thereupon he dismissed the assembly. As Theron was led away, a great part of the crowd followed. He was crucified in front of Callirhoe's tomb, and from his cross he looked out on that sea over which he had carried as a captive the daughter of Hermocrates, whom even the Athenians had not taken.

5     Now, everybody else thought they should wait for the sailing season and put to sea at the first gleam of spring, because at the time it was still winter, and it seemed quite impossible to cross the Ionian Sea. But Chaereas was eager to go—his love was such that he was quite prepared to knock a raft together, launch out onto the sea, and let the winds carry him where they would; so the ambassadors too were reluctant to put things off, out of embarrassment with regard to him and especially Hermocrates, and got ready to sail. The Syracusans made it an official expedition, to give the embassy additional prestige; so they launched the famous flagship, which was still flying the standards of the victory. On the appointed day of departure the people all hurried to the harbor, not just men, but women and children too; and prayers were joined with tears, groans of despair, words of consolation, fear, confidence, despair, hope. Chaereas's father, Ariston, who was in the grip of extreme old age and disease, flung his arms round his son's neck and clung to him, weeping. "My child," he said, "to whom are you abandoning me? I am old, and half-dead already; I shall clearly never see you again. Wait just a few days so that I can die in your arms; then bury me and leave." His mother grasped his knees. "I beg you, my child," she said, "do not leave me here all by myself! Take me on board your ship—I shall be a light cargo; if I am heavy and too much for you to carry, throw me into the sea you are sailing on!" As she spoke, she tore at the front of her dress and thrust forward her breasts. "My child!" she cried.

"Respect these breasts and pity me, if ever I offered you my breast
to calm your sorrows."[56]

Chaereas broke down at his parents' appeals and threw himself from the ship into the sea; he wanted to die, so as not to have to choose between abandoning the search for Callirhoe and causing grief to his parents. The sailors quickly leapt overboard and just managed to bring him out of the water. Then Hermocrates told the crowd to disperse and ordered the pilot to set sail finally. Another noble act of friendship took place too. Chaereas's friend Polycharmus was not to be seen among them at the time. He had actually said to his parents, "Chaereas is my friend, my dear friend—but not so dear that I will risk my life with him, so I shall stay out of the way until he sails." But when the ship had cast off, it was from her stern that he said farewell to his parents, so that by then they could not hold him back.

56. *Iliad* 22.82–83 (Hecuba begging Hector not to meet Achilles in battle).

As he left harbor, Chaereas looked towards the open water. "Sea!" he cried. "Take me over the same route as you took Callirhoe! Poseidon! Grant, I beg you, that either she return with us or I too not come back, without her! If I cannot recover my wife, I want to be with her even as a slave!"

A following wind caught the trireme, and it ran as if in the tracks of the cutter; they reached Ionia in the same number of days and moored at the same beach on Dionysius's estate. The rest of the ship's company, after landing exhausted, hurried to see to their own well-being, pitching tents and getting a meal ready; but Chaereas, walking about with Polycharmus, said: "How can we find Callirhoe now? I am very much afraid that Theron lied to us, and the poor girl is dead. Then again, even if she really has been sold, who knows where? Asia is big." In their wandering they happened upon the temple of Aphrodite, so they decided to offer worship to the goddess. Chaereas threw himself at her feet: "Lady," he said, "you were the first to show me Callirhoe, at your festival; give me back now the woman you granted me." As he rose, he saw beside the goddess's statue a golden image of Callirhoe which Dionysius had offered.

And then his limbs gave way, his heart felt faint.

He felt dizzy and fell to the ground. The attendant saw him, brought water, and revived him. "Don't be frightened," she said. "Many other people have been scared by the goddess besides you; she appears in person, you see, and lets herself be distinctly seen. But this is a sign of great good fortune. You see the golden image? That woman was a slave, and Aphrodite has made her mistress of all of us." "Why, who is she?" asked Chaereas. "The mistress of this estate, my child, the wife of Dionysius, the leading man in Ionia." When Polycharmus heard this, he would not let Chaereas say another word—*he* had his wits about him—but raised him up and took him away; he did not want it to be known who they were before they had thought about the whole situation carefully and come to agreement about it. Chaereas said nothing in the presence of the attendant but forced himself to keep silence—although he could not stop tears from coming to his eyes. When he was some distance away, he threw himself on the ground, alone, and cried: "Kindly sea! Why have you preserved me so far? Is it so that after my fair voyage I may see Callirhoe another man's wife? I did not think that would ever happen, even if Chaereas died! What shall I do, in my misery! I expected to get you back from a master; I was sure I would win over the man who bought you, by offering ransom for you. In fact I have found you wealthy, perhaps even a queen. How much more fortunate I should be if I had found you begging! Am I to go up to Dionysius and say, 'Give me back my wife!' Who can say that to a man who has married her? Why, I cannot even go up to you if I meet you! I cannot even offer you the most ordinary of greetings—as my fellow citizen! Perhaps I shall even risk death as the debaucher of my own wife!" Such were his laments; and Polycharmus tried to comfort him.

7    Meanwhile Dionysius's steward Phocas, when he saw a warship, felt a certain alarm. Ingratiating himself with one of the crew, he found out from him who they really were and where they were from and the reason for their journey. So he realized that this trireme brought real disaster for Dionysius and that he would not live if he were separated from Callirhoe. He was fond of his master and wanted to forestall trouble and extinguish a war that would not be a big affair, certainly, nor widespread, but affected Dionysius's household alone. So he rode off to a Persian garrison and told them that an enemy trireme was riding at anchor in a secluded spot, perhaps with a view to spying, perhaps for piracy, and that it was in the King's interest that it be seized before it did any harm. He convinced the Persians and led them out in battle order. So they fell on the ship in the middle of the night, set it on fire, and destroyed it; they chained all the men they took alive and drove them back to the garrison. When the prisoners were shared out, Chaereas and Polycharmus begged to be sold to one master. The man who got them sold them into Caria; there, trailing heavy chains, they worked the land of Mithridates.[57]

Chaereas appeared to Callirhoe in a dream, in chains, trying to approach her but unable to do so. She uttered in her sleep a loud, piercing cry of distress, "Come to me, Chaereas!" That was the first time Dionysius had heard the name of Chaereas. To his wife's consternation he asked, "Who is it you are calling to?" Her tears gave her away; she could not hold her grief in check but gave voice to her sorrow. "A poor unfortunate man," she said, "my first husband, unhappy even in my dreams— I saw him in chains. O my poor husband, in looking for me you have found death—it is your death that the chains signify—while I am alive and living in luxury, lying on a bed of beaten gold with another husband! But before long I shall come to you; even if in life we could not enjoy each other, we shall possess each other in death!" When he heard this, Dionysius was assailed by conflicting sentiments. He was seized with jealousy, that Callirhoe loved Chaereas even dead; with fear, that she would kill herself. Yet still, he was heartened by the thought that his

57. Caria is the region east and southeast of Miletus, the southwest of Asia Minor. Mithridates is not a historical person, but his name is typically Persian; this is true in general of the names Chariton gives to his Persian characters, which can usually be found somewhere in Persian history.

wife thought her first husband dead, for he supposed that she would not leave Dionysius if Chaereas was no longer alive. So he consoled his wife as best he could, and for many days he watched over her in case she did herself some harm. Callirhoe's grief was dissipated by the hope that perhaps Chaereas was alive and her dream had been a deceptive one, and most of all by the child in her womb. Seven months after the wedding she gave birth to a son, ostensibly Dionysius's child, but in reality that of Chaereas. The town mounted a great festival, and delegations came from all over as people shared in Miletus's happiness at the addition to Dionysius's family. The master, in his joy, yielded to his wife in everything and made her mistress of his house. He filled the temples with votive gifts and invited the whole town to sacrificial banquets.

Callirhoe was worried that her secret would be betrayed, so she asked   8 for Plangon to be freed. Plangon was the only person besides herself who knew she was pregnant when she came to Dionysius, and Callirhoe wanted to make sure of having her loyalty, not just as a matter of sentiment but on the basis of her material position. "I will gladly recognize the help Plangon has given us in our courtship," said Dionysius, "but we are acting wrongly if, when we have rewarded the servant, we are not to show gratitude to Aphrodite, in whose temple we first saw each other." "I want to more than you do," said Callirhoe, "since my debt to her is greater than yours. For the moment I am still recovering from the birth; it will be safer if we wait a few days before we go to the country."

She quickly recovered from the birth and grew stronger and bigger, no longer a girl, but now a mature woman. When they reached the estate, Phocas arranged magnificent sacrifices—a large crowd had followed them from town. As he began the public offering, Dionysius said: "Lady Aphrodite, you are the source of all my blessings; it is you who gave me Callirhoe, you who gave me my son; you have made me a husband and a father. I was satisfied to have Callirhoe—she is sweeter to me than country or parents—but I love my child, for making his mother more surely mine; I have a guarantee of her goodwill. I beg you, my lady, keep Callirhoe safe for my sake and keep my son safe for her sake." The crowd of people standing round said amen to his prayer and pelted them with roses or violets or whole garlands, so that the temple grounds were filled with flowers. Well, Dionysius had voiced his prayer in the hearing of everyone, but Callirhoe wanted to speak to Aphrodite alone. First she took her son in her own arms; that formed a beautiful sight, such as no painter has ever yet painted nor sculptor sculpted nor poet recounted, since none of them has represented Artemis or Athena holding a baby in her arms.[58] Dionysius wept for joy when he saw it and quietly addressed a propitia-

58. Because both were virgin goddesses.

tory prayer to Nemesis.[59] Callirhoe told Plangon alone to stay with her and sent everyone else ahead to the house. When they had left, she stood near to Aphrodite and held up her child. "On his behalf I am grateful to you, mistress," she said. "On my own behalf I am not sure. I should be grateful to you for myself as well if you had watched over Chaereas for me. But you have given me an image of my dear husband; you have not taken Chaereas from me altogether. Grant, I pray you, that my son be more fortunate than his parents, and like his grandfather. May he too sail on a flagship—and when he is in action, may people say, 'Hermocrates' grandson is greater than he was!' His grandfather too will be happy to see his courage inherited; and we shall be happy, his parents, even if we are dead. I beg you, mistress, be at peace with me now; I have had enough misfortune! I have died and come to life again. I have been taken by pirates and made an exile; I have been sold and been a slave; and I reckon my second marriage a greater burden yet than all this. I beg one favor of you, and of the other gods through you, to requite all: preserve my fatherless child!" She would have said more but could not for her tears.

9     After a short time she called the priestess. The old woman came when called. "Why are you crying, child," she asked, "when you have such good fortune? Why, foreigners are actually worshiping you as a goddess now. The other day two handsome young men sailed by here, and one of them almost fainted when he saw your image—that is how famous Aphrodite has made you." These words struck at Callirhoe's heart; she stared as though she had gone out of her mind and cried: "Who were the foreigners? Where had their ship come from? What story did they tell you?" The old woman was frightened and at first stood there speechless; then she managed to speak. "I only saw them," she said. "I didn't hear anything." "What did they look like? Try to recall their appearance." The old woman told her, not in detail, but Callirhoe suspected the truth all the same—people always believe what they want to be the case. She looked at Plangon. "Perhaps poor Chaereas has wandered to these parts and is here now," she said. "What then has happened to him? Let us look for him—but say nothing about it."

Now when she joined Dionysius she told him only what the priestess had told her; she knew that love is naturally inquisitive, and that Dionysius would try of his own accord to find out what had happened. That was just how it turned out. Dionysius did find out and was immediately seized with jealousy; it never occurred to him to think of Chaereas, but he was afraid that someone was hiding on the estate plotting to seduce his wife. Her beauty led him to suspect and fear anything—and not only

59. Nemesis was originally the concept of retribution, then was personified as the goddess of divine vengeance.

human assaults on her; he half expected a god, even, to come down from heaven and compete with him for her love. So he called Phocas to him and questioned him thoroughly. "Who are these young men? Where do they come from? Are they rich and handsome, I wonder? Why were they worshiping *my* Aphrodite? Who told them about her? Who said they could do so?" Phocas tried to hide the truth of the matter, not because he was afraid of Dionysius, but because he realized that if Callirhoe found out what had happened, she would ruin him and his family, so he said that there had been no visitors. Thereupon Dionysius, not knowing why he was acting in that way, began to suspect that a more serious design was being woven against himself. He grew very angry and called for whips and the wheel, to use on Phocas; and he sent for everybody else on the estate as well as him, convinced that it was a case of seduction he was investigating. Phocas saw the danger he was in whether he spoke or not. "Sir," he said, "I will tell you truth—to you alone." Dionysius sent everyone away. "There you are," he said, "We are alone. Don't tell any more lies—tell me the truth, even if it is ugly." "Ugly, no, sir," he said, "In fact I have very good news for you; the beginning may sound rather grim, but don't let that worry you or distress you; wait till you've heard the whole story—you'll find it has a happy ending." Dionysius was excited at the promised news and hung on Phocas's words. "Hurry up," he cried. "Tell me at once!" So Phocas began his story. "A trireme arrived here from Sicily with ambassadors on board, sent by the Syracusans to demand Callirhoe back." Dionysius fainted when he heard that; darkness spread over his eyes. In his mind's eye he saw Chaereas standing over him tearing Callirhoe away from him. So he lay there inert and pale as a corpse; Phocas did not know what to do, and did not want to call anyone because he did not want anyone to know his secret. Gradually and with difficulty he managed to revive his master himself. "Don't be distressed," he said. "Chaereas is dead; the ship is destroyed; there's nothing to be afraid of now." Dionysius took heart at what he said; gradually he came back to himself and began to ask about all the details. Phocas told him about the sailor who had given him the information—where the ship was from, the purpose of their journey, who was on board; he told him also about his own tactics of involving the Persians and about that night—how the ship was attacked and burned, and the crew killed or captured. So the dark cloud lifted from Dionysius's mind;[60] he embraced Phocas and said: "You are my benefactor, you are my true guardian, the most faithful partner in my secrets. It is through you that I possess Callirhoe and my son. I would not have told you to kill Chaereas—but now that you have done it, I do not find fault with you, because you did

---

60. The text is corrupt; the translation gives the general sense.

wrong out of loyalty to your master. You were careless in only one thing—you did not find out whether Chaereas was among the dead or the prisoners. You should have searched for his body; he would have had burial, and I should have better grounds for confidence. As things are, I cannot enjoy my good fortune without anxiety, because of the prisoners; we don't even know where any of them has been sold."

10    He instructed Phocas to report publicly everything else that had happened, but to say nothing about two matters: his own tactics and the fact that some of the men from the trireme were still alive. Then he went to Callirhoe, looking sad. Next he called together the countryfolk and interrogated them,[61] so that his wife could learn what had happened and consequently be confirmed in her despair over Chaereas. They all came and reported what they knew. "Barbarian brigands swept down from somewhere during the night and burned a Greek trireme that had anchored offshore the day before; at daybreak we saw the sea stained with blood and dead bodies being tossed about by the waves." When his wife heard that, she tore her clothing, beat at her eyes and cheeks, and ran into the house she had first entered when she was sold. Dionysius let her emotions take their course; he was afraid he would make a nuisance of himself if he forced his presence on her. So he told everyone to leave; Plangon alone was to sit with her, to make sure she did herself no harm. When Callirhoe managed to be by herself, she sat on the ground, poured dust over her head, tore her hair, and began to utter her lament. "I prayed to die before you or with you, Chaereas; I must in any event die after you, for what hope is left now that would keep me in life? Until now, in my misery I reckoned: 'Some day I shall see Chaereas and tell him all I have suffered for him—that will make me more precious to him. How full of joy he will be when he sees our son!' It is all pointless now! Even my child is a useless burden now—he is fatherless, an addition to my troubles! Aphrodite, you are unjust! Only you have seen Chaereas—you did not show him to me when he came! You have given that fair body into robbers' hands! He sailed across the sea for your sake, and you did not take pity on him! Who could pray to such a goddess, who killed her own suppliant? On a night of fear you saw a fair young man, a lover, being murdered near you—and did not help him! You have robbed me of my comrade and countryman, my lover and beloved, my bridegroom! Give me back at least his body! I grant that we were born ill starred above all others—but what wrong had the trireme done? Even the Athenians could not take it—and it has been burned by barbarians! At this moment our parents are sitting by the sea, waiting for us to come back home; at every ship that appears on the horizon they say,

---

61. The text is corrupt; the translation gives a suitable sense.

'Chaereas is coming with Callirhoe!' They are preparing our marriage bed; our bridal chamber is being decked out—and we do not even have a tomb of our own! Hateful sea! You brought Chaereas to Miletus to be murdered—and me to be sold!"

## Book Four

So Callirhoe spent that night weeping and wailing, mourning for Chaereas while he was still alive. But for a short time she slept, and she dreamed she saw a band of barbarian robbers bringing torches, and the ship ablaze, and herself rescuing Chaereas. Dionysius was distressed to see his wife wasting away, because of course he was afraid her beauty might suffer; and he began to think that it would serve his own love if she abandoned all thought of her former husband for good. So to show his affection and magnanimity he said to Callirhoe: "Get up, my dear, and erect a tomb for the poor fellow! Why yearn for what cannot be, and neglect what has to be done? Imagine that he is standing over you saying,

'Bury me so that I may pass through the gates of Hades as soon as possible!'[62]

For even if the poor man's body cannot be found, it is an old Greek custom to offer the honor of a tomb even to those who are lost."

He soon persuaded her, since his suggestion was to her liking. As the idea sank in, her grief abated, and she got up from her bed and began to look for a place to erect the tomb. She was attracted by the area near Aphrodite's temple; that way, posterity too would be reminded of their love. But Dionysius did not want Chaereas to be so close to the temple, and he wanted to keep that spot for himself. At the same time he wanted to keep her thoughts occupied, so he said, "Let us go to the city, my dear, and erect in front of it a lofty tomb, clearly visible,

so that it may be seen by men far off, from the sea.[63]

Miletus has fine harbors, and even Syracusans often anchor in them, so your credit will even reach the ears of your countrymen." Callirhoe liked the idea and restrained her eagerness for the moment. But once she was in town, she began to construct a tomb on an elevation by the shore; it was like her own tomb in Syracuse in all respects—shape, size, costliness—and like hers it was built for someone who was still alive! Thanks to the money lavished on it and the abundance of labor, the work was soon completed; and then she also staged a mock funeral for Chaereas. A

62. *Iliad* 23.71 (Patroclus's soul to Achilles).
63. *Odyssey* 24.83 (of Achilles' tomb).

date was decided and announced, and on that day the population not only of Miletus but of practically all Ionia came together.

There were also present two satraps who were visiting Miletus at the time, Mithridates of Caria and Pharnaces of Lydia.[64] They were there ostensibly to show respect to Dionysius, but in fact to see Callirhoe; her reputation was indeed great throughout all Asia, and by now her name had reached the King of Persia and was more celebrated than that of Ariadne or Leda.[65] On that day she looked even lovelier than she was reputed to be. She appeared dressed in black, with her hair let down; with her shining countenance and her arms bared she looked more beautiful than Homer's goddesses of the "white arms" and "fair ankles."[66] In fact no one present could stand the radiance of her beauty. Some turned their eyes away, as if the sun's rays had fallen on them; some even fell to the ground in worship; even children were affected. Mithridates, the governor of Caria, was speechless with astonishment. He fell to the ground like someone struck unexpectedly by a slingshot, and his attendants could scarcely hold him up. At the head of the procession was an image of Chaereas, modeled from the seal of Callirhoe's ring; but handsome as it was, no one looked at it, because Callirhoe was there—she alone drew all eyes to her. How could the end of the procession be fitly described? When they reached the tomb, those who were carrying the bier set it down. Callirhoe went up onto it and embraced Chaereas, kissing his image. "First you buried me, in Syracuse, and now I am burying you in Miletus. Our misfortunes are not merely great, they are also hard to believe—we have buried each other! Yet neither of us even has the other's dead body! Malicious Fortune! You do not let us even share a tomb in death! You have exiled even our dead bodies!" The crowd broke out in lamentation; everyone pitied Chaereas—not for dying, but for being deprived of such a wife.

2      So Callirhoe was burying Chaereas in Miletus while Chaereas was working in Caria in chains. He was soon physically worn out with digging, for many things weighed on him: weariness, neglect, his chains—and above all his love. He wanted to die but was kept from doing so by a faint hope that perhaps someday he would see Callirhoe. Then Polycharmus, the friend who had been captured with him, since he saw that Chaereas could not work and was being beaten and shamefully mistreated, said to the overseer, "Apportion a special area to us, so that you

64. Lydia is the region on the west coast of Asia Minor to the north of Miletus. Pharnaces is another nonhistorical figure with a typical name.

65. Leda was visited by Zeus in the shape of a swan and became by him the mother of Helen.

66. These formulaic epithets are applied by Homer to various females, not all goddesses; "white arms" is frequently applied to Hera; Leucothea, Danae, and Hebe all have "fair ankles."

do not set the other prisoners' laziness to our account, and we will do our own share each day." The overseer agreed and assigned their share. Polycharmus, a strapping young man who was not enslaved to Love—a cruel master!—completed both their allotted portions of work practically single-handed; he gladly took on most of the work to save his friend. So they were in this miserable situation and eventually had to realize they were no longer free. Meanwhile the satrap Mithridates returned to Caria. He was a different man from when he had gone to Miletus; he was pale and thin, because he had a burning, smarting wound in his heart. Consumed with passion for Callirhoe, he would have perished altogether if he had not found some consolation in the following way. Some of the men in Chaereas's chain gang—there were sixteen of them all told, shut in a dark hut—broke their chains in the night, murdered the overseer, and tried to escape. They failed because the dogs' barking gave them away; they were caught that night and all imprisoned more carefully, in stocks, and the next day the estate manager reported the incident to his master. Without even seeing them or hearing their defense the master at once ordered the crucifixion of the sixteen men in the hut. They were brought out chained together at foot and neck, each carrying his cross—the men executing the sentence added this grim public spectacle to the inevitable punishment as an example to frighten the other prisoners. Now Chaereas said nothing when he was led off with the others, but Polycharmus, as he carried his cross, said: "Callirhoe, it is because of you that we are suffering like this! You are the cause of all our troubles!" The supervisor heard what he said and concluded that some woman was their accomplice in their bold enterprise; so to get her punished too and have an investigation made into the plot, he at once detached Polycharmus from the chain that bound them all and took him to Mithridates. Mithridates was lying in a garden, beside himself with despair, picturing Callirhoe to himself as he had seen her in her grief; absorbed in the thought of her, he was displeased to see even his servant. "Look, why are you bothering me?" he asked. "It is necessary, sir," was the reply. "I have discovered the origin of that dreadful crime. This damnable villain knows an accursed woman who was an accomplice in the murder." At these words Mithridates frowned menacingly. "Tell me who this woman is," he said, "who was in this plot and helped you commit this crime!" Polycharmus said he did not know—he had had no part in the business at all. They called for whips; fire was brought; preparations were made for torture. Now one of them laid hands on Polycharmus. "Tell us the name of the woman," he said, "who you said was the cause of your troubles." "Callirhoe," said Polycharmus. Mithridates was startled at the name; he thought that by some unfortunate coincidence the women had the same name. So he was no longer very eager to pursue the investigation, in case he eventually found himself obliged to do violence to that sweet name. But when his friends and household urged him to conduct the search more carefully, he said, "Get Callirhoe here." So they started hitting Polycharmus and asking him who she was and where they were to fetch her from. Poor Polycharmus was distressed, but he did not want to bring a false accusation against any woman. "Why are you making this pointless fuss," he said, "trying to find a woman who isn't here? It is Callirhoe of Syracuse I was talking about, the daughter of the general Hermocrates." At these words Mithridates blushed violently and burst into sweat; in fact a tear even dropped from his eye in spite of himself; whereupon Polycharmus himself fell silent, and nobody knew what to do. Eventually Mithridates managed to pull himself together. "What have you to do with that Callirhoe?" he asked. "Why did you speak her name when you were going to be executed?" "Sir, it is a long story," replied Polycharmus, "and it will not do me any good now. This is not the time to bother you with my chatter. Besides, I am afraid that my friend will be gone before me if I take too long, and I want to share his death too." His audience's mood softened; their anger changed to pity. Mithridates was more overcome than anyone. "Don't be afraid," he said. "You won't be bothering me with your story—I am a sympathetic man. Take courage and tell me everything—don't leave anything out. Who are you? Where are you from? How did you get to Caria? Why are you working the fields in a chain gang? Above all, tell me about Callirhoe— and tell me who your friend is."

3 So Polycharmus began his story. "We—the two prisoners—are Syracusans. The other young man was once preeminent in Sicily, in rank and wealth and appearance; as for me, I am of no consequence, but I am his companion and friend. Well, we left our parents and sailed away from Syracuse. I went for his sake; he, because of his wife, Callirhoe; he thought she was dead and had given her a costly funeral, but tomb robbers found her alive and sold her in Ionia. We got this information from the pirate Theron when he was publicly questioned under torture. So Syracuse sent a trireme and a delegation to look for the woman. This ship was set on fire by barbarians at night as it lay at anchor. They killed most of us but made prisoners of me and my friend and sold us to your estate. Now we put up with our misfortune patiently, but some of our fellow prisoners—whom we do not know—broke their chains and committed a murder; and you ordered us all to be taken off and crucified. Well, my friend didn't utter a word against his wife, even when the execution was under way; but I was moved to speak her name and call her the cause of our troubles, because she was the reason we sailed." Before he had finished, Mithridates cried, "It is Chaereas you mean?" "He is my friend," said Polycharmus. "Sir, please tell the executioner not to sepa-

rate even our crosses." This story was greeted with tears and groans, and Mithridates sent everybody off to reach Chaereas before he died. They found the rest nailed up on their crosses; Chaereas was just ascending his. So they shouted to them from far off. "Spare him!" cried some; others, "Come down!" or "Don't hurt him!" or "Let him go!" So the executioner checked his gesture, and Chaereas climbed down from his cross— with sorrow in his heart, for he was glad to be leaving a life of misery and ill-starred love. As he was being brought, Mithridates met him and embraced him. "My brother, my friend!" he said. "Your silence almost misled me into committing a crime! Your self-control was quite out of place!" Straightaway he told his servants to take them to the baths and see to their physical well-being, and when they had bathed, to give them luxurious Greek clothes to wear. He himself invited men of rank to a banquet and offered sacrifice for Chaereas's rescue. They drank deep, and there was generous hospitality and cheerful rejoicing. As the feasting went on, Mithridates became heated with wine and passion. "Chaereas," he said, "it is not your chains and your cross that I pity you for—it is losing such a wife!" Chaereas was thunderstruck. "But where have you seen my Callirhoe?" he cried. "She is not yours any more," said Mithridates. "She belongs to Dionysius of Miletus —she is his legally married wife. And now they have a child as well." When he heard that, Chaereas could not endure it. He fell at Mithridates' feet. "Sir," he cried, "I implore you, put me back on the cross! It is worse torture to force me to live after such news! Faithless Callirhoe! Wickedest of all women! I have been sold into slavery on account of you; I have dug the earth; I have carried my cross; I have been handed over to the executioner—and you were living in luxury, you were celebrating your marriage, while I was in chains! And you were not satisfied to become another man's wife while Chaereas was still alive—you became a mother too!" Everyone began to weep; the banquet became a scene of gloom. Mithridates alone was pleased at this; it gave him some hope in his passionate love, since he could now talk and take some action about Callirhoe, ostensibly to help a friend. "Well," he said, "it is night now, and time to break up. We can think about all this tomorrow, when we are sober; it needs time to look into it." With that he rose and brought the banquet to an end. He himself retired as usual; as for the young Syracusans, he gave them their own room and servants to look after them.

Throughout the ensuing night a score of preoccupations gripped them 4 all; no one could sleep. Chaereas was angry; Polycharmus tried to console him. Mithridates, for his part, was basking in the hope of getting a bye, so to speak,[67] as in athletic games, while Chaereas and Dionysius

---

67. The translation is an approximation to the institution here referred to (*ephedreia*, "sitting by").

competed for Callirhoe, then himself carrying off the prize without a struggle. The next day, when the discussion began, Chaereas at once asked to be allowed to go to Miletus and ask Dionysius to give him his wife back—Callirhoe herself, he said, would not stay there once she had seen him. "As far as I am concerned," said Mithridates, "you can go. I don't want you to be separated from your wife even for one day. I wish that you had never left Sicily and that no trouble had ever befallen the two of you. But Fortune is capricious, and she has involved you in a grim drama, so you must be very careful what you decide about the next step. At the moment you are rushing ahead emotionally, not rationally; you are not looking ahead. Do you propose to go alone, and a foreigner, to a very big city, and try to tear away his wife from a wealthy man who is the most prominent citizen of Asia, when she is specially linked to him?[68] What power have you on your side? Hermocrates and Mithridates will be a long way away, and they are your only allies; they can grieve for you, but they cannot help you. Besides, I am afraid Miletus is an unlucky spot for you. You have already suffered badly there, but what you have suffered will seem like privileged treatment to you—Miletus was kinder to you in the past than it will be in the future.[69] You were put in chains, true; but your life was spared. You were sold as a slave—but to me. But this time, if Dionysius catches you trying to wreck his marriage, what god will be able to save you? You will find yourself in your rival's power—and his power is absolute. Perhaps he won't even believe you *are* Chaereas—and if he does, that will be even more dangerous for you! Do you not know what Love is like? You must be unique. Love revels in tricking people, setting traps. I think you had better try the woman out first by letter. Find out whether she remembers you, whether she is prepared to leave Dionysius or

wants to make thrive the house of the man who weds her.[70]

Write her a letter; make her grieve, make her rejoice; make her search for you and call you to her. I'll find a way to get the letter to her. Go off and write to her." Chaereas took this advice. When he was alone, with no one near, he tried to write, but his tears flowed and his hand trembled and he could not. He wept deeply over his sad lot; then he managed to start this letter.

68. By the child, that is.

69. I have departed from Blake's text and given what I think is the meaning of the original text, which may now be impossible to recover. Jackson's proposed emendation ("the past will seem golden to you—Miletus was kinder then") is probably similar to what Chariton wrote.

70. *Odyssey* 15.21.

From Chaereas to Callirhoe. I am alive, alive thanks to Mithridates, my benefactor—and yours, I hope. I was taken to Caria and sold by barbarians who set on fire that splendid trireme that was your father's flagship—the state had sent off a delegation in it, to recover you. I do not know what has happened to the other Syracusans, but my friend Polycharmus and I were on the point of being executed when our master took pity on us and we were spared. But all of Mithridates' kindness is counteracted by the distress he has caused me in telling me of your marriage. Death I expected—I am human; but I never thought to find you married. Change your mind, I beseech you—this letter of mine is drenched with the libation of my tears and kisses! I am your Chaereas—that Chaereas you saw when you went to Aphrodite's temple as a virgin, that Chaereas who caused you sleepless nights! Remember our bridal chamber and that night of initiation—when you first knew a man, and I a woman! You will say I showed jealousy. That is the mark of a man who loves you. I have made amends to you: I was sold, enslaved, put in chains. Do not harbor malice against me for kicking you, in my temper—in my turn I ascended the cross because of you and did not say a word against you. Oh, if you should still remember me, my sufferings are nothing; but if you are minded otherwise, you will be passing sentence of death on me!

Mithridates gave this letter to Hyginus, a very trusted man who administered all his possessions in Caria; he had revealed his own passion to him as well. He also wrote to Callirhoe himself, expressing his goodwill and concern for her and saying that it was for her sake that he had reprieved Chaereas. He advised her not to treat her first husband cruelly and promised that he would personally see to it that they recovered each other, if he had her agreement too. He sent three attendants with Hyginus, and expensive gifts and a large amount of gold; to avoid suspicion, the other servants were told that they were destined for Dionysius. He instructed Hyginus to leave the others at Priene[71] when he got there and to go on to Miletus by himself in the guise of an Ionian—he spoke Greek—and reconnoiter; when he had found out how to handle the situation, then he was to bring the Priene party to Miletus. So Hyginus went

71. Priene lay slightly to the north of Miletus: Plepelits, *Chariton*, 179 n. 118, points out that the geography of Hyginus's journey makes it likely that Mithridates' headquarters were east rather than south of Miletus; hence Chariton was probably thinking of his own city, Aphrodisias (in the valley of the Maeander), as his seat. This would constitute another anachronism, since Aphrodisias's heyday was in the early imperial period, Chariton's own time. Priene, on the other hand, was no longer an active town after the first century B.C., when the Maeander silted up.

off and set about carrying out his instructions. But Fortune ordained an issue different from what was intended; she set on foot matters of greater moment. When Hyginus left for Miletus, the slaves were left without any supervision; with abundant money at their disposal, they launched on a bout of dissolute living. In a small town, where in true Greek fashion everybody was inquisitive, this extravagance on the part of visitors attracted general attention; a group of unknown fellows living luxuriously, they struck people as probably robbers and at least runaway slaves. So the chief magistrate came to their inn and made a careful search; he found gold and precious jewelry. Thinking they were stolen, he interrogated the servants, asking them who they were and where these things came from. Fear of torture induced them to disclose the truth, that Mithridates, the governor of Caria, had sent them as gifts to Dionysius; and they showed him the letters as well. As they were fastened with seals, the magistrate did not open them; he handed everything over to the public officials, along with the servants, and sent them to Dionysius, thinking to earn his gratitude thereby. At that moment Dionysius was entertaining the leading citizens at a sumptuous party; a flute was just beginning to play, and voices were raised in song. At that point the letter was handed to him.

> From Bias, Chief Magistrate of Priene,[72] to his benefactor Dionysius. Greetings! Gifts and letters being sent to you by Mithridates, the Governor of Caria, were being damaged by worthless slaves, whom I have seized and sent on to you.

Dionysius read this letter in the middle of the party and preened himself on the royal gifts. Then he ordered the seals to be broken and set about reading the letters. So he saw the words "From Chaereas to Callirhoe. I am alive." "His legs and heart gave way"; then darkness spread over his eyes. But even as he fainted, he kept hold of the letters—he was afraid someone else might read them. People bustled about him; he came to his senses, realized what had happened to him, and told his servants to carry him to another room—he wanted peace and quiet, he said. The party broke up in dismay—people imagined Dionysius had had a stroke; left to himself, Dionysius read the letters over and over again. He was gripped by emotions of all sorts—anger, despair, fear, disbelief. As for Chaereas being alive, that he did not believe (it was the last thing he wanted). It was rather an excuse for procuring adultery, he suspected, on the part of Mithridates, who was trying to seduce Callirhoe by encouraging her to think she could recover Chaereas.

72. One of the "Seven Wise Men" of antiquity was a Bias of Priene.

The next day he kept his wife under careful surveillance, to make sure 6
no one approached her or told her anything of the news from Caria. For
himself, he thought of the following way of defending his interests. At
just that time Pharnaces, the governor of Lydia and Ionia, was on a visit
there; he was considered the most important of the governors appointed
by the King over the coastal regions. Dionysius went to him—he was a
personal friend—and asked for a private interview. "Sir," he said, "please
help me and yourself. Mithridates, who is a wretched villain and jealous
of you, was my guest; now he is trying to destroy my marriage—he has
sent letters to my wife, along with money, to provoke her to adultery."
Then he read the letters and explained Mithridates' design. Pharnaces
was glad to hear his story—partly on Mithridates' account, no doubt,
since their proximity had several times caused friction between them, but
mainly because of his passion. For he too was ardently in love with Callirhoe; it was on her account that he kept on visiting Miletus and inviting
Dionysius to banquets, along with his wife. So he promised to help him
as much as he could and wrote a confidential letter.

Pharnaces, the Satrap of Lydia and Ionia, sends greetings to his
Master Artaxerxes, the King of Kings. Dionysius of Miletus is your
slave, like his ancestors before him, and a loyal and zealous friend
to your house. He has complained to me that Mithridates, governor of Caria, who has been his guest, is trying to seduce his wife.
This is bringing great discredit on your government—in fact it is
causing disturbance; any improper behavior in a satrap is reprehensible, but this is particularly so. Dionysius is the most powerful of
the Ionians, and his wife's beauty is celebrated, so this outrageous
behavior cannot escape notice.

When this letter arrived, the King read it to his friends and discussed
with them what to do. Different views were expressed. Those who were
envious of Mithridates or coveted his satrapy thought that a design on
the wife of a man of distinction should not be overlooked. The more
phlegmatic among them, and those who respected Mithridates—and
they were numerous and highly placed—did not like the idea of ruining a
respected man on the basis of a report of misbehavior. Opinions were
evenly balanced; the King made no decision that day and postponed the
inquiry. When night came, a feeling of righteous repugnance came over
him, as he kept in mind the dignity of his royal position, but he was
moved also by caution as he considered the future—this could encourage
Mithridates to treat him with disrespect. So he was moved to summon
him to trial. But a different sentiment urged him to send for the beautiful
woman as well; in his solitary state, wine and darkness played on the

King's mind and reminded him of that part of the letter too. In addition, he was excited by the rumor that someone by the name of Callirhoe was the most beautiful woman in Ionia; the only reproach the King had to make against Pharnaces was that in his letter he had not added the woman's name. Still, on the chance that another woman might turn out to be even more beautiful than the one so much talked about, he decided to summon the wife as well. He wrote to Pharnaces, "Send my slave, Dionysius of Miletus"; and to Mithridates, "Come and defend yourself on the charge of plotting to destroy Dionysius's marriage."

7    Mithridates was astonished and could not imagine what had given rise to this accusation. Then Hyginus returned and reported the incident with the servants. So Mithridates, now that he had been betrayed by the letters, began to turn over in his mind the idea of not going up to court; he was afraid of animosity against him and of the King's anger. Rather, he would seize Miletus, kill Dionysius, the cause of his troubles, carry off Callirhoe, and revolt from the King. "Why rush," he said to himself, "to surrender your liberty to your master? If you stay where you are, you may even end up on top. The King is a long way away, and his generals are incompetent; besides, even if he does mark you down for destruction, nothing worse can happen to you. In the meantime, don't give up the two greatest blessings, love and power: authority is a glorious winding-sheet, and with Callirhoe beside you death would be sweet." Even as he was turning these thoughts over in his mind and getting ready to revolt, a message reached him that Dionysius had set out from Miletus and had Callirhoe with him. This news caused Mithridates more pain than the order summoning him to trial. He wept bitterly over his own misfortune. "What have I to hope for now if I stay here?" he asked himself. "Fortune is playing me false at every turn. After all, perhaps the King will take pity on me—I have not done anything wrong; and if I am to die, I shall see Callirhoe again. And in the trial I shall have Chaereas with me, and Polycharmus—they will speak for me and prove that I am telling the truth too." So he ordered all his household to follow him and set out from Caria. He was in good heart, because he did not expect to be convicted of any wrongdoing, so he was escorted at his departure not with tears at all but with sacrifice and festive procession. Now as Eros was dispatching this procession from Caria, another left Ionia—more distinguished, for it contained more conspicuous and regal beauty. Rumor sped ahead of the lady, announcing to all the world that Callirhoe was at hand: the celebrated Callirhoe, nature's masterpiece, "like Artemis or golden Aphrodite."[73] The report of the trial increased her fame still

73. *Odyssey* 17.37 and 19.54 (of Penelope).

further. Whole cities came to meet her; people flocked in and packed the streets to see her; and all thought her still lovelier than report had made her out. The felicitations Dionysius received caused him distress, and the extent of his good fortune only increased his fears, for he was an educated man and was aware how inconstant Love is—that is why poets and sculptors depict him with bow and arrows and associate him with fire, the most insubstantial, mutable of attributes. He began to recollect ancient legends and all the changes that had come over their beautiful women. In short, Dionysius was frightened of everything. He saw all men as his rivals—not just his opponent in the trial, but the very judge; he ended up, in fact, wishing he had never rashly revealed the affair to Pharnaces,

when he could have slept and kept his loved one.[74]

Keeping watch over Callirhoe in Miletus was one thing; in the whole of Asia, it was another matter. Nonetheless, he kept his secret to the end; he did not tell his wife the reason for the journey but pretended that the King had summoned him to consult him about affairs in Ionia. Callirhoe was distressed to be taken far from the Greek sea; as long as she could see the harbors of Miletus, she had the impression that Syracuse was not far away; and Chaereas's tomb in Miletus was a great comfort to her.

## Book Five

How Callirhoe, the most beautiful of women, married Chaereas, the handsomest of men, by Aphrodite's management; how in a fit of lover's jealousy Chaereas struck her, and to all appearances she died; how she had a costly funeral and then, just as she came out of her coma in the funeral vault, tomb robbers carried her away from Sicily by night, sailed to Ionia, and sold her to Dionysius; Dionysius's love for her, her fidelity to Chaereas, the need to marry caused by her pregnancy; Theron's confession, Chaereas's journey across the sea in search of his wife; how he was captured, sold, and taken to Caria with his friend Polycharmus; how Mithridates discovered his identity as he was on the point of death and tried to restore the lovers to each other; how Dionysius found this out through a letter and complained to Pharnaces, who reported it to the King, and the King summoned both of them to judgment—this has all been set out in the story so far. Now I shall describe what happened next.

As far as Syria and Cilicia, then, Callirhoe found her journey easy to bear: she heard Greek spoken; she could see the sea that led to Syra-

74. A line from Menander's play *Misoumenos*.

cuse.[75] But when she reached the Euphrates, beyond which there is a vast stretch of unending land—it is the threshold of the King's great empire—then longing for her country and family welled up in her, and she despaired of ever returning. She stood on the bank of the river, told everyone to leave her except Plangon, the only person she could trust, and began to speak. "Malicious Fortune! Insistently attacking a lone woman! You shut me up alive in a tomb, then let me out—not from pity, but to hand me over to pirates! The sea and Theron, between them, brought me into exile; I, the daughter of Hermocrates, was sold as a slave; and harder for me to bear than having none to love me, I aroused a man's love, and so, while Chaereas was still alive, married another. And now you grudge me even this. Now it is not Ionia where you keep me exiled; the land you allotted me up to now was admittedly a foreign country, but it was Greek, and there I could take great comfort in the thought that I was living by the sea. Now you are hurling me from my familiar world—I am at the other end of the earth from my own country. This time it is Miletus you have taken from me; before, it was Syracuse. I am being taken beyond the Euphrates, shut up in the depths of barbarian lands where the sea is far away—I, an island woman! What ship can I hope will come sailing after me from Sicily now? I am even being torn from your tomb, Chaereas; who shall pour libations over you, benevolent spirit?[76] Bactra and Susa[77] are my home from now on, and my tomb. Once only, Euphrates, am I going to cross you—it is not the length of the journey that frightens me, but the fear that there too someone will think me beautiful!" With these words she kissed the ground, stepped on board the ferry, and crossed the river. Now Dionysius's own entourage was large, as he wanted to make an impressive show of his wealth to his wife, but the attentions of the local people made their progress even more royal. One community escorted them to the next; one satrap gave them into the care of his neighbor; her beauty won all hearts. The Persians were encouraged too by the expectation that this woman would acquire great power, so they all eagerly offered gifts or tried in some way to secure her goodwill for the future.

2       That was how things were on their side. Mithridates, for his part, took the route through Armenia and traveled more energetically, mostly because he was afraid the King might hold it against him if he followed in Callirhoe's footsteps, but also because he was anxious to get there first and prepare for the trial. When he reached Babylon, then (that was

---

75. Cilicia is the coastal area in the southeast of Asia Minor, bordering on Syria; there were Greek settlements all along the coast.

76. This looks like a reflection of the Latin term *di manes,* "spirits of the departed."

77. Two of the major cities of the Persian Empire. Bactra was the chief city of Bactria (northern Afghanistan); Susa, to the west of Babylon, was the location of one of the royal residences.

where the King was staying), he spent that day quietly in his own quarters—all the satraps have residences set aside for them. The next day he went to the palace and greeted the Persian peers. Then he paid his respects to the eunuch Artaxates, the greatest and most powerful man at court, offering him gifts, and said, "Inform the King that his slave Mithridates has come to refute the slanderous charge of a Greek and to do homage." The eunuch soon returned from the King's presence and said: "It is the King's hope that Mithridates is innocent. He will pass judgment when Dionysius too arrives." So Mithridates made his obeisance and left. When he was by himself, he called Chaereas and said to him: "I am being put on trial. Because I tried to restore Callirhoe to you I am being accused of a crime. That letter you wrote to your wife—Dionysius says I am the author of it, and thinks he can prove I am trying to seduce his wife. He is convinced you are dead. Well, let him remain convinced until the trial; you can appear out of the blue. I ask you, in recognition of my generosity to you, to stay in hiding; steel yourself not to see Callirhoe and not to ask about her." Much against his will Chaereas accepted this. For all his efforts to avoid notice, tears ran down his cheeks. "Sir," he said, "I will do as you bid me"; and he went off to the room where he was staying along with his friend Polycharmus, threw himself on the ground, tore his clothing, and

with both hands he took dark dust and poured it over his head, defiling his lovely countenance.

"Callirhoe," he sobbed, "we are so close and may not see each other! It is not your fault—you do not know that Chaereas is alive. It is I who am the most godless man on earth. I am forbidden to look at you—and coward that I am, so enamored of life, I submit to such gross tyranny! If *you* had had such an order, you would not have chosen to live!"

Well, Polycharmus tried to console him; but by now Dionysius too was near Babylon, and Rumor was overrunning the city in anticipation, proclaiming to all the imminent arrival of a woman of superhuman, divine beauty, such as did not exist anywhere else under the sun. Barbarians are naturally passionately fond of women, so every house, every alley was filled with report of her beauty. The reports reached the King himself, and he actually asked the eunuch Artaxates whether the woman from Miletus had arrived. As for Dionysius, he had long been troubled by his wife's celebrity—it made him feel insecure. Now that he was on the point of entering Babylon, he burned still more with anxiety. With a sigh he said to himself: "Dionysius, this is no longer your own city, Miletus—and even there you were constantly on the alert for plots against you. Rash, shortsighted man—bring Callirhoe to Babylon, which is full of men like Mithridates? Menelaus could not keep Helen in security in virtuous Sparta. King though he was, a barbarian shepherd supplanted him; and there is many a Paris among the Persians. Can you not see the dangers? Can you not see them already coming upon you? We are welcomed by cities, entertained by satraps. She has already grown more proud, and the King has not yet seen her. Clearly my only hope of security lies in smuggling her into the city. She will be safe if I can keep her out of sight." On coming to that conclusion he mounted his horse but left Callirhoe in the carriage and closed the curtains. And perhaps he would have succeeded in his aim if events had not taken the following turn.

3      The wives of the most eminent Persians went to the King's wife, Statira, and one of them said: "Madam, a Greek female is attacking our households. Everybody has been admiring her beauty for some time; now that we are involved, the reputation of Persian women is at risk. So we should consider how to prevent this foreign woman from scoring over us." The queen laughed; she did not believe the rumors. "Greeks are boastful, impoverished creatures," she said. "That is why they are so easily impressed. They claim that Callirhoe is beautiful as they claim that Dionysius is rich. Rest assured—when she arrives, let just one of us appear in her company and that will put this wretched slave woman in the shade." They all made an obeisance to the Queen and voiced due admiration of her judgment. At first they cried out as with one voice, "If only you could show yourself, Madam!" After that, different views were expressed as they put forward the names of the women most admired for their beauty. A vote was taken, as in a civic assembly,[78] and the first choice was Rhodogune, the daughter of Zopyrus and wife of Megabyzus and a celebrated beauty; what Callirhoe was to Ionia, she was to Asia. The women took her and dressed her up, each of them contributing something of her own to her adornment; the Queen too gave her bracelets and a necklace.

So when they had enhanced her beauty for this meeting with her rival, she appeared on the scene, ostensibly to receive Callirhoe—there were suitable grounds for this in that she was the sister of Pharnaces, the man who had written to the King about Dionysius. All Babylon poured out to see the spectacle; the people crowded round the city gates. Rhodogune, royally escorted, took up her position in full public view. She stood there luxuriating in her beauty, as if challenging comparison; everyone gazed at her, and as they gazed, they said to each other; "We have won! Our Persian will outshine that foreign woman! Let her stand the comparison if she can! Let Greeks learn that they are mere braggarts!" At this point Dionysius arrived. When he was told that Pharnaces' relative was there, he leapt down from his horse and approached her in friendly

78. Literally "in a theater"; but what that meant in Hellenistic times was "in the assembly," which was held in the theater.

greeting. She blushed. "I want to welcome my sister," she said; and as she spoke, she moved towards the carriage.

It was impossible for Callirhoe to stay hidden any longer. Against his will, and groaning to himself at this embarrassment, Dionysius asked Callirhoe to step forward. Now everyone strained their eyes, indeed their very souls, almost falling over each other in their desire each to be the first to see and to get as close as possible. Callirhoe's countenance shone forth in splendor; a dazzling light fell on everyone's eyes, as if bright daylight had suddenly blazed out at dead of night. The Persian people were awestruck and fell to the ground in homage to her; they all acted as if Rhodogune were not there. Even Rhodogune realized she had been worsted. Unable to leave, but unwilling to be looked at, she entered the carriage with Callirhoe, surrendering to her superior. So the carriage moved on with curtains drawn; and the crowd, unable now to see Callirhoe, kissed the wagon.[79] When the King heard that Dionysius had arrived, he ordered his eunuch Artaxates to convey the following message to him: "Since you are bringing an accusation against a man entrusted with high office, you should not have traveled so slowly; but I am setting aside that charge since you were traveling with a woman. I am at present conducting a religious festival and am busy with the ceremonies. I shall hear the case thirty days from now." Dionysius made obeisance and left.

So both sides began to prepare for the trial as if it were the greatest of wars. The Persian population was divided. The satraps and their parties sided with Mithridates—he was originally from Bactra and had only moved to Caria later. The ordinary people sympathized with Dionysius; they thought he had been treated badly and unlawfully in that an attempt had been made to seduce his wife—and what a wife! That was the most important thing! Nor was the Persian women's side unaffected; there too, sympathies were divided. Those among them who prided themselves on their beauty were jealous of Callirhoe and hoped the trial would result in some harm to her reputation; but the ordinary women, out of ill feeling to these local beauties, joined in praying that the foreign woman's standing would be enhanced. Each of the two men thought victory was in his grasp. Dionysius's confidence reposed in the letter Mithridates had written to Callirhoe in Chaereas's name (he never expected Chaereas to be living). Mithridates, since he could produce Chaereas, was convinced that he could not be convicted; but he pre-

4

---

79. The kissing gesture is perhaps not so much romantic as religious in nature, like *proskynesis* ("kowtowing"). The episode does, however, recall a more romantically intended kiss bestowed on a carriage by Abradates' wife, Panthea, in Xenophon *Cyropaedia* 6.4.9ff. (in the whole account of this Persian episode in the present story there are a number of echoes of this work of Xenophon and also of his *Anabasis*).

tended to be afraid and consulted advocates, to enhance the effect of his defense by the element of surprise. For the thirty days ordained, men and women alike in Persia talked of nothing but this trial; if the truth be told, Babylon was nothing but a law court. Everyone found the appointed interval too long, including the King himself. What Olympic Games, what Eleusinian nights[80] ever promised such passionate interest?

When the appointed day came, the King took his seat. There is a special room in the palace which is designated as a law court, an unusually big and beautiful room. In the middle stands the King's throne; on each side are places for the King's friends, those who in rank and ability count among the very first in the land. Around the throne stand captains and commanders and the most distinguished of the King's freedmen—one could well say of such an assembly,

The gods, sitting at Zeus's side, held debate.[81]

Those involved in the case are brought in in silence and trepidation. Well, on this occasion Mithridates was the first to appear, early in the morning; he was escorted by his friends and relatives, and was far from bright and cheerful in appearance, but rather, as befitted a man under examination, pathetic to behold. Dionysius followed; he was dressed in Greek style, wearing a Milesian robe, and had the letters in his hand. Once in court they made their obeisance. Then the King ordered the clerk of the court to read out the letters—that of Pharnaces and his own reply—so that his fellow judges should know how the matter had come to court. When his letter was read out there was a great burst of applause—people approved the King's moderation and sense of justice. When silence was restored Dionysius, as the plaintiff, was due to speak first. All were looking to him when Mithridates said: "Sir, I am not trying to put my own case out of turn, but I know the proper disposition of affairs. Everyone necessary to the trial should be present before the speeches begin. Where, then, is the woman the case is about? You judged her necessary because of the letter; you wrote that she should be present; and she is present. So Dionysius should not conceal the main element and cause of the whole affair." Dionysius replied as follows. "This is another proof of adulterous intention—trying to expose another man's wife to public view against her husband's wishes, when she herself is neither plaintiff nor defendant. Now if she had actually been compromised, she would be under examination and would have to appear. In fact she knew nothing of your designs on her, and I am not calling my wife either as

80. The reference is to the very famous annual celebration of the mysteries of Demeter at Eleusis, near Athens.
81. *Iliad* 4.1 (the gods debating the fate of Troy).

witness or to assist me in my case. So why should she have to appear?
She has no part in the case." Dionysius's argument was legally a good
one but was not likely to carry weight with anyone—everybody was
desperately eager to see Callirhoe. The King, however, was embarrassed
about giving a direct order, so his friends found a plausible justification
in the letter he had written: she had been summoned as being essential to
the proceedings. "Why," they said, "it would be ridiculous for her to
come all the way from Ionia and then when she is in Babylon to stay in
the background!" It was decided, then, that Callirhoe should also appear
in court. But Dionysius had so far told her nothing; all the way he had
concealed the reason for this journey to Babylon. So now he was afraid
to bring her into court without warning, when she did not know what
was happening—she would probably be angry at having been misled;
and he asked for the case to be postponed to the next day.

In this way, then, the session broke up. When he returned home
Dionysius, like the sensible, educated man he was, spoke to his wife in
the most convincing way possible in the circumstances, explaining everything tactfully and gently. For all that, Callirhoe could not refrain
from weeping as she heard the story. At the mention of Chaereas she
burst into a flood of tears and spoke bitter words about this trial. "Oh,"
she cried, "that was all I needed, in my misfortunes—to be taken to
court! I have died and been buried; I have been stolen from my tomb; I
have been sold into slavery—and now, Fortune, on top of that I find myself on trial! You were not satisfied with traducing me to Chaereas; you
have led Dionysius to suspect me of adultery! The first time, your slander led me to the tomb; now it brings me to the royal court of justice!
Asia and Europe tell tales about me! How can I face my judge? What
must I hear said about me? Treacherous beauty, given to me by Nature
for one purpose only—that I be overwhelmed by slanders against me![82]
Hermocrates' daughter is on trial and does not have her father to defend
her! When other people go into court, they pray for goodwill and kindness; what I am afraid of is finding favor with the judge!"

She spent the whole day lamenting despondently to herself like this;
Dionysius was in even worse state. When it came night, she had a dream:
she saw herself in Syracuse entering Aphrodite's shrine, still a maiden;
then returning from there and seeing Chaereas and her wedding day. She
saw Syracuse all decked out with garlands and herself being escorted by
her father and mother to the bridegroom's house. She was on the point
of embracing Chaereas when she suddenly started up from her dream.
She called Plangon—Dionysius had got up before her, to rehearse for the
trial—and told her about the dream. Plangon replied: "Take courage,

82. There is a textual problem here; I give the apparent general sense.

madam—you should be glad! That is a good dream that you have had; you will be freed from all your worries; what you dreamed is what will happen in reality. Go off to the King's courtroom as if it were Aphrodite's temple; recall your real self and recover the beauty you had on your wedding day." As she was speaking, she began to dress Callirhoe and make her beautiful; and Callirhoe instinctively felt cheerful, as if divining what was to come.

Well, the next morning the crowd milled around the palace; the streets were packed, overflowing the city. Everybody was crowding together, ostensibly to hear the trial but in fact to see Callirhoe; and Callirhoe surpassed herself in beauty as much as she had earlier surpassed the other women. So she entered the courtroom looking like Helen when the divine Homer describes her as appearing among the elders

> around Priam and Panthous and Thymoetes.[83]

Her appearance produced stunned astonishment and silence;

> everyone prayed to lie in bed beside her.

If Mithridates had had to speak first, he would have been unable to utter a word; it was as if, on top of the wound he had already received at Love's hand, he had now been struck another blow even more violent than his original passion.

6    Dionysius began his speech as follows. "Sir, I am grateful to you for according respect to me, to virtuous behavior, and to the institution of marriage. You would not allow a private individual to be the victim of a governor's intriguing; you summoned him here in order to punish wanton and arrogant behavior as it has affected me, and to forestall it as it may affect others. And the offense deserves punishment all the heavier for the culprit's being who he is: it is Mithridates—not my enemy, but my guest and my friend—who has designs against me. And he aims not just at some other of my possessions but at what is more precious to me than body and soul: my wife. This is a man who, had anyone else offended against me, ought himself to have come to my assistance—if not for my sake, who am his friend, then for your sake, who are the King; for you put in his hands the highest office; in proving unworthy of it he has brought shame on—nay, he has betrayed—him who entrusted him with that office. I am well aware that I cannot rival Mithridates in groveling or in the power and resources he is deploying in this suit. But I have confidence in your justice, sir, and in the institution of marriage, and in the law, whose integrity you preserve for all alike. If you are go-

---

83. *Iliad* 3.146; the following quotation, from *Odyssey* 1.366 and 18.213, refers to Penelope and her suitors.

ing to acquit him, it would have been much better never to summon him here in the first place; because in that case all would have been in fear and trembling, knowing that wanton behavior would be punished if brought to judgment. But now people who are brought to judgment and not punished will feel contempt.

"My case is clear and brief. I am the husband of Callirhoe here present, and already a father by her. She was not a virgin when I married her; she had been married before, to a man called Chaereas, long since dead—in fact his tomb is in Miletus. Now, Mithridates came to Miletus and saw my wife in the course of normal hospitality. Thereafter he behaved neither as a friend nor as a man of restraint and decency such as you require in those entrusted with the government of your cities. Rather, he showed himself wanton and lawless. Knowing my wife to be chaste and loyal to her husband, he judged her impervious to words or gifts, and he devised what he thought would be a very convincing means of advancing his designs. What he did was pretend that her former husband, Chaereas, was alive; he forged a letter in his name and sent it to Callirhoe by means of slaves. But Fortune appointed a king worthy of the name,[84] and the providence of the other gods brought the letters to light. Bias, the governor of Priene, sent the slaves and letters to me; I discovered the plot and reported it to Pharnaces, the satrap of Lydia; and he reported it to you.

"I have told you the story of the matter you are judging. My argument is incontrovertible: either Chaereas is alive or Mithridates is guilty of adulterous intent—no other conclusion is possible. He cannot even say he did not know Chaereas was dead; he was in Miletus when we erected his tomb, he joined us in mourning him. No, when Mithridates wants to commit adultery, he resuscitates the dead! I close by reading the letter he sent by his own slaves to Miletus from Caria. Take it and read it.[85] 'From Chaereas ... I am alive.' If Mithridates can prove that, he should be acquitted. But think, sir, what a shameless adulterer it is who even tells lies about a dead man!"

Dionysius's speech aroused his audience; they were on his side at once. The King was moved to anger and looked at Mithridates in a threatening, ominous way. Well, Mithridates showed no sign of distress. 7 "Sir," he said, "you are a just, humane man; I beg you not to condemn me before you have heard the arguments on both sides. Do not let a mere Greek who has craftily put together a tissue of slanderous lies about

84. The text here is corrupt, probably incurably. The translation may give the approximate sense; another possibility is that Dionysius is attributing the King's sense of justice to his (the King's) "fortune," or guardian spirit.

85. Chariton is again following real legal procedure: the text of such a document would be read aloud (by a court official—Dionysius's injunction is not addressed to the King himself) but would not appear in the published speech.

me carry more conviction for you than the truth. I realize that the woman's beauty contributes heavily to directing suspicion against me, since no one would find it surprising that a man should try to seduce Callirhoe. But I have always lived a respectable life; this is the first charge that has ever been laid against me. But even if I were a dissolute, licentious man, I should have been reformed by your entrusting me with the government of so many cities. Who could be so foolish as to deprive himself of such blessings, by his own choice, in favor of a solitary pleasure—a disgraceful pleasure at that? And after all, even if I were conscious of misconducting myself, I could in fact have raised legal objection to the suit:[86] Dionysius's accusation is not based on a legally valid marriage—his wife was offered for sale, and he bought her; and the law against adultery does not apply to slaves. He will have to read you the title of emancipation before he can talk of marriage. Are you actually calling her your wife—a woman sold to you by a pirate, Theron—who had snatched her from a tomb at that? 'Ah, but,' he will say, 'it was a freeborn woman that I bought.' Then you have kidnapped her, not married her.

"But I will answer your charges as though you were her husband. Consider the purchase a marriage; consider the price you paid for her a dowry. She is a Syracusan, but for today let her count as Milesian. I shall demonstrate, sir, that I have committed no crime against Dionysius either as her husband or as her owner. To start with, he accuses me of an act of adultery that has not taken place, but according to him was intended to take place. Being unable to quote facts, he reads out letters devoid of content. But what the law punishes is deeds. You produce a letter. I could say: 'I did not write it. That is not my writing. It is Chaereas who is trying to find Callirhoe—he is the one you should be bringing to court.' 'Ah yes,' he will say, 'but Chaereas is dead. It is you who used a dead man's name to try to seduce my wife.' Dionysius, you are throwing down a challenge to me. It is not at all in your interest. I swear to you—I am your friend, I am bound to you by ties of hospitality. Retract this charge; it is in your interest to do so. Ask the King to dismiss the case. Recant; say, 'Mithridates is not guilty—my accusation was irresponsible.' If you persist, you will regret it; you will be condemning yourself. I am warning you: you will lose Callirhoe! The King will find you the adulterer, not me!"

After this speech he fell silent. Everybody looked at Dionysius to see whether he would withdraw the charge, now that he had been given the choice, or persist in it. They had no idea what these mysterious words of

---

86. The legal objection would be a *paragraphe,* "demurrer," contesting the legal validity of the plaintiff's case. Throughout this episode Chariton is using his technical knowledge of precedure to produce a realistic effect.

Mithridates meant, but they supposed Dionysius did know. He did not. It never occurred to him that Chaereas could be alive. His response was: "Say what you will, you will not fool me with your clever arguments and plausible-sounding threats. Dionysius will never be shown to be fabricating accusations."

"Taking up from there,"[87] Mithridates raised his voice, and as if in a divinely inspired frenzy, called out: "Royal gods, gods of heaven and underworld, help a virtuous man! I have often prayed to you in proper observance and offered you magnificent sacrifices; reward me for my piety, falsely accused as I am! Accord me Chaereas, be it only for this trial! Appear, noble spirit! Your Callirhoe summons you! Stand between the two of us, myself and Dionysius, and tell the King which of us is the adulterer!"

While he was still speaking—that is how they had arranged things— 8 Chaereas himself stepped forward. When she saw him, Callirhoe cried out, "Chaereas! Are you alive?" and made to run to him. But Dionysius held her back, blocked the way, and would not let them embrace. Who could fitly describe that scene in court? What dramatist ever staged such an astonishing story? It was like being at a play packed with passionate scenes, with emotions tumbling over each other—weeping and rejoicing, astonishment and pity, disbelief and prayers. How happy all were for Chaereas! How glad for Mithridates! For Dionysius, how sorrowful! As for Callirhoe, they did not know what to think. She was in total confusion and stood there unable to utter a word—she could only gaze wide-eyed at Chaereas. I think the King himself, at that moment, would have liked to be Chaereas. When men are rivals for a woman's love, they are always easily provoked to violence. In this case, the sight of the prize made them even readier to fight; but for the King's presence they would have come to blows. But they limited themselves to words. "I am her first husband," said Chaereas. "And I am a more reliable one," replied Dionysius. "Did I put away my wife?" "No, you buried her." "Show me the divorce papers!" "You can see her tomb." "Her father married her to me." "She married me herself." "You aren't fit for Hermocrates' daughter!" "You're even less fit—Mithridates had you in chains!" "I demand Callirhoe back!" "And I am keeping her!" "You're laying hands on another man's wife!" "And you killed your own!" "Adulterer!" "Murderer!" Such was their argument—and the audience enjoyed it. Callirhoe stood there with her eyes cast down, crying: she loved Chaereas; she respected Dionysius. The King dismissed everyone and discussed the matter with his friends. He was not now considering Mithridates' case— he had produced a brilliant defense; the question now was whether he

87. A Homeric tag (*Odyssey* 8.500) that Chariton uses elsewhere too.

should arbitrate about Callirhoe. Some held that that was not a matter for the King to decide. "You were quite right to hear the charge against Mithridates—he was a satrap"; but the people involved now were all private individuals. But the majority advised the opposite course, partly on the grounds that Callirhoe's father had done the royal household no little service, and also because this was not a separate case that he was bringing to his court, but virtually part of the case already before him. They did not want to admit the real reason—that they could not tear themselves from the sight of Callirhoe's beauty. So he recalled those he had dismissed. "I acquit Mithridates," he said. "Tomorrow he shall receive gifts from me, and he is to return to his own satrapy. Chaereas and Dionysius are each to set out their claims to the woman, because I must make proper provision for the daughter of Hermocrates, who defeated the Athenians, my and Persia's worst enemy." On pronunciation of this decision Mithridates made an obeisance, but the others found themselves quite at a loss. The King saw their perplexity. "I am not hurring you," he said. "I will give you the chance to make your preparations before you come for the trial. I grant you an interval of five days. During that time my wife Statira will look after Callirhoe. It would be wrong for her to appear for trial in the company of a husband when the purpose of the trial is to determine who is her husband." So they left the courtroom. Everybody else was downcast; only Mithridates was smiling. He collected his gifts, stayed that night, and set out for Caria the next morning, more radiant than ever.

9     As for Callirhoe, eunuchs took charge of her and brought her to the Queen, without any advance warning—when the King sends, no announcement is made. Seeing her so suddenly, Statira jumped up from her couch; she thought it was an apparition of Aphrodite, to whom she was especially devoted. But Callirhoe made an obeisance. The eunuch perceived Statira's astonishment, "This is Callirhoe," he said. "The King has sent her for you to look after until the trial." Statira was delighted to hear this. She set aside all the jealousy a woman might feel, and her goodwill towards Callirhoe was increased by the honor done to her—she was proud to have Callirhoe entrusted to her. She took her by the hand and said: "Don't cry, my dear—you have nothing to worry about. The King is a good man. You will have the husband you want; you will celebrate your wedding with greater honor after the judgment. Go and rest now. I can see that you are worn out and still distressed." Her words were welcome to Callirhoe, who was longing for peace and quiet. When she had lain down, and they had left her to herself to rest, she touched her eyes. "Have you really seen Chaereas?" she said. "Was that my Chaereas? Or is that too an illusion? Perhaps Mithridates called up a spirit for the trial; they say there are magicians in Persia. But he actually

spoke—everything he said showed he knew the situation. Then how could he bear not to embrace me? We parted without even a kiss!" As she was communing with herself in this fashion, the sound of footsteps could be heard, and the loud cries of women; they were all hurrying to the Queen, thinking it a splendid opportunity to see Callirhoe. But Statira said: "We should let her be; she is indisposed. We have four days to see her, and to listen to her and talk to her as well." They left, sadly, and came early the next day; and they eagerly repeated the process every day—the palace filled up with people. The King, too, visited the women more frequently, ostensibly to see Statira. Expensive gifts were sent to Callirhoe; she refused all of them and maintained her appearance of a woman oppressed by misfortune, sitting there dressed in black and unadorned; but that only made her look more striking. When the Queen asked her which man she wanted as her husband, she made no answer but burst into tears.

This, then, was Callirhoe's situation. As for Dionysius, he tried to endure what was happening to him in a spirit of nobility, drawing on his natural stability of character and his disciplined good breeding. But the unbelievable disaster that had befallen him might have driven even the bravest man out of his mind, for he was more ardently in love than he had been in Miletus. When his passion first began, it was just her beauty he was in love with, but by now much else was contributing to that love: familiarity, the blessing of children, her lack of gratitude, his jealousy, and above everything the unexpectedness of it all.

Suddenly he began to cry repeatedly: "What Protesilaus is this who has come back to life to plague me?[88] What god of hell have I offended that I should find a rival in a dead man—dead, and buried on my land? Aphrodite, you have trapped me—me, who built you a temple on my estate, who sacrifice to you so often! Why did you show me Callirhoe, when you did not intend to let me keep her? Why did you make me a father when I am not even a husband?" Amid these lamentations he took his son in his arms. "Poor child!" he sobbed. "Until now I thought myself blessed by your birth; now it seems untimely! You are your mother's heritage to me, a memorial to my ill-fated love. Little child as you are, you are not wholly unaware of what your father is suffering. It was a disastrous journey; we should never have left Miletus; Babylon has been our ruin. I have lost the first case—Mithridates turned the accusation against me. But I am more afraid of the second. The risk is greater, and the way the case has begun has left me pessimistic: I have had my wife taken away from me without a trial; I am having to fight for my own wife with another man—and what is worse, I do not know whom Cal-

10

88. Protesilaus was the first Greek to be killed in the attack on Troy. His wife, Laodamia, grieved so much for him that she was allowed to return to life for some hours.

lirhoe prefers. But you can find out, my child—she is your mother. Go now and intercede for your father. Cry and kiss her and say, 'Mother, my father loves you!' but do not reproach her. What is that you are saying, pedagogue?[89] We are not allowed to enter the palace? What cruel tyranny—preventing a son from going to his mother to set out his father's claims!"

So Dionysius's time, right up to the trial, was spent trying to arbitrate the struggle between passion and reason. Meanwhile, Chaereas was in the grip of inconsolable grief. So he pretended to be ill and asked Polycharmus to accompany Mithridates, the benefactor of both of them. When he was alone he tied a noose, and as he was on the point of stepping up and putting his neck in it, he said: "I should be dying a happier death if I were ascending the cross set up for me by a false accusation when I was a prisoner in Caria, for I should be leaving this life under the delusion that Callirhoe loved me. As things are, I have lost not only life but that which would have consoled me for my death. Callirhoe saw me and did not come to me, did not embrace me; I was there, and she wanted to spare another man's feelings. She need not feel embarrassed; I will forestall the decision; I am not going to wait for an inglorious end. I know I am a negligible rival for Dionysius—foreigner that I am, poor, already estranged from you. Good fortune go with you, my wife! I call you wife, though you love another. I am leaving you; I will not disturb your marriage. Enjoy your wealth and luxury! Revel in Ionia's rich living! Have the husband you want! Now, as Chaereas is really dying, I beg one last favor of you, Callirhoe: when I die, approach my body and—if you can—shed a tear; that will mean more to me than immortality. Bend over my gravestone and say—even if your husband and child are watching—'You are gone now, Chaereas, gone for good; you are dead now: I was going to choose you in the King's court!' I shall hear you, my wife; perhaps I shall even believe you. The gods of the underworld will respect me the more for your action.

Even if in Hades people forget the dead, even there I shall remember you, my dear."[90]

With such expressions of distress he kissed the noose. "You are my consolation, my advocate," he said. "I am the victor thanks to you; you show more affection for me than Callirhoe." As he was stepping up and

89. The child is here represented—perhaps merely rhetorically—as accompanied by a *paedagogus*, or male counterpart of a nanny or governess, as would befit a child of affluent parents.

90. *Iliad* 22.389–90 (an adaptation of Achilles' words about the dead Patroclus).

fitting his neck into the noose, his friend Polycharmus burst in; unable any longer to comfort him, he restrained him forcibly, out of his mind as he was.

And now the day appointed for the trial was upon them.

## Book Six

The day before the King's intended decision as to whether Callirhoe was    1 to be Chaereas's wife or Dionysius's, all Babylon was up in the air about it. When talking to one another at home, and when they met in the streets, people said: "Tomorrow is Callirhoe's wedding day! Who is going to end up the lucky man?" The city was split in two. Those on Chaereas's side said: "He was her first husband; she was a virgin when he married her; he loved her, and she loved him. Her father gave her to him; her fatherland buried her. He did not abandon his wife and was not abandoned by her. Dionysius did not win her; he did not marry her; pirates sold her, but he could not buy a freeborn woman." Dionysius's supporters replied: "He rescued her from a crew of pirates when she was going to be murdered. He paid a talent to save her life. First he saved her, then he married her. When Chaereas married her, he killed her. Callirhoe should remember her marriage. And the biggest thing in favor of Dionysius's victory is the fact that they also share a child." That was what the men said. As for the women, they not only made speeches, they gave Callirhoe advice as if she were there. "Do not abandon your first husband," they said. "Choose the man who first loved you, your own countryman, so that you can see your father too; if you do not, you will live an exile in a foreign land." Those on the other side said: "Choose your benefactor, your savior, not the man who killed you. What if Chaereas has another fit of anger? Will that mean another burial? Do not betray your son! You should respect your child's father!" This is how you could hear people talking—you would have thought Babylon was one big courtroom!

The last night before the trial had arrived. The royal couple lay abed with different thoughts passing through their minds. The Queen was praying for the day to come more quickly so that she could put from her the burden of her charge—the woman's beauty could be compared with hers at close quarters, and that was a trial to her. Besides, she was suspicious of the King's frequent visits and unseasonable attentions. Up till now he had rarely entered the women's quarters, but ever since she had had Callirhoe there with her, he had been a constant visitor; and she repeatedly caught him glancing surreptitiously at Callirhoe, even when he was talking to her, his eyes wandering unconsciously in her direction as he kept stealing a look at her. So Statira was looking forward to the next day with pleasure. But the King was not. He lay awake all night,

Lying now on his side, now on his back, now face down,[91]

preoccupied, saying to himself: "The moment of judgment has arrived; I was too hasty; I set too early a date. What am I going to do tomorrow? Callirhoe will soon be leaving for Miletus or Syracuse. Unhappy eyes! You have one hour left to enjoy that fairest of sights; and after that my slave will be happier than I! My soul, consider what you should do. Search within yourself; you have no one else to advise you; only Love can advise a lover. So first answer your own question, Who are you? Callirhoe's lover or her judge? Don't deceive yourself. Though you may not realize it, you are in love; it will be all the more evident when she is gone from your sight. Then why deliberately hurt yourself? The Sun, your ancestor, has chosen this creature specially for you, the fairest of all he surveys—and are you driving the god's gift away? Much I care for Chaereas and Dionysius—my humble slaves—to arbitrate their marriages! I, the Great King, acting as marriage broker like an old woman! But no, I was the one who took it on myself to judge this case, and everybody knows it. And above all I could not look Statira in the eye. Well, then, neither broadcast your love nor bring the trial to an end. It is enough for you just to see Callirhoe. Postpone your decision—even an ordinary judge can do that."

2 So when day dawned, the servants set about getting the royal courtroom ready; the crowds rushed to the palace, and all Babylon was in commotion. Just as you can see the competitors at Olympia arriving at the stadium escorted by a procession, so you could see these contestants. The Persian nobility escorted Dionysius; the people, Chaereas. The supporters of each sent up prayers and innumerable cries. "You are the better man!" they shouted in encouragement. "You are the winner!" But the prize was not a wreath of wild olive or fruit or pine, but supreme beauty, for which the gods themselves might fitly have contended. The King called the eunuch Artaxates, who was highly in favor with him, and said: "The royal gods have appeared to me in a dream and are demanding sacrifice. I must carry out my religious duty; that is my first obligation. So give the order for all of Asia to observe a sacred month of festival for thirty days; all lawsuits and business are to be set aside." The eunuch issued the order as he had been instructed, and immediately the whole country was full of people garlanded and offering sacrifice. There was the sound of the flute, of the syrinx piping, of people singing; incense burned in the entries of houses; every street held a banqueting party;

91. *Iliad* 24.10–11 (Achilles after Patroclus's death).

the savor rose to heaven, swirling in the smoke.[92]

The King set magnificent sacrifices by the altars. Then for the first time he sacrificed to Eros, and repeatedly called on Aphrodite to help him propitiate her son.

In this general rejoicing three people only were sad: Callirhoe, Dionysius, and above all Chaereas. Callirhoe could not show open distress in the royal palace, but secretly she sighed to herself under her breath, cursing the festival. As for Dionysius, it was himself he cursed, for leaving Miletus. "Miserable wretch," he said, "you will have to put up with this disaster—it is your own fault, it is you who are responsible for what is happening. You could have kept Callirhoe even though Chaereas was alive. You were master in Miletus—the letter would never even have reached Callirhoe against your will. Who would have seen it? Who would have had access to Callirhoe? But you rushed to throw yourself among your enemies! And if only it were just you—but it is a possession more precious to you than your life! That is why you find yourself attacked on all sides! What do you expect, you fool? You have Chaereas as your opponent in this trial, and you have made your lord and master your rival in love! Now the King is having dreams, on top of everything else; the gods he sacrifices to every day are demanding sacrifices from him! The shamelessness of it! Dragging out the trial while he has another man's wife in his palace! And a man like that claims to be a judge!" Such were Dionysius's complaints. But Chaereas would not touch food; he had lost all desire to live. His friend Polycharmus tried to stop him from committing suicide. "You pretend to be my friend," he said, "but you are my worst enemy· you are holding me down while I am tortured; you like to see me punished! If you were my friend you would not grudge me my liberty, persecuted as I am by some evil power! How many times have you destroyed my chance of happiness? I would have counted myself happy to be buried in Syracuse with Callirhoe when she was being buried—but then too you prevented me from killing myself and robbed me of her sweet company on the way to the tomb; indeed, perhaps she would not have left the tomb if it meant leaving my body behind. In any event, I should be lying there now; I should have been spared what followed—being sold, attacked by robbers, put in chains, crucified—and a king more cruel than the cross! How sweet death would have been after I heard that Callirhoe had married again! And again, what an opportunity you spoiled for me of doing away with myself after the trial! I saw Callirhoe and did not go to her, did not embrace her! It is unheard of; it passes belief—Chaereas on trial to determine whether he is Callirhoe's husband! And even this question—for what it is worth!—the malicious

92. *Iliad* 1.317.

deity will not allow to be decided. In dream and in reality alike, the gods hate me!" With these words he made to seize his sword; but Polycharmus managed to restrain him and watched him very closely, almost to the point of tying him up.

3    The King called the eunuch to him. He was his most trusted servant, but at first the King was embarrassed even with him. Artaxates saw that he was blushing deeply and had something to say. "Sir," he said, "what are you hiding from your slave? I am your friend, and I can hold my tongue. What is this terrible thing that has happened? I am worried in case some plot—" "A plot, yes,"[93] cried the King, "a massive plot—but laid by a god, not by human beings. I had heard what Love is like before now, in stories and poems; I had heard that he is master of all the gods, even of Zeus, but all the same I did not believe that anybody could be more powerful than me at my own court. But the god is upon me. Love has taken up residence in my heart, in his power and violence. It is hard to confess, but I am truly his prisoner." As he said this, he was overwhelmed by a flood of tears and could say nothing more. But despite his silence Artaxates knew at once the source of his wound. Even before this he had had his suspicions and had seen the fire smoldering; besides, it was clear beyond any shadow of doubt that with Callirhoe there he would not have fallen in love with anyone else. Still, he pretended not to know. "What beauty can overcome your heart, sir?" he said. "Everything beautiful is in thrall to you: gold, silver, clothing, horses, cities, peoples; you have countless beautiful women—why, Statira is the most beautiful woman under the sun, and she is yours alone to enjoy. When you can have whatever you want, that overthrows Love. Or has some goddess come down from heaven? Has a second Thetis risen up from the sea? For I am sure that even gods yearn for your society." "What you say may be true," replied the King. "This woman may indeed be a goddess—her beauty is superhuman. But she says she is not; she claims she is a Greek, from Syracuse. And that suggests she is deceiving us: she is trying to avoid being shown up, in not naming any city in my empire, but rather setting her story beyond the Ionian Sea, far across the ocean. She has come to attack me, under cover of a trial; she is the one who has stage-managed this whole drama. But I wonder how you can call Statira the most beautiful woman in the world when you can set your eyes on Callirhoe. Well, we must think of some way to rid me of my distress. Look everywhere to see if it is possible to find some remedy." "It exists already, Your Majesty," said Artaxates, "among Greeks and non-Greeks alike, this remedy you are looking for. The only remedy for Love is the loved one; that, after all, is what the famous oracle said—'He who hurt

93. The anacoluthon is probably genuine (I adopt Jackson's text), but there may be a longer lacuna.

shall heal.'"[94] The King was greatly embarrassed by what he said. "Don't suggest any such thing—that I should defile another man's wife!" he said. "I am mindful of the laws I myself established and the justice I practice among all men. Don't ascribe such lack of self-control to me! I am not as far gone as that." Artaxates was frightened; he felt he had spoken rashly, and changed his approach to words of praise. "These are truly noble thoughts, Your Majesty," he said. "Do not heal Love's wound as other men do. Apply another remedy, one worthy of a king: wrestle with yourself! For you—and you alone—can master even a god; divert your own mind, then, with pleasures of all kinds. You are extremely fond of hunting in particular—indeed, I know you can go without food or drink all day when you are hunting, you like it so much. Better to spend your time hunting than in the palace close to the fire."

The King accepted the suggestion, and a magnificent hunt was proclaimed. Horsemen rode out splendidly got up, Persian nobles and the pick of the army generally. Every one of them was a sight worth seeing, but the most spectacular was the King himself. He was riding a huge, magnificent Nisaean horse whose trappings—bit, cheekpieces, frontlet, breastpiece—were all of gold, and wearing a cloak of Tyrian purple, woven in Babylon, and his royal hat was dyed the color of the hyacinth; he had a golden sword at his waist and carried two spears, and slung about him were a quiver and bow of the costliest Chinese workmanship.[95] He was an impressive sight in the saddle—it is characteristic of Love to indulge in display. He wanted Callirhoe to see him surrounded by people; on his way out, throughout the entire city, he kept looking around to see whether she was perhaps watching the procession. Soon the mountains were full of people shouting and running, dogs barking, horses neighing, game fleeing. The excitement and the noise they were making would have driven Love himself out of his senses; delight was mixed with anguish, joy with fear, danger with enjoyment. But the King saw no horse, though so many horses were galloping alongside him; no animal, though so many were being pursued; he heard no dog, when so many were barking; no man, though all were shouting. All he could see was Callirhoe—who was not there; he could hear her, though she was not speaking. For Love had come out to hunt with him; he is a god who will have

4

94. In a skirmish on the journey to Troy Achilles wounded Telephus, king of Mysia. The wound would not heal, and the Delphic oracle told Telephus that "the one who wounded you will heal you." In the event Telephus was cured by rust from Achilles' spear.

95. Contact with China is attested from the latter part of the first century B.C.—the Greek word for "silk" is *serikon*, i.e., the product of the Seres, or Chinese. This description of the King's luxurious appearance and equipment is one of the very few examples of *ecphrasis*—descriptive writing—in Chariton (cf. the description of Tyre in 7.2 and of Persian mobilization in 6.8). Other novelists (Achilles Tatius, Heliodorus) revel in such word pictures. Artaxerxes' hat is the "tiara," worn only by the king; not a crown, but a conical felt hat not unlike a turban.

his own way, and when he saw someone opposing him with carefully planned resistance—as he thought—he turned his own devices against him, using the remedy itself to inflame his heart. Love entered the King's thoughts, whispering to him, "How wonderful it would be to see Callirhoe here, her tunic tucked up to her knees, her arms bared, face flushed, breast heaving, a very

> Artemis the archer as she moves on the mountain, high Taygetus or Erymanthus, delighting in boars and swift deer."[96]

Painting this scene in his imagination, the King burned with passion ... [97] When he said this, Artaxates replied; "Sir, you are forgetting what has happened. Callirhoe has no husband. The decision remains to be made as to whom she should marry. So remember that you are in love with a woman who has lost her husband. That means that you need not be afraid of breaking the law—the law applies to married people—or of committing adultery; because first there has to be a husband who would be the injured party—only then can there be an adulterer to commit the injury." The King approved this argument, because it tended to his pleasure. He put his arm round the eunuch and embraced him. "I am right to hold you in esteem beyond all others," he said. "You are the most well disposed to me; you protect me well. Go, then, and bring Callirhoe. But with two injunctions: do not bring her against her will and do not bring her openly. I want you to win her consent, and I do not want anyone to know about it." So at once the agreed signal was given for recalling the hunt, and everyone turned back. The King's hopes were exalted, and he rode into the palace in high spirits, as if he had caught the finest game. Artaxates was in high spirits too; he thought that he had undertaken a valuable service[98] and would be holding the reins at court from now on, since both would be grateful to him, especially Callirhoe. He judged that it would be an easy matter to handle; he was thinking like a eunuch, a slave, a barbarian. He did not know the spirit of a wellborn Greek— especially Callirhoe, chaste Callirhoe, who so loved her husband.

5   Well, he waited for the chance to approach her when she was by herself. "I have brought you a wealth of great benefits, lady," he said. "Do remember my services to you; I am sure you have a grateful nature." At his first words Callirhoe's heart filled with joy. Human beings are constituted to believe what they want to happen, so she thought she was about to be restored to Chaereas; she was eager to hear that and readily

---

96. *Odyssey* 6.102–4 (of Nausicaa).

97. There is a lacuna in the manuscript; evidently the King discussed Callirhoe with the eunuch Artaxates.

98. The sense is approximate; the manuscript appears to be defective at this point.

promised to reward the eunuch for his good news. He began again with a preliminary opening. "Lady," he said, "you have been blessed with divine beauty; but you have not gained any great benefit or distinction from it. Your name is known and famous all over the world; but up till now it has not got you a husband or lover worthy of you—it has lit on two men, one a poor islander, the other a slave of the King. What great or glorious benefit has come to you from them? What fertile land do you own? What costly jewels? What cities do you rule over? How many slaves bow down before you? Women in Babylon have servants who are wealthier than you. But you have not been completely forgotten. The gods are looking after you; and that is why they have brought you here—ostensibly for the trial—so that the Great King may see you. And this is your first piece of good news: it has given the King pleasure to see you. I remind him of this, too; I speak well of you to him." This, of course, was his own addition; any slave, when he is talking to someone about his master, will bring himself into the story in the hope of profiting personally from the conversation. Artaxates' words struck at Callirhoe's heart like a sword. She pretended not to understand. "May the gods continue gracious to the King," she said, "and he to you, for taking pity on an unfortunate woman. Let him release me all the sooner from my worry, I beg, by deciding the issue, so that I may no longer be a burden to the Queen either." The eunuch thought that he had not made his meaning plain and that Callirhoe had not understood; and now he spoke more clearly. "This is just where you are lucky," he said. "It is not slaves and poor men who are your lovers now, but the Great King—who can give Miletus itself to you as a present, and the whole of Ionia, and Sicily, and other nations greater than those. So make sacrifice to the gods and count yourself happy! Try to please him still more! And when you are rich, remember me." Callirhoe's first impulse was to dig her nails into the eyes of this would-be pimp and tear them out if she could; but being a well-brought-up and sensible woman, she quickly remembered where she was, who she was, and who it was who was talking to her. She controlled her anger and from that point spoke hypocritically to the barbarian. "Oh," she said, "I hope I am not so deranged as to let myself believe I am fit for the Great King. I am like the servants of Persian women. I beg you, please do not talk about me to your master anymore. You can be sure that even if he is not angry with you straightaway, he will be later on, when he realizes that you have thrown the ruler of the whole world to Dionysius's slave girl. I am surprised that with all your intelligence you fail to recognize how humane the King is: he is not in love with an unfortunate woman, he is taking pity on her. We had better stop this talking; someone may misrepresent us to the Queen." With that she hurried off, leaving the eunuch standing there all agape; he had been brought up in a highly despotic society and could not conceive that there was anything impossible—even for himself, let alone the King.

6      Left by himself like that, not even deemed worthy of an answer, Artaxates went away, seething with all kinds of emotion: he was angry with Callirhoe, sorry for himself, and frightened of the King—who perhaps would not even believe that he had spoken to Callirhoe at all, even though without success, but might think he was betraying his charge to please the Queen. He was also afraid that Callirhoe would even report their conversation to the Queen and that Statira would be angry and devise some serious trouble for him, thinking he was not just serving the King's passion but actually promoting it. The eunuch, then, for his part fell to wondering how he could safely report to the King what had happened. As for Callirhoe, when she was by herself, she said: "That is what I foresaw would happen! Euphrates, you are my witness: I said I should never cross you again! Good-bye, my father, and you, my mother, and Syracuse, my home! I shall never see you again! Now Callirhoe truly is dead! I left my tomb once; not even the pirate Theron will take me from here now. My beauty, my treacherous beauty, you are the cause of all my troubles. It was because of you that I was carried off and sold; because of you that I married another after Chaereas; because of you that I was taken to Babylon and brought into a courtroom. How many times have you handed me over—to pirates, to the sea, to the tomb, slavery, judgment! But the heaviest burden I have had to bear is the King's love. And I have not even mentioned the King's anger yet; to me, yet more frightening is the Queen's jealousy. Not even Chaereas could endure jealousy, man though he is and Greek though he is; what will it do to a woman, an Oriental queen?[99] Come, Callirhoe, conceive some plan of noble kind, worthy of Hermocrates: kill yourself! But no, not yet! So far this is the first approach you have had, and it comes from a eunuch. If some more violent thing happens, that will be the time to show Chaereas, in his presence, how loyal you are!"

The eunuch went to the King and tried to hide the truth about what had happened. He gave the excuse that he had been busy and had been keeping careful watch on the Queen; as a result, he had not even been able to approach Callirhoe. "You told me to make sure no one saw me, sir. And you were quite right to do so: you have assumed the very dignified role of judge, and you want to have the good opinion of Persia; that is why everyone sings your praises. But Greeks find fault over trifles, and they gossip. They will spread this business all over—Callirhoe will boast that the King loves her, and Dionysius and Chaereas will give vent to their jealousy. Besides, it is not fair to cause pain to the

99. I adopt Jackson's emendation.

Queen, whom the trial has made more beautiful than she was already reputed to be."[100] He began to insert this recantation into his words in the
hope that he could turn the King away from his passion and remove a
difficult duty from his own shoulders.

Well, for the moment he managed to persuade him. But when night 7
came, the King was once more inflamed with passion; Love kept on reminding him what eyes Callirhoe had, how lovely her face was. He
commended her hair, her walk, her voice; the way she entered the courtroom, the way she stood; her manner of speaking, her manner of not
speaking; her blushes, her tears. He lay awake most of the night, and
when he snatched a little sleep, it was only to dream of Callirhoe. The
next morning he sent for the eunuch. "Go and be on the alert near her all
day," he said. "You are bound to find a chance to talk to her, even if
only for a moment, without anyone noticing. If I wanted to slake my desire openly and by force, I have guards available." The eunuch made
obeisance and promised to do so; when the King commands, none may
argue. He knew that Callirhoe would not give an opening but would
evade any conversation by purposely staying in the Queen's company,
and in order to deal with just that maneuver he shifted the responsibility
from the woman thus protected to the one protecting her. "Sir," he said,
"please send for Statira and say that you want to talk privately with her;
her absence will give me access to Callirhoe." "Act accordingly," said the
King. Artaxates went to the Queen, made obeisance, and said, "Madam,
your husband summons you." On hearing this Statira signified her obedience with a bow and hurried off to the King. The eunuch saw Callirhoe left by herself, took her hand in a manner suggesting his goodwill
towards Greeks and all mankind, and led her away from the crowd of attendant women. Callirhoe knew what he wanted. She at once went pale
and fell silent; but she followed him. When they were alone, he said to
her: "You have just seen how the Queen bowed in obedience when she
heard the King's name, and went off with all speed. But you—his
slave—cannot accept your good fortune; you are not satisfied that he invites you where he could command. But I respect you, and I have not reported your crazy behavior to him. On the contrary: I have made a
promise on your behalf. So you have two ways open to you; choose
which you will take; I will tell you what those two ways are. Either you
do what the King wants, in which case you shall have magnificent presents and the husband of your choice—for I hardly imagine he is going
to marry you himself; you will merely afford him momentary
gratification. Or else, if you do not do what he wants, you know what
happens to the King's enemies: they are the only people who are not per-

100. This is what the manuscript says; there may be something wrong with the text.

mitted to die even when they want to." Callirhoe laughed in his face at this threat. "It will not be my first experience of suffering," she said. "I am acquainted with misfortune. What disposition can the King make for me that would be worse than I have already suffered? I have been buried alive; the tomb is narrower than any prison cell. I have been delivered into the hands of pirates. And now I am suffering the worst of my torments: Chaereas is near me and I cannot see him." The last remark betrayed her; the eunuch was an intelligent man and saw that she was in love. "Foolish woman!" he cried. "Do you prefer a slave of Mithridates to the King?" Callirhoe bridled at the insult to Chaereas. "Hold your tongue, you wretch!" she cried. "Chaereas is nobly born! He is the foremost man in a city that even Athens could not overcome—and Athens overcame that Great King of yours at Marathon and Salamis!" As she said this, she burst into tears, and the eunuch pressed her harder. "The delay is your own fault," he said. "It is assuredly better to gain the judge's goodwill,[101] so as to win your husband back as well. Chaereas may never even know what happened; even if he does, he will not be jealous of his superior—you will be all the more precious to him for pleasing the King." This last remark was not meant to persuade Callirhoe; it was what he himself really thought. All barbarians, you see, stand in complete awe of the King; they think he is a god come among mankind. But Callirhoe would not have welcomed Zeus himself as a husband, or preferred immortality to one day with Chaereas. The eunuch, then, unable to make any headway, said: "Lady, I will give you a chance to think about it. But you should not consider yourself alone, but Chaereas as well. He is in danger of dying a miserable death; the King will not tolerate being outdone in love." With that he left; but Callirhoe took his final words to heart.

8      Then Fortune brought about a rapid change in the situation, banishing all thought and all discussion of love, and events took a quite different turn. A report came to the King of a major rebellion in Egypt: the Egyptians, he learned, had murdered the royal satrap and elected a king from among themselves. He had marched out from Memphis and passed through Pelusium[102] and was already overrunning Syria and Phoenicia, to the point where their cities were offering no more resistance; it was as though a river in spate, or a fire, had suddenly assailed them. The King was thrown into panic by this report, and the Persians were terror-stricken; a deep gloom settled over the whole of Babylon. Then the gos-

---

101. Adopting Wifstrand's emendation, πῶς οὐκ εὐμενῆ τὸν δικαστὴν σχεῖν κάλλιον; (Eikota, K. Humanistiska Vetenskapssamfundets i Lund Årsberättelse, 1944–45, 2 [Lund, 1945], 1–9.)

102. Memphis is thought of as the capital of Egypt; Pelusium is the area around the easternmost branch of the Nile Delta.

sips and seers began to maintain that the King's dream had foretold the future: by demanding sacrifice, they said, the gods were foretelling danger but also victory. The usual speeches were made, and the usual measures were taken—everything you would expect when war breaks out suddenly; all Asia, indeed, was in a ferment. Thus, the King called together the Persian peers and all the heads of the constituent nations who were in Babylon—men with whom he habitually discussed important questions—and considered the situation that had arisen. They all had different suggestions, but everybody agreed that urgent measures were necessary and that there should be no delay, not even a day if possible. There were two reasons for this: to check the growth of the enemy's power and to revive their friends' spirits by showing them that help was at hand. If they delayed, on the other hand, the opposite would happen in every respect: the enemy would think they were afraid and would hold them in contempt, and their own side would think they were being neglected and would give in. It was very lucky for the King that the news had reached him in Babylon, near to Syria, rather than in Bactra or Ecbatana, since he had only to cross the Euphrates to come to grips with the rebels. So he decided to march out with the troops already at hand, and to send the order throughout his empire for the army to gather at the river Euphrates. Persia can mobilize its forces very easily. The system has been in force since the time of Cyrus, the first king of Persia. It is established which nations have to supply cavalry for a war, and how many; which are to supply infantry, and how many; who is to supply archers; how many chariots each people is to supply (both ordinary and scythed); where elephants are to come from, and how many; and from whom money is to come, in what currency, and how much. Everybody participates in these preparations, and they take no more time than one man takes to get ready.

The King marched out from Babylon on the fifth day after this 9 proclamation; there was a general order for all men of military age to follow him. Dionysius was among them; he was an Ionian, and none of the King's subjects was allowed to stay behind. He armed himself magnificently and formed a by no means negligible company from his own followers, and stationed himself in a conspicuous position in the front ranks. It was clear that he would distinguish himself; he had an ambitious nature, and did not consider courage a merely secondary virtue—on the contrary, he esteemed it one of the noblest. Furthermore, on this occasion he also had some slight hope that if he showed himself useful in the war, the King would give him Callirhoe as a reward for his valorous service, without even making a decision in the case.

As for Callirhoe, the Queen did not want her to be taken along. For that reason she did not even mention her to the King or ask what he wanted done with the foreign woman. Artaxates too kept his peace; his excuse was that now that his master was in a dangerous situation he did not dare remind him of an amorous dalliance, but the truth was that he was glad to be rid of her, as he would be of a wild beast. In fact, I rather think he was actually grateful to the war, for having broken this passionate attachment on the King's part—it was feeding on lack of occupation. But the King had by no means forgotten Callirhoe; the recollection of her beauty came back to him even in that indescribable confusion. But he was too embarrassed to mention her; he did not want to be thought altogether adolescent, thinking of a pretty girl in the middle of a war like that. Still, his impulses made themselves felt. He did not say anything to Statira herself, or even to the eunuch, since he knew about his love; but he devised the following plan. It is customary for the King himself and the Persian nobility, when they go off to war, to take along with them their wives and children and gold and silver and clothing and eunuchs and concubines and dogs and dining-room furniture and their costly treasures and luxuries. So he summoned the man in charge of this. After much preliminary talk, and first giving instructions for the disposition of everything, he ended up by mentioning Callirhoe with a well-counterfeited expression meant to convey that it did not matter to him. "Oh," he said, "that foreign girl whose case I undertook to judge—she can come along with the other women." And so Callirhoe left Babylon—not to her displeasure, because she thought that Chaereas would be leaving too. Now, she thought, war brings many unforeseeable events in its train, including improvement in the fortunes of those in distress, so perhaps peace would soon be concluded and bring with it an end to the trial.

## Book Seven

1 When they all went off with the King to the war against the Egyptians, no one gave any orders to Chaereas, since he was not a slave of the King—in fact he was the only free man in Babylon at the time. He was glad of that, expecting Callirhoe also to be staying behind. So the next day he went to the palace to try to find his wife. Finding it closed and the gates heavily guarded, he started hunting throughout the city, incessantly asking his friend Polycharmus, like a man out of his mind: "Where is Callirhoe? What has happened to her? *She* can't have gone off to fight!" Failing to find Callirhoe, he began to look for his rival Dionysius, and went to his house. Somebody duly came out, as if by fortunate coincidence, and told Chaereas what he had been instructed to say. Dionysius, you see, wanted to deprive Chaereas of all hope of marrying Callirhoe and discourage him from waiting any longer for the outcome of the trial, so he thought up the following scheme. When he went off to fight, he left someone behind to tell Chaereas that the Persian King, needing allies,

had sent Dionysius to collect an army to fight Egypt, and that to ensure his faithful and energetic service he had adjudged Callirhoe to him. When he was told that, Chaereas believed it at once—it is easy to deceive a man in misery. He rent his clothes, tore his hair, and beat his breast, crying: "Treacherous Babylon! Inhospitable city—a very desert to me! A fine judge—prostituting another man's wife! A wedding in wartime! When I was preparing my case, I was convinced it would be just—and I lose it by default! Dionysius has won without saying a word! But he will gain nothing by winning; Callirhoe will not live if Chaereas is near and she is separated from him; even the first time, she was misled by the thought that I was dead. Then why delay—why not cut my throat in front of the palace and pour out my blood at the judge's door? Let the Persians and Medes know how the King passed judgment there!"

Polycharmus saw that he could bring no consolation in this disastrous turn of events. Chaereas was beyond help. "My dearest friend," he said, "for a long time now I have been trying to bring you comfort. Time after time I have held you back from suicide. But this time I think you are right. Far from holding you back, this time I am ready to die with you. But we should think carefully about what would be the best way to die. The way you have in mind will no doubt cause some ill feeling against the King and make him feel ashamed thereafter, but does not offer much satisfaction for our sufferings. I think that once we have settled on dying we should use our death to avenge ourselves on the despot. It would be a noble thing to do him so much harm that he really regrets his actions, and to leave behind for future generations a glorious tale of how two Greeks who were unjustly treated paid out the Great King by the suffering they caused him, and died like men." "Yes," said Chaereas, "but how can the two of us by ourselves, poor as we are, and in a foreign country, do any harm to a man who rules so many great nations and possesses the resources we have seen? He has bodyguards, and other guards before those. Even if we kill one of his people, even if we set fire to some of his property, he will not even notice the damage." "What you say would be correct," replied Polycharmus, "if there were no war; but we have learned that Egypt has rebelled, Phoenicia has fallen, and Syria is being overrun. The war will come to meet the King before he has even crossed the Euphrates. So we are not just two men by ourselves; all the Egyptian king's troops are our allies, all his weapons, all his resources, all his ships. Let us use the strength of others to avenge ourselves!" "Before he had finished speaking" Chaereas cried out: "Quick, let us be off! I shall get judgment against this judge from the war!"

They quickly set out, then, in the King's tracks, claiming to want to join his army; they hoped that this excuse would get them across the Euphrates without danger. They caught up with the army at the river, attached themselves to the rearguard, and followed along; but when they

2

reached Syria they deserted to the Egyptian side. The guards seized them and began to interrogate them to find out who they were; because they did not look as if they were on an official mission they were suspected of being, on the contrary, spies. At that point they would have been in considerable danger had it not been for a Greek who happened to be there and understood their language. They asked to be taken to the king since they had something greatly to his advantage to offer him. When they were brought before him, Chaereas said: "We are Greeks; we are of noble family in Syracuse. My friend here came to Babylon because of me; I came because of my wife, the daughter of Hermocrates—you may have heard of Hermocrates, a general who defeated the Athenians at sea?" The Egyptian king nodded to say he had; the whole world had heard of the disaster Athens suffered in the war with Sicily. "Artaxerxes has behaved tyrannously to us," he said, and they told him the whole story. "We have come of our own accord," said Chaereas, "to offer you our loyal friendship; we have the two strongest possible motives for acting bravely: we passionately want to die and we passionately want revenge. I should be dead already, such are my misfortunes, but I am staying alive solely to make my enemy suffer.

No, let me not die without effort, without glory, but after some great exploit that even our descendants will know about!"[103]

The Egyptian was delighted to hear this and extended his hand to Chaereas. "You have come at the right time for both of us," he said. So at once he ordered them to be given arms and a tent; soon afterwards he invited Chaereas to share his table, then formally appointed him his adviser. For Chaereas was showing good sense and courage, and loyalty as well, true to his noble nature and upbringing.

But what spurred him on and distinguished him even more was his hostility to the Persian King and his desire to show that he was not a man to take lightly, but deserved respect. So he soon had a major achievement to his credit. So far the Egyptians had had an easy success. They had seized Coele-Syria in their rapid invasion, and Phoenicia was in their power as well.[104] But Tyre held out. The Tyrians are by nature a very warlike people who desire a reputation for courage; they do not want to be thought to be bringing shame on Hercules, who is their most prominent god and to whom the city is dedicated almost exclusively.[105] Fur-

---

103. *Iliad* 22.304–5 (Hector's final words before engaging in combat with Achilles, who kills him).

104. Roughly speaking, Phoenicia was the coastal strip including Tyre and Sidon (say, Israel and Lebanon), and Coele-Syria was its hinterland.

105. The local god Melkart was identified by the Greeks with Hercules. The siege here recounted by Chariton is intended to recall Alexander's seven-month siege of the city in 332. There is, however, some obscurity in Chariton's description of the topography and situation of the city, and the text may be faulty. See Plepelits, *Chariton*, 17ff. Chariton may be working from an early version of the *Alexander Romance*.

thermore, the site is secure, and that adds to their confidence. The city is
built in the sea; a narrow causeway joins it to the land and keeps it from
being an island; it is like a ship at anchor that has let down its gangplank
onto the land. So the inhabitants can easily shut out hostile action from
any direction: an infantry attack since it has to come from the sea, and
one gate is enough; and a naval assault by means of their walls, since the
city is solidly built and is closed off like a house by harbor installations.

All the surrounding area, then, had been captured, and the Tyrians 3
alone were defying the Egyptians and remained well disposed and loyal
to Persia. Irritated by this, the Egyptian king summoned his council; that
was the first time he called Chaereas into his circle of advisers. He made
the following speech. "My allies!—for I am not going to call my friends
slaves—you see the problem. We are like a ship that has had fair sailing
for a long time and now is caught in an adverse wind. Tyre, impregnable
Tyre, is holding back our swift advance; and we hear too that the King is
hard upon us. So what should we do? We cannot take Tyre; nor can we
pass it by; it is like a wall that stands in our way, shutting us out of the
whole of Asia. My view is that we should get away as soon as we can,
before the Persian forces join the Tyrians. It would be dangerous for us
to be caught in enemy territory. Pelusium, on the other hand, is secure.
There we need not fear attack from Tyrians or Medes or the whole
world. The desert is impassable, the entrance is narrow, the sea is ours,
and the Nile is the Egyptians' friend." At this overcautious speech all fell
silent and were downcast. Chaereas was the only one with enough spirit
to say anything. "Your Majesty," he said, "for it is with you that true
majesty lies, not with the Persian, who is the vilest of human beings—I
am sorry you are considering retreat at a time when we should be celebrating victory, for we are on the road to victory, if the gods so will; and
it is not just Tyre we are going to capture, but Babylon itself. Many obstacles arise in a war; we should not shrink from them but come to grips
with them, with good hope as a constant shield. These Tyrians who are
now laughing us to scorn—I shall set them before you naked and in
chains. If you do not believe me, then leave—but sacrifice me first; for I
shall not share your retreat while I live. But if you insist on going, leave
a few volunteers with me;

I and Polycharmus will fight, for it is at a god's behest that we have
come."[106]

They were all too ashamed not to accept Chaereas's proposal; the king
applauded his spirit and granted him permission to select as large a force

---

106. Adapted from *Iliad* 9.48–49, where Diomedes similarly rejects Agamemnon's proposal to leave Troy, in face of imminent defeat.

as he wanted. He did not make his choice immediately but went about among the troops encamped there, telling Polycharmus to do the same, and began first to search out any Greeks in the camp. There were a number to be found, serving as mercenaries; he picked out Spartans, Corinthians, and men from the Peloponnese generally, and also found a score or so of Sicilians. When he had formed a group of three hundred, he addressed them as follows. "Greeks! The king gave me the chance to pick the best men in the army; I have picked you; I am Greek myself, from Syracuse, Dorian by race. We must surpass the others in courage as well as in noble origin. Now, no one should panic at the operation I am asking you to undertake; we shall find it feasible and easy—it looks more difficult than it will prove to be. The same number of Greeks resisted Xerxes at Thermopylae. There are not five million Tyrians;[107] there are only a few of them; they are disdainful and arrogant, not spirited and sensible. Well, they shall find out how superior Greeks are to Phoenicians. I have no passionate desire to be your leader. I will follow anyone among you who wants to be in command; he will find me obedient—it is not my own fame but that of all of us that fires my ambition." They all cried out, "*You* be our general!" "You want me to be your leader—I will," he said. "You have given me the command, so I shall do all I can to ensure that you do not regret showing this goodwill to me and this trust in me. Rather, with the help of the gods you shall become famous and celebrated in our own time, as well as the richest of the allies, and for the future you shall leave behind you an undying reputation for courage. Everyone will sing your praises; as they do with Othryades' three hundred men or those of Leonidas, so they will with Chaereas's band."[108] Before he had finished speaking, they all cried out, "Be our leader!" and they all ran for their weapons.

4       Chaereas equipped them with the best of arms and armor and led them to the king's tent. The Egyptian was surprised to see them; he thought it was not his familiar troops, but some others, that he was looking at, and he promised them great rewards. "We are sure of that," said Chaereas, "but keep the rest of your troops in arms, and do not move on Tyre until we have it in our power and climb up on the walls

---

107. Herodotus (7.186) gives this as the number of Persians (counting camp followers) at Thermopylae, though no one now believes him. The reference in the preceding sentences to three hundred troops is of course to the famous three hundred Spartans who stayed with King Leonidas at Thermopylae in 480, after Leonidas had sent all the other Greek forces home. They were killed to the last man by the advancing Persians.

108. I here translate the text as modified by Lucke-Schäfer, after D'Orville, at 7.3.11: πάντες ὑμνήσουσιν ὡς τοὺς μετὰ Ὀθρυάδου τριακοσίους ἢ τοὺς μετὰ Λεωνίδου. For Othryades, the manuscript mentions Mithridates (sheer confusion). He is mentioned by Herodotus (1.82), in an account of a conflict between Argos and Sparta that does not seem nearly as appropriate as the Thermopylae story. Perhaps Chariton is gilding the lily with rather pale paint, or possibly there is an interpolation in the text.

and call you in." "May the gods bring that to pass!" said the king. Chaereas drew his men up in close order and then led them against Tyre; they looked far fewer than they were—in fact it really was a case of

> Shield pressed against shield, helmet against helmet, man against man.[109]

At first they were not even seen by the enemy, but when they were close, the men on the wall caught sight of them and signaled to those inside. The last thing they expected was that they were hostile troops; who would ever have thought that so small a force would approach an extremely powerful city to attack it—a city that not even the whole Egyptian army had ever dared to attack? When they came close to the walls, the Tyrians wanted to know who they were and what they wanted. Chaereas replied: "We are Greek mercenaries. We are not getting our pay from the Egyptians—in fact, they are plotting to kill us. So we have come to you to join you, so as to get our revenge on our common enemy." This information was passed on to those inside. The gates were opened and the garrison commander came out with a handful of men. Chaereas killed him first and rushed at the others

> And smote about him on every side; and a hideous groaning rose from them.[110]

Others slew others, like lions falling on an unguarded herd of cattle; and the whole city was in the grip of wailing and lamentation as few could see what was happening and everyone was in a panic. A disordered mass of people poured out at the gate to see what had happened. That more than anything else was what brought about the destruction of the Tyrians; for those inside kept trying to force their way out, while the people outside, being struck and stabbed by swords and spears, tried to escape back inside; they collided with each other in a confined space, and this gave their slaughterers an excellent opportunity. It was not even possible to close the gates, because the entry was piled high with corpses.

In this indescribable confusion Chaereas was the only one who kept his head. He forced his way through those in his path, got inside the gates, leapt up onto the walls with nine others, and from up there signaled to the Egyptians to come. They arrived at lightning speed, and Tyre was captured. Its capture was the signal for general festivity; Chaereas alone neither offered sacrifice nor put a garland on his head. "What use is it to me to celebrate victory if you are not there to watch, Callirhoe? I will never wear a garland again, after our wedding night; if

109. *Iliad* 13.131 and 16.215.
110. *Odyssey* 22.308 and 24.184 (the slaughter of the suitors) and elsewhere—especially *Iliad* 10.483ff., where the simile of the lion follows at once, as here.

you are dead, it is sacrilege; and even if you are alive, how can I be festive if I am separated from you?"[111]

Well, that was the situation they were in. As for the Persian King, he had crossed the Euphrates and was hurrying as fast as he could to get to grips with the enemy; for when he heard that Tyre had been captured, he was afraid for Sidon and the whole of Syria, since he could see that the enemy were now a match for him. He decided for this reason not to take all his train along with him on the march anymore, but to travel light so that nothing would impede his rapidity of movement. He took with him the best of his army and left behind the age group unsuited for service, along with the Queen, his possessions, his clothing, and the royal treasure. Since everything was a mass of confusion and disorder, and since the cities as far as the Euphrates were in the grip of the war, he thought it would be safer to put the people who were being left behind on Aradus for security.

5      Aradus is an island three or four miles from the mainland.[112] It contains an old shrine of Aphrodite; the women lived there as in a house, feeling completely secure. Callirhoe stood in front of Aphrodite, looking at her. At first she said nothing but wept; her tears reproached the goddess. Then she managed to find her voice. "So now it is Aradus; a small island instead of great Sicily—and there is no one here of my own people. My lady, that is enough. How long are you going to be at war with me? I may really have given you offense; but you have punished me for it. Perhaps my ill-starred beauty evoked your indignation; but it has been my ruin. Now I have experienced the one misfortune I had never known—war. Compared to my present situation, even Babylon was charitable to me. There Chaereas was near at hand. Now he is assuredly dead; he would not have stayed alive when I left the city. But I do not know from whom I can find out what has happened to him. All are strangers to me, all are foreigners; they envy me, they hate me—and worse than those who hate me are those who love me! My lady, reveal to me whether Chaereas is alive!" With these words on her lips she went away. Rhodogune came to her to comfort her;[113] she was the daughter of Zopyrus and the wife of Megabyzus—both father and husband were Persian nobles; she had been the first Persian woman to meet Callirhoe on her entry into Babylon.

When the Egyptian heard that the King was close, and had made preparations both on land and at sea, he called Chaereas to him and said: "I have not had the chance to reward you for your first success—putting

111. I accept Jackson's emendation.
112. Aradus was north of Tyre and Sidon and east of Cyprus.
113. I accept Morel's emendation ("Some Remarks on the Text of Chariton," *Classical Quarterly* 33 [1939]: 212).

Tyre into my hands; but I ask you to help me with the next stage. We must not lose the advantages we now possess, which I shall share with you: I am satisfied with Egypt, Syria shall be yours. We must consider what to do. The war is at its height in both elements. I give you the choice: you command the land or the naval forces, whichever you wish. I think you will feel more at home on the sea: you Syracusans overcame even the Athenians at sea. Today it is the Persians you are fighting, and they were beaten by the Athenians. You have Egyptian warships available; they are bigger than the Sicilian ships, and there are more of them. Do as your kinsman Hermocrates did at sea!" "Any danger is sweet to me," replied Chaereas. "I will undertake this war for you, and also against the King, who is my detested enemy. But along with the warships give me my three hundred men as well." "Take them," said the king, "and as many more as you want along with them." These words were at once translated into action; the need was pressing. So the Egyptian made ready to meet the enemy with the infantry, while Chaereas was appointed admiral. The infantry were at first somewhat discouraged that Chaereas was not in their ranks, because he had now won their affection and they were full of optimism if he was to lead them; so it was as if a great body had had an eye removed. On the other hand, the navy's morale rose high, and they were filled with fighting spirit at the thought of having the bravest and finest of men as their commander. "No ignoble thought entered their minds":[114] captains, helmsmen, crew, marines, all set out eagerly to see who would be the first to display to Chaereas his zealous devotion.

Battle was joined on land and sea the same day. For a long, long time the Egyptian infantry held out against the Medes and Persians; then they were overwhelmed by sheer numbers and gave in. The King rode after them. The Egyptians tried hard to effect an escape to Pelusium; the Persians were eager to catch them before they got there. The Egyptians might actually have got away had not Dionysius produced a remarkable achievement. He had performed brilliantly in the engagement, always fighting near the King so as to catch his eye, and was the first to rout those ranged against him. Now, when the retreat proved a long one, with no respite night or day, he saw that the King was worried by that. "Don't worry, sir," he said. "I will stop the Egyptians from getting away if you give me some picked cavalry." The King commended him and gave him the cavalry. He took five thousand men and completed two

---

114. This translates an emendation of a not very suitable phrase in the manuscript, "they had little or no grief." The translation quotes a phrase from Thucydides describing the state of mind of Athenians and Spartans at the beginning of the Peloponnesian War; if the emendation is correct, the reference can be added to some other passing reminiscences of Thucydides in this passage (the great sea fight in the harbor at Syracuse in 413, which ended in the defeat of the Athenian fleet).

days' journey in one day; he fell on the Egyptians unexpectedly at night, took many of them prisoner, and killed more. The Egyptian king, who was going to be taken alive, killed himself; Dionysius took his head back to the King, who, when he saw it, said: "I shall list you as a benefactor to my house. Here and now I give you the most pleasing of gifts, one that you yourself desire above all others: I grant you Callirhoe to be your wife. The war has decided the case; you have the finest possible prize for your brave deeds." Dionysius made obeisance; he counted himself the equal of the gods, for he was convinced that he was now firmly established as Callirhoe's husband.

6    That was what happened on land. At sea Chaereas was victorious. The enemy fleet was no match for him at all: they could not take the ramming of the Egyptian triremes and would not face head-on attacks at all.[115] Some of them turned tail immediately; others were forced ashore, and Chaereas captured them, crews and all. The sea was full of shipwrecked Median vessels. But the King did not know about the defeat of his own naval forces; equally, Chaereas did not know about the Egyptian defeat on land; each thought his own side had been victorious in both elements. So on the day of his victory Chaereas sailed to Aradus to put in there; he ordered his fleet to circle round the island and keep it under surveillance ... [116] to report in person to their master. They collected the eunuchs and maidservants and all the less valuable personnel into the town square, which offered an extensive area. There were so many there that they spent the night not only in the colonnades but in the open air. Those of some value they took into a building in the square where the town council usually transacted its business. The women sat on the ground around the Queen. They neither lit a fire nor ate any food; they were convinced that the King had been captured, that Persia was ruined, and that the Egyptians had won everywhere.

That night both ecstasy and misery held Aradus in their grip. The Egyptians were glad to be rid of war and enslavement to Persia; the Persian prisoners were expecting chains, whipping, humiliation, slaughter, and—the kindest fate of all—enslavement. Statira laid her head in Callirhoe's lap and wept; Callirhoe, like a cultivated Greek woman with her own experience of sorrow, did her best to comfort the Queen. What happened was as follows. An Egyptian soldier who had been given the job of guarding the people in the building discovered that the Queen was

115. The usual naval maneuver consisted of rowing between the enemy lines and then turning to ram an enemy ship on its beam with a strengthened prow. Sometimes head-on attacks were made. In any case the tactics consisted of ramming, after which "marines" would board the enemy ship.

116. There is a lacuna in the text here, which presumably described Chaereas's capture of Aradus and the Persians who were there but did not include his recognition of who the captives were; probably not a lot is missing.

inside. Given the innate superstition that barbarians feel towards the royal title, he could not bring himself to approach her; but he stood by the closed door and said: "Do not be afraid, my lady. At present the admiral does not know that you too have been shut up here with the prisoners, but when he finds out, he will look after you kindly. He is not only brave but ... [117] will make you his wife—he has a liking for women." When she heard that, Callirhoe broke out in loud lamentation and tore her hair. "Now I really am a prisoner! Slay me, but do not make me such a promise! Marriage I cannot endure—I pray rather for death! They can torture me—goads and fire will not make me rise from here; this spot is my tomb! If your commander is as kind as you say, let him grant me this favor—let him kill me here!" The Egyptian renewed his pleas, but she refused to get up; rather she sank to the floor and lay there, her head covered. The Egyptian had to consider what to do: he could not bring himself to use force, but on the other hand could not persuade her to do as he said. So he went back to Chaereas with a gloomy expression. When he saw him Chaereas said: "What has happened now? Are there people stealing the best of the spoils? They won't get away with it!" "There is no harm done, sir," replied the Egyptian. "It is that woman; I found her lying on the floor;[118] she refuses to come. She has thrown herself on the ground; she is asking for a sword to kill herself with." Chaereas laughed. "What a fool you are!" he said. "Don't you know how to deal with a woman? Appeal to her, flatter her, make promises to her! Above all, let her think she is loved! You probably tried to force her to come and treated her harshly." "No, sir, I didn't," he said. "I have  done everything you said—in fact I've gone a lot farther: I've taken your name in vain and said you would marry her—and that made her angrier than ever." "What a charming, irresistible man I must be," said Chaereas, "if she rejects me and hates me before she has even seen me. She seems to be a woman of dignity. No one is to offer her violence; let her do as she pleases; self-respect deserves my respect. Perhaps she is mourning a husband herself."

117. There is an altogether bigger lacuna in the text here. Apparently Chaereas learns that the Queen is among the prisoners (but of course has no idea that Callirhoe is with her) and gives orders to treat her with all respect. In the course of carrying out his orders, one of his Egyptian adjutants sees an extraordinarily beautiful woman (but of course does not know who she is) and reports this to Chaereas. Chaereas sends for her, and it is while on this errand that the Egyptian promises her favorable treatment, including marriage, from Chaereas (without naming him); this is the position when the text begins again. There are strong echoes, even in what is preserved of this scene, of Alexander's magnanimity to the family of the defeated Darius after the battle of Issus in 333 (see Arrian *Anabasis* 2.7—but Chariton is using an earlier Alexander-history) and of Xenophon's *Cyropaedia* 5.1.6, where Cyrus is described by one of his staff as being similarly generous in comparable circumstances. See Plepelits, *Chariton*, 18f. and n. 181.

118. The text is badly corrupted here; the translation gives a suitable sense.

## Book Eight

I How Chaereas, suspecting that Callirhoe had been handed over to Dionysius, determined to avenge himself on the King and so went over to the Egyptian side; how he was appointed admiral and gained control of the sea; how after his victory he seized Aradus, where the King had placed his own wife for security, and along with her all his train and Callirhoe too—all of that has been described in the previous book. But Fortune was minded to do something as cruel as it was paradoxical: Chaereas was to have Callirhoe in his possession and fail to recognize her; while taking others' wives on board his ships to carry them off, he was to leave his own behind, not like Ariadne asleep, and not for Dionysus to be her bridegroom, but as spoils of war for his own enemies. But Aphrodite thought this too harsh; she was growing less angry with him. At first she had been incensed by his misplaced jealousy: she had given him the fairest of gifts, fairer even than the gift she had accorded to Alexander Paris,[119] and he had repaid her kindness with arrogance. But now that Chaereas had made honorable amends to Love, in that he had wandered the world from west to east and gone through untold suffering, Aphrodite took pity on him; having harassed by land and sea the handsome couple she had originally brought together, she decided now to reunite them. And I think that this last chapter will prove very agreeable to its readers: it cleanses away[120] the grim events of the earlier ones. There will be no more pirates or slavery or lawsuits or fighting or suicide or wars or conquests; now there will be lawful love and sanctioned marriage. So I shall tell you how the goddess brought the truth to light and revealed the unrecognized pair to each other.

It was evening,[121] and much of the captured material was still left on shore. Worn out as he was, Chaereas got up to make his arrangements for the ships' departure. As he was passing through the town square, the Egyptian said to him: "Sir, there is the woman who wouldn't come to you but wants to kill herself. Perhaps you can persuade her to get up— why leave behind the choicest of the spoils?" Polycharmus added his weight to the suggestion; he wanted to push Chaereas into a new love affair if at all possible, to console him for the loss of Callirhoe. "Let's go in

119. The gift, of course, was Helen. In imperial authors Paris is sometimes, as here, called by both his names; earlier, by one or the other. (Paris is not a Greek name; Alexander, "he who fights men off," is its Greek translation.)

120. It is of some interest that the word Chariton uses for "cleanses away," *katharsion,* is the adjectival form of the noun *katharsis* (*catharsis* in Latin transliteration) made famous by Aristotle in his *Poetics,* of the operation of tragedy; there it is usually translated either "purge" or "purify" (i.e., "refine"). We cannot be sure whether or not Chariton is referring to Aristotle; in any event, the idea here is clearly "getting rid of," "obliterating."

121. See note 10 above for this reference to a familiar dramatic passage in Demosthenes.

to her, Chaereas," he said. So he went in the door. When he saw her stretched out on the ground with her head covered, he felt his heart stirred at once by the way she breathed and the look of her, and felt a thrill of excitement; he would certainly have recognized her had he not been thoroughly convinced that Dionysius had taken Callirhoe for himself. He went up to her quietly. "Don't be frightened, lady," he said, "whoever you are. We are not going to use force on you. You shall have the husband you want." Before he had finished speaking, Callirhoe recognized his voice and threw the covering from her face. They both cried out at the same time: "Chaereas!" "Callirhoe!" They fell into each other's arms, swooned, and fell to the ground. At first Polycharmus too could only stand there, struck speechless by this miracle. But after a time he said: "Get up! You have recovered each other; the gods have granted your wishes, both of you; but remember that you are not in your own country, you are in enemy territory, and the first thing to do is to deal with that situation, so that no one separates you again." He had to shout; they were like people plunged deep in a well who could scarcely hear a voice calling from above. Slowly they came to themselves; then, when they saw each other and embraced, they were overcome again; and this happened a second time and a third time. All they could say was: "You are in my arms—if you really are Callirhoe!" "If you really are Chaereas!"

The rumor spread that the admiral had found his wife. Not a soldier stayed in his tent, not a sailor on his ship, not a lodgekeeper at his door. People poured together from all sides, saying to each other, "What a lucky woman, to win such a handsome husband!" But when Callirhoe appeared, no one praised Chaereas anymore; they all turned their gaze on her, as if she alone existed. She moved with dignity, escorted on either side by Chaereas and Polycharmus. They had flowers and wreaths showered on them; wine and myrrh were poured out at their feet as they walked; the sweetest fruits of war and peace were joined in celebration of victory and marriage.

Chaereas was in the habit of sleeping on board ship, since he was busy night and day. Now, however, he handed everything over to Polycharmus, and himself went into the royal bedroom without even waiting for night to fall (in every town there is a special house set aside for the Great King). In it was a bed of beaten gold covered with cloth of Tyrian purple, of Babylonian weave. Who could describe that night? They told each other their countless adventures; they wept endlessly; they embraced endlessly. It was Callirhoe who began, with her story: how she had come back to life in the tomb; how she had been carried off by Theron; how she had crossed the sea; how she had been sold. Up to that point Chaereas had wept as he listened, but when she reached Miletus in her account of her adventures, Callirhoe became embarrassed and fell silent, and Chaereas' natural jealousy rose up in him again; he was consoled, however, when he heard about the child. But before he had heard the whole story, he said: "Tell me how you came to Aradus, and where you left Dionysius, and what you have had to do with the King." She at once swore that she had not seen Dionysius since the trial; the King, she said, was in love with her, but she had had no contact with him, not even a kiss. "Then I have been unjust and quick-tempered in doing the King so much damage when he was not harming you; when I was separated from you, I thought I had to go over to his enemy's side. But I have not disgraced you; I have filled land and sea with trophies of victory." And he told his whole story in detail, taking pride in his successes. But when they had had enough of weeping and describing their adventures, they fell into each other's arms and

Gladly turned to the pact of their bed as of old.[122]

2      But before day broke, an Egyptian of high rank landed, and as he stepped ashore from the cutter he began to ask urgently where Chaereas was. So he was taken to Polycharmus; but he said he could not deliver his secret message to anyone else, and his mission was very urgent. For a long time Polycharmus tried to put off his meeting with Chaereas, because he thought it was no time to intrude on him. But since the man kept on insisting urgently, he half-opened the bedroom door and told Chaereas of the emergency. Like a good general, Chaereas said: "Tell him to come in. War brooks no delay." It was still dark when the Egyptian was shown in. He stood by the bed. "I have to tell you," he said, "that the Persian King has killed the Egyptian king. He has sent part of his army to Egypt to establish order there and is bringing all the rest here—in fact he is almost here now. He has heard that Aradus has been taken and is very anxious about all the wealth he has left here, but particularly distressed about his wife, Statira." At this news Chaereas leapt up, but Callirhoe caught hold of him. "Where are you rushing off to," she said, "before thinking about the situation? If you broadcast this news, you will cause a great insurrection—once everybody knows, they will pay no heed to you. We shall be captured again and shall be worse off then ever." Chaereas was soon convinced by what she said, and had a plan in mind when he left the bedroom. He took the Egyptian by the hand and called all his force together. "Men," he said, "we have beaten the King's forces on land as well! This man has brought us the good news and letters from the Egyptian king. We are to sail as soon as we can where he tells us; so all of you get ready and board ship."

122. *Odyssey* 23.296 (the reunion of Odysseus and Penelope).

At these words the trumpeter sounded the call for reembarkation. They had loaded the spoils and prisoners the previous day, and there were only heavy or useless objects left on the island. Then they began casting off and weighing anchor; the harbor was full of shouting and confusion, with everybody busy at something. Chaereas went from ship to ship, giving the captain of each a secret signal to set course for Cyprus—they must seize it, he said, while it was still without a garrison. The next day they had a favorable wind and put in at Paphos, where there is a temple of Aphrodite.[123] When they anchored, before anyone disembarked, Chaereas sent heralds to proclaim peace and make a treaty with the inhabitants. They accepted the proposal, and he landed his whole force and paid honor to Aphrodite with offerings; then, collecting a large number of animals for sacrifice, he held a feast for his army. While he was considering his next move, the priests, who are also prophets,[124] reported that the sacrifices augured well. Cheered by this news, he called together the ships' captains and his three hundred Greeks[125] and all the Egyptians whom he saw to be well disposed to him and spoke as follows.

"Fellow soldiers and friends! You have shared great successes. To me, peace is fairest and war least dangerous when you are with me. Experience has shown that harmony among us has made us masters of the sea. And the critical moment is now on us when we must consider our future course, for our own security. I have to tell you that the Egyptian king has been killed in battle; the King of Persia is in possession of all the land; and we are caught in the midst of our enemies. So now, does anyone suggest that we go off to the King and throw ourselves unreservedly into his hands?" They immediately shouted that that was the last thing they should do. "Then where shall we go? Everything is hostile to us. We cannot even rely on the sea anymore, now that the land is in the hands of our enemies. We cannot fly away!" These words were greeted with si-

123. Paphos is the name of a settlement in southwestern Cyprus where there was indeed a famous shrine of Aphrodite. But it is some miles inland. It was only after the dramatic date of the story, in the early Hellenistic period, that a *port* was built near Paphos; and the port usurped the name, the original Paphos becoming Old Paphos. Chariton is here conflating the two places—which admittedly are not very far apart—and thus killing two birds with one stone: finding a suitable launching pad for the last stage of his heroes' journey and reestablishing contact between them and Aphrodite. It thus seems likely that this anachronism is a conscious narrative device on his part. See Plepelits, *Chariton*, 187–88 n. 184.

124. As Plepelits, *Chariton*, 188 n. 185, observes, it is interesting that Chariton evidently thought that his own audience would need this footnote; in earlier classical times it would not have been necessary.

125. Through a printer's error the three hundred Greeks are omitted from Blake's Greek text, although they appear in his translation, *Chariton's Chaereas and Callirhoe* (Chicago and Oxford, 1939).

lence. A Lacedaemonian, a relative of Brasidas,[126] who had had to leave Sparta as a result of a crisis, took it on himself to speak first. "Why are we looking for somewhere to go to get away from the King?" he said. "We have the sea; we have ships; between them they can take us to Sicily and Syracuse, and there we need not be afraid of the Persians or even the Athenians." Everyone applauded these sentiments. Chaereas alone pretended not to agree; the reason he gave was that it was a long way to sail, but he really wanted to test their firmness of purpose. But they insisted and were all for sailing at once. "Well, my Greeks," he said, "it is good advice you are giving; I am grateful to you for your goodwill and your loyalty. I shall see to it that you do not regret it, if the gods take you into their care. But the Egyptians—there are many of them whom we cannot compel against their will; they have wives and children, most of them, whom they do not want to be torn from—so circulate among their numbers and start asking around, each one of them, as quickly as you can, to make sure we take along only those who want to come."

3    His instructions were carried out. But Callirhoe took Chaereas by the hand and led him aside by himself. "What have you decided to do, Chaereas?" she asked. "Are you going to take Statira and the beautiful Rhodogune to Syracuse as well?" Chaereas blushed. "It is not for myself that I am taking them," he said, "but as servants for you." "May the gods never make me so mad," cried Callirhoe, "as to have the Queen of Asia as my slave! Especially as she has shown me hospitality! If you want to please me, send her to the King; she kept me safe for you as if it were her own brother's wife she had in her charge." "There is nothing I would not do for you," said Chaereas. "You are mistress of Statira and all I have won from the enemy—and, above all, of my heart." Callirhoe was delighted. She kissed Chaereas and at once told her servants to take her to Statira. Statira was in the hold of a ship, along with the highest-ranking Persian women. She knew nothing at all of what had happened, not even that Callirhoe had found her Chaereas, since she was heavily guarded and no one was allowed to approach her or tell her anything of what was happening. When Callirhoe came on board, with the captain escorting her, everyone immediately panicked and began running all over in their confusion. Then one man said quietly to another, "The admiral's wife is here." Statira gave a loud, profound sigh and began to weep. "Fortune!" she cried. "You have preserved me to this day so that I, a queen, may look upon my mistress! Perhaps she has come to see what sort of slave she has acquired!" At this she raised a loud lament; at that moment she found out what it is for a noble person to be a captive.

126. A Spartan general during the Peloponnesian War.

But it was a rapid change of fortune that the god brought about: Callirhoe entered quickly and embraced Statira. "Be of good heart, Queen!" she said, "for Queen you are and always shall remain. It is no enemy whose hands you have fallen into, but your dear friend, whose benefactor you have been. It is my Chaereas who is admiral; it was his anger against the King that made him admiral of the Egyptian fleet, because of the delay in recovering me. But his anger is past; he has made his peace and is no longer Persia's enemy. Get up, my dear, and go in good heart. You too shall have your own husband, for the King is alive, and Chaereas is sending you to him. And you get up too, Rhodogune, the first Persian woman to be my friend, and go to your own husband; and as many other women as the Queen wishes. And remember Callirhoe!" Statira was astonished to hear this; she could neither believe it nor disbelieve it. But Callirhoe's character was such that no one could think she would mislead people in so serious a situation; and the emergency called for immediate action. Now there was among the Egyptians a man called Demetrius, a philosopher who was known to the King of Persia; he was advanced in years and superior to the other Egyptians in culture and character. Chaereas called this man to him and said: "I wanted to take you with me, but instead I am asking you to undertake an important mission for me: I am sending the Queen in your charge to the Great King. This will also give you greater standing with him and will assure a pardon for the rest." At this he appointed Demetrius commander of the ships that were being sent back.

Everybody wanted to go with Chaereas; they thought more of him than of their countries and their children. But he chose only twenty ships, the biggest and best, because he was going to cross the Ionian Sea; on board these he put all the Greeks who were there and all the Egyptians and Phoenicians he found to be most energetic; many Cypriots embarked too as volunteers. All the rest he sent home; he gave them a share of the spoils so that they could look forward to returning to their families, because their standing would be improved. No one who asked anything of Chaereas failed to get it. Callirhoe brought all the royal jewels to Statira. She would not take them, however. "No," she said, "you wear them; beauty like yours deserves to be royally adorned. You need presents for your mother and offerings for your country's gods. I have left in Babylon more than there is here. May the gods grant you a good journey safe home and may you never again be separated from Chaereas. You have behaved properly to me in every way; you have shown a noble character, worthy of your beauty. It was a fine treasure that the King left in trust with me!"

Who could describe all the different activities of that day? There were 4 people praying, saying good-bye, rejoicing, sorrowing, giving each other instructions, writing home; Chaereas, too, wrote a letter, to the King, as follows.

You were going to decide the case, but I have already been declared the winner by the fairest of judges: war is the best arbiter between stronger and weaker. War has given me back Callirhoe; and it has given me not only my wife but yours as well. But I am not as slow to act as you; I am restoring Statira to you rapidly, though you have not even asked for her return; she is undefiled, and even in captivity has remained a queen. You should know that it is not I who am sending this gift, but Callirhoe. We ask you to repay us by pardoning the Egyptians; more than anyone, a king should show forbearance. You will have good soldiers who will feel affection for you; they have chosen to stay with you in friendship rather than come with me.

That was what Chaereas wrote. Callirhoe too thought it proper to show her gratitude to Dionysius by writing to him. This was the only thing she did independently of Chaereas; knowing his jealous nature, she was anxious to prevent him learning of it. She took a writing tablet and wrote the following.

From Callirhoe: greetings to Dionysius, my benefactor—for it was you who freed me from pirates and slavery. Please do not be angry: I am with you in spirit through the son we share; I entrust him to you to bring up and educate in a way worthy of us. Do not let him learn what a stepmother is like. You have a daughter as well as a son; two children are enough for you. Marry them to each other when he comes of age;[127] and send him to Syracuse so that he can see his grandfather too. Plangon, my greetings to you; this letter is written in my own hand. Fare you well, good Dionysius, and remember your Callirhoe.

She sealed the letter and hid it in a fold of her dress. When the time came to put to sea, when everyone had to embark, she personally gave her hand to Statira and led her to the ship. Demetrius had set up a royal tent on the ship, with its sides made of purple, gold-stitched Babylonian cloth. Callirhoe, with the most flattering attentions, helped her to dispose herself on the couch. "Good-bye, Statira," she said. "Remember me and write to me often in Syracuse—anything is easy for the King. I shall tell my parents and the gods of Greece how grateful I am to you. I commit my child to your goodwill—you too liked to see him; tell yourself that you have him entrusted to you in place of me." At these words

127. In Greece half siblings with the same father (but not those with the same mother) could marry and often did. (Dionysius of course thinks that he is the father of both children.)

Statira's eyes filled with tears and she set her attendant women weeping and wailing. As she was leaving the ship, Callirhoe leaned a little towards Statira, blushed, and gave her the letter. "Give this to poor Dionysius," she said. "I recommend him to your care and the King's. Comfort him. I am afraid that now he is separated from me he may kill himself." The women would have gone on talking and weeping and embracing each other if the helmsmen had not given the order to put to sea. Just before she went on board, Callirhoe made an obeisance to Aphrodite. "I thank you, lady," she said, "for what is happening now. You are reconciled to me now; grant that I see Syracuse too! A great stretch of sea separates me from there; an ocean is waiting for me that is frightening to cross; but I am not frightened if you are sailing with me." None of the Egyptians would embark in Demetrius's ships without saying good-bye to Chaereas, kissing his head and hands; such affection did he inspire in everyone. And he let Demetrius's fleet put out to sea first, so that until it was far out cries of praise for him could be heard mixed with prayers for his well-being.

So they were off on their journey across the sea. Meanwhile, now that 5 the Great King had overcome his enemies, he sent a man to Egypt to restore order and stability there, while he hurried to Aradus to recover his wife. When he had reached Chios[128] and Tyre and was celebrating his victory by sacrificing to Hercules, a messenger arrived with the news that Aradus had been sacked and was now deserted, and that everything on the island was being carried away in the Egyptian ships. Of course this news caused the King deep distress—he thought the Queen was lost. The Persian nobles were in anguish too,

Apparently for Statira, but in fact each for his own sorrows;[129]

one mourned his wife, another a sister, another a daughter, everyone some relative. The enemy had sailed off, but no one knew in what direction. The next day the Egyptian ships were seen approaching. Not knowing what the situation really was, they were surprised to see them. They were even more puzzled when the royal standard was broken from Demetrius's ship; usually it was flown only when the King was aboard. This caused confusion, since they were thought to be enemy ships. They ran at once to tell Artaxerxes. "Perhaps it will turn out to be a king of Egypt," they said. The King jumped up from his throne, rushed to the shore, and gave the signal for battle; he had no warships but posted all

128. Manifestly not the large island off the west coast of Asia Minor; Chariton, who lived in Caria, could hardly make such a mistake in geography. Either the text is corrupt or the name here refers to a locality near Tyre.

129. *Iliad* 19.302 modified (women weeping, ostensibly for Patroclus but in fact for themselves).

his forces on the harbor ready for battle. They were already drawing their bows and were ready to throw their spears, had not Demetrius realized the situation and reported it to the Queen. Statira came out of her tent and showed herself. At once they threw down their arms and made obeisance. The King could not control himself but was the first to leap on board the ship, before it had even put in properly to shore. Throwing his arms round his wife, he wept in his joy. "What god has restored you to me, my dearest wife?" he said. "I cannot believe either that the Queen should be lost or that being lost she should be found again! How is it that when I left you behind on land, I recover you from the sea?" Statira replied, "I am a gift to you from Callirhoe." The sound of that name, to the King, was like a fresh blow on an old wound. He looked at the eunuch Artaxates. "Take me to Callirhoe; I want to thank her." "I will tell you the whole story," said Statira; and at that they went from the harbor to the palace. Then she told everyone to go away, allowing only the eunuch to stay, and told him what had happened on Aradus and in Cyprus; she ended by giving him Chaereas's letter. The King was filled with countless emotions as he read it: he was angry at the capture of his dear ones, he regretted making Chaereas go over to his enemies, and then again he was grateful to him that he could not see Callirhoe anymore.[130] But above all he was envious. "Happy Chaereas!" he said. "He is luckier than I!"

When they had described their experiences to their satisfaction, Statira said, "King, console Dionysius—Callirhoe asks you to do so." Artaxerxes turned to the eunuch. "Tell Dionysius to come," he said. He came at once, his hopes buoyed up; he knew nothing of what Chaereas had done, and thought that Callirhoe had come with the other women and that the King was calling him to give her to him as he had promised, as a reward for his courageous behaviour. When he came in, the King told him everything that had happened. It was at this critical moment above all that Dionysius showed his good sense and excellent upbringing. As if a man were to remain undisturbed by a thunderbolt landing at his feet, so Dionysius, when he heard words more distressing to him than any bolt from the blue—that Chaereas was taking Callirhoe away to Syracuse— remained steady; he did not think it prudent to give way to grief when the Queen had been saved. "If I could," said Artaxerxes, "I would have restored Callirhoe to you, Dionysius; you have shown yourself entirely devoted and loyal to me. But since that is impossible, I am appointing you to govern all Ionia, and you will be given the title of Principal Benefactor of the Royal House of Persia. Dionysius made obeisance, thanked

130. There may be some words missing in the text, to the effect that the King "was grateful to him that [he had treated the queen well, but sorry that] he could not see Callirhoe anymore."

the King, and made haste to leave so as to be able to give rein to his tears. As he left, Statira unobtrusively gave him the letter.

Dionysius went back to his quarters and shut himself in. When he recognized Callirhoe's handwriting, he first kissed the letter, then opened it and clasped it to his breast as if it were Callirhoe present in the flesh. He held it there for a long time, unable to read it for crying. After copious tears he began to read it, with difficulty; and the first thing he did was kiss the name "Callirhoe." When he came to the phrase "to Dionysius, my benefactor," he groaned: "Ah, no longer 'my husband!' No, it is you who are *my* benefactor—what have I done for you to deserve that name?" But he was pleased with the plea that the letter contained, and read the same passage time and time again, for it seemed to suggest that she had left him unwillingly; Love is such an irresponsible thing and can easily persuade a lover that he is loved in return! He gazed at the child and "rocked him in his arms."[131] "You too will leave me someday, my son," he said, "and go to your mother; that is what she herself asks. And I shall live all alone. It is all my own fault! It is my futile jealousy that has ruined me—and you, Babylon!" With these words he got ready to return to Ionia as quickly as possible, thinking he would find great consolation in a long journey, authority over many cities, and the likenesses of Callirhoe in Miletus.

This, then, was the situation in Asia. Meanwhile, Chaereas completed 6 the journey to Syracuse successfully; he had a following wind all the time. Since he had big ships, he took the route across the open sea, terrified as he was of once more being a target for some cruel deity's attack.[132] When Syracuse appeared on the horizon, he gave the order to the captains to decorate their ships, and also to sail in close formation since the sea was calm. The inhabitants saw them, and someone said: "Warships? Where are they coming from? They aren't Athenian, are they? We had better tell Hermocrates." He was told at once. "General," they said, "consider what you are going to do. Should we close the harbors? Or should we put out against them? We do not know whether a bigger fleet is following and the ones we can see are only an advance squadron." Hermocrates hurried down from the main square to the shore and sent a rowboat to meet them. The man he sent, when he drew near, asked who they were. Chaereas instructed one of the Egyptians to reply, "We are merchants from Egypt, with a cargo that will delight the Syracusans." "Well, do not all sail in together," said the Syracusan, "until we find out whether you are telling the truth. I cannot see any

131. Chariton here adapts a phrase from a famous scene in the *Iliad* (6.474) where Hector plays with his son, Astyanax, for the last time before going, as he knows, to meet his death at the hands of Achilles.

132. The direct route (cf. note 52 above) would be quickest, although for smaller ships it would also be dangerous sailing.

cargo ships—only naval vessels, which look like warships that have been in action. Most of you will have to stay at sea outside the harbor; one ship can come in." "We will do as you say."

So Chaereas's ship sailed in first. On its upper deck was a tent covered with Babylonian tapestries. When the ship docked, the whole harbor was full of people; a crowd is naturally an inquisitive thing, and on this occasion they had several other reasons for collecting. When they saw the tent, they thought that it contained not people but rich cargo; they made various conjectures about it, but guessed everything except the truth. For since they were already convinced that Chaereas was dead, it was quite out of the question that they should expect him to land back home alive, and amid such luxury. So Chaereas's parents did not even come out of their house. Hermocrates was active in the city's affairs but was also in mourning; on this occasion he was present but stayed in the background. No one knew what to make of it, and they were all straining their eyes, when suddenly the tapestries were drawn back. Callirhoe could be seen reclining on a couch of beaten gold, dressed in Tyrian purple; Chaereas, dressed like a general, sat beside her. Thunder never so stunned the ears nor lightning the eyes of those who beheld them, nor did anyone who had found a treasure of gold ever cry out as did that crowd then, when beyond all expectation they saw an indescribable sight. Hermocrates leapt on board, ran to the tent, and threw his arms around his daughter. "Are you alive, my child," he cried, "or is this too an illusion?" "I am alive, Father! I am really alive now that I have seen you!" They all wept for joy.

Meanwhile, Polycharmus was sailing in with the other ships—it was he who had been entrusted with the rest of the fleet since they left Cyprus, because Chaereas could no longer give his attention to anyone but Callirhoe. So the harbor quickly filled up; it looked like the scene after the sea fight with Athens—these ships too were sailing back from battle decorated with garlands and with a Syracusan commander. The crews of the ships joined their voices to those of the people on shore in mutual greeting; the air was thick with blessings, cries of praise, and prayers, exchanged by both sides. Chaereas's father came too, fainting with the unexpected joy. Chaereas's friends from young men's club and playing field jostled to welcome him. The women crowded round Callirhoe, who seemed to them to be lovelier than ever; you truly would have thought you were looking at Aphrodite herself as she arose from the sea.[133] Chaereas went up to Hermocrates and his father. "Accept from me," he said, "the riches of the Great King!" There and then he

133. According to one legend Aphrodite was born of the sea foam; indeed, that is what the name itself suggests. There was a famous painting "Aphrodite rising from the sea" by Apelles.

gave orders to unload an untold quantity of silver and gold; after that he displayed to the Syracusans ivory and amber and clothing and all sorts of costly material and craftsmanship, including a bed and table belonging to the Great King; so that the whole city was filled, not, as previously, after the Sicilian war, with the poverty of Attica, but—a real novelty—with Persian spoils, in time of peace!

With one voice the throng cried out, "Let us go to the assembly!" for they were eager both to see and to hear them. More quickly than words can tell the theater was filled with men and women. When Chaereas came in by himself, they all cried out, men as well as women, "Call Callirhoe in!" In this too Hermocrates did what the people wanted: he brought his daughter in too. First the people lifted their eyes to heaven and praised the gods, more thankful for that day than for the day of their victory. After that, for a time they divided, the men uttering praise of Chaereas, and the women of Callirhoe; but then they turned to praising them both together—and that pleased the couple better. As soon as she had expressed her greetings to her country, Callirhoe was taken home from the theater after her journey and the distress she had suffered. But the crowd kept Chaereas there; they wanted to hear the whole story of his journey. Chaereas started at the end, since he did not want to cause the people sorrow by telling them of the grim episodes at the beginning. They kept on insisting, however. "Begin at the beginning, we beg you— tell us the whole story, don't leave anything out." Chaereas was reluctant to do so; he felt it would be embarrassing to talk about many events that had not turned out to his satisfaction. But Hermocrates said: "Do not be embarrassed, my boy, even if you have painful or unpleasant things to tell us. It has ended brilliantly, and that overshadows all the earlier events; whereas if you do not tell us, your very silence will make our suspicions worse. It is your own people and your own parents you are talking to, and they love you both equally. As for the first part of the story, the people themselves already know that—it was they themselves who brought about your marriage. We all know how you fell into unfounded jealousy because of the intrigue the rival suitors mounted,[134] and how you groundlessly struck your wife, and how she was thought dead and given a costly funeral, and how when you were tried for murder you condemned yourself to death out of your own mouth because you wanted to die along with your wife; but the people realized that what had happened was involuntary on your part and acquitted you. As for what happened after that—how the tomb robber Theron broke into the tomb at night, found Callirhoe alive among the funeral offerings, put her on his pirate ship, and sold her in Ionia; how you went out to search for

7

134. The text appears to be defective; I have adopted Jackson's emendation.

your wife, did not find her, but fell in with the pirate vessel at sea, and found all the rest of the pirates dead of thirst and only Theron still alive; how you brought him into the assembly and he was tortured and questioned and then crucified; how the city sent a ship and a delegation to bring back Callirhoe, and your friend Polycharmus volunteered to sail with you—all this we know. Now you tell us what happened after you sailed from here."

"Taking up the tale from there," Chaereas began his account. "We crossed the Ionian Sea safely and landed on the estate of a citizen of Miletus called Dionysius, a man preeminent throughout Ionia for his wealth, lineage, and distinguished reputation; he was the man who had bought Callirhoe from Theron for a talent. Do not be afraid; Callirhoe did not become a slave! At once he made the woman he had bought for money the mistress of his own heart. Loving her as he did, he would not bring himself to force his affections on a freeborn woman, but he could not bear to send back to Syracuse the woman he loved. When Callirhoe realized that she was pregnant by me, she found herself compelled to marry Dionysius, because she wanted to preserve your fellow citizen; she disguised the child's parentage so that it should be thought that Dionysius was the father, and so that it should be brought up in a worthy manner. Yes, Syracusans! There is growing up in Miletus one who will be a Syracusan; a wealthy one, and reared by a distinguished man—for Dionysius is indeed of distinguished Greek lineage. We should not grudge him his great inheritance!

8     "This, of course, I learned only later. At the time, when I had landed on this estate, I saw only Callirhoe's statue in a temple, and that gave me great confidence. But during the night a band of Phrygian brigands made a lightning raid on the shore, set fire to our ship, slaughtered most of us, tied me and Polycharmus up, and sold us in Caria."[135] The crowd broke out in lamentation at this. "Allow me to pass over in silence what happened next," said Chaereas. "It is grimmer than the beginning of the story." "Tell us the whole story!" cried the assembled people. Chaereas continued. "The man who bought us, a slave of Mithridates, the governor of Caria, ordered us to be put in chains and set digging. When some of the chain gang murdered their guard, Mithridates ordered us all to be crucified. I was taken away. Polycharmus, on the point of being tortured, spoke my name, and Mithridates recognized it—while staying

---

135. Chariton commits some inconsistencies in this final recapitulation. Here Chaereas speaks of Phrygian brigands; in 3.7 we are told that it was a "barbarian" (i.e., Persian) army unit that destroyed Chaereas's ships. A little farther on Chaereas says that Polycharmus uttered his (Chaereas's) name; in fact it was Callirhoe's (4.2). It is true that Chaereas himself could have no direct knowledge of these details, but it seems pointless for Chariton consciously to make him get them wrong; more probably Chariton himself is in some haste to finish his story.

with Dionysius in Miletus he had been present at Chaereas's funeral—Callirhoe had heard about the ship and the brigands, thought I had been killed, and constructed a costly tomb for me. So Mithridates at once ordered that I be taken down from the cross—I was practically finished by then—and put me among his closest friends; he was anxious to restore Callirhoe to me, and got me to write a letter to her. But through the carelessness of Mithridates' agent in the matter Dionysius got hold of the letter himself. He did not believe I was alive; he did believe that Mithridates had designs on his wife, and he immediately wrote to the King, accusing Mithridates of adulterous intentions. The King decided to hear the case and summoned everyone to him. So we went up to Babylon. Dionysius took Callirhoe with him and made her celebrated, the wonder of all Asia; Mithridates took me along with him; and when we got there we pleaded our cases in a great trial before the King. Well, he acquitted Mithridates at once and announced his intention of arbitrating between me and Dionysius over Callirhoe, whom he placed in the charge of Queen Statira in the meantime. How often, Syracusans, do you think I determined to kill myself, separated from my wife? Except that Polycharmus, the only friend to remain faithful to me throughout, saved my life. Furthermore, the King had quite disregarded the case—he was passionately in love with Callirhoe. But he could not win her, and he did not offer her violence.

"At the critical moment there was a rebellion in Egypt; that started a great war, which however brought me great benefits. The Queen took Callirhoe with her, and I heard a false report—someone told me she had been awarded to Dionysius. To get my revenge on the King I went over to the Egyptians and brought off great feats: by my own actions I subdued Tyre, which was very difficult to take; then I was appointed admiral, beat the Great King at sea, and captured Aradus, where the King had left the Queen for safety, along with the riches you have seen. So I was able to set up the Egyptian king as lord of all Asia, only he was killed fighting in a separate battle where I was not present. Finally, I secured the Great King's friendship for you by making a present to him of his wife and by sending to the Persian nobles their mothers and sisters and wives and daughters. I have brought back here with myself the best Greek troops and those of the Egyptians who wanted to come. Another fleet of yours will come from Ionia too, and it will be commanded by the descendant of Hermocrates."

This account brought cries of well-wishing from everyone. Chaereas checked the applause and said: "I and Callirhoe express, in your presence, our gratitude to my friend Polycharmus. He has shown devotion and true loyalty to us; with your agreement, let us give him my sister as his wife—and he shall have a share of the spoils as his dowry!" The assembly acclaimed his words. "The people are grateful to you, noble Polychar-mus, their loyal friend! You are a benefactor of your country! You are worthy of Hermocrates and Chaereas!" After this Chaereas spoke again. "The three hundred men here," he said, "Greeks, my brave company—I ask you to grant them citizenship!" Again the assembly cried, "They are worthy to be citizens of Syracuse—let us have that voted!" A decree was passed, and they took their places at once as members of the assembly. Chaereas also made a present of a talent to each one, and Hermocrates distributed land to the Egyptians for them to farm.

While the crowd was in the theater, Callirhoe went to Aphrodite's temple before entering her house. She put her hands on the goddess's feet, placed her face on them, let down her hair, and kissed them. "Thank you, Aphrodite!" she said. "You have shown Chaereas to me once more in Syracuse, where I saw him as a maiden at your desire. I do not blame you, my lady, for what I have suffered; it was my fate. Do not separate me from Chaereas again, I beg of you; grant us a happy life to-gether, and let us die together!"

That is my story about Callirhoe.

# XENOPHON OF EPHESUS

# AN EPHESIAN TALE

## TRANSLATED BY
## GRAHAM ANDERSON

## Introduction

The main interest of Xenophon's *Ephesian Tale of Anthia and Habrocomes*, to give it its full title, is as a specimen of penny dreadful literature in antiquity; it exhibits in vintage form the characteristics of the melodrama and the popular novel as it portrays the tribulations of a pair of lovers harassed by misfortune. The narrative exemplifies the basic pattern of late Greek romance: initial felicity rudely broken by journey and separation; danger to life, limb, and chastity; rescue by divine agency; and eventual reunion through similar means. The story thus offers a model against which more developed examples may be measured. Of its author we know next to nothing; a notice in the *Suda* tells us only that he also wrote a history of Ephesus and that the *Ephesian Tale* is in ten books, rather than the five we now have—a matter to which we shall return. His very name may be a pen name, borrowed from a more famous Xenophon. Of the work's date we know even less; suggested *termini* are inconclusive, and the most likely guess is the second century A.D.

But the *Ephesian Tale* has its own interest, which lies principally in the rich repertory of stories, variously exciting and moving, contained in its many episodes, subsidiary tales, and incidents: Anthia plunged by a drug into apparent death (a theme in *Romeo and Juliet*), or forcibly married to a poor goatherd, who, however, respects her chastity (a theme in Euripides' *Electra*); the enduring love of a fisherman for his dead wife; hero and heroine each repeatedly brought to the verge of spectacular death or disaster, only to win a last-minute reprieve just as spectacular. It was assuredly this basic narrative material, these perennial themes, that consti-

125

tuted the story's appeal, rather than the way the author fits them into a sequential structure. For the tale cannot be called sophisticated, and scholars have readily succumbed to the temptation of bombarding it with uncomplimentary adjectives: crude, clumsy, simplistic, cliché-ridden. It is undoubtedly all of these. But that is not all it is. These are characteristics of folktale; Xenophon's story, along with *The Story of Apollonius of Tyre,* is closer to folktale than the other ideal romances, and should be judged by the conventions of folktale rather than those of a more complex literary aesthetic. It is also in some respects similar to Chariton's novel, which Xenophon is now generally thought to be imitating, and comparison of the two is rewarding for both. Conspicuous elements in common include, for instance, the incident of the tomb robbery (Chariton 1.7–10, Xenophon 3.8) and the fact that both marry off their heroines before the start of their adventures. But the two authors approach this material differently. Chariton is concerned with the overall structure of his story, and creates tension from such elements; Xenophon's interest is focused on individual scenes and incidents, which he presents in strong colors, and his construction is correspondingly lax. Similarly, Xenophon's characters are depicted melodramatically. His hero, Habrocomes, is passive, even for a Greek novel; but his minor characters are generally either benign, sentimental, and sympathetic, or else patently villainous, with the power of simple excitement that villains evoke; for instance, he produces some fiercely predatory females to endanger Habrocomes. The unifying secondary character, Hippothous, is allowed to go to extremes in both directions—great kindness towards Habrocomes, brutal torture and sadistic murder attempts on Anthia; and he becomes a gigolo in order to repair his fortunes. The narrative qualities of the *Ephesian Tale* are those that still excite us in westerns. Such stories, if we will surrender to them, embody a primitive and satisfying view of the world.

One explanation that has been offered of the shortcomings of the work is that it is an epitome of a longer novel, and that some portions of the original ten books mentioned in the *Suda* have been summarized, notably in the short Book 4.[1] Those who are wholly convinced of this, however, must still acknowledge inadequacies in the parts they think have not been so abridged, such as Book 1. Another kind of reworking has also been adduced to explain inconsistencies in the religious content of the book: it has been suggested that the role played by Helius in our version has been superimposed on an original novel centered on the in-

---

1. See K. Bürger, "Zu Xenophon von Ephesos," *Hermes* 27(1892): 36–67; against this theory, Tomas Hägg, "Die *Ephesiaka* des Xenophon Ephesius: Original oder Epitome?" *Classica et Mediaevalia* 27(1966): 118–61.

tervention of Isis. But Xenophon is not interested in controlling the variety of his divine forces; he is content to make the couple worship the local deity wherever they happen to be. In so doing he produces a vivid picture of contemporary popular religious attitudes; syncretizing tendencies and apparent contradictions were certainly not less common in his day than they are now, when practicing Christians observe New Year's Day and avoid walking under ladders.

Furthermore, some of the problems of this text may have to be reconsidered in the light of recent research about the origin of the novel plots. Since (in my view) significant analogues for other novels have now turned up in oriental fiction, there is at least the possibility that such an origin will explain some of the features of Xenophon's plot.[2] It is certainly true that substantial sections of it survive in modern Greek folktale as well as in oriental sources.[3] What we may well find is that our version is one of not two but a multiplicity of retellings of a familiar story, whose relationships to Xenophon are not easily identifiable—one modern Greek version in effect makes Hippothous the hero! But we should be wise to wait for the appearance of an ancient oriental analogue rather than try to imagine one from the dubious indications in Xenophon's story.

Although the story may have been popular in antiquity, it was not noticed in academic circles. Nor are there any papyri of it, and there is only one manuscript—the one that also contains the only complete text of Chariton's novel. Xenophon himself, however, was not without literary aspirations, which he imposes on the simple basis outlined above. In particular, he tries to accommodate Hellenistic prose to "atticizing"—the attempt to write in the manner of the classical age. It is not easy to strike the right balance in translating his language. I have tried for the most part to retain the characteristic monotony and slightly pedantic ethos of Xenophon's style and narrative manner, but have occasionally enlivened it, for instance by the use of indirect speech or narrative to replace the most un-English emotional outbursts. But it should be said that a lively, polished translation would credit Xenophon with qualities that he does not possess. The translation is based on A. D. Papanikolaou's text, with a few divergences from it. The hero's name may well be Abrocomes (as Papanikolaou thinks), but I have preferred to keep the more familiar Habrocomes. Occasional lacunae in the text are indicated as ... or are supplemented in parentheses.

2. See Graham Anderson, *Ancient Fiction: The Novel in the Graeco-Roman World* (London and Totowa, N.J., 1984).

3. See G. Dalmeyda in his introduction, xxvii–xxxi, to Xenophon d'Ephèse, *Les Ephésiaques* (Paris, 1924).

## Bibliography

TEXT

Xénophon d'Ephèse. *Les Ephésiaques.* Edited by G. Dalmeyda. Paris, 1924 (Budé).

Xenophon Ephesius. *Ephesiacorum Libri V.* Edited by A. D. Papanikolaou. Leipzig, 1978 (Teubner).

GENERAL

Gärtner, H. "Xenophon von Ephesos." In *Realencyclopädie der classischen Altertumswissenschaft* 9A.2 (1967), 2055–89.

Schmeling, Gareth L. *Xenophon of Ephesus.* Boston, 1980.

# AN EPHESIAN TALE

## Book One

I AMONG THE MOST influential citizens of Ephesus was a man called Lycomedes. He and his wife, Themisto, who also belonged to the city, had a son Habrocomes; his good looks were phenomenal, and neither in Ionia nor anywhere else had there ever been anything like them. This Habrocomes grew more handsome every day; and his mental qualities developed along with his physical ones. For he acquired culture of all kinds and practiced a variety of arts; he trained in hunting, riding, and fighting under arms. Everyone in Ephesus sought his company, and in the rest of Asia as well; and they had great hopes that he would have a distinguished position in the city. They treated the boy like a god, and some even prostrated themselves and prayed at the sight of him. He had a high opinion of himself, taking pride in his attainments, and a great deal more in his appearance. Everything that was regarded as beautiful he despised as inferior, and nothing he saw or heard seemed up to his standard. And when he heard a boy or girl praised for their good looks, he laughed at the people making such claims for not knowing that only he himself was handsome. He did not even recognize Eros as a god; he rejected him totally and considered him of no importance, saying that no one would ever fall in love or submit to the god except of his own accord. And whenever he saw a temple or statue of Eros, he used to laugh and claimed that he was more handsome and powerful than any Eros. And that was the case: for wherever Habrocomes appeared, no one admired any statue or praised any picture.

Eros was furious at this, for he is a contentious god and implacable   2
against those who despise him. He looked for some stratagem to employ
against the boy, for even the god thought he would be difficult to capture. So he armed himself to the teeth, equipped himself with his full armory of love potions, and set out against Habrocomes. The local festival
of Artemis was in progress, with its procession from the city to the temple nearly a mile away. All the local girls had to march in procession,
richly dressed, as well as all the young men of Habrocomes' age—he was
around sixteen, already a member of the Ephebes,[1] and took first place in
the procession. There was a great crowd of Ephesians and visitors alike
to see the festival, for it was the custom at this festival to find husbands
for the girls and wives for the young men. So the procession filed past—
first the sacred objects, the torches, the baskets, and the incense; then
horses, dogs, hunting equipment ... some for war, most for peace. And
each of the girls was dressed as if to receive a lover. Anthia led the line of
girls; she was the daughter of Megamedes and Euippe, both of Ephesus.
Anthia's beauty was an object of wonder, far surpassing the other girls'.
She was fourteen; her beauty was burgeoning, still more enhanced by the
adornment of her dress. Her hair was golden—a little of it plaited, but
most hanging loose and blowing in the wind. Her eyes were quick; she
had the bright glance of a young girl, and yet the austere look of a virgin. She wore a purple tunic down to the knee, fastened with a girdle
and falling loose over her arms, with a fawnskin over it, a quiver attached, and arrows for weapons; she carried javelins and was followed by
dogs. Often as they saw her in the sacred enclosure the Ephesians would
worship her as Artemis. And so on this occasion too the crowd gave a
cheer when they saw her, and there was a whole clamor of exclamations
from the spectators: some were amazed and said it was the goddess in
person; some that it was someone else made by the goddess in her own
image. But all prayed and prostrated themselves and congratulated her
parents. "The beautiful Anthia!" was the cry on all the spectators' lips.
When the crowd of girls came past, no one said anything but "Anthia!"
But when Habrocomes came in turn with the Ephebes, then, although
the spectacle of the women had been a lovely sight, everyone forgot
about them and transferred their gaze to him and were smitten at the
sight. "Handsome Habrocomes!" they exclaimed. "Incomparable image
of a handsome god!" Already some added, "What a match Habrocomes
and Anthia would make!"

1. The *ephebia* appears to have existed from early times in Athens as a form of military
service, although it was not formalized as an institution until the late fourth century B.C. In
the Hellenistic period it evolved into a social institution for well-to-do youths, with some
educational function. Similar bodies existed in other Hellenistic cities. The institution was
still flourishing at the time this novel was probably written (second century A.D.), although
it declined later.

These were the first machinations in Love's plot. They quickly learned each other's reputation. Anthia longed to see Habrocomes; and Habrocomes, up till now impervious to love, wanted to see Anthia.

3 And so when the procession was over, the whole crowd went into the temple for the sacrifice, and the files broke up; men and women and girls and boys came together. Then they saw each other, and Anthia was captivated by Habrocomes, while Love got the better of Habrocomes. He kept looking at the girl and in spite of himself could not take his eyes off her. Love held him fast and pressed home his attack. And Anthia too was in a bad way, as she let his appearance sink in, with rapt attention and eyes wide open; and already she paid no attention to modesty: what she said was for Habrocomes to hear, and she revealed what she could of her body for Habrocomes to see. And he was captivated at the sight and was a prisoner of the god.

Then after the sacrifice they parted in dismay and were annoyed at being separated so soon. They still wanted to look at each other; they turned back and stopped and found a host of excuses for delay. And when each of them arrived home, they realized then what troubles had befallen them. Both felt their minds infiltrated by the image of the other; both of them were aflame with love, and the rest of the day they fueled their desires; when they went to sleep, their misery was total, and neither could contain their love any longer.

4 Habrocomes pulled at his hair and tore his clothes; he lamented over his misfortunes and exclaimed: "What catastrophe has befallen me, Habrocomes, till now a man, despising Eros and slandering the god? I have been captured and conquered and am forced to be the slave of a girl. Now, it seems, there is someone more beautiful than I am, and I acknowledge love as a god. But now I am nothing but a worthless coward. Can I not hold out this time? Shall I not show my mettle and stand firm? Will I not remain more handsome than Eros? Now I must conquer this worthless god. The girl is beautiful; but what of it? To your *eyes,* Habrocomes, Anthia is beautiful; but not to *you,* if your will holds firm. You must make up your mind to that. Eros must never be my master."

At this the god pressed on him all the more; he dragged him along as he resisted, and tortured him against his will. So when he could hold out no longer, he threw himself to the ground. "You have won, Eros," he said. "You have set up a great trophy over the self-possessed Habrocomes; he is your suppliant. In his desperation he has come for refuge to you, the master of all things. Do not abandon me or punish my arrogance too hard; because I had not felt you, Eros, I paid no attention to you as yet. But now give me Anthia. Do not be only a vengeful god against the man who has resisted you, but a help to the man you have conquered."

But even after this prayer Eros was still angry and intended to take a terrible revenge on him for his arrogance. Anthia too was in a bad way; when she could bear it no longer, she pulled herself together as she tried to hide her plight from those around her. "What has happened to me?" she commiserated with herself. "I am in love, although I am too young, and I feel a strange pain not proper for a young girl. I am madly in love with Habrocomes; he is handsome, but he is proud. Where will this desire end, what will end my misery? This man I love is disdainful, and I am a girl kept under watch; whom shall I find to help me? To whom shall I confide everything, and where shall I see Habrocomes?"

Each of them lamented like this all night. They saw each other before    5 their eyes, as they impressed their mental image on each other. When it was day, Habrocomes went off to his usual exercises, while Anthia went as usual to worship the goddess. Their bodies were worn out after the previous night; their eyes weary; their complexion changed. And this went on and on, and matters went no further. But in the meantime they spent day after day looking at each other in the temple, ashamed and afraid to tell each other the truth. But Habrocomes got as far as moaning, weeping, and praying in a pitiful fashion while Anthia was within earshot; she felt the same way, but her misery was more extreme; when she saw other girls or women looking at him (and they all looked at Habrocomes), she was visibly distressed, in case some rival would outdo her. Each of them privately prayed the same prayers to the goddess.

As time went on, the boy was unable to go on; already his whole body had wasted away and his mind had given in, so that Lycomedes and Themisto were very despondent, not knowing what had happened to Habrocomes, but afraid at what they saw. Megamedes and Euippe were just as afraid for Anthia, as they watched her beauty wasting away without apparent cause. At last they brought in diviners and priests to Anthia to find a remedy to her plight. They came and performed sacrifices, made libations of all sorts, pronounced foreign phrases, alleging that they were placating some demons or other, and pretended that her malady came from the underworld. Lycomedes' household too kept offering prayers and sacrifices for Habrocomes. There was no relief for either of them from their malady, but their love burned still more fiercely. Both, then, lay ill; their condition was critical, and they were expected to die at any moment, unable to confess what was wrong. At last their fathers sent to the oracle of Apollo to find out the cause of their illness and the antidote.

The temple of Apollo in Colophon is not far away; it is ten miles' sail    6 from Ephesus. There the messengers from both parties asked the god for a true oracle. They had come with the same question, and the god gave the same oracle in verse to both. It went like this.

Why do you long to learn the end of a malady, and its beginning?
One disease has both in its grasp, and from that the remedy must be
accomplished.
But for them I see terrible sufferings and toils that are endless;
Both will flee over the sea pursued by madness;
They will suffer chains at the hands of men who mingle with the
waters;
And a tomb shall be the burial chamber for both, and fire the destroyer;
And beside the waters of the river Nile, to Holy Isis
The savior you will afterwards offer rich gifts;
But still after their sufferings a better fate is in store.[2]

7 When this oracle was brought to Ephesus, their fathers were at once at a loss and had no idea at all what the danger was, and they could not understand the god's utterance. They did not know what he meant by their illness, the flight, the chains, the tomb, the river, or the help from the goddess. So they decided after a great deal of deliberation to palliate the oracle as far as they could and marry the pair, since the god implied by his prophecy that this was his will too. They decided this and determined to send them on a trip abroad for a time after their marriage.

Already the revelry filled the city; there were garlands everywhere, and the impending marriage was on everyone's lips. Everybody congratulated Habrocomes on the prospect of marrying such a wife as Anthia; they congratulated her in turn because she was to be the bride of such a handsome young man. When Habrocomes found out the prophecy and heard about the marriage, he was overjoyed at the prospect of marrying Anthia. He was not at all afraid of the prophecies; the present seemed much more pleasant than all the dangers. In the same way Anthia too was delighted at the prospect of marrying Habrocomes. What the flight or the disasters meant she did not care, since she had Habrocomes to console her in all future perils.

8 And so the time for their marriage arrived; there were all-night celebrations and a feast of sacrifices to the god. And when these had been performed, night came (everything seemed too slow for Habrocomes and Anthia); they brought the girl to the bridal chamber with torches, sang the bridal hymn, shouted their good wishes, brought the couple in, and put them on the couch. The chamber had been prepared: a golden couch had been spread with purple sheets, and above it hung an awning with an embroidered Babylonian tapestry. Cupids were playing, some attending Aphrodite, who was also represented, some riding on

---

2. The text of this oracle is disputed at some points, but the general sense is clear.

Nabataean ostriches,[3] some weaving garlands, others bringing flowers. These were on one half of the canopy; on the other was Ares, not in armor, but dressed in a cloak and wearing a garland, adorned for his lover Aphrodite.[4] Eros was leading the way, with a lighted torch. Under this canopy they brought Anthia to Habrocomes and put her to bed, then shut the doors.

Both of them felt the same emotions and were unable to say anything 9 to each other or to look at each other's eyes but lay at ease in sheer delight, shy, afraid, panting—and on fire. Their bodies trembled and their hearts quivered. And at last Habrocomes recovered and took Anthia in his arms. And she wept, as she poured forth the tears that symbolized her inward desire. And Habrocomes spoke: he sighed at the arrival of the night he had longed for and reached with such difficulty after many previous nights of misery. "Girl sweeter to me than the light of day, and luckier than anyone in any story—you have as husband the man who loves you! God grant that you live and die with him a chaste wife!" With this he kissed her and caught her tears, and they seemed to him a sweeter drink than nectar, more powerful a remedy than any other against pain. She said only a few words: "Is it true, Habrocomes? Do you really think I am beautiful? Do I really please you even after your own handsome appearance? Unmanly coward! How long did you delay your love? How long did you neglect it? I know what you have suffered from my own miseries. But look, here are my tears; let your beautiful hair drink a cup of love; and as we lock together, let us embrace and wet the garlands with each other's tears so that these too may share our love." With this she kissed him all over his face, pressed all his hair to her own eyes, and took off the garlands and joined his lips to hers in a kiss; and their feelings passed through their lips from one soul to the other. Anthia kissed Habrocomes' eyes and said to them: "It is you who have often brought me grief, you who first implanted the goad in my heart; then you were full of pride, now you are full of desire; you have served me well, and well have you brought my love into Habrocomes' heart.[5] So I kiss you again and again, and let my eyes meet his, for mine are the servants of Habrocomes. May you always look on the same objects and not reveal

3. "Nabataean" translates Papanikolaou's reading. If it is correct, it is not clear what the connection of these birds is with Aphrodite. The word used by Xenophon for the bird in question is *strouthos*, generally translated "sparrow"; sparrows were thought of as lustful and hence were associated with Aphrodite. Elsewhere the *strouthos* can be the swan, another bird associated with Aphrodite; see J. R. T. Pollard, *Birds in Greek Life and Myth* (London, 1977), 29 and 147. The Nabataean (i.e., Arabian) *strouthos* is a (now extinct) species of ostrich. The reading of the manuscript is *anabatai*, "mounted," which seems redundant.

4. See *Odyssey* 8.266–332.

5. The thought is that the eyes can serve as a channel for the physical transmission of emotions. This is a reflection of Hellenistic theories of sense-perception.

anyone else's beauty to Habrocomes, nor may anyone else appear beautiful to me; accept the hearts that you yourselves set on fire; and preserve them both in the same way." With this they relaxed in each other's arms and enjoyed the first fruits of Aphrodite; and there was ardent rivalry all night long, each trying to prove they loved the other more.

10     When it was day, they got up much happier, and much more cheerful, after fulfilling the desires they had had for each other for so long. Their whole life was a festival, everything was full of enjoyment, and already they had forgotten even the oracle. But fate had not forgotten, nor had the god overlooked his plans. After a little while their fathers decided to carry out their decision and send them away from the city; they were to see some other land and other cities, and palliate the effect of the divine oracle as far as they could by leaving Ephesus for a while.[6] And so all the preparations went ahead for their departure; they had a great ship with its crew ready to sail, and all they needed was being put aboard: a large selection of clothes of all kinds, a great deal of gold and silver, and a great abundance of food. There were sacrifices to Artemis before they set sail; the whole population prayed and wept at the impending loss as if they regarded the children as their own. They had prepared to make the voyage to Egypt. And when the day came for their departure, many of the servants and handmaidens went aboard; when the ship was about to sail, the whole population of Ephesus came to see them off, including many of the priestesses with torches and sacrifices. Meanwhile Lycomedes and Themisto remembered everything at once: the oracle, their child, and the voyage; and they lay on the ground in despair. Megamedes and Euippe had the same experience, but they were more cheerful, looking forward to the final outcome of the oracle. Already, then, the sailors were making a commotion, the mooring ropes were being loosened, the steersman was taking his place, and the ship was under way. There was a great confusion of shouts from ship and shore, with parents and children anxiously asking if they should see one another again; so there were tears and lamentations, as each of them hailed a loved one by name, and they left their names as reminders to one another. And Megamedes took a cup, poured a libation, and prayed so as to be heard aboard ship. "Children," he cried, "may you be ever so happy and escape the hard words of the oracles, and may you reach Ephesus again safe and sound and recover your own dear country. But if anything else should happen, know that we will not go on living; we are sending you away on a journey that is sad but necessary."

6. There has been speculation as to the meaning of παραμυθεῖσθαι, here translated as "palliate"; the parents certainly seem to be looking for trouble, given the contents of the prophecy. Probably, unless this version of the novel is indeed an epitome of the original (see the Introduction), this is simply a clumsy way of getting the adventures started.

Even as he spoke, his tears choked back his words. The parents re-   11
turned to the city, with everyone trying to console them, while Habrocomes and Anthia lay embracing each other and turning a host of things
over in their minds: pitying their parents, longing for their homeland,
fearing the oracle, and feeling uneasy about the voyage. But the fact that
they were sailing with each other consoled them for everything. And
that day they had a favorable wind; they finished this stage and reached
Samos, the sacred island of Hera. There they sacrificed and took a meal,
and after offering many prayers they put out to sea the next night. Once
more the sailing was easy, and they talked a great deal to each other.
"Will we be allowed to spend our whole lives together?" At this Habrocomes gave a loud groan, at the thought of what was in store for him.
"Anthia," he said, "more dear to me than my own soul, my fondest
hope is that we live happily and survive together; but if it is fated that we
suffer some disaster and be separated, let us swear to one another, my
dearest, that you will remain faithful to me and not submit to any other
man and that I should never live with another woman." When she heard
this, Anthia gave a loud cry. "Habrocomes," she said, "why are you
convinced that if I am separated from you, I will still think about a husband and marriage, when I will not even live at all without you? I swear
to you by the goddess of our fathers, the great Artemis of the Ephesians,
and this sea we are crossing, and the god who has driven us mad with
this exquisite passion for each other, that I will not live or look upon the
sun if I am separated from you even for a short time." That was Anthia's
oath; Habrocomes swore too, and the occasion made their oaths still
more awesome.

Meanwhile the ship passed by Cos and Cnidus, and already the great
and beautiful island of Rhodes was coming into view; here they all had to
disembark, for the sailors said that they had to take on water and rest in
preparation for the long voyage ahead.

So the ship put into Rhodes, and the sailors disembarked; Habro-   12
comes too came off, hand in hand with Anthia. All the Rhodians gathered, amazed at the young people's beauty, and no one who saw them
passed by in silence: some said that it was a visitation of auspicious gods;
some offered them worship and adoration; and soon the names of
Habrocomes and Anthia had traveled all through the city. Public prayers
were offered to them; the Rhodians offered many sacrifices and celebrated their visit as a festival. So they toured the whole city and gave as
an offering to the temple of Helius[7] a gold panoply and inscribed on a
votive tablet an epigram with the donors' names.

7. The multiplicity of deities involved in the action is one of the problems—or matters
of interest—in this text. Usually a Greek novel employs one principal divinity. On the
theme of Helius, see the Introduction.

THE STRANGERS OFFERED YOU THESE WEAPONS OF BEATEN GOLD,
ANTHIA AND HABROCOMES, CITIZENS OF HOLY EPHESUS.

After making these offerings, they stayed a few days on the island, but at
the sailors' insistence they took on supplies and put to sea. The whole
population of Rhodes saw them off. At first they were carried along by a
favorable wind and enjoyed the voyage; and that day and the following
night they sailed along, making headway over the Egyptian sea. The
next day the wind had dropped; there was a calm, and they could make
little headway; the sailors relaxed into a drinking bout; and the prophecies began to take effect: Habrocomes dreamt that a woman stood over
him, fearful in appearance and superhuman in size, and dressed in a
bloodred robe; and the vision seemed to set the ship alight; the rest perished, but he swam to safety with Anthia. As soon as he dreamt this, he
was in a panic and expected his dream to portend some dreadful outcome, as indeed it did.

13    It so happened that in Rhodes there were Phoenician pirates moored
alongside them in a large trireme. They were posing as merchantmen,
and they were a large and daredevil crew. These men found out that
there was gold and silver and a large quantity of valuable slaves aboard
Habrocomes' ship. So they decided to attack and kill those who resisted,
but to sell the rest in Phoenicia with the booty. They regarded their
quarry as weaklings not likely to put up a fight. The pirate chief was
Corymbus, a tall young man with a fearsome look; his hair hung loose
and unkempt. And when the pirates had decided their plan, they at first
sailed quietly alongside Habrocomes' ship. It was around midday, and all
the ship's company were lying down, some asleep and others the worse
for drink and off their guard; then at last Corymbus and his crew went
into the attack, driving their vessel at high speed. When they got
alongside, they leapt into the ship, armed to the teeth, with their swords
drawn; and at this some threw themselves in terror into the sea and perished; others who were prepared to defend themselves were slaughtered.
But Habrocomes and Anthia ran to the pirate Corymbus, took hold of
him by the knees, and said: "Take the goods, master, and take us as your
slaves, but spare our lives and do not kill those who submit to you of
their own accord. By the sea itself, by your own right hand, we implore
you: take us where you will; sell us as your slaves; only take pity on us
and sell us to the same master."

14    When he heard this, Corymbus at once gave orders to his men to
spare them from slaughter; he transferred the more precious part of the
cargo, along with Anthia and Habrocomes and a few of the servants, and
set fire to the ship: all the rest were burned to death, for he could not
take them all, nor did he think it safe to do so. It was a pitiful spectacle,

some of them being taken off in the trireme, others burning in the ship, stretching out their hands and moaning. And some said: "Where on earth will you be taken, masters? What land will receive you; what city will you live in?" Others exclaimed, "Happy are those who will be lucky enough to die without suffering the pirates' chains and seeing themselves the slaves of pirates!" With this, they were taken away by ship, while the rest died in the fire.

Meanwhile Habrocomes' tutor, already an old man, venerable in appearance and a pitiful sight in his old age, was unable to bear Habrocomes' being taken away; he threw himself into the sea and swam in an attempt to catch up with the trireme. "Where are you going my child," he exclaimed, "without your aged paedagogus? Where, Habrocomes? Kill this poor wretch yourself and bury me, for what is life to me without you?" After this plea, despairing of seeing Habrocomes ever again, he finally gave himself up to the waves and died.[8] For Habrocomes this was the most pitiable sight of all; and so he kept stretching out his hands to the old man and pleaded with the pirates to take him on board. But they took no account of him; they completed their voyage in three days, putting in at Tyre in Phoenicia, where the pirates had their base. They did not bring them to the city itself, but to a place nearby; the man in charge of the pirate lair was Apsyrtus; Corymbus himself was only his lieutenant, who received a wage and a share of the booty from him. Corymbus was passionately in love with Habrocomes from seeing him so often daily during the course of the voyage, and his contact with the boy inflamed him all the more.

Now in the course of the actual voyage he did not consider it possible to win over Habrocomes, for he saw that he was in a bad way in his despair and that he loved Anthia. Besides it also seemed difficult to use force, for he was afraid that Habrocomes would do himself some injury. But when they reached Tyre, he was no longer able to contain himself but first of all took care of Habrocomes and tried to console him and gave him every attention. Habrocomes for his part thought that Corymbus's attentions were only out of pity. Next Corymbus confided his love to one of his fellow pirates, Euxinus, and asked him to help and advise him how to succeed in bringing Habrocomes round. Euxinus was glad to hear of Corymbus's affair, for he himself was madly in love with Anthia and was totally infatuated with her; so he confessed his own love to Corymbus and advised him not to be frustrated any longer but to take the matter in hand. "For it would not be right at all," he argued, "for us

8. This episode appears to be an imitation of Chariton 3.5. For Xenophon's imitation of Chariton see A. D. Papanikolaou, *Chariton-Studien* (Göttingen, 1973), 153ff. See the Introduction.

to take risks and expose ourselves to danger and not enjoy with impunity what we have obtained by effort. But we will be able to choose them as our share and have them as a gift from Apsyrtus." With this he was able to persuade him easily, in his lovesick state, and so they each agreed to put in a good word for the other; Euxinus was to win over Habrocomes; Corymbus, Anthia.

16 Meanwhile Habrocomes and Anthia were prostrate in despair, full of apprehension, as they talked to each other, and constantly swore to honor their agreement. So Corymbus and Euxinus came to them and said that they wanted to say something in private; Corymbus took aside Anthia while Euxinus spoke to Habrocomes. Their hearts were palpitating, and they suspected no good would come of it.

Euxinus, then, spoke to Habrocomes on behalf of Corymbus. "My boy, you must expect to come off badly in this catastrophe, now that you are a slave instead of a free man, and a poor man instead of a rich one. But you must put everything down to fortune, accept the fate that rules over you, and be friends with those who have become your masters. You must know that it is in your power to recover your happiness and freedom if you are willing to obey your master, Corymbus, for he is madly in love with you and is prepared to make you master of all he possesses. Nothing unpleasant will happen to you, and you will make your master still more kindly disposed to you. Think of your position. There is no one to help you; this is a strange land, your masters are pirates, and there is no escape from their vengeance if you arrogantly reject Corymbus. What need have you for a wife or domestic ties, and why should a  man of your age need to love a woman? Throw all that away. You must look only to your master and obey his command." Habrocomes listened and at once was dumbfounded and could find no answer, but wept and wailed when he saw the plight he was in. And so he said to Euxinus, "Let me think about it for a little while, master, and I will give you an answer to everything you have said."

And Euxinus went away. But Corymbus had been speaking to Anthia about Euxinus's love for her and her present plight, and had been telling her that she must implicitly obey her masters. And he kept showering her with promises, a legal marriage, money, and prosperity if she obeyed. But she gave him the same kind of answer and asked for a short time to consider it. And so Euxinus and Corymbus both waited for their answers, but expected to win them over without difficulty.

## Book Two

1 When Habrocomes and Anthia came back to their usual quarters and told each other what they had heard, they threw themselves down and wept

and wailed. They invoked their parents, the homeland they loved so much, and their household and family. At last Habrocomes recovered and lamented their misfortune. "What will happen to us," he exclaimed, "now that we are in a savage land, handed over to lustful pirates? The oracles are beginning to be fulfilled. Already Eros is taking his revenge on me for my arrogance: Corymbus is in love with me; Euxinus with you. Our good looks are proving untimely for both of us! Was it for this that I kept myself chaste up to now, to submit to the foul lust of an amorous pirate? And what are my prospects in the future, reduced from a man to a prostitute, and deprived of my darling Anthia? But I swear by the chastity that has been with me from childhood till now, I could not submit to Corymbus. I will die first and prove my chastity with my own dead body!" With this he broke down. Anthia too lamented their plight. "How quickly," she exclaimed, "we are being forced to remember our oaths! And how soon we are experiencing slavery! A man is in love with me and has been expecting to win me over and come to my bed after Habrocomes; he expects to sleep with me and satisfy his lust. But I hope never to be so much in love with life; I hope not to survive to face the daylight after my degradation. Let us be resolved on that. Let us die, Habrocomes. We shall have each other after death, with no one to molest us."

And that was their decision. But meanwhile Apsyrtus, the robber 2 chief, had heard that Corymbus and his men had arrived with a marvelous hoard of booty; he came to their lair and saw Habrocomes and Anthia, was struck by their appearance, and at once realizing that they would bring a huge profit, claimed them for himself. The rest of the money, goods, and young girls that had been captured he distributed to Corymbus and his band. Euxinus and Corymbus were reluctant to give up Anthia and Habrocomes to Apsyrtus, but were forced to nevertheless, and left. But Apsyrtus took Habrocomes and Anthia and two slaves, Leucon and Rhode, and brought them to Tyre. People gazed at them on the way; everyone was amazed at their beauty. And barbarians who had not previously set eyes on such radiance thought they were gods, and congratulated Apsyrtus on having acquired such slaves. He brought them home, gave them to a trusted slave, and told him to take good care of them, since he hoped to make a large profit if he could sell them at their market value.

And so this was the predicament in which Habrocomes and Anthia 3 found themselves. But a few days later Apsyrtus went off on another venture to Syria, and his daughter Manto fell in love with Habrocomes. She was beautiful and already of marriageable age, but not nearly as beautiful as Anthia. Through her day-to-day contact with Habrocomes this Manto became uncontrollably infatuated, and she did not know what to do. For she did not dare to speak to Habrocomes; she knew that he had a wife, and never expected to win him round; nor did she dare to tell any of her own household for fear of her father. Because of all this her feelings were all the more inflamed and she was in a bad state. Unable to contain herself any longer, she decided to confess her love to Rhode, Anthia's companion, a young girl of her own age; she was the only one she thought would help her attain her desire. So she found a suitable opportunity, took the girl before the family shrine, and asked her on oath not to betray her; she confessed her love for Habrocomes, begged her to cooperate, and promised her a great deal if she did. And she added, "You must realize that you are my slave and that if you hurt me, you will experience the anger of a barbarian woman!" With that she sent Rhode away; the girl was in an impossible dilemma. She loved Anthia and so could not bring herself to speak to Habrocomes; but she was terrified of the barbarian girl's anger. So she decided that it would be wise to confide to Leucon beforehand what Manto had said. They had been lovers even in Ephesus, and so she had an understanding with him. So at that point she found him alone and said: "Leucon, we're really done for; now we're about to lose our companions. The daughter of our master, Apsyrtus, is madly in love with Habrocomes and is threatening to do us terrible harm if she does not succeed. So consider what we must do. It is dangerous to thwart this barbarian woman but impossible to come between Habrocomes and Anthia." At this Leucon burst into tears, expecting terrible consequences. But when he finally pulled himself together, he told her to keep quiet and he would arrange everything.

4     With this assurance he went to Habrocomes. Now he was preoccupied with his love for Anthia and hers for him, with talking to her and hearing her speak. Leucon approached them and asked them as friends and fellow slaves what their course of action was to be. "Habrocomes," he explained, "one of our masters thinks you are handsome. Apsyrtus's daughter is madly in love with you, and it is dangerous to turn down a barbarian girl in love. So decide what you should do, but save us all and don't let us fall victim to our masters' anger." The moment Habrocomes heard this he flew into a rage; he looked Leucon straight in the eye and said: "You villain, worse than these Phoenicians! You have dared to speak like this to Habrocomes, and you talk about another woman in front of Anthia? I am a slave, but I know how to keep vows. They have power over my body, but my soul is still free. Now let Manto threaten me if she pleases—with swords, the noose, fire, and everything that the body of a slave can be made to bear, for she could never persuade me to do wrong against Anthia of my own free will." That was his answer; Anthia for her part was dumbfounded and speechless at their misfortune; at length and with difficulty she came round and said: "You love me,

Habrocomes, and I believe that you could not love me more. But I ask you, master of my soul, do not betray yourself or subject yourself to a barbarian's anger, but submit to your mistress's desire. And I will kill myself and not stand between you. Only this will I ask of you; that you bury me with your own hands, kiss me as I lie dead, and remember Anthia."

All this made Habrocomes' plight still more poignant, and he did not 5 know what was to become of him. While they were in this predicament, Manto could hold out no longer when Rhode kept her waiting, and wrote a note to Habrocomes. Its contents went like this.

> From his mistress to the fair Habrocomes, greeting. Manto is in love with you and can no longer contain herself, improperly perhaps for a girl, but inevitably for a girl in love. I beg you, do not spurn or humiliate the girl who has shown you her favor. For if you agree, I will persuade my father, Apsyrtus, to give me to you in marriage; we will get rid of your present wife, and you will be rich and prosperous. But if you say no, think what will happen to you when the woman you insulted takes her revenge, and what will happen to the accomplices who advised you in your arrogant action.

She took this letter and sealed it, then gave it to one of her own barbarian servants, telling her to give it to Habrocomes. He took it and read it and was upset at everything in it; he was particularly aggrieved at the part about Anthia. He kept the writing tablet, wrote the reply on another, and gave it to the servant.[9] The letter went like this.

> Mistress, do as you will and use my body as the body of a slave; and if you want to kill me, I am ready; if you want to torture me, torture me as you please. But I could not come to your bed, nor would I obey such a request even if you ordered me.

When she received this letter, Manto could not control her anger. All her feelings were confused: she felt envy, jealousy, grief, and fear, and was planning how to take her revenge on the man who was turning her down.

Now it was at this moment that Apsyrtus returned from Syria with a Syrian bridegroom, Moeris, for his daughter. As soon as he arrived, Manto contrived her plot against Habrocomes. She disheveled her hair and tore her clothes, went off to her father, and fell at his knees. "Have pity, father," she exclaimed, "on your daughter, wronged by a slave, for

---

9. Manto's letter would be written on a wax-coated tablet (*pinax*); normally the message would be erased and the same tablet used for the reply.

the 'chaste' Habrocomes tried to rob me of my virginity, and in saying that he loved me he betrayed you as well. So you must take just vengeance on him for such a dreadful outrage; but if you let your daughter fall into the hands of your slaves, I will kill myself first."[10]

6     Apsyrtus listened and thought she spoke the truth. He did not investigate the matter further, but sent for Habrocomes and called him a depraved villain. "Did you dare," he cried, "to insult your masters? Did you try to corrupt a girl, and you a slave? But you will not get off with it, for I will have my revenge on you, and your torments will serve as an example to the other slaves." And after this he would not allow himself to hear a single word but gave orders to his slaves to tear off Habrocomes' clothes, bring fire and whips, and flog the boy. It was a pitiful sight. For the tortures disfigured his whole body, unused to servile tortures, his blood drained out, and his handsome appearance wasted away. Apsyrtus submitted him to fire and tortured him assiduously, demonstrating to his prospective son-in-law that he would be marrying a chaste virgin. Meanwhile Anthia fell at Apsyrtus's knees, pleading on Habrocomes' behalf. "On the contrary," he replied, "for your sake he will be punished all the more, because he wronged you too by loving another woman when he had a wife." Then he gave orders to tie him up and imprison him in a dark cell.

7     And so Habrocomes was bound and imprisoned. He was dreadfully despondent, especially since he could not see Anthia. He kept looking for any number of ways of killing himself but found none, since he was heavily guarded. But Apsyrtus held his daughter's wedding, and the celebration went on for days on end. But for Anthia all was misery, and whenever she could persuade the prison guards, she went to Habrocomes in secret and lamented their plight. And already preparations were being made to go to Syria: Apsyrtus sent his daughter off loaded with gifts and gave her Babylonian fabrics and plenty of gold and silver. And he made her a gift of Anthia, Rhode, and Leucon. So when Anthia realized this and found out that she would be taken to Syria with Manto, she found a way of going to the prison, embraced Habrocomes, and said: "Master, I am being taken away to Syria as a gift for Manto; soon I will be in the hands of the girl who envies me. But you are still in prison and dying miserably, with no one even to lay out your corpse. But I swear by our mutual guardian angel that I will still be yours as long as I live, and even if I have to die."

8     With this she kissed him, embraced him, clung to his chains, and rolled at his feet. But at last she left the prison, while he threw himself to

10. Manto's accusation recalls Anteia's accusation of Bellerophon in the *Iliad* (6.163–65)—and, of course, Potiphar's wife. This novel recalls several folktales (see the Introduction).

the ground just as he was, and wept and wailed. He invoked the father he loved and his mother, Themisto. "Where is the happiness," he cried, "that we once thought we enjoyed in Ephesus? Where are the radiant Anthia and Habrocomes, the beautiful people admired by all? She has gone as a prisoner to some far-off land, and I have been robbed of my one and only consolation and will die in prison miserable and alone." As he said this, sleep overtook him, and he had a dream. He dreamt that he saw his father, Lycomedes, dressed in black, wandering over every land and sea, stopping at the prison, freeing him, and letting him leave his cell; and that he himself took the form of a horse, went through many lands in pursuit of a second one—a mare—and finally found her and became a man again. When he dreamt this, he leapt up and was a little more hopeful.

So he was shut up in the prison, while Anthia, Leucon, and Rhode    9
were taken to Syria. And when Manto and her train reached Antioch (for that was where Moeris came from), she bore a grudge against Rhode but hated Anthia. So she at once ordered Rhode to be put on a ship together with Leucon, to be sold as far away from Syria as possible, and planned that Anthia should live with a slave, one of the meanest at that, a goatherd in the country; that way she hoped to get her revenge on her. She sent for the goatherd, Lampon, gave him Anthia, and told him to make her his wife; and if she refused, his instructions were to use force. And so she was taken to the country to live with the goatherd. And when she got to where Lampon pastured his goats, she went down on her knees and implored him to take pity on her and respect her chastity. She told him who she was, how she had once been a lady, had had a husband, and had been taken prisoner. When Lampon heard her story, he took pity on her and swore that indeed he would not molest her, and tried to reassure her.[11]

So she was in the country with the goatherd, always weeping for   10
Habrocomes. Meanwhile Apsyrtus, searching the cramped quarters where Habrocomes had been living before his punishment, came across Manto's note to Habrocomes, recognized the writing, and realized that his punishment was unjust. So immediately he gave orders to set Habrocomes free and bring the young man before him. After his terrible and pitiful sufferings Habrocomes fell down at Apsyrtus's knees. But the latter brought him to his feet and said: "Courage, my boy; I believed my daughter's accusations and condemned you unjustly; but now I will make you a free man instead of a slave. I am putting you in charge of my household, and I will give you a free citizen's daughter for a wife. You must not bear a grudge because of what has happened, for I did not mean

11. The theme of chastity respected in such circumstances occurs in Euripides' *Electra*.

to do you wrong." To this proposal from Apsyrtus Habrocomes replied, "I thank you, master, for finding out the truth and rewarding me for my continence." In fact the whole household was glad for Habrocomes and thanked the master on his behalf. But he himself was very distressed over Anthia and kept thinking about her to himself. "What use is freedom to me? What is the point of being rich and looking after Apsyrtus's possessions? Such a life is not for me; if only I could find Anthia, dead or alive!"

This, then, was his plight, as he managed Apsyrtus's household but wondered when and where he would find Anthia. But Leucon and Rhode had been taken to Xanthus in Lycia, a town some distance from the sea, and there they were sold to an old man who gave them every attention and treated them as his own children (for he himself had none). And they enjoyed every comfort during their stay, but sorely missed the sight of Anthia and Habrocomes.

11 Anthia lived for some time with the goatherd; while Moeris, Manto's husband, made frequent visits and fell passionately in love with her. At first he tried to hide it, but finally he confided his love to the goatherd and promised him a great reward in return for his cooperation. The goatherd made an agreement with Moeris, but for fear of Manto he went to her and told her about Moeris's feelings. She flew into a rage. "I am the most miserable woman on earth!" she exclaimed. "Will I be bringing my rival everywhere I go? Because of her I was first robbed of a lover in Phoenicia, and now I am in danger of losing my husband. But Anthia will not get away with attracting Moeris as well, for I will take my revenge on her for what happened in Tyre at the same time." For the moment then she said nothing; but while Moeris was away she sent for the goatherd and ordered him to seize Anthia, take her into the thickest part of the wood, and kill her, and promised him a reward. The goatherd for his part was sorry for the girl, but for fear of Manto went to Anthia and told her her fate. She let out a cry and lamented: "Ah, this beauty conspires against both of us at every turn! Because of his all too attractive appearance Habrocomes has perished in Tyre, and I here. But I ask you, Lampon the goatherd, who have treated me with respect up till now, if you kill me, give me at least a token burial in the ground nearby, put your hands on my eyes, and keep calling out Habrocomes' name as you bury me; this would be a happy burial for me, in Habrocomes' presence."

The goatherd was moved to pity by this plea, since he thought that he would be committing an unholy act by killing so beautiful a girl who had done no wrong. He took hold of her, and yet he could not bring himself to kill her but said this to her: "Anthia, you know that my mistress, Manto, has ordered me to take you and kill you. But I fear the gods and have pity on your beauty; I am willing instead to sell you far away from here, in case Manto finds out that you are not dead and takes her malice out on me." She cried and clung to his feet. "Gods," she prayed, "and you, Artemis, goddess of Ephesus, reward the goatherd for this act of kindness"; and she begged him to sell her. The goatherd took Anthia and went to the harbor. And there he found Cilician merchants to whom he sold the girl; he took the price and returned to the estate. The merchants took Anthia, put her aboard, and sailed at nightfall for Cilicia. But they were caught by an adverse wind, and the ship broke up; some of the crew survived with great difficulty and came ashore on planks with Anthia among them. There was a thick wood there, so that night as they wandered in the wood they were captured by Hippothous's robber band.[12] Meanwhile a servant came from Syria from Manto with the following message to her father, Apsyrtus.

> You gave me a husband in a foreign country; but Anthia, whom you gave me with the other slaves as a present, I ordered to live in the country for her many wicked deeds. Your fine Moeris kept seeing her there and is in love with her. I could not bear this any longer; I sent for the goatherd and ordered her to be sold again in some city in Syria.

When he heard this, Habrocomes could not bear to stay any longer. So unknown to Apsyrtus and all his household, he went in search of Anthia. So when he came to the estate where Anthia had been living with Lampon the goatherd, who had been given her as a wife by Manto, he took him along the shore and asked Lampon to tell him if he knew anything about a girl from Tyre. The goatherd said that her name was Anthia; he told him about the marriage and how he had respected her; he told him about Moeris's love, the order to execute her, and the journey to Cilicia. And he said that the girl kept talking about someone called Habrocomes. Habrocomes did not say who he was but got up at dawn and rode for Cilicia, hoping to find Anthia there.

That night Hippothous's robber band spent their time roistering; the next day they set about their sacrifice. They busied themselves with all the preparations: statues of Ares, wood, and garlands. The sacrifice had to be performed in their usual manner, which was to hang the intended victim, human or animal, from a tree and throw javelins at it from a distance. The god was considered to accept the sacrifices of all who hit; those who missed tried to appease him a second time. Anthia had to be

12. This brusque introduction of Hippothous has been thought to be evidence of epitomizing. It may, however, arise merely from a brief lacuna in the text. There are unexplained sudden appearances of characters in other novels: see Achilles Tatius 1.16 (Satyrus and Clio). Cilicia—the southeast coast of modern Turkey—was an area noted for brigands.

sacrificed in this manner. And when all was ready, and they were on the point of hanging her up, they heard the woods rustling and the sound of marching. It was the eirenarch of Cilicia, Perilaus, one of the foremost men in the land.[13] This man fell on the robbers with a large force and killed them all, except for a few he took alive. Only Hippothous was able to take his weapons and get clean away. Perilaus took Anthia and felt sorry for her when he found out the dreadful fate that had been about to overtake her. But his pity for her was the beginning of another terrible calamity. He took her, together with his robber captives, to Tarsus in Cilicia. The frequent sight of the girl led him to fall in love with her, and little by little Perilaus was captivated by Anthia. When they got to Tarsus, he put the robbers in prison and devoted his attentions to her. He had neither wife nor children, but a considerable fortune. So he told Anthia that she would be all things to him: she would be his wife, his mistress, and his children. At first she refused, but when he pressed her and kept insisting, she had no alternative but to agree to marriage, since she was afraid he would try something more desperate; but she begged him to hold off and wait a little while, as much as thirty days, and not touch her during that time; Anthia made some excuse, which Perilaus accepted, and he gave an oath to respect her during the interval.

14    So she found herself in Tarsus with Perilaus, awaiting the time for her marriage. Meanwhile Habrocomes was making for Cilicia. And not far from the robbers' cave (for he too had lost his way), he met Hippothous, fully armed. When the latter saw him, he ran to meet him and greeted him and asked to join him on the road. "For I see, my lad, whoever you are, that you are handsome and manly too. Someone must have done you an injury for you to be wandering about like this. So let us leave Cilicia and make for Cappadocia and Pontus, for they tell me that wealthy men live there." Habrocomes did not mention his quest for Anthia. But at Hippothous's insistence he agreed: each swore to help and assist the other. Habrocomes also hoped in the course of their long travels to find Anthia. For that day they went back to the cave and used any provisions they had left to recoup their energies and refresh the horses (for Hippothous too had a horse hidden in the wood).

## Book Three

1    The next day they left Cilicia and made for Mazacus, a fine big town in Cappadocia, for from it Hippothous intended to recruit able-bodied young men to reconstitute his band. And as they went through the large

13. This mention of an "eirenarch" (peace officer) is one of the few indications of Xenophon's date: the office is first mentioned, as far as is known, in an inscription of A.D. 116–117 found not very far from Ephesus.

settlements they had a plentiful supply of provisions of all kinds, for Hippothous was able to speak Cappadocian, and everyone accepted him as a native. In ten days they reached Mazacus; there they took lodgings near the gates and decided to relax for a few days after the rigors of their journey. And it was as they were carousing that Hippothous let out a moan and began to weep. Habrocomes asked him why he was weeping. "It's a long story," he replied, "and a very tragic one." Habrocomes asked him to tell it and promised to tell his own as well. As they were alone, Hippothous told his story from the beginning.

"I belong," he said, "to one of the leading families of Perinthus, a city close to Thrace. And as you are aware, Perinthus is an important city and its citizens are well-to-do. There while I was a young man I fell in love with a beautiful youth, also from Perinthus, called Hyperanthes. I first fell in love with him when I saw his wrestling exploits in the gymnasium and I could not contain myself; during a local festival with an all-night vigil I approached Hyperanthes and begged him to take pity on me. He listened to me, took pity on me, and promised me everything. And our first steps in lovemaking were kisses and caresses, while I shed floods of tears. And at last we were able to take our opportunity to be alone with each other; we were both the same age, and no one was suspicious. For a long time we were together, passionately in love, until some evil spirit envied us. One of the leading men in Byzantium (the neighboring city) arrived in Perinthus: this was Aristomachus, a man proud of his wealth and prosperity. The moment he set foot in the town, as if sent against me by some god, he set eyes on Hyperanthes with me and was immediately captivated, amazed at the boy's beauty, which was capable of attracting anyone. When he had fallen in love, he could no longer restrain himself but first made overtures to the young man; when that brought no result (for Hyperanthes would let no one near him because of his relationship with me), he won over the boy's father, a villainous man not above bribery. And he made over Hyperanthes to Aristomachus on the pretext of private tuition, for he claimed to be a teacher of rhetoric. When he first took the boy over, he kept him under lock and key, then took him off to Byzantium. I followed, ignoring all my own affairs, and kept him company as often as I could; but that was seldom, there were few kisses, and he was difficult to talk to: too many were watching me. At length I could hold out no longer. Nerving myself, I went back to Perinthus, sold everything I had, got my money together, and went to Byzantium; I took a sword (Hyperanthes had agreed to this as well), made my way into Aristomachus's house during the night, and found him lying in bed with the boy. I was enraged and struck him a fatal blow. All was quiet, and everyone asleep: I left secretly with Hyperanthes without further ado; traveling all through the night to Perinthus, I

2

at once embarked on a ship for Asia, unknown to anyone. And for a while the voyage went well. But a heavy storm struck us off Lesbos and capsized the ship. I swam alongside Hyperanthes, gave him support, and made it easier for him to swim. But night came on, and the boy could not hold on any longer, gave up his efforts to swim, and died. I was only able to rescue his body, bring it to land, and bury it. I wept and wailed profusely and removed the relics. I could only provide a single stone to serve as a memorial on the grave, and inscribed it in memory of the unfortunate youth with a makeshift epigram.

> HIPPOTHOUS FASHIONED THIS TOMB FOR FAR-FAMED HYPERANTHES,
> A TOMB UNWORTHY OF THE DEATH OF A SACRED CITIZEN,
> THE FAMOUS FLOWER SOME EVIL SPIRIT ONCE SNATCHED FROM THE
>    LAND INTO THE DEEP,
> ON THE OCEAN HE SNATCHED HIM AS A GREAT STORM WIND BLEW.[14]

After this I decided not to return to Perinthus but made my way through Asia to Phrygia Magna and Pamphylia. And there, since I had no means of supporting myself and was distressed at the tragedy, I took to brigandage. At first I was only one of the rank and file, but in the end I got together a band of my own in Cilicia; it was famed far and wide, until it was captured not long before I saw you. This, then, is the misfortune I am telling you about. But you, Habrocomes, are my best friend; tell me your own story, for I am sure that there was some pressing reason that forced you to take to the road."

3    Habrocomes told him that he was an Ephesian and that he had fallen in love with a girl and married her; he mentioned the prophecies, the voyage, the pirates, Apsyrtus, Manto, his imprisonment, his flight, the goatherd, and the journey to Cilicia. While he was still speaking, Hippothous joined his lamentations: he mourned the loss of his parents and homeland, which he would never see again, and he mourned for Hyperanthes, his dearest friend of all. "Now you, Habrocomes," he went on, "will set eyes on your beloved and recover her in time; but I shall never be able to set eyes on Hyperanthes again." And as he spoke, he showed him the lock of Hyperanthes' hair and wept over it. And when both of them had had their fill of mourning, Hippothous looked hard at Habrocomes and said: "I have left out another story. A short time before my band was captured, a beautiful girl who had lost her way came upon our cave; she was the same age as you and said she came from Ephesus. I did not find out any more. We decided to sacrifice her to Ares; and in fact everything was ready when our pursuers came upon us; and I for my part took to flight, but I don't know what happened to her. She was very

14. This story of a homosexual love affair ending in a tragic accident is similar to one in Achilles Tatius (2.34).

beautiful, Habrocomes, and simply dressed; her hair was golden, and she had lovely eyes." While he was still speaking, Habrocomes exclaimed: "It was my Anthia you saw, Hippothous! Where then has she escaped to? And where is she now? We must turn back to Cilicia and look for her; she cannot be far from the pirate lair. I earnestly beg you, by the soul of your own dear Hyperanthes; do not willfully wrong me, but let us go where we shall be able to find Anthia." Hippothous promised to do all he could, adding only that he would have to collect some men as a bodyguard for their journey.

So there they were, planning their return to Cilicia. Meanwhile Anthia's thirty days were up, and Perilaus was making preparations for the wedding. Animals for sacrifice were being brought in from the countryside, and there was a lavish supply of everything else. Perilaus's friends and relations had joined him, and many of the local population too were celebrating Anthia's wedding.

While Anthia, taken from the robbers' lair, (waited in Perilaus's 4 household), an old doctor from Ephesus called Eudoxus arrived in Tarsus. He had been shipwrecked on a voyage to Egypt. This Eudoxus went round all the local aristocracy of Tarsus, begging for clothes or money and describing his misfortune; among them he approached Perilaus in turn and told him that he was an Ephesian and a doctor by profession. Perilaus took him and brought him to Anthia, thinking she would be glad to see someone from Ephesus. She was sympathetic to Eudoxus and tried to find out whether he could tell her anything about her own family. But he told her that he knew nothing, since he had been away from Ephesus for a long time. But Anthia was still pleased to see him, since he reminded her of the people back home. And so he had become a familiar visitor to the household and came to see Anthia each time, enjoying every comfort and always asking her to send him back to Ephesus, for he had a wife and children there.

Now when Perilaus had made all the preparations for the wedding, 5 and the day had arrived, a sumptuous dinner was ready for them, and Anthia had been dressed in a bridal dress. But she did not stop weeping night or day but always had Habrocomes before her eyes. And she reflected on a host of things at once: her love, her vows, her country, her parents, her plight, and her wedding. And so when she was by herself, she took her opportunity, and disheveling her hair, she exclaimed: "How unjust and wicked I am in everything I do: for I do not suffer for Habrocomes as he does for me. He endures chains and tortures, and perhaps has even died, so as to remain my husband; while I forget his sufferings and marry, unhappy creature that I am; and someone will sing my bridal hymn, and I will go to Perilaus's bed. But, my own dearest darling Habrocomes, do not be at all aggrieved over me, for I would never wrong you of my own free will. I will come to you and still be your bride even unto death."

After this outburst, Eudoxus, the Ephesian doctor, called on her. She took him to a private room, fell at his knees and implored him to report none of their conversation to anyone, and bound him by an oath by their ancestral goddess, Artemis, to cooperate in everything she asked.

Eudoxus made her get up, as she poured out her laments; he told her to cheer up and swore on oath to do it all. So she told him of her love for Habrocomes, her vows to him, and their pact of chastity. And she added: "If it was possible for me to live and recover Habrocomes alive or to run away from here unnoticed, I would make plans to do so. But since he is dead and it is impossible to flee and impossible to endure my impending marriage, for I will not transgress my vows to Habrocomes or disregard my oath, you must help me and find me some drug to release my wretched life from its miseries. Before I die, I will pray repeatedly to the gods on your behalf, and they will give you a great reward for this service; I myself will give you money and see to your return to Ephesus. You will be able to take ship for home before anyone finds out; and when you arrive, find my parents, Megamedes and Euippe, and tell them the news of my death and the whole story of my travels; tell them too that Habrocomes has perished."

With this she groveled at his feet and begged him not to refuse but give her the poison; and she brought out twenty minas of silver and her necklaces, which she gave to Eudoxus (she had plenty of everything, for she had the free run of Perilaus's estate). Eudoxus gave the matter a great deal of thought and was sorry for the girl's plight; he wanted to return to Ephesus; and won over by the money and the gifts, he promised to give her the poison and went away to get it. In the meantime she lamented a great deal, distressed at the fact that she was so young, and depressed that she was to die before her time; she kept calling Habrocomes as if he was there. Meanwhile after a short delay Eudoxus arrived, not with a lethal drug but with a sleeping-potion, so that nothing should happen to the girl, while he would get his fare and arrive safely home. Anthia took the drug, thanked him profusely, and sent him away. He immediately embarked and went off to sea, while she looked for a suitable opportunity to drink the poison.[15]

6    And already it was night, and the bridal chamber was being made ready; and those whose duty it was arrived to escort Anthia. She went out in tears against her will, hiding the potion in her hand; and as she approached the bridal chamber, the household struck up the bridal song. But Anthia wept and wailed: "This is how I was once led to my bride-

15. This whole major episode of Anthia's apparent death and its consequences is very similar to what happens to Callirhoe in Chariton's story; see the Introduction.

groom Habrocomes; the fire of love was our escort, and the wedding song was being sung for a happy marriage. But now what will you do, Anthia? Will you wrong Habrocomes, your husband, your loved one, who died for your sake? I am not so weak or cowardly in adversity. My mind is made up: I must drink the poison; Habrocomes must be my only husband; I want only him, even if he is dead." And with this she was led to the bridal chamber.

Now at this point she was alone, while Perilaus was still carousing with his friends. She made an excuse that the tension had made her thirsty and ordered one of the servants to bring her water to drink. And when a cup was brought, she took it while no one was in the chamber with her, threw in the poison, and wept. "Habrocomes, my darling," she cried, "as you see I am discharging my promises and am on my way to you; it is a sad road, but an inevitable one; welcome me gladly and make my life with you in the other world a happy one." With this she drank the drug and immediately fell into a deep sleep; she collapsed to the ground, and the drug took its full effect.

When Perilaus came in and immediately saw Anthia lying there, he   7 was dumbfounded and cried out, and there was a great deal of commotion in the household: they felt a welter of emotions—grief, fear, and terror. Some pitied the girl who had apparently died; others shared Perilaus's grief; while all mourned the tragedy. Perilaus tore his clothes and fell on the body. "My poor dear girl," he exclaimed, "you have deserted your lover before your marriage, after only a few days as the promised bride of Perilaus. What kind of bridal suite will I take you to—the tomb! Happy Habrocomes, whoever he was; a fortunate man, indeed, to receive such gifts from his beloved!" Perilaus lamented in this fashion, fondly embracing her body all over and clinging to her hands and feet. "Poor bride," he exclaimed, "and still more unhappy wife." He laid her out in all her finery and surrounded her with a great quantity of gold. And no longer able to bear the sight, when day came he put Anthia on a bier (she was still lying insensible) and took her to the tombs near the city. And there he laid her in a vault, after slaughtering a great number of victims and burning a great deal of clothing and other finery.

When he had carried out the accustomed rites, he was taken back to   8 the city by his household. But Anthia, left in the tomb, recovered her senses, realized that the poison was not fatal, and moaned and wept. "The poison has played me false!" she exclaimed. "It has barred the way of happiness back to Habrocomes. My misery is total; I have been cheated, even of my own wish to die. But by remaining in the tomb I can still do the poison's work by starving to death. No one would take me from here, nor could I look upon the sun nor will I go to the light." With this she strengthened her resolve and steadfastly waited for death.

Meanwhile some pirates had found out that a girl had been given a sumptuous burial and that a great store of woman's finery was buried with her, and a great horde of gold and silver. After nightfall they came to the tomb, burst open the doors, came in and took away the finery, and saw that Anthia was still alive. They thought that this too would turn out very profitable for them, raised her up, and wanted to take her. But she rolled at their feet and kept pleading with them. "Whoever you are, take away all this finery; take all there is and everything that is buried with me, but spare my body. I am a sacrifice to two gods, Love and Death. Leave me to devote myself to them in peace. By the gods of your own country, do not expose me to the daylight, when my misfortunes deserve night and darkness." So she pleaded, but she could not persuade the pirates: they brought her out of the tomb, took her down to the sea, put her into their skiff, and brought her to Alexandria. And they looked after her on the ship and tried to console her. But she took to moping once more over her dreadful misfortunes, as she wept and wailed. "Once again," she cried, "pirates and sea! Once again I am a prisoner! But now it is worse because I am without Habrocomes. So what land will have me? And who will I see there? Not Moeris again or Manto or Perilaus or Cilicia! My only prayer is that I may go where I shall at least see the tomb of Habrocomes." She lamented in this fashion time after time and refused to touch food or drink, but the pirates forced her.

9      Now they completed their lengthy voyage and arrived in Alexandria.[16] There they made Anthia disembark and decided to give her over to some slave dealers. But Perilaus, learning that the tomb had been broken into and the body had gone, was grief-stricken and inconsolable. Meanwhile Habrocomes was searching and making enquiries if anyone had heard any news of a foreign girl who had been brought in by pirates. And when he found out nothing, he came wearily back to their quarters. Hippothous's men prepared dinner for themselves: the rest were taking their meal, but Habrocomes was deeply distressed, threw himself on his bed and wept, and lay there without taking any food. As the band went ahead with their drinking, an old woman named Chrysion who was with them started to tell a story. "Listen, strangers," she said, "to a tragic event that happened not long ago in the city. One of the most prominent men in the city, Perilaus, was elected eirenarch of Cilicia; he went out to hunt for robbers and brought back some he had captured, together with a beautiful girl, whom he persuaded to marry him. Everything was ready for the marriage. She came into the bridal chamber, and either because she was mad or because she was in love with someone else, she

16. This is of some interest as establishing a vague dramatic date for this story: it takes place at least after the foundation of Alexandria in 332–331 B.C. (the detail about the eirenarch—see note 13—is probably an unconscious reflection of the author's own period).

drank a poison she had somehow obtained. This is how people said she died." Hippothous listened and said, "This is the girl Habrocomes is looking for!" Habrocomes had been listening to the tale but had been too depressed to notice. But at length and with difficulty he leapt up when he heard Hippothous and exclaimed: "Now it is clear that Anthia is dead! Perhaps her tomb is here, and the body is still intact!" He asked the old woman Chrysion to bring him to Anthia's tomb and show him the body. But she cried aloud: "This is the saddest part of the poor girl's story. Perilaus certainly gave her a sumptuous burial and provided her grave with ornaments, but pirates found out what was buried with her, opened the grave, took the treasure, and spirited away the body. And on that account Perilaus is searching far and wide."

When he heard this, Habrocomes tore his tunic to shreds and in a loud voice mourned Anthia's chaste and noble death, and her unhappy disappearance afterwards. "What pirate," he exclaimed, "is so much in love as to desire your corpse and even take your body away? I, poor wretch that I am, have been deprived of your body, my only consolation. So I am absolutely determined to die. But first I will go on until I find your body, embrace it, and bury myself with you." So he mourned, as Hippothous and his band tried to console him.

So for the moment they rested all that night. But Habrocomes kept turning everything over in his mind: Anthia, her death, the tomb, and her disappearance. And he came to the point where he could restrain himself no longer; while Hippothous's band was still prostrated with drink, he excused himself and slipped out; then he went clean away and made for the sea and found a ship weighing anchor for Alexandria. He went aboard and sailed off, hoping to catch in Egypt the pirates who had plundered everything. It was a forlorn hope that drove him to this. He made the voyage to Alexandria, but when day came Hippothous's band were upset at Habrocomes' departure; after a few days they recovered their morale and decided to embark on raids on Syria and Phoenicia.

Meanwhile the pirates handed over Anthia to merchants in Alexandria for a large sum. They looked after her at great expense and lavished attention on her appearance, always looking for a buyer at a suitable price. And sure enough someone did come to Alexandria, an Indian ruler, to see the city and do business. His name was Psammis. This man saw Anthia at the merchants' quarters, was ravished at the sight of her, paid the merchants a large sum, and took her as a maidservant. The moment he bought her the barbarian tried to force her and have his will with her. She was unwilling and at first refused, but at length gave as an excuse to Psammis (barbarians are superstitious by nature) that her father had dedicated her at birth to Isis till she was of age to marry, which she said was still a year away. "And so," she said, "if you offend the goddess's ward, she will be angry with you and take a terrible revenge." Psammis believed her, paid homage to the goddess, and kept away from Anthia.

12    She was still secluded in Psammis's household, regarded as consecrated to Isis. But the ship for Alexandria with Habrocomes on board went off course and was wrecked at the Paralian mouth of the Nile Delta, next to the Phoenician coast. And when they were cast ashore, men from the herdsmen who lived there attacked them and plundered their cargo, bound the men and took them on a long desert road to the Egyptian city of Pelusium, and there sold them to various buyers.[17] An old retired soldier called Araxus bought Habrocomes. He had a wife who was hideous to look at and much worse to listen to; she was amazingly insatiable, and her name was Kyno. This Kyno fell in love with Habrocomes the moment he was brought to the house and could not contain herself any longer; she was terribly passionate and determined to indulge her lust. Now Araxus for his part was kind to Habrocomes and treated him like a son, but Kyno made suggestions and tried to win him over, promising to kill Araxus and make him her husband. This proposal horrified Habrocomes, and he thought hard about a number of things at once: Anthia, his oath, and the chastity that had done him so much harm in the past. Kyno kept pressing him, and at last he agreed. When night came she killed Araxus, intending to have Habrocomes as her husband, and told Habrocomes what she had done. But he could not tolerate the woman's shameless act and left the house, leaving her behind, saying that he would never sleep with a vile murderess. When she came to her senses, she went at dawn to the assembly at Pelusium, lamented over her husband and accused their newly bought slave of murdering him, put up a great show of grief, and persuaded the assembly that she was speaking the truth. They at once arrested Habrocomes and sent him in chains to the current prefect of Egypt. He was brought to Alexandria for punishment for the alleged murder of his master, Araxus.

## Book Four

1    Meanwhile Hippothous's band moved off from Tarsus and made their way to Syria, forcing any opposition in their path to submit. They burned villages and slaughtered large numbers. In this way they reached Laodicea in Syria, and there they took up lodgings, not as pirates this time, but posing as tourists. There Hippothous made repeated enquiries

17. These "herdsmen" were robbers who existed historically in the Nile Delta and rose against the Romans in 172–173 (Dio Cassius 71.4). Xenophon here calls them *poimenes,* "shepherds"; the more usual name is *boukoloi,* "herdsmen," and that is what they are called by Achilles Tatius (3.9ff.) and Heliodorus (3.5ff.), in whose stories they play a much larger part.

in the hope of somehow finding Habrocomes. When he drew a blank, they took a rest and made for Phoenicia, and from there to Egypt, for their plan was to overrun the country. They gathered a large band of robbers and made for Pelusium; sailing on the Nile to the Egyptian Hermopolis and Schedia, they put in to Menelaus's canal and missed Alexandria. They arrived at Memphis, the shrine of Isis, and from there traveled to Mendes. And they recruited natives to serve in their band and act as guides. Going through Tawa, they reached Leontopolis, and passing a number of towns, most of them of little note, they came to Coptus, which is close to Ethiopia. There they decided to do their robbing, for there was a great crowd of merchants passing through for Ethiopia and India. Moreover, their band was now five hundred strong. And when they had taken the heights of Ethiopia and got their caves ready, they decided to rob the passing travelers.[18]

Meanwhile Habrocomes came before the prefect of Egypt.[19] The Pelusians had made him a report of what had happened, mentioning Araxus's death and stating that Habrocomes, a household slave, had been the perpetrator of so foul a crime. When the prefect heard the particulars, he made no further effort to find out the facts but gave orders to have Habrocomes taken away and crucified. Habrocomes himself was dumbfounded at his miseries and consoled himself at his impending death with the thought that Anthia, so it seemed, was dead as well. The prefect's agents brought him to the banks of the Nile, where there was a sheer drop overlooking the torrent. They set up the cross and attached him to it, tying his hands and feet tight with ropes; that is the way the Egyptians crucify. They then went away and left him hanging there, thinking that their victim was securely in place. But Habrocomes looked straight at the sun, then at the Nile channel, and prayed: "Kindest of the gods, ruler of Egypt, revealer of land and sea to all men: if I, Habrocomes, have done anything wrong, may I perish miserably and incur an even greater penalty if there is one; but if I have been betrayed by a wicked woman, I pray that the waters of the Nile should never be polluted by the body of a man unjustly killed; nor should you look on such a sight, a man who has done no wrong being murdered on your territory." The god took pity on his prayer. A sudden gust of wind arose and struck the cross, sweeping away the subsoil on the cliff where it had been fixed. Habrocomes fell into the torrent and was swept away; the water did him no harm; his fetters did not get in his way; nor did the river creatures do him any harm as he passed, but the current guided him along. He was

18. Xenophon's geography, here and elsewhere, is not to be taken too seriously, although he shows some fragments of knowledge.

19. Mention of a "prefect" of Egypt (*archon* in the Greek) appears to be another reflection of contemporary Roman rule.

carried to the delta where it meets the sea, but the guards on duty there arrested him and took him before the prefect as a fugitive from justice. He was still angrier than before, took Habrocomes for an out-and-out villain, and gave firm orders to build a pyre, put Habrocomes on it, and burn him. And so everything was made ready, the pyre was set up at the delta, Habrocomes was put on it, and the fire had been lit underneath. But just as the flames were about to engulf him, he again prayed the few words he could to be saved from the perils that threatened. Then the Nile rose in spate, and the surge of water struck the pyre and put out the flames. To those who witnessed it the event seemed like a miracle:[20] they took Habrocomes and brought him before the prefect, told him what had happened, and explained how the Nile had come to his rescue. He was amazed when he heard what had happened and ordered Habrocomes to be kept in custody, but to be well looked after till they could find out who he was and why the gods were looking after him like this.

3      And so Habrocomes remained in prison. But Psammis, who had bought Anthia, decided to make for home and was making preparations for the journey. He had to go through upper Egypt and make for Ethiopia, where Hippothous had his lair. Everything was ready, a host of camels, asses, and packhorses. There was a great deal of gold, silver, and clothing, and he was taking Anthia along with him. When she had left Alexandria and arrived in Memphis, she stood before the temple and prayed to Isis. "Greatest of goddesses," she pleaded, "until now I have remained chaste, since I was regarded as sacred to you, and I preserve my marriage to Habrocomes undefiled. But from this point I go to India, far from the land of Ephesus, far from the remains of Habrocomes. So either deliver this poor woman from here and give me back to Habrocomes if he is still alive, or if it is absolutely fated that we should die apart, bring it about that I remain faithful to his corpse." After this prayer they set out on the road, and already they had gone through Coptus and were reaching the boundaries of Ethiopia when Hippothous fell on them, killed Psammis himself and many of his followers, took his goods, and took Anthia prisoner. He gathered the booty they had taken and put it in the cave they had set apart for the purpose. There Anthia went too; neither recognized the other; whenever he asked who she was and where she was from, she did not tell the truth but said she was a native Egyptian called Memphitis.

4      So Anthia stayed with Hippothous in the robbers' cave. Meanwhile the prefect of Egypt sent for Habrocomes and interrogated him about himself. He found out his story, felt sorry for his misfortune, gave him

---

20. Perhaps the gods of the Nile had read Herodotus, who reports that Croesus escaped a similar fate in a comparable manner (1.87).

money, and promised to send him to Ephesus. Habrocomes thanked him profusely for saving his life but asked instead to be allowed to continue his search for Anthia. And so he accepted an abundance of gifts, went aboard ship, and sailed for Italy, hoping to hear something there about Anthia.[21] Meanwhile the prefect of Egypt found out the truth about Araxus, sent for Kyno, and had her crucified.

While Anthia was in the cave, one of her robber guards, Anchialus, 5 fell in love with her. He was a native of Laodicea, one of the band who had come with Hippothous from Syria: the latter had a high opinion of him, since he was a spirited and influential member of the band. Anchialus, then, fell in love with Anthia, started making suggestions to win her over, and expected to talk her round and ask her from Hippothous as a gift. But she turned down all his pleas, undismayed by the cave, the fetters, or the robber's threats; she was still saving herself for Habrocomes, even if it seemed he was dead, and often when she was out of earshot, she would exclaim, "I pray that I may remain the wife of Habrocomes, even if I have to die or suffer still more than I have already." This made Anchialus's misery still worse, and the sight of Anthia every day fanned his passion. When he could take no more, he tried to use force. One night, when Hippothous was away with the others on a raid, he got up and tried to rape her. In desperation she drew a sword that was lying beside her and struck him. The blow proved fatal: while he was trying to embrace and kiss her, he had leant right on top of her; she held the sword underneath him and drove it into his chest.

Anchialus had paid the price for his wicked passion; but Anthia began to be afraid over what had happened and kept wondering whether to kill herself (yet she still had some hope for Habrocomes) or to flee from the cave (but that was impossible: she could scarcely travel alone, and there was no one to show her the way). So she decided to wait in the cave and take whatever Providence had in store.

That night, then, she waited, unable to get any sleep, and with a great 6 deal on her mind. When day came, Hippothous arrived with his band. When they saw Anchialus dead and Anthia beside the body, they guessed what had happened, interrogated her, and found out everything. They were furious about it and decided to take revenge for their dead companion. Different suggestions were made for Anthia's punishment, one man telling them to kill her and bury her with Anchialus's body, another to crucify her. Hippothous for his part was distressed over Anchialus and

21. We are not told why Habrocomes chooses Italy as his next destination—but we may observe that it is Sicily that he reaches. Possibly Xenophon is remembering that Chariton's heroes came from Sicily; more probably the reason is that Habrocomes has not yet wandered enough for the story's needs, and has not yet been in the western Mediterranean. Hippothous's journey to Sicily (5.3) *is* motivated. Or this lack of motivation may be a further result of epitomizing.

decided on an even harsher penalty. So he gave orders to dig a large, deep trench and throw Anthia in it with two dogs beside her, to make her pay dearly for her daring. The robbers obeyed, and she was brought to the trench. The dogs were huge and particularly fearsome-looking Egyptian hounds. When they threw them in, they shut the trench with large planks and piled earth on top—the Nile was not far away—and put one of the robbers, Amphinomus, on guard. Now he had already fallen in love with Anthia, so that he now felt all the more sorry for her and sympathized with her plight. So he found a way of keeping her alive and stopping the dogs from molesting her; every so often he would remove the planks from over the trench and throw in bread, give her water, and so keep her spirits up. By feeding the dogs he prevented them from doing her any harm; soon they were tame and docile. But Anthia thought about herself and her current plight. "What perils! What a revenge!" she exclaimed. "To be shut in a ditch as a prison, with dogs—and even they are not nearly as fierce as the robbers. I share your own fate, Habrocomes, for you were once in the same straits; and I left you in prison in Tyre. If you are still alive, then my plight is nothing; for some day, perhaps, we shall be together; but if you are already dead, it is in vain that I struggle to live, and in vain this man, whoever he is, is taking pity on my miserable life." She kept mourning and moping in this vein; and so there she was, shut in the trench with the dogs, while Amphinomus kept consoling her and pacifying the dogs with his feeding.

## Book Five

1    Meanwhile Habrocomes completed his voyage from Egypt but did not reach Italy itself; for the wind drove the ship back, blew it off course, and brought it to Sicily, and they disembarked at the large and splendid port of Syracuse. There Habrocomes decided to go round the island and search for any more news of Anthia. So he took lodgings near the sea with an old man, Aegialeus, a fisherman by trade. This man was a poor stranger who just scraped a living from his work. But he gladly took Habrocomes in, treated him as his own son, and was exceptionally kind to him. Soon they were great friends, and Habrocomes told him his story—about Anthia, his love for her, and his wanderings—and Aegialeus in turn began his own story.

"Habrocomes, my child, I am neither a settler nor a native Sicilian, but a Spartan from Lacedaemon, from one of its leading families. I was very prosperous, and when I was a young man enrolled in the ephebes, I fell in love with a Spartan girl called Thelxinoe, and she with me. We met at an all-night festival in the city (a god guided both of us), and we found the fulfillment of the desire that had brought us together. For some time our relationship was a secret, and we often made pacts to be faithful unto death. But one of the gods, I suppose, was envious. While I was still an ephebe, her parents arranged to marry her to a young Spartan by the name of Androcles, who was also now in love with her. At first she kept making excuses and putting off the wedding, until finally she was able to meet me and agreed to elope with me by night. So both of us dressed as young men, and I even cut Thelxinoe's hair. We left Sparta the very night of the wedding for Argos and Corinth, where we took ship for Sicily. When the Spartans found out we had gone they condemned us to death. We spent our lives here in Sicily, poor but happy, since we thought we were rich because we had each other. Thelxinoe died here in Sicily not long ago; I didn't bury her body but have it with me; I always have her company and adore her." At this he brought Habrocomes into the inner room and showed him Thelxinoe. She was now an old woman but still seemed beautiful to Aegialeus. Her body was embalmed in the Egyptian style, for the old fisherman had learnt embalming as well. "And so, Habrocomes, my child," he explained, "I still talk to her as if she were alive and lie down beside her and have my meals with her, and if I come home exhausted from fishing, the sight of her consoles me, for she looks different to me than she does to you; I think of her, child, as she was in Sparta and when we eloped; I think of the festival and the compact we made."[22]

While Aegialeus was still speaking, Habrocomes broke into a lament. "Anthia," he exclaimed, "the unluckiest girl of all! When will I ever find you, even as a corpse? The body of Thelxinoe is a great comfort in the life of Aegialeus, and now I have truly learnt that true love knows no age limits; but I wander over every land and sea, and yet I have not been able to hear about you. How doom-laden were the prophecies! I pray you, Apollo, who gave us the harshest oracles of all, have pity on us now and bring your prophecies to their final fulfillment."

And so Habrocomes lamented like this, while Aegialeus tried to console him, and lived in Syracuse, where he now helped Aegialeus with his fishing. Meanwhile Hippothous's band was already a large one, and they had plans to leave Ethiopia and now attack more ambitious targets, for Hippothous was not satisfied with robbing individuals rather than attacking villages and towns. So he collected his followers and had everything loaded for his expedition (he had a host of pack animals and a large number of camels). He left Ethiopia and made for Egypt and Alexandria, and had plans to return once more to Phoenicia and Syria. As for Anthia, he thought that she was dead. But Amphinomus, who was guarding her in

2

22. There seems to be another literary reminiscence here: in Euripides *Alcestis* 348–353 Admetus promises his dying wife, Alcestis, that he will keep a likeness of her in his bedroom.

the trench, could not endure to be separated from the girl, because of his love for her and her impending peril. So he did not follow Hippothous, but escaped attention in the crowd and hid in a cave with the stores he had gathered. After nightfall Hippothous's band came to the Egyptian village of Areia, intending to plunder it. Meanwhile Amphinomus opened up the trench, brought Anthia out, and tried to console her. But she was still afraid and diffident, so he swore an oath by the sun and the gods of Egypt to respect her and preserve her chastity, until such time as she should agree to sleep with him of her own free will. Anthia was convinced by Amphinomus's oath and followed him. And the dogs were not left behind but fawned on them as faithful companions.

So they came to Coptus, and there they decided to spend some days until Hippothous's band had gone ahead; and they took care to feed the dogs.

Meanwhile Hippothous's band attacked the village of Areia, killed many of the inhabitants and burned the houses, and withdrew not by the same route but by the Nile. They took all the barges from the intervening villages, embarked and sailed for Schedia, and disembarking there they continued their journey through the rest of Egypt beside the banks of the Nile.

3    Meanwhile the prefect of Egypt had received word of what had happened in Areia; he was informed of Hippothous's band and its march from Ethiopia. So he got ready a large force of soldiers and put in charge of them one of his kinsmen, Polyidus, a handsome and courageous young man, and sent him against the bandits. This Polyidus took the army and met Hippothous's force at Pelusium, and at once there was a battle beside the riverbanks; many fell on both sides. When night fell the bandits were routed, and all were slaughtered by the soldiers, except for some they took alive. Only Hippothous threw away his weapons, escaped during the night, and reached Alexandria. From there he was able to escape unnoticed, went aboard a ship that was putting out, and sailed off. His great aim was to reach Sicily, for there he thought he was most likely to escape detection and make a living; for he heard that the island was large and prosperous.

4    Polyidus was not satisfied with defeating the robber band in battle; he decided it was necessary to conduct a thorough investigation and clean out Egypt in the hope of finding either Hippothous or any remaining companions. He took with him a detachment of his troops and the robber captives, so that if any appeared, they would tell him; he sailed up the river, made thorough enquiries in the cities, and intended to go as far as Ethiopia. And so they came to Coptus, where Anthia was staying with Amphinomus. Now as it happened, she was in their quarters, but the robber captives recognized Amphinomus and told Polyidus; Amphi-

nomus was captured and on being questioned told them all about Anthia. When he heard, Polyidus gave orders for her to be brought to him; when she arrived, he made enquiries as to who she was and where she came from. But she did not tell him any of the truth, but said she was an Egyptian captured by the robbers.

Meanwhile Polyidus, who had a wife in Alexandria, fell passionately in love with Anthia. In his passion he at first tried to persuade her with great promises; but at length when they reached Memphis on their way down to Alexandria, Polyidus tried to use force on Anthia. She was able to escape, went to the temple of Isis, and took refuge as a suppliant. "Mistress of Egypt," she exclaimed, "who have helped me often, save me yet again. Let Polyidus spare me as well, since I am keeping myself chaste for Habrocomes, thanks to you." Polyidus revered the goddess, but he also loved Anthia and pitied her fate. He came to the temple alone and promised never to use force on her or commit any insult against her, but to respect her chastity as long as she wished, for in his infatuation he would be content only to look at her and talk to her.

Anthia was persuaded by his oaths and left the temple. And when they decided to rest in Memphis for three days, she went to the temple of Apis. This is the most illustrious shrine in Egypt, and the god gives oracles to those who wish them. For whenever a person comes and prays and makes an enquiry to the god, he comes out, and the Egyptian children in front of the temple foretell the future, sometimes in prose, sometimes in verse. So Anthia too came and prostrated herself before Apis. "Kindest of gods," she prayed, "who have pity on all strangers, have pity on me too in my misery and make me a true prophecy about Habrocomes. For if I am to see him again and have him as my husband, I will remain alive. But if he is dead, it is well that I too should depart this unhappy life." With this prayer she wept and left the temple. But meanwhile the children playing in front of the precinct shouted out in chorus,

Anthia will soon recover her own husband, Habrocomes.

When she heard this she took heart and prayed to the gods. And at once they left for Alexandria.

The wife of Polyidus had found out that he was in love with a girl and 5 bringing her home; afraid that he would prefer the newcomer to herself, she said nothing to Polyidus but made plans of her own to take revenge on the woman who seemed to be threatening her marriage. Now Polyidus had been making his campaign report to the prefect and was now engaged in his duties at headquarters. While he was away, Rhenaea (that was the name of Polyidus's wife) sent for Anthia, who was in the house at the time; she tore her clothes and disfigured her body. "Shameless woman," she said, "plotting against my marriage! You have attracted Polyidus in vain, for you will gain nothing from your good looks; perhaps you were able to entice the pirates and sleep with a horde of young drunkards, but you will not get away with insulting Rhenaea's bed!" With this she cut off Anthia's hair and tied her up. Handing her over to a loyal servant, Clytus, she ordered him to put Anthia aboard a ship, take her to Italy, and sell her to a brothelkeeper. "For in that way, my beauty," she told Anthia, "you will be able to satisfy your lust." Anthia was taken away by Clytus, weeping and wailing. "My beauty conspires against me; my charms are fatal! Why do they keep me company and harass me; why are they the cause of so many ills? Were the tombs, murders, bonds, and pirates' lairs not enough? But now will I be made to stand up in a brothel, and will a brothelkeeper force me to lose the virtue that I have been preserving till now for Habrocomes? But master," she said, falling at Clytus's knees, "do not take me to suffer *that* punishment but kill me yourself. I will not endure a brothelkeeper for a master. Believe me, I have always been chaste." So she pleaded, and Clytus had pity on her.

Anthia, then, was on her way to Italy, but Rhenaea said to Polyidus when he came back that Anthia had run away; and because of what had already happened, he believed her, while Anthia was brought to the city of Tarentum in Italy. And there Clytus, for fear of Rhenaea's instructions, sold her to a brothelkeeper, who saw her beauty, of a kind he had never before set eyes upon, and thought the girl would earn a great deal. He rested her for some days, as she was weary from her voyage and Rhenaea's tortures; Clytus returned to Alexandria and informed Rhenaea of what had been done.

6      Now Hippothous had completed his voyage and put in to Sicily, not at Syracuse, but at Tauromenium, and was looking for a chance to support himself. And now that Habrocomes had spent a long time in Syracuse, he was terribly distressed and in despair, because he could neither find Anthia nor reach his homeland again, so he decided to sail from Sicily to Italy, and from there, if he could find no trace of what he had been looking for, to make the unhappy voyage back to Ephesus. By this time the couple's parents and all Ephesus were in great distress, since no messenger and no letters had come from them. They sent out men to look for them everywhere. And in the despair of old age the parents of both were unable to endure and took their own lives. Meanwhile Habrocomes was en route for Italy; but Leucon and Rhode, the companions of Habrocomes and Anthia, decided to return to Ephesus now that their master had died in Xanthus and had left his large estate to them; they thought that their masters had already reached home safely; and they had had their fill of the rigors of exile. They put all their goods in a ship and sailed for Ephesus, and after only a few days reached Rhodes. And when

they found out there that Habrocomes and Anthia had not yet been rescued, while their parents had died, they decided not to return to Ephesus but to stay some time there, until they could hear some news of their masters.

Meanwhile the brothelkeeper who had bought Anthia forced her after a while to exhibit herself in front of his establishment. So he dressed her in a beautiful costume, loaded her with gold, and brought her to take her position in front of the brothel door. But she lamented bitterly over her misfortunes. "Are my previous disasters not enough," she exclaimed, "the chains and the bandits' lair? Must I now be a prostitute as well? My beauty is justly disgraced, for it remains with me to my cost; but why do I lament like this and not find some way to guard the chastity I have preserved till now?" As she said this, she was brought to the brothel, while the brothelkeeper sometimes tried to console her and sometimes threatened her. And when she arrived and was put up for hire, a crowd of admirers surged forward, most of them ready to pay money to satisfy their desires. She was in an impossible plight but found a means of escape. She fell to the ground, let herself go, and pretended to be afflicted with the divine disease.[23] The bystanders felt pity and fear and no longer wanted to satisfy their desires but tried to attend to her. And the brothelkeeper, realizing the disaster that had befallen him and thinking that the girl really was ill, brought her home, made her lie down, and looked after her, and when she seemed to have come to, he asked her the cause of the disease. Anthia replied: "I wanted to tell you in fact before my illness and explain what happened. But I was embarrassed and covered it up. But now it is not hard to tell you, since you have already found out everything about me. While I was still a girl, I was at an all-night festival; I got separated from my companions and came to the tomb of a man who had recently died. And there someone seemed to leap up from the tomb and tried to take possession of me. I kept screaming and tried to run away. The man was frightful to look at, and his voice was a great deal worse; at last, when it was already day, he let me go but struck me on the chest and said that this disease had come upon me. And from that time onward I have been afflicted by the disease in different ways at different times. But I ask you, master, do not be angry with me, for this is not my fault; you could still sell me and lose none of the price you paid." The brothelkeeper was not pleased to hear this, but he was sympathetic, on the grounds that it was not her fault that she was afflicted.

So she was being looked after as a sick woman at the brothelkeeper's. Meanwhile Habrocomes returned from Sicily and put in at Nuceria in

7

8

23. The "divine disease" is epilepsy. The motif of evasion of a prostitute's duties plays a major role in *The Story of Apollonius of Tyre*, along with the theme of recognition of the heroine in the capacity of a prostitute.

Italy; he had now nothing to live on and did not know what to do; but first of all he went round looking for Anthia. For this woman was the reason for his wandering and his whole existence. And when he found nothing (for the girl was in Tarentum at the brothelkeeper's), he took work in the quarries. For him the work was arduous, for he had not been used to subjecting himself to hard or rigorous physical work; he was in a bad way and often lamented his fate. "See, Anthia," he exclaimed, "how your Habrocomes works at a laborious task and has submitted his body to slavery. And if I had any hope of finding you and sharing your life in the future, this would console me better than anything; but as it is perhaps I am laboring in my misery to no purpose. You must have died for love of Habrocomes; but I am sure, my dearest, that never, not even in death, would you have forgotten me."

So he mourned and bore his troubles in misery, but Anthia had a dream as she slept in Tarentum. She dreamed she was with Habrocomes, and both were beautiful, and it was the time when they were first in love. Some other beautiful woman appeared and was dragging Habrocomes away from her; and at last, when he cried out and called her by name, she started up and the dream came to an end. When she had this dream, she at once leapt up and cried out and thought the dream was true. She lamented her plight. "I undergo every misery," she exclaimed, "and suffer all kinds of misfortune, poor wretch, and invent ways of keeping chaste beyond a woman's capacities, for Habrocomes' sake; but perhaps you prefer the sight of another woman; for that is the import of my dream. Why then do I stay alive? Why do I distress myself? Better then to die and escape from this miserable life, and be rid of this degrading and perilous slavery. But even if Habrocomes has broken his vows, may the gods not punish him; perhaps he was forced to; but for me the noble course is to die chaste." This was how she lamented, as she tried to find a way to kill herself.

9     Meanwhile Hippothous of Perinthus was in Tauromenium. At first he was in a bad way, for lack of means; but as time went on an old woman fell in love with him, and poverty forced him to marry her. After he had lived with her a short time she died, and he inherited her great wealth and luxury. He had a huge retinue of servants, a large wardrobe, and sumptuous effects. So he decided to sail to Italy, to buy attractive young servants and maidservants, and all the other extravagances of a man of means. And he always kept Habrocomes in mind and prayed that he would find him; he was determined to share with him his whole way of life and his wealth.

And so he took ship and reached Italy, taking with him a young Sicilian aristocrat named Cleisthenes; he was a handsome young man who shared all Hippothous's possessions. But now Anthia's brothelkeeper had it in mind to sell her, since she seemed to have recovered. So he brought her to the market and was exhibiting her to prospective buyers. Meanwhile Hippothous was going round the city of Tarentum in the hope of buying something elegant; and he saw Anthia, recognized her, and was amazed at the coincidence. He reflected a great deal to himself. "Is this not the girl I once buried in a trench in Egypt in revenge for the death of Anchialus, and shut up with dogs? So what change of fortune is this? How has she been rescued? How did she escape from the trench? How could she possibly have survived?" With this he went up as if he wanted to buy her, stood beside her, and said, "Tell me, my girl, aren't you familiar with Egypt, and did you not fall among bandits and suffer some other misfortune there? Don't be afraid to tell me, for I recognize you from there." When she heard of Egypt and remembered Anchialus, the bandit lair, and the ditch, she wept and wailed, looking hard at Hippothous; for she could not recognize him at all. "I did suffer many terrible things in Egypt, stranger," she replied, "whoever you are, and I did fall among bandits. But how do you know my story? How can you say you know a wretch like me? It is true that my sufferings are well known and spread abroad, but I do not recognize you at all." When Hippothous heard this and recognized her still better from what she said, he kept silent for the moment and bought her from the brothelkeeper; he took her home and tried to console her. He told her who he was, reminded her of what had happened in Egypt, and told her of his own wealth and his flight. She asked him to forgive her, explained in turn that she had killed Anchialus because of his outrageous behavior, and told him about the trench and about Amphinomus; she explained how the dogs were soothed and how she had escaped to safety. Hippothous was sorry for her, but had not yet discovered who she was; from daily contact with the girl he too fell in love with her, wanted to sleep with her, and offered her many inducements. At first she refused him, saying that she was not worthy of her master's bed.

At last, when Hippothous insisted, she was at a loss what to do and thought it better to tell him all her secrets rather than break her vow to Habrocomes. So she mentioned Habrocomes, Ephesus, their love, their vows, their misfortunes, and the bandits' lairs; and she kept lamenting over Habrocomes. But when Hippothous heard she was Anthia and the wife of his dearest friend, he embraced her, told her not to be afraid, and explained his friendship with Habrocomes. And he kept her in his house and gave her every attention out of regard for Habrocomes. And he for his part made all the enquiries he could in the hope of finding Habrocomes.

Now Habrocomes at first struggled hard in Nuceria, but at last he  10
could not bear his labors and decided to take ship for Ephesus. One night

he went down to the sea and just caught a ship sailing. He boarded her and sailed back to Sicily, with a view to making for Crete, Cyprus, and Rhodes, and from there to Ephesus; he also had hopes of hearing some news of Anthia during the course of his long voyage. He sailed with few provisions and completed the first part of the journey to Sicily, where he found his former host, Aegialeus, dead. When he had poured a libation for him and wept copiously, he set sail again; he passed Crete and arrived in Cyprus; after a few days there and a prayer to the ancestral goddess of the Cyprians, he sailed off and arrived in Rhodes. There he took quarters near the harbor. And now he was near Ephesus and thought of all his perils; he thought of his country and parents; he thought of Anthia and their servants. And he lamented over his misfortunes. "I shall arrive in Ephesus alone," he exclaimed. "My parents will see me without Anthia, and in my misery I will make a pointless voyage and tell tales that are perhaps incredible, without anyone who has shared my sufferings. But persevere, Habrocomes, and when you arrive in Ephesus, endure just long enough to raise a tomb for Anthia and mourn her and pour libations and then bring yourself to lie beside her." So he lamented and wandered round the city, demented; he still had no news of Anthia, and he was destitute.

Meanwhile Leucon and Rhode, who were staying in Rhodes, had made an offering to the temple of Helius beside the gold panoply that Anthia and Habrocomes had dedicated. They put up a pillar inscribed in gold to commemorate Habrocomes and Anthia, with their own names, Leucon and Rhode, inscribed as donors. Habrocomes had come to pray to the god and noticed the pillar. He read the inscription, recognized the donors, and realized how thoughtful his servants had been. And when he saw the panoply nearby, he sat down beside the pillar and moaned loudly: "I am unlucky in everything! I come to the end of my life and remember my own misfortunes. Here before me is the very panoply I set up with Anthia; I sailed away with her, and now I come back without her. And if this is the offering set up by our companions for both of us, what is to become of me now that I am alone; where will I find those dearest to me?"

So he lamented, and meanwhile Leucon and Rhode suddenly appeared; they prayed as usual to the gods, and saw Habrocomes sitting beside the pillar and looking at the panoply. They did not recognize him, but wondered who would stay beside someone else's offerings. And so Leucon spoke to him. "Why are you sitting weeping, young man, and lamenting beside offerings that have nothing to do with you? What concern of yours are these? And what do you have in common with the people named here?" Habrocomes replied, "I am the very person the offerings of Leucon and Rhode are for, and after Anthia it is them I am praying to see; I am the unfortunate Habrocomes!" When Leucon and Rhode heard this they were immediately dumbfounded, but gradually recovered and recognized him by his appearance and voice, from what he said, and from his mention of Anthia; and they fell at his feet and told their own story—their journey to Syria from Tyre, Manto's anger, the sale to Lycia, their master's death, their wealth, their arrival in Rhodes. And so they took him with them and brought him to their lodgings, made over their possessions to him, took care of him, looked after him, and tried to console him. But to him there was nothing more precious than Anthia, and time after time he mourned for her.

And so he lived in Rhodes with his companions, thinking over what to do. Meanwhile Hippothous decided to take Anthia from Italy to Ephesus, to restore her to her parents; he also hoped to find out something about Habrocomes there. And so he put everything he had into a large Ephesian ship and set sail with Anthia; they put in during the night in Rhodes after a few days' welcome voyage, and there took lodgings with an old woman called Althaea, near the sea; he brought Anthia to his hostess and himself rested that night. The next day they were already getting ready to sail, but a magnificent public festival was being celebrated by the whole population of Rhodes in honor of Helius with a procession and sacrifice, and a great crowd of citizens was taking part in the revels. Leucon and Rhode were there, not so much to take part in the festival as in an attempt to find out something about Anthia. Now Hippothous came to the temple with Anthia. And she looked at the offerings and remembered the past. "O Helius," she exclaimed, "who look over the affairs of all men and pass over only me in my misery, when I was in Rhodes before I worshiped you in happiness and made sacrifices with Habrocomes, and at the time people thought I was happy; but now I am a slave instead of a free woman, a captive wretch instead of that happy girl, and I am going to Ephesus alone and will appear before my family without Habrocomes."

She said this and shed many tears and asked Hippothous to let her cut off a lock of her hair, as an offering to Helius, and put up a prayer about Habrocomes. Hippothous agreed; cutting off what she could of her hair and choosing a suitable opportunity, when everyone had gone away, she offered it with the inscription

ON BEHALF OF HER HUSBAND HABROCOMES
ANTHIA DEDICATED HER HAIR TO THE GOD.

When she had done this and prayed, she went away with Hippothous.

But Leucon and Rhode, who had been at the procession up to this point, stopped at the temple, looked at the offerings, and recognizing the names of their masters, first kissed the hair and lamented as much as if they were looking at Anthia, but finally went round to see if they could find her anywhere (the names were already familiar to the Rhodian crowd from their previous visit). That day they could find nothing and went away and told Habrocomes what was in the temple. His heart was disturbed at this unexpected event, but he had high hopes of finding Anthia.

The next day Anthia again arrived at the temple with Hippothous, since they were unable to sail. She sat by the offerings and wept and wailed. Meanwhile Leucon and Rhode came too, leaving Habrocomes at home, since he was depressed for the same reasons as before. They came and saw Anthia but as yet did not recognize her; but they reflected on everything: the girl's love, her tears, the offerings, the names, and her appearance; and in this way they gradually recognized her. Falling to their knees, they lay dumbfounded. But she wondered who they were and what they wanted, for she never expected to see Leucon and Rhode. But when they recovered, they said: "Mistress Anthia, we are your slaves, Leucon and Rhode, who shared your voyage and the pirate lair. But what chance brings you here? Have courage, mistress; Habrocomes is safe; and he is here, always mourning for you." When Anthia heard this she was amazed at the news: she came to herself with difficulty, recognized them, embraced them and greeted them, and learned in the greatest detail all about Habrocomes.

13     When the Rhodians heard that Anthia and Habrocomes had been found, they all surged together. Hippothous too was among them; he was recognized by Leucon and Rhode, and learned in turn who they were. And now they had everything they wanted, except that Habrocomes still did not know the news. They ran to the house just as they were. And when he heard from one of the Rhodians that Anthia had been found, Habrocomes ran through the middle of the city like a madman, shouting, "Anthia!" And so he met Anthia near the temple of Isis, followed by a great crowd of Rhodians. When they saw each other, they recognized each other at once, for that was their fervent desire. They embraced each other and fell to the ground. A host of different emotions took hold of them at once—joy, grief, fear, memory of past events, and anxiety for the future. The Rhodians cheered and shouted in their excitement, hailing Isis as a great goddess and exclaiming, "Now once again we see Habrocomes and Anthia, the beautiful pair!" They recovered, sprang up, and came into the temple of Isis, saying, "To you, greatest goddess, we owe thanks for our safety; it is you, the goddess we honor most of all, who have restored us." Paying homage before the precinct they fell down before the altar. Then they betook themselves to Leucon's house, Hippothous transferred his belongings there, and they were ready for the voyage to Ephesus. And when they sacrificed that day and

feasted, there were many different stories from all of them: each of them told all that had happened to them and all they had done; and they carried on their party till late, since they had found each other at long last. When night came, all the others lay down as they were—Leucon with Rhode, Hippothous with the handsome Cleisthenes, who had followed him from Sicily to Italy. But Anthia lay down with Habrocomes.

And when all the rest had fallen asleep and there was complete stillness, Anthia put her arms around Habrocomes and wept. "Husband and master," she said, "I have found you again, after all my wanderings over land and sea, escaping robbers' threats and pirates' plots and pimps' insults, chains, trenches, fetters, poisons, and tombs. But I have reached you, Habrocomes, lord of my heart, the same as when I first left you in Tyre for Syria. No one persuaded me to go astray: not Moeris in Syria, Perilaus in Cilicia, Psammis or Polyidus in Egypt, not Anchialus in Ethiopia, not my master in Tarentum. I remain chaste, after practicing every device of virtue. But did you, Habrocomes, remain chaste, or has some other beauty eclipsed me? Has no one forced you to forget your oath and me?" With this she kept kissing him, but Habrocomes replied, "I swear to you, by this day that we have longed for and reached with such difficulty, that I have never considered any other girl attractive, nor did the sight of any other woman please me; but you have found Habrocomes as pure as you left him in the prison in Tyre."

They made these protestations of innocence all night and easily persuaded each other, since that was what they wanted. And when day came, they went aboard ship, put aboard all their belongings, and set sail; the whole population of Rhodes saw them off. And Hippothous too went with them, with Cleisthenes and all his belongings. And after a few days' voyage they put in to Ephesus. The news had already reached the whole city that they were safe. And when they disembarked, they immediately went just as they were to the temple of Artemis, offered many prayers, and made their sacrifice, and among their offerings they set up an inscription in honor of the goddess, commemorating all their sufferings and all their adventures. When they had done this, they went up into the city and built large tombs for their parents (for they had already died from old age and despair), and they themselves lived happily ever after; the rest of their life together was one long festival. Leucon and Rhode shared everything with their companions; and Hippothous too decided to spend the rest of his life in Ephesus. He now erected a great tomb for Hyperanthes in Lesbos, and adopting Cleisthenes as his son, he spent his life in Ephesus with Habrocomes and Anthia.

# ACHILLES TATIUS

# LEUCIPPE AND CLITOPHON

## TRANSLATED BY
## JOHN J. WINKLER

*Introduction*

> Nothing is as consubstantial with literature and its
> modest mystery as the questions raised by a translation.
> J. L. BORGES, "Las versiones homericas," DISCUSIÓN

It is fairly certain that his name was Achilles Tatius, rather than Achilles Statius (as the *Souda* and several manuscripts give it), and it is marginally more likely that Tatius should be regarded as an ordinary Latin name (like Longus) rather than a theophoric Egyptian name honoring the god Thoth (Greek, Tat). Evidence of papyri on the one side and of Hellenic hairstyles and Alexandrian topography on the other suggests that *The Adventures of Leukippe and Kleitophon* (*Leukippe,* for short) was written in the third quarter of the second century C.E. The *Souda* also relates that Achilles Tatius was an Alexandrian (which is possible), that he became a Christian bishop (wishful thinking), and that he wrote three other works—on the heavenly sphere (possible), on etymology, and a historical miscellany about famous people (no trace of the latter two survives).[1]

*Leukippe* seems to have been one of the most popular Greek novels, at least in Greco-Roman Egypt, the only land for which papyrus gives us evidence in such matters. Seven papyri are known, dating from the second to the fourth century;[2] no trace at all has been found of Xenophon or

---

1. More extensive discussion of the author and his work can be found in *Achilles Tatius: Leucippe and Clitophon,* ed. E. Vilborg, 2 vols. (Stockholm, 1955–62); and particularly K. Plepelits, *Achilleus Tatios: Leukippe und Kleitophon* (Stuttgart, 1980).

2. See Vilborg, *Leucippe and Clitophon,* 1:xv–xvii; and J. N. O'Sullivan, *A Lexicon to Achilles Tatius* (London and New York, 1980), xv–xvi. Further fragments from one of the papyri have been identified subsequently.

Longus, and there is only one papyrus of Heliodorus. My starting point as a translator has been the assumption that though other ancient novels are superb in their own various ways, *Leukippe* at least was fun to read and had enough appeal to win for itself what we would nowadays call a mass market.

In one sense the translator of an ancient novel is forced to read it rather as the ancient critics did than as modern ones do. That is to say, modern critics and readers wonder, What is it? and give answers such as comedy, parody, an antiplatonic essay on *eros,* and so on.[3] The ancient reader, to judge by the extant remarks of Photios and Psellos[4] and by analogous second-century literary discussions, placed the accomplishments of style and the excellence of individual, excerptible sentiments first in their program of reading. To us this is part of a larger problem, that ancient literary criticism seems to be, with few exceptions, a territory dominated by scholars interested primarily in formal classification rather than by analysts of culture such as now control the field. But the translator is occupationally bound to approach the text asking not the modern question What does this *mean* (in a large sense)? but the ancient litterateur's question How does this *read?*

There is, of course, another activity, prior to translation proper, in which the question What does this mean? is taken narrowly and seriously: its product is the crib and its point is to construe the Greek for a watchful schoolmaster. The reader who wants such a thing can find it in the Loeb version.[5] The work before you, however, is a different thing—not a crib but a translation. It aims to give the late twentieth-century English-speaking reader direct and immediate pleasures analogous to those experienced by Achilles Tatius's second-century readers. A crib is properly printed on pages facing the original, which stands as an exacting tribunal ready to condemn each single word. A translation, by contrast, is meant to be read, not used as an answer book, and read with a continuity and pleasure comparable to the original. A translation carries a broader kind of responsibility—to the style and esthetic of the *whole* rather than to individual words in isolation. The limit of this responsibility is that a translation should not be misleading: it should be a reliable and informative guide for people who want to know what Achilles Tatius was like. I emphasize "was *like.*" "If we grant that in their nature all translations of any kind are basically absurd, we can then be stimulated by the myriad possibilities of simulacra, by the tension of challenge, by the act of re-

3. The views respectively of Arthur Heiserman, *The Novel Before the Novel* (Chicago, 1977); D. B. Durham, "Parody in Achilles Tatius," *Classical Philology* 33(1938): 1–19; and G. Anderson, *Eros Sophistes: Ancient Novelists at Play* (Chico, Calif., 1982).

4. Cited in Vilborg, *Leucippe and Clitophon,* 1:163–68.

5. *Achilles Tatius,* ed. S. Gaselee (London, 1917; rev. ed., 1969).

creation itself and its occasional accomplishments."[6] What then was *Leukippe* like? How does Achilles Tatius read?

His style displays a curious variety. It includes both the boldly poetic and the baldly prosaic (and not a little alliteration—it has about the same degree of mild euphuism as *The Unfortunate Traveller*). *Leukippe* is by turns terse, exotic, punning, limpid, and baroque; usually interesting, sometimes grotesque, often challenging. An English translation which is not these is not good. Greek, with a verb system so highly inflected and word order so free, can manage effects of devastating elegance with a minimal vocabulary: μεστὸς γὰρ ἥλιος ἡδονῆς, 5.8.2; οὐκ ἀκίνδυνον δὲ ἐπιφαρμάσσειν τὰ σπλάγχνα ἤδη πεφαρμαγμένα, 4.16.2. English, to have a similar charm, to be readable as the Greek is readable, must often substitute an interesting range of words, achieving by variation of vocabulary what Greek conveys by the flexible complexity of its syntax. I have exercised the responsibility of my freedom as a translator with far less liberty than the great Elizabethans; within a single sentence I have sometimes rearranged the parts, doubled one conceptual element or reduced another, but the elements are substantially the same. The untranslatable effects of Achilles' Greek must be imitated, but I could not always imitate them in the same place as in the Greek. I take it that Achilles *redivivus,* if he were producing this version himself, would (like Nabokov) employ the resources of English wordplay in about the same proportion as he did for his original. In the nature of things he would have to sacrifice some of his best effects, but he would be able to invent similar ones which in Greek were not yet possible. For example, I could not reproduce the sound of *paidōn de philēmata men apaideuta* (2.37), and I did not like the dull clunk of "that they may turn aside the voluntary aspect of shame by the appearance of compulsion" for *hina tēi doxēi tēs anankēs apotrepōntai tēs aischunēs to hekousion* (2.10); so I used the lost alliteration of the one passage in rendering the nonalliterative neatness of the other: "that they may avert the shame of consent by the sham of constraint." Swings and roundabouts. At 5.5 Achilles employs an etymologizing echo that escapes our ears: *Tēreus/tērousin.* The sentence could be cribbed as "Tereus goes up with them and becomes a bird; they still preserve a likeness of their suffering." My English for this loses the two *tēreus/ tērous-,* but adds sounds and concepts which occur elsewhere in the novel and whose introduction here is not misleading: "And Tereus ascends with them, a bird. Even now they enact a shadowy dream of that shameful drama." This is a rather florid example of a kind of verbal pleasure which is *like* that often found in *Leukippe.* My general rule was: if my "likeness" did not directly and immediately give the reader an Achillean

6. K. Friar, *Modern Greek Poetry* (New York, 1973), 651.

pleasure or wince, it would not do. (Clearly, then, the reader should not draw any conclusions from single words, such as *drama* in the last-cited example. My English is not Greek, my translation is not a crib, though it never knowingly misrepresents what Achilles Tatius says.) A similar problem is that of familiar tags from classical literature. A footnote does not give the same *frisson* as direct recognition. My solution has been to allow about the same number of half-echoes of Shakespeare, Keats, Conan Doyle, and others to hover in the background, where Fortune made that possible.

The insouciance of mentioning Keats and Conan Doyle in the same category raises another matter. The translator's attention to the question How does this read? includes at many points decisions about the larger meaning, the seriousness, the important themes, and the organization of the whole. Certain awkwardnesses might have been smoothed out so as to downplay the startling differentiation of *Leukippe*'s parts, the odd amalgamation of incompatible elements. The novel seems to draw on many different generic resources: travel adventure, love story, psychological study, picaresque narrative, paradoxography, and description of paintings, any one of which could determine the dominant perspective and contents of an ancient composition. The translation can reflect, by its control of tone, whether this "miscellaneous" quality is to be read as studied or inept. The majority of modern critics have judged *Leukippe* incompetent, but I think rather that we need to reexamine our own reading habits, our conditioning to a certain type of fictional organization of the world.[7] I have in mind the studies of B. Uspensky and E. Ermarth, which broadly trace the correspondences between the Renaissance invention of rules for a single, fixed perspective in painting and the conventions of "realistic" narrative.[8] By standards of unifocal realism, which insist on plausibility of action, relevance of detail, consistency of character, and uniformity of perspective, Achilles Tatius's novel is a multifocused miscellany. As with medieval, Byzantine, and ancient painting, the framed field contains objects and scenes seen from a variety of perspectives, answering to different interests, and not necessarily coordinated to provide one "meaning" (the modern critic's question). At any moment the author may redirect our attention to something entirely different. The novel's fundamental rule of composition seems to be sophisticated eclecticism, of the sort known from Kallimachos's *Aitia* to Aulus Gellius's *Attic Nights* and Aelian's *Poikilē Historia* (*Miscellany*). Charm, el-

7. E. Vinaver has done this brilliantly for chivalric narrative of the twelfth and thirteenth centuries in *The Rise of Romance* (Oxford, 1971).

8. B. Uspensky, *A Poetics of Composition,* trans. A. Savarin and S. Wittig (Berkeley and London, 1973); E. Ermarth, *Realism and Consensus in the English Novel* (Princeton, 1983).

egance, and utter diversity are the goals: the story and characters, though consistently developed, are just an occasion. The recent discovery of Lollianos's *Phoinikika* made certain resemblances between *Leukippe* and Petronius's *Satyrika* fall into place as marks of what we might call sophisticated criminal fiction.[9] But even that cannot integrate the mélange of *Leukippe*'s materials into a single type of thing, for which there might be a generic name. At best we can perhaps locate a certain sensibility, not a genre or a "meaning," but an esthetic.

We may characterize it as an esthetic of unresolved stresses. Achilles Tatius specializes in the creation of exquisite tensions, like the pleasure of pressing on a tooth that hurts. He is quite unmatched for sheer staginess (using not only the conventions but the apparatus of melodrama: the Homerist's sword, 3.20); for killing the action by analytic asides that dissect the physiology of emotions; and for something like sadism, in the slow-motion examination of beautiful pain (tears, 6.7; terror, 1.1; dying flesh, 3.7; a forced embrace, 6.18). *Leukippe* pushes its readers into marginal areas of experience, cultivating the hypocritical, the mimetic, the incredible, and the inauthentic. From this we could extrapolate certain theories of life, love, desire, and art—whose being is mimetic, self-divided, and unreal—but *Leukippe* should not be made a vehicle for something else. The unanswerable enigma of its contradictory styles should be enjoyed directly as a lascivious surface and nothing more, making us conscious that the quest for depth, for meaning, and for unity is a fraud of the ages. That cannot quite be the author's intention, since he could not have foreseen the time when tentative endeavors for unity of meaning, perspective, and point of view would one day have succeeded in creating a system of seeing and reading that knew no other possibility, but as children of that system it must be part of the author's meaning for us. Otherwise we will misread his stressful irresolutions as bad rather than purposely ineffable. *Leukippe* should astonish, beguile, repel, and linger with a peculiar aftertaste. If my English does that to you, I will have served "these lusty saints"[10] well.

9. See J. J. Winkler, "Lollianos and the Desperadoes," *Journal of Hellenic Studies* 100(1980): 155–81, esp. 166–75; for another treatment of this material see C. P. Jones, "Apuleius' *Metamorphoses* and Lollianus' *Phoinikika*," *Phoenix* 34(1980): 243–54.
10. The acid taste of love combined with chastity
    is pictured in the tale of Kleitophon.
    Chaster still the all-astounding heroine:
    Leukippe beaten, shaved, and much abused.
    But, most astounding!—she endured three executions.
    And if you too, my friend, are so inclined to chastity,
    Ignore the incidental glitter of his style
    And fix your mind upon the termination of the tale
    which joins these lusty saints in holy wedlock.
*Anthologia Palatina* 9.203, sometimes attributed to the patriarch Photius (see Vilborg 1, *Testimonia* I, p.163).

The Greek text used for this translation is Vilborg's, with only slight modifications. Like a sailor shipwrecked and saved, I owe deep thanks to the three readers who rescued me from howling errors: Stanley Lombardo, the masterful translator of Parmenides, Empedokles, Aratos, Kallimachos, and Hesiod; James N. O'Sullivan, a sharp-eyed lexicographer and expert on this text;[11] and the editor. Where I stubbornly balked, I take the blame.

## Bibliography

### TEXT

*Achilles Tatius.* Edited by S. Gaselee. London, 1917. Rev. ed., 1969 (Loeb Classical Library).

Achilles Tatius. *Leucippe and Clitophon.* Edited by E. Vilborg. 2 vols. Stockholm, 1955–62. Text and commentary.

### GENERAL

Hägg, Tomas. *Narrative Technique in Ancient Greek Romances: Studies of Chariton, Xenophon Ephesius and Achilles Tatius.* Stockholm, 1971.

Plepelits, K. *Achilleus Tatios: Leukippe und Kleitophon.* Stuttgart, 1980. Translation with extensive introduction and commentary.

Sedelmeier, D. "Studien zu Achilleus Tatios." *Wiener Studien* 72 (1959): 113–43 (reprinted in H. Gärtner, ed., *Beiträge zum griechischen Liebesroman* [Hildesheim, 1984]). Literary study.

# LEUKIPPE AND KLEITOPHON

## Book One

SIDON IS A CITY beside the sea. The sea is the Assyrian;[1] the city is the metropolis of Phoenicia; its people are the forefathers of Thebes.[2] Nestled in its bosom, discreetly refusing the ocean's advances, is a broad double harbor: where the bay curves round on the right, a second entrance has been channeled, a further inlet for the tidewater, a harbor within the harbor. There the great freighters calmly wait out the storms of winter and in the summer ply the harbor's forebay.

11. O'Sullivan's lexicon to Achilles Tatius embodies discussion of the text and on pages xvi–xix includes a bibliography of contributions to the text.

1. It was a mark of archaizing elegance to use "Assyria" for Syria: Lucian *Syrian Goddess* 1, Philostratos *Life of Apollonios of Tyana* 1.16; so also "satrap" for Roman rulers (see note 58).

2. Kadmos of Tyre, searching for his daughter Europa, founded Thebes.

Arriving at this port after a violent storm, in thanks for my safe arrival I offered a sacrifice to the Phoenicians' great goddess, who in Sidon is known as Astarte.[3] Then touring the rest of the city to see its memorial offerings, I saw a votive painting whose scene was set on land and sea alike: the picture was of Europa; the sea was Phoenicia's; the land was Sidon. On the land were represented a meadow and a chorus of maidens, on the sea swam a bull, and on his back was seated a beautiful maiden, sailing on the bull towards Crete.

The meadow was in full flower, with trees and shrubs standing guard: adjacent trees wove a lattice roof of leaves, an intertessellation of green branches, a shaded vault for the flowers. The artist had sketched the shadows cast below the leaves, and sunshine filtered in soft splashes onto the meadow through fissures left by the artificer in the leaves above. A colonnade enclosed the meadow on every side: within its cloistered covering the meadow rested secure. At the foot of luxuriant bushes grew beds of flowers in neat rows—narcissus, roses, myrtle. And in the very middle of this picture garden was a flow of water, first bubbling up from deep in the earth and then spreading out over the surface for the flowers and plants. An irrigator bent down over one rivulet with hoe in hand, depicted in the very act of making a channel for the stream.[4]

At the far end of the meadow, where the land jutted out into the sea, the artist had placed the maidens. Their pose expressed both joy and fear. Their heads were bound with garlands; their hair flowed freely down over their shoulders; their legs were quite bare—no skirt hampered their calves, no sandal their feet, for their cinctures drew the skirts up to the knee. Their faces were blanched, a wry twist at the corners of their mouths, eyes wide and staring out to sea. Their mouths were slightly open, as if a moment later they would actually scream in fear; they reached out their arms towards the bull. They stood on the margin of the sea where the line of the waves rose just ever so slightly above the line of their soles: one could almost see they wanted to run after the bull but were afraid of entering the water.

The sea itself was dichromatic—it had a red tinge near land, but it was dark blue towards the deep. Then a composition of foam and rocks and waves: rocks rising above the land, foam splashing the rocks white, waves swelling to peaks that shattered into foam around the rocks.

A bull was painted in midsea, riding on the waves, which ascended like a steep hill under the bent curve of the bull's foreleg. The maiden sat on his back, not astride but sidesaddle, with her feet together towards the right, and on the left her hand holding the horn as a charioteer would

3. The content of the sentence, as often in the novel, shows that its audience is assumed to be Greek and strangers to Phoenicia.
4. This detail recalls *Iliad* 21.257–59.

hold the reins. And the bull in fact had turned his head somewhat in the direction of the pressure of her guiding hand. There was a chiton over the maiden's chest down to her modesty; from there on a robe covered the lower part of her body: the chiton was white, the robe red, and the body showed subtly through the clothing—navel well recessed, stomach flat, waist narrow, but with a narrowness that widened downward towards the hips. Breasts gently nudging forward: a circumambient sash pressed chiton to breasts, so that it took on the body's form like a mirror.

Both her arms were outstretched, one to the horn and one towards the tail; connecting them from either side was her veil, which fluttered behind her in a long arc above her head. The bosomy folds of this garment billowed out in all directions, puffed full by a wind of the artist's own making. She rode on the bull as if on board a cruising ship, using her veil as a sail. Around the bull dolphins danced and Loves cavorted: you would have said their very movements were visibly drawn.

And Eros was leading the bull: Eros, a tiny child, with wings spread, quiver dangling, torch in hand. He had turned to look at Zeus with a sly smile, as if in mockery that he had, for Love's sake, become a bull.

Though the entire painting was worthy of admiration, I devoted my 2 special attention to this figure of Eros leading the bull, for I have long been fascinated by passion, and I exclaimed, "To think that a child can have such power over heaven and earth and sea."[5]

At this point a young man standing nearby said, "How well I know it—for all the indignities Love has made *me* suffer."

"And what have you suffered, my friend? You have the look, I know it well, of one who has progressed far in his initiation into Love's mysteries."

"You are poking up a wasps' nest of narrative. My life has been very storied."

"Well sir, by Zeus and by Eros himself, please don't hesitate. The more storied the better." I clasped his right hand and we walked to a grove nearby where many plane trees grew in dense array and a stream meandered, cold and clear as if from fresh-melted snow. When we had found a low bench to sit on, I said, "See, here we have the perfect spot for your story—as delightful place and a setting most appropriate for tales of love."[6]

5. For Love's power viewed in paintings, see Petronius *Satyrika* 83. The votive painting of Europa's rape seems to be in a temple; for similar discussions beginning in public temples, see Varro *On Agriculture* 1.2 (prompted by a painting) and Pausanias 7.23.6 (meeting with a Phoenician from Sidon).

6. A clear reminiscence of the setting of Plato's *Phaidros* (229–30); the text abounds in such covert references.

3 And he began to speak as follows.[7]

*the start of*
*a stranger's story*

I was born at Tyre in Phoenicia. My name is Kleitophon. My father
and his brother are named Hippias and Sostratos—they are not full
brothers; they had the same father, but my uncle's mother was a lady of
Byzantium, and my father's mother was from Tyre. My uncle Sostratos
indeed spent all his time in Byzantium, where his mother had left him a
considerable estate. My father dwelt in Tyre. I never knew my mother;
she died when I was a baby. My father then remarried, and his second
wife bore him a daughter, my sister, Kalligone. My father decided that
Kalligone and I should marry,[8] but the powers above were reserving
someone else to be my wife.

Often the celestial powers delight to whisper to us at night about what
the future holds—not that we may contrive a defense to forestall it (for
no one can rise above fate) but that we may bear it more lightly when it
comes.[9] The swift descent of unforeseen events, coming on us all at once
and suddenly, startles the soul and overwhelms it; but when the disaster
is expected, that very anticipation, by small increments of concern, dulls
the sharp edge of suffering. I was in the ninth year of my teens, and my
father was making plans for my marriage in the coming year, when Fortune began her drama.

*bad dream*

In a dream I saw my sister's body and mine grown together into a single body from the navel down and separating into two above. Over me
there hovered a huge, fearsome woman who glowered at me savagely:
eyes shot with blood, rough cheeks, snakes for hair, a sickle in her right
hand, a torch in her left. In a wild attack she aimed her sickle at our groin
where the two bodies joined, and severed the girl from me.

Waking up from sheer fright, I decided to tell no one but brooded
over my troubles privately.

It was at this time that the following event took place: my father's
brother, as I mentioned, was Sostratos. A messenger arrived on the boat
from Byzantium with a letter that read as follows.

Sostratos to his brother Hippias:
Greetings! This is to announce the arrival of my daughter Leukippe
and Pantheia, my wife. War with Thrace has put Byzantium in
severe straits. Protect my dear family until the fortunes of war are
decided.

---

7. The story here entered on by the young man constitutes the remainder of the novel.
8. In Greek cities the laws on consanguinity often allowed marriage between half
brother and half sister.
9. Dreams and their interpretation were of much interest to contemporary readers, and
there are many examples in the novels. For the view that dreams allow us time to adjust
ourselves to imminent disasters, see Artemidoros *Oneirokritika* 1.2.

When my father had read this letter, he got up at once and hurried 4 down towards the shore. He returned shortly, and behind him there came a great crowd of attendants and maidservants whom Sostratos had sent with his wife and daughter. In the center of the crowd stood an imposing woman, richly dressed. While I was directing my attention to her, there appeared on her left a young maiden. Her face flashed on my eyes like lightning. Such beauty I had seen once before, and that was in a painting of Selene on a bull: delightfully animated eyes; light blond hair—blond and curly; black eyebrows—jet black; white cheeks—a white that glowed to red in the center like the crimson laid on ivory by Lydian craftswomen.[10] Her mouth was a rose caught at the moment when it begins to part its petal lips. As soon as I had seen her, I was lost. For Beauty's wound is sharper than any weapon's, and it runs through the eyes down to the soul. It is through the eye that love's wound passes, and I now became a prey to a host of emotions: admiration, amazement, trembling, shame, shamelessness. I admired her generous stature, marveled at her beauty, trembled in my heart, stared shamelessly, ashamed I might be caught. My eyes defied me. I tried to force them away from the girl, but they swung back to her, drawn by allure of her beauty, and finally they were victorious.

The women were conducted to our house, where my father designated 5 a suite of rooms for their use and then oversaw preparations for dinner. When the dinner hour came, we took our places at table as my father arranged us, two on a couch—he and I on the middle couch, the two mothers on the left, the two maidens on the right.[11] When I heard him announce this arrangement, I almost went over and kissed him for displaying her thus before my eyes. As to what we had for dinner, by all that's holy, I really didn't know: I ate like a man in a dream. With one elbow resting on the pillow and putting myself at an angle for a better view, I watched her directly, though without ever seeming to stare. She was my entire meal.

When we had finished with dinner, one of my father's household servants entered and tuned a lyre. For a while he simply strummed chords, his bare hands playing idly over the strings. Then, as his fingers caressed the instrument, a melody gradually emerged. He began to use a pick on the strings and after playing a while he added lyrics to the melody. The song was Apollo's complaint at Daphne's running away from him, his pursuing and almost capturing, how she was transformed to a tree and he wove her leaves into a wreath for himself.

10. The phrase is reminiscent of *Iliad* 4.141–42.

11. The diners occupy couches in front of three tables placed at right angles, with the fourth side left open for servants. They recline on their left side, leaving the right hand free to eat with.

This lyrical interlude fanned higher the fire in my soul, for stories of love stir feelings of lust. In spite of all our admonitions to moderation, models excite us to imitation, particularly a pattern set by our betters. And more, the shame we feel at wrongful deeds is changed by the good repute of superior people to saucy freedom of speech. So I said to myself: "Look here, Apollo himself loves a maiden; unashamed of his love, he pursues her—while you hesitate and blush: untimely self-control! Are you better than a god?"

6    When evening came the women retired to sleep, and slightly later we did, too. The others gauged their pleasure's fullness by their stomachs,[12] but my banquet had been in my eyes: a surfeit of her face, a champagne vision drunk down till I could drink no more. I went away tipsy with love.

When I reached my bedroom, I was unable to fall asleep. For all diseases and wounds are usually more severe at night; they attack us more at our rest and increase our pain. When the body is relaxed, then a wound is free to fester. And when the body is inactive, wounds of the soul are all the more painful. During the day the eyes and ears are absorbed in many activities and help take the edge off illness by giving the soul no leisure in which to suffer. But once the body is constrained in quietude, the soul is set adrift in a sea of troubles. For then begins to stir all that till then slept: woes of the sorrowing, worries of the careworn, imperiled men's fears, the fires of men in love.

About dawn, a sleep of sorts took pity on me at last and gave me a brief rest. But even then the girl would not leave my soul. All my dreams were of Leukippe. I spoke with her, played with her, ate with her, touched her—I had more good sensations than during the day. Yes, I even kissed her, and truly it was a kiss—so that when the servant roused me, I snapped at him for his untimely interruption that lost me so sweet a dream.

So I got up and purposefully strolled about within the house where I could see her, holding a book and lowering my head to read. Whenever I passed the doorway, my eyes rolled up to watch her, and after a few such circuits I felt so drenched in love from my seeing her directly that I departed sick at heart. These fires continued to smolder for three days.

7    I had a cousin named Kleinias, whose parents both were dead; he was two years older than myself and already an initiate in the rites of love. His boyfriend was a lad whom he loved to distraction. Recently, when the boyfriend admired a horse he had just bought, Kleinias said, "It's yours," and gave it to him outright. I used to joke with him about his carefree attitude, that he devoted all his time to friendship and was a

12. The phrase is borrowed from Demosthenes *On the Crown* 296.

slave to the pleasures of Eros, and he would smile, shaking his head, and say, "Some day, believe me, you will be such a slave, too."

I went to him now and with a greeting sat down beside him and said: "I am paying the penalty for my jokes: I, too, am Love's slave." With a clap of his hands and a laugh he stood up and kissed me right on the face, where the signs of love's insomnia were all too clear. "You're in love. You're really in love. Your eyes tell the tale."

At that moment Charikles (this was the name of his boyfriend) came running up in great agitation and cried, "O Kleinias, I'm done for!" Kleinias groaned too, and now wholly rapt in Charikles' soul, with a trembling voice said: "You will kill me with silence. Tell me what is hurting you. Who is your enemy?"

And Charikles replied: "My father has arranged a marriage for me, and a marriage with an ugly maiden, so that I have two evils to live with. A wife is a troublesome thing, even a pretty one; but if she also has the bad luck to be ugly, the disaster is doubled. But Father is eager for the match because she is wealthy. I'm being sold for her money. O awful fate—to be a bought husband, married for money!"

At these words Kleinias went pale. Then he sharpened Charikles' will to refuse the marriage with a diatribe against the female sex.[13]

"So your father has arranged a marriage, eh! What crime have you committed to deserve these chains and fetters? Remember the words of Zeus.

> In lieu of flame I have a gift for men:
> an evil thing and still their heart's delight,
> so all men will embrace their own destruction.[14]

Such is the pleasure of women, like that of the Sirens, who lead men to destruction by the pleasure of their song.

"The extent of the disaster you can understand from the wedding ceremony itself—flutes whining, doors banging, torches waving: noticing such an uproar, someone will say, 'Pity the prospective groom, it looks as if they're sending him off to war.'

"If you were a stranger to culture, you would not know about the dramas involving women, but as it is you could tell others how many plots women have contributed to the stage: Eriphyle's necklace, Philomela's banquet, Stheneboia's accusation, Aerope's theft, Prokne's slaughter. Agamemnon desires the beautiful Chryseis, and it brings a

13. Misogyny and debates on marriage among Greek males have a long history; the classic example is Semonides 7 (on the types of woman). A different but related topos is the male debate on whether young men or women are better sex partners (see below, 2.35–38, and Pseudo-Lucian Amores).

14. Hesiod Works and Days 57–58.

*speech against women*

plague on the Greeks. Achilles desires the beautiful Briseis and introduces himself to sorrow. Grant that Kandaules' wife be fair, yet this same wife killed Kandaules.[15] The fiery torch, lit for Helen's marriage, lit another fire hurled against Troy. The wedding of Penelope, chaste creature, was the death of how many suitors? Phaidra loved Hippolytos and killed him; Klytemestra hated Agamemnon and killed him. Oh, women, women, they stop at nothing! They kill the men they love; they kill the men they hate. Was it right that handsome Agamemnon be slain, whose beauty was celestial, 'eyes and head like to thundering Zeus'[16]—and a woman, O Zeus, lopped off this fair head.

"All this can be said against beautiful women. They are a sort of mitigated disaster, for beauty does offer some consolation in the midst of calamity, a stroke of luck in a losing streak. But if, as you say, she is not even pretty, it is a catastrophe redoubled. Could any man at all endure this, much less a young man of your beauty? No, Charikles, by all the gods, not you—you'll be a slave and prematurely old, the bloom of your beauty crushed before its time. For marriage has this afterclap as well: the prime of your youth will wither. Please, Charikles, do not wither on the vine; don't let an ugly gardener pluck your lovely rose."

And Charikles replied: "The gods and I will look after this. The wedding is still some days off, and much can happen in a single night. We will discuss it thoroughly at our leisure. But now, I'm off to ride, to enjoy for the first time the wonderful horse you gave me. The exercise will lighten my sorrow." So it was that Charikles departed for his last ride, his first and final feat of horsemanship.

9    I then told Kleinias about the drama that was in progress in my heart: the events, my sentiments, what I had witnessed, my aunt's arrival, the dinner party, the beauty of Leukippe. Finally, I felt myself losing all control in what I said. "Kleinias, I can't continue in such pain. Eros has attacked me with all his forces and drives the very sleep from my eyes. Fantasies of Leukippe face me everywhere. No man on earth has ever experienced such cruel misfortune: my torment is living with me in the same house."

"Nonsense!" said Kleinias. "You're lucky in love. Why, you don't

15. This passage refers to the following stories: Eriphyle—bribed by Polyneikes with a golden necklace to persuade her husband to join the expedition of the Seven against Thebes; Philomela and Prokne—see below, 5.5; Stheneboia—her advances rejected by Bellerophon, she slandered him to her husband (*Iliad* 6.155–70, where she is called Anteia); Aerope—wife of Atreus, she stole his golden fleece for her lover, Thyestes; Chryseis and Briseis—*Iliad* 1; Kandaules' wife—King Kandaules of Lydia forced his bodyguard Gyges to hide behind the bedroom door and witness his wife's naked beauty, but she noticed that he was there and later forced him to choose between dying on the spot or killing Kandaules to avenge her honor (Herodotos 1.7–12). The stories of Helen, Penelope, Phaidra, and Klytemestra are familiar.

16. *Iliad* 2.478.

even have to walk to another house or hire a go-between. Fortune has not only delivered you a mistress but carried her right inside and installed her. Other lovers must be content with occasional glimpses of some well-guarded virgin, and they consider just catching sight of her a great blessing. A happier class of lovers may hear a word from her lips. But you are at liberty continuously to look and to listen; you share food and drink with her. You must not rail against felicity nor despise these favors of Eros.

"You have no idea how marvelous a thing it is to look on one's beloved. This pleasure is greater than that of consummation, for the eyes receive each others' reflections, and they form therefrom small images as in mirrors. Such outpouring of beauty flowing down through them into the soul is a kind of copulation at a distance. This is not far removed from the intercourse of bodies—it is in fact a novel form of intimate embrace, and soon (I predict) you will experience the act itself.

"The quickest way to win a girl's heart is persistent exposure: eyes are the ambassadors of love, and the habit of daily sharing encourages reciprocity. Habit reduces wild beasts to domesticity: the same method works even better on women.

"The fact that you are both young gives you a certain advantage with a maiden. The instinctive urgings of youth and a consciousness that she is loved often beget in a young girl's heart a corresponding love. Every maiden wants to be beautiful, and she is glad of a lover's love as a testimony to her own charm. Until some man declares his love for her, she has no confidence that she is truly lovely. So my one piece of advice is this: let her feel sure that she is loved, and soon enough she will imitate your love with her own."

"But just how is this prophecy to be fulfilled?" I asked. "Show me where to begin. You, remember, were initiated into these mysteries long before me and speak now as an adept in the divine service. But what do I say? What do I do? How can I reach my beloved? I flounder in ignorance of method."

"Don't look to learn this from anyone else," said Kleinias. "This god is a self-taught scholar. Who teaches newborn babies where to look for food? No one; but they spontaneously discover a banquet ready in the breasts. So too when a young man feels the first stirrings of love within him, he needs no instruction in how to bring it to birth. When you feel the pangs of labor and your day of delivery is at hand, even if it's your first time, you will follow the right path and discover how to deliver, with Cupid himself as your midwife.

"Now, as far as general principles are concerned and without requiring favorable circumstances, listen to this: never mention anything Aphrodisiac in her presence, but try to reach the real thing without mentioning it. Boys and girls have the same sense of modesty: when it comes to gratifying their Aphrodisiac instincts, even those who feel ready would rather not have their feelings named aloud. The shame of it, they think, consists in mentioning the words. Now experienced women like the words as well as the deeds; a maiden, on the other hand, will submit the distant volleys of lovers to examination and then suddenly gives her assent. But if you approach her with a direct request for the physical act, the words fall on her ears like shock waves, she blushes, is appalled by the suggestion, thinks herself insulted. Even if she wants to say yes, she is too embarrassed by the words, for she takes the moderate tingle of pleasure that accompanies the suggestion of sex to be equivalent to the act itself.

"If your application of seductive effort is rewarded with a sweet advance on your part and a more compliant attitude on hers, then you must—as in the mysteries—stay almost wholly silent. Just approach her and kiss her gently. A lover's kiss is an unspoken message: if she is willing to accommodate him, she understands it as a tacit request; if she is unwilling, as his entreaty.

"Now, when there is some sort of agreement to go all the way, even then women complaisant to the deed prefer to appear compelled, that they may avert the shame of consent by the sham of constraint. Therefore, do not give up when you see her resist somewhat, but carefully note the tenor of her resistance. This is a moment that calls for fine discrimination: if her refusal has an edge of insistence, do not use force, for she is not yet fully persuaded; but if you sense a mounting softness in her will, spare nothing in staging whatever elaborate production will bring your drama to its intended climax."

11   "Kleinias," I said, "these are helpful directions for my project, and I hope it will be successful. Yet I'm apprehensive that good luck now will only be the beginning of greater trouble, an inflammation leading to greater passion. For suppose this strange power surges ever higher, what will I do? I couldn't marry her: I'm already promised to another—a marriage my father insists on, and not unreasonably, for he is not bartering me to increase his fortune (as is the case with Charikles) nor giving me to a woman either remote or repugnant, but to his own daughter, a beautiful girl, or so (good God!) I thought before I met Leukippe. Now I am blind to her beauty, and I have eyes for the loveliness of Leukippe alone.

"I am in a combat zone between two opponents: Eros and my father are at war. My father is armed with the respect I owe him; Eros attacks with his fire. How can I fairly decide between them? It is a court battle between Duty and Nature. I would take your side in the suit, Father, but the opposition's case is stronger. The judge is being tried by torture, pelted with weapons, braised by his own torch. If I don't give a verdict in favor of Eros, I'll burn at the stake."

While we were thus rapt in deep philosophy concerning the god, one   12
of Charikles' slaves suddenly ran toward us. The expression on his face
gave advance warning of bad news. When Kleinias saw him, he exclaimed, "Something has happened to Charikles." Simultaneously the
slave exclaimed, "Charikles is dead."

Kleinias froze, stunned and speechless at the news, like a man caught
in the eye of a tornado. The slave told the story.[17]

"He mounted on your horse, Kleinias, and rode for a while at a gentle
pace. After two or three laps he reined to a halt and began wiping the
sweat off the horse, still seated on it and dropping his hold on the reins
without a thought. While he was wiping its back, there was a noise from
behind, and the horse gave a startled leap straight up into the air and then
began to run crazily. Stung to terror, he tossed his head upwards, with
the bit still between his teeth, and he performed aerobatic maneuvers,
mane flying in the wind. As he ran, it seemed as if his back legs were trying to outrace the front legs, so closely did they follow in pursuit, leap
for leap. This persistent bucking up and down of his legs, vying most
energetically to outjump each other, made his back arch in rising and
falling curves like stormy waves tossing a ship. Poor Charikles bounced
to and fro on the alternate surges of this bronco-billow, sliding towards
the tail or flung headfirst towards the neck. While trying to ride out the
squall, he lost control of the rein straps and surrendered himself to the
hurricane of his mad career, a plaything of Chance. The horse in headlong flight galloped away from the road towards the woods and suddenly knocked poor Charikles against a tree. He was hurled from his seat
as from a catapult, and his face was pelted by the branches, gashed with
as many incisions as there were points on the broken wood. The rein
thongs were wrapped about his waist and did not pull free but dragged
him along, leaving a trail of death. The horse was frightened still further
by the falling body, and when it got in the way of his legs, he kicked at
the poor corpse, trampling it as an impediment to his progress. He is no
longer recognizable as Charikles."

Kleinias was stunned silent for a time. Recovering his senses, he gave   13
a loud moan and started off running towards the body. I followed along,
offering such consolation as I could. Charikles was being carried home, a
pitiful and grievous spectacle. He was one continuous wound, at the
sight of which no bystander could hold back his tears. His father began
the mourning with the following distracted outcry.

"O my son, the difference of state between your departure and return!
Curses on such riding! Alas for this uncommon death! Alas for your un-

17. For other tragic gay subplots, see 2.34, Xenophon of Ephesos 3.2, Iamblichos *Baby-
loniaka* 17.

comely corpse! Other cadavers preserve at least the trace of their familiar features; they lose the bloom of freshness but retain a recognizable resemblance, consoling our grief by the semblance of sleep. Death takes away the inner life but not its human encasement. Yet Fortune has robbed you of this too, decreeing death (alas!) for body as well as for soul. Even your profile and outline have disappeared. Your soul has fled and I can find no trace of you in these—oh—too mortal remains.

"And when will you marry, my son; when will I make the offerings to sanctify your wedding, O groom and bridegroom—unconsummated bridegroom, unlucky chevalier. Your bridal chamber is the grave, your wedlock is with death, your wedding march a funeral hymn, your marriage song this dirge. I looked to light a different torch for you my son, but envious Fortune extinguished my hope along with your life. Instead she lights these firebrands of disaster. Oh, how these torches keep wickedly burning—to light the consummation not of your love, but of your life."

14    So the father spoke his sorrow, while not far off Kleinias uttered his grief privately—lover and father in mournful competition.

"I have lost my master. Why did I give him such a gift? It should have been a golden bowl that he might drink from it and pour libations and use my gift for his revels. Instead—O twisted fate—I gave the lovely boy a wild animal and even decorated the sinful beast with breastplate and frontlet, with silver cheekplates and golden bridle. O Charikles, I put golden trinkets on your murderer. O monstrous horse, you brute insensitive to beauty! He wiped your sweaty withers, promised extra fodder, praised your gait—and you killed him while he flattered you. Did you not love the touch of such a body; weren't you proud to be ridden by such a rider? No, you heartless beast, you trampled his beauty in the dust. O, cruel fate! I bought you your murderer and gave him to you as a gift!"

15    As soon as the funeral was over, I hurried back to the girl. She was in a formal garden adjoining the house. It was in fact a grove of very pleasant aspect, encloistered by a sufficiently high wall and a chorus line of columns that together formed a covered portico on all four sides of the garden. Protected within the columns stood a populous assembly of trees. A network of sturdy branches interlaced to form an intricate pattern wherein petals gently embraced their neighbors, leaves wound round other leaves, and fruits rubbed softly on other fruits. Thus far the world of plants knows intercourse.

Ivy and bindweed raveled their way around some of the massy trunks: the bindweed clung to the plane tree by a soft reticulation of tendrils, while the ivy spiraled intimately among the pine boughs. This symbiosis provided support for the ivy and ivy wreaths of honor for the tree.

Grapes grew on trellises on either side of the tree, thick-leaved, ripe with fruit whose clusters tumbled through the trelliswork like locks of curly hair. When the highest, sunlit leaves fluttered in the wind, the earth took on a dappled look, with yellow patches in the shade.

The flowers of various colors displayed their beauty in turn—violet, narcissus, rose—the earth's dyed stuffs. The calyx of the rose has the same contour as that of the narcissus—a natural drinking cup. The petals opening about the rose's calyx have two colors—of blood at the edge, of cream at the base—but the narcissus's calyx has throughout the same cream color as the heart of the rose. The violet's calyx is nowhere to be seen; its color is like that of sunlight flashing on a still sea.

Among the flowers, a spring bubbled up within a rectangular pool constructed to contain the flow. The flowers were reflected in the water as in a mirror, so that the entire grove was doubled—the realm of truth confronting its shadowy other.

Some birds, because they took their food from men and were amenable to human company, nested in the woods, and others that flew free played around the treetops. The songbirds were singing; the others silently displayed the splendor of their plumage. The singers were crickets and swallows: these sang of Dawn's divan; those of Tereus's table.[18]

The tame birds were peacocks, swans, and parrots: the swans were feeding around the springs of water; the parrots rested in their cages suspended in the trees; the peacocks trailed their plumes among the flowers. The splendor of the flowers competed in brilliance with the color of the birds, whose very wings seemed to flower before our eyes.

To lay the ground for Leukippe's more amorous inclination, I began   16
speaking to Satyros,[19] taking as my text the timely presence of the bird, for Leukippe in her walk with Kleio happened to be standing in sight of the peacock, who at that very moment (as luck would have it) spread his beautiful tail and showed the amphitheater of his feathers.

"He does this by design," I said, "for he is a lover. He uses his gorgeous resources thus when he wishes to arouse his mistress. Do you see her near that plane tree?" I said, pointing to the peahen. "For her benefit he shows off his beauty, a field of flowers in his feathers. The peacock's meadow by comparison blossoms more richly, for even gold grows nat-

18. Dawn (Aurora) loved many mortal men, among them Tithonos, for whom she asked the gift of immortality but forgot to ask for eternal youth as well: he dwindled away till the only strength left in him was his voice (*Homeric Hymn to Aphrodite* 218–38). Hellanikos (*FGrH* 140), perhaps thinking of the old men on Troy's walls with voices like crickets (*Iliad* 3.151), says Dawn finally changed Tithonos into a cricket. Tereus raped his wife's sister and was tricked into eating his own son at a banquet, after which all three (Tereus, Prokne, Philomela) were transformed into birds.

19. Satyros and Kleio, introduced here without explanation, are slaves of the household.

urally on his plumes, and a ring of sea blue surrounds the gold in the form of an eye."

17    And Satyros, understanding the reason for my speech, prompted me to continue by asking, "Is Eros so powerful that he makes his fire felt even by the birds?"

"You are wrong to say 'even by the birds.' Since he too has wings, his influence on them is no surprise—but say rather, 'even by reptiles and plants,' and if you ask my opinion, even by the stones.

"There is a stone of Magnetia that has a strong desire for iron. If she but sees and barely touches a piece of iron, she draws it to herself, as if by the power of an erotic fire within. This is a marvelous kiss between erotogenic stone and erotopathic iron.

"Wise men give an account of plants that I would call a myth if it weren't common knowledge among farmers, too. It goes as follows.

"There is such a thing as plant-life passion, and it is particularly pressing in the case of the palm, a species whose members (they say) are distinguished as male or female. The male desires the female: if the female is too far away in the plantation's arrangement, the male lover begins to droop. The farmer understands what the plant is suffering and climbs up to a vantage point to see in which direction the palm is nodding, for it declines in the direction of its desire. When this is discovered, he tends the tree in its sickness by grafting into its heart a shoot of the female palm. And the tree's life revives; its dying body is renewed and stands upright, joyful at the embrace of his beloved. And so may plants be wed.

18    "And then there is the transoceanic wedding of waters: the lover is a river from Elis, the mistress a spring in Sicily. This lover flows across the sea as he would across a plain, and the sea does not absorb the lover's sweet waters in her briny waves but parts herself for him to flow along her surface: this crack in the sea is the river's bed. And so she escorts Alpheios the bridegroom to Arethousa the bride. When the games at Olympia are celebrated, many toss gifts into the streams of this river, and he carries them to his mistress, love tokens from a suitor.

"There is among reptiles another sacred mystery of love, drawing not only members of the same but members of different species together. The viper, a land snake, lusts for the eel: the eel is a different kind of reptile altogether, living in the sea, a snake in form but a fish in function. When they wish to make love, he comes down to the beach and hisses a secret song for the eel; she recognizes the sound and rises from the waves. But she does not approach her bridegroom directly, for she knows that he carries death in his fangs. She slithers onto a rock and waits for her lover to detoxify his mouth. They stand there gazing at one another—a continental lover and his island sweetheart. When the viper has vomited the poison that frightens his bride, and she sees the deadly serum spilled onto the sand, she descends from the rock, swims to the mainland, and coils around her lover, no longer afraid of his kisses."

I was looking at the young lady to see how she reacted to my erotic lesson. She discreetly indicated that she had not been displeased by my discourse. The radiant beauty of the peacock struck me less forcefully than that glance from Leukippe. The beauty of her body challenged the flowers of the field: her face was the essence of pale jonquil; roses arose on her cheeks; her glance was a revelation of violet; her hair had more natural curls than spiral ivy. Such was the meadow of Leukippe's face.

Shortly thereafter she went away, summoned by the hour for her lesson on the lyre. Yet she seemed to stay with me, for as she left, she committed her features to my eyes. Satyros and I congratulated ourselves, me for my mythology, him for his timely prompting.[20]

## Book Two

We made our way to the girl's quarters, still full of self-congratulation, on the pretext of listening to her play. I was unable to control, even for the shortest time, my desire to see her. First she sang Homer's passage about the boar fighting a lion,[21] then a more lyrical song in praise of the rose. The gist of the song, in plain language, without the modulations of the music, would be as follows.

If Zeus had wanted to place one flower as king over all the rest, the rose would reign supreme: jewel of the earth, a prodigy among plants, most precious of all flowers, the meadow's blush, a stunning moment of beauty, the fragrance of Eros, invitation to Aphrodite; the rose luxuriates in fragrant petals, surrounded by the most delicate leaves, that ripple laughter as the West Wind strokes them.

While she sang, I indulged a fantasy of her lips as a rose whose cup was reshaped in the form of a mouth.

She finished her song just when it was time for dinner.[22] As the drinking progressed, I began staring at her without embarrassment. When Eros and Dionysos, both powerful gods, take hold of the soul, they drive it on to the wilder reaches of immodesty, for the gift of Dionysos

20. All manuscripts here add "And after a short while it was time for dinner, and again we drank together as before." This clearly interrupts the sequence from self-congratulation in the garden (1.19) to music lesson (2.1) and must be removed as a mistake. Its resemblance to the phrases introducing 2.2 and 2.9 might suggest that it is an accidental by-product of whatever editorial work altered the position of 2.2.

21. *Iliad* 16.823–26.

22. On the evidence of a fourth-century papyrus, the description of the origin of wine (2.2.1–2.3.2 in the manuscripts) has been placed between 2.8 and 2.9. See M. D. Reeve, "Hiatus in the Greek Novelists," *Classical Quarterly* 21(1971): 538–39; and M. Laplace, "Achilleus Tatios, Leucippé et Clitophon: P. Oxyrhynchos 1250," *Zeitschrift für Papyrologie und Epigraphik* 53(1983): 53–59

fuels the well-known fires of Eros. Wine is the aliment of love. Already
she too was daring to look at me with more than casual interest.

4 And so it went for ten more days: a circumscribed audacity, a limited
enjoyment—we dallied with our eyes and nothing more. I then confided
all my feelings to Satyros and asked that he be my accomplice. He admitted he had known about it long before I told him but had refrained from
prying into my affair as long as I wished to keep it quiet. For when a
lover is acting with any sense of stealth, he assumes that unsolicited inquiries are a form of criticism and resents being asked.

"Circumstance," he said, "has played things in our favor. Her trusted
chambermaid Kleio has paired up with me and regards me as her lover. I
will bring her round in stages to our point of view, to help us with our
task. And you must pursue your siege with more than eye contact. Speak
to her with a greater sense of urgency. Then come at her with a second
battery: touch her hand; squeeze her fingers; sigh deeply. If she submits
to this and allows you to continue, your next step is to call her your lady
and kiss her neck."

"By the goddess Athena," I said, "you are a persuasive coach. But I
still have lingering doubts that, as Love's athlete, my nerve may fail, and
I will falter in the contest."

"Look here, young master, Eros does not tolerate the fainthearted.
Any picture of him will show you he is geared for active war—bow and
quiver and arrows and fire—these are the weapons of manly courage,
bristling with audacity. With this god inside you how can you be cowardly or frightened? Don't make a liar of him. I'll arrange an opportunity
for you. I will divert Kleio from her post when I see a timely moment
for you to be left alone with the maiden."

5 Satyros went outside, and, left to myself, I took his advice to heart. I
tried to whip up my courage to face the maiden.

"How long will you keep silent, sissy boy? What use is a spineless soldier in the service of a virile god? Are you waiting for her to make the
first move?"

Then I answered myself: "Come to your senses, you fool. Aim your
love shafts at the proper target. You have another lovely maiden in your
own family: desire *her*, gaze at *her*; marriage with her is in your power."

I thought I had convinced myself, but the voice of Eros replied from
deep down in my heart: "Such insubordination! So, you would take up
position and fight against me? How can you escape when I attack from
the skies with arrows and fire? If you dodge my arrows, you won't
evade my fire. And even if you douse that with your high-minded self-
control, I will catch up with you on my wings."

6 At the end of this conversation, I realized to my surprise that
Leukippe was nearby; seeing her so suddenly I blanched and then
blushed. She was alone, not even Kleio was with her. Yet like one not

*a kiss*

knowing what to say in my confusion, I said, "Greetings, my lady." She smiled a winsome smile; though her amusement said clearly that she understood why I called her "my lady," she asked, "I? Your lady? Don't say that!" "Ah, but a certain god has sold me into your service as surely as Herakles was sold as slave to Queen Omphale."[23] "You mean Hermes? Whom Zeus ordered to sell Herakles?" And again she smiled. I replied, "Hermes? Nonsense! You know very well what I mean."

While the conversation was shuttling back and forth like this, circumstances came to my assistance. On the previous day, around noon, she 7 had happened to be playing her lyre; Kleio had been sitting there with her, and I was walking by. Suddenly a bee had come buzzing out of nowhere and stung Kleio on the hand. She cried out; Leukippe started up and, putting aside her lyre, diagnosed the wound and comforted her, telling her not to worry, for she could stop the pain with a simple two-line spell, taught her once by an Egyptian woman as a remedy for bee and wasp stings. She chanted her formula over the sting, and after a little while, Kleio said she felt better. Well, as chance would have it, at this very moment a wasp or a bumblebee was circling round my head with a menacing *zzzzzzzz*. In a moment of inspiration, I clapped my hand to my face and pretended that I had just been stung and was in pain. The girl came close and took my hand, asking where I had been stung. "On my lip," I said. "Why don't you recite your spell, dearest?" She moved closer and put her mouth near mine in order to mumble her charm over the wound. In whispering the formula, she lightly grazed my lips with hers. I silently kissed her in return, just suppressing the noise kisses make. And as she formed the words, opening and closing her mouth, she transformed that incantation into a steady stream of kisses. Then I took her in my arms and really kissed her. She stepped back. "What are you doing?" she cried. "Is that some spell you know?" "I'm kissing my enchantress," I replied, "because you have relieved my pain." Since she understood my meaning and even smiled, I went on boldly. "Oh dear, my dearest, I'm stung again and still more harshly. The wound has spread to my heart and still needs your magical remedy. There must be a bee inherent in your lips, for they taste as sweet as honey, and their kiss leaves a wound. Say the spell again, but this time don't run through it so hastily, for that merely irritates the wound."

I put my arms around her more securely and kissed with greater abandon. She allowed me this freedom with only a token resistance. But 8 when we saw her servant in the distance coming towards us, we broke apart, with reluctance and regret on my side; I don't know with what feeling on hers. This episode relieved some tension and raised my hopes. I could feel her kiss still resting on my lips like a foreign body, and I

23. Herakles was forced, in punishment for a crime, to serve Queen Omphale of Lydia, an episode often associated with cross-dressing.

carefully guarded it as a secret store of pleasure. For a kiss is a premier pleasure, love child of the mouth, and the mouth is the loveliest member of the body, for it is the organ of speech, and speech is a shadow of the soul itself. The union and commingling of two mouths radiates pleasures down into the bodies and draws up the souls towards the kissing lips. I cannot remember any previous experience when my heart was happier. I learned then for the first time that for sheer pleasure nothing can compete with a lover's kiss.

2    When evening came, we dined together again. It was the feast of Dionysos of the Harvest. Since the myth of Kadmos is a living part of Tyrian tradition, they regard Dionysos as one of their own gods, and this is the myth they tell about the origin of the feast.

No wine ever existed among men before the Tyrians had it—not "the *noir* of fine bouquet," not "the vine of Biblia," not "the Thracian vintage of Maron," not "the Chian from a Lakonian cup," not "the island wine of Ikaros."[24] All of these are colonies sent out by Tyrian wines, where the mother of all vintages first grew.

There was once a hospitable shepherd of Tyre—just like the Athenian tale of Ikarios: in fact, *he* was the one who transferred the story to an Attic milieu. Dionysos visited this herdsman and was served produce from the field and the dairy. They drank water—the same as the cattle drank outside. The Age of Wine had not yet arrived.

Dionysos thanked the shepherd for his kindness and offered him a cup to pledge their friendship—the drink was wine. As he drank it down, he felt a strange surge of pleasure and said to the god: "Sir, where did you tap this water dyed with red, this delectable blood? This is not what flows on the face of the earth. What flows on the earth, as it descends into my breast, brings only a flicker of pleasure, but this liquid delights my nostrils even before I drink. Though cold to the touch, it races to my stomach and lights there a bonfire of beautiful feelings."

And Dionysos replied, "This is the water of my harvest; this is the blood of my grapes." Then the god led the herdsman to the vine, and he took a cluster and crushed it and showing it to him said, "This is that water; this is the fountainhead."[25] And so it was that wine came to

24. These are all wines referred to in familiar passages of literature, e.g., *Odyssey* 9.197, where Odysseus makes the Cyclops drunk with "Maron's wine." Other references here are to passages in Hesiod, Theokritos, Aristophanes, and other writers (see Achilles Tatius, *Leucippe and Clitophon,* ed. E. Vilborg, 2 vols. [Stockholm, 1955–62], for details and for associated textual problems).

25. If the resemblance of Dionysos's words ("This is...my..., this is...my....") and gesture ("he took...and crushed....") to the Christian eucharistic rite is not accidental, it must surely be interpreted as parody. The legend of Achilles Tatius being a Christian bishop (*Souda*) is as fanciful as the legend that Leukippe and Kleitophon had a child who became a Christian saint; see H. Dörrie, "Die griechischen Romane und Christentum," *Philologus* 93(1938): 273–76. The recipient of Dionysos's gift, Ikarios—not to be confused with Ikaros (see text at previous note)—gave some wine to his fellow shepherds; they drank it, thought they had been poisoned, and killed Ikarios.

mankind, according to the Tyrians' account, and they celebrate a feast on    3
that day in honor of that god.

My father, in an expansive mood, made more than usually lavish arrangements for the dinner. Of particular note was a sacred bowl, of great expense, second only to that of Glaukos on Chios.[26] It was crystal, and on it was carved long coils of grapevine that seemed to grow from the bowl itself. Their clusters hung at random on all sides. When the bowl was empty, the carved grapes were green and immature, but as you filled it with wine, the clusters slowly grew darker, and the grapes ripened. Dionysos was engraved near the grapes like a farmer who would tend their growth with wine.

When we came to the wine course, we all drank as usual, but Satyros    9
was in charge of the wine, and he arranged an erotic sleight of hand: exchanging cups, he set mine before the girl and hers in front of me. After pouring the wine and mixing in the water he offered them to us. I took note of the place on the rim where her lips had touched the cup when she drank, and put my lips to the same place. So I kissed the cup itself and left a vicarious kiss for her. She saw me and understood that I was thrilled even by the trace of her lips. Then I saw her mimic my action, drinking as I had done, which made me even happier. This happened a third time, and a fourth time, and so we pledged our love, drinking and kissing for the rest of the day.

After dinner Satyros came up to me and said: "Now is the time for    10
you to play the man. As you know, the girl's mother is in poor health and stays in bed in her own room. So the girl will be alone on her usual promenade before bedtime, with only Kleio to keep her company. I shall engage Kleio in a conversation and divert her from the path."

So we lay, as it were, in ambush: he would take Kleio; I would get the girl. And that's what happened. Kleio was inveigled elsewhere; the maiden was left by herself in the colonnade. As the last rays of daylight were fading, I made my advance, somewhat bolder after my first sally, like a soldier who has won a battle and makes light of war. I had numerous inducements to fight the good fight—wine, lust, hope, a quiet place. Without a word, without any preliminaries, as if setting to an assigned task, I embraced her tightly and gave her a long kiss. Just as I was about to try something a little more advanced, there was a noise behind us. We jumped apart in consternation. She hurried off towards her room; I went in the other direction. I was quite upset that such a good operation had misfired, and I cursed that noise. Satyros came up to me beaming: it seems that he had been watching us from behind a tree and keeping a lookout for intrusive presences, and it was he who had made the noise when he saw someone coming.

26. Herodotos 1.25.

11     A few days later my father began organizing the plans for our wedding, sooner than he had originally said. For a recurring dream had made him apprehensive: he was conducting the service, he had just lit the nuptial torch, and suddenly the fire went out. But this made him all the more determined to bring us together, and he fixed the following day for the ceremony.

He bought Kalligone her wedding dress and jewelry. Her necklace was of various gems; her dress was all of finest crimson cloth. Where other dresses may have a crimson trim, this one was hemmed in gold. The gemstones competed for attention: the beryl was like a rose frozen in stone; the amethyst caught violet highlights from the reflected gold. A central pendant was composed of three precious stones, juxtaposed for their colors: the base stone was jet, joined by a thread-line seam to a white one in the middle and surmounted by a flame-red jewel above. The pendant was surrounded with a ring of gold like a pigeon's eye. The color of the gown was not a coarse derivative dye but a *ne plus ultra* violet, pure porphyry such as the Tyrians traditionally claim was found by a shepherd's dog, and which they use to this day for the royal robe of Aphrodite.

Once upon a time the elegance of porphyry was a secret kept from all mankind: a small mollusk kept it hidden in the inmost chamber of his spiral shell. A fisherman casting his net caught this shellfish; he hoped for fish, and when he saw its spiny shell, he cursed his catch and tossed it aside as sea trash. A dog, coming upon this lucky find, began gnawing on it, and as the juice trickled through his mouth, it made his jaws seem to run with blood. The blood stained the dog's jaws and dyed its mouth purple. The shepherd, seeing the dog's jowls stained with blood, thought he was injured. So he tried to wash it with seawater, but the blood only glowed a deeper crimson, and when he touched it, his hand too was stained. The shepherd realized that it was something in the nature of the shell, some powerful ingredient of natural beauty. He took a handful of wool and pushed it into the winding interior, seeking to reveal the mysteries of the mollusk, and like the dog's jaw it turned bloodred. He had discovered the source of the color purple.[27] Using stones to break through the wall enclosing the elixir, he opened the sacred shrine of the porphyry and exposed a treasure chamber of dye.

12     When I heard that my father had begun to perform the prenuptial rites, I nearly died. I had to find some way to postpone the marriage. While I was pondering this problem, there was a commotion in the men's quarters. This is what happened: when my father had sacrificed the animal, and the meat lay on the altar, an eagle swooped down and snatched it up. It was no good trying to shoo it away, the bird was gone

27. The text says "He had discovered the image (*eikona*) of purple," possibly meaning the "archetype." No one has explained this, but the general sense is clear.

with his catch. They decided this was a bad sign, so they put off the
wedding for that day, while my father called in priests and interpreters
and told them about the ominous incident. They said that since the bird
had flown towards the sea, he must go to the seashore at midnight and
there offer sacrifice to Zeus as God of Hospitality.[28] When this happened,
I praised the eagle extravagantly—truly the king of all birds. The fulfillment of this marvelous sign was not far off.

There was a young man from Byzantium named Kallisthenes. He was    13
wealthy and without parents, in fact an extravagant wastrel. He heard
people speak of Sostratos's daughter as a beautiful woman, and though
he had never seen her, on this basis alone he wanted her for his wife. He
was, in short, a hearsay suitor. Such is the insolence of men with no re-
straints on them! They can fall in love with a rumor and suffer with their
ears the agonies usually experienced by the soul from love's wounds in
the eye.

So he approached Sostratos some time before Byzantium was locked
in war and asked for her hand, but Sostratos disliked his insolent ways
and therefore refused. Kallisthenes grew angry at what he considered the
dishonor cast on him and the bafflement of his desire. By indulging fantasies of her beauty and dreaming of her whom he had never seen, he
sank by imperceptible degrees into a miserable state. Well, he began plotting to revenge himself on Sostratos for his rejection and to fulfill his
own desire. His strategy was dictated by a Byzantine law, to the effect
that if a man kidnapped a maiden and made her his wife before he was
caught, his only penalty was to stay married to her. So he waited for an
opportunity to launch such an adventure.

Then the war broke out, and the girl was sent to us. Kallisthenes kept    14
track of each development and was not dissuaded from his plan. He was
helped by the following turn of events: the Byzantines received an oracle
that said

> Both island and city, people named for a plant,
> Isthmus and channel, joined to the mainland,
> Hephaistos embraces grey-eyed Athena,
> Send there an offering to Herakles.

They were all puzzling over the meaning of the prophecy when Sostratos (who, as I mentioned, was one of the generals in this war)[29] said:
"We should send to Tyre a sacrifice in honor of Herakles.[30] Tyre holds
the solution to every one of these riddles. The god spoke of a people

---

28. The manuscripts here add a sentence that seems to be intrusive: "The event quickly
came to pass; for it happened that the eagle flew out to sea and was seen no longer." Both
of these clauses are variants of material that occurs immediately before and after; the "for"
(*gar*) that connects them makes no sense.

29. A joke or a mistake: Sostratos's generalship has not been mentioned before this.

30. Herakles was the patron deity of Tyre; see Herodotos 2.45 and Chariton 7.2.

named for a plant. Tyre is an island of Phoenicia, and the phoenix is a species of palm. Land and sea are locked in combat around her; the sea claims her on one side, the land on the other—in fact she physically belongs to both. She rests on the sea but has not severed her connection with the land. A narrow neck joins her to the mainland, like the island's throat. But she has no foundation in the sea, and the water flows freely under her. Below the isthmus lies the channel crossing. It is a novel sight: a sea-city and a mainland-island.

" 'Hephaistos embraces Athena': a riddle about the olive and the fire, which live in close community in Tyre. There is an enclosed holy precinct where olive trees grow with gleaming branches, accompanied by fire that ignites spontaneously and plays abundantly along the boughs. The smoky vapors from the fire husband the plant. This is the friendly affection of fire and tree: Athena welcomes the attentions of Hephaistos."[31]

Chairephon, also a general but of higher rank, himself Tyrian on his father's side, thought this an almost divine display of divination and said: "You interpreted the oracle well in every point. I invite you to admire not only the nature of fire but that of water as well. I have witnessed these mysteries with my own eyes. In Sicily there is a spring whose water is shot through with fire. You can see the flames flickering upwards from the depths. If you touch the water, it is cold as snow. Neither the fire is quenched by the water nor the water burned by the fire, but they fraternize in the fountain under conditions of truce.

"And there is an Ismaric river[32] that to all appearances is just an ordinary river, but if you would hear the voice of the waters, wait awhile and listen closely. If a small breeze disturbs the eddies, the water gives out musical notes: the wind acts like a plectrum, and the stream sings like a lyre under its touch.

"A certain Libyan lake borrows a trick from India, and the Libyan maidens know the secret: there is wealth in the water. But it is locked up in the mud as in a treasure vault: a gold mine in the slime. They plunge a barge pole smeared with pitch into the water to rob the river's stronghold. The pole draws out the gold as a fishhook draws the fish, but the bait in this sport is pitch. Gold nuggets that touch it ever so slightly are trapped and then drawn to land. That is how they fish for gold in a Libyan river."[33]

31. This is a Tyrian legend; it is interesting that in the standard Athenian legend about Hephaistos and Athena she *rejects* his advances. Achilles Tatius is here, as elsewhere, offering a recherché version of legend.

32. Ismaric = Thracian. The manuscripts give "Iberian," which, if correct, would be a unique, and unsupported item in the paradoxography of waters. See M. Laplace, "Achille Tatius, *Leucippé et Clitophon,* II.14.8: sur un fleuve prétendument 'ibérique'," *L'Antiquité Classique* 52(1983): 243–45.

33. The story is also told in Herodotos 4.195 and Ktesias *Indika* 4.

After speaking, he urged that sacrifices be sent to Tyre, and the city 15
approved. Kallisthenes maneuvered an appointment as one of the envoys, whereupon he promptly sailed to Tyre, learned which house was my father's, and kept a watch for the women.

The women went out to see the sacrifice, which was to be a lavish affair. The offerings were splendidly arrayed; the flowers were intricately intertwined. The offerings were cassia, frankincense, and saffron; the flowers were amaryllis lilies, roses, and sprigs of myrtle. The scent of the blossoms competed with the odor of the offerings. The breezes skirred upwards, blending the various perfumes in the air; it was a draft of pleasure. The sacrificial objects were many and varied, but outstanding among them were the cattle of the Nile.

The Egyptian ox is a striking animal, both in size and color. It is quite large, has a solid neck, broad back, full stomach. Its horns are not small like the Sicilian cattle nor ill formed like the Cypriot but rise up from the temples and gradually curve in from either side till the tips are just as far apart as the bases. Their shape is exactly that of the crescent moon. The color of these cattle is that of Thracian horses, whose praises have been sung by Homer.[34] The bull walks in procession with head held high as if to show that he is king of the other cattle. If the myth of Europa be true, surely Zeus took the form of an Egyptian bull.

It so happened that my mother was not feeling well. Leukippe pretended to be sick too and stayed at home—for we had agreed to come together whenever most of the people were out of the house. So my sister went out with Leukippe's mother to see the procession. Now Kallisthenes had never seen Leukippe, so when he saw my sister, Kalligone, and recognized Sostratos's wife with her, he thought she was Leukippe.

He was so struck with the sight of her beauty that he made no inquiries but pointed her out to his most trusted servant: he told him to gather a band of men, and explained to him in detail how to carry out the kidnapping. A holiday was coming during which (he had been informed) all the young women would gather on the beach. He then performed the religious duties for which he had been sent, and departed.

He had his own ship, which he had outfitted at Byzantium with a 17
view to this adventure. The other Byzantine officials sailed away, but he waited some distance from the land so as to seem to be following the others, and so as not to become suspect after the kidnapping because his ship was seen in the neighborhood of Tyre. When he reached Sarapta, a coastal village of Tyre, he launched a cockboat under the command of Zeno (the trusty servant to whom he had assigned the kidnapping). He was a robust seaman, a born pirate: he quickly rounded up some felonious fishermen from that village and sailed back to Tyre. An island not

34. *Iliad* 10.437.

far from Tyre, called Rhodope's Tomb by the local people, has a small anchorage; that was where the cockboat lay in wait.

18 Before the holiday that Kallisthenes was waiting for, there occurred the episode of the ominous eagle. We made preparations at night for the sacrifice due to take place the next day—none of which escaped the watchful eyes of Zeno. When the time came, late in the evening, we started down to the beach, and he followed. As soon as we reached the edge of the sea, he gave a signal to the cockboat, which immediately began rowing towards us, and when it came near, we could see ten young fellows in it. Eight more were hiding on the shore: they were wearing women's clothes and had shaved their beards clean.[35] They carried weapons under their dresses; each of them also brought something for the sacrifice so as not to arouse suspicions. We thought they were women.

We had already constructed the pyre when suddenly they ran at us, shouting, and extinguished our torches. We were terrified, scattering in all directions. They pulled out their swords, grabbed my sister and put her in the boat, and took to flight quick as a bird. Some of us were still running and neither knew nor had seen anything, but those who had seen what happened cried out, "They've kidnapped Kalligone." But by that time the boat was already out in midsea.

When they reached Sarapta, Kallisthenes received their signal from a distance and sailed out, took the girl aboard, and headed for the high seas. I breathed a sigh of relief at this curious solution to the problem of my wedding, yet I was not without grief at the fate that had befallen my sister.

19 I waited a few days and then said to Leukippe: "How long will we stop at mere kisses, dearest? The overture is delightful, but now let us add erotic grace notes. We can exchange promises to be faithful to each other. Once Aphrodite has initiated us into her mysteries, no other power can contravene her will."

By repeating this charm frequently enough I persuaded her to admit me to her bedroom at night, with the cooperation of Kleio, her chambermaid. Her room was situated as follows: one wing of the house had four rooms, two on the right, two on the left. A narrow hallway ran down the middle, which was closed by a single door at one end. This was where the women lodged. The farther two rooms were occupied by the girl and her mother, directly opposite each other; the rooms near the entrance were Kleio's (on the same side as the girl's) and a storeroom. Each night Leukippe's mother tucked her in bed and locked the door of the

35. K. Plepelits, *Achilleus Tatios: Leukippe und Kleitophon* (Stuttgart, 1980), 11, notes that this detail would hardly have been included before the widespread readoption of beards as a male fashion following the example of Hadrian (117–138). This may thus be a pointer to the date of the text.

wing from the inside. She had someone else lock the door from the outside and pass the key to her through the opening. She kept the keys with her all night until the next morning, when she called the servant and passed him the key again to open the door.

Satyros made duplicates of these keys and tested them. When he found that they worked he persuaded Kleio, with the girl's full knowledge, not to interfere with our scheme. Such was the plan.

One of the visitors' servants was a busybody, a gossip, a nosey parker, and every name you could think of. His name was <u>Nat</u>.[36] I thought he was observing our doings at a distance, and since he suspected that we were going to act under cover of nightfall (as indeed we were), he began staying up until far into the night, keeping the door of his room wide open, so that it was a problem to sneak past him. Satyros wanted to win him over to our side, so he tried joking with him, calling him in fun a pesky gnat. But Nat saw through his plan and only pretended to respond to Satyros's playful banter, using a silly little story to signal his firm intention not to collaborate. "Since my name amuses you, let me tell you a story about a gnat.

"The lion frequently criticized Prometheus: for though he had made him big and handsome and had lined his jaws with sharp teeth and fortified his feet with claws and had in general made him mightier than the other creatures, 'yet, with all this strength, I am still afraid of a cock.'[37] Prometheus stood over him and said: 'Don't waste your time blaming me. You have everything I was able to create, but your soul is soft on this one point alone.' So the lion went away, indulging in self-pity and calling himself a coward and eventually contemplating suicide. In this frame of mind he met an elephant, said hello, and stood there talking for a while. He noticed that the elephant's ears were continuously moving back and forth, back and forth. 'Is there something wrong with your ears? Why do they never rest, even for a little while?' At that moment a gnat happened to be zooming by, and the elephant replied: 'You see that little buzzer there? If he gets in my ear canal, I'm dead.' And the lion thought to himself: 'Why should *I* meditate death? Compare my size to a cock's, and then an elephant's to a gnat's—why, that's how much better off I am than the elephant!'

"So you see how strong the gnat is, that even an elephant is afraid of him." — a veiled threat

Satyros understood that under this scabby story there festered an ugly meaning, and said with a trace of a smile on his lips: "Now I have a tale for you, which I heard from a certain philosopher. Its characters are also

36. His Greek name is Konops, which means "gnat" or "mosquito." A second pun occurs at 2.23: Kyklops (Cyclops)/Konops.

37. A familiar belief, reported by other authors, e.g., Aelian *Nature of Animals* 3.31 and Pliny *Natural History* 8.52.

a lion and a gnat: I don't need the elephant for my story; I'll give him to you as a present.

22    "One day a bragging gnat said to the lion: 'You may be king of the other beasts but not of me. You are really no handsomer than I, nor stronger nor larger. Consider: what is always your first line of attack? Scratching and biting. Women's weapons! What is your claim to size and beauty? A broad chest, sturdy shoulders, and a lot of hair on your neck. Have you noticed that your hindquarters are a laughingstock? My size is limited only by the dimensions of the air itself, wherever my wings take me. The meadow flowers are my beauty for I put them on like clothes whenever I don't feel like flying. It would be pointless to run through the complete catalogue of my courage: I am a whole arsenal in myself. I stand in the ranks with my trumpet, but my mouth is a weapon as well as a trumpet—which puts me in the archery squadron as well as the bugle corps. I am my own bow and arrow: my wings send me flying through the air, and when I land I leave a wound like a lance. The injured enemy cries out and looks for his assailant. I'm an absent presence. I escape, but I don't run away. I surround him on all sides like the cavalry, riding on my wings. I laugh to see him dancing about with all his wounds. But why even discuss it? *En garde!*'

"So saying, he attacked the lion, diving towards his eyes and the hairless parts of his face, then circling round and sounding his buzz-bugle. The lion was enraged. He turned every which way and snapped at the air, but the gnat made sport of his anger and stung him on his very lips. Wherever he was stung, the lion would bend back to that part of his body and try to bite the gnat, but the gnat, like a wrestler shifting his weight before the clinch, would dodge aside, escaping the lion's jaws by flying right through his teeth, which missed their prey and came crashing together like castanets. At length, the lion was exhausted by this shadowboxing against the air and stood there helpless with anger. The gnat flew around his mane, piping a victory tune. As he swung in ever-widening circles, crassly exaggerating his triumph, he failed to notice that he was flying straight into a spider's web. But the spider noticed. When he was entangled and helpless, he exclaimed: 'What a fool I was! I challenged a lion to battle, but now I'm defeated by a small spiderweb.'

"So you too should look out for spiders," said Satyros with a smile.

23    A few days later Satyros bought a sleeping potion and invited Nat to dinner, knowing that he was a slave to his appetite. Nat hesitated at first, suspecting a trick, but when his own dear stomach startled rumbling in anticipation, he accepted. He came over to Satyros's room, and after dinner, when he was just about to leave, Satyros poured some of the drug into his last cup. He drank it down, and in a little while—in fact, just enough time to reach his own room—he collapsed on his bed in a

drugged stupor. Satyros ran to me and said, "Your Cyclops is fast asleep; now you prove yourself a good Odysseus."

A moment later we were at my mistress's door. Satyros waited outside while Kleio received me without a sound, and I entered, feeling counter-tremors of joy and fear at the same time: my fear of the dangers threw my cherished hopes into confusion, while on the other hand my hopes of attaining Leukippe spread a sweet icing of pleasure over my fear. Thus my very hopes threw me into a fright, and my distress brought a kind of delight.

Just as I was entering the girl's bedroom, something was happening across the hall to her mother. She was being disturbed by a dream, in which she saw a bandit with a naked sword seize her daughter, drag her away, throw her down on her back, and slice her in two all the way up from her stomach, making his first insertion at her modest spot. Pantheia was so distressed and frightened that she leaped up just as she was and ran the few steps to her daughter's bedroom, just as I was lying down.

I heard the noise of the door opening; I sprang to my feet. She was already near the bed. Realizing that the situation was desperate, I jumped aside and hurled myself through the door, running. I collided with Satyros, who held me still trembling and shaken. We ran through the dark until we reached our room.

Her mother fell down in a faint. When she recovered, she slapped    24
Kleio across the face and grabbed her by the hair, crying out to her daughter: "You've ruined all I ever hoped for, Leukippe. O Sostratos! While you're fighting for other men's marriages in Byzantium, you have been defeated in Tyre, and someone has despoiled your own daughter of *her* marriage. You pitiful thing: I had hoped for something better in the way of a wedding. Why did you ever leave Byzantium? Better you were a wartime atrocity, better raped by a victorious Thracian soldier than this. That would have been a disaster but not a disgrace, if force was used. Wretched girl! This way you lose your reputation along with your happiness. My dream misled me: the truth was worse than I saw. That incision in your stomach is much more serious: he pricked you deeper than a sword could have. But I didn't see the man who did it; I don't know how the disaster happened. Oh, dear me! What if it was a *slave!*"

The girl was glad to hear that I had escaped. "Don't find fault with    25
my virtue, Mother. I have done nothing to deserve this tongue-lashing, and I have no idea who it was—a god or a spirit or a burglar. I just lay there terrified, too frightened even to scream. Really fear is the perfect muzzle. Of one thing though I am sure: no one has disgraced my virgin body."

Pantheia sank to the floor in a heap, sobbing and groaning.

Satyros and I were alone, planning our next move, and we decided that it was best to run away, before morning, when Kleio might make a full confession under torture.

26    We set about our plan, first lying to the porter that we were going out to a girlfriend's house, and soon we arrived at Kleinias's house. It was now after midnight, and the porter there was reluctant to admit us. Kleinias from his bedroom on the second floor heard us talking and ran down to let us in, all excited. Just then we saw Kleio running up in a great hurry: she had decided to escape.

So at one and the same time Kleinias heard what we had done, we heard Kleio's decision to run away, and she in turn heard our plans. Going indoors, we described to Kleinias in greater detail what had happened and how we had decided to run away. Kleio said: "I'm going with you. If I wait here till morning, I will be sentenced to death or, worse, torture."

27    Kleinias led me by the hand to the other side of the room, out of Kleio's hearing. "I think I know just what to do: send Kleio away secretly, wait for a few days, and if everyone still agrees, pack up and go. According to you, the girl's mother even now does not realize whom she surprised in the bedroom, and if Kleio is out of the picture, there will be no one to inform on us. Possibly you will persuade the girl too to elope with us." He promised to join in our escape. We agreed to this plan.

He entrusted Kleio to one of his servants, telling him to put her on board ship. We waited there a while, thinking through the contingencies. Finally we decided to ask the girl: if not, we would remain here, and let fate take its course. We tried to get a little rest for the few remaining hours of the night and at dawn returned home.

28    Pantheia, immediately on rising, began to prepare the tortures for Kleio and gave orders to fetch her. When she was nowhere to be found, she returned to her daughter and said: "Will you not confess the plot of your little drama? Now Kleio has disappeared."

Leukippe reacted boldly. "What more can I say? What kind of proof would satisfy you that I'm telling the truth? If there is a virginity test, I'll take it."

"That's all we need now, for everybody to know about our disgrace!" And with that she turned and marched out of the room.

29    Left to herself and with her mother's words still ringing in her ears, Leukippe was caught in emotional chaos. She was vexed, ashamed, angered: vexed at being caught, ashamed at being criticized, angered at not being believed. Shame, grief, and anger are three waves rising in the soul. Shame enters at the eyes, where it takes away their freedom of movement; grief lodges in the breast, where it dampens the soul's glow; anger barks around the heart, where it overwhelms reason with its foaming insanity. Speech is the father of all three: like arrows aimed at a target

and hitting it dead center, words pierce the soul and wound it in many places. One verbal arrow is insult, and the wound it leaves is called anger: another is exposure of one's misfortunes, and this arrow causes grief; a third is lectures on one's faults, and this wound is known as shame. One quality common to all these weapons is that they pierce deeply but draw no blood. The only remedy for them is counterattack with the same weapons. The wound caused by one sharp tongue is healed by the razor edge of another. This softens the heart's anger and assuages the soul's grief. If one is prevented by *force majeure* from uttering one's defense, the wounds silently fester. Unable to eject their foam, the waves swell up in labor, distended by the puffing breath of words within. Under the stress of so many afflictions, Leukippe did not put up with her mother's attack.

It was just then that I dispatched Satyros to her to sound her out about   30 an elopement. But before he could get a word in, she said: "I beg you, by all the gods—ours and anyone else's, get me out of my mother's sight, anywhere you like. If you go and leave me behind, I will hang myself."

When I heard this, I cast most of my troubles to the wind. We waited two more days while my father was out of town, all the while preparing for our escape.

Satyros had some of the sleeping potion left that he had used on Nat.   31 While waiting at table he secretly poured some into the last cup that he served to Pantheia. She rose from the table, went to her room, and instantly fell asleep. Leukippe had a second chambermaid, whom he drugged with the same potion (he had pretended to be in love with her too, from the day she joined the household). His third quarry was the porter, whom he bagged with the same brew.

Kleinias had arranged for a carriage to be waiting for us at the gates, and he was already there with it, waiting for us. When the whole city was asleep, at about the first watch of the night, we set out without a sound, Satyros guiding Leukippe by the hand. (Nat, our vigilant enemy, chanced to be out of town that day on an errand for his mistress.) Satyros opened the door, and we started on our way. When we arrived at the gates, we climbed into the carriage. There were six altogether: ourselves, Kleinias, and two of his servants. We drove along the road to Sidon, and when about two-thirds of the night had passed, we arrived at the city and immediately set our course for Beirut, expecting to find a ship docked there. Our luck had not run out: just as we reached the harbor in Beirut, we found a vessel setting sail, in fact ready at that moment to throw off its stern cables. Without even inquiring its destination, we transferred ourselves from land to sea, only minutes before sunrise. The ship was sailing to Alexandria, the great city of the Nile.

32 The sight of the sea was at first very heartening. That was while the ship was still lying in the harbor and not running on the high seas. As soon as the wind was clearly favorable for weighing anchor, the entire ship became a pandemonium of sailors running back and forth, the skipper barking orders, rigging being hauled up. The yardarm was heaved around; the sail unfurled; the ship got under way; the anchors were raised; the harbor was left behind. From the ship we watched the land recede by slow degrees, as if it were setting sail instead of us. There were many hymns and prayers, invocations and moments of reverent silence, appealing to the seaman's gods to protect this our journey and make it truly auspicious, amen.

A stronger wind sprang up, the sail bellied out, and the ship went spanking along.

33 When it was breakfast time, a young man who had settled his belongings next to ours very kindly asked us to eat with him. Satyros was already serving our breakfast, so we put what we had together in the middle and shared both food and conversation.

I spoke first. "Where do you come from, my young friend, and what is your name?"

"I am Menelaos, born in Egypt. And you?"

"I am Kleitophon, and this is Kleinias, both from Phoenicia."

"Why are you traveling?"

"We'd like to hear your story first: then we will tell you ours."

34 "The principal cause of my travels is the jealousy of Eros and a fateful safari. I was in love with a handsome young man who had a passion for hunting. Often I tried to hold him back, but I could never control him. When he wouldn't be persuaded, I joined him in the chase. We were both on horses, and at first the hunt was successful, as we pursued only smaller creatures. But suddenly a wild boar bolted from the underbrush, and the lad took off in hot pursuit. The boar wheeled about, leveled his tusks at him, and ran straight at him. My boyfriend didn't turn aside, though I called and screamed, 'Hold back; rein aside; he's dangerous.'

"The boar was moving in fast, covering ground by leaps and bounds, making straight for my lover. They were on a collision course, and I was shaking with fright as I watched. Afraid that the boar would strike first and gore the horse, I wound the thongs on my javelin[38] and hurled it at the target without taking careful aim. My lover veered straight into its trajectory and intercepted the weapon.

"What do you think my feelings were then? If I had any feelings at all, they were those of a man dying though still alive. Saddest of all, he

38. The Greek and Roman method of javelin throwing involved winding a leather thong along the haft with a loop at the end through which the thrower placed his first finger. This imparted a spinning motion to the javelin, aiding in distance and accuracy. Strabo (*Geography* 4.4.3) notes that the Gauls throw their spears "by hand, not by thong."

reached out his arms to me, just barely breathing, embraced me, and as he lay there dying of that blow I had dealt him, he felt no hatred for me—murderer most foul. And he died in the embrace of the very arms that had killed him.

"The young man's parents brought me to court, and I did not resist. I took the stand and made no defense. Rather I demanded the death penalty for myself. The judges favored clemency and sentenced me to three years in exile, a period that is just now ending. And so I am returning to my own land."

Kleinias wept as he was speaking, "outwardly for Patroklos,"[39] remembering Charikles.

Menelaos said, "Are you weeping for me, or has a similar experience sent you into exile?"

Heaving a great sigh, Kleinias told him all about Charikles and his horse, and I in turn related my story.

Since Menelaos was visibly depressed at the memory of his misfortune, and Kleinias silently wept at the thought of Charikles, to liven their spirits and turn their minds from sorrow I turned the discussion in the direction of *jeu d'amour*.[40] Leukippe of course wasn't present: she was asleep in a corner of the ship.

I said with a sly smile: "Kleinias always comes out ahead of me. I know he was looking for an opportunity to deliver his diatribe against women as usual, which he could easily do now that he has found a companion who shares his view of love. It does look as if male-directed love is becoming the norm."

"But surely it is much preferable to the alternative," said Menelaos. "Young men are more open and frank than women, and their handsome bodies offer a sharper stimulus to pleasure."

"How can it be sharper? Their beauty no sooner peeps out than it is gone, before the lover has had time to savor it. It often vanishes like Tantalos's pool in the very act of drinking, and the lover goes away thirsty. It is snatched away in the midst of his drinking, before he is satisfied. A lover cannot come to the end of an affair with a boyfriend feeling unqualified gratification, for he is invariably left thirsty for something more."

And Menelaos replied: "Kleitophon, you don't know the principal fact about pleasure: to be unsatisfied is always a desirable state. Constant re-

39. *Iliad* 19.302, where captive Trojan women are forced to mourn for Patroklos; in reality they weep for their own woes. The expression became proverbial.

40. Chapters 35–38 have caused a good deal of anxiety to translators, who have often dealt with them by dubious methods, such as translation into the indecent obscurity of a learned language (Latin in the first edition of the Loeb) or more radical surgery (removal of the passage or changing the sexes). Anthony Hodges (1638) condenses everything into two lines: "So at last we fell in a large discourse concerning the dignity of their sex, which I list not here to set down."

course to anything makes satisfaction shrivel into satiation. What can only be snatched is always fresh and blooming—its pleasure never grows old. And as much as beauty's span ₁is diminished in time, so is it intensified in desire. The rose for this reason is lovelier than other plants: its beauty soon is gone.

"There are, I think, two kinds of beauty current among mortals, one heavenly, one vulgar, just like the two goddesses who represent these types of beauty.[41] The heavenly beauty is oppressed at her implication in mortal beauty and seeks quickly to mount to heaven; the vulgar gravitates downwards and luxuriates among bodies. If you would like a poetic testimony to the heavenly ascent of beauty, listen to Homer.

> The gods caught up Ganymede to pour wine for
> Zeus because he was beautiful and they were
> glad to have him among them.[42]

No woman has ever ascended to the heavens because of her beauty. (Zeus *has* been known to resort to women.) Alkmene became a tearful fugitive; Danae was consigned to the sea in a chest; Semele fed the fire.[43] But when Zeus desired a Phrygian youth, he gave him the sky, that Ganymede might live with him and serve his nectar. The previous occupant of that post was rudely ousted. It was, I believe, a woman."[44]

37      "One can argue," I said, "that the beauty of women is the more heavenly in that it does not so quickly fade. Timelessness is next to godliness. Anything that changes and fades reflects its mortal nature, and is vulgar rather than heavenly. Zeus lusted indeed for a Phrygian youth and brought this Phrygian youth to heaven; but the loveliness of women brought Zeus himself down to earth. To win a woman Zeus has mooed, has capered the satyric high step, has transformed himself to gold.[45] Let Ganymede serve the nectar; let Hebe drink with the gods; let the woman be served by the youth. His rape was not even stylish: a carnivorous bird swooped down, made the snatch, rode roughshod over him—all very undignified, and rather a tasteless spectacle—a young man dangling from those talons. Semele's escort to heaven is nothing to be surprised at. It got Herakles there. You laugh at Danae's chest, but you didn't mention little Perseus in there with her. Alkmene was more than satisfied that Zeus had shanghaied three whole days and spent them all on her.

41. Cf. Plato *Symposion* 180D–182A.
42. *Iliad* 20.234f.
43. Alkmene: mother of Herakles by Zeus; her sorrow and flight evidently refer to her later persecution by Eurystheus, who drove her to Trachis and then to Athens. Danae: mother of Perseus by Zeus; her father, Akrisios, locked her and her baby in a chest and cast it into the sea. Semele: mother of Dionysos by Zeus; Hera tricked Semele into asking her secret lover to reveal his true form, whose fiery glory killed her.
44. Hebe.
45. Zeus accomplished various rapes by changing his form to that of a bull (Europa), a satyr (Antiope), a golden shower (Danae).

"If we might pass from this heroic casuistry to speak of the real pleasures involved, though I am only a novice in my experience of women, and that has been restricted to commercial transactions with women of the street, and though another more deeply initiated into their secrets might well have more to say, yet I will speak in their behalf, even though I have no very wide experience.

"A woman's body is well lubricated in the clinch, and her lips are tender and soft for kissing. Therefore she holds a man's body wholly and congenially wedged into her embraces, into her very flesh; and her partner is totally encompassed with pleasure. She plants kisses on your lips like a seal touching warm wax; and if she knows what she is doing, she can sweeten her kisses, employing not only the lips but the teeth, grazing all around the mouth with gentle nips. The fondled breast, too, is not without its special pleasure.

"When the sensations named for Aphrodite are mounting to their peak, a woman goes frantic with pleasure; she kisses with mouth wide open and thrashes about like a mad woman. Tongues all the while overlap and caress, their touch like passionate kisses within kisses. Your part in heightening the pleasure is simply to open your mouth.

"When a woman reaches the very goal of Aphrodite's action, she instinctively gasps with that burning delight, and her gasp rises quickly to the lips with a love breath, and there it meets a lost kiss, wandering about and looking for a way down: this kiss mingles with the love breath and returns with it to strike the heart. The heart then is kissed, confused, throbbing. If it were not firmly fastened in the chest, it would follow along, drawing itself upwards to the place of kisses.

"Schoolboys are hardly so well educated in kissing; their embraces are awkward; their lovemaking is lazy and devoid of pleasure."

And Menelaos replied: "You seem less like a novice and more like an old, a very old pro at Aphrodite's business, bombarding us with all these fancy refinements devised by women. Now listen to a rebuttal on behalf of boys.

"Women are false in every particular, from coquettish remarks to coy posturing. Their lovely looks are the busy contrivance of various ointments: they wear the borrowed beauty of myrrh, of hair dye, even chemical preparations. If you strip them of their many false attractions, they would be like the fabled jackdaw who lost his feathers.[46] A boy's beauty is not carefully nurtured by the odor of myrrh nor enhanced by other scents of insidious intent. Sweeter than all a woman's exotic oils is the honest day's sweat of an active lad.

---

46. A jackdaw stuck some peacock feathers into his own and went proudly strutting among the peacocks. They pecked at him, pulling at his feathers, and drove him out. In his dilapidated condition his own flock refused to allow him back (Phaedrus 1.3).

"And young men have the privilege, before wrestling under Aphrodite's rules, of grappling on the mat, publicly locking bodies in the gym; and no one says these embraces are immodest. The softer sex are flabby opponents in Aphrodite's ring, but boys' bodies compete on equal terms, striving like athletes whose mutual goal is pleasure.

"His kisses, to be sure, are not sophisticated like a woman's; they are no devastating spell of lips' deceit. But he kisses as he knows how—acting by instinct, not technique. Here is a metaphor for a boy's kiss: take nectar; crystallize it; form it into a pair of lips—these would yield a boy's kisses. You could not have enough of these: however many you took, you would still be thirsty for more, and you could not pull your mouth away until the very excess of pleasure frightened you into escaping."

## Book Three

1   After three days of clear sailing, a sudden gloom materialized around us, and the daylight abruptly ended. A wind gusting up from the sea came straight against the prow, and the pilot ordered the yardarm to be swung around. The sailors hustled to their jobs: one detail bunched the sail to one side of the mast, inching it by sheer force over the yardarm, for the wind was hitting it too strongly for easy hauling; the detail on the other side was watching how far forward to swing the yardarm so that the wind would catch the sail from behind.[47]

The deck started slanting as one side sank and the other rose into the air, almost on its beam-ends. Most of us thought the ship was about to somersault altogether if the wind gave it just a push. So we all moved over to the higher part of the ship to lighten the submerging side and by transferring our weight to force the ship a little closer to an even keel. But our efforts accomplished nothing. The rising deck simply moved us up more than we forced it down. We struggled for some time to bring the ship down to a level as it teetered in the waves' balance. Suddenly the gale reversed directions, and the ship was almost swamped: the side sloping into the waves swung up with a sharp kick; the other side, which had been suspended in the air, crashed down into the sea. A great cry arose from the crowd on deck: there was a mass migration, all shouting and

47. The text, if correct, evidently describes a navigational operation in response to a head wind, a two-part maneuver described by Aristotle (*Mechanical Problems* 7). First, the sail is shortened on one side of the mast; second, the yardarm is rotated so that the side where the sail is still full and slack moves forward until it catches some wind, while the other side of the yardarm, where the sail is somewhat furled, goes back towards the pilot. Aristotle's explanation for the first part of the maneuver is that the rudder is ineffective when the wind is too strong, so the sail must be reefed to catch less wind; for the second part, that the pilot can convert the unfavorable direction of the wind to his advantage by catching its force so that it drives the ship to one side while he steers the rudder in the opposite direction.

running back to our original location. This happened a third time, a fourth time, and many more. The ship seesawed in the waves, and so did the passengers. Before we could finish a lap in one direction, we had to start racing back the other way.

Oh, how we ran in that all-day marathon, back and forth over the ship's deck, dragging our baggage, always expecting death; and it was in all likelihood not far off. At about noon the sun was utterly extinguished; we saw each other as by moonlight. Lightning's fire danced through the air, thunder bellowed from the skies, the air was alive with the sounds of moaning, and the waves in civil war answered them from below. Somewhere between the sky and the sea the winds were having a cat fight, spitting and snarling; a resonance as of muted horns echoed in the air. The mast ropes flailed about, screaming through the air and whipping against the sail. As the ship's timbers cracked and shivered, we were afraid that the nails would tear loose one by one, and the hull would soon be wide open. Wicker shields had been set up on all sides of the ship, for the storm water was flooding over; we crawled under their shelter as if into a cave and waited there, abandoning ourselves to fortune and giving up all hope.

Three-decker waves rose up on all sides—from the bow, from the stern—and crashed into each other. The ship by turns was either elevated to the very apex of a swelling sea-dome or sliding down sudden chutes between the waves, which seemed at one moment like mountains, then like canyons. But the waves that struck us amidships from either side were even more frightening. The sea came onto the ship, washed through the wicker shields, and covered the whole deck. The billows rose high and seemed to touch the very clouds. At a distance from the ship they seemed the size of mountains, but watching them advance you were sure the ship would be swallowed up. Wind and waves were at war. We could not stay in any one place, so violently did the deck quake and heave beneath us.

It was a pandemonium of noise: roaring waves, blustering wind, the shrill shouts of women, the hoarser cries of men, the sharp commands of sailors, an utter welter of various wailings.

The pilot gave orders to jettison all cargo: no distinction was made between gold or silver and other valuables, all alike was tossed over the rails. Many of the merchants laid hands on their own goods and energetically heaved their hopes for profit overboard. By now the ship was stripped of all its cargo, but the storm had not yet spent its force.

At last the pilot gave up. He abandoned the rudder, surrendered the ship to the sea, got the lifeboat ready, told the crew to get in, and started down the gang-ladder. They hustled down at once, right on one another's heels.

Then followed a fearful scene of fighting hand to hand. The men in the lifeboat tried to cut the cable that tied it to the cargo vessel; the passengers were all eager to jump down into it at the spot where they had seen the pilot hauling in the cable, but those in the lifeboat refused to let them on, threatening with swords and axes to strike anyone who tried to board. Many on the ship tried to arm themselves with makeshift munitions—fragments of an old oar, pieces of bench planking. The sea had now made force its natural order, and a most novel naval encounter ensued. For fear that the lifeboat would swamp under the added weight of more passengers, the crew hacked away at potential boarders with knives and hatchets; the other side leaped over the rails, swinging clubs and bats. Some just got their fingers on the lifeboat, but slipped off into the sea; others scrambled aboard and struggled with those already there.

Ties of friendship and decency were no longer operative as each man sought only his own safety and suppressed his more generous impulses. Momentous crises have a way of making one's philanthropy flag.

4     Then a muscular young man on the ship caught the towboat's cable and started tugging. As it came nearer everyone prepared to jump. Two or three succeeded, though not without bloodying themselves, but many more failed in the attempt and rolled head over heels into the sea. The sailors soon set their boat free by cutting the rope again with an axe, and they drifted as the wind took them. The passengers on the ship cursed and prayed that the boat would sink.[48]

As the ship skipped and spun about in the waves, it crashed without warning against a submerged rock and shivered its timbers. As it rebounded, the mast fell in the other direction, shattering part of the hull and driving the rest under water.

Those who were engulfed by the sea at once and swallowed the salty water met a relatively mild fate in these terrible circumstances—they were spared the prolonged terror of a slow sea death, which kills you a thousand times before you die. Fear is infinitely multiplied by the ocean's endless vista; death of this sort is worse than any other, for it is as frightening as the sea is wide. Some tried to dive away from the wreckage, but the surge raked them across the rocks to their death; many were impaled on points of shattered planking, like speared fish. Still others, half-dead, swam on.

5     When the vessel broke in pieces, some good deity rescued a section of the prow for Leukippe and me to float on wherever the sea's movement took us. Menelaos and Satyros and other passengers had reached the mast and were swimming while holding onto it. We saw Kleinias nearby swimming with his arm over the yardarm, and we heard him shout,

48. Reading with some manuscripts ἐπηρῶντο rather than Vilborg's ἐπειρῶντο ("They tried to sink the boat").

"Take hold of the spar, Kleitophon." Just as he said this a wave rolled up behind and engulfed him. We screamed: at this moment a billow was bearing down on us, too. But by a stroke of luck its surge rolled up under us as it passed, so that our timber merely rose in the air to crest the wave, and we once again glimpsed Kleinias.

In a breaking voice I prayed: "O Lord Poseidon, grant in your clemency final peace to these final pieces of your shipwreck. In our fear and trembling we have lived through many deaths. If it be your will to destroy us now, spare us at least from isolation in death: let a single wave overwhelm us together. If we are doomed to feed the fish, let a single monster engorge us together, a single stomach accommodate us as one, so that even among the fish we may share a sepulcher."

Shortly after I finished my prayer, most of the wind died down, and the angry waves subsided. The sea was littered with corpses. The tide carried Menelaos and company to land first: it was somewhere along the Egyptian seaboard, in a region then controlled by pirates.

Later that afternoon Leukippe and I were lucky enough to float to  shore at Pelousion, where we embraced the land with glad relief and sang hymns of mourning for Kleinias and Satyros, on the presumption that they had died.

In Pelousion there is a holy statue of Zeus Kasios, representing him as 6 a young man, closer in age to Apollo. In his outstretched hand he holds a pomegranate, symbol of a religious mystery.[49] We were told that this god could be consulted as an oracle, so we prayed to him, asking for a sign as to the fate of Kleinias and Satyros. We walked to a back chamber of the temple and saw there a representation of two figures, signed by the artist.

The artist was Euanthes; the figures were Andromeda and Prometheus. Both were prisoners (this was obviously what led the painter to link them), and their situations corresponded in various particulars: both were chained to rocks; both were tormented by a wild beast, one from the air, the other from the sea. They were rescued by Argive heroes of the same family—Prometheus by Herakles, who shot down Zeus's eagle; Andromeda by Perseus, who fought off Poseidon's sea monster. But Herakles aimed his bow with his feet planted firmly on the ground, while Perseus was hovering in the air on his winged sandals.

The girl was placed in a recess of the rock which was just her size. It 7 seemed to suggest that this was not a man-made but a natural hollow, a concavity drawn by the artist in rough, irregular folds, just as the earth produced it. Looking more closely at her installed in her shelter, you might surmise from her beauty that she was a new and unusual icon, but

49. The region and the temple were famous, but the statue described by Achilles is of Harpokrates rather than Zeus. Pomegranates with "mystical" meanings were also associated with Demeter at Eleusis and Hera at Argos.

the sight of her chains and the approaching monster would rather call to mind an improvised grave.

There is a curious blend of beauty and terror on her face: fear appears on her cheeks, yet a bloomlike beauty rests in her eyes. Her cheeks are not quite perfectly pale, but brushed with a light red wash; nor is the flowering quality of her eyes untouched by care—they seem like violets in the earliest stage of wilting. The artist had enhanced her beauty with this touch of lovely fear.

Her arms were spread against the rock, bound above her head by a manacle bolted in the stone. Her hands hung loose at the wrist like clusters of grapes. The color of her arms shaded from pure white to livid, and her fingers looked dead. She was chained up waiting for death, wearing a wedding garment, adorned as a bride for Hades. Her robe reached the ground—the whitest of robes, delicately woven, like spiderweb more than sheep's wool, or the airy threads that Indian women draw from the trees and weave into silk.

The sea monster rose from below the sea, parting its surface directly in front of the girl. Most of him was hidden in the water; only his head emerged, but the dim outline of his body was drawn below the surface, as were the scaly laminations and sinuous laps of his neck, the spiny crest, and loops of tail. His jaws were long and large, opening wide from a point of intersection at the shoulders, and all the rest was gullet.

Between the monster and the girl, Perseus was drawn descending from the air, in the direction of the beast. He was entirely naked but for a cloak thrown over his shoulders and winged sandals on his feet. A felt cap covered his head, representing Hades' helmet of invisibility. In his left hand he held the Gorgon's head, wielding it like a shield. Even as a painting it was a frightening object, with eyes starting out of their sockets, and serpentine hair about the temples all writhing and erect: a graphic delineation of intimidation. This was his left hand's weapon of war; his right was armed with a twin-bladed implement, a scythe and sword in one. The single hilt contains a blade that divides halfway along its extent—one part narrows to a straight tip, the other is curved; the one element begins and ends as a sword, the other is bent into a sinister sickle, so a single maneuver can produce both a deadly lunge and a lethal slash. This was Andromeda's drama.

8    The sequel was Prometheus. Prometheus's bonds are iron and stone; Herakles' weapons are bow and spear; a bird is enjoying a visceral banquet. Poised at mid-incision, his beak continues to cut an already gaping wound, deeply inserted in the gastrointestinal trench, excavating for liver, which the artist has slightly revealed through the abdominal slit. His talons grip the giant's thigh.

Prometheus is caught in a painful convulsion: one side of his torso is contracted as he draws up his thigh towards himself, actually pressing the eagle deeper into his wound; his other leg is tautly stretched out, pointing downwards, narrowing to a point at the toes. Signs of his agony are etched on his face: arching brows, lips twisted to expose the teeth. You would have pitied the pain in this painting.

But Herakles comes to the rescue: he aims his bow at Prometheus's executioner. The arrow is fitted to the bow; his left arm is held straight, gripping the handle of the bow; his right arm is bent at the elbow, drawing back the bowstring to his right nipple. The design is an arrangement of interdependent angles, of bow, string, and arm: the bow is drawn back by the string; the string is plucked to a point by the arm; the arm is folded against the breast.

Prometheus is further torn by hope and despair: he stares both at his own wound and at Herakles, wanting to concentrate on the hero but forced to focus at least half of his attention on his own agony.

After two days of rest and recuperation we hired an Egyptian boat, 9 using the little bit of money we had tucked away under our belts, and sailed along the Nile to Alexandria, where we had decided to stay in hopes of locating our friends.

As we were sailing past one city, we suddenly heard a great outcry. Our sailor said, "Rangers,"[50] and swung the boat around to sail back in the opposite direction. All at once the shore was full of wild frightening men, all large and black (not deep black like Indians but as black as, say, a half-Ethiopian might be), bareheaded, heavyset but quick on their feet. They all shouted in a foreign language. The pilot said, "We're done for," and stopped the boat. (The river was very narrow at that point.)

Four of the bandits boarded and took everything on the boat including our bit of money. They tied us up and took us to a hut and left us under guard. They said they would bring us later to the bandit chief, whom they referred to as the King. This would involve a two-day journey, as we heard from those who were captured with us.

When it was night and the guards were asleep, as we lay there fettered 10 and forlorn, I at last felt free to weep for Leukippe. Thinking over all the troubles I had caused her, I groaned deep in my soul, concealing its actual sound within me.

"O gods and spirits, if you do exist and hear our prayers, what great crime did we commit, to be overwhelmed by this avalanche of adversities? Now you have put us in the hands of Egyptian bandits to deprive us even of sympathetic hearing. A Greek bandit would respond to our

---

50. *Boukoloi* ("Rangers") is both an ordinary word for cowherds and a proper name for Egyptian brigands (perhaps insurgents against foreign domination), who occupied the northwest wastelands of the Nile Delta. They figure both in history (Cassius Dio 71.4) and in fiction (Heliodoros, Lollianos), though the line between historical report and fictionalized account is hard to draw. See J. J. Winkler, "Lollianos and the Desperadoes," *Journal of Hellenic Studies* 100(1980): 155–81.

speech, and his hard heart might melt at our prayers. Speech often succeeds on its mission of mercy. The tongue as go-between serves the beleaguered soul, conveys its point of view to the listener, and mollifies his angry spirit. But now in what language will we frame our requests? What solemn oaths can we offer? If I were as persuasive as a Siren, still the butchers would not listen. I can only communicate my cause by expressive gestures, display my desires in sign language. O massive misfortunes! Must I pantomime my miseries?

"But I feel less sorrow for my own troubles—overwhelming though they be—than for yours, Leukippe. My mouth cannot mourn, my eyes cannot weep as they ought. You are faithful in the hard circumstances of love, a support to your lover in his trials. What a resplendent wedding: your bedroom is a prisoners' cell; your mattress is the ground; your garlands and bracelets are hawsers and wrist ropes; the bride's escort is a brigand sleeping at the door! Instead of the wedding march we hear a funeral song.

"We confessed our gratitude too soon, O sea. I reject your philanthropy: you were more humane to your dead victims than to us whom you saved only for a worse death. You spitefully decided that our death would be incomplete without bandits."

11 Such was my silent soliloquy; I could not weep. Eyes are known to have this property in the larger disasters of life. During moderate disasters, tears flow freely—interceding with the persecutors for their victims and relieving those who suffer, rather like lancing a boil. But on occasions of overwhelming unhappiness, tears simply fail, deserting the battle and leaving the eyes alone; for as the tears rise from within, they are met by grief, which checks their progress along the path to the eyes and carries them down again, condensing in a steady stream, into the soul. There they aggravate the wound.

I said to Leukippe, who was keeping utterly quiet: "Why are you silent, dearest? Why don't you say something to me?"

"Because, Kleitophon, my voice has died even before my soul."

12 Dawn crept up on us while we were talking. Then a man with a large and unruly mane of hair rode up on horseback. The horse also had a large mane. He was without caparison, not even a saddle blanket or cheekpieces. (Bandits' horses are always ridden bareback.) The man came with a message from the head pirate. "If any of the captives is a virgin, bring her to the god as a purification sacrifice for the group."

All eyes turned towards Leukippe, who clung fiercely to me and screamed. The pirates then began yanking and slugging: they yanked Leukippe and slugged me. They picked her up and carried her away on their shoulders; the rest of us were led more slowly in a chain gang.

13 When we had marched about a quarter of a mile from the village, we heard a great shouting and the sound of bugles, and a phalanx of the

Egyptian army appeared, all infantrymen. The bandits spotted them and halted, ready to fight them off. They put us in the center of the group. Soon they were upon us, fifty in number, some carrying full-length shields, others with light round shields. The outlaws, who greatly outnumbered them, took up clods of earth to hurl at the soldiers. An Egyptian clod is harder than any stone—heavy and rugged and irregular: its irregular surface contains sharp flinty edges, and it wounds two ways, by contusion from the heavy impact and by laceration from the sharp points. But this made little difference to the army, who warded off the clods with their shields.

When the effort of hurling the clods had left the bandits exhausted, the soldiers parted formation, and a company ran from their midst, armed with spears and swords, and as they ran they hurled javelins, and all hit their targets. Then the regular infantry advanced and closed battle, trading blows, wounds, and death. The soldiers' greater experience made up for what was lacking in their numbers.

We captives looked for the weakest point in the bandits' line of defense and, gathering ourselves in a tight body, made a run for it. We broke through their line and escaped to the opposition. The soldiers, initially unaware of what was happening, raised their weapons as if to cut us down, but when they noticed that we were unarmed and had our hands tied behind our backs, the truth dawned on them, and they allowed us to enter their ranks. We were sent to the rear to rest.

Reinforcements now arrived, namely, the Egyptian cavalry. As they drew near, they spread out on both sides and rode around either flank of the fighters, hemming them in and making a quick massacre. Soon the dead lay in heaps, the nearly dead still trying to fight; the rest were taken alive.

It was late afternoon when the battle ended. The commanding officer    14 summoned us for interrogation to learn who we were and how each of us had fallen into the hands of the bandits. We all told our tales in turn. When he had heard all our stories, he invited us to stay with him and offered to outfit us as soldiers. His plan now was to wait for the rest of the army and then make a concerted attack on the great City of the Bandits. They were said to number in the thousands.

I requested a horse, since I was an accomplished rider. When one was brought, I took him through his paces in a graceful display of the cavalry drill, and won high praise from the commander himself. He invited me to his table that day, and during dinner I responded to his inquiries by relating my entire history, to which he listened sympathetically. Compassion is a natural human response to a recital of wretched reversals, and pity is prompt to promote rapport. Feelings of sorrow soften the soul while troubles are being told, and by gradual degrees the auditor's pity mellows to amity, his grief to compassion. He was so moved by my story that he wept, but there was nothing more we could do as long as Leukippe was in the clutches of the outlaws. He assigned an Egyptian orderly to me to look after my needs.

15     The next day he made preparations to move forward by first filling the great trench that lay in the path of our march. We could in fact see brigands aplenty and fully armed standing on the opposite side of the trench. They had improvised an altar of earth and near it a coffin. Two of them were leading a girl to the altar with her hands tied behind her back. I couldn't see who they were in their armor, but I did recognize that the maiden was Leukippe. They poured a libation over her head and led her around the altar to the accompaniment of a flute and a priest intoning what I guessed was an Egyptian hymn—at least, the movements of his mouth and the distention of his facial muscles suggested that he was chanting.

Then at a signal they all moved far away from the altar. One of the attendants laid her on her back and tied her to stakes fixed in the ground, as sculptors picture Marsyas bound to the tree. He next raised a sword and plunged it into her heart and then sawed all the way down to her abdomen. Her viscera leaped out. The attendants pulled out her entrails and carried them in their hands over to the altar. When it was well done they carved the whole lot up, and all the bandits shared the meal.[51]

As each of these acts was performed, the soldiers and the general groaned aloud and averted their eyes from the sight. But I, contrary to all reason, just sat there staring. It was sheer shock: I was simply thunderstruck by the enormity of the calamity. Perhaps the myth of Niobe was no fiction after all: faced with the carnage of her children, she felt just as I did, and her emotional paralysis had given the appearance of petrifaction.

When the ceremony was concluded, so far as I could tell, they placed her body in the coffin, covered it with a lid, razed the altar, and ran away without looking behind them. All this was done according to the rubrics sanctioned by the priest.

16     By evening the trench was entirely filled in. The soldiers crossed over and camped a little way beyond. While they were at dinner, the general attempted to console my bitter grief.

At some point during the first night watch, having waited until everyone was asleep, I went out with my sword, intending to kill myself by the coffin. When I reached it, I drew my sword and said: "O poor Leukippe, least happy of all human beings! I do not mourn merely the fact of your death, nor its alien milieu, nor its violence, but rather the

---

51. Human sacrifice and cannibalistic communion occur together in Lollianos's *Phoinikika* (see later in this volume); for an argument that this is simply an extreme form of what all the novels cultivated, see Winkler, "Lollianos and the Desperadoes," esp. 166–75.

farce your murderers made of your misfortune, that you were an expia-
tion for those execrable bodies, that they slit you (alas!) alive, witnessing
your own incision. They took communion of the secrets of your stomach and left what was left of you on an abject altar and bier. Your body
is laid out here, but where will I find your vitals? Oh, far less devastating
had the fire devoured them, but no—your insides are inside the outlaws,
victuals in the vitals of bandits.

"Oh, wicked votive candles! Oh, strange communion service! The
gods above observed this sacrifice—yet the fire was not extinguished; the
flame burned on and wafted the savor upwards to their nostrils. And
now, my Leukippe, receive this appropriate libation."

I held my sword up, poised to plunge it down through my throat. In    17
the light of the full moon I saw two men running quickly towards me.
Thinking they were bandits, I waited for them to come and kill me, but
as they came nearer they began to shout. It was Menelaos and Satyros.
And yet, in spite of the unexpected discovery that two close friends of
mine were alive, I could not bring myself to embrace them or feel any
real joy, my mind was so numb with grief. They grabbed my hand and
tried to take away the sword.

"By all the gods," I cried, "do not deny me this noble death, this
medicine, rather, to heal my misery. I cannot continue living, even if
you try to force me, now that Leukippe has died such a death. You can
take away this sword, but the sword of grief is even now driven into my
heart and cuts deeper every moment. Would you have me linger forever
on the edge of death?"

Menelaos replied: "If this is your reason for dying, hold your sword.
Leukippe will now come to life again."

I stared at him and said: "How can you mock me in my misery?
That's a fine tribute, Menelaos, to the god who watches over strangers
abroad."

Then he tapped on the coffin. "Since Kleitophon doesn't believe me,
tell him yourself that you're alive, Leukippe." As he said this he tapped
on the top of the coffin a second and a third time, and I heard a delicate
voice from under the lid. I began to tremble all over and looked at
Menelaos, wondering whether he was a magus. He opened the coffin,
and Leukippe rose up, a frightening (O gods!) and blood-chilling sight.
The entire length of her stomach hung open, and the visceral cavity was
hollow. She fell into my arms' embrace, we pressed close, and then we
both collapsed.

When I gradually came to, I asked Menelaos: "Tell me what's going    18
on. This is Leukippe, isn't it—her body I hold, her voice I hear? Then
what was all that I saw yesterday? One or the other has to be a dream.
But this kiss is real and alive; its sweetness is none other than
Leukippe's."

"And now," said Menelaos, "she will recover her innards, her frontal gash will grow together, and you will see her once more sound. But cover your eyes, for I am summoning Hekate to the deed."

I trusted him and covered my face. He began some hocus-pocus and recited some magic words. Then, as he spoke, he removed a contraption from her stomach and restored her to her original condition.

"Open your eyes," he said.

I was very slow and fearful about doing so, for I did indeed think Hekate was there, but finally I removed my hands from my eyes and saw Leukippe intact and sound.

Still more amazed, I asked Menelaos, "My dearest friend, if you are some servant of the gods, I beg you to tell me where in the world I am and what am I seeing."

And Leukippe said: "Menelaos, stop frightening him. Tell him how you fooled the bandits."

19 Menelaos said: "Well, you know that I am Egyptian; I told you all about that on board the ship. Most of my property was in the vicinity of this village, and I know the important men of the town. After the ship was wrecked, the waves tossed me onto the Egyptian coast, where Satyros and I were captured by the bandits who patrol this region. As I was being led to the bandit chief, some of the men suddenly recognized me and untied me with encouraging remarks to buck up and join the bandits, since I was practically one of the family. I asked for Satyros as my attendant. 'But first,' they said, 'you must prove you've got guts.' Just then an oracle was received to sacrifice a virgin for the purification of the bandits' citadel, to partake of her immolated liver, to consign her remains to a coffin and leave the area so that the enemy army would cross the place of sacrifice. Tell him the rest, Satyros: from here on it's your story."

20 And Satyros continued: "While I was being dragged towards their camp, I wept and mourned, master, for I had learned the fate of Leukippe, and I begged Menelaos to save her by any and every means. Some kind god came to our help.

"It was the day before the sacrifice, and we happened to be sitting by the sea, feeling very depressed and mulling over our dilemma. Some of the bandits spotted a ship that had innocently wandered that way and set out after it. The men on the ship realized who it was they had run into and tried to back water, but when the bandits caught up with them, they made a stand. One of the passengers was a professional stage actor who gave dramatic readings from Homer.[52] He armed himself and his fellow passengers with some props from his Homeric act and tried to fight. In fact they acquitted themselves rather well against the first line of assault.

52. Such performers are mentioned by Achilles' contemporaries Athenaios (*Deipnosophistai* 14.620B) and Artemidoros (*Oneirokritika* 4.2).

But more and more bandit vessels sailed against the ship and sank it, and they killed the survivors in the water.

"But in the wreckage of the ship a chest was diverted and carried to shore at our feet. Menalaos took it up and we carried it some distance away, thinking it might contain something important. He opened it, and we discovered therein a tragic robe and a sword with an eight-inch hilt but an extremely short blade, no more than an inch and a half. As Menelaos was handling it, without any special thought he happened to point it downwards, and the insignificant blade suddenly shot out from its hiding place in the hilt, adding that extra eight inches to its length. When it was pointed upwards, the blade slid back in again. This was obviously one of that poor man's props, used for staging a spurious slaughter.

"I said to Menelaos: 'If you are willing to do a good deed, god will fight on our side. We now have the means to save the girl and elude the bandits. Listen to my plan. We take an animal hide, as soft a one as we can find, and sew it into a pouch about the size of a human stomach. Then we fill it with other creatures' bloody entrails and resew the pseudo-stomach tightly enough so the viscera won't drip. We tie it onto the girl and then dress her in an outer garment with sashes and girdles to hide the paraphernalia. The oracle's prescription is propitious for deception. It requires a long robe to be rent in the midriff. Now, you see this trick sword? If you press it against a body, it retreats into the hilt as into a sheath. The audience believes the blade is penetrating the body, but actually it retires into the recessed hilt, leaving just enough point to cut the deceptive diaphragm and let the hilt itself rest flush against the victim. And when you draw the blade from the wound, the sword emerges from its recess exactly as the hilt is drawn upwards, and again misleads the spectators, for the blade appears to plunge down into the wound as far as it protrudes from the gadget. If we use this, the bandits will never perceive the ruse. The skin will be concealed, the guts will eject on cue, and we will take them to the altar for the sacrifice. From this point on, the bandits are not to come near the body, but we will lay it in the coffin. You heard the bandit chief just a little while ago say that we had to show our courage: now you can go to him and promise just such a show.'

"After outlining this plan I earnestly entreated him to help me, invoking Zeus Patron of Travelers, reminding him too of our common meals and shared shipwreck.

"And this worthy gentleman answered, 'It is a large undertaking, but in the name of friendship, the risk is surely right, and even if we must die in the doing, such a death would be sweet.'

"'I believe,' I said, 'that Kleitophon too is still alive. While I was making my inquiries, the girl said that when she left him the original captors still held him bound, but some of that band have since come to the ban-

21

22

dit chief and reported that all the captives escaped on the march to the camp. So you will be earning Kleitophon's gratitude at the same time that you show compassion for a poor girl in desperate straits.'

"This speech convinced him, and Fortune acted as our co-conspirator.

"I set to work preparing the equipment. Menelaos was on the point of speaking to the bandits about the sacrifice when by a bit of inspired luck the chief anticipated him. 'We have a tradition that sacrifices, especially human sacrifices, must be performed by newly initiated bandits. Prepare yourselves to carry out tomorrow's sacrifice. Oh yes, and your servant will be initiated with you.'

" 'Yes sir! We are ready to live up to the highest standards of banditry. We will personally undertake that the girl be suitably dressed for her dissection.'

" 'The ceremony is entirely in your hands,' said the chief.

"Privately then we equipped Leukippe as we told you and encouraged her to be brave, explaining each phase of the mission, especially how she had to stay inside the coffin as long as it was daylight and not try to come out even if she woke up early. 'If we run into any hitch, make a dash for the army camp and save yourself.' And so we led her to the altar. You know the rest."

23 Their tale left me helpless with various emotions, and I was at a loss what to do to show my gratitude to Menelaos. I did the most obvious thing: fell into his arms with a tremendous hug and then knelt in humble adoration, as if he were a god. My soul was swamped in pure rapture. Now that Leukippe's safety was assured, I asked, "And what became of Kleinias?"

Menelaos replied: "I do not know. After the ship went down I saw him clinging to a spar, but where it took him I do not know."

Overjoyed as I was, I cried out in distress. Some power above, it seemed, had resented the perfection of my happiness. Kleinias—gone from the face of the earth, and all because he had tried to help me; Kleinias—my mentor, after Leukippe; Kleinias—out of all the rest, he alone was swallowed by the sea, losing not only life but proper burial.

"O senseless sea, out of pure jealousy you refused to let your drama of human kindness reach a perfectly happy ending!"

And so we went back together to the camp and passed the rest of the night in my tent. Our adventure soon became common knowledge.

24 At dawn I took Menelaos to the general and explained everything. He was very pleased and treated Menelaos as a friend. He asked him about the size of the enemy forces. Menelaos said that the entire population of the next inhabited area were desperadoes, a robbers' nest numbering in the tens of thousands. The general said: "The five thousand we have can handle twenty thousand of them. An additional force of two thousand

men will presently arrive, drawn from the troops stationed along the delta and at Heliopolis against these barbarians."

As he said this, a slave ran in to announce that a messenger from the camp on the delta had arrived and that the two thousand men would not leave for five more days. The barbarian incursions had been repelled, but just as the force was about to set out the sacred bird had arrived bearing his father's bier. So the expedition had to be put off for five days.

"What is this bird," I asked, "who commands such respect? And what   25 sort of casket did you say he was carrying?"

"The bird is Phoenician in name, but Ethiopian in origin. He is about the size of a peacock but surpasses the peacock in the beauty of his plumage, a blend of gold and deepest red. He proudly claims the Sun as his master, and this is confirmed by the shape of his head, crowned (as it is) by a stately circle, an image of the sun itself: deep crimson in color, comparable to a rose, a beautiful arrangement of projecting rays which are actually rudimentary feathers.

"The Ethiopians claim the honor of his lifetime residence, the Egyptians of his death. For when he dies (which happens only after a very long lifetime), his son brings him to the Nile, constructing from his own resources a burial box. He collects a lump of the most fragrant myrrh, of a size sufficient to contain his father, and digs it hollow with his beak to form a resting place for the corpse. He tucks the body into this coffin and seals it with a lump of mud. Then he delivers his handiwork to the banks of the Nile.

"A chorus of other birds accompanies him like a guard of honor, and the young phoenix is like nothing so much as a great king out on an expedition. He unerringly proceeds to the City of the Sun, Heliopolis, the migratory goal of the deceased phoenix. He rests on high, surveying the city, and allows the representatives of the god to approach. An Egyptian priest brings a book from the inmost tabernacle and examines the bird according to the holy writ. The phoenix knows that his authenticity is being questioned and points to the ineffable symbols of his physical identity, proudly displays the corpse, and puts on a funeral ceremony. The priests of Helios receive the dead phoenix and give it burial. Ethiopia gave him sustenance in life; Egypt gives him sepulture in death."

## Book Four

The general, on learning of the enemy's preparedness and the allies' de-   1 lay, decided to turn back to the village from which we had set out, until his reinforcements should arrive. A house was assigned to me and Leukippe a short distance up the street from the general's headquarters.

When I went in I embraced her and felt in myself certain stirrings of

manly energy. But she shied away, and I said: "How long are we to defer the rites of Aphrodite? Consider the incredible adventures we have already gone through—shipwreck, pirates, human sacrifice, ritual murder.
Let us use this opportunity while Fortune is smiling from clear skies: this
may be the calm before a greater storm."

And she replied: "But it would still be wrong to do that. The day before yesterday, when I was crying because I was going to be butchered,
Artemis appeared, standing above me in my sleep, and said, 'Do not be
sad, you shall not die, for I will stand by you and help you. You will remain a virgin until I myself give you away as a bride. No one but
Kleitophon will marry you.' Of course I was upset at the postponement
but very glad of our expectations."

When I heard her dream, I remembered having a similar one myself.
On the previous night I had dreamed about a temple of Aphrodite, and
inside the temple was a statue of the goddess. When I approached to
pray, the doors slammed shut. I was disappointed, but a woman appeared who looked just like the statue in the temple and said, "You are
not allowed to enter the sanctuary at this time; but if you wait a short
while, I will not only open the doors for you but make you a high priest
of the goddess of love." I related this dream to Leukippe and made no
further attempt to ravish her. When I carefully considered the implications of Leukippe's dream, I was more than a little upset.[53]

2      Meanwhile Charmides (that was the general's name) began to cast his
eye on Leukippe. This came about in the following way. Some men had
captured a remarkable river creature, which the Egyptians call the Nile
horse. The term *horse* might properly be applied to its belly and legs, except that it has a cloven hoof; but in size it is closer to the largest of cattle, with a short, hairless tail; and indeed the hide is hairless on every part
of its body. Its head is rounded, ears minute, cheeks somewhat horselike,
great flaring nostrils breathing out a smoky exhalation as from a hidden
fire; jaws as wide as its cheeks are long; the mouth open all the way back
to the temples; curved canines, in form and position like a boar's but
three times as big.

3      The general invited us to view the catch. Leukippe too went along.
While we were eyeing the animal, the general was eyeing Leukippe, and
suddenly he was trapped. Desiring to prolong our presence as long as
possible so he could feast his eyes on her, he searched out topics of conversation, telling first what he knew of the species, then how it is
hunted, about its insatiable appetite, which makes it devour whole fields
of grain, and the trick that traps it.

The hunters carefully note its haunts and dig there a pit, hidden by a
clay-and-wattle cover. Below the fragile facade of reeds is placed a

53. Artemidoros discusses dreams of marriage with his section on death, "since marriage is like death and is signified by death" (*Oneirokritika* 2.65).

wooden cage with doors open on top facing the trench roof, just waiting for the beast to drop in. As soon as he sets hoof on the roof it chutes him into the cage like a cubbyhole, and the hunters run up and close the doors. This is the only way he can be hunted, since no one can bring him to bay by force or direct confrontation. "His defenses are formidable, especially his hide, which you see is quite thick and renders him indifferent to injury from weapons. He is a sort of Egyptian equivalent of the elephant of India, which is perhaps the only creature mightier than he is."

And Menelaos said, "Oh, have you ever seen an elephant?"

"I have indeed," said Charmides, "and I have heard experts describe its incredible gestation."

"We have never yet seen one," I said, "except in pictures."[54]

"I'd be glad to tell you all about it; we have plenty of time. The mother conceives and carries her offspring for the longest period—a full ten years of intrauterine development.[55] Finally, at the end of this long decade, she gives birth, when the fetus is almost senile. From this fundamental fact we can explain its great size, its nonaggression, its long life span and tardy demise. They claim that it lives longer than Hesiod's fabled crow.[56]

"The elephant's jaw is the size of an ox's head, and to look at it you would think it had two horns growing in its mouth: these are its curved tusks. Between them grows the trunk, something like a long trumpet in shape and size, a multipurpose tool of great value. It forages for food and any edible that comes within reach. The trunk reaches out to the staples of his diet, plucks them, and curls up from below and offers them to his mouth. When he spots a delicacy, he lassos it with a tight knot of his trunk and lifts it up whole above his head as an offering to his master, for an Ethiopian keeper rides on his back—a strange sort of pachyderm jockey. The elephant's behavior is ingratiating and timorous; he attends to the intonations of his master's voice and patiently endures the goad, which is an iron ankus.

"Once I saw an incredible thing: a Greek man inserted his own head right up into the head of an elephant, who had opened wide his mouth and was breathing around the human intrusion. Both were quite amazing—the man's courage and the elephant's tolerance. The man said that he had given the creature a reward, for the following reason: its exhaled breath is almost indistinguishable from Indian spices and is an excellent

4

---

54. For a roughly contemporary interest in exotic beasts known through pictures: Herodian (1.15.45) describes Commodus's fights in the amphitheater with strange animals brought from India and Ethiopia and hitherto known "only from pictures."

55. Both accurate and fantastic reports of elephant gestation were current. Achilles Tatius's preference for folklore over more accurate information is part of the same mischievous attitude that refuses to use Roman political terms in referring to the Roman offices (see note 58).

56. Hesiod frag. 304 Merkelbach-West (Plutarch De defectu oraculorum 415C).

remedy for headaches. Now the elephant is aware of the value of his services and does not open its mouth *gratis,* but like a quack doctor insists on prior payment. So if you give it to him, he agrees and keeps his part of the bargain, opening his jaws wide and waiting as long as the man wants. He knows he has bartered his breath."

5 "And how," I asked, "does this great hulking beast come to have such fragrant breath?"

"Alimentary, my dear Kleitophon: the solution lies in his diet," continued Charmides. "India is situated near the sun: they are the first to see the god's ascent, his light shines more warmly on them, and their bodies absorb his fiery rays. Now in Greece there grows a flower of Ethiopian color that in India is a nonflowering shrub, like our leafy bushes. It hides its fragrance and conceals its scent; either it is too well bred to make a point of its own excellence in company already aware of it, or else it resents sharing anything with its fellow citizens. But once it crosses the border and gets a little way from its own country, it discloses hidden aromatic resources, emerges from mere foliation to full flowerhood, and revels in its own scentuality.

"This is the dusky rose of India—their elephant fodder, as grass is for our cattle. Since this is the constant nourishment of every elephant from birth, a certain wholesome spiciness is a natural by-product of their nutrition: they generate an intensely fragrant inward vapor that is the perfumifacient principle of their breath."[57]

6 When we finally left the general's company and conversation, he waited only a short while (a man so wounded can scarce endure the pressure of his fever). He summoned Menelaos and, grasping his hand, said: "I know the depth and quality of your friendship from your services to Kleitophon. You will find me no less grateful. I now must ask of you a favor, a mere nothing to you, but it will save my life if you accept. Leukippe holds my life in her hands: you must be my savior. She is still obligated to you for saving her life. Fifty gold pieces are yours for your service in this matter, and gold to her heart's content for her."

Menelaos answered: "Keep your money for those who sell their favors. I will see what I can do as your friend."

Then he came and told me everything. We racked our brains for a plan and decided to mislead him. Outright refusal would run the risk of provoking violence; escape was out of the question, as there were bandits everywhere, and he had such a large force under him.

7 So a little while later Menelaos went back to Charmides and said: "It's all set. At first, of course, she refused in the most strenuous terms, but when I persisted and reminded her of all I had done for her, she con-

---

57. No one has identified the plant described in chapter 5; clove, cinnamon, and *Althaea rosea* (hollyhock) have all been suggested.

elephants

Charmeus employs Menelaos to seduce Leukippe

sented. But she does have one small and quite reasonable request, that you grant her a few days' grace until she gets to Alexandria: for in a village like this, everyone knows what is going on; nothing is secret."

"That's a long delay to ask for," said Charmides. "War doesn't allow a man leisure to postpone desires. How can a soldier with a war on his hands have any idea of how long he will live? There are so many ways to die. Ask Fortune to grant me a safe-conduct, and I will wait. I am about to battle against the Rangers, but another battle is being waged in my soul. The enemy within is besieging me with his bow, harassing me with arrows: I have lost the fight; I am bristling with his shafts. Call the doctor, sir, and quickly; my wounds demand immediate attention. True, I fight mortal enemies with fire, but Eros hurls his own burning brands at me. O Menelaos, quench this fire first. Premartial sex is a good omen for success. Let Aphrodite set me up for Ares."

And Menelaos replied, "But you see it's not easy for her to avoid her boyfriend, not to mention the fact that he is madly in love with her."

"We can dispose of Kleitophon: that's no problem."

Menelaos, realizing that Charmides was serious and that I was in danger, thought up a reasonable excuse *ex tempore.*

"Well, do you want to know the real reason for her delay? She had her period just yesterday, and it is not decent for her to be that close to a man."

"In that case we'll wait," said Charmides, "three or four days. That should be enough. For now, I'd like her to go as far as decency does allow: let me look at her and talk with her. I want to hear her voice, hold her hand, touch her body: such foreplay has some satisfaction. And then too we might kiss: her female problems are no obstacle to that, I trust."

When Menelaos came back and reported all this, I cried out in response that I would rather die than stand by and witness this alienation of osculation.                                                                                          8

"Is there anything more delicious than a kiss? Aphrodite's consummation is a fully filling finale; take away kisses and it's nothing. For a kiss has no moment of satiation, no point of no return, the novelty never wears off.

"The mouth has three exciting features: breath, voice, and kiss. Though only the lips come in contact, a geyser of pleasures spouts up from the very soul. Believe me when I say, Menelaos (for even in the midst of misery I shall reveal our mysteries), that I myself have tasted nothing of Leukippe's love beyond her lips. She is a virgin to this day: my spouse in kisses only. If someone snatches these as well, I will not bear the loss. They're *my* kisses, and I won't let them be adulterated by another man."

"Then we need a good plan," said Menelaos, "and we need it now. A lover can wait as long as he has his hopes up—his desires aroused for a rousing denouement. But once he has given up hope, his desire changes, and he applies his passion, as far as he can, to inflicting similar pain on whatever is blocking his path. And if he has the force to impose penalties with impunity, his feeling of security intensifies with resentment. We have a problem, and every minute makes it worse."

9    While we were talking this over, someone ran in bursting with excitement and said that as Leukippe was walking along, she had suddenly fallen down, and her eyes were rolling in their sockets. We ran over and found her sprawled on the ground. I went up to her and asked what was the matter. When she saw me, she leaped up and hit me in the face, staring at me with bloodshot eyes. When Menelaos tried to restrain her, she kicked him in the shins. Surmising that her problem was some mental derangement, we grabbed her and tried to pin her down. She wrestled with both of us, oblivious to all the conventions of womanly modesty. There was an uproar around the tent: the general himself ran in and took in everything at a glance. At first he had suspicions that it was merely a trick attack staged for his benefit, and he glowered at Menelaos. But as he gradually realized the truth, he too was moved to pity. They brought ropes and tied up the unfortunate woman.

When I saw her arms tied I begged Menelaos (after the crowd had left): "Release her, I beg you, release her. These tender arms should not be cramped by cords. Leave me alone with her: I will hold her tightly in my embrace and take the place of these straps. Let all her rage vent itself on me. Why should I continue to live if Leukippe does not recognize me? She lies here lashed and bound, and I, heartless brute, who could release her, won't.

"Did Fortune rescue us from robbers for you to become dementia's pawn? Our good fortune in each case has proved bad luck: we have escaped domestic danger only to suffer shipwreck; we have survived the sea and eluded the outlaws, yes—because we were being groomed for delirium. And if you ever do recover your wits, my dearest, I can only fear that god must have some other calamity in store. Who could be more disaster-prone than we, who are even frightened of good fortune? But if only you would return to sanity and self-possession, let Fortune begin a new round of her game."

10   Menelaos tried to console me, claiming that such seizures were not a permanent disability but were in many cases a normal side effect of youthful exuberance: young blood seething in its own strength may boil over the veins and rise inside the head, where by flooding it impedes the circuits of rational thought; so we should send for doctors and nurse her back to health. Menelaos approached the general and asked that the army surgeon be assigned to her case, which he was glad to do (as a lover loves to make arrangements that affect his *affaire*).

The doctor arrived and said: "We must make her rest, to calm the manic energy now at its peak. Sleep is a remedy that suits every malady. When the crisis is past, we will see to her further treatment."

Then he dispensed a small amount of medication about the size of a bitter vetch seed, with instructions to dissolve it in oil and dab it on the top of her head. He said he would prepare another drug to purge her stomach. We did as he said, and a short while after the treatment, Leukippe fell asleep and did not awake until morning.

I kept watch through the entire night, weeping by her bedside, watching the ropes that bound her. "Dearest Leukippe, even asleep you are tied; not even your sleep is free. What fancies are running through your head? Are you sane in your sleep, or is your dream life wild as well?" When she awoke, her cries again were unintelligible. The doctor returned and applied further treatments.

In the meantime a messenger from the satrap[58] of Egypt arrived with a 11 letter to the general. It must have contained directions to prosecute the campaign, for he immediately gave orders for all his men to arm themselves for a battle with the Rangers. Each man leaped instantly to action, running at top speed to his own equipment and then back in a moment to his squadron leader. At that point the general announced the password and gave orders to bivouac, then retired to his own quarters. At dawn the next day he led the army out against the enemy.

Now, to describe the enemy's settlement: the Nile flows northward from Egyptian Thebes and maintains the same breadth until Memphis or a little beyond. The village Kerkasoros marks the end of the great stream. There it divides into three rivers, the two outer ones forming the sides of the delta and the central one flowing on as before. Nor do any of these reach the sea intact, but each divides into further branches, as it reaches one town after another; and even so these subdivided streams are greater than what are called rivers in Greece. Its waters, though parted, are never exhausted but suffice for sailing and drinking and irrigation.

The mighty Nile is everything to them: a river, a land, a sea, a lake— 12 affording to the eye novel conjunctions of ships and spades, paddles and plows, rudders and sickles, where sailors consort with farmers and cattle are neighbors to fish. You sow where once you sailed, and the field you sow is a sea brought under cultivation. The river, you see, keeps to a schedule of visits; an Egyptian may sit and wait for the river's arrival,

58. The use of an archaizing Persian term, familiar from classical Attic literature, is a stylistic elegance rather than an attempt to set the story in early times; see H. J. Mason "The Roman Government in Greek Sources: The Effect of Literary Theory on the Translation of Official Titles," *Phoenix* 24(1970): 150–59. Plepelits, *Achilleus Tatios*, 18ff., demonstrates that the story is set in the period of the Roman Empire, although it is difficult to be more precise.

counting the days. And the Nile never forgets its obligations, but watches for deadlines and measures out its water. It is a river unwilling to be found unpunctual. River and land can be seen to strive in friendly competition, the river turning so much land into a sea, the land in turn absorbing so great and sweet a sea. Their victories show perfect equality—neither is ever the loser; the water and land are always coterminous.

In the region where the Rangers dwell the river is always abundant. When all the land is inundated, lakes are formed; and even when the Nile retreats, the lakes remain, holding less water but full of mud from the water. On these lakes the Rangers can both walk and sail. No boat can make any headway other than a boat carrying one person only—the mud impedes and holds all nonlocal vessels, but they have small light boats requiring only a little water. And if it is utterly waterless, they portage their boats until they come to water again.

In these lakes are scattered islands, some of which have no houses but are overgrown with papyrus reeds. The rows of papyrus grow close together, with just enough room in between for a man to stand; these corridors between close-set ranks are covered above by the papyrus fronds, so the Rangers run under them and there hold council or lie in ambush or concealment behind walls of papyrus. Some of the islands have huts and look like rough imitations of cities, encircled by lake waters in place of walls, and these are where the Rangers reside.

One of the nearby islands is larger and has more huts (I believe its name is Nikochis). They all assembled here, thinking it their strongest position, confident both of their numbers and its geography. Only a narrow belt of land keeps it from being a perfect island. It is six hundred feet long and seventy-five feet wide. The settlement was surrounded by marshes on all sides.

13 When they saw the general approaching, they devised the following plan: all the old men assembled in a body, carrying fronds of palm like suppliants, while behind them were stationed the strongest of the younger men with shields and spears. The old men were to hold their branches high as a leafy cover for the men behind, who dragged their spears along the ground for minimal visibility. If the general gave in to the old men's prayers for mercy, the spearmen would initiate no violence; otherwise they would pretend to submit to execution but inveigle him back to their city, and in the middle of the narrow causeway the old men at a signal would drop off their branches and run while the armed men would charge forward and wreak what havoc they could.

So the old men got themselves ready according to the plan and met the general, begging him to respect their advanced age, respect their suppliant branches, and spare their city. They offered him a personal gift of

the Rangers trick
the Egyptian general

a hundred silver talents and promised that a hundred of their men, who were willing to sacrifice themselves for the benefit of the city, would go with him to the satrap's palace as a prize of war. This was not a false offer, but one they would have honored if the general had been willing to accept it. But he would make no such agreement. "Very well," said the old men, "if that is your decision, we will bear our fate. But grant us one favor in our last extremity: do not kill us outside our gates and far from our city, but take us to the land of our fathers, the hearths where we were born. Let our city be our tomb: behold, we will lead our own funeral procession." The general then relaxed his battle readiness and ordered his troops to follow at their ease.

All this was being watched by distant scouts whom the Rangers had ordered, if they saw the enemy crossing the causeway, to break down the dikes and let a flood of water swamp them. Each water channel running from the Nile has an earthen barrier built by the Egyptians in case the river rises and floods the land before the time when it is most needed. Whenever they need to water the plain, they open the barrier a little until the river starts to flow. Now, behind the village there was just such a conduit, large and broad. When the men assigned this task saw the enemy coming, they quickly cut through the dam. Everything happened at once: the old men in front suddenly parted; the spearmen ran forward; the water flooded in; the standing lakes began to swell, getting bigger on all sides; the isthmus was awash; everything in effect was sea. The Rangers attacked and speared the front ranks of the army and the general himself, all of whom were caught off guard as they watched the strange event.

The deaths of the others passed all description: some died in the first assault without so much as brandishing a spear; others hadn't a moment to defend themselves but felt the blow as they saw it coming. Some felt it before they knew what hit them; others stood in shocked horror, waiting for their death. Some made a single move and slipped in the water, as the river took their legs from under them; others, trying to escape, tumbled down into the depths of the lake and were swept under. The water, now as high as the waists of the men who stood on land, surged against their shields and exposed their stomachs to attack; the levels in the lake were well over the head of a man everywhere. It was impossible to discriminate what was lake and what was ground: those who ran away went slowly for fear of slipping off the land and so were swiftly taken, and those who mistook lake for land in their flight sank beneath the waters.

Novel accidents and shipwreck everywhere without a ship: both were new and paradoxical—land troops fighting in water and shipwreck on the land. The bandits exulted in their triumph, thinking it due to their courage rather than to a deceitful trick. Egyptians are quite cowed by cowardice in moments of fright, but when they feel brave their bravado knows no bounds. Both reactions are extreme: they accept disaster in a very despondent spirit, and display rashness in victory.

15    Leukippe had now suffered through ten days of fitful dementia with no improvement. Then one night in her sleep she cried out in a frenzy, "I am mad because of you, Gorgias." When morning came, I reported her remark to Menelaos, and we began to search the village for a man named Gorgias. As we were walking along the streets, a young man came up to us. "I have come to be your savior," he said, "and your wife's too."

Startled, I supposed that he had been sent by the gods and said, "Your name wouldn't happen to be Gorgias?"

"Oh, no," he replied. "My name is Chaireas. It is Gorgias who destroyed you!"

"Gorgias!" said I, now even more distraught. "Destroyed? How? Who is this Gorgias? Some spirit pronounced his name to me in the night. Interpret that divine message for me!"

"Yes, Gorgias was an Egyptian soldier—*was:* he is dead now; the Rangers finished him. He lusted after your wife, and used his pharmaceutical genius to concoct an aphrodisiac which he then persuaded your Egyptian valet to mingle in Leukippe's cup. But by mistake he administered it full strength and the undiluted dose brought insanity. You see, I learned all this yesterday from Gorgias's own orderly, who was on campaign with him against the Rangers. Fortune, it seems, has saved him to help you. He now requests a fee of four gold pieces for Leukippe's cure. He claims he has a recipe for another elixir that will counteract the effects of the first."

"A thousand blessings on you," I said, "for your kindness. This man you mentioned—bring him to us."

Chaireas departed. I went inside to the valet and struck him in the face with my fist, then again, and then again. I shouted at him: "Tell me what you gave Leukippe? What made her go crazy?"

He was so frightened that he made a complete confession of everything, just as Chaireas had told us. We kept him in custody under lock and key.

16    Meanwhile, Chaireas arrived with Gorgias's attendant. I said to them: "You've already earned your four gold pieces for giving good information. But as to further pharmacy—well, hear me out. Clearly drugs were responsible for her present plight; it is risky to add medication to a system already drugged. You must therefore tell me exactly what you are putting into the remedy and prepare it in our presence. Another four gold pieces are yours if you do it."

"Your caution is justified. In fact all the ingredients are common ones and perfectly edible. I myself will drink an equal portion of the drug I give her."

He then listed each ingredient for someone to buy and bring back to him. As soon as everything was assembled, we gathered around, and he mortar-and-pestled it all together and then divided it into two equal portions. "I'll drink one of these first, then give the other to your wife. When she has taken it, she will sleep soundly all night long, and around dawn she will awake to the real world and to her right mind."

He quaffed one cup and told us to give her the other in the evening. "I'm going home to sleep, as the prescription requires."

He left with a payment of four gold pieces. "I'll give you the rest," I said, "if she recovers."

When the time came for her to drink the potion, I filled the cup and prayed: "O drug, born of Earth, boon of Asklepios, prove true to your prescription. Be a safer, more effective remedy than I was. Bring quick relief to my darling Leukippe. Drive that other wild and barbarous drug out of her head and down to defeat!" After these words of cordial encouragement to the elixir, I kissed the brim and gave it to Leukippe to drink. Just as the man had said, she soon lay sleeping. I sat by her bedside and talked on as if she were listening.

"Will ever your mind uncloud, Leukippe? Will you ever recognize me? Will I hear that voice again? Give me a sign in your sleep. Yesterday your word was 'Gorgias,' and that oracle proved true. Your luck seems to improve when you're unconscious. Your waking hours are hysterical, but your dreams at least show sense."

While I talked on as if she were listening, gradually the dawn, so long desired, arose, and then Leukippe spoke and the word she said was "Kleitophon."

I leaped up and drew near to her, asking how she felt. She seemed to have no awareness of anything she had done but was amazed at being in bondage and asked who had tied her up. I saw that she was perfectly sane, and with a great whoop of joy I untied her and then explained at some length all that had passed. She was embarrassed to hear what she had done, and blushed as if it were happening now. I began to comfort her, and cheerfully paid the man for his restorative. All of our travel monies were intact: Satyros had his money belt on when the ship went down, and both he and Menelaos had kept their money safe from the bandits.

In the meantime a stronger force against the bandits arrived from the capital, and their entire citadel was razed to the ground.

Now that the river was once again secure from the violence of the Rangers, we prepared to sail to Alexandria. Chaireas was traveling with

17

18

us, for he had become a friend since he had given us information about the drug. His home was the island of Pharos, and he was a fisherman by trade. He had joined the navy as a mercenary for the campaign against the Rangers, so that now the war was over he was free to leave.

Because of the long embargo, there were vessels crowding everywhere—and in all directions a colorful scene was spread before your eyes: choruses of sailors singing chanteys, passengers clapping hands, a naval oratorio. The river was one unending holiday; our sailing a celebration of the river.

And then I took my first taste of the Nile, unadulterated by wine, to see how sweet that water was; for water wanes when wine intervenes. I scooped some up in a clear glass goblet and watched the water and its vessel compete for clarity: the glass lost. The water was sweet and cold, though not unpleasantly cold—I know some comparable streams in Greece whose cold can cut your tongue. Accordingly the people of Egypt are not afraid to drink this water neat, disdaining Dionysos. And I was struck, too, by their drinking style: they scorn all use of bucket or cup, when nature has fashioned a drinking instrument right at hand—the hand. If anyone is cruising down the stream and feels a little thirsty, he pokes his head over the side, leans towards the water, lowers hand, forms cup, aims a fistful mouth-wards, and launches it on target—the gaping mouth awaits the shot, receives it, closes, and doesn't spill a drop.

19     And I saw another creature of the Nile, a beast celebrated as being more ferocious than the river horse. Their name for it is crocodile. Nature has crossed categories to breed this fish-animal. Its body is huge from head to tail, but disproportionately thin and narrow. Its hide is a wrinklework of scales, black rocky back, white underbelly, walking on four bowlegged buttresses like a tortoise; long, bulky tail like a solid body, not simply an omissible appendage as in other animals, but the continuation of its single spinebone, and a functional limb. The upper side rises into ugly spines like saw teeth. When hunting food and wrestling down victims, it lashes them with its tail as with a whip, inflicting multiple lacerations with a single blow. The head is directly joined to the line of the back: nature has robbed it of a neck; the head is more ferocious than the rest of the body, stretches endlessly along the jaws, and all of it opens. At other times, when the mouth is not gaping, it is only a head, but when it opens its jaws to prey, it becomes all mouth. Only the upper jaw moves; the lower one stays fixed in place. The span is incredible—a chasm as far back as the shoulders, opening directly onto the stomach. Inside, infinite vistas of teeth—according to popular belief, the crocodile has as many teeth as the year has days of god's own sunshine—a vigorous crop flourishing on the broad field of its jaws. When it comes

out of the water onto the land, it so drags its body that you would surely underestimate its force.

## Book Five

We sailed into Alexandria three days later. As I was coming up to the 1 city entrance whose gates are dedicated to Helios, suddenly the beauty of the city struck me like a flash of lightning. My eyes were filled to the brim with pleasure. A double row of columns led straight across the entire city from this entrance of Helios to the opposite entrance of Selene, Sun and Moon being the guardians of the city gates. Between the columns there lay the city's open area. Crossing it is such a long journey that you would think you were going abroad, though you are staying at home.

Proceeding a little distance into the city, I came to the quarter named for Alexander himself, where I saw a whole other city, one whose beauty was split up in separate sections: for a row of columns went in one direction, and another just as long crossed it at right angles. My eyes tried to travel along every street, but I was left an unsatisfied spectator. The totality of its beauty was beyond my eyes' scope. At every moment when I was actually glimpsing some parts, I was on the point of seeing more and pressing on to others still but reluctant to pass some by. The things to see outstripped my sight; the prospects lured me on. Turning round and round to face all the streets, I grew faint at the sight and at last exclaimed, like a luckless lover, "Eyes, we have met our match."

But then I saw two new and unheard-of contests. The city's very largeness challenged its loveliness, and the populace vied with the city for size. Both won. This city was more massive than any mainland; this populace was more numerous than any nation. If I considered the city, I well might doubt that any swarm of men could fill it; but if I looked at the populace, I was amazed that any urban space could contain them. So evenly balanced were the scales.

As it happened, this was the holy month of the high god whose Greek 2 name is Zeus, but who in Egypt is known as Serapis. For this celebration, there was a torchlight procession, a sight to surpass any other in my experience—for evening had come, and the sun was set, yet night was nowhere, only a second sunrise of light in shimmering fragments, as if Alexandria meant to surpass the very heavens in splendor.

I also visited the Beneficent Zeus and the temple of Zeus Celestial. After praying as suppliants to the high god that he would add no further chapters to our tale of perils, we went to the lodgings that Menelaos had rented for us. But the god, I suppose, did not listen to our prayers, and further trials were in store for us on Fortune's obstacle course.

3    For, unbeknownst to us, Chaireas had long been lusting after Leukippe, and the real reason he had disclosed to us the secret of the drug
was that he wanted an opportunity to become a familiar acquaintance,
and of course also to keep her alive for his own enjoyment. Once he realized that her virtue was impregnable, he laid his plans as follows: collecting a band of fellow seamen of his own sort and instructing them what
to do, he invited us to a party at his home on Pharos to celebrate (he
said) his birthday. As we were just going out the door, an evil omen befell: a hawk pursuing a swallow collided with Leukippe, striking her
head with its wing. I was quite upset, and raising my eyes to heaven,
said: "O Zeus, what are you trying to tell us by this sign? If you have really given us this bird as a warning, please send your message again in a
still more perspicuous sign."

Then, turning around, I happened to face an artist's studio and saw a
painting on display whose allusions could but confirm the ominous bird.
It showed the rape of Philomela, Tereus attacking her, her tongue cut
out. The plot of the drama was there in every detail—the robe, Tereus,
the banquet. A maid was holding the unfolded robe; Philomela stood beside her and pointed to the pictures she had woven; Prokne nodded that
she understood; her eyes glowed fiercely and angrily at the picture. King
Tereus of Thrace was embroidered there, wrestling Philomela to his lust;
her hair had been torn, her waistband broken, her dress ripped open, one
breast exposed; she planted her right hand against his eyes and with her
left tried to hold the torn shreds of her garment across her breasts.
Tereus held Philomela tightly in his arms, drawing her body as close as
he could to his own and tightening his embrace on her flesh—so deftly
the artist designed this figured weft. The rest of the icon showed the
women showing Tereus his dinner—scraps in a basket—the head and
hands of his infant son. They are laughing, at the same time terrified.
Tereus is shown leaping up from his couch and drawing his sword
against them. He plants one leg on the table, which is neither standing
nor fallen, a picture of impending collapse.

4    Menelaos then remarked: "I suggest we put off our trip to Pharos.
You see these two unfavorable signs: the bird's aggressive wing and the
threat implicit in this painting. Interpreters of signs tell us to consider the
story of any painting we chance to see as we set out on business, and to
plot the outcome of our action by analogy with that story's plot. Well,
just look at the disasters proliferating in this scene: lawless sex, adultery
without shame, women degraded! I therefore advise that we go no further."

This seemed perfectly reasonable to me, and I excused us to Chaireas
for that day. He was very upset indeed and went away saying he would
come back tomorrow.

Then Leukippe asked me (for there's something in the nature of women that dearly loves a tale): "What does this picture mean? In the story, who are these birds, and the women, and that *awful* man?"

And I began to tell their tale: "Nightingale, swallow, hoopoe—each a human being, each a bird. The man is the hoopoe; the two women are Philomela the swallow and Prokne the nightingale; their city, Athens. Tereus was the husband; Prokne, Tereus's wife. But it seems the sexual appetite of barbarian men is not satisfied by a single wife, especially when the situation offers scope for sadistic luxury. In the case of this Thracian the opportunity to give rein to his nature was afforded by Prokne's familiar affection; for she sent her husband, Tereus, to fetch her sister. He departed Prokne's husband; he returned Philomela's lover. Along the way he made Philomela another Prokne. He feared Philomela's tongue, and his wedding present to her was the gift of silence. He snipped off the blossom of her voice. But even this was ineffectual, for Philomela's skill discovered voiceless speech. She wove, you see, a robe as messenger, and she threaded the drama into her embroidery, hand imitating tongue; she conveyed the ears' message to Prokne's eyes, telling her what she suffered by means of her shuttle. Prokne, learning the rape from the robe, exacted an exorbitant revenge on her husband: the conspiracy of two women and two passions, jealousy and outrage, plan a feast far worse than his weddings. The meal was Tereus's son, whose mother *had* been Prokne before her fury was roused and she forgot the pain of giving birth; for the pains of jealousy are stronger than those of the womb. Women in love who hurt a man in return for his affront, even if they must endure as much harm as they impose, weigh the pain of their suffering against the pleasure of taking action. It was a feast of Furies set for Tereus. And then, laughing with terror, they brought in the basket with the child's remains. Tereus, when he saw the fragments of his son, grieved over what he had eaten, and recognized himself as father of the meal. This knowledge drives him mad; he plucks his sword, runs after the women, who rise into the air. And Tereus ascends with them, a bird. Even now they enact a shadowy dream of that shameful drama: the nightingale flees, Tereus pursues. His hate is still intact, even as a bird."[59]

So for the time being we escaped the snares of his plot. But our margin of grace was only a single day—for early the next morning Chaireas was back again, and we were too embarrassed to refuse. We boarded a skiff and sailed out to Pharos. Menelaos stayed behind, saying he felt unwell. Chaireas first led us to the lighthouse and gave us a guided tour

59. This is the Greek version of this famous story; in Latin versions Philomela is the nightingale and Prokne the swallow.

around the foundation, explaining what a feat of engineering genius it was—a mountain erected in midsea, a skyscraper rising from the very waves and poised in suspension above them. And, towards the pinnacle of the mountain, there rose another helmsman[60] for the ships at sea. Next he brought us to his house, right on the ocean at the outermost part of the island.

7      That evening Chaireas went outside, to satisfy (he said) the needs of nature. A short while later there was suddenly shouting at the door and a band of huge men ran in with swords drawn, and all of them made for Leukippe. When I saw my darling being carried off, I couldn't stand it and rushed among the swords. Someone struck me on the thigh with a knife and I slumped down, blood streaming as I lay there. They put Leukippe on a boat and began to make their escape. Because the commotion and cries sounded like a pirates' attack, the marshal of the island appeared on the scene, a man I knew from the recent campaign. I showed him my wound and begged him to follow the kidnappers. Many ships were moored in the harbor. The marshal, along with his guards on duty, commandeered one of these for the chase; I went on board with them, though I had to be carried bodily.

When the pirates saw our vessel closing in and us prepared to fight, they stood Leukippe on the top deck with her hands tied behind her, and one of them cried out in a loud voice, "Here's your prize!" and so saying, he cut off her head and toppled the rest of the body into the sea. When I saw that, I uttered a loud groan and tried to throw myself overboard. The crew held me back, and I begged them to stop where we were so someone could jump in and recover her body for burial. The marshal agreed and stopped the vessel, and two sailors plunged over the side and soon were swimming back with the torso in tow.

Meanwhile the pirates were trying even harder to get away, but as we were once more closing the gap, they spotted another vessel containing men they recognized and called to them for support. These were purple-fishers who doubled as marauders. The marshal, seeing there were now two enemy ships, had second thoughts and ordered his men to reverse direction. The pirates stopped fleeing and taunted us to fight.

Eventually we reached land, and I disembarked and fell to weeping, holding her body in my arms. "This time, Leukippe, you are without doubt dead twice over, divided in death between land and sea. I hold a headless relic; I've lost the real you. Oh, what an unfair division between land and sea: I have been left the smaller part of you in the guise of the greater, whereas the sea, in a small part of you, possesses all of you. Yet

---

60. I.e., the light of the lighthouse (presumably); the text has been suspected, and some would write "another sun as helmsman."

now, since Fortune denies me the kisses of your lips, come then, let me kiss your butchered neck."

After lamenting in this vein, I buried the body and returned to Alexandria, where I reluctantly let my wound be treated. But eventually with Menelaos's encouragement I resolved to keep on living.

Six months had now passed, and the vivid impressions of sorrow were just beginning to fade; for time cures grief and soothes the heart's wounds. Sunlight is full of pleasure. Even extreme grief seethes for only a short time, as long as the soul is aflame; it cools when it is overcome by the soothing passage of time. As I was strolling in the agora, someone behind me suddenly seized my arm, whirled me around, and without a word embraced me heartily and kissed me repeatedly. At first I had no idea who this was and stood amazed, the passive object of his friendly pummelings, the target of his kisses.

When he paused a moment and I saw his face—it was Kleinias! With a shout of joy I started a whole new round of hugs and kisses. Then we adjourned to my lodgings where he told me his story, how he had survived the shipwreck, and I told him all about Leukippe.

"As soon as the ship had cracked open," he said, "I leaped towards the yardarm, which was already so crowded that I could barely cling to one end, but I wound my arms around it for dear life. We had only been bobbing like this for a short time when a huge wave raised the beam high and dashed it directly against a submerged rock. It was the other half, not the end I was dangling from, that hit, but the spar sprang back from this downward impact like the released arm of a catapult and propelled me through the air like a missile from a sling. For where I landed I swam on as long as there was daylight, no longer expecting to be rescued. My strength had run out, and I was consigning myself to fate when I saw a ship ahead of me. I raised my arms as best I could and signaled for help. And they, either out of pity or because the wind carried them that way, sailed towards me, and a sailor dropped a rope as the ship moved past. I grabbed it, and they hauled me up from death's door. The ship was bound for Sidon, and some of the crew recognized me and nursed me back to health.

"We reached the city in two days, and I asked the Sidonians on board, Xenodamas the merchant and Theophilos, his son-in-law, to keep my shipwreck and rescue a secret from any Tyrians they might run into, so that none would know I had eloped with you. For I hoped to avoid detection if only the disaster could be kept quiet, seeing that a mere five days had elapsed since I was last seen. I had forewarned the servants (as you know) to tell all who inquired that I was off to the country for a good ten days, and I found on my return that this had been accepted without question. Your father too was still away in Palestine, and when

the reaction
a home
(a reaction
at home)

he returned two days later, he found a letter from Leukippe's father which had arrived the day after our departure, and in which Sostratos announced Leukippe's engagement to you. He was in a pretty pickle when he read this letter and heard of your flight, vexed to lose this happy match and that Fortune had let it come so close. For none of this would have happened if only the mail had come a little quicker.

"He decided not to tell his brother what had happened and asked Leukippe's mother to keep the secret for the present. 'Perhaps we will find them. There is no need for Sostratos to know of this unfortunate escapade. No matter where they may be, they will surely come back when they hear they have been betrothed and that they can enjoy with our blessing the pleasures they eloped for.'

"He spent a great deal of time and energy inquiring where you might have gone, and a few days ago a Tyrian named Diophantos sailed from Egypt with the news that he had seen you there. As soon as I heard it, I instantly set sail, and I've been combing Alexandria for the past seven days. Now it is up to you, since your father is almost certainly on his way here."

11    On hearing this I lamented Fortune's practical joke. "O God, now at last Sostratos gives me Leukippe; now comes news from the front that we can be married—but the days were counted so that the news would not precede our elopement. O tardy tidings! My happiness was delivered one day late. Marriage *post mortem*! Wedding after wake! Now Fortune presents me with a bride whose corpse she once refused to let me have in its entirety."

"This is not the time for a dirge," said Kleinias. "We must decide whether you should return to your homeland or perhaps wait for your father here."

"Neither," I said. "How could I look my father in the eye, after I not only ran away from home in such dishonorable circumstances but caused the death of the niece entrusted to his care? The only thing left is to escape from here before he arrives."

Meanwhile Menelaos came in, and Satyros with him. They embraced Kleinias, and we told them the new developments.

"Well, the solution is obvious," said Satyros. "You can solve your own problem and also do a favor for that poor soul who is burning for you. Kleinias should hear this. Aphrodite has put a magnificent opportunity in his grasp, and he refuses to hold out his hand. She has driven a woman insane with love for him, a very beautiful woman, a living work of art. She's an Ephesian lady named Melite, rich and still young. Her husband just recently died at sea. She wants this fellow here, I won't say as her husband merely, but rather as her lord and master. She wants to surrender herself and her entire fortune to him. She has spent the last

a love interest

four months here begging him to come back with her.[61] <u>I don't know what's gotten into this young man. He ignores her, nourishing fantasies that Leukippe will come back to life."</u>

And Kleinias said, "I think Satyros has a point. The combined offer of beauty, wealth, and love requires no consultation, no procrastination. Her beauty promises pleasant nights; her wealth, luxurious days; her love, a faithful wife. Heaven hates the haughty and prostrates the proud; so listen to Satyros and do what God wants." 12

And I cried: "Lead on—since Kleinias agrees, <u>I'll go wherever you say, but on one condition: the woman must stop bothering me with her constant sexual innuendos and invitations, until we reach Ephesos. I have already taken a vow never to copulate in this part of the world, where I lost Leukippe."</u>

Satyros ran to Melite with this good news and soon returned, saying that she had fainted almost dead away for delight and requested that I come to dinner that day with her as a formal inauguration of our union. I agreed and went.

When she saw me, she jumped up, embraced me, and covered my whole face with kisses. She really was beautiful; her skin you would have said was bathed in milk, and her cheeks the natural essence of rose. The gleam in her eye was unmistakably erotic. Her hair was long and thick and of a light golden color, and again I had to admit she was very pleasant to look at. The meal itself was lavish, but she barely touched the food in front of her and only seemed to eat. She could not take in real food but was wholly focused on me. To a lover nothing is savory save only the beloved. Love occupies the soul in its entirety, leaving no room for thoughts of food. The pleasure of this vision slides through the eyes into the breast and there attracts the beloved's image, catching it on the soul's mirror-plate and printing its picture there. Beauty's effluence, drawn on unseen rays to the erotic heart, imprints a shadow image in its depths. 13

I understood her feelings and said: "You've hardly touched your food. You sit there like some still unnourished bride of quietness."

And she, <u>"What rare venison, what vintage rarer still, could satisfy me like the vision of you?" And then she kissed me—kisses I took with pleasure—and after a pause said, "This is all the nourishment I need."</u>

And there for the time matters rested. But as evening was drawing on, she tried to prevail on me to sleep with her, but I begged off, re- 14

---

61. This was not the usual way of things in ancient Greece. But there are contemporary accounts of such phenomena. The frame tale of Plutarch's *Amatorius (Dialogue on Love)* is the pursuit of a handsome young man by a wealthy widow. She kidnaps him, and they live together happily! Artemidoros (*Oneirokritika* 5.29) records the case of a woman who pressured a man into marrying her against his will.

minding her of the conditions I had spoken of to Satyros. Reluctantly, regretfully, she let me go.

On the next day we had agreed to meet at Isis's temple to speak further and to exchange vows with the goddess as our witness. Menelaos and Kleinias accompanied us. I pledged to cherish her without guile; she pledged to name me her husband and declare me master of all her properties.

"Our arrival at Ephesos," I said, "will inaugurate the contract. Here, as I said, you take second place to Leukippe." A rich dinner was then served, a wedding supper in name only, the consummation being stored away for a future occasion. I recall a witty remark of Melite's during that banquet. As the guests were wishing our union well, she leaned over to me and said quietly, "How unique! This is rather like the ceremony for persons whose bodies can't be found: I've heard before of a tomb without a tenant, but not of a bride's empty bed." A joke of course, but she was serious.

15 On the following day we prepared to leave, and by chance even the wind seemed to invite us. Menelaos came as far as the dock, hugged us good-bye, wishing us a safer voyage than our previous seas, and then turned away—a fine young man he was, and deserved every blessing from heaven. I noticed that tears were welling in his eyes, and indeed we all began to weep freely. Kleinias decided not to leave me but to sail with us to Ephesos and after spending some time in the city to return home, once he was sure that I was well settled.

The wind was carrying us along in the right direction; it was evening, and after supper we were lying down to sleep. Melite and I had our own private cabin on the ship. She held me in her arms, kissed me, and asked again that we consummate our union. "Now at last we have gone beyond Leukippe's boundaries and entered the territory of our promises. The day we contracted for is here. Why should I wait until Ephesos? The moods of the sea are fickle; the winds cannot be trusted. Trust me, Kleitophon; I am on fire. Would that I could show you the flame; would that my combustion like the element itself could lick along your flesh and ignite you in a sheet of flames. But with its other properties this fire alone has its own fuel—it smolders in the secret places where lovers' bodies intertwine, and however incandescent glows the furnace of their love, they are not burned away. O mystic fire! O torch for private handling only! O flame refusing to leave your proper hearth! My dearest, let us enter Aphrodite's inner sanctum and initiate ourselves into her mystic liturgy."

16 And I said: "Do not pressure me to break my solemn undertaking to the dead. We have not left her region until we reach another shore. Have you not heard that she died at sea? Then I am still sailing over Leukippe's

grave. Perhaps her ghost is circling about the ship even now. They say that souls who die in the sea never descend to Hades but wander over the water. And is this an appropriate place to consummate any marriage? Our wedding night on choppy waves? Our first time on a rocking boat? Surely you want our bridal bed to stay in one place?"

"Darling," she replied, "you're splitting hairs. For lovers every location is a bedroom. No place is inaccessible to that god. The sea in fact is quite appropriate for Eros and his mother's mysteries—Aphrodite is a daughter of the sea. Let us gratify the goddess of unions and please the sea her mother by our marriage. The ship itself is hinting at our matrimony: above our heads swings the crossyoke, and ropes are knotted on the yardarm. O my master, good omens! We will be yoked in holy wedlock and linked by bonds of love. The helmsman's rudder is hard by our bed: Fortune is steering us to our union. Poseidon and his chorus of Nereids will be our entourage, remembering his own marine marriage to Amphitrite. And the wind, as it whistles through the rigging, sounds to my ears like a flute picking out the notes of the wedding melody. And how I laugh to see the sail conceive and grow big-bellied—prophesying here and now a blessed eventuality. Soon you will be a father too."

Seeing how insistent she was, I said: "I vote for the ascetic life until we land. I promise you, in the name of the sea itself and our safe passage, that my eagerness is a match for yours. But the sea too has its mores, and often have I heard old salts agree that ships and sex should never mix, whether in reverence for the ships' own holiness or to keep the tars taut for danger. The sea itself, my darling, might grow angry at our insolence: desire and apprehension are uneasy bedfellows. Let us keep our pleasure unadulterated by other feelings." I sweetened my argument with kisses, and she let herself be convinced. We slept that night in innocence.

After five days of continuous sailing we reached Ephesos and then her 17 house, one of the finest in the city, crowded with servants and richly furnished. She ordered them to prepare a truly memorable meal. "In the meantime," she said, "we will take a tour to inspect the estate."

Her farmlands were four stades away from the city, so we climbed into a carriage and drove out. When we got there, we were strolling through the orchards, and suddenly a woman threw herself at our feet! She had heavy irons bound around her ankles, a workman's hoe in her hands, her head was shaved, her body was all grimy, her miserable clothing was hitched up for work, and she cried out: "Have mercy on me, m'lady, as one woman to another. I am free by birth, though now a slave, as Fortune chooses." And so saying, she fell silent.

Melite said: "Stand up, woman. Tell me your name and country and who put these shackles on you. Even in fallen circumstances, your beauty proclaims you a person of no mean birth."

"It was the bailiff," the woman replied, "because I would not submit to his lechery. Lakaina is my name, ma'am, born in Thessaly. I humbly beg your generous ladyship, free me from this awful condition, keep me somewhere safe until I can pay back the two thousand gold pieces that Sosthenes gave the pirates for me. I'll pay it off quick, I promise you. Else I'll wait on you hand and foot, m'lady. Just look here, now, how he's been swinging his lash at my poor back!" And she slipped down part of her dress to show her back cruelly striped with welts.

When we heard her plea, I was profoundly shaken, from a certain resemblance this wretched creature bore to Leukippe. Melite said: "Cheer up, woman. We will free you of these chains and send you to your original home with no payment required. Someone fetch Sosthenes here at once!"

The woman was unshackled and the bailiff appeared, cowering and unnerved. Melite said: "You filthy swine! Have you ever seen any slave in our household, even the most worthless, treated so despicably? Who is she? Tell me the entire truth!"

"All I know, my lady," replied the bailiff, "is that some merchant named Kallisthenes sold her to me, claiming that he had bought her from pirates and that she was a freeborn woman. The merchant called her Lakaina."

Melite divested him of his responsibilities as bailiff and handed the woman over to her maidservants, with instructions to wash her, dress her in clean clothes, and take her to town. Disposing of certain matters about the estate that she had traveled to see, she mounted the carriage with me, and we returned to the city and went in to dinner.

18 While we were eating, Satyros signaled me with his eyes to come away, and his expression indicated it was something serious. Pretending to answer a natural need, I rose from the table and excused myself. When I had gone to him, without a word he handed me a letter. Before I could read a single sentence, my jaw dropped in astonishment: I recognized the handwriting as Leukippe's. The letter read as follows.

From Leukippe to her master Kleitophon:
It is "Master" I must call you, for you are my mistress's husband. You know well all that I have suffered for you, yet now I am obliged to refresh your memory. For your sake I left my mother and undertook a life of wandering. For your sake I went through shipwreck and captivity at the hands of pirates. For your sake I have been a sacrificial victim, an expiatory offering, and twice have died. For your sake I have been sold and shackled in iron; I have wielded the hoe, scraped the earth, endured the lash—and was all this in order to become another man's wife, as you are now another

woman's husband? God forbid! But while I have struggled through one disaster after another, here are you, unsold, unlashed, now married. If there is any gratitude left in your heart for all the trials I have undergone for you, beg your wife to send me home as she promised. Lend me the two thousand gold pieces that were the price Sosthenes paid for me and assure Melite that I will make it good. Byzantium is not far. If you have to pay the money yourself, you may regard it as a payment for my long-suffering devotion to you. Farewell; be happy in your new marriage. I write this letter still a virgin.

On reading this, my feelings exploded in all directions—I turned red; I    19
went pale; I wondered at it; I doubted every word. I was rapt with joy and racked with distress. I said to Satyros: "Did you carry this letter from Hades? What does it mean? Has Leukippe come to life again?"

"She has indeed," he said. "She is the woman you saw in the fields. At that time no one else could have recognized her either—she had become so much the young man. The mere cropping of her hair transformed her utterly."

"Why do you stop," I said, "with this good news and satisfy my ears alone? My eyes demand their share of this happiness. Show me Leukippe in person!"

"Hold on," said Satyros. "Be patient for a short time, or you'll destroy us all. We need some time to make a safe plan. After all, the first lady of the Ephesians is madly in love with you, and we are all alone, surrounded by snares."

"I can't do it," I said. "Joy is flooding along every pathway of my body. But look how she lambasts me in this letter!"

Returning to the text, I scrutinized each word, as if seeing her through the letters. I said: "Your charges are all too true, my dearest. You suffered all for me. I caused you untold troubles." When I got to the part about the whips and tortures applied by Sosthenes, I wept as if I were witnessing them myself. Thinking about it set my mind's eyes working on what the letter said and made the visible tangible. I flushed at her criticism of my marriage, like an adulterer caught in the act. The letter itself made me feel ashamed.

"Oh, no! How will I defend myself, Satyros?" I said. "I'm caught.    20
Leukippe condemns me. Probably she hates me already. But how was she saved, tell me? Whose body did we bury?"

"She will tell you herself when the time comes. As for now," said Satyros, "you must reply to her letter and try to win her back. I swore to her that you married against your will."

"You said I actually married her? You've destroyed me!"

*an unconsummated marriage—his way out?*

"Don't be silly; the whole city knows that you're married."

"Yes, but I haven't gone through with the marriage, Satyros; no, by Herakles and by my present lot."

"You're joking, sir; you do sleep with the lady!"

"I know it's incredible, but we've never done *it*. Kleitophon remains pure to this day as far as Melite is concerned. But tell me what to write. I'm so upset by what has happened that I can't think."

"I'm no cleverer than you," said Satyros. "Eros himself will supply your words. But do it now." I began to write.

> Greetings to Leukippe, mistress of my heart!
> I languish in my luxury, noting the absence of your presence, visibly missing in the letters of your letter. If only you will wait for the truth to be told! Don't condemn me without a trial. You will learn that I have imitated your virginity, if that word has any meaning for men as it does for women. If your heart is already hard against me before I plead my case, I swear by the same gods who saved your life that it will take only a short time for me to explain my action. Good-bye, my darling, and may you be happy.

21    I gave this letter to Satyros to hand to Leukippe, and I asked him to say a few appropriate words in my favor. Then I went back to our dinner party, bubbling with happiness and heartache together, for I knew Melite would not let that night go by without demanding that we consummate our marriage, but now that Leukippe was recovered, I could not even look at another woman.

Back at the table I tried to control my face to betray no new emotion, but at this I was not entirely successful. When I was overcome, I quickly pretended that it was only a shiver: Melite realized that I was showing signs of reneging on my promise, but she did not have enough evidence to accuse me outright. Without having eaten I rose to retire; she, with her meal half-finished, rose at once and was right after me. When we reached the bedroom, I exaggerated my sick act still further. She, however, was very insistent and said: "Why are you doing this to me? How long are you going to torture me? So we've crossed the sea. Look, this is Ephesus: here we celebrate our marriage. Are we waiting for a special day? How long are we to sleep together as if in a temple? You lead me to water, and you won't let me drink! So long a time I've had this water near me, and still I thirst; I even have to sleep in the bed of the stream! My bed is as satisfying to me as Tantalos's nourishment was to him."

So she complained and began to weep, resting her head so forlornly against my chest that I began to sympathize in earnest. I was rapidly losing my self-possession, for I did feel her complaints had merit. So I said, "Darling, I swear by the ancestral gods, yea verily, that I urgently want to respond to your enthusiasm. But I just don't know," I said, "what is wrong with me. I have caught some illness that strikes without warning. You know that infection drives out affection."

So saying, I wiped away her tears and vowed with still other oaths that she would get all she wanted in the not too far distant future. So at last and with the utmost reluctance she ceased to press me.

On the next day she summoned the maidservants to whose care she had entrusted Leukippe and first inquired if they had treated her handsomely. They replied that she wanted for nothing. Melite bid them bring the person to her. When she arrived, Melite said: "It would be superfluous to remind you of my generosity, of which you are well aware. I have treated you fairly; now I ask an equal favor in return, if it is in your power. I hear that you women of Thessaly can bewitch the man you love so that he never looks at another woman and finds in you his all. Provide me, my dear, with such a philter to satisfy my fire of passion. Did you notice the young man who was walking with me yesterday?"

"You mean your husband?" replied Leukippe, maliciously. "I heard who he was from the other women."

"Some husband!" said Melite. "I might as well be married to a rock. He's more interested in some dead woman. He's always talking about her; at meals, in bed, it's 'Leukippe this' and 'Leukippe that.' (Her name was Leukippe.) My dear, I spent four whole months in Alexandria chasing him. I came right out and asked him; I begged him; I promised him anything; I tried every possible line and did all I could to please him. And do you think he listened to me? Like iron or wood or some lump of inanimate matter. Well, in time he agreed—agreed, that is, to look at me. But as Aphrodite is my witness, I've slept with him these five nights, and I might as well have been sleeping with a eunuch. I think it's a statue I'm in love with; in appearance only is he my lover. Now I'm asking you as one woman to another—the same request you made to me yesterday: help me against this proud monster. You will be saving my soul, which already I can feel ebbing away."

When Leukippe heard this, she was thrilled that I had not done anything with that woman. She said she would go out, with her ladyship's permission, into the fields of her country estate and hunt for the proper herbs; and go she did, for she thought that if she denied her witchcraft she would not be believed. This, I presume, was the premise of her promise. Melite felt easier with something to hope for; for pleasures, even absent, please in prospect.

For my part, knowing nothing at the time of these details, I was in despair, casting about for a way to postpone my wedding night for one more night and to meet Leukippe. It seemed that Leukippe was just as

eager to get away from Melite by going into the country and would return about evening. We went in to drink. Just as we had reclined at table,
a great clamor and scrambling about occurred in the men's quarters, and
one of the servants ran in, panting and exclaiming, "Thersandros is alive;
he's here now!" This Thersandros was Melite's husband, who she
thought had died at sea. What really happened was that some of his servants, who were saved when the boat overturned, thought their master
had gone down, and they had circulated this report when they returned.

No sooner had the servant spoken than Thersandros ran in behind
him, for he had learned everything about me on his way here and was
eager to catch me. Melite leaped up in astonishment at the incredible turn
of events and tried to embrace her husband. He shoved her roughly aside
without a thought, and catching sight of me, he muttered, "There's the
adulterer!" and sprang forward, punching me on the temple. I felt a full
load of fury in his fist. Dragging me by the hair, he pounded my head
against the floor and falling on me he began punching me right and left.
I, like one being initiated into a mystery, knew nothing at all—who was
this person? Why was he striking me? Yet, as I had a notion that something here was not quite right, I forebore to defend myself, though it
was well within my power. When we at last grew tired—he of beating
me steadily, and I of bearing it philosophically—I got up and said, "Who
in the world are you, sir, and why have you treated me so disgracefully?" He became even more enraged at the fact that I had dared to
speak, and pummeled me again, calling now for chains and fetters. They
then tied me up and took me to a little room.

24    I failed to notice, while all this was going on, that Leukippe's letter
had slipped out of my clothes. I had been carrying it inside my chiton,
tied there by a tassel. And Melite picked it up without being observed,
for she was afraid that it was one of her letters to me. When she started
to read it in a private moment, she saw the familiar name "Leukippe,"
and her heart skipped a beat; her next thought was that this couldn't be
*her*—the same woman she had so often heard spoken of as dead. But
when she read on, the rest of the letter told her the whole story, and she
felt her soul torn apart by conflicting emotions: shame, anger, love, and
jealousy—she was ashamed to face her husband; the letter made her angry, but her anger withered away before her love, which was in turn
inflamed by her jealousy. In the end her love prevailed.

25    It was towards evening, and Thersandros, in the first flush of anger,
had stormed away to one of his comrades in town. Coming to the guard
who was stationed at my door, Melite spoke with him briefly and then
slipped surreptitiously into the room, leaving two of her servants outside. She found me lying on the ground and came over to my side, as all
her many feelings struggled to find expression simultaneously. I could

read each change of feeling in her face as she tried to express all she wanted to say.

"Oh, what misery is this, that I cannot even look at you without reliving all my pain! I loved you first, a love that never reached its goal, an utterly foolish love; now, though you hate me, I still love you though you hurt me. I pity you; not even your insolent rejection can stop me from loving you. Oh, you two are yoked in devilish magic, conspiring against me, this man who never tires of reenacting my humiliation, that woman who has gone to fetch a charm to satisfy my love. I didn't realize, ill starred as I am, that I was asking my worst enemy to use her skill against me."

And with that she threw Leukippe's letter towards me. When I saw it and recognized what it was, I shuddered and turned my eyes down to stare at the ground, feeling the full force of her indictment. She resumed her declamation.

"Ah! Wretched woman, wretched life! Now I have lost my husband on your account, and I have no hope of keeping you with me any longer, not even just to look at, which is all you have been good for.

"I know that my husband despises me and holds me guilty of adultery with you, a fruitless adultery, a sexless affair; all I have to show for it is the disgrace. Other women have at least the pleasure of their passion to compensate for their scandalous fall, but it is my bad luck to reap all the shame and none of the pleasure.

"You treacherous, savage man! How could you, a devotee of Love yourself, let a woman who loved so strongly burn away in Love's own fire? Were you not afraid of his retaliation? Weren't you in awe of his fire? Did you not feel respect for his sacred mysteries? Did the tears in these eyes never touch your heart? You are more pitiless than any desperado; even a common cutthroat has some respect for tears.

"But nothing stirred your feelings to a single consummation of Aphrodite's ritual, no earnest prayer, no passage of time, no overlapping of limbs. You offered me the supreme insult: you held me close, you kissed me, and then you rose from my bed as would another woman. What phantom shadow of a marriage was this? You were not sleeping with an old crone or one who rejected your embraces, but a young and loving bride, and as anyone else would add, beautiful too. Eunuch! Effeminate! Evil eye of beauty! On your head I pronounce this most fitting curse: may Eros condemn you to the same fate as I." She ceased and broke into tears.

As I stood silent with my eyes cast down, she paused a while and then spoke in a new spirit. "All that I just said, my darling, was uttered from my anger and my grief. In what I am about to say my love is speaking. However angry you make me, I still burn with love for you; however scornfully you reject me, I still cherish you. Make a truce with me at least for now; pity me. I no longer ask for length of days and a permanent marriage, that foolish dream I dreamed of you. A single consummation will be enough. It is a small remedy I ask for so great an illness. Quench a little of my fire. If I spoke some rash and hasty words against you, forgive me, dearest. Disappointed love goes wild. I realize how indecent it is to make this request, but I am not ashamed to proclaim the holy mysteries of Love. You are an initiate; you already know what I am going through. To the uninitiated the god's arrows are invisible, and none of them could display his archery. Only lovers know these wounds in others as in themselves.

"I have only this day left. I hold you to your promise. Remember Isis and the vows you made then. If you are willing to live with me as you swore, I would disregard a thousand Thersandroses. But since you have found Leukippe, and marriage is impossible with any other woman, I willingly concede this. I realize I have lost the fight. I do not demand more than I am able to receive.

"The problems I face are all new ones. Even the dead rise up against me. O sea, you spared my life when I was sailing across you, but after saving me you destroyed me by sending two corpses to haunt me—Leukippe alone was not enough (let her live so Kleitophon will grieve no more), but now the wild Thersandros is with us too.

"You were struck while I watched, miserably unable to help. Punches landed on this dear face, O gods! I think Thersandros was blind. I beg you, Kleitophon, my master (for you are my soul's own master), give yourself to me today, the first time and the last. This brief moment feels like many days to me. So may you never lose Leukippe anymore, so may she never die again, not even in sham.

"Do not scorn my love, which brought you such great happiness: my love brought Leukippe back to you. If I had not fallen in love with you, if I had not brought you here, Leukippe would still be just a corpse to you. Fortune has her generous moods from time to time. And if a man stumbles on a treasure, he honors the site of his discovery—erects an altar, brings a sacrifice, wreathes the spot with flowers. You discovered your treasure of love right here through me, and now you dishonor your benefactor.

"Listen to Love: can't you hear him speaking through me—'I ask this favor, Kleitophon, as your mystic mentor. Do not go away without showing Melite our secret rites. My fire is burning in her shrine too.'

"And listen to what else I mean to do for you. You will be immediately released from bondage, even against Thersandros's will. You will be sheltered for as many days as you wish with my foster brother. You may expect Leukippe to be at your side by tomorrow morning. She told me she would spend the night in the fields gathering herbs so she might pluck them by moonlight. She was secretly laughing at me, for I asked her as a Thessalian woman to give me a love potion for you. What else could I do in my despair but look for herbs and potions? They are the refuge of the lovelorn.

"As for Thersandros, to set your mind at ease about him, he has charged off to a friend's house, angrily leaving me alone in the house. I think some god arranged to drive him away so that you could administer to me these last rites. All I ask is that you give me yourself."

When her philosophical discourse was concluded—for Love also     27
teaches us what to say—she unfastened my bonds and kissed my hands and touched them to her eyes and heart, saying: "You see how it beats, how it is pounding under the pressures of agony and hope: may it soon throb with pleasure too! Its very beat sounds like an insistent request."

When she released me and embraced me, weeping, I had a normal human reaction. And I was genuinely afraid that the god Love might exact a terrible vengeance; and in any case I had now recovered Leukippe, and very soon I would be separated from Melite, and the act could no longer be considered precisely a marital one but was rather a remedy for an ailing soul. So when she embraced me, I did not hold back; when our limbs drew close, I did not refuse the touch. Everything happened as Love willed. We had no need of bedding or of any of Aphrodite's accoutrements; for Love is handy and resourceful, and a clever *bricoleur,* who can turn any place into a chapel for his mystic liturgy. The casual in sex is far more sweet than the carefully prepared: its pleasure springs up like an untended plant.

## Book Six

When I had successfully treated Melite's complaint, I said to her, "Now     1
grant me a safe escape and keep your promises about Leukippe." "Don't worry on her account," she said. "You may regard her as already in your possession. Now put on my clothes and hide your face with my veil. Melantho will guide you to the door, where a servant will be waiting for you: I've instructed him to bring you to the house where you will find Kleinias and Satyros, and Leukippe will join you there."

As she said this, she was dressing me as herself, and then she kissed me, saying: "How much more lovely you have become in this dress. I once saw such an Achilles in a painting.[62] But save yourself, my dearest, and keep this dress as a remembrance. Leave your own clothes with me

---

62. Achilles was dressed as a maiden by his mother and made to live with the daughters of King Lykomedes on Skyros to avoid being drafted for the Trojan War.

so that I can feel your embrace when I put them on." She also gave me a hundred pieces of gold and called Melantho, who was one of her confidential maids and was keeping watch now outside the door. When she entered, Melite told her our agreement and bade her return when I was outside the door.

2  In this fashion I slipped out. The guard of the chamber stepped aside, thinking I was his mistress as Melantho gave him a nod. I passed through the deserted rooms of the house till I came to a certain door that did not let onto the main street, and the servant whom Melite had stationed here took me in hand. He was a freedman who had sailed with us, and I was on friendly terms with him. When Melantho returned, she found the guard just having locked the door, and she told him to open it again. When he did, and she had entered and told Melite of my departure, she called the guard. And he, as one might surmise, on seeing a most paradoxical sight—like the deer in place of a maiden in the story[63]—was astonished and stood there in silence. So she said to him: "It was not because I distrusted your willingness to release Kleitophon that I employed this deception, but rather that you might be provided with an exonerating alibi in Thersandros's eyes as not being aware of what was happening. These ten pieces of gold are a gift for you—a gift, that is, from Kleitophon if you stay here; otherwise it will help you on your way if you decide it is better to run away." Pasion—for so the guard was called—said, "Lady, what pleases you pleases me." Melite then decided that it was better for him to disappear for the present, and only when she had settled matters with her husband, and his anger had grown calm, would he return. Pasion did as she directed.

3  But as for me, my usual bad luck set her sights on me once again and arranged a novel drama to undo me. For whom did she bring onto the scene, just as I was leaving the house, but Thersandros! He had been persuaded by the friend he had visited not to spend the night away from his own bed, and so after dinner he was returning to his house. It was the festival of Artemis, and drunken people were roaming everywhere, so that all night long a crowd filled the entire agora. I thought that this was the only danger, not realizing that another, far more serious plot had been hatched against me. For Sosthenes—who had purchased Leukippe and whom Melite had ordered to give up his management of the fields—learning that the master was present, refused to give up the fields and decided to get back at Melite. His first step was to inform Thersandros about me—Sosthenes had been my accuser—and then he told a very persuasive lie about Leukippe too. For when he realized that he was not to have her, he turned pander to his master to separate him from Melite. "I

63. Iphigeneia at Aulis.

have purchased a maiden, O master, who is beautiful, quite an incredible thing of beauty. Trust my words that she is so, as you would trust your own eyes. I have been keeping her for you, for I had heard it said that you were alive, and my wish gave credence to the tale. But I told no one, so that you might catch your lady red-handed and no longer be mocked by an adulterer of low degree and foreign birth. Your lady had this slave girl removed yesterday and was going to send her away. But Fortune has kept her for you as a choice morsel of loveliness for the taking. She is in the country at this moment, sent there on some pretext or other by Melite. Before she returns, I will get her under lock and key, if you wish, so that she too may be in your control."

Thersandros approved and bade him go ahead. Sosthenes therefore 4 went in great haste to the country. Seeing the cabin where Leukippe was going to spend the night, he took two workmen aside and told them to trick the maids who were with Leukippe, to get them as far away as possible, and to hold them in conversation. Then he brought two others, and when he saw Leukippe alone he jumped out at her, covered her mouth, and dragged her away in the opposite direction from where the maids had been induced to go. He brought her to a secret little shack and, setting her down, said: "I am here to heap happiness on you, and all that I ask is that you not forget me in your good fortune. Have no fear at being carried away; do not think it happened to your harm. It is just my master's way of introducing himself as your lover."

At this unexpected twist of fate Leukippe was stunned and silent. Sosthenes returned to Thersandros and told him what he had done, meeting him just at the moment when he was returning to the house. At Sosthenes' account of Leukippe's situation, which included lyrical descriptions of her beauty, Thersandros was filled by his words with a sort of image of beauty; and since it was an all-night festival and the fields some four stades distant, he bade Sosthenes to lead the way to her and was just setting off.

I had changed into Melite's clothes while this was going on, and without looking carefully where I was going I bumped into them face-to-face. Sosthenes recognized me first and said, "Well, what have we here: the adulterer coming at us like a bacchant and bearing the spoils of your wife." The young man who was leading me had seen them coming and ducked away, afraid even to take the time to warn me. When they caught sight of me, they grabbed me. Thersandros started shouting, and a crowd of people out for the festival began to gather around us. Thersandros, with an audience, indulged himself in an orgy of personal suffering, crying out speakable and unspeakable accusations—"adulterer," "thief." He hauled me to the jailhouse and turned me in on a charge of adultery. Now, actually none of this really upset me, neither the indignity of bondage nor the verbal harassment, for I was confident that I would survive the trial by arguing that I was no adulterer but had been quite openly married to her. Yet fear gripped me for Leukippe's sake, since I still had not actually reclaimed her. Our souls by nature have a prophetic instinct for evil in the offing; seldom does our fortune-telling tell good fortune and true. My thoughts then for Leukippe were all morose; everything seemed to me suspicious and fraught with terror. Thus I languished, ill at heart.

6     Meanwhile Thersandros, after throwing me into jail, made for Leukippe with all speed. When they reached the hut, they found her lying on the ground, her thoughts occupied with the fate described by Sosthenes, displaying in her features grief mixed with fear. For I believe it is incorrect to say the mind is utterly invisible: it shows itself accurately in the face as in a mirror. When glad, it lights up an image of joy in the eyes; feeling pain, it tightens the face to a picture of suffering. So when Leukippe heard the doors opening (there was already a light inside), she raised her head a moment and then cast her eyes down again. Thersandros glimpsed her loveliness for a fleeting second, like a lightning flash (for beauty resides especially in the eyes), and his soul went out to her. He stood fixed by the sight, waiting for the moment when she would look up again to him. As she kept her head lowered, he said: "Why do you look downwards, woman? Why let the loveliness of your eyes spill onto the earth? Let it flow rather into these eyes of mine."

7     On hearing this, she welled up into tears, and even so her tears had their own peculiar loveliness. For a tear arouses the eye and makes it more prominent; if it be a dull, unlovely eye, a tear only increases its unattractiveness. But say it be a sweet eye, a deep saturation of black smoothly encircled by white; when such an eye grows moist with tears, it is like the swelling nipple of water in a bubbling spring; as the saltwatery tears flow into the outer rim, the white glistens, the black takes on a purple tint, like a violet next to a narcissus; tears held swimming in the eyes seem to smile. Such were Leukippe's tears, snatching from her very grief a sudden victory of beauty. If they could have been congealed as they fell, the earth would have possessed a new kind of amber.[64] Thersandros was dumbfounded by her beauty, driven made by her grief, and his own eyes were pregnant with tears. It is in the nature of tears to elicit pity from those who see them, especially a woman's tears; inasmuch as they are more abundant, so are they more beguiling; and if the woman weeping be beautiful, as well as the viewer a lover, his eye is not immobile but imitates her tears. For when the loveliness of lovely people lives in their eyes and flows from there to rest in the eyes of viewers, it makes

64. Amber was supposedly formed by the tears of Phaethon's sisters as they wept for his death (Hesiod frag. 311 Merkelbach-West).

a spring of tears well up as well. The lover, receiving both, hurries the loveliness into his soul but keeps the tear in his eyes. He prays to be seen, and though he could wipe it away, he doesn't, but rather guards the tear as long as he can, and is afraid it will fall too soon. He even refuses to let his eye move lest the tear fall before the beloved has seen it. This he believes attests that he is indeed in love. Such was the state of Thersandros; he cried to display his tears—feeling (one may presume) some natural emotion, yet making himself look good in Leukippe's eyes, as a man who wept for no other reason than that she was crying.

Then he leaned over and said to Sosthenes: "Take care of her for now, for you see how grief-stricken she is. I shall leave her presence—the last thing I want to do—in order not to burden her. When her mind is more at peace, then I will talk with her. As for you, woman, be of good cheer. Soon enough I will heal your tears." Then on his way out he spoke again to Sosthenes. "See that you speak well of me. Come to me tomorrow morning with everything arranged." With this he left.

While this was going on, it happened that Melite after her interview    8 with me had at once sent a young man to the estate to get Leukippe. He was to prompt her to return home, since Melite had no need of further cure. When he reached the estate, he discovered the maids looking for Leukippe and very upset. As she was nowhere to be found, he ran back and reported the news. When Melite heard what happened to me, that I had been thrown into jail, and then about Leukippe, that she had disappeared, a dense fog of grief settled over her. She had no way of finding the truth, but she suspected Sosthenes. Wanting to conduct her search for Leukippe openly through Thersandros, she then constructed a clever account that blended truth with sophistry as follows. ~ a Cu

When Thersandros entered the house and started shouting again: "It    9 was you who smuggled out the adulterer; you set him free and sent him out of the house. Why don't you follow him? Why do you stay here? Go on; go to your boyfriend, so that you can see him chained up now in still heavier shackles." "What adulterer?" Melite said. "What's wrong with you? Please, stop acting crazy; listen to the whole story. The truth is easy to explain. I ask only one thing first: be a fair judge, forget the accusation you heard, dismiss the anger from your heart, make reason the honest judge of this case, and listen.

"This young man is no adulterer and no husband to me. He is a Phoenician, second to no other Tyrian. He too sailed a luckless voyage, and all his goods became the sea's property. When I heard of his unhappy fate, I felt pity for him; I remembered you, and I offered him hospitality, thinking, 'Perhaps Thersandros too is wandering somewhere just like this. Maybe,' I said to myself, 'some woman will take pity on him too. And if he has really died at sea, as rumor reports, come let us pay honor to all shipwrecks as if they were his.' Many the shipwrecked men I nursed, many the sea's corpses I buried; whenever a piece of flotsam from a wrecked ship came to shore, I would pick it up and say, 'Perhaps Thersandros sailed on this ship.' This man was simply one of those many survivors I helped, and the last. In honoring him I was paying my respects to you. He sailed the seas as you did: in him, my dearest, I was honoring an image of your misfortune. Why then did I bring him here with me, you ask? The tale is true. He was mourning the death of his wife, but unbeknownst to him she was still alive after all. Someone passed this information on to him and said she was here with one of our overseers. He specifically named Sosthenes. And it turned out to be true. We came and found the woman. This was the reason he followed me. You have Sosthenes; the woman is on our country estate. Test each one of my statements. If I have told a single lie, I am taken in adultery."

10    So she spoke, pretending not to know of Leukippe's disappearance, and further having in reserve that if Thersandros sought to discover the truth, she would bring forward the maids who had accompanied her, if Leukippe did not appear by morning, and they would say (which was the truth) that the maiden was nowhere to be seen. Thus it would be possible for her to conduct her own search for Leukippe publicly, and also to force Thersandros to cooperate.

With that piece of persuasive acting behind her, Melite added the following: "Trust me, husband. You have never had anything to hold against me, dearest, throughout the years of our marriage. Don't begin to harbor such suspicions now. The rumor went into circulation because of the honor I paid to the young man, since most people were ignorant of the reason for our association. If rumor be believed, you yourself were dead. Rumor and Slander are two kindred iniquities: Rumor is Slander's daughter. Slander is more sharp than a sword, more powerful than fire, more persuasive than Sirens; Rumor spreads more elusively than water, is more fleet than a breeze, swifter than wings. When Slander takes aim with a story, it speeds like an arrow and wounds the targeted person, who may be far away. The person who hears it soon believes it, a fire of anger is lit in him, and he rages against the wounded victim. Rumor is born from the bow shot: she spreads extensively and instantly, her sound waves reverberating in the ears of passersby; she comes up like a sudden squall of windy words, and she flies lightly on the wings of people's tongues. These two powers are at war with me. They have occupied your soul and barred the gates of your ears to my words."

11    As she said this, she touched his hand and tried to kiss it. He had calmed down somewhat, the plausibility of her speech warming his heart, and the agreement of her story about Leukippe with Sosthenes' account took away some part of his suspicion. Yet he did not entirely trust

her. Once jealousy has invaded the soul, it is hard to evict. He was upset at hearing that the maiden was my wife, and therefore hated me even more. For the time being, then, he merely said he would look into her story and went off to sleep by himself. Melite was sick at heart, since she had failed to keep her promise to me.

Sosthenes, after accompanying Thersandros for a little way and promising in no uncertain terms to bring Leukippe round, returned once more to her. Putting on a pleasant face, he said: "We have triumphed, Lakaina. Thersandros is in love with you, and he is driven to distraction, so much so that quite probably he will even make you his wife. This victory is mine, for it was I who repeatedly revealed to him the marvels of your beauty and filled his mind with fantasies of you. Why are you weeping? Get up, sacrifice to Aphrodite for your blessings, and in your prayers remember me!"

And Leukippe replied, "May you receive such blessings as you have 12 brought to me." Missing her irony, Sosthenes thought she was speaking in earnest and added in a kindly tone: "I want to tell you just who Thersandros is, to make you even happier. He is the husband of Melite, whom you saw on the estate. He is the noblest born of all Ionians; his wealth surpasses his pedigree, and his virtue his wealth. You saw his age and appearance, how young and handsome he is, qualities which particularly please a woman."

At this Leukippe could no longer put up with Sosthenes' chatter. "You wicked beast! How long will you pollute my ears? What has Thersandros to do with me? Let his good looks exist for Melite, his wealth for the city, his virtue and generosity for those who need it. These mean nothing to me, not even if he is nobler than Kodros and richer than Kroisos. Why this recital of irrelevant virtues? I will praise Thersandros as a good man when he stops forcing himself on other men's wives."

And Sosthenes replied in all seriousness, "You're joking!" 13

"Why would I be joking?" she answered. "Leave me to my slow erosion by Fortune and the evil genius who haunts me. I know I have fallen into a den of iniquity."

"I think you are incurably insane," he replied, "to regard all this as something bad—wealth, marriage, luxury, a husband offered you by Fortune whom the gods so love that they saved him from the gates of death itself!" Then he recounted the shipwreck, exaggerating the miraculous rescue as if it were a wonder beyond Arion's dolphin. When Leukippe refused to utter a word in response to his fairy tales, he said: "Consider carefully what is your better course; see that you say nothing like this to Thersandros lest you rouse that fine man's anger. When he is angry, he is unendurable. A noble nature treated with compliance grows nobler still, but the irritation of being rebuffed rebounds to wrath. The superabundant energy employed in philanthropy can be rerouted just as surely to revenge." And such for the moment was Leukippe's situation.

14     When Kleinias and Satyros learned that I had been locked up in jail (for Melite had sent them the news), they promptly appeared at my cell while it was still night. They wanted to wait there with me, but the man in charge of prisoners would not let them and told them to go away instantly. Though he chased them away against their will, I managed to say to them that if Leukippe were to turn up, she should come to me at daybreak with all speed. I told them too about Melite's promises. My divided soul was teetering then, its parts being apportioned between the balance pans of hope and fear: each new bit of hope found a gram of fear to balance it; each particle of fear was counterpoised by hope.

15     When day at last arrived, Sosthenes hastened to Thersandros, Satyros and Co. to me. When Thersandros saw Sosthenes, he asked how things stood with the maiden: was she persuaded to accept him? The account he then gave was not the truth on all counts; instead he devised an artful and persuasive dodge. "She still refuses, but I do believe her 'no' is not a pure and simple negative, rather she suspects (I think) that you will use her once and cast her aside. Such indignity she'll not endure."

    "As far as that goes," replied Thersandros, "she has nothing to worry about. My feelings towards her are as good as undying. My only grounds for fear (and this I am eager to discover from the maid), is whether she is truly married to the young man, as Melite related." Thus conversing, they reached Leukippe's hut. When they were near the doors, they heard her lamenting aloud, so they stood silently behind the door.

16     "Oh, dear, oh, dear, O Kleitophon, my dear." (She repeated this a lot.) "You don't know where I've gone, where I am imprisoned, neither do I know what fate has befallen you. We suffer an identical agony of ignorance. I hope that Thersandros didn't discover you in his house. I hope he hasn't done something outrageous to you too. I often wanted to ask Sosthenes but had no pretext for asking. If I inquired about you as my husband, I was afraid of causing you some harm, provoking Thersandros against you. If I asked about you as a stranger, that too would look suspicious. For what business has a woman to pry beyond her proper sphere? So many times I tried to force myself but could not persuade my tongue to speak. All I could say was, 'Kleitophon, my husband, husband of Leukippe alone, faithful and secure, whom not even a woman sleeping beside you could persuade to be unfaithful, though I was loveless enough to believe that you had. When I saw you on the estate after so long a time, I did not kiss you.' Now if Thersandros comes inquiring, what am I to say? Shall I disclose the roles in our play and explain the truth? 'Thersandros, case to regard me as a slave. I am the daughter of a Byzan-

*Thersandros now hears this*

tine general, and wife of one of the leading men of Tyre. I am not Thessalian, and my name is not Lakaina. This is an insult imposed by pirates who robbed me even of my name. My husband is Kleitophon; my country, Byzantium; Sostratos is my father, and Pantheia my mother.' But you wouldn't believe me even if I told you, and I'm afraid that if you did believe me about Kleitophon, my untimely exercise of free speech would spell my lover's doom. Come, I shall return again to my play; come, I shall put on again the mask of Lakaina."

When Thersandros heard this, he stepped a little distance away and said to Sosthenes: "Did you hear that incredible speech, so full of passion! Oh, her words, her grief, her self-accusation! That adulterer triumphs over me everywhere. I think he is not only a brigand but a wizard. Melite loves him; Leukippe loves him. O Zeus, would that I were Kleitophon."

"But you mustn't be weak, master," said Sosthenes, "when there's a job to be done. You must face the maid yourself. She may indeed love this cursed adulterer now, yet up to now she has known only him and has not been intimate with any other man: her soul is shaped by him alone. But once you come together with her—you being a far handsomer man than he—she will forget him entirely. A new passion makes the old one wither. A woman especially loves what is present and remembers what is absent only so long as she has not found something new. When she takes a new lover, she erases the previous one from her soul."

Thersandros was stirred by these words, for an optimistic speech about achieving one's passion is easy to believe. Desire, choosing its allies carefully, whips up expectations.

Leaving a little interval of time after Leukippe's speech so as not to seem to have overheard what she said, Thersandros made his entrance, putting on his most seductive look (as he thought). When he saw Leukippe, his soul burst into flame, and she seemed to have become even more beautiful. For he had nurtured that fire the whole night through, as long as he was away from the girl, and now her visible presence was like dry kindling thrown on it: the flame came suddenly to life, and he all but threw himself on her. Keeping control, however, he sat down beside her and began to make conversation, skipping from one subject to another in a way that made no sense at all. Such is the way with lovers when they try to talk with their girlfriends: they don't let logic rule their words but rather, since their soul is entirely focused on the loved one, their tongue alone does the talking, unrestrained by its charioteer logic.

While he was talking, he placed his hand on her neck and then tried to embrace her for a kiss. She foresaw the path along which his hand was moving and bent forward, putting her face in her lap. He embraced her nonetheless and tried to force her face upwards. She plunged further down and concealed her kisses. As this wrestling went on longer and longer, Thersandros was gripped by a strong feeling of erotic competition: he put his left hand down under her face, his right hand taking hold of her hair, and with the one drew her head backwards, with the other pressed on her chin and forced her face up.

When he abated his force for a moment, whether this was by chance or by design or simply from exhaustion, Leukippe said to him: "You are not acting like a free man, much less a gentleman. You have merely copied Sosthenes, a slave to match his master. Desist from this course and do not hope to consummate it, unless you become Kleitophon."

19    On hearing this, Thersandros no longer knew just who he was, for he felt both desire and rage at once. Anger and love are two burning lamps. The fire of anger is matched by another fire, opposite in nature but equally violent. The one kindles hatred; the other compels love. The source of each fire lies very close to the other: one is seated in the liver; the other about the heart. When both take hold of a person, the soul becomes a pair of scales, the fire of each emotion is weighed against the other; they fight to make the scales turn. Often love prevails, when it succeeds in achieving its desire. But if the beloved scorns his love, it invites anger to an alliance. Good neighbor anger accepts, and they light their fires in tandem. When love has left its own seat and gone wholly into anger's service, anger (which of its nature will never treat for peace) no longer fights as an ally along with love to achieve desire but binds love as a slave and represses desire. It will never allow love to make a truce with the beloved, however much it wants to. Love is drenched in anger, sinks down into it, and though it may want to return to its original sphere, it is no longer free but is compelled to hate the beloved. But when the bubbling vat of anger reaches a full boil and in the fullness of its power overflows, it then grows tired from sheer indulgence and begins to weaken. Love then takes the offensive, gives arms to desire, and stands victorious over anger, which is by now sleeping soundly. Love surveys the battlefield, and when it sees the damages it has inflicted on the loved one by its own senseless orgy, it grieves and tries to make excuses to the beloved, arranges a meeting to discuss their differences, and undertakes to soften anger with pleasure. When its goal is achieved, love is hilariously happy; but when rejected once again it descends to the seat of sleeping anger, wakes it up, and repeats the old pattern. Anger is ever the ally of scorned love.

20    Thersandros, who at first had hopes that this love would be successful, had for a while been Leukippe's slave entire. But in his present disappointment he let slip the reins of anger. He slapped her across the cheek and said: "You wicked little baggage! You *are* lovesick—literally! I heard

everything you said. You should be thrilled that I even speak to you; you should think it a great blessing to kiss your master; instead you behave like a prude and put on a despondent pose. In very truth you must be just a whore; certainly the man you love is an adulterer. But since you are unwilling to feel my passion as your lover, you shall feel my power as your lord!"

Leukippe replied, "Since you mean to be master, be mastered I must, but I will not be taken by force." And looking towards Sosthenes, she said, "Witness how I act in the face of injury, for you have done me an even worse injustice."

Humiliated by the truth of the indictment, Sosthenes said, "We must shred her, master, with whiplashes and a thousand other torments, until she learns not to despise her lord."

"Take his advice," said Leukippe. "He is a good counselor. Bring on    21
the instruments of torture: the wheel—here, take my arms and stretch them; the whips—here is my back, lash away; the hot irons—here is my body for burning; bring the axe as well—here is my neck, slice through! Watch a new contest: a single woman competes with all the engines of torture and wins every round. And you call Kleitophon an adulterer, an adulterer yourself! Tell me, aren't you afraid of your goddess Artemis? You rape a virgin in the virgin's own city? Lady goddess, where are your arrows?"

"A virgin?" said Thersandros. "Ridiculous impudence! A virgin after nights with all those pirates? Did the desperadoes become eunuchs just for you? Was the pirates' lair a school of philosophy? Did none of them have eyes?"

Leukippe responded: "Yes, a virgin, even after Sosthenes! Ask him    22
yourself. He is my principal despoiler. The rest were more moderate than you two; none of them was such a rapist. Look at what you're doing; you are the real pirates! Aren't you ashamed to do what even brigands have not dared? You may not realize it, but your shameless behavior is giving me even greater glory: even if you kill me in your senseless rage, someone will say, 'Leukippe was a virgin after the Rangers, a virgin after Chaireas, a virgin even after Sosthenes.' These are modest claims; the greater encomium is 'a virgin even after Thersandros, a more wanton sinner than any cutthroat. Whom he cannot rape he kills.' Arm yourself, then; take up the whips against me, the rack, the fire, the sword. Let Sosthenes, your counselor, join the campaign too. I am unarmed, alone, a woman. My one weapon is my freedom, which cannot be shredded by lashes, dismembered by sharp blades, or burned away by fire. It is the one thing I shall never part with. If you try to set it on fire, you will not find the fire hot enough."

## Book Seven

1    On hearing this, Thersandros reacted in several ways at once: he grieved, he raged, he plotted. He raged as a man insulted; he grieved as a man rejected; he plotted as a man in love. His soul split among various passions, he said nothing to Leukippe but simply ran out. He seemed to be charging off in a fury but actually was giving himself time to separate out the three waves of feeling that battered him. After taking counsel with Sosthenes, he approached the warden of the jail and asked him to kill me with poison. When the jailer refused (he was afraid of the community: a warden before him had been caught doing the same thing and had been executed), Thersandros made a second request—to put someone into the same cell where I was shackled, as if he were a fellow prisoner, pretending that he would merely use this decoy to learn more about me. The jailer agreed and admitted the man. The plan was that this man, on instructions from Thersandros, was very artfully to introduce the news that Leukippe had been killed and that Melite had masterminded the murder. This fiendishly clever strategy was devised by Thersandros to throw me into despair at the death of my beloved so that even if I was judged innocent at the trial, I would not set out to find her. He added Melite to the murder plot so that I would not, thinking Leukippe dead, try to marry Melite (given that she was in love with me) and so remain there as a constant threat to his safe enjoyment of Leukippe; if (as was likely) I hated Melite as Leukippe's murderess, I would in all likelihood leave the city at once.

2    When the man had been placed near me, he began to play his part. The deceitful knave began to groan and said: "What life is left for me to live! How will I ever protect myself against the pitfalls endangering my life? An honest career is no guarantee. Bad luck attacks and overwhelms us. I ought to have guessed who it was who was traveling with me and what he had done." He said all this and more to himself, angling for an entree for his deceitful message to me, hoping I would ask what he had suffered. But I was worrying about my own problems and gave little thought to his woes. But another of our fellow prisoners (for a person in misery, you see, is a creature curious to hear other people's troubles; this can act as a drug for the sorrow of his own suffering—bonding with another in his misery) said: "What happened to you at the hands of Fortune? It seems that though you did no wrong, you fell foul of a wicked deity. I'm just guessing from my own experiences." And with that he launched into a recital of his own adventures, which had landed him in jail. I was paying no attention to any of this.

3    When he finished, he asked for the corresponding tale of woe. "Please tell your story too." And the other answered: "I happened to be walking

yesterday along the road that leads out of the city. I was making the journey to Smyrna. After I had gone about four stades, a young man approached me from the fields, saluted me, and walked beside me for a while. 'Where are you going?' he said. 'To Smyrna,' I replied. 'I am going the same way, good luck to us!' he said. We traveled together from that point and conversed as one does on a journey. When we came to an inn, we decided to eat together. Meanwhile four men sat down near us; they pretended that they were eating too, but they were glancing at us continually and gesturing to each other. I suspected they had some design against us, but I couldn't interpret what their gestures meant. My companion turned pale by degrees and was eating in slow motion; he had even begun to tremble. When they noticed this, they leaped up, grabbed us, and bound us with thongs. One struck him across the head. Reeling from the blow as if he had endured a thousand tortures, he started talking, though no one asked him any questions. 'I killed the girl. I received a hundred pieces of gold from Melite, Thersandros's wife. She hired me to do the murder. But look, here are the hundred gold pieces, they're yours: why ruin me and deprive yourselves of a profit?'"

I had not been paying attention previously, but when I overheard the names of Thersandros and Melite, it was as if the words had nipped my soul like a gadfly. I stirred to attention and turning to him said, "Who is this Melite?"

"Melite," he replied, "is one of the leading women here. She fell in love with some young man. A Tyrian, I think they said he was. He happened to have a girlfriend whom he discovered sold as a slave in Melite's household. She was on fire with jealousy, so she tricked this woman, arrested her, and handed her over the man who was (as I said) by evil fortune my companion on the road, with orders to kill her. He actually did this unholy deed, while I, a poor wretch who neither saw him nor participated in word or deed, was bound and dragged away with him as a partner in crime. Worst of all, when they had gone a little way from the inn, they took the hundred pieces of gold from him, let him escape, and led me to the magistrate."

When I heard this tale of my unhappiness, I did not groan, I did not cry. I had no voice, no tears. A tremor at once spread over my body, my heartbeat slowed to nothing, and only a small spark of consciousness survived. Then after I had recovered a little from the drunken daze brought on by his narrative, I asked, "How did this hireling murder the girl, and what has he done with her body?" But once he had let the gadfly bite me and so done the job that he was there to do, he was silent and said nothing. When I asked again, he said: "Do you think I helped him kill her? All I heard from the murderer was that he had killed the girl. He didn't tell me where or how!" Then at last my tears came and granted my eyes their grief. For just as when a bruise from a blow to the body does not rise at once, and the blow at first creates no mottled flower on the skin, but shortly afterwards it rises to the surface; and just as when a person slashed by a boar's tusk looks for the wound and cannot see it, for it goes down deep, and its slow-motion effect is hidden, but suddenly a thin white line appears, harbinger of blood, and after a pause blood arrives and flows abundantly—just so the soul struck by an arrow of grief shot from a story is already wounded and cut, but because the injury occurred with such velocity, the wound did not open at once, and the tears from the eyes followed far behind; for a tear is the blood from a wound in the soul. As the tooth of sorrow slowly gnaws at the heart, the soul's wound breaks open, in the eyes a door opens for tears, and a short while later they flow out. So it was that the first hearing of his story, striking my soul like an arrow's sudden impact, left me silent and stopped my tears at their source; but afterwards they flowed, when my soul's tense attention to its shock had relaxed.

5    So I said: "Which deity deceived me with a brief bout of joy? What god put Leukippe on display in this new plot of disasters? I did not even satisfy my eyes—yet they gave me the only happiness I had. I did not take my fill even of looking. All my pleasure was just a dream! O my Leukippe, how many times you have died on me! Have I ever had a rest from mourning? I am always at your funeral, as one death hastens to replace another. But those were practical jokes that Fortune played on me; this is no longer one of her tricks. Well then, Leukippe, how did you really die? In the case of those sham deaths I always had some consolation, however small: in the first, your whole body was left me; in the second, I lacked only your head (as it then seemed) for a proper burial. But now you have died twice over—soul and body both are gone. You escaped from two gangs of cutthroats, but Melite's pirates have killed you. Oh the unholiness and sacrilege of it: how many times I kissed your butcher, how our limbs intertwined in defilement, and the ultimate gift of Aphrodite I gave to her, not you!"

6    While I was wailing, Kleinias entered. I told him everything, and that I had made up my mind to die. He tried to console me. "Who knows whether she is alive this time too. Hasn't she died many times before? Hasn't she often been resurrected? Why be hasty about your death? You'll always have time for that, after you're clear about her death."

"You babble. How can one be more sure than this? I think I have come up with the perfect way to die, a plan from which that accursed Melite cannot escape unscathed. Hear me out. I prepared, as you know, a defense against the charge of adultery, if the case came to trial. Now I have decided to do the exact opposite—to confess to the adultery and say that Melite and I killed Leukippe because we were so in love with each *revenge*

other. Thus she too will be punished, and then I hope to quit this cursed life."

"Bite your tongue," said Kleinias. "Would you actually dare to be executed on the most shameful of charges, thought by all to be a convicted murderer—and what's more, of Leukippe!"

"Nothing is shameful," I replied, "that hurts your enemy."

And so we were conversing when the jailer after a while released that man, the man who reported the sham murder, saying the magistrate had ordered him to come and make a statement about the charges against him. Kleinias and Satyros tried to advise me, hoping they could persuade me not to say to the court what I had planned. But they did not succeed. So for that day they rented rooms, so as not to be with Melite's foster brother any longer.

On the following day I was led to the court.[65] The attack mounted 7 against me by Thersandros was elaborate and included a corps of no less than ten rhetors. Melite's side was equally well prepared for a vigorous defense. When they had finished their speeches, I demanded a hearing and said: "All these speakers, both Thersandros's and Melite's, are talking nonsense. I will tell you the whole truth. I had long ago a girlfriend, Byzantine by birth, Leukippe by name. Thinking her dead (for she had been captured by cutthroats in Egypt), I met Melite, and we traveled as a couple to Ephesos, where we discovered Leukippe enslaved to Sosthenes, bailiff for the estates of Thersandros. I will let you make your own judgement as to how Sosthenes came to hold this free woman as a slave and what relation he had to the cutthroats. When Melite learned that I had found my former wife, she was afraid that my devotion would incline to her, and so she plotted to do away with her. I agreed to the plan—why should I hide the truth?—since she promised to make me master of all her wealth. I hired someone to do the job. His price for murder was a hundred pieces of gold. After he had done the deed, he left and has not been seen since. But love took revenge on me at once. As soon as I learned that she was dead, I repented, I wept, I felt my love for her, and I love her now. This is why I accuse myself, so that you will send me to join my beloved. I cannot bear to go on living—a murderer and still in love with her whom I killed."

After my speech everyone was in shock at the astounding twist in the 8 case, especially Melite. While Thersandros's rhetors joyfully chanted a victory song, Melite's were asking her what this all meant. Her answer

*Klitophon's defense*

65. Courtroom scenes and debates such as those in the following scene are familiar features in Greek novels (Chariton 5.4–8, Longus 2.15–16). They may even represent different styles of forensic speech: Kleinias's speech in 9 is sober in style; that of Sopatros in 8.10, florid. This reflects different fashions in literary style (simple "Atticism," ornate "Asianism") in Achilles' own day.

was compounded of troubled exclamations, of denials, of explanations that were hasty and unclear: she admitted to knowing about Leukippe and the rest of my story, but totally denied the murder. Since most of her admissions were in harmony with my version of events, they too became suspicious of her and professed themselves at a loss for a useful line of defense.

9    At this point, amidst great confusion in the courtroom, Kleinias stepped forward and said: "May I be allowed to address the court? A man's life is at stake." When he had been given permission, his eyes filled with tears, and he began to speak. "Men of Ephesos, be slow to pass a sentence of death on a man who wants to die, for death is naturally a welcome drug to the desperate. He has falsely accused himself of the crime alleged by those criminals. He wants to reap the reprisal of the miserable. The cause of his despair is briefly told. He had a girlfriend, as he said. This, at least, was no lie. And that cutthroats caught her, the affair of Sosthenes, all that he recounted leading up to the murder, happened as he said. But she disappeared suddenly, and it is not clear whether someone has killed her or if she has been kidnapped and is still alive. The only fact I am sure of is that Sosthenes is in love with her and has racked her with a thousand torments because he could not have her, and his cronies are cutthroats. This poor fellow here thinks his wife is dead and therefore no longer wants to live. This was his motive for self-incrimination as a murderer. His deep desire for death we know from his own confession, and that the reason is sorrow for his wife. Now think whether a man who has murdered someone would truly wish to join his victim in death, would find life too painful to bear. Was there ever a murderer so compassionate? What is this tender hatred? No, by the gods, do not believe him; do not execute a person who needs sympathy rather than sentencing. If he plotted the murder, as he says, let him name the man who was hired to do it, let him show us the corpse. But if there is no killer and no victim, who ever heard of such a murder? 'I was in love,' he said, 'with Melite. That is why I killed Leukippe.' How then can he accuse Melite, whom he loves, of murder, but want to die for Leukippe, whom he killed? Can anyone so hate what he loves and love what he hates? Would he not far rather have denied the murder, even when convicted, in order to spare his beloved and avoid a meaningless death because of the dead woman?

"Why then did he accuse Melite, if she really has done no such thing? I will explain this too; and by the gods, do not think I speak my piece in order to slander the woman—it is to explain how it all happened. Melite had felt a certain passion for him and had spoken about marriage before this corpse from the sea came back to life. But Kleitophon had no such feeling and strongly rejected the marriage, and meanwhile, rediscovering his beloved (as he said), whom he thought dead, alive in Sosthenes' clutches, he was even more estranged from Melite. And she, before she learned that the woman with Sosthenes was Kleitophon's girlfriend, pitied her, released her from her bondage under Sosthenes, received her into her household, and favored her in other ways appropriate to a freeborn woman in distress. When she learned who she was, she sent her to the country to do some service for her. After this they report that she disappeared. Melite will confirm that I am telling the truth, and the two maids whom she sent to the fields with Leukippe. This one circumstance makes Kleitophon suspect that Melite might have had Leukippe killed out of jealousy. Something else happened in prison that confirmed his suspicion and made him so ferocious against himself and against Melite. One of the prisoners, bemoaning his misfortune, said that he had innocently kept company on the road with a murderer who had killed a woman for pay. The names he mentioned were Melite, who hired him, and Leukippe, the victim. Whether that really happened I can hardly say, but it is within your power to find out. You have the prisoner. Then there are the maids, and then there is Sosthenes. He will tell from whom he got Leukippe as a slave; they will tell how she disappeared. And the other will testify about the hired killer. Until you have investigated each of these, it would be unholy and sacrilegious to execute a miserable young man, trusting the testimony of his insanity, for he has been driven mad by grief."

Kleinias's speech seemed persuasive to most of the court, but Thersandros's rhetors and friends present cried out that the killer who by god's providence had condemned himself should be executed. Melite handed over her maidservants and demanded that Thersandros hand over Sosthenes, saying that he was the most likely suspect in Leukippe's murder. Her counselors earnestly put this forward as a challenge. Thersandros took fright and secretly sent one of his men to the estate to Sosthenes, with orders for him to disappear at once, before the officers arrived for him. The man mounted a horse, rode wildly to Sosthenes, and told him the danger and how he would be put to torture if he were caught in the district. Sosthenes happened to be in Leukippe's hut, trying to charm her. Hearing his name called by the man when he arrived, with a shout and a great commotion, he went out and, hearing the news, was filled with fear. Already thinking the torturers were after him, he jumped on a horse and made for Smyrna with all speed. The messenger returned to Thersandros. There is evidently some truth in the saying "Fear shatters memory."[66] Sosthenes, at least, was so afraid for himself that in the shock of it he entirely forgot what was right there before him—he did

66. Thucydides 2.87.4.

not lock the door of Leukippe's hut. When a member of the servile class takes it into his head to be frightened, he really is an exemplary coward.

11    Meanwhile Thersandros was stepping forward in response to this first challenge by Melite. "We have heard quite enough silly fairy tales from this fellow, whoever he is. I find your insensitivity extraordinary: a murderer caught red-handed (for an explicit confession is stronger than an arrest on the spot), and you do not consign him at once to the executioner but sit enthralled by a wizard of words, a plausible actor, yes, and a plausible man with a tear. In my opinion he is an accomplice in the killing, afraid now for himself. So I cannot imagine what possible need there could be for torture in a case so clear and convincing.

"I further believe that he has committed a second murder. The very Sosthenes whom they are demanding from me has been missing for three days now, and the obvious suspicion is that he too has been claimed as a victim of their conspiracy. It was he who revealed to me the adultery. So probably they killed him and, knowing that I would not be able to produce him, have entered an unscrupulous challenge to bring him forward. I only wish that he could appear and not be found dead. Though even if he were present, what is there to learn from him? Whether he purchased a certain girl? Very well, say that he purchased her. Whether Melite took her on? Sosthenes, speaking through me, admits she did. Then Sosthenes' testimony is finished.

"Now I take up the argument against Melite and Kleitophon. What have you done with the slave you took? For she was my slave; Sosthenes purchased her. And if she were alive and had not been killed by them, she would still be my slave, pure and simple." (Thersandros inserted this argument into the record quite unscrupulously so that if Leukippe were later discovered alive, he could take her into slavery. Then he proceeded.) "Kleitophon then has confessed to the murder and has his judgment. Melite still denies her part. In her case we will have the torture of the maids. If it turns out that they took the girl from Melite but never brought her back, what has become of her? Why was she sent to the country in the first place? And to whom? Is it not obvious that they set up some people to kill her? The maidservants, I should guess, did not know these people, to keep the number of conspirators at a minimum and reduce the risk of exposure. They left her where their gang of cutthroats was hiding, so that not even the maids saw what actually happened.

"He also babbled about some prisoner who talked about the murder. Who was this prisoner who said nothing to the magistrate but only confided his mysterious knowledge of the crime to this man alone? Who else but someone who recognized him as a part of the plot! Do you suppose that the hand of god is not evident in this man's voluntary confession?"

After Thersandros had spoken and sworn that he did not know what    12
had happened to Sosthenes, it was decided by the president of the
judges—he was of the royal house[67] and sat in judgment of cases of murder (according to law he was advised by elders whom he took as arbiters
for each decision)—the president, then, decided in consultation with his
advisers to pass a sentence of death against me, in accordance with the
law which directed that self-confessed murderers must die. For Melite
there would be a second trial when the maids were tortured. Thersandros
was to take an oath in writing that he did not know what had happened
to Sosthenes. I, as a convicted criminal, was now to be tortured about
Melite's part in the murder. At the moment when my arms had been tied
and the clothes had been stripped from my body and I was hanging in
the air on ropes and the torturers were bringing on the whips and fire
and rack, while Kleinias was groaning and calling on the gods, the priest
of Artemis was seen advancing towards us, crowned with laurel. This is
a symbolic gesture that an embassy to the goddess has arrived. Whenever
this happens, there must be a moratorium on all punishments for however many days the ambassadors are making sacrifice. So at that point I
was let down and untied. The leader of the embassy was Sostratos,
Leukippe's father. The Byzantines, you see, had experienced an apparition from Artemis during their war against the Thracians, and after their
victory they reckoned that they should send her a sacrifice to acknowledge her help in their military triumph. The goddess had also appeared
to Sostratos personally one night: the vision indicated that he would find
his daughter in Ephesos and his brother's son as well.

Meanwhile Leukippe had noticed that the door of the hut was un-   13
locked and that Sosthenes was not in evidence. She peeked out to see if
he was outside the hut. Since he was nowhere, her usual courage and optimism returned, for her memory of having been so often and unexpectedly saved from present dangers encouraged her to use this opportunity.
And so, since the sanctuary of Artemis was close to the estate, she ran to
it and took refuge in the temple.

From ancient days this temple had been forbidden to free women who
were not virgins. Only men and virgins were permitted here. If a non-
virgin woman passed inside, the penalty was death, unless she was a
slave accusing her master, in which case she was allowed to beseech the
goddess, and the magistrates would hear the case between her and her
master. If the master had in fact done no wrong, he recovered his maidservant, swearing that he would not bear a grudge for her flight. If it was
decided that the serving girl had a just case, she remained there as a slave
to the goddess. Within moments after Sostratos set off to the court to

---

67. The situation is comparable, perhaps, to that in Athens, where cases of murder were
tried before a "royal archon."

halt the trials, taking the priest with him, Leukippe arrived at the temple, so that she just barely missed meeting her father.

14 When I had been released from the tortures, the court adjourned, and a crowd gathered around me, a confused mixture of sympathizers, miracle mongers, and the merely curious. Then Sostratos came near, saw me, and recognized me, for, as I said at the beginning of my narrative, he was once in Tyre to celebrate a feast of Herakles and had in fact spent a considerable amount of time there long before our elopement. So he quickly recognized me from my appearance, especially since he was naturally expecting to discover us because of his dream. Coming up to me, he said: "Here is Kleitophon. Where then is Leukippe?"

I recognized him and just stared at the ground. The others relayed to him my testimony of self-incrimination. He groaned aloud, beat himself about the head, and then went for my eyes and nearly gouged them out; for I made no attempt to defend myself but rather offered my face to his violence. In an attempt to stop him, Kleinias went up and addressed him. "What are you doing, man? Why this stupid outburst against a man who loves Leukippe more than you do? He set himself up to suffer death because he thought that she was dead." He said much more as well in the way of consolation.

Sostratos wept and wailed, invoking Artemis. "Is this why you led me here, O Lady? Is this the kind of prophetic message you send in dreams? And to think I trusted your dreams and expected to find my daughter in your city. A fine present you hand me! All you have helped me find is her murderer!"

Kleinias, however, on hearing of the dream of Artemis, was overjoyed and said: "Courage, Father; Artemis does not lie. Your Leukippe is alive. Have faith in my predictions. Don't you see how she just saved this man too, snatching him from the torturers as he hung in the ropes?"

15 At this point one of the temple attendants came running very quickly up to the priest and said in the hearing of all, "A foreign maiden has sought sanctuary with Artemis." As I heard this, my heart spread its wings, I lifted my eyes from the ground, and I began to come to life again. Kleinias said to Sostratos, "My prophecies have come true, Father." And he turned to the messenger: "She is beautiful?"

"I have never seen another like her," he replied, "second only to Artemis."

At this I leaped up and shouted, "It must be Leukippe!"

"Why, yes, exactly," he said. "She said that was her name, that her country is Byzantium and her father is Sostratos."

Kleinias started clapping his hands and singing the paean; Sostratos collapsed for joy. I jumped into the air, chains and all, and flew to the temple as if hurled from a catapult. The guards chased after me, thinking

I was trying to escape, and kept shouting to passersby to grab me. But then I had wings for feet. However, some people just managed to stop me in my mad career, and the guards caught up and tried to thrash me. But I had now regained my courage and defended myself. They started dragging me back to jail.

Then Kleinias and Sostratos appeared on the scene. Kleinias cried out: 16 "Where are you taking him? He has not committed the murder for which he was judged guilty." Sostratos in turn said the same and added that he was the father of the supposed victim. The people around who heard the whole story praised Artemis. They surrounded me and prevented the guards from taking me to prison. The guards kept claiming that they had no authority to release a person condemned to death, until the priest, at Sostratos's request, gave assurances that he would keep me and present me to the public when it was required.

And so I was released from my bonds, and I quickly pressed on to the temple. Sostratos was at my heels—I would suppose with joy similar to my own. Yet no one can run so fast that the wings of rumor will not outrun him. In this case too she reached Leukippe before us, bringing her the whole story of Sostratos and myself. Seeing us, she leaped from the temple and embraced her father, keeping her eyes the while on me. Embarrassment before Sostratos keeping me from leaping on her, I stood there looking all the time into her face. Thus we fondly greeted each other with our eyes.

## Book Eight

Just as we were about to seat ourselves and discuss all that had happened, 1 Thersandros charged madly up to the temple, bringing some witnesses, and said to the priest in a stentorian voice: "I call these people to witness that you have improperly removed from death row a person condemned to legal execution. You hold my female slave as well, a lascivious woman, a nymphomaniac. You had better keep her for me!"

The words "female slave" and "lascivious woman" upset me terribly. I did not put up with his wounding words but interrupted him in mid-insult. "And you, sir, are a slave from a long line of slaves, a lunatic and a lecher. She is a free woman, a virgin and worthy of the goddess."

When he heard this, he replied, "And you even insult me, you convict and crow bait!" He struck me one very forceful blow across the face and then added a second. Gushers of blood spurted out of my nostrils, for he put all his rage into the punch. As he struck me a third time, rather carelessly, he accidentally hit his knuckles against my teeth. This wounded his fingers; he managed painfully to withdraw his hand, groaning. Thus my teeth avenged the wounded honor of my nose. They struck a blow against his bashing knuckles and made his fist get as good as it gave. He nursed his hand and groaned involuntarily. That was the end of the affray.

Seeing the extent of his injury, I pretended not to notice it at all but instead made the temple resound with a high tragic lament on the subject of Thersandros's tyrannous treatment of me.

2 "Whither further may we flee violence? Where may we seek shelter? To whom of the gods after Artemis? We are attacked in the very temples; we are struck in the sanctuaries! In desert places only do such things occur, where no man is and no witness watches. Yet you act the tyrant in the gods' own sight. Even to the wicked the temples' security gives refuge, but I who never a wrong have done, a refugee of Artemis, am knocked about at her own altar, while the goddess (alas!) looks on. Against Artemis the blows are struck!

"His drunken violence stops not at striking blows but even draws blood from my face, as if this were a battlefield and we at war. This sacred floor is stained with human gore. Who makes such libation to the goddess? Is this not the way of barbarians, of Taurians before the Artemis of Skythia? Only they have a temple that runs with blood like this. You have transformed Ionia into Skythia; blood that flows among the Taurians now flows in Ephesos as well. Draw your sword against me too. Though what need have you of iron? Your hand has done the sword's work. That man-slaughtering, blood-letting hand has produced effects like those of murder!"

3 While I was screaming this, a crowd of people in the temple gathered round. They cursed Thersandros, and the priest himself was indignant that Thersandros was not ashamed to do such things so openly and in the very temple. I felt emboldened to say: "This is what I have suffered, gentlemen, I a free man and citizen of a not insignificant city, a victim of this man's plot against my life, though saved by Artemis, who revealed him as a false accuser. Now I must go out and wash my face away from the temple. I wouldn't do it here, lest the holy water too be polluted by the blood of violence."

They dragged him struggling from the temple, and as he left, he shouted: "Your case has already been decided, and you will presently suffer punishment. As for that pseudo-virgin prostitute, the flute will punish her."

4 When he finally left, I went out and cleansed my face. It was dinnertime, and the priest entertained us very cordially. I was unable to look Sostratos straight in the eyes, knowing what I had put him through. And Sostratos as well, noticing the scratches around my eyes that I had suffered at his hands, felt embarrassed to look at me. Leukippe too stared at the ground most of the time. Our entire symposium was embarrassing.

But as the drinking proceeded, and Dionysos (who is, after all, the father of candor) gradually loosened up our embarrassment, the priest began the conversation by saying to Sostratos: "Why not tell us, stranger, your tale, whatever it may be? It appears to me to contain some pleasant complications. Such stories are best told over wine."

Sostratos gladly made use of the opportunity. "My part in the story is a simple one. Sostratos is my name, Byzantine by birth, uncle to this man, father to this woman. As for the rest, which is the real tale, tell us, Kleitophon, my boy, and don't be ashamed. Even if some of it should be such as to distress me, it is certainly not your doing, but the god's. Furthermore, once deeds are over and done with, one who suffered through them now finds their telling brings more pleasure than pain."

I then narrated all of the adventures on our expedition away from Tyre—the voyage, the shipwreck, Egypt, the Rangers, the capture of Leukippe, the sham stomach at the altar, Menelaos's trick, the general's passion and Chaireas's medicine, the kidnapping by cutthroats and the wound in my thigh (showing my scar). When I reached the chapters about Melite, I modified my account of my behavior to emphasize my chastity (though I told no positive lies): Melite's passion and my self-control; her oft repeated pleas, disappointments, promises, and fits of melancholy. I included in my narrative the ship, the voyage to Ephesos, our sleeping together, and, "I swear by Artemis here present," how she rose from bed as a woman from another woman. I omitted only one scene from my synopsis, the fact that I subsequently discharged my obligation to Melite. When I had given them the banquet scene and the false-confession sequence and brought the story up to the arrival of the Byzantine embassy, I said: "That is my side of the story; Leukippe's is much more intense: she was sold, enslaved; she hoed the ground; her beautiful hair was ravaged. You see how she's shorn." I went through each event as it happened. Here too, when I got to the part about Sosthenes and Thersandros, I elaborated her tale even more than my own, my lover's gift to her, since her father was listening. I told how she bore every indignity and insult to her body save one, and how for the sake of this one she submitted to all the others. "And she has remained up to the present day, Father, in the same condition in which you sent her from Byzantium. Credit for this belongs not to me, that I chose to elope but did not consummate what we were eloping for, but rather to her, that even in the midst of bandits she remained a virgin, and conquered that great bandit, I mean Thersandros the Shameless, Thersandros the Violent. We have acted like sage philosophers, Father, while we have been away from home. Passion was hot on our trail; we fled as lover and beloved, but in our exile we were like brother and sister. If one can speak of such a thing as male virginity, this is my relationship to Leukippe up to now. For she has long been longing for Artemis's temple. Lady Aphrodite, do not be angry with us as if we had insulted you. We did not want to wed without a father present. The father is here now. Be with us too and shed your grace on us. Amen."

The priest was quite astonished, marveling at each episode; Sostratos cried as well, whenever the drama focused on Leukippe. When I reached the end, I said: "You have heard our tale. Now there is just one thing I would like to learn from you, Reverend. What in the world did Thersandros mean by his parting shot at Leukippe—the flute?"

"A good question," he replied. "It is only right and fitting that we who know the secret of the syrinx should impart it to our guests. I shall pay you in kind for your tale.

6   "You see this grove here at the back of the temple. Here there is a cave forbidden to women except those who enter as pure virgins. A little way inside the doors of the cave hangs a syrinx. If they play such an instrument back home in Byzantium, you already know what I mean. But just in case any of you is less familiar with this form of music, I will explain its nature and the whole story of Pan that goes with it.

"The syrinx consists of a number of pipes, each made from a reed; the set of pipes plays like a single flute. They are lined up in a row, side by side and joined. The front and back are identical. The reeds that are somewhat shorter are placed before the longer in such a way that the second, say, is as much longer than the first as the third is longer than the second, and the proportion determines the place of each succeeding reed in the chorus, each a step above the one before it, and the middle one is the mean between extremes. The reason for such a ranking is the distribution of notes. The pipes at the ends have the highest and lowest notes. Between these extremes are the intervals of the scale, each of the intervening reeds bringing the pitch down to its neighbor on the line until it reaches the final low note.

"The sounds that in the case of the Athena-flute are produced within the body of the instrument the Pan-pipes produce at the ends of the reeds. In the flute, it is the fingers that produce the music; in the Pan-pipes, the musician's mouth serves the function of the fingers. The flautist closes all the openings but one, through which the breath flows forth; here the player leaves all the other reeds free and only puts his lips on the one that does not want to be silent, and jumps about from one to another, wherever the notes will produce a happy harmony. So the mouth dances along the reeds of the Pan-pipes.

"Originally the syrinx was neither a flute nor a reed but a virgin as lovely as you could wish. Pan pursued her in a race for love; a thick wood received her in her flight. At that moment, Pan, who was right on her heels, reached out his hand to seize her. He thought he had caught her and was holding her by the hair, but the tresses in his hand were reeds. They say that she sank into the earth and that the earth produced reeds in her place. Pan cut the reeds angrily for concealing the object of his desire. But when he was unable to find her, he thought the maid had been changed into the reeds and wept that he had cut her, supposing his beloved had been slashed. Gathering up the severed bits of reed as if they were the limbs of her body and joining them together as a single body, he held in his hands the cut ends of the reeds and kissed them as if they were the maiden's wounds. He groaned as he put his lover's lips to them and so breathed into the flutes from above as he kissed them. His breath flowed through the narrow reed passages and made flutelike sounds: the syrinx had a voice.

"They say, then, that Pan dedicated this syrinx here and locked it up in a cave, and that he frequents the place and is in the habit of playing on the pipes. At a later date the area was presented to Artemis, Pan having struck an agreement with her that no woman not a virgin was to enter it. Whenever a woman is accused of not being a virgin, the populace accompanies her up to the doors of the cave and lets the syrinx pass judgment. The girl enters, dressed in the proper attire, and someone else closes the cave doors. If she be a virgin, a delicate, ethereal melody is heard—either the place itself has a musical breath that plays on the pipes or perhaps it is actually Pan himself playing. Shortly afterwards the doors of the cave open of their own accord, and the virgin appears crowned with sprigs of pine. If she has lied about her virginity, the syrinx is silent, and instead of music a scream is heard from the cave. At once the populace quits that place, leaving the woman in the cave. On the third day a virgin priestess of the place enters and finds the syrinx lying on the ground, with no trace of the woman. So decide what your situation is and prepare yourselves in consequence. If she is a virgin, as I hope and pray, go your way rejoicing to meet the blessing of the syrinx, for it would never deliver a false decision. But if not—well, you know as well as anyone that a girl trapped in such toils, no matter how she resists, is all too likely to have been—"

Before the priest could complete his sentence, Leukippe exclaimed: 7 "Well I think you can stop right there! I'm quite prepared to walk into the cave of the syrinx and to be shut up in it, whether formally challenged to do so or not."

"A good response," the priest said, "and I rejoice with you in your chastity and your lot."

Then, since it was evening, each of us went off to sleep where the priest had prepared quarters for us. Kleinias had not joined us for dinner, so that we would not strain the hospitality of our host, but remained that day where he had lodged the day before. I noticed that Sostratos was a bit shaken by the story of the syrinx, thinking we might have been too ashamed before him to tell the truth about her virginity. I signaled to Leukippe with a discreet nod that she should allay her father's anxiety, for she would know how best to convince him. It seemed to me that she had the same intuition about him—she took my meaning at once, and even before I nodded she had been considering what action to reassure him would be most tactful. So when she was on the point of retiring to sleep, she gave her father a hug and said to him quietly: "Have confidence in me, Father; trust what you have heard. By Artemis, neither of us has told any lie."

On the following day, Sostratos and the priest were occupied with the embassy, and the sacrifices had been performed. The city council was present, too, to take part in the liturgy. The goddess was frequently invoked in suitably sacred terms. Thersandros, who also happened to be present, approached the president and said, "Put our case on the docket for tomorrow, for certain parties have already set free the man you condemned to death yesterday, and Sosthenes is nowhere to be found." The case was accordingly scheduled for the next day. We readied ourselves meticulously to meet the charges.

8 When the moment arrived, Thersandros spoke as follows. "It is hard to know where to begin, which crime should take precedence, whom I should accuse first and whom second. The outrages are so daring, the outragers so numerous, and no one of them takes second place to any other. Each is independent of the others, and it might well happen that I leave some untouched in my accusations, for if my emotions get the upper hand, I am afraid the argument may be incomplete, as the fresh thought of other crimes keeps leading my tongue to a new subject. The urge to state what is yet unsaid impairs the completion of what is begun. For when an adulterer murders another man's bailiff, and a murderer adulterates another man's wife; when a brothelkeeper dissipates our embassies, and a whore pollutes our most sacred temple; when such people can determine the trial date for a slave woman and her master—what have they left undone? Their lawless behavior has been compounded with adultery, with sacrilege, and with murder!

"You sentenced a man to death on certain charges (it makes no difference what they were) and sent him off in chains to jail to await execution. Here he stands before you, wearing not chains but a white robe, a prisoner standing in the ranks of the free. Perhaps he will even be so bold as to say something, to give a fine oration against me—or rather against you and your verdict. Read here the decree of the presidents and their counselors." *******[68]

68. As in real forensic speeches, the text of such a document is not given; the document is "taken as read," as it were.

"You hear then how you voted and the verdict you reached in my favor against him: 'It is the sentence of this court that Kleitophon must die.' Then where is the executioner? Let him take this man away. Administer the hemlock. He is already legally dead. His doom is overdue.

"What do *you* have to say for yourself, most reverend and proper priest! In what holy laws is it written that you should snatch from execution men condemned by the council and prytanies, men already consigned to bondage and death, to loose their bonds, to arrogate to yourself higher authority than the presidents and courts? Get up from the bench, Mr. President, yield your court and your authority to him. You no longer have any power at all. You have no right to cast a vote against the wicked; today's decrees are tomorrow's dead letters. Why do you stand here with us, priest, as if you were one of the multitude? Step up and set yourself on the president's throne; conduct the rest of our trial; no, tell us like a tyrant what to do! Don't wait for any law to be read or jury to reach a verdict and don't consider yourself a mere human being. Be worshiped along with Artemis, since you have grabbed some of her prerogatives too. She alone has the right to rescue those who seek sanctuary with her, but only provided the court has not passed its sentence. The goddess has never released a prisoner from his shackles nor freed a condemned man from the death penalty. Her altars are for the wretched, not the wicked. But you actually free the bound prisoner and absolve the condemned. So you think yourself superior to Artemis!

"Who has treated a temple as a prison cell? A murderer and adulterer, living in the house of the goddess of purity! Oh, an adulterer dwelling with the Virgin! And with him an immoral woman who ran away from her master. We noticed that you took her in too and that you shared with them a common feast and symposium. Perhaps you slept with them too, eh, Reverend? You have made the sacred shrine a common bawdy house, the home of Artemis a bedroom for adulterers and whores. Such things hardly happen in a brothel. This one complaint is directed at both of them: I demand that the priest be punished for his willful presumption and that the convict's sentence be carried out.

"My second case is against Melite for adultery, and I need present no arguments against her. The court has already determined to examine the maids under torture. I demand that they be presented, and if even under torture they deny any knowledge that this convict lived for a prolonged period of time with her in my house in the role of a husband, not merely of an adulterer, I dismiss all charges against her. If, however, they testify to the opposite, I claim that she should according to the law relinquish her dowry to me and that he should undergo the punishment allotted to adulterers, namely, death—so that however this man dies, *qua* adulterer or *qua* murderer, since he is guilty of both, he will not have paid for his crime when he has paid for his crime. Dead, he will owe another death!

"My third case is against my slave girl and her pious impostor of a father, whom I shall keep for later, after you have sentenced this batch." With these words, he stopped.

9    The priest stepped forward. He was by no means an incompetent speaker, an emulator in particular of Aristophanic comedy.[69] He began to speak in the urbane style of comedy, attacking the sexual integrity of Thersandros.[70] "To insult the goddess by such an uncontrolled harangue against her clean-living servants is the work of an impure mouth. Not only here but everywhere he goes, this man's tongue is coated with rank insolence. As a youth he was on intimate terms with many well-endowed men, spending his youthful beauty all on them. His looks exuded piety; he acted the role of chastity, pretending a very hot desire to be cultivated. When he found men who would exercise him to this end, he would kneel at their feet and bend over double to please them. He left his father's house and rented a little bedroom where he set up shop, specializing in the old Greek lays (Homer, I mean), and was receptive to all who might serve him and give him what he wanted. He was supposed to be developing his mind, but this was just a cover for a dissolute life. In the gymnasiums we couldn't help but notice how he oiled his body, that special way he shinnied on the pole, and how in wrestling with the boys he always clung more tightly to the ones who were more manly. So much for his physical activities.

"This went on while his youthful beauty lasted. When he became a man, he exposed everything that he had concealed before. He neglected the rest of his body, which was worn out anyway, and concentrated on the tongue, whetting it for disgusting activities, and used his mouth in shameless ways, insulting everyone, parading his shamelessness on his very face. This man was not ashamed to slander in your presence (and so inelegantly at that!) a man whom you have honored with the priesthood. If I had lived in some other land and not with you, I would have to defend myself and my ways of life. But since you know that my behavior is very far removed from his blasphemies, let me speak to you instead about the specific accusations.

"'You released,' he says, 'the man condemned to death.' He waxed bitterly indignant about this, calling me a tyrant and other pompous-sounding names. But the tyrant is not he who saves a man falsely

---

69. Menander was still the most popular writer of comedy with the Atticists of Hadrian's time. Phrynichos, who lived later in the second century, is said to have been the first Atticist to try to put Aristophanes on Menander's pedestal. This detail may offer further evidence for the date of the novel.

70. It was a licit and familiar tactic in the Athenian trials known from fourth-century orators to attack not merely an opponent's case but his entire life. Aischines *Against Timarchos* offers a splendid example, charging Timarchos with youthful sexual conduct unbefitting a citizen (and incidentally mentioning a dissolute Thersandros, 1.52).

charged; the tyrant is he who locks up the innocent before council or populace have condemned them. By what laws, tell me, did you lock up this young foreigner in prison the first time? Which magistrate had sentenced him? What court had bound him over to prison? Even granting that he had committed every crime you mentioned, let him be tried first, let him be examined and given a chance to speak. Let the law, which has authority over you and everyone, bind him. Without a judgment passed, no man has more rights than another. Close the courts! Abolish the councils! Throw out the magistrates! All that you said to the chief magistrate would in truth be more justly said against you. Get up and give your seat to Thersandros, Mr. President. You hold your office in name alone. This man performs your functions, or rather exceeds them, for you have advisers and may never proceed without them, and you would never exercise any part of your authority before you had taken your seat on this bench. Nor have you condemned a person to prison in your home. But this noble man is all things unto himself: populace, council, president, magistrate. In his own house he punishes, holds court, remands to custody, and hears his cases in the evening: a nocturnal juror is a fine thing![71] And now he cries out repeatedly 'You set free a convict sentenced to death.' What death? What conviction? Tell me the grounds for his death sentence. 'He has been judged guilty of murder,' he says. He has committed murder then? Tell me who it was. The woman whom he killed and who you said had been murdered you see here alive. You would not be so foolhardy as still to accuse the same man of her murder. For this is not a ghost of the girl; Aidoneus has not sent the murdered woman to haunt you.

"We now hold you accountable for two murders: you killed her verbally; you tried to kill him in reality; and further you were going to kill her too, for we heard about your drama on the estate. But the great goddess Artemis saved them both, snatching her from the clutches of Sosthenes, him from yours. You yourself have snatched off Sosthenes to prevent your incrimination. For shame! You charge the strangers with crimes, and it turns out that you framed them both. Let me end here my defense against this man's blasphemous charges; the defense of the strangers I will turn over to themselves."

A rather prominent rhetor, a member of the council, was rising to speak on behalf of me and Melite, when another rhetor named Sopatros, a counselor for Thersandros, leaped up ahead of him. "It is my turn to speak against these adulterers, my dear Nikostratos," (this was our

---

71. It is not clear what is objectionable about conducting public business in the evening; perhaps it was felt that normally such business was for the daytime, and Thersandros was upsetting the normal order. Any stick is good enough to beat your opponent with in this kind of legal speech.

rhetor's name) "and then yours. For Thersandros's speech was directed only at the priest and merely touched on—barely grazed really—the case against the prisoner. After I have demonstrated that he is responsible for two deaths, then you will have an opportunity to rebut the charges."

With these words he made some grand flourishes, rubbed his face, and began as follows. "We have listened to this priest's bawdy routine, his shameless and shocking jibes at Thersandros's expense. His opening remarks in particular were nothing but the very criticism leveled against himself redirected against Thersandros. In point of fact, none of Thersandros's accusations against him was untrue—he did release a prisoner; he did entertain a prostitute; he did condone adultery. His shameless lies, told to discredit Thersandros's life, stop short of no dishonesty. A priest should, above all, keep his speech pure and unblemished by insult. (I shall use his own argument against him.) After his burlesque routine, he shifted up to tragedy, speaking plainly now and not in innuendos. He took umbrage that we arrested and held an adulterer. It boggles the mind to imagine what price could have bought his zeal. One can suspect the truth—he took one look at the faces of these filthy reprobates, the adulterer and his whore. She is young and lovely; the lad too is lovely, still easy on the eyes and still serviceable for the pleasures of our priest. Which of these two has bought you off? You all slept together, you got drunk together, and all night long there was no one to watch you. I am afraid you have rededicated Artemis's temple to Aphrodite, and we must have a hearing on your priesthood to see if you should hold this office.

"Everyone knows that Thersandros's life from his earliest boyhood has been chaste and decent and that when he reached manhood he took a wife, observing all the proper forms. His only mistake has been the woman he chose, for he did not find her to be as he hoped, having unwisely trusted in her social position and wealth. It is likely that she has been sinning with other men for a long time past and has been more successful at hiding those lovers from her noble husband. For the last act of her performance she has thrown off her veil of respectability and wallowed in her shameless behavior. When her husband embarked on a long voyage away from home, she thought the time was timely for adultery and found a young hustler (this was her great misfortune, that her lover was the sort who imitates a man with women but becomes a woman with men). She was not content with the security of coupling with him openly in a foreign land but brought him here, sleeping with him on that long sea voyage and on the ship disporting herself lasciviously for all to see. O adultery that spreads itself over land and sea! O adultery that stretches from Egypt to Ionia! Some women commit adultery, but only for a single day. If the crime is repeated, they hide the act and deceive everyone. But this woman hires a brass band and a herald to announce her sin. All Ephesos knows the adulterer. She shamelessly brought home this cargo from her travels, as if she had purchased a job lot of loveliness and had set up an importer's market for adultery.

"'But I thought,' she says, 'that my husband was dead.' Consider the implications. If on the one hand he were dead, she would be free of the charge, for no one exists to suffer the injury of the adultery, and when a marriage lacks the man, it cannot be insulted. But if on the other hand the marriage has not been annulled, because the husband is still alive, then a stranger corrupting the wife has poached on another man's property. The propositions are equally valid: if the husband were not alive, the adulterer as such would not exist; but he *is* alive, and Kleitophon *is* an adulterer!"

While Sopatros was still speaking, Thersandros interrupted him. "There is no need for speeches. I have two challenges to issue—one against Melite and one against this alleged daughter of the pious ambassador (I no longer intend to have her tortured, as I said a short while ago), who is in reality my slave." And he read out, "Thersandros challenges Melite and Leukippe (for I heard that this was the whore's name): if Melite has not celebrated the communion rites of Aphrodite with this stranger during the period of my absence, and if she enters the waters of the holy Styx and swears to that, she will be acquitted of all charges. The other one, if she is not a virgin, must reenter her master's service—for only slaves who are not virgins may enter the temple of Artemis—but if she claims to be a virgin, she must be enclosed in the cave of the syrinx."

We instantly accepted the challenge, for we had known that it was coming. Melite was confident because during the time Thersandros was away, the closest we had come to each other was words. "I do indeed accept this challenge and will myself add still more to it—principally, I never allowed any man at all, whether citizen or stranger, to have intercourse with me during the specified period. But what penalty will you pay if you are proved a liar?"

"Whatever the judges decide to assess," he said. With this the court was adjourned, the following day being assigned for us to comply with the challenges.

The water of the Styx worked as follows. There was a beautiful virgin named Rhodopis who had a passion for the hunt and chase. Her feet were swift; her hands were sure; she wore a cincture and headband, for she hitched her chiton up to her knees and clipped her hair like a man. Artemis saw her, liked what she saw, invited her over, and made her a companion in the chase. From then on they usually hunted together. She further swore to remain with her always, to flee from intercourse with men, and not to endure the outrage of sex. Rhodopis so swore; Aphrodite heard, turned angry, and wanted to punish the maid for her disdain. There was a young man of Ephesos, as handsome among the youths as Rhodopis was among the virgins. They called him Euthynikos. He was a hunter like Rhodopis and like her preferred to have no thoughts of Aphrodite. So the goddess proceeded against them both by bringing their hunting paths together. Hitherto they had had no contact whatsoever, but that day Artemis was absent. Aphrodite stood beside her son the archer and said, "My child, you see that loveless pair, who hate us and our mysteries. The virgin, even bolder, has sworn an oath against me. You see them running towards each other, pursuing the doe. You take the first shot; begin with the haughty maid. Your arrow always hits its mark." Both drew their bows back simultaneously: Rhodopis aimed at the doe; Eros aimed at the virgin. Both hit their target; and the huntress, after her catch, was caught. The doe had an arrow in her back; the virgin in her heart. The arrow was love for Euthynikos. Eros let go a second shot in his direction. Euthynikos and Rhodopis saw each other. At first their eyes froze at the other's sight; neither wished to turn his glance aside. Gradually their wounds became inflamed, and Eros herded them to this cave, where the spring is now, and here they broke the oath. Artemis saw Aphrodite laughing and understood what had happened, and she remade the maid into a springhead of water on the very spot where she had sprung her maidenhead. This is why when someone is accused in affairs of Aphrodite, she enters the spring to bathe. The fountain is a small one, reaching only to the mid-calf. The ordeal is this: she writes the oath on a tablet and ties it around her neck with a string. If she has not been false to her oath, the spring remains in place. If she is lying, the water seethes and rises to her neck and covers the tablet. After a discussion of these things, since it was well into evening, we parted company to sleep, each person separately.

13    On the next day the entire populace showed up. Thersandros was up in front, beaming, and looking at us with a smile. Leukippe was outfitted in a religious robe: an ankle-length chiton, made of fine linen, belted at the waist. There was a red fillet around her head; her feet were unsandaled. She entered the cave with a stately walk. As I watched her, I stood trembling and said to myself: "I have utter faith in your virginity, Leukippe, but Pan, my dear, throws me into a panic. This god has a penchant for virgins, and I fear you may become a second syrinx! She fled his pursuit on a plain, she was chased on open ground, but we have shut you in behind closed doors like a city under siege, so that if he should pursue, you could not flee. Lord Pan, be kind and do not violate the law of this place. We have observed it. Let Leukippe come back to us a virgin. You made an agreement with Artemis. Do not play this virgin false!"

As I was mumbling this to myself, a melody began to be detected, 14 and it was said that never before had such delicate music been heard. At once we saw the doors had opened. As Leukippe ran out, the people gave a loud cry of joy and started abusing Thersandros. There is no way I could put in words my feelings at that moment. Having won this glorious first round, we went to the second ordeal, that of the Styx. The populace reassembled for this spectacle, and the procedure was followed to the letter there too. Melite was wearing the tablet; the spring lay clear and low. She walked into the waters and stood there with a beaming face. The water did nothing at all! It stayed in its place without the slightest surge from its usual level. When the allotted time for her stay in the spring had passed, the magistrate held out his hand and helped her out of the water. Thersandros had lost the second round.

He was about to fall a third time but slipped away to his house and disappeared, afraid the crowd would stone him. For just at that moment four young men were dragging Sosthenes forward, two relatives of Melite and two slaves. Melite had sent them off to search for him. Thersandros could see what was coming: he knew that Sosthenes under torture would reveal all. So he disappeared first and left the city under cover of night. The archons remanded Sosthenes to prison, now that Thersandros had fled. At last we were free, victorious in our cause and cheered by one and all alike.

The next day the warders assigned to Sosthenes brought him to the 15 archons. When he saw himself being led to the instruments of torture, he confessed everything without ambiguity, all the crimes of Thersandros and his own role as accomplice. He even included the private conversation between Thersandros and himself about Leukippe outside the door of her hut. Then he was thrown back into jail to serve his sentence, and Thersandros was condemned to banishment *in absentia*.

The priest entertained us again in what had now become the customary manner. During dinner we told again the same stories as the day before and filled in little blanks that had been left. Leukippe, no longer embarrassed before her father, since her virginity had been established beyond doubt, narrated her adventures with gusto. When she had reached Pharos and the pirates, I said: "Tell us the tale of the cutthroats at Pharos and the riddle of the severed head. Your father should hear this too. This is the only scene missing from the whole drama."

"The bandits deceived a woman," she said, "one of those unfortunate 16 creatures who sell their favors for money. They told her they had a sea captain on board who would take her on as his woman and brought her onto the ship; she did not know why she was really there and was waiting quietly with one of the pirates. The cutthroat was her ostensible lover. When they kidnapped me, as you saw, and put me on the skiff and spread their oars like wings to get away, they noticed your ship in pursuit and gaining on them. Removing that poor woman's ornaments and clothes, they dressed me as her and put my modest little shift on her. Stationing her on the stern, where you in pursuit would see her, they sliced off her head and hurled the body (as you saw) down into the sea, but the head, as it fell, they caught and kept on the ship. A little later they got rid of this too, tossing it overboard when they were no longer being pursued. I do not know whether they had arranged to have the woman on board for this eventuality or whether they had originally planned to enslave and sell her, as they later sold me. But during the chase they slew her in my place to deceive their pursuers, thinking they would stand to gain more profit from my sale than from hers.

"The same considerations led to Chaireas's downfall, and I saw him pay for his crimes as he richly deserved. It was he who urged them to kill the woman and throw her overboard in my stead. The rest of the bandit band then refused to hand me over to him alone; he had now used up another body that might have been sold and brought them an initial profit. In place of the dead woman I was to be sold to benefit the common purse and not just Chaireas alone. When he objected, bringing up legal points and referring to their contractual obligations, how they were commissioned to kidnap me for his passion, not their profit, and even ventured to use some strong language, one of the cutthroats, standing behind him, cut off his head—and a good job too! And so, having paid a penalty that none could find fault with for his kidnapping, he too was tossed into the sea. The pirates sailed on for two days, brought me to some place or other, and sold me to a dealer they knew, who in turn sold me to Sosthenes."

17 "Now that you have told me your tales, children," said Sostratos, "listen while I tell you what happened back at home to Kalligone, your sister, Kleitophon. I don't want to be left out of the storytelling entirely."

At the mention of my sister's name, I focused my attention all on him and said: "Come, Father, tell us. I only hope your story's subject is still alive."

He began to tell what I have earlier recounted—Kallisthenes, the oracle, the embassy, the boat, the kidnapping. Then he added: "When Kallisthenes learned during the voyage that she was not my daughter and that all his work had been a mistake, he loved Kalligone nonetheless, and very passionately too. He went down on his knees and said: 'Lady, do not think me a common criminal or cutthroat, for I am nobly born, a Byzantine second to none. Eros has made me act the role of a robber and weave this plot against you. From this day forward you must think of me as your slave. I shall present you with a dowry, in the first place myself and thereafter more than your father would have given you. I shall respect your virginity for however long you please.' With these words and yet others, he laid the ground for the girl to be more pliant and appreciative. He was in fact a handsome man to look at and eloquent and most persuasive. And when he reached Byzantium, he drew up a contract for an immense dowry and made lavish preparations, clothes and gold and all the appurtenances of a fine lady. He treated her well and kept her untouched as he promised. As a result, he had by now captured her heart. In every other respect too he showed himself a proper gentleman, considerate and modest: this was a sudden and amazing transformation in the young man. He rose from his chair when his elders entered the room; he was the first to say hello when meeting people in the street. His reckless extravagance up to that point changed from prodigality to prudence. His generosity was a bulwark for those whom poverty constrained to receive help from others. Everyone was amazed at the suddenness of his transformation from wastrel to gentleman. I must say I was even more impressed than most, loved him like a son, and came to think his early sottish ways were just the marvelous exuberance of his nature, not a real lack of self-control. And I was reminded of what they say about Themistokles, that in his youth he broke every rule, but later on he outdid every Athenian in intellect and virtue. I don't mind saying I heartily repented having told him to go to blazes when he first proposed marrying my daughter. He became very attentive to my needs, called me 'Father,' acted as my escort in the marketplace, and was diligent about his military training; he was particularly outstanding among the horse guards. You see, he had always enjoyed this sort of thing and kept at it even during his prodigal period, but only as an idle sport or game. Yet all the while his manliness and experience were developing in secret. The final result was that he became a superior soldier, strong and many-talented. He also donated a good deal of money to the city. They elected him a general along with me, after which he was even more considerate to me, making himself my subject in all matters.

"When we won the war by an epiphany of the gods, we returned to Byzantium, praising Herakles and Artemis, and the two of us were delegated as ambassadors—I to Artemis here, he to Herakles in Tyre. At that point he took me by the right hand and told me everything he had done about Kalligone. 'But those deeds, Father,' said he, 'were done by the natural violence of youth; what follows was done by choice. For I kept the girl a virgin up to now, even though I was a soldier at war, a time when no man defers his pleasures. Now I have decided to take her to Tyre to her father and to seek from him her hand in lawful marriage. If he is willing to give her to me, I shall take her as my wife, and may For-

18

tune favor us. If he is angry and resentful, he will receive her back a virgin. I would gladly bestow on her a not inconsiderable dowry and take her in marriage.' I shall read you the statement that I drew up before the war broke out, asking your father to marry his daughter to Kallisthenes; in it I tell about his family tree and his fortune and his valor in battle. This is our agreement. If we win our acquittal, I have decided that I will sail first to Byzantium and after that to Tyre." After trading these stories we retired to bed in the usual fashion.

19     The next day Kleinias came by and said that Thersandros had run away during the night; he had appealed the case, not really intending to contest it but rather wishing to use any pretext to postpone the indictment for his crimes. We waited then for three days, the period appointed, and went before the president and read out the laws according to which Thersandros had no further case against us. Embarking on a ship and sailing with a fair wind, we put in at Byzantium. There we celebrated our long-awaited marriage and then set off for Tyre. Arriving two days after Kallisthenes, we found my father preparing to celebrate my sister's wedding on the next day. We attended the ceremony, sacrificing along with him and praying to the gods that both my marriage and Kallisthenes' be preserved in good fortune. We decided to spend the winter in Tyre and then make our way to Byzantium.[72]

72. As noted in the Introduction, consistency is not high on the list of Achilles Tatius's goals, and minor or suspected loose ends have not been annotated throughout. That there is no closure of the framing narrative in which Kleitophon's long tale is set is more likely to be a deliberate act, for which there was precedent in Plato's *Symposion*.

# LONGUS

# DAPHNIS AND CHLOE

## TRANSLATED BY
## CHRISTOPHER GILL

### Introduction

Almost nothing is known of the author of *Daphnis and Chloe,* although his home is generally thought to be the island of Lesbos, the location of the novel. What is completely clear, however, is that he is a writer of considerable sophistication; and his work is often placed in the period of the Second Sophistic, a renaissance of Greek prose writing in the second century A.D. Certainly, Longus's book is as artistically conceived and skillfully written as any of the Greek novels we now possess.

Much of what is distinctive about *Daphnis and Chloe* derives from the fact that it is a *pastoral* novel (its full title in the manuscript tradition is *A Pastoral Story of Daphnis and Chloe*). What this means is that Longus has tried to merge the narrative form of the Greek romantic novel (a form that seems to have been fairly well developed by this time) with elements of the genre of pastoral poetry created by Theocritus in the third century B.C. This merging—in many ways an extraordinary one—has far-reaching implications for the social world and locale, as well as the style and tone, of the novel Longus has written.

The central fiction of pastoral poetry is that there exists somewhere (in remote places such as the mountains of Sicily or Arcadia) a society of herdsmen and shepherds who live in harmony with each other, and with the world of nature, its scenery, animals, and gods. These herdsmen combine a life of rustic simplicity (and simplicity of thought and emotion) with the desire and skill to express this simplicity in music, in piping and in song. Their happiness is sometimes disrupted by sadness, especially that of unsatisfied love. But this too is converted into song, and the beauty of the song somehow restores the sense of pastoral harmony.

The central figures of Longus's novel, Daphnis and Chloe, are taken directly from pastoral poetry. They want nothing but to live in idyllic simplicity with each other, and with their goats and sheep, in their familiar meadows, hills, and woods, worshiping the pastoral gods, especially Pan and the Nymphs. Their characteristic mode of activity is loving attention (to each other, the animals, and their gods), an attention often expressed in musical form or in songlike speech. In return for this, when their capacities for understanding or action fail, they are helped out by each other, by their pastoral gods (and, beyond them, by Dionysus and Eros), and sometimes too by their own animals acting in concert with the gods. (See, for example, 1.28–30 and 2.20–30.)

Daphnis and Chloe exist, then, in a kind of charmed circle, which is defined by contrast with a series of wider circles. The immediately surrounding circle is that of the local countrypeople, including Daphnis's and Chloe's own foster parents. This circle is rustic rather than pastoral, consisting of relatively mundane, unidealized farmers. At its best, the circle supports and frames Daphnis's and Chloe's magical existence. At its worst, it threatens to destroy that existence by cruder instincts and reactions, brute lust expressed in seduction or violence, or small-minded desire for profit (as in 1.20–21, 2.2, 3.15ff., and 4.27–29). Outside this circle, in turn, is the world of the city, which also has two faces. Its violent face is that of pirates from a nearby city, a vicious and marauding army, irresponsible young aristocrats, or an opportunistic homosexual parasite. (See 1.28, 2.12ff., 2.20ff., 4.11–12, and 4.16ff.) Its benign face only appears in the fourth book, with the rediscovery of the true parents of Daphnis and Chloe. This rediscovery transfers Daphnis and Chloe to the world of the city—but only temporarily, for now they choose to resume the life that was formerly the result of accident (or rather of divine providence), their pastoral coexistence. Their final state (like that of the pastoral genre itself) is thus one of deliberate simplicity.

Longus's decision to make his novel a pastoral one has significant and rather paradoxical implications for its structure and style. What is characteristic of the Greek novel in general is the forward thrust of its narrative movement, as the hero and heroine survive a succession of unpredictable episodes that delay—till the end—their goal of a life of mutual love. What is typical of pastoral poetry, on the other hand, is its intensely static quality. The characteristic pastoral moment is midday, when, shaded from the immobilizing heat, the shepherds relax with songs that are themselves expressions of mood and of the pastoral context, rather than narratives of events. What is formally distinctive in Longus's novel derives from its alternation of narrative (often narrative of events that in some way jeopardize the peace of the pastoral world) with passages of description, dialogue, or monologue, in which the pastoral present is reestablished. In the second type of passage, Longus slows up the narra-

tive pace by adopting the verbal pattern typical of pastoral poetry: a series of short word-groups, linked by assonance and anaphora, and giving
a repetitious, often incantatory effect. (A striking example is found at
2.7; see also 1.14, 1.16–18, 1.25, 2.3, and 2.5.) An alternation between
fast-moving narrative of events and more fully realized, "dramatic" passages is not uncommon in the Greek novels. But rarely are the "high
spots" static and timeless in the way they are in *Daphnis and Chloe*. There
is, of course, one continuing movement in the novel, the gradual development of Daphnis's and Chloe's sexual maturity. But this—like the cycle of the seasons that provides a temporal background for the action—
has a certain inbuilt inevitability. Sooner or later, we know, Daphnis and
Chloe *will* find out how to make love! But this movement does not give
the novel the tension and mobility provided in other novels by the violent vicissitudes of circumstances, which frequently keep the lovers physically apart. Daphnis and Chloe achieve companionship and feelings of
mutual love from a quite early stage in the novel; and this provides a relatively stable context for their sexual exploration.

The pastoral mode of the novel also determines the narrative tone of
voice and the authorial attitude to the figures. Whatever may be the ultimate origins of pastoral song, the genre of pastoral poetry, as we know
it, is a product of a sophisticated sensibility, characteristic of Alexandrian
culture of the third century B.C. Theocritus and his successors chose to
write in a deliberately simple way, to convey naive, rustic emotions; but
the achievement of this simplicity involved a good deal of literary skill,
restrained so as not to spoil the overall effect. In the same way, Longus
keeps the style of his narrative and dialogue simple in vocabulary and
sentence structure, as well as in content and sentiment. But behind the
surface simplicity there is a perceptible sophistication. This is sometimes
indicated by discreet but unmistakable literary allusions, sometimes by
moments when the narrator distances himself from his rustic creatures.
Indeed (given these indications of sophistication), the carefully maintained simplicity is itself an index of authorial control. Our awareness of
an author slightly removed from his work tends to distance us also from
the central figures and their preoccupations. It is hard to enter *fully* into
Daphnis's sexual puzzlement and his periodic distress at being separated
from Chloe—especially as some agency (human, divine, or animal) tends
to appear promptly to resolve these problems. But then Longus is not really aiming to elicit full emotional involvement in the characters but
rather a more conscious attention to the literary project itself, and appre-
ciation of its sophisticated simplicity. Like the author himself, in his pro-
logue, the reader is invited to view "others' passions" while he keeps his
own "self-control." In this sense, the novel is a virtuoso piece, though
the virtuosity is not so obtrusive as to destroy completely the fragile
world of pastoral simplicity that lies at its center.

I am grateful to Michael Reeve for supplying me with a copy of the text of his Teubner edition of *Daphnis and Chloe* in advance of its publication. This text has been used throughout as the basis for the present translation (except for two minor variations; see notes 3 and 8 in the translation). I am much indebted to him too for reading an earlier version of the translation and giving me in numerous acute comments the benefit of his unique familiarity with the text. Karen, my wife, has helped me by her frank and constructive reactions to my attempts at producing readable English, as well as in preparing the typescript. Remaining errors and infelicities are mine alone.

## Bibliography

TEXT

Longos. *Daphnis und Chloe*. Edited by O. Schönberger. Berlin, 1960 (2d ed., 1973).

Longus. *Daphnis and Chloe*. Edited by J. M. Edmonds. London, 1916 (Loeb Classical Library). With a revised translation by George Thornley, 1657.

Longus. *Daphnis and Chloe*. Edited by M. D. Reeve. Leipzig, 1982 (Teubner).

Longus. *Pastorales (Daphnis et Chloé)*. Edited by G. Dalmeyda. Paris, 1934 (Budé).

GENERAL

Chalk, H. H. O. "Eros and the Lesbian Pastorals of Longus." *Journal of Hellenic Studies* 80(1960): 32–51 (reprinted in H. Gärtner, ed., *Beiträge zum griechischen Liebesroman* [Hildesheim, 1984]).

Hunter, R. L. *A Study of Daphnis and Chloe*. Cambridge, 1983.

McCulloh, W. E. *Longus*. New York, 1970.

# DAPHNIS AND CHLOE

## Prologue

WHEN I WAS HUNTING in Lesbos, I saw the most beautiful sight I have ever seen, in a grove that was sacred to the Nymphs: a painting that told a story of love. The grove itself was beautiful—thickly wooded, flowery, well watered; a single spring nourished everything, flowers and trees alike. But the picture was lovelier still, combining great artistic skill with an exciting, romantic subject. Many people were attracted by its fame and came, even from abroad, to pray to the Nymphs and to look at the picture.

The picture: women giving birth, others dressing the babies, babies exposed, animals suckling them, shepherds adopting them, young people pledging love, a pirates' raid, an enemy attack—and more, much more, all of it romantic. I gazed in admiration and was seized by a yearning to depict the picture in words.

I searched out an interpreter of the picture and produced the four volumes of this book, as an offering to Love, the Nymphs, and Pan, and something for mankind to possess and enjoy. It will cure the sick, comfort the distressed, stir the memory of those who have loved, and educate those who haven't. For certainly no one has ever avoided Love, and no one will, as long as beauty exists, and eyes can see. As for me—may the god Love let me write about others' passions but keep my own self-control.[1]

## Book One

There's a city in Lesbos called Mytilene, a big and beautiful one, divided 1 by canals through which the sea flows gently, and decorated with bridges of white, polished stone. You would think you were looking at an island, not a city.[2] About twenty miles from this city of Mytilene a rich man had an estate, a very fine property.[3] There were hills covered with game, plains rich in wheat, slopes with many vines, pastures stocked with sheep, and the soft sand of a long beach, washed by the sea.

A goatherd called Lamon, who grazed his flocks on this estate, found 2 a child being suckled by one of his she-goats. There was a copse of oaks,

---

1 In educated prose writings of the second century A.D., a common feature is the use of the *ekphrasis*, the description or interpretation of a visible object, such as a picture. Longus presents his whole story as an *ekphrasis*. He gives emotional impact to this literary device by presenting it autobiographically: he claims to have found the picture and been inspired by it to tell the story.

Longus indicates the genre of his work, the romantic novel, by repeated use of the key term *eros*, "passionate love," and its cognates, such as *erotikos*, "romantic." In Greek, *eros* is also a god; when the god is intended, he is presented as Love (with a capital letter) in the translation, and Eros in the notes. (In both translation and notes, all Greek names are given in their conventional, Latinate form, whereas other Greek terms are transliterated exactly.) Longus ascribes to his book both a religious and a pleasurable objective; his comment hints at the close connections between divine influence and the gradual unfolding of human love that is one of this novel's distinctive features.

2. Longus's description of Mytilene is slightly romanticized; other ancient accounts speak of *one* canal, not a whole network of them.

3. Here, I follow the manuscript reading "two hundred stades" (= twenty-two miles) instead of the "twenty stades" adopted by Reeve. Longus's topography has been much discussed recently, by H. J. Mason, "Longus and the Topography of Lesbos," *Transactions of the American Philological Association* 109(1979): 149–63; P. Green, "Longus, Antiphon, and the Topography of Lesbos," *Journal of Hellenic Studies* 102(1982): 210–14; and E. L. Bowie, "Theocritus' Seventh Idyll, Philetas and Longus," *Classical Quarterly* 35(1985): 67–91. These scholars differ about the location of the estate but agree that Longus' picture of the topography of Lesbos is generally accurate.

with brambles and wandering ivy, and soft grass, on which the child was lying. The goat kept on running to this spot and often disappeared from view, leaving her kid alone while she stayed with the newborn baby. Lamon felt sorry for the neglected kid and kept an eye on the goat's comings and goings. It was midday; he followed her closely and saw the goat standing carefully over the child (so that she wouldn't hurt it by treading on it with her hooves) and the child sucking her milk as though from its mother's breast. Naturally, he was amazed; he went up close and found a baby boy, big and beautiful, and dressed in baby clothes finer than you would expect to find on a child that had been exposed—he had a purple cloak with a gold clasp, and a dagger with an ivory handle.

3      His first plan was to ignore the baby and to take only the tokens of its identity. Then he felt ashamed at failing to match even a goat's humanity; waiting for nightfall, he took everything to his wife, Myrtale—tokens, child, and goat too. She was amazed at the thought of goats producing children—but he explained it all to her: how he found the child exposed, how he saw it being suckled, how he felt ashamed at leaving it to die. She agreed with him about what they should do. They hid the things left with the baby, called the child their own, and handed over the job of nursing him to the goat. To make sure the child's name sounded pastoral, they decided to call him Daphnis.[4]

4      Two years went by. A shepherd called Dryas, from the neighboring fields, made the same discovery and saw the same sight. There was a cave sacred to the Nymphs, formed from a big rock that was hollow on the inside and curved on the outside. The images of the Nymphs themselves had been made of stone: their feet were bare; their arms were bare to the shoulder; their hair hung loose over their necks; they had belts on their waists, smiles on their faces—the whole appearance was that of a group of dancers. In the very middle of the cave formed from the big rock, water bubbling up from a spring flowed out in a stream; and so a very smooth meadow spread out in front of the cave, with thick, soft grass fed by the moisture. Various things were tied up there: milk buckets, transverse flutes, Pan-pipes, reed pipes, the offerings of shepherds in the past.

5      An ewe who had recently lambed kept going repeatedly to this shrine and often gave Dryas the impression that she was lost. He wanted to punish her and bring her back to her previous good conduct; so he twisted a green shoot into a loop, to make a kind of halter, and went to the rock, hoping to catch her there. But when he got close, he saw something quite different from what he had expected. He saw the ewe acting

4. The name Daphnis is "pastoral" because Daphnis is a key figure in earlier pastoral poetry and the myths it draws on. Traditionally, Daphnis is the inventor of pastoral music, and the victim, in various ways, of love's power. Many of Longus's names are symbolic or associative.

in a very human way, giving her teats to a child to suck as much milk as it wanted, and the child, without crying, greedily putting its mouth to each of her teats. The child's mouth was clean and shining, because the ewe licked its face with her tongue when it had had enough milk. This child was a girl; and like the other it had tokens of identity lying beside it: a belt threaded with gold, gilded sandals, and golden anklets.

Dryas thought he had found a gift from the gods. Learning from the ewe to feel sorry for the child and love it, he lifted the baby in his arms and put the tokens away in his bag. He prayed to the Nymphs to foster the child that had taken refuge with them and favor it with good luck. When the time came to drive the flock home, he went to his farm, told his wife what he had seen, showed her what he had found, and urged her to treat the child as their little daughter and to bring it up as their own, without telling anyone the truth. Nape (this was his wife's name) became a mother instantly and began to love the child, as though frightened of being outdone by the ewe. She too gave the child a pastoral name— Chloe—to make people believe it was her child.[5] 6

These children grew up very quickly and became more beautiful than country children usually are. He was fifteen years old, and she was two years younger, when Dryas and Lamon, in a single night, both had a dream like this. They dreamed that the Nymphs—the ones in the cave where the spring was, where Dryas found his child—were handing Daphnis and Chloe over to a very pretty boy, with a very arrogant manner, who had wings growing from his shoulders and carried little arrows and a miniature bow. The boy touched both of them with a single arrow, and for the future told Daphnis to look after the herd of goats, and Chloe to look after the flock of sheep. 7

*CUPID*

When the two men had this dream, they were upset at the thought that the children were to become shepherds and goatherds, although their tokens had promised greater things. Indeed, because of this, they had brought the children up rather delicately, teaching them to read and write and to do everything that was regarded as elegant in the country. But they thought they should obey the gods' instructions—for, after all, the children had only survived by divine providence. After telling each other their dreams and making a sacrifice in the Nymphs' shrine to "the winged boy" (they did not know his name),[6] they sent the children out as shepherds with the flocks. But first they gave them detailed instructions: how to graze the animals before midday, how to graze them again when the midday heat had died down, when to lead them to drink, when 8

5. Chloe, in Greek, means "the first green shoot of plants in spring"; it is an epithet of Demeter, protectress of young plants.

6. The "winged boy" is Eros, or Love. An important theme in the story is the general ignorance in the rural population of the divine nature and power of Love (cf. 1.13, 2.7; and contrast the urban sophistication of Gnathon, 4.16–17).

to drive them home to rest, which animals they needed to use a stick on, which could be controlled by using the voice only. The children greatly enjoyed this and felt they were taking over a position of great responsibility. They loved the goats and sheep more than herdsmen usually do, because she attributed her survival to a sheep, and he remembered he had been suckled by a goat when he was exposed.

9   It was the beginning of spring, and all the flowers were in bloom, in the woods, in the meadows, and on the hills. Now there was the hum of bees, the sound of sweet-singing birds, the skipping of newborn lambs. The lambs skipped on the hills; the bees hummed in the meadows; the birds filled the copses with the enchantment of their song. Everything was possessed by the beauty of spring; and Daphnis and Chloe, impressionable young creatures that they were, imitated what they heard and saw. They heard the birds singing, and they sang; they saw the lambs skipping, and they leapt about nimbly; they copied the bees and gathered flowers. They scattered some of the flowers in the folds of their clothes; and they used the rest to weave little garlands, as offerings to the Nymphs.

10   They did everything together, grazing their flocks near each other. Often Daphnis rounded up those of her sheep that wandered off, and often Chloe drove the more adventurous of his goats down from the crags. Sometimes one of them looked after both the flocks, while the other was absorbed in some toy. Their toys were of a pastoral and childish type. She picked stalks of asphodel from here and there and wove a trap for grasshoppers, and while she was working on this, she paid no attention to her sheep. He cut slender reeds, pierced them at their joints, fastened them together with soft wax, and practiced piping until nightfall.[7] They also shared their drink of milk or wine, and they divided whatever food they brought from home. You would have been more likely to see the sheep and the goats separated from each other than Chloe and Daphnis.

11   While they were playing these games, Love contrived to make things serious, in this way. A she-wolf carried off many of the sheep from the other flocks in the neighborhood; she was raising young cubs and needed a great deal of food to rear them. The villagers got together at night and dug some pits, six feet wide and twenty-four feet deep. They carried off most of the soil that was dug up and scattered it some distance away; but over the opening of the pits they stretched long pieces of dry wood and sprinkled the rest of the soil over them, to make the ground look the same as before. The pieces of wood were more fragile than dry stalks; and so even a hare, if it ran onto them, would snap them—and then it would have the chance to find out it was not earth but just looked like it.

---

7. This is the *syrinx,* or Pan-pipes, the most typically pastoral instrument.

They dug a number of pits like this in the hills and the plains. They didn't succeed in catching the she-wolf (a wolf can tell when ground has been meddled with), but they did kill a number of goats and sheep—and almost killed Daphnis too.

What happened was this. Two he-goats got excited and started to 12 fight. In a violent clash one of the goats had a horn broken and ran away snorting and leaping with pain. The victor followed him closely and kept up the chase continuously. Daphnis was upset about the one goat's horn and annoyed by the other's audacity; he took a club and his shepherd's staff and pursued the pursuer. As you might expect when one is trying to get away and the other is chasing in anger, they didn't pay close attention to what was at their feet, and they both fell down a pit, first the goat and then Daphnis. Indeed, what saved Daphnis's life was his using the goat to break his fall.

Daphnis wept and waited in the hope that someone might pull him out. Chloe had seen the accident, and now she came running up to the pit; finding he was still alive, she called to a cowherd from the fields nearby for help. He came and looked for a long rope so that Daphnis could hold onto it and be pulled out of the pit. No rope was to be found, but Chloe took off her breast band and gave it to the cowherd to let down.[8] So the two of them stood on the edge and pulled, and he climbed up with his hands as they pulled the band. They also pulled out the poor goat, who had *both* of his horns broken—so he was punished harshly for his defeat of the other goat. As a reward for helping to save Daphnis's life, they gave the cowherd the goat to be sacrificed. If anyone at home missed the goat, they planned to make up a story about an attack by wolves. They went back and checked the flock of sheep and herd of goats; when they found the goats and sheep were grazing in an orderly manner, they sat down at the foot of an oak tree to see if there was blood anywhere on Daphnis's body from his fall. He hadn't been wounded, and there was no blood to be found, but his hair and the rest of his body were streaked with earth and mud. He decided to wash before Lamon and Myrtale realized what had happened.

He went with Chloe to the shrine of the Nymphs and gave her his tu- 13 nic and bag to look after while he stood beside the spring and started to wash his hair and his whole body. His hair was dark and thick, and his body was tanned by the sun; you could have imagined that his body was taking its dark color from the shadow of his hair. It seemed to Chloe, as she gazed at him, that Daphnis was beautiful; and she thought that since he hadn't seemed beautiful to her before, the bathing must be the cause

8. The "breast band" was a long piece of material that was wrapped around the body, covering the breasts. (Reeve reads "*a* breast band" or other piece of material, not "*her* breast band.")

of his beauty. She washed his back, and as she did so, his flesh yielded so gently to her touch that she surreptitiously felt her own several times to see if his was more delicate than hers. And then, since it was nearly sunset, they drove their flocks home: and all the time Chloe had felt nothing but the desire to see Daphnis bathing again.

The next day, when they came to pasture, Daphnis sat under the usual oak tree and played the pipes while he kept an eye on his goats, which were lying down and seemed to be listening to his tunes. Chloe sat near him, and while she kept an eye on her flock of sheep, she paid more attention to Daphnis. He seemed beautiful to her again as he played the pipes, and this time she thought the music must be the cause of his beauty. So, when he had finished, she took the pipes herself, in the hope that she too might become beautiful.

She also persuaded him to have another bath; and as he bathed, she watched him, and after watching she touched him; then she went away, thinking again how handsome he was. And that thought was the beginning of love. She didn't know what was happening to her: she was a young girl brought up in the country and hadn't even heard anyone speak of love. Her heart ached; her eyes wandered uncontrollably; she kept repeating "Daphnis." She took no interest in food; she lay awake at night; she disregarded her flock. Now she laughed; now she cried; one moment she sat down; the next she jumped up; her face went pale and then, in turn, blushed red. Even a cow stung by a gadfly does not behave so madly.[9] When she was on her own, she said to herself:

14 "Now I feel ill, but I don't know what my illness is; I feel pain, although I've not been injured; I feel sad, although I've lost none of my sheep; I feel hot, although I'm sitting in deep shade. How many times I've been scratched by brambles, and I've not wept! How many times I've been stung by bees, and I've not cried out! But the thing that's stinging my heart now is sharper than all those things. Daphnis is beautiful— but then so are the flowers. His pipes make a beautiful sound—but then so do the nightingales. And yet I care nothing for those things. I wish I were his pipes, so he could breathe into me. I wish I were his goat, so I could be led to graze by him. You wicked stream! You only made Daphnis beautiful; I bathed in you, and nothing happened. I'm dying, dear Nymphs; and even you are doing nothing to save the girl who has grown up at your side. Who will put garlands on you when I am gone? Who will bring up the poor lambs? Who will look after the chattering grasshopper I took such trouble to catch so that it could put me to sleep by singing in front of the cave? But now I cannot sleep because of Daphnis, and the chattering of the grasshopper does me no good."

9. Here and elsewhere, Longus's description of the symptoms of the "sickness" of love recalls Greek love poetry, esp. Sappho; cf. notes 14 and 59.

This was what she felt and said; the word she was looking for was  15
"love." Now Dorcon, the cowherd, was the one who had pulled Daphnis and the he-goat out of the pit; he was a young man, whose beard had
just started growing, and he knew about love—what it's called as well as
what it makes you do. He fell immediately in love with Chloe on that
very day, and his feelings became more and more inflamed as the days
went by. He didn't take Daphnis seriously, regarding him as a child, and
determined to have his way either by giving presents or by using force.

First of all, he brought presents for them both: for Daphnis, Pan-
pipes, the nine reeds fastened together with bronze instead of wax; for
Chloe, a bacchant's fawnskin, whose colors looked as if they'd been
painted on. From then on they regarded him as their friend, but gradually he stopped paying attention to Daphnis, while every day he brought
Chloe a soft cheese, a garland of flowers, or a ripe apple. One day, he
brought her a newly born calf, a wooden cup with ivy tendrils carved on
it and inlaid with gold, and some chicks of mountain birds. She had no
experience of a lover's wiles, and she took the presents with pleasure; indeed, her pleasure was greater because she now had something that she
could give to Daphnis.

One day (since Daphnis too, in his turn, had to learn what love makes
you do) a beauty contest took place between Dorcon and him. Chloe
was the judge, and the prize set for the winner was giving Chloe a kiss.[10]
Dorcon spoke first.

"I'm bigger than Daphnis, my girl, and I'm a cowherd, while he's a  16
goatherd; so just as cows are better than goats, I'm better than him. My
complexion is white like milk, and my hair is auburn like the summer
corn ready for harvesting.[11] And it was my mother, not an animal, that
suckled me. But he's small, beardless like a woman, and dark like a wolf.
He looks after he-goats, and he's picked up their terrible smell. He's so
poor he can't keep a dog. And if, as people say, a she-goat gave him her
milk, he's no better than a kid."

This was the sort of thing that Dorcon said, and then Daphnis spoke.

"I was suckled by a she-goat, and so was Zeus.[12] I look after he-goats
that are bigger than his cows. I don't pick up their smell any more than

10. The idea of a contest in which the speakers compete in self-praise recalls Theocritus
*Idyll* 5. Longus gives poignancy to the situation by making Chloe the judge, instead of another shepherd. The judge is loved by one of the competitors already, and the prize for the
competition—Chloe's kiss—makes the other fall in love with her too.

11. "Auburn" is *pyrros* (or *pyrrhos*) in Greek, and so is "red-haired" in Daphnis's riposte.
*Pyrros* is actually reddish-gold and thus comparable to ripe corn, if one wants to make
it sound attractive. Golden hair was typically preferred to dark hair in Greece; hence
Daphnis's excitement at realizing that Chloe's hair was golden (1.17). The term for
"golden," *xanthos,* can also denote a reddish-gold color and is thus compared to fire in 1.17
and 2.4.

12. Zeus was brought up in a cave in Crete, in concealment from his father, Cronus,
and was suckled by the goat-nymph Amaltheia.

Pan does, although he's more goat than man. I've plenty of cheese, bread baked on a spit, and white wine—which is as much as even rich country dwellers have. I don't have a beard, but neither does Dionysus; I'm dark, but so is the hyacinth. Dionysus is better than the satyrs, just as the hyacinth is better than lilies.[13] But Dorcon is red-haired like a fox and bearded like a he-goat and white-skinned like a woman from the town. If you have to kiss me, it's my mouth you'll kiss, but if it's him, you'll kiss the hairs on his chin. And remember, my dear girl, that an animal suckled you too, and yet you are beautiful."

17 Chloe waited no longer. She was pleased at his compliment, and in any case she had longed to kiss Daphnis for ages. She leapt up and kissed him; it was a simple, unsophisticated kiss, but it was quite capable of setting a heart on fire. Dorcon was hurt and ran off, looking for another route to love. But Daphnis, as though he had been stung, not kissed, immediately looked distressed; he shivered repeatedly; he tried without success to control his pounding heart; he wanted to look at Chloe, but when he looked, he blushed deeply.

Then, for the first time, he realized with admiration that her hair was golden, that her eyes were as big as a cow's, and that her face was really even whiter than the goats' milk. It was as if he had then, for the first time, acquired eyes, and had been blind before. He ate none of his food except just a taste; when he had to drink, he did no more than moisten his lips. He was silent, although before he had chattered more than the grasshoppers; he did nothing, although before he had been more energetic than the goats. Even the flock was neglected; even the pipes were discarded; his face was paler than the grass in summer.[14] Only with Chloe was he talkative; and whenever he was on his own, away from her, he rambled away to himself like this.

18 "Whatever is Chloe's kiss doing to me? Her lips are softer than rose petals, and her mouth is sweeter than honeycombs, but her kiss is sharper than the bee's sting. I've often kissed kids; I've often kissed newborn puppies and the calf that Dorcon gave her—but this is a new kind of kiss. My breath comes in gasps; my heart leaps out of my breast; my spirit dissolves—and yet I want to kiss her again. Oh, what a terrible victory! Oh, what a strange disease! I don't even know what to call it! Did Chloe take poison before she kissed me? But then why didn't she die? How the nightingales sing while my pipes are silent! How the kids jump around while I sit still! How the flowers bloom while I make no gar-

13. The term "hyacinth" in Greek always suggests a blue flower (either a larkspur or a kind of bluebell) and so is a good example of a dark flower.

14. Chapters 17 and 18 echo Greek erotic poetry, especially Theocritus and Sappho. The striking phrase "paler than grass" for instance, comes from Sappho 31 LP (= *Poetarum Lesbiorum Fragmenta,* ed. Edgar Lobel and Denys Page [Oxford, 1955]).

lands! But while the violets and hyacinth flourish, Daphnis wastes away. Will even Dorcon come to seem more attractive than me?"

This is what our noble Daphnis felt and said, as you would expect of someone who was tasting for the first time what love makes you do and say. Dorcon, however, the cowherd who was in love with Chloe, waited until Dryas was planting a vine plant nearby and went up to him with some excellent small cheeses. He gave these to Dryas as a present, being an old friend of his from the time when Dryas used to do his own grazing. This was his first move; and then he raised the question of marrying Chloe. Being a cowherd, he said he could offer many valuable gifts if he took her as his wife: a pair of oxen for ploughing, four hives of bees, fifty apple trees, a bull's hide for cutting up into sandals, and, every year, a weaned calf. Dryas was nearly enticed by these gifts into giving his consent. But he reckoned that the girl was worth a better bridegroom; and he was frightened that if he did give his consent, this would be found out one day and would get him into really bad trouble. So he refused the match, asked Dorcon to excuse him, and declined the presents offered.

Now Dorcon had been cheated of his hopes twice—and had wasted some good cheeses too. He decided to make a physical assault on Chloe when she was on her own. He noticed that Daphnis and the girl led the flocks to drink on alternate days, and he worked out the sort of plan a herdsman would think of. He took the hide of a big wolf that a bull had gored to death once fighting for its cows and stretched it over his back, all the way down to his feet. He wrapped the hide around him in such a way that he had the front paws spread over his hands, and the back paws spread over his legs down to the heels, and the gaping mouth covering his head like a soldier's helmet. When he had done all he could to make himself a beast, he went to the spring where the goats and sheep drank after grazing. The spring was in a deep hollow in the ground, and the whole area round it grew wild with thorns, brambles, dwarf junipers, and thistles; so a real wolf could easily have waited there in ambush without being seen. Dorcon hid himself there, waiting for the drinking time; he was sure that he could frighten Chloe by his appearance and get his hands on her.

A little time went by, and then Chloe drove the flocks to the spring, leaving Daphnis cutting green leaves as fodder for the kids after they had finished grazing. The dogs who went with her to guard the sheep and goats were busy sniffing things out, as dogs usually are, and they caught Dorcon moving to attack the girl. They pounced on him, barking shrilly, taking him for a wolf; they surrounded him before his terror allowed him to get up fully, and bit him as hard as they could. For a time he lay quietly in the bushes, ashamed of being found out, and protected by the hide that covered him. But when Chloe, terrified at the first sight of him, called to Daphnis for help, and the dogs dragged the hide off and got their teeth into Dorcon's own body, he gave a great cry and begged for help from the girl and from Daphnis, who had now arrived. They gave the usual call to the dogs to come back and quickly brought them under control. The dogs had bitten Dorcon's thighs and shoulders, and they took him to the stream, washed him where he'd been bitten, chewed up some green elm bark, and smeared it on his wounds. Because they had no experience of lovers' recklessness, they thought Dorcon had put on the hide as a pastoral game; they were not at all angry but were sympathetic to him, and gave him a helping hand before seeing him off.

22    Dorcon, after being on the brink of such danger and escaping from the jaws of a dog (not of the proverbial wolf),[15] took care of his wounded body. But Daphnis and Chloe were hard at work till nightfall, rounding up their goats and sheep. These were terrified by the hide and upset by the barking dogs, and some of them ran up to the rocks, while others ran down all the way to the sea. They had been trained to obey the voice, to calm down when they heard the pipes, and to form a herd when they heard a handclap. But on this occasion fear made them forget everything; and it was only with difficulty that Daphnis and Chloe tracked them down, like hares, by their footprints, and drove them back to the farms. That was the only night that they both had a really deep sleep, and exhaustion cured the pain of love. But when it was day again, they had the same feelings once more. They felt pleasure at seeing each other and pain at leaving each other. They wanted something, but they didn't know what they wanted. The one thing they knew was that he had been destroyed by a kiss and she by a bath.

23    The time of year inflamed them too. It was the end of spring and the beginning of summer, and everything was in its prime. The fruit was on the trees; the crops stood in the fields. The chirping of the cicadas was pleasant; the smell of the fruit was sweet; the bleating of the sheep was delightful. You could have imagined that the rivers were singing as they flowed gently, that the winds were playing the pipes as they blew in the pines, that it was from passion that the apples were falling to the ground,[16] and from love of beauty that the sun was making everyone undress. Daphnis, inflamed by all this, kept plunging into rivers. Sometimes he washed himself; sometimes he tried to catch the swirling fish; often he drank the water, trying to put out the fire inside him. Chloe,

15. To escape "from the jaws of a wolf" is proverbial in Greek for an unexpected piece of good fortune.

16. Longus suggests, rather preciously, that one could imagine that the apples fell not from natural causes but from a passionate attraction to the ground, in harmony with the erotic atmosphere of the season. Apples have erotic connotations elsewhere in the novel; cf. 1.24 (throwing apples at someone was taken to be a declaration of love in ancient pastoral) and note 60.

when she had milked the ewes, and most of the she-goats too, spent a long time and had a lot of trouble thickening the milk into cheese—for the flies were terrible, bothering her and biting her if she didn't chase them off. But then she washed her face, put on a garland of pine twigs, wrapped her fawnskin around herself, and, filling a bucket with wine and milk, she shared a drink with Daphnis.

When midday came, their eyes were captivated. Chloe, seeing Daph- 24 nis naked, was lost in gazing at his beauty and felt weak, unable to find fault with any part of him. Daphnis, seeing her in a fawnskin and garland of pine holding out the bucket, thought he was seeing one of the Nymphs from the cave.[17] He snatched the pine garland from her head and put it on his own, after kissing it first. She put on his clothes when he was bathing and naked, and she too kissed them first. Sometimes they threw apples at each other, and tidied themselves up by combing each other's hair. She said his hair was like myrtle berries, because it was dark; he said her face was like an apple, because it was pink and white. He taught her how to play the pipes too; and when she started to blow, he snatched the pipes and ran his lips along the reeds. He gave the impression of correcting Chloe's mistakes, but really it gave him an excuse for kissing her by means of the pipes.

When he was playing his pipes at midday, and the flocks were lying in 25 the shade, Chloe drifted into sleep. Daphnis noted this, and, dropping his pipes, he gazed at her, all of her, insatiably, shamelessly, and as he did so, he said, under his breath:

"What eyes are sleeping there, what a sweet breath comes from her mouth! Apples do not give off such fragrance, nor do pears. But I'm frightened of kissing her. Her kiss stings my heart and, like new honey, makes me mad. And if I kiss her, I'm frightened I shall wake her up. Oh, these chattering cicadas! With their loud chirping they won't let her go on sleeping! And the he-goats are fighting, with crashing horns! Oh, you wolves—more cowardly than foxes—why haven't you carried them off?"

While he was saying this, a cicada, running away from a swallow that 26 wanted to catch it, slipped down the front of her clothes. The swallow came after it; it wasn't able to catch the cicada, but it came close in its pursuit and touched Chloe's cheeks with its wings. Chloe didn't know what had happened; giving a loud shriek, she woke up with a start. When she saw the swallow still flying near her and Daphnis laughing at her fear, she stopped being frightened and rubbed her eyes, which were still sleepy. The cicada chirped from inside her clothes like someone who had taken refuge there and was thanking her for rescuing him. Chloe

17. Chloe resembles a maenad or bacchant, a devotee of Dionysus, and so do the danc-ing Nymphs in 1.4. On the Dionysus theme in the novel, see note 26.

gave another loud shriek, and Daphnis laughed. Taking this opportunity, he put his hands between her breasts and took out that obliging cicada, which did not go quiet even when it was in his hand. Chloe enjoyed seeing this; she took hold of the cicada, kissed it, and put it back, chirping, inside her clothes.

27    One day, a wood pigeon pleased them by singing a pastoral song from the wood. When Chloe wanted to know what its song meant, Daphnis taught her, telling her a story that had often been told.[18]

"There was a young girl, young girl, as beautiful as you are; and she had a herd, like you, keeping many cows in a wood. She was a beautiful singer too, and her cows enjoyed her singing. She managed her herd without hitting them with a stick or prodding them with a goad; sitting under a pine and garlanded with pine, she sang the story of Pan and Pitys,[19] and the cows stayed close to hear her voice. There was a boy who kept a herd of cows not far away, who was also beautiful and had a beautiful voice like the girl. He competed with her in singing, and, displaying a voice that was stronger like a man's but still sweet like a boy's, he lured her eight best cows into his herd and led them away. The girl was distressed at the loss to her herd and at her defeat as a singer, and prayed to the gods to turn her into a bird before she arrived home. The gods granted her prayer and made her into a bird, a mountain dweller like the girl, and a lovely singer like her. Even now she tells of her misfortune, in her song, and says she is searching for cows that have gone astray."

28    These were the kinds of pleasure summer gave them. But when autumn was at its height, and the grapes were now turning dark, some pirates from Pyrrha, using a light Carian boat (so that they might seem foreigners),[20] landed at those fields. They disembarked with cutlasses and breastplates and swept off everything that fell into their hands: wine with a sweet bouquet, masses of wheat, honey still in the combs. They drove off some cows from Dorcon's herd too.

They also took Daphnis, who was wandering beside the sea. (Chloe drove out Dryas's sheep later in the day; being a young girl, she was

18. Daphnis's story, like the wood pigeon's song, is pastoral, since it is based on the theme of contest between singer-herdsmen (see note 10). The story itself is a stock mythological type, explaining a bird's song and involving a metamorphosis (cf. the following note).

19. This story tells how a nymph (Pitys) became a pine (*pitys,* in Greek) as an unfortunate result of Pan's love (cf. the stories of Syrinx, 2.34, and Echo, 3.23). Thus, both Daphnis's story and the story within the story end in an unhappy metamorphosis. The pine was closely associated with Pan's worship.

20. Pyrrha was a city on the coast of Lesbos, on the southern shore of the gulf of Kalloni, while Caria was on the southwest coast of Asia Minor, i.e., modern Turkey. (The reading "from Pyrrha" is Reeve's suggestion. Other editors read "from Tyre," i.e., also from Asia, which seems to make less sense.)

frightened of the other shepherds, who were bullies.) When the pirates saw a young man who was tall and handsome and worth more than the plunder from the fields, they didn't waste any more energy on the goats or on the rest of the fields but drove him down to the ship weeping and desperate and calling out "Chloe" in a loud voice. The pirates had just untied the mooring rope and were thrusting the oars in the water and moving out to sea when Chloe drove down her flock of sheep, carrying a new set of pipes as a present for Daphnis. Seeing the goats in confusion and hearing Daphnis, whose cries of "Chloe" grew ever louder, she forgot her sheep, threw down the pipes, and ran to Dorcon to ask for help.

Dorcon was lying on the ground, battered by the pirates' violent     29 blows and scarcely breathing, streaming with blood. When he saw Chloe, he recovered a little of the fire of his former love and said:

"Chloe, I shall die soon—those unholy pirates butchered me like a cow when I was trying to defend my cows—but I want you to rescue Daphnis, give me revenge, and destroy them. I've trained my cows to follow the sound of the pipes and to chase its tune, however far away they are grazing. So come on, take these pipes, and play on them that tune I taught Daphnis once and Daphnis taught you. Then it'll be up to the pipes themselves and the cows out there. And take these pipes as a present from me; with them I've won competitions with many cowherds and goatherds. In return, kiss me while I live and mourn for me when I die and if you see anyone else grazing my cows, remember me."

Dorcon said this and kissed his last kiss; with that kiss and those     30 words he let out his final breath. Chloe took the pipes, and, putting them to her lips, she blew as loudly as she could. The cows heard and recognized the tune; moved by a single impulse, they all mooed and jumped into the sea. Since the cows made this violent jump on one side of the ship and created a deep trough in the sea as they fell in, the ship rolled over and sank as the waves met over it.[21] Those aboard all fell out—but not with the same chance of survival; for the pirates had cutlasses hanging at their side and were wearing breastplates covered with metal scales and greaves that reached halfway up their shins. But Daphnis had bare feet—as you'd expect of someone grazing on the plain—and he was half-naked, as the weather was still burning hot. So the pirates were only able to swim a little way before their armor carried them down to the depths, while Daphnis got out of his clothes easily. He still swam only with a struggle, since he had swum only in rivers before. But then necessity taught him what to do: he plunged into the middle of the cows, and, taking hold of two cows, with each hand on one horn of each cow, he was

21. This bizarre incident seems to be based on an actual event recorded by Aelian (*Nature of Animals* 8.19) and Pliny (*Natural History* 8.208), although that incident involved pigs, not cows.

carried along in the middle, painlessly and effortlessly, as though he were driving a cart. Cows, in fact, are even better at swimming than men; they are inferior only to water birds and fish themselves. A swimming cow would never drown unless its hooves got soaked through and dropped off. A proof of this point is the fact that many parts of the sea are called Bosporus to this day.[22]

31     In this way Daphnis was saved, escaping against all hope from two dangers, piracy and shipwreck. Coming out of the water, he found Chloe on land laughing and crying at the same time and fell into her arms, asking her what her reason was for playing the pipes. She told him everything: how she had run to Dorcon, how he had trained the cows, how he told her to play the pipes, how Dorcon was dead. The only thing she did not mention was the kiss—she was too embarrassed. They thought they should honor the memory of their benefactor, and so they went with his relatives and buried poor Dorcon. They piled a great mass of earth on his grave, planted many garden trees, and hung up the firstfruits of their labors in his honor. They also poured out libations of milk, squeezed some grapes, and smashed a number of pipes. They heard the cows mooing sadly and saw them running wild while they mooed. And they supposed, cowherds and goatherds as they were, that this was the cows' way of mourning for the dead cowherd.

32     After the burial of Dorcon, Chloe led Daphnis to the Nymphs, brought him into the cave, and washed him. And then for the first time, she washed her body while Daphnis was looking. It was white and pure in its beauty and needed no washing to make it beautiful. Then, after gathering all the flowers that were in season at that time, they put garlands on the images and hung the pipes of Dorcon from the rock as a thank-offering. Then they went and checked on the goats and sheep. They were all lying down, neither grazing nor bleating—I think they were missing the absent Daphnis and Chloe. At any rate, when those two came into view and gave their usual cry and played their pipes, the sheep got up and started grazing, and the goats skipped around, snorting as though they were pleased at the rescue of their usual goatherd. But Daphnis could not bring himself to feel any pleasure now that he'd seen Chloe naked and seen the beauty revealed that had been hidden before. He felt a pain in his heart, as though it was being eaten by poisons; sometimes he panted as though someone was chasing him, and some-

---

22. Bosporus means "cow-crossing" in Greek. Erudite pieces of information are not uncommon in Greek novels (cf. the comments on Lesbian vines in 2.1) and suit the taste of Longus's period, the Second Sophistic. This passage, however, seems to be an ironic pastiche of such erudition rather than a serious example, as indicated by the incredible idea of horn hooves becoming soaked through. After having the effrontery to save his hero by the quasi-miraculous behavior of a herd of cows, Longus pretends to substantiate the incident by pseudo-erudition.

times he was short of breath, as though it had all been used up in the at-tacks he had just survived.[23] The bath seemed more terrible than the sea. He thought he must have left his life behind with the pirates—for he was young and a country boy and still ignorant of the piracy of love.

## Book Two

Now the fruit season was at its height, and the grapes were ripe for har-     1 vesting. Everyone was working in the fields: some were getting wine-presses ready for use; some were cleaning out wine jars; some were plait-ing wicker baskets. One man was attending to a small reaphook for cutting the bunches of grapes; another to a stone for squeezing the juice out of the grapes; another to a dry willow twig that had been battered into shreds to make a torch so that the sweet new wine could be drawn off at night.[24] Daphnis and Chloe too stopped looking after their goats and sheep and gave the others a helping hand. He carried bunches of grapes in baskets, put them in the winepresses and trod them, and drew off the wine into the jars. She prepared food for the grape pickers, poured out drinks of mature wine for them, and picked the grapes off the vines that were nearer the ground. In Lesbos all the vines are low; they do not grow up high and are not trained on trees, but they let their shoots hang down and are spread out like ivy. In fact, a baby who'd only just got his hands out of his shawl could reach a bunch.[25]

As is only natural at a festival celebrating Dionysus and the birth of     2 wine, the women called from the neighboring fields to help with the work made eyes at Daphnis and paid him compliments, saying he was as beautiful as Dionysus. One of the cheekier ones even kissed him—which excited him and hurt Chloe. Meanwhile the men in the winepresses hurled all sorts of comments at Chloe and jumped madly around her like satyrs excited by a bacchant.[26] They prayed to be turned into sheep and to be led to pasture by her—so this time she was pleased, and Daphnis was hurt. They both prayed that they would finish the grape harvest

23. The erotic symptoms echo those of 1.18.

24. The stone seems to be used for squeezing the residual juice of the grapes after they have been trodden by human feet. "Sweet new wine" is what is sometimes called must, wine in its unfermented or partly fermented state, whose sugar has not yet been used up in fermentation.

25. A puzzling aside: if *all* the vines in Lesbos are low, what sense does it make to say that Chloe picks the grapes nearer the ground? Presumably, while all the vines are low in comparison to those grown elsewhere (which are trained on trees and allowed to grow to some height), some are lower than others. The smallish Chloe picks the grapes left by the taller men; while some grapes are so low even a baby could pick a bunch.

26. These comments hint at the recurrent Dionysus motif; cf. notes 17, 46, 62, and 68. Dionysus, like Eros, is a god who is specially associated with the mysterious workings of divine power in human life, especially in human minds and emotions, a pervasive theme in the novel.

quickly so that they could go back to their usual haunts again and hear the pipes and their own flocks bleating instead of this disharmonious chatter.

A few days later, the vines were harvested, the sweet new wine was in jars, and there was no longer any need for many hands. Daphnis and Chloe drove their flocks down to the plain and, in a happy mood, worshiped the Nymphs, bringing them bunches of grapes still on the shoots as firstfruits of the grape harvest. Not that they ever went past them and neglected them before; they always visited them when they went to pasture and worshiped them when they left the pasture and without fail brought them some kind of offering, a flower or a fruit or some green leaves or a libation of milk. For this, they received a reward from the goddesses later on. But at that time, as people say, "The dogs were let off the lead": they jumped, played the pipes, sang, and wrestled with their goats and sheep.

3     While they were enjoying themselves, an old man came up to them. He was dressed in a goat's-hair cloak and had rawhide sandals on his feet and a bag hanging from his shoulder, a very old one. He sat down beside them and spoke in this way.

"My children, I am old Philetas.[27] I sang many songs to these Nymphs here, I played many tunes on the pipe to that Pan over there, and I led a herd of many cows by the power of music alone. I've come to tell you what I've seen and to pass on to you what I've heard.

"I have a garden that I made with my own hands. I've worked at it ever since I stopped being a herdsman because of my age, and each season it grows everything that the season brings. In spring, there are roses, lilies, hyacinths, and violets, both light and dark; in summer there are poppies, pears, and all sorts of apples; at this time of year there are vines, figs, pomegranates, and green myrtle berries. Flocks of birds gather in this garden early in the morning; some come for food, and some to sing. They come here because it is overhung with trees, shady, and watered by three springs. If you took away the fence, you'd think you were looking at a grove of trees.[28]

4     "As I went there today around midday I saw, under the pomegranates and myrtles, a boy, with myrtle berries and pomegranates in his hands. His skin was white like milk, and his hair was reddish-gold like fire, and his body glistened as though he'd just bathed. He was naked and alone, and he was enjoying himself fruit picking, as though it was his own gar-

---

27. Longus gives this herdsman-musician the name of a famous Alexandrian poet, who was regarded as a poetic model by Theocritus and the Latin love elegists. His description of Eros is verbally reminiscent of that given by the pastoral poets Theocritus and Moschus.

28. For another example of the motif of the marvelously fertile garden, see 4.2 and note 61.

den. I pounced on him to try and catch him, frightened that he'd break down the myrtles and pomegranates in his naughtiness. But he escaped from me easily, with quick, light movements, sometimes running under the rosebushes and sometimes hiding under the poppies like a young partridge. I've often had trouble chasing unweaned kids, and I've often got tired running after newborn calves; but this was something tricky and impossible to catch. Tired (I'm an old man) and leaning on my stick while still watching that he didn't escape, I asked which of the neighbors was his father and what he meant by picking fruit in someone else's garden. He didn't reply, but standing near me he gave a very soft laugh and threw myrtle berries at me and—somehow or other—he charmed me out of my anger. I begged him to come into my arms and not to be frightened anymore; and I swore by the myrtle berries that I'd let him go and give him some apples and pomegranates too and let him pick the fruit and pluck the flowers at any time—if I got just one kiss from him!

"At that, he gave a very loud laugh and spoke in a voice sweeter than    5
a swallow's, a nightingale's, or a swan's (even a swan as old as me).[29]

" 'It's no trouble for me to kiss you, Philetas; for I want to be kissed more than you want to be young again. But consider whether the gift is a suitable one at your age. Your age won't save you from chasing me after your one kiss. And I'm hard to catch, even for a hawk and an eagle and any bird faster than these. I'm not really a boy, even though I look like one, but I'm even older than Cronus and the whole of time itself.[30] I've known you when, as a lusty young man, you used to graze your large herd of cows on that mountain there, and I've been with you while you played the pipes beside those oaks when you were in love with Amaryllis. But you didn't see me, although I was standing very close to the girl. Well, I gave her to you, and now you have sons who are good cowherds and farmers. At the moment, Daphnis and Chloe are the flock I am looking after. And when I've herded them together in the morning, I come into your garden and enjoy your flowers and trees and bathe in these springs. That's why the flowers and trees are beautiful—because they're watered by the springs I bathe in. Look and see whether any of your trees has been broken down, whether any of your fruit has been picked, whether any of the stems of your flowers has been trampled on, whether any of your springs has been muddied; and be happy that you're the only man who's seen this boy in your old age.'

29. In the ancient world, the swan was associated with old age (because of its white plumage) and was thought to sing melodiously, particularly before its death (the swan song).

30. Longus here combines the long-standing conception of Eros as a primeval cosmic force (going back to Hesiod *Theogony* 120–22) with the typical portrayal of Eros in poetry and art as a young boy.

6    "He said this and then hopped like a young nightingale into the myrtles and, moving from branch to branch, worked his way through the leaves to the top. I saw wings growing from his shoulders and a little bow between his wings, and then I saw neither them nor him. If it's not for nothing that I've grown these grey hairs, and if I haven't grown feebleminded in my old age, you are consecrated to Love, my children, and Love is looking after you."

7    Daphnis and Chloe enjoyed this very much, treating it as a story rather than as fact, and they asked whatever this "Love" was—a boy or a bird—and what power he had.

"Love is a god, my children; he is young, beautiful, and winged; and so he enjoys youth, pursues beauty, and makes souls take wing. Zeus has not so much power as he has: he rules the elements; he rules the stars; he rules his fellow gods—more completely than you rule your goats and sheep. All the flowers are the work of Love; all the plants are his creation; thanks to him, the rivers flow, the winds blow. I have seen a bull in love, bellowing as though stung by a gadfly, and a he-goat in love with a she-goat, following her everywhere.

"I was young myself once and fell in love with Amaryllis. I forgot to eat; I didn't drink; I couldn't sleep. My soul was in pain; my heart pounded; my body was frozen. I cried out as though being hit; I was silent as though dying; I plunged in rivers as though on fire. I called on Pan to help me, since he himself had been in love with Pitys. I praised Echo for calling after me the name of Amaryllis. I smashed my pipes because they charmed the cows, but they failed to draw Amaryllis to me. There is no medicine for Love, no potion, no drug, no spell to mutter, except a kiss and an embrace and lying down together with naked bodies."[31]

8    Philetas taught them all this and went away, after accepting from them some cheeses and a kid that already had its horns. When they were left on their own, now that they'd heard for the first time the word "love," they felt a spasm of pain in their souls; and when they went home to their farms at night, they compared their own experiences with what they'd heard.

"Lovers feel pain—and so do we. They neglect their food—and we've neglected ours in the same way. They cannot sleep—and that's happening to us at this moment. They seem to be burning up—and there's a fire inside us. They long to see each other—and that's why we pray for the day to come more quickly. Surely this is "love"; and we are "in love".

31. This chapter is a kind of prose poem, a series of short "verses," linked by rhyme or assonance—a suitable form for Philetas to use; cf. note 27. The first half forms a kind of hymn, the second a kind of erotic poem, and both parts are strongly reminiscent of Greek and perhaps Latin literature on the subject.

with each other without realizing it. Or is it that this is love and that I
alone am in love? But then why do we feel the same pain? Why do we
look for each other's company? Everything that Philetas said is true. The
boy in the garden was also seen by our fathers in that dream, and he was
the one who told us to graze the flocks. How could anyone catch him?
He is small, and he'll escape you. And how could anyone escape him? He
has wings, and he'll catch you. We must run to the Nymphs in search of
help. And yet Pan didn't even help Philetas when he was in love with
Amaryllis. We must try the remedies he mentioned—kissing and embracing and lying naked on the ground. It is cold, but we shall put up
with it, as Philetas did."

This was the lesson the night taught them. The next day, driving their 9
flocks to pasture, they kissed each other when they met—something
they'd never done before—and threw their arms round each other in a
close embrace. But they shrank from the third remedy—stripping naked
and lying down together. This was too bold an act for a young girl—or
even a young goatherd. Then again they passed a sleepless night, thinking about what they'd done and blaming themselves for what they'd
failed to do.

"We kissed, and that was no use. We embraced; and that did no more
good. Lying down together must be the only cure for love; we must try
that too. It will certainly have more power than a kiss."

After these thoughts—as you might expect—they had passionate 10
dreams about kisses and embraces. And what they hadn't done in the
day, they did in their dreams: they lay with each other naked. When the
next day came, they got up still more possessed by Love's power and,
whistling, drove their flocks down to pasture, eager for the kisses; when
they saw each other, they ran together smiling. Kissing took place, of
course, and embraces followed; but the third remedy was delayed, because Daphnis didn't dare to speak about it, and Chloe didn't want to
make the first move—until, by accident, they did this too.

They were sitting beside each other at the foot of an oak tree and, 11
having tasted the delight of kissing, were taking their fill of the pleasure
insatiably. They also embraced, crushing their bodies against each other
to match the impact of their lips. As Daphnis drew Chloe rather violently towards him, she somehow slipped over on her side, and he, following her kiss, slipped down with her. Recognizing what they had seen
in their dreams, they lay down for a long time as though tied together.
They did not know what to do next and thought that this was the limit
of love's satisfaction. So they spent most of the day in this futile way,
and then separated, and drove their herds back, hating the night. Indeed,
perhaps they might have really done something if a disturbance hadn't
gripped the whole countryside, in this way.

12    Some rich young men from Methymna wanted to spend the harvest-time on a pleasure trip away from home.[32] So they launched a small boat, putting in their domestic slaves as oarsmen, and sailed round those parts of the Mytilenean countryside that are near the sea. The coast has good harbors and is well equipped with rich houses. There is a continuous row of bathing places, parks, and woods, some the product of nature, others of human art. All in all, it's a good place to be young in.

They sailed along and made landings; they did no harm and enjoyed various sports. Sometimes they tried to catch fish in pools from a rock projecting into the sea, using hooks attached to rods with fine threads. Sometimes, with dogs and nets, they hunted hares that were running away from the din in the vineyards. Sometimes they turned to hunting birds, and with snares they caught wild geese, ducks, and bustards. So their sport also provided for their table. If they needed anything else, they got it from the countrypeople, paying several obols more than it was worth. All they needed was bread, wine, and a roof over their heads; for now that autumn had begun, they did not think it was safe to sleep at sea, and so they used to drag their boat up onto land, frightened of a stormy night.

13    One of the local farmers needed a rope to haul up the stone used to crush the grapes after they had been trodden, as the rope he had before was broken. He went furtively to the sea, approached the unguarded boat, untied the mooring cable, carried it home, and used it for what he needed. In the morning, the young men from Methymna made a search for the rope; when no one owned up to stealing it, they complained a bit about their hosts and sailed on. After sailing round the coast for three or four miles, they put in near the fields where Daphnis and Chloe lived. The plain looked to them a good spot for hunting hares. They didn't have a rope to tie up as a mooring cable, so they twisted a long, green willow shoot into a rope, and with that they secured the boat, by its stern end, to the land. Then, letting the dogs free to sniff out the scent, they laid out nets on the paths that looked most promising. The dogs ran around barking and frightened the goats; then the goats left the hilly areas and rushed towards the sea. Having nothing to gnaw at in the sand, the more adventurous ones went to the boat and ate up the green willow shoot the boat had been moored with.

14    The sea had also become rather rough because of a wind blowing from the hills. So, now that the boat was floating free, the backwash of the waves very soon lifted it up and carried it out to the open sea. When the Methymneans realized this, some ran towards the sea while others

32. Methymna was the second largest city on Lesbos, just under forty miles by road from Mytilene, and the center of an independent city-state.

called the dogs together. They all shouted, so that all the people from the neighboring fields heard them and came in a group. But it was no use. The wind was blowing its hardest, and the boat was being carried away on the current at an uncontrollable speed.

Now that they had lost something worth a good deal, the Methymneans looked for the herdsman of the goats; and when they found Daphnis, they hit him and stripped off his clothes. One of them picked up a dog lead and started twisting Daphnis's hands behind his back to tie him up. While he was being hit, Daphnis shouted out, begging for help from the local farmers; he called out especially to Lamon and Dryas. These fought back well, being tough old men, strong from farm laboring. They demanded the chance to debate the matter before a judge.

Since the other side agreed to this, they appointed Philetas the cowherd as judge; for he was the oldest of those there, and he had a reputation among the villagers for being exceptionally fair. The Methymneans put the case for the prosecution first, putting it in clear and concise terms, since they had a cowherd for a judge.[33]

"We came to these fields wanting to go hunting. We left the boat tied to the shore with a green willow shoot while we used our dogs to look for game. Meanwhile, this man's goats came down to the sea, ate the shoot, and let the boat loose. You saw the boat carried away on the sea; but have you any idea how many valuables it contains? What good clothes we've lost, what fine equipment for the dogs, how much silver! Anyone who had all that could buy up these fields. In return for our losses, we demand to take this man with us. He must be a terrible goatherd, since he puts his goats to graze on the sea like a sailor!"[34]

This was the Methymneans' case for the prosecution. Daphnis was in a bad way because of his beating. But when he saw Chloe there, he rose above everything and spoke in this way.

"I am a goatherd and a good one. Not one of the villagers has ever held me responsible because a goat of mine has been feeding on anyone's garden or has broken down a young vine. But these men are bad hunters and have dogs that are badly trained, which run all over the place, barking noisily. These dogs were like wolves chasing the goats down from the hills and plains to the sea. They say the goats ate up the willow shoot. Yes, they did; but in the sand they didn't have any grass, wild strawberry, or thyme to eat. They say the boat's been lost because of the wind and the sea. Well, that's the work of the weather, not my goats.

33. Trial scenes are quite common in the Greek novels and are often handled rhetorically. In this trial, the style of the speeches is unusually simple and pastoral, though, paradoxically, the rustic Daphnis (rising to the occasion and inspired by Chloe's presence) is more rhetorical than his urban accusers.

34. The sentence seems to contain a pun: the Greek word for "goats" can also mean "waves."

They say it contained clothing and silver. But what man with any sense will believe that a boat holding so much stuff had a willow shoot for its mooring cable?"

17    At this, Daphnis burst into tears and made the villagers feel very sorry for him. So Philetas, the judge, swore by Pan and the Nymphs that Daphnis had done no wrong, nor had the goats, but the sea and the wind—which had other judges than him. This statement by Philetas did not convince the Methymneans. They made an angry rush and dragged Daphnis away again, wanting to tie him up. At this the villagers got excited and swooped down on them like starlings or jackdaws.[35] They soon removed Daphnis from their grasp (he was fighting himself now), and they soon sent them packing, hitting them with clubs. They didn't leave them alone until they had driven them out of their boundaries and into someone else's fields.

18    While they were chasing the Methymneans, Chloe was completely at peace, leading Daphnis to the Nymphs. She washed his face, which was covered with blood because his nose had been broken by a blow. And she took out from her bag a piece of bread and a portion of cheese and gave them to him to eat. But what most revived him was a honey-sweet kiss that she gave with her soft lips.

19    So on that occasion, Daphnis came close to disaster. And the matter did not end there. When the Methymneans managed to get home—now that they had become footsloggers instead of yachtsmen and wounded veterans instead of luxury tourists—they called an assembly of the citizens. They laid a petition before the people, begging to be granted fitting vengeance. They didn't tell the truth about a single thing. Apart from anything else, they didn't want to appear ridiculous at having suffered so badly and so much at the hands of shepherds. And so they accused the people of Mytilene of taking their boat and plundering their possessions and acting as if they were at war. The citizens believed them, because of their wounds, and thought it was right to take revenge in support of young men from their leading families. They voted for war against the Mytileneans, without even a declaration of war—and they ordered their general to launch ten ships and make destructive raids on the seashore. Because winter was near, they didn't think it was safe to put a bigger force to sea.

20    Right away, the next day, the general put to sea with soldiers at the oars and attacked the coastal regions of Mytilene. They carried off many sheep, a great deal of corn and wine (for the grape harvest had just been completed), and a number of people who were working there. Among the fields they attacked were the ones where Chloe and Daphnis lived;

35. Longus highlights the conflict with an epic touch; the simile is Homeric (*Iliad* 17.755).

they made a sudden landing and then drove off as booty whatever they found. Daphnis was not grazing his goats but had gone up to the wood and was cutting green leaves so that he would have fodder for the kids in winter. So he saw the raid from up there and hid in the hollow trunk of a dry beech. But Chloe was with the flocks. When she was chased, she ran to the Nymphs looking for sanctuary and begged the men, in the name of the goddesses, to spare both her flocks and herself. But it was no good; the Methymneans jeered a good deal at the images and then drove off the flocks and took her too, treating her like a goat or sheep and beating her with willow shoots.

Now they had filled their ships with all sorts of plunder, they decided 21 not to sail any further but started to make their journey home, worried about the winter and their enemies too. So they sailed off, working very hard at their oars because there was no wind. Now that things were quiet, Daphnis went to the plain where they used to graze. But he did not see the goats, nor did he find the sheep, nor did he discover Chloe, but instead everywhere was deserted, and the pipes that Chloe used to enjoy were thrown on the ground. He gave a great shout, and, crying pitifully, he ran first to the oak where they used to sit, then to the sea, in the hope of seeing her there, then to the Nymphs, where she herself had run for refuge when she was being chased. Here he threw himself on the ground and blamed the Nymphs for betraying them.

"Chloe was snatched away from you: and could you bear to see this— 22 the girl who used to weave garlands for you, who used to pour you libations of the freshest milk, who offered you these very pipes there? Not a single goat of mine was ever snatched off by a wolf, but now enemies have snatched off the herd and the girl who helped me look after them. They will skin the goats, sacrifice the sheep—and Chloe will spend the rest of her life in a city! How can I take the steps that will lead me back to my father and mother, without the goats, without Chloe, to be out of work? For I have nothing left to graze. No, I shall lie here and wait for death—or a second war. And you too, Chloe, do you feel like this? Do you remember this plain, these Nymphs, and me? Or are you comforted by the sheep and the goats taken prisoner with you?"

While he was talking in this way, a deep sleep took him out of his 23 tears and pain. The three Nymphs appeared to him as tall, beautiful women, half-naked and barefooted, their hair flowing free—just like their images. First of all, they seemed to be feeling sorry for Daphnis. Then the eldest spoke, encouraging him.

"Don't blame us, Daphnis. We care about Chloe even more than you do. We were the ones who took pity on her when she was a child, and when she was lying in this cave, we saw to it that she was nursed. Even now we have paid attention to her situation and made sure she won't be

*Eros*

carried off to Methymna to become a slave and won't become part of the spoils of war. You see Pan over there, his image set up under the pine, who's never received from you even the honor of some flowers—well, we've asked him to be Chloe's protector. He's more used to army camps than we are, and he's already left the country and fought a number of wars.[36] And when he attacks the Methymneans, they won't find him a good enemy to have. Don't make yourself anxious. Get up and show yourself to Lamon and Myrtale. Like you, they're lying on the ground, thinking that you are part of the plunder too. Chloe will come to you tomorrow, with the goats and with the sheep, and you will graze together and play the pipes together. All your other affairs will be taken care of by Love."

24 Seeing and hearing this, Daphnis jumped up out of his sleep; weeping with pleasure and pain, he kneeled down before the images of the Nymphs and promised that if Chloe were rescued, he would sacrifice the best of the she-goats. He also ran to the pine where the image of Pan was set up, goat-legged, horned, holding pipes in one hand and a leaping he-goat with the other. He kneeled before him too and prayed for Chloe and promised to sacrifice a he-goat. It was only around sunset that he could bring himself to stop crying and praying. He picked up the leaves he had cut and went back to the farm and Lamon's family, freeing them from grief and filling them with joy. He had some food and fell asleep; but still he couldn't stop crying, while he prayed to see the Nymphs again in a dream and prayed for the day to come quickly, the day on which they promised him Chloe. Never did any night seem as long as that one; and on that night this is what happened.

25 After traveling for about a mile, the Methymnean general wanted to give his soldiers a rest, because they were tired from their raid. So he made for a headland that jutted out in the sea, forming a long crescent shape; inside this crescent the sea made a natural anchorage that was calmer than any harbor. There he anchored the ships, in deep water, so that none of the countrypeople could damage any of the ships from the land, and he let his men relax and enjoy the pleasures of peace. They had plenty of everything from their plunder; and so they drank and played around and held a kind of victory celebration. The day was just coming to a close, and the night was bringing their enjoyment to an end, when suddenly the whole earth seemed to blaze with fire, and they heard the noise of splashing oars, as though a huge fleet was sailing against them.

36. Pan is not only a god of the countryside; he is also associated with warfare and with the "panic" that can overwhelm armies in war (see 2.25–26). A number of details in the following account are based on earlier myths involving gods other than Pan: e.g., the ivy sprouting on the goats (cf. *Homeric Hymn to Dionysus*), the role of a dolphin as pilot (2.29, cf. *Homeric Hymn to Apollo*).

Someone shouted out that they should arm themselves; someone else called for the general; someone looked as if he had been wounded; and someone else lay there looking like a corpse. You would have thought you were seeing a night attack—but there was no enemy there.

After a night like that, the day came; and this was much more terrify-  /26
ing than the night. Daphnis's he-goats and she-goats had flowering ivy on their horns, while Chloe's rams and ewes howled like wolves. Chloe herself was seen with a garland of pine on her head. Also, many bizarre things happened in the sea itself. The anchors stuck to the seabed when they tried to lift them up; the oars broke off when they lowered them into water to row; dolphins, leaping out of the sea, hit the ships with their tails and loosened the joints in the ships' timbers. Above the steep cliff that lay under the headland a sort of piping sound was heard; but it did not give pleasure to those listening, as pipes usually do, but terrified them, like a war trumpet. They were panic-stricken, ran to take up arms, and spoke of enemies although they could not see any. In fact, they prayed for night to come again, in the hope that they would get a truce then.

Now it was clear to everyone with any sense that these apparitions and noises were the work of Pan and that he had some grudge against the sailors. But they couldn't work out the reason; for they hadn't plundered any shrine of Pan. But then, around midday, the general fell asleep (not without divine prompting), and Pan himself appeared to him and spoke in this way.

"Most unholy and impious of men, what madness has driven you to  27
act so recklessly? You've filled the countryside I love with war; you've driven off herds of cows, goats, and sheep that are under my care; you've dragged from the altars a girl whom Love wants to make the subject of a story; and you showed no shame before the Nymphs when they watched what you did, or before me—Pan. If you sail on with these spoils, you'll never see Methymna, nor will you escape this piping that has made you so panic-stricken. Instead I shall sink your ship and make you food for the fish unless, immediately, you hand back Chloe to the Nymphs and the flocks to Chloe, both the goats and the sheep. So get up and put the girl ashore, together with the animals I spoke of. I myself will be your guide on sea, and hers on land."

Bryaxis (that was the general's name) was very disturbed. He jumped  28
up, summoned the ships' captains, and ordered them to look for Chloe among the captives as soon as possible. They were quick to find her and bring her into his sight; for she was sitting with a pine garland on her head. Taking this as a sign that tallied with what he had seen in his dream, Bryaxis carried her on his own flagship to land. Chloe had only just stepped out of the ship when the sound of pipes was heard again

from the cliff. But now it was no longer warlike and frightening but pastoral, like the sound that leads flocks to pasture. And indeed, the sheep started to run down the gangways, slipping on their horny hooves, and the goats came too, much more confidently, as you would expect of animals used to walking on steep rocks.

29    Now these animals were standing in a circle around Chloe like a chorus, jumping and bleating and showing signs of happiness. But the goats of the other goatherds, and the sheep and the cows, stayed in the hold, as though the tune had no magical effect on them. Everyone was gripped by amazement and shouted out in praise of Pan; but then they saw things taking place, on both elements, that were more amazing still. Before the Methymneans had pulled up the anchors, the ships started to sail, and the flagship was piloted by a dolphin that jumped up out of the sea. Meanwhile the goats and sheep were led by the sweetest piping sound, although no one saw the piper; both sheep and goats moved forward in unison and grazed, responding with pleasure to the tune.

30    It was about the time of the second grazing when, from a high lookout, Daphnis saw the flocks and Chloe and shouted out loud, "O Nymphs and Pan!" He ran down to the plain, threw his arms around Chloe, and fell down in a faint.

When he was, with difficulty, brought back to life by Chloe's kisses and the warmth of her embraces, he went to their usual oak tree and, sitting at the foot of the trunk, he asked how she had escaped from such a large enemy force. She told him everything: the ivy on the goats, the howling of the sheep, the pine that grew on her head, the fire on land, the noise at sea, the two kinds of piping—the warlike and the peaceful— the night of terror, and how although she did not know her way home, music pointed the way. Daphnis recognized his dream of the Nymphs and the work of Pan; and he told her what he had seen, what he had heard, how he intended to die but was kept alive by the Nymphs. Then he sent her to fetch Dryas and Lamon and their families and to bring what they needed for a sacrifice. Meanwhile he caught the best of the goats and put a garland of ivy on it, just as the goats had appeared to the enemy. Then he poured a libation of milk on its horns, sacrificed it to the Nymphs, and after hanging it up and skinning it, he presented the skin as a thank-offering.

31    Now that Chloe and the others had arrived, he lit a fire, boiled some of the meat, and roasted the rest. He made the first offerings to the Nymphs and poured out a mixing bowl full of sweet new wine as a libation. He spread out beds of leaves and then turned to eating, drinking, and playing. At the same time he kept an eye on the flocks to make sure no wolf fell on them and did what the enemy had done. They also sang some songs to the Nymphs, the compositions of shepherds of old. When

night came, they slept there in the field, and on the next day they gave their attention to Pan. They put a pine garland on the he-goat that was the leader of the herd, led him to the pine, poured a libation of wine, and shouted in celebration of the god, before sacrificing, hanging up, and skinning the goat. After roasting and boiling the meat, they placed it nearby on the leaves in the meadow. But they tied the skin, together with its horns, to the pine beside the image, a pastoral offering to a pastoral god. They made the first offerings of the meat to Pan and poured out libations from a larger mixing bowl.[37] Chloe sang, and Daphnis played the pipes.

After this day they lay down and were eating when the cowherd 32 Philetas appeared, bringing, by a coincidence, some little garlands to Pan and also some bunches of grapes still on the leafy shoots. His youngest child, Tityrus, accompanied him—a boy with red hair, blue eyes, pale skin, and plenty of cheek; he bounded along lightly as he walked, like a kid.[38] So they jumped up, and together they put the garlands on Pan and tied the vine shoots onto the foliage of the pine. Then they made Philetas lie down beside them and join in the drinking. As old men do, when they've had a few drinks, they talked a lot to each other; saying how they used to graze when they were young, and how many pirates' raids they had escaped from. One of them boasted that he had killed a wolf; another that he had played the pipes better than anyone except Pan: this was the boast of Philetas.

So Daphnis and Chloe used every kind of appeal to make him share 33 his skill with them and to play the pipes, since they were celebrating a god who took pleasure in the pipes. Philetas promised he would (though he complained that old age made him breathless) and took hold of Daphnis's pipes. But they were too small for a great artist, because they were made to be played in a boy's mouth. So he sent Tityrus for his own pipes from his farm, which was about a mile away. The boy threw off his cloak and, wearing just a tunic, swept off, running like a fawn. Meanwhile Lamon promised to tell them the story of the pipes, which a Sicilian goatherd sang to him once for the price of a he-goat—and a set of pipes.[39]

37. The sacrifices described here follow the usual ancient procedure. The differences of detail between the two sacrifices seem to reflect the ritual associations of the gods (e.g., Pan's victim has a pine garland, not an ivy one), and the special honor due to Pan for his role in the recent rescue (his victim is the leader of the goat herd; his libations are of fully fermented wine and made from a larger mixing bowl).

38. Tityrus is another name with pastoral associations. This is confirmed by the descriptions of his movements: he bounds like a kid, runs like a fawn (2.33).

39. The "Sicilian goatherd" seems to be an allusion to Theocritus of Sicily; the practice of exchanging gifts for songs is common in pastoral poetry. The story of Syrinx (the Greek word for "Pan-pipes") is a common one (it is retold by Achilles Tatius 8.6.7–11). For this type of story, cf. note 19.

*love as violence — cures — transformation*

34    "These pipes were originally not an instrument but a beautiful girl with a lovely singing voice. She grazed goats, played with the Nymphs, and sang—as she does now. While she was grazing, playing, and singing, Pan approached her and tried to talk her into doing what he desired, promising to make all her she-goats have twins. But she laughed at his love and said that she'd never accept as a lover a creature who wasn't completely goat or completely man. Pan started to chase her, intending to use violence. Syrinx ran away from Pan and his violence. When she got tired in her running, she hid among some reeds and vanished completely into a marsh. Pan angrily cut down the reeds, but he couldn't find the girl. When he understood what she had suffered,[40] he invented the Pan-pipes: he blew into the reeds, after fastening together reeds of unequal length because their love had been ill matched. So what was then a beautiful girl is now a sweet-sounding set of pipes."

35    Lamon had just finished his storytelling, and Philetas was praising him for telling a story sweeter than any song, when Tityrus arrived, bringing his father his pipes. The instrument was a big one, with big reeds, and decorated with bronze where the reeds were fastened with wax. You could have imagined it was the very instrument that Pan first put together. Philetas got up and sat upright on a chair. First he tried the reeds to see if he could blow through them properly. Once he'd found that his breath ran through them unimpeded, he then blew a loud and lusty note. You would have thought you were hearing several flutes playing together, so strong was the sound of his piping. Gradually reducing his force, he modulated the tune to a sweeter sound and displayed every kind of skill in musical herdsmanship:[41] he played music that fitted a herd of cows, music that suited a herd of goats, music that flocks of sheep would love. For the sheep the tune was sweet; for the cows it was loud; for the goats it was sharp. Altogether, that one set of pipes imitated all the pipes there are.

36    The others lay in silence and enjoyed listening to the music; but Dryas got up and told him to play a Dionysian tune, and danced a dance of the grape harvest for them. Sometimes his movements were those of someone picking the grapes, sometimes carrying the baskets, then treading the grapes, then filling the jars, then drinking the sweet new wine. Dryas danced all this so gracefully and vividly that they seemed to see the vines, the press, the jars—and Dryas really drinking.

---

40. The Greek seems to refer to the old idea of "learning through suffering" (cf. Aeschylus *Agamemnon* 177). Pan learns—from the girl's suffering rather than his own—and reflectively turns their ill-matched love into a musical instrument.

41. In the word *eunomia*, Longus puns on the two ideas of "harmony" and "good herdsmanship," thus fusing the two ideas of shepherd and musician that make up the pastoral ideal.

*realism*
*chastity*)

So he became the third old man to win applause, this time by dancing. 37
He kissed Chloe and Daphnis, who got up right away and danced out
Lamon's story. Daphnis took the part of Pan, and Chloe the part of Syrinx. He begged and tried to talk her round; she smiled indifferently. He
gave chase, running on tiptoe to give the impression of having hooves;
she acted as if she were tired from running away. Then Chloe disappeared into the wood, as though into the marsh; and Daphnis took Philetas's big pipes and piped a plaintive tune, like one in love, then a romantic tune, like one who tries to win his love, and then a tune that sounded
a rallying call,[42] like one looking for his lost love. Philetas was amazed at
this; he jumped up and kissed Daphnis, and, kissing him, he gave the
pipes as a present and prayed that Daphnis too would leave them to a
successor as good as himself.

Daphnis gave his own little pipes as an offering to Pan. Kissing Chloe, 38
as though he had found her again after a real chase, he drove his herd
home, piping, since night was now falling. Chloe drove her flock home
too, and she too used the tune of the pipes to keep her flock together.
The goats walked beside the sheep, and Daphnis walked close to Chloe.
They took their fill of each other in this way till night came, agreeing to
drive the herds out earlier than usual the next day.

And this they did. The day was only just breaking when they went to
pasture. They saluted first the Nymphs and then Pan, and then sat under
the oak, playing the pipes. Then they kissed each other, embraced, lay
down together, and—after doing nothing more—got up again. They also
thought about food and drank some wine mixed with milk.

All this made them hotter and more audacious. They started compet- 39
ing with each other about who loved the other more, and gradually
reached the point of swearing oaths to their fidelity. Daphnis went to the
pine and swore by Pan that he would never live alone, without Chloe,
not even for a single day. Chloe went to the cave and swore by the
Nymphs that all she wanted was to be with Daphnis, in life or in death.
But such was Chloe's girlish simplicity that as she left the cave, she demanded to have a second oath as well.

"Daphnis" she said, "Pan is a romantic god and an unreliable one. He
fell in love with Pitys; he fell in love with Syrinx; he never stops pestering the Dryads and bothering the Nymphs that guard the flocks. If you
fail to keep the oaths you swear by him, he'll fail to punish you, even if
you go after more women than there are reeds in the pipes. Swear to me,
by this herd of goats and the she-goat that suckled you, not to abandon
Chloe as long as she remains faithful to you. But if she does wrong to
you, and to the Nymphs, avoid her, hate her, and kill her like a wolf."

42. The term is a military one; cf. 4.15.

Daphnis was pleased at her distrust. Standing in the middle of the herd, holding a she-goat with one hand and a he-goat with the other, he swore to love Chloe while she loved him. And if she ever preferred another man to Daphnis, he swore to kill himself instead of her. She was delighted and trusted him, being a shepherd girl, who regarded the goats and sheep as the patron gods of shepherds and goatherds.

## Book Three

1 When the Mytileneans learned of the expedition of the ten ships, and some people came from the fields and gave reports of the ravages there, they thought it was intolerable that they should be treated like that by the Methymneans and decided to make war on them as soon as possible. So they enrolled three thousand infantry and five hundred cavalry and sent them off, under the command of their general, Hippasus, by land, because they were nervous of the sea in winter.

2 Hippasus set off; but he did not make raids on the fields of the Methymneans, nor did he plunder the herds and property of the farmers and shepherds, regarding this as the act of a pirate rather than a general.[43] He moved quickly towards the city itself, in the hope of breaking through the city gates while they were still unguarded. But when he was about twelve miles away from the city, an envoy came to meet him, bringing terms for peace. For the Methymneans had learned from their prisoners that the people of Mytilene knew nothing of the original incidents, which were the reaction of some farmers and shepherds to a group of irresponsible young men. The Methymneans now regretted their action against a neighboring city, regarding it as impetuous rather than sensible. They proposed a settlement in which they divested themselves of all their spoils and restored safe communications by land and sea.

Hippasus responded by sending the envoy to the people of Mytilene, although he had been elected as a general with full power to take decisions; meanwhile he pitched camp about a mile from Methymna and waited for his city's orders. Two days later, a messenger came and told him to recover the booty and return home without doing any damage. Being in a position to choose between war and peace, they found peace more profitable.

3 And so the war between Methymna and Mytilene came to an end, finishing as suddenly as it had begun. But winter arrived, and this was more bitter for Daphnis and Chloe than the war had been. Suddenly a heavy snowfall blocked all the roads and shut all the farmers in their

---

43. In this brief war, Hippasus, and the Mytileneans generally, come out as more sensible and scrupulous than Bryaxis and the Methymneans; Mytilene also turns out to be the original home of Daphnis and Chloe and so has a special significance in the novel.

homes. Swollen rivers rushed down violently. The ice was rock hard, and the trees looked as though they were breaking down under the weight. The ground was completely invisible except around some springs and streams. No one drove a herd to pasture or went out of doors himself. They lit big fires at cockcrow, and some spent their time spinning flax, others combing out goat hair, others making ingenious traps for birds. Sometimes too they saw to it that the cows at the mangers had bran to eat, that the goats and sheep in the pens had leaves, and that the pigs in the sties had acorns.

Now that they all had to stay at home, the other farmers and herds- 4 men enjoyed the short holiday from their work and liked having meals in the morning as well as the evening and sleeping late, so that winter seemed to them sweeter than summer, autumn, and even spring. But Chloe and Daphnis remembered the pleasures they had left behind—how they kissed, how they embraced, how they took their meals together— and spent sleepless nights and painful days and waited for spring as if it were a rebirth from death. They were upset if they handled a bag they had taken their food from or saw a milk bucket they had both taken a drink from or pipes thrown carelessly down that had been a love gift. They prayed to the Nymphs and Pan to release them from these miseries too and to show the sun, at last, to them and their flocks. While they prayed, they also searched for some way of seeing each other. Chloe was terribly helpless and could think of nothing, for her supposed mother was always with her, teaching her how to card wool and turn spindles and going on about marriage. But Daphnis had spare time—and was in any case cleverer than a girl—and he came up with this plan for seeing Chloe.

In front of Dryas's farm, right next to the farmyard itself, two myrtles 5 and some ivy had grown up; the myrtles were near each other, and the ivy lay between the two of them. The ivy spread its tendrils into each of the myrtles, like a vine, and made a kind of cave with the interwoven leaves, while the clusters of ivy berries hung down, as numerous and as big as grapes on vine shoots. There were a great number of winter birds gathered around the ivy because of the shortage of food outside. There were lots of blackbirds, lots of thrushes, wood pigeons, starlings, and all the other birds that eat ivy. Claiming that it was these birds he wanted to hunt, Daphnis started out, filling his bag with honey cakes and carrying birdlime and snares, to look convincing. The distance between the two places was no more than a mile, but the snow hadn't melted yet and gave him a lot of trouble. But love can fight its way through anything—fire, water, or Scythian snow.[44]

44. The sentiment—and the detail of *Scythian* snow—are typical of ancient erotic po-etry. However, winters on Lesbos can be severe, especially on the hills.

6     He ran to the farm, and after shaking the snow from his legs, he set the snares, smeared the birdlime on some long twigs, and then sat down to wait for birds—and Chloe. A large number of birds came, and he caught enough to give him plenty of trouble, collecting them, killing them, and plucking them. But none came out of the farm, not a man, not a woman, not a farmyard fowl—they were all shut up inside, sticking close to the fire. So Daphnis was completely at a loss and thought his trip there was ill omened.[45]

He screwed up his courage to make some excuse and push his way through the doors; and he asked himself what was the most convincing thing he could say.

"I've come to get a light for a fire."

"But didn't you have neighbors two hundred yards away?"

"I've come to ask for some bread."

"But your bag's full of food."

"I need some wine."

"But it was only the other day you had the grape harvest."

"A wolf chased me."

"And where are the wolf's footprints?"

"I came to hunt the birds."

"Well, you've caught them; why don't you go away?"

"I want to see Chloe."

"Who'd admit that to a young girl's father and mother?" Stumbling against obstacles on every side, he said to himself:

"All of these remarks sound suspicious. It'll be better to say nothing. I'll see Chloe in the spring, since it doesn't seem fated for me to see her in the winter."

Thinking along these lines and silently collecting his catch, he was starting to go off, when (as though Love had taken pity on him) this happened.

7     Dryas's family was sitting round the table. The meat was being carved; the loaves were being put out; the wine was being mixed. Then one of the sheepdogs, waiting for an unguarded moment, snatched some meat and ran out through the door. Dryas was annoyed; for it was his own helping. He picked up a club and ran on its heels, like a dog himself. Reaching the ivy in his chase, he saw Daphnis, who had just hoisted his catch onto his shoulders and decided to clear off. Dryas instantly forgot about the meat and the dog, and, giving a great shout—"Hello, my boy"—he put his arm around him, kissed him, took his hand, and led him indoors.

45. The Greek contains a pun: the phrase "ill omened" (literally "with inauspicious birds") hints at the birds Daphnis has caught—that have failed to help him gain his real objective in the hunt.

*What? is this foreplay? not chaste*

When they saw each other, they nearly collapsed onto the ground, but, finding the strength to stay upright, they greeted each other and kissed; this gave them some sort of support and stopped them falling down.

Daphnis had found more than he hoped for—not only Chloe but a kiss. He sat down by the fire and unloaded the wood pigeons and blackbirds from his shoulders onto the table. He told them how he got fed up of staying at home and went out hunting, how he took some of the birds with snares and some with birdlime while the birds were trying to get at the myrtle berries and the ivy. They complimented him on his enterprise and told him to help himself to what the dog had left behind. They also told Chloe to pour out something to drink. She was pleased and served the others first and Daphnis last: for she was pretending to be annoyed because he had come there and then planned to run away without seeing her. But before passing him his wine, she drank some of it herself and then gave it to him. Although he was thirsty, he drank it slowly and gave himself a longer pleasure in this way.

The table was quickly emptied of bread and meat, but they stayed sitting there and asked about Myrtale and Lamon. They congratulated them on their good fortune in having someone like Daphnis to look after them in their old age. Daphnis enjoyed being complimented while Chloe was listening, but when they asked him to stay, as they were going to make a sacrifice to Dionysus the next day, he was so delighted he almost kneeled down to worship them instead of the god.[46] At once, he took out of his bag a large number of honey cakes and the birds he'd caught, and they started to prepare these for their evening meal. A second mixing bowl was set on the table, and a second fire was lit, and after night had fallen early, they fed well on this second meal. Afterwards they told some stories and sang some songs until they went to bed, Chloe sleeping with her mother, and Dryas with Daphnis. For Chloe, there was no advantage in this arrangement except that she was going to see Daphnis the next day. But Daphnis enjoyed an empty pleasure: he thought it pleasant to sleep even with Chloe's father, so he embraced him and kissed him often and dreamed he was doing all this to Chloe.

When day came, it was extraordinarily cold, and the north wind was scorching everything up. They got up and sacrificed a year-old ram to Dionysus, built a big fire, and prepared a meal. While Nape was making bread, and Dryas was boiling the ram, Daphnis and Chloe took advantage of this free time and came out of the farm to the place where the ivy was. They set up traps again and smeared on birdlime and hunted a con-

46. The winter sacrifice to Dionysus accompanied prayer for new life in the spring. On the role of Dionysus in the novel, see note 26.

siderable number of birds. They also enjoyed continuous kissing and took pleasure in talking to each other.

"It was because of you I came, Chloe."

"I know, Daphnis."

"It's because of you I'm killing these poor blackbirds."

"What do you want me to do then?"

"Remember me."

"I do remember you, by the Nymphs—the Nymphs whose cave I visited once to swear by—the cave we'll go to as soon as the snow melts."

"But there's lots of snow, Chloe, and I'm afraid I shall melt before the snow does."

"Cheer up, Daphnis; the sun is quite hot."

"If only, Chloe, it were as hot as the fire that burns my heart."

"You're joking and mocking me."

"No—by the goats you told me to swear by."[47]

11    Chloe gave these responses to Daphnis like an echo; then, as Nape was calling them, they ran inside, bringing a much bigger catch than that of the day before. After making an offering to Dionysus of the first drops from the mixing bowl, they put garlands of ivy on their heads and ate their meal. When it was time, they shouted "Iacchus" and "Evohe"[48] and sent Daphnis on his way, after filling his bag with meat and bread. They also gave him the wood pigeons and thrushes, to take to Lamon and Myrtale, saying that they would catch others for themselves as long as the winter continued, and the ivy berries lasted. He went off, kissing them all—and Chloe last, so that her kiss might remain pure on his lips. He made many other journeys on different pretexts, so that their winter was not entirely deprived of love.

12    Now spring was starting, the snow was melting, the earth was being exposed, and the grass was beginning to grow. The other shepherds drove their flocks to pasture: but Chloe and Daphnis were the first to do so—as you might expect, since they were slaves to a more powerful shepherd.[49] They ran at once to the Nymphs and the cave, then to Pan and the pine, then to the oak tree, under which they sat and grazed their flocks and kissed each other. They also looked for flowers, wanting to put garlands on the gods. These were only just coming out, nourished by the west wind and warmed by the sun. But still they found violets, narcissi, pimpernels, and all the firstfruits of the spring. They also took fresh milk from some of the she-goats and ewes, put the garlands of flowers on the images, and poured the milk out as a libation. They also

47. This dialogue is a kind of parallel to the imaginary dialogue in 3.6. Chloe gives the kind of tart replies Daphnis imagines he will receive from her family.

48. These are standard ritual cries to Dionysus.

49. The shepherd is Eros; cf. 2.5 and 4.39.

made a musical offering, the firstfruits of the pipes, as though they were
challenging the nightingales to sing. And the nightingales did start to call
softly in the bushes, gradually perfecting their dirge for Itys, as though
they were remembering the song after a long silence.[50]

Over here the sheep bleated; over there the lambs jumped around,    13
then kneeled under their mothers, and sucked away at the teats. As for
the ewes that had not yet lambed, the rams chased them until each got
his ewe in position and mounted her. The he-goats were even more passionate in chasing the she-goats and jumping on them. They also fought
over the she-goats; for each he-goat had his own wives and was on his
guard against secret adulteries. Even old men would have been excited to
desire by such sights. But Daphnis and Chloe, blooming with youthful
energy, who had long since been searching for love, were inflamed by
what they heard and felt faint at what they saw and looked for something
more than kissing and embracing for themselves—especially Daphnis.
He had been wasting his youth in the winter, sitting at home doing nothing, and now he was hot for kisses, eager for embraces, more vigorous
and ready for anything.

He asked Chloe to give him all he desired and to lie naked beside his    14
naked body on the ground for longer than they used to before. This, he
said, was the one thing left untried in Philetas's instructions for producing the sole cure and antidote for love. She asked what more there was
than kissing and embracing and actually lying down, and what he proposed to do when they were lying down naked together. "What the rams
do to the ewes," he replied, "and the he-goats to the she-goats. After
they've done it, don't you see how the females stop running away from
the males, and the males don't have the trouble of chasing the females?
But from then on they graze together as though they've enjoyed mutual
pleasure. What they're doing must be something sweet that overcomes
the bitterness of love."

"But don't you see, my dear Daphnis, that he-goats and rams do it
standing up, and she-goats and ewes have it done to them standing up.
The males jump on the females, and the females are jumped on, from behind. But do you propose that I should do this lying down, and naked
too—although these hairy animals are much more well covered than I
am even in my clothes?"

Daphnis was convinced by this. After getting down on the ground
with her and lying there for a long time (but not knowing how to do
what he wanted so hotly), he made her stand up and clung to her from
behind, copying the he-goats. He felt more puzzled and sat down and

50. This refers to a well-known myth in which the nightingale's song is treated as the
lament of a metamorphosed woman (Procne) for the son she has killed (Itys); for this type
of myth, cf. 1.27.

wept at the thought that he was more stupid than the rams at making love.[51]

15 He had a neighbor called Chromis who farmed his own land and who was now physically past his prime. He had imported a wife from town who was young, pretty, and rather sophisticated for the countryside; her name was Lycaenion.[52] She saw Daphnis every day, driving his goats to pasture in the morning and driving them back at night. She wanted to acquire him as a lover by seducing him with presents; and one day she ambushed him when he was on his own, and gave him as a present a set of pipes as well as honey in a honeycomb and a deerskin bag. But she shrank from saying anything, sensing his love for Chloe; she saw he was completely devoted to the girl. She had guessed this already from their nods and laughter; but then she went out early in the morning, pretending to Chromis that she was visiting a neighbor who was having a baby. She followed Daphnis and Chloe, keeping close behind; and, hiding in some bushes so as not to be seen, she heard everything they said and saw all they did. She didn't even miss Daphnis's outburst of crying. She sympathized with their trials and saw a twofold opportunity—for rescuing them and satisfying her desire; so she worked out this plot.

16 The next day, pretending to go to the woman having a baby, she went—openly this time—to the oak tree where Daphnis and Chloe were sitting and gave an accurate imitation of a woman in distress.

"Rescue me, Daphnis," she said. "I'm in a bad way. An eagle snatched off the finest of my twenty geese. As it was so heavy to carry, he couldn't carry it right up to his usual high rock over there but fell down into the wood down here, still holding it. Please—by the Nymphs and Pan there—come into the wood with me (I'm frightened to go by myself), rescue my goose, and don't let my flock lose one of its number. Perhaps you'll be able to kill the eagle too, and he'll stop snatching off so many of your lambs and kids. In the meantime, Chloe will look after the herd; the goats certainly know her well, since she is your constant companion in grazing."

17 Without any suspicion of what was going to happen, Daphnis got up at once, took his shepherd's staff, and followed behind Lycaenion. She led him as far as possible from Chloe, and when they were in the thickest part of the wood, she told him to sit down by a spring and said:

"Daphnis, you're in love with Chloe: I found this out from the Nymphs last night in a dream. They told me how you wept yesterday

---

51. In this novel, humans often imitate animals in a way that is beneficial (see, for example, 1.3, 1.6, 1.9)—this illustrates the pastoral harmony of men and animals. Here Longus, rather slyly, points out a significant dissimilarity between humans and animals that his pastoral lovers have not yet appreciated (cf. also 3.17).

52. The name is the diminutive form of "she-wolf," the herdsman's predatory enemy.

and told me to rescue you by teaching you how to make love. This isn't just kissing and embracing and doing what the rams and he-goats do. It is a kind of leaping that is sweeter than theirs, for it takes longer and gives a longer pleasure. If you want to get rid of your troubles and try out the pleasures you are searching for, come and give yourself to me as a pupil, and I will give you a lesson, as a favor to those Nymphs."

Daphnis did not resist but was delighted. Being a rustic, a goatherd,   18
in love and young, he threw himself at the feet of Lycaenion and begged her to teach him, as soon as possible, the skill that would make him able to do what he wanted to Chloe. In fact, he acted as if he was going to be taught something great and really superhuman and promised to give her a kid brought up in the fold, some soft cheeses made from a she-goat's first milking, and the she-goat too. So Lycaenion found Daphnis even more of a goatherd (and more generous too) than she expected. She started to educate him in this way. She ordered him to sit beside her, just as he was, to kiss her, in his usual way, and as often as usual, and, as he kissed her, to embrace her at the same time and lie down on the ground. When he had sat down, kissed, and lain down, and she discovered that he was capable of action and was swollen with desire, she lifted him up from where he was lying on his side, slipped her body underneath, and guided him skilfully on the road he had been searching for until now. After that, she did nothing exotic; from then on, nature herself taught him what had to be done.

When the lesson in lovemaking was over, Daphnis still had a shep-   19
herd's understanding and was eager to run to Chloe and do what he'd been taught right away, as if frightened that he would forget it if he waited. But Lycaenion held him back and told him this.

"You've still got this to learn, Daphnis. Because I happen to be an experienced woman, I didn't suffer any harm just now (long ago another man gave me this lesson and took my virginity as his reward). But if Chloe has this sort of wrestling match with you, she will cry out and weep and will lie there, bleeding heavily. But don't be afraid of the blood; when you talk her into giving herself to you, lead her to this spot so that if she cries out, no one can hear her, and if she weeps, no one can see her, and if she bleeds, she can wash in the spring. And remember—I made you a man before Chloe did."

This was what Lycaenion advised him; she then went off to another   20
part of the wood, as though she was still looking for her goose. Daphnis thought about what she had said and lost his previous impulse, and shrank from pestering Chloe for more than kisses and embraces. He did not want her to cry out at him as though he was an enemy or weep as if she was hurt or bleed as if she was wounded. Having only just learned about the blood, he was frightened of it and thought it was only from a

wound that blood came. So he decided to take only his usual pleasures with her. He left the wood and came to where she was sitting, weaving a little garland of violets; he told a false story abut snatching the goose from the eagle's talons,[53] and, clinging to her, he kissed her just as he had kissed Lycaenion when they were enjoying themselves. This was all right, he thought, as it involved no danger. She fitted the garland to his head, kissed his hair, and said it was better than violets. She took a piece of fruitcake and some bread from her bag and gave them to him to eat; and as he ate, she snatched them from his mouth and ate them herself, like a young bird.

21      While they were eating—and kissing more than they ate—a fishing boat came into view, sailing past them. There was no wind, and the sea was calm, and so the sailors had decided to row and were rowing vigorously. They were hurrying to get their freshly caught fish to the city in good condition for one of the rich men there. As they lifted their oars, they did what sailors usually do to take their minds off their tiring work: one man was acting as cox and singing sea chanteys to them, while the rest behaved like a kind of chorus and shouted out in unison, taking their time from his voice. When they did this in the open sea, their shout vanished, as their voices were dispersed in a great expanse of air. But when they ran under a particular headland and rowed into a crescent-shaped bay surrounded by land, a louder shout was audible, and the coxes' songs traveled clearly to the land;[54] for there was a rounded glen lying above the plain, which acted like a musical instrument, taking the sound into itself and reproducing every noise, both the sound of the oars and also, quite distinctly, the sailors' voices. It was pleasant to listen to; the sound from the sea came first, and then the sound from the land started and finished correspondingly later.

22      Daphnis knew what was going on and gave his attention only to the sea; he enjoyed watching the boat as it ran past the plain faster than a bird, and he tried to retain some of the songs to make them into tunes on the pipes. But for Chloe this was her first experience of what is called an echo: sometimes she looked at the sea when the sailors were calling out the time; sometimes she turned to the wood, looking for the choir that sang in response. When they had sailed past, and there was silence in the glen, she asked Daphnis if, behind the headland, there was another sea and another ship sailing past and other sailors singing the same songs and all of them going quiet together. Daphnis laughed at her sweetly and

53. Daphnis's only lie to Chloe in the novel; cf. Chloe's reticence about Dorcon's dying kiss (1.31).

54. At first it seems as though there is one cox in the boat while the rest are his crew-chorus. Here it becomes clear that the sailors take it in turn to act as cox and call out the time by singing (cf. 3.22, "the sailors were calling out the time"). The location here is presumably the site of the Methymneans' "panic" (2.25).

gave her a kiss that was sweeter still. Then he put the garland of violets on her and started to tell her the story of Echo, asking her for a reward of ten more kisses if he taught her it.

"My dear girl, there is a great family of Nymphs: there are Nymphs   23 of the Ash, Nymphs of the Oak, and Nymphs of the Meadow. All of them are beautiful, and all of them are sweet singers. One of them had a daughter called Echo, who was mortal because she had a mortal father, but was beautiful because she had a beautiful mother. She was brought up by the Nymphs and taught by the Muses to play the pipes, the flute, the lyre, and the cithara, and to sing songs of every kind. When she grew up and flowered into a lovely girl, she danced with the Nymphs and sang with the Muses. But she shunned all males, both human and divine, loving her virginity. Pan was angry with the girl, because of his jealousy of her musical artistry and because of his failure to enjoy her beauty; so he sent the shepherds and the goatherds mad, and, like dogs or wolves, they tore her apart and scattered her limbs—which were still singing—over the whole earth.[55] As a favor to the Nymphs, Earth hid all her limbs and preserved their music; and by the will of the Muses, Earth has the power of speech and copies everything, just as the girl did then—gods, men, instruments, beasts. It copies Pan himself, when he plays the pipes; and when he hears it, he jumps up and chases over the mountains. All he wants now is to know who his invisible pupil is." When he told this story, Chloe gave him not only ten kisses but very many; for the echo had repeated almost everything he said, as though confirming that he hadn't told a lie.

The sun was growing hotter every day—for spring was coming to an   24 end and summer was starting—and again they found new pleasures, those of summer. He swam in the rivers; she bathed in the springs. On his pipes he competed with the whistling of the pines, while she sang in contest with the nightingales. They hunted talkative grasshoppers; they captured chirping cicadas. They gathered flowers, shook trees, ate fruit. And now, one day, they lay down together naked, covering themselves with a single goatskin; and Chloe would easily have become a woman if the thought of the blood had not disturbed Daphnis. He was understandably frightened that one day he might not be able to control himself, and so he did not allow Chloe to undress often. Chloe was amazed at this, but she was ashamed to ask the reason.

This summer, there were a great number of suitors after Chloe; many   25 of them, from many different places, visited Dryas, asking to marry her; some brought a present with them; others promised big presents if they

---

55. There is a pun in the Greek: *mele* can mean "songs" as well as "limbs." The Echo story is a common one, though there are a number of variants; for the type, cf. notes 18 and 19.

won her. Nape was buoyed up by hopes; her advice was to give Chloe away and not to keep a girl of her age at home. Chloe, she said, would very soon lose her virginity while grazing and make a man of some shepherd in return for some apples or roses. Instead, they should make her mistress of a house and make a good deal of money themselves and keep it for their own real son (a boy had been born to them a little before this). Dryas was sometimes attracted by these arguments; for gifts were being named by each of the suitors that were greater than one would expect for a shepherd girl. But at other times he reflected that the girl was better than her farmer suitors, and that if he ever found her real parents, she would make Nape and him very rich. So he put off an answer and made delay after delay, and while doing so made a considerable profit in gifts.

When Chloe learned about this, she spent a very miserable time. For quite a while, she avoided Daphnis, not wanting to hurt him. But when he insisted and pressed her for an answer and was more upset through not knowing than he was likely to be if he knew, she told him everything: how she had many rich suitors, how Nape was arguing that she should be married quickly, how Dryas did not refuse but had put the question off till the grape harvest.

26 Daphnis went out of his mind at this and sat there, weeping. He said he would die if Chloe stopped grazing with him—and not only he but also the sheep would die, deprived of a shepherdess like her. Then he recovered and cheered up and formed the plan of trying to win round her father. He started counting himself as one of the suitors and hoped he would beat the rest easily. One thing troubled him. Lamon was not a rich man. This was the only thing that made his hope a slender one. Yet he thought he should ask if he could marry her, and Chloe thought so too. He didn't dare say anything to Lamon, but he found the courage to speak to Myrtale, revealed his love for Chloe, and made a proposal of marriage; and Myrtale passed this on to Lamon at night.

Lamon reacted harshly to her suggestion; he abused her for acting as the go-between in matching a shepherd's little daughter with their son. He pointed out that Daphnis gave promise of great good fortune in the tokens he had as a child, and if the boy found his own parents, he would give him and Myrtale their freedom and make them masters of a bigger estate. Myrtale was afraid that if Daphnis was completely disappointed in his hope of marriage, he might try to kill himself because of his love. So she gave him different reasons for his father's refusal.

"We are poor, my boy, and we want a bride who'll bring in some money rather than ask for it. But they're rich people and want a rich bridegroom. But come on, talk Chloe round, and get her to talk her father round so that he'll give you her as a wife without asking for much of a present. At least Chloe loves you too and wants to sleep with a poor but handsome man rather than a rich ape."

Myrtale didn't suppose for one minute that Dryas would agree to this proposal, when he had rich suitors, but she thought it was a plausible way of putting off the marriage. Daphnis could not find fault with what she said. But now that he had fallen far short of what he'd asked for, he did what poverty-stricken lovers generally do—he wept; and he also made another appeal to the Nymphs to rescue him. They appeared to him while he was sleeping at night, in the same form as before, and again it was the eldest who spoke. 27

"Another god is taking care of Chloe's marriage. But we shall give you a present that will bring Dryas round. The boat that belonged to the young Methymneans—the one whose willow shoot your goats once ate—was blow far out to sea on that memorable day. But in the night a wind from the sea made the water rough, and the boat was cast ashore on the rocks of the headland. The boat itself and the bulk of its cargo were destroyed. But a purse, with three thousand drachmas in it, was thrown out by the waves and is lying, covered with seaweed, near a dead dolphin; that's why none of the passersby even goes near it, because they're keeping away from the stench of the decay. But you go up to it, and once you're there, pick it up, and once you've picked it up, use it as a present. For the time being, it is enough for you not to seem poor; later on, you will actually be rich."[56]

Saying this, they vanished with the night. Now that it was day, Daphnis jumped up cheerfully and, with a lot of whistling, drove his goats to pasture.[57] He kissed Chloe, paid his respects to the Nymphs, and went to the sea as if he wanted to splash himself with water, and then walked on the sand near the place where the waves break, looking for the three thousand. It didn't seem that he would have much trouble finding it. He was met by the terrible smell of the dolphin, which was flung up on shore and was clammy with decay; and, using its smell of decay to guide his path, he went straight to it, removed the seaweed, and found the purse, which was full of silver. He picked it up and put it in his bag; but he didn't go away until he had shouted out in celebration of the Nymphs and the sea itself. Goatherd though he was, he now thought 28

56. After the mid–third century A.D., because of inflation, three thousand drachmas would not have been enough to make someone "not...seem poor." This suggests the novel was written before this date.

57. Another Homeric echo (cf. note 35), this time of the Cyclops, Polyphemus, whistling as he drove his flock to the mountain (*Odyssey* 9.315).

the sea was sweeter than the land, because it was helping him to marry Chloe.

29    Now that he'd got hold of the three thousand, he waited no longer; as though he were the richest, not only of the farmers there, but of all mankind, he went straight to Chloe, told her the dream, showed her the purse, told her to look after the herds until he came back, and rushed eagerly to Dryas. He found him with Nape threshing some corn, and made a very bold proposal of marriage.

"Give me Chloe as my wife. I know how to reap well and to prune the vine and plant trees. I also know how to plough a field and winnow grain in the wind. And Chloe can witness how I graze a flock; I took over fifty she-goats, and I've made them into twice that number. I've also reared some fine big he-goats; before, we used to mate our she-goats with other people's he-goats. I'm young too and a good neighbor to you. And I was nursed by a she-goat—just as Chloe was nursed by an ewe. I'm better than the others in these ways, and I won't be beaten as far as presents go either. The rest will give you goats and sheep and a couple of mangy oxen and corn that couldn't even keep farmyard fowls alive. But this is my present to you—three thousand drachmas. Only, don't let anyone know this, not even Lamon, my father."

As he gave it to them, he put his arms round them and kissed them. When they saw all that money—far more than expected—they promised to give him Chloe and undertook to talk Lamon round. Nape stayed there with Daphnis, driving the oxen round and grinding the ears of corn in the threshing machine, while Dryas stored the purse away where the tokens were kept. Then he swept off quickly to Lamon and Myrtale, intending to do something entirely novel—to ask for a son's hand in marriage. He found them measuring the barley they too had just been winnowing, and feeling depressed because it was almost less than the seed that had been sown. He encouraged them about this, agreeing that the shortage was the same everywhere. Then he asked for Daphnis as a husband for Chloe. He said that although others were offering to give him a lot of money, he would take nothing from them; instead, he would give Lamon and Myrtale something from what he owned. He said the two young people had been brought up with each other, and that by grazing together they had become linked with a bond of affection that could not easily be broken; and that they were old enough to sleep with each other now. Dryas said this and much more, as you'd expect of a man who stands to win three thousand if he convinces his listeners.

Lamon could not plead poverty as an excuse (for the other couple were not looking down on them) nor Daphnis's youth (for he was already a young man). Even so, he did not speak out what he was really thinking—that Daphnis was superior to such a marriage—but after a short silence he answered in this way.

"You're right to prefer neighbors to strangers and right not to value 31 wealth above honest poverty. May Pan and the Nymphs love you for this! I'm eager for this marriage too—indeed, I'd be mad, now that I'm getting older and needing an extra hand for the work, if I didn't take this opportunity of uniting our families—something that's very advantageous. Chloe is much sought after too, a lovely girl in the bloom of youth and good at everything. But as I'm a slave, I'm not in charge of my own affairs; my master must learn of this and give his consent. Come, let's put off the wedding till the autumn. Those who've come here from town say that he's coming then. Then they'll be man and wife. For the present they must love each other like brother and sister. There's just one thing, Dryas, you should know: the young man you're keen about is better than us." As he said this, he kissed him and offered him a drink, for midday was now at its height, and, after treating him with every friendliness, he walked with him part of the way home.

Dryas had listened to Lamon's last remark with an attentive ear; as he 32 walked home, he reflected about Daphnis's identity.

"He was nursed by a she-goat, as if the gods were taking care of him. He's handsome and quite unlike that snub-nosed old man and his balding wife. He could afford three thousand drachmas too, although you wouldn't expect a goatherd to have three thousand wild pears! Did someone expose him too, like Chloe? Did Lamon find him, just as I found her? Were there any tokens lying beside him like those I found?[58] If this is really right (and I pray it is, Master Pan and my dear Nymphs), perhaps Daphnis will find out something about Chloe's mysterious origin if he finds his own parents." These thoughts and dreams passed through his mind all the way back to the threshing floor. When he got there, he found Daphnis in suspense for news; he encouraged him by calling him son-in-law, promised to celebrate his marriage in the autumn, and, shaking his hand, he swore that Chloe would belong to no man but Daphnis.

Quicker than thought, neither drinking nor eating, Daphnis ran to 33 Chloe and found her doing the milking and making cheese. He told her the good news about the marriage and kissed her openly, as his future wife, and shared her work. He milked the ewes into the buckets, set the

58. Dryas seems already to know *something* about Daphnis's origins. The fact that he was nursed by a she-goat seems to be public knowledge (cf. 1.16); Daphnis also knows that Chloe was nursed by an ewe (3.29; cf. 1.16). But other details of the origin of the children, such as the tokens, seem to be family secrets (cf. 1.3, 1.6), to be revealed dramatically later in the novel (4.18ff., 4.30ff.).

cheeses in the baskets to dry, put the lambs and kids underneath their mothers to feed. When all this was in order, they washed, fed, drank, and walked around, looking for ripe fruit. There was plenty available because it was the time of the year when everything is ripe. There were lots of wild pears and lots of cultivated ones; lots of apples, some of which had already fallen, some still on the trees. Those on the ground were more fragrant; those on the branches were fresher in color. The former smelt like wine; the latter shone like gold.

One apple tree had been stripped and had neither fruit nor leaves; all the branches were bare. But it still had one apple hanging at the very top of the highest branches—a big and beautiful one, and one that by itself had more fragrance than all the rest put together. The apple picker must have been frightened to climb up there and failed to take it down; also, perhaps, the lovely apple was being preserved for a shepherd in love.[59]

34    When Daphnis saw this apple, he was eager to climb up and pick it and ignored Chloe when she wanted to stop him. She was annoyed at being ignored and went away to the flocks. Daphnis climbed quickly and achieved his goal of picking it and taking it to Chloe as a present; although she was angry, he spoke to her in this way.

"My dear girl, fine seasons gave birth to this apple, and a fine tree nursed it while the sun ripened it, and chance looked after it. As long as I had eyes, I wasn't going to leave it to fall on the ground so that some herd of animals could trample it underfoot as they grazed, or some snake could poison it as it crawled along, or time could destroy it as it lay there, being looked at and praised. Aphrodite took this as a prize for her beauty; and I am giving it to you as a prize for your victory. You have the same kind of witness of your beauty as she did: he was a shepherd, while I'm a goatherd."

Saying this, he put the apple in her lap, and as he came close, she kissed him, so that Daphnis did not regret having dared to climb so high; for he got a kiss that was better than an apple—even a golden one.[60]

---

59. This passage is based on Sappho 105 LP, in which the lovely apple seems to have been used as a simile for the beloved; cf. the following note.

60. Daphnis's speech implies an analogy between Chloe and the apple; both Chloe and the apple are too beautiful for Daphnis to abandon to an uncertain future. (In addition, Chloe, like the apple, had a nurse who was different from her parents, and was preserved by good fortune.) The apple's erotic implications have already been touched on in this novel (cf. note 16); Longus now pursues these implications in myth. Paris, when a shepherd (after being exposed by his parents, like Daphnis), gave an apple as the prize to Aphrodite, after "the judgment of Paris" (that Aphrodite was more beautiful than Hera or Athena). The golden apple probably refers to those dropped by Atalanta to distract her suitors, who had to beat her at running to win her hand in marriage. Chloe's kiss is better even than one of those golden apples—and in any case Chloe is not running away from her suitor but rewarding him for reaching his goal.

*Garden*

## Book Four

One of Lamon's fellow slaves arrived from Mytilene and brought the    1
news that their master would be coming there just before the grape harvest, to check whether the Methymnean raid had done any damage to his
fields. And so, since summer was passing now, and autumn was approaching, Lamon got his master's country house ready to please the eye
in every way. He cleaned out the springs so that they could have clean
water, carted the dung out of the farmyard so that it wouldn't annoy
them with its smell, and worked on the enclosed garden so that it could
be seen in all its beauty.

The garden was a very beautiful place and bore comparison with royal    2
gardens. It was two hundred yards long, lay on elevated ground, and
was over a hundred yards wide. You would say it was like a long plain.
It had every kind of tree—apple, myrtle, pear, pomegranate, fig, and
olive. On one side, it had a tall vine, which spread over the apple and
pear trees with its darkening grapes, as if it was competing with their
fruit. These were the cultivated trees; and there were also cypresses, laurels, planes, and pines. These were all overgrown, not by the grape but
by the ivy, while the clusters of ivy berries, which were big and turning
dark, looked just like bunches of grapes. The fruit-bearing trees were on
the inside, as though protected by the others. The other trees stood
around them like a man-made wall, but these were enclosed in turn by a
narrow fence. Everything was divided and separate, with each trunk at
some distance from its neighbor. But, higher up, the branches joined and
intertwined their foliage. This was the work of nature, but it also seemed
to be the work of art. There were beds of flowers too, some produced by
the earth itself, and some by art. Roses, hyacinths, and lilies were the
work of human hands; violets, narcissi, and pimpernels were produced
by the earth itself. There was shade in the summer, flowers in the spring,
grapes for picking in the autumn, and fruit in every season.[61]

From there the plain was clearly visible, so you could see people graz-    3
ing their flocks; the sea was visible too, and people sailing past were open
to view. This too contributed to the luxurious feel of the garden. At the
midpoint of the length and breadth of the garden was a temple and altar
to Dionysus. Ivy surrounded the altar, and vine shoots surrounded the
temple. Inside, the temple had paintings of subjects related to Dionysus:

61. This description of an enclosed garden (*paradeisos*, cf. *paradise*)—to be distinguished
from the simple yard around the house mentioned elsewhere—is a fine example of an
*ekphrasis* (cf. note 1), with echoes of the first and most famous of such gardens in Greek literature, that of Alcinous in Homer's Phaeacia (*Odyssey* 7.114ff.). In the description, Longus
repeatedly stresses the harmonious collaboration of human art and nature, thus exemplify-
ing a general feature of the pastoral world of the novel.

Semele giving birth, Ariadne asleep, Lycurgus in chains, Pentheus being torn apart; there were also Indians being conquered and Etruscans changing shape. Everywhere satyrs were treading the grapes; everywhere bacchants were dancing. And Pan was not forgotten; he sat there too on a rock, playing the Pan-pipes himself, as though he were providing an accompaniment both for the treaders and the dancers.[62]

4    This was the garden that Lamon started to work on, cutting away the dry wood and tying up the vine shoots. He put a garland on Dionysus and watered the flowers from a spring that Daphnis had found for the flowers: the spring was reserved for the flowers, but even so it was called Daphnis's spring. Lamon also encouraged Daphnis to fatten up the goats as much as possible, saying that the master would certainly look at them, since he hadn't been there for so long. Daphnis was sure he would be complimented on them; he had doubled the number he had taken over, not a single one had been snatched by a wolf, and they were fatter than the sheep. But wanting his master to be more favorable to his marriage, he gave them every care and attention. He drove them out very early in the morning and drove them back very late in the evening. He led them to drink twice a day and looked for the best grazing places. He also equipped himself with new milk bowls, a number of milk buckets, and larger cheese baskets. In fact, he was so attentive that he started putting oil on their horns and combing their hair; you would think you were looking at a flock that was sacred to Pan. Chloe shared in all the work that was done on them. Neglecting her own flock, she gave up more of her time to his goats, so that Daphnis began to think that they seemed beautiful because of her.

5    While they were busy in this way, a second messenger came from town and told them to strip the vines as soon as they could. The messenger said he would stay until they had made the grapes into sweet new wine; then he would go back to the city and bring his master to make his visit, with that autumn's grape harvest completed. They gave a very warm welcome to this man (he was called Eudromus)[63] and started at once to strip the vines, carry the grapes to the winepresses, and draw off the sweet new wine into the jars. They also set aside the grapes with the

62. The *ekphrasis* of pictures on temple and other walls was a notable feature of writing of the second Sophistic. We find it in Lucian, Philostratus, and Achilles Tatius (3.7ff.), and there is a famous predecessor in Virgil (*Aeneid* 1.446ff.). The paintings represent Dionysus's birth (to Semele), his marriage (to Ariadne), and his vengeance on enemies, both individuals (such as Pentheus) and groups (such as the kidnapping Etruscan pirates he turned into dolphins). The owner of all these pictures of Dionysus is called, significantly, *Dionyso*phanes (see note 68). Pan is associated closely with Dionysus, as he often is in the novel (cf. note 36 and 4.26).

63. The name means "good runner," corresponding to his function (4.6).

best bloom on them and kept them on the shoots, so that even the people coming from the city could have the pleasure of picking the grapes and seeing what the harvest was like.

Eudromus was now about to run to town, and Daphnis gave him a 6 number of presents, including the sort of gifts a goatherd can make: firm cheeses, a kid born late in the year, and a shaggy white goatskin so that he would have something to put on when running messages in the winter. Eudromus was delighted; he kissed Daphnis and promised to put in a good word for him with his master.

So Eudromus went off, very well disposed towards him, while Daphnis anxiously grazed his flock with Chloe. She was also very frightened. A young man who was used to looking at goats, a hill, farmers, and Chloe, was about to have his first sight of his master, when before he had only heard his name. She worried on his behalf, wondering how he would be when he met the master, and her feelings were agitated about the marriage, in case they were dreaming of something that would never happen. They kissed continuously, and they embraced like two people who had grown into one. Their kisses were timid too, and their embraces were gloomy, as though the master was already there, and they were frightened or trying not to be seen. They were also disturbed by another source of anxiety.

There was a cowherd called Lampis, who was a bully. He had also 7 asked Dryas if he could marry Chloe and had already given him a large number of presents in his eagerness for the marriage. He heard that if Daphnis got his master's consent, he would marry her, and looked for some way of making the master antagonistic to Daphnis and Lamon. He knew that the master took pleasure in his garden and decided to do what he could to damage it and spoil its beauty. If he cut down the trees, he was likely to get caught because of the noise; so he made the flowers his target for destruction. He waited for night; then he crossed the fence, dug some up, broke others off, and trampled the rest down like a pig. He got away without being seen. When Lamon came to the garden the next day, intending to draw water for the flowers from the spring, he saw the whole place devastated—in a way an enemy, not a thief, would have gone to work. At once he ripped his tunic in pieces and called on the gods with a great shout, so that Myrtale dropped what she was doing and ran out, and Daphnis left his goats and ran up. Seeing it, they shouted, and, shouting, they wept: a new kind of mourning—for flowers.

They cried from fear of what their master would do; but even a 8 stranger would have cried if he had been there, for the place was completely ruined, and all the ground was now a muddy mess—except that any flowers that had escaped the assault still kept some bloom and shine and were still lovely even as they lay on the ground. The bees hung over them too, making a continuous, ceaseless humming, as though mourning. Lamon was shocked and said:

"Oh, the bed of roses—how they've been broken down! Oh, the bed of violets—how they've been trampled down! Oh, the hyacinths and narcissi, that some evil man has dug up! Spring will come, and they will not flower. Summer will come, and they will not reach full bloom. Another autumn will come, and they will not form a garland for anyone. Lord Dionysus, didn't you feel sorry for these poor flowers? You used to live beside them and look at them, and I often made you garlands with them. How shall I show the garden to the master now? And what will be his reaction when he sees it? There's an old man he'll string up on one of the pines, like Marsyas;[64] and perhaps he'll think that goats did this and string up Daphnis too!"

9 At this there were even hotter tears, and now they were not mourning for the flowers but for their own bodies. Chloe mourned too at the thought that Daphnis would be strung up, and prayed that their master might no longer come, and lived through days of utter misery, as though she was already seeing Daphnis being whipped. When night was already falling, Eudromus brought them the news that the older master would arrive in three days' time, but that his son was coming first and would be there the very next day. They discussed what had happened and brought Eudromus in to join their deliberations. He regarded Daphnis as his friend; and he advised them to admit what had happened to the young master first, promising to help them in this. He said he was respected by the young man because they had been nursed at the same breast.

10 When it was day, that was what they did. Astylus came on horseback, with a hanger-on of his, who was also on horseback. The young man had the first growth of beard on his chin, while Gnathon (the name of the hanger-on)[65] had been shaving for some time. Lamon, together with Myrtale and Daphnis, fell at Astylus's feet and begged him to take pity on an unfortunate old man and to snatch from his father's wrath someone who had done no wrong; at the same time he told him all the facts. Astylus was moved by their appeal. He went to the garden and saw the destruction of the flowers. He said he would appeal to his father himself and put the blame on the horses, saying that they had been tied up there and stampeded and when they got loose, had broken some things off,

64. Marsyas was a Phrygian satyr who was unwise enough to challenge Apollo to a music contest; after his defeat, Apollo had him tied to a tree and flayed alive. Tying to a tree (or "stringing up") is the usual preliminary to whipping (cf. 4.9) in Greek practice.

65. The name means "full mouth" in Greek. The hanger-on (*parasitos*) is a stock comic figure whom Longus introduces as an alien element in the pastoral world. The name Astylus suggests "urban" or "urbane"; cf. 4.11.

trampled others down, and dug others up. At this, Lamon and Myrtale prayed that he should have every happiness, while Daphnis brought him some presents—kids, cheeses, birds and their young chicks, bunches of grapes on shoots, and apples on branches. They also gave him some wine with a fine bouquet—and the wine of Lesbos is the best of all wines to drink.

Astylus complimented them on these things and turned his attention 11 to hunting hares, as you'd expect of a rich young man who spent all his time amusing himself and had come to the country to find a new type of pleasure. But all Gnathon knew how to do was to eat and to drink till he was drunk and to have sex when he was drunk. He was nothing but a mouth and a stomach and what lies underneath the stomach. He had paid close attention to Daphnis when he brought the gifts. He had homosexual inclinations, and now that he'd found beauty of a kind you don't get in the city, he decided to make advances, thinking it would be easy to win over Daphnis, who was a goatherd.[66] Having reached this decision, he didn't join Astylus on the hunt but went down to where Daphnis was grazing his herd. He pretended he had come to look at the goats, but actually he was looking at Daphnis. To soften him up, he complimented him on the goats, asked him to play a goatherd's tune on the pipes, and said he would quickly make him a free man, being a person of immense power.

When he saw Daphnis was amenable, he lay in wait for the boy at 12 night when he was driving the goats from the pasture. Gnathon ran up to Daphnis, kissed him first, and then tried to talk him into letting himself be used as he-goats use the she-goats. Daphnis slowly realized what he meant and said that it was all right for he-goats to mount she-goats, but that nobody had ever seen a he-goat mounting a he-goat or a ram mounting a ram instead of an ewe or cocks mounting cocks instead of hens.[67] Gnathon then got ready to take him by force and was putting his hands on him, but Daphnis pushed him away and threw him to the ground (the man was drunk and could hardly stand up). Daphnis scampered off like a puppy and left him lying on the ground, needing a man, not a boy, to give him a helping hand. After that Daphnis didn't let Gnathon come near him at all but grazed his goats in different places at different times, avoiding him and looking after Chloe. But Gnathon didn't meddle with him anymore, having found out that he was not only handsome but also strong. But he started looking for an opportunity to

66. For homosexuality as a theme in the Greek novel, cf. Xenophon of Ephesus 1.16, 3.2; Achilles Tatius 2.34ff.

67. Here, as elsewhere, Daphnis takes animals as his standard of conduct (cf. note 51). The argument from nature against homosexuality is one we find elsewhere in Greek writing; cf. Lucian Amores 22. For Gnathon's counterarguments, see 4.17.

talk to Astylus about him and formed the hope of getting him as a present from the young man, who was often willing to do great favors.

13 But he wasn't able to do this just then; for Dionysophanes was arriving with Cleariste,[68] and there was the noise and confusion of pack animals and servants, men and women. Later, however, he started putting together a long passionate speech. Dionysophanes was getting greyhaired now, but he was tall and handsome and a match for any young man. Few men were as rich as he, and none as good. On the first day he came, he sacrificed to the patron gods of the countryside, Demeter, Dionysus, Pan, and the Nymphs, and set up a mixing bowl for everyone there to share. On the following days, he inspected Lamon's work. He saw the plains ploughed, the vine shoots trimmed, and the garden looking beautiful (for, as far as the flowers went, Astylus had taken the blame). Dionysophanes was very pleased, praised Lamon, and promised to set him free. After that he went down to the goat pasture to look at the goats and their herdsman.

14 Chloe ran away to the wood, embarrassed and frightened at such a big crowd. But Daphnis stood there, with a shaggy goatskin wrapped round him, a newly sewn bag hanging from his shoulders, holding in one hand some freshly made cheeses, and with the other some unweaned kids. If Apollo ever did work as cowherd for Laomedon, he must have looked just as Daphnis looked then.[69] Daphnis himself said nothing but blushed deeply and looked down, holding out the presents, while Lamon said:

"Master, this is the herdsman of your goats. You gave me fifty she-goats to graze and two he-goats; he has made them into a hundred she-goats and ten he-goats for you. Do you see how sleek they are, with shaggy hair and unbroken horns? He has even made them lovers of music! At any rate, when they hear the pipes, they do everything required."

15 Cleariste, who was present at these remarks, wanted to test what he said and told Daphnis to pipe to the goats in his usual way, promising that if he did this, she would make him a present of a tunic, a cloak, and a pair of sandals. Daphnis made them all sit down like the audience in a theater, while he took his stand under the oak tree. Producing his pipes from his bag, he first of all gave a gentle blow on them: the goats stood

68. The name Dionysophanes means "Dionysus made manifest" and indicates his role as a kind of human *deus ex machina* who resolves the problems and obscurities in the plot (on the Dionysus theme, see note 26). Cleariste's name suggests "fairest fame." Like Alcinous's wife, Arete, in the *Odyssey* (6.305–15, 7.54ff.), she plays a significant role in deciding events (see 4.15); cf. note 61 on the garden as a link between Dionysophanes and Alcinous.

69. Apollo was said to have worked for a year as shepherd for Laomedon, king of Troy, as punishment for joining a revolt against Zeus; he is always represented as a handsome young man in Greek literature and art. This allusion, like that to Paris (cf. note 60), may hint at the fact that Daphnis's period as a shepherd is also a temporary one.

still and raised their heads. Then he blew the grazing tune: the goats low-ered their heads and started to graze. Then he struck up another tune, clear and sweet: they all lay down together. He piped a high-pitched tune: they ran away into the wood as if a wolf was coming. A little later, he sounded a rallying cry: they came out of the wood and ran together near his feet. You wouldn't see human slaves so obedient as this to the orders of their master.[70] They were all amazed, especially Cleariste, who swore that she would indeed give him the presents, since he was a fine musician as well as a fine goatherd. They went up to the farm and had lunch and sent Daphnis some of what they were eating. He shared it with Chloe and enjoyed having a taste of urban cuisine; he felt confident now of talking round his masters and of winning the marriage.

Gnathon, on the other hand, was still more inflamed by what had 16 happened at the goat pasture, and thought that life was not worth living if he didn't get Daphnis. He waited until he could catch Astylus walking around the garden, then brought him to the temple of Dionysus, and started kissing his hands and feet. Astylus asked him why he was doing that, told him to say what was on his mind, and swore that he would help him.

"Master," the other said, "this is the end of your poor Gnathon. The one who, until now, only loved your table, who swore that nothing had a finer bloom than a vintage wine, who said that your cooks were better than the young men of Mytilene—now the only thing that I find beauti-ful is Daphnis! I've lost my taste for expensive food—although there's such a lot being prepared every day, meat, fish, honey cakes—and I'd enjoy turning into a she-goat and eating grass and leaves as long as I was listening to the pipes of Daphnis and was led to pasture by him. Rescue your Gnathon and defeat unconquerable Love. If you don't, I swear by you, my own god, that I will take a dagger, and, filling my stomach with food, I shall kill myself in front of Daphnis's door; and then you'll no longer call me—as you used to, jokingly—'my sweet little Gnathon.' "

Astylus was a generous young man, who had some experience of the 17 pain of love himself, and he could not resist Gnathon when he cried and kissed his feet again. He promised to ask his father to give him Daphnis, and to take the young man to the city as a slave for himself and as a boyfriend for Gnathon. But wanting to induce in the man himself some misgivings, he asked, with a smile, if he wasn't ashamed at being in love with the son of Lamon and at being eager to lie with a young man who looked after goats; and as he said this, he made a gesture of disgust at the

70. The presentation of animals as intensely responsive to music is a feature of pastoral poetry and a recurrent motif in this novel. Daphnis's power approximates here to Pan's (2.28–29; cf. 1.29–30).

stink of the goats. But Gnathon had learned all about love talk in debauched drinking parties; and he did not fail to hit the mark, in his defense of himself and Daphnis.

"Master, nobody in love makes a fuss about things like that. Whatever the body he finds beauty in, he is still captured. That's why some people have fallen in love with a tree, a river, and a wild animal—though who could help feeling sorry for a lover who had to be frightened of the one he loved? I am in love with someone who has the body of a slave but the beauty of a free man. Don't you see how his hair is like a hyacinth, his eyes shine under his brows like a jewel in a golden setting, his face is very rosy, while his mouth is full of white teeth like ivory? What lover would not pray to take sweet kisses from someone like that? And if I've fallen in love with a herdsman, I've done what the gods have done. Anchises was a cowherd; and Aphrodite had him as her lover. Branchus used to graze goats; and Apollo loved him. Ganymede was a shepherd; and the king of the universe snatched him away. We shouldn't look down on a boy who, as we've seen, is obeyed even by his goats, as though they loved him. Instead we should be grateful to the eagles of Zeus for allowing such beauty to remain on earth."[71]

18    Astylus laughed sweetly, especially at this last remark, and said that Love made men into great orators; then he looked out for an opportunity to speak to his father about Daphnis. Eudromus had been secretly listening to this whole conversation. He liked Daphnis, regarding him as an honest young man; and he was annoyed at the thought of such a handsome man becoming the object of Gnathon's drunken lust. So he told everything to Daphnis and Lamon. Daphnis was horrified and resolved to risk an attempt at running away with Chloe or to take her as his companion in death. But Lamon called Myrtale outside the farm and said:

"Wife, we're finished. The time has come to reveal the secrets. You and I will spend our life deserted if I do; the goats will be deserted, and everything else too. But, by Pan and the Nymphs, even if I'm to be left like an ox in the stall (as they say),[72] I won't keep silent about Daphnis's origin. I shall tell how I found him exposed; I shall reveal how I found him being suckled; I shall show the objects left out with him. That revolting Gnathon must know the sort of person he's in love with. Just get the tokens ready for me."

19    Agreeing on this plan, they went inside again. When his father was unoccupied, Astylus sidled up to him. He asked to be allowed to take

71. Gnathon's first speech (4.16) is reminiscent of comedy. In his second speech he adopts a higher tone and ransacks Greek mythology to justify his lust. The lover of a "wild animal," for instance, is probably Pasiphae, who fell in love with a bull and produced the Minotaur; Ganymede, snatched off by Zeus's eagles, became the gods' beloved cupbearer.

72. "An old ox left in the stall" was a proverbial expression for something useless.

Daphnis back to the city; Daphnis, he said, was handsome, too good for the country, and he could quickly be taught the ways of the town by Gnathon. His father gave Daphnis to him with pleasure, and, sending for Lamon and Myrtale, he told them the good news that in future Daphnis would serve Astylus instead of she-goats and he-goats, and promised to give them two goatherds in his place. All the slaves were now crowding round and were pleased that they would have such a handsome fellow slave when Lamon asked permission to speak and started in this way.

"Master, hear the truth from an old man. I swear by Pan and the Nymphs that I shall tell no lies. I am not Daphnis's father, nor has Myrtale ever had the good fortune to be a mother. This child had different parents, who exposed him, perhaps because they had enough older children.[73] I found him exposed, being suckled by my she-goat; when the goat died, I buried it in the yard, loving it because it did the work of a mother. I also found some tokens left out with him—I admit this, master—and I have kept them till now. They are signs of his fortune in life, which is higher than ours. It isn't that I think it's beneath him to become the slave of Astylus, a fine servant for a fine gentleman. But I can't let him become the object of Gnathon's drunken lust—for Gnathon's keen to take him to Mytilene to do the job of a woman."

After saying this, Lamon stopped talking and cried a great deal, while Gnathon blustered and threatened to beat him. Dionysophanes was startled at this statement. He told Gnathon to keep quiet, shooting fierce glances at him, while he questioned Lamon again, telling him to tell the truth and not to make up fabulous tales in an attempt to keep his son with him. But Lamon stood firm and swore by all the gods and offered himself for torture to test if he was lying. So, asking Cleariste to sit on one side and leave him alone, Dionysophanes reviewed what Lamon had said. 20

"Why should Lamon be lying, when he stands to get two goatherds instead of one? In any case, how could a rustic have made this up? In fact, wasn't it incredible from the start that such a handsome son could have been produced by an old man of that sort and his shabby wife?"

The best thing seemed to be to stop guessing and to look at the tokens to see if they gave signs of a splendid origin and one that was more distinguished than Daphnis's present situation. Myrtale went away to bring all the things, which had been put in an old bag for safekeeping. When she had brought them, Dionysophanes saw them first, and once he had seen a purple cloak, a gold clasp, and a dagger with an ivory handle, he gave a great shout of "Oh, Lord Zeus!" and called his wife to come and look. She saw them and also gave a great cry. "Oh, the dear Fates! 21

73. This guess turns out to be true; cf. 4.24.

Aren't these the things we left out with our own child? Wasn't it to these very fields we sent Sophrone, when we told her to carry him off? Yes, these things are nothing other—they are the very things. Dear husband, the child is ours. Your son is Daphnis, and he has been grazing his father's goats."[74]

22    While she was saying this, and Dionysophanes was kissing the tokens and weeping from the intensity of his joy, Astylus realized that Daphnis was his brother, threw off his cloak, and ran down from the garden, wanting to be the first to kiss Daphnis. When Daphnis saw him running with a crowd of people and shouting "Daphnis," he thought that Astylus was running to catch him and take him off. He threw down his bag and his pipes and rushed to the sea to throw himself off the big rock. And perhaps—strangest of all fates—Daphnis would have been lost as soon as he'd been found[75] if Astylus hadn't realized what Daphnis was thinking and cried out again:

"Stop, Daphnis. Don't be afraid. I am your brother, and those who were your masters before are now your parents. Lamon has just told us about the she-goat and shown us the tokens. Turn round and see how they're coming—beaming with joy and laughing! But kiss me first. I swear by the Nymphs I'm not lying."

23    Finally, after this oath, Daphnis stopped and waited for Astylus as he ran towards him, and kissed him as he came up. While Daphnis was kissing him, the rest of the crowd came streaming up—menservants, maidservants, his father himself, and his mother at his side. They all started throwing their arms around him, kissing him, happy and weeping at once. But he embraced his father and mother before the others; he held them to his breast and was unwilling to leave their arms, as if he had known the truth for a long time. So quickly can nature win our trust! He even forgot about Chloe for a moment. Going to the farm, he put on expensive clothes, and, sitting beside his real father, he listened to him as he said this.

24    "My sons, I married when I was quite young, and, after a short time, I had become, as I thought, a very lucky father. First, a son was born to me, and then a daughter, and thirdly, Astylus. I thought I had a big enough family, and when this child here was born to me, on top of all the others, I exposed him, putting these objects out with him not as tokens of his identity but as funeral ornaments. But Fate had other plans.

74. The motif of recognition by signs or tokens is one of the oldest in Greek literature, treated in different ways in tragedy, New Comedy, and the novel (see Heliodorus, for example). Cf. also the following note.

75. Longus perhaps has in mind here the most famous of such unfortunate recognitions, that of Oedipus. See, for instance, Sophocles *Oedipus the King* 438, "This day will give birth to you and destroy you."

For my oldest son and my daughter died on a single day from the same illness, while you were rescued by divine providence so that we could have more hands to guide us in old age. Daphnis, don't hold it as a grudge against me that I exposed you; it was from no desire of mine that I formed this plan. And you, Astylus, don't be upset at receiving part of my property instead of the whole; to sensible men nothing is more valuable than a brother. Both of you, love each other; as far as wealth goes, you can compete even with kings. For I shall leave you both a great deal of land, a large number of useful servants, gold, silver, and all the other possessions that rich men have. This estate alone I am giving exclusively to Daphnis—and I also give him Lamon and Myrtale and the goats he grazed himself."

Even while he was still speaking, Daphnis jumped up. 25

"You were right to remind me, Father. I'm off to take the goats for a drink. They're probably thirsty now and waiting for the sound of my pipes while I'm sitting here." They all laughed pleasantly at him because although he'd become a master, he still remained a goatherd; and someone else was sent to look after the goats, while they sacrificed to Zeus the Preserver and started organizing a party. The only person who didn't come to this party was Gnathon, who was staying, terrified, in the temple of Dionysus, night and day, like someone seeking refuge. The news quickly got around to everyone that Dionysophanes had found a son, and that Daphnis the goatherd had been discovered to be the master of his fields. So, at dawn, people ran there, from all over the place, sharing in the young man's pleasure and bringing presents to his father. The first of them was Dryas, Chloe's foster father.

Dionysophanes kept them all there to share his happiness as well as his 26 banquet. A great deal of wine had been got ready, a great deal of wheatmeal bread, waterfowl, sucking pigs, and various kinds of honey cakes; and a great many animals were sacrificed to the gods of the locality. Then Daphnis collected all his pastoral possessions and gave them, as offerings, to different gods. To Dionysus he dedicated his bag and goatskin; to Pan his pipes and transverse flute; to the Nymphs his shepherd's staff together with the milk buckets he had made himself. Familiar things give us even greater pleasure than prosperity, when that is strange to us. And so Daphnis wept over each of these things as he parted with them. Nor did he offer up the buckets until he'd used them for milking, nor the goatskin until he'd wrapped it round himself, nor the pipes until he'd played on them; he also kissed all of them and spoke to the she-goats and called the he-goats by name. He also drank from the spring, because he had done this often with Chloe. But he did not admit his love yet, waiting for the right opportunity.

27 While Daphnis was busy with his offerings, this was what was happening to Chloe. She was sitting and weeping, grazing the sheep, and saying what you'd expect.

"Daphnis has forgotten me completely. He's dreaming about a rich marriage. Oh, why did I tell him to swear by the goats instead of the Nymphs? He's abandoned them as he's abandoned Chloe.[76] Even when he was sacrificing to the Nymphs and Pan, he didn't feel any desire to see Chloe. Perhaps he's found some of his mother's maids more attractive than me. Well, good-bye to him. But I shan't go on living."

28 While she was saying and thinking this sort of thing, Lampis the cowherd came up with a gang of farm workers and carried her off—thinking that Daphnis wouldn't want to marry her anymore and that Dryas would be happy to have him as her husband. She was taken away crying out piteously; someone who saw what had happened told Nape; she told Dryas; and Dryas told Daphnis. He went out of his mind; but he didn't dare to speak to his father; nor could he bear it either, and so he went to the yard and expressed his misery in these words.

"How horrible it is that I've been recognized! How much better it was for me to be a herdsman! How much happier I was when I was a slave! Then I looked at Chloe; then I listened to Chloe chattering. Now Lampis has carried her off and gone away with her; and when night comes, he'll sleep with her too! While I'm drinking and living in luxury—and my oath to Pan and the goats is worth nothing."

29 Gnathon, who was hiding in the garden, heard Daphnis saying this and thought his chance had come to get on good terms with him again. So he took some of Astylus's young men, chased after Dryas, and told him to lead them to Lampis's farm. He ran there eagerly and caught Lampis just as he was bringing Chloe in; he took Chloe away and gave the farmers a thorough beating. He was keen to tie Lampis up and lead him off like a prisoner of war—but Lampis ran away first. After his success in this great exploit, he came back as night was beginning.[77] He found Dionysophanes asleep, but Daphnis sleepless and still weeping in the yard. He brought Chloe to him, and as he gave her to him, he told him everything. He asked Daphnis not to bear a grudge against him anymore, but to treat him as a slave who was not without his uses, and not to banish him from his table—which would lead to his death from hunger. When Daphnis saw Chloe and held her in his arms, he was reconciled with Gnathon, seeing him as his benefactor, while he defended himself to Chloe for his neglect of her.

76. Cf. 2.39 and contrast the true situation (4.28).
77. Gnathon is portrayed here as the "braggart soldier" type common in ancient comedy.

They considered what to do and decided that Daphnis should conceal 30
their intention to marry and keep Chloe hidden, except for admitting his
love to his mother. Dryas did not agree; he thought Daphnis should tell
his father, and promised to talk him round himself. When it was day,
with the tokens of Chloe's identity in his bag, Dryas approached
Dionysophanes and Cleariste, who were sitting in the garden; Astylus
and Daphnis himself were there too. When they were all quiet, he began
to speak.

"Like Lamon, I'm compelled to say things that have been kept secret
till now. I am not the father of Chloe here, nor was she suckled in my
house. She is the child of different parents; and she was suckled by an
ewe, while she lay in a cave sacred to the Nymphs. I saw this myself and
was amazed to see it; and because of my amazement, I gave her a home.
Her beauty bears witness to the truth of this (for she is quite unlike us),
and so do the tokens (which are more valuable than any shepherd could
own). Look at them and make a search for the girl's relations—in case
she may turn out to be a match for Daphnis."

Dryas did not throw this last comment out without an end in view, 31
nor did Dionysophanes fail to take the point. Looking at Daphnis and
seeing him turning pale and surreptitiously weeping, he quickly detected
that he was in love. And so—more anxious now about his own son than
about someone else's daughter—he examined Dryas's statements with
great exactness. When he saw the tokens that Dryas had brought, the
golden sandals, the anklets, the belt, he called Chloe to him and encouraged her to cheer up, saying that she already had a husband and would
quickly find her father and mother. Cleariste took charge of her and
dressed her up for the part of her son's future wife, while Dionysophanes
asked Daphnis to come aside on his own and asked him if Chloe was a
virgin. Daphnis swore that nothing more had taken place between them
than kissing and vows; so Dionysophanes was pleased and made them sit
down at the banquet.

Then you could learn what beauty is like, when it is properly pre- 32
sented. For when Chloe was dressed and had put her hair up and washed
her face, she seemed so much more beautiful to everyone that even
Daphnis scarcely recognized her. Even without the tokens anyone would
have sworn that Dryas was not the father of a girl like that. Yet Dryas
was there too, feasting with Nape and having Lamon and Myrtale as
drinking companions on their own couch. Again, on successive days,
victims were sacrificed and mixing bowls were put on the table. Chloe
too dedicated her own things—the pipes, bag, goatskin, milk buckets.
She also mixed wine with the water of the spring in the cave, because she
had been brought up beside it and had often bathed in it. She also put

garlands on the grave of the ewe, when Dryas showed it to her. Like
Daphnis, she played on the pipes to her flock, and after she had played,
she prayed that she would find that the parents who had exposed her
were good enough for her to marry Daphnis.

33     When they had had enough of country festivals, they decided to go to
the city and look for Chloe's parents and not to hold up their wedding
any longer. At daybreak they got themselves ready. They gave Dryas
another three thousand drachmas, and they gave to Lamon a half share in
the harvest and fruit picking on the estate, as well as the goats (together
with the goatherds), four pairs of oxen, and winter clothes; they also
gave freedom to him and his wife. Then they drove to Mytilene on
horseback or in carriages, in great luxury.

They arrived back at night and so were not observed by the citizens.
But the next day a crowd of men and women formed around their door.
The men shared Dionysophanes' pleasure at finding his son—and did so
all the more when they saw how handsome Daphnis was. The women
shared Cleariste's joy at gaining at once a son and a bride for her son.
Chloe astonished them too by her incomparable beauty. The whole city
was excited about the boy and girl. Already they congratulated them on
their marriage and prayed that the girl's family would be found to be
worthy of her beauty. And many wives of very rich husbands prayed to
the gods that it should be believed that they were the mother of such a
beautiful daughter.

34     Dionysophanes, after a great deal of thought, fell into a deep sleep and
had this dream. It seemed to him that the Nymphs were begging Love to
give his consent at last to their marriage and that Love unstrung his little
bow and took off his quiver.[78] Love then told Dionysophanes to ask all
the best of the Mytileneans to come to a party, and when he had filled
the last mixing bowl, to show each person the tokens of Chloe's identity—and then sing the wedding song. After seeing and hearing this,
Dionysophanes got up at daybreak and gave orders for the preparation of
a glittering feast—drawing on the resources of the land and the sea, the
marshes and the rivers—and invited as his guests all the best of the
Mytileneans. When it was already night and the mixing bowl had been
filled to make the libation to Hermes,[79] a servant brought in the tokens
on a silver tray and carried them round from left to right, showing them
to everyone.

78. Eros appeared in a dream to Lamon and Dryas to initiate the romance of Daphnis
and Chloe (1.7). Now that the romance is to culminate in marriage, Eros lays down the
weapons he uses to provoke passion.

79. The last libation of the night at a party was regularly made to Hermes, who con-
ducts men to sleep.

Nobody else recognized them, but someone called Megacles, seated in  35
the place of honor because of his age, and so the last to see them,[80] recognized the tokens and gave a very loud and lusty shout.

"What is this I see? What has happened to you, my daughter? Are you
still alive—or has some shepherd found these things, without the child,
and picked them up? I beg you, Dionysophanes, tell me. Where did you
get the tokens of my child? Don't begrudge my finding something, after
you've found Daphnis."

Dionysophanes told him to speak first about his exposure of the child;
and Megacles said this, without lowering his voice.

"At one time in the past, I had very little money to live on; for what I
did have, I spent on public services, paying for dramatic choruses and
warships.[81] At that time, a little daughter was born to me. Shrinking
from bringing this child up in poverty, I fitted her up with these tokens
and exposed her, knowing that many people are eager to become parents
even by this means. So the child was exposed in the cave of the Nymphs,
placed in the trust of the goddesses; meanwhile I became more affluent
every day—now that I had no heir—for I haven't had the good luck to
have any more children, even a daughter. In fact, the gods seem to make
fun of me, sending me dreams at night that show a sheep making me a
father!"

Dionysophanes gave a shout that was even louder than Megacles had  36
produced. Jumping up, he brought in Chloe, who was very beautifully
dressed, and said:

"This is the child you exposed. This girl of yours was suckled by an
ewe, thanks to divine providence, just as my Daphnis was suckled by a
she-goat. Take the tokens and your daughter too; and after taking her,
give her back as a bride for Daphnis. We've exposed them both; we've
found them both; they've both been cared for by Pan, the Nymphs, and
Love."

Megacles agreed wholeheartedly with what he said. He sent for his
wife, Rhode, and held Chloe to his breast. They stayed and slept there,
for Daphnis swore that he wouldn't give up Chloe to anyone—not even
her father.

When it was day, they all decided to drive back to the country. Daph-  37
nis and Chloe had begged for this, not being able to bear life in town;
and their parents too thought it right to give their wedding a pastoral
character. They went to Lamon's house and introduced Dryas to Megacles and presented Nape to Rhode, and made splendid preparations for

80. Megacles was seated on the right hand of the host in the place of honor. His name
suggests "great fame"; cf. *Cle*ariste (see note 68).
81. This was a kind of tax imposed on rich men at Athens and elsewhere.

the feast. Chloe's father gave her away in the presence of the Nymphs, and he presented the tokens as offerings, along with many other things; and he gave Dryas what he needed to make up a total of ten thousand drachmas.

38    The weather was fine, and so Dionysophanes spread out beds of green leaves, right there, in front of the cave, and invited all the villagers to sit down and feasted them lavishly. Lamon and Myrtale were there, and so were Dryas and Nape, the relatives of Dorcon, Philetas and his children, Chromis and Lycaenion; even Lampis was there, for they had forgiven him. As you would expect of such guests, everything was agricultural and rustic. One man sang the sort of songs reapers sing; another made the sort of jokes that are made at the winepress; Philetas played the pipes; Lampis played the flute; Dryas and Lamon danced; Chloe and Daphnis kissed each other. The goats grazed nearby as if they too were joining in the feast. This was not entirely pleasing to the guests from town. But Daphnis called some of the goats by name and gave them green leaves and took them by the horns and kissed them.

39    Not only then but for as long as they lived, Daphnis and Chloe spent most of their time living the pastoral life. They worshiped as their gods the Nymphs, Pan, and Love, owned numerous flocks of sheep and goats, and thought that fruit and milk were the sweetest kind of food. When they had a baby boy, they put him under a she-goat for nursing, and when their second child was born to them, a little girl, they had her suck the teat of an ewe. They called the boy Philopoemen, and the girl Agele.[82] They also decorated the cave and set up images in it and established an altar to Love the Shepherd, and gave Pan a temple to live in instead of the pine, calling him Pan the Soldier.[83]

40    But it was later that they gave these names and did these things. At that time, when night came, everyone conducted them into the bedchamber, some playing the pipes, some playing the flute, others holding up great torches. And when they were near the door, they sang with harsh, rough voices, as though they were breaking up the earth with forks, not singing a wedding hymn. Daphnis and Chloe lay down naked together, embraced and kissed, and had even less sleep that night than the owls. Daphnis did some of the things Lycaenion taught him; and then, for the first time, Chloe found out that what they had done in the woods had been nothing but shepherds' games.

82. Philopoemen suggests "friend of shepherds" (or "friendly shepherd"); Agele means "herd."

83. These cult names (which have parallels elsewhere in cult or myth) have special appropriateness to this story; cf. 2.5, 2.7, 3.12, and (with reference to Pan) note 36.

# HELIODORUS

# AN ETHIOPIAN STORY

## TRANSLATED BY
## J. R. MORGAN

## Introduction

To a reader about to embark on the *Aithiopika*[1] the most obvious fact
about it is its length. This is a work on an altogether grander scale than
any other extant Greek novel, a work whose structure and execution express an ambition to be considered at the highest level.

The narrative opens with a band of Egyptian bandits peering over a
hilltop in the Nile Delta. Through their eyes and with their bewilderment we see a macabre and memorable tableau: a deserted ship, the remains of a banquet, a host of dead bodies. What has happened? What
does it mean? You must read the story yourself to find the answers, but
in one sense it means this: the author has thought hard about the weaknesses of the traditional romance plot, which consists, in essence, of a
falling in love, a loss of felicity, and its eventual recovery after a series of
ordeals. There are two unsatisfactory features about this. The adventures
that interrupt felicity give the author his greatest opportunity to excite
and entertain his reader, but they can easily degenerate into an infinitely
extendable concatenation of organically unconnected and randomly arranged episodes. Secondly, at the end of all their adventures hero and
heroine find themselves back where they started; ultimately nothing has
changed. Heliodoros has tackled these weaknesses by starting his narration in the middle of the story, with the result that the reader is not just

---

1. The work is known variously as the *Aithiopika* (*Ethiopica*) (*Ethiopian Story*), as *The
Story of Theagenes and Charikleia*, and as *Charikleia*.

349

passively bombarded with a series of sensational happenings but is drawn into a hermeneutic quest to account for what he already knows. Part of the riddle concerns the heroine's identity, and the solution to that question gives the plot a new sense of ending. For this couple there is a goal, and life *will* be different at the end of the journey. The plot has acquired unity, direction, complexity.

The opening paragraph alerts us also to another feature of this novel. The narrator knows what the scene on the beach means, but he is not telling. The reader is compelled to share the ignorance of the bandits; their eyes are our eyes. So throughout the novel the narrator stays very much in the background. The truth emerges dramatically from the characters, and their learning is our learning. This quality in its turn entails another of the *Aithiopika*'s greatest delights: its sheer convolution and intricacy. As connections emerge, seemingly of their own accord, over long spans of text, as plot and subplot slowly mesh together, as subsidiary narrators successively play with the partial knowledge of their audience, we are invited to admire the virtuoso skill of the self-concealing author who has engineered the whole complex mechanism.

The same opening paragraph raises yet another point. For all its theatricality the tableau is set precisely in a real place: at the Heracleotic mouth of the Nile, whose reality is secured by being viewed from a perspective outside the narrative frame ("that *men call* the Heracleotic"). Heliodoros has gone to great pains to anchor his story to reality, or at least to Greco-Roman perceptions of reality. Real places are brought to life by authentic details. Even racial characteristics conform to reality as the author aligns himself with traditions of crafty Egyptians, degenerate Persians, pious Ethiopians, and noble Greeks. In a subtler way that opening paragraph also gives us a temporal setting: the scene is close to the site of Alexandria, but there is no mention of the city in the text. We are in a period before its foundation, and this hint is confirmed by later indications of a date in the late sixth or early fifth century B.C. The dramatic date remains imprecise, and it has to be said that there are anachronisms (some of which are indicated in the notes), but the impression at least is conveyed that the story took place in real time and in real places. Verisimilitude is enhanced by certain narratorial mannerisms, such as admitting limitations of knowledge or inability to determine causes or motives. For all the self-conscious artistry, we are being asked to assume that the story is in some sense "true."

The *Aithiopika* is also a very religious, or rather religiose, text. References to supernatural agencies of various kinds abound: gods, the god, the powers above, the divine, spirits, chance, fate, destiny, and so on. And at the end we are left with the satisfying feeling that everything has been accomplished under the guidance of Providence. But in a work of fiction Providence is only Plot in disguise. I cannot find any consistency in the attribution of events to nonhuman agencies and am inclined to think the whole divine apparatus a literary device to give the plot a sense of direction, purpose, and eventual closure, rather than a statement of belief intended to instruct its readers in the ways of god. It is striking that virtually the whole plot is motivated sufficiently at a human level. Thus, although the opening tableau is initially ascribed to the stage management of the deity, we are eventually given an entirely rational account of it. I have not, therefore, been overscrupulous about maintaining a one-to-one equivalence of Greek and English vocabulary in naming the divine: rhetoric matters more than precision.

In particular, it has often been suggested that the *Aithiopika* was written in praise of the sun-god of Heliodoros's hometown, Emesa in Syria—a particularly tempting idea in view of the author's statement in his colophon that he was a descendant of the sun. But this is an identification, not a credo, and it is very hard either to find a role for the sun-god in the economy of the plot or to trace any connection between the theology and rather strict morality of the narrative and those of the cult of the sun, whether in its orgiastic form as introduced to Rome by the Syrian emperor Elagabalus (reigned A.D. 218–22) or in its more universalized and sanitized form as instituted by Aurelian in A.D. 274.

The *Aithiopika* is as ambitious in its texture and diction as in its construction. It is, firstly, a very literary piece of writing, permeated by allusions to earlier literature, especially the Homeric epics and Euripidean tragedy. Some of these allusions I have indicated in the notes, but often they consist of a characteristic word or turn of phrase whose distinctiveness cannot be translated. The author's penchant for the theater makes itself felt also in comparisons to dramatic techniques and equipment. This is a double ploy: an admission of the work's theatricality, and simultaneously a claim to a realism outside theatrical convention, like a character in a film saying, "If this were a movie, I wouldn't believe it."

Heliodoros wrote wonderful Greek. To try to translate it is a humbling experience. Much of its effect is lost in a noninflected language like English, which lack Greek's ability to hold together a periodic structure with case forms and combine them into an intricate pattern of balance and rhyme. The style is florid and artificial, but exuberant and alive, employed with a zest and love of words and the games that can be played with them. The vocabulary is wide and highly nuanced. I discovered at an early stage that to translate Heliodoros literally is not to translate him at all. Sometimes one has to overtranslate simply to convey everything that is there in the Greek. Some attempt has to be made to reproduce the jingles, puns, and wordplays, even at the cost of insignificant inaccuracy of detail. So, for instance, at 3.10, I have used a pun on the word *spirit(s)* that anachronistically attributes the drinking of distilled liquor to the Greeks, but better that than to lose the punning banter so essential to the passage. Nevertheless, I am only too aware that this translation is a pastel version of the stained-glass colors of the original. I only hope that the reader can follow what is going on and can get an occasional sense, as through a glass, darkly, of the music and rhetoric of the set pieces and the flashes of sardonic wit in the narrative.

Although Heliodoros emerges as a very distinct personality, paradoxically given his recessive stance, we know next to nothing about him. A report by the ecclesiastical historian Sokrates says that he was a Christian bishop at Trikka in Thessaly who enforced celibacy on his clergy; Byzantine historians elaborate the story by telling how he was forced to choose between disowning the novel of his youth and resigning his see: romantically, he chose the latter. It is difficult to know how much truth there is in any of this, though attempts to find traces of Christianity in the novel are certainly misguided. We do not even know when it was written. My own inclination is to date it to the fourth century on the strength of similarities between the siege of Syene in the ninth book and the siege of Nisibis by the Parthians in A.D. 350, but others would like to put it a hundred years earlier. The *Aithiopika* was a favorite work at Byzantium, made respectable reading by a belief in its author's Christianity, and exerted considerable influence on writers as different as Sidney, Cervantes, and Racine. Although he was once ranked alongside Homer and Virgil, Heliodoros has seemed too artificial, too precious for the taste of more recent centuries. I hope that this translation may persuade modern readers that his novel is more than a historical curiosity.

I have used the Budé text; substantial departures from it are indicated.[2] For the lengthier quotations from Homer I have used the now standard translations of Richmond Lattimore. Heliodoros is an erudite writer; for fuller annotation than was possible in the present volume the reader is referred to the Budé edition, to which I acknowledge my indebtedness. Omissions are indicated by ...

## Bibliography

TEXT

Héliodore. *Les Ethiopiques* (*Théagène et Chariclée*). Edited by R. M. Rattenbury and T. W. Lumb. 3 vols. Paris, 1935–43 (Budé).

Heliodorus. *Aethiopica*. Edited by A. Colonna. Rome, 1938.

---

2. For Books 9 and 10 those who are interested in the text may refer to my discussion in "Noctes Aethiopicae," *Philologus* 127(1983): 87–111.

GENERAL

Morgan, J. R. "History, Romance and Realism in the Aithiopika of Heliodoros." *Classical Antiquity* 1(1981): 221–65.

Sandy, G. N. *Heliodorus*. New York, 1982.

Winkler, J. J. "The Mendacity of Kalasiris and the Narrative Strategy of Heliodoros' *Aithiopika*," *Yale Classical Studies* 27(1982): 93–158.

# AN ETHIOPIAN STORY

## *Book One*

T HE SMILE OF DAYBREAK was just beginning to brighten the sky, the sunlight to catch the hilltops, when a group of men in brigand gear peered over the mountain that overlooks the place where the Nile flows into the sea at the mouth that men call the Heracleotic.[1] They stood there for a moment, scanning the expanse of sea beneath them; first they gazed out over the ocean, but as there was nothing sailing there that held out hope of spoil and plunder, their eyes were drawn to the beach nearby. This is what they saw: a merchant ship was riding there, moored by her stern, empty of crew but laden with freight. This much could be surmised even from a distance, for the weight of her cargo forced the water up to the third line of boards on the ship's side. But the beach!—a mass of newly slain bodies, some of them quite dead, others half alive and still twitching, testimony that the fighting had only just ended. To judge by the signs this had been no proper battle. Amongst the carnage were the miserable remnants of festivities that had come to this unhappy end. There were tables still set with food, and others upset on the ground, held in dead men's hands; in the fray they had served some as weapons, for this had been an impromptu conflict; beneath other tables men had crawled in the vain hope of hiding there. There were wine bowls upturned, and some slipping from the hands that held them; some had been drinking from them, others using them like stones, for the suddenness of the catastrophe had caused objects to be put to strange, new uses and taught men to use drinking vessels as missiles. There they lay, here a man felled by an axe, there another struck down by a stone picked up then and there from the shingly beach; here a man battered to death with a club, there another burned to death with a brand from the fire. Various

1                                                                                            

---

1. The westernmost of the seven principal mouths of the Nile.

were the forms of their deaths, but most were the victims of arrows and archery. In that small space the deity had contrived an infinitely varied spectacle, defiling wine with blood and unleashing war at the party, combining wining and dying, pouring of drink and spilling of blood, and staging this tragic show for the Egyptian bandits.

They stood on the mountainside like the audience in a theater, unable to comprehend the scene: the vanquished were there, but the victors were nowhere to be seen; the victory was unequivocal, but the spoils had not been taken, and the ship lay there by herself, crewless but otherwise intact, riding peacefully at anchor as if protected by a great force of men. But although they were at a loss to know what it all meant, they still had an eye for plunder and a quick profit. So they cast themselves in the role of victors and set off down the hillside.

2     They had reached a point a short distance from the ship and the bodies when they found themselves confronted by a sight even more inexplicable than what they had seen before. On a rock sat a girl, a creature of such indescribable beauty that one might have taken her for a goddess. Despite her great distress at her plight, she had an air of courage and nobility. On her head she wore a crown of laurel; from her shoulders hung a quiver; her left arm leant on the bow, the hand hanging relaxed at the wrist. She rested the elbow of her other arm on her right thigh, cradling her cheek in her fingers. Her head was bowed, and she gazed steadily at a young man lying at her feet. He was terribly wounded and seemed to be barely conscious, coming round from the verge of death as if from a deep sleep. Even so he had a radiant, manly beauty, and his cheek appeared more gleaming white because of the red streak of blood running down it. His pain made his eyes heavy, but the sight of the girl drew them upwards to her. What forced them to see was that it was her they saw. He gathered his breath and sighed deeply.

"My darling," he whispered, "are you really alive, or were you another victim of the fighting and now cannot bear to be separated from me, even after death? Does even your ghost, your soul, still care what befalls me?"

"It depends on you," replied the girl, "whether I live or die. Do you see this?" She indicated a sword that lay on her knees. "Till now it has been idle, stayed so long as you draw breath."

As she spoke, she leapt up from the rock. Thunderstruck with wonder and terror at the sight, the bandits on the hillside scattered and dived for cover in the undergrowth. When she stood up, she seemed to them larger and more godlike, her weapons rattling at the sudden movement,[2] the gold thread in her robe flashing in the sun, her hair tossing under her

2. An allusion to the description of Apollo descending from Olympos near the beginning of the *Iliad* (1.46–47).

crown like a bacchante's and cascading over her back. They were terrified; but their incomprehension of the scene caused them greater terror than the mere sight of it. Some said she must be a god—the goddess Artemis, or the Isis they worship in those parts;[3] others said she was a priestess possessed by one of the gods and that she was responsible for the carnage before them. That is what they thought, but they did not yet know the truth.

Suddenly, the girl threw ' rself down onto the young man and embraced him bodily, weeping, kissing him, wiping his face, sobbing, unable to believe that she held him in her arms. When they saw this, the Egyptians began to have second thoughts. "How could a god behave like that?" they said. "How could a divine being kiss a corpse with such passion?" They urged one another to be brave and to go closer and find out the truth. So they pulled themselves together and ran down the hill. When they reached her, the girl was still intent on the young man's wounds. They stood stock-still behind her, too scared to speak or act. Their movements produced a loud noise, and the shadows they cast fell across the girl's eyes; she looked up, saw them, and looked down again, quite unperturbed by the strange color and robberlike appearance of these armed men, quite single-minded in tending the wounded man. So it is that genuine affection and wholehearted love disregard all external pains and pleasures and compel the mind to concentrate thought and vision on one object: the beloved.

The bandits moved round and stood in front of her. They seemed to be on the point of taking some action when the maiden looked up again and saw their dark skins and unkempt faces.

"If you are the ghosts of those who here lie dead,"[4] she said, "you are wrong to trouble us. Most of you died at one another's hands. Those that we slew we slew in self-defense and in retribution for your outrage against chastity. But if you are living men, you lead the life of brigands, it seems. Your appearance is timely. Set us free from the woes that beset us! Kill us and so bring our story to a close!"

But of this tragic outburst they could understand not a word. So they left them there under the strong guard of their own weakness and ran to the ship and began to unload its cargo. There was great quantity and great variety, but they passed over everything except gold, silver, precious stones, and silk, each man taking off as much as he could carry. When they had as much as they wanted—and there was enough to satisfy

3. The bow and quiver suggest Artemis, goddess of hunting and, significantly, chastity; the girl's pose recalls the Egyptian goddess Isis tending the dead body of her husband, Osiris. These associations of divine purity and love would be implicit for an ancient reader in the iconography of the description of the heroine at this her first appearance in the novel.
4. In Greek popular belief at least some types of ghost had black faces.

even a bandit's greed—they laid out their booty on the beach and began to divide it into separate bundles, making their division not according to the value of each item but so that each share was of equal weight. They were going to deal with the young man and woman later.

At that moment a second band of brigands came on the scene, led by two men on horseback. When they caught sight of them, the first band put up no resistance but ran off as fast as they could, empty-handed to avoid pursuit. There were ten of them, and they could see that the newcomers were three times that number. So the young couple was taken prisoner for a second time without yet having been taken prisoner once. Despite their haste to be at the plunder, the brigands stopped for a moment, puzzled and disturbed by the sight that confronted them. They guessed that all the carnage was the work of the first bandits, but when they saw the girl in her strange and splendid attire, disregarding the horrors that beset her as if they did not even exist, totally occupied in treating the young man's wounds and feeling his pain as if it were her own, they were taken aback by her beauty and courage. They wondered too at the wounded man, so tall and handsome he lay there, for he had already recovered a little of his strength, and his face had taken on its usual expression once more.

4      After a while the bandit chief walked up to the girl. He grabbed her and told her to get up and come with him. She could not understand a word he said, but guessed what it was that he was commanding her to do. As she rose to her feet, she also drew up the young man, who clung tightly to her, and, pointing to the sword at her breast, she threatened to kill herself unless the brigands took them both. The chief understood what she meant, partly from her words, but mainly from her gestures. He also hoped to have in the young man, if he lived, a valuable addition to his band. So, dismounting from his horse and making his henchman do the same, he set the prisoners on horseback, and, with a word of command to the others to follow on when they had finished loading the spoils, he set off running on foot beside the horses, supporting his captives whenever either of them was unsteady. There was something remarkable in the sight: the master appeared as a servant; the captor chose to minister to his captives. Thus may nobility of appearance and beauty of countenance vanquish even a brigand heart and triumph over the harshest of natures.

5      They rode along the beach for some four hundred yards, then left the track and headed straight up the mountainside with the sea on their right. After a stiff climb they passed over the crest of the hill and pressed on down towards a lake that lay outspread below them on the other side of the mountain. Its nature was as follows: the Egyptians call the whole area

the Land of Herds;[5] there is a natural bowl into which the floodwater from the Nile pours; thus a lake has formed, immeasurably deep at the center but shallowing off at the edges into a marsh, for as beaches are to seas, so marshes are to lakes. This is the home of the entire bandit community of Egypt, some of them building huts on what little land there is above water, others living on boats that serve them as both transport and dwelling. On these boats their womenfolk work at their weaving; on these boats their children are born. Any child born there is fed at first on its mother's milk, later on fish from the lake dried in the sun. If they see a child trying to crawl, they tie a cord to its ankles just long enough to allow it to reach the edge of the boat or the door of the hut. A strange way to keep children in hand, to tie them by the feet![6]

Many a Herdsman has been born here and reared as I have described, and has come to look upon the lake as his homeland. It affords a secure stronghold for bandits, and so that class of person flocks there. The water encircles the entire settlement like a wall, and instead of a palisade they are protected by the vast quantities of reeds growing in the marsh. By cutting devious and intricately winding paths through the reeds, and so constructing passages that are easy enough for themselves, as they know the way through, but quite impossible for anyone else, they have contrived for themselves an impregnable fastness to safeguard them against any attack.[7] Such, more or less, are the lake and the Herdsmen who live on it.

It was just about sunset when the chief and his men reached the lake. They pulled their young captives down from their horses and began to unload their booty into their boats. Most of the bandits had stayed at home and now began to appear from various parts of the marsh; they ran to welcome their chief, greeting him almost as if he were their king. When they saw the huge quantities of booty and looked upon the girl, whose beauty seemed to exceed that of humankind, they thought that their comrades must have looted a holy place, a temple full of gold; had they carried off the priestess too, they wondered, or was this girl the statue of the goddess, a living statue? Poor fools!

Extolling their chief's excellence at great length, they escorted him to

---

5. In Greek, *Boukolia*. The marshes of the Nile Delta provided a refuge for brigands and outlaws at all periods. The *Boukoloi*, "Herdsmen," whose life Heliodoros here describes, are attested in several classical sources, rising to particular prominence as a result of their uprising against Roman rule in A.D. 172. There is thus a kernel of fact here, but the Nile Delta bandits are generally part of the romantic furniture of novel plots, and there is no way of telling how authentic Heliodoros's detail is.

6. This and several other details of life on the lake are borrowed from Herodotos's account (5.16) of the lake-dwelling Paionians.

7. Here a long phrase is taken from Demosthenes 21.138 (*Against Meidias*).

his dwelling, which was a small, secluded island, set aside as a residence for him and his few closest followers. On reaching it he sent most of his men home, bidding them all to come to him the next day. Only his few usual companions remained with him. He entertained the company to a hasty meal, of which he too partook; his young prisoners he placed in the care of a young Greek who had been captured not long before, so that they might have someone to talk to. He assigned them a hut not far from his own and gave instructions that care should be taken of the young man, and particularly that no one should be allowed to treat the girl with disrespect. He himself was so fatigued after his journey, so beset by pressing cares, that he had already fallen asleep.

8    Silence enveloped the marsh. It was the time of the first watch. For the girl and her companion the absence of people to interrupt them presented a good opportunity for voicing their sorrows. In my opinion, the very darkness aggravated their misery, for there was no sight or sound to distract them, and they could devote themselves solely to their grief. So the girl, with many a solitary sigh (she lay apart from the others, as had been commanded, on a pallet bed), and amid a flood of tears, cried: "Apollo, you punish us too much and too harshly for our sins! Do you think we have not already suffered punishment enough—separation from our families, capture by pirates, a thousand dangers at sea, now a second capture by bandits on land, and a future even bitterer than the past? What end will you bring to our torments? If it is an inviolate death, then my end will be sweet. But if someone is to have his way with me—as not even Theagenes has—then I shall forestall the outrage by hanging myself, preserving myself as pure as I now preserve myself, even unto death. My chastity will make me a fine shroud! Yours is the cruelest court in which I shall ever stand trial!"

Theagenes interrupted her. "Enough, my darling, my soul, Charikleia. Your lamentations may be justified, but you provoke the godhead more than you think. You should plead, not reproach; the powers above are made propitious by prayers, not by accusations."

"You are right," she said. "How are you now?"

"Better," he replied, "now the evening has come. And the treatment the young lad gave me has soothed and comforted the agony of my wounds."

"You will be more comfortable yet, come the morning," said the man who had been given the task of looking after them. "I shall bring you an herb that will heal your wounds in three days. I know; I have used it before. Ever since I was brought here as a prisoner, any of those serving this leader who have returned wounded from a skirmish have not taken many days to recover if they use this herb I mentioned. You should not be surprised if I am concerned about you, for you seem to share the same fate as I do. I feel sympathy for you because you are Greek, and I am a Greek myself."

"A Greek! Heaven be praised!" exclaimed the strangers in joyful unison. "Truly a Greek in birth and speech! Perhaps now there will be some respite from our suffering."

"What name should we call you by?" asked Theagenes.

"Knemon," he replied.

"And where are you from?"

"Athens."

"And what is your story?"

"Stop," he said. "Why do you batter and prize open these doors, to borrow a phrase from the tragedians?[8] This is no time to introduce a new theme into your own tragedy in the form of my misfortunes. Besides, what is left of the night would not be time enough for the telling, especially as you need sleep and rest after all that you have been through."

But they pressed their request and by all means besought him to tell his tale, thinking that the story of woes like their own would be a great consolation. So Knemon began.

"My father was Aristippos, an Athenian by birth, a member of the Upper Council,[9] fairly well-to-do. After the death of my mother, he was disposed to marry a second time, thinking it ill to anchor all his hopes on me, his only child. So he took to wife a woman, pretty enough, but the cause of much evil for his house. Her name was Demainete. From the moment she entered the house, she had my father in her power, obedient to her every whim. She exploited her charms to win the old man's affections and lavished attentions on him. If ever a woman knew how to drive a man mad with passion, she did, so extraordinarily well versed was she in the arts of allurement. When my father went out, she sighed, and when he came in, she ran to meet him; when he was late home, she complained and said she would have died if he had been a second later; and with every word she kissed him, and with every kiss she wept. By all this my father was ensnared: he lived for her, had eyes for her alone.

"At first she pretended to look on me as a son, though this was only another trick to win her way to Aristippos's heart. Sometimes she would come up to me and kiss me, and she was forever requesting the pleasure of my company. I did not object, for I had no inkling of the truth. I was simply surprised that she showed a mother's affection towards me. But

8. To be precise, from Euripides' *Medeia* (1317). There is a concealed anachronism here, since the novel is actually set at a date rather earlier than the lifetime of Euripides.

9. The Council of the Areiopagos, named after the Hill of Ares in Athens, where it sat. It was composed of all former holders of the office of *archon*, the highest office of state at Athens, and, until the democratic reforms of the fifth century B.C., formed a center of aristocratic and conservative influence in the Athenian state. Its prestige survived its loss of power. Aristippos is thus a man of some standing, socially and politically.

when her advances became bolder, her kisses grew warmer than they
ought to have been, and the far from chaste look in her eyes aroused my
suspicions, then I avoided her for the most part, and when she came near
me I kept her at arm's length. Why should I bore you with all the details
of what ensued? Her repeated attempts at seduction, her repeated promises? Sometimes she would call me her child, at others her darling. She
would address me as her son and heir, and then, a minute later, as her
beloved. In short, she intertwined decent names with seductive ones and
observed carefully which I responded to best. With the more respectable
names she was masquerading as a mother, but with those unnatural en-
dearments she revealed all too plainly that she was aflame with desire.

10      "In the end this is what happened. It was during the festival of the
Great Panathenaia,[10] when the people of Athens escort a ship overland to
Athene. I had just come of age,[11] and, after singing the traditional hymn
to the goddess and taking part in the ritual procession, I went home still
dressed in my short mantle and garlands. The moment she saw me, she
was beside herself. She no longer made any attempt to disguise her passion; her desire was quite blatant. She ran to me, threw her arms around
me, and cried, 'My young Hippolytos!'[12]

"You can imagine my reaction if even now I blush in the telling. That
evening my father was dining out in the Council Hall and was going to
be away all night, as is the way with such ceremonies and public merrymaking. She came to me in the night, seeking satisfaction for her unnatural desires. But I was not to be seduced, and rebuffed all her attentions,
promises, and threats, until at last she left, with a deep sigh. She waited
only for morning before she started her devilish web of intrigue against
me.

"Her first step was not to leave her bed that morning. When my father came home and asked her what was wrong, she pretended to be unwell and at first would not answer his question. However, he persisted
and asked her again and again what had happened until she replied: 'That
paragon of piety, that son of ours, yours and mine, to whom—as the

10. The festival of the Panathenaia was celebrated every summer to mark the birthday
of the goddess Athene. Every fourth year it was observed with much more pomp and ceremony: this was the Great Panathenaia. The center point of the festival was a procession to
convey to the cult statue of Athene on the Akropolis a specially embroidered robe (peplos),
which was carried through the streets of Athens hoisted on the mast of a ship with wheels.

11. Knemon was an ephebos. Young men were registered in the college of epheboi on
their eighteenth birthday, at least from the fourth century B.C., although the institution was
less formalized before that time. Knemon took part in the procession as a member of a formal group, wearing a sort of uniform.

12. The text is uncertain here, but the point is clear enough. Hippolytos, the son of
Theseus, was the object of the desire of his stepmother, Phaidra, just as Knemon is of Demainete's. In the myth Phaidra killed herself after revealing her love to Hippolytos and being rebuffed by him; but before she died, she left a note accusing him of attempting to rape
her; Theseus, ignorant of the truth, cursed his son and so caused his death. See the Hippolytos of Euripides.

gods are my witness—I have often shown more affection than you have, discovered somehow that I was pregnant, which I was hiding from you until I knew for certain. He waited until you were out of the house and then, when I was giving him my usual advice, urging him to behave himself and not to waste so much time drinking and whoring—these tendencies of his had not escaped me, though I said nothing to you for fear you would think I was acting like a typical stepmother—when I was saying all this to him in absolute privacy to spare his blushes, well, I cannot bring myself to repeat all the outrageous things he said about you and me, but he kicked me in the belly, which is the cause of my present condition.'

"In reply he said not a word, asked no question, gave me no opportunity to defend myself, but without more ado, taking it for granted that one who was so well disposed to me would not have told lies about me, immediately found me somewhere about the house and, much to my surprise, set about me with his fists and then called his slaves and had me soundly whipped. I did not even have the usual consolation of knowing the reason for this flogging. When he had sated his anger, I said, 'Perhaps now, Father, if not before, I might know the reason for this beating?' 11

"This question only added to his exasperation. 'The hypocrite!' he exclaimed. 'He wants me to explain his depravity to him!'

"With that he turned away and hurried off to Demainete. But her spite was not yet glutted, and she set in motion a second scheme against me. This is what it was. She had a slave girl by the name of Thisbe, a not unattractive creature who could sing to the harp. She set Thisbe on to me, told her to fall in love with me—yes, to fall in love with me!— which Thisbe, of course, immediately did! And although she had often rejected my advances, she now began to lead me on in every way she could, with looks, gestures, and various other tokens. Like an idiot, I was convinced that I had suddenly become good-looking, and in the end she came to my room one night, and I let her in. She came a second and a third time, and after that she would come to me every night.

"One night, when I warned her at some length to take care not to let her mistress find out, she said; 'Knemon, I think you must be very naive. If you think that it is wrong for a bought slave like me to be caught having intercourse with you, what punishment would you say that woman deserves who claims to be of a good family, who is lawfully wedded to a husband, who knows that death is the penalty for such an offense,[13] but nevertheless takes a lover?'

13. In classical Athens a husband had the right to kill his wife's lover if he caught him in the act (as Knemon, acting for his supposedly absent father, proposes to do at 1.12). This right, however, seems not to have extended to killing the wife, nor did an adulterous wife face death if the case came to law. Many of Heliodoros's legal details in this episode are vaguely plausible inventions rather than historical facts.

" 'Stop!' I cried. 'I cannot believe what you are saying.'

" 'Nevertheless, if you wish, I shall deliver her lover to you in the act.'

" 'If only you would,' I said.

" 'Indeed I will,' she replied, 'not just for your sake, because she has treated you so outrageously, but equally for my own: every day I suffer to the limits of endurance because of an unfounded jealousy she nurses against me. Be sure not to let me down.'

12     "I promised that I would not, and for that night she left me. But two nights later she roused me from my sleep, whispering that the lover was in the house; my father, she said, had gone off to the country on unexpected business, and the lover—such was the arrangement he had with Demainete—had not long since stolen his way in. She told me I must steel myself for vengeance and burst in, blade in hand, so that the villain should not get away. I did as she said, and armed with a dagger I made my way to the bedroom, Thisbe leading the way and lighting the lamps as we went. When we reached the room, there was lamplight glimmering from inside. The doors were closed, but in my anger I burst them open and sprang into the room, shouting, 'Where is the scoundrel, this fine lover of that paragon of chastity?'

"And with these words I stepped forward to dispatch the pair of them. But—heaven have mercy!—it was my father who slid from the bed and fell at my feet, pleading: 'My child, stay your hand a while! Have pity on your father! Have mercy on the grey head that raised you! I have done you wrong, but I do not deserve to die. Do not lose control of your temper and stain your hands with your father's blood.'

"To these pitiful pleas he added others of the same kind. I stood there, thunderstruck in incoherent horror. I looked for Thisbe, but somehow she had slipped away. I stared at the bed and gazed round the room, lost for words, incapable of action. The blade dropped from my hand, and Demainete darted forward and grabbed it. Now that my father was safe, he seized hold of me and ordered me to be thrown into chains. Demainete fueled the flames of his anger, shouting: 'Is not this what I warned you of? I told you to beware of the boy. I said he would attack you if he had the chance. I saw the look in his eye, and I knew what he was thinking.'

" 'Yes,' he replied, 'you did warn me, but I did not believe you.'

"And for that night he had me locked up, and although I tried to explain to him how things really were, he refused to hear a single word. As
13   soon as it was light, he took me, still in my chains, before the popular assembly. His head begrimed with dirt,[14] he began to speak.

14. To arouse the pity of the jurymen.

" 'It was with higher hopes than this, men of Athens, that I reared this boy. From the hour of his birth I expected him to be a support in my old age; I gave him the upbringing that befits a free man; I gave him an excellent education; I had him enrolled in my phratry and my clan;[15] I entered his name in the register of ephebes; I proclaimed him a fellow citizen of yours according to the laws; I anchored the whole of my life on him. But he shows no gratitude for all I have done for him. He began by insulting me and assaulting my lawful wife here, and ended up by drawing his sword on me in the night. He was prevented from becoming a father-killer only by Chance, which made him drop his weapon in sudden panic. So I have come to seek your protection, and I now denounce him before you. The laws allow me to put him to death myself, but I do not choose to do so. Rather I leave everything in your hands, preferring to see justice done in my son's case by due process of law rather than by summary execution.'

"As he spoke, he wept. Demainete began to sob loudly too, making a great but insincere show of sympathy for me, calling me an unfortunate boy who was going to die deservedly but before his time, who had been turned against his parents by malevolent powers. She was not lamenting so much as using her lamentations to testify against me and confirming the truth of the accusation with her tears.

"When I asked leave to speak, the secretary stepped forward and asked me one simple question: Had I drawn a sword on my father?

" 'I did,' I replied, 'but let me explain.'

"There was a general outcry, and they decided that I did not even have the right to speak in my own defense. Some held that I should be stoned to death, others that I should be handed over to the public executioner and cast into the Pit.[16] Throughout this uproar, and all the time they were engaged in casting their votes about my punishment, I kept shouting: 'Stepmother! I am being done to death by my stepmother! My stepmother is destroying me without a trial!'

"Many of them took note of my words and began to suspect the truth. But even then I was not given a hearing, for the assembly was by now in such a furor that nothing could be done to stop it.

"When the votes were counted, those in favor of the death penalty numbered about seventeen hundred, some of whom advocated stoning, 14

15. The phratry (*phratria*, "brotherhood") was a broad kinship group; membership of a phratry was the essential qualification for Athenian citizenship, at least until the reforms of Kleisthenes in 508–507 B.C. The clan (*genos*) was a group of men claiming descent from a common ancestor; it was a narrower grouping than the phratry and had definite aristocratic connotations.

16. The *barathron*, a gully to the west of the Akropolis where people condemned for crimes against the state were hurled to their death. Stoning was never an official method of execution at Athens.

others hurling me into the Pit; those against were around a thousand, who, swayed by their suspicion of a stepmother, condemned me to perpetual exile. Even so, it was their judgment that carried the day, for although they numbered less than the total opposition, the opposition was divided as to the proper penalty, and so the thousand were the largest single group. Thus I was banished from my family home and the land of my birth; but that she-devil Demainete did not escape the punishment that was her due. How this came about I shall tell you another time, but now you must sleep. We are far into the night, and you badly need rest."

"But it will only add to our misery," said Theagenes, "if the wicked Demainete is left unpunished in your story."

"Very well then," replied Knemon. "If that is what you wish, I shall tell you."

"After the trial I did not tarry but went straight down to the Peiraeus. There I found a ship on the point of setting sail and made the crossing to Aigina, where I knew my mother had relations. After landing I found the people I was looking for, and to begin with the time passed quite pleasantly.

"About three weeks later, in the course of my customary stroll, I went down to the harbor. A cutter was just coming into port, and I lingered a while, curious to see where she was from and who her passengers were. Even before the gangplank was properly fixed, a man leapt ashore, ran up to me, and threw his arms around me. It was Charias, a contemporary of mine.

" 'I have good news for you, Knemon,' he said. 'Justice is done. Your foe has paid the price. Demainete is dead!'

" 'Greetings, Charias,' I said, 'but why do you hurry past this piece of good news as if the tale you had to tell were something appalling? Tell me just how she died, for I am very much afraid that she may have died some run-of-the-mill death and so escaped the end she deserved.'

" 'Justice,' replied Charias, 'has not altogether departed from this world as Hesiod says.[17] Small transgressions she may sometimes overlook, delaying her reprisals long, but on the truly wicked her eye falls keen. So she pursued the sin of Demainete. I knew everything that was done or said, for, as you know, I am intimate with Thisbe, and she told me all. After the sentence of exile was imposed on you, little though you deserved it, your poor father began to regret what he had done. He removed himself to some remote place in the country, and there he lived, devouring his heart, to use Homer's phrase.[18] As for Demainete, the Fu-

17. Charias seems to have in mind a passage of Aratos's *Phainomena* (96–136). The lines of Hesiod usually cited here (*Works and Days* 197ff.) concern not Justice (Dike) but Shame (Aidos) and Divine Retribution (Nemesis).

18. *Iliad* 6.202.

ries were on her trail at once. She loved you even more madly now you were gone; her tears of sorrow never ceased: they were for you, she said, but really they were for herself. "Knemon," she cried night and day, calling you her darling little boy, her very soul. Her lady friends who came to visit her were astonished and impressed that a stepmother showed a mother's feelings, and tried to comfort her and raise her spirits. But she said that the pain was beyond comforting and that no one else could know what barbs had pierced her heart.

" 'Whenever she was alone, she would complain at length that Thisbe 15 had not served her as a servant ought. "She is interested only in doing harm," she would say. "She did nothing to help me in my love, but when it came to robbing me of my darling, it was no sooner said than done; she did not even give me a chance to change my mind!"

"It was quite clear that she meant Thisbe no good, and when Thisbe realized that she was nursing such a burden of resentment and was so racked with the pain of her grief that she might strike at any moment, particularly as her fury and desire had undermined her reason, she decided to forestall her mistress: she would strike the first blow and thus secure her own safety. So she went to Demainete and said: "What is the meaning of all this, mistress? Why blame your poor servant for something she did not do? Your wish has always been my command; this business is no exception. If all has not gone as you wished, then you must put it down to Chance. I am ready and able to devise you a way out of your predicament. You only have to say the word."

" ' "My dear girl," replied Demainete, "what way out can there be when the one man who could provide it is out of reach? It is the unexpected clemency of the court that has done for me. If he had been stoned or put to death, then at any rate the pain in my heart would have died with him. For once something is beyond hope, it is erased from the soul, and when there is no longer any prospect of achieving its desires, then the grieving heart may cease to suffer. But, as it is, I fancy I see him; I delude myself that I can hear his voice; I blush to hear him rebuke my wicked scheme. I dream that one day I shall find him come to me by stealth and take my pleasure of him, or that I shall go to him, wherever in the world he may be. These thoughts fan the flames of desire and drive me mad with longing. Oh, gods! I deserve my torment! Why did I not use gentle persuasion instead of underhand schemes against him? Why did I not cast myself on his mercy instead of hounding him? He repelled my first advances—but so he ought: he was shrinking not merely from adultery but from adultery with his own father's wife. But perhaps in time he might have been induced to soften; perhaps gentle handling might have brought him round. Instead, I behaved like a savage beast, more like a tyrant than a lover. I took offense because he would not do exactly as I said but thought nothing of Demainete, though his charms far surpass hers. But, sweet Thisbe, what is this way out you mentioned?"

" ' "An easy one, mistress," she replied. "For all most people know, Knemon has left the city and gone abroad in accordance with the verdict of the court; but I have been busy on your behalf, and I have discovered that he is in hiding somewhere near the city. I am sure you have heard of Arsinoe the flute girl. She was Knemon's mistress. After his fall from fortune she took him in and promised to go away with him. She is keeping him in her house until she is ready to leave."

" ' "What a lucky woman Arsinoe is," exclaimed Demainete. "She was already Knemon's lover, and now she is off to foreign parts with him. But what might all this have to do with me?"

" ' "A great deal, mistress," answered Thisbe. "I shall pretend to be in love with Knemon and ask Arsinoe, who is an old professional acquaintance of mine, to let me go to him in the night in her place. If she agrees, then you must play the part of Arsinoe and take her place in his bed. I shall make sure that he has had a drink or two before he goes to bed. If you get what you want, it is more than likely that your passion will abate; for most women one consummation is enough to dowse the fires of their desire; performance of the act slakes lust. If (which heaven forfend) your desires persist, we must think again: if at first you don't succeed, try, try again, as they say.[19] For the moment, though, let us attend to the matter in hand."

16 " ' "Demainete thought this a good plan and begged her to put the scheme into effect with all speed. Thisbe asked her mistress to allow her one day to bring the plan to completion. Then she went to Arsinoe and said, "You know Teledemos?" Arsinoe said she did, and Thisbe went on. "Let us have a room for the day. I promised that I would sleep with him. He will come first, and I shall join him when I have put my mistress to bed."

" ' "Then she hurried to Aristippos in the country and said: "I have come to make a confession, sir. Do to me what you will. It is partly my fault that you have lost your son. I did not mean it to happen, but nevertheless I am partly to blame. You see, I discovered that my mistress's conduct was not all it should be, that she was dishonoring your bed. I was both afraid for my own sake that it would be bad for me if this state of affairs was brought to light by someone else, and distressed for yours if this treatment was all the thanks you got for the love you showed your wife; but, being unable to summon the courage to tell you face to face, I

19. Literally "there will be a second setting sail," a proverb used most notably by Plato (*Phaidon* 99C) and explained by a late commentator as referring to those who take to their oars when they find the wind fails.

went to the young master, in the night for secrecy's sake, and revealed all to him, saying that there was a lover sleeping with the mistress. As you know, he had an old score to settle with her and, thinking that I meant that the lover was in the house at that very moment, he was seized with a fit of uncontrollable anger. He seized his dagger and, ignoring all my attempts to restrain him, all my protestations that nothing of that kind was going on at that moment, or else suspecting that I had had second thoughts, he rushed to her bedroom in a fury. You know what happened next. Now, if you care to take it, you have an opportunity to show your son, even though he is in exile at present, that you regret what has happened, and at the same time to take vengeance on the woman who has done you both wrong. This very day I shall show you Demainete in bed with her lover in a house—not even her own house, mark you!—outside the town."

"'"If you show me this as you promise," replied Aristippos, "you will be rewarded with your freedom. Perhaps vengeance on a hated foe would breathe new life into me. For a long time now I have nursed smoldering suspicions, but I have taken no action for lack of proof. What do I have to do?"

"'"You know the garden where the Monument of the Epicureans[20] is?" she said. "Go there this evening and wait for me."

"'With these words she hurried off the Demainete and said: "Make yourself attractive. You must look your prettiest when you get there. I have made all the preparations, just as I said I would."

"'Demainete embraced her and did as she said. Evening was already closing in; Thisbe took her by the hand and led her away to keep her assignation. When they were still a little way distant, she told her mistress to wait a moment and went on ahead by herself to ask Arsinoe to take herself off to another room and not interrupt her: the boy, she said, was shy, having only recently begun his initiation into the mysteries of Aphrodite. Arsinoe did as she was asked, and Thisbe returned to collect Demainete, took her into the house, and laid her down on the bed, removing the lamp to avoid, she said, Demainete being recognized by you—though of course you were in Aigina all the time.

"'After making her promise to consummate her desire without uttering a sound, she said: "I am going to fetch the young man; I shall bring him to you. He is drinking in a neighbor's house not far from here."

"'She slipped out and found Aristippos in the appointed place. In response to her urgent exhortations to catch the lover in the act and arrest

17

20. There is a serious anachronism here. Epikouros the philosopher died in 270 B.C., much later than the dramatic date of the plot. This garden was the headquarters of his school of philosophy; here it is sited, authentically, outside the walls of Athens on the road to the Akademia.

him, he went with her and burst suddenly into the room. Finding the bed with some difficulty in the dim moonlight, he cried, "You are caught, damn you!"

" 'The very instant that he uttered these words, Thisbe slammed the doors as loudly as she could and exclaimed: "Calamity! Her lover has got away! Be careful not to lose them both, master."

" ' "Don't worry," he replied. "I have the godforsaken woman. She was the one I really wanted." And seizing Demainete, he led her off towards the city.

" 'Demainete, of course, saw her predicament in a flash: her hopes had come to nothing, her reputation was lost forever, the law would take its course, and punishment awaited her. Smarting at the way she had been trapped, furious at the way she had been tricked, when she reached the Pit in the Akademia (you must know the place; it is where the polemarchs perform the traditional sacrifices to the Heroes),[21] she suddenly wrenched her hands free of the old man and hurled herself in, head first. Thus she died, a fitting death for one so evil. Aristippos said only, "You have given me satisfaction, even before the laws took their course."

" 'The next day he apprised the people of all that had taken place, and, securing a pardon only with some difficulty, he set about canvassing his friends and acquaintances in the hope of obtaining your recall. Whether or not he succeeded I cannot tell you, for before a decision was reached I set sail for Aigina, as you see, on private business. Nevertheless you can expect the people to agree to your recall and your father to come to fetch you. That was what he declared he would do.'

18 "That was the news that Charias brought me. What happened next, how I came here, what adventures I have had is a long story, and there is not time enough to tell it."

And he wept. The strangers wept too, ostensibly at his story but in fact in remembrance of their own. They would not have ceased from sorrowing, had not sleep, drawn by the pleasure they took in weeping, come fluttering down to staunch their tears.

So they slept, but Thyamis (this was the name of the robber chieftain), after sleeping soundly most of the night, had been disturbed by certain fleeting visions that appeared to him in his dreams and startled him from his slumbers. Unable to divine their meaning, he lay awake, wrapped in thought. It was about the time that cocks crow, possibly (so the theory runs) because their instinctive perception of the sun's course

21. The *polemarchos* (literally "war commander") was the third in rank of the nine annually appointed *archontes,* or magistrates. By the classical period the office no longer entailed military command, its functions being mainly ritual. The pseudo-Aristotelian *Constitution of the Athenians* (58) tells us that one of the duties of the polemarch was to make offerings to the tyrannicides Harmodios and Aristogeiton, who were regarded as heroes; Pausanias (1.29.15) adds the information that they were buried in the Akademia.

around the earth moves them to salute the god, or else because a combination of warmth and urgent desire to stir and feed causes them to issue
their distinctive summons to the men who share their lives, and rouse
them to work. The dream that visited him was god-sent; this is what it
was. He was in Memphis, his hometown, and found himself at the temple of Isis, which he dreamt was all ablaze with torchlight; the altars and
sacred hearths were drenched with the blood of all kinds of animals; the
gates and colonnades were teeming with people, who filled the whole
place with a confused babble of chatter. When he went inside the shrine
itself, he dreamt the goddess came to him, gave Charikleia into his
hands, and said, "Thyamis, this maiden I deliver to you; you shall have
her and not have her; you shall do wrong and slay her, but she shall not
be slain."

This dream caused him great perplexity, and he turned the vision over
and over in his mind, wondering what it could mean. Eventually, in desperation he forced the interpretation to conform with his own desires.
The words "you shall have her and not have her" he took to mean as a
wife and no longer a virgin; "you shall slay her" he guessed was a reference to the wounds of defloration, from which Charikleia would not die.

That was how he interpreted the dream, for that was how his desires
expounded it to him. At dawn he summoned his lieutenants, and, digni-
fying their plunder with the title of spoils of war, he ordered it to be laid
out where all could see. He also sent for Knemon, telling him to bring
his charges as well.

"What fate awaits us?" they cried on their way to the meeting, and
pleaded with Knemon to do what he could to help them. He pledged his
aid and urged them not to despair, the robber captain, he assured them,
was not a complete savage but had a gentle side to his nature; he came
from a distinguished family and had taken up his present way of life only
out of necessity. By this time they had reached the meeting place, and
the rest of the company had assembled. Thyamis took his seat on a
mound and declared the island to be a parliament. Instructing Knemon
to interpret to the prisoners what he was about to say—for Knemon
could by now understand Egyptian, whereas Thyamis was not fluent in
Greek—he began his speech.

"Comrades, you know how I have always felt towards you. As you
know, I was born the son of the high priest at Memphis, but I did not
succeed to the priesthood after my father's disappearance, since my
younger brother illegally usurped the office.[22] I took refuge with you in
the hope of gaining revenge and regaining my position. You chose me to

22. By the classical period, Egyptian priesthoods had become almost family possessions, passing as a rule to the eldest son on the decease of the father; compare Herodotos
2.37.

be your leader, and to this day I have made a practice of not giving myself a larger share than the rest of you. If it has been a case of sharing money, then I have been content with an equal portion, and if it has been a matter of selling prisoners, I have contributed the proceeds to the common fund in the belief that a leader as good as I hope I am should undertake the largest share of the work but receive only an equal share of the profits. As for prisoners, I have enrolled into our number those men whose physical strength was likely to be of use to us, and sold the weaker ones; I have never misused a woman, but I have set free the wellborn, either for ransom or from simple pity at their misfortune, while those of humble extraction, for whom slavery was a normal way of life rather than a condition imposed on them by their capture, I have distributed among you all as servants.

"But in the present case I am asking you for one item of our spoils: this foreign girl. I could present her to myself, but I think it better to take her with the consent of you all; it would be silly to take the prisoner by force and thus stand revealed as acting against the will of my friends. Furthermore, I am not asking you this as a free favor: I shall repay you by taking no share in the rest of the booty. As the priestly caste despises common sex, it is not for bodily pleasure that I have decided she should be mine, but for the continuation of my line.

20 "Let me explain my reasons to you. In the first place she seems to me wellborn. This I surmise from the treasure that was found with her, and the fact that rather than submitting to her present misfortunes she has retained a pride befitting her original station. Next, I estimate that her soul is good and chaste: since in beauty she excels all women but by the modesty of her expression she compels respect from those that look upon her, is it not inevitable that she should inspire the best opinion about herself? That is only right. But, most important, she seems to me to be the priestess of some god. Even in dire adversity she thinks it altogether wrong to remove her sacred crown and robe. I put it to you, my friends:
21 what better match could there be than one between high priest and consecrated priestess?"

They all cheered and gave their blessing to the marriage.

"Thank you," he continued, "but we must also ask the young lady what her feelings are in this matter. If this were simply a case of exercising authority, my will would be quite sufficient: for those with power to compel, polite inquiry is superfluous. But in the case of marriage the consent of both parties is needed."

Turning to the girl, he asked, "What are your feelings, my dear, about becoming my wife?" At the same time he asked her to explain who they were and whence they came.

For a while she stood with her eyes fixed on the ground, repeatedly shaking her head, apparently gathering her thoughts to say something.

Eventually she looked Thyamis full in the face. Her beauty dazzled him even more now, for her reflections had brought a special blush to her cheeks, and there was fire in her eyes. With Knemon interpreting, she said: "It would have been more fitting for my brother Theagenes here to speak, for I think that silence becomes a woman,[23] and it is for a man to respond among men. But since you have included me in the discussion, and give the first evidence of your kindness in trying to obtain your rights by persuasion rather than force, and particularly since the matter in hand bears entirely on me, I feel compelled to pass beyond the bounds of my normal maidenly conduct and reply to my master's question, even though it concerns marriage and was put before such a crowd of men.

"Our story is this: by race we are Ionians; we belong to the nobility of Ephesos. Our parents are both still alive, and as tradition calls upon such people to undertake divine service, I became priestess of Artemis, and my brother here priest of Apollo.[24] The office is held for a year, and as our tenure was drawing to an end, we were taking a sacred embassy to Delos,[25] where we were to organize musical and athletic competitions and lay down our office as dictated by ancestral custom. So a boat was loaded with enough gold, silver, vestments, and so forth for the games and public entertainment, and we put to sea. Our parents are well on in years and stayed at home from fear of the sea voyage, but many of our fellow citizens came with us, some on board the same vessel, others in their own craft.

"Our voyage was almost done, when the ship was caught by a sudden swell, a lashing gale, a welter of storm winds and tempests howling over the sea that blew it off course. In the face of such overwhelming adversity, there was nothing the helmsman could do but abandon the rudder to the storm and let fortune steer the ship. For seven days and seven nights we ran before the gale, until eventually we ran ashore on the beach where you found us. You saw the slaughter there; during the feast which we held to celebrate our deliverance, the sailors set on us, planning to kill us for our money. In the end we won the upper hand, but only after a bitter struggle that cost the lives of all our own people as well as the aggressors as each side slew and was slain.[26] From all that number we were the sole, pitiful survivors: I wish it were not so! Among so many ills our one piece of good fortune is that some god has put us into your hands. Fear for our lives has changed to thoughts about marriage, which I have not the least intention of refusing. For a woman cap-

23. Virtually a proverb, certainly a commonplace in tragedy, e.g., Sophokles *Aias* 293.
24. Ephesos was famous for its temple of Artemis (Diana of the Ephesians). Apollo and Artemis were twins, which accounts for the paired priesthoods.
25. A small island in the Cyclades, famous as the birthplace of Apollo and Artemis and sacred to Apollo, in whose honor an annual festival of song, dance, and athletic contests was held there.
26. A tag lifted from the *Iliad* (4.451, 8.65).

tured in war to be thought worthy of her master's bed is already the pinnacle of good fortune, and for one who is herself dedicated to the gods to become the wife of the son of a high priest—who, god willing, will soon be a high priest himself—this certainly seems to bear the mark of heaven's care.

"Just one grace I beg you, Thyamis. First allow me to go to a town or some other place where there is an altar or shrine to Apollo, and there lay aside my priesthood and its insignia. It would be better to go to Memphis when you resume your rightful place as high priest, for then the marriage would be celebrated with better cheer, linked with victory, and consummated in success. But I leave it to you to decide whether it should be sooner. Only let me perform our traditional rite first. I know you will agree, for, as you say, you have been destined for divine service since childhood and attach great importance to religious observance."

23     As she finished speaking, she started weeping. The whole assembly pronounced their blessing on her request and urged Thyamis to do as she asked, shouting that they had no objection. Thyamis pronounced his blessing too, though his feelings were mixed. So aflame was he with desire for Charikleia that even one hour's postponement seemed an eternity of waiting, but her words worked a siren spell on him and compelled his assent. And besides, he thought back to his dream and felt sure that the marriage was destined to take place at Memphis. He dismissed the assembly after distributing the plunder, himself receiving many of the choicest items, which his men were pleased to grant him.

24     He told them to be ready to march on Memphis in ten days' time. To the Greeks he allocated the same cabin as before, and again, by his command, Knemon shared it with them, but henceforward he was appointed not their warder but their companion. Thyamis saw to it that they passed their days in conditions of rather greater comfort than hitherto, and even invited Theagenes to share his table occasionally, out of respect for his sister. As for Charikleia herself, however, he decided to avoid seeing her as far as possible, for fear that the sight of her might fuel the craving flame that burned within him and make him break the resolutions he had made, the promises he had given. For these reasons Thyamis shunned the sight of his bride, for he thought that he could not look upon her without yielding to temptation.

The bandits dispersed to their quarters in various parts of the lake, and as soon as they were gone, Knemon ventured out a short distance from the lake in search of the herb that he had promised to Theagenes the previous day.

25     Meanwhile, Theagenes took advantage of his absence to break into tears and loud sobbing. Not a word did he speak to Charikleia, but over and again he called on the gods to be his witness; and when she asked

him whether these tears were caused by the same woes that had caused them both so many tears before, or whether some unfamiliar affliction had befallen him, he answered, "What affliction could be less familiar, more unrighteous than oaths and vows transgressed, than Charikleia putting me out of her thoughts and assenting to marriage with another?"

"Do not say such things," the girl said. "Do not doubt me: that would be harder to bear than any misfortune. When experience has given you such ample proof of my love in the past, do not become suspicious now because of a few expedient words uttered in need. Otherwise it will be just the opposite of what you say: the change in you will seem far greater than any change you will find in me. I admit that we are in a sorry plight, but no peril could ever be so dire as to induce me to compromise my virtue. Only once to my knowledge have I been less than virtuous— in my original passion for you. But even that was honorable, for from the start I gave myself to you not like a woman yielding to her lover, but like a wife pledging herself to her husband. To this day I have kept myself unstained by carnal contact, even with you. Many times have I repelled your advances, looking to the day when the union we pledged at the outset—a vow that has bound us through all adversity—will be legally solemnized. It would be quite absurd if you really thought that I preferred a savage to a Greek, a robber to my beloved."

"Then what was the meaning of that fine speech of yours?" said Theagenes. "Making out that I am your brother was an exceedingly clever ruse: it prevents Thyamis becoming jealous of us and allows us to keep each other's company without fear. And I realized that the story about Ionia and losing our way to Delos was a way of concealing the truth, intended to make those who heard it lose their way indeed! But why you should so readily agree to marry him, accept his proposal so unambiguously, and even fix the date, that surpassed both my power and my desire to comprehend. I prayed for the earth to open and swallow me up rather than have all my hopes, all the ordeals I have faced for your sake, end like this!"

Charikleia threw her arms around Theagenes, smothered him with kisses, showered him with tears. "It gives me great joy," she said, "to hear you voice such fears about me, for they prove that your love for me has not been diminished by all our misfortunes. But let me tell you, Theagenes, that we should not be talking together like this now if I had not made the promises I did; for, as you know, immovable resistance only aggravates the force of irresistible passion, whereas a meek answer and swift submission can curb the first eruption of desire and soothe away the pangs of lust with the sweet taste of a promise given. Lovers of a coarser grain, it seems to me, consider a declaration of intent as the first act of love: a promise makes them think they own you, and thenceforth,

26

secure in the haven of their hopes, they act with much more composure. It was with this end in mind that I went through the motions of engaging myself to him. Now our future is in the hands of the gods and the power that from the beginning has been allocated the responsibility of overseeing our love.[27] A day or two can often do much to deliver us from peril, and chance can bring to pass what all the plans of men have failed to achieve. So in this affair my intention was to fend off the certain dangers of the present with the uncertainties of the future. My deception is our protection, my love, and we must maintain it and say nothing, not just to the others but to Knemon too. I know he has been kind to us, I know he is a Greek, but he is a captive and will try to ingratiate himself with his master, if so he may. We have neither a long friendship nor a close connection to give us a firm guarantee of his reliability, so even if his suspicions lead him to light upon the truth about us, our first reaction must be to deny it. Sometimes even a lie can be good, if it helps those who speak it without harming those to whom it is spoken."

27    Charikleia was still propounding these suggestions and others similarly intended to win them the advantage, when Knemon ran through the door in breathless haste, his alarm and consternation evident on his face. "I have brought you the herb, Theagenes," he said. "Lay it on your wounds and heal them. Now we must gird ourselves for more wounds and another crop of killings.

   "There is no time to explain now," he went on, when Theagenes appealed to him to say more clearly what he meant. "Events might overtake my words. Hurry now, come with me—Charikleia too!"

   And seizing them both by the arm, he took them to Thyamis, whom he found polishing a helmet and sharpening a lance.[28] "You have chosen the right time to be busy with your weapons," he cried. "Put on your own gear and tell the others to do the same. The biggest enemy force I have ever seen is upon us. I saw their heads coming over the ridge not far from here—that's how close they are!—and I have run all the way here at top speed to warn you of the attack, and on my way across the lake I told as many as I could to prepare for action."

28    Thyamis sprang to his feet. "Where is Charikleia?" he demanded, apparently more concerned for her safety than for his own. Knemon pointed to where she stood, not far away, modestly inconspicuous in the doorway.

    27. Here, as often elsewhere in the novel, we have the notion of a personal spirit (*daimon*), more often than not malevolent, which has had an individual allocated to it as its portion.

    28. This seems to be modeled on a scene in the *Iliad* (6.321ff.), where Hektor, who has left the battlefield to fetch his brother Paris, discovers him preparing his weapons in his bedroom and then encourages him to come out and fight.

"Take her to the cave," whispered Thyamis so that only Knemon could hear, "where we hoard our treasure away for safekeeping. Put her in, my friend, close the entrance with the stone in the normal way, and then come back to me as soon as you can. The fighting will be my concern.[29]

He ordered his henchman to bring a sacrificial animal so that they could make an offering to their native gods before entering battle. Knemon set off on his appointed errand, and though Charikleia cried loud and long and kept turning back towards Theagenes, he brought her to the cave and shut her in. This cave was no work of nature like the many caverns that form spontaneously above and below ground: it was created by brigand handiwork in mimicry of nature, a warren dug by Egyptian hands for the safekeeping of plunder. It was fashioned somewhat as follows: it was entered through a narrow, lightless opening concealed beneath the doorway of a secret chamber in such a way that the stone threshold acted as a second door, giving access to the underground passage when need arose; this stone dropped effortlessly into place and could be opened just as easily. Beyond the opening was a maze of irregularly winding tunnels. The shafts and passages leading to the heart of the cave in some places ran separately, with cunning twists and turns; at others they met and crisscrossed like roots, until in the nethermost depths they merged and opened into a broad gallery lit by a feeble shaft of light from a fissure near the lake's edge. It was down here that Knemon brought Charikleia, using his knowledge of the path to guide her steps to the innermost recesses of the case, where, after doing what he could to lift her spirits and giving her his word that he would return that evening with Theagenes—whom he would not allow to come to close quarters with the enemy but would keep clear of the fray—he left her. Not a sound passed Charikleia's lips; this new misfortune was like a deathblow to her, separation from Theagenes tantamount to the loss of her own life. Leaving her numbed and silent, Knemon climbed out of the cave, and as he replaced the threshold stone, he shed a tear in sorrow for himself at the necessity that contrained him, and for her at the fate that afflicted her; he had virtually entombed her alive and consigned Charikleia, mankind's brightest jewel, to darkest night.

He ran back to Thyamis, whom he found spoiling for the fight; he and Theagenes were both fitted out in fine array, and Thyamis was haranguing those of his men who had already assembled, rousing them to even greater fury. He was standing in their midst, saying: "Comrades, I am not sure that there is any need of long speeches to put heart into you. War is a way of life to you, and you do not need me to refresh your

29

29. This is a near quotation of Hektor's words to his wife at *Iliad* 6.492.

memories of it. Besides, the suddenness of our enemies' attack precludes a long-winded speech; those whose enemies are already taking action must act equally swiftly to defend themselves: to fail to do so is to be culpably dilatory. We all know that it is not wives and children that are at issue, although for many these are by themselves incentive enough to fight—to us these things are of little importance, and we shall be able to replace them whenever victory is ours.[30] No, it is our very lives that are at stake; no brigand war has ever ended in a formal truce or been concluded by a treaty of peace—victory means life, and defeat inevitable death. With these thoughts to give edge to our strength and spirit, let us join battle with our bitterest enemies!"

30    His speech concluded, he looked round for his henchman and called him by name several times, "Thermouthis!" But Thermouthis was nowhere to be seen. With a torrent of menaces, Thyamis hurried to his dinghy as fast as he could run. Fighting had already broken out, and, even at a distance, one could see those who lived by the inlets along the lake's edge falling into enemy hands. As the lake dwellers fell fighting or took to their heels, the attackers set fire to their boats and cabins, the flames from which carried in the wind the short distance to the marsh, where they hungrily devoured the reeds that grew there in such abundance. Words cannot describe the blinding sheet of flame that assailed the eyes, the deafening noise that assaulted the ears. War in all its forms was loudly raging: the inhabitants of the lake put up a stout and spirited resistance, but their opponents had the immense advantages of strength of numbers and suddenness of attack; some they slew on land; others they sent to the bottom of the lake with their very boats and homes. From this scene a welter of noise rose skywards, the sounds of battle on land mingling with those of fighting on the water, the cries of killing with the cries of dying,[31] the groans of men staining the lake scarlet with their blood with the screams of men trapped by fire and water.

The sight and sound of all this reminded Thyamis of the dream in which he had seen Isis and her whole temple full of torches and sacrifices: this, he thought, was nothing other than the scene that now confronted him. Now he interpreted his dream quite differently from before: he would "have and not have" Charikleia because war robbed him of her; he would "slay but not wound" her by the sword, and not in the act of love. He cursed the goddess again and again for her deceit. Unable to bear the thought of Charikleia becoming the property of another man, he told his men to wait for a moment, explaining that they must hold their ground and carry on the battle by lying low around the islet and mount-

---

30. Reading ὁσάκις for the manuscripts' ὅσα καί.
31. Taken from the *Iliad* (4.451, 8.65).

ing surprise attacks from the cover of the surrounding swamps—though even with these tactics they would be lucky to hold out against the enemy's superior numbers. Then, on the pretext that he was going to find Thermouthis and make an offering to the gods of the hearth, he forbade any to follow him and made his way back to the chamber in a state of frenzy.

Once embarked on a course of action, the heart of a savage brooks no turning back. And when a barbarian loses all hope of his own preservation, he will usually kill everything he loves before he dies,[32] either in the deluded belief that he will be reunited with it beyond the grave or else to save it from the shameless clutches of his enemies. So it was that Thyamis did not spare a thought for any of the dangers that beset him, even though the enemy were all around him like a circle of nets, but, crazed with love and jealousy and anger, he went to the cave as fast as he could run and jumped down into it, shouting long and loud in the Egyptian tongue. Just by the entrance he came upon a woman who spoke to him in Greek. Guided to her by her voice, he seized her head in his left hand and drove his sword through her breast, close to the bosom. With a last, piteous cry, the poor creature fell dead.

Thyamis scrambled out of the cave, and after replacing the threshold stone and sprinkling a little earth over it, he wept as he said, "This is my bridal gift to you."

On his return to the boats he found the others planning to make a run for it, for now the enemy was close enough to be clearly visible. Thermouthis had returned and was in the act of dispatching the sacrificial animal. Thyamis heaped abuse on him: he had already sacrificed the most beautiful of victims, he said. Then he clambered into his rowboat with Thermouthis and his oarsman. Being made in one piece, rather crudely hollowed out from a single, thick log, these lake boats are unable to carry more than three people. Theagenes followed in another boat with Knemon, as did the rest in their various craft.

When they were a little distance from the island, which they had not so much rowed away from as rowed round, they stilled their oars and drew their boats up in line to receive the enemy's attack full on. This was close enough for most of them; even the splashing of the oars was more than they could endure; at the very first sight of the enemy they all turned tail, some of them not brave enough even to withstand the martial din of war. Theagenes and Knemon backed off too, though their withdrawal was not entirely due to fear. Only Thyamis, who was per-

32. Shakespeare alludes to this passage in *Twelfth Night* 5.1.121ff.:

Why should I not, had I the heart to do it,
Like to the Egyptian thief at point of death,
Kill what I love?

haps too proud to run away, or even possibly unable to bear the thought of life without Charikleia, hurled himself into the midst of the foe.

32    They were just on the point of coming to grips when someone shouted: "That is him, that is Thyamis! Take care, everyone!" And with that they formed their boats into a circle around him. Thyamis tried to fend them off and inflicted a number of casualties, some of them fatal, with his spear. This was a quite incredible scene: not a single sword was raised against Thyamis, not a single arrow shot at him; the efforts of each and every one were directed at taking him alive. He held out for some time, until, faced with a concerted attack, he lost his spear and also his henchman, who had given him stout support but after sustaining an apparently fatal wound had given way to despair and flung himself overboard into the lake; being an experienced swimmer, he had swum underwater until he was out of range and then, with no little difficulty, had succeeded in getting away to the marsh. It did not occur to anyone to pursue him, for by this time they had taken Thyamis, the capture of which individual they considered a full-scale triumph. Although they had lost so many of their friends, they felt more joy in forming a respectful escort for the man who had slain them and yet lived than pity at the death of their comrades. So much more precious, evidently, do brigands consider money than life itself: friendship and kinship are defined solely in terms of financial gain. This was certainly the case here.

33    They were in fact from the same band of brigands who had fled from Thyamis and his men by the Heracleotic mouth of the Nile. Angered at being robbed of other people's property and resenting the loss of the plunder as much as if it actually belonged to them, they had mustered their comrades who had been left at home and called upon the aid of the surrounding villages, offering a fair and equal division of the spoils they expected to take. Thus they were the leaders of the assault, but their reason for taking Thyamis alive was this. He had a younger brother, Petosiris, at Memphis, who had treacherously and in defiance of ancestral usage usurped the office of high priest from Thyamis. Petosiris's inquiries had revealed to him that his elder brother was the leader of a band of outlaws, and he was afraid that Thyamis might one day seize an opportunity to take action against him; besides, he could see that he was generally suspected of having murdered the missing Thyamis. And so he had sent word round the bandit villages, offering cattle and large sums of money as a reward for anyone who brought his brother to him alive. This was what motivated the robbers, who, even in the heat of battle, were not oblivious to financial gain. So when Thyamis was recognized, they took him alive, though it cost many lives to do so.

Detailing half their number to guard him, they escorted him to dry land cursing their apparent mercy and crying that he preferred death to these detestable shackles. The rest made their way to the island, expecting to find there the treasure and spoils they had come to collect. But though they scoured the place and left not an inch unsearched, they found nothing of what they had been hoping for, apart from a few small items that had been left lying around and not secreted in the underground cave. By this time evening was drawing in, which made them afraid of staying on the island lest they be surprised by those who had escaped the slaughter. So they set fire to the cabins and rejoined their comrades.

## Book Two

Thus the island became an inferno. But as long as the sun was in the sky, I Theagenes and Knemon were unaware of the catastrophe, for in the daytime firelight is dulled and outshone by the beams of the sun-god. But when sunset ushered in the night, the flames took on a glaring brilliance that lit the sky for miles around. Darkness brought confidence to the two Greeks; they emerged from their hiding place in the marsh, only to see the island by now well and truly in the grip of the blaze.

Theagenes smote his brow and tore his hair. "Let this day be my last!" *histrionics* he cried. "Let this be the end and undoing of all things—fear, danger, anxiety, hope, love. Charikleia is dead, and Theagenes is no more. Fate is against me. I played the coward, but in vain. In vain did I betray my manhood in abject flight, trying to save my life for your sake, my love. But, my darling, I shall not live if you are dead. The hardest thing to bear is that it was no natural death you died, that you did not breathe your last in the arms you would have wanted to enfold you as you died. Fire has consumed you; no wedding torches did heaven light for you, but these flames instead. That incomparable beauty has been reduced to ashes, so that not even your dead body remains to preserve a trace of your perfect loveliness. How cruel the divinity is! I cannot find words to express its jealous malice. Even a last embrace is denied me. I am cheated even of a final, lifeless kiss!"

With these words, he looked round for his sword. Quick as a flash, 2 Knemon knocked it from his hand. "What are you doing, Theagenes?" he cried. "Why mourn the living? Yes, Charikleia is alive. She is not dead! Take heart!"

But Theagenes replied; "Tell that to fools and children, Knemon. You have cheated me of the balm of death; you have done for me!"

Knemon, however, swore that he was speaking the truth and told him the whole story: Thyamis's command, the cave, how he had thrust Charikleia in with his own hands; he described the cave, adding that there was no likelihood of the fire having penetrated to its deepest recesses, as the endlessly labyrinthine tunnels would have kept it at bay. At this Theagenes' spirits revived. Now he was in a hurry to get across to the island: Charikleia was not with him, but in his thoughts he saw her and pictured the cave to himself as a bridal chamber. Little did he know what sorrow awaited him there!

So they pushed off with a will, though they had to do their own rowing, as their boatman had flung himself over the side the moment the fighting started, as if the shouting had catapulted him overboard. This way and that they veered, for, having little skill in oarsmanship, they were not pulling together—and besides, there was a wind blowing

3   against them. However, their determination was more than a match for their incompetence, and eventually, though with some difficulty and much exertion, they managed to beach their boat on the island and ran as fast as they could to the cabins. They found them already reduced to ashes, identifiable only by their position; but the threshold stone that concealed the entrance to the cave was clearly visible.

The wind had got up behind the flames and blown them on to the huts, which, being flimsily constructed from woven reeds (from the marsh, of course), had been burned to ashes as the wind gusting past fanned the flames, leaving the ground more or less flat. The blaze had quickly burned itself out and died back to a bed of glowing embers, but most of the ash had then blown away in the strong wind, while the little that was left had been almost completely doused by the breeze and was now cool enough to walk on.

Knemon and Theagenes found some half-burned torches and scraps of reed, which they lit. They opened the entrance and hurried in, Knemon leading the way. They had gone only a few steps when Knemon suddenly cried out, "O Zeus, what is this? We are done for! Charikleia is dead!"

He dropped his torch to the ground, where it went out, and sank sobbing to his knees, his hands clasped over his eyes. As if pushed forcibly from behind, Theagenes sprawled over the body of the dead woman and lay pressing her to his bosom in a long, clinging embrace. Knemon sensed that he was conscious of nothing but his grief, that he was drowning in the sea of his troubles. Fearing that Theagenes might do himself some mischief, he stealthily removed the sword from the scabbard that hung at his friend's side, and then left him there alone while he hurried outside to rekindle the torches.

4   Meanwhile, Theagenes cried aloud in tragic sorrow; "Pain beyond enduring! Horror wrought by heaven's curse! What persecuting Fury was this that took such insatiable delight in our misery after imposing on us exile from our homeland, exposing us to peril on the sea, peril in pirate

lairs, throwing us upon the tender mercies of brigands, and more than once robbing us of all we had? One thing alone had it left me, and now that too has been snatched away! Charikleia is dead; my beloved has fallen victim to an enemy's hand. Obviously she was protecting her chastity and keeping herself for me. For me! She is no less dead for all that, poor girl! She had no joy of her beauty; nor did I. My darling, speak to me just once more as you used to. If you have an atom of breath left in you, tell me your last wishes. But alas! You do not speak. That prophetic, god-inspired voice is silent! Darkness has snuffed out the bringer of light! Oblivion shrouds the attendant of the inner shrine! Those eyes that dazzled everyone with their beauty have lost their light; your murderer did not see them, of that I am sure. What is one to call you? Bride? But you will never marry! Wife? But you are forever a virgin! What shall I call you? How shall I address you now? By the sweetest name of all—Charikleia! Rest easy, Charikleia. Your lover is true. Soon I shall be with you again. See, on your grave I shall pour a libation: my lifeblood; I shall offer you my blood, the blood you love. Here in this cave we shall lie: it will serve as our tomb. At least we shall be able to find union after death, even if heaven did not vouchsafe us it in life!"

With these words he reached down to draw his sword. It was gone! 5 "Knemon!" he cried, "you have done for me! And you have wronged Charikleia too by a second time depriving her of the company of the one she loves."

Even as he uttered these words, a voice came echoing back from the depths of the cave. "Theagenes," it called.

He was not in the least disconcerted. "I am coming, beloved spirit," he responded. "Evidently you still haunt the earth; you cannot bear to depart from the beautiful body from which you were forcibly expelled, or perhaps the ghosts of the underworld refuse you admittance because you are unburied."[33]

At that moment Knemon returned with a lighted torch. Again came the same voice, and again the word it spoke was "Theagenes."

"Gods above!" exclaimed Knemon. "That is Charikleia's voice, is it not? She is safe, I think, Theagenes! For the voice that falls upon my ears comes from the furthest depths of the cave, from the very part where I know I left her."

"I have had enough of your continual deceptions," replied Theagenes.

"If I am deceiving you," said Knemon, "I am deceiving myself as well, if it turns out that this dead woman is in fact Charikleia."

33. It was common belief that until the body was buried, the soul of the dead was not allowed to cross the rivers of the underworld and find its eternal resting place.

And with these words, he turned the body over to see its face. But at the sight of it he exclaimed: "What is this? O gods, you have brought about the impossible! This is Thisbe's face!"

He reeled backwards and stood shivering in dumb amazement. At this
6 turn of events, Theagenes, however, came to life and felt a new optimism. He brought Knemon round from his faint and begged him to lead the way to Charikleia as quickly as he could. Knemon took a moment to collect himself and then had another look at the body. It really was Thisbe! Beside her had fallen a sword, which he recognized by its hilt: Thyamis, in the haste of his passion, had left it in the body at the time of the murder. Protruding from her breast was a writing tablet that was tucked under her arm. Knemon picked it up and tried to make out what was written on it, but Theagenes was too pressing to let him read it. "Let us rescue my beloved first," he said, "in case even now some malign power is making fun of us. There will be plenty of time to read that later."

Knemon could see the sense of this. They picked up the sword and, taking the tablet with them, made their way quickly towards Charikleia, who had been crawling on her hands and knees towards the light. She ran to meet Theagenes and flung her arms around his neck.

"I have found you, Theagenes!" she said.

"You are alive, Charikleia!" he replied.

They continued in this vein, until in the end they collapsed, both at once, to the ground, where they lay clasped in a mute embrace that seemed to fuse their very beings—but brought them close to death. So it is that excess of joy has time and again turned to grief, that pleasure passing beyond its due proportion has given rise to self-induced sorrow. That is how it was with Theagenes and Charikleia: contrary to all expectations they had escaped death, but now they were in mortal danger, had not Knemon scratched in the earth to make a well of sorts and, cupping his hands to scoop up the moisture that trickled into it, splashed their faces and tickled their noses until they regained consciousness.

7     They came to to find themselves lying on the ground, which was not at all the posture of their meeting! They leapt to their feet, blushing (especially Charikleia) in shame that Knemon should have witnessed such an exhibition, and begged his forgiveness. But Knemon merely smiled and dispelled their anxiety by replying: "I thought your behavior was quite admirable—as would anyone else who has ever tasted the pleasure of defeat in a tussle with Love and meekly submitted to those holds of his from which there is no escape. But there was one thing, Theagenes, that I could not find it in myself to admire—to be honest, I found it a disgusting spectacle—and that was when you threw yourself onto a com-

plete and utter stranger and wept abjectly over her despite my protestations that your beloved was alive and safe!"

"Knemon," replied Theagenes, "please stop maligning me in front of Charikleia. I was weeping for her in another's body, for I thought that the dead woman was she. But now that some god has been kind enough to reveal that I was deceived, it is time for you to be reminded of your own remarkable display of bravery: you wept for my griefs before I did, and when you found that the dead woman was who you least expected it to be, you took to your heels as if she were some evil spirit in a play; though you were armed and had a sword in your hand, you fled from a woman, and a dead one at that! The intrepid Athenian warrior turned tail and ran!"

They laughed a little at this, but their laughter was forced and not without sadness; in fact, naturally enough in such adversity, there was more grief than mirth in it. Charikleia paused a moment, then, scratching her cheek just beneath her ear, she said: "My felicitations to the woman Theagenes grieved for, or even, as Knemon said, kissed—whoever she may be. Please do not suppose that love is making me feel pangs of jealousy, but who was that lucky woman whom Theagenes favored with his tears? How were you misled into bestowing on this stranger kisses that were meant for me? I should dearly like to know the answers to these questions, if you have them!"

"This will surprise you," he replied. "Knemon here says she is Thisbe, that Athenian harp-girl who plotted the downfall of him and Demainete."

Charikleia was astounded. "It is not possible, Knemon!" she said. "How can someone suddenly be spirited away by a sort of theatrical special effect,[34] out of the heart of Greece to the remotest parts of Egypt? How did it happen that we did not meet her on our way down here?"

"That I cannot tell you," answered Knemon. "But what I do know of her story is this. After Demainete had been caught in Thisbe's trap and had thrown herself to her death in the Pit, my father reported to the assembly what had happened. Pardon was no sooner sought than given, whereupon he began to make arrangements for procuring the people's assent to my return and for undertaking a voyage to find me. He was so busy that Thisbe found herself with plenty of time on her hands and felt no compunction about hiring out herself and her musical talents for drinking parties. Eventually her nimble harp-playing and stylish singing to the lyre made her more in demand than Arsinoe, whose flute playing

34. Heliodoros here specifies the *mechane,* a sort of crane used in the fifth-century Athenian theater to stage the miraculous appearance of a god (*deus ex machina*) and for similar purposes.

was rather lackluster. Unawares she had made herself the object of a courtesan's bitter jealousy, the more so when she became the mistress of a rich merchant from Naukratis,[35] Nausikles by name, who had previously been Arsinoe's lover but had discarded her after seeing her playing the flute, her cheeks bulging with the force of her breath and grotesquely protruding as far as her nose, her eyes bloodshot and popping out of her head.

9     "In a boiling fever of jealous rage, Arsinoe approached Demainete's relations and told them of Thisbe's plot against her mistress, combining the suspicions she had formed herself with what Thisbe had told her as friend to friend. Demainete's family closed ranks against my father and at great expense secured the services of the most formidable public speakers to bring charges against him. They declared that Demainete had been killed without a trial and without a conviction; they maintained that the story of her adultery was merely a cover for her murder; they requested him to produce her lover, dead or alive, and insisted that he should at least reveal the lover's name; and finally they demanded Thisbe for interrogation under torture.[36] My father promised to hand her over to them, but was unable to do so, for Thisbe had foreseen this turn of events before the case even came to court, and had made a compact to elope with her merchant. The people now lost their temper with my father. He was convicted not of murder, for he was able to give a full account of what had happened, but he was adjudged to have been an accessory to the intrigue against Demainete and to my wrongful banishment; he was exiled from the city, and his property was confiscated. Such was the joy that his second marriage had brought him!

    "And so it was that Thisbe—curse her!—set sail from Athens; now, before my very eyes, she has paid the penalty for her crimes. More than that I do not know; this much was told me in Aigina by a man called Antikles, with whom I later sailed to Egypt, hoping to discover Thisbe at Naukratis and take her back to Athens so as to put an end to the suspicions and allegations against my father and demand justice for the intrigues against my whole family. And now here I am, facing the same predicament as you! Why and how this came about, all my adventures in the meantime, I shall tell you some other time. How Thisbe came to be in the cave, and who killed her here, we may never know, unless some
10 god reveals the answers to us. But perhaps we should take a close look at the writing tablet that we found in her bosom. It probably has something further to tell us."

35. A Greek city in Egypt which became the sole channel for Greek commerce in Egypt soon after 570 B.C. under the pharaoh Amasis.
36. The regular way of obtaining evidence from slaves; they were presumed to be naturally liars, who would not tell the truth except under duress.

They agreed that they should. Knemon opened the tablet[37] and began to read. This is what was written there.

To Knemon, my lord and master, from your enemy and benefactress, Thisbe. First I have some good news for you: Demainete is dead. It was I who brought this about, out of love for you. How it happened I shall tell you face-to-face if you will agree to see me. Next I bring you the news that I have been on this island for ten days now, the captive of one of the bandits who live here; he boasts that he is their captain's right-hand man. He is keeping me under lock and key and does not allow me even to put my head outside the door, claiming that he has incarcerated me like this because he loves me, though in my estimation he is afraid that someone might take me away from him. But by the grace of some god I saw you walk past, my lord, and I recognized you. I am sending you this tablet secretly, by way of the old woman who shares my dwelling. She has instructions to deliver it into the hand of the captain's handsome Greek friend. Deliver me from the clutches of these brigands! Do not abandon your servant! Help me, please; for the wrongs I appear to have done I was compelled to do, but the revenge I took on your enemy I took voluntarily. But if you are too full of anger to heed my prayers, then vent your hatred on me however you please. My one wish is to be yours, even if it means my death. Better to die at your hands and be buried like a Greek than to endure a life worse than death and suffer the torment of a savage's love, which causes me, as an Athenian, more pain than any hatred.

Such was the information that Thisbe gave of herself on the tablet. "Thisbe," said Knemon, "I am glad you are dead, that you were yourself the messenger who brought us word of your misfortunes, for it was your very corpse that delivered your narrative to us! It seems indeed that an avenging Fury pursued you over all the world and did not still her whip of Justice until she had brought you to Egypt, where I, the victim of your crimes, happened to be, and presented me with the spectacle of the retribution she exacted from you. I wonder what new scheme you were concocting against me beneath the cloak of this letter, when Justice preempted your plans with death. Even dead I regard you with suspicion, and I am haunted by the fear that the story of Demainete's death is untrue, that the friends who brought me the news were deceiving me, and that you have come across the sea to make me the victim of another Attic tragedy, but in an Egyptian setting!"

11

37. A writing tablet consisted of two pieces of wood coated with wax and hinged together so that they could be closed to protect the inscribed wax.

"Enough," exclaimed Theagenes, "of your superhuman courage! And of your dread of ghosts and phantoms! You cannot say that Thisbe has cast a spell on me and my power of sight, for I have no part in your tragedy. She is well and truly dead, I assure you. So take heart on that score at least, Knemon! But what puzzles and astounds me most is this: who could this friend and benefactor of yours possibly be who slew her? How and when had she been brought down into this cave?"

"All I can say with any certainty," replied Knemon, "is that the person who killed her was Thyamis, if we are to judge by the sword that we found beside the body. I recognize it as his by this device of an eagle carved on the ivory hilt."

"So," asked Theagenes, "can you say how he committed this murder—and from what motive?"

"How should I know?" he replied. "This cave has not given me the power of second sight, like the shrine of Pytho!"[38]

Theagenes and Charikleia gave a sudden cry of sorrow. "O Pytho! O Delphi!" they sobbed. Knemon was quite startled and had no idea why they should be so affected by the name of Pytho.

12 Meanwhile, Thermouthis, Thyamis's henchman, who had swum to land after being wounded, had, after the fall of night, discovered a boat from the wreckage drifting around the marsh. He clambered in and at that very moment was hastening towards the island to find Thisbe.

A few days previously, while she had been traveling in the company of Nausikles the merchant, Thermouthis had waylaid them on a narrow road through the foothills and carried her off. In the confusion of the battle that followed the enemy's assault, he had been sent by Thyamis to fetch the victim for sacrifice and had taken the chance to put Thisbe where no weapon could touch her, hoping to keep her alive for himself. No one had seen him as he shut her in the cave, but in his frantic haste he had left her close by the entrance. Once sealed in, Thisbe had not ventured far from the cave mouth, for she was terrified by her predicament and had no knowledge of the paths that led to the depths of the cave; there Thyamis had found here and slain her in the belief that she was Charikleia.

It was to Thisbe that Thermouthis was hurrying, confident that she had escaped the perils of war. He landed on the island and ran as fast as his legs would carry him to the huts, of which nothing now remained but ashes. With some difficulty Thermouthis located the entrance to the cave by the stone that lay across it. Making a torch from the few, still smoldering reeds that were left, he scrambled down into the cave as quickly as he could, calling Thisbe by name—for her name was the one

38. An archaic and poetic name for the sanctuary at Delphi, where Apollo killed the serpent Python.

word of Greek he knew. But the sight of her dead body struck him dumb. A long time he stood there, but eventually he became aware of the hum and murmur of voices floating upwards from the bowels of the cave, for Theagenes and Knemon were still engaged in conversation. He concluded that these were Thisbe's murderers, but now he was in a quandary: on the one hand he had the hot blood of all brigands and the quick temper of all savages, which, aggravated by his frustrated passion, impelled him to close with the supposed culprits there and then; on the other hand he had no weapon, no sword. Reluctantly he was constrained to control his impulses: better, he thought, to conceal his hostile intentions for the first encounter, then to wreak vengeance on his foes the moment he could lay his hands on a weapon. Thus resolved, he presented himself to Theagenes and the others. But the wild and cruel way he regarded them made all too plain the purpose hidden in his heart.

At the unexpected appearance of this naked, wounded man with blood streaming down his face, Charikleia withdrew into the bowels of the cave, partly from caution perhaps, but mainly because her modesty was offended by the naked and indecent appearance of this new arrival. Knemon also took a step or two backwards, for he recognized Thermouthis, whom he had not expected to see and who he thought might turn nasty. But Theagenes was undismayed at the sight. Indeed, it spurred him to action, and he brandished his sword, ready to strike Thermouthis dead if he tried anything untoward.

"Stay where you are!" he cried, "or you are a dead man! The only reason you are not already dead is that you seem vaguely familiar and your intentions are not yet clear."

Thermouthis fell pleading at his feet, but his supplication was the product of circumstances rather than of natural inclination. He entreated Knemon to come to his assistance and said it would be wrong for them to take his life, he meant them no harm, he maintained: he had always been a friend of theirs before the day of the attack, and it was as friends that he had come to them now.

These protestations had their effect on Knemon. He stepped forward and helped Thermouthis, who was clinging to Theagenes' knees,[39] to his feet, plying him with questions as to the whereabouts of Thyamis. Thermouthis told the whole story: how he had closed with the foe and hurled himself into their midst, fighting with no quarter for them and no thought for himself; how he slew all who came within his reach but was himself under the protection of a strict order that no one was to lay a finger on Thyamis. He could not say what had become of Thyamis in the end, but he himself had managed to swim to land despite his wounds

13

14

39. The classic posture of supplication.

and now had come to the cave in search of Thisbe. In response to their questions as to what interest he had in Thisbe and how she came to be the object of his search, Thermouthis went on to relate how he had stolen her from merchants and fallen madly in love with her, how he had kept her hidden right up to the time of the enemy attack, when he had concealed her in the cave, only to return now to find her slain by persons unknown, whose identity he would dearly like to learn so as to discover why they had done this thing.

In his eagerness to exculpate himself, Knemon blurted out with unseemly haste, "It was Thyamis who killed her!" And to prove it he held up the sword that they had found at the scene of the crime. When Thermouthis saw the blade still dripping with gore, dribbling blood so recently shed that it was still warm, he knew it belonged to Thyamis and groaned from the depth of his being. Unable to account for what had happened, he made his way back up to the entrance of the cave in stunned silence, and when he came to the dead girl's body, he laid his head on her breast and murmured, "Thisbe, my Thisbe!" Over and over he intoned her name; no other words could he find, until, dividing the word into separate syllables and pronouncing it less and less distinctly, he lulled himself to sleep.

15 Theagenes and Charikleia, and Knemon too, suddenly took stock of all the troubles that beset them. They seemed to want to form a plan, but the extent of their past woes, the hopelessness of their present predicament, the uncertainty of the future, clouded their intellects. For a long time they stared at one another, each expecting the other to speak; but meeting only with silence, they averted their eyes towards the ground, then raised their heads and drew a deep breath, easing with a sigh the pain that pressed heavy on their hearts. Finally Knemon lay down on the ground, Theagenes slumped onto a rock, and Charikleia flung herself on top of him. For as long as they could they kept at bay the sleep that assailed them, for they wanted desperately to devise a strategy against their present plight; but eventually they were compelled to obey the law of nature and yield to their lassitude and fatigue. They slipped into a sweet slumber, so intense was their sorrow. Thus it is that sometimes the conscious mind consents to accede to bodily pain.

16 But only a few moments' sleep were they able to snatch, and scarcely had their weary eyelids closed, when a dream of the following form appeared to Charikleia: a man with matted hair, with cunning in his eyes and blood on his hands, with one stroke of his sword struck out her right eye, whereupon she screamed and called to Theagenes, saying that her eye had been plucked out. No sooner did she call than he was at her side, in as much anguish at her distress as if he shared even her dreams.

Charikleia put her hand to her face and felt all over to find what she had lost in her dream. But it was only a dream.

"It was only a dream," she said. "My eye is still there. It is all right, Theagenes."

At these words, Theagenes heaved a sigh of relief. "I am glad that your eyes still shine with a radiance as bright as the sun," he said. "But tell me what has happened to you. What was it that so terrified you?"

"A wicked, evil-hearted man, undaunted even by your invincible strength, tried to ravish me as I slept on your knees, and I dreamt that he put out my right eye with the sword he held in his hand. I wish that the apparition had been real, Theagenes, and not a mere dream!"

"Do not speak such wickedness!" he exclaimed, and asked her why she said such a thing.

"Because," she answered, "I should prefer to have lost one of my eyes than to feel such dread for your sake. I have a horrible fear that you might be the object of my dream, for I count you my eye, my soul, my all."

"Enough of such talk!" interrupted Knemon, who, having been awakened from his sleep by Charikleia's initial scream, had overheard this entire exchange. "It seems plain to me that the dream has a quite different meaning. Answer me this: Are your parents still alive?"

"Yes," she replied, "if ever they were."

"Then you must presume that your father is dead," said Knemon. "The way I reach this conclusion is as follows. We all know that our parents are responsible for our coming into the world and partaking of the light of day. So it is not implausible for dreams to use our two eyes to symbolize our mother and father, for it is through them that we perceive the light and are presented with images of the visible world."[40]

"Even this is bad news," said Charikleia, "but I would rather your version were true than the alternative. May the tripod that inspires you to oracular utterance[41] prevail, and I be exposed as a false prophet."

"It will be as I say," said Knemon. "Have no doubt. But we really do seem to be in a dreamworld! Here we are analyzing dreams and figments of the imagination and not pausing for a moment to think how to solve our own problems! This is the ideal opportunity, too, while this

40. The interpretation of dreams was a developed art in antiquity. Identical reasoning and significance for the loss of the right eye are to be found in the standard textbook on the subject, Artemidoros's *Oneirokritika* (1.26).

41. The Delphic priestess delivered her oracles seated on a tripod sacred to the oracular god Apollo, from which she was supposed to derive her mantic inspiration. Originally this simply made visible her role as the god's proxy, but later ages devised a more "scientific" view of the priestess perching on her tripod above a chasm from which issued intoxicating vapors. This is pure fiction.

Egyptian"—he was referring to Thermouthis—"is out of the way, indulging in romantic fantasies about the dead and weeping over the body
of his beloved."

17     "Very well, Knemon," retorted Theagenes. "Some god has brought
us together and made you our companion in adversity, so let us hear
your advice first. You know these parts and speak the language; and besides, we are sunk deep in a flood of misfortunes greater than yours, and
our wits are too dulled to know what is required."

Knemon paused a moment before replying: "I am not sure whose
misfortune is the greater, Theagenes. The divinity has been no niggard in
filling my cup of misery, too. But you asked me, as the elder, to say
something about our position. This is how I see it: this island, as you see,
is completely deserted, apart from us. There is gold, silver, and clothing
aplenty, for Thyamis and his men stole these things in great quantities
from you and other victims of their banditry. But of food and other necessities there is not so much as a whisper left. If we stay here, we are in
danger of starving to death, and also of becoming the victims of an attack either by the enemy, who may return, or by our erstwhile colleagues, who may regroup and be drawn back by the treasure that they
know is here. In that case we should be killed before we could escape, or
else (and this is the best treatment we could hope for) we should find
ourselves at the mercy of their brutality. These Herdsmen are a treacherous crew, particularly now that they have lost their leader, who was able
to exert a moderating influence on them. This island is a trap, a prison
cell: we must get away from it; but first let us get rid of Thermouthis on
the pretext of sending him off to make inquiries and busy himself trying
to find some news of Thyamis. It would be easier to make our plans and
carry them out without him; and anyway it would be good to be rid of a
man who is congenitally unreliable and has the acrimonious temperament of all brigands, particularly as he harbors some suspicion against us
over Thisbe, which he will not let drop until he has perpetrated some villainy—should the opportunity arise."

18     Knemon's plan met with their approval, and they decided to act upon
it. They could already see the first glimmers of dawn, so they hurried
back to the mouth of the cave, where they found Thermouthis sound
asleep. They woke him and told him as much of their intentions as they
thought he should know; he was a rather gullible individual, and they
had no difficulty in convincing him. They laid Thisbe's body in a hole
and, in place of earth, sprinkled ash from the huts over her. For piety's
sake they performed the customary offices as best the occasion allowed,
offering tears and mourning in place of all the proper funeral sacrifices.
Then they sent Thermouthis off on the errand they had planned for him,
but after a few steps he turned back and refused to go by himself or to

undertake such a dangerous reconnaissance unless Knemon was prepared to accompany him on this mission. Knemon's dismay as he reported the Egyptian's words was all too plain, and Theagenes could see that he had no stomach for the task.

"Your intellect may be formidable, but your heart is puny," he said, "as your present behavior reveals more plainly than ever! Sharpen your resolve! Lift up your heart and act like a man! For the moment I think you have no choice but to agree to his demands, or he may begin to suspect that we are planning to steal away. You must go along with him for the first part of the way. He is completely unarmed, while you have a sword and armor to protect you; so you have absolutely no reason to be afraid of going with him. Then, at the first opportunity, you can sneak away and leave him to his fate, and join us at some agreed place. If you have no objection, let us agree upon some village near here. Do you know one where the people are friendly?"

Knemon thought this was good advice and suggested a village called Chemmis,[42] a prosperous and populous settlement on a hill by the banks of the Nile, which served as a stronghold against the Herdsmen; it was about eleven miles distant, he said, once they had crossed the lake; they must head due south.

"It will not be easy," answered Theagenes, "at least for Charikleia, who is not used to walking long distances. All the same we shall get there. We shall disguise ourselves as beggars, vagabonds who beg for a living."

"Of course!" said Knemon. "Your faces are hideously ugly, Charikleia's even more so now she has just had her eye cut out! It seems to me that beggars like you will not ask for scraps but for swords and cauldrons!"[43]

This brought a smile to their faces, but it was forced and did not come from the heart. After confirming under oath that they would do as they had agreed and calling on the gods to witness their vows that they would never of their own free will forsake one another, they began to put their plan into effect.

At daybreak Knemon and Thermouthis crossed the lake and started to make their way through a thick wood, so overgrown as to be virtually impenetrable. Thermouthis led the way, at the suggestion of Knemon, who employed Thermouthis's knowledge of the difficult terrain as a pre-

19

42. Apparently invented; the name is authentically Egyptian, but neither of the two places for which it is attested would suit this context.

43. This reverses *Odyssey* 17.222, where Odysseus, disguised as a beggar, is described by the arrogant Melanthios as "begging only for handouts, never for swords or cauldrons" (the kind of thing that any self-respecting member of epic society would desire as a gift of friendship). Knemon means that, despite their disguise, Theagenes and Charikleia will appear too noble for beggars.

text for letting him go first, though in reality he was making sure of his own safety and engineering an opportunity to make good his escape. On their way they came across a flock of sheep, whose shepherds ran off and hid in the thicker part of the forest. They slaughtered one of the rams that led the flock and greedily devoured the meat, which they roasted over the fire the shepherds had already built; but their hunger was so ravenous that they could not even wait for the meat to be cooked properly. So, like wolves or jackals,[44] they gobbled each morsel as it was cut from the carcass, though the fire had barely had time to singe it; and as they ate, the blood from the half-cooked flesh dribbled down their cheeks. Their appetites sated, they took a drink of milk before pressing on with their journey.

Now it was about the time when oxen are unyoked after a day's ploughing,[45] when Thermouthis said that on the other side of the ridge they were climbing was the village where he thought Thyamis was being detained after his capture, unless he had already been put to death there. At this moment Knemon began to complain that he had eaten too much and had a stomachache, adding that the milk was causing him terrible diarrhea. He told Thermouthis to go on ahead and said he would catch up with him. By repeating this performance a second and a third time, he convinced Thermouthis that he was in earnest, and said that he had been hard put to it to catch up with him again. Eventually the Egyptian grew so used to Knemon's disappearing that he failed to notice that he had not returned—actually he was making good his escape, careering full tilt down the hillside to where the wood was too thick for anyone to follow him.

20      When Thermouthis reached the top of the hill, he sat down on a rock to rest and wait for nightfall, for they had agreed to enter the village after dark and start probing for information about Thyamis. He kept a constant watch for Knemon, from whatever direction he might appear, for he was plotting mischief against him. There still lingered in his mind the suspicion that it was Knemon who had killed Thisbe, and he was considering how he might dispose of him; then, with Knemon out of the way, he had deranged visions of attacking Theagenes and Charikleia too. However, Knemon was nowhere to be seen, and it was now the dead of night. Thermouthis lay down to sleep, but the sleep he slept was the final sleep, the brazen sleep of death, for he was bitten by a viper. Perhaps it was destiny's will that his life should end in a way so befitting his character.[46]

44. Heliodoros is here turning two Homeric similes into narrative· see *Iliad* 16.156ff. and 11.474ff.

45. An epic way of telling the time: see *Iliad* 16.779 and *Odyssey* 9.58.

46. According to Aelian (*Nature of Animals* 10.31), there was a variety of asp that the Egyptians called *thermouthis,* whose bite was supposed to be fatal only to the wicked. So there is a peculiar aptness in the manner of Thermouthis's death.

From the moment he deserted Thermouthis, Knemon kept running and did not stop to take breath until night fell and the darkness put a brake on his haste. He concealed himself just where he was when the night overtook him, heaping as many leaves as he could over himself.[47] And beneath his blanket of leaves he spent a miserable night. He hardly slept at all: every sound, every gust of wind, every rustling leaf he thought was Thermouthis; and if ever, in spite of himself, he fell asleep for a moment, he dreamed he was running, constantly turning back and looking over his shoulder for a pursuer who was not there. And though he longed to sleep, he prayed that the gods would not grant him what he longed to have, for his dreams were even less pleasant than the reality. He felt it was the longest night there had ever been, and he seemed ready to curse it for being so protracted, but at length, to his great relief, day dawned. First, so as not to inspire terror or distrust among those he met, he trimmed his hair, which he had grown long among the Herdsmen so as to look more the part of a brigand. The Herdsmen cultivate an alarming appearance, particularly as regards their hair, which they pull forward to meet their eyebrows and toss violently as it falls over their shoulders, for they are well aware that long hair makes lovers seem more alluring but robbers more alarming. But even a dandy will wear his hair shorter than a bandit, and it was to this measure that Knemon trimmed his, before pressing on with all speed towards Chemmis, the village where he and Theagenes had agreed they should meet.

As he drew close to the Nile, which he had to cross to reach Chemmis, he saw an old man walking aimlessly along the riverbank, pacing to and fro, to and fro, beside the river, like an athlete in a long-distance race running length after length of the track, apparently confiding his cares to the river. His hair was long, like a priest's, and pure white; his beard grew long and thick, lending him an air of dignity, while his cloak and the rest of his clothes were of a Greekish appearance. Knemon waited a moment, but the old man continued striding to and fro, so entirely wrapped up in his thoughts, his mind so closed to everything but his reflections, that he seemed not even to be aware that he was not alone, until Knemon stood full in front of him and opened the conversation by bidding him good day.

The old man replied that he could not have a good day, since fate refused to grant him one.

"This stranger is a Greek!" exclaimed Knemon in astonishment.

"No, not a Greek," said the other. "I come from hereabouts. I am an Egyptian."

"How do you come to be dressed like a Greek then?"

"I owe this fine change of clothes to my misfortunes!"

47. Knemon in his bed of leaves is intended to recall Odysseus in his, after his shipwreck at the end of the fifth book of the *Odyssey*.

Astonished that anyone should be prompted to dress up in bright apparel by his sorrows, Knemon asked the old man to tell him what these misfortunes were.

"It is an Odyssey of woe,"[48] came the reply. "You are disturbing a hornets' nest of sufferings that will buzz and drone in your ears for an eternity. But where are you off to, young man? Where have you come from? How does a man who speaks Greek come to be in Egypt?"

"This is ridiculous!" exclaimed Knemon. "You have told me nothing about yourself, even though I asked first, and now you want to know my story!"

"Well, then," said the other, "you seem to be a Greek, compelled by fate, no doubt, to disguise yourself thus. You have an irresistible desire to hear my story, and I am desperate to tell it to someone—if I had not met you, I might even have told it to these reeds, as in the myth.[49] So, let us leave the Nile and its banks, for a spot under the scorching midday sun is not the most agreeable of places for listening to long tales. Let us adjourn to the village that you can see on the other bank, unless you have more pressing business. I cannot offer you the hospitality of my own house, but I shall entertain you in the home of a good man who has given me sanctuary. There you can hear my story if you wish and tell me yours in return."

"Let us go," said Knemon. "I am anxious to reach the village in any case, as I have arranged to wait for some dear friends there."

22    So they clambered into one of the small boats that were moored in great numbers along the bank waiting to ply for hire across the river, and crossed to the village on the other side. On reaching the lodgings where the old man was staying, they found that the master of the house was not at home, but they were given the warmest of welcomes by their host's daughter, a young lady of marriageable age, and by all the serving women of the house, who treated their guest just like a father, for such, I imagine, had been their master's instructions. While one washed his feet and cleaned the dust from the lower part of his legs, another busied herself with the couch, making sure that it was comfortable for him to lie on; a third brought a jug of water and lit a fire, while a fourth came in with a table set high with wheat bread and all sorts of seasonal fruit.

---

48. Literally "you are carrying me from Troy," an allusion to the words with which Odysseus begins his retrospective narrative in the *Odyssey* (9.39).

49. Midas, king of Phrygia, had to judge a musical contest between Apollo and Pan. Having declared Pan the winner, he was punished by Apollo, who gave him ass's ears in token of his lack of musical discrimination. The only person to know about the king's ears was the royal barber, who, unable to keep the secret, whispered it into a hole in the ground. However, the reeds that grew when the hole was filled in whispered the story whenever the wind blew through them. See Ovid *Metamorphoses* 11.153ff.

Knemon exclaimed in amazement, "We seem to have come to the court of Zeus, the God of Hospitality, so generous and obviously full of affection has been our reception!"

"Not to the court of Zeus," replied the old man, "but to the house of a man who is scrupulous in his respect of Zeus, the God of Hospitality and Supplication. He is a merchant, my son, and, like me, leads a nomadic existence; he has visited many cities and seen into the hearts and minds of many men. For this reason, I suppose, he has opened his house to many people, including myself just a few days ago when I was lost and in despair."

"What do you mean when you say you were lost, Father?"

"Robbers have taken my children. I know who they are who do me wrong, but there is nothing I can do in retaliation. So I hover around this place trying to assuage my sorrow with tears. I suppose I am rather like a bird whose nest is plundered and chicks devoured by a snake before her very eyes; she dare not go near but cannot bear to fly away; her heart is torn between desire and despair, and she twitters and flutters around the sack of her home, but her pleas and the grief she feels for her young are wasted on cruel ears that nature has left unacquainted with compassion."[50]

"Would you like to tell me how and when you fell victim to this atrocity?" asked Knemon.

"Later," he answered. "Now it is time to attend to the stomach. Homer knew how the belly subordinates everything to itself, and that is what he had in mind when, in that memorable passage, he called it 'accursed.'[51] But first we must make our libation to the gods according to the custom of the wise men of Egypt. Even hunger could not induce me to neglect this observance. May my grief never be so great as to make me forget my duty to the divine."

With these words he poured from his drinking bowl a libation of the water, unmixed with wine, that formed his drink, and said, "Let us make this offering to the gods of this land and of Greece, particularly Pythian Apollo, and also to Theagenes and Charikleia, the noble and fair, for they count as gods in my book." And as he spoke, he wept, and his tears were like a second libation he poured them.

23

50. This simile derives ultimately from the description of an omen of a snake eating a nest of birds in the *Iliad* (2.311ff.), but Heliodoros's immediate inspiration seems to have been a passage from *Megara* (21ff.), a poem attributed to Moschos:

> But even as a bird that waileth upon her young ones' perishing when her babes be devoured one by one of a dire serpent in the thicket, and flies to and fro, the poor raving mother screaming above her children, and cannot go near to aid them for her own great terror of that remorseless monster. (J. M. Edmonds trans.)

51. The word is quoted from *Odyssey* 17.287; but cf. *Iliad* 19.155ff., 19.216ff; *Odyssey* 7.215ff.

At the sound of those names Knemon froze. He looked the old man up and down and asked: "What do you mean? Are Theagenes and Charikleia really your children?"

"They are my children," he replied, "though they were born to me motherless, since it is by chance that the gods have declared them mine. They are the offspring of my soul's agony, and the love I have for them in my heart has made them as the children of my flesh. For this reason they have come to look on me and talk of me as their father. But tell me, please, how you come to have made their acquaintance."

"Not only have I made their acquaintance," replied Knemon, "but I am the bringer of good news: they are alive and safe."

"Apollo!" exclaimed the old man. "And gods! Where in the world are they? Tell me. I shall account you my savior and on a level with the gods."

"What shall I gain from it?"

"For the moment, my gratitude," he answered, "which I think any man with any sense would consider the finest gift that friendship can offer. I know of many men who have locked it away in their hearts as if it were a priceless treasure. But if we reach the land of my birth—which the gods foretoken will soon come to pass—you shall drink as deep as you may at the well of wealth."

"What you promise is far in the future and uncertain," said Knemon, "though you have the wherewithal to pay me now."

"If you see anything here, name it. I should even be prepared to give you part of my body!"

"There is no need for the amputation of any limbs! I shall consider myself paid in full if you would consent to tell me all about them— where they come from, who their parents are, how they came here, what adventures they have had."

"Very well," replied the old man, "though there is no greater reward you could have requested, even if you had demanded all the money in the world. But first let us take a little sustenance, for a long task lies ahead of us—for you to listen to the tale, and for me to tell it."

So they ate a meal of nuts, figs, dates fresh from the tree, and other fruits of this kind, which formed the old man's customary diet, for he refused to take the life of any living thing for the sake of food; he washed his food down with water; Knemon, with wine. After a short pause Knemon said, "You know, Father, how Dionysos delights in stories and enjoys an entertaining tale. Now the god has taken up residence in me,[52]

52. Dionysos, as god of wine, is now metaphorically present inside Knemon, who has had a drink. The telling of stories was a staple form of entertainment at drinking parties, but Knemon, as a good Athenian, is also playing on the fact that Dionysos was patron of the dramatic festivals at Athens.

easing my heart and putting me in a mood for listening; and he is pressing me to demand the payment you promised. The time has come for you to set the stage and present your tale."

"Hear it you shall," replied the old man, "but I wish my friend Nausikles could have been here with us. Time and again he has pestered me to initiate him into my secrets, but I have always found some excuse to postpone my narrative."

"Where might he be at the moment?" asked Knemon, for he recognized the name of Nausikles. 24

"He has gone hunting."

Knemon asked what game he was hunting, and the old man replied: "The most dangerous of all beasts: men they are called, Herdsmen, though the life they lead is one of brigandry, and it is almost impossible to run them to ground, as they retreat into their dens and lairs in the marsh."

"What complaint does he have against them?"

"The theft of an Athenian girl with whom he was in love. He said her name was Thisbe."

Knemon gasped and suddenly fell silent, as though he had had to check himself from saying more.

"What is wrong?" asked the old man, but Knemon changed the subject.

"I am wondering how he came to conceive the plan of attacking them and what force of arms he has to rely on."

"My friend," explained the old man, "the Great King's satrap[53] in Egypt is Oroondates; by his ordinance Mitranes, a commander of guards, has been assigned this village, and Nausikles has paid him a large sum of money to accompany him with a large detachment of cavalry and men-at-arms. He is smarting at the theft of his Athenian girl, not just because he loves her or because she is an excellent musician, but because, so he said, he intended to take her to the king of Ethiopia to be his wife's confidante and companion in things Greek. Having been robbed of the large profit he expected her to bring him, he is now setting in motion every available expedient to get her back. I must confess that I encouraged him in this undertaking, hoping against hope that he might also save my children's lives."

"Let us have no more of Herdsmen, or satraps or Great Kings either!" interrupted Knemon. "You very nearly succeeded in bringing me straight to the ending of the story with your talk, before I realized what you were up to, wheeling on this subplot which, so the saying goes, has

53. The Great King is the king of Persia. Egypt was conquered by Kambyses in 525 B.C. and became a satrapy, or province, of the Persian Empire, governed by a satrap, or viceroy.

nothing to do with Dionysos.[54] So take your narrative back to what you promised. So far I have found you just like Proteus of Pharos, not that you take on false and shifting forms as he did, but you are forever trying to lead me in the wrong direction!"[55]

"Very well," said the old man. "But first I shall tell you briefly about myself. This is not, as you think, a sophist's trick to avoid telling the story, but the logical way to present my narrative and an indispensable preliminary.

"My home is Memphis. My name is Kalasiris,[56] as was my father's before me. Now I lead the life of a rover, but it was not always so: once I was a high priest. By the law of my city I took a wife, and by the law of nature I lost her. After her release from this life, I lived untroubled for some time, complacently proud of the two sons she had borne me; but before many years had passed the preordained celestial cycle of the stars turned the wheel of our fortunes; the eye of Kronos lit upon my house and brought a change for the worse.[57] My science had given me warning of this, but not the ability to escape it, for while it is possible to foresee the immutable dispensations of Fate, it is not permitted to evade them. Insofar as such circumstances admit a comfort, it is foreknowledge that dulls the agony of misfortune; for in calamity, my child, what is unexpected is unbearable, since it reduces the mind to cringing terror; but what is foreknown is easier to endure, since we can think rationally about it, and by becoming accustomed to the prospect of disaster we are better able to handle it.

"In my case this is what occurred. A Thracian woman, in the full bloom of youth, second in beauty only to Charikleia, Rhodopis by name,[58] was touring Egypt. I know not whence or how she came there, but she brought evil to all she met, until one day she came carousing into Memphis with every imaginable luxury and extravagance in her train. She was fully equipped for the sexual hunt: any man who crossed her path was trapped, for there was no escaping or resisting the net of sensuality that she trailed from her eyes. She became a frequent visitor to the

54. A proverbial phrase, meaning "not to the point." Heliodoros is here playing with theatrical terms, alluding in particular to the *ekkyklema*, a kind of trolley used to reveal interior scenes by literally wheeling them on stage.

55. A sea god with the power of changing shape. Menelaos in the *Odyssey* (4.383ff.) could only make him reveal his secrets by holding onto him tightly through all his shifts of form.

56. An Egyptian word that Herodotos refers to a long linen garment (2.81) and also to one section of the warrior caste (2.164).

57. Kronos, father of Zeus, was identified with the Roman Saturn. The eye of Kronos is a poetic way of describing the planet Saturn, whose malign influence was generally recognized by astrologers.

58. A famous and historical courtesan of Naukratis, whose story is told by Herodotos (2.134–35). She was loved by Charaxos, brother of the poetess Sappho, which would make her career predate the Persian occupation of Egypt by fifty years or so.

temple of Isis where I was high priest, performing constant devotions to the goddess with hugely expensive sacrifices and dedications.

"It shames me to tell you this, but tell it I shall. The constant sight of her proved too much even for me; the self-control I had practiced all my life fell before her assault. For a long time I pitted the eyes of my soul against the eyes of my flesh, but in the end I had to admit defeat and sank beneath the weight of carnal passion. This woman, I discovered, was the start of the ordeals that heaven had predicted awaited me; it was clear to me that she was but acting a part in the drama of destiny, a mask, as it were, worn by the malign power that guided my fate at that time.[59] I decided not to bring disgrace on the priesthood with which I had grown up, resolved not to defile the gods' temples and precincts. I referred my case to the court of reason and imposed upon myself a penalty that befitted the sins I had committed not in fact (heaven forfend!) but merely in inclination. Exile was the sentence I pronounced on my concupiscence, and so, driven by relentless fate, I left the land of my birth.

"In doing so I was not only surrendering to the decrees of destiny and entrusting my fate to its whims, but also escaping from that abomination, Rhodopis. You see, my friend, I was afraid that under the pressure of the star that was then in the ascendant I might be driven against my will actually to perform acts of shamelessness. But, above and besides all else, it was my children who were the cause of my exile, for the god-sent wisdom of which I may not speak predicted to me on many occasions that they would take up swords and fight one another. Even the sun, I think, would hide his beams in cloud and turn away from so cruel a sight; and it was in an attempt to avoid seeing it, to spare a father's eyes the spectacle of his sons' fratricide, that I banished myself from the home and land of my fathers. I told no one of my departure, but pretended that I was making a visit to Great Thebes to see the elder of my two sons, who at that time was living there with his grandfather. His name, my friend, was Thyamis."

Again Knemon started back: the name of Thyamis rang in his ears like a blow to the head, but he checked himself from speaking, for he wanted to hear what came next. Kalasiris went on as follows.

"I shall say nothing of my ensuing travels, for they have no bearing on what you want to know, my young friend. But I learned that in Greece there was a city called Delphi, sacred to Apollo but a holy place for the other gods too, a retreat where philosophers could work far from the madding crowd. Here I made my way, for it seemed to me that a town devoted to holy rites and ceremonies was a place of refuge well suited to a member of the priestly caste.

26

59. Greek drama was performed by actors wearing masks. Rhodopis is nothing more than a supernatural power acting out a part in the drama of destiny.

"I sailed along the Krisaian Gulf and came to anchor at Kirrhaia, where I left my ship and hastened up to the city. As I entered the town, the place's own oracular voice sang in my ears in tones that truly were heaven-sent. The city seemed like an abode fit for the lords of heaven, especially as regards the nature of its surroundings: Parnassos towers above the city exactly like a fortress or a natural citadel, enfolding the town in the fond embrace of its foothills."

"An excellent description!" exclaimed Knemon. "You have truly felt the breath of the oracle's inspiration. It was exactly so that my father described the setting of Delphi to me when the city of Athens sent him as a representative to the Holy Council."[60]

"Were you from Athens then, my boy?"

"Yes indeed," replied Knemon.

"What is your name?"

"Knemon," he answered. "I shall tell you more about myself another time, but now please go on with your story."

"I shall," said Kalasiris, returning to Delphi. "After admiring the town with its streets, squares, and fountains and visiting the famous spring of Kastalia, with whose waters I performed the ritual of ablution, I hastened to the temple in a state of high excitement, for the crowd was abuzz with the rumor that it was time for the prophetess to awake. I entered the temple, and as I knelt in private prayer, the Pythian priestess broke into speech.

> From Nile's corn-rich banks your path has led
> As you flee from far-reaching Fate's spun thread.
> Fear not. The hour is near when I shall lead you home
> To black-soiled Egypt. For now, friend, welcome!

27     "When she had delivered this oracle, I prostrated myself on the altar and besought the god's favor in all things. The large crowd of onlookers were loud in their praises of the god for granting me an oracle the very first time I approached him. They pronounced me blessed and thereafter lavished all kinds of attention on me: they said that only one person had ever been more warmly received by the god—a certain Lykourgos from Sparta.[61] They consented to my wish to make my home in the temple precinct and voted to pay me an allowance from the public purse. In short, my happiness was complete, for I spent my time either perform-

60. The Amphiktyonic Council, composed of representatives (hieromnemones) from member states, was responsible for administering the shrine at Delphi and the Pythian Games, which were held there every four years.

61. The semimythical Spartan lawgiver, said by some to have designed the unique Spartan social system according to instructions received from the Delphic oracle. His reception by the priestess is recounted by Herodotos (1.65).

ing holy ritual or taking part in sacrifices, which a host of people, both native and foreign, perform each and every day in great numbers and in many forms to win the god's favor; or else in discussions with philosophers, for that type of person congregates in great numbers around the temple of Pythian Apollo; the whole city is literally a palace of the Muses, permeated by the Apolline spirit of the god who leads them.

"To begin with, our inquiries ranged over a variety of topics: one would ask me how we worship our native gods in Egypt, while another might ask me to explain why different races venerate different animals and what myth is attached to each case; and a third might inquire about the construction of the pyramids, and a fourth about the underground maze.[62] In short, their questions covered everything there is in Egypt, for Greeks find all Egyptian lore and legend irresistibly attractive.

"And so the days passed, until one day one of the more sophisticated 28 ones started to question me about the Nile: What are its sources, what unique property does it have that makes it so different from other rivers, and how is it that, unlike all others, it floods in the summer? I told him everything I knew, all that is recorded about this river in sacred texts, things of which none but members of the priestly caste may read and learn. I explained that the river rises on the furthest boundaries of Ethiopia and Libya, where the East ends and the South begins. The reason that it floods in the summer is not, as some have thought, that its flow is impeded by the Etesian winds blowing against its current,[63] but that these selfsame winds blow around the time of the summer solstice and sweep all the clouds from the north southwards, until they converge on the torrid zone, where their forward impulse is checked by the immense heat of that region, and all the moisture that has hitherto gradually accumulated and condensed in them is turned into vapor, which is the source of violent rainstorms. The Nile swells: not content with being a river, it bursts its banks and turns Egypt into a sea, cultivating the fields as it goes. And thus the water of the Nile is sweeter to drink than that of any other river, since it is supplied by the rains of heaven, and also more pleasant to the touch, for it has lost most of the heat of the area where it rises but still retains some warmth redolent of its origins. This is also the reason why the Nile, alone of all rivers, does not give off breezes, which it certainly would do, I think, if, as I gather some eminent Greeks have suggested, its flood were caused by the melting of snow.

"While I was expounding these and similar ideas, the priest of Pythian 29 Apollo, with whom I had struck up a close acquaintance—Charikles was

---

62. The burial vaults of the pharaohs near Egyptian Thebes.

63. Etesian winds blow from the northwest in summer. The cause of these floods was a matter of perennial interest to classical writers.

his name—said to me: 'Excellent! That is exactly my own view. That is what I was told by the priests of the Nile at Katadoupoi.'[64]

" 'You have been to Egypt then, Charikles?' I asked.

" 'Yes indeed, Kalasiris, my wise friend.'

" 'What took you there?' was my next question.

" 'A domestic tragedy,' he replied, 'which has turned out to be a source of great happiness to me.'

"I expressed my surprise at this paradox.

" 'You would not be so surprised,' said Charikles, 'if I told you how it has come about. And tell you I shall, whenever you wish.'

" 'Then now is the time for you to tell your tale,' I said. 'I want to hear it straightaway.'

"Charikles sent the crowd away, and then he said: 'Listen then. Actually for some time I have wanted to tell you the story of my past, because I think you may be able to help me.

" 'After my marriage we had no children, but I never ceased to pray to the god, and eventually, when I was well on in years, I was pronounced the father of a baby girl. But the god foretold that her birth would bring me no happiness. She reached the age to be wedded, and of the many who sought her hand I gave her in marriage to the one whom I adjudged the best. But on the very night that she first lay with her husband, my poor child's life ended. A fire broke out in her chamber—whether heaven-sent or deliberately started I cannot say—and before the wedding anthem was finished, it modulated into a funeral dirge; she was borne from her marriage bed to her place of eternal rest; the same torches that had shone so brightly at her nuptials served to light the pyre at her funeral. But malevolent Fate was planning a second act to my tragedy: the child's mother, broken by her death, was also taken from me.

" 'Such divinely imposed suffering was more than I could endure, but I did not put an end to my life, for religious teachers had convinced me that such an act is sinful. Instead I stole away from the land of my birth, fled from the desolation that had once been my home: one's troubles are easier to forget if the eyes cannot remind the heart so sharply of them. Through many lands I wandered, until eventually I came to Egypt, your country, and visited Katadoupoi to find out about the cataracts of the Nile.

30 " 'So now you know the reasons for my visit, my friend. But there is a sequel to this story—or to be more accurate, its climax—that I should like you to hear. As I was wandering around the town, whiling away my

---

64. Literally "down-crashers"; strictly speaking, this is the name of the first cataract of the Nile, modern Aswān. Heliodoros is the only classical writer to apply the name to a town, clearly mistakenly.

time and buying a few things that it is hard to find in Greece—for with the passage of time the pain of my grief had begun to lose its edge, and now I was hankering to return home—I was accosted by a man of imposing appearance, whose intelligence in particular was plain to see in his expression; he had not long come of the age of manhood, and his skin was as black as it could be. In faltering Greek he said he would like a word with me in private. I readily agreed, and he took me aside into a temple close by.

" ' "I have been watching you buying a number of the herbs and roots that grow in India, Ethiopia, and Egypt," he said. "If you were interested in buying such things unadulterated and with no suspicion of sharp dealing, I would be pleased to supply them for you."

" ' "I am interested," I said. "Show me your wares."

" ' "I shall let you see them," he replied, "but give me your word that you will not haggle over the price."

" ' "You must make sure then," I answered, "that the price you ask is not extortionate."

" 'He drew out a little pouch that he carried beneath his arm and opened it to reveal a prodigious display of precious stones: pearls the size of small nuts, perfectly spherical and glistening the purest white; emeralds and sapphires, the former as green as grass in springtime, their depths glowing with a luster as clear and soft as olive oil, the latter exactly the color of the sea[65] in the shadow of a tall cliff, sparkling on the surface and a deep violet beneath. In short, all these gems, with their blend of many scintillating hues, were a sight to gladden the eye. But one glance was enough.

" ' "My friend," I said, "it is time you started looking for another customer. All that I am and possess would hardly be enough to pay for just one of the stones you have shown me."

" ' "But even if you are unable to buy them," he said, "you are perfectly capable of taking them as a gift."

" ' "Of course I could afford them if they were given me," I answered. "But for some reason you are making fun of me."

" ' "This is no joke," he replied. "I am very much in earnest. In the name of the god in whose temple we stand, I swear that I shall give you all these jewels, on condition that, in addition to what you see, you will agree to accept another gift much more precious than these."

" 'At this I burst into laughter, and when he asked why, I replied, "Because it is absurd for you to promise to give me a gift of such great value and then to offer me payment for accepting it far in excess of the value of the gift itself!"

65. The text is corrupt at this point; the translation suggests the most probable sense.

" ' "Trust me," he said. "But now you too must swear an oath, to put my gift to the best possible use and to follow my instructions to the letter."

" 'I was thoroughly bewildered, but the thought of such riches led me to take his oath, exactly as he prescribed. That done, he took me to his house and showed me a little girl, lovely beyond telling, sublimely beautiful. He said she was seven years old, but to me she seemed nearly of an age to be married, such is the impression of increased stature given by surpassing beauty. I stood there bemused, not comprehending what had happened, unable to take my eyes off the scene in front of me. He began to speak as follows.

" " "The child you see before you, my friend, was, for a reason which you will learn shortly, exposed by her mother in her swaddling clothes, and her fate entrusted to the uncertainties of fortune. I chanced upon her and took her up, for once a soul had taken human form it would have been a sin for me to pass it by in its hour of peril—this is the sole precept of the naked sages of my country,[66] to whose teaching I had recently been admitted. Besides, even at so tender an age, there was something special, something godlike, about the light in the baby's eyes, so piercing yet so enchanting was the gaze she turned on me as I examined her. Beside her had been laid the necklace of gemstones that I showed you just now and a waistband of woven silk embroidered in native characters with a narrative of the child's circumstances. It was her mother, I imagine, who had had the foresight to provide the baby with these signs and tokens of recognition. When I read the embroidery and learned the truth of her origins and parentage, I took her to a country estate far away from the city and gave her to my shepherds to raise, warning them to speak of this to no one, under threat of punishment. The tokens that had been laid beside her I kept myself, from fear that they might be the cause of some mischief against the child.

" ' "So for several years she passed unnoticed, but, as time went by, and she grew into the full blossom of youth, it became clear that her beauty was quite out of the ordinary. It would have been impossible to keep her loveliness hidden even by burying it in the ground: even then, I think, her radiance would have shone through! I was afraid that the child's secret would be revealed, resulting in death for her and consequences none too pleasant for me either. So I contrived to have myself sent as an ambassador to the satrap of Egypt, and I have brought her here with me, with the aim in mind of securing her future. Very soon I shall discuss with the satrap the business on which I have come; he has

66. These naked sages, or gymnosophists, were usually supposed to live in India; but Heliodoros is here following the lead of Philostratos, who in his biography of Apollonios of Tyana located some gymnosophists in Ethiopia.

promised me an audience this very day. I commit this child to your care and that of the gods who willed it thus. I do this on conditions that you are under oath to me to honor: she is freeborn—preserve her so and give her in marriage to a freeborn husband; and as her dowry give her this band that you now receive from me, or rather from the mother who laid it beside her when she exposed her child. I feel sure that you will honor our compact to the letter: I have your oath, and throughout your long stay here I have kept you under scrutiny and found your character to be that of a true Greek. For the moment I have been able to tell you this story only in an abbreviated form, for I have urgent business connected with my official mission. Meet me tomorrow by the temple of Isis, and I shall tell you about the child in more detail and at greater length."

"'I did as he said; I took the child from him and, covering her face    32 with a veil, conveyed her to my lodgings, where for that day I tended her with much love, and in my heart I felt deep gratitude to the gods. From that day forward I thought of her, and spoke of her, as my own daughter.

"'The next morning at daybreak I set out in great haste for the temple of Isis, where I had arranged to meet the stranger, but after several hours of restless waiting there was still no sign of him, so I went to the satrap's palace and asked if anyone had seen the Ethiopian ambassador. There I was told that he had left, or rather had been expelled, for the satrap had threatened to have him put to death if he was not across the border by sunset. When I asked the reason, my informant said, "Because he told the satrap to keep his hands off the emerald mines,[67] claiming that they belong to Ethiopia."

"'I trudged home with heavy heart, stunned and reeling from the heavy blow of not having been able to hear all about the girl—who she was, where she came from, who her mother and father were.'"

"It is not surprising," interrupted Knemon. "I am dismayed myself not to have heard. But perhaps I shall."

"Indeed you will," said Kalasiris, "but first I must tell you the rest of    33 Charikles' tale.

"'When I reached my rooms,' he said, 'the child ran to meet me. Without uttering a word—for she did not yet know Greek—she clasped my hand in welcome. The mere sight of her was enough to dispel my gloom. I was impressed by the way that, just as puppies with a good pedigree will show affection to anyone after only a moment's acquaintance, she too had been so quick to sense the warmth of my feelings towards her and to behave towards me as a father.

67. These mines really existed, in the mountains near the border between Egypt and Ethiopia.

" 'I decided not to tarry at Katadoupoi, lest some supernatural malevolence should once again rob me of a daughter. I sailed down the Nile to the sea, where I found a ship and embarked for home. And now the child lives here with me: she is my daughter, she bears my name and is the mainstay of my life. In nearly every respect she is better than I could ever have hoped: she rapidly acquired Greek; like a vigorous young plant,[68] the bud of her childhood burst rapidly into the flower of youth; in physical beauty she is so superior to all other women that all eyes, Greek and foreign alike, turn towards her, and wherever she appears in the temples, colonnades, and squares, she is like a statue of ideal beauty that draws all eyes and hearts to itself. Yet, for all her qualities, she is, for me, the source of a pain that will not heal. You see, she has renounced marriage and is resolved to stay a virgin all her life; she has dedicated herself to the sacred service of Artemis and spends most of her time hunting and practicing archery. Life is a torment to me: I had hoped to marry her to my sister's son, a pleasant young man with nice manners and a civil tongue, but his hopes have been thwarted by her cruel decision. I have tried soft words, promises, and reasoned arguments to persuade her, but all to no avail. But the worst part is that I am, as the saying goes, hoist with my own petard: she makes great play with that subtlety in argument whose various forms I taught her as a basis for choosing the best way of life. Virginity is her god, and she has elevated it to the level of the immortals, pronouncing it without stain, without impurity, without corruption. But Eros and Aphrodite and all nuptial revelry she curses to damnation.

" 'This is the problem on which I am seeking your advice, and this is why I seized my opportunity and, when an opening somehow arose of its own accord, told you my tale at some length. Bear with me, Kalasiris, my dear friend. Use your magic and cast an Egyptian spell on her.[69] Induce her by word or deed to acknowledge her own nature. Make her realize that she is a woman now. It is something you could do with no difficulty if you set your mind to it, for she is not shy of men of learning—in fact she has passed most of her virgin life in their company—and she shares your dwelling—inside the temple precinct, I mean. I come to you as a suppliant. Do not reject my prayer; do not condemn me to live out my life without children, without comfort, without heirs, old and miserable. By the great god Apollo and by the native gods of Egypt I implore you.'

68. Alluding to and expanding the phrase used of Achilles by Thetis in the *Iliad* (18.437).

69. Egyptians were renowned as practitioners of magic, both black and white; also as crafty and duplicitous. These twin perceptions explain a great deal about the attitudes of Charikles and, later, Theagenes towards Kalasiris; and also his reaction in conforming to their stereotypes.

"He wept as he made his entreaty, and I wept to hear it, Knemon, and promised to give him whatever assistance I could.

"We were still pondering this problem when a man burst into the 34 room and announced that the leader of the Ainianes' sacred mission was at the door and had for some time been asking with some impatience for the priest to come out and commence the ceremony. I asked Charikles who the Ainianes were and what was this sacred mission and sacrifice they were performing.

"'In the whole of the province of Thessaly,' he replied, 'there are none of more noble ancestry than they. They are Hellenes in the truest sense of the word,[70] for they trace their descent from Hellen, the son of Deukalion.[71] They dwell all along the coast of the Gulf of Malis, but take particular pride in their capital, Hypata, whose name, according to them, is derived from the verb *hypateuein,* "to have rule over others," although the generally accepted view is that the town is so named simply because it is built at the foot of Mount Oite, *hyp' Oitei.* As for the sacrifice and sacred mission, the Ainianes send it to Neoptolemos, the son of Achilles, once every four years to coincide with the Pythian Games, which, as you know, are being held at the moment; for it was in Delphi that Neoptolemos was treacherously murdered by Orestes, the son of Agamemnon, at the very altar of Pythian Apollo.[72] This year the mission is especially splendid, as its leader prides himself on being a descendant of Achilles. I met the young man yesterday, and he struck me as a truly worthy member of the clan of the Sons of Achilles, so tall and handsome to behold that the mere sight of him is proof of his ancestry.'

"I confessed my astonishment that a man of the race of the Ainianes could proclaim himself a son of Achilles, for the works of the Egyptian poet Homer make it quite plain that Achilles came from Phthia.

"'The young man contends,' answered Charikles, 'that Achilles was an out-and-out Ainianian, for he maintains that Thetis rose from the Gulf of Malis to marry Peleus, and that the country along this coast has been called Phthia from time immemorial.[73] Other nations, he says, have invented fictitious claims on Achilles because of the high regard in which the hero is held. Furthermore, he also reckons himself among the descen-

---

70. *Hellenes* was the name which classical Greeks applied to the whole Greek nation, though originally, as in Homer, it was confined to a small tribe in southern Thessaly. Their eponymous ancestor, Hellen, seems to have been a later invention.

71. The Greek version of Noah, with his wife the sole survivor of a world flood.

72. There were many versions of the death of Neoptolemos; Heliodoros is here following that found in Euripides' *Andromache.*

73. In the *Iliad* Achilles is a native of Phthia. In classical times that name was given to the area around Pharsalos in Thessaly. The claim here is that in Homer the name refers to a different district, further south, which can thus claim Achilles as its own.

dants of Aiakos[74] by citing as an ancestor Menesthios, Spercheios's son by Polydora, the daughter of Peleus—the same Menesthios who was one of the foremost of Achilles' companions in the expedition against Troy and commanded the first brigade of the Myrmidones by virtue of his kinship with Achilles. There is one final piece of evidence that he offers in his efforts to substantiate a claim on Achilles and win him for the Ainianes, and that is the offering of propitiation sent to Neoptolemos; the peoples of Thessaly, he claims, unanimously renounced any claim on this in favor of the Ainianes, thus furnishing further proof of their closer ties of kinship.'

" 'I have no desire to challenge their claims,' I replied, 'be they true or be they simply wishful thinking. But please have the leader of their sacred mission shown in. I am all agog and aflutter to see what he is like.'

35     "Charikles nodded his assent, and in came the young man, who really did have something redolent of Achilles about him in his expression and dignity. He carried his head erect,[75] and had a mane of hair swept back from his forehead; his nose proclaimed his courage by the defiant flaring of his nostrils; his eyes were not quite slate blue but more black tinged with blue, with a gaze that was awesome and yet not unattractive, rather like the sea when its swelling billows subside, and a smooth calm begins to spread across its surface. After the customary exchange of courtesies, he said that the time had come to make sacrifice to Apollo so that the subsequent offering of propitiation to the hero and the procession in his honor could be performed punctually.

" 'Very well,' said Charikles, leaping to his feet. Then he turned to me and said, 'Today you will see Charikleia, if you have not already done so, for it is ancestral custom for the acolyte of Artemis to attend the procession and offering of atonement to Neoptolemos.'

"Actually, Knemon, I had seen his child many times before, for she had participated with me in sacrifices and had occasionally asked me questions about the scriptures. But I held my tongue and waited to see what would happen. Without more ado, we set off towards the temple, where the Thessalians had already made all the arrangements for the sacrifice. We had reached the altar, the priest had spoken the introductory prayer, the young man was on the point of commencing the ceremony, when from the inner shrine the voice of the priestess of the oracle rang forth.

74. Achilles' grandfather. The genealogy of Menesthios derives from *Iliad* 16.173ff., where he is introduced as commander of the first brigade of Myrmidones that accompany Patroklos to battle.

75. This and several other details in the description that follows bear a remarkably close resemblance to a description of Achilles by Philostratos (*Heroikos* 19.5): both probably reflect a well-known work of art.

One who starts in grace and ends in glory, another goddess-born:[76]
Of these I bid you have regard, O Delphi!
Leaving my temple here and cleaving Ocean's swelling tides,
To the black land of the Sun will they travel,
Where they will reap the reward of those whose lives are passed in
    virtue:
A crown of white on brows of black.

"So spake the god, but the bystanders were completely nonplussed 36
and quite at a loss to explain the meaning of the oracle. They each tried
to extract a different interpretation from it; each understood it in a sense
that matched his own wishes. As yet not one of them had discovered its
real meaning, for by and large the interpretation of dreams and oracles
depends on the outcome. In any case, the people of Delphi were in too
much of a hurry, for they were highly excited at the prospect of this
pageant for which such magnificent preparations had been made: no one
took the time to investigate exactly what the oracle signified.

## Book Three

"When the procession and the rest of the ceremony of propitiation had 1
come to an end—"

"Excuse me, Father," interrupted Knemon, "but they have not come
to an end at all. You have not yet described them so that I can see them
for myself. Your story has me in its power, body and soul, and I cannot
wait to have the pageant pass before my very eyes. Yet you hurry past
without a second thought. I feel like the proverbial guest who has turned
up too late for the feast! You have rung up the curtain and brought it
down again all in one phrase!"

"The last thing I want to do, Knemon," replied Kalasiris, "is to bore
you with such irrelevancies, so I was confining myself to the central
theme of my tale and the answers to your original questions. But your
interest in incidental spectacle only confirms my impression that you are
a true Athenian! So I shall give you a brief description of this pageant,
one of the most remarkable there has ever been, both in itself and in its
sequel.

"At the head of the procession came the sacrificial animals, led on the
halter by the men who were to perform the holy rites, countryfolk in

76. This line plays untranslatably on the names of the hero and heroine. Charikleia's
name is formed from *charis*, "grace," and *kleos*, "glory"; while Theagenes' consists of *thea*,
"goddess," and the suffix *-genes*, meaning "born from."

country costume. Each wore a white tunic, caught up to knee length by a belt. Their right arms were bare to the shoulder and breast, and in their right hands they each brandished a double-headed axe. Each and every one of the oxen was black: they carried their heads proudly on powerful necks that thickened to a hump of perfect proportions; their horns were flawlessly straight and pointed, on some gilded, on others wreathed with garlands of flowers; their legs were stocky, their dewlaps so deep that they brushed their knees. There were exactly one hundred of them—a hecatomb in the true sense of the word. Behind the oxen came a host of different sorts of beasts for the sacrifice, each kind separate and in its due place, while flute and pipe began a solemn melody as prelude to the sacred ceremony.

2     "After the animals and the cowherds came some Thessalian maidens, in beauteous raiment girdled deep,[77] their hair streaming free. They were divided into two companies: half—the first company—carried baskets full of flowers and fresh fruit, while the others bore wickerwork trays of sweetmeats and aromatics that breathed a sweet fragrance over the whole place. They balanced their baskets on their heads, leaving their hands free to link arms in a formation of diagonal rows; thus they were able to dance and process simultaneously. They were given the signal to begin by the second group launching into the introduction to the ode, for this group had been granted the privilege of singing the hymn through from beginning to end. The hymn was in praise of Thetis and Peleus, and their son and finally their son's son. After them, Knemon—"

"What do you mean 'Knemon'?" interrupted Knemon. "For a second time, Father, you are trying to cheat me of the best part of the story by not giving me all the details of the hymn. It is as if you had only provided me with a view of the procession, without my being able to hear anything."

"Listen then," replied Kalasiris, "if that is what you want. The hymn went something like this.

> Of Thetis I sing, the golden-haired goddess,
> Daughter of Nereus, the Lord of the Ocean,
> Married to Peleus at mighty Zeus's wishing,[78]
> The star of the sea waves, our own Aphrodite.
> The child of her womb was the noble Achilles,
> Who fought like the War God and raged in the battle,
> Whose spear flashed like lightning, whose fame lives forever.

77. Homeric; see *Iliad* 9.594; *Odyssey* 3.154, etc.
78. In some versions of the myth Zeus would have had Thetis for himself but for a prophecy that she would bear a son stronger than his father. Fearing loss of his throne, Zeus married her to a mortal man, Peleus, who thus became a byword for felicity.

Neoptolemos, the son Pyrrha bore him,[79]
Death-dealer to Trojans but Greece's salvation,
Neoptolemos, we pray you, be gracious;
Showered with blessings in your tomb here in Delphi,
Smile and accept the offering we bring you.
From all tribulation deliver our city.
Of Thetis I sing, the golden-haired goddess.

"To the best of my recollection, then, Knemon, the hymn was along 3
these lines. So exquisite were the harmonies of the singers, so exactly did
the rhythms of the sound of their steps keep time with the music, that
one's ears charmed one's eyes to be blind to what they saw; and as the
procession of maidens passed, the onlookers moved in step with them, as
if drawn by the cadences of the song, until behind them the troop of
young horsemen and their captain rode up in splendor to prove the vision of beauty more potent than any sound.

"The young men numbered fifty, divided into two groups of twenty-
five to escort the leader of the sacred mission who rode at their center.
They wore boots woven from straps of crimson leather and bound
tightly above their ankles. Their cloaks were white, fastened across their
chests with a golden clasp and hemmed all around with a band of dark
blue. Their mounts were all Thessalian steeds,[80] and the light of the freedom of the plains of Thessaly shone in their eyes; they resented the mas-
tery of the bit, foaming and champing and trying to dislodge it, yet they
allowed their riders' thoughts to guide them. The horses were capari-
soned with silver and gold frontlets and cheekpieces so splendid that you
might have thought that the young men had held a competition on this
point.

"But splendid though they were, Knemon, the crowd hardly spared
them a second glance. Every eye was turned towards their captain—my
beloved Theagenes; it was as if a flash of lightning had cast all they had
seen before into darkness, so radiant he was in our eyes. He too was on
horseback, in full armor and brandishing a spear of ash wood tipped with
bronze.[81] He wore no helmet but led the procession bareheaded, cloaked
in a flowing crimson mantle with gold embroidery depicting the battle of
Lapiths and Centaurs[82] and a clasp with, at its center, an amber figure of

79. Neoptolemos is normally described as the son of Deidameia. Pyrrha seems to have
been introduced here to allude to and explain the hero's other name, Pyrrhos.
80. Thessaly, virtually the only flat area of any size in Greece, was famous for its fine
horses and the horsemanship of its inhabitants.
81. Recalling the famous ash-wood spear of Achilles in the *Iliad*.
82. This battle took place when the Centaurs became drunk at the wedding of the
Lapith king Peirithoos at Larisa. This is thus an appropriately Thessalian legend.

Athene with her Gorgon's head talisman on her breastplate. A sweetly blowing breeze added to the charm of the scene, for its gentle breath tenderly caressed the hair that cascaded over his neck and parted the curls on his forehead, and also swept the hem of his mantle over his horse's back and shanks. The very horse seemed to understand what a fine thing it was to carry such a fine rider on his back, so proudly he flexed his neck and carried his head high with ears aprick; there was arrogance in the way his brows arched over his eyes, and pride in his step as he pranced along with his master on his back; he obeyed the rein's every command, and with each pace he paused for an instant in perfect balance with one leg uplifted, gently clipping the ground with the tip of his hoof so as to give a smooth and gentle rhythm to his gait. The sight took everyone's breath away, and they all awarded the young man the prize for manhood and beauty. And all those women of the lower orders who were incapable of controlling and concealing their emotions pelted him with apples and flowers in the hope of attracting his goodwill.[83] The verdict was unanimous: nothing in the world could surpass the beauty of Theagenes.

4    "But when rosy-fingered Dawn, the child of morning, appeared (as Homer would say),[84] when from the temple of Artemis rode forth my wise and beautiful Charikleia, then we realized that even Theagenes could be eclipsed, but eclipsed only in such measure as perfect female beauty is lovelier than the fairest of men. She rode in a carriage drawn by a pair of white bullocks, and she was appareled in a long purple gown embroidered with golden rays. Around her breast she wore a band of gold; the man who had crafted it had locked all his art into it—never before had he produced such a masterpiece, and never would he be able to repeat the achievement.[85] It was in the shape of two serpents whose tails he had intertwined at the back of the garment; then he had brought their necks round under her breasts and woven them into an intricate knot, finally allowing their heads to slither free of the knot and draping them down either side of her body as if they formed no part of the clasp. You would have said not that the serpents seemed to be moving but that they were actually in motion. There was no cruelty or fellness in their eyes to cause one fright, but they were steeped in a sensuous languor as if lulled by the sweet joys that dwelt in Charikleia's bosom. They were made of gold but were dark in color, for their maker's craft had blackened the gold so the mixture of yellow and black should express the roughness and shifting hues of their scales. Such was the band round the maiden's

---

83. The apple was a symbol of Aphrodite, and thus of sexual desire.

84. This is a formulaic line that occurs twice in the *Iliad* and twenty times in the *Odyssey*.

85. This passage echoes *Odyssey* 11.613–14, where Odysseus describes the baldric worn by the ghost of Herakles.

breast. Her hair was neither tightly plaited nor yet altogether loose: where it hung long down her neck, it cascaded over her back and shoulders, but on her crown and temples, where it grew in rosebud curls golden as the sun, it was wreathed with soft shoots of bay that held it in place and prevented any unseemly blowing in the breeze. In her left hand she carried a bow of gold, the quiver was slung over her right shoulder, and in her right hand she held a lighted torch. But as she was that day the light in her eyes shone brighter than any torch."

"It's them!" exclaimed Knemon. "It's Charikleia and Theagenes!"

"Where are they? In the gods' name, show me!" implored Kalasiris, supposing that Knemon could actually see them.

"They are not here, Father," replied Knemon, "but your description portrayed them so vividly, so exactly as I know them from my own experience, that they seemed to be before my eyes."

"I doubt," said Kalasiris, "that you have seen them as Greece and the sun gazed upon them that day, universally admired, universally acclaimed. Men lost their hearts to Charikleia, and women theirs to Theagenes. To know the love of one of them, people thought, must be very heaven, although the people of Delphi were rather more lost in admiration of the young man, and the Thessalians of the maiden, each being more struck by what they were seeing for the first time; for an unfamiliar sight is generally more impressive than one well known to us.

"Such a sweet deception, such a pleasant mistake, Knemon! My heart was all aflutter when I thought you could see my beloved children and were telling me they were here. But I think you have been deceiving me all along, because at the beginning of my story you gave me your word that they were on their way and would appear any second—and, what is more, you demanded payment in the form of their history. Now it is evening, the sun has set, and still you cannot produce them!"

"Have no fear," answered Knemon. "They will come; you can be assured of that. As it is, something may have happened to detain them, so that they will arrive later than we had arranged. Anyway, even if they were here, I should not tell you, for I have not yet been paid in full! So, if you really do long to see them, keep your side of the bargain and tell me how the story ends."

"I am loath," said Kalasiris, "to broach a subject so full of painful memories for me, especially as I thought I must be wearying you beyond the point of surfeit with my prattling. But I can see that you enjoy listening and have an insatiable appetite for good stories, so, come, let us pick up the narrative where I left it. But first let us light a lamp and pour the last libation of the day to the gods of night. Then, when the traditional respects have been paid, we shall be able to pass the night in storytelling without fear."

5    With these words the old man motioned to a serving girl, who
brought in a lighted lamp. Then he began his libation, invoking all the
gods, but Hermes in particular,[86] and prayed for a night free from unpleasant dreams and entreated that his loved ones should appear to him,
if only in sleep.

This done, he went on. "So now, Knemon, when the procession had
wound three times around the tomb of Neoptolemos, and the young
men had ridden three times around it, the women cried aloud and the
men raised a loud cry; whereupon, as if at one preconcerted signal, cattle,
sheep, and goats began to be sacrificed, almost as if they were all being
slaughtered by a single hand. On an enormous altar they heaped countless twigs, and on top they laid all the choicest parts of the sacrifices, as
custom demanded. Then they asked the priest of Pythian Apollo to commence the libation and light the altar fire. Charikles replied that it was his
office to pour the libation, 'But the leader of the sacred mission should be
the one to light the fire, with the torch that he has received from the
hands of the acolyte. This is the usage laid down by ancestral custom.'

"With these words he began the libation, and Theagenes made to take
the fire; and in that instant it was revealed to us, Knemon, that the soul is
something divine and partakes in the nature of heaven. For at the moment when they set eyes on one another, the young pair fell in love, as if
the soul recognized its kin at the very first encounter and sped to meet
that which was worthily its own. For a brief second full of emotion they
stood motionless; then slowly, so slowly, she handed him the torch and
he took it from her, and all the while they gazed hard into one another's
eyes, as if calling to mind a previous acquaintance or meeting.[87] Then
they smiled a fleeting, furtive smile, discernible only as a slight softening
of their expressions. And then they blushed, as if they were embarrassed
at what had occurred, and a moment later—I suppose as their passion
touched their hearts—the color drained from their faces. In short, in the
space of an instant, an infinity of expression passed across both their
faces, as every imaginable alteration in complexion and countenance bore
witness to the waves that pounded their souls.

"No one but me seemed to see any of this; they were all taken up with
their own concerns and thinking their own thoughts. Even Charikles
failed to notice, as he was pronouncing the traditional prayer and invocation. But I was concerned solely to watch the young couple, for at the
moment, Knemon, when the oracle sang through the temple as Theage-

86. This recalls the bedtime libation of the Phaiakians in the *Odyssey* (7.137f.). Hermes,
as guide of the souls of the dead, was also responsible for preventing their haunting the living in the shape of dreams.

87. This equation of falling in love with memory derives from Plato's discussion of love
in the *Phaidros*. The whole scene is rich in echoes of Plato.

nes made his offering, I had recognized the allusion to their names and so formed some notion of what lay ahead. But as yet I had no clear idea as to what the rest of the oracle meant.

"Eventually, and with what appeared a great effort of will, Theagenes 6 wrenched himself away from the maiden, and used the torch to light the altar fire. The ceremony was at an end: the Thessalians went off to celebrate, while the rest of the assembly dispersed, each to his own home. Charikleia threw a white shawl around her shoulders and set off, with her usual few companions, towards her lodgings in the temple precinct. She did not live with her so-called father, as considerations of ritual purity demanded that she live in absolute seclusion.

"My curiosity had been whetted by what I had seen and heard, and I was pleased when I ran into Charikles, who asked, 'Did you see her, my pride and joy, and Delphi's too, Charikleia?'

"'Yes, indeed,' I replied, 'although this was not the first time. I have seen her on many occasions before today, when we have met in the temple; we have a more than passing acquaintance, as they say, for we have frequently joined in offering sacrifice, and I have answered the problems that she has put to me on matters human and divine.'

"'What did you think of her today then, Kalasiris my friend? Did she not add a certain luster to the ceremony?'

"'Mind your words, Charikles,' I said. 'That is like asking whether the moon shines more brightly than the other stars!'

"'There were those, though,' he said, 'who sang the praises of that young man from Thessaly.'

"'They were only awarding second and third prizes,' I replied. 'Everyone admitted that the crowning glory, the real jewel of the pageant, was your daughter.'

"Charikles was delighted, and I too was making real progress with my objective of winning his absolute confidence in me. He smiled.

"'I am on my way to her at the moment,' he said. 'If you do not mind, let us both show our concern and go together to make sure that she has come to no harm from that horrid crowd of common people.'

"I gladly accepted his invitation and assured him that I deemed his affairs of more pressing importance than any other business I might have. But when we reached Charikleia's residence, we entered and found her 7 tossing restlessly on her bed, her eyes moist with love. She embraced her father as normal, but when he asked her what was wrong, she said she was suffering from a headache and would be grateful if she might be left in peace. Charikles was much alarmed; instructing her serving girls that she was not to be disturbed, he tiptoed out of her room; I followed.

"Once outside the house, he said, 'What is the matter with her, Kalasiris? What malady is this that my daughter has contracted?'

"'You must not be surprised,' I replied, 'if, by taking part in a procession before such a huge crowd of people, she has attracted the attention of an evil eye.'

"'So,' said Charikles, with a mocking laugh, 'you share the vulgar belief that there is such a thing as the power of the evil eye?'

"'Of course,' I replied. 'It is as real as it could be. Let me explain.[88] We are completely enveloped in air, which permeates our bodies by way of our eyes, nose, respiratory tract, and other channels, bringing with it, as it enters, various properties from outside, thus engendering in those who take it in an effect corresponding to the properties it introduces. Thus, when a man looks maliciously upon beauty, he imbues the air around him with the quality of malevolence, and disperses his own breath, charged as it is with spite, towards his neighbor. Being composed of such fine particles, it penetrates to his bones, to his very marrow. So in many cases disease is caused by malice, and this effect is quite properly spoken of as the power of an evil eye.

"'Here is another instance, Charikles. Many people contract ophthalmia or some infectious disease without having touched the patient at all or shared a bed or table with him, merely by breathing the same air. Conclusive proof of my point is furnished by the genesis of love, which originates from visually perceived objects, which, if you will excuse the metaphor, shoot arrows of passion, swifter than the wind, into the soul by way of the eyes. This is perfectly logical, because, of all our channels of perception, sight is the least static and contains the most heat, and so is more receptive of such emanations; for the spirit which animates it is akin to fire, and so it is well suited to absorb the transient and unstable impressions of love.

8    "'If you want another example, let me furnish you with an instance from the world of nature, one recorded in the sacred texts on animals.[89] There is a species of plover[90] that can cure jaundice: a person suffering from that disease has only to look the bird in the eye to be cured. However, the bird keeps its eyes firmly shut, turns tail, and runs away, not because, as some have suggested, it begrudges its healing powers, but because it has a natural tendency to attract and divert the current of the disease towards itself, simply by looking upon it. So the sight of jaundice is like a physical injury, and the bird avoids it. You may also have heard of a serpent called the basilisk, whose mere breath and regard are

88. The explanation that follows and the examples cited correspond closely, sometimes word for word, to a passage in Plutarch's *Table Talk* (680Cff.). Either Heliodoros has taken this material from Plutarch or, more probably, they share a source.

89. Despite this claim to privileged information, what follows is common knowledge, and Heliodoros is still using the same source.

90. The text specifies the *charadrios;* perhaps the Norfolk or thick-knee plover, *Charadrius oedicnemus.*

sufficient to wither and cause serious damage to anything that crosses its path.

"'So if some people have a malignant effect even on their nearest and dearest, we should not be surprised: they are congenitally malevolent, and the effect they have is the result not of volition but of an innate characteristic.'

"Charikles paused a moment before replying: 'Your solution to the 9 problem is brilliant and completely convincing. I only hope that one day Charikleia will get a glimpse of love's craving; in that case my diagnosis would not be one of sickness but of restored good health. You know that it was to achieve precisely that that I enlisted your aid. As things are, there is no chance of anything of that kind having befallen her, for she abhors sex and detests love. It really is the evil eye that has made her unwell, it seems, but I am sure you will agree to break the spell, for you are a good friend and nothing is beyond your powers.'

"I promised to give her such assistance as I was able, if I found her to be the victim of any affliction. This discussion was still in progress when 10 we were accosted by a fellow in a great hurry who said: 'Gentlemen, the way you are dawdling anyone would think you had received an order to go into battle rather than an invitation to a banquet thrown by Theagenes, the finest of men, under the patronage of Neoptolemos, the greatest of heroes. Come along! Do not keep the party waiting all day! All the guests are there but you.'

"Charikles leaned towards me and whispered in my ear: 'This is a man who believes in carrying a big stick when he issues his invitations! Not the right spirit at all—although he is obviously no stranger to spirits! But we had better go, or else he might resort to violence.'

"'You are joking, of course,' I replied. 'But, yes, let us go.'

"When we arrived at the party, Theagenes gave Charikles the place on the couch next to himself and treated me with respect too, for Charikles' sake. There is no point in boring you with all the details of the celebration—the dances of the maidens, the flute girls, the war dance that the young men performed in full armor,[91] everything else that Theagenes had arranged to complement the magnificence of the banquet in his determination to make the party convivial and memorably merry.

"But there is something that it is of the utmost importance for you to hear and that gives me especial pleasure to relate, which is this: Theagenes kept up the pretense of being in high spirits and forced himself to be hospitable to his guests, but he could not disguise the true tendency of his thoughts from me. At one moment he would stare into space and the

91. This war dance is named as the *pyrriche,* sometimes said to have been invented by and named after Neoptolemos/Pyrrhos, and thus particularly appropriate entertainment for a feast held in the hero's honor.

next heave a deep sigh for no apparent reason; he would be gloomy, seemingly lost in thought, and then the next minute he would seem to become conscious of his state, recall his thoughts, and affect a more cheerful expression; it seemed to take very little to produce these changes of mood, which covered the whole spectrum of emotions. The mind of a person in love is rather like that of a drunkard: volatile and completely unstable, since in both cases the soul is riding on a tide of emotional fluidity, which is why lovers are prone to heavy drinking, and drunkards to falling in love.

11     "But eventually the listless melancholy that filled his heart could be concealed no longer, and then it became obvious to the rest of the company that he was unwell. Even Charikles noticed his malaise and whispered to me, 'The evil eye must have lighted on this fellow as well. I think the same has happened to him as to Charikleia.'

    "'It is the same, by Isis!' I replied. 'Though that was only to be expected, considering that he, like her, played a prominent part in the pageant.'

    "While we were talking, the time came for the wine cups to be passed around the table. Theagenes drank a toast of friendship to each guest, though with rather bad grace, but when it came to my turn, I thanked him for his kind wishes but declined to take the cup.[92] He glared at me angrily, supposing that my refusal of the cup was meant as a slight, but Charikles realized what was happening and said, 'He does not drink wine nor eat any creature that is endowed with a soul.'

    "Theagenes asked the reason for this, and Charikles explained, 'He comes from Memphis, in Egypt, where he is a high priest of Isis.'

    "On hearing the words 'Egypt' and 'high priest,' Theagenes suddenly flushed with joy, like a man who has stumbled on hidden treasure. He leapt to his feet and called for water, which he drank, saying: 'Wisest of men, please accept this cup of fellowship in which I have drunk your health with your favorite drink. May this shared table be a pledge of our friendship.'

    "'So be it,' I answered, 'though, my dear Theagenes, my friendly feelings towards you are of long standing.' Then I took the cup and drank.

    "With this the party came to an end, and we each departed to our own homes. Theagenes bade me good night with a long embrace whose warmth belied the brevity of our acquaintance. After returning to my lodgings, I lay awake in bed for the first part of the night, examining every facet of the question of the young couple, hunting for the meaning of the last lines of the oracle. Then, in the small hours, Apollo and Artemis appeared to me, so I imagined—if indeed I did imagine it and not see

---

92. The toast comprised both parties drinking to one another from the same cup.

them for real. Apollo entrusted Theagenes to my care; Artemis, Charikleia. They called me by name and said: 'It is time now for you to return to the land of your birth, for thus the ordinance of destiny demands. Go then and take these whom we deliver to you; make them the companions of your journey; consider them as your own children. From Egypt conduct them onward wherever and however it please the gods.'

"With these words they departed, and in so doing they demonstrated 12 that my vision had been real and no mere dream. I understood most of what I had seen but was at a loss to know to what race of men or what land it might please the gods for the young couple to be conducted onward."

At this point Knemon interrupted. "I am sure you learned the answer afterward, father, and will tell me in due course. But you said that the gods demonstrated to you that they had not come in a dream but had manifested themselves in physical form. How?"

"In the way that Homer, the wise poet, alludes to, although the ignorant majority miss the allusion. Somewhere he says

for I knew
easily as he went away the form of his feet, the legs' form
from behind him. Gods, though gods, are conspicuous.[93]

"I seem to be one of the ignorant majority then, and perhaps, Kalasiris, your purpose in referring to those verses was to prove that! I know that I was taught the superficial purport of the lines when the text was first expounded to me, but I am totally unaware of the religious teaching embedded in them."[94]

Kalasiris paused for a moment until he had achieved the exalted state 13 of mind appropriate to the contemplation of holy mysteries. Then he said: "Knemon, when gods and spirits descend to earth or ascend from earth, they very occasionally assume the form of an animal, but generally they take on human shape: the resemblance to ourselves makes their theophany more accessible to us. They might pass unperceived by the uninitiated, but they cannot avoid recognition by the wise, who will know them firstly by their eyes, which have an extraordinary intensity and never blink, but more especially by their method of locomotion, which is not accomplished by the displacement or transposition of their feet, but by a sort of smooth, gliding motion and without touching the ground, so that they cleave rather than walk through the circumambient air. This is why the Egyptians make their statues of the gods with the two feet connected and carved virtually as one form. Homer was well

93. *Iliad* 13.71–72.
94. It was not uncommon in late antiquity for allegorical meanings to be extracted from literary texts, particularly the Homeric poems.

aware of this too, for he was an Egyptian and well versed in our holy lore. So he included enigmatic references to these phenomena in his epics, leaving their discovery to those who were capable of interpreting them. Thus of Athene he says, 'Her eyes were terribly shining,'[95] and of Poseidon,

> I knew
> easily[96] as he went away the form of his feet, the legs' form
> from behind him,

as if he were gliding along: that is the meaning of 'easily as he went away,' although some misconstrue the sentence and interpret 'I knew easily.'"

14     "You have initiated me into one mystery, reverend sir," said Knemon, "but several times you have referred to Homer as an Egyptian, a suggestion which, it may well be, no one in the whole world has heard made before today. I have no doubt that what you say is true, but I am most surprised, and should be very grateful if you could spare a few minutes to explain this point fully."

"This is not the moment, Knemon," he replied, "to discuss the question in depth, but nevertheless let me give you a brief answer.

"Different nations may make different claims about Homer's origins, my friend;[97] and it may be true that the wise man is a native of every city. But the fact of the matter is that Homer was a compatriot of mine, an Egyptian, and his hometown was Thebes, 'Thebes of the hundred gates,' to borrow his own phrase.[98] Ostensibly he was the son of a high priest, but in actual fact his father was Hermes, whose high priest his ostensible father was: for once when his wife was sleeping in the temple in the performance of some traditional rite, the god coupled with her and sired Homer, who bore on his person a token of this union of human and divine, for, from the moment of his birth, one of his thighs was covered with a shaggy growth of hair. Hence, as he begged his way around the world, particularly through Greece, performing his poetry, he was given the name *ho meros,* 'the thigh.' He himself never spoke his true name, never mentioned his city or his origins, but the name Homer was coined by those who knew of his physical deformity."[99]

"What was his purpose in concealing the land of his birth, Father?"

---

95. *Iliad* 1.200.

96. Kalasiris's interpretation involves taking the adverb "easily" (*rheia*) with the verb "went" rather than with "knew," and connecting it with the verb *rhein,* "to flow" or "to glide." Such a reading is just about possible, as in the English, but highly unnatural; the etymological point is impossible to reproduce.

97. The truth of Homer's identity was lost in the mists of time, and various Greek states competed to prove themselves Homer's birthplace. Despite Knemon's surprise, the theory that Homer was actually an Egyptian was not a particularly novel one.

98. *Iliad* 9.383.

99. Many etymologies were offered for Homer's name; this is among the most fanciful.

"It may be that he felt the disgrace of being an exile particularly keenly, for he was banished by his father after the mark he bore on his body had led to the realization of his illegitimacy at the time when he came of age and was being enrolled as an ordinand. Or possibly this may be another example of his wisdom, and by concealing his true place of origin he was claiming the whole world as his own."

"I find what you have to say completely convincing, bearing in mind 15 not only the typically Egyptian combination of concealed meanings and sheer enjoyment in his poetry but also his extraordinary genius, which would not have so far excelled everyone else, had there not been a literally divine and superhuman element in his begetting. But now, Kalasiris, having detected the gods by the Homeric method, tell me what happened next."

"Much the same as what had gone before, Knemon: renewed sleeplessness, deliberation, and the apprehensions that go hand in hand with darkness. I was happy, because I hoped that I had found something that I had not expected to find, and could now look forward to returning home; but I was saddened to think that Charikles would have his daughter taken from him; I was perplexed when I tried to work out how to bring the young pair together and arrange our departure; I was tormented with worries about how we could make our escape undetected, what direction we should take, whether we should go by land or sea. In short, I was tossed on a sea of anxiety and passed the rest of the night in sleepless anguish.

"At the very crack of dawn there was a knocking at the inner door, 16 and I heard someone calling for the slave boy. When the servant asked who it was hammering at the door and what his business was, the caller replied, 'Tell your master that Theagenes the Thessalian is here!'

"I was delighted by the news that the young man was at the door and told them to show him in. It seemed to me that my plans were already afoot without my having lifted a finger, for I inferred that, having heard at the party that I was from Egypt and a high priest, he had come to enlist my help with his love, laboring, I suppose, under the common misapprehension that the wisdom of Egypt is all of one and the same kind. On the contrary: there is one kind that is of low rank and, you might say, crawls upon the earth; it waits upon ghosts and skulks around dead bodies; it is addicted to magic herbs, and spells are its stock-in-trade; no good ever comes of it; no benefit ever accrues to its practitioners; generally it brings about its own downfall, and its occasional successes are paltry and mean-spirited—the unreal made to appear real, hopes brought to nothing; it devises wickedness and panders to corrupt pleasures. But there is another kind, my son, true wisdom, of which the first sort is but a counterfeit that has stolen its title; true wisdom it is that we priests and members of the sacerdotal caste practice from childhood; its eyes are raised towards heaven; it keeps company with the gods and partakes of the nature of the Great Ones; it studies the movement of the stars and thus gains knowledge of the future; it has no truck with the wicked, earthly concerns of the other kind, but all its energies are directed to what is good and beneficial to mankind. And this wisdom was the cause of my timely departure from the land of my birth, for, as I explained to you before, I hoped to avert the ills it foretold and to prevent the battle my sons were to fight with one another. But let us lay all this in the lap of the gods, especially the Fates, who have the power to bring things to pass or not. Now it seems that they sentenced me to exile from the land of my birth not so much for this reason as that I should find Charikleia. How this came about the next stage of my story will tell.

17    "Theagenes entered, and, having exchanged courtesies, I made him sit next to me on the bed.

"'What brings you here so early in the morning?' I asked.

"He sat there for a while running his hand over his face before replying, 'I am in terrible trouble, but I am too ashamed to tell you what it is.' These were the only words he could speak.

"The situation, I decided, called for a spot of showmanship; I would divine what I knew already! So, gazing at him with a benign expression, I said, 'You may hesitate to confess, but all things are known to my wisdom and the gods.'

"Then I paused a moment, performed some meaningless calculations on my fingers, tossed my hair around, and pretended that the spirit was upon me.

"'You are in love, my son!' I pronounced.

"At this oracular utterance he started, but when I added, 'with Charikleia,' he thought that the voice of god really was speaking through me, and would have prostrated himself at my feet, had I not restrained him. He moved closer and showered my head with kisses. He gave thanks to the gods; his hopes, he said, had not been disappointed. He begged me to save him: he needed my help, he said, and needed it now, otherwise he would die, so terrible was the evil that had struck him, so fiercely burned the flames of passion in a heart that had never felt love before now. He claimed that he had never been intimate with a woman and swore many oaths to that effect; he had never felt anything but contempt for their whole sex, he said, and even for married love, if it was ever mentioned to him; but now Charikleia's beauty had exposed the falseness of his pretensions: it was not that he was naturally proof against temptation, simply that until yesterday he had never set eyes on a woman worthy of his love. He wept as he spoke, as if to make it clear that it was only under compulsion that he admitted defeat at the hands of a girl.

"I comforted him, saying: 'Now that you have come to seek my aid, all will be well. She will not be able to resist my power now. She may be pitiless, she may fight hard against love's dominion, she may sneer at the merest mention of Aphrodite and marriage, but on your behalf all resources must be mobilized. Art can bend even nature to its will. Just take heart, and when I tell you what you must do, be sure to do it.'

"He promised to carry out whatever orders I might give him, even if I were to command him to walk over swords. He was still making his appeals and promising to give me all he had in payment for my services when a messenger arrived from Charikles.

"'Charikles asks you to join him,' he said. 'He is in the temple of Apollo, not far from here, offering up a hymn to the god, for he has had a dream that has rather alarmed him.'

"I rose to my feet at once and said good-bye to Theagenes. When I reached the temple, I found Charikles sitting on a seat, slumped in melancholy and sighing continuously. I stood beside him and asked, 'Why so glum and pensive?'

"'How else do you expect me to be?' he replied. 'I have had a most alarming dream, and, I am told, my daughter's condition has deteriorated—she has not slept a wink all night. Her ill health is causing me great distress, especially because tomorrow is the day when the games are due to be held, a day when tradition demands that the holy acolyte should display the torch to the view of the competitors in the race in armor and decide the winner. We have a choice of evils: either she must miss the race, which would be an affront to tradition, or else she must attend it despite herself, which would aggravate her sickness.

"'So, if you have not already done so, help us now and effect a cure. That would be the proper thing to do for a friend like me, and would also be an act of piety towards the gods. As you said yourself, it is only a matter of curing the effect of the evil eye, something you could do easily if you put your mind to it: high priests are quite capable of putting even the greatest wrongs to right.'

"I concealed my true thoughts from him also by confessing that I had been remiss and asking him to allow me that day, for, I said, I had a certain preparation to see to in order to effect a cure.

"'But now,' I said, 'let us visit the girl in order to make a closer examination and set her mind at rest, so far as we are able. Also, Charikles, I should like you to speak to your daughter on my behalf and tell her that I am a close and trusted friend, so that she will be more at ease and respond in better heart to my physicking.'

"'Very well,' he said, 'let us be on our way.'

"When we reached Charikleia—but why mince words? She was completely enslaved by her passion; the bloom was leaving her cheeks, and it was as if the fire in her eyes were being doused by the water of her tears. Nevertheless, she composed herself when she saw us and did her best to assume her normal countenance and way of speaking. Charikles embraced her and covered her with kisses beyond numbering; he displayed every possible sign of tenderness towards her.

"'My daughter, my child,' he said, 'are you trying to hide your suffering from me, your father? You have fallen under the evil eye, so why hold your tongue as if you are the one who are doing wrong rather than the one who have been wronged by the eyes that looked with malice upon you? Take heart: I have asked the wise Kalasiris here to find a cure for you. I am sure he will succeed, for he is more skilled than anyone else in the divine art. You see, he is a high priest who has dedicated the whole of his life to the service of the gods; and, more important, he has the warmest of feelings towards us. So, please, feel no inhibitions in making him welcome. He wishes to make an incantation and try some other remedies, so please cooperate with him. It is not as if you are unused to the company of scholars!'

"Charikleia said not a word, but she nodded, as if to say that she was glad to receive my assistance. With that we parted, but not before Charikles had urged me not to forget his earlier entreaties and to see if I could find a way to arouse in Charikleia some appetite for men and marriage. I promised him that it would not be long before his wish was fulfilled, and he took his leave of me in high spirits.

## Book Four

1 "The following day was the last of the Pythian tournament, but for the young couple another tournament was still at its height, one presided over and refereed, it seems to me, by Love, who was determined to use these two contestants, in the only match he had arranged, to prove that his particular tournament is the greatest of all.

"What happened was this: the whole of Greece had gathered to watch the games, which were supervised by the Amphiktyones. The other events—footraces, wrestling bouts, boxing matches—had been completed in magnificent style when finally the herald proclaimed, 'Let the men in armor step forward!'

"At that moment, Charikleia, the holy acolyte, appeared in all her glory at the end of the racetrack. So she had come! Her disinclination had been outweighed by tradition, or rather, I think, by her hopes of catching a glimpse of Theagenes. In her left hand she held aloft a lighted torch, in her right at arm's length a branch of palm.[100] Her appearance

---

100. A symbol of victory; the prizes in the Pythian Games usually consisted of wreaths of laurel.

caused every eye in the crowd to turn towards her, but perhaps no eye was quicker than that of Theagenes. A lover is so swift to espy the object of his desires! He must have been told what was to happen, for he was so keyed up to the moment of her appearance that he was quite unable to sit there in silence. He turned to me—he had deliberately sat next to me—and whispered: 'That is her! That is Charikleia!' I told him to calm down.

"In response to the herald's summons, a man in light armor stepped 2 forward. He clearly had a high opinion of himself and considered himself the star of the show. He had won many victories in the past, but on this occasion there was no one to oppose him; I suppose no one felt he had a chance of beating him. The Amphiktyones were on the point of dismissing him, as the rules did not allow the crown of victory to be awarded to anyone who had not taken part in a contest, but he asked that the herald should invite all comers to race against him. The umpires gave the word, and the herald proclaimed that anyone who would contest the race should come forward.

"'It is me that he is calling!' Theagenes said to me.

"'What do you mean?' I said.

"'You will see, Father,' he replied. 'While I am here watching, no one else shall carry off the prize of victory from Charikleia's hands.'

"'But what if you fail?' I said. 'Do you not care about the humiliation you will incur?'

"'I shall not fail,' he replied. 'Who is so insanely eager to see and be near Charikleia that he could outrun me? Is there anyone else to whom the mere sight of her can give wings and draw him to her without his feet touching the ground? Do you not know that painters give Love wings to symbolize the mercurial state of his victims? Besides, if you will allow me to boast a little, to this day no one has ever had the satisfaction of beating me in a footrace.'[101]

"With these words, he leapt to his feet and strode out into the center 3 of the stadium, where he gave his name and stated his nationality and then drew lots for the lane in which he was to run. He donned the full set of armor and stood on the starting line, panting in his eagerness for the race, so impatient that he could scarcely wait for the trumpet's starting signal, an awesome, magnificent sight, exactly like Achilles as Homer presents him contesting the battle with the river Skamandros.[102] The whole of Greece thrilled with emotion at this dramatic turn of events and prayed for Theagenes to win as fervently as if each man were running the

101. Theagenes' prowess in running reflects that of his mythical ancestor, Achilles, whose standard epithet in Homer is "swift-footed."

102. *Iliad* 21.203–384. Another instance of Theagenes' assimilation to Achilles. This episode depicted Achilles confronting an elemental force stronger than himself, a useful image for heroic endeavor against the odds.

race himself; for there is nothing to compete with beauty for winning the sympathy of those who behold it. Charikleia's emotion passed all bounds; I had been observing her carefully for some time and saw every conceivable expression pass in succession over her face.

"The herald proclaimed the names of those entered for the race for all to hear, 'Ormenos[103] of Arkadia and Theagenes of Thessaly.' The starting gate opened, and they were off, running at such a speed that the eye could barely keep pace with them. Now the maiden could stay still no longer: her feet began to skip and dance, as if, in my estimation, her soul were flying beside Theagenes and sharing his passion for the race. Who would win? There was no one there who was not affected by the suspense—myself particularly, now that I had been charged to love Theagenes as my son."

"It is not surprising," interrupted Knemon, "that those who were there watching should have felt the suspense; even now my heart goes out to Theagenes. So, I beg you, make haste and tell me whether he was proclaimed the victor."

4   "The race was half-run, Knemon, when, with a slight turn of his head, Theagenes glared at Ormenos, then lifted his shield high, threw back his head, and, fixing his eyes on Charikleia and on her alone, shot forward like an arrow to its mark, and finished several yards ahead of the Arkadian, the margin of victory being measured afterwards.[104] He ran on towards Charikleia, and, unable (or so he made out) to control his momentum, deliberately fell bodily into her arms. And as the maiden presented him with the palm branch, I saw him kiss her hand."

"That victory and that kiss have saved my life!" exclaimed Knemon. "What happened then?"

"Not only do you have an insatiable appetite for tales, Knemon, but you also seem proof against sleep. Here we are in the small hours of the morning, yet you are still wide awake and not at all fatigued by the inordinate length of my story."

"I cannot agree with Homer, Father, when he says that there is satiety of all things, including love.[105] In my estimation, one can never have a surfeit of love, whether one is engaged in its pleasures or listening to tales of it. And if the story being told is the love of Theagenes and Charikleia, who could be so insensitive, so steely-hearted, that he would not be spellbound by the tale, even if it lasted a whole year? So please continue."

103. Literally "speeding," an appropriate name.
104. Something must be wrong here! But no satisfactory emendation of the Greek text has ever been proposed.
105. From *Iliad* 13.636–37:

> there is satiety in all things, in sleep, and love-making,
> in the loveliness of singing and the innocent dance.

"So it was, Knemon, that Theagenes received the crown and was proclaimed victor. Everyone there cheered him on his way, but Charikleia was now utterly vanquished, even more a slave to her passion than before, after seeing Theagenes a second time. For when lovers look one another in the eye, their ardor is reawakened; the sight rekindles their hearts and fuels the flames of love.

"She went home and passed a night as anguished as those that had gone before, if not more so. I spent another sleepless night too, pondering which direction we should take to avoid apprehension, wondering to what land the god was conducting the young couple. All I was sure of was that we should make our escape by sea, reckoning that this was our best chance of success from the lines of the oracle where it said that

cleaving Ocean's swelling tides,
To the black land of the Sun will they travel.

"To the problem of where they were to be conducted I could see but 5 one solution: somehow I had to see the band that had been abandoned with Charikleia and on which Charikles said he had been told her history was embroidered. From the band I could probably discover the girl's homeland and the identity of her parents, though I had already formed my suspicions on this point. Perhaps that was where destiny was leading them.

"So early the next morning I went to call on Charikleia, but I found the whole household in tears, especially Charikles. I accosted him and asked, 'What is all this commotion?'

"'My daughter's sickness has worsened,' he replied, 'Last night was the most uncomfortable she has had.'

"'Wait outside,' I said. 'And the rest of you, leave us. Just have them fetch a tripod, some laurel, fire, and some incense. Then no one whatsoever is to disturb us until I call you.'

"On Charikles' instructions they did as I asked. Having secured our privacy, I launched into a sort of stage performance, producing clouds of incense smoke, pursing my lips and muttering some sounds that passed for prayers, waving the laurel up and down, up and down, from Charikleia's head to her toes, and yawning blearily, for all the world like some old beldam.[106] I kept this up for some time, until, by the time I came to an end, I had made complete fools of both myself and the girl, who shook her head again and again and smiled wryly as if to tell me that I was on quite the wrong track and had no idea what was really wrong with her.

106. Similar spells against the evil eye are still practiced in Greece, usually by old women. The yawning is an important part of the proceedings, the idea apparently being that the healer draws the malignity of the evil eye out of the victim into herself and then dispels it by yawning.

"I sat down beside her and said, 'Take heart, my daughter. Your sickness is trifling and easily cured. You have been touched by an evil eye, possibly while taking part in the procession, but probably while umpiring the race. And I have an idea who was chiefly responsible for casting the evil eye upon you—it was Theagenes, the one who ran the race in armor. I clearly saw him staring at you on several occasions and eyeing you quite forcefully.'

"'Whether he looked at me like that or not,' she replied, 'much joy may it bring him. But what are his origins? Where is he from? Because I noticed that he caused quite a stir.'

"'That he comes from Thessaly,' I said, 'you have already heard from the lips of the herald when he proclaimed his name. The young man traces his lineage back to Achilles, and I think he may well be right, if his stature and looks are anything to go by; they are a sure sign of a pedigree worthy of Achilles—except that Theagenes has none of his conceit or arrogance;[107] his character has a gentle side to temper his pride. But, however great his qualities, I hope he suffers worse pain than he has inflicted, for he has an eye full of envy and has bewitched you with his stare.'

"'I thank you, Father,' she said, 'for your concern on my behalf, but what is the point of baseless maledictions against a man who may have done no wrong? You see, it is not the evil eye that ails me but some other disease, I think.'

"'Why keep it secret then, my child? Why not trust me and tell me so that we can find a way to help you? Am I not old enough to be your father? And, more important, do I not love you like a father? Am I not a friend and soul mate of your father? Reveal what it is that ails you. I will respect your confidence, under oath if you like. So speak without fear and do not feed your pain by refusing to tell of it. Any wound that is quickly diagnosed is easily healed, but one that is allowed to fester is virtually beyond curing. Silence nurtures sickness, but a trouble shared is a trouble halved.'

6 "My words were followed by a short silence, but the look in her eyes was enough to tell me that her mind was a turmoil of shifting impulses. Then she said: 'Give me one day's grace. Then I shall tell you the truth—that is, unless you discover it first, for you do claim to have powers of divination.'

"I rose and left without a word, allowing the girl an interval in which to come to terms with her sense of shame. Charikles hurried to my side.

"'What do you have to report?' he asked.

"'Everything is fine,' I answered. 'By tomorrow she will be free of the complaint that is troubling her, and in its place will come something

107. This recalls Diomedes' assessment of Achilles at *Iliad* 9.699.

*tricks*

else very much to your liking. There is nothing to stop you calling in a physician.'

"And with that I hurried away to prevent Charikles asking any more questions. I had barely left the house when I saw Theagenes pacing around the temple precinct, talking to himself and apparently quite happy simply to keep watch on the house where Charikleia lived. I averted my eyes and walked past, pretending not to have noticed him.

"'Good day, Kalasiris!' he called. 'I was waiting for you. I must talk to you.'

"I turned round with a start. 'Theagenes, my handsome friend!' I exclaimed. 'I did not see you.'

"'How can you call me handsome,' he said, 'if Charikleia does not find me attractive?'

"I made a show of annoyance. 'I shall thank you to stop slandering me and my art,' I said, 'which has already ensnared her and compelled her to love you. Now she is praying to catch a glimpse of you as if you were one of the gods.'

"'What do you mean, Father?' he exclaimed. 'Is Charikleia in love with me? Then why are we not already on our way to her?'

"And with that he set off at a run. But I grabbed his cloak and said: 'Hey there! I know you are a good runner, but wait a minute! Our undertaking is not plunder taking! These are not goods openly on sale at a cheap price to anyone who cares to buy them. This is something that requires a great deal of forethought to achieve a proper result and a great deal of preparation to carry it off successfully. Are you not aware that the girl's father is the most important man in Delphi? Do you not realize that the laws impose the death penalty on people who do what you have in mind?'

"'Death does not matter to me,' he said, 'so long as Charikleia is mine; but still, if you think it best, let us go to her father and ask for her hand in marriage. I shall be a son-in-law for Charikles to be proud of.'

"'He would refuse,' I said, 'not that he could find anything to object to in you, but many years ago Charikles engaged the girl to his own sister's son.'

"'I shall make him pay, whoever he may be!' exclaimed Theagenes. 'No one else shall take Charikleia to wife while I am alive. My hand and my sword will not stand idly by and let it happen!'

"'Hold on!' I said. 'There is no need of anything like that. Just do as I say and take whatever action I tell you. Go home now and take care not to be seen in my company all the time. Come to me alone and in private.'

"He took his leave with heavy heart. The following day I happened to meet Charikles. No sooner did he see me than he ran to my side and showered me with kisses, exclaiming repeatedly: 'That is what I call wisdom! That is what I call friendship! You have won a great victory! She was unconquerable, but she has succumbed! She was invincible, but you have triumphed over her! Charikleia is in love!'

"Whereupon I started strutting about self-importantly, hoisted an eyebrow, and said: 'Of course, there was never any question of her withstanding my first assault, even without my invoking any of the greater powers. But how did you discover that she is in love, Charikles?'

"'By taking your advice,' he replied. 'I called in the most eminent physicians, as you suggested, and took them to examine her, with promises to pay them everything I possessed if they could find any remedy. As soon as they entered her room, they asked her what the matter was, but she turned her face to the wall and refused to say a single word in reply; only she kept repeating a verse of Homer out loud,

Son of Peleus, far greatest of the Achaians, Achilles.[108]

"'The learned physician Akesinos[109]—you must know who I mean— seized her wrist, despite her protests, and appeared to diagnose her complaint from the pulse; I suppose because it indicates the movements of the heart. He spent some time in scrutinizing her closely, examining and reexamining her from head to toe, then said: "It was a waste of time bringing us here, Charikles. There is nothing at all that medicine can do for her."

"'"Good heavens!" I exclaimed. "What do you mean? Is my daughter done for? Is there no hope for her?"

"'"There is no need to be alarmed," he replied. "Let me explain."

"'He took me aside, away from Charikleia and the others. "Our science," he continued, "professes to treat disorders of the body, and not, in theory, those of the soul, except when it is affected by the disorders of the body and derives benefit as the body is treated. What your daughter has is certainly a disease, but not one of the body. You see, there is no excess of any humor, she is not troubled by headaches, she is not feverish, and there is nothing else physically wrong with her, either in part or as a whole. So we are driven to a different diagnosis."

"'I persisted with my questions and asked him to tell me if he had discovered anything.

"'"Is it not plain even to a child," he said, "that her disorder is one of the soul and that we have here a clear case of love sickness? Can you not see the dark rings under her eyes, how restless her eyes are, how pale her

108. The line is quoted from *Iliad* 16.21, where Patroklos explains to Achilles the dire effects his refusal to fight is having on his Greek comrades. Charikleia, as an educated young lady, no doubt intends her hearers to recall this context.

109. The name is formed from the verb *akeisthai,* "to heal."

face is, although she does not complain of any internal pain? Her concentration wanders; she says the first thing that comes into her head; she is suffering from an inexplicable insomnia, and has suddenly lost her self-confidence. There is only one person that can cure her, Charikles, and that is the man she loves. He is the one you must find."

"'With these words he took his leave, but I have run to you as fast as I could. You are my savior, my god! Even Charikleia recognizes that you are the one person who can assist us. I implored her, I entreated her to tell me what was wrong, but only one thing did she reply: she did not know what was wrong, but she did know that only Kalasiris could cure her. She begged me to summon you to her side. From which, more than from anything else, I deduced that she has succumbed to your powers.'

"'So, we know she is in love,' I replied, 'but can you say with whom?'

"'No, by Apollo!' he replied. 'How could I know that? Who could have told me? But more than all the world I pray that she is in love with Alkamenes, my sister's son, who is the husband I chose for her many years ago, insofar as it is a matter for my choosing.'

"I said that he could easily put his hopes to the test by taking the young man to visit her and letting her see him. The suggestion met with his approval, and off he went. Later I met him again, at the time when the marketplace is full.[110]

"'I have distressing news for you,' he said. 'I think my child must be possessed, she is behaving so queerly. I took Alkamenes to see her, as you suggested, and presented him to her looking his best. But it was as if she had seen the Gorgon's head or something even more horrible. With a piercing scream she averted her eyes to the other side of the room and fastened her hands around her neck like a noose, threatening and swearing to do away with herself unless we went away instantly. We left her more quickly than it takes to tell; what else were we to do in the face of such extraordinary conduct? For a second time I come to you on bended knee. Do not leave her to die and me to be cheated of my heart's desire.'

"'Charikles,' I replied, 'you were quite correct when you said that she is possessed, for she is beset by powers that I myself called down upon her, powers not inconsiderable but strong enough to compel her to act in a way contrary to both her nature and her wishes. There must be a divine counter-power blocking my efforts and combating the spirits that are in my service. So, now or never, you must show me the band that you said was abandoned with the child and passed on to you along with the other tokens of recognition. You see, I fear that it may be steeped in

110. A fairly standard way of indicating the hours before midday, when trade was conducted.

sorcery of some kind, that it may be inscribed with occult spells that are enraging her soul. Perhaps some enemy schemed at her birth that she should live a life without love and die without child.'

8    "Charikles agreed and soon returned with the band. I said I needed peace and quiet, which I persuaded him to allow me; then I returned to my lodgings, where, without a moment's delay, I began to read the band—it was embroidered in the Ethiopian script, not the demotic variety but the royal kind, which closely resembles the so-called hieratic script of Egypt.[111] As I perused the document I discovered that it contained the following narrative.

> I, Persinna, Queen of the Ethiopians, inscribe this record of woe as a final gift to my daughter, mine only in the pain of her birth, by whatever name she may be called.

I froze at the mention of Persinna's name, Knemon, but nevertheless I continued reading. This is what came next.

> That it was not from guilt, my child, that I exposed you at birth as I did and concealed all sight of you from your father, Hydaspes, I swear as the Sun, the founder of our race, is my witness. Nevertheless, I here one day plead my case before you, my daughter, if you live, before the man who saves your life, if heaven vouchsafe you a deliverer, and before the whole human race, by revealing my reason for abandoning you.
>
> Our line descends from the Sun and Dionysos among gods and from Perseus and Andromeda[112] and from Memnon[113] too among heroes. Those who in the course of time came to build the royal palace decorated it with scenes from the stories of these figures: they painted the likenesses and exploits of the others in the men's quarters and the colonnades, but made use of the romance of Perseus and Andromeda to adorn the bedchambers. It was there one day that your father and I happened to be taking a siesta in the drowsy heat of summer. Ten years had passed since Hydaspes

111. According to Herodotos (2.36), the Egyptians had two kinds of writing, sacred and demotic. Diodoros (3.3) adds that in Egypt only members of the priesthood could read the sacred script, whereas everyone in Ethiopia could. The Meroitic peoples of Ethiopia did in fact use two kinds of script, one an adaptation of Egyptian hieroglyphs to their own language, the other a stylized, cursive form that would have been indecipherable to an Egyptian. The latter, however, simply evolved over time from the former and was not reserved for special groups or contexts.

112. Perseus married Andromeda, the daughter of King Kepheus of Ethiopia, after rescuing her from a sea monster.

113. Son of the goddess Dawn (Eos) by Tithonos, and king of Ethiopia. This is a vestige of an archaic view of the world that located the Ethiopians to the east, near the rising sun, which was responsible for their blackened skins (Ethiopian means "scorched-face"). As the Greeks learned more of the real world, these mythical Ethiopians were increasingly identified with the negroid peoples of sub-Saharan Africa, and the eastern legends were transferred to the south.

made me his wife, and still no child had been born to us. But that day your father made love to me, swearing that he was commanded to do so by a dream, and I knew instantly that the act of love had left me pregnant.

The time before the birth was a period of universal celebration and sacrifices of thanksgiving to the gods, for the king hoped for an heir to continue his line. But you, the child I bore, had a skin of gleaming white, something quite foreign to Ethiopians. I knew the reason: during your father's intimacy with me the painting had presented me with the image of Andromeda, who was depicted stark naked, for Perseus was in the very act of releasing her from the rocks, and had unfortunately shaped the embryo to her exact likeness.[114] I was convinced that your color would lead to my being accused of adultery, for what had happened was so fantastic that no one would believe my explanation. So I decided to save myself from a dishonorable death and to do you the kindness of laying you on fortune's uncertain mercies, which were preferable to certain death or, at best, the stigma of illegitimacy. I lied to my husband that you had died at birth, and, in the utmost secrecy, I laid you by the roadside.[115] Beside you I laid as much wealth as I could afford as a reward to the person who saved your life; but chief among the treasures with which I bedecked you was this band that I wrapped around you, the history of your sorrow and mine, written in the blood and tears shed for you by a mother whose first childbearing was the occasion of such grief.

But, my beloved, my daughter of an hour, if you live, be sure not to forget your royal blood. Honor chastity: it is the sole mark of virtue in a woman. Maintain the demeanor of a princess in memory of those who gave you life. Above all, be sure to find among the treasures that I laid beside you a certain ring. Keep it by you always: it was a gift that your father gave me during our courtship, engraved all around with the royal crest and set with a pantarbe jewel[116] that endows it with holy, mystic powers.

This message was the only way I could find to convey all this to you, since heaven has robbed me of your living presence and the

114. This theory of "maternal impression," whereby images seen by the mother were imprinted on her unborn child, was widely recognized by Greek (and later) medical writers. Andromeda, though an Ethiopian princess, was usually depicted with white skin (see Achilles Tatius 3.7; Philostratos *Imagines* 1.29), a sign that the myth was localized in Africa only at a comparatively late stage.

115. It was common for embarrassing, defective, or unwanted (usually female) children to be exposed and left either to die or be rescued. Tokens might be left with them as a reward for anyone who saved the child's life and to allow identification later. The unexpected recognition of abandoned children is a staple of the plots of New Comedy.

116. A precious stone, red in color, impossible to identify. Various magic powers are ascribed to it by various writers. The name *pantarbe* literally means "all-fear."

opportunity to tell you to your face. Perhaps my story will remain unread and useless, but perhaps it will one day work to your advantage. The secrets of fortune cannot be read by men. If you live, my child whose futile beauty served only to expose me to false allegations, what I have written will be a token of your recognition; but if that occurs which I pray never to hear of, then it will take the place of a mother's tears and sorrow at your graveside.

9     "On reading this, Knemon, I perceived the hand of the gods and marveled at the subtlety of their governance. I was filled with a mixture of pleasure and sadness and had the peculiar experience of being moved simultaneously to joy and tears. My heart was thankful that the mystery had been explained, that the riddle of the oracle had been solved, but it was sorely troubled about the course the future might take and filled with pity for the life of man, whose instability and insecurity, whose constant changes of direction were made all too manifest in the story of Charikleia. My mind was filled with the contemplation of many things: whose child she was and whose she had passed for, how far from the land of her birth her exile had brought her, and how she was called the daughter of a man who was not her father after losing her legitimate place in the royal family of Ethiopia. For a long time I stood there, torn between pity for past sorrows and despair for future happiness, until, clearing my mind of such intoxicating thoughts, I decided to set to work to do what I had to do. I went to Charikleia, whom I found alone. She had now ceased to fight her passion, for struggle as she might mentally, her physical distress was too great, her body having quite succumbed to

10 the disease and being now too weak to resist the pain. I ordered her attendants out of the room with instructions that no one was to disturb us, as I was going to employ certain prayers and invocations on the girl.

"'Well, Charikleia,' I said, 'the time has come for you to tell me what is wrong with you, for that was what you promised yesterday. You must stop hiding the truth from one who cares about you and has the power to know everything even if you refuse to speak.'

"She took my hand, kissed it; her tears fell on it. 'Wise Kalasiris,' she said, 'let this be the first kindness you do me. Diagnose my sickness how you will, but do not force me to speak of my distress; allow me at least to spare myself dishonor by concealing that which it is shameful to suffer but even more shameful to divulge. Although I am caused great pain by the malady which is now at its height, I am caused even more pain by not having overcome that malady at the outset, but having instead succumbed to a passion whose temptations I had hitherto always resisted, and the very mention of which is an affront to the august name of virginity.'

"'My daughter,' I said reassuringly, 'for two reasons you are right not to speak of your plight: there is no need for you to tell me what my science told me long ago, and it is quite natural that you should blush to speak of something that it is more seemly for women to conceal. But now that you have had a taste of love, and Theagenes has captured your heart at first sight—this was revealed to me by a voice from heaven—you must realize that you are not the first or the only woman ever to have experienced this pain; it has been felt by many noble ladies and many maidens who were otherwise paragons of virtue. Love is the greatest of the gods, and stories are told that on occasion he masters even gods. You must consider how to make the best of your situation: never to have felt love's touch is a blessing, but once caught it is wisest to keep one's thoughts on paths of virtue. If you are willing to believe this, you may rid yourself of this slur of carnal desire and make your objective the lawful contract of wedlock, so transforming your malady into matrimony.'

"At these words, Knemon, rivers of perspiration began to run down her face, and there could be no doubt that she was prey to all kinds of emotion: joy for what she heard, anguish for what she hoped, shame for what had been detected in her. A long silence; then she said, 'Father, you speak of marriage, and urge me to make that my aim, as if we could be sure either that my father would consent or that my adversary would reciprocate.'

"'As far as the young man is concerned,' I replied, 'we need have no fears. His feelings are identical to yours, and if anything, he is even deeper in love's power than you are. The moment you set eyes on each other, it seems, your souls in some way recognized partners worthy of one another and were affected in precisely the same way. I have played my part too, because of the love I bear you, by using my science to intensify his desire. But your supposed father has another husband in mind for you—Alkamenes, with whom you are not unacquainted.'

"'As for Alkamenes, I had rather my father had my death in mind than my marriage to him,' she exclaimed. 'If I cannot be Theagenes' wife, then I shall go to my fated end! But please tell me how you discovered that Charikles is not really my father, merely supposed so.'

"'From this,' I said, holding up the band.

"'How did you come by that? Who gave it you? After he took me from my guardian in Egypt, however it was done, and brought me here, he took that band from me and ever since has kept it locked away in a casket to protect it from the ravages of time.'

"'How I came by it,' I replied, 'I shall tell you later. For the moment tell me whether you know what is written on it.'

"She replied that, obviously, she did not.

"'It contains the truth about your birth, your nationality, and your station,' I said.

"She begged me to reveal all I knew, so I told her everything, reading through the document in detail and translating it word by word.

12    "When she learned who she was, a pride befitting her birth was awakened in her. She ran to embrace me and asked, 'What should I do?'

"At last the moment had come for me to drop my pretense and offer her my counsel in earnest. I concealed nothing from her.

"'My daughter,' I said, 'my travels took me as far as the land of the Ethiopians, whose wisdom I was eager to learn. There I met your mother, Persinna, for the royal court is ever the home of wise men, and I was held in particular honor for bringing about the apotheosis of the wisdom of Egypt by supplementing it with the wisdom of Ethiopia.[117] When Persinna saw that I was about to depart for home, she told me the whole of your story, having first sworn me to secrecy. She did not dare speak to the wise men of her own land, she said, but begged me to ask the gods first whether you had been rescued after she abandoned you, and then where in the world you might be; for despite searching far and wide she had not been able to discover anyone of your description in Ethiopia.

"'From the gods I learned the whole truth, and I told Persinna both that you were alive and where you were living, whereupon she renewed her pleas for me to search you out and persuade you to return to the land of your birth, for, she said, since the pains of your birth she had lived a sterile and childless existence and was ready, if ever you were found, to confess to your father what had occurred; she was sure that he would believe her as the long years of their life together had given him ample proof of her virtue and because his wish for a child to succeed him was being so unexpectedly granted.

13    "'Such was the favor Persinna begged of me, calling upon me repeatedly to undertake this mission in the name of the Sun, an oath which any wise man is duty-bound to respect. So I have come here to do as she implored me to do, in discharge of my sworn undertaking. Although this was not the reason for my eagerness to visit Delphi, it is a substantial compensation for my banishment, set in store for me by the gods. As you are aware, I have been dancing attendance on you for some time, and all that time I have never omitted to pay you the respect that is your due. But I have kept the truth secret, biding my time for the right moment, waiting until, one way or another, I could get hold of the band to confirm the truth of what I had to tell you. So, if only you will put your

117. Philostratos (*Life of Apollonios* 6.6) says that the wisdom of the sages of Ethiopia surpassed that of the Egyptians, though it fell short of that of the Indians.

trust in me and join me in getting away from here before you are compelled to submit to something distasteful—for Charikles has set his heart
on marrying you to Alkamenes—you may be restored to your kinsfolk,
to your homeland, to your parents, and be wedded to Theagenes, who is
ready to follow us wherever in the world we choose to go. Thus you
may exchange the life of an outcast in a foreign land for the throne that is
yours by right, where you will reign with your beloved at your side—
that is, if one is to put any trust in the gods, in particular in the oracle of
Pythian Apollo.'

"And then I reminded her of the oracle and explained what it meant.
It was very familiar to Charikleia, for many were reciting it and trying to
interpret it. She froze at my words.

"'You say that this is the gods' will,' she said, 'and I believe you. So
what am I to do, Father?'

"'Pretend to consent to marry Alkamenes,' I told her.

"'It is hard, even repugnant, to so much as speak of preferring another
to Theagenes,' she said, 'but since I have put myself in your hands and
the gods', tell me what is the purpose of the deceit, and how will it be
prevented from being made reality?'

"'Events will reveal all,' I replied. 'When a plan is disclosed to a
woman in advance, it can sometimes cause her alarm, and often an enterprise is executed more boldly if it is carried through without forethought.
Just do as I say: in particular, in the present instance you must go along
with Charikles' plans for your wedding; everything he has done has been
with my guidance.' She gave me her word and was in tears as I left.

"Scarcely had I left the house when I saw Charikles, looking exceed- 14
ingly unhappy and thoroughly dejected.

"'What a strange man you are,' I said to him. 'This is a time when
you should be wearing garlands in your hair and joyfully offering
sacrifices of thanksgiving to the gods. Your constant prayer has been
granted! It needed a great deal of my magic art, but at long last Charikleia's resolve is broken, and she desires to marry. Yet, at the very moment of triumph, here you are, gloomy and glum and almost in tears for
some reason or other.'

"'Of course I am in tears,' he replied, 'when my darling daughter is
possibly about to depart this life rather than enter into marriage, as you
claim—at least if one is to pay any heed to dreams, in particular those
that struck such fear into me last night. I dreamed that an eagle, released
from the hand of Pythian Apollo, suddenly swooped down and, alas,
snatched my poor daughter from my arms and flew off with her to one
of the world's remotest extremities, a place teeming with dark and shadowy phantoms. I do not know what he did to her in the end, for my vi-

sion was obstructed from keeping pace with the bird's flight by the immensity of space between us.'

15    "The import of the dream he described was clear, but in an effort to dispel his despondency and deflect him from any intimation of what was to ensue I said: 'For a priest, and the priest of the god with the greatest powers of prophecy at that, you strike me as a pretty poor interpreter of dreams, if, when your dreams foretell your child's coming marriage by using the eagle to symbolize the bridegroom who will take her from you and give you the glad assurance that this will come to pass (for Pythian Apollo signifies his approval and, so to speak, produces her future husband from his hand), you are nevertheless distressed by your vision and force a pessimistic interpretation on your dream. Therefore, Charikles, let us keep our tongues from words of ill omen and comply with the will of the gods by redoubling our efforts to win the girl round by persuasion.'

"He asked what he should do to make her more compliant, and I replied: 'If you have a valuable heirloom, such as a robe woven with gold thread or a necklace of precious stones, present it to her as a wedding gift from her bridegroom and soften Charikleia's heart with this present. Gold and jewels exert an irresistible spell on women. And you must complete all the other arrangements for the ceremony; the wedding must be held before the effect of my magic in forcibly arousing the girl's desire can wear off.'

" 'You can be sure that I shall play my part,' said Charikles and hurried away, his joy so great that he could not wait to act upon my suggestion. I learned afterward that in fact he lost no time in doing as I had advised, and presented Charikleia, under the guise of wedding gifts from Alkamenes, with the Ethiopian necklaces that Persinna had laid beside her to prove her identity.

16    "Then I found Theagenes and asked him where his fellow participants in the procession were lodging. He replied that the girls were already on their way home; being unable to make such good speed, they had been sent on ahead; the young men too were homesick and becoming importunate in their demands to be homeward bound. On hearing this, I instructed him what to tell them and what steps to take himself and told him to watch until I gave him a sign that the time had come. Then I took my leave of him and hurried to the temple of Pythian Apollo to entreat the god to make known to me in an oracle how I was to make my getaway with the young couple.

"But, as ever, the divine had outrun any human wit. Heaven speeds those enterprises that are according to its will, and frequently in its benevolence grants our prayers before we have had time to form them. So it was then. Before I could pose my question, Pythian Apollo gave

*Kalasiris uses religion as a band yet is he a v. religious man?*

me a response and made his guidance manifest in events. With no thought for anything but the cares that were weighing on my mind, I was, as I said, hastening to consult the prophetess when I was halted in my tracks by a voice.

"'Join our libations, sir!' called a group of strangers, who were offering a festal sacrifice to Herakles, to the accompaniment of flute music. On hearing this, I checked my haste, for it would have been wrong for me to pass by and ignore a religious summons. I took incense and offered it in sacrifice, then poured a libation of water; the strangers seemed taken aback by the lavish scale of my oblations,[118] but nevertheless they invited me to join them in their feast. Again I complied, and lay down on the couch which they had strewn with myrtle and laurel in honor of their guests. Having partaken of my usual food and drink, I said to them, 'My friends, I have no lack of most excellent food, but I still have no information about you; so it is time for you to tell me who you are and where you are from, for I think it is vulgar and the height of bad manners to join someone's libations and share his table, to sprinkle the sacred salt that is the seed of friendship, and then to depart without even an exchange of introductions.'

"They replied that they were Phoenicians from Tyre, merchants by trade, sailing to Carthage in Libya[119] with an argosy of merchandise from India and Ethiopia, as well as Phoenicia. At the moment they were celebrating this victory feast in honor of Herakles of Tyre,[120] for this young fellow—indicating the man reclining at the head of the table—had been awarded the victor's crown in the wrestling competition at the games here, and so, through him, Tyre had won a resounding victory on Greek ground.

"'We ran into contrary winds as we rounded Cape Malea,'[121] they continued, 'and had to put in at Kephallenia, where this fellow swore that this ancestral god of ours appeared to him in a dream and predicted his coming victory in the Pythian Games. He persuaded us to turn aside from the course we had laid and land here; and now his success has proved the prophecy correct, and he, who before this day was a mere merchant, is now proclaimed a champion of high renown. He is celebrat-

---

118. Sarcastic, of course. Kalasiris, as we have seen, abstains on religious grounds from animal sacrifice and libations of wine.

119. Originally a Phoenician trading colony founded from Tyre, with which it retained strong links throughout its history.

120. The Phoenician god Melkart, venerated in Tyre, was identified with the Greek Herakles.

121. The southeastern promontory of the Peloponnese, notorious for its changeable winds. The Phoenicians had been unable to make progress westwards and had obviously hugged the coast until they reached the island of Kephallenia at the mouth of the Corinthian Gulf, through which they would have easy access to Delphi.

ing this sacrifice in honor of the god who revealed the future to him, a sacrifice of victory and thanksgiving, but also of departure, for we mean to set sail at dawn, my friend, if the direction of the winds is the same as that of our intentions.'

"'Is that really what you mean to do?' I asked.

"'Indeed it is,' they replied.

"'Then, if you will allow me, I shall travel with you. I have to go to Sicily on business, and, as you know, the quickest route to Libya will take you close by that island.'

"'If you will consent to come with us,' they replied, 'then we shall think our happiness complete, for we shall have the company of a man who is wise, a Greek, and also perhaps, to judge from our short acquaintance, a favorite of the gods.'

"'I shall be pleased to come with you,' I said, 'if you will allow me one day to make ready.'

"'We shall let you have tomorrow,' they said, 'only you must be down by the sea by evening without fail, for there is much to be said for setting sail at night, when the land breezes still the waves and speed vessels on their way.'

"I agreed to do as they asked, having first been given their sworn word that they would not put out to sea before the agreed hour. And so I left them there, still enjoying their music and dancing, which consisted of cavorting to a gay tune played by the pipes in the Assyrian style: at one moment they would leap nimbly high into the air, the next squat on their haunches close to the ground, spinning and whirling their entire bodies like dervishes.

"After leaving them I went to pay a call on Charikleia, whom I found staring at Charikles' treasures, which still lay in her lap, and after her on Theagenes. I told each of them what was to be done and when; then I returned home and awaited events. The next day the following incident occurred: in the middle of the night, when the city was immersed in sleep, an armed band of revelers stormed Charikleia's house. The commander in this campaign of love was Theagenes, who had formed the young men from the procession into a squadron of soldiers. With a sudden outburst of loud shouting they banged their shields, which filled all who heard anything at all of the noise with terror. They had no difficulty in forcing the gate to the courtyard, for the bolts had been tampered with so that it could be opened easily. Torches ablaze, they burst into Charikleia's room and snatched her away. She submitted willingly to this violent assault, which came as no surprise to her, for she knew in advance exactly what was to take place. They also made off with such items as the girl wished to take with her, not a few. Once outside the house, they raised their battle cry and clattered their shields with a fearful din, then ran the length and breadth of the town, arousing in the inhabitants a terror beyond the power of words to describe: they had chosen to act at the dead of night precisely so as to cause greater alarm, and the echoes of Parnassos[122] redoubled their cries and the din of clanging bronze. And as they ran through the streets of Delphi, endlessly in turn they cried aloud the name of Charikleia.

"When they were outside the town, they rode off as fast as they could go towards the mountains of Lokris and Oita. But Theagenes and Charikleia, in pursuance of our preconcerted plan, did not accompany the Thessalians; instead, taking care not to be seen, they made their way to seek refuge with me. Together they fell at my feet and for some length of time clasped my knees, trembling and quaking and intoning over and again, 'Save us, Father!' That was all that Charikleia could say; her head was bowed, and she was overcome by shame at the extraordinary events that had just taken place.

"Theagenes, however, had further entreaties to make. 'Save us, Kalasiris,' he said. 'We come to you in supplication, strangers in a foreign land, with no home to go to, who have lost everything in order to win one another, the only thing in the world that we desire. Save us! Now our persons are mortgaged to fortune, bound by the chains of a chaste love, cast into an exile self-imposed but innocent. On you depends our only hope of deliverance.'

"His words made my heart bleed. I shed an inward tear for my young friends, a tear of the mind rather than of the eyes, to them invisible, but to me a relief in my sorrow. I raised them to their feet and tried to comfort them, holding out high hopes for the future, for our enterprise had been started with divine blessing.

"'I must go and see to the next stage of our plan,' I said. 'Stay here and wait for me and make absolutely sure that no one sees you.'

"With these words I began to hurry away, but Charikleia seized my cloak and held it tight.

"'Father,' she said, 'it will be the beginning of iniquity, or should I say betrayal, if you go off and leave me alone in Theagenes' care, without stopping to think what an untrustworthy guardian a lover makes when he has the object of his desires in his power, particularly when those who could touch his sense of shame are elsewhere. The flames of his passion burn higher, I think, when he sees his beloved defenseless, with none to protect her. So I shall not let you go until I have Theagenes' sworn word as a guarantee of my safety both on this occasion and, even more importantly, in the future. Let him swear that he will have no carnal knowledge of me before I regain my home and people; or else, if heaven

122. The mountain above Delphi.

prevents this, that he will make me his wife with my full consent or not at all.'

"I found this speech quite admirable and decided without demur that it should be done as she asked. I lit a fire in the grate to serve as an altar and made an offering of incense, after which Theagenes swore his oath, protesting that it was not fair that by a preemptive oath aspersions should be cast on his probity of character before it could be put to the test; he would not be able to display the power of moral choice, for people would think that he was acting under the compulsion of fear of heaven's wrath. Nonetheless, he swore by Pythian Apollo, by Artemis, by Aphrodite herself and her Erotes,[123] that he would in all things do exactly as Charikleia willed and bade him.

19 "While they were calling upon the gods to witness these and certain other vows, I hastened to Charikles and arrived to find the house full of commotion and lamentation. Servants had already brought Charikles the news of his daughter's abduction, and a throng of townspeople had also gathered and was pressing around Charikles in his grief, uncertain what had happened and unsure what to do next.

"'My poor friends,' I shouted, 'how long will you sit here like dummies, saying nothing, doing nothing, as if in this calamity your wits had been stolen too? Will you not take up arms and set off in pursuit of the foe? Will you not apprehend and punish those who have perpetrated this outrage?'

"'There is probably no point,' replied Charikles, 'in trying to do anything about this situation. I see now that this is a punishment imposed by the gods' wrath: once I entered the inner shrine before the proper time, and my eyes beheld that which it is a sin to behold; on that day Apollo foretold that this would come to pass, that in requital for seeing that which ought not to be seen I should be deprived of the sight of that which I loved most. Nonetheless, there is nothing to stop us taking up arms even in the face of divinity, as the saying goes,[124] if only we knew whom to pursue, who is responsible for this appalling act of violence.'

"'It was that Thessalian you thought so much of,' I replied, 'whose friendship you tried to thrust on me too. It was Theagenes and his young companions. Until last night they were visitors to your town, but you

---

123. Personifications of love (*eros*), usually conceived as small children, like Roman Cupids. All the gods named have some interest in the matter: Apollo as overseer of Delphi and the games and giver of the oracle; Artemis as Charikleia's patron and also as protector of chastity; Aphrodite as personification of the force that might lead Theagenes to act in a way distressing to Charikleia.

124. *Iliad* 17.103–4, where Menelaos, forced to retire from Patroklos's body by Hektor, who has Apollo's assistance, says that if Aias were at hand, he would be prepared to confront the god.

will not find a single one of them there now. On your feet, then, and call a meeting of the people!'

"And that is what he did. The chief magistrates proclaimed a special session of the assembly, and the proclamation was made known to the town by the sound of a trumpet. No sooner was this done than the populace gathered, and the theater became a midnight council chamber. Charikles stepped forward. The mere sight of him at once moved the crowd to tears, wrapped as he was in a black cloak, his head and face smothered with dust and ashes. This is what he said.

"'Men of Delphi, I have suffered more than one man can bear, and this may lead you to think that I have called this assembly and come before you to announce my intention to end my life. But it is not so. True, I suffer enough misfortunes to die many times over; I am alone in the world and under god's curse; my home is now a mere shell, emptied of all the loved ones who shared it with me. All the same, hope, vain hope, the deceiver of all humankind, whispers to me that there is a chance that my daughter may yet be found, and so seduces me into perservering. But the main reason for my continuing to live is this city: I shall not die until I have seen her exact retribution from those who have so wickedly wronged her—unless of course those Thessalian puppies have also robbed you of that pride that tolerates no master and your sense of outrage on behalf of the land of your birth and gods of your fathers. The hardest thing to stomach is that a handful of dancing boys in the service of the sacred mission should with impunity have trampled underfoot the foremost city of Greece and robbed the temple of Pythian Apollo of its most priceless treasure—Charikleia (alas!), the light of my life. How mercilessly heaven hounds me! You know how it extinguished the life of my first child, my own true daughter, along with the light of her wedding torches, how it snatched away her mother to join her before my pain had had time to heal, and banished me from the land of my birth. But after I found Charikleia it was all bearable. Charikleia was my life, my hope, the continuation of my line; Charikleia was all I had to console me, a sort of anchor to hold me fast. But now this anchor has been shorn away and swept aside by this tide of misery; whatever the truth behind it, that is my lot; once again, with fiendish subtlety, it has chosen the cruelest time to make me its plaything, not at a random moment, but from her very bridal chamber, more or less, when her forthcoming marriage had just been made public to you all.'

"He abandoned himself to his grief, but before he could finish what he had to say, he was interrupted by Hegesias,[125] the chief magistrate, who

20

125. The name is derived from the verb *hegeisthai*, "to lead."

thrust him aside and said: 'Gentlemen, Charikles may lament now and hereafter, but let us not drown in the sea of his grief and find ourselves carried along by the current of his tears and thus passing up the time for action, something which is of decisive importance in all things, especially in war. If we leave this assembly now, there is a chance of catching our enemies while they are proceeding with little sense of urgency, secure in the belief that we shall have to make preparations for pursuit. But if by succumbing to self-pity—or should I say by behaving like women—we allow them a greater start through our indecisiveness, then we must inevitably be made a laughingstock, and, what is worse, at the hands of mere striplings. I say we should apprehend them as quickly as may be, impale them alive, and then extend our vengeance to their offspring by stripping their descendants of their privileges. This could easily be done if we can excite the indignation of the Thessalians against any of these miscreants who might escape us, and against their descendants, by passing a decree banning them from taking part in the sacred mission and the propitiation of the hero, and resolving to bear the cost of this ceremony from our own exchequer.'

21  "Even before the applause that greeted this proposal had died away, even while it was still being ratified by popular vote, the chief magistrate said: 'Here is another proposal to vote on, if you will: the holy acolyte should no longer display the torch to those who are competing in the race in armor, for it is my guess that this was the flame that kindled Theagenes' wickedness. Apparently he conceived the idea of abducting her at the very first sight of her. We should do well to eliminate for all time the possibility of anyone ever committing such an act again.'[126]

"Everyone raised their hands, and this motion too was passed unanimously. Then Hegesias gave the signal to commence the expedition, the trumpet sounded a call to arms, and the audience left the theater to go to war; no one could have stopped them as they rushed out of the assembly and into battle. It was not only those of the strength and age to bear arms who went, but a number of children and lads barely out of childhood, making up in zeal what they lacked in years, were bold enough to take part in this expedition. Many women too had men's hearts, despite their sex; they seized whatever came to hand as a weapon and ran after the men, but to no avail, for they could not keep up and had to admit the inherent weakness of the female sex. You would have seen old men too, fighting against age, sheer willpower dragging their bodies along, their zeal railing against their decrepitude. Thus the whole city smarted under the affront of Charikleia's abduction, and a single pain stirred the hearts

126. There is no evidence that the priestess of Artemis was in reality expected to attend the games as Charikleia did. This decree has the effect of providing an aetiology for the usual practice, which might have been familiar to Heliodoros's readers.

of all her citizens. There and then, without even waiting for the day to dawn, Delphi launched itself in a mass pursuit.

## Book Five

"Such was the state of affairs in Delphi: they did what they did, but what it was I have no idea. The hue and cry they raised was my cue for flight; so, collecting the young couple, I took them down to the sea, dead of night though it was, and there I put them aboard the Phoenician ship, which was on the very point of casting off, for as the first glimmer of daybreak was at that moment beginning to light the sky, the Phoenicians considered that they had kept their oath to me, having pledged themselves to wait just one day and one night. They greeted our arrival most joyfully and without further ado cleared the harbor, making way under oar to begin with. But when a gentle breeze began to blow off the land, and a low swell started to run under the ship, splashing merrily against her stern, then they stopped rowing and allowed the vessel to proceed under sail. The Gulf of Kirrha, the foothills of Parnassos, the headlands of Aitolia and Kalydon, slipped past as the ship sped by like a bird in flight, and just as the sun was setting, the Oxeiai—the Pointed Islands, whose name describes their appearance—and the Sea of Zakynthos came into view.

"But what am I doing prolonging my tale further at this time of night? Here I am without thinking literally launching my narrative upon a vast sea of ensuing events! Let us break the story at this point and snatch a little sleep. However indefatigable a listener you may be, Knemon, however valiantly you may resist sleep, I think that even you must be wilting by now, for my tale of woe has dragged on far into the night. And I for my part am beginning to feel the burden of my years, my son; and the remembrance of my sorrows numbs my heart and lulls it to sleep."

"Stop then, Father," said Knemon, "though not because I want no more of your story. I do not think that would ever happen, even if you were to go on telling it for dozens of nights and scores of days without a break, for like the Sirens' song it only leaves one hungry for more. But for some time a sort of noise and hubbub of many voices in the house has been ringing in my ears, but though I was somewhat alarmed, I forced myself to say nothing, for my desire to go on hearing what you had to tell me next was irresistible."

"I heard nothing," said Kalasiris, "possibly because the years have dimmed my hearing—for age affects the ears particularly—perhaps also because I had thoughts for nothing but my story. Nausikles, the master of the house, must be back. How has he made out, by heaven?"

"Exactly as I hoped," said Nausikles, appearing suddenly in the room. "Your interest in my undertaking was obvious, my dear Kalasiris, and I could see that in spirit you were with me on my quest; this was apparent from your whole attitude towards me, and the words I caught you speaking just now as I came in confirm it. But who is this stranger?"

"A Greek," replied Kalasiris. "I shall tell you all about him later. But make haste and tell me whether you have had any success, so that we can share your happiness."

"I shall tell you everything in the morning," said Nausikles. "For tonight suffice it to say that Thisbe is mine, but better than before. Now I am fatigued from my journey and by everything else on my mind. I must sleep awhile and refresh myself."

2      With these words Nausikles bustled off to do as he had said he would do. Knemon, however, had been stunned to hear Thisbe's name; he racked his brains in bewilderment and despair to make sense of it; sigh after heavy sigh he sighed, and the rest of the night was a torment to him, so that in the end even Kalasiris, despite having been in a deep sleep, became aware of his distress. The old man raised himself up and, leaning on one elbow, asked Knemon what was wrong with him and what was the reason for his tossing and turning in such an extraordinary manner that he seemed for all the world like a madman.

"I am mad; I must be" replied Knemon. "I have heard that Thisbe is still alive."

"Who is Thisbe?" asked Kalasiris. "How do you come to recognize her name, and why does the news that she is alive cause you such distress?"

"You will hear all about her one day when I tell you my story," said Knemon, "but the point is that with my own eyes I saw and recognized her lifeless body, and with my own hands I buried her on the Herdsmen's island."

"Go to sleep," said Kalasiris. "We shall not have long to wait to learn the truth of this matter."

"I could not," replied Knemon. "You stay here and rest, but I shall surely die if I do not slip out here and now and discover somehow or other what this delusion might be to which Nausikles has fallen victim, or how it is that Egypt is the only place on earth where the dead come back to life."

This drew a little smile from Kalasiris, who then returned to his slumbers. Knemon left the room and, considering that he was lost in a strange house at night, with no light, had exactly the kind of experience one might have expected. Nevertheless, so eager was he to allay the awful suspicion that Thisbe's name had stirred in him that he was prepared to face any ordeal. Eventually, after spending some time wandering round and round in circles in the mistaken belief that he was all the time exploring new places, he heard the sound of a woman's voice, softly and sadly sorrowing in the darkness, like a nightingale's song of grief in springtime.[127] Her lamentations guided his steps to her room, where he put his ear to the crack between the doors and listened. She was still pouring forth her sadness, and this is what he heard.

"My misery is complete! I thought that I had escaped from the clutches of robbers and eluded certain death by the sword, that I could live out the rest of my days in my beloved's company: it would have been a homeless life in foreign lands, but his presence would have made it the sweetest of all lives. There is no ordeal so terrible that, with him by my side, I could not face it. But now the spirit that from my birth has guided my destiny, its spite still unsatisfied, has given me a short taste of happiness, only to deceive me later. I thought that I had escaped slavery—and I am a slave once more. I thought that I had escaped my prison cell—and I am under lock and key again. I was imprisoned on an island, in a place without light; my present plight is identical, or, truth to tell, even more parlous, for I have lost the one person who had the power and the will to comfort me. Until today a robbers' cave was my dwelling place; a deep abyss, a veritable grave, my home. But my predicament was made easy by the presence of him whom I love more than all the world. There he grieved for me while I yet lived and wept for me when he thought me dead; he mourned me in the belief that I was slain, but now I am deprived even of that consolation; I have lost my comrade in adversity, who ever shared my burden of pain. I am alone and forsaken, a prisoner and full of grief, a victim of the whims of cruel fate. Indeed, my hope that my beloved yet lives is the only reason I have to endure life any longer. My heart, I wonder where you are, what fate awaited you. Perhaps you too are in slavery, alas!—you who were so singularly proud and free and acknowledged no master, save only Love. I pray only that you are alive and that one day you will see your Thisbe; for by that name must you call me, detest it as you may!"

This was more than Knemon could endure; having heard this much, he could not bring himself to stay and hear the rest of what she had to say. Although her first words had encouraged him to think otherwise, the latter part of her outpouring had convinced him that this was indeed Thisbe, and he very nearly fell into a swoon right there by the door. With a great effort he clung to consciousness, and, terrified that someone

127. King Tereus of Thrace raped Philomela, sister of his wife, Prokne, then cut her tongue out to prevent her telling. Prokne discovered the truth nonetheless and in revenge killed Itys, her son by Tereus, and served him cooked as a meal for his father. Tereus was metamorphosed into a hoopoe; Prokne, into a nightingale, which sings perpetually in sorrow for Itys.

might find him there, for the cocks were already crowing for the second time, he took to his heels, tripping and stumbling, blundering into walls and cracking his head time and again against door beams or such objects as were hanging from the roof, until, after taking many wrong turnings, he reached the room where he and Kalasiris were staying and there collapsed on his bed, shaking all over uncontrollably, his teeth chattering loudly. His very life might have been in danger, had not Kalasiris, seeing instantly that all was not well, brought him round by keeping him warm and speaking many a word of comfort to him. Knemon revived a little, and Kalasiris asked him why he was in such a state.

"I am done for," he replied. "Thisbe really is alive, damn her!"

4    With these words he lapsed back into unconsciousness, and once again Kalasiris's attempts to bring him back to life cost him much effort. In fact, however, a supernatural power, whose habit it is in general to make mock of all human life and use it as its plaything, was playing with Knemon and refusing to allow him great happiness without also making him feel some pain. In a short while Knemon was going to experience joy, which heaven therefore was now combining with sorrow, perhaps simply giving another demonstration of its habitual malice—though possibly human nature cannot admit of pure joy without a taint of sadness. Thus it was that that day Knemon was turning away in fear from that which he wanted above all else, and that that which was sweetest to him of all things caused him such terror. For the woman he had heard lamenting was not Thisbe, but Charikleia!

This is what had happened to her: after Thyamis had fallen into his enemies' hands and become their prisoner, and the island had been set alight and evacuated by the Herdsmen whose home it had been, Knemon and Thermouthis, Thyamis's henchman, sailed across the lake at dawn on a mission of reconnaissance to discover what the enemy had done with their captain; their adventures have already been narrated. Theagenes and Charikleia were left alone in the cave, but the extremity of their plight they counted the greatest boon. Now, for the first time, they were alone in one another's company with no one to interrupt them as they hugged and kissed to their heart's content with nothing to restrain or distract them. They instantly forgot their plight and clasped one another in a prolonged embrace so tight that they seemed to be of one flesh. But the love they consummated was sinless and undefiled; their union was one of moist, warm tears; their only intercourse was one of chaste lips. For if ever Charikleia found Theagenes becoming too ardent in the arousal of his manhood, a reminder of his oath was enough to restrain him; and he for his part moderated his conduct without complaint and was quite content to remain within the bounds of chastity, for though he was the slave of love, he was the master of pleasure.

But eventually they fell to thinking of what they should do, and reluctantly they had to consider their appetite for kisses satisfied. Theagenes was the first to speak.

"To live in union with one another, Charikleia, to possess that which we have come to value above all things and for which we have undergone so many travails, such is our prayer, which I pray the gods of Greece may grant. But the human condition is full of uncertainty and subject to constant change; we have endured much and can expect to endure more; now we are obliged to make our way to the village of Chemmis with all haste according to the promises we made Knemon, and what fate awaits us thereafter none can tell; a long and seemingly infinite distance still separates us from the land we hope to reach. Wherefore, come, let us agree upon some signs that will enable us to pass secret messages while we are together, and by which we may track one another down if ever it should happen that we are separated. For when one is on the road, a sign agreed with one's friends for the purpose of finding one another again is a very good thing to have in reserve."

This suggestion met with Charikleia's approval, and they decided, if they were parted, to scratch the following message on shrines, conspicuous statues, sculpted pillars,[128] or stones at crossroads: The Pythian (in the masculine form for Theagenes, the feminine for Charikleia) has gone to the right, or the left, in the direction of such and such a town or village or district, adding a precise indication of time and date. If they were reunited, it would be enough, they said, simply to lay eyes on one another, for all eternity would be too short a time to efface the tokens of recognition that love had engraved upon their hearts. Nevertheless, as a more tangible token Charikleia produced the ring from her father that had been exposed with her, and Theagenes showed her a scar on his knee that he had got hunting boar.[129] They also agreed upon certain verbal signs: Charikleia chose the word "torch;" Theagenes, "palm."[130]

Thereupon they began embracing one another again and weeping, as if (it seems to me) they were offering libations in their tears and swearing oaths in their kisses. Their plans laid, they left the cave. Of all the treasures that were stored there they touched nothing, for they considered riches acquired by robbery to be contaminated; the only items they put in their packs were those they themselves had brought from Delphi and

128. *Hermai,* stone pillars topped with a bust of Hermes and often adorned with a phallus.

129. This assimilates Theagenes to the second great epic hero, Odysseus, whose nurse, Eurykleia, recognizes him by a scar given him by a hunted boar, the acquisition of which is recounted in a lengthy and famous digression (*Odyssey* 19.392–475).

130. The two objects held by Charikleia on the occasion of their first kiss at the armored race at Delphi.

been robbed of by the bandits. Charikleia changed her clothes and stowed her necklace, crown, and sacred robe away in a small bag, concealing them beneath other objects of lesser value; her bow and quiver she handed to Theagenes to carry, a burden which gave him great joy, for the bow was the special attribute of the god they served.[131]

6 But just as they reached the lakeside and were about to climb into a small boat, they saw a large number of armed men coming across the water towards the island. Their heads swam with horror at the sight, and they stood rooted mutely to the spot, as if fortune's never-ending cruelty no longer had the power to hurt them. It was not until the attackers were virtually on the point of putting ashore that Charikleia finally began to urge Theagenes to make a run for it and hide in the cave in the hope of escaping detection. So saying, she began running, but Theagenes held her back and said: "How much longer shall we flee from a destiny that pursues us wherever we turn? Let us yield to fate! Let us embrace the current that sweeps us along! What do we have to lose? A life of exile and vagrancy! Heaven's incessant mockery! Can you not see the glee with which it forges the chain of our misfortune? After exile come pirates' dens, after the horrors of the sea come worse horrors by land, and in a moment after bandits will come war! A short time ago it held us captive, then it arranged for us to be alone and forsaken; it offered us deliverance and an escape to freedom, but now it has produced men to slay us. To wage this campaign against us is heaven's sport, as if our lives were a drama played on stage for its pleasure. So why do we not cut short its tragic plot and give ourselves up to those whose desire it is to kill us? Otherwise heaven in its desire to bring our play to a melodramatic conclusion may compel us to die by our own hands!"

7 Charikleia was not in total accord with what he said: fate was thoroughly deserving of his abuse, she said, but she could not support his suggestion that they should put themselves voluntarily into their enemies' hands, for they could not be sure that death would follow capture—the power against which they were struggling was not so kind as to permit them a swift release from their misfortunes; no, it was quite possible that the enemy would want to spare their lives and make them their slaves, a fate worse than any death; in which case, they faced the prospect of ill-treatment too appalling to name at the hands of barbarian cutthroats.

"This we must do our very utmost to avoid," she went on. "Our past experiences do offer us some hope of success, for on many occasions before now we have emerged unscathed from situations even more hopeless than this."

131. Apollo, the archer god.

"Let us do as you wish," replied Theagenes and followed reluctantly as Charikleia led the way. But it was too late! They were unable to reach the cave, for while their attention was fixed on those of their assailants in front of them, they were encircled from behind and trapped unawares by a detachment of the enemy that had landed on another part of the island. They were too dismayed to move; Charikleia ran to Theagenes' side so that if she had to die it would at least be in his arms. A couple of the attackers raised their arms to strike them dead, but when the young lovers turned their eyes towards them, their beauty so dazzled their assailants that their anger subsided and their arms dropped to their sides; for even the hand of a savage, it seems, is overawed by beauty; even the eye of a heathen is subdued by the sight of something so love-worthy.

So seizing Theagenes and Charikleia, they took them to their leader, most eager to be the first to bring him the finest piece of booty. In fact this was the only booty that they were to bring him, for no one found anything else, although they searched the length and breadth of the island, and armed men stood all around it like a circle of huntsmen's nets. It had been totally devastated by fire in the earlier fighting. The only thing left was the cave, which was a secret unknown to the newcomers. So Theagenes and Charikleia were brought before the commander, who was none other than Mitranes, the commander of guards in the service of Oroondates, the Great King's satrap in Egypt, who, as we have seen, had been paid a great deal of money by Nausikles to come to the island in search of Thisbe. At the sight of Theagenes and Charikleia being led past him, continually imploring the gods to deliver them, Nausikles, with his merchant's eye for profit, had a bold idea: he leaped to his feet and ran forward. "That's her! That's Thisbe!" he shouted at the top of his voice. "Those damned bandits took her from me, but now, thanks to the gods and to you, Mitranes, I have her back!"

He seized hold of Charikleia and was to all appearances overjoyed, but beneath his breath he whispered to her in Greek so that his companions would not know what he was saying, suggesting that if she wished her life to be spared, she should concur that she was Thisbe. The ruse worked. Hearing him speak Greek, Charikleia guessed that his ploy might work to her advantage and so connived in his scheme, so that when Mitranes asked her her name, she confirmed that she was called Thisbe. Thereupon Nausikles ran to Mitranes' side and showered his head with kisses. He professed great admiration for Mitranes' achievement: the success he had won in today's operation was, Nausikles suggested, outstanding even in his long record of military prowess. Nausikles' words made the barbarian swell with pride, and his compliments turned his head, so that the deception over the girl's name took him in completely. Even so, he was struck by her loveliness, which shone forth even in her shabby garments like a moonbeam from behind a cloud. However, the trick was too quick for his meager intelligence, and there was no time for second thoughts.

"She is yours. Take her away," he said. And with these words he handed her over to Nausikles, though the way he stared at her so fixedly was ample proof that he was parting with the girl reluctantly and only because he had already accepted payment for her. "But this man, whoever he is"—he was referring to Theagenes—"is to be my prize. Put him under guard and let him come with me. He will be sent up country to Babylon, for he is fit to wait at the Great King's table!"

9    Following this exchange they rowed back across the lake and took their leave of one another. Nausikles went on to Chemmis with Charikleia, while Mitranes took a different road leading towards other settlements subject to him and wasted no time in sending Theagenes, together with a letter, to Oroondates, who was at Memphis. This was the text of the letter.

> Mitranes the Commander of Guards to Oroondates the Satrap. I am sending you a young Greek I have taken prisoner. He is too handsome to remain in my service, too excellent to come before or wait upon anyone but his Divine Majesty, the King of Kings. I humbly accept that you should have the honor of conveying to him who is master of us both a gift of such value and splendor, a jewel the like of which the royal court has never beheld before and will never behold again.

10    Such was his letter, but at the very crack of dawn Kalasiris went with Knemon to find Nausikles, eager for information. He asked Nausikles what success he had had, and Nausikles told him everything: how he had gone to the island and found it deserted; how at first he had not encountered a soul; how he had outwitted Mitranes and won possession of some girl they had discovered by pretending that she was Thisbe; he had done better, he said, by finding her than he would have done by recovering Thisbe, for there was a vast difference between the two, a difference as great as that between man and god. Her beauty was beyond compare and beyond his power to describe in words—particularly as she was in the house, and he could easily show them her.

11    No sooner did they hear this than they began to suspect the truth. They implored Nausikles to command the girl to be brought straightaway, for this indescribable beauty they recognized as that of none other than Charikleia. She was brought to them and at first stood with her head bowed and a veil covering her eyes, but when Nausikles assured her that there was nothing to be afraid of, she raised her head a little. She saw them; they saw her—though they had despaired of ever seeing one

*recognition*

another again. In the same instant they all burst into tears and cried aloud, as though a single sign had been given them all, or one blow had been dealt them all. For some time all that was to be heard were cries of "Father!" "Daughter!" and "Truly it is Charikleia and not Thisbe!"

Nausikles was dumbfounded as he watched how Kalasiris wept as he embraced Charikleia, and tried in bewilderment to make sense of the theatrical recognition scene being played before him, until Kalasiris clasped him in a fond embrace, kissed him, and said: "Most excellent friend, may the gods reward you for this by granting you the satisfaction of all your desires.[132] You have rescued the daughter whom I had despaired of finding, and you have granted me to see the one sight that gives me more pleasure than any other! But Charikleia, my daughter, where did you leave Theagenes?"

At this question Charikleia cried aloud in grief and paused a moment before replying, "He is a prisoner and was taken away by whoever it was that presented me to this man."

So Kalasiris implored Nausikles to tell them what he knew about Theagenes, who his new master was, and where he was taking him. Nausikles realized that these were the children of whom the old man had often spoken to him, and in quest of whom he knew that he roamed the world in grief. He told Kalasiris everything but added that there was nothing to help them in what he had to say, beyond knowledge of the facts: they were destitute, and he would be surprised if Mitranes would consent to release their young friend, even in return for a large ransom.

"We do have money," Charikleia whispered to Kalasiris. "Promise him as much as you like! I have kept safe the necklace you know of, and I have it with me now."

Her words gave Kalasiris new heart, but he was anxious that Nausikles should have no idea of the truth, or of the treasures that Charikleia had about her person.

"My dear Nausikles," he said, "a philosopher never wants for anything. His will is a thing of substance. He knows what he may properly ask of the gods, and he receives all that he asks. So all you have to do is tell us where we may find the man who has Theagenes in his power: divine concern will not disregard us; heaven will provide however much we may require to sweep aside the greed that the Persians have for money."

Nausikles smiled and said: "You will only convince me that you can become rich all of a sudden, as if by magic, if you start by paying me the price of this girl's release. You must be well aware that merchants have just as great a passion for money as do Persians!"

12

132. A close verbal echo of *Odyssey* 6.180, apparently partially disguised by textual corruption.

"I know," replied Kalasiris. "You will have what you ask, of course you will, for your kindness towards us leaves nothing to be desired. You agree to our requests before we have time to make them and consent to return my daughter to me without my having to ask. But first I must pray."

"Certainly," replied Nausikles, "but I am going to make a sacrifice of thanksgiving to the gods, and if you preferred, you could join me in the ceremony—for you are a holy man—and make your devotions then. Ask them to send me some wealth, and get some for yourself too!"

"Do not mock; be not of such little faith," said Kalasiris. "You go ahead and make your preparations for the sacrifice. We shall join you when everything is ready."

13 That is what they did, and it was not long before someone came from Nausikles to summon them to make haste to the sacrifice. They had already agreed on a plan of action and set off with a light heart, the two men walking with Nausikles and the rest of his numerous guests (it was a public sacrifice he had organized), and Charikleia with Nausikles' daughter and the other women, who had only prevailed on her to join them with much coaxing and persistent persuasion; though perhaps she would never have been prevailed upon had she not formed the intention of using the occasion of the sacrifice to pray for Theagenes' safety. They arrived at the temple of Hermes, whom Nausikles considered as his patron god, since of all gods he is the most concerned with markets and commerce, and to whom therefore the sacrifice was being offered. The rite was quickly performed. Kalasiris briefly inspected the entrails: the play of expressions on his face showed that the future he saw foretold was one of alternating joy and sorrow. Then he passed both his hands over the altar, all the while pronouncing an invocation, and drew—or pretended to draw—from the altar fire what he had had in his hand all along.

"This is the price of Charikleia's release, Nausikles," he said, "which the gods convey to you by way of me."

As he spoke, he pressed into Nausikles' hand one of the royal rings. A magnificent, sublime thing it was, its hoop inset with amber, its bezel aflame with an Ethiopian amethyst as big in circumference as a maiden's eye and in beauty far surpassing the amethysts of Iberia and Britain,[133] in which the bloom of crimson is pale and weak: they are like rosebuds just breaking into flower and blushing pink for the first time in the sunlight,

133. According to Pliny (*Natural History* 37.121) the finest amethysts were produced in India. Neither Ethiopia nor Britain is attested elsewhere as supplying these stones. We know, however, that some amethysts came from the area corresponding to Soviet Georgia, called Iberia in antiquity. It seems from the present passage that Heliodoros has misunderstood his source and confused this eastern Iberia with a completely different region of the same name, modern Spain and Portugal.

but from the heart of an Ethiopian amethyst blazes a pure radiance, fresh as springtime. If you held one and turned it in your hands, it would throw off a shaft of golden light that did not dazzle the eye with its harshness but illuminated it with its brilliance. Furthermore, there resides in it a power more authentic than in the stones of the west: its name is no misnomer, it truly is *amethysos*, "proof against intoxication," and keeps its owner sober at drinking parties.[134]

Every amethyst from India or Ethiopia is as I have described, but the   14 stone that Kalasiris was now presenting to Nausikles was far superior to all others, for it had been incised and deeply carved to represent living creatures. The scene depicted was as follows: a young boy was shepherding his sheep, standing on the vantage point of a low rock, using a transverse flute to direct his flock as it grazed, while the sheep seemed to pasture obediently and contentedly in time to the pipe's melody. One might have said that their backs hung heavy with golden fleeces; this was no beauty of art's devising, for art had merely highlighted on their backs the natural blush of the amethyst. Also depicted were lambs, gamboling in innocent joy, a whole troop of them scampering up the rock, while others cavorted and frolicked in rings around their shepherd, so that the rock where he sat seemed like a kind of bucolic theater; others again, reveling in the sunshine of the amethyst's brilliance, jumped and skipped, scarcely touching the surface of the rock. The oldest and boldest of them presented the illusion of wanting to leap out through the setting of the stone but of being prevented from doing so by the jeweler's art, which had set the collet of the ring like a fence of gold to enclose both them and the rock. The rock was a real rock, no illusion, for the artist had left one corner of the stone unworked, using reality to produce the effect he wanted: he could see no point in using the subtlety of his art to represent a stone on a stone! Such was the ring.

Nausikles' amazement at the miracle was exceeded only by his delight   15 at the value of the gem, which he estimated to be worth as much as all that he possessed.

"My dear Kalasiris," he said, "I was only jesting; my request for payment for her release was not meant seriously; I intended to release your daughter to you without payment. But, as you say in Egypt,[135] 'Never to be cast away are the gifts of the gods, magnificent'; so I accept this jewel that the gods have sent me, firm in the belief that this unlooked-for treasure comes to me from Hermes, who with his customary generosity

134. This etymology is specifically rejected by Pliny and Plutarch (*Table Talk* 647C), who suggests that the amethyst was so called because its color was like that of wine so watered down as to remove any threat of inebriation.

135. This must be the meaning of the second person plural verb φατέ. The words that follow are actually a quotation from Homer (*Iliad* 3.65), so it seems that Nausikles too has received a lecture on the Egyptian origins of the greatest Greek poet.

conveyed this gift to you through the agency of the flames. It is true! Look, you can see how the fire still burns in it! Besides, I think that a benefaction that enriches the recipient at no cost to the donor is the best kind there is!"

Acting on these words, he led the way to the feast. The inside of the temple had been set aside specially for the ladies, while tables had been laid for the men in the temple forecourt. When their appetites for the pleasures of the table were satisfied, the tables were removed to make way for wine bowls, and the men sang and poured a libation of departure to Dionysos, while the women danced a hymn of thanksgiving to Demeter. But Charikleia found a private place to perform her own rites, and there she prayed to the gods to preserve her life for Theagenes' sake, and his for hers.

16    The revelries were at their height, the guests had turned to various forms of amusement, when Nausikles held out a bowl of water with no wine added to it and said: 'My dear Kalasiris, we drink your health in pure water, as is pleasing to you, water that has had no intercourse with Dionysos, the god of wine, but retains its virgin purity. If, in return, you were to toast us with the story we long to hear, we could want no finer draught for our entertainment. As you can hear, the ladies have begun to dance to entertain themselves as they drink, but we, if you are agreeable, could want no finer accompaniment to our revels than the story of your travels, far sweeter than any dancing or flute music. As you know, you have many times put off telling me the tale because you were drowning in a sea of troubles; but you cannot keep it back for a better moment than the present—there will never be one! One of your children, your daughter, is here before your eyes, safe and sound, and, with the gods' help, you will see your son very soon indeed, particularly if you do not annoy me by postponing your narrative yet again!"

"Blessings be upon you, Nausikles!" interrupted Knemon. "At your behest all sorts of musical instruments are in attendance at our festivities, yet now you do not give them a second thought and leave them to people with less taste, preferring to hear of things that are truly mystical and imbued with a pleasure that is indeed divine. You are, in my view, showing a very fine understanding of the ways of the gods when you ensconce Hermes beside Dionysos[136] and spice the wine you pour us with the sweet flow of words. I was much impressed by the great expense you had been to in your sacrifice, but I am sure that there is no better way to propitiate Hermes than by bringing as your contribution to the festivities that which is his own special concern—words."

136. Besides being the patron of merchants, Hermes was regarded in late antiquity as the god of eloquence, Hermes Logios. What Nausikles intended as a trader's ritual has become, for Knemon, an appropriate occasion for storytelling under the patronage of the same god. Dionysos, of course, stands for wine.

*Is Kalasiris a reliable storyteller?*

*story re-started*

*17*

Kalasiris assented, partly to please Knemon, partly to place Nausikles under an obligation for the future. He told the whole story; the first part, that Knemon had already heard, he told briefly and, as it were, in outline, deliberately omitting some details that he deemed it best Nausikles should not know. Then he went on with the sequel, as yet untold, to his earlier narration, taking the story up from the point where they had boarded the Phoenician merchantman in their flight from Delphi.[137] At first, he went on, the voyage had gone just as they wished, with a gentle wind blowing astern and carrying them along; but when they reached the straits of Kalydon,[138] they had run into the rough waters generally characteristic of that place and received a severe buffeting.

Even on this point, Knemon insisted that Kalasiris omit nothing but tell them the explanation, if he had found one, for the turbulence that is so prevalent in that vicinity.

"At that point," replied Kalasiris, "the wide expanse of the Ionian Sea is compressed into a narrow passage and flows into the Gulf of Krisa[139] through a sort of bottleneck. The pressure drives the water forward to unite with the Aegean Sea, but its onward thrust is stopped short by the Peloponnesian isthmus; divine providence, it seems, has placed that narrow strip of land there to block the sea's way and keep its flood tide from sweeping over the coasts that lie in its path. Naturally enough this creates a backwash of water, which is subjected to greater compression in the vicinity of these straits than elsewhere in the gulf; also, the water running in often collides with that washing back, so that the sea seethes and boils, arching up to the sky in huge, angry waves at the shock of the impact."

This explanation was received with enthusiastic approval by the company, who declared it to be true. Then Kalasiris went on with his story.

"After passing through the straits and leaving the Pointed Islands in the distance behind us, we caught our first glimpse—though we could not be certain—of the heights of Zakynthos, barely visible on the horizon, like a vague cloud. The helmsman gave orders to lower some of the sails, and when we asked why he was trimming the ship's speed when she had such a fair wind behind her, he explained: 'Because if we ran before the wind under full sail, we should come to anchor at Zakynthos in the early hours of darkness, and there would be a risk of our running aground in the dark on one of the many reefs and rocks along this coast. So it is better to spend the night at sea and proceed with lowered sails,

137. This transition is modeled exactly on the beginning of Demodokos's song of the fall of Troy in the *Odyssey* (8.499ff.).

138. The narrows at the entrance to the Gulf of Corinth.

139. Strictly speaking, the Gulf of Krisa (or Kirrha) is the branch of the Gulf of Corinth running up to the port that serves Delphi. Heliodoros here uses it as a synonym for the whole of the larger gulf, apparently unaware that it is identical with the Gulf of Kirrha he located more accurately at 5.1.2.

calculating just how much wind we need to catch to reach the land at daybreak.'

18    "The helmsman did not say this, Nausikles, without it happening as he had said. Day dawned to find us in the very act of dropping anchor. Those of the island's inhabitants who lived around the harbor (which was a short distance from the town) flocked down to the quayside to stare at us, as if they had never seen the like before. They were clearly impressed that a vessel whose construction combined grace with immense size and height should also handle so responsively: it was clear, they said, that such a masterpiece of the shipwright's art could only be Phoenician. But they were even more astounded at our extraordinary good fortune in having made the voyage in winter, when the Pleiades were already beginning to set,[140] without running into foul weather or coming to any harm.

"Even before the stern ropes had been made fast, virtually the whole crew left the ship and hurried off to the town of Zakynthos to buy and sell in the market there. I had been told by the helmsman that they intended to rest up on the island for the winter, so I set off to look for lodgings somewhere near the seashore, rejecting the ship's own accommodation as improper because of the hurly-burly of the sailors, and that of the town as too dangerous, since my two young charges were on the run. I had not gone far when I saw an old fisherman sitting at the door of his house repairing the mesh of a torn net. I accosted him and said: 'Good morning, my friend. Could you please tell me where one might find lodgings?'

" 'Just here, by the headland,' he replied. 'It got snagged on a sunken rock yesterday, and now it is full of holes!'

" 'That is not what my question was about,' I said, 'but it would be very helpful of you if you could find room for us yourself, or tell me someone else who might.'

" 'It was not me,' he replied. 'I was not out with them. No! I hope Tyrrhenos never gets so old and silly as to do such a stupid thing. It is those young whippersnappers who are to blame: they do not know their way around the reefs and put down their nets in the wrong place.'

"Eventually it dawned on me that he was somewhat hard of hearing, so I bellowed at the top of my voice: 'Good day to you! We are strangers here. Please tell us where to find lodgings.'

" 'Good day to you too!' he replied. 'If you like, you can stay with us, unless you are one of those people who insist on grand houses and bring a huge crowd of servants with them.'

140. The reference is to the so-called cosmical setting, when the constellation disappears beneath the horizon just before sunrise. In Greece this occurs around the end of October, which coincides with the onset of wintry, stormy weather. The setting of the Pleiades was thus widely taken as marking the suspension of navigation until the return of spring.

"I told him that there were just three of us, myself and my two children.

"'That is nice,' he said, 'nearly the same as us. You will find us just one more in number. I still have two sons living at home, you see; the older ones are married now and have homes of their own to run. The boys' nurse makes four; their mother died not long ago, you see. So, my good sir, do not hesitate. You can be sure that we shall be pleased to welcome someone who, even on a first acquaintance, is obviously a well-bred gentleman.'

"I accepted his invitation and soon returned with Theagenes and Charikleia. The old man greeted us warmly and allocated us the sunnier side of the house. To begin with the winter passed pleasantly enough: we spent our days with our hosts, parting from them only when it was time to go to bed. Charikleia shared a room with the nurse, Theagenes and I had a room to ourselves, while Tyrrhenos and his sons slept in another. We ate our meals together; we provided most of the food, though Tyrrhenos regaled his young guests with huge quantities of fish from the sea. Usually he would go out fishing by himself, but sometimes we would while away an idle hour by joining him on one of his expeditions. He was a master of his craft in all its forms, with a technique to suit every season. The fellow was so successful and always had such a good catch that his patiently acquired skills were generally taken for the favoritism of fortune.

"But, as the saying goes, the unfortunate can nowhere escape their 19 misfortune.[141] Even in that lonely spot Charikleia's beauty attracted unwelcome attention. Our shipmate, that Tyrian merchant turned Pythian champion, came to me many times in private and wearied me to the point of annoyance with his persistent entreaties that I—whom he took for Charikleia's father—should grant him her hand in marriage. He loudly sang his own praises, in turns reciting his noble pedigree and reckoning up the riches he had with him: the ship was his own private property, he said, and he was the owner of most of the cargo she was carrying—gold, priceless gems, and silken raiment; he also spoke of his victory in the Pythian Games, which he considered as greatly enhancing his standing, and of much else besides. I used our penurious circumstances as an excuse and said that I could never bring myself to marry my daughter to a man who lived in foreign parts and in a country so far removed from Egypt, but he replied: 'Let us have no more of this, Father! In the girl's person I shall consider myself to have received a magnificent dowry worth many talents, worth all the world's riches. And I shall adopt your nation and homeland as my own, abandoning my voyage to Carthage and sailing with you wherever you choose to go.'

141. Source unknown.

20    "Seeing that far from abandoning his suit he in fact continued to press it with excessive fervor, not a single day passing without his tedious entreaties on the same subject, I decided to stall the Phoenician for a while with fair promises, for I was afraid that we might even become the victims of an act of violence on the island. I gave him my word that all would be accomplished when I reached Egypt.

"But I had scarcely won a moment's respite from his attentions when, as the saying goes, wave upon wave of evil fortune broke over me:[142] a few days later Tyrrhenos took me to a certain headland that jutted out into the sea like a bent arm and said: 'Kalasiris, I swear to you by Poseidon, Lord of the Ocean, and by the other gods who inhabit the sea, that I love you as a brother, and your children as much as my own children. I have come to tell you of a certain matter that has arisen. Unpleasant it may be, but it would be wrong for me to keep quiet about it now after having shared my hearth and home with you, while for you it is of the utmost importance to know about it. There is a gang of pirates lying in wait for the Phoenician merchantman, lurking out of sight in the bay formed by the crook of this point, with lookouts posted in relays to watch for the ship to leave harbor. So keep your eyes open, be on your guard, and decide what is to be done, for you, or rather your daughter, are the object of this typically vicious scheme of theirs.'

" 'May the gods make you the recompense you deserve for this information,' I replied. 'But how have you got wind of this plan, Tyrrhenos?'

" 'I'm known to these people through my trade,' he answered. 'I supply them with fish, for which they pay me above the going rate. Yesterday I was lifting my lobster pots by the cliffs when the pirate captain accosted me and asked, "Do you by any chance know when the Phoenicians are going to leave harbor?"

" 'I realized the point of his question, disguised though it was, and replied, "I cannot tell you exactly, Trachinos,[143] but I think they are going to set sail as soon as spring comes."

" ' "And the girl who is lodging with you," he said, "will she be sailing with them?"

" ' "I am not sure," I said. "But why are you so curious?"

" ' "Because I am madly in love with her," he replied. "I have only seen her once, but it was enough. I cannot remember ever having seen such beauty, though plenty of women who were pretty enough have been my prisoners."

---

142. Perhaps from Euripides *Ion* 927ff.:

> for just when
> I banished from my heart a wave of trouble
> A second rose at the stern.

143. The name is connected with the adjective *trachys,* "rough," "savage," "cruel."

" 'In an attempt to inveigle him into revealing the whole of his plans, I asked: "So why do you have to get entangled with the Phoenicians at all? Why not snatch her from my house, and so get her without spilling a drop of blood before they put out to sea?"

" ' "Even pirates," he replied, "retain a certain conscience and consideration for their friends. I am sparing you all the unpleasantness you would be caused when people started asking awkward questions about the disappearance of your guests; and besides, at a single stroke I intend to win the two prizes I want above all else—the riches of the ship and the hand of the girl. I should certainly lose the first of these if I attempted the job on land. In any case, anything of that kind would be risky close to the town, for people would raise the alarm and give chase in no time at all."

" 'I warmly commended his good sense and took my leave of him, but in revealing to you the plot that these brutes are hatching I implore you to give your mind to the question of how to safeguard yourself and your children.'

"Having heard his story, I went away in the depths of despair. I racked my brains to find a way out of our predicament, until a solution presented itself unbidden in the shape of the merchant, who accosted me yet again and began talking on his usual subject, thus unknowingly giving me the inspiration for a plan. Concealing from him such parts of Tyrrhenos's information as I chose not to tell him, I revealed to him no more than that one of the local people had it in mind to kidnap the girl and that he was too formidable an opponent for the merchant to contemplate open resistance.

" 'But,' I went on, 'I would far rather betroth my daughter to you, partly because of our previous acquaintance, partly because of your great wealth, but above all because I already have your word that you will live in Egypt if you win her hand. So, if you really do want to marry her, we must make haste to set sail and leave this place, before it is too late, and we become the victims of something that we are powerless to resist.'

"He was overjoyed to hear my words. 'Excellent, Father!' he exclaimed, moving closer and kissing me on the head. He asked when I wanted them to put out to sea, explaining that though it was not yet the season for sailing, it was nevertheless possible for us to avoid the plot that was hatching against us by moving to another anchorage and awaiting the arrival of spring there.

" 'Well then,' I answered, 'if it is to be my word that counts, I should like to leave this very night.'

" 'Then that is what we shall do,' he replied, and departed.

"Returning to our house, I said not a word of this to Tyrrhenos but told my children that we should have to go back on board our ship that evening after dark. They were taken aback by the suddenness of this an-

nouncement and asked the reason for it. But I put off telling them to another time, saying only, 'In the circumstances this is the best course of
action for us to take.'

22    "After a light supper we retired for the night, but as I slept, a vision of
an old man appeared to me. Age had withered him almost to a skeleton,
except that his cloak was hitched up to reveal a thigh that retained some
vestige of the strength of his youth. He wore a leather helmet on his
head, and his expression was one of cunning and many wiles; he was
lame in one leg, as if from a wound of some kind.[144] He stood by my
bed and said, with a sinister smile: 'You, my fine friend, are the only
man who has ever treated us with such utter contempt. All others whose
ships have passed by the island of Kephallenia have paid a visit to our
home and deemed it a matter of importance to learn of my renown.
You, on the other hand, have been so neglectful as to grant me not even
the common courtesy of a salutation, despite my dwelling in the vicinity.
But your omissions will be visited on you very soon. Ordeals like mine
shall you undergo; land and sea you shall find united in enmity against
you. However, to the maiden you have with you my wife sends greetings and wishes her joy, since she esteems chastity above all things.
Good tidings too she sends her; her story has a happy ending.'

"I woke with a start, shivering in fright at my dream. Theagenes
asked me what was wrong.

"'We may be too late to board our ship before she sails,' I replied. 'I
awoke in panic at the thought. Get up now and pack our things while I
fetch Charikleia.'

"The child came when I called, but the noise had awakened Tyrrhenos
too, and he got out of bed to ask what we were doing.

"'What we are doing,' I said, 'is acting on your advice and trying to
escape from those who have evil designs on us. You have been the
kindest of men to us: heaven preserve you for it! One final favor I ask of
you: take your boat over to Ithake and make an offering to Odysseus on
our behalf. Ask him to temper his wrath against us, for he has appeared
to me this very night and told me that he is angry at having been
slighted.'

"Tyrrhenos promised to do as I asked, and walked with us as far as
our ship, weeping bitterly and wishing us a safe and successful voyage.

144. This description contains a number of Homeric allusions that would have the effect, for an educated reader, of identifying the apparition before Kalasiris solves the riddle
by naming him at 5.22.5. The withering of age refers to the disguise given by Athene at
*Odyssey* 13.398ff.; the strong thigh comes from *Odyssey* 18.66ff.; the leather helmet from *Iliad* 10.261ff.; the Homeric words for "cunning" and "of many wiles" from *Odyssey* 13.332
and 1.1, respectively; the wound in the leg is the boar-inflicted scar from *Odyssey* 19.392ff.

"Why bore you with too many details? We put out to sea just as the morning star appeared in the sky. To begin with the crew had been vehemently opposed to our departure, but eventually they were won round by our Tyrian merchant, who told them that he had had forewarning of an attack by pirates and was taking evasive action. He thought this was a fiction: did he but know it, his words were true! Buffeted by gales, lashed by a storm too violent to resist, pounded by a sea swell that words are not adequate to describe, we narrowly escaped with our lives and beached our ship on a headland in Crete, one of our rudders gone[145] and most of our rigging smashed. We decided to stay on the island for a few days to repair the vessel and recover our own strength.

"This done, the resumption of our voyage was fixed for the day of the moon's reappearance after her conjunction with the sun. This time we set sail to the sound of gentle spring breezes and sailed night and day while the steersman held the ship on a course for the land of Libya. He said that with such a favorable wind we could sail straight across the open sea without touching land, and he was anxious to reach the safety of a haven on the mainland, for he suspected that the cutter visible off our stern was a pirate ship.

"'Ever since we put out from the headland in Crete,' he said, 'she has been following in our wake and pursuing a course identical to our own, as if on tow. And on a number of occasions, when I have deliberately steered our ship off a straight course, I have seen her change tack to match.'

"Some of those on board were alarmed at his words and urged that we make ready to defend ourselves, but others made light of the danger, suggesting that it was perfectly normal on the open sea for small craft to tail those of great tonnage, using their superior navigational expertise to show them what course to follow, as it were.

"These arguments continued on both sides until the time of day when the yeoman looses his ox from the plough, when the blustery wind began to ease, slackening little by little until it was blowing in our sails with ineffectual weakness, merely rippling the canvas with no forward thrust. Eventually it subsided into complete calm, as if it were departing with the setting sun, or, more truthfully, as if it were collaborating with our pursuers. For as long as we were running before the wind, the cutter and her crew lagged far astern of our merchantman, as one might have expected with our larger sails catching more of the wind; but when we were becalmed upon a smooth sea and forced to take to our oars, they were upon us quicker than it takes to tell, for the whole crew was row-

23

---

145. Ancient ships used two *pedalia*, steering paddles.

ing hard, I imagine, to propel their cutter, which was a nimble craft and more responsive to the oar than our vessel.

24 "They were almost alongside when one of our crew who had joined ship at Zakynthos yelled: 'The game is up, my friends! It is a gang of pirates! I recognize the cutter. It is Trachinos's!'

"A tremor ran through the merchantman at this announcement. Though she was becalmed, a storm raged on board her, and she was buffeted by a welter of cries of alarm and despair and disordered running in all directions; as some members of the crew sought refuge in the bowels of the ship, others encouraged one another to put up a fight on deck, while others again resolved to jump into the ship's dinghy and escape. But in the end, while they vacillated, they were forestalled by the onset of fighting, which forced them to make a reluctant stand and defend themselves with whatever came to hand. Theagenes was ablaze with eagerness to join the fray, but Charikleia and I threw our arms around him and restrained him, though only with difficulty. Charikleia did not want to be parted from him even in death, she said, and wished one sword and one thrust to deal the same fate to them both; but I had recognized that our assailant was Trachinos, and was already devising an expedient that would work to our advantage in what ensued—as indeed it did.

"The pirates came alongside, then cut across our bows. In an attempt to take the merchantman without bloodshed, they held their fire and circled around us, forcing us to a standstill. They were like a besieging army, eager to negotiate the capitulation of the ship.

"'You fools!' they shouted. 'It is madness to put up any resistance against such superior and invincible might as ours. Why run the risk of certain death? We are not yet without mercy: you may get into your dinghy and seek safety wherever you wish.'

"Such was their offer, but the merchantman's crew, courageous so long as they were fighting a battle with no dangers, a war with no 25 bloodshed, refused to abandon her. But then one of the pirates, bolder than the rest, leapt aboard the ship and started cutting down all who crossed his path, giving a clear indication that war is decided only by bloodshed and death. As the rest swarmed aboard, the Phoenicians had a change of heart and fell at the knees of the enemy, pleading for their lives and promising to do whatever they were told.

"Although the pirates were already engaged in spilling blood—and the sight of blood tempers an iron heart to steel—they unexpectedly spared the lives of their cowering foe, on Trachinos's orders. But what ensued was an armistice with no formal guarantees, actually warfare of the cruelest imaginable kind, suspended in name only for a peace that was in truth no peace at all: the terms imposed were even more horrible than the fighting had been. Notice was served on them to leave the ship with just

Charikleia's
cunning

one short tunic apiece, with a threat of death for any who did not comply. But it seems that there is nothing so precious to men as life.[146] So now the Phoenicians, though robbed of whatever hopes they had had of the ship's rich cargo, acted like men who had lost nothing and actually stood to show a profit by scrambling into the dinghy ahead of their fellows, each vying with his shipmates in a race to reach the certainty of survival before they did.

"As we filed past, submissive and obedient, Trachinos caught hold of   26 Charikleia and said: 'It was not in any sense against you, rather because of you, that I have fought this battle, my beloved. I have been following you ever since the day you left Zakynthos, and it was for love of you that I dared undertake such a lengthy and hazardous voyage. Take heart then! I tell you now that by my side you shall be queen of all my men.'

"Charikleia, the clever little minx, ever quick to turn a situation to her own advantage, but also in part taking her cue from what I had told her, discarded the downcast expression that her ordeals had brought to her face, and composed her features into an alluring smile.

"'Thanks be to the gods who inspire your heart with such kindness towards us,' she said. 'But if you wish me to be truly of good heart, and to remain so, then grant me this first proof of your affection. Save my brother here and my father from death; prevent them leaving the ship. If they are taken from me, I cannot possibly go on living.'

"And as she spoke, she fell and clasped his knees in prolonged supplication, while Trachinos luxuriated in the sensual pleasure of her embrace and deliberately took his time before giving her his word. Her tears moved him to pity, and her eyes reduced him to abject slavery. Raising the girl to her feet, he said, 'Your brother's life is a gift I give you with great pleasure, for I can see that he is a young man full of courage and well fitted to share our way of life. This old man is a dead weight, but simply to please you he may live!'

"Meanwhile the sun had completed its daily cycle and set in the west.   27 In the resultant twilight, that no-man's-land twixt day and night,[147] the sea suddenly started to turn rough. This alteration may have been the spontaneous product of the moment, or perhaps the change was due to the whim of some fate. There was a thunderous noise as the gale came sweeping towards us, and in an instant the full force of the blast had struck the pirates almost without warning and filled them with surprised alarm. They had left their own cutter and now were trapped on board the merchantman, whose cargo they were engaged in pillaging, with no idea of how to handle a vessel of her size. All the tasks involved in sailing

146. Alluding to Euripides *Alkestis* 301.
147. The phrase alludes perhaps to Aischylos *Choephoroi* 64.

a ship were performed *ad hoc* by whoever chanced to be at hand, and they tackled various skilled duties for which they had no qualification but rash courage. Some tried to reef the sails, but with no semblance of coordination, while others tried to work the rigging, but with no knowledge of its operation. One incompetent individual stationed himself in the bows, while another, equally incompetent, took charge of the stern and the tiller. We were brought to the edge of destruction, not so much by the force of the storm, which had not yet reached the climax of its fury, as by the incompetence of the helmsman, who stayed at his post so long as there was a glimmer of daylight left in the sky, but deserted it once the darkness reigned supreme.

"We were awash and close to sinking when some of the pirates first attempted to reboard their own vessel, then gave up the attempt, finding themselves rebuffed by the heavy seas, to say nothing of the arguments of Trachinos, who convinced them that they would be able to afford many thousands of such cutters if only they could bring the merchantman and the treasure in her hold safely to land. In the end he sliced through the hawser attaching her to the ship, asserting that this was just another storm they had in tow and urging them to take thought for their future safety: they would be open to suspicion if they put into any port with both ships, for questions would inevitably be asked as to what had happened to the crew of the other one. This seemed good advice, and for a while the one stroke won him double credit. After the cutter was cut loose, they did experience a respite, but not for long. They were by no means out of danger yet, and, pounded by wave after gigantic wave, they began to jettison much of the ship's equipment. Every peril imaginable confronted them, but eventually that night passed, though it seemed never-ending, the next day too, and we ran ashore in the evening on a promontory near the Heracleotic mouth of the Nile.

"Thus, poor wretches, we landed in Egypt willy-nilly. They were all happy to have reached land, but we were downcast and reproached the sea bitterly for sparing our lives; she had begrudged us a death free from outrage and instead had given us up to the land, where even worse horrors seemed to await us, exposed as we now were to the evil whims of pirates. Those scoundrels had barely set foot on land before our worst fears were confirmed: saying that they intended to make a sacrifice of thanksgiving—thanksgiving indeed!—to Poseidon, they began to unload Tyrian wine and other items from the ship and dispatched some of their number to buy cattle from the surrounding district, giving them vast amounts of money and telling them to pay the first price asked.

28    "Very soon they were back, with a whole flock of sheep and pigs. They were welcomed by their comrades who had stayed behind, who

now set about lighting an altar fire, skinned the sacrificial animals, and
started to prepare the banquet. But Trachinos took me to one side, out of
earshot of the others.

"'Father,' he said, 'I have sought and won your daughter's hand in
marriage. I intend to celebrate the wedding today, as you can see,
combining that most joyful of festivities with this sacrifice in honor of
the gods. I do not want you sitting among the revels with a scowl on
your face because no one told you what was happening; but I do want
your daughter to hear from you what the future holds for her and welcome it gladly. So I have decided that I ought to give you prior warning
of my intentions, not because I want you to confirm them—my position
is sufficient guarantee that my will will be done—but simply because I
consider it right and proper to secure my bride's compliance by having
her father tell her beforehand that she is to be married.'

"I commended his words and feigned joy and all possible gratitude to
the gods who had turned my daughter's master into her husband. I withdrew for a minute, and, after some private rumination on our best course
of action, I returned to Trachinos and appealed to him for greater ceremony in the celebration of the rite; I asked him to designate the ship as
the girl's bridal chamber and command that there be no intrusion, no interruption, so that as much care might be taken over her bridal apparel
and general appearance as circumstances allowed.

"'It would be the absurdest thing I have ever heard of,' I went on, 'for
one so proud of her birth and wealth, one who is, most important, to be
the bride of Trachinos, not even to make use of what finery is available
to her, even if time and place do not admit the full dignity of the marriage ceremony.'

"My words put Trachinos in a good humor, and he happily promised
that he would command his men to do as I had asked. He commanded
that they should unload immediately everything that they would need
and thereafter stay away from the ship. This order was obeyed, and they
began to off-load tables, wine bowls, rugs, screens, handiwork of Tyre
and Sidon,[148] and lavish quantities of everything else necessary for a
feast, humping it all unceremoniously off the ship on their shoulders. All
this treasure, which it had taken so much hard work and thrift to accu-
mulate, fate had abandoned to be dissipated in a drunken orgy.

"I took Theagenes with me to see Charikleia, whom we found in
tears.

148. Compare *Iliad* 6.289ff.:

> There lay the elaborately wrought robes, the work of Sidonian
> women, whom Alexandros himself, the godlike, had brought home
> from the land of Sidon.

29

"'My child,' I said, 'you are indeed no stranger to unhappiness, but tell me: is the cause of your weeping the same as before or something new?'

"'I weep,' she replied, 'for the whole of my life, but above all for my fears about Trachinos's abominable affection for me, which circumstances will probably intensify. Unexpected prosperity has a way of turning men's thoughts in improper directions. But a plague on Trachinos and his loathsome love! I shall cheat him of his desires by taking my own life first; but it was the thought of being parted from you and Theagenes before I die that reduced me to tears.'

"'Your inference is correct,' I said. 'Trachinos does aim to turn this celebration from a sacrifice into a wedding between you and him. Believing me to be your father, he has told me his intentions, though I have known of his insane infatuation for you ever since Tyrrhenos told me of it on Zakynthos; but I said nothing of it to either of you so as to save you premature anguish over sorrows that were still in the future.[149] There was always a possibility that we might escape his schemes. But since heaven has thwarted that hope, and we are now plunged in adversity, come, let us stake our all on a resolute venture! Let us confront the danger head-on! Thus we shall either win a life of honor and freedom or else at least have the consolation of a courageous and chaste death.'

30    "They gave me their word that they would do whatever I told them, and, after explaining to them what they had to do, I left them to make their preparations and went to find the pirate who was Trachinos's second-in-command; his name was Peloros,[150] I think. I said I had something to tell him that was very much to his advantage. He raised no objection and took me to one side where we should not be overheard.

"'I must be brief, my son,' I said. 'Time is too short for a long speech. My daughter is in love with you—and I am not a bit surprised: she has succumbed to your superior quality. But now she suspects that your chief is preparing to turn this celebration into a wedding. Indeed, he has already hinted as much by commanding that she be arrayed in especial finery. So think how you can scotch this scheme of his and win the girl for yourself instead, for she says she will die before she will wed Trachinos!'

"'Have no fear,' he replied. 'For some time I too have felt drawn to the girl and have long been praying for a chance to gain my ends. So Trachinos will either stand aside of his own choice and grant me this bride as the prize to which I am entitled as the first to have boarded the

149. The thought and the diction are drawn from Thucydides (2.39.4).
150. "Monstrous."

merchantman, or else he will find his wedding has a bitter taste,[151] and my right arm will inflict on him the death he so richly deserves!'

"Having listened to this speech, I hurried away so as not to arouse any suspicions. I went to the young couple and encouraged them with the good news that my plan was under way.

"A little while later we were at table. When I saw that the pirates were very much the worse for drink and that their behavior was passing the bounds of moderation, I turned to Peloros—I had deliberately placed myself next to him at table—and whispered, 'Have you seen how beautiful the girl looks in all her finery?'

"'Of course not,' he replied.

"'You can see her now, if you like,' I said. 'You only have to go into the ship, but you must make sure that you are not seen, for, as you know, this is something Trachinos has expressly forbidden. You will see Artemis herself sitting there! But, for the moment, restrain yourself from doing any more than just looking, otherwise you will bring down death on yourself and on her.'

"Without a moment's delay he jumped to his feet, saying that he had to answer an urgent call of nature, and ran stealthily to the ship. And there he saw Chariklea with a crown of laurel on her head, refulgent in her gown of golden weave (she had dressed herself in her sacred robe from Delphi, to be either the mantle of victory or else a funeral shroud); everything around her was radiantly beautiful, creating the illusion of a nuptial bedroom. At the sight of her he was, of course, consumed by a fire of passion; desire and jealousy flooded over him, and the instant he rejoined us it was clear from the look on his face that there was madness in his heart. Scarcely had he resumed his place before he said, 'Why have I not received my reward for being the first aboard?'

"'Because you have not asked for it!' responded Trachinos. 'In any case we have not had time yet to share out our takings.'

"'Well,' said Peloros, 'I claim the girl we captured.'

"'You may have whatever you wish, apart from her,' answered Trachinos.

"But Peloros interrupted him. 'Then you are overturning the pirate law that allows whoever is the first aboard an enemy vessel and the first to brave the danger of combat on behalf of all his comrades to choose whatever he pleases from the spoils.'

"'My dear fellow,' said Trachinos, 'I am not overturning that law, but I base my claim on another rule which says that subordinates must give

151. The unusual word *pikrogamos*, "bitter marriage," is Homeric: see *Odyssey* 1.266, 4.346, 17.137.

way to their superiors. The girl has won my heart, and I demand that my right of precedence be honored and that I be given her for my wife. As for you, if you do not do as you are told, you will soon regret it—I shall smash your head in with this wine bowl!'

"Peloros turned to the company. 'Do you see how hard work is rewarded?' he said. 'One day each one of you will have his prize taken from him like this; one day you will all be the victims of this arbitrary and autocratic law.'

32      "Well, what a spectacle ensued, Nausikles! Like a sea lashed by a sudden squall, you might have said, they were whipped into indescribable turmoil by an irrational impulse, for drink and anger had now taken full possession of them. Some sided with Trachinos, bawling that the leader must be respected; others with Peloros, clamoring that the law must be upheld. In the end Trachinos raised his bowl above his head, intending to brain Peloros with it, but Peloros was ready for him and got in first with a dagger thrust through the heart. Trachinos fell, mortally wounded. For the rest of them this meant open war, with no quarter asked or given. They fell on one another, raining blow after blow, one side claiming to be defending their captain, the other to be championing Peloros and the cause of right. There was one confused howl as sticks, stones, wine bowls, blazing torches, and tables flew through the air and found their marks. I had withdrawn to a safe distance and found myself a spot on a hill where I could watch the fighting well out of harm's way, but neither Theagenes nor Charikleia held back from the action. Acting upon the plan we had agreed, Theagenes armed himself with a sword and to start with joined one of the two parties, fighting like a man completely berserk; and when Charikleia saw that hostilities had commenced, she began shooting arrows from the ship: every shaft found its mark, and she spared none but Theagenes. Her shots were not confined to one side or the other, but she slew whoever was the first to cross her line of vision. She herself was out of sight, but the firelight made her enemies easy targets. They, on the other hand, had no idea what this mischief was, and some even supposed that their wounds were divinely inflicted.

"Eventually they all lay dead, and Theagenes was left to fight one against one with Peloros, a man of enormous courage and a practiced killer, who had butchered victims beyond number. Not even Charikleia's bowmanship could help him now: she longed desperately to come to his aid but was afraid of missing her aim, for now they were locked in a hand-to-hand tussle. But in the end Peloros had to admit defeat, for Charikleia, unable to give Theagenes any material assistance, sent words winging to his aid instead. 'Have courage, my beloved!' she called.

"From that moment Theagenes had much the better of Peloros. It was as if her voice had brought him new strength and new heart and proved that the prize for which they were contending was still his for the winning. With renewed vigor he hurled himself upon Peloros, despite the pain of his numerous wounds, and aimed a sword stroke at his head. Peloros ducked a little to one side; the blade missed its mark but, grazing past the pirate's shoulder, severed his arm at the joint of the elbow.[152] Peloros had had enough; he turned tail and ran, with Theagenes in hot pursuit.

"What happened after that I cannot say, except that I did not see  33 Theagenes return, for I stayed on my hilltop, too timid to venture across a battlefield in the dark. But Charikleia saw him sure enough. Day dawned to reveal him lying at her feet like a dead man, with Charikleia sitting over him, weeping, obviously wanting to take her own life but dissuaded from doing so by a faint hope that the young man just might come through alive. But to my sorrow I did not have time to speak to them, to hear of their woes, to ease their distress with words of comfort, to do what I could for them in their hour of need; for, without a moment's respite, perils from the sea were succeeded by perils from the land. I was just making my way down the hillside, having seen day dawn, when a troop of Egyptian bandits came racing down, evidently from the mountain overlooking the beach. The young couple were already in their power, and in a minute or two they were leading them away, also taking with them as much of the ship's cargo as they could carry. Vainly, pointlessly, I tried to follow them at a safe distance, lamenting their fate and mine. There was nothing I could do to help, and I thought it best not to tangle with the bandits but to husband my strength in the hope of being able to come to my children's aid. But my strength failed me, of course! My age prevented me from keeping up with the fast pace the Egyptians set over the steep hill-paths, and I fell behind. And it is only thanks to the gods' favor and your kindness, Nausikles, that I am now reunited with my daughter: I have had no part to play in her deliverance; my only contribution has been my lamentations and ceaseless tears for her."

His story concluded, he began to weep, and the entire company wept with him. The festivities had turned to sadness, not unmixed with a kind of pleasure; for wine disposes men to tears. Finally Nausikles tried to raise Kalasiris's spirits, saying: "Father, you can be of good cheer from now on. You already have your daughter back, and it is only the night that prevents you from seeing your son. At daybreak we shall go to Mitranes and try every means at our disposal to secure the release of your excellent Theagenes."

---

152. Intended to recall the killing of Hypsenor by Eurypylos in the *Iliad* (5.79ff.).

"That is what I should like," replied Kalasiris. "But now it is time to break up the party. First let us remember the spiritual powers and let us each in turn pour a libation for our deliverance."

34    Thereupon the libation was passed around the table, and the guests dispersed. Kalasiris was looking out for Charikleia; he watched the people go past but could not see her in the throng. Eventually a woman told him where she was, and he went through into the shrine, where he found her clinging fast to the feet of the holy statue. Exhausted by her protracted prayers and by the ravages of sorrow, she had slipped into a deep sleep. Kalasiris shed a tear or two and implored the god to let her life take a happier turn. Then, gently, he woke her and led her back to their lodgings. She blushed, apparently at having allowed sleep to get the better of her without realizing. Then she withdrew into the privacy of the women's room, but, lying in bed beside Nausikles' daughter, she was unable to sleep for all the fears and anxieties preying on her mind.

## Book Six

1    Kalasiris and Knemon retired to bed in a room in the men's part of the house. The remainder of the night passed more slowly than they wished, but more quickly than they expected, for the greater part of it had already been spent in feasting and the telling of stories whose length only left their hearers hungry for more. Too impatient even to wait for the day to dawn fully, they went to wake Nausikles and begged him to tell them where he thought Theagenes might be and to take them to him as quickly as he could. He made no demur, and they set off together. Charikleia pleaded again and again to be allowed to accompany them, but was reluctantly persuaded to stay behind by Nausikles' assurances that they did not have far to go and would be back in no time with Theagenes. So they left her there, tossed on a tide of conflicting emotions, midway between sorrow at being parted from them and joy at her hopes for the future.

They were walking along the banks of the Nile soon after leaving the village when they saw a crocodile scuttle across their path from right to left and plunge full tilt into the waters of the river. For two of them this was a common sight and occasioned them no alarm—except that Kalasiris said it was a sign portending some impediment to their mission. Knemon, however, was much perturbed by what he had seen: he had not had a clear view of the creature but had merely glimpsed a dark shape close to the ground slither past him; he very nearly turned tail and ran, much to Nausikles' amusement.

"Knemon," said Kalasiris, "I thought it was only at night that you suffered from a faint heart, and that your attacks of timidity were confined to the hours of darkness. But it seems that your courage was just as heroic in the daytime all along! And it is not just the sound of names that causes you such agitation, but the sight of everyday, harmless objects too!"

"Which god or spirit-being is it," asked Nausikles, "whose name our bold friend here cannot endure to hear?"

"I cannot say," replied Kalasiris, "whether the names of gods and spirit-beings have the same effect on him; this is the name of a human being—and, what is more, not of a man or any famous hero but of a woman, and a dead one at that, according to him! But he shakes with fear if anyone so much as mentions it. That night when you, my friend, brought back Charikleia safe and sound from the Herdsmen, somehow or other and somewhere or other he had heard a passing reference to this name I am talking about, and he did not let me get a wink of sleep; he was at death's door with fright all night, and I had quite a job to bring him round. And if it were not for the fact that it would cause him great distress and terror, I should tell you the name this very minute, Nausikles. Then you would laugh even more!"

And so saying, he let fall the word "Thisbe."

Nausikles had stopped laughing now; taken aback by what he had heard, he stood awhile lost in thought, wondering what the name of Thisbe meant to Knemon, what association he had had with her to cause him to react in such a way.

Now it was Knemon's turn to roar with laughter. "My dear Kalasiris," he said, "now do you see just how great the power of this name is? I am not the only one for whom it holds the terrors of hell[153]— it has affected Nausikles in the same way now. Or rather there has been a complete reversal of roles: now it is my turn to laugh, for I know that she is dead, while our valiant friend Nausikles, who laughs so heartily at other people's expense, has become long-faced and glum."

"Please stop!" said Nausikles. "You have had your own back on me, Knemon; that is enough now. In the name of the gods of hospitality and friendship, by the salt and food with which, I believe, I made you so welcome in my home, tell me, both of you, how you know the name of Thisbe and how you have come either to fear it or use it to make fun of me."

"The tale is yours to tell, Knemon," said Kalasiris. "You have often promised to tell it me, but until now you have always found an excuse of one kind or another to put off doing so. Now is the time for you to tell it, and in so doing you will not only be granting the request of Nausikles

153. Literally "for whom it is a *mormolykeion*," a mythical bogey used to frighten naughty children.

here but also making our journey less arduous and helping us on our way with your story."

Knemon consented, and he briefly told them all that he had already recounted to Theagenes and Charikleia: that his home was in Athens, his father was called Aristippos, and Demainete had become his stepmother. He told them also of Demainete's illicit infatuation with him, and how, when she was thwarted of her desires, she devised a scheme against him, using Thisbe as the instrument of her intrigue. He went on to describe the nature of the trap she had laid, how he was banished from the land of his birth, this being the penalty imposed on him by the popular assembly as a father-killer; how, while he was staying on Aigina, first Charias, one of his contemporaries, had brought him the news of Demainete's death and how it had come about after Thisbe had set a trap for her too, and then Antikles had told him how Demainete's family had united against Aristippos and induced the people to suspect him of murder, with the result that he had been subjected to the confiscation of his property, while Thisbe had eloped from Athens with her lover, the merchant from Naukratis. Knemon ended his tale by telling how he had sailed off to Egypt with Antikles in search of Thisbe, hoping to find her and take her back to Athens, where he would clear his father's name and bring her to book. In the period that followed he had faced many dangers and experienced many adventures, finally being captured by buccaneers; but he had managed to escape, only to be captured for a second time as soon as he set foot in Egypt by the bandits called Herdsmen. That was how he had met Theagenes and Charikleia; he told them also of the killing of Thisbe and everything thereafter, until he reached the part of his story that was already familiar to Kalasiris and Nausikles.

Knemon's story left Nausikles in a state of utter indecision, by turns disposed to admit the truth about himself and Thisbe and then inclined to put off doing so to another time. In the end he kept his own counsel, though only with difficulty, partly by his own decision, partly because something else occurred to prevent his telling all. They had come just about seven miles, and were drawing close to the village where Mitranes was stationed when they ran into an acquaintance of Nausikles and asked him where he was going to in such a desperate hurry.

"Nausikles," he replied, "you ask the reason for my haste as if you did not know that at the moment my whole life is directed towards a single end—namely, doing as I am bidden in the service of my lady, Isias of Chemmis: I work my land for her; I supply her every need; she allows me no rest by day or night; whatever service Isias demands of me, be it great or small, I accept, whatever the cost to me in money or hardship. Now I am on my way to my beloved posthaste with a particular bird she demanded I should bring her—this Nile flamingo you can see here."

"What a considerate mistress you have got yourself involved with," said Nausikles. "How modest her demands are if it is only a flamingo that she has demanded of you and not the phoenix itself that comes to us from Ethiopia or India."[154]

"This is typical of her," he replied. "It is her way to make fun of me and what I do for her. But where are you going? What is your business?"

"We are in a hurry to see Mitranes," they replied.

"Then your haste is pointless and futile," he said. "Mitranes is not there at the moment. This very night he went off to fight the Herdsmen who live in the village of Bessa;[155] he had sent some young Greek he had captured to Oroondates in Memphis—to be taken on from there, I suppose, as a gift to the Great King—but the men of Bessa and their newly chosen leader, Thyamis, mounted a surprise attack and seized the young man, who is now in their possession."

Even before these words were out of his mouth, he was hurrying on his way. "I must not keep Isias waiting," he called. "At this very moment she may be peering around impatiently for me, and I should not want the progress of my love to be obstructed by unpunctuality. She is forever making trumped-up complaints and accusations against me at the slightest provocation and pretending to be indifferent to my attentions."

On hearing these words, they stood awhile rooted in dumb dismay at the way their hopes had been so unexpectedly dashed, but eventually Nausikles tried to raise their flagging spirits by pointing out that there was no need to abandon their enterprise completely because of a momentary setback: now they would have to return to Chemmis and give some serious thought to what they should do next; then they must equip themselves for a trip further afield and go in search of Theagenes among the Herdsmen, or wherever else their inquiries might lead them, secure wherever they went behind a shield of confidence[156] that they would be reunited with him. The hand of god was manifest in what had just happened, for a fortuitous meeting with one of his acquaintances had brought them information guiding them to the place where they must seek Theagenes; their target was the Herdsmen's village, and that was the direction their path should point.

---

154. There is an untranslatable pun here: the word for "flamingo" is *phoinikopteros* ("crimson-wing"), which suggests the comments on the phoenix. The flamingo is a very easy bird to catch; the phoenix, much harder as (a) it was supposed to appear in Egypt only once every five hundred years, and (b) it is purely mythical. There are several versions of its origins. Herodotos (2.73) says it comes from Arabia; for Ethiopia see Achilles Tatius 3.25; for India, Philostratos *Life of Apollonios* 3.49.

155. The name is attested for a town in southern Egypt, but not for anywhere that would fit with Heliodoros's narrative.

156. This curious metaphor is taken almost verbatim from a speech by Demosthenes (*On the Crown* 97).

5    They were quite happy to fall in with this suggestion, both because his words had, it seems to me, shown them new cause for hope and because Knemon whispered to Kalasiris that he had no doubt that Thyamis would ensure no harm came to Theagenes. So they decided to return—which they did, to find Charikleia in the porch of the house, scanning all points of the compass for their appearance in the distance. When she saw that there was no sign of Theagenes, she gave a piercing scream of sorrow. "So you have come back without him, Father!" she said. "Three of you left this house, and the same three have returned! Theagenes must be dead then! If you have anything to tell me, then in the name of the gods tell it me quickly. Do not make my sorrow more painful by not coming straight to the point. Not to mince words in breaking bad news is a kindness, for it enables the soul to come to grips with its anguish and find a swift remedy for its sorrow."

Knemon cut short her distress. "That is an annoying habit of yours, Charikleia," he said. "You are always inclined to divine the worst,[157] and you are always wrong—I am glad to say in this case. Theagenes is alive and well, by the gods' grace." And then he explained briefly what had happened and where Theagenes was.

"It is obvious from your words that you have never been in love, Knemon," said Kalasiris. "Otherwise you would have known that for lovers even perfectly innocent things are full of fear. They trust no evidence but that of their own eyes where their sweetheart is concerned, and separation from the object of their love brings instant dread and anguish to a lover's heart. The reason is that they are convinced that their beloved would never fail to come to them unless there were a horrible obstacle preventing him from doing so. So, my friend, let us forgive Charikleia, who is displaying all the classic symptoms of love! Let us go indoors and consider our next step."

6    And with that he took Charikleia by the hand and, with a tenderness betokening a love like that of a father for his child, led her inside. Nausikles, who wished to ease the burden of their cares for a time—though he had a certain other matter in mind too—prepared a banquet of extraordinary splendor, a party at which the only guests were they and his own daughter, whom he had made lovelier to behold than she normally was and had arrayed in exceptionally lavish finery. When he judged them to be of sufficiently good cheer, he started to speak as follows.

157. Compare Agamemnon's words to Kalchas in the first book of the *Iliad* (106–8):
Seer of evil: never yet have you told me a good thing.
Always the evil things are dear to your heart to prophesy,
but nothing excellent have you said nor ever accomplished.

"My friends—and may the gods bear witness to the truth of what I am going to say—it would be much to my liking if you were to decide to stay and live here in my house forevermore, sharing my possessions and all that I hold most dear. You see, I have come to think of you not just as guests staying awhile in my home but as true friends, who reciprocate my feelings, and thus nothing you may ask of me shall I consider in the slightest as an imposition. I am ready to help you in whatever way I can in your search for your friends, while I am here. But I must tell you quite plainly that my life is that of a merchant: trade is the field I work in. For some time past the west winds have been blowing fair, opening up the sea to navigation and bringing traders the good news that the sailing season has arrived. The clarion call of business beckons me away to Greece. So I should much appreciate it if you could let me know what your intentions are so that I can arrange my own affairs to fit in with your plans."

Kalasiris paused awhile in silence before replying. "Nausikles," he said, "may your sailing be blessed by divine favor. May Hermes the God of Profit and Poseidon the God of Safe Passage be your companions and guides. May their attendance bring you favorable tides and winds on every sea you sail and ensure that you find a safe haven in every port and a warm welcome for merchants in every town. You have discharged the duties of hospitality and friendship to the full, treating us as honored guests while we were staying with you and not seeking to detain us now that we wish to be on our way.[158] Though it is painful to part from you and your home, which you have allowed us to think of as our own, we cannot evade our duty to do everything possible to recover those whom we love most in the world. Such is the intention of Charikleia here and myself, but what Knemon's thoughts are, whether he is willing to give us the pleasure of his company on our long and winding road or has come to some other decision, he is here to tell us himself."

Knemon was on the point of speaking when his intended reply was cut short by a fit of violent sobbing, and a flood of warm tears ran down his cheeks, rendering him incapable of speech, until eventually he gathered his breath and, with a deep sigh, said, "O wheel of human fortune, you are forever turning, never stable! Many men have suffered on many occasions from the delight you take in making misfortune ebb and flow

158. Echoing Menelaos in the *Odyssey* (15.69ff.):
I would disapprove of another
hospitable man who was excessive in friendship,
as of one excessive in hate. In all things balance is better.
It is equally bad when one speeds on the guest unwilling
to go, and when he holds back one who is hastening. Rather
one should befriend the guest who is there, but speed him when he wishes.

so violently, but none more than I. You took from me my family and my father's home, dispossessed me of my homeland and the city of my loved ones; you drove me ashore in Egypt (to say nothing of what intervened) and delivered me into the clutches of the bandits known as Herdsmen. Then you let me see a glimmer of hope when through your agency I met some people who for all their sorrows were at least Greek. I hoped to live out what was left of my life with them, but now, it seems, you are cutting short even this solace. Which way should I turn? What ought I to do? Am I to abandon Charikleia before she has been reunited with Theagenes? What a cruel and sinful thing to do, O Earth![159] Should I go with her then and join her quest? If we were assured of finding him, efforts spent in the expectation of success would be efforts well spent. But on the other hand if the future is uncertain and merely holds yet more misfortune, then it is also uncertain what end there will ever be to my wanderings. Why do I not crave forgiveness from you and from the gods of friendship and, at long last, begin to think about returning to my homeland and my family? Particularly as, thanks to one of the gods, it seems, such an excellent opportunity has presented itself, Nausikles here having voiced his intention of sailing for Greece. Otherwise something might happen to my father while I tarry here, and then my home would be left with no one at all to inherit in due line of succession. Even if I am to be destitute, it is a proper and sufficient end in itself that at least some remnant of my family should survive in me.

"Charikleia—for it is to you above all that I am seeking to justify myself—I offer you my apologies, which I beg you to accept. If Nausikles will agree to wait a little longer, despite his urgent haste, I shall go with you as far as the Herdsmen, in the hope that I shall be able to return you to Theagenes in person. Then he would be able to see that I have conscientiously looked after the charge he entrusted to my safekeeping, and I should be able to take my leave of you with a clear conscience and high hopes for the future. But if—which heaven forfend—we do not find him, even then I could still be excused, for even then I should not be abandoning you to a lonely fate but entrusting you to the sure protection and fatherly love of Kalasiris here."

A lover is quick to discern another who has fallen prey to the same passions as himself; many signs had already led Charikleia to suspect that Knemon was enamored of Nausikles' daughter, and now Nausikles' words had made it clear to her that he would welcome the match and had busily been working to this end for some time, expending all man-

159. Knemon invokes Ge, a personification of earth, regarded as protector of oaths and often linked with Themis (Right); here the word translated "sinful" is *athemiton,* "against *themis.*" Knemon feels himself bound to Charikleia by obligations as strong as sworn oaths and overseen by the same powers.

ner of inducements to purchase Knemon's compliance. In any case she thought that Knemon was no longer a seemly or wholly trustworthy traveling companion.

"As you please," she said. "I am grateful and deeply indebted to you for your kindness in doing what you have done for us. But as far as the future is concerned, you are under no obligation whatsoever to concern yourself about us or to stay with us against your will and face the dangers of a destiny that is not your own. I hope you will win back Athens, your home and family, and embrace with all your heart our friend Nausikles and the pretext which, to use your words, has presented itself to you in his person. Whatever befalls, Kalasiris and I shall fight on until we reach the end of our wanderings, confident that even if no human being should join our quest, we have the gods as our traveling companions."

At this point Nausikles intervened. "May Charikleia's prayers be granted," he said, "and may the gods go with her as she asks; may she be reunited with her kin, as she deserves, for she is spiritually noble and intellectually able.

"As for you, Knemon, you must not be disappointed if you are returning to Athens without Thisbe, especially as you have found in me the culprit responsible for abducting her and spiriting her out of Athens. Yes, the merchant of Naukratis, Thisbe's lover, is none other than myself! And you need not think that you will have to beg for a living and bewail your penury. If you are as agreeable to the idea as I am, I shall make you a rich man and restore you to your home in your own country; if you will consent to marry her, I betroth my daughter, Nausikleia here, to you; she brings with her a magnificent dowry from me, and I ask nothing in return, for I consider that your obligations were met on the day that you told me of your family, your standing, and your nationality."

Knemon did not hesitate an instant in accepting this proposal. Everything that he had long prayed for and desired but never expected to have was now, contrary to all expectation, being granted him in a manner surpassing his prayers. "Consider it done," he said. "I accept everything you offer with great joy."

As he spoke, he held out his right hand, whereupon Nausikles presented him with his daughter and formally pronounced the betrothal. Then, instructing his servants to sing the marriage hymn, he led off the dance himself, turning the festivities they were already enjoying into an impromptu wedding feast.

Everyone was dancing; in festive procession they went to sing an extemporaneous marriage hymn at the door of the bridal chamber; the lights of the wedding vigil illuminated the house. Only Charikleia did

8

not join in; she stole away from the company and withdrew to her room; she locked the doors securely behind her; now she could be sure that no one would disturb her. Possessed by a frenzy of despair, she untied her hair without inhibition; she tore her dress and said: "Come then, let us dance too, in a manner befitting the malign power that controls our destiny. Let us sing him a song of mourning and dance him a dance of sorrow! Let us smash this lamp to the ground and veil our performance in the black gloom of night! So this is the nuptial chamber our guiding deity has built for us! This is the bridal room he has appointed for us! There is no one in it but me, no husband beside me. The room is empty, widowed of Theagenes, my husband in name only. Knemon is getting married, but Theagenes is wandering the world, a prisoner what is worse, perhaps even in chains. Even that would be a supreme happiness, so long as he were alive. Now Nausikleia is a bride, and I am parted from her who until this night shared my bed; Charikleia is alone and forsaken. It is not on their account that I reproach you, Destiny divine—I hope that they will achieve the happiness they wish for—rather on our own, because you have not been as kind to us as you are to them. The drama in which you have cast us is infinitely protracted, more tragic than anything on stage.

"But what am I doing? This is not the time for such an outcry against the gods: may their will be done in what ensues. Theagenes, the thought of whom is the one thought that brings me any joy, if you are dead, if I am brought to believe the news that I pray never to hear, I shall not hesitate to join you in death. For the present I make you this offering"—as she spoke, she tore her hair and laid the tresses on the bed[160]—"and I pour you this libation from the eyes that you love"—and straightway the rain of her tears watered her bed. "But if you are alive, as I hope, come and sleep beside me, my love; appear to me in my dreams at least. But even then respect me, my friend, and preserve your bride's virginity for lawful wedlock. See, I pretend I can see you here with me, and I embrace you!"

9    And so saying, she flung herself face downwards on the bed. She held the mattress clasped tight in her arms, sobbing and moaning from the depths of her heart, until her sorrow grew past bearing, and a swirling mist stole over her, plunging her conscious mind into darkness and causing her to slip, despite herself, into a slumber in which she remained till long after daybreak. Her failure to appear as normal surprised Kalasiris, whose search for her led him to her room. He knocked loudly on her door and called Charikleia repeatedly by name until he roused her from sleep. She awoke so abruptly that she had no time to collect her wits and

160. Hair was given as an offering to the dead (most notably offered by Elektra on the tomb of Agamemnon), but hair-offerings were also connected with marriage ritual (Herodotos 4.34; Pausanias 1.43.3, 2.32.1). Charikleia's action thus has a double aspect.

mend her appearance: she hurried to the door, drew back the bolt, and opened the door to let the old man in; but when Kalasiris saw her hair disheveled, her dress hanging in tatters over her breasts, her eyes still swollen and bearing the marks of the delirium that had preceded her sleep, he understood the cause and led her straight back to the bed, where he sat her down and wrapped a mantle around her.

Now that she was decently covered, he said: "What is the meaning of this, Charikleia? Why this extravagant and unseemly anguish? Why this senseless submission to adversity? Till now I have always admired your stalwart devotion to propriety in the face of circumstances, but now I hardly know you. Please, let us have no more such silliness! Kindly remember that you are a human being, a creature of change, subject to rapid fluctuations of fortune for good or for ill. So why hasten yourself to an untimely death when possibly a brighter future awaits you? My child, have pity on me; have pity, if not on yourself, at least on Theagenes, who has no desire to live if he cannot share his life with you, who counts his existence a gain only if your life is preserved."

Charikleia blushed, partly at Kalasiris's words, but more at the thought of the condition in which he had found her. For a long time she made no reply, but as Kalasiris pressed her for an answer, she said: "Your censure is well founded, father, but perhaps I may be forgiven; for it is no depraving desire such as ordinary people feel that makes me act as I did in my distress, but rather a pure and chaste longing for one who, in my eyes, is nonetheless my husband for never having consummated our love, for a man of Theagenes' quality. His absence from my side causes me anguish, but, even more than that, doubt as to whether he is alive or not fills me with dread."

"On that count," replied Kalasiris, "you need have no fears. He is alive and will soon be beside you. Such is the gods' will, if we are to believe—as we must—the prophecies that have been made about you, and the man who told us yesterday that Theagenes had been captured by Thyamis while being taken to Memphis. If he has been captured, then he must be safe, for there already exist ties of acquaintance and friendship between him and Thyamis. Now we have no time to lose. We must hurry as fast as we can go to the village of Bessa, where you must search for Theagenes, and I must in addition seek my son—for you know full well from what you have already heard that Thyamis is my son."[161]

Charikleia grew pensive and said, "If Thyamis really is your son, if this is your Thyamis and not a different son of a different father, then we are headed towards a most dangerous situation."

Kalasiris was taken aback and asked her why she said that.

---

161. We must presume that Kalasiris has on some unnarrated occasion mentioned to Charikleia that he has a son named Thyamis.

"You know," she answered, "that I was taken prisoner by the Herdsmen; while I was with them, my physical beauty, the possession of which seems to bring me nothing but ill fortune, provoked Thyamis too to desire me. Now I am afraid that if we meet him in the course of our search, the sight of me might remind him that I am the woman he loved, and he might consummate by force the marriage that he proposed to me then and that, by various artifices, I managed to fend off."

Kalasiris replied: "I hope that he would never succumb so far to carnal desire as to pay no heed to the visible presence of his father, so far that a father's look could not shame his son into repressing whatever illicit desire he might have. All the same, there would be no harm in your devising some ploy to circumvent your fears. You seem to be adept at thinking of clever ways to deflect and defer unwelcome advances."

10    Charikleia brightened a little at these words and said: "At this moment I shall not pause to ask whether you are being serious or just poking fun at me! Theagenes and I tried a ruse once before, though the events of that day cut it short. I propose that we make use of it again, with better hopes of success this time. Having determined to make good our escape from the Herdsmen's island, we decided to change into the shabbiest clothes we could find and disguise ourselves as beggars before venturing into the towns and villages. If you do not object, let us adopt this guise now and start begging for a living. That way we shall have less to fear from the people we meet, for in circumstances like ours there is a certain security in slender means, and penury is a closer neighbor to compassion than to envy. And we shall find it easier to obtain our daily bread,[162] for in a foreign land food to buy is hard for strangers to find, but food requested is given generously by those who feel compassion."

11    This suggestion met with the approval of Kalasiris, who was now impatient for their wayfaring to begin. So when they met Nausikles, Knemon, and the others, they informed them of their intention to depart. Two days later they set off, having dispensed with the offer of a pack animal and with all human company. Their departure was attended by Nausikles, Knemon, and everyone else in the house, including Nausikleia, who had pleaded incessantly with her father to be allowed to join the throng, for the modesty she felt as a newly wedded bride was outweighed by the spell of love that Charikleia had cast on her.

Half a mile outside the village, they embraced for the last time, Kalasiris the men, Charikleia the women, and clasped right hands, praying, amid a flood of tears, that better fortune would attend their parting. Knemon asked them to forgive him for not accompanying them, having but recently embarked upon the estate of matrimony; he said he would

162. The whole phrase is taken from Thucydides 1.2.2.

*artist*

catch up with them if the opportunity arose—but he did not mean it. Then they parted. Knemon, Nausikles, and the rest returned to Chemmis, but the first action of Charikleia and Kalasiris was to change their clothes and adopt the guise of beggars, using rags they had ready for this purpose to turn themselves into paupers. Then Charikleia befouled her face, smearing soot and daubing mud on it to make it dirty, and arranged a filthy shawl skew-whiff on her head so that the edge of it hung down over one eye like a crazy veil. Under her arm she slung a pouch, apparently to serve as a receptacle for bits of bread and scraps of food, though in fact it had the more important function of containing her sacred Delphic robe and crown and the treasures and tokens of recognition that her mother had laid beside her when she was abandoned. Kalasiris wrapped Charikleia's quiver in some tattered bits of sheepskin and carried it slung crosswise over his shoulders as if it were merely another bit of baggage. He unstrung her bow, and, as soon as it had straightened out, he held it like a staff, leaning on it with all his weight; and whenever he saw that he was about to encounter someone on the road, he assumed a stoop even greater than his years compelled and developed a limp in one leg; sometimes he had Charikleia lead him by the arm.

When they had applied the finishing touches to their charade, they teased one another a little, telling each other in jest how well the costume became them, and entreated the power that guided their destinies to make these rags the limit of their suffering and inflict no further pain on them. Then they set off in haste towards the village of Bessa, where they hoped to find Theagenes and Thyamis. But it was not to be.

It was nearly sunset, and they were close to the outskirts of Bessa when they saw a host of newly slain bodies lying on the ground. Most could be identified as Persians by their apparel and equipment, but there were a few Egyptians too. The scene was clear evidence that there had been fighting, but who the adversaries had been they could not guess. But as they picked their way through the corpses, looking at them closely as they went in case there was someone close to them among the dead—for the heart is ever in dread for those it loves the most, ever quick to divine the worst about them—they came upon a little old woman clasping one of the Egyptian dead in her arms, making all manner of mournful lamentations. They decided to try to get some information from the old woman, if they could; so they sat down beside her and began by trying to console her and reduce the excesses of her grief. This produced the desired effect; so they asked the old woman (Kalasiris speaking to her in the Egyptian tongue) who it was she was grieving over and what this fighting had been about. In a few words she told them everything: her grief was for her son, who was among the dead, and she had come to the battlefield in the express hope that someone would run her through and release her from life. In the meantime, however, she was making her son the customary offerings, so far as circumstances permitted, though she had nothing to give but tears and lamentation.

13      What she told them about the fighting was this. "A foreigner, an exceptionally tall and good-looking young man, was being taken to Oroondates, the Great King's governor-general in Memphis; I think he had been taken prisoner by Mitranes, the commander of guards, who had sent him as some sort of special gift, so they say. The men of our village here"—pointing to the nearby settlement—"seized him in a holdup. They said he was a friend of theirs, though I do not know whether they were telling the truth or inventing a pretext. When Mitranes got to hear what had happened, he was naturally very annoyed and so, the day before yesterday, mounted an assault on the village. Now, the people of the village are great fighters: brigandage is a way of life to them, and they hold death in all its forms in contempt, because of which they have many times over left many women without their husbands or sons, as has happened now to me. There had been signs that the attack was imminent; so they laid a number of ambushes in advance. When the enemy attack came, our men emerged victorious, some fighting the foe directly, face-to-face, while those in the ambuscades, with a great yell, surprised the Persians from behind. Mitranes died fighting valiantly, and virtually all of his men died with him, for they were completely encircled and had no way of escape. A few of our men were also killed, and it was heaven's stern decree that my son should be among those few, with, as you can see, a Persian arrow through his heart. And now in sorrow I weep over his dead body, but I think I shall soon be weeping too for the only son who is left me, for yesterday he marched off with the rest against the city of Memphis."

Kalasiris asked the reason for this expedition, and the old woman, adding that this was what she had been told by her surviving son, explained that the men of Bessa, having killed some royal troops and one of the Great King's commanders of guards, could see all too clearly that as a result of their regrettable action this affair would have dire consequences, imperiling their very existence; for as soon as the news reached Oroondates, the governor-general at Memphis with a whole army of men at his disposal, he would brush all opposition aside, subject the village to the "dragnet,"[163] and exterminate the entire population in reprisal.

"Seeing that their lives were at stake, they decided to attempt to find the cure for their rash action in an action even rasher, namely, by pre-

163. This Persian technique is described by Herodotos (6.31):

The men join hands and make a chain right across the island from north to south, and then move from one end to the other, hunting everyone down.

empting Oroondates' preparations, mounting a surprise attack, and if
they found the satrap at Memphis, adding his blood to that already spilt;
but if he happened to be out of town—for there is a rumor that at present
he is busy fighting a war of some kind with the Ethiopians—it would be
relatively easy for them to compel the city's submission when there was
nobody there to defend it, thus winning themselves a temporary respite
from danger and incidentally achieving a second success by restoring to
their leader, Thyamis, the office of high priest, which had been usurped
by his younger brother. Should they fail, they intended at least to die in
battle rather than endure the ignominy of capture, followed by humiliation and torture at the hands of the Persians.[164] But, strangers, where are
you headed for now?"

"To the village," replied Kalasiris.

"It would not be safe," said the old woman, "for you, as total
strangers, to present yourselves at this hour of the night to the villagers
who were left behind."

"If you came with us to introduce us," answered Kalasiris, "our safety
would be guaranteed."

"I cannot at the moment," replied the old woman. "I have certain rites
for the dead to perform that can be performed only at night. But if you
care to wait—though in fact you have no choice in the matter—move off
a little way, find some spot not too far away clear of dead bodies, and
wait there. At daybreak I shall accompany you to the village, and my
protection will ensure your safety."

Kalasiris repeated to Charikleia all that the old woman had said, and
together they moved away. After stepping over the corpses for a short
distance, they found a little hillock, and there Kalasiris stretched himself
out, pillowing his head on the quiver, while Charikleia sat, using her
pouch as a seat. The moon had just risen and was bathing the whole
scene in bright light, for it was the second night after full moon.
Kalasiris, naturally enough for an old man, especially one fatigued by his
travels, lay fast asleep, but the anxieties that beset Charikleia kept her
awake; and thus she found herself witnessing a performance which,
abominable as it may be, is common practice among the women of
Egypt.

Supposing herself now secure against any intrusion or observation,
the old woman began by digging a pit, to one side of which she lit a fire.
After positioning her son's body between the two, she took an earthenware bowl from a tripod that stood beside her and poured a libation of
honey into the pit, likewise of milk from a second bowl, and lastly of

164. Persian punishments and executions were notorious for their prolongation and cruelty.

wine from a third.[165] Then she took a cake made out of fine wheat flour
and shaped into the effigy of a man, crowned it with bay and fennel, and
flung it into the pit. Finally she picked up a sword and, in an access of
feverish ecstasy, invoked the moon by a series of grotesque and out-
landish names, then drew the blade across her arm. She wiped the blood
onto a sprig of bay and flicked it into the fire. There followed a number
of other bizarre actions, after which she knelt over the dead body of her
son and whispered certain incantations into his ear, until she woke the
dead man and compelled him by her magic arts to stand upright.

Even before this Charikleia had been somewhat alarmed by the scene
she was observing, but now her horror at this appalling ritual became so
great that she began to tremble with fear. She shook Kalasiris awake so
that he was able to see with his own eyes what was taking place. Positioned as they were in the darkness, they were invisible but could observe with little difficulty all that took place in the light cast by the fire,
and were also close enough to hear distinctly what was being said, particularly as the old woman had now begun to question the corpse in a
somewhat louder voice. What she wanted to know was whether the
corpse's brother, her one surviving son, would live to return home.

The dead man made no reply, merely nodded his head in a way that
left some doubt as to whether his mother could expect her wishes to be
fulfilled or not. Then he suddenly collapsed and fell flat on his face. The
old woman rolled the body over onto its back and persisted with her
questions. Employing apparently more powerful spells of compulsion
this time, she repeated her string of incantations into his ears, and, leaping, sword in hand, from fire to pit, from pit to fire, she succeeded in
waking the dead man a second time and, once he was on his feet, began
to put the same questions to him as before, forcing him to use speech as
well as nods of the head to make his prophecy unambiguous.

While the old woman was engaged in this, Charikleia desperately
sought Kalasiris's permission to draw closer and put a question themselves concerning Theagenes. But he refused, saying that the mere sight
of such things was unclean and that he could only tolerate it because he
had no alternative; it was not proper for a priest either to take part in or
to be present at such rites; the prophetic powers of priests proceeded
from legitimate sacrifices and pure prayer, whereas those of the profane

---

165. This scene is intended to recall the episode in the *Odyssey* (11.24ff.) when Odysseus
summons the spirits of the dead:

> I, drawing from beside my thigh my sharp sword,
> dug a pit, of about a cubit in each direction,
> and poured it full of drink offerings for all the dead, first
> honey mixed with milk, and the second pouring was sweet wine,
> and the third, water, and over it all I sprinkled white barley.

were obtained literally by crawling upon the ground and skulking among corpses, as the accidents of circumstances had permitted them to see this Egyptian woman doing.

Before Kalasiris could finish, the corpse spoke, its voice a hoarse whisper, sinister and cavernous, as if rising from some infernal abyss. 15

"Till now I have been merciful to you, Mother," it said. "I tolerated your transgression of the laws of man's nature, your affront to the ordinances of destiny, your use of the black arts to move the immovable, for even in the afterlife we continue to respect our parents so far as we may. But the respect I had for you is now forfeit by your own actions: not content with the first sin of compelling a dead body to stand upright and nod its head, you are taking your sinfulness to the extreme of extorting speech from me as well. With no thought for anything but your own concerns, you neglect the rites that are my due in death and keep me from the company of the other souls. Learn now what I have hitherto kept from telling you! Your son shall not return alive, nor shall you escape death by the sword. The whole of your life you have spent in sinful practices such as this, but soon you will meet the violent end that awaits all such as you. These are forbidden mysteries, cloaked in secrecy and darkness, but you have had the audacity to perform them, not in solitary privacy but in the presence of others, and you even parade the secrets of the dead before witnesses such as these: one is a high priest—and in his case the offense is of lesser importance, for he is wise enough to lock such secrets away in the silence of his heart and never divulge them; besides, the gods love him: his sons are armed; they are facing one another ready to fight to the death, but if he makes haste, his arrival will stay their hands on the very point of joining single combat. What is worse is that a young girl is also witness to your necromancy and can hear every word that is spoken, a young lady distraught with love and wandering over virtually the whole face of the earth in search of some loved one; but after hardships and dangers beyond counting, at earth's farthest boundaries, she will pass her life at his side in glorious and royal estate."

With these words the corpse fell limp to the ground. The old woman realized that it was the strangers that had been spying on her, and there and then she launched herself after them, sword in her hand and madness in her heart. She scoured the battlefield, suspecting that they were hiding among the dead bodies and meaning to kill them if she discovered them, for she presumed that they had spied on her necromancy from malicious and hostile motives. But her fury was so great that she did not look where she was going as she hunted through the corpses, and ended by accidentally impaling herself through the groin on a broken spear that stood upright in the ground. So she died, bringing instant and fitting fulfilment to the prophecy that her son had given her.

## Book Seven

1  Kalasiris and Charikleia had had a narrow escape, and it was with a new urgency that they now pressed on towards Memphis; not only were they concerned to put a safe distance between themselves and the terrors of that place, but their haste was also born of the prophecies that they had heard. Even as they drew close to the city, the predictions wrung from the dead man were already beginning to be fulfilled within its walls.

The appearance of Thyamis at the head of his army of bandits from Bessa had been narrowly anticipated by the inhabitants of Memphis, who had closed the city gates just in time, after the alarm had been raised by one of Mitranes' solders, who had escaped from the battle at Bessa and seen that this attack on Memphis was imminent. Thyamis commanded his men to ground arms beside a section of the wall, where he allowed them to recover from the exertions of their forced march. He intended—incredible though it seems—to put the city under siege. At first the people of Memphis had been terrified, for they had supposed the force moving against them to be a large one, but after observation from the walls revealed that in fact their assailants were few in number, they could not wait to muster the few archers and cavalrymen who had been left to protect the city, arm the populace with makeshift weapons, and go outside the walls to join battle with the foe. However, they were prevented by an elderly and widely respected man, who reminded them that although, as chance would have it, the satrap Oroondates was not at that time in Memphis, having marched off to war against the Ethiopians, it was nevertheless right and proper to notify his wife, Arsake,[166] before they took action, for if she gave her approval, such soldiers as were to be found in the city would be more inclined to cooperate.[167] This advice was well received, and they hastened *en masse* to the palace, which, in the absence of the king, the satraps used as their residence.

2  Arsake was a tall, handsome woman, highly intelligent and arrogant and proud by reason of her noble birth, naturally enough for one who had been born the sister of the Great King. But the life she led was disreputable: in particular she was a slave to perverted and dissipated pleasure. Her crimes included being in part responsible for Thyamis's banishment from Memphis. It was just after Kalasiris had, without a word to anyone, removed himself from Memphis as a result of the prophecy concerning his sons that he had been given by the gods. The old man having disappeared and being presumed dead, the office of high priest fell upon

166. An archetypal Persian name, recalling Arsakes, founder of the Arsakid dynasty of Parthia.
167. Reading συλλαμβάνοι with the majority of the manuscripts.

Thyamis as his elder son. While he was performing public sacrifices to
mark his assumption of the office, Arsake chanced to see him in the temple of Isis: a comely young man, in the flower of his manhood, and arrayed in especial splendor because of the ceremony in which he was engaged. She cast on him eyes of lust and made him signs to hint at her
obscene intentions. This, however, elicited no response at all from
Thyamis, whose character and upbringing were devoid of all unchastity;
far from suspecting the true meaning of her actions, he may have been so
absorbed in his holy rites that he attributed them to an entirely different
cause. However, his brother, Petosiris, in whom had been festering for
many years a jealous desire for the office of high priest, had observed Arsake's advances. Her illicit approaches provided him with the basis of a
plot against his brother. In a secret audience, he not only informed
Oroondates of Arsake's infatuation but compounded his story with the
false insinuation that Thyamis had complied with her desires. Oroondates already entertained suspicions about his wife and needed little convincing. In the absence of firm proof, however, he took no steps against
her; besides, the awe and respect in which he held the royal house compelled him to keep to himself such suspicions as he had. But he issued a
number of proclamations threatening Thyamis with death, and did not
cease until he had driven him into exile, whereupon he created Petosiris
high priest in his stead.

That was all past history now. To return to our story, Arsake responded to the crowd that had gathered at her residence to inform her of
the enemy attack—something she was already well aware of—and request her permission for such troops as were available[168] to join them in a
sortie, by refusing to grant this permission without proper consideration
and before she had ascertained the size of the enemy's force, who they
were, or where they came from, or had even learned the reason for their
attack; their first action should be to go over to the city walls and make a
thorough reconnaissance of the situation from there, and then, with additional assistance, they could pursue a course that was both feasible and
expedient.

This was adjudged good advice, and without further ado they hastened to the wall, where Arsake gave orders for a pavilion to be erected
beneath a canopy of purple embroidered with gold. Then, exquisitely arrayed, she took her seat on an elevated throne, encircled by her bodyguard in their gilded armor. Holding aloft a herald's staff to signify that
she wished to negotiate peace, she called upon the enemy's leaders and
men of note to draw close to the wall. Thyamis and Theagenes were
chosen by their men and stepped forward. They stood at the foot of the

3

168. Reading παροῦσι for οὖσι.

wall, in full armor, except that their heads were bare, while the herald proclaimed: "Hear the words of Arsake, wife of Oroondates the supreme satrap, and sister of the Great King. Who are you? What is your purpose? What reason do you adduce for venturing to attack this city?"

They replied that their army was composed of men of Bessa. Thyamis identified himself and said that he had been wronged by his brother, Petosiris, and Oroondates, who had conspired to rob him of the office of high priest, to which the men of Bessa were now restoring him. If he was now reinstated in his priesthood, hostilities would be at an end, and the men of Bessa would return home without inflicting any harm on anyone; otherwise, war and the force of arms would have to decide the matter. If Arsake had any concern for propriety, Thyamis continued, she should avail herself of this opportunity to punish Petosiris for his schemes against her and the wicked and lying slanders about her that he had uttered to Oroondates, which had caused her to be suspected by her husband of an illicit and degraded passion and him to be banished from his homeland.

4    This caused universal consternation among the people of Memphis. They recognized Thyamis, and, although previously, at the time of his departure, they had been unaware of the reason for his banishment, Thyamis's words now aroused their suspicions, and they had no doubt as to the truth of what he said. Most confounded of all was Arsake, who was trapped in a maelstrom of emotion. She was filled with anger against Petosiris, and as she recalled past events, she began to plan her revenge; and as she looked upon Thyamis and then upon Theagenes, her heart was rent in two, torn asunder by the desire she felt for each of them: in one case it was the revival of an old passion, in the other a new and more painful shaft piercing her heart. Her anguish was plain, even to those around her. Nevertheless, after a moment's silence, she regained her composure, like one recovering from an attack of epilepsy, and said: "The whole of Bessa must have been infected by an insane desire for war, particularly you, my friends: such handsome young men, in the first bloom of manhood, wellborn too, as is obvious from your appearance, yet facing certain death just for the sake of a gang of bandits—for if it came to a battle, you would be unable to withstand even the first onset. May the Great King's strength never be so weakened that, even in the absence of his satrap, the merest leftovers of his army in Egypt would not be sufficient to sweep you, to a man, off the face of the earth!

"However, there is no need for extensive bloodletting, I think: the reason for this aggression is a private one that is of no concern to the people at large. I can see no reason why the dispute should not also be settled privately and be brought to whatever end the gods and justice herself shall decide. This is my command," she said. "The people of Memphis and Bessa shall be at peace and shall not wage war on one another when they have no cause to do so. But those who are in dispute over the office of high priest will face one another in single combat, with the priesthood as prize for the victor."

Arsake's words were greeted with a roar of approbation by all the inhabitants of Memphis, partly because they had been induced to suspect Petosiris of dishonest dealings, and partly because they all rather liked the idea of escaping from obvious and imminent danger by letting someone else do the fighting. The majority of the men of Bessa, on the other hand, seemed unhappy with the proposal and disinclined to abandon their leader to risk his life on their behalf, until Thyamis persuaded them to agree to the idea by pointing out Petosiris's lack of strength and martial experience; in combat, he assured them, the odds would be overwhelmingly in his favor. This thought, it seems was exactly what had prompted Arsake to propose the single combat, for she realized both that her ends would be accomplished without any suspicion falling on herself and that, in fighting to the death with Thyamis, who was much the better man, Petosiris would pay a penalty befitting his offense against her.

There ensued the spectacle of Arsake's orders being put into effect more quickly than it takes to tell: Thyamis, on the one hand, all eagerness to take up the challenge, was completing his arming systematically and joyfully, while Theagenes, with many a word of encouragement, placed on his head his helmet, surmounted by a splendid crest and glinting with the brilliance of polished gold, and secured the straps on the rest of his equipment; Petosiris, on the other hand, was being manhandled out of the city gate in compliance with Arsake's command and, cry as he might for mercy, was being forcibly prepared for battle.

On seeing him, Thyamis exclaimed, "Theagenes, my dear friend, do you not see how Petosiris is quaking with fear?"

"I do indeed," replied Theagenes, "but how are you going to act in this situation? It is not just an enemy you are fighting against—it is your brother!"

"Quite right," said Thyamis. "Your words have flown unerringly to the mark of my own thoughts. My purpose is to defeat him, god willing, but not to kill him. I hope I should never be such a prey to anger and resentment over past wrongs as to be prepared to purchase vengeance for the past and a degree of honor for the future by spilling my own brother's blood and polluting my hands with the killing of one born from the same womb as I."

"Your words," replied Theagenes, "show you to be a man of nobility and well aware of the bonds of nature. What charge do you have to lay upon me?"

"It would be easy," Thyamis answered, "to make light of the contest that awaits me, but the fortunes of men often have a way of producing strange and unexpected results. If I win, then you will accompany me

into Memphis, where we shall live together as brothers; but should anything untoward occur, then you must take command of these men of
Bessa, who are devoted to you, and endure the ordeals of life as a brig-
and, until god allows you to glimpse a happier ending to your story."

6    Thereupon they embraced and kissed one another tearfully. Without
moving from that spot, Theagenes sat down, still in his armor, to watch
what happened. Thus, did he but know it, he was affording Arsake the
sensual pleasure of looking upon him as she studied his every feature and
allowed her eyes to indulge their desire awhile.

Thyamis rushed at Petosiris, who made no attempt to withstand the
onslaught but, at the first step that Thyamis made towards him, took to
his heels and ran to the gates in a desperate effort to get back into the
city; but it was to no avail. He was repulsed by the men posted on the
gates, and wherever his frantic flight took him, the people on the walls
refused to allow him back in. And so he threw down his weapons and,
for the moment, went on running, as fast as his legs would carry him,
around the perimeter of the city. Keeping pace behind them ran Theagenes, who, full of apprehension for Thyamis's safety, was determined not
to miss anything that happened. He carried no weapons, however, so
that no one could suspect him of intending to assist Thyamis in the fight;
his spear and shield he had left lying by the section of the wall where he
had been sitting beneath Arsake's gaze, thus affording her the consolation
of having them, if not his person, in her sight while he joined in the pursuit. Running for his life, Petosiris managed to stay ahead of Thyamis,
but only by a very short distance; at every moment it looked as if he was
on the point of being caught, but he always eluded Thyamis's grasp by
just that margin by which one might have expected a man in full armor
to lag behind a man in none. Round the walls they sped, once, twice, but
towards the end of their third circuit, with Thyamis leveling his spear at
his brother's back and threatening to strike him dead if he did not stand
and fight, with the entire population of the city lining the walls,[169]
watching like the presiding judges in a theater[170]—at that very moment
either some divine power or some fortune that arbitrates over human
destiny made the drama take a new and tragic twist, almost as if bringing

169. The pursuit around the city walls is meant to recall the pursuit of Hektor around
Troy by Achilles in the *Iliad* (22.137ff., esp. 199ff.):

> As in a dream a man is not able to follow one who runs
> from him, nor can the runner escape, nor the other pursue him,
> so he could not run him down in his speed, nor the other get clear.

Likewise the single combat between the brothers Thyamis and Petosiris for the high priesthood of Memphis reminds the reader of that between Eteokles and Polyneikes, sons of
Oidipous, for the throne of Thebes.

170. At the festivals where Attic tragedy and comedy were performed the plays were
ranked in order of merit by a panel of judges, and prizes were awarded accordingly.

a second drama on stage to compete with the one already in progress: by a miracle of stagecraft[171] it brought Kalasiris onto the scene on that very day, at that very hour, to join the race and, alas for him, to behold his sons fight to the death. Many ordeals had he endured, every imaginable expedient had he contrived—even to the point of sentencing himself to banishment and exile in foreign lands—in the hope of avoiding this dreadful sight. But he was no match for destiny, and he was compelled to behold that which the gods had foretold long before.

He was some way off when he first espied the chase, but, from the many prophecies he had received, he realized that the combatants must be his own sons and forced his aged body to a spurt of speed remarkable for a man of his years in the hope of forestalling their fatal conflict. Now he had caught up with them and was running alongside them. "What are you doing, Thyamis and Petosiris?" he called over and over again. "What are you doing, my children?" he cried repeatedly.

But as yet they did not recognize their father, for he was still clad in his beggar's rags, while they had thought for nothing but their contest, so that they paid him no attention whatever, taking him for a vagabond or some other kind of lunatic. Some of those on the walls were impressed by the way he sought to interpose himself between two armed men with such selfless courage, but others thought he must be deranged, and laughed at such irrational exertions.

But finally the old man realized that it was his shabby appearance that was preventing his sons from recognizing him, whereupon he threw off his disguise of rags, untied his priest's mane of hair, cast aside the pack from his back and the staff from his hands, and confronted them, revealed in all his sacerdotal dignity. Then, slowly, he sank to his knees, his hands outstretched in supplication. "My children," he cried through his tears, "it is Kalasiris you see before you, none other than your own father. Run no more. Cease from this lunacy that destiny has caused in you. Your father is restored to you; honor him as you should!"

At these words their strength failed them, and they very nearly swooned. Then they both knelt before their father and clasped his knees. At first they gazed upon him hard and long to make sure they were not mistaken, but then, having assured themselves that what they saw was no illusion but reality, they experienced many contrary emotions at one and the same time: joy at the unexpected restoration of their father, sorrow and shame at the business in which he had surprised them, and finally anguish over the uncertainties of what might ensue. And before the people of Memphis could recover from their amazement, as silent as if they had been struck dumb with bewilderment, as still as figures in a

171. The *mechane* again; see note 34. Kalasiris is like a *deus ex machina*.

painting, so engrossed and moved were they by this spectacle, the drama was interrupted by another unexpected entry:[172] Charikleia! She was following hard on Kalasiris's heels and had recognized Theagenes from afar—for a lover's eyes are so quick to recognize the object of their love that often the merest movement or gesture, even if seen from a great distance or from behind, is enough to suggest an imaginary resemblance. Now, as if the sight of him had stung her to a frenzy, she threw herself upon him, flung her arms around his neck, and hung in a clinging embrace, tearfully sobbing out her greeting.

But of course the sight of her face hideously disguised with filth and of her tattered and ragged garments led him to suppose that she truly was some mendicant vagabond, and he tried to push her away and elbow her aside. But she refused to let him go and made such a nuisance of herself, blocking his view of what was happening to Kalasiris, that eventually he cuffed her round the head.

"O Pythian," she whispered, "have you forgotten the torch?" Her words pierced Theagenes' heart like an arrow, for he recognized the torch as one of the signs that they had agreed upon. He gazed hard at Charikleia and was dazzled by the brilliance of her eyes, as if by a shaft of sunlight shining out between the clouds. He took her in his arms and held her tight, with the result that all the people thronging the section of the wall where Arsake, already swelling with jealousy at the spectacle of Charikleia, had her throne were enraptured by this miracle of theatrical art.

8    So this sinful war between brothers was at an end, and the struggle, which had seemed set to be settled by the spilling of blood, changed at its denouement from tragedy to comedy. The father who had beheld his sons engaged in single combat, their swords drawn against one another, who had come within an ace of the misery of having his children die within the sight of the eyes that gave them birth, himself became the agent of peace. He had proved unable to escape destiny's ordinance, but his arrival in the nick of time to witness what had been preordained had brought him happiness. The two sons now had their father restored to them after his ten years of homeless wandering. He had been the cause of a quarrel over the priesthood for which they had been prepared to shed one another's blood, but the very next moment with their own hands they garlanded his head and crowned him with the insignia of his holy office, before escorting him into the city. But all were agreed that the high point of the drama was its romantic side, in the shape of Theagenes and Charikleia, two charming young people in the full bloom of their

---

172. Heliodoros here uses (or possibly misuses) an obscure technical term of the theater, *parenkyklema:* this seems to describe the use of the *ekkyklema* (see note 54) to interrupt the action taking place on stage.

youth, who against all expectation were now reunited: the eyes of the city were turned upon them more than upon any of the other participants.

The entire population came pouring out through the gates and began to pack the plain that lay before the walls. All ages were there: the youthful element of the city, those on the verge of manhood, flocked to Theagenes, while those of maturer years, fully adult males who were able to recognize him, gathered around Thyamis; the maidens of Memphis, those already dreaming of their bridal bed, clustered around Charikleia, while the whole tribe of priests and elders formed an escort for Kalasiris. Spontaneously a kind of religious procession formed. Thyamis dismissed the men of Bessa after expressing his heartfelt thanks for their zeal, with a promise that, in a few days' time, when the moon was waxing full, he would send them one hundred head of cattle, a thousand sheep, and ten drachmas for each man. Then he placed his father's arm around his neck to take the old man's weight and support him as he walked, for the joyful surprise had left him somewhat unsteady on his legs. On the other side Petosiris did likewise, and so, by the light of flaming torches, Kalasiris was conducted to the temple of Isis, while all around the crowd cheered and clapped him on his way, and massed pipes and temple flutes played a rousing tune that had the more ebullient of the young people dancing in an intoxication of high spirits.

Arsake was not to be left out of the action but paraded self-importantly in a grandiose procession of her own, made up of her private bodyguard, to the temple of Isis, where she dedicated jewelry and a vast quantity of gold, ostensibly from the same motives as the rest of the city, though in reality her eyes were fixed only on Theagenes, and none looked upon him more hungrily than she. However, her pleasure was not unalloyed, for the sight of Theagenes taking Charikleia by the arm and protecting her from the crush of the crowd stung Arsake with the sharp pain of jealousy.

On entering the shrine, Kalasiris prostrated himself and embraced the feet of the cult statue. He remained in that position for some length of time and very nearly expired there. With great difficulty, and only with the help of the bystanders, he rose to his feet and offered a libation and a prayer to the goddess. Then he took the crown of priestly office from off his own head and set it upon the head of his son Thyamis, explaining publicly that he was now well advanced in years and could foresee, moreover, that his end was at hand, while Thyamis, as the elder of his sons, was legally entitled to the insignia of the priesthood and had the spiritual and physical strength to perform the duties of that office. The people showed their approval with an eruption of clamorous applause. Then Kalasiris retired to a room in the temple set aside for the high priests, and there he remained, along with his sons and Theagenes and Charikleia.

The rest departed, each to his own home, including Arsake, though she found it hard to tear herself away and turned back many times and loitered in the temple, pretending to pay further pious homage to the goddess. But depart she eventually did, with many a backward glance at Theagenes as long as he remained in view. When she reached the royal court, she rushed straight to her chamber and hurled herself onto her bed, where she lay fully clothed in silent misery. She was a woman generally addicted to ignoble pleasure, but now her passion was fired as never before by Theagenes' peerless beauty, before which everything else in her experience paled into insignificance. All night she lay there, ceaselessly tossing from side to side, ceaselessly sighing from the depths of her being: one moment she would sit bolt upright, the next slump back on the bedclothes; she would remove part of her clothing and then suddenly collapse back on her bed, or, occasionally, summon a maidservant for no apparent reason and then send her away again without asking her to do anything.[173] In short, her desire was degenerating imperceptibly into insanity, until an old woman by the name of Kybele, one of the chambermaids who were in the habit of abetting Arsake in her love affairs, bustled into her mistress's room. Understanding perfectly what had happened—for there was a light burning in Arsake's room whose flame, as it were, shared in the fire of her love—she asked: "What is the matter, mistress? What is this new pain that makes you suffer so? Whom has my baby seen that causes her such heartache? Who could be so presumptuous or so deranged as not to capitulate before your beauty or not to consider union in love with you to be very bliss? Who dares disregard your will and pleasure? You have only to tell me, my darling child; there is no heart so hard that it is proof against my spells. You have only to tell me, and you will have your heart's desire in an instant. My past achievements have given you proof enough of my abilities, I think."

10   And while she intoned these and many other words of the same kind, Kybele fawned and whined at her mistress's feet, coaxing Arsake by every means she knew to tell her what was wrong.

After a short silence, Arsake said: "I am stricken more deeply than ever before, Mother, and though many times in the past you have served

173. Arsake's restless sleeplessness is one of the familiar symptoms of love in literature, but Heliodoros also wishes to call to mind Homer's picture of Achilles grieving sleeplessly for Patroklos (*Iliad* 24.4ff.):

> nor did sleep
> who subdues all come over him, but he tossed from one side to the other
> in longing for Patroklos....he let fall the swelling tears, lying
> sometimes along his side, sometimes on his back, and now again
> prone on his face; then he would stand upright.

me well in matters of this sort, I doubt whether this will be another of your successes on my behalf. Today before the city walls a war nearly broke out, but peace was quickly restored: as far as everyone but myself is concerned this peaceful result was achieved without a drop of blood being spilled, but for me it has become the start of a war in greater earnest, an injury not just to some limb or member of my body but to my very soul; for, alas, it gave me a sight of that young stranger who ran beside Thyamis in the duel. You must know the man I mean, Mother: his beauty was like a lightning flash, easily eclipsing all others. Even some old gaffer with no concern for things of beauty could not have failed to notice him—let alone you with your wide experience of the world. There now, my dearest, you know by what shaft I am pierced, and now you must try every device you know, all the charms and insinuations at which old woman are so adept, if you value your baby's life—for there is no way I can go on living if I do not make him mine at all costs."

"I know the young man," replied the old servant, "a broad-chested, broad-shouldered fellow, who held his head high with an extraordinary pride and stood taller than all the rest; his eyes were of the clearest blue, and his expression at one and the same time attractive and imposing. He was the one with the lovely long hair and the first growth of golden down on his cheeks. Some foreign female, quite pretty but far too forward, I felt, suddenly ran up, threw her arms around him, and clung fast in his embrace. Or is that not the man you mean, mistress?"

"That is the one, Mother" she said, "and thank you for reminding me of that disgusting spectacle, that damned little whore, with her head swollen with the idea of her own meager, vulgar charms that she got out of a jar! But all the same she is a luckier woman than I to have a lover like that."

At these words a sly smile flickered over the old woman's lips. "Take heart, mistress," she said. "Her days of seeming fair in the stranger's eyes are over. If I can induce him to turn his attention to you and your charms, he will reject that little trollop with her delusions of beauty and unfounded conceit, and, as the saying goes, will exchange bronze for gold."[174]

"If only you could, my dear old Kybele. You would cure me of two sicknesses at one stroke—love and jealousy, by satisfying the one and ridding me of the other."

174. Referring to the famous exchange of weapons between Glaukos and Diomedes in the sixth book of the *Iliad* (234–36):

> but Zeus the son of Kronos stole away the wits of Glaukos
> who exchanged with Diomedes the son of Tydeus armour
> of gold for bronze, for nine oxen's worth the worth of a hundred.

"I shall play my part," replied Kybele. "What you must do now is rest and regain your strength, keep up your spirits and not let despair exhaust your strength too soon."

11 With these words she removed the lamp and locked the bedroom door, before departing. At the first faint glimmer of dawn, she took one of the royal eunuchs and another serving maid, whom she told to follow with sacrificial cakes and certain other offerings, and hurried to the temple of Isis. At the temple door she announced that she was bringing a sacrifice to the goddess on behalf of her mistress, Arsake, who had been alarmed by certain dreams and wished to make a placatory offering to avert her vision. But one of the sacristans refused her admittance and told her to go home, since, he said, the whole sacred precinct was shrouded in sorrow. Returned home after long years of absence, Kalasiris the high priest had spent the evening partaking of an excellent dinner in the company of those he loved best, and had indulged himself to the full in the pleasures of relaxation and conviviality. At the end of the meal he had poured a libation and prayed long to the gods and then had told his sons that this would be the last time they saw their father. He had laid a solemn charge on them to make the best provision they could for the two young Greeks he had brought with him and to render them whatever assistance they could in whatever they chose to do. Then he had retired to bed. Concerned by their father's intimations of the future, his sons had kept vigil all night at his bedside, and at cockcrow the old man had been found to be dead: possibly his enormous joy had caused the muscles of his respiratory tract to become excessively dilated and flaccid consequent upon the sudden exhaustion of his aged body; or else perhaps he had prayed for death, and the gods had granted his prayer.

"We have just now dispatched messengers," he continued, "to summon hither the whole of the remaining hierarchy of Memphis to pay his body the customary respects according to ancestral tradition. Now get you gone: for seven whole days henceforward none save those ordained into the priesthood may offer any sacrifice or even set foot inside the temple."

"So what will become of those strangers you mentioned?" inquired Kybele.

"Thyamis, the new high priest," he replied, "has commanded that accommodation be provided for them nearby, outside the temple grounds. Look, here they come now, quitting the holy places for a time in obedience to the law."

Kybele seized on the opportunity offered by this turn of events and began to stalk her quarry. "Most blessed of temple servants," she said, "here is a chance for you to do a good turn for the strangers and for me too—or rather for Arsake, the sister of the Great King. You know how

*Kybele's scheme*

she loves all things Greek and how very ready she is to open her house to strangers. Tell these young people that by order of Thyamis accommodation has been arranged for them in my lord's palace."

The sacristan did as Kybele suggested, for he suspected nothing of the schemes hatching in the darkness of her heart but supposed that he would be doing the strangers a kindness if by his agency they were received into the satrap's court, and also that he stood to earn the gratitude of those who were making this request, which seemed to cost nothing and harm no one.[175] Seeing Theagenes and Charikleia coming towards him downcast and weeping, the sacristan said: "In mourning and lamenting the passing of a high priest, despite an express warning that this was forbidden, you are transgressing our rules and contravening our traditions: rather, according to the precepts of divine and sacred lore, he should be conducted to his grave with rejoicing and blessings[176] for having entered upon a better estate and joined heaven's elect. However, you may be forgiven, for you have lost one whom you called Father, your protector and sole support. Nevertheless, you must not lose heart completely, for along with the priesthood Thyamis appears to have inherited his father's concern for your well-being. His first command was that good care be taken of you. Splendid accommodation has been arranged for you, such as might be the envy of a wealthy native of this country, to say nothing of foreigners whose present state seems less than prosperous. Go with this lady"—he pointed to Kybele—"and think of her, both of you, as your mother. She will take care of you. Do as she says."

The two lovers did as the sacristan told them, partly because they were too deeply sunk in a tide of unexpected misfortune to think clearly, partly because they were happy to find shelter and refuge anywhere in their present plight. But had they had any inkling of the fatal pride that dwelt in the palace and of the harm it would cause them, they surely would never have entered it. Now the fate that presided over the tournament of their destiny had ceased its persecution for a few hours and smiled on them, but their happiness was to be short-lived, its brief day succeeded by new sorrows that destiny was already preparing. Fate was delivering them like willing captives into the hands of their foe, imprisoning, by a semblance of kindness and hospitality, two young people, strangers in a foreign land and unsuspecting of what lay in store for them. For thus it is that a life of wandering imposes on travelers sojourning in foreign parts a lack of awareness that is tantamount to blindness.

On reaching the satrapal residence, they were immediately confronted by an impressive gateway of a grandeur far exceeding that of a private

12

175. The Greek text is corrupt at this point; the translation gives the probable sense.
176. This is quoted word for word from a famous passage of Euripides' lost play *Kresphontes* (frag. 449 Nauck).

dwelling, lined with a magnificent array of guardsmen and teeming with a pretentious retinue of other household servants. They were filled with a mixture of awe and dismay at the sight of this palace that was in such marked contrast to their own present condition. They followed Kybele, who was at great pains to encourage and reassure them and kept calling them her darling little children and assuring them that they need have no fear concerning what awaited them. Eventually the old woman showed them to her quarters, which were in a secluded and private part of the palace. She asked the attendants to leave, and now she had Theagenes and Charikleia to herself.

She sat down beside them and said: "My children, I know the cause of the depression that oppresses you today: you are grieving for the death of the high priest Kalasiris, who was as a father to you. But I think I have a right to know who you are and where you are from. I know that you are Greek, and the evidence of my own eyes tells me that you are of noble family, for the brilliance of your eyes and an appearance that combines elegance and charm are positive proof of good breeding. But I should like very much to know what part of Greece, what city you hail from, who you are, and how your travels have brought you to Egypt. Please tell me. It will be greatly to your advantage, for then I shall be able to tell my mistress, Arsake, the sister of the Great King and wife to Oroondates, the greatest of satraps, a lover of refinement and all things Greek, and known for her kindness to strangers, all about you; and she will receive you with especial honor, as is your due. You will be telling someone who has much in common with you, for I am a Greek myself: Lesbos was my home;[177] I was taken prisoner in a war and brought here, where I am much better off than those who stayed at home. I am everything to my mistress; you might say I am the very air she breathes; I am her eyes, her mind, her ears, her all. She relies on me to introduce the right sort of people to her, and I know and keep all her most intimate secrets."

Theagenes was beginning to associate Kybele's words with Arsake's extraordinary behavior towards him the previous day. He recalled how she had stared at him with such intensity and lack of modesty, never taking her eyes off him, so that her dishonorable intentions were all too plain. He had a premonition that no good would come of all this. But just as he was on the point of replying to the old woman, Charikleia leaned over and whispered softly in his ear, "Remember your sister in whatever you say!"

13    Theagenes understood the hint. "Mother," he said, "you seem to have

177. The place is chosen for its erotic associations. It was the home of the poetess Sappho, writer of passionate love poetry; and the women of Lesbos were widely regarded as experts in oral sex, giving rise to the verb *lesbiazein,* "fellate."

discovered for yourself that we are Greeks. We are in fact brother and sister, who set off in search of our parents, who had been abducted by pirates. But our misfortunes have been even crueler than theirs, for we became the victims of men even more brutal than those pirates. We were robbed of all we had—and it was a great deal—and barely escaped with our lives. But then, through some benevolence of heaven, we met our dear, departed Kalasiris and so came to Egypt, where we hoped to spend the rest of our lives in his company. Now, as you can see, we have nothing; we are alone and forsaken, for besides everything else we have now lost the one whom we considered—indeed who was—our father. There, now you know our story. We are very grateful to you for your present kindness and hospitality, but the greatest kindness you could show us would be to arrange for us to live together far from the eyes of the world and to say no more of the kind offer you were making a few moments ago to introduce us to Arsake. She is rich and happy; we are homeless, wretched strangers in a foreign land; do not impose our sorrows on her. I am sure you understand that it is best for introductions and acquaintances to be made between people whose situations are similar."

On hearing this Kybele was unable to prevent a broad smile spreading over her face, clear indication of her joy at hearing that they were brother and sister, for she envisaged that Charikleia would not pose any sort of obstacle to the affairs of Arsake's heart.      14

"My dear young man," she said, "you will not speak like that about Arsake when you have seen at first hand what she is like. She is not one to stand aloof, whatever your station, and, moreover, she is generous to those who, despite their merits, are less well off than she. Although she is a Persian by race, she is very much a Greek at heart and very partial to people from that country. She is fond to a fault of Greek ways and the company of Greeks. You can feel confident then that you will be treated with all the honor appropriate to a man, while your sister will be my mistress's intimate companion. What should I tell her your names are?"

They said they were called Theagenes and Charikleia. "Wait for me here," said the old woman and hurried off to Arsake, though not before giving strict instructions to the doorkeeper, another old woman, to refuse admittance to anyone wishing to enter the room and not to allow the two young people to leave.

"Not even if your son, Achaimenes,[178] turns up?" asked the doorkeeper. "Just after you set out for the temple he went out to get some ointment for his eyes—you know that they are still giving him a bit of trouble."

178. Another typically Persian name, recalling the eponymous founder of the Persian royal house.

"Not even him," replied Kybele. "Lock the door, keep the key yourself, and tell him that I have taken it with me!"

Her bidding was done. But no sooner had Kybele departed than Theagenes and Charikleia, finding themselves alone, remembered their sorrowful plight and began to weep. The words and substance of their lamentations were virtually identical. "O Theagenes!" she wailed and wailed, and each time he responded, "O Charikleia!"

"What new chance has made us its victims?" he cried, while she sobbed, "Whatever lies in store for us?" And with each thought they embraced and renewed their kisses through their tears. And finally the loss of Kalasiris came to mind and turned their lamentation into grief at his passing, particularly for Charikleia, who had known him for a longer time and benefited more from his affectionate attentions.

"O Kalasiris!" she cried mournfully. "No more may I call anyone Father, the best of names, for heaven has made it its sport at every turn to deny me the right to address anyone as my father. My natural father I have never seen; my adoptive father, Charikles, alas, I have betrayed; now I have lost the man who took me into his care, cherished me, and saved my life. And the rules of his priestly office do not even permit me to perform the usual rituals of grief over his dead body. But come now, my guardian and my savior—and I shall add the name of Father even though heaven denies it me—in such place and such manner as I may, I pour you a libation—of my own tears!—and bring you an offering—of my own tresses!"

With these words she began to tear out great handfuls of her hair. Theagenes seized her hands, restrained her, begged her to stop, but she went on with her tragic scene, saying: "What is the point of going on living? What hope do we have to guide us? Kalasiris is dead, he who led us by the hand through foreign lands, who was our rod and staff in our wanderings, our guide on our journey to the land of my birth, the key to my parents' recognition, our solace in distress, our help and salvation in perplexity, the anchor on whom our whole destiny was fastened. He is dead, and the two of us are left beset by sorrows in a strange land with no eyes to discern what we should do next. All routes by land and sea are closed to us by our lack of knowledge. That noble and kindly heart, that wise and truly venerable soul, has passed away, and even he was not allowed to see the end to which all his kindnesses were directed."

15    While she was still piteously lamenting in this vein, Theagenes both echoing her grief with sorrows of his own and at the same time choking back his tears so as to spare Charikleia further pain, along came Achaimenes, only to find the doors locked and bolted.

"What is going on?" he asked the doorkeeper, who replied that it was his mother's doing. As he was standing mystified at the door, he became

*[margin note: lost w/o father figure]*

aware of Charikleia's lamentations, bent down to peer through the holes through which the chains that held the bolts were fastened, and saw what was taking place. Turning back to the doorkeeper, he asked her who the people in the room were. She replied that all she knew was that they were a young man and woman—foreigners she would guess—whom his mother had brought home with her not long before.

He bent down again and tried to identify the people he could see. Charikleia he had never seen before, though he was greatly struck by her beauty and pictured to himself what she would look like if she were not in mourning; and imperceptibly admiration led to love. Theagenes, on the other hand, he fancied was vaguely familiar, though he could not be sure.

At this point Kybele returned and caught him peering through the door. She had reported her interview with the young couple to Arsake and congratulated her warmly on the good fortune that unprompted had produced a happy result one might have despaired of ever achieving by countless ploys and stratagems: she had the object of her affections ensconced in the house, where they could meet in complete security. She had added much else of similar import, thus fanning the flames of Arsake's passion so high that Kybele had had some difficulty in checking her eagerness to see Theagenes there and then: she would not like the young man, she had said, to see her mistress now, with her face pale and eyes red from her sleepless night, but tomorrow when she had had a day's rest to restore her normal beauty. Having thus raised Arsake's spirits and made her confident of achieving her heart's desire, Kybele had instructed her on the appropriate way to behave towards her guests.

When, to resume our story, she found Achaimenes at the door, she    16
exclaimed, "What are you being so inquisitive about, my child?"

"The strangers in there," he replied. "Who are they? Where are they from?"

"You must not ask, my son," Kybele told him. "Hold your tongue. Keep your thoughts to yourself and mention this to no one. Have as little to do with our guests as possible. This is our mistress's will."

Achaimenes obeyed his mother without demur and left, surmising that Theagenes was just one more of those young men who came to minister to Arsake's sexual appetite. But as he left, he said to himself: "Is not that the man that Mitranes, the commander of guards, gave me the other day to take to Oroondates so as to be sent on to the Great King? Thyamis and the men of Bessa took him from me, and I came within an inch of losing my life—in fact, I was the only one of the escort party that managed to get away. Or are my eyes playing tricks? No, they are better now, and my vision is almost back to normal. Besides, I have heard that Thyamis turned up yesterday and was restored to the office of high priest

*[margin note:]* Achaimenes recognizes Theagenes

after fighting a duel with his brother. Yes, this is the man; I am sure of it! But for the moment I must keep it to myself that I know who he is, and wait and see what my mistress's intentions are towards the strangers."

17     Such was his soliloquy. As Kybele burst into the room, she found the traces of the young couple's sorrow still fresh; for although, as the doors banged open, they tried to compose themselves and did their utmost to feign normality of bearing and expression, they were unable to conceal their sadness from the old woman, for their eyes were still full of tears.

So Kybele exclaimed: "My darling children, why are you weeping? This is no time for tears, but rather for joy and jubilation at your good fortune. Arsake's feelings towards you are as warm as you could wish. She has agreed to grant you an audience tomorrow, and in the meantime it is her wish that you be treated with all possible attention and hospitality. But first you must stop this silly weeping. It really is childish. The time has come for you to attune yourselves to your situation and submit obediently to Arsake's bidding."

"Mother," replied Theagenes, "it was recollection of the passing of Kalasiris that made us grieve and weep for the loss of his fatherly affection."

"Stuff and nonsense!" retorted Kybele. "Kalasiris, who was your father only in your imaginations, was just an old man who has gone the way of all flesh when his years grew too many for him. Now, at a stroke, you have everything: position, wealth, luxury, indulgence in all the pleasures of youth. In short, you must realize that Arsake is the goddess of your fortune and prostrate yourself before her.[179] All you have to do is follow my instructions on how you should enter her presence and in what manner you should look upon her when she grants you an audience, how you should conduct yourself and perform whatever she asks of you. As you know, she has the imperious pride of a queen, which her youth and beauty do nothing to moderate. She will not tolerate defiance of her commands."

18     Theagenes made no reply, but in his heart he realized that Kybele's words hinted at some horrible villainy. Shortly afterward, some eunuchs came in, bearing on golden dishes what purported to be leavings from the satrap's table—but leavings of unimaginable extravagance and delicacy!

"With these gifts," they said, "our lady bids the strangers welcome and pays them her first respects." Then they set down the dishes beside the young pair and withdrew immediately. Partly in response to Ky-

179. It was customary for Persians to prostrate themselves (proskynein) before their rulers. The Greeks, however, reserved this gesture of respect for their gods and regarded with horror what they interpreted as divine honors being paid to a living man. Hence prostration (proskynesis) became in Greek eyes a symbol of the servile condition of the Persian, and refusal to perform it a proclamation of their own status as free men.

bele's urgings and partly from a prudent wish not to appear so rude as to reject Arsake's hospitality, Theagenes and Charikleia nibbled the food before them, though without appetite. The same thing happened in the evening and on each of the succeeding days.

The next morning, at about the first hour of the day, the same eunuchs came to Theagenes and said: "Sir, you are blessed among men; your presence is commanded by our lady, and we are bidden bring you to an audience. Come and enjoy the privilege that she bestows seldom and on but few."

Theagenes was silent for a moment, then rose reluctantly to his feet as if under duress. "Are your orders that only I should come," he asked, "or my sister here as well?"

They replied that only he should come; Charikleia would be granted a separate audience, but at the moment Arsake was in conference with some Persian dignitaries, and in any case it was her habit to receive men and women in separate audiences.

Theagenes leaned towards Charikleia and whispered: "I do not like this. It is very suspicious."

But when Charikleia replied that he should make no resistance but respond favorably to begin with and give the impression that he would do just as Arsake wished, he followed the eunuchs who had been sent to escort him. They explained how he should behave on being presented to Arsake and how he should address her, adding that it was customary to abase oneself on entering her presence. Theagenes said not a word, but when he entered and found her enthroned on high, resplendent in a gown of purple shot with gold, flaunting the conspicuous value of her jewelry and the majesty of her crown, her bodily charms accentuated by all the means at the disposal of cosmetic art, with her bodyguard flanking the throne and her noble counselors sitting in state on either side of her, he was nothing daunted. He seemed to have forgotten the compact he had made with Charikleia to feign servility; the hollow pomp and show of Persia served merely to strengthen his indomitable spirit. He neither knelt nor abased himself, but, with his head held high, he said, "Greetings to you, Arsake, lady of the blood royal!"

The court was outraged and muttered menaces against Theagenes for his failure to prostrate himself, calling him an insolent upstart. But Arsake smiled and said: "You must forgive him. He is a stranger and does not know our ways. He is every inch a Greek and is afflicted with the scorn that all Greeks feel for us."

And with that she took off the crown from her head, despite repeated protests from her courtiers, for the Persians consider that this is a token that a greeting is returned. "Welcome, stranger," she said through her interpreter, for although she understood Greek, she could not speak it. "Tell me what you desire, and you shall have it."

Then, with a nod to her eunuchs to signify her will, she dismissed him. As the bodyguards escorted Theagenes away, Achaimenes saw him a second time, and now he was even more certain that he knew who he was. He could guess the reason why such inordinate honor was being paid Theagenes, and was lost in amazement. But still he held his tongue, in pursuance of the decision he had taken.

Arsake entertained the leading Persians to dinner, ostensibly as the customary mark of honor to them, though, truth to tell, it was her meeting with Theagenes that she was celebrating. And she sent to Theagenes and Charikleia not only their usual portion of the meal but also a number of rugs and counterpanes, handiwork of Sidon and Lydia. Besides, she sent two slaves to wait on them, a little girl for Charikleia and a little boy for Theagenes; they were both Ionian by birth, and neither had yet reached puberty. She pressed Kybele to make haste and achieve her goal as quickly as she could, for she was unable to bear her pain any longer—not that Kybele was idle; in fact she was doing her best to close the trap on Theagenes. Without ever making Arsake's intentions explicit, she tried to make Theagenes understand them by hinting at them indirectly and ambiguously. She made much of her mistress's affection for him and employed a number of plausible pretexts to allow him a glimpse not just of Arsake's readily apparent beauty but of the charms concealed beneath her clothes as well. She described Arsake's character as attractive and accessible, and recounted the pleasure her mistress derived from the company of vigorous and sophisticated young men. With every word she said she was probing to see if Theagenes had any inclination to the joys of love. He responded by echoing her praise of Arsake's generosity and love for Greece and suchlike and expressing his gratitude to her. But he deliberately ignored Kybele's efforts to lure him into immorality and pretended not even to have begun to understand them. The old woman felt as if the frustration was throttling her, and her heart went into palpitations, for she surmised that Theagenes understood her pandering well enough, and it was obvious that he was rebuffing all her efforts with insulting lack of ceremony. What is more, she was beginning to find Arsake's incessant pestering intolerable, for she kept saying she could wait no longer and demanding the satisfaction she had been promised. Kybele fobbed her off with a series of different excuses, on one occasion suggesting that the young man was ready enough but nervous of the consequences, on another inventing the story that he had fallen victim to some disorder.

20 Five or six days or so went by, during which time Arsake summoned Charikleia once or twice and, to ingratiate herself with Theagenes, received her with respect and kindness. Kybele now had no choice but to speak more plainly to Theagenes; without further dissimulation she told

him of Arsake's love and assured him that benefits beyond counting would be his if he complied.

"Why so timid? Why so frigid?" she went on. "A handsome young man like you, in the full vigor of his manhood, rejects a woman of equal attractions who is dying of love for him! He does not look upon this as an unexpected stroke of luck, his for the taking, even though there is no risk involved: her husband is away, and I, who suckled her and am privy to all her secrets, am here to abet your union. There is nothing at all standing in your way, no wife or bride-to-be here to stop you! Besides, many men have been able to overcome even that kind of inhibition, at least if they were sensible enough to recognize that this was something in which they would do no harm to their loved ones but much good to themselves by way of financial gain and sensual gratification."

She ended with a veiled threat. "Women of quality who have a fancy for young men are apt to become bitter and vindictive if they do not get their own way. They regard rejection as an insult and, reasonably enough, take reprisals. Remember too that Arsake is a Persian, by birth a lady of the blood royal (to quote your own salutation), richly endowed with wealth and power and thus able to reward devotion and punish opposition at will; whereas you are alone in a foreign land with no one to protect you. Have pity—on her as well as on yourself! She deserves your pity, for her misbehavior is the consequence of her insane infatuation with you. Take care! Beware the wrath of spurned love, the vengeance that will follow if you snub her. Many I know who have come to regret their obduracy. I have more experience than you in the affairs of Aphrodite. This grey head before you has taken part in many such contests, but I have never known anyone as callous and hard-hearted as you."

Then she turned and spoke to Charikleia, in whose hearing she had been compelled to venture this desperate plea. "My child," she said, "add your weight to my appeals to this—I am not sure what to call him!—this brother of yours. You too will profit from this business: you will have just as much affection and more honor; you will have as much money as you could wish for, and you will be able to contract a splendid marriage for yourself. These are prospects that even the prosperous might envy, let alone strangers whose present condition is one of penury."

Her eyes smoldering like coals, Charikleia shot a wry glance at Kybele. "I should have preferred," she replied, "the excellent Arsake never to have fallen victim to such a passion: that would have been best. Failing that, the next best would have been for her to endure love's pain with self-control. However, since, according to you, she has succumbed to an all too human affliction and is a slave to her desires, I would join you in urging Theagenes here to consent to the undertaking, so long as there is no danger in it for him. But I pray that he does not do unwitting harm,

both to himself and to her, if this business ever comes to light, and somehow the satrap gets to hear of these illicit goings-on."

At this Kybele leapt to her feet, hugged Charikleia, and showered kisses on her. "Well spoken, my child!" she exclaimed. "You are right to have felt compassion for your fellow woman, and you are also right to be concerned for your brother's safety. But on that score you need have no worries. Not even the sun will know, as the saying goes."

"That is enough for the moment," said Theagenes. "Allow us some time to think it over."

Kybele left the room at once, whereupon Charikleia said: "So, Theagenes, this is the kind of good fortune that heaven vouchsafes us—good fortune in which there is more adversity than anything resembling happiness. Nevertheless, sensible people ought to make the best they can of their misfortunes. I have no idea whether you intend to carry this business through to its end; and indeed I should not blame you too much if it were the one issue on which our life or death depended. But even if, to your credit, you consider this request abhorrent, nevertheless pretend to agree to it. Feed this barbarian woman's desire with promises; play her along and so ensure that she does not turn spiteful; allay with hope the wound that festers in her heart; ease her pain with fair words. With the gods' help it is not impossible that the time you buy might bring about our deliverance. But please, Theagenes, do not allow the role you play to become the first step to shameful reality."

Theagenes smiled and replied: "Even in the most dangerous predicament you are not immune to the congenital sickness of womankind— jealousy! But let me assure you that I could not even pretend to have such intentions: to speak immoral words is just as wrong as to commit immoral acts. Besides, a point-blank rejection of Arsake will have one pleasant result at least: she will stop making such a nuisance of herself. I may be made to suffer for it, but fate and my resolve have, through many ordeals, equipped me to endure whatever may befall."

All Charikleia said in reply was, "Take care not to land us both unwittingly in great danger."

22    While Theagenes and Charikleia were engaged in these deliberations, Kybele had once more set Arsake aflutter with expectation and told her that she should be optimistic of success, for Theagenes had given some indication to that effect. Then she had returned to her quarters. She did not raise the subject again that evening, but during the night she appealed at length to Charikleia, who from the start had been sharing her room, to lend her assistance; and at daybreak she again began to ask Theagenes what he had decided. His reply was a blunt refusal that ruled any hope of his compliance out of the question. In deep gloom Kybele hurried to Arsake, who, on being told of Theagenes' obduracy, had the old woman

thrown out on her ear, then withdrew hastily into her chamber, where she lay on the bed, clawing at herself.

Kybele was barely through the door of the women's quarters when her son, Achaimenes, saw her, weeping forlornly. "What has happened, Mother?" he asked. "Nothing untoward, I hope? Nothing unpleasant? Has the mistress had some news that has upset her? Not word from the army of a reverse, I hope? I trust the Ethiopians are not getting the better of our lord Oroondates in the war he is fighting."

He maintained a barrage of such questions, but Kybele merely replied, "What drivel you talk!" and hurried away. Nothing abashed, Achaimenes ran after her, seized her by the hands, embraced her, and begged her to tell her own dear son what was making her so sad.

Taking him by the hand, she led him to a quiet corner of the garden. 23 "I would never have told anyone else," she said, "of the evils that beset my mistress and myself; but now she is quite lost in a sea of troubles, and I can foresee that my own life is in danger, for I know that Arsake's sadness and madness will not leave me unscathed. So I am left with no choice but to tell you everything in the hope that you can think of a way to help the mother who bore you, who brought you forth into the light of day and suckled you at these very breasts. Our lady is in love with the young man who is staying with us. She loves him with a love too strong to resist, a love that is not of the ordinary kind, a love that has no cure. Until today she and I were both deluded enough to believe that we could bring it to a successful consummation—hence all the various courtesies and evidences of affection that have been extended to the strangers. But that young man is such a hot headed and hard hearted fool that he has rejected our advances, and I know for certain that now Arsake will put an end to her life and have me killed as well for having deceived and humiliated her with my promises. There you have it, my son. If there is any help you can give me, give it. Otherwise give your mother a proper burial when she is dead."

"What reward shall I get, Mother?" he asked. "I can see this is no time for me to play coy, so I must come straight to the point and not beat around the bush in offering to help, for you are almost passing out with anxiety."

"Anything you want," replied Kybele, "you may be sure of having. She has already made you head steward as a mark of her regard for me, but if you have some more exalted office in mind, tell me. Riches you would receive in quantities beyond counting if you saved our poor lady."

"I have suspected this for some time," he said, "but although I realized what was afoot, I held my tongue and bided my time to see what would transpire. I have no aspirations to office or wealth. If Arsake gives me the girl who is called Theagenes' sister to be my wife, then she shall have her heart's desire. You see, Mother, I love that girl; I love her to distraction. The mistress will know from her own feelings what the pain is like, how severe it is, and it would be only right for her to help a fellow victim of that sickness, particularly one who is offering to accomplish as great a feat as I am."

"Do not worry," replied Kybele. "The mistress will leave no doubt as to her gratitude if you become her benefactor and savior—and besides, there might be something we could do ourselves to win the girl's assent. Tell me just how you can help."

"I shall say nothing," he replied, "until the mistress has sworn a binding oath to keep this promise to me. And don't you make any premature attempts to talk the girl round either! I can see that she is nearly as proud and haughty as her brother, and I do not want you inadvertently upsetting the whole business."

"Just as you say," said Kybele, and ran off to Arsake in her chamber. Falling at her knees, she said: "Be of good heart. Thanks be to the gods, everything is coming right. All you have to do is give word for my son, Achaimenes, to be summoned to your presence."

"Let him be summoned," said Arsake, "—unless this is another of your tricks."

24     In came Achaimenes, and after the old woman had explained how things stood, Arsake gave her solemn pledge that she would reward him with the hand of Theagenes' sister. Then Achaimenes said, "Mistress, Theagenes is your slave, and I think he should stop playing hard to get with his own mistress!"

"What do you mean?" asked Arsake, whereupon Achaimenes told her the whole story: how Theagenes was captured and made a prisoner, as men are in war; how Mitranes sent him to Oroondates in order for him to be sent on to the Great King; how he himself was given charge of the prisoner to take him to the satrap but lost him when Thyamis and the men of Bessa mounted a daring assault; how he had barely escaped with his life. As final proof he showed Arsake Mitranes' letter to Oroondates, which he had had the foresight to bring with him, and added that if she required further proof, Thyamis would corroborate what he said.

At these words, Arsake began to revive. Without pausing even for a moment, she hurried out of her chamber to the hall where it was her custom to sit in state and grant audiences. There she commanded that Theagenes be brought before her. On his arrival, she pointed to Achaimenes, who was standing at her side, and asked Theagenes whether he recognized him. He said he did. A second question followed. "Were you not taken prisoner, and were you not being brought here under his supervision?"

Theagenes again had to admit that this was true.

*religion as a language tool* A

"Then know that you are my slave! You will perform the duties of a household servant and obey my every nod, much though it galls you. Your sister I betroth in marriage to Achaimenes here, whom we hold in the highest esteem, both for his mother's sake and for his general devotion towards us. The marriage will take place just as soon as a date can be fixed and preparations made for an exceptionally magnificent celebration."

These words had wounded Theagenes to the heart, but nevertheless he decided not to cross swords with Arsake but to sidestep her onslaught like that of a wild animal.

"My lady," he said, "thanks be to the gods that people of such high nobility as ourselves have at least had the good fortune to find in the midst of adversity the consolation of being slaves to none but you, who looked upon us with such gentleness and kindness even when we appeared to be mere strangers and no concern of yours. As regards my sister, who is not a prisoner of war, and therefore not your slave, but chooses of her own free will to serve you and to accept whatever status you may be pleased to grant her, act howsoever, after due consideration, you deem correct."

"He shall be assigned to wait at table," said Arsake. "Achaimenes shall teach him to pour wine. So, even in this outpost of the empire, he shall become accustomed to the king's service."

And so they left the room, Theagenes frowning pensively as he wondered what to do now, Achaimenes gloating and taunting Theagenes. "Well now, our fine, proud, swaggering fellow of an hour ago;[180] our lone, stiff-necked champion of liberty, who refused to bow his head in veneration, perhaps now you will bow it—or else you will feel my knuckles on it to teach you the art!"

Arsake dismissed all her attendants except Kybele. "So now, Kybele," she said, "there will be no more excuses! Go to our haughty friend and tell him that if he obeys me and behaves as I wish, he will enjoy a measure of freedom and live a life of ease and plenty. But if he persists in the contrary course, he will incur the combined wrath of a lover slighted and a mistress displeased, and find himself reduced to a condition of the most abject and contemptible servitude and subjected to punishments of every imaginable variety."

Kybele went and told him what Arsake had said, with many embellishments of her own such as she thought might be helpful in persuading him to submit. Theagenes asked her to allow him a moment's grace, and, taking Charikleia to one side, he whispered: "We are done for, Charikleia! Our mooring ropes have all snapped, as the saying goes; the

25

180. A quotation from Menandros's play *Perikeiromene* (172 Sandbach).

anchors on which our hopes were fastened have all been torn irretrievably loose. We may not even face our misfortunes with the status of free persons; we have been made slaves again"—and here he explained how this had come about—"and now we are the defenseless prey of barbarian cruelty and must either submit to our masters' whims or else account ourselves gallows' meat. Even this I could endure, but the heaviest burden to bear is that Arsake has pledged to give you to Kybele's son, Achaimenes, to be his wife. This will not happen, or if it does, I shall not be alive to see it—that much is beyond doubt, so long as life permits me access to a sword and a way of escape. What can we do? What plan can we devise to frustrate these abhorrent unions between Arsake and me and Achaimenes and you?"

"One only," replied Charikleia. "By consenting to the one you will be able to prevent mine."

"You must not speak like that!" he answered. "May the god who has us in his power never be so cruel that I, who have never known Charikleia, am compelled to defile myself in illicit intimacy with another woman! But I think I have an idea that may work. Necessity is the mother of invention!"

And so saying, he returned to Kybele and said, "Tell milady that I should like a word with her alone and in private."

26    Imagining that Theagenes had, at long last, submitted, the old woman took the news to Arsake, who told her to bring the young man to her after dinner. Kybele did so, and, after giving strict instructions to Arsake's entourage not to disturb their mistress or do anything to incommode the occupants of her chamber, she ushered in Theagenes. The palace was shrouded in the darkness of night; the only light burning was the one in Arsake's chamber: thus the deed was done unobserved. Having let Theagenes into the room, Kybele made to withdraw, but he held her back and said: "I should like Kybele to stay for a moment, my lady. I know that you trust her to keep all your secrets."

So saying, he took Arsake's hands in his and went on. "My lady, it is not from stubborn defiance of your will that I have until now been reluctant to do as you ask; rather I was trying to procure its accomplishment without risk. But now since fate has made me your slave—which perhaps is for the best—I feel far fewer qualms about doing whatever you wish of me. You have promised me many and great rewards, but consent to grant me one thing only: cancel the marriage between Achaimenes and Charikleia. For, to say nothing of all the other considerations, it would be quite wrong for a woman who takes such pride in the high nobility of her birth to become the wife of one born and bred to slavehood. If you refuse me this, I swear to you by the gods, and in particular by the Sun, the fairest of them all, that I shall never comply with your wishes and that if force is used against Charikleia, you will see me dead by my own hand before I submit to you."

"Please believe me," replied Arsake, "I am ready to give you anything you desire, just as I am willing to give you myself. But I am bound by a previous oath to give Achaimenes your sister in marriage."

"Good, my lady!" exclaimed Theagenes. "Give him my sister, whoever she may be, but I am sure you will not choose to give him my betrothed, my bride, one who must be accounted my wedded wife—nor will you do so even if you so choose."

"What are you saying?" she asked.

"No more than the truth," he answered. "Charikleia is no sister to me, but my bride, as I said. So your oath is no longer binding. If you want conclusive proof, you can get it by celebrating my marriage to her whenever it so pleases you."

Arsake felt a pang of jealousy on hearing that Charikleia was not his sister but his bride, but nevertheless she said: "So be it. We shall find Achaimenes another match to console him."

"And now that that is settled," said Theagenes, "I shall make good my side of the bargain."

And with these words he took a step forward to kiss her hands. But Arsake leaned forwards and, offering him her lips rather than her hands, kissed him. So Theagenes departed, the recipient and not the bestower of a kiss. As soon as he had the opportunity, he told Charikleia everything, although some parts of his story aroused jealousy in her as well. He went on to explain his purpose in making such an immoral promise: the single act served many aims.

"Achaimenes' plan to marry you has been confounded, and a pretext has been established to keep Arsake's desires waiting for a while. And, most important, we can now expect Achaimenes to throw the whole situation into confusion, both from vexation at the frustration of his hopes and from anger that Arsake's favor towards me has so diminished his own standing with her. He is certain to hear every detail, for a full account will be given him by his mother, whose presence at our interview I engineered for precisely this purpose: I wanted my confidences to be betrayed to Achaimenes, and I was also ensuring that I had a witness that my intercourse with Arsake was purely verbal. It may be enough to keep one's conscience clear and pin one's hopes on the benevolence of heaven, but it is right too to demonstrate one's innocence to the people among whom one lives, and so pass one's brief sojourn in this world in candid honesty."

He went on to say that there was every likelihood that Achaimenes would go so far as to form hostile designs against Arsake: he was a man born to slavery (and a man subject to a master tends to hate the master to whom he is subject); a man wronged, a solemn pledge to whom had been set at nought; a man in love who had discovered that another had been preferred to himself; a man with intimate knowledge of the most illicit and immoral goings-on, who had no need to invent falsehoods with which to attack Arsake (as on many occasions men have been emboldened by their grievances to do) but had only to reveal the truth to exact his vengeance.

27    By elaborating on this theme at some length, he imparted some measure of confidence to Charikleia. The next day Achaimenes took him to wait at table, as Arsake had commanded. He changed into the sumptuous Persian apparel she had sent him and, with a mixture of delight and disgust, bedecked himself with bangles of gold and collars studded with precious gems. Achaimenes then tried to demonstrate and explain to him something of the art of cup bearing, but Theagenes ran to one of the tripods on which the cups stood, picked up one of the precious vessels, and exclaimed: "I have no need of teachers! I shall use my instinct in serving my mistress and not erect a mystique around something so simple. It is your lot in life, my friend, to know how to do such things, but in my case natural ability and the requirements of the moment tell me what is to be done."

With these words he mixed a delicious draught and conveyed the bowl to Arsake, balancing it with exquisite grace in his fingertips. The drink raised her to new heights of Dionysiac ecstasy. As she quaffed the cup, she kept her eyes fixed steadily on Theagenes; and she drank deeper of the cup of love than of the wine. She made a point of not draining the bowl dry but leaving a little wine in the bottom, as an ingenious way of drinking Theagenes' health.[181]

Achaimenes, for his part, had suffered a wound of a different kind. The rage and envy that filled his heart were so obvious that even Arsake noticed him scowling and muttering something under his breath to his companions.

At the end of the banquet Theagenes said, "The first favor I crave, my lady, is this: command me to wear these clothes only when I am waiting on you."

Arsake nodded her assent, and, changing into his normal clothes, he left. Achaimenes left with him, berating Theagenes at length for his forwardness and saying that his casual manner was pure childishness; although to begin with the mistress might overlook the behavior of a newcomer who did not know the ways of the court, he would not go unpunished if he persisted in such self-opinionated insolence; he was giv-

181. Normally one would drink from a bowl and then pass it, with words of friendship, to the other person for him to drink from too. By leaving some wine in the bottom of her cup, which is then taken away by Theagenes, Arsake is able to perform her side of the toast ritual.

ing him this advice as a friend—or, rather, as one who was shortly to become his kinsman, for their mistress had promised him that he could marry Theagenes' sister. Achaimenes continued in this vein at great length, but Theagenes had the appearance of not listening to a word he said, walking beside him with his eyes fixed on the ground, until they ran into Kybele, who was on her way to put her mistress to bed for her siesta. Noticing the sour expression on her son's face, she inquired what the reason for it was.

"That young foreign whippersnapper," he replied, "is held in greater esteem than we are. He has only been here a couple of days, and he is allowed to pour wine at table. Then he bids us, the headwaiters and chief butlers, good day, hands milady a bowl, and stands next to the royal person, without so much as a by-your-leave to us and our superior rank—so called! That this fellow should be promoted above our heads and made intimate to our lady's inmost secrets through our own mistaken silence and connivance is the least of our misfortunes, bad though it is. But it might at least have been possible for this to be done without humiliating and insulting those of us who have aided and served her in all her honest dealings."

"We must talk about this again later, but at the moment, Mother, I should like to see my betrothed, my dearest darling Charikleia, in the hope that in the sight of her I can find a cure for the hurt that has stung my soul." 28

"What betrothed, my child?" replied Kybele. "It seems to me that what vexes you is the least of your grievances; of the greater ones you appear blissfully unaware. You are no longer engaged to marry Charikleia!"

"What do you mean?" he exclaimed. "Am I not worthy to marry my own fellow slave? What is the reason, Mother?"

"We ourselves are to blame," she replied. "We and our loyal service to Arsake in an unlawful cause. We esteemed her above our own safety; we thought her lust more important than our own lives; we served her pleasure devotedly; and the result is that this noble fellow, this wonderful lover of hers, has had to worm his way into her chamber just once for the mere sight of him to induce her to break all the oaths she swore you and to pledge Charikleia to him, because now he claims that she is not his sister but his bride-to-be."

"Has Arsake really made that promise, Mother?"

"She has, my child," replied Kybele. "I was there, and I heard her. She is going to hold a splendid celebration to mark their wedding in a few days' time, and she has undertaken to find you a different wife."

Hearing this, Achaimenes groaned in despair and wrung his hands. "I shall make sure that they all find that this wedding has a bitter taste," he said. "The only help I ask of you is that you arrange for the wedding to

be postponed for as long as need be. And if anyone asks after me, tell
him I am somewhere in the country, laid up after a fall. Our fine friend
calls his sister his bride-to-be! As if we were too stupid to realize that this
is a tale made up simply to thwart me! If he were to take her in his arms
and kiss her as other men do, or, better still, were to share her bed, that
would be proof positive that she is not his sister but his bride-to-be! I
shall see to this, with the help of the oaths she has transgressed and the
gods she has disregarded."

29     So he spoke. Anger, jealousy, love, and disappointment combined to
goad him to fury: emotions capable of turning anyone's mind, let alone a
savage's. An idea formed in his mind, and he decided immediately to act
on it, without any rational consideration of the consequences. That
evening he managed to make off with one of the Armenian horses that
were kept in the satrap's stables for ceremonial purposes, and rode away
to find Oroondates, who at that time was in Great Thebes, mustering an
expeditionary force against the Ethiopians, collecting material for every
conceivable kind of fighting and troops of all descriptions; even now he
was making ready to march out against the foe.

## Book Eight

1     The king of Ethiopia had succeeded in outwitting Oroondates and had
seized one of the prizes for which the war was being fought by mounting
a preemptive strike to take possession of the city of Philai, a perennial
object of dispute. In so doing, he had reduced the satrap to impotence
and left him no alternative but to dispatch an expedition at short notice
and, for the most part, with no prior organization. The city of Philai lies
on the river Nile,[182] a little above the Lesser Cataracts, some twelve miles
from Syene and Elephantine. It was once occupied and settled by Egyptian exiles, who thus rendered it a bone of contention between the
Ethiopians and the Egyptians, for the former maintain that the boundary
of Ethiopia lies at the cataract, whereas the Egyptians claim that the city
is rightfully theirs on the grounds that its original occupation by refugees
from Egypt constituted an act of conquest.[183] The city has changed hands
continually, belonging to whichever of the two sides has been able to
make themselves masters of the place by preempting the other. At the
period in question it was manned by a garrison of Egyptians and Per-

---

182. Philai is actually an island in the Nile.
183. This historical sketch is largely fiction. Strabo (17.1.49) suggests that the place was
settled jointly by Egyptians and Ethiopians, while Ailios Aristeides tells us that Ethiopian
soldiers were stationed there in the second century. The Egyptian exiles are presumably to
be identified with the "Deserters" mentioned by Herodotos (2.30) and others, although the
area they were supposed to have settled lay much further to the south.

sians, but the king of Ethiopia was demanding the return both of Philai and of the emerald mines (which had been the subject of unsuccessful representations by him some years previously, as has already been related) and had sent a deputation to Oroondates. He allowed his emissaries a few days' start, then set off after them. He had made his preparations well in advance, under the guise of some quite different campaign, and had not revealed the objective of his expedition to anyone. When he calculated that the delegation would have passed Philai and put its inhabitants and garrison off their guard with its pronouncements that its mission was to seek peace and possibly even friendship, he suddenly attacked the city in person and expelled the garrison, which held out for some two or three days but was eventually overcome by the sheer weight of the enemy's numbers and his siege engines. Thus he gained possession of the city without harming a single one of its inhabitants.

It was in the state of confusion caused by these events that Achaimenes found Oroondates, who had learned exactly what had happened from those who had managed to escape. Achaimenes' unexpected and unbidden arrival only heightened the satrap's alarm: he asked whether something untoward had occurred concerning Arsake or the rest of his household. Achaimenes replied that it had, and asked to speak to him in private. As soon as they were alone, Achaimenes told him everything: how Theagenes had been taken captive by Mitranes and sent to Oroondates for him to send on as a gift to the Great King, if he thought fit— and indeed the young man was of a quality fit for the royal court and table; how the men of Bessa had snatched him away, killing Mitranes in the process; how subsequently he had come to Memphis (at which point Achaimenes digressed to relate events concerning Thyamis). Finally, he told of Arsake's infatuation with Theagenes and how Theagenes had been brought to live in the palace, the attentions that had been lavished on him, and the episode of his waiting at table and pouring the wine; maybe nothing illicit had occurred as yet, for the young man had so far proved stubborn and recalcitrant, but there was a distinct possibility of its occurring if the stranger were subjected to duress, or the passage of time in some way weakened his resolve—unless immediate steps were taken to remove him from Memphis before it was too late and thus to deprive Arsake's infatuation of all its substance. This was why he had stolen away and come in such haste to bring word to Oroondates: his devotion to his master was such as to compel him to speak out about the wrongs being done to his master.

Achaimenes' story filled Oroondates' heart with rage; he was consumed with anger and thoughts of vengeance. But then Achaimenes went on to tell him about Charikleia and lit new fires, fires of passion, in the satrap's breast. He sang her praises loudly (though he said nothing unmerited by the reality); he did his best to convey the divine glory of her beauty and grace: her like had never been seen before and could never occur again.

"You must imagine that all your concubines are as nothing to her—not only the ones you left in Memphis but even those that have come on campaign with you," he said and added much more in the same vein, hoping that if Oroondates bedded Charikleia, it would not be long thereafter before he could request her hand as the reward for his information, and so make her his own wife.

By now the satrap's whole being was aroused; he was aflame, enmeshed in the twin nets of rage and desire. There and then he summoned Bagoas, one of his trusted eunuchs,[184] gave him command of fifty horsemen, and dispatched him to Memphis with orders to bring Theagenes and Charikleia to him as quickly as possible, in whatever place he was to 3 be found. He also handed him two letters. One was to Arsake and read as follows.

> Oroondates to Arsake. Send me Theagenes and Charikleia, the brother and sister who were taken captive and are now slaves of the Great King; I shall send them on to the king. Send them to me of your own free will; if you refuse, they shall be brought to me all the same, and Achaimenes' allegations will be confirmed.

The second was to Euphrates, the head eunuch at Memphis.

> As regards your negligence over my household, you will have to account to me. For the moment deliver to Bagoas the Greek strangers who are prisoners of war so that they may be conveyed to me, whether Arsake consents or not. Be sure to deliver them to him; otherwise, know that I have given orders for you to be put in chains and flayed alive.

The satrap sealed these letters with his own seal so that the people in Memphis should have proof of their authority and release the young couple instantly. Then Bagoas and his party departed to execute their master's bidding. Oroondates departed also, for the war against the Ethiopians. He commanded Achaimenes to go with him and had him watched discreetly, without his knowledge, until he could prove the veracity of his information.

During these same days at Memphis the following events took place. Soon after Achaimenes' disappearance, Thyamis, who was now securely reinstated as high priest and was thus a person of some consequence in

184. This name was borne by several historical Persian eunuchs; according to Pliny (*Natural History* 13.41) the word actually meant "eunuch." It became a typical eunuch's name in literature.

the city, having performed the rites of Kalasiris's funeral and paid his father all the traditional respects for the prescribed number of days, began to give some attention to the question of finding Theagenes and his companion, now that the rules of his office permitted him to have contact with people outside the temple. After exhaustive inquiries, he discovered that they had become residents of the satrapal palace, and he hurried immediately to Arsake to demand the return of the young strangers, with whom he said he had many ties, in particular the fact that the last words of his father, Kalasiris, had been to charge him to protect and provide for the strangers to the best of his ability. He acknowledged his gratitude to her for showing such kindness to the young pair, Greeks in a foreign land as they were, and taking them into her house during the days since his father's death when it was forbidden for the unconsecrated to dwell within the temple; but at the same time he demanded as his right the return of those who had been placed in his care.

"I find it beyond belief," replied Arsake, "that with one breath you can testify to our generosity and humanity and with the next accuse us of inhumanity in suggesting that we are likely to be unable or unwilling to provide for the strangers and treat them as is their due."

"That is not what I meant," said Thyamis. "I am quite well aware that their life would be much more comfortable here than with me, should they choose to stay here. However, they are members of a noble family who have been subjected to every kind of indignity that fortune can inflict and are now destitute and homeless; their one desire is to be reunited with their family and return to the land of their birth. My father has bequeathed me the responsibility of assisting them in this, though the strangers have other claims besides on my friendship."

"I am glad," replied Arsake, "that you are no longer casting aspersions and now rest your case on equity. In fact, though, equity is clearly on my side, inasmuch as ownership is a stronger claim to possession than mere concern."

Thyamis was taken aback. "How do you own these people?" he asked.

"By the rules of war," she replied, "according to which captives taken in war become slaves."

Thyamis recognized this as a reference to the incident concerning Mitranes. "But Arsake," he said, "this is a time not of war but of peace. And while it is in the nature of war to make slaves, it is in the nature of peace to set them free; the former act is a tyrant's whim; the latter shows the judgment of a true king. The true distinction between peace and war resides less in the inherent meaning of the words than in the deportment of the agents concerned. Your interpretation of equity would seem stronger if you accepted this principle. Concerning propriety and expediency, on the other hand, there is no question: how can it possibly be right or in your interests for you to demonstrate and profess such a passionate attachment to young foreigners?"

5    Arsake could contain herself no longer. Her reaction was one typical of lovers: as long as they think that no one knows of their love, they blush with guilt, but as soon as they are found out, they lose all sense of shame: the lover undiscovered lacking boldness, the lover detected having rather too much. So it was with Arsake: her guilty conscience led her to betray her guilt. She assumed that Thyamis had guessed something of her predicament and, with no respect for the high priest or the dignity of his priestly office and no thought for the modesty proper in a woman, she exclaimed: "You will pay for what you did to Mitranes, too. One day Oroondates will bring to book those who murdered him and his men. I will *not* release them! For the moment they are my slaves, and soon they will be sent up to my brother, the Great King, as the law of Persia requires. You can make all the fine speeches you like, with your meaningless definitions of equity, propriety, and expediency. He who holds absolute power needs none of these things: his will serves for them all. Now get out of our palace at once! Go of your own accord, otherwise you may find yourself being forcibly ejected."

So Thyamis left, but not before calling the gods to witness; he confined himself to declaring that she would regret her behavior, for he was resolved to inform the city of what had happened and call upon the assistance of the people.

"I do not give a damn for your holy orders!" exclaimed Arsake. "The only holy order that love knows is its consummation!"

And with that she withdrew to her chamber and, summoning Kybele, fell to reflecting upon her situation. She had already begun to feel vaguely apprehensive that Achaimenes, who was nowhere to be seen, had run away, but whenever she raised the subject and asked where Achaimenes was, Kybele would invent a whole succession of various excuses, trying to induce her to believe anything rather than that he had gone to Oroondates; but ultimately she did not quite convince her mistress, who began to doubt her word as the days went by.

So now she said: "What are we to do, Kybele? How can I escape from my predicament? Far from abating, my love is more intense than ever, and the young man is like fuel to its raging fire. He is cruel and hardhearted, and he showed more humanity at the beginning than he does now: then at least he afforded me the comfort of false promises, but now he rejects my suit utterly and unambiguously—which disturbs me the more because I am afraid he may have got wind of what I suspect myself concerning Achaimenes, and so have even less stomach for the performance of the deed. Achaimenes is the biggest worry of all. He has gone to inform Oroondates, has he not? What he says may be believed, or at least not seem beyond belief. If only I could see Oroondates! One caress, one tear from his darling Arsake, would finish him! The eyes of a woman, of a wife, possess a powerful magic of persuasion against her husband. What a cruel twist it would be if I were accused of having my way with Theagenes before I could actually do so—or if, as it may be, I were punished for it, as might happen if Oroondates were convinced of my guilt before he saw me. So, Kybele, leave no stone unturned; try everything you know, for you can see that my situation is critical, poised on a razor's edge. Remember too that if I despair of my own life, there will, of course, be no possibility of my sparing others. You will be the first to enjoy the fruits of your son's schemes. In fact I cannot understand how you were not aware of them."

"You are quite wrong about my son and about my own devotion to you, my lady," replied Kybele, "as events will show you. When your own approach to your love is so supine, when you really are behaving like a woman, you must not try to throw the responsibility onto others who are not to blame. You are not acting like a mistress with power to make the young man do her will; you treat him with as much consideration as if *you* were *his* slave. That may have been the right thing to do at the beginning when we thought he was a dainty fellow whose spirit could easily be broken. But since he is unresponsive when you play the lover, let him learn what you can be like as a mistress; let whip and rack make him submit to your will. It is in the nature of young men to react arrogantly to kindness but to yield to compulsion. That is how it will be with him: punishment will succeed where blandishment failed."

"That is good advice, I think," said Arsake. "But in god's name, how could I bear to watch with my own eyes that beautiful body being flogged or punished in any way at all?"

"You are playing the woman again," replied Kybele. "Can you not understand that a few lashes will be enough to bring him to his senses, and that after a moment's distress you will have your heart's desire? You need not even pain your eyes with the sight: you can hand him over to Euphrates and tell him to punish him for some misdemeanor, and so spare yourself the distress of watching the punishment being done—hearing about something causes less pain than seeing it; then, if we hear that he has had a change of heart, you can say that he has been reprimanded sufficiently and have him released."

This was enough to convince Arsake, for a love that has been thwarted in its hopes shows no mercy to its beloved, and failure very often turns to a wish for revenge. She sent for her chief eunuch and gave him her orders. Temperamentally afflicted with jealousy (as eunuchs are), he had long nursed a smoldering hatred of Theagenes as a result of what he had seen and conjectured. He immediately loaded him with iron chains and locked him up in a dark cell, where he made him suffer the pains of starvation and torture. Theagenes knew why he was being treated like this, but pretended not to and pointedly asked the reason; but the eunuch answered never a word. He daily increased the severity of the punishment, exacting a retribution harsher than Arsake desired or had commanded, and allowed no one to visit his prisoner, with the single exception of Kybele, in whose case he had received specific instructions. She paid continual visits, on the pretense of smuggling food in to Theagenes. She affected compassion and a sympathy born of their former intimacy, but, in fact, she had come to gauge his reaction to his present condition and see whether the rack had brought about any submission or softening of his resolve. But on the contrary he was more of a man than ever and rebuffed her advances with redoubled firmness. Though his body was in torment, his spirit had the strength of virtue, and he refused to bow his head to fortune, proclaiming proudly that despite her hostility in all else she had shown him kindness in the one thing that mattered by presenting him with an opportunity to display his love and devotion to Charikleia; he counted it the supreme happiness if only she knew of his ordeals, and never ceased from calling Charikleia his life, his light, his soul.

Seeing this, Kybele, despite being told by Arsake that she wanted Theagenes' suffering to be slight, as the purpose of her sentence had been to apply pressure to him, not to kill him, told Euphrates on the contrary to increase the severity of the punishment. But it was soon apparent to her that this was to no avail and that this approach too had ended in disappointment and failure. She realized that her position was desperate: on the one hand she could expect imminent retribution from Oroondates, should he hear from Achaimenes what was going on; on the other, Arsake might well destroy her before he could, on the grounds that her assistance to her mistress in her love had succeeded only in making a fool of her. So she decided to bring the crisis to a head and by the perpetration of one great crime either bring Arsake's desires to a successful consummation and so avert for the moment the threat posed by her mistress, or else destroy the evidence for the whole affair by contriving the deaths of all the participants at one fell swoop.

So she went to Arsake and said: "Our efforts are all in vain, my lady. He has a heart of stone and will not give in. His insolence grows day by day. Charikleia's name is forever on his lips, and he seems to derive comfort and healing merely from speaking it. If you agree then, let us use our anchor of last resort,[185] as the saying goes: she is in our way, so

185. A Greek ship would carry several anchors, the last of which would be employed only when all the others had failed. Hence a proverbial expression denoting a final, desperate fling on which all hopes were pinned.

we must remove her. If he hears that she is dead, it is quite likely that he will have a change of heart and fall in with our wishes, once he realizes that his love for her is hopeless."

Arsake pounced on these words. The jealousy she had long felt to- 7 wards Charikleia was now augmented by her rage at what she had just heard. "You are right!" she exclaimed. "I shall make it my business to give orders for the accursed creature to be killed."

"And who will obey those orders?" replied Kybele. "You may hold absolute power, but the laws forbid the taking of life unless sentence has been passed by the Persian judiciary. So you will be obliged to invent some charge or other to bring against the girl, which will be a bothersome and unpleasant business—and, what is more, there is no guarantee that our accusations will be believed. I have a better idea: I am prepared to do anything for you, whatever the cost. With your permission, I shall use poison to carry this scheme through for you and eliminate our adversary with a witch's potion."

Arsake agreed and told her to proceed. Kybele lost no time. When she came to Charikleia, she found her weeping and lamenting, mourning, in fact, as for one dead, and considering how to put an end to her own life, for by now she was aware of Theagenes' fate, although all along Kybele had done all she could to throw her off the scent and had invented a whole series of explanations for his disappearance and failure to pay his usual visits to her room.

"My poor child," she said, "please stop this. You are worrying yourself to death for no reason. See now, Theagenes has been released. He will be here this evening. He offended the mistress in some way while waiting at table, and in a moment of anger she ordered him to be locked up. But today she has promised to release him, for she is about to celebrate some traditional feast day; besides, my appeals have won her round. On your feet then, and break your fast by having something to eat with me now."

"Why should I believe you?" asked Charikleia. "Your never-ending lying makes me doubt every word you utter."

"By all the gods," replied Kybele, "I swear to you that this day will see the end of all your misfortunes and your deliverance from all anxiety—just so long as you do not starve yourself to death first. It is days since you have eaten; let me persuade you to take a mouthful of this food that has arrived from the kitchens so opportunely."

Charikleia consented only with reluctance, but consent she did. Although she had grown used to suspecting treachery, the oaths had gone some way to winning her trust, and she was only too happy to believe such pleasant promises, for the heart is prone to believe in that for which it craves. So, taking their places at table, they began to eat. One of Arsake's favorite slaves was waiting on them, and when she offered them cups of wine mixed with water, Kybele motioned to her to serve Charikleia first, then took the second cup herself and started to drink. But before she could drink it dry, it became plain that the old woman's head was swimming. She dashed the last few drops of her wine to the ground and glared ferociously at the maid; then a fit of the most violent convulsions and paroxysms racked her body.

8     Charikleia was astounded and attempted to revive her; the rest of the company was astounded too. The poison, so it seemed, was more deadly than any arrow dipped in death-dealing venom, and powerful enough to dispatch a young person in the prime of his strength; and thus now its effect on a body that age had reduced to mere skin and bones was even more drastic. The poison reached her vitals more quickly than it takes to tell. The old woman's eyes bulged, and, as the convulsions ceased, her limbs became paralyzed and rigid, and her skin took on a blackish hue. But the treachery in her heart was, I think, more vicious than any lethal drug, for, even in her death throes, Kybele did not forget her evil tricks: with a combination of gestures and gasped words she indicated that Charikleia was her murderer.

Even as the old woman was breathing her last, Charikleia was manacled and brought immediately before Arsake, who demanded to know whether she had brewed the poison herself, and threatened her with punishment and torture if she refused to confess the truth. Then Charikleia presented an extraordinary sight to those who were there to see her: with no sign of despondency or cowardice, she clearly viewed her predicament as a matter for derision, partly because a clear conscience allowed her to feel nothing but contempt for such a false accusation, partly from joy at the prospect of being united in death with Theagenes, with the added benefit of being spared the pollution of bloodshed if others did to her what she had already determined to do to herself.

"Your Excellency," she said, "if Theagenes is alive, then I too am innocent of murder; but if anything untoward has happened to him as a result of your pious counsels, then you have no need to torture a confession out of me. I confess that it was I who poisoned the woman who nursed you and educated you to such virtue. Kill me without more ado: that would be the dearest wish of Theagenes, who so morally scorned your immoral counsels."

9     In furious rage at Charikleia's words, Arsake gave orders for her to be soundly beaten, then said: "Take the accursed creature down to the cells. Leave her chains on her. Let her see that wonderful sweetheart of hers receiving the same treatment as herself—as he so richly deserves. Shackle her hand and foot and give her too to Euphrates to keep under guard until tomorrow, when the Persian magistrates will sentence her to pay with her life for what she has done."

But as she was being led away, the young slave who had served the wine to Kybele (she was one of the two Ionians whom Arsake had presented to wait on the young couple when they first arrived in the palace) burst into tears, possibly touched by an affection for Charikleia that sprang from the shared intimacy of daily life, or possibly even enacting the will of heaven. "The poor thing!" she sobbed. "She is quite innocent!"

Puzzled by her words, the assembled company wrung from her an explanation of what precisely she meant. She confessed to having given the poison to Kybele, who had herself given it to her to give to Charikleia; but, before she could do so, possibly because she was flustered by the enormity of the crime or else because Kybele's gesture to serve Charikleia first had muddled her, she had switched the cups and presented the old woman with the one with poison in it. She was taken straight to Arsake, for they all considered this evidence of Charikleia's innocence a remarkable stroke of luck: compassion for a noble heart and a fair countenance can be felt even by a race of barbarians. But the only result of the maidservant repeating her story was for Arsake to say, "This person appears to be an accomplice," and command that she should be put in chains and held under guard to await the trial. She then sent word to the Persian lords in whom power was vested to discuss matters of state, to pronounce judgements and decide sentences, summoning them to hear the case the following day.

The judges arrived at daybreak and took their seats on the bench. Arsake conducted the prosecution, omitting no detail of fact in her account of the poisoning. Throughout the proceedings she wept for her erstwhile nurse and the loss of one more devoted to her and more esteemed by her than any other, and called upon the judges to verify that this was the way her kindness in welcoming a stranger into her house and lavishing affection on her had been reciprocated. In short, she mounted a damning case for the prosecution. In defense Charikleia said nothing; she repeated her admission of guilt and made no attempt to contest the charge of poisoning, adding among other things that she would gladly have done away with Arsake also, had she not been prevented. She abused Arsake forthrightly and did all she could to provoke the judges into condemning her. This was because the previous night in her prison cell, after telling Theagenes all that had happened and hearing in turn of his ordeals, she had made a compact with him to accept voluntarily any death that might be inflicted on them, and so be rid forever of a life without hope, an exile without end, and a fate without pity. For what she thought would be the last time she had embraced him. She always took care to have the necklaces that had been exposed with her concealed about her person, but today she wore them as a kind of burial shroud, fastened around her waist beneath her clothes. None of the charges brought against her did she contest, and where no charge was brought she invented one.

Her judges had no hesitation; they very nearly sentenced her to the excessive cruelty of a Persian execution, but, touched perhaps by the sight of her youth and peerless beauty, they condemned her instead to be burned at the stake. At once she was seized by the executioners and taken to a place just outside the city wall. All this time a crier was proclaiming that she was being led to the stake as a poisoner, and a large crowd of other people from the city had joined the procession: some had actually seen her being led away, others had heard the story that raced through the town, and had hurried to watch. Arsake was there too, watching from the wall, for she would have been most disappointed not to feast her eyes on the sight of Charikleia's punishment.

The executioners built a gigantic bonfire and then lit it. As the flames took hold, Charikleia begged a moment's grace from the guards who held her, promising that she would mount the pyre without the use of force. She stretched her arms towards that quarter of the sky whence the sun was beaming, and prayed in a loud voice: "O Sun and Earth and you spirits above and beneath the earth who watch and punish the sins of men, bear me witness that I am innocent of the charges laid against me and that I gladly suffer death because of the unendurable agonies that fate inflicts on me. Receive me mercifully, but with all possible speed exact retribution from that she-devil, that evil adulteress—Arsake—who has contrived all this to rob me of my beloved."

At these words there was general uproar. While some of the crowd were still making up their minds to halt the execution for a second trial, others were already moving to do so, but, before they could act, Charikleia climbed onto the pyre and positioned herself at the very heart of the fire. There she stood for some time without taking any hurt. The flames flowed around her rather than licking against her; they caused her no harm but drew back wherever she moved towards them, serving merely to encircle her in splendor and present a vision of her standing in radiant beauty in a frame of light, like a bride in a chamber of flame.

Charikleia was astounded by this turn of events but was nonetheless eager for death. She leapt from one part of the blaze to another, but it was in vain, for the fire always drew back and seemed to retreat before her onset. The executioners did not let up but redoubled their efforts, encouraged by threatening signs from Arsake, hurling on logs and piling on reeds from the river, fueling the flames by whatever means they could, but all to no avail. The city was now in even greater uproar; this deliverance seemed to show the hand of god. "She is innocent," they yelled. "She has done nothing wrong!" The crowd surged forward and tried to drive the executioners away from the pyre. Their leader was Thyamis, who had joined them after being alerted to what was happen-

ing by the deafening tumult. He tried to embolden the people to go to
Charikleia's assistance; but for all their eagerness to rescue her they did
not have the courage to approach the fire, but instead urged the girl to
leap out of the flames: anyone who could stand unscathed in the blaze
had nothing to fear if she decided to come out.

Charikleia too had come to the conclusion that she owed her salvation
to the gods, and when she saw what the people were doing and heard
what they were calling to her, she decided not to show ingratitude to
heaven by rebuffing its munificence. She leapt down from the pyre
whereupon, as with one voice, the city exclaimed in joyful awe and invoked the gods' majesty. But it was more than Arsake could bear: she
hastened down from the wall and, emerging at a run through a postern
gate, escorted by a phalanx of bodyguards and Persian lords, laid hold of
Charikleia with her own bare hands. Glaring fiercely at the populace, she
said: "Do you feel no shame in trying to save an evil poisoner, a wicked
and self-confessed murderess, who was caught red-handed, from just
punishment? Not only are you rendering assistance to a heinous criminal,
but you are flouting the laws of Persia, and the Great King himself too,
with his satraps, lords, and judges. Perhaps you have been gulled into
feeling sympathy for her and ascribing her deliverance to the gods because she did not burn in the fire. But come to your senses, and you will
see that this is yet further proof of her sorcery! She is so steeped in the
black arts that she can withstand even the power of fire! Come, if you
please, to the council meeting tomorrow. It will be a public session expressly so that you can hear her admit her guilt and listen to the damning
evidence of her accomplices, whom I have under lock and key."

So saying, she grasped Charikleia firmly by the neck and began to
lead her away, ordering her attendants to clear a path through the crowd.
Some people angrily considered resistance, but others gave way, being
both influenced by the suggestion that she was a sorceress and, in some
cases, intimidated by Arsake and the might of her entourage. So Charikleia was returned to the custody of Euphrates, and this time was fettered
with even heavier chains than before to await a second trial and execution. But desperate though her plight was, she found in it one compensation that outweighed all her suffering: she was with Theagenes and could
tell him what had happened. This was something else that Arsake had
devised to spite and make cruel fun of them. She thought that it would
cause the young couple more pain if they were shut up in the same cell so
that they could see one another in chains and being subjected to corporal
punishment, for she knew that a lover feels his beloved's pain more
deeply than his own. But, on the contrary, this proved a great solace to
them, and they were glad that they were both enduring identical hardships, for each felt that to undergo less severe punishment would have
been a defeat at the other's hands, a sign of deficiency in love. Besides,

they were able to be together, to provide mutual consolation, to inspire in one another the courage to face with resolution and bravery whatever befell them, and not to flinch from the struggle for their chastity and devotion.

10    Deep into the night they talked of many things, naturally enough for two people who believed that after tonight they would never see one another again and who were enjoying one another's company as long as they might. Eventually they fell to considering the miracle at the stake. Theagenes was inclined to attribute it to the benevolence of the gods, who had been incensed by Arsake's iniquitous allegations and taken pity on her innocent and blameless victim. Charikleia seemed to be less certain.

"My bizarre deliverance," she said, "certainly bears all the marks of a supernatural or divine intervention to save me. But the fact that we are so beset by one misfortune coming directly after another and subject to such various and excessive torments suggests that we are under heaven's curse and the victims of divine malevolence—unless it is the divinity's way of working miracles to plunge us deep in despair and then deliver us from the abyss!"

11    Theagenes entreated her to keep her tongue from blasphemy and advised her to set even greater store by piety than by chastity,[186] but Charikleia continued her tirade until she suddenly broke off to exclaim: "Heaven have mercy on us! Such a dream I dreamed last night—if dream it was and not reality! At the time it somehow slipped from my thoughts, but now it comes back to me. The dream was in the form of a line of verse, and it came from the lips of Kalasiris, most blessed among men. Either I fell asleep without realizing, and he came to me in a dream, or else I saw him in the very flesh. It went something like this, I think:

If you wear pantarbe fear-all, fear not the power of flame:
Miracles may come to pass: for Fate 'tis easy game."

Theagenes shook like a man possessed and, so far as his chains permitted, sprang to his feet. "May heaven look kindly upon us!" he cried. "Memory is making a poet of me too! I have an oracle from the selfsame prophet; be it Kalasiris or a god in Kalasiris's shape, he appeared to me and seemed to speak these words:

Ethiopia's land with a maiden shalt thou see:
Tomorrow from Arsake's bonds shalt thou be free.

Now, I can guess the meaning of the prophecy as it affects me: by 'Ethiopia's land' it signifies, I think, the netherworld,[187] 'with a maiden'

186. Reading πλέον ἢ καὶ σωφρονεῖν.
187. Because both were inhabited by beings with black faces.

means I shall be with Persephone,[188] and the release from bonds is the departure of my soul from my earthly body. But what sense do your lines make? They are full of contradictions! The word *pantarbe* means 'fearing all things,' but then the commandment requires you not to be afraid of the pyre."

"My darling Theagenes," replied Charikleia, "misfortune has been so constant a companion that you have grown used to putting the worst construction on everything, for people are apt to allow their circumstances to shape their thoughts. But it seems to me that the words of the prophecy presage a brighter future than you are disposed to see. Perhaps 'the maiden' is me, and you are being given an assurance that, at my side, you will come to Ethiopia, my fatherland, free of Arsake and her bonds. How this will come to pass we are not told, and it is not easy to credit. But to the gods it is possible; they gave us this prophecy, and they will see that is is fulfilled. Their prediction concerning me at any rate has, as you know, already been effected as they willed it. Death seemed certain, but see! Here I am alive still. I carried my salvation with me, though I did not know it at the time; but now I think I understand. Even in the past, I have made a point of always keeping about my person the tokens of recognition that were exposed with me, but yesterday I was especially careful to do so, for I was about to stand trial, and I thought that day would bring my death. So I girded them around my waist out of sight: if I lived, they would assure me of the necessities of life; and if anything happened to me, they would serve to adorn me in the final sleep of the grave. They consist of precious necklaces and priceless gems from India and Ethiopia, and among them, Theagenes, is a ring, a gift that my father gave my mother when he asked her to be his bride. It is set with a jewel called pantarbe and inscribed with certain sacred characters; it is full, it seems, of a supernatural and mystic property, which I think must have endowed the stone with the power to repel fire and bestow immunity from the flames on its wearer. This it was that saved my life no doubt, by the gods' grace. So much is suggested and confirmed by what I was told by Kalasiris, that most blessed of men; on more than one occasion he related to me that this is described and explained by the writing embroidered on the band that was laid beside me—and which is now wound around my waist."

"That is plausible enough to be true—or at least consistent with what has occurred," said Theagenes. "But what new pantarbe will there be to deliver us from tomorrow's dangers? Unfortunately, it does not bestow immortality as well as immunity to fire, and we can presume that that

188. The daughter of Demeter, abducted by Hades to be queen of the underworld. Persephone was also known as Kore, "the Maiden"; this is the same word for "maiden" as that used in the first line of Theagenes' dream prophecy and facilitates his misinterpretation.

she-devil Arsake is at this very moment devising some different and more exquisite form of execution for us. May she condemn the two of us to a single death in a single hour. That I should not count death at all, but merely rest from all our sorrows."

"Take heart," replied Charikleia. "We have a second pantarbe in the prophecy the gods have made us. So let us trust in the gods: that way our deliverance will bring us greater joy, and we shall endure whatever ordeals we must with purer hearts."

12 So Theagenes and Charikleia passed the night in reflections of this kind, alternating between, on the one hand, lamentations and proud avowals that each felt more pain and anguish on the other's behalf than on his own and, on the other, the exchange of last wishes and oaths, sworn in the name of the gods and their present fortune, that they would remain true to one another in love so long as they lived.

Meanwhile, at the dead of night, when the whole town was asleep, Bagoas and his fifty horsemen reached Memphis. With hardly a sound they woke the sentries, spoke their names, and were recognized. Then quickly and noiselessly they made their way through the city to the satrap's residence. There Bagoas left the horsemen posted in a ring around the palace, ready to come to his aid if he encountered any resistance, and then entered alone through a small side-gate, whose existence was not public knowledge. The door was not strong, and he had little difficulty in forcing it. He made himself known to the gatekeeper, whom he ordered not to say a word, and then hurried to Euphrates; he knew the palace like the back of his hand, and besides there was a little moonlight that night to light his way. Euphrates was asleep in bed and leaped up in alarm when Bagoas woke him.

"Who is it?" he cried.

"It is Bagoas," he replied, and told him to keep quiet. "Have a light brought to us."

Euphrates called one of the slave boys who were sleeping in the next room and told him to light a lamp without waking any of the others. The boy returned, set the lamp on a stand, then withdrew.

"What is going on?" asked Euphrates. "What bad news have you got for us, suddenly turning up without warning like this?"

"That is soon told," replied Bagoas. "Take this letter and read it, but before you open it, examine the device on the seal and satisfy yourself that these orders come from Oroondates. Then do as he commands: you have the advantage of darkness and surprise; exploit it before anyone knows what is happening. Whether it would be a good idea to give Arsake the letter addressed to her before you do anything else, you must decide for yourself."

13 Bagoas handed the letters to Euphrates, who read them both. "This spells trouble for Arsake," he said, "though her condition is desperate

enough already: yesterday she suddenly developed a high fever, a punish-ment from the gods, it seems. Hot flushes spread over her entire body and still have not subsided. There seems little hope of her recovering. But even if she had been in the best of health, I should not have given her this letter; she would sooner have died and taken us all to perdition with her than have agreed to release the young couple. You have arrived in the nick of time, I can tell you. Take the strangers and go. Do whatever lies within your power to help them. Take pity on them, I beg you. They are hapless victims of ill fortune, who have been subjected to indig-nities and torments beyond counting, not that I enjoyed what I had to do but such were Arsake's orders. Besides, they seem to be nobly born and, as I know from what I have seen of their behavior, they are utterly pure of heart."

With those words he led Bagoas to their cell. The young couple were in chains, and the torture inflicted on them had begun to take its toll, but Bagoas was nevertheless impressed by both their stature and their beauty. Theagenes and Charikleia assumed that their end was at hand and that Bagoas and his men had come before time to take them on that final journey that led to death. For a moment their spirit failed them, then they collected themselves, and their faces broke into a broad smile that made it quite plain to all present that they felt less fear of death than joy at its approach. Euphrates and his men drew close and, seizing them roughly, began to release them from the planks to which their chains were fastened.

"My compliments to that she-devil Arsake!" exclaimed Theagenes "She thinks to shroud her wicked deeds in the darkness of night. But the eye of Justice sees clear; it can detect and bring to light the most darkly kept wicked secrets. Do as you have been commanded. Whatever is or-dained for us, be it fire, water, or the sword, the one grace that we ask of you is to let us both die the same death at the same time."

Charikleia added her pleas to his, and the eunuchs wept, for they could understand a little of what was said. They led them outside, still in their chains. Euphrates remained behind, but once Bagoas and his horse- 14 men were clear of the satrap's palace, they relieved the young couple of most of their chains, the few remaining being intended to prevent them escaping rather than to cause any suffering. They set each of them on a horse, then, forming a protective circle around them, they rode off posthaste towards Thebes.

For the rest of the night they rode without a break, and throughout the following day too they did not stop anywhere to rest, until, at about the third hour, the scorching heat of the sun blazing from the summer sky of Egypt grew too hot to bear. They were exhausted from lack of sleep and could see that so long a time in the saddle had pushed Chari-kleia in particular beyond the limits of her endurance. So they decided to bivouac just where they were, to get their breath back, give their horses a rest, and allow the girl to refresh herself.

There was a sort of promontory in the bank of the Nile, where the water, prevented from flowing straight ahead, meandered through a semicircle, until it returned to a point in line with the place where the detour began. The area thus enclosed formed, as it were, an inland bay, which, the whole tract being well watered, was covered in lush meadows and produced, unworked by human hand, a rich profusion of grass and herbiage, where animals could graze to their hearts' content beneath a shady canopy of persea trees,[189] sycamores, and other plants whose natural habitat is the banks of the Nile. Here Bagoas and his men made their camp, the canopy of trees serving them for a tent. He divided his food between himself and Theagenes and Charikleia, whom he forced to eat despite their initial refusal: they said there was no point in eating when they were going to be dead within the hour, but they were won round by his assurances that nothing of the kind was going to happen and by the information that they were being taken not to execution but to see Oroondates.

15    The intolerable noonday heat was now beginning to abate: the sun was no longer beating down directly overhead, but its rays fell aslant as it began to sink in the west. Bagoas and his men were making ready to move on when a man on horseback rode up: he appeared to have been riding hard and was fighting for breath; his horse was streaming with sweat and nearly collapsing beneath him. He whispered something to Bagoas, then rested from his exertions. For a moment the eunuch gazed at the ground, apparently lost in thought at what he had been told. Then he said "Take heart, my friends. Your foe has paid the penalty: Arsake is dead. When she learned that we had taken you away, she hanged herself in a choking noose,[190] choosing to die by her own hand rather than wait for a death she could not hope to avoid, for she would not have escaped punishment by Oroondates and the Great King: either her throat would have been slit, or else she would have lived out the rest of her life in abject degradation. Such is the import of the message that the man who has just arrived has brought me from Euphrates. So take heart and be of good spirit: I am satisfied that you have done no wrong, and now you are rid of the woman who wronged you."

Bagoas said this in an attempt to make the young couple well disposed towards himself, but he spoke in a faltering Greek with many grammati-

---

189. *Mimosus schimperi,* a tree producing succulent pearlike fruit and regarded as holy by the Egyptians. Theophrastos (*Inquiry into Plants* 4.2.1) names the persea and the sycamore as distinctively Egyptian.

190. The phrase is quoted from Euripides *Hippolytos* 802, where the chorus breaks to Theseus the news of Phaidra's suicide.

cal errors[191] and a thick accent. His words were inspired in part by his own joy, for he had detested Arsake's tyrannous excesses while she was alive, in part by a wish to reassure and encourage the young couple, for he hoped, not without reason, to win great credit and favor with Oroondates if he could bring to him alive a young man who would eclipse the rest of the satrap's retinue and a girl of peerless beauty to be Oroondates' wife, now that Arsake was dead and gone. The news brought joy to Theagenes and Charikleia too. They acclaimed the power of divine justice, and it seemed to them that nothing could hurt them now, even if the worst of fates befell them, for their bitterest enemy lay dead. So it is that sometimes even death may be sweet, if one can see one's foes die first.

By now the cool of the evening was dispelling the suffocating heat and making traveling possible again. They remounted and rode on through the evening, all through the night and the morning of the following day, making all possible speed in the hope of reaching Oroondates before he left Thebes. Without success, however: on the road they met a man from the army, who told them that the satrap had already departed from Thebes; he himself had been dispatched to rally every single soldier and man-at-arms, including those left behind on guard duty, to assemble in haste at Syene, for everything was in uproar, and there was a danger that the satrap was too late and the town had already fallen to the Ethiopian army, which had pressed home its attack with a speed that beggared description. So Bagoas turned off the road to Thebes and headed for Syene.

He had nearly reached the town when he was surprised by an  16 Ethiopian ambuscade, a large number of well-armed young men who had been sent as an advance party to reconnoiter and make sure that the way ahead was secure for the whole army by testing it themselves. But, not knowing the area, they had lost their way in the dark and strayed so far ahead of their comrades that they thought it unwise to go any further. So they had concealed themselves in one of the reed beds on the Nile bank, which they had spent a sleepless night in securing as a strong point for themselves and a trap for the enemy. At the crack of dawn they saw Bagoas and his detachment of horsemen ride past. Having established that they were few in number, they allowed them to proceed a little way and then, having satisfied themselves that there were no others coming along behind, suddenly emerged from the marsh with a loud cry and gave chase.

Bagoas and the other horsemen were filled with alarm at this sudden shouting. They recognized their assailants as Ethiopians by the color of

---

191. There is no attempt to reproduce these errors in the Greek spoken by Bagoas.

their skin and could see that there were too many of them to stand and fight—the reconnaissance party comprised a thousand men, though not heavily armed. The mere sight of them was too much for the Persians, who turned and fled, though at first they withdrew at a rather more leisurely pace than they were capable of so as not to make it too obvious that they were running away. The Ethiopians set off in pursuit, throwing into the first line of attack all the two hundred or so Troglodytai[192] who were with them.

The Troglodytai form one of the constituent parts of Ethiopia. They are a nomadic people whose lands are adjacent to those of the Arabs. Naturally swift runners, they cultivate this gift by training from childhood. They have never learned to use heavy armor but in battle employ slings, which they use at long range: this can cause great damage to the enemy, but if they see that their opponents are getting the upper hand, they take to their heels, whereupon the enemy immediately gives up the chase, being well aware that the Troglodytai can run as swiftly as birds on the wing and conceal themselves in narrow cracks and hidden crevices in the rocks.

So on this occasion the Troglodytai on foot outran the horsemen and succeeded in causing a number of casualties with slingshot. But when the Persians turned and counterattacked, they did not stand their ground but ran back pell-mell to the main body of their friends, who were coming up some distance behind. Observing this and feeling nothing but contempt for such a paltry adversary, the Persians pressed home their counterattack with confidence and, having thus won a short respite from hostile attention, resumed their efforts to get away, spurring on their horses and giving them free rein to gallop as hard and as fast as they could. Most of them escaped by running into the shelter of a bend in the river Nile, which formed a sort of headland whose protruding banks enabled them to get out of sight of the enemy. Bagoas, however, was taken prisoner after falling to the ground when his horse stumbled and sustaining an injury to one leg that left him unable to move. Theagenes and Charikleia were captured too, partly because they had not the heart to abandon Bagoas, a man whose kindness towards them already had been such as to lead them to expect more; so they dismounted and stood by him when they might have got away. But in greater part this was a voluntary surrender, for Theagenes said to Charikleia that this was what his dream

192. This name was applied to cave-dwelling tribes from various places, but in particular to a people living on the coast to the south of Egypt. They were the subject of travelers' tales, and much legendary material accumulated around them, particularly concerning their speed of foot, which is first mentioned by Herodotos (4.183). Heliodoros has edited out some of their more implausible attributes, but his description of them, and of other exotic nations, reflects literary tradition rather than fact.

had foretold, that these were the Ethiopians to whose land it was their destiny to go after being taken prisoner; so it was right to place themselves in their hands and trust to the uncertainties of fortune rather than the certain dangers posed by Oroondates.

Charikleia knew now that Destiny was guiding her steps. She felt sure  17
that their fortune was about to take a turn for the better, and looked upon her assailants as friends, not foes. But of these thoughts she said nothing to Theagenes and pretended that it was his advice alone that had induced her to submit. When the Ethiopians drew near, they could see simply by looking that Bagoas was a eunuch and no soldier, and also that Theagenes and Charikleia carried no weapons but were prisoners—though prisoners of extraordinary beauty and nobility. They detailed one of their number, an Egyptian who could also speak Persian, to ask them who they were, hoping that they would understand one or other of these languages, if not both. Spies and scouts, I should explain, are dispatched to reconnoiter what is being said as well as what is being done, and experience has taught them to take with them people who speak the language of the local inhabitants and of the enemy.

The question was simple, and Theagenes had long been familiar with the Egyptian tongue. He replied that Bagoas was a person of some importance to the satrap, while he and Charikleia were Greeks, who until now had been traveling as prisoners of the Persians but whom a kinder fate perhaps was now delivering into the hands of the Ethiopians.

The Ethiopians decided to spare them and take them back alive. This was their first catch, as it were, and it was a fine one for them to present to their king: on the one hand, the most prized of the satrap's possessions (for eunuchs act as eyes and ears to the courts of Persian royalty, since they have no children or family, love for whom might divide their loyalties, but are entirely dependent on him who places his trust in them); on the other, the young couple, who would be a gift to adorn the retinue and court of their king.

So without a moment's delay they led them away, after mounting them on horseback, Bagoas because he was hurt, Theagenes and Charikleia because their chains made them unable to keep up with the rapid pace that was set. The scene was like the preliminary appearance and introduction of the actors in the theater before the play begins:[193] strangers in a foreign land, prisoners in chains who a moment ago had been haunted by a vision of their own violent death, were now being not so much led as escorted in captive state, guarded by those who were soon to be their subjects. Such was the position of Theagenes and Charikleia.

193. The technical terms used here (*proanaphonesis, proeisodion*) are obscure, and so the exact point of the comparison is unclear.

## Book Nine

1 Syene meanwhile had been put under tight and complete siege: the Ethiopian army was staked out around the town like a ring of hunting nets; for when Oroondates realized that the Ethiopians had passed the cataracts and were almost upon him as they drove towards Syene, he had made a dash for the town, which he had managed to enter just ahead of them. Then he had barricaded the gates and lined the walls with spears, swords, and engines of war, and now was sitting tight, waiting to see what would happen next. Hydaspes, the Ethiopian king, had been in time to observe from a distance the Persian dash for Syene, but despite a vigorous pursuit had arrived too late to engage them before they entered the town. Thereupon he had unleashed his forces against the city, whose walls they encircled like a river, in numbers so vast that the mere sight of them made resistance inconceivable. The siege had begun, as the countless thousands of Hydaspes' men, weapons, and beasts combined to reduce the open plains of Syene to a narrow, crowded passage.

It was here that the scouting party found him and presented their prisoners to him. Joy welled in him at the sight of the young pair; he felt an instant attraction to his own flesh and blood, as, did he but know it, the prophetic intuition of his heart exerted its power over him. But he derived even greater joy from the omen afforded by the presentation of these bound prisoners.

"Excellent!" he exclaimed. "In the first spoils of war, the gods deliver our enemies bound into our hands! Let these, our first prisoners," he went on, "be kept safe for the victory sacrifices as the firstfruits of the war, for so Ethiopian law requires. They are to be kept under guard to be an offering to the gods of our homeland."

He rewarded the scouting party with gifts and sent them and their prisoners away to the supply train. He detailed a complete detachment of Greek-speakers to stand guard over the young pair and gave them instructions to spare no pains in catering to their needs and stint nothing in their care, but above all to keep them clean of all impurity, for they were now being kept as a pair of sacrificial victims. He also gave orders that their fetters were to be replaced with chains of gold, for in Ethiopia gold is customarily employed for the purposes for which other nations use iron.[194]

2 The guards put these orders into effect. The removal of the first set of chains raised hopes in the two lovers that they were to be given their

194. The wealth of Ethiopia is part of the literary tradition:

The king [of Ethiopia] conducted them to a prison in which all the prisoners were bound with gold chains, for in Ethiopia the rarest and most precious metal is bronze. (Herodotos 3.23) freedom, but these hopes were dashed when their guards loaded them with new chains, chains of gold. Theagenes could not contain his laughter. "A great improvement, I must say!" he exclaimed. "What kindness fortune is showing us! We change iron for gold,[195] captivity brings us riches, and now we are aristocrats among prisoners!"

Charikleia smiled too and tried to brighten Theagenes' mood by reminding him of what the gods had foretold and beguiling him with happier hopes for the future.

Meanwhile Hydaspes attacked Syene, which he expected to capitulate with its walls intact before a blow was struck. However, he suffered a temporary rebuff, since the defenders not only put up a spirited military resistance but also assailed him with outrageous and exasperating verbal abuse. Furious that they had so much as contemplated resistance rather than voluntarily delivering themselves into his hands at the first onslaught, he resolved not to exhaust his army by a lengthy siege, nor to make use of [196] his siege engines, which would inflict many casualties but at the same time afford a few a means of escape. Instead he decided to reduce the city by a spectacular siege tactic that would take less time and make no exceptions.

This is what he did. He divided the circuit of the wall into sections, allocated lengths of ten fathoms to groups of ten men, and told them to dig a trench whose dimensions he specified as being as broad and as deep as possible. While they dug, others removed the loose earth, and a third group heaped it up into a high mound, thus constructing a second wall to face the one under siege. No one attempted to prevent or disrupt the walling off of the town, for no one had the courage to make a sortie from the city to attack an army so immeasurably strong; and everyone could see that it was futile to shoot arrows from the battlements, for Hydaspes had taken the precaution of computing the distance between the two walls so as to ensure that his men would be out of range as they worked. He had countless hands at work to hurry the job along, so that it was completed more quickly than words can say; whereupon he commenced a second operation, which was as follows. He had left a section of his encirclement, about fifty feet wide, flat and unmounded, and from the two terminal points of his earthworks he now extended two arms to connect his excavations to the Nile, following the gradient from lowlying to elevated ground with each of these arms. One might compare the result to Long Walls.[197] The fifty-foot gap remained constant along the whole length, which was equal to the distance between Syene and the

195. Homeric allusion as at note 174.
196. Reading ἀποπειρᾶσθαι for ἀποπειρώμενος.
197. Defensive walls linking a city to the sea. The best-known were those connecting the city of Athens to its port, Peiraeus.

*keeping the Egyptians in*

Nile. When the dike reached the riverbanks, he cut an inlet for the river and channeled the outflow into the canal formed by the two arms. The water was dropping from a raised position to lower ground,[198] from the immense breadth of the Nile into a cramped channel whose artificial banks kept it narrowly confined, and thus, around the inlet, it generated a thunderous and ear-splitting din, while along the canal it made a low rumbling that was audible for a great distance.

The sight and sound of all this was enough to bring home to the people in Syene just what a desperate predicament they were in: the purpose of the encirclement was to flood them out; escape from the city was impossible, since the earthworks and the water, which was drawing ever closer, barred the way out; but the dangers of doing nothing were equally obvious. So they took such steps as circumstances permitted to safeguard their own position. First, they packed the cracks between the planks in the city gates with oakum and pitch; then they strengthened the walls and reinforced their foundations, everyone carting along such materials as he had to hand—earth, stones, timber. No one was idle: women, children, and old men alike all joined in the work, for mortal danger is no respecter of age or sex. The fittest and those of age for military service were assigned to dig a narrow underground tunnel running
4 from the city to the enemy's earthworks, the operation being conducted in the following manner: first they sank a shaft about five fathoms deep close to the wall; once they had passed beneath the foundations, they began to dig horizontally and, by the light of torches, excavated an underground passage leading straight towards the earthworks. Those in front passed the loose soil to those behind, and thus it was handed back along the line and taken away to be dumped in an area of the city that for many years had been a public park. Here a great mountain of earth was accumulated. This was a precaution to allow the water, if it ever reached that point, to escape harmlessly along the empty passage, but for all their precaution[199] the calamity was too quick for them. The Nile had already passed along the long canal and now was flooding into the circular section, which it filled entirely, turning the space between the two walls into a lake. In an instant, Syene was an island, an inland town surrounded by water, washed by the waves of the flooding Nile.

To begin with, the wall held up for a short part of the day. But as the water level rose, the pressure increased, and the water began to seep deep into the ground through the fissures that the heat of summer had caused to open up in the black and fertile soil, and found its way underneath the base of the wall. At that point the soil beneath could no longer support the weight and gave way; and wherever the earth had become spongy

198. The river would be embanked to control the summer flood.
199. Reading προμηθίαν for προθυμίαν.

and had subsided, the wall began to settle too, with a shudder that made the danger all too plain, as the battlements tottered, and the defenders were thrown off their feet by the shock.

But as evening drew in, a section of the wall between two turrets did   5 actually collapse, not to such a degree that the level of the breach was lower than that of the lake or that water came in; but the wall now stood only five cubits or so clear of the water and seemed liable to succumb to the flood at any moment. This was greeted with a wail of despair from every mouth in the city, audible even to the enemy. They raised their hands to heaven and, for this was the only hope left to them, called upon the gods to deliver them. They also pleaded with Oroondates to open negotiations with Hydaspes. To this he agreed, for, little though he liked it, he was fate's slave. But walled in as he was by water, he had no way of communicating with the enemy, until necessity suggested an idea.

He wrote down what he wanted to say, and then, fastening this message to a stone, used a sling to try to conduct negotiations with the enemy, firing his entreaties across the waves. But it was to no avail, for the shot was not long enough and fell into the water short of its mark. He repeated the attempt, shooting the same message, but again failed; and although every bowman and every slinger competed to reach the mark— for the mark they were all trying to reach was their own salvation—not one succeeded. Finally they stretched out their hands towards the enemy, who were standing on the earthworks watching their distress like an audience watching a play, and with pitiful gestures indicated as best they could the meaning of their shooting, in turns holding out their hands with the palms uppermost to signify their earnest entreaty, and then, in acceptance of enslavement, crossing them behind their backs, ready to receive the manacles.

Hydaspes realized that they were begging for their lives, which he was ready to grant them, for a good man has an obligation to show mercy to an enemy who submits; but for the moment there was nothing he could do, and so he decided to subject his enemy's intentions to a further test. He already had a number of ferryboats from the river standing by, which he had allowed to drift along the canal from the Nile and had made fast when they reached the circular earthworks. He selected ten of these that were newly built and manned them with bowmen and foot soldiers whom he sent to treat with the Persians after giving them strict instructions what to say.

They made the crossing fully armed so as to be ready to defend themselves should the people on the walls try anything untoward. This was a most extraordinary spectacle: a ship crossing from one wall to another, a sailor sailing over the countryside, a ferry plying over ploughed fields! War is a constant producer of surprises, but on this occasion it excelled itself to conjure forth a quite unprecedented situation, bringing shipborne troops into conflict with wallfighters, making a soldier on dry land take up arms against another sailing the lake.

For when the men in the city saw the boats and the armed men in them heading towards the very place where the wall had been breached, they assumed, being distraught with terror at their perilous plight, that those who were in fact coming to their rescue were hostile (for when one is in an extremity of danger, nothing is without fear or suspicion), and began to hurl javelins and shoot arrows at them from the walls. So it is that even men who have despaired of their lives count every second's postponement of death a profit. They were not even shooting to inflict casualties, merely to prevent a landing. The Ethiopians returned their fire; they did not yet understand what was in the Persians' minds, and their aim was surer, so that they shot dead a couple or more, some of whom were catapulted headfirst from the walls into the water beneath by the force of the unexpected impact.

Indeed, the fighting might have flared up even further, for though the Persians were shooting only to hinder, rather than to kill, the Ethiopians were retaliating angrily—had not one of the prominent elders of Syene gone to the troops manning the wall and said: "You imbeciles! Has our predicament robbed you of wits completely? Hitherto we have been consistently imploring and beseeching them to come to our aid, but now when, beyond all our hopes, they have come, are we not going to allow them to land? If they come in friendship with proposals of peace, they will be saviors to us. On the other hand, if their intentions are hostile, it will be easy enough to overwhelm them even after they have landed—though I do not know what good it would do us if we did destroy these few when such a host encircles the city by land and water! Let us make them welcome and discover what their intentions are."

Everyone, including the satrap, thought that this was good advice. They stood away on either side from the breach in the wall and waited quietly with their weapons grounded.

6      The stretch of wall between the turrets was now cleared of the troops who manned it, and the populace began waving linen cloths to show that they would allow the Ethiopians to land. Only then did the Ethiopians venture nearer, and from the forum of the boats they addressed their beleaguered audience as follows. "Persians and those Syenians here present, Hydaspes, King of the Ethiopians who dwell to the East and to the West,[200] and now your sovereign also, has the capacity to destroy his en-

200. Compare *Odyssey* 1.22:

> Aithiopians, most distant of men, who live divided,
> some at the setting of Hyperion, some at his rising.

This reflects an archaic tradition placing Ethiopians in the regions of the world closest to the sun, the places where it rises and sets; cf. note 113.

emies utterly but is naturally inclined to take pity on suppliants. While he adjudges the former course a mark of strength befitting the act of a soldier, he considers the latter to show a love of humanity germane to his own character. He has it in his power to decide whether you live or die; but in response to your entreaties, he grants you relief from the obvious and indisputable danger that threatens you as a result of these hostilities. As for the terms on which you may obtain a welcome release from your predicament, he does not define them himself but leaves the choice to you. For he does not play the tyrant in his hour of triumph; rather he so regulates the fates of men as to avoid the wrath of the gods."

To this the Syenians replied that they surrendered themselves, their wives, and their children to Hydaspes to do with as he pleased: he was now master of their city, should it survive; but at the present time its situation was insecure and hopeless, unless the gods, or Hydaspes, came up with some immediate expedient for its preservation. Oroondates promised to abandon his claims on the places over which and for which the war had been fought, by recognizing Hydaspes as the rightful master of the city of Philai and the emerald mines. He requested to be put under no compulsion to surrender either himself or his men: if Hydaspes wished to demonstrate the full extent of his clemency, he should allow them to depart to Elephantine, on condition that they did no damage and offered no resistance. It was all one to him, he said, whether he died here and now or won an apparent reprieve only to be condemned later by the Persian king for having betrayed the army; in fact the former alternative was preferable, for he could probably look forward to some simple and conventional form of death, whereas in the latter case his execution would be of a most barbaric kind and specially devised to make his punishment as agonizing as possible.

Using arguments of this kind, he requested that two Persians be permitted to come aboard the boats, on the pretense that they would go to Elephantine and, if the troops there would join in submitting to enslavement, he for his part would surrender immediately. The envoys responded by taking two Persians on board before returning to Hydaspes, to whom they made a full report. He laughed and berated Oroondates in no uncertain terms for his stupidity in presuming to negotiate on equal terms when his very prospects of life and death rested not on himself but on another.

"But it would be absurd," added Hydaspes, "for one man's folly to entail the loss of so many lives."

So he allowed Oroondates' emissaries to proceed on foot to Elephantine,[201] for the possibility of the troops there conspiring to oppose him

201. Heliodoros apparently did not realize that Elephantine is an island.

never occurred to him. Then he assigned some of his own men to dam the inlet that had been dug for the Nile, others to cut a second channel through the earthworks; thus the inflow would be stopped, while the outflow would drain the flooded area, so speeding the process of clearing the water from around Syene and making the ground dry enough to walk over. Those who had been allocated this task only had time to make a start on it before adjourning its completion to the following day, for no sooner had the order been given than night fell.

8 Those inside the city meanwhile continued to work for their salvation by whatever means were available to them, for they had not despaired of the possibility, remote though they knew it to be, of being rescued from their plight. Those who were digging the underground tunnel were now close to the earthworks, or so they judged by estimating by eye the distance from the wall to the dike and then measuring the same distance along the tunnel with a rope. Meanwhile others rebuilt by torchlight the section of the wall that had collapsed; this was an easy task, for the stones at the breach had rolled inwards. They thought that they had achieved a temporary security, but even so the night did not pass without a fresh alarm. About midnight a section of the dike where the previous evening the Ethiopians had begun to dig an outlet ruptured without warning: it may be that the earth in that section had been piled up loosely and not properly tamped down, so that the base gave way as the water soaked into it; or those excavating the tunnel may have created an empty space into which the base of the dike could collapse; or possibly the workmen had left the place where they had started their digging somewhat lower than the rest of the dike, so that as the water level rose during the night, causing a fresh influx, the water was able to find a way out through the place where the earth had been shoveled away, and, once that happened, the channel grew deeper without anyone being aware of the fact;[202] alternatively one might ascribe the event to divine intervention. The rupture was accompanied by such a thunderous crash, the mere sound of which was sufficient to fill men's hearts with dread, that although they did not know exactly what had happened, both the Ethiopians and the Syenians themselves jumped to the conclusion that the greater part of the city and its walls had fallen down.

The Ethiopians, who had nothing to fear, stayed quietly in their tents, waiting for daybreak to learn just what had happened. But those inside the city made a complete circuit of their wall; they each found their own section still intact and concluded that the damage had occurred elsewhere, but when the light of day dawned, it dispelled the fog of doubt and fear. The rupture in the dike was plain to see, and the water had sud-

202. I have modified the text of this long sentence in two places. The rise in water level is caused by the onset of the annual flood.

denly receded, for the Ethiopians were already at work blocking off the inlet that fed the lake, lowering sluice gates made of planks fastened together and buttressed with thick timbers on the landward side, and plugging the gaps with loose earth and brushwood. Many thousands of men were engaged in this operation, some working from the banks, others on boats. Thus the water receded, but it was still not possible for either side to reach the other, for the ground was covered by a thick layer of mud, and though the surface appeared dry and firm, a quagmire lurked beneath, waiting to suck under man and horse alike, if any ventured to set foot on it.

This situation continued for some two or three days. The Syenians had thrown open their city gates, while the Ethiopians had laid down their weapons, both sides thus indicating that hostilities were at an end. It was in effect an armistice with no contact between the two sides. Neither side bothered to post guards anymore, while those inside the city in particular gave themselves over to merrymaking, for, by an odd coincidence, it happened to be the time of the Neiloa, the greatest of all festivals in Egypt. This feast is celebrated around the time of the summer solstice,[203] when the river shows the first signs of rising in flood, and is the most important in the entire Egyptian religious calendar, for the following reason: the Egyptians apotheosize the Nile and consider it the greatest of all divinities, hallowing the river as the exact counterpart of heaven: for without clouds or celestial precipitation it brings moisture to their fields and waters the ground like rain with the utmost regularity each year.[204]

This is the popular version, but the substance of their belief in the river's divinity is this: they believe that human life and existence derive principally from the conjunction of moist and dry elements, and their theory is that all other elements are subordinate to these two and occur only in combination with them; the Nile embodies the moist element; their own land, the dry. This much they disclose to all and sundry, but to initiates they reveal the truth that the land is Isis and the Nile Osiris, with these titles imparting a deeper meaning to the material objects. The goddess longs for her husband when he is away and rejoices at his return, mourns his renewed absence and abominates Typhon like a mortal enemy.[205] There is, I imagine, a school of natural philosophers and theologians who do not disclose the meanings embedded in these stories to lay-

203. Around 21 June. Many classical writers use this way of dating the start of the Nile flood.

204. This paragraph is taken, in great part verbatim, from a passage in the *Life of Moses* by the hellenized Jew Philon of Alexandria (2.195). Such comparisons are found in many classical authors.

205. Typhon (or Seth), the slayer of Osiris, in this allegory is identified with the desert sun and drought.

men but simply give them preliminary instruction in the form of a myth. But those who have reached the higher grades of the mysteries they initiate into clear knowledge in the privacy of the holy shrine, in the light cast by the blazing torch of truth.[206]

10 · Well, may the gods pardon me for saying this much. The greatest mysteries may not be spoken of: let us respect their sanctity[207] as we continue our story of the events at Syene.

So it was the time of the feast of the Neiloa, and the local people were occupied with sacrifices and religious ceremonies. Physically they were exhausted by their terrible predicament, but spiritually they did not neglect their duty to reverence the gods, so far as the situation permitted. Oroondates waited until midnight, when the Syenians were sunk in a deep slumber as a result of their festivities, and stealthily led his army out of the town. He had previously given the Persians secret notification of a particular time and gate through which they were to make their escape. Each decurion had received orders to leave their horses and pack animals behind so as to avoid difficulties and prevent any disturbance that might lead to the detection of their enterprise; they were to collect their weapons and procure a plank or length of wood, and to bring nothing else.

11     When they had assembled at the appointed gate, Oroondates laid the lengths of wood brought by each decury crosswise on top of the mud, edge to edge with no gaps between them. Thus, with those in the rear continually handing the planks to those in front, he constructed a kind of bridge, across which he was able to take his army without difficulty or delay. After reaching dry land, he slipped past the Ethiopians, who had not foreseen anything like this and had not even bothered to mount a guard: they were sleeping, without a care as to what might happen. Then he led his army in one movement towards Elephantine at a speed that had them panting for breath. No one tried to prevent him entering the town; the two Persians who had been sent on in advance from Syene were on the lookout for his arrival every night (as they had been instructed), and when he gave the agreed password, they immediately threw open the gates.

As day broke, it began to dawn on the Syenians that the Persians had got away. First they each found individually that the Persians billeted in their homes were nowhere to be seen, next they conferred in groups, and

206. The metaphor is chosen to remind the reader of the torch-lit processions and ceremonies of the Isiac mysteries (Herodotos 2.62; Apuleius *Metamorphoses* 11.10, 11.27).

207. This pose of "religious silence" is modeled on Herodotos's practice in his account of the mysteries of Egyptian religion. Heliodoros's comments on the Isis myth are for the most part common knowledge and do not reveal any degree of personal acquaintance with the cult.

finally they were even able to discern the bridge. They were prey to renewed anxiety and fully expected to be charged with new crimes more
serious than before: that, despite Hydaspes' magnanimity, they had
demonstrated their treachery by conniving at the Persian escape. They
resolved to make a massed exodus from the city and throw themselves
on the Ethiopians' mercy, swearing solemn oaths to deny their complicity and hoping thus to move them to compassion. Young and old alike
they collected, holding branches as a token of supplication, carrying
lighted candles and torches. They placed the priestly caste and the images
of the gods at the head of the procession like so many flags of peace and
walked across the bridge towards the Ethiopians; but before they reached
them, they fell to their knees in entreaty and with one accord and one
voice set up a mournful and piteous wail of supplication. To excite even
greater compassion they set their little babies on the ground in front of
them and allowed them to go wherever chance took them, so using the
most innocent and least culpable section of the population to mollify the
ire of the Ethiopians. Terrified and unable to understand what was happening, the babes fled from those who had borne them, those who
nursed them, and, guided perhaps by their fear of the deafening cries behind them, took the path that led towards the enemy, some crawling,
others toddling unsteadily, all whimpering pathetically. It was as if
chance were using them to stage an unscripted scene of supplication.

*Supplication*

When Hydaspes saw this, he imagined that they were simply reinforc-   12
ing their earlier entreaties and acknowledging their submission in such a
way as to leave no room for doubt; so he sent to ask them what they
were about and why they had not brought the Persians with them. The
Syenians told him everything: the Persians had escaped, but they themselves were entirely innocent; they had been celebrating a traditional festival and had been performing their religious duties so single-mindedly
that they had not observed the Persians make their getaway while they
were sleeping off their festivities; but they would probably still have escaped even if the Syenians had known what was afoot, for having no
weapons they would have been powerless to stand in the way of armed
men.

When this was reported to him, Hydaspes began to suspect the truth,
that Oroondates was planning to deceive and surprise him somehow. He
asked the priests to come to him unaccompanied, and after making obeisance to the images of the gods that they carried with them so as to
heighten their feeling that they were under an obligation to tell him the
truth, he asked whether they had any further information to give him
about the Persians—what direction they had taken, who they were rely-
ing on, where they intended to attack. The priests replied that they knew
nothing but surmised that they were headed for Elephantine, where the

greater part of their forces had assembled, including the armored cavalry,
on whom Oroondates placed particular reliance. Then they earnestly en-
13  treated him to come into the city—for it belonged to him, they said—
and to put away the anger he felt against them.

Hydaspes did not think that this was the time to enter the city in person, but he sent two regiments of heavily armed infantry to discover
whether his suspicions that this was a trap were correct and, if they were
not, to garrison the town. Then he dismissed the Syenians with generous
guarantees and formed his own army into battle array so as to withstand
the Persian onslaught, or alternatively to mount an attack on them himself if they squandered the initiative. But before his deployments could
be completed, scouts came galloping up to report that the Persians were
on their way in battle formation. To recapitulate, Oroondates had issued
instructions for the rest of his army to assemble at Elephantine, but when
he observed the Ethiopians bearing down on him unexpectedly, he had
been obliged to make a dash for Syene with a few troops; there he had
been walled in by the earthworks and compelled to beg for his life; Hydaspes had promised to spare him, but then Oroondates had proved the
most treacherous of men: he had arranged for two Persians to cross the
water with the Ethiopians and dispatched them ostensibly to canvass
opinion at Elephantine as to the conditions on which they would be prepared to make terms with Hydaspes, though in reality their mission was
to discover whether they would rather make ready for battle at whatever
time he himself might be able to make good his escape. He put this
treacherous plan into effect: he found his men ready and waiting and
marched out of the city with them at once, refusing to set his attack back
by one minute but moving so quickly as to leave the enemy no time to
make proper preparations—or so he thought.

14    By now he was within sight, his army drawn up ready for battle.
Even from afar the pomp and show of Persia compelled the attention of
every eye. From their gold and silver weapons lightning flashed and
flickered over the plain, for the sun was not long risen and was shining
full on the Persians' faces, so that their armor shone back with its own
inherent brilliance, broadcasting an awesome coruscation into the furthest distance.

The right wing of Oroondates' line was held by Persians and Medes
of native birth, heavily armed infantry in front with all the archers
marching behind them so that, despite their lack of body armor, they
would be able to shoot their arrows from a safe position behind the
shield of the infantry. On the left wing he stationed his battalions of
Egyptians and Libyans and all his foreign troops, and alongside them, as
on the right, he placed javelin throwers and slingers with orders to make
rapid sallies from the line and direct their fire at the enemy's flanks. He
took the center himself, conspicuous in a scythed chariot, with a regi-

ment on either side to escort and protect him. The only troops he stationed ahead of himself were the armored cavalry, and it was largely because of his reliance on these that he ventured to fight at all. Of all the Persian formations these are generally the most effective, ranged before the line like a wall, impervious to the tides of war.

The form of their armor is as follows.[208] A man chosen for his exceptional physical strength dons a close-fitting helmet, beaten from a single piece of metal and cunningly crafted into a realistic representation of a human face, like a mask. This covers his head completely from crown to neck, apart from slits over the eyes so that he can see. His right hand is armed with a lance somewhat longer than a spear, leaving his left free to work the reins. A scimitar hangs at his side. His body armor covers not just his breast but the whole of the rest of his body as well. It is constructed in the following way. They take rods of bronze and iron and beat them into squares about a span in size; these are then fitted together so that they overlap at the edges, each plate riding over the one beneath and the one beside it so as to leave no gaps. This contexture is then fastened together with stitches underneath the overlaps, thus producing a garment of plate-mail that sits comfortably on the body, yet fits tightly all over, shaping itself onto every limb and contracting and expanding so as to allow unimpeded movement. The armor also has sleeves and extends from head to knee, the only opening being at the thighs, where it is necessary for the rider to bestride his horse. This, then, is their body armor, impervious to arrows and resistant to all injury. Their greaves reach from the soles of the feet to the knee, where they meet the body armor.

The horse too is protected by armor of a very similar kind: shinplates are fastened round its legs, its head is totally sheathed in tight-fitting frontlets, and a skirt of iron mail is draped over its back, down to its belly on either side, thus affording the animal protection while at the same time being loose enough not to hamper its galloping. Equipped and virtually encased[209] in armor of this kind, the rider bestrides his steed, though he is so heavy that he cannot mount it by himself but has to rely on others to lift him on. Then, in the hour of battle, he gives his horse its rein, digs in his spurs, and bears down at full tilt on the enemy, looking just like a man of steel or a hammer-worked statue come to life.[210] The

208. Although the Persians did employ armored cavalry of a kind, the description that follows is based on the cataphracts introduced into the Roman imperial army from the East by Alexander Severus, and has many points of contact with similar descriptions in other writers of the third and fourth centuries. We are therefore dealing with a literary commonplace, not firsthand observation.

209. Retaining the manuscript reading ἐσκευασμένος . . . ἐμβεβλημένος. The printed text makes these participles refer to the horse rather than its rider.

210. A statue made by beating sheets of metal onto wooden shapers rather than by casting. The indentations left by the hammer blows resemble the plates making up the suit of armor.

sharp end of the lance projects some way ahead horizontally and is supported by a clasp on the horse's neck, while the butt end is fastened into a loop on the animal's flank. Thus the lance is held firm against the force of impact and does not act against the rider's hand, which has only to direct the thrust as the rider braces himself and lunges forward to increase the force of the impact—which is so violent that the lance transfixes everyone in its path, often impaling two or more opponents at a single blow and carrying them along, skewered.

16     With these cavalry forces and with his army deployed as I have described, the satrap advanced to meet the enemy face-to-face, keeping his back to the river all the while. He was heavily outnumbered by the Ethiopians, but his plan was to use the river to prevent himself being encircled. Hydaspes moved forward to meet him. To face the Persians and Medes on the right wing he deployed the men of Meroe, heavy infantry and expert in hand-to-hand combat at close quarters. The men from the country of the Troglodytai and those who live near the Land of Cinnamon,[211] lightly armed but swift of foot and excellent bowmen, he assigned to harass the slingers and javelin throwers on the enemy's left. He reacted to the information that the Persian center boasted the armored cavalry by stationing himself and his squadron of turret-bearing elephants to face them; but in front he positioned the infantry of the Blemmyes and the Seres,[212] whom he had given special instructions to put into effect when the action began.

17     The standards were raised on both sides, and the signal was given for battle, by clarion calls on the Persian side, on the Ethiopian with bull-roarers and tom-toms. Oroondates called to his men and led his forces forward at the double. Hydaspes, on the other hand, told his troops to make their advance at a somewhat more measured pace to start with, accelerating gradually with each stride, so that the elephants would not lose touch with the front line and also so that the intervening distance would dissipate the impetus of the enemy's cavalry charge. The two armies were less than a bowshot apart now, and the Blemmyes could see the armored horsemen spurring on their steeds to the charge. Now they did as Hydaspes had instructed them, and, leaving the Seres to act as shield and defense to the elephants, they sprang forward some distance from their own lines and charged towards the armored cavalry as fast as they were

211. Modern Somalia; it was believed that cinnamon was produced in this area, though in fact it was imported from further east.
212. The Blemmyes were a nomadic tribe living to the south of Egypt. They acquired a semimythical status in classical literature and are often described as having no heads. From the third century onward they posed a continuing threat to the security of Egypt. The name Seres usually denotes Eastern silk-producers, i.e., the Chinese. The Seres are another exotic people of literary tradition. Their presence in Hydaspes' army perhaps derives from the tendency to identify Ethiopia with the east as much as with the south.

able. To all who saw them it seemed like madness for them to take the initiative in attacking an enemy so superior in numbers and so heavily armored. The Persians more than ever gave their horses their heads and thundered towards the foe, reckoning their impetuous courage an unlooked-for stroke of luck and confident that they would annihilate them the instant the charge struck home.

Now the Blemmyes were on the very point of closing with the enemy, were within inches of the points of their lances, when, all of a sudden and with one accord, they dropped to the ground and ducked underneath the horses, whose flying hooves brushed within a hair's breadth of their backs and heads. No one could have foreseen their next action: as the horses charged past, they stabbed upwards with their swords, causing terrible injuries to the animals' bellies. Many men fell there, as the horses in their pain ignored the reins' commands and threw their riders, who lay waiting on the ground, as helpless as lumps of wood, for the Blemmyes to finish them off with a thrust of the sword through the groin, for without someone to help him a Persian armored cavalryman is incapable of movement.

Those who escaped with their horses unscathed rode on towards the Seres, who held their ground until the enemy were almost upon them, then withdrew behind the elephants, as if the beasts afforded a refuge like that of a hilltop or fortress. There ensued a massacre, the virtual annihilation of the cavalry; for the horses had never seen an elephant before, and when they were suddenly confronted with the sight of them in all their grotesque[213] hugeness, it threw them into panic. Some tried to go back the way they had come; others collided with one another and threw their formation into instant disarray. Meanwhile the archers in the turrets on the elephants' backs (each turret was manned by six men, two shooting from each side with only the rear left idle) kept up such a constant barrage of accurately aimed arrows from the bastion of their turrets that to the Persians it seemed as dense as a cloud blotting out the sun,[214] especially as the Ethiopians directed their aim particularly at their enemies' eyes: to them it was more like an archery contest than an evenly matched battle, and their aim was so unerringly true that the horsemen who had been hit plunged in utter disarray through the melee, with the arrows protruding from their eyes like the twin pipes of a double flute.[215]

Any who were carried clear by the unstoppable momentum of their horses' charge were unable to prevent themselves being hurled upon the

18

213. I have modified the text.

214. Alluding to Herodotos (7.226), who says that at the battle of Thermopylai the Persian arrows were so numerous that they hid the sun. There is a satisfying irony here in that the Persians are now on the receiving end of a famous historical occurrence.

215. The musical instrument the *aulos* is depicted as two pipes (one for the melody, one for a drone bass), played simultaneously and held at an angle to one another.

elephants. Thus some of them were finished off there and then by the elephants, who tossed them in the air and trampled them underfoot; others by the Seres,[216] who sallied out from behind the cover of the elephants, where they had been lurking, wounded some with well-aimed arrows and grappled others off their steeds onto the ground. All those who survived withdrew without having made any impression whatsoever on the elephants, for the animal is clad in iron when it goes into battle, and nature has in any case endowed it with a hide like tempered steel whose surface is covered with a layer of scales so tough and impervious that it simply shatters any spear that strikes it.

19    The remainder of the army turned and fled, but the most dastardly act of cowardice was that of the satrap Oroondates, who immediately abandoned his chariot and mounted one of his Nisaian horses in an attempt to save his own skin.[217] The Egyptians and Libyans on his left wing, who were unaware of all this, battled on with great courage and, although they were getting the worse of the exchange, stood their ground stalwartly. The men from the Land of Cinnamon, who had been posted to oppose them, gave them a terrible time of it and caused them great embarrassment. Whenever the Egyptians and Libyans advanced, they would take to their heels and outrun them by some margin, though even as they ran they would shoot arrows backwards over their shoulders; then, when the Egyptians and Libyans retreated, they would move to the attack, some peppering the enemy's flanks with slingshot, while others sniped at them with little arrows smeared with serpent's venom, so causing an instant and agonized death. When the men from the Land of Cinnamon engage in archery, they seem to be playing a game rather than shooting in earnest. They tie a sort of circular mesh around their heads, through which they poke their arrows, all around the circle, with the flights nearest their heads and the tips pointing outward, like the rays of the sun. In battle all they have to do is to pull the arrows out of their headdress, as if from a quiver. And as they loose them against the foe, they prance and cavort, frolic and caper like satyrs, stark naked except for their wreath of arrows.[218] They have no need of iron to tip their shafts, for they take a bone from the spine of a serpent, make the body of it straight and true to act as the arrow shaft, and hone the tip to a very sharp point, so producing an arrow that is all of one piece. In fact it is not impossible that the Greek word for "arrow" (*oistos*) derives from the word for "bone" (*osteon*).[219]

216. Excising the intrusive words ὑπό τε τῶν Βλεμμύων.
217. Oroondates' flight is intended to recall that of the Persian king Dareios after his defeat by Alexander at Gaugamela.
218. This is verbally very close to a passage of Lucian's (*On Dancing* 18), with which it clearly shares a source. Ethiopian bowmen with arrows in their hair are depicted in the frieze of the Arch of Constantine in Rome.
219. This etymology is Heliodoros's own.

The Egyptians preserved their line intact for some time, locking shields to protect themselves from the arrows. They were naturally doughty warriors, who affected an indifference towards death, not that they stood to gain anything thereby except glory, though it may well be that they anticipated some awful punishment if they deserted their positions. But when they discovered that the armored cavalry, which was supposed to be the strongest contingent of their army and their greatest hope, had been destroyed, that the satrap had run for his life, and that the much-vaunted Median and Persian heavy infantry had followed all the others, without having performed anything of note in the battle but instead having come off much the worse from their exchange with the men of Meroe who confronted them, then the Egyptians too gave up the struggle and fled headlong from the field.

To Hydaspes from the vantage point of his turret it was apparent now that he had won a decisive victory. He sent heralds to tell his pursuing troops to refrain from bloodshed and to take as many prisoners as possible alive and bring them to him, but first and foremost Oroondates. And that is exactly what happened. The Ethiopians redeployed their formation into a line … shields deep,[220] converting the great depth of their ranks into a long extension of their line on either side. Then they swung their wings inward, encircling the Persian forces and leaving only one way for the enemy to run—the way that led to the river. The majority were forced into the water by the melee of horses, scythed chariots, and the rest of the army. Thus they learned to their great cost that what had seemed a clever stratagem on the satrap's part was in fact a tactical blunder that had rebounded on them. His original dread of encirclement had led Oroondates to position his forces with their backs to the Nile and thus unwittingly block his own line of escape.

It was by the river that he was himself taken prisoner: Achaimenes, the son of Kybele, had now been informed of everything that had occurred at Memphis and, repenting of his allegations against Arsake—which he had not had time to substantiate before the evidence for them was destroyed—had formed the scheme of forestalling trouble by killing Oroondates in the general chaos. However, he failed to strike a mortal blow, and his misdeeds were instantly punished by a fatal shot from one of the Ethiopian archers, who not only recognized the satrap and meant to save him from death, as had been ordered, but was also much affronted by the criminality of a man in flight from the enemy attacking his own side and welcoming such an extremity in order to settle what appeared to be a personal score.

220. The printed text means "they extended their line on the shield side" (i.e., the left), which is immediately contradicted. I therefore read ἐπ' ἀσπίδας and suppose the omission of a numeral.

21 Oroondates' captor took him to Hydaspes, who, at the sight of him streaming with blood and at the very point of death, had his wounds staunched by means of an incantation performed by those expert in such practices. He resolved to save Oroondates' life, if he could, and tried to lift his spirits with reassuring words.

"My friend," he said, "your life will be safe: such is my will, for it is right that we should overcome our enemies with the sword while yet they stand and with kindness when they are fallen. But what did you mean by such a blatant act of perfidy?"

"My act of perfidy to you," replied Oroondates, "was one of loyalty to my own master."

"And what punishment do you consider appropriate for yourself in defeat?" was Hydaspes' next question, to which the satrap replied, "Whatever punishment my king would have demanded for one of your commanders who refused to betray his loyalty to you."

"I am sure," said Hydaspes, "that if he is a true king and no mere tyrant, he would have commended him, rewarded him, and allowed him to go free, aiming with such a commendation of another's servant to inspire his own to act in the same way. But, my dear friend, though you claim to have been loyal, even you would have to admit that it was folly so rashly to have ventured battle against such countless thousands."

"Perhaps it was not such folly," replied Oroondates, "to have gauged the way my king's mind would work. His rigor in punishing any who show themselves cowards in war tends to exceed his generosity in honoring the brave. So I decided to confront the danger head-on: either I would win a great and unexpected victory, which is the kind of miracle that the crises of war often produce, or else if I was lucky enough to get away with my life, the way would be clear for me to say in my own defense that I had done all that it was in my power to do."

22 Hydaspes concluded the interview by commending Oroondates and then having him conveyed into Syene, but not before instructing the physicians to lavish all their skill on him. Then he entered the town himself, accompanied by the flower of his army. The whole city, young and old alike, turned out to greet him, showering his soldiers with garlands and Nile blossoms and singing Hydaspes' praises in victory hymns. No sooner had he entered the walls—an elephant substituting for the triumphal chariot—than he turned to the sacred duty of offering thanks to the gods for his victory. He inquired of the priests what the origin of the Neiloa was and whether there were any curiosities in the city that they could show him.

They took him to see the well that measures the Nile, which is almost identical to the one at Memphis: it is constructed of close-fitting blocks of polished stone and has an engraved scale marked in cubits; the river water seeps underground into the well, where its level against the markings registers the rise and fall in the level of the Nile for the benefit of the inhabitants of the area, who are able to gauge the degree of inundation or shortage of water by the number of divisions covered or exposed.[221] They also showed him the sundials that cast no shadow at noon, for in the latitude of Syene[222] the light of the sun is perpendicularly overhead at the summer solstice and thus throws equal illumination on all sides of an object, precluding the casting of a shadow. Likewise the water at the bottom of wells is directly illuminated. Hydaspes, however, was not much impressed by these sights, which were already familiar to him: exactly the same occurred, he said, at Meroe in Ethiopia.

Next the priests claimed that their festival was celebrated in a god's honor, for to such status did they exalt the Nile, to which they gave the title of Horos, Giver of Grain and Giver of Life, Lord of all Egypt, Savior of the South, Father and Creator of the North,[223] who each year brings fresh silt (in Greek *nea ilys*, which, they suggested, is the origin of the name *Neilos*,[224] or Nile), who marks the seasons of the year—the summer by its flooding, the autumn by its recession, and the spring by the flowers that bloom on its banks and the hatching of the crocodiles' eggs; the Nile, they said, is actually the year incarnate, as is confirmed by its name—for if the letters in its name are converted to numerals, they will total 365, the number of days in the year.[225] They ended by describing the peculiarities of the local fauna and flora, and much else besides.

"But all these things of which you speak so proudly belong not to Egypt but to Ethiopia," replied Hydaspes, "for this river, this god as you call it, and every creature in it, comes to you from the land of Ethiopia, which thus in fairness should be the object of your worship, for it is the mother of your gods!"

"Then worship it we do," exclaimed the priests, "especially since it is responsible for the epiphany of you, our god and savior!"

---

221. This whole passage is extremely close to the description of the Nilometer at Elephantine by Strabo (17.1.48). No doubt Heliodoros and Strabo derive their information from the same source. Devices of this kind were essential in a country whose agriculture depended entirely on the annual inundation of the Nile.

222. Syene lies almost exactly on the Tropic of Cancer, where the sun is directly overhead on the day of the summer solstice—which, of course, is the time of year when this section of the novel is set. The shadowless sundial and illuminated well bottom are often mentioned in connection with the city.

223. Horos was the son of Isis, born after the death of his father, Osiris, at the hands of Typhon/Seth. He was called Savior of the South because the Nile flood waters an otherwise arid land, and Creator of the North because it was widely believed that Lower Egypt was formed by the alluvial mud deposited at the mouth of the Nile.

224. This fanciful etymology is depressingly widespread.

225. The letters of the Greek alphabet did double duty as numerals. If the letters of the Greek word Neilos are read as numerals and added together, we have the sum $50 + 5 + 10 + 30 + 70 + 200 = 365$.

23    Remarking that their compliments ought to fall short of blasphemy, Hydaspes retired to his tent, where he passed the remainder of the day resting after his exertions. He threw a banquet for distinguished Ethiopians and the priests of Syene, and gave the rest of his men permission to do likewise. The people of Syene supplied his army with many a herd of cattle and flock of sheep, and flocks of goats and droves of swine[226] in even greater numbers, along with a vast quantity of wine. What they did not give as a gift, they sold to the Ethiopians.

The following day, seated on a lofty throne, Hydaspes distributed to his army the horses and beasts of burden and all the other material taken as spoils both in the town and in the course of the battle, carefully weighing the merits of each man's actions. When it came to the turn of the man who had captured Oroondates and saved his life, Hydaspes said to him, "Ask for whatever you wish."

"I have no need to ask, my liege," replied the man. "If you will approve what I have done, I have sufficient reward already in what I took from Oroondates when I saved his life as you commanded."

So saying, he held up the satrap's sword belt, a magnificent object studded with gems, which must have cost many talents in the making. Many of the bystanders exclaimed that it exceeded the estate of a private individual, that it was rather a kingly treasure. But Hydaspes smiled and said: "What could be more kingly than that my magnanimity should not fall short of this fellow's cupidity? Besides, the conventions of war permit anyone who takes a prisoner to take spoils from his captive. So let him have with my blessing what he could easily have had without, had he chosen to keep it secret."

24    Next came the turn of the captors of Theagenes and Charikleia. "Sire," they said, "the spoils we brought you were not gold or precious stones. These things are cheap in Ethiopia and lie in heaps in the storerooms of your palace. Rather we have presented you with a maiden and a young man, Greeks, brother and sister, surpassing all mankind (save only yourself) in stature and beauty. In return we ask not to be excluded from  your generosity."

"You did well to remind me," said Hydaspes. "It was a hectic time when you presented them to me, and I was too busy to spare them more than a passing glance. Someone go and fetch them; and let the rest of the prisoners be brought too."

This was done immediately: a runner was sent to the baggage train outside the walls and told their warders to take them to the king as quickly as they could. They asked one of their guards, a half-caste Greek,

226. This list is couched in Homeric terms and echoes *Iliad* 11.678–79.

where they were being taken now. He replied that King Hydaspes was inspecting his prisoners.

"We are saved! The gods be praised!" the young couple exclaimed in unison, for they recognized the name Hydaspes, though to that moment they had had no proof that he had not been succeeded by another king.

Theagenes whispered to Charikleia: "Obviously, my love, you will tell the king the truth about us. This is indeed Hydaspes, who you have often told me is your father!"

But Charikleia replied: "My darling, great ends can only be achieved by means of equal greatness. A story whose beginnings heaven has made convoluted cannot be quickly resolved. In particular it may be dangerous to reveal abruptly things that the passing years have made obscure, especially when the central figure of our entire story, the key to the whole tangled web of complexity and recognition, is missing. I refer, of course, to my mother, Persinna, whom we know to be yet living, by heaven's grace."

"But what if we are sacrificed before we see her?" interrupted Theagenes. "What if we are given away as booty of war and so prevented from ever reaching Ethiopia?"

"We shall not be; quite the reverse," said Charikleia. "You have often heard the guards say that we are being nurtured as sacrificial victims to the gods of Meroe. There is no chance of our being given away or killed too soon, for we are dedicated to the gods by a solemn promise that it would be wrong for men with such a deep respect for piety to break. But if we let ourselves be carried away by our joy and reveal the truth about ourselves before the time is right, when those who could recognize and corroborate the truth of our story are not present to do so, then we run a risk of unwittingly annoying our hearer and becoming the objects of his justifiable anger, for he might well think it wicked claptrap for a couple of prisoners marked out for slavery to concoct some incredible tale and dramatically impose themselves on the king as his own children."

"But the recognition tokens," said Theagenes, "which I know you keep safe about your person, will corroborate that we are more than a tale or an imposture."

"The recognition tokens," replied Charikleia, "are tokens only to those who know them or to those who laid them beside me. For those who do not know them or do not recognize every item, they are mere precious trinkets, which might well bring their bearer under suspicion of being a thief or a robber. And even if Hydaspes should recognize one of them, who is there to prove to him that it was Persinna who gave them to me, to prove that she gave them to me as mother to daughter? The one incontrovertible token of recognition, Theagenes, is maternal instinct, which, by the workings of an unspoken affinity, disposes the parent to feel affection for her child the instant she sets eyes on it. Let us not deprive ourselves of the one thing that would make all the other tokens convincing."

25 In the course of this exchange they had reached the king's presence: Bagoas had been brought too. When he saw them standing before him, Hydaspes leapt from his throne for a moment.

"Heaven have mercy!" he exclaimed, then sank back, lost in thought. The dignitaries at his side asked him what was wrong.

"I dreamed that a daughter just like this girl had been born to me this very day," he replied, "and had matured instantly to just such a youthful beauty. I paid no attention to the dream, but now I am reminded of it by the identical appearance of the person I see before me."

His courtiers replied that this was an image generated by the soul, which frequently prefigured the future and gave it form in dreams. So he pushed his vision to the back of his mind for the moment and inquired who they were and where they were from. Charikleia said nothing, but Theagenes replied that they were brother and sister and came from Greece.

"Well done, Greece!" exclaimed the king. "Her sons are men of sterling worth, and, most important, she has presented us with noble and auspicious victims for the sacrifices to mark our victory."

Then, turning to his entourage, he said with a smile: "How was it that a son was not born to me too in my dream? If this young man, the girl's brother, was to appear before me, he ought also, by your account, to have been prefigured in my dreams."

Then he addressed himself to Charikleia and asked in Greek (for this language is cultivated among the naked sages and rulers of Ethiopia): "As for you, girl, why do you say nothing? Why do you make no answer to my questions?"

"At the altars of the gods, for whom we know we are being kept as sacrifice," she replied, "there shall you know who I am and who are my mother and father."

"And just where in the world are your mother and father?" asked Hydaspes.

"They are here," she answered. "They will be there at my sacrifice, have no doubt!"

Hydaspes smiled again. "My dream child really is a creature of dreams," he said, "if she imagines that her mother and father will be transported from Greece to the heart of Meroe! Bring them with us and pay them the customary attentions; they must want for nothing if they are to grace our sacrifice. But who is this standing here? He looks like a eunuch."

"He is indeed a eunuch," replied one of the attendants. "His name is Bagoas, and he is Oroondates' most-valued possession."

"Let him go with them too," ordered Hydaspes, "not as a sacrificial victim but to protect one of the victims: this girl, who is so young and beautiful that much careful thought is required to keep her free from stain until the hour of our sacrifice. Jealousy is endemic in eunuchs: they are employed to prevent others enjoying the pleasures of which they are themselves deprived."

So saying, he continued his inspection of the prisoners as each came in 26 turn before him, and decided their fates. Those whom fortune had marked as born to be slaves he gave away, while those who were well-born he allowed to go free. He selected ten young men and an equal number of girls from those who were notable for their youthful beauty, and commanded that they should be taken south with Theagenes and his companion, to serve the same purpose. All requests made of him he granted, until finally he came to Oroondates, who had been summoned and fetched on a litter.

"I am now master of the places for which the war was fought," he said. "The original reasons for our enmity, namely Philai and the emerald mines, are now in my possession. However, I resist the all too human temptation to turn success to excess. I do not exploit my victory to extend my dominions indefinitely. I am content with the boundaries that nature drew when she first made the cataract to divide Egypt from Ethiopia. I have that for which I came north, and now I shall respect what is right and return home. If you live, govern your original satrapy and write this message to the king of Persia: 'Your brother Hydaspes, having overcome you by force of arms, has in his wisdom allowed you to keep all that is yours. He welcomes your friendship if you are prepared to give it, for of all human things friendship is the fairest; but he will not refuse to fight, should you begin hostilities again.' To these people of Syene I grant ten years' exemption from payment of their appointed tribute, and I charge you to give this effect."

These words were greeted with an acclamation of praise by the assem- 27 bled townsfolk and soldiers, who cheered and clapped as one, so loudly that the noise was audible far into the distance. Oroondates held out both his hands, crossed his right arm over his left,[227] bowed his head, and made obeisance, though it is unlawful among the Persians to reverence any king but their own in this fashion.

"Gentlemen," he said, "I do not consider that I am transgressing our traditional principle if I recognize as king the man to whom I owe my satrapy, nor that I am breaking any law in making obeisance to the man

227. In a symbolic invitation to bind his hands; apparently authentic.

who has more respect for law than all mankind. It was in his power to kill me, but in his mercy he gave me life: fate had made me his slave, but he allowed me to be a satrap. Wherefore, if I live, I give my word that there will be unbroken peace and everlasting friendship between Ethiopia and Persia, and I promise to uphold your edict concerning Syene. But if anything should happen to me, then I pray that the gods may reward Hydaspes, his house, and his nation for his noble actions towards me."

## Book Ten

1 Let this be the end of our narrative of events at Syene: from so perilous a predicament the city had passed in an instant to such felicity, owing to the righteousness of one man.

Hydaspes sent the larger part of his army on ahead and then set off for Ethiopia himself, escorted for a considerable distance by the entire population of Syene and the entire Persian army, both hymning his praises. To begin with he followed the banks of the Nile and kept to the areas watered by the river, but when he reached the cataracts, he sacrificed to the Nile and the gods of Egypt and then turned away from the river and marched inland instead, until he came to Philai, where he rested his army for two days or so. Then he sent most of his army on ahead once more, while he stayed at Philai to strengthen the city's defenses and install a garrison, having done which, he departed. He selected two horsemen, who were to ride ahead, changing to fresh horses at every town and village so as to accomplish their mission with all possible speed: to these he gave letters announcing the good news of his victory to the people of Meroe.

2 To the wise men, known as gymnosophists, or naked sages, who form a cabinet that the king consults on matters of policy, he wrote as follows:

King Hydaspes to the most reverend Council.
I write to you with the glad tidings of our victory over the Persians, not in boastfulness at my triumph, for I have no wish to provoke the changeability of fortune, but to pay my prompt respects in this letter to your powers of prophecy, which have proved correct now as ever. Wherefore I invite and implore you to come to the accustomed place, where your presence will sanctify for the Ethiopian commonalty the sacrifices to be performed in thanksgiving for my victory.

To his wife, Persinna, he wrote as follows:

I write to inform you that I am victorious and, which is of more concern to you, that I am safe. Make preparations for magnificent pageants and sacrifices to render thanks. Add your own invitation to the sages to that contained in my letter. Then make haste with them to the glade outside the city walls[228] that is consecrated to our ancestral deities, the Sun, the Moon, and Dionysos.

When these letters were delivered, Persinna exclaimed: "This explains the dream I saw in my sleep last night. I dreamed I was with child and that I gave birth at the same instant: the child was a daughter, who grew in a trice to womanhood. The dream must have been using the pains of birth to symbolize the anguish of the war, and the daughter to represent victory. Now go to the city and make it resound with your glad tidings."

The advance riders did as they were told. Crowning their heads with the lotus that grows along the Nile, and waving palm fronds in their hands, they rode through the main streets of the city, where their mere appearance was sufficient proclamation of victory. In an instant Meroe was filled with joy as night and day, in their families, in their communities, in their clans, the people danced and offered sacrifice to the gods, festooning their sanctuaries with flowers and rejoicing not so much at the victory as at the safe return of Hydaspes, whose righteousness, combined with his civility and graciousness towards his subjects, had instilled an almost filial devotion in his people's hearts.

Persinna had herds of oxen, horses, and sheep, of zebras and griffins[229] and other creatures of every variety, taken across the river to the sacred glade to await the ceremony. There were enough for a hecatomb, a hundred victims of each and every species to be offered in sacrifice, while the remainder would provide a feast for the populace. Next she went to the gymnosophists, who had their abode in the temple of Pan;[230] she handed them the letter from Hydaspes and joined him in begging them to accede to the king's request by gracing the ceremony with their presence, which she would also consider a personal honor to herself.

They asked her to wait a moment and withdrew into the inner sanctum to pray to the gods as was their wont and ask them what they should do. After a few minutes they returned and stood in silence while Sisimithres, the president of their college, said: "We will come, Persinna. The gods give us their leave. But the divine power warns that the

228. Alluding to Herodotos's story (3.18) of the Table of the Sun, "a meadow situated in the outskirts of Meroe," where a plentiful supply of sacrificial meats was kept perpetually replenished.

229. Reading ὠρρύγγων (Colonna). Griffins were mythical beasts, half lion, half eagle; see note 246.

230. The worship of Pan is mentioned nowhere else in the novel, though Heliodoros may be alluding here to a tradition that Pan was worshiped in Ethiopia, attested by Diodoros (3.9) and Strabo (17.2.3). But perhaps it would be more appropriate to read here "Pantheion" (temple of all the gods) for "Paneion" (temple of Pan).

*Prophecy*

sacrifices will be disrupted by some commotion or disturbance, the outcome of which, however, will be good and joyful: you have lost a limb, the royal house has lost a member, but in that hour destiny will enable you to find that which you seek."

"Your mere presence," replied Persinna, "will be sufficient to transform any danger whatsoever into a blessing. When I hear that Hydaspes is at hand, I shall inform you."

"There is no need to inform us," said Sisimithres. "He will arrive tomorrow morning. A letter will come shortly to tell you so."

*?*

This was exactly what happened. Persinna was on her way back to the palace and had nearly reached the gates when a man on horseback handed her a letter from the king, which informed her that he would arrive the following day. Heralds immediately proclaimed this information throughout the city, but only those of the male sex were permitted to greet the returning king: women, they announced, were excluded. As the sacrifice was to be performed in honor of the Sun and the Moon, the purest and most resplendent of the gods, it was forbidden for the female sex to take part, lest the sacrificial victims be polluted by any uncleanness, however involuntary. The only woman allowed to be present was the Priestess of the Moon: this was Persinna, for by law and tradition the king was Priest of the Sun, and the queen Priestess of the Moon. Charikleia also was to be present at the rite, but not as an onlooker—she was to be sacrificed to the Moon-goddess.

An irresistible thrill of anticipation swept the city. Unable to wait for the appointed day to dawn, people began crossing the river Astaborrhas the previous evening, some by the bridge, others in riverboats made out of reeds. These craft were moored in great numbers up and down the riverbanks to facilitate the crossing for those whose homes were too far from the bridge. They are very nippy little vessels, being constructed from such a light material and incapable of taking any weight other than two or three men. They are in fact no more than a reed split down the middle, each half forming a boat.

5    Meroe is the capital of Ethiopia.[231] In form it is a triangular island bounded on all three sides by navigable rivers: the Nile, the Astaborrhas, and the Asasobas.[232] The first of these, the Nile, breaks upon the apex of

231. The ruins of the city of Meroe, center of the powerful Ethiopian kingdom, lie beside the Nile in the Sudan, south of the Nile's confluence with the Atbara. The tract of land bounded by the Atbara, the Blue Nile, and the Nile is known as the island of Meroe, although it is not really an island. Many classical authors, however, conceived of it as literally an island in the Nile. Though wildly inaccurate in absolute terms, Heliodoros's geography is passably in harmony with Greco-Roman beliefs, especially in its stress on the fertility of the region.

232. These names are authentic, but classical writers do not agree about their application to particular rivers.

the triangle, where it splits into two; the other two rivers run along either side of the island until they rejoin to form one river, the Nile, which subsumes their names as well as their waters. In size Meroe is so vast that, despite being an island, it presents the impression of being a continent; its length comprises 345 miles; its breadth, 115.[233] It provides a habitat where enormous animals, including elephants, can flourish, and is so fertile that it produces the tallest trees in the world. Apart from gigantic palm trees that bear massive, succulent dates, the ears of corn and barley grow so high there that they can completely conceal even the tallest man on horseback—or even, occasionally, on camelback!—and are so prolific that the seed sown is increased 300-fold. The size of the reeds that grow there has already been touched upon.

So throughout the night in question people crossed the river by their 6 various means, and in the morning they welcomed Hydaspes back, meeting him on the road and paying him godlike respects. The people at large traveled some distance along the road to meet him, but the gymnosophists waited to greet him at the edge of the holy glade, where they clasped his hands, embraced, and kissed him. The last person to welcome him home was Persinna, who was waiting at the temple gate, inside the sacred precinct. After prostrating themselves in homage to the gods and discharging their vows of thanksgiving for his victory and safe return, they left the precinct and turned their attention to the public sacrifice, taking their seats in the pavilion that had been erected in readiness in the plain. This was a square structure, whose weight was borne by four freshly cut reeds which stood like columns, one in each corner; their upper sections were arched over and connected to make, with the addition of palm fronds, a dome that formed a canopy over the space beneath. There was a second pavilion close by, where, on an elevated dais, had been set images of their national gods and likenesses of the heroes whom the kings of Ethiopia regard as the founders of their house: Memnon and Perseus and Andromeda. Beneath these, on the lower step of the dais, sat the gymnosophists, so that the gods appeared to stand over them. All this was ringed by a regiment of foot soldiers, resting on their shields, which they held vertically, with no gaps between them, so creating an unobstructed space in the middle from which the crowd was excluded and where the ceremony could be performed.

After a short address to the people, in which he reported his victory and the successes he had won on behalf of the state, Hydaspes commanded the officiants to commence the sacrifice. A total of three lofty al-

233. These measurements are not invented but are taken from a source used also by Diodoros (1.33) and Strabo (17.2.2), who, however, describe the island as shield-shaped rather than triangular. In one manuscript of Heliodoros a scribe's comment has been incorporated into the text: "Totally wrong if you reckon accurately"!

tars had been erected, two of which, those to the Sun and the Moon, were adjacent to one another and separate from the third, which stood by itself in a different place: this altar was dedicated to Dionysos, to whom the Ethiopians customarily sacrificed animals of every kind, propitiating him with such all-embracing variety in token, I presume, of his benevolence to all without distinction of class. As for the other two altars, to the Sun they offered a team of four white horses, dedicating to the swiftest of the gods, it seems, the swiftest of all mortal creatures;[234] and to the Moon a pair of bullocks, probably choosing to sacrifice creatures that help us to work the land in recognition of the goddess's own association with the earth.

7      But before the ceremony could be completed, it was interrupted by an outbreak of shouting, as incoherent and disorderly as one might expect from so immense and nondescript an assembly. "Perform the traditional rite!" shouted the crowd. "Now make the time-honored offerings for the nation's safety! Offer the gods the firstfruits of the war!"

Hydaspes understood that they were demanding the human sacrifice that was always performed to celebrate victories over foreign foes, though on no other occasions, the victims being supplied from the prisoners captured. Waving his hand and nodding his head to indicate that their request would be granted without delay, he gave orders for the prisoners who had long ago been marked out for this purpose to be fetched. So they were all brought before the king, including Theagenes and Charikleia. Their chains had been removed, and wreaths placed upon their heads. They all looked dejected, naturally enough—though Theagenes somewhat less than the rest—with the exception of Charikleia, whose countenance was radiant and smiling and who stared so long and so hard at Persinna that the queen suffered some distress at the sight of her and said, with a deep sigh: "O husband, what a girl you have selected for the sacrifice! Never to my knowledge have I seen anyone so beautiful. How noble her expression is! With what dignity she confronts her destiny! What pity I feel for her youth and beauty! If the only child I ever bore, the little daughter that was so cruelly taken from me, had been allowed to live, she would now be about the same age as this girl. I wish, husband, that there were some way to give her exemption. It would be a great comfort to have one such as her to wait on me. The poor child might even possibly be a Greek: her features are not those of an Egyptian."

234. An allusion to Herodotos 1.216:

> The only god they worship is the sun, to which they sacrifice horses; the idea behind this is to offer to the swiftest of the gods the swiftest of mortal creatures.

I have inserted the word θνητῶν into the text of Heliodoros, as the allusion requires.

"She *is* a Greek," replied Hydaspes. "As for her mother and father, the moment has come for her to tell us who they are: she could scarcely produce them before our eyes. Of course not! Though that is what she promised.

"It is not possible to save her from sacrifice, though I should be only too happy if it were, for I too am touched in some indefinable way and feel great pity for her. But, as you are aware, convention demands that we offer human sacrifice, male to the Sun, female to the Moon. This girl was the first prisoner brought before me and was marked out for the ceremony we must perform today. The crowd would never countenance a replacement for her. There is just one thing that might save her, and that would be if, when she stepped onto the gridiron that you know of, she were discovered to be not altogether clean of the taint of intercourse with men, for the law commands that the woman presented to the goddess should be undefiled, and likewise the man offered to the Sun, though it makes no such distinction as regards the sacrifice to Dionysos. But consider this: if the gridiron were to convict her of having had intercourse with a man, it would not be proper for us to receive such a person into our palace."

"Let her be convicted," answered Persinna, "so long as her life is spared. Captivity, war, and exile so far from the land of her birth are sufficient excuse for such conduct, particularly in the case of this girl, whose very beauty is an incitement to violence against her—if indeed she has suffered anything of that kind—which accompanies her everywhere she goes."

While Persinna was still speaking, and trying to conceal her tears from 8 the assembled company, Hydaspes gave orders for the gridiron to be fetched. The attendants selected prepubertal children from the crowd, for these are the only people who can touch the gridiron without risk of injury,[235] and with their help carried it out of the temple and set it down where all could see. Then they commanded the prisoners to step onto it one by one. As each of them set foot on it, the soles of his feet were immediately scorched; some could not even endure the first instant of contact. The gridiron is made from a lattice of gold bars and is imbued with a power so strong that it can incinerate anyone who is unclean or in any other way perjured, while allowing those of the opposite condition to walk painlessly over it. Apart from a couple of young women who were shown to be virgins by walking over the gridiron, they were all allocated to Dionysos and the other gods.

But then Theagenes stepped onto the gridiron: he was shown to be 9

235. Because only in prepubertal children can virginity be guaranteed. Young children were in fact employed in cult for precisely this reason.

without stain. Everyone was impressed, not simply by his beauty and stature, but more especially by the fact that a young man such as he, in the full vigor of his youth, was ignorant of the joys of Aphrodite. As they began to prepare him for sacrifice to the Sun, he whispered to Charikleia: "A life of virtue earns a fine wage in Ethiopia: sacrificial slaughter is chastity's reward! But why do you not make your identity known, my love? What are you waiting for now? For someone to slit our throats? Speak out, I implore you, and reveal your true status. Once you are recognized for who you are, you may be able to intercede for my life too. But even if you cannot obtain that grace, you, at least, will assuredly be spared. If I know that, I can die happy."

"The hour of my trial is at hand," replied Charikleia. "Even now destiny is weighing our fate in the balance."

Then, before the people supervising the test could tell her what to do, she produced, from a little pouch that she was carrying, her Delphic robe, woven with gold thread and embroidered with rays, and put it on. She let her hair fall free, ran forward like one possessed, and sprang onto the gridiron, where she stood for some time without taking any hurt, her beauty blazing with a new and dazzling radiance as she stood conspicuous on her lofty pedestal; in her magnificent robe she seemed more like an image of a goddess than a mortal woman. A thrill of wonder ran through the crowd, who in unison made the heavens resound with their cry, wordless and unmeaning, but expressive of their astonishment. What they found expecially awesome was that she had preserved pure and undefiled a beauty so far surpassing that of humankind, even in the springtime of its years: visible proof had been furnished that, for all her youthful charms, the greatest ornament to her beauty was chastity.

The crowd as a whole was saddened by this confirmation that she was meet for the sacrifice, and, despite their religious scruples, they would have been glad to see some miracle occur to save her. But none was more grieved that Persinna, whose distress was so great that she turned to Hydaspes and said: "Poor, unhappy child. This proud show of chastity is ill timed and will cost her dear. Death will be her only reward for such virtue. What can be done, my husband?"

"It is pointless to press me," he replied. "Your pity is wasted on one who cannot be saved, one who, it seems, has been reserved from birth for the gods by reason of her natural excellence."

Then, turning to the gymnosophists, he said; "All-wise ones, everything is ready. Why do you not begin the ceremony?"

"Do not speak such words," answered Sisimithres, in Greek so that the people should not understand what he was saying. "Our eyes and ears are defiled enough by what we have already witnessed. Now we shall withdraw into the temple,[236] for neither can we ourselves approve of anything as barbaric as human sacrifice nor do we believe that is pleasing to the divinity. I only wish it were possible to put an end to all animal sacrifice as well and be satisfied with offerings of prayers and incense such as we make.[237] But you stay here—for a king must serve the wishes of his people, misguided though they sometimes are—and perform this sacrifice which, for all its uncleanness, is nonetheless required of you by the traditional ordinances of Ethiopian law. Later you will need purification—though perhaps you will not, for I do not think that this sacrifice will reach its consummation, a prediction I base on signs given by the godhead, particularly the halo of light around the strangers, a sure sign that they are under the protection of one of the lords of heaven."

With these words he and the rest of the high council rose to their feet and made as if to withdraw. But Charikleia leapt down from the gridiron, ran to Sisimithres, and threw herself at his feet, although the attendants tried their hardest to restrain her, for they imagined that her supplication was nothing more than an appeal for her life to be spared.

"All-wise ones," she said, "wait a moment. I have an action to bring, a suit to plead against those who hold sovereign power, and I am told that you alone have judicial authority over such people. For me it is a question of life and death, and you must decide it. I shall demonstrate to you that it is neither possible nor proper for me to be sacrificed to the gods."

The gymnosophists gladly took up her plea. "Your Majesty," they said, "do you hear the appeal to law made by this stranger and her demands for her rights?"

Hydaspes laughed. "What kind of suit, on what basis, can this person have against me? On what grounds and with what entitlements is it brought?"

"To learn that we must hear what she has to say," replied Sisimithres.

"Would it not seem more like a case of outrageous insolence than a case at law if I, the king, have to defend myself against charges made by a captive woman?" said Hydaspes.

"Justice does not stand in awe of station," Sisimithres replied. "At law there is but one king: he who has the stronger case."

"The law permits you to judge cases only between the crown and its native subjects," said Hydaspes, "not foreigners."

---

236. This episode is apparently modeled on one in Philostratos's *Life of Apollonios* (1.31), where the sage withdraws from the sacrifice of a horse after making an offering of incense.

237. Reading νόμον and repunctuating as necessary.

"For a wise man," retorted Sisimithres, "a person's character is as important as the color of his face in reaching a judgment."

"We can be sure that she will say nothing worth listening to," said Hydaspes. "She will just give us a string of fictions to buy herself time, typical of people whose lives are in danger. Nevertheless, let her speak, to please Sisimithres!"

11    The prospect of deliverance from her besetting woes had already lifted Charikleia's spirits, but her joy was compounded when she heard the name of Sisimithres; for he it was who had taken her up when she was abandoned by her mother so long ago, and who had entrusted her to Charikles' keeping ten years previously when he was sent to Katadoupoi as an envoy to Oroondates over the issue of the emerald mines; at that time he had simply been a member of the college of gymnosophists, but now he had risen to become their president. Although Charikleia did not recollect his face, for she had been a mere child, no more than seven years old, when she was parted from him, she nevertheless recognized his name, and her joy was compounded, for she hoped to have his collaboration and corroboration to assist her recognition.

She stretched her arms towards the sky and cried so all could hear: "O Sun, forefather of my ancestors, and you other gods and heroes who founded our race, I call on you to bear me witness that I shall speak no untruth, and to render me your aid in the trial that now awaits me. I shall begin my case with this question: Does the law enjoin on you, sire, the sacrifice of aliens or of your own countrymen?"

"Aliens," he said.

"Then it is time for you to find a new victim to sacrifice," she said, "for you will find that I am a native of this land of ours!"[238]

12    In spite of Hydaspes' astonished assertions that she was not speaking the truth, Charikleia continued: "You evince surprise at the least important part of my revelation: the most important is yet to come. Not only am I an Ethiopian, but I am of the royal house and bound to you by the closest ties of kinship."

Once more Hydaspes dismissed her words as arrant nonsense, but then she said, "Please, Father, no more of this abuse of your own daughter!"

It was now obvious that the king's dismissal of Charikleia's questions was giving way to anger and that he considered the whole business wicked claptrap.

"Sisimithres," he exclaimed, "and the rest of you, do you see the consequences of your tolerance? The girl is downright insane, telling blatant lies in an attempt to avert death, casting herself in the role of my daugh-

238. Retaining the manuscript reading.

ter to resolve a hopeless situation like a *deus ex machina* in the theater, when in fact, as you well know, I have never known the joy of father-hood, except once, when in a single instant I was given the news of my child's birth and lost her. Take her away, someone! Let us have no more of her schemes to delay the sacrifice!"

"No one shall take me away," exclaimed Charikleia, "until the judges so decree. You are a party in the case before the court; it is not for you to reach a verdict. The law may permit you, sire, to kill aliens, but neither law nor nature allows you, Father, to murder your own child! For today the gods shall proclaim you a father, deny it as you will. In every case that comes to trial, sire, two types of evidence are recognized as most conclusive: documentary proof and corroboration by witnesses. Both types I shall adduce to demonstrate that I am your daughter. The witness I shall call is no ordinary member of the public, but the very person who is hearing the case—and I think that a speaker can produce no proof more conclusive than the judge's own acquaintance with the facts—while the document I present is this narrative of my own destiny—and yours!"

And with these words she brought forth the band that her mother had 13 laid out beside her and that she wore around her waist, unfolded it, and presented it to Persinna. The instant she saw it, the queen was struck dumb with amazement, and some time passed while she scrutinized first the writing on the band and then the girl; she was seized with a fit of pal-pitations, perspiration streamed from every pore, as joy at the return of what had been lost combined with perplexity at this incredible and un-looked-for turn of events, and with fear that Hydaspes might be suspi-cious and incredulous of these revelations, possibly even angry and vengeful; so that even Hydaspes became aware of his wife's anguished astonishment and said: "What is this, wife? Why are you so affected by the appearance of this document?"

"Sire," she answered, "lord, husband. I have nothing more to say. Take the band and read it. It will tell you all there is to tell."

She handed it to him and relapsed into forlorn silence. Hydaspes took the band and called on the gymnosophists to stand beside him and read it with him. As he read, he was filled with wonderment and could see that Sisimithres was equally astounded, for his expression testified to an infinity of shifting emotions and his gaze was fixed on the band and on Charikleia. Hydaspes read of the exposure of his child and the reasons for it, but at last he said: "I know now that a girl-child was born to me: at the time I heard from Persinna's own lips that the baby was dead, but I see now that it was abandoned at the wayside. But who was it who took her up, saved her, and fed her? Who was it who took her to Egypt where she has now become my captive? Indeed, how can we be sure that this is she, that the child did not perish after being abandoned, that someone did not chance upon the tokens of recognition and has not made use of the gifts of fortune[239] by bestowing them on this girl and using her as a kind of mask, so exploiting my desire for a child and imposing upon us a false and supposititious line of succession, clouding the light of truth with this band?"

14     At this point Sisimithres intervened. "The first of your questions is easily answered: the man who took her up after she had been abandoned, who concealed her and brought her up, who took her to Egypt when you sent me there on a diplomatic mission, is none other than myself: and you know from experience that our code forbids the telling of lies. Furthermore, I recognize the band, which, as you can see, is inscribed in the Ethiopian royal script, proving beyond any shadow of doubt that it originated here and nowhere else. That it is embroidered in Persinna's own hand, you yourself are best qualified to confirm. But there were other tokens exposed with the child, which I gave to the man who took over responsibility for the girl. He was a Greek, and evidently a person of good character."

"They are safe too," said Charikleia, whereupon she produced the necklaces, the sight of which threw Persinna into a deeper state of shock, so that when Hydaspes asked her what these objects were and whether she had anything more to tell him, the only answer she made was that she recognized them, but it would be best to examine them in the privacy of the palace.

Once again her words produced an obvious unease in Hydaspes, and Charikleia added, "These tokens might be for my mother to recognize, but this ring is specially for you," and she showed him the pantarbe. Hydaspes recognized it, for he had given it to Persinna as a gift when he asked her to be his wife.

"Madam," he said, "these are tokens that I recognize, but that you who bear them are my child, not merely someone who has chanced upon them, I do not yet recognize. Apart from anything else, your skin has a radiant whiteness quite foreign to Ethiopian women."

"The child I rescued," said Sisimithres, "was white when I rescued her; and besides, the number of years tallies with the girl's present age, for some seventeen years in all have passed since the exposure, and she is seventeen years old. There is a striking similarity in the expression of the eyes; and the whole stamp of her features, the excellence of her beauty, are familiar to me: what I see now is in accord with what I knew then."

"This is all very well, Sisimithres," retorted Hydaspes, "the kind of thing one might expect from an impassioned advocate rather than from a judge. But beware lest, in answering one point, you raise another ques-

---

239. I have followed the alternative manuscript tradition here in omitting a phrase.

*[handwritten margin note: What is the significance of Charikleia being the image of Andromeda?]*

tion, a serious one that is far from easy for my consort to answer: how could we, Ethiopians both, produce, contrary to all probability, a white daughter?"

Sisimithres shot him a wry glance and said with a slightly condescending smile: "I do not know what is wrong with you. It is not like you to criticize me for an advocacy that I see no reason to regret. We define the true judge as the one who advocates justice. In the end you will probably think me as much your advocate as the girl's, for, with god's help, I shall prove that you are a father, and I shall not forsake the daughter whom I preserved for you in her cradle now that she is safely restored in adulthood. But think what you will about us, for we attach no importance to it. We do not live to please others: our only goal is perfect virtue, and if our own consciences are satisfied, it is enough.

"In any case, the solution to the problem about the color of her skin is contained in the band, where Persinna here admits to having absorbed certain images and visual forms of resemblance from the picture of Andromeda that she saw while having intercourse with you.[240] If you desire further confirmation, the exemplar is to hand. Take a close look at Andromeda, and you will find that she is reproduced in this girl exactly as she appears in the painting."

At a word of command from the king, the attendants went to take 15 down the picture, which they brought and set up next to Charikleia. This occasioned universal cheering and acclaim: those members of the crowd with the slightest understanding of what was being said and done explained it to their neighbors, and the exactitude of the likeness struck them with delighted astonishment. Even Hydaspes could hold out no longer in his disbelief but stood motionless awhile, possessed by a mixture of joy and amazement.

"There is one point remaining," said Sisimithres, "for we are talking about the throne and its legitimate line of succession—and, most important, about truth itself. Bare your arm, girl: she had a black birthmark on her upper arm. There is nothing indecent in laying bare that which will confirm your parentage and descent."

Straightway Charikleia bared her left arm, and there was a mark, like a ring of ebony staining the ivory of her arm![241] Persinna could contain herself no longer. Suddenly she leapt from her throne, ran to Charikleia, 16 and threw her arms around her. As she held her tight, she burst into tears and, unable to control herself for joy, set up a sort of animal howling (for a surfeit of pleasure very often gives rise to mournful wailing) and very nearly bore Charikleia to the ground.

240. The Greek text is mangled here; the translation follows Toup's emendations.
241. Alluding to *Iliad* 4.141, where blood running down Menelaos's leg calls forth the simile of colored ivory.

The sight of his wife's distress touched Hydaspes, and his heart was moved to compassion, but he stood with his eyes fixed as unblinkingly on the scene before him as if they had been of horn or steel, fighting back the welling tears.[242] His soul was buffeted by waves of fatherly love and manly resolve that fought for possession of his will, which was pulled in two directions by their opposing tide races. But finally he bowed to all-conquering nature: not only was he convinced that he was a father, but he also betrayed a father's feelings. Persinna was on the ground, clasping her daughter, and as Hydaspes raised her to her feet, he visibly embraced Charikleia and poured out a libation of his tears to acknowledge his fatherhood.

Nevertheless, he was not altogether deflected from what he had to do. For a moment he stood and looked at his people, whose emotions were no less than his own and who were weeping from a mixture of delight and pity at destiny's stage management of human life. An unearthly clamor rose from their lips to make the heavens resound, and, call as the heralds might for silence, the people paid no attention, though they did not make the meaning of this uproar plain. Hydaspes raised his arm and with a motion of his hand stilled the tempest that raged in the people.

"My people," he said, "as you can see and hear, the gods, beyond all expectation, have shown me to be a father. Abundant evidence identifies this girl as my daughter. But so all-surpassing is my devotion to you and the land of my birth that, without a second thought for either the continuation of my line or the joy of being called father—all of which she would have brought me—I am resolved to sacrifice her to the gods for your sake. I see your tears; I see your perfectly natural emotions; your regret that she must die so young, your regret that my hopes for the continuation of my line are to be dashed, is clear to me. And yet I have no choice: though possibly you might prefer me not to, I must obey the law of our fathers and put the interests of the nation above my own. Whether it is the gods' wish to bestow her on me and take her from me in the space of a single instant—a blow that fell on me once before at her birth and that falls on me again now at her return—I cannot tell, nor do I know whether they will accept the return to them through sacrifice of one whom they exiled from the land of her birth to the uttermost ends of the earth and then miraculously brought home in the condition of a prisoner of war and restored to the bosom of her family; these are questions I leave you to ponder.

242. From *Odyssey* 19.209ff.:

> but Odysseus
> in his heart had pity for his wife as she mourned him,
> but his eyes stayed, as if they were made of horn or steel,
> steady under his lids.

"When she was my foe, I did not slay her. When she was my prisoner, I did not abuse her. But now that this same girl is revealed as my daughter, I shall not flinch from offering her up in sacrifice, for it is your will that I should. I shall not succumb to feelings that any other father might be forgiven for succumbing to. I shall not falter. I shall not kneel before you and entreat you to indulge me by this once merely going through the motions of compliance with the law while in reality attaching greater importance to the emotions that spring from parenthood, making the excuse that the godhead can be served equally well by other means. Your evident sympathy for us, your obvious involvement in our agony, have only increased my concern for your welfare. I care little for my own loss, little for the sorrows of poor Persinna here, whom a single hour has made a mother for the first time and then childless. So then, if you will, cease your tears, put away your empty commiserations, and let us proceed with the ceremony.

"And you, my daughter—now for the first and last time I call you by the name I have yearned so long to speak—you who have gained nothing from your beauty, have gained nothing by returning to your parents, who have found a worse fate in your own country than in foreign parts (for in other lands you found deliverance; in the land of your birth, only death), do not confuse my heart with sorrow,[243] but now if never before conduct yourself with the pride and courage befitting a king's daughter. Come with your father: he has not been able to robe you in a bridal gown, it is not to marriage torches and a bridal chamber that he has brought you, but it is for sacrifice that he adorns you now, and the torches he lights are not those of the wedding ceremony but those that burn on the altar of sacrifice, to which he brings your peerless and supreme beauty as an offering.

"And gods, if in the coils of passion I have uttered any word that offends against piety, forgive me, for I am the man who has to slay his child in the very instant of calling her by that name!"

So saying, he laid hold of Charikleia and made as if to lead her towards the altars and the fire that burned on them, though the fire of sorrow that smoldered in his own heart was hotter than any altar fire. And all the while he prayed that his oration, whose rhetoric he had contrived to ensure its ineffectiveness, would fail to carry its point. But his words jolted the Ethiopian assembly into activity: they would not allow Charikleia to take so much as a single step towards the altar, and exclaimed loudly, as with one voice: "Let the girl live! Let the blood royal live! The

243. This is quoted almost exactly from Achilles' reply to the appeals of Phoinix at *Iliad* 9.612:

Stop confusing my heart with lamentation and sorrow.

gods have preserved her; you must do the same! We are satisfied; the requirements of the law have been met as far as we are concerned. We recognized you as our king; now recognize yourself as a father! May the gods forgive this apparent infringement of the law; it would be a greater infringement if we opposed their will. No one must slay her whose life they have saved! You are father of the people; now be a father in your own house!"

These cries were accompanied by countless others of a similar nature, until finally the people made it plain that they were prepared physically to prevent the sacrifice, by blocking Hydaspes' path, barring his way to the altars, and demanding that the gods' favor be won by sacrificing any victim but her.

Hydaspes was only too glad to admit defeat: he had prayed for his hand to be forced, and he complied willingly. It was clearly going to take some time for the exultant and unremitting chanting of the people to die away, with such exuberance were they prancing and cheering; so he made no attempt to cut short their jubilation and waited for them to calm down in their own good time.

18 He moved to Charikleia's side and said: "My dearest child, that you are my daughter is proven by the tokens of recognition and confirmed by the testimony of Sisimithres, though it is the benevolence of the gods that is most responsible for the revelation. But who is this man who was taken prisoner with you and set aside to be offered to the gods in our victory sacrifices, and who is now at the altar awaiting immolation? How did you come to call him your brother when you were first presented to me at Syene? Surely he will not be discovered to be our son! Persinna was with child once only—and that was you!"

Charikleia blushed and lowered her eyes. "I lied when I said he was my brother," she said, "but the falsehood was the product of necessity. It would be better if he told you himself who he really is, for he is a man and can explain himself with less shame and embarrassment than I could as a woman."

Hydaspes did not grasp the true sense of what she said. "Forgive me, little daughter," he said, "if the question I asked you about the young man offended your virgin modesty and brought a blush to your cheeks. Go into the pavilion and sit with your mother. Indulge her pleasure at your return, for even the labor of your birth cost her less agony than the impatience she now feels to enjoy your company. Tell her about yourself; comfort her. I shall see to the sacrifice once we have selected the girl to be sacrificed in your stead, alongside the young man, if we can possibly find one fit to take your place."

19 Charikleia almost wailed aloud in her anguish at this reference to Theagenes' immolation; it was with some difficulty that she refrained

from anything so inopportune and forced herself to subdue the frenzy of her emotions to the exigences of her situation. Once more she tried to work round stealthily to her goal.

"My lord," she said, "in sparing me the people may have consented to forgo the female sacrifice altogether, thus relieving you of any further obligation to find a girl. If anyone insists that the sacrifice must be performed without subtraction, with victims of both sexes, then you must look not only for another girl, but for another young man as well. Otherwise you will have to kill not another girl, but me, as you originally intended."

"Be careful what you say," said Hydaspes, and asked her reason for saying this.

"Because," she replied, "it is my god-given destiny to live while this man lives and die when he dies."

But still the truth had not dawned on Hydaspes. "Daughter," he said,   20
"I commend your kindliness. It is right that you should feel compassion for this Greek stranger and try to find a way to spare his life: you and he are of an age, you have endured captivity together, and there has grown up between you the intimacy of exile in foreign lands. But it is absolutely impossible for him to be exempted from the sacrifice. For one thing, it would be sacrilegious for the ancestral rite of offering sacrifices in thanks for victory to be dispensed with entirely; and, most important, the people would not stand for it. It was only with great difficulty and through the benevolence of the gods that they were moved to countenance your reprieve."

"Your Majesty," replied Charikleia, "—for it may be impossible for me to call you father—if it is through the benevolence of the gods that my body has been saved from death, then it would be part of that same benevolence to save from death my soul also, which the gods know they fated to be my soul in very truth. But if this turns out to be contrary to the will of destiny, and the stranger must definitely grace the ceremony with the sacrifice of his life, at least grant me one wish: bid me slay the victim with my own hand; bid me take the sword in my hand as a treasure beyond price and earn undying renown among the Ethiopians for my courage!"

Hydaspes was thoroughly perplexed by this request. "I cannot under-   21
stand your complete change of heart," he said. "A moment ago you were trying to shield the stranger; now you are seeking leave to be his killer, as if he were your bitterest enemy. To my eyes, there would be nothing noble or meritorious in such an act, at least for a girl of your age. And even if there were, it is not possible. This function is traditionally confined exclusively to those ordained to serve the Sun and the Moon, and these are not chosen at random but must have, respectively, a wife

or a husband. Thus your virginity prevents me granting this extraordinary request of yours."

"There is no obstacle on that count," whispered Charikleia, bending close to Persinna's ear. "There is a man I can call husband, if you will give your consent."

"You shall have our consent," replied Persinna with a smile, "and if the gods approve, we shall lose no time in marrying you to a husband chosen as being a fit match for you and ourselves."

"There is no need," replied Charikleia, raising her voice, "to choose a husband I already have."

22    She was on the point of explaining herself more fully, for the urgency of the situation compelled her to speak out boldy, and the danger all too visibly threatening Theagenes forced her to ignore the qualms of a virgin's modesty, when she was interrupted by Hydaspes, who could contain himself no longer.

"O gods!" he exclaimed, "you seem to have mixed ill fortune with the good. You gave me unlooked-for happiness, but now you seem to prevent me enjoying it to the full. You have shown me a daughter I never expected to see, but she seems to be mad. She talks such nonsense that her mind must be unhinged. She spoke of a brother, who does not exist. When I asked her who this stranger, who does exist, was, she said she did not know. But then she made every effort to save the life of this unknown stranger, as if he were a friend. And then, when she was told that her request could not be granted, she begged on bended knee to be allowed to sacrifice him with her own hands, as if he were her bitterest enemy. When we told her that was forbidden, as there is only one woman, a woman with a husband, who is sanctioned to perform this kind of sacrifice, she claimed to have a husband, without saying who he is: how could she when he does not exist and has been shown by the gridiron never to have existed? Unless of course in her case and her case alone the test of chastity that has never yet lied to the Ethiopians is not telling the truth, lets her step on and off it without being burnt, and graces her with a kind of bastard virginity; unless of course she has a license denied the rest of us to call the same people friend and foe in the same breath and invent nonexistent brothers and husbands for herself!

"Go into the pavilion then, wife, and try to clear her head. Either she has been intoxicated by the presence of one of the gods at this ceremony, or else the surprise of her good fortune has caused such a surfeit of joy that it has addled her brain! For my part, I shall give someone the task of seeking and finding the woman to be sacrificed in her stead, and in the meantime I shall occupy myself in receiving the embassies from the provinces of our empire and accepting the gifts they bring in honor of our victory celebration."

And with these words he seated himself on a high throne beside the pavilion and commanded the ambassadors to come forward and present any gifts they might have brought. Whereupon Hermonias the chamberlain inquired whether it was his will that he should present them all together or in turn, separate and distinct, one nation at a time. Hydaspes 23 replied that he wished to see the embassies in order, individually, so that each might be accorded the honor they deserved.

"In that case, sire," replied the chamberlain, "the first to be presented will be Meroebos, your brother's son. He has just arrived and is waiting at the entrance to the assembly for his name to be announced."

"What!" exploded Hydaspes. "You idiot! You half-wit! Why did you not inform me immediately? You knew that it was not a mere ambassador who had arrived but a king and, furthermore, the son of my recently deceased brother. It was I who secured him his place on the throne, and I love him as my own son."

"I was aware of all this, my lord," replied Hermonias, "but I was also aware of the paramount importance of gauging the right moment to announce him: this function demands more circumspection on the part of a chamberlain than any other. Pardon me therefore if, observing that you were in conference with the royal ladies, I forebore to interrupt their charming conversation."

"Let him come forward now at least," said the king, and, thus bidden, Hermonias scuttled off and returned immediately with his master's bidding: Meroebos strode into view. He was a striking example of young manhood, who had but recently passed the threshold of adulthood, his age being seven years and ten. Yet he stood taller than almost everyone there. A magnificent retinue of shield bearers escorted him, and the Ethiopian army in reverence and deference parted to let him pass through the circle of soldiers without obstruction. Nor did Hydaspes remain 24 seated on his throne, but he rose to greet Meroebos, whom he embraced with fatherly affection and seated next to himself.

Clasping his hand, he exclaimed: "You have come just in time, my boy, to join our victory festivities and to celebrate the rite of marriage. Our ancestral gods and heroes, founders of our race, have discovered a daughter for us and, it seems, a bride for you! I shall tell you the full tale later on, but now, if you wish me to hear any petition on behalf of the subjects of your kingdom, speak out."

At the mention of the word "bride" Meroebos flushed red from a mixture of joy and embarrassment, and even in his black skin he could not conceal the blush that suffused his countenance like a flame licking over soot.

After a moment's silence he replied: "Father, the other embassies here today will each present you with the choicest gifts their land produces to crown your glorious victory. I, on the other hand, have thought it proper to give you something appropriate to your valor in war and of a kind with your heroic renown. Therefore I bring you a man who is a master without rival of the art of bloodletting on the field of battle and a champion without peer at wrestling and boxing in the dust of the arena."

25 So saying, he nodded his head as a sign for the man to come forward, and he strode into full view and prostrated himself at Hydaspes' feet. So huge, so primordially titanic, was he that even as he knelt to kiss the king's knee he was almost as tall as those seated on elevated thrones. Without even waiting for the command, he threw off his clothes and stood stark naked, challenging all comers to combat with weapons or bare hands. But no one came forward to take up the challenge, though time and again the king had his herald urge them to do so.

"Then you will receive the appropriate prize from my hands," said Hydaspes, and ordered an enormous, fully mature elephant to be brought him. When the creature arrived, the man accepted it with pleasure, and the populace erupted into laughter, delighted by the king's jest, and consoled for what was in their eyes a humiliation by his satirical deflation of the fellow's conceit.

Next to be presented were the ambassadors of the Seres; the gift they brought consisted of two robes, one dyed crimson, the other of the purest white, woven from the gossamer webs spun by the spiders that

26 live in their land. The king graciously accepted these gifts and acceded to their request for the release of a number of men who had served long sentences in jail. Next came the ambassadors of the Wealthy Arabs[244] with their gift of incense leaves, cassia, cinnamon, and the other spices that scent the land of Arabia, each to the value of many talents: their delicious perfume pervaded the entire area. They were followed by the delegation of the Troglodytai, who presented ant gold[245] and a pair of griffins[246] harnessed with chains of gold. Next in line was the embassy of

---

244. Wealthy Arabia, Arabia Eudaimon, corresponds roughly to modern Aden. The Wealthy Arabs were the people who supplied spices to the Mediterranean civilizations. It was widely believed that the spices originated in Arabia, but in fact the Arabs shipped them from the Far East. It may be that Heliodoros identified the Arabs, who did not fight in the battle, with the inhabitants of the Land of Cinnamon, who fought but are missing from the list of embassies.

245. Gold supposedly extracted from the dust ejected from the ant heaps of a particular species of giant ant (Herodotos 3.102). These ants were usually located in India, but Heliodoros seems once more to be following the lead of Philostratos (*Life of Apollonios* 6.1) in transferring them to Ethiopia.

246. Griffins were originally conceived of as guardians of the gold of the Hyperboreans in the far north. However, gold-guarding griffins tended to be confused with gold-digging ants and were relocated accordingly.

the Blemmyes, with a crown they had woven of bows and snake-bone arrowheads.

"These are the gifts we bring you, sire," they said. "Their price may be less than those of other nations, but they proved their value beside the river against the Persians, as you can testify."

"Then they are more precious than the costliest of gifts," said Hydaspes, "for it is because of them that all these other presentations are now being made to me."

So saying, he gave them leave to make any request they chose. They asked for a reduction in their taxes, whereupon he waived payment altogether for a period of ten years.

Almost all the visiting embassies had been received: the king had shown his gratitude for their gifts by presenting gifts of his own in return, in no case of less value than those he had received, in the majority of cases of rather more. The last envoys to come forward were those of the Auxomitai,[247] who were not subject to tribute but partners in a treaty of friendship. To convey their compliments on his recent successes they too brought various gifts, including a specimen of an unusual and bizarre kind of animal: in size it stood as tall as a camel, but its hide was marked with garish leopard spots. Its hindquarters and rear parts were squat and leonine, but its withers, forelegs, and chest were disproportionately taller than the rest of its anatomy. Notwithstanding the bulk of the rest of its body, its neck was as slender and elongated as the crop of a swan. In appearance its head was like a camel's, in size not quite twice that of a Libyan ostrich. Its eyes were rimmed with a black line like mascara and darted hither and thither with an expression of pompous disdain. Even its method of locomotion was unique, since it rolled from side to side like a ship at sea, in a manner quite unlike any other creature, terrestrial or aquatic: it did not advance each of its legs individually, in rotation, but its two right legs moved forward in unison, separately from the two left legs, which also functioned as a distinct pair, thus leaving each side of its body in turn without support. It was so halting in its gait and so docile in its temperament that its keeper could lead it on a slender cord wound around its neck, and it obeyed the directions of his will as if it were a chain that brooked no disobedience.

The arrival of this beast produced universal amazement. The people spontaneously invented a name for the creature derived from the most

27

247. The people of Axum, a city in the mountains of northern Ethiopia. Insignificant at the dramatic date of the novel, Axum had become a city of great importance by the time of Heliodoros, eclipsing the older power of Meroe. Some hint of this later importance may be intended in the exceptional status of Axum among Hydaspes' allies.

prominent features of its anatomy: *camelopard*.[248] But it threw the ceremony into total disarray.

28      What happened was this: at the altar of the Moon was standing a pair
of bulls, at the altar of the Sun a team of four white horses, ready to be
sacrificed. Their alarm at the sight of this strange and unfamiliar monster, whose like they had never seen before, was as great as if they had
seen a ghost. Panic-stricken, one of the bulls (the only one, apparently,
to have caught sight of the creature) and two of the horses jerked their
halters out of their keepers' hands and bolted. There was no holding
them. Unable to break through the ring of soldiers, whose locked shields
formed a wall totally enclosing the central space, the animals careered
blindly around, galloping and wheeling all over the enclosure and upend-
ing everything in their way, inanimate object and living creature alike.
Uproar ensued, screams of fear from the people in the creatures' path
mingling with cries of delight from others, who derived much mirth and
merriment from seeing them collide with someone else and flatten anyone who got in their way. The noise was such that Persinna and Charikleia were unable to stay quietly in the pavilion but drew the curtain
aside a little way so as to be able to see what was happening.

I cannot say whether what Theagenes did next was the product of his
own innate courage or the inspiration of some god or other. Hitherto he
had been kneeling at the altar, expecting the sacrificial blow to fall at any
moment, but now, observing that the guards who flanked him had scattered in the general confusion, he suddenly leapt to his feet and, seizing
one of the sticks that lay on the altars, grabbed hold of one of the horses
that had not bolted and leapt onto its back. He grasped its mane, and, using the hair to steer it, he dug his heels like spurs into the horse's flank,
whipped on his steed with his stick, and rode off in pursuit of the runaway bull. At first the onlookers assumed that Theagenes was attempting
to escape, and each started shouting at his neighbor not to let him break
through the cordon of soldiers. But as the exploit proceeded, they saw
that they had been wrong, that this was no pusillanimous attempt to escape being sacrificed.

In a trice Theagenes had caught up with the bull, and for a while he
rode just behind it, prodding it and goading it to run even faster; through
all the twists and turns of its frantic career he stayed with it, cautiously
29      sidestepping its charges and rushes, until it had grown accustomed to the
sight of him and what he was doing. Now he was riding alongside it, so
close that flesh touched flesh, that the bull's breath and sweat mingled
with the horse's. So precisely did he correlate the speed of the two racing

248. A giraffe, of course.

animals that from a distance the spectators were presented with the illusion that the creatures' two heads sprang from a single neck, and they acclaimed Theagenes as a hero who had brought so strange a team, a hippotaur, a creature half bull, half horse, beneath the yoke.

Such was the popular response, but Charikleia as she watched was seized with a fit of palpitations, for she was quite bewildered as to the purpose of this exploit and felt the pain of any injury to Theagenes, should an accident occur, as keenly as if it were her own life at stake. So great was her anguish that it even became apparent to Persinna, who said: "What is wrong, my child? Tell me, do. You seem to be facing the danger in proxy for the stranger. I am affected too: it is sad that he must die so young. But I pray that he will escape danger and be preserved for the sacrifice; otherwise our duty towards the gods will be completely neglected."

"How absurd," exclaimed Charikleia, "to pray that he is not killed in order to be killed! Mother, if you can, save this man's life. Do this as a favor to me."

Persinna did not realize the true motive for Charikleia's request: she took it for a mere infatuation.

"To save his life is out of the question," she said. "But I am your mother; you can confide in me. Tell me what connection you have with this man that makes you so anxious on his behalf. Even if it is some improper passion, something unworthy of your virginity, a mother's natural love can keep her daughter's lapse secret, a woman's fellow feeling can mask another woman's sin."

Charikleia wept long and bitterly. "This is my greatest misfortune," she said. "Even people of intelligence find my words unintelligible and are deaf when I speak of my misfortune. Now I am compelled to resort to an explicit and undisguised denunciation of myself."

So she spoke, only to find her resolve to reveal the truth frustrated for 30 a second time as the heavens resounded to an outburst of cheering from the crowd. Theagenes gave his steed its head: with its last ounce of speed it inched ahead till its chest was level with the bull's head. Then, leaving the horse to career along riderless, Theagenes leapt from its back and hurled himself onto the bull's neck. He planted his own face between its horns and locked his forearms like a crown around the animal's head, with his fingers knotted in a wrestling grip on its forehead, and allowed the rest of his body to hang suspended clear of the ground alongside the bull's right shoulder. For a moment or two he was borne along dangling like this, flung this way and that as the bull bucked and leapt. But when he felt the animal gasping for breath beneath his weight and its muscles losing their last degree of tautness, just as it passed the place where Hydaspes sat in state, he swung his feet round to the front so that they hung just ahead of the bull's legs, and kicked and hacked at its hooves until it tripped and stumbled. Its forward impetus obstructed, its strength broken by that of the young man, the bull's legs buckled at the knees, and suddenly it catapulted forward onto its head and turned a somersault to land on its back and shoulders. And there it stayed, flat on its back, with its horns stuck in the ground and so firmly rooted that its head could not move, while its legs flailed ineffectually and pawed the empty air in helpless rage at its defeat.[249]

Theagenes pressed home his victory, and, using only his left hand to pin the bull to the ground, he stretched his right hand heavenwards and waved and waved, beaming at Hydaspes and the assembled multitude. His smile was an invitation to share his joy, and the bellowing of the bull was like a trumpet call to sound his victory. The populace responded with a tumultuous ovation: no distinct words could they articulate to praise him, but they just opened their mouths and let the sound come straight from their vocal chords to give voice to their wonderment, which wafted heavenwards as their cheering continued for some length of time without any diminution of its volume.

At a word of command from the king, attendants leapt into action. Some lifted Theagenes to his feet and brought him to the king, while others looped a rope around the bull's horns and dragged it crestfallen back to the altar, where they tethered it, along with the horse, which they had also recaptured. Hydaspes was on the point of speaking to Theagenes and of dealing with him when he was interrupted by the populace: they were delighted with the young man, with whom they had sympathized from the moment they first saw him; they were impressed by his strength, but, more important, they were still smarting with resentment against Meroebos' Ethiopian champion.

"Let him be matched against Meroebos' man!" they all yelled with one accord. "Let us have a contest between the winner of the elephant and the captor of the bull!" they chanted.

Eventually Hydaspes acceded to their demands, and the Ethiopian was brought into the center of the circle, glaring around him with arrogant disdain and with a swagger in his step as he strutted along, swinging his forearms across his body, so that his crooked elbows jutted out first one side, then the other. As he approached the place where the king and his cabinet were sitting, Hydaspes turned to Theagenes and said in Greek: "Stranger, this is the fellow you must fight. The people command it."

31

249. This description of the technique of bull throwing (taurokathapsia) accords fairly closely with that found in other references to the sport. It was practiced particularly in Thessaly, which is Theagenes' home.

"Let their will be done," replied Theagenes. "But what form will the contest take?"

"Wrestling," said Hydaspes.

To which Theagenes replied: "Why not armed combat with swords? Then I might strike some blow—or receive one—that would jolt Charikleia out of her complacency, for till now she has resisted the temptation to speak the truth about us or else, most probably, has forgotten about me altogether."

"Your purpose in dropping Charikleia's name into this conversation," said Hydaspes, "you alone know. Be that as it may, you must wrestle and not spar with swords. The sight of spilt blood is forbidden before the moment of sacrifice."

Theagenes realized that Hydaspes was afraid he might be killed before the sacrifice, and said: "You are right to preserve me for the gods. They will take care of us."

And so saying, he took a handful of dust and sprinkled it over his shoulders and forearms, which were still dripping with perspiration from the bull chase. Then, shaking off what had not adhered to him, he put up his guard, planted his feet in a firm stance, flexed his knees, hunched his shoulders and the broad of his back, lowered his head a little, tensed every muscle in his body, and stood in impatient anticipation of the grips and holds of a wrestling bout. The Ethiopian glared at him and smirked; he shook his head sarcastically to make clear his low estimation of his opponent. Suddenly he darted forward and brought his forearm crashing down like a sledgehammer onto Theagenes' neck. The sound of the blow reverberated, and the Ethiopian resumed his posturing and broke into arrogant laughter.

Theagenes, who was a lifelong devotee of the gymnasium and athletic endeavor and a past master in the art of combat whose patron god is Hermes,[250] decided to give ground to start with: he had already experienced the power of his opponent and was resolved not to come to grips with such a monstrous hulk of a man in the full spate of his bestial fury, but rather to use skill to outwit brute force. So, although he was only slightly dazed by the blow, he feigned to be worse affected than in fact he was, and offered the other side of his neck to be struck. The Ethiopian delivered another blow, but Theagenes rolled with the punch and pretended nearly to fall flat on his face.

The Ethiopian thought him beaten and was confident of victory. As he advanced to strike the third blow, he dropped his guard. He had

32

250. Hermes was the god of the gymnasium and particularly of the wrestling arena. In this aspect his cult title was Enagonios, god of combat, to which Heliodoros has contrived an allusion in the previous phrase.

raised his forearm again and was on the point of swinging it down, when suddenly Theagenes ducked to evade the swing and closed with his adversary; with his own right forearm he pushed back the Ethiopian's left arm, thus unbalancing his antagonist, who was also drawn groundwards by the swing of his own arm as it descended into empty space. Theagenes came up beneath his armpit and leaped onto his back.[251] With some difficulty he got his arms around the Ethiopian's enormous stomach and with his heels kicked and hacked at his ankles with all his might, not ceasing until he had prized his feet off the ground and forced him to his knees. Then, straddling his opponent, he forced his thighs apart with his legs, knocked away the Ethiopian's wrists, which were taking the weight of his body and holding his torso clear of the ground, knotted his arms around his head, and wrenched them backwards towards his back and shoulders, so sending him sprawling on his belly on the ground.

At this, with one voice, the people erupted into a clamor even more deafening than before. Even the king could not restrain himself: he leapt from his throne crying, "O Destiny, what a man the law obliges us to sacrifice!"

Then he called Theagenes to him and said: "Young man, the traditional crown of sacrifice already awaits you, but now receive another crown to mark your glorious victory—though it will last but a moment and profit you nothing. Much as I wish to, I am powerless to reprieve you from the end that now awaits you, but I shall grant you such reward as I am permitted. If you know of anything that could give you pleasure while yet you live, ask it."

With these words he set a crown of gold set with precious stones on Theagenes' head, and as he did so, he could not hide his tears.

"I do have a request," replied Theagenes, "which I ask you to grant as you have promised. If it is quite beyond your power to grant me a reprieve from sacrifice, at least bid it be done by the hand of your newly discovered daughter!"

33 These words stung Hydaspes, and he was reminded of the selfsame request made by Charikleia. However, he did not think he could halt the ceremony at so critical a juncture to resolve this mystery.

"My friend," he said, "I gave you leave to ask and pledged myself to give only what it is possible to give. She who wields the sacrificial knife must be a married woman, not a virgin. The law demands it."

"But she does have a husband!" answered Theagenes.

"Nonsense!" exclaimed Hydaspes. "You talk like someone whose

251. The maneuver Heliodoros proceeds to describe is an authentic wrestling ploy known as the *klimakismos,* "ladder hold."

mind is wandering in the face of death, which is just what you are! The gridiron has proved that the girl has no experience of marriage or a man's intercourse—unless by her husband you mean Meroebos here, though I have no notion how you know! But he is not yet her husband; the only title he has received from me is that of husband to be—"

"Finish your sentence," interrupted Theagenes, "by saying he never will be her husband, not if I know anything of Charikleia's heart. And you will have to believe my predictions, for I am a sacrificial victim!"

"It is not while victims are alive that they can foretell the future, my friend," interposed Meroebos, "but when they have been slaughtered and cut open so that soothsayers can read the signs in their entrails! So you were quite right, Father, to say that the stranger is talking nonsense because his mind is wandering in the face of death. Now, if such be your command, let him be taken to the altars. Do whatever business you have left to do, and proceed with the ceremony."

Theagenes was led back to the appointed place, and Charikleia, whose spirits had revived a little at his victory, found her optimistic hopes dashed and began to weep as he was led away again. Persinna made every effort to console her and said, "The young man could probably be saved if only you could bring yourself to tell me more plainly what you have so far left unsaid about yourself."

Charikleia had no alternative. She could see that the situation was such that she could put it off no longer, and so she proceeded straight to the heart of her tale.

Hydaspes meanwhile was asking his chamberlain whether any of the 34 embassies had not yet been given an audience.

"Only those from Syene, sire," replied Hermonias. "They arrived but a moment or two ago and bear a letter and gifts of friendship from Oroondates."

"Let them be presented then," said Hydaspes, and the ambassadors came forward and handed him the letter, which he opened and read. This is what it said:

Oroondates, satrap of the Great King, to Hydaspes, gracious and blessed king of the Ethiopians.

You have shown yourself my superior in battle, and even more so in wisdom. Unprompted, you relinquished an entire satrapy to me: I anticipate therefore that you will not refuse me one further small request now. A certain girl was on her way to me from Memphis when she was caught up in the war. Those who were with her and escaped danger on that occasion have told me that she was captured and, on your orders, sent to Ethiopia. This person I petition you to release and to make me a present of her. I ask this partly because I am myself attracted to the child, but mainly because I wish to restore her to her father. He has wandered the face of the earth and in the course of his search for his child was interned in the garrison town of Elephantine after the outbreak of war. I came across him there afterward, when I was inspecting my surviving troops, and he asked to be given a passage to Your Gracious Majesty. He stands before you now, among the other ambassadors: his manners are sufficient indication of his breeding; his appearance, sufficient claim on your compassion. Send him back to me in joy, sire, a father in fact, not merely in name.

When he had finished reading, Hydaspes asked, "Which of you is it who is looking for his daughter?"

They pointed to an old man, and the king said: "My friend, there is nothing I would not do to oblige Oroondates. But I had only ten young female captives brought here. One of these, we have just discovered, is not your daughter. Still, have a look at the others and if you find her, say who she is, and she will be yours."

The old man prostrated himself before the king and kissed his feet. The girls were brought, and he looked at them; but when he did not find the child he sought, his gloom returned.

"She is not one of these, sire," he said.

"You have my sympathy," replied Hydaspes. "If you cannot find the child you seek, you must blame fate. I give you permission to look around and satisfy yourself that no girl was brought here apart from these and that there are no others in the camp."

35 The old man smote his brow and wept. Then, raising his head, he ran his eyes all around the assembly. Suddenly he darted forward like a lunatic, ran to the altar, and, looping the hem of the threadbare cloak[252] in which he was clad into a noose, he threw it around Theagenes' neck[253] and started to drag him away from the altar, yelling at the top of his voice: "You are mine now, you villain! You are mine now, you accursed scoundrel!"

Try as the guard might to restrain him and to release Theagenes from his clutches, the old man refused to let go and clung so tight to Theagenes that they seemed inseparable. Finally, he suceeded in bringing him before Hydaspes and the council.

---

252. The man is wearing a *tribonion,* a cloak of rough material worn by the poor and those who affected asceticism. Here it is worn to arouse pity.

253. This peculiar action can be paralleled as a form of citizen's arrest, and the words that the old man speaks also echo a legal formula.

"Sire," he said "this is the man who kidnapped my daughter. This is the man who left my home desolate and childless, who stole my soul from the very heart of Apollo's sanctuary at Delphi; and now here he is, seated at the gods' altars as if he bore no stain of guilt."

This incident gave rise to general consternation: the few who could understand his words were no more astounded by what he said than were the rest by what they saw.

Pressed by Hydaspes to explain more clearly what he meant, the old 36 man (who was none other than Charikles) suppressed the full truth of Charikleia's origins, for he had no wish to attract the hostility of her true parents if she had in fact disappeared during her flight southwards before ever reaching Meroe. So he simply summarized the harmless parts of her story and said: "I had a daughter, sire. Her intelligence and beauty were such that any description would seem incredible unless you had seen her with your own eyes. She lived a virgin life as acolyte of Artemis at Delphi, until this paragon, a Thessalian who came to my city of Delphi as the leader of a sacred mission to perform some ancestral rite, stole her slyly away and looted the holy shrine of Apollo. And so you might with justice consider yourselves the victims of his sacrilege, for he has desecrated the person and the holy precinct of Apollo, who is one and the same as the Sun, the god of your fathers. His accomplice in this act of sin was a charlatan priest from Memphis. I scoured Thessaly and demanded his extradition by the people of Oita, his fellow citizens, but he was nowhere to be found. However, they disowned this fellow here as one polluted by sin and gave me a free hand to put him to the sword, wherever he was to be found. Surmising that the goal of their flight was Memphis, Kalasiris's hometown, I made my way there, only to find Kalasiris already dead, as he so richly deserved. However, his son Thyamis told me everything there was to tell about my daughter, including the fact that she had been dispatched to Oroondates at Syene. But though I went to Syene, I was unable to reach Oroondates or to enter the town, and was overtaken by the war in Elephantine.

"Now I have come to you and kneel before you in supplication, just as the letter has explained. You have the abductor; now take up the search for my daughter. Your charity to me, a man who has suffered much, will also give you the satisfaction of demonstrating your regard for the satrap who is treating with you on my behalf."

His voice trailed away into silence, and he sobbed bitterly at his story. 37 Hydaspes turned to Theagenes and said, "What do you have to say to these accusations?"

"They are all true," he answered. "I am a thief, a robber, a vicious criminal to him, but to you I have done good service."

"Give him back his daughter then," said Hydaspes. "She is his property, not yours. As you have already been consecrated to the gods, you will die the honorable death of sacrifice, not the judicial death of just execution."

"It is not the man who committed the crime," said Theagenes, "but the man who has the proceeds of the crime in his possession who should do the giving back. That man is you! Give her back then, unless this man too will admit that Charikleia is *your* daughter!"

Nobody could restrain himself now: there was pandemonium. From the very start all the words and actions had made sense to Sisimithres, but he had resisted the impulse to intervene, waiting for the gods to bring their revelation to the fullness of its clarity. Now he ran to Charikles and embraced him.

"The child you regarded as your daughter, the child I committed to your keeping all those years ago, is safe," he exclaimed, "though in truth she is, and has been discovered to be, the child of parents whose identity you know!"

38    Now Charikleia came running from the pavilion and, oblivious of the modesty incumbent on her sex and years, raced like a maenad in her madness towards Charikles and fell at his feet.

"Father," she said, "to you I owe as much reverence as to those who gave me birth. I am a wicked parricide; punish me as you please; ignore any attempts to excuse my misdeeds by ascribing them to the will of the gods, to their governance of human life!"

A few feet away, Persinna held Hydaspes in her arms. "It is all true, my husband," she said. "You need have no doubts. Understand now that this young Greek is truly to be our daughter's husband. She has just confessed as much to me, though it cost her much pain."

The populace cheered and danced for joy where they stood, and there was no discordant voice as young and old, rich and poor, united in jubilation, for though they had understood very little of what was said, they were able to surmise the facts of the matter from what had already transpired concerning Charikleia; or else perhaps they had been brought to a realization of the truth by the same divine force that had staged this whole drama and that now produced a perfect harmony of diametric opposites: joy and sorrow combined; tears mingled with laughter; the most hideous horror transformed to celebration; those who wept also laughed; those who grieved also rejoiced; they found those whom they had not sought and lost those whom they thought to have found; and finally the offering of human blood, which all had expected to see, was transformed

39    into a sacrifice free of all stain, for Hydaspes turned to Sisimithres and said: "What are we to do, all-wise one? To refuse the gods their due

*[handwritten marginalia at top: their entrance to the priesthood mirrors Kalasiris' abstaining from live sacrifice — is there a connection — is the author making a point about purity?]*

sacrifice would be irreverent; to put those who are the gods' gifts to the knife would be sacrilegious. We must consider carefully what to do."

"Sire," replied Sisimithres, speaking Greek no longer, but Ethiopian for the whole assembly to understand, "it seems that a surfeit of joy can cloud even the most intelligent of minds. You ought to have realized long ago that the gods have no desire for the sacrifice you are making ready to offer: first, on the very altar of sacrifice, they revealed the blessed lady Charikleia to be your daughter and dramatically transported her foster father here from the heart of Greece; then they cast fright and panic among the sacrificial bulls and horses and so gave a sign that those sacrifices that are thought superior would also be cut short; and now, to make our happiness complete, as a theatrical climax they have revealed that this young stranger is betrothed to the maiden. Let us not be blind to the miracles the gods have wrought; let us not thwart their purpose; let us abolish human sacrifice forevermore and hold to purer forms of offering!"

Sisimithres proclaimed this loud and clear for all to hear. Now Hy-   40
daspes too spoke in the native tongue. Laying his hands on Charikleia and Theagenes, he said, "My people, these things have been brought to pass by the gods' will: we must not oppose them. So now, calling to witness both the gods who have spun the thread of this destiny, and you whose obedience to their decrees is amply proven, I declare that this couple has been joined by the laws of matrimony, and I give them leave to pass their lives together in accordance with god's ordinance for the bearing of children. With your permission, let us make our sacrifice to confirm this decision; let us turn our minds to the gods' service."

The army cheered their approval of this speech and clapped their   41
hands in thunderous applause, as if the marriage were being solemnized then and there. Hydaspes stepped to the altar and, before making the first offering, said, "Our Lord the Sun, the Moon our Lady, since by your decrees Theagenes and Charikleia are proclaimed man and wife, they now have the right to serve in your priesthood."

And so saying, he removed his miter, the insignia of the priesthood, from his own head, and Persinna's from hers, and placed his own on Theagenes, Persinna's on Charikleia. And thereupon Charikleia recalled to mind the oracle at Delphi and found the prophecy that the gods had given long ago fulfilled in fact: it had said that the young pair would flee from Delphi and

To the black land of the Sun will they travel,
Where they will reap the reward of those whose lives are passed in
    virtue:
A crown of white on brows of black.

And so, Theagenes and Charikleia, crowned with their white miters, invested with holy office, offered the sacrifice with their own hands, and the omens were good. Then, by the light of torches, to the melody of flute and pipe, they rode into Meroe, Theagenes beside Hydaspes in a chariot drawn by horses, Sisimithres in a second beside Charikles, Charikleia with Persinna in a carriage pulled by white oxen. The people cheered and clapped and danced as they escorted them into the city, where the more mystic parts of the wedding ritual were to be performed with greater magnificence.

So concludes the *Aithiopika*, the story of Theagenes and Charikleia, the work of a Phoenician from the city of Emesa, one of the clan of Descendants of the Sun, Theodosios's son, Heliodoros.

# PSEUDO-LUCIAN

# THE ASS

## TRANSLATED BY J. P. SULLIVAN

## Introduction

This erotic novella (also known variously as *Lucius or The Ass, Asinus,* or *Onos*) is included in the manuscripts of Lucian, but despite many Lucianic touches in its often pedestrian, almost vulgar, Greek, it is unlikely to be the direct product of his own pen. Photius, patriarch of Constantinople in the latter half of the ninth century, made the attribution in his *Bibliotheca* (Migne 129), suggesting that Lucian had plagiarized a longer work, the *Metamorphoses* of an otherwise unknown Lucius of Patras. But since the suffering narrator, Lucius by name, hails from Patras, probably Photius or someone earlier had foisted on the Roman antihero of *The Ass* the actual authorship of the much longer work. The most plausible theory is that of B. E. Perry, who argues cogently that Lucian himself wrote the longer and presumably more artistic work, perhaps utilizing earlier materials. The story itself of the lady who loves an ass long predates Lucian, who flourished in the second century A.D. Some of the other amusing and bawdy episodes from this lost original may be incorporated in Apuleius's *Metamorphoses,* however different the basic theme and purpose of the latter, since there are a number of parallel incidents in Apuleius and our condensed *Onos,* not always in sequence, and we may reasonably infer that more of the same material was taken by Apuleius from the longer work. I have indicated a few of these parallels in the notes, partly to demonstrate the somewhat cavalier attitude of the excerpter towards his original. The whole question is exhaustively examined by H. van Thiel.

The plot of *The Ass* is straightforwardly picaresque. A young businessman with an insatiable curiosity, particularly about magic and the supernatural, finds himself in Thessaly, an area notorious for witchcraft;

and his hosts's wife happens to be an adept. By seducing the maid he manages to witness her mistress's metamorphosis into an owl. His curiosity impels him to try the same experiment, but he uses the wrong lotion and turns into an ass, and only eating roses can restore him to his proper shape. That same night, however, he is stolen by bandits; and so begins the long saga of his misfortunes (and occasional triumphs), as he is transferred in rapid succession from one set of owners to the next. The denouement occurs at a public spectacle, when he manages to snatch some roses and dramatically regains his human shape, after which, much relieved, he sails back home to Patras.

The moral of the story is made quite explicit: curiosity about the occult is foolhardy and dangerous, and nemesis always follows. Wisdom will come through suffering (*pathos mathos*), and only then will heaven come to the rescue. In the last few lines of the work Lucius makes sacrifice to the gods for his escape from his asinine curiosity.

The psychologist will of course find nothing strange in the close association of curiosity, witchcraft, and sexuality in the basic tale. It is prominent also in such novelists as Petronius. According to Freudian theory, the initial ground of curiosity is an interest in the nature of sexuality, the desire to see what is forbidden, the sexual act or the private parts of one's parents and others. This desire, which in its basic form is fraught with the threat of punishment, may then transmute itself into an overwhelming interest in the occult in general: in ghosts, witches, and other supernatural phenomena, as may be seen in the child's delight in fairy tales and ghost stories. Fortunately this curiosity is later directed towards science, scholarship, or intelligence work, to unlocking the secrets of nature, the past, or the enemy.

But to return to the hero of *The Ass*. Lucius's punishments, naturally enough, are those appropriate for his new shape. He is overburdened and overworked; he is sadistically beaten by various masters and narrowly escapes butchery several times. The author, however, alleviates this dreary catalogue of afflictions by introducing other traditional motifs: the rescue of a heroine, a major theme in other Greek novels; satire on the avarice and perverted license of Eastern religious cults; and, finally, the blatant sexuality and audacity of almost all women. This misogyny is traditional in Greek and Roman fiction and satire and reflects standard ancient attitudes. In our tale it shows itself in the portrait of the wealthy foreign lady who falls in love with Lucius as an ass, but rejects him with contumely when he is human once more.

Apuleius in the *Metamorphoses* (10.19–22) heightens and lengthens considerably the account of the ass's sexual encounter with a similar rich and oversexed lady. He does the same with most of the bizarre adventures common to the two works, but it is impossible to determine how much or how little he owed to the lengthier lost original.

In this common use of sadistic and lecherous episodes the resemblance ends. *The Ass* is not multidimensional like the *Metamorphoses*. Nor is this a question of a jejune style contrasting with lavish linguistic exuberance, or an impression that one author just wants to get on with the story, whereas the other, like Cervantes, delights in his digressions and the twists he brings to the plot. For Apuleius the bare story is a peg on which to hang several hats. He is interested in more than merely narrative purposes. The vulgar curiosity of the hero about the supernatural, common to all three works, slowly develops through suffering and learning into a search for what is transcendentally supernatural, into a quest for the divine. And Apuleius's hero finds this in Isis, the mother of all things, the primal generating principle of the universe. The hero of *The Ass* loses his ass's skin and perhaps his foolish curiosity, but Apuleius's Lucius sloughs off not merely his bestial hide but also his unregenerate self. This salvation had been foreshadowed earlier in the narrative by the famous tale of Cupid and Psyche. Its recital by a disreputable old crone symbolizes the upward momentum of the whole work. The unredeemed hero, turned into a pathetic beast, finally becomes a neophyte of Isis, and his vulgar and perilous superstition becomes true religion and salvation. So in the prefiguring fable, Psyche is bedeviled by curiosity and must suffer like Lucius. For all their dogged endurance through their ordeals, both need divine help to reach their ultimate goals: for Psyche reunion with Cupid, and self-knowledge and purification for Lucius.

The language of *The Ass* rarely rises above the adequate except in the sexual scenes, where it becomes detailed and complex even to the point of obscurity. Here, perhaps, the excerpter was following his original more closely. In general the style is basically simple, consisting of coordinate clauses with a plethora of unnecessary connectives and strings of participles, and showing little attempt at verbal variation in its descriptions of actions and things. This normally jejune vocabulary and rapid movement from sentence to sentence, along with the overfrequent deployment of the vivid present tense, seem intended to present us with the portrait of a naive, helpless hero hurled through a series of bewildering and distressing events over which he has little control. To attempt an absolutely literal translation would make the narrative too graceless and redundant for the twentieth-century reader. I have therefore hewed closely to the meaning, but felt free to adapt the sentence structure and vary the monotonous vocabulary in the light of modern English norms. Similarly I have omitted unnecessary connectives or adversatives. The use of the vivid present is retained only where it is appropriate. The author is no Apuleius, but with such a racy little story unfolding, there is clearly no need to leave the reader breathless.

I have used Van Thiel's text but occasionally adopted readings from M. D. Macleod's Oxford text or Loeb edition; the major instances are indicated in the notes. I acknowledge also my debt to the notes in the Loeb edition, to which the reader may be referred for further information.

## Bibliography

TEXT

*Der Eselsroman.* Edited by H. van Thiel. Vol. 1, *Untersuchungen;* Vol. 2, *Synoptische Ausgabe.* Munich, 1971–72.

*Lucian.* Vol. 8. Edited by M. D. Macleod. London, 1967 (Loeb Classical Library).

*Lucian. Opera.* Vol. 2. Edited by M. D. Macleod. Oxford, 1974 (Oxford Classical Texts).

GENERAL

Perry, B. E. "The *Metamorphoses* Ascribed to Lucius of Patrae." Ph.D. diss., Princeton University, 1920.

————. *The Ancient Romances: A Literary-Historical Account of Their Origins.* Berkeley, 1967. See chapter 6.

See also H. van Thiel's text edition above.

# THE ASS

1    I WAS ONCE on my way to Thessaly.[1] I was involved in some business deal of my father's there with a man of that country. A horse provided transport for me and my gear, and one servant came along with me. Well, I was following my planned itinerary, and it happened that there were others also en route back to Hypata, a city in Thessaly, where they came from. We broke bread,[2] and so, making short work of that uncomfortable road, we were already close to the city when I asked the

---

1. Thessaly, in northern Greece, had been the traditional home of witchcraft long before Plato's time.
2. Literally "we shared salt."

Thessalians if they knew a man living in Hypata by the name of Hipparchus. I was bringing him a letter of introduction from home so I might stay with him. They said they knew this Hipparchus and his address in the city; he had money enough, and he kept only one maid and his wife, as he was frightfully stingy.[3] When we got close to the city, there was a garden and in it a nice little house, where Hipparchus lived.

So the others gave me a farewell hug and went on, while I approached  2
and knocked on the door; slowly and reluctantly a woman answered the door and then came out. I inquired if Hipparchus was at home.

"He is," she said, "but who are you, and why do you want to know?"

"I've come with a letter to him from Professor Decrianus of Patras."

"You wait here for me," said she, and, locking the door, she went back in again. After a while, she told us to come in. Going into the house, I greeted the master and gave him the letter. He happened to be starting dinner and was reclining on a cramped little couch, with his wife seated near him and a table laid with nothing on it. After going through the letter, he said: "But Decrianus is a very dear friend of mine, the most outstanding person in Greece. He's really kind in confidently sending his very own associates to stay with me. You see how small my little place is, Lucius, but we're courteous enough with a guest here. And you will make it a palace if you'll show a little tolerance during your stay."

He called the young maid. "Palaestra,[4] give him the guest bedroom and take whatever baggage he has to it, then direct him to the baths, as he's come quite a long way." At these words, the slip of a girl Palaestra  3
led me off and showed me to a charming little room. "You'll sleep on this bed," she says, "and I'll lay out a mattress there for your slave, and I'll put a pillow on it." Once she'd told us this, we went off to have our baths, after giving her the price of some barley for the horse. She fetched everything in and stowed it away.

After the bath we returned and went straight inside. Hipparchus shook my hand and invited me to take a place beside him. The dinner wasn't at all stingy, and a sweet vintage wine was served. When we had dined, there was drink and the usual conversation one has after dinner with a guest, and so, after devoting that evening to drinking, we retired to bed. The next day Hipparchus inquired where I would be off to now and whether I'd be staying with him for the whole time. "I'm going to Larissa,"[5] I told him, "but I'd like to spend three to five days here."

3. Apart from another reference in chapter 4, nothing in the plot hinges on this supposed parsimony of Hipparchus. It is one of the many signs of inexpert excerption from a longer original. Apuleius makes much of this aspect of the host's character (*Metamorphoses* 24 and 26).

4. Palaestra in Greek means "wrestling school." The appropriateness of this choice of name for the character will soon become evident.

5. Larissa was the principal town in Thessaly.

4    But this was a pretext. I very much wanted to stay there to find one of those women versed in the magic arts and see something incredible, like a man flying or being turned to stone. So abandoning myself to my passion for such a spectacle, I wandered around the town. I was at a loss where to begin my search, but I went all the same. In the course of this, I observed a woman approaching, still young and, to guess from seeing her on the street, very comfortably off; for she had brightly decorated clothes, lots of slaves, and more than enough gold on her. As I got nearer, the woman hailed me, and I responded in like fashion. She then said: "I'm Abroea, a friend of your mother's, if you've heard the name, and I love all you sons of hers like my very own. So why won't you stay with me, my boy?"

"Well, many thanks to you," I said, "but I'm embarrassed to leave a friend's house when I have no complaints about him. Nevertheless, my dear lady, I am staying with you in my heart."

"Where have you moved in?" she asked.

"With Hipparchus."

"With the skinflint?"

"Don't say that, mum," I broke in. "He's such a splendidly lavish host to me that you might even accuse him of extravagance."

Smilingly, she took me by the hand, led me further off, and said to me: "For my sake, watch out for Hipparchus's wife and take every care, for she's an expert witch, a loose woman, and she has her eyes on all the young men. Anyone of them who turns a deaf ear to her she punishes through her magic art, and she has turned many of them into animals, and some she has done away with altogether. You are both young and handsome, my boy, enough to attract a woman immediately, and, as a stranger, you are a thing of no concern."[6]

5    For my part, discovering that the object of my long quest was there at my house, I paid no more attention to her. When after a while I got away from her, I went off home, saying to myself along the road: "Come on then, you're the one who says he has a craving for this strange spectacle; pull yourself together and think up some crafty scheme to gain access to what you're longing for. Strip for action with Palaestra the maid at once—you have to keep away from the wife of your host and friend. Try a roll over her, have a good workout, and get to close grips with her—you can be sure that you'll easily get your information. Slaves know it all, the good and the bad."

Talking to myself like this, I went into the house. I discovered neither Hipparchus nor his wife at home, but Palaestra was occupied round the

6    fireplace, preparing the dinner for us. I immediately "took it from

6. Again, nothing is made of the lechery of Hipparchus's wife in the plot.

there"[7] and said, "Palaestra, you beauty, how rhythmically you twist and tilt your buttocks in time with the saucepan, and your loins flow as they move. Happy the man who gets a dip in there."

Said she—for she was a very pert little hussy and a bundle of charms: "You'd scamper, my lad, if you had any common sense and wanted to go on living, since it's full of hot fire and steam. If you were to as much as touch it, you'd be sitting here with a shocking burn, and no one can cure you, not even the God of Healing, except me who burned you. And the strangest thing of all, I shall make you yearn[8] for more, and though flaming from the pain of the treatment, you'll always put up with it, and even if you are pelted with stones, you won't run away from the delicious pangs. What are you laughing at? You're looking at a real cannibal-cook, for it's not only these common dishes I prepare, but now this great lovely dish called man. I know how to butcher him, skin him, and chop him, and the sweetest part is getting hold of his very innards and heart."

"You're right when you say that," I responded, "for even when I was away off and nowhere nearby, you hit me not with just a burn, by God, but with a whole firestorm, and by sending your invisible flame through my eyes down into my innards you are roasting me even though I've done nothing amiss. So, for heaven's sake, heal me with these bitter-sweet treatments you speak of, and now that I'm already butchered, take me and skin me how you like."

A loud, sweet, sweet laugh followed this, and after that she was mine, and it was agreed between us that when she had got her master and mistress to bed, she would come into my room and sleep there.

When Hipparchus eventually came back, after our baths we had din- 7 ner, and there was lots of wine as we chatted. Then, on the pretext of sleep, I got up and in fact went to my bedroom. Everything inside had been beautifully arranged. Bedding was spread for my slave on the floor outside, and a table with a cup stood at my bedside. Wine was set out there, and there was hot and cold water at hand. All of this was furnished by Palaestra.

Over the coverlets quantities of roses were scattered, some in their natural state, some pulled apart, some twined into garlands. Finding the drinking party all arranged, I waited for my drinking companion. Once 8 she had put her mistress to bed, she came hastily to my room, and we had a rapturous time toasting each other with wine and kisses. When, thanks to the drinks, we had nicely braced ourselves for the night, Palaestra said to me: "This above all you've got to remember, my lad, you're into a fall with Palaestra, and now you must show me if you were a demon with the boys and picked up a lot of wrestling tricks."

7. One of the few classical quotations in the work, here Homer *Odyssey* 8.500, etc.
8. Macleod's reading (OCT).

"Well now, you wouldn't see me shrinking from *this* test. So strip off, and let's begin the wrestling now."

"You must put on the exhibition," she said, "the way I want it. *I* will follow the rules of a trainer and manager, and I'll call out the names of the holds I want as I think of them: you've got to be ready to follow orders and do everything you're told."

"Then give me the orders," I said, "and watch how prompt, agile, and tight my holds will be."

9     She stripped off her clothes and, standing up stark naked, started her orders then and there. "Off with them, my lad, and rub on some of the scented oil from over there, then get a grip on your opponent. With a snatch hold on my two thighs, drop me on my back, then, from the on-top position, slip through my thighs; once you have them apart, lift up my[9] legs and stretch them high, then relaxing them and setting them in place, stay glued to the thing. Get closer and hit it; pushing forward, stab it in every which way till you're flagging, and let your tenderloin show its strength. Then pulling out level, put the thing right through the groin, and push again to the wall and then thump it. When you see some relaxing, at that point come on with a clinch to the waist and grip with a tight lock. And try not to rush it, but have a bit of self-control and match your speed to mine. Now you can leave the ring."

10     On my side, since I had easily followed all the instructions, and our wrestling bouts had quietly ended, I said to Palaestra, laughing: "You see, coach, how handily and obediently I've got through the wrestling. But watch that you aren't out of order when you propose your holds. For you demand different ones all the time."

But she smacked me on the side of the face, saying: "What a babbler I've taken on as an apprentice! Now watch out that you don't get more smacks for using other wrestling holds than those signaled."[10] With these words, she got out of bed, and after taking care of herself, she said, "Now you'll prove whether you're young and in shape as a wrestler and if you know how to wrestle and make it in the kneeling position."

She dropped to the bed on one knee. "Let's go, wrestling champ, you're centered, so flaunt yours; *then,* with a sharp push in, get it down deep. You see it here laid bare; make full use of it. First of all, going by the book, get a stranglehold on me; then, bending me backwards, throw yourself forward and hold me tight, with no space between us. But if there's any slack, lift faster, move it higher, bend over[11] with a bang, and

9. The Greek is not clear as to whose legs are being so positioned. One commentator (Macleod) in his translation (Loeb) takes it to be Lucius's legs; this would be quite a strain and to little erotic purpose.
10. Macleod's reading (OCT).
11. Macleod's reading (OCT).

see that you don't pull away faster than you're told. Instead, arching well over, take it out, and after getting me down again with the trip technique, cling close and move it vigorously; then let it out, since it's down and limp, and your opponent has completely turned to water."

I was now having a big laugh and said: "I'd like to press for a few holds myself, coach, where *you* have to listen to me. Well, get up and sit down, and then give me some water for my hands; rub the rest of the oil on yourself and wipe it off. Now, by Heracles, keep hugging me and send me off to sleep."

Such were the pleasures and frolics we had, competing in our nightly bouts of wrestling and winning our laurels. There was a great deal of self-indulgence in this. Consequently, I entirely forgot about my trip to Larissa. At some time, though, there came to my mind the thought of the knowledge for the sake of which I'd been so athletic. I thereupon said to Palaestra: "Darling, give me a look at your mistress performing magic or changing her shape. I've long had a desire for this strange spectacle. Better, if you have the knowledge, do some magic yourself, so that you appear to me in one manifestation after another. I think that you too are not without experience in this art. I know this not from any other source but from my very own soul, since I who have long been like adamant, so the women say, and have never directed these eyes with love on any woman, have been trapped by this art of yours, and you hold me captive by your enchantments in the war of love."

Palaestra said: "Stop your teasing. For what spell can conjure up love, when he's master of the art? Darling, I know nothing of these things—I swear by your very life and this blessed bed. I haven't learned to read, and the mistress is very jealous when it comes to her own art. But if the opportunity turns up, I'll try to let you see the mistress changing shape."

Then, after our agreement, we fell asleep. Not many days later Palaestra announced to me that her mistress was going to turn into a bird and fly to her beloved.

I said, "Now's the right time, Palaestra, to do me the favor I'm begging you for, by which you can set to rest an age-old longing."

"Don't you worry," she said.

When it was evening, she took me and guided me to the door of the room where those two slept and told me to put my eye to a tiny chink in the door and observe what was happening inside. I now saw the woman undressing. Then she approached the lamp naked, and, taking two lumps, she put the frankincense on the flame of the lamp, and, standing there, she recited at length over the lamp. Then, opening a sturdy chest holding a great many containers, she picked one of them up and brought it out. It contained I don't know what, but from the look of it, it appeared to be olive oil. Taking some of this, she smeared herself all over, beginning with her toenails, and suddenly feathers grew on her, and her nose became horny and hooked, and she had all the features and signs of a bird. She was nothing less than a long-eared owl.[12] When she saw herself all feathered, with a fearsome croak, just like those ravens of the night, she rose and flew out through the window.

13     Thinking I was dreaming, I rubbed my eyelids with my fingers, not trusting my own eyes to be either seeing this or even awake. As I slowly and gradually became convinced that I was not asleep, I then begged Palaestra to put feathers on me and smearing me with some of that powerful lotion let me fly; for I wished to find out by experiment whether, changed from my human shape, I would have the soul of a bird also. Quietly opening the bedroom, she brought out the container. In my eagerness I was already undressed, and I smeared myself all over, and tragically I didn't become a bird; instead a tail grew from my backside, and all my fingers vanished I don't know where. All I had was four nails, and these were nothing but hooves; my hands and feet had become the feet of an animal, and my ears were long, and my face huge. When I turned and looked myself over, I saw I was an ass, but I no longer had a human voice to curse at Palaestra.

But I pulled down my lip, and, given my very appearance, I looked angrily at her in the way an ass would, accusing her, as far as was in my power, for my changing into an ass instead of a bird. Hitting herself in the face with both hands, she said: "Misery me, I have done a lot of harm. In my hurry I made a mistake due to the similarity of the boxes, and I took a different one, not the one that brings out[13] the feathers. But don't worry, my dearest; the cure for this is really simple. If you just eat roses, you'll immediately shrug off the beast from you, and you'll give me back again my very own lover. However, please, dearest, this one night stay inside the ass, and at dawn I'll run and bring you roses, and after eating them, you'll be restored." This she said, while stroking my ears and the other parts of my hide.

15     I was in other ways an ass, but in heart and mind I was a man, still that same Lucius, apart from the voice. Therefore blaming Palaestra severely to myself for the mistake and biting my lip, I went off to where I knew my horse was stalled, as well as a real ass belonging to Hipparchus. When they sensed me entering, afraid that I was coming in to share their fodder, they laid back their ears and made ready to protect their bellies with their feet. I understood, and, moving further away from the feedbox, I stood there laughing, though my laugh came out as a bray. Then I thought to myself: "Oh, what mistimed meddling! What if

12. *Nuctikorax,* to which the author alludes, means literally "night raven."
13. Macleod's reading (OCT).

a wolf or some other savage beast should get in? I'm running a risk, even though I've done nothing wrong." For all these thoughts, I didn't know in my misfortune about the impending disaster. For when it was now 16 deepest night, and profound silence and sweet sleep prevailed, there was a noise from the outside of the wall as though it were being broken through. It was indeed being broken through, and a hole now appeared large enough to let a man in. Immediately a man was in through it, and another likewise, until there were a great number inside and all holding swords. Thereupon, once inside, they tied up Hipparchus, Palaestra, and my servant in their rooms and then calmly went about emptying the house of money, clothes, and furniture and carrying them outside. When nothing else was left indoors, they took me, the other ass, and the horse, saddled us, and then tied on our backs all they had hauled out. Despite such a heavy load, they drove us, beating us with sticks, towards the mountain, attempting to escape by an unused path. I can't say what the other animals felt, but I myself, feet unshod and unused to such travel, moving over sharp rocks and carrying such heavy stuff, I was practically dead. I often tripped, but I wasn't allowed to fall down, as one of them would immediately hit me from behind on my rump with a stick. I often wanted to cry out "Oh, Caesar," but I managed nothing but a bray. The "Oh" I would shout out loud and clear, but the "Caesar" wouldn't follow. Nevertheless I was thrashed for this too, because I was giving them away by my braying. Finding then that my shouts were useless, I learned to proceed in silence and gain the advantage of not being beaten.

By this time it was already daylight, and we had traveled up many 17 mountains. Our mouths were muzzled with chains to prevent us grazing and taking up traveling time for breakfast. And so for that day too I remained an ass. When it was absolutely the middle of the day, we made a halt at some farm, which, to judge from what went on, belonged to acquaintances of theirs, for they hugged and kissed one another, and the people at the farm invited them to stop awhile, and they served them breakfast and flung down some barley for us animals. The others ate their breakfast, but I remained miserably hungry. Since, however, I had never breakfasted on raw barley before, I looked out for something to eat. I spotted a garden there behind the courtyard, and it had lots of beautiful vegetables, and above them appeared roses. Avoiding the notice of all those inside occupying themselves over breakfast, I went into the garden, partly to gorge myself on raw vegetables, partly because of the roses; for I calculated that by eating the flowers, I'd become a human again. Going into the garden then, I glutted myself on lettuce, radishes, and celery, the sort of things a man eats raw, but the roses were not real roses, but the flowers of the wild laurel tree. People call them rhododen-

drons,[14] a poor breakfast this for any ass or horse; for they say that if you
18 eat them, you drop down dead. Meanwhile the gardener, perceiving
what was going on, grabbed a stick and came into the garden, where seeing his foe and the destruction of his vegetables, like some highly respectable personage catching a thief, he banged me with his stick, sparing
neither my ribs nor my haunches, and in fact he battered my ears and
pulped my face. Putting up with it no longer, I kicked away at him with
both hind hooves, and, sending him flying on his back into the vegetables, I rushed off up the mountain. When he saw me running off, he
yelled for the dogs to be set loose on me. There was a whole pack of
dogs, huge in size and capable of fighting bears. I knew that when they
got me they'd tear me apart. So after running around awhile, I decided,
as the saying goes, "to run back rather than run into trouble."[15] I therefore went back and entered the courtyard again. They grabbed the dogs
who were racing down on me and tied them up. As for me, they started
beating me and did not give up until in my agony I got rid of all the vegetables through my back passage.

19 What is more, when it was time to proceed on our way, they dumped
on me the heaviest and largest parts of their loot, and we moved on from
there. Soon, when I was exhausted by my beatings and the weight of my
burden, and my hooves were worn away by the road, I made up my
mind to fall down then and there and never get to my feet again, even if
they butchered me with their blows, as I was hoping to do myself a great
service by this plan. I thought that they would give up completely, dis-
tribute my articles among the horse and the mule, and leave me lying
there for the wolves. But some evil demon, aware of my designs, turned
them right around. The other ass, perhaps with the same thoughts as
mine, fell down in the road. They first ordered the poor thing to get up,
beating it with a stick, but when it wouldn't respond to their blows, they
took it, some by the ears and some by the tail, and tried to get it up.
When they were unsuccessful, and it lay stone cold in the road, deciding
among themselves that their labors were in vain and they were using up
their escape time by attending to a dead ass, they divided all the goods he
was carrying between me and the horse. As for my unlucky partner in
captivity and drudgery, they took him, chopped off his legs with their
swords, and pushed him, still gasping, over the precipice. Down he
went, dancing his way to death.

20 Seeing the outcome of my schemes in the case of my traveling companion, I resolved to accept what was ahead of me like a gentleman and

14. Probably not the modern rhododendron but *Nerium oleander*. The Greeks used the
names *nerion*, *rhododaphne*, and *rhododendron* for the same poisonous shrub, which Lucius believed was fatal to grazing animals.
15. A line from some lost drama.

keep on walking cheerfully in the hopes that some time I'd surely come upon the roses and, saved from all this, become myself. And I heard the bandits saying that there wasn't much of the journey still left and that they would be staying where they unpacked. So we carried all this stuff at a trot, and we arrived at their home base before dusk. An old woman was seated inside, and a huge fire was burning. The bandits unloaded all the things that we'd been carrying and stowed them away inside. They then asked the old woman, "Why are you sitting there like that instead of getting a meal ready?"

"But everything's ready for you," said the old woman. "There's lots of bread, jars of mature wine, and I've cooked some game for you." They complimented the old woman; then, stripping off, they oiled themselves in front of the fire, and, drawing hot water from a cauldron and pouring it over themselves, they had a makeshift bath.

Then just a little later a gang of young men arrived, carrying great 21 quantities of gold and silver vessels as well as clothes and a good deal of female and male jewelry. These were all partners. And when they had brought all this stuff inside, these washed themselves in the same way. After this there was a plentiful meal and a lot of conversation among the murderers over their cups. The old woman set out some barley for me and the horse. But he gulped the barley down hastily from the reasonable fear that I was to be his companion at supper. I, however, ate bread from what was around whenever I saw the old lady go outside. The next day, leaving only one young man to the old woman, all the rest went off to their work. I then groaned over my situation and the strict watch being kept. It was possible to disregard the old woman and get out of her sight, but the young man was big and had a terrifying look; he always carried his sword and always kept the door closed.

Three days later, about the middle of the night, the bandits returned, 22 bringing neither gold nor silver nor anything else, but just a young woman, extremely beautiful, who was crying, with her clothing and hair in tatters. Putting her down inside on the straw, they told her not to be frightened and ordered the old woman to stay inside at all times and keep the girl in custody. The girl didn't want either to eat or drink, but she wept incessantly and tore at her hair. As a result I myself wept in concert with the lovely girl from where I stood near the feedbox. Meanwhile the thieves were eating their meal outside in the forecourt. Towards evening one of the lookouts assigned to watch the roads come in with the news that a stranger was just about to pass by their way and he was carrying a lot of valuables. Getting up just as they were, they put on their weapons, saddled me and the horse, and led off.

In my misery, knowing that I was being driven to combat and fighting, I proceeded nervously, for which I was beaten with sticks as they pressed on hard. When we came to the road where the stranger was going to ride by, the bandits fell on the convoy, killing the master and his servants, and, picking out all of the most precious items, loaded them on the horse and me. The rest of the stuff they concealed there in the wood. Then like this they started to drive us back, but, being goaded on and thrashed with cudgels, I struck my foot against a sharp rock and got a painful wound from the impact. I walked on, limping the rest of the way. They began saying to each other: "What's the good of our feeding this ass when he's always falling down? Let's pitch him over the cliff— he's bad luck." "Yes," said one, "let's pitch him over as a scapegoat for the crimes of our whole group." And they began closing in on me, but, hearing this proposal, I traveled the rest of the journey as though the wound belonged to someone else, the fear of death making me unconscious of the pain. When we came back to where we were staying, they took down those articles on our shoulders and carefully stowed them away. They themselves took their places and ate dinner. At nighttime they came out to recover the rest of the things. "This miserable ass!" said one of them. "Why do we drag him along, when he's useless because of his hoof? We'll carry some of the things ourselves, and the horse will carry the rest." They went off with the horse in tow. It was a very bright night because of the moon, and I then said to myself: "You pathetic creature, why are you still staying here? The vultures and their young will eat you for dinner. Don't you hear what they've planned? Do you want to be thrown over the cliff? It's now night, with a full moon, and they've gone off somewhere. Run away; save yourself from your bloodthirsty masters."

I was thinking all this to myself when I saw that I wasn't tethered to anything, but the thong for pulling me down the road was dangling by my side. This was the greatest possible incitement to flight, and I went off at a gallop. The old woman, when she saw me ready to run away, took hold of me by the tail and clung on. I told myself that to be caught by an old woman well deserved the cliff and any other form of death, and I began dragging her with me. She screeched loudly to the captured girl inside. Coming out and seeing this aged Dirce[16] hanging from an ass, she performed an heroic act of daring, worthy of a crazy youth: she leaped up on me, seated herself on my back, and rode me away. What with my desire to escape and the girl's eagerness I galloped off like a horse, and the old woman was left behind. The girl prayed to heaven to save her by letting her get away, and to me she said, "If you get me to

16. Dirce was tied to the tail of a bull by the sons of Zeus, Amphion and Zethus, for her maltreatment of their mother, Antiope, deserted by King Lycus of Thebes in Dirce's favor. The bull dragged her around until she died.

my father, you beautiful beast, I'll let you go free from all work, and there'll be a big bushel[17] of barley each day for your breakfast."

As for me, determined to escape from my killers and hoping for some generous assistance and care from the girl I'd saved, I raced on ignoring my injury. When we came to where the road split into three,[18] our enemies, now on their way back, caught up with us; in the moonlight they immediately recognized their unlucky prisoners from a distance, and, running up to us, they grabbed me and said: "Hey you fine young lady! Where are you going at such a strange time, you miserable wretch? Aren't you even frightened of unearthly powers? However, come here to us, and we'll give you back to your family." They said this laughing sarcastically, then turned me around, and dragged me behind. Remembering now my foot with the injury, I began limping. "Are you lame now?" they said. "When you've been caught running away? But when you decided to escape, you were in good shape, running faster than a horse and putting on wings." After these words came the stick, and by this time I had an open sore on my thigh from their castigations. When we got back to the house again, we found the old woman hanging by a rope from the rock; for in fear of her masters, as well she might be, on account of the girl's escape, she had hanged herself with a strangle knot round her neck. They expressed their admiration of the old lady's good sense, and, bringing her down, they pushed her over the cliff, still in the noose. The girl they tied up inside; then they had dinner, followed by heavy drinking. During this they began discussing the girl with each other. "What shall we do with the runaway?" asked one of them. "What else," said a second, "but throw her down after the old lady there? She was going to steal a lot of money from us if she could, and she was going to betray our whole gang. You ought to realize, my friends, that if she had reached her folks, not one of us would have been left alive. We'd all have been captured once our enemies had got organized and come down on us. So let's avenge ourselves on the woman—she's our enemy. Yet don't let her die too easily in a fall on the rocks, but let us think up for her the most excruciating and lingering death and one that will keep her alive a long time in agony until it finally destroys her."

Then they considered what should be her death, and one said: "I'm sure you'll approve of this masterly scheme. We need to kill the ass, since

24

25

---

17. The Attic corn-measure, *medimnus,* was equivalent to one and a half modern bushels.

18. The crossroads, pointless here, was probably more important in the original. In Apuleius (*Metamorphoses* 6.29) it is the pair's indecision about the fork to take that allows the thieves to catch up with them. There are various other infelicities in the narrative due to careless abridgment of the original.

it's a shirker and is now pretending to be lame, and, what's more, it was the helper and the accomplice in the girl's escape. So at dawn, after we slaughter it, let's cut open its belly and throw out all its guts, and let's lodge the fine young lady inside the ass, with her head sticking out of the beast so that she wouldn't suffocate immediately, but with all the rest of her body concealed inside; once she's put there, we'd sew them up really well and throw both of them out for the vultures—this'll be a novel breakfast set for them! Think, my friends, of the horror of the torture, first to be lodged in an ass's carcass, then to be broiled in the searing summer sun inside the beast, to die by the lingering death of starvation, while not being able even to choke herself. As for the other things she'll suffer as the ass goes rotten, and she's in the middle of the stench and the worms, I refrain from describing them. In the end the vultures will make their way through into the ass and rip her to bits like him, perhaps while she's still alive."

26     All yelled approval of this monstrous scheme, as though it were a fine idea, but I sobbed for myself, as I would be butchered, and not even as a corpse would I rest happy; instead, I'd play the host to the hapless girl and become the tomb of the innocent lass.

But it was still daybreak when a large detachment of troops suddenly turned up, having come to get these fiends; they tied them all up on the spot and led them off to the governor of the territory. The girl's fiancé also came with the soldiers, for he was in fact the one who had told the authorities about the thieves' hangout. So taking the girl and seating her on my back, he led her home like that. The villagers, when they saw us, realized even from a distance that all had turned out happily for us, since I had brayed out the good news to them, and they ran up, hugged us, and led us indoors.

27     The young girl was most considerate towards me, doing the proper thing for her fellow prisoner, who had escaped with her and had run the risk of sharing that dreadful death with her. A large bushel of barley would be set before me by my mistress for breakfast and enough hay for a camel. At those times I cursed Palaestra heartily for changing me by her arts into an ass and not a dog, for I watched the dogs sidling into the kitchen and wolfing down quantities of the tidbits served at the weddings of rich couples.

Not many days after the wedding,[19] when my mistress expressed her gratitude towards me in the presence of her father, he, in a desire to recompense me with my just reward, gave instructions for me to be set free under the open sky and to graze with his brood mares. "For he'll live the

---

19. This abrupt information about the wedding is perhaps another sign of epitomization.

life of pleasure as though in freedom," he said, "and he'll mount the mares." This seemed a most just reward at the time, if the matter were being judged by an ass. Thereupon, calling one of his herdsmen, he handed me over to him, and I was very happy at the prospect of carrying no more loads. When we came to the range, the herdsman put me among the mares and led the herd of us to pasture. Then too the same        28
thing had to happen to me as had to Candaules,[20] for the man in charge of the mares dropped me at home for his own wife, Megapole.[21] She would harness me to the mill to grind wheat and barley. This would have been a reasonable burden for a grateful ass, to grind for his own masters, but that best of women also hired out my miserable neck to the other countryfolk—and they were very numerous—asking for flour as payment. The barley meant for my breakfast she would roast and force me to grind, and then, making cakes of it, she would gulp them down whole, and the husks became my breakfast. Whenever the herdsman did drive me out with the mares, I was almost killed by the blows and bites of the stallions, for they were always suspecting me as a possible seducer of their own mares and would chase me away, kicking at me with both hooves, till I couldn't bear their equine jealousy. So in a short time I became thin and unsightly, since I had no comfort indoors at the mill nor in grazing outdoors, being at constant war with my pasture companions.

What's more, I was often sent up into the mountains and hauled wood        29
on my shoulders. This was the crowning peak of my misfortunes. First I had to go up a high mountain by a fearfully steep road, and, to add to this, the mountain was stony for my unshod hooves. And they sent along with me as a mule driver an unholy little urchin, and every time he would find new ways of hounding me to death. First he used to beat me, even though I was running fast, and not with a plain stick, but one that was studded with numerous sharp knots, and he always struck me on the same part of the thigh, so at that spot on my thigh there was a constant open sore from the rod, and it was the wound he always struck at. Then he would pile on me a load that would be difficult for an elephant to carry. The descent was steep, and even then he would beat me, and if he saw the load slipping and leaning to one side or another, when he should have[22] removed some of the wood, to add it to the lighter side, and so make it balance, he never did that, but, picking up great stones from the mountainside, he'd heap them on the lighter and higher side of the load. And I descended in a pitiable state, hauling useless rocks along with the

20. Candaules was a king of Lydia who was assassinated by his wife and her lover. Herodotus (1.8ff.) comments that he was a man doomed to misfortune.

21. Megapole means literally "much-turning" or "busy miller," a reference to the tasks to which she will assign Lucius.

22. Macleod's reading (OCT).

wood. There was a perennial river at one point on the road, and, to save his shoes, he forded it by sitting on me behind the wood.

30    If ever I fell down exhausted and overburdened, then the horror was unbearable. Here was no bending down to give me a hand, raise me from the ground, and remove some of my load; he never offered me even a hand, but from up there, beginning with my head and ears, he would beat on me with his stick, until the blows forced me to get up. In addition, there was another nasty and unbearable trick he'd play on me. Gathering a bundle of the thorniest acanthus[23] and knotting a thong around it, he'd hang the thorns behind my tail, and these, as you might expect, dangling there as I went down the road, banged against me, stabbing and lacerating my hindquarters all over. Protection was impossible, for the pricking spikes always followed me and stayed tight to me; for if I went forward steadily, wary of the onslaught of the thorns, I was battered to death by his sticks; if I dodged the switch, then the prickly horror behind swung into me. In short, it was my driver's aim to kill me.

31    Once in my terrible sufferings, unable to bear them any longer, I took a kick at him, and this kick always stayed in his memory. Another time he was told to transport some flax from one place to another place. So taking me and putting together a great load of flax, he tied it on me and fastened it to me very tightly with an excruciating piece of rope, churning up a lot of pain in me. When we had to move ahead finally, he sneaked a still glowing piece of firewood from the hearth, and when we were some way from the farm, he secreted it in the flax. This immediately ignited—what else was possible?—and from there on I was lugging just one huge fire. Realizing then that I would be roasted in no time and coming across a deep swamp by the roadside, I flung myself into the wettest part of it. Then rolling the flax in it and twisting and turning myself, I extinguished my hot stinging load, and so I was able to finish the rest of the journey without further danger; for it was no longer feasible for the boy to rekindle the flax, as it was mixed with wet mud.

On arrival the brazen lad slandered me by claiming that I had deliberately banged against the hearth in passing. So on that occasion I escaped from the flax, though hardly expecting to.

32    But the imp thought up another and far worse trick to play on me. He took me out to the mountain, and, piling on me a massive load of logs, he sold it to a farmer who lived in the neighborhood, and, bringing me home barebacked and logless, he falsely charged me before his master of iniquitous behavior. "This ass, master, I don't know why we feed him, as he's terribly lazy and slow. What's more, he's now taken up another bad habit. Whenever he sees a beautiful young woman or girl or boy, he

23. *Acanthus spinosus,* or bear's breech.

kicks up his hooves and makes off after them at a run, like a real man in
love, making advances to his beloved lady, and he bites them under the
appearance of a kiss and struggles to get near them, and because of this
he'll bring on you lawsuits and harassments, with people everywhere being assaulted, and being knocked down all over the place. Just now,
while carrying wood, he saw a woman going off into a field. He shook
off and scattered all the wood on the ground, and he knocked the woman
down on the road and wanted to make her his, until different people ran
up from different directions and defended the woman from being ripped
apart by this fine lover here."

His master, informed of this, said, "Well, if he's not willing to walk      33
or haul and feels human passions in his lust for women and boys, slaughter him and give his guts to the dogs and keep his meat for our workers,
and if the question comes up as to how he died, blame it on a wolf."
Then that young fiend, my driver, was jubilant and wanted to slaughter
me right away. But one of the neighboring farmers happened to be there
at the time, and he preserved me from death with an awful plan he proposed for me.

"Surely," he said, "you shouldn't kill an ass that can grind and haul.
And it's no big matter. Since he's attracted to human beings by passion
and a relentless urge, take him and castrate him. Once relieved of this
erotic drive, he'll at once become gentle and fat and will carry a heavy
load without protest. If you're inexperienced personally in this surgery,
I'll come back in three or four days time and hand him over to you tamer
than a sheep after my excision."

Of course all those there approved of his sound advice, but I was already in tears at the thought of the instant loss of my manhood in my
ass's skin and told myself that I had no wish to go on living if I were to
become a eunuch. So I became determined to refuse all food from then
on or throw myself from the mountain, where, although falling to a
most pathetic death, I would die with my body whole and intact.

When it was deep night, a messenger came to the estate and farm      34
from the village with a report about the newly wed bride, the one who
had been captured by the robbers, and her groom. Around late evening
they had been taking a walk on the seashore, and suddenly the sea had
risen and carried them away out of sight, and they had met their end in
disaster and death. Since the house had been bereaved of its young owners, they decided to remain in slavery no longer, but after looting everything inside, they escaped to safety. The one who cared for the horses
took me and, grabbing everything he could, tied it on me and the other
horses and animals. I was angry at carrying a real ass's load, but on the
other hand I was happy to get this reprieve from castration.

Traveling the whole night on an uncomfortable road, we came to the end of it after three more days and arrived in Beroea, a large and well-populated city of Macedonia.[24]

35    There our drivers decided that we and they should settle there; a sale of us animals was arranged and a strong-voiced auctioneer stood in the middle of the marketplace and shouted for bids. Those who came up wanted to open and examine our mouths, and calculated each one's age from his teeth. The others were purchased by different people, but when I was the last left, the auctioneer told them to lead me back home. "As you see," he said, "this is the only one who hasn't found an owner." But constantly whirling and changing Nemesis[25] steered a master to me also, although not the sort I would have prayed 'for. For he was an old pervert, one of those who carry the Syrian goddess[26] around the villages and the countryside and force her to play the beggar. I was sold to this creature for the very high price of thirty drachmas.[27] Groaning inwardly, I now followed behind my master.

36    When we came to where Philebus[28] lived—for this was the name of the buyer—he immediately gave a loud shout in front of the door. "Girls, I've bought you a beautiful, strong slave of Cappadocian birth." These "girls," however, were a crowd of perverts, Philebus's coworkers, and they all clapped their hands at his yell, for they thought that what he had purchased was a real man. When they saw that the slave was an ass, they mocked Philebus now, saying: "This is no slave, but a new husband for yourself; so where did you bring him from? We hope you'll get some assets[29] out of this fine match and that you'll soon produce foals like
37    him." And they laughed. The next day they assembled for work, as they themselves termed it, decked out the goddess, and placed her on my

24. Now Verroia, about forty miles from Thessalonica.

25. Goddess of vengeance, who restores equilibrium in human affairs, dealing out happiness and unhappiness, and in particular humbling the proud or the too fortunate. "Whirling Nemesis" sounds like a quotation.

26. "Syrian goddess" was the Hellenistic description of the Semitic mother-goddess Atargatis, also identifiable with the Phoenician Astarte or with Cybele, the mother-goddess of Asia Minor. The cult involved ritual castration (cf. the legend of Attis), self-flagellation, and a close association with beasts, hence the appropriateness of the ass's addition to the company.

27. Thirty drachmas was obviously a high price. The next time the ass is sold (chapter 46) he goes for twenty-five *Attic* drachmas, regarded by the new owner as a reasonable price. The value of the Aeginetan drachma, which must be in question here, compared to the Attic drachma was 5:3; so the ass is bought for twice its market value. Probably in the original story much was made of the fact that it was bred in Cappadocia, a country famous for its sturdy pack animals and strong, if stupid, slaves. The corresponding passage in Apuleius (*Metamorphoses* 8.24–25) has the auctioneer make much of his origin, strength, and tameness.

28. As we have seen already, the names of the characters often have significance for the future action. Philebus, "lover of youth," will later participate in a sexual attack on a young villager (chapter 38).

29. To represent a possible pun in the Greek.

back. Then we drove out of the city and circulated through the countryside. Whenever we came to some village, I, as the vehicle of the goddess, would stand there, while the throng of flautists blew their inspired
strains, and the others ripped off their turbans; and, twisting their heads
down from their necks, they would lacerate their forearms with their
swords, and each would thrust his tongue through his teeth and cut this
too, so that in a moment everything was full of effeminate blood. When
I saw this, at first I stood trembling in case the goddess might develop a
need for ass's blood also. Whenever they cut themselves up like this, they
would collect obols and drachmas from the bystanders watching. Others
contributed dried figs, a jar of wine, and cheeses, as well as a big bushel
of wheat and barley for the ass. It was on these they subsisted and served
the goddess who was carried on my back.

One time we dropped in on a village in the region, and they hunted  38
down a hefty young man, one of the villagers, hauling him off to the
place where they happened to be staying. Then they passively underwent
from the villager all the usual things so much enjoyed by such evil perverts. I was deeply anguished by my change of shape, and I wanted to
shout, "Hard-hearted Zeus, what limits of degradation I have reached!"
But it wasn't my natural voice that came from my throat, but that of an
ass, and I let out a mighty bray. Some villagers at that time happened to
have lost an ass and in their search for the missing animal, hearing my
loud bellow, they came inside without speaking to anyone, under the
impression that I belonged to them, and they caught the perverts inside
at their unspeakable activities. A great laugh arose among the newcom
ers. Running outside, they went into details to the whole village about
the filthy behavior of the priests. They were dreadfully ashamed that
their goings-on had been unmasked, and the ensuing night they immediately moved out.

When they came to a deserted part of the road, they vented their indignation and rage at me for betraying their secret rituals. Grim enough
though it was to listen to their verbal abuse, it was tolerable, but what
followed became intolerable. Taking the goddess down from me and
laying her on the ground and snatching all the covers from me, they now
tied me bare to a large tree, and, lashing me with that knucklebone whip
of theirs, they must have come close to killing me, as they directed me
from now on to be a silent conveyance for the goddess. Indeed they were
planning to slaughter me after the whippings, as I had exposed them to a
great deal of abuse, and I had forced them out of the village before they
had done their work. But an obstacle to their killing me was the goddess,
lying on the ground with no way to travel, and she made them feel terribly guilty. After my whipping, then, I took up my lady and traveled on,  39
and now towards evening we stopped at a rich man's manor. He was at

home and received the goddess into his house very eagerly and brought her sacrificial offerings. There I discovered myself in great danger; for a friend of the lord of the manor had sent him as a gift a wild ass ham. The cook had taken it to prepare but through carelessness had lost it when a lot of dogs had sneaked in. In fear of a great whipping and torture because of the loss of the ham he decided to string himself up by the neck. His wife, however, was to be my ruin. "Don't die, darling, and don't abandon yourself to such deep despair. If you listen to me, you'll make everything turn out all right. Take the perverts' ass away to a lonely spot, then slaughter him and, cutting off that part, the ham, bring it here and serve it up to the master all prepared, and drop the remains of the ass into a ditch someplace. It'll look as though he's run off somewhere and vanished. You see what good meat he has on him, altogether superior to that wild ass." The cook praised his wife's idea, saying: "This notion of yours is excellent, my dear wife, and only by doing this can I escape a whipping. It's already as good as done."

40  Now this unholy scoundrel, my self-appointed cook, was standing near me as he plotted all this with his wife. Foreseeing already what was going to happen, I decided it would be the best thing to save myself from the knife, and, breaking the halter by which I was led and kicking up my hooves, I went running inside to where the perverts were dining with the master of the manse. Then, as I ran in, I overturned the lamp, tables, and everything with my kicking. I thought I had found a smart way of ensuring my safety and that the lord of the estate would immediately order me locked up somewhere and safely guarded as a high-spirited ass. This smart trick, however, brought me into extreme danger. Thinking I was crazy, they now snatched up a great number of swords and spears and long staves to set upon me, and so they got ready to kill me. Seeing the extent of the threat, I ran inside the room where my masters were going to sleep. When they saw this, they closed the doors very

41  tightly from outside. When dawn came, taking the goddess up once more, I went off with the charlatans, and we arrived at another village, large and well populated, where they introduced a strange new procedure whereby the goddess was not to stay in any mortal's house but was to have her abode in the temple of the local deity most revered among them. The inhabitants were delighted to welcome the foreign divinity and set her up in the home of their own goddess, but showed us to a house belonging to some paupers. After spending many days there, my masters wanted to leave for the city nearby and asked the townspeople for the return of the goddess, and, going themselves into the sacred precinct, they brought her out and, placing her on my back, drove away. Now, as it happened, the ungodly fellows, when they went into that sacred enclosure, filched a golden bowl, a votive offering, which they took away in the keeping of the goddess. When the village folk discovered

this, they immediately set off after us; then as they drew near, they jumped down from their horses, arrested the priests on the road, and began calling them sacrilegious temple robbers and demanding the return of the stolen votive offering. They searched everything and found it in the bosom of the goddess. Then tying up the pansies, they led them back and threw them into prison. The goddess who was riding on my back they took and presented to another temple and returned the gold vessel to the deity of their city.

The next day they decided to sell off the thieves' property, including   42 me, and they handed me over to a man from a nearby village, whose trade was baking bread. This fellow took me and, after buying ten large bushels of wheat, placed them on my back and drove me and himself home along a hard road. When we got there, he led me to the mill, and I saw inside a large pack of animals, my fellow slaves. There were a great number of mills, all being turned by them, and everywhere was full of flour. Then, as I was a new slave and carried a very heavy load along a hard road, they let me rest in there, but the next day they covered over my eyes with a piece of linen and yoked me to the spoke of the mill and then set me going. I knew how one was to grind from frequent experience, but I pretended ignorance; my hopes, however, were in vain. A lot of those working there, taking up cudgels, stood around me, and, just as I wasn't expecting it because I couldn't see, they whacked me in a concerted action, so that I suddenly whirled like a top from the blow. And I learned from experience that a slave should not wait for his master's hand before doing what he has to do.

Consequently I became very thin and physically weak, so that my   43 master decided to sell me, and he got rid of me to a market gardener, who had a patch to cultivate. This was our work schedule. At dawn the master loaded me with vegetables and took me to the market, and when he had handed them over to his customers, he took me back to his market garden. Then he used to dig, plant, and water his produce, while I stood around doing nothing. But life then was terribly irksome, first because it was now winter, and the master could not afford bedding for himself, let alone for me, and I was walking unshod on wet clay or rough, sharp ice,[30] and the only food for us both was bitter and stringy lettuce.

One day when we were leaving for the nursery, a gentleman in mili-   44 tary uniform came up to us. First[31] he spoke to us in Latin and asked the gardener where he was taking his ass, namely, me. He, through igno-

30. Macleod's reading (OCT).

31. The excerpter has omitted to specify the second language used in the original: probably broken or incomprehensible Greek. It should be remembered that the Roman armies of occupation often treated the provincials badly, and since they were under military and not local jurisdiction, it was hard, though not entirely impossible, for natives to get redress.

rance of the language, I suppose, made no reply. The other got angry, taking this as an insult, and struck the gardener with his whip. The latter then grappled with him, tripped him up and laid him flat on the road, and then struck at him lying there with hands, feet, and a rock from the roadside. At first the soldier fought back and threatened to kill him with his sword if he got to his feet again. My master, so forewarned by the soldier himself, to be really on the safe side, drew the soldier's sword and flung it into the distance and then resumed beating his prostrate opponent, who, faced now with an unbearable predicament, pretended he was dead from the beating. Scared by this, my master left him lying there as he was and, making me carry the sword, proceeded to the city.

45    When we got there, he entrusted his market garden to a colleague to care for, and he himself, afraid of the risk on the return road, went into hiding with me at the house of one of his friends in the town. The next day, after mulling it over, what they did was this. They hid my master in a chest; then taking me by the feet, they carried me up the ladder to an attic and there locked me up. The soldier, having just managed to get himself up from the road, so they reported, and with his head aching from the blows, had got to the city and, encountering his army mates, told them of the demented behavior of the nurseryman. They accompanied him and found where we were hidden and brought along the city authorities. They sent inside one of their subordinates and ordered all the occupants to come outside. When they came out, the nurseryman was nowhere to be seen. Thereupon the soldiers insisted that the nurseryman, as well as I, his ass, was in there. The occupants, however, said there was nothing left inside, neither nurseryman nor ass. With all this confusion and their loud shouting in the alley, brassy and always curious and wanting to know who was doing the shouting, I shoved my head down through the window. On sight of me, the soldiers immediately raised an uproar, and the occupants were trapped in their lies. The authorities went in and, after a complete search, discovered my master in the chest. Arresting him, they sent him to prison to face charges for his disorderly behavior. Me they carried down and handed over to the soldiers. They all laughed uncontrollably at the informer from upstairs, who had turned in his own master. Therefore, because of me, there originated that common saying among people "from the snooping of an ass."[32]

46    What happened the next day to my master, the market gardener, I don't know, but the soldier decided to put me up for sale and got twenty-five Attic drachmas for me.[33] The buyer was the servant of a

---

32. A tag from Menander's comedy *The Priestess* (frag. 246 Kock). According to our ancient sources, it was applied to lawsuits brought on ridiculous grounds. Here it is applied, reasonably enough, to a ridiculous informant.

33. See note 27 above.

very wealthy man from Thessalonica, the largest city in Macedonia. This man's occupation was preparing his master's meat courses, and he had a brother, a fellow slave, whose expertise was bread baking and honey confectionery.[34] These brothers were always inseparable; they lodged in the same place and kept the tools of their trades thrown together, and from then on, they put me up where they lodged. After their master had dinner, both of them would bring in quantities of leftovers, one of meat and fish, the other of bread and cakes. Then locking me up inside with all of this and putting me in the most delectable custody, they went off for a bath. I bade a fond farewell to the barley laid in front of me and would concentrate on the products of my masters' skills, and I would stuff myself on human food at long last. When they would return, at first they didn't notice at all my gourmet diet because of the amounts of food lying about, and I was stealing my meals nervously and cautiously. But finally, realizing their unawareness, I used to gobble down the nicest bits and a lot more besides, and when they did become wise to their losses, at first they both looked at each other suspiciously, and one called the other a thief and a shameless pilferer of their common property. After this, they were both very careful, and an account was kept of the delicacies.

But I continued my life of pleasure and luxury, and on this normal 47 diet my body became handsome once more, and my hide regained its luster as the hair grew out again. These respectable fellows, seeing me big and fat and the barley not depleted but remaining at the same level, developed a suspicion about my bold behavior, and, going out as though off to the baths, they then closed the doors, and, putting their eyes to a chink in the door, they watched what went on inside. Then, completely unaware of their trick, I went and ate my meal. At first they laughed at my unbelievable repast, then they called over their fellow slaves to look at me, and there was such hearty laughter that their master heard it because of the din outside his quarters, and he asked what was causing such amusement among those outside. When he heard, he got up from the party, and, peering in, he saw me devouring a piece of wild boar, and came running in bellowing with laughter. I took it very hard that I had been caught out in my master's presence as a thief as well as a glutton, but he guffawed loudly at me and first commanded me to be brought to the party and then ordered a table to be set up in front of me and on it to be put a lot of things that no other ass could stomach: meat, shellfish, soups, fish, some marinated in fish sauce[35] and olive oil, some smothered in mustard. Seeing that fortune was fondly smiling on me and realizing that only this piece of comedy would save me, I stood by the table, and

---

34. Such refined divisions of labor were common in wealthy Greco-Roman households.

35. The Roman *garum*, a pungent sauce of rotted fish entrails, somewhat similar to the Southeast Asian fish sauce, *nuoc nam*, which is made in the same manner.

although I was already bloated, I dined away nevertheless. The party went into peals of laughter, and someone said, "This ass will drink wine if someone will mix it and give it to him." The master gave the instructions, and I drank what I was offered.

48  Seeing in me, naturally enough, an incredible acquisition, he told one of his household staff to give the man who bought me my purchase price and as much again, and he entrusted me to the care of a young freedman on his staff and told him to train me in all the things that I could do that would most amuse him. Everything was easy for him, for I promptly obeyed him at every lesson. First he made me recline on a couch on my elbow, just like a man, then wrestle with him, even dance upright on my two legs, and nod assent or dissent when asked a question, and do all the things I could have done without instruction. The whole business became widely talked about, an ass devoted to his master, a wine bibber, a wrestler, an ass that danced, and the biggest thing still was that I nodded agreement or disagreement at the right time in response to questions. And whenever I wanted a drink, I would nudge the waiter and ask for it with my eyes. They were all astonished at this extraordinary feat, little realizing that there was a man underneath the ass, but I made their ignorance provide my high living. What's more, I learned to parade with my master on my back and to run at a speed that was very comfortable and imperceptible to my rider. I had an expensive outfit and the coverlets thrown on me were purple, and I was given bridles inlaid with silver and gold, and the bells fastened to me produced a most melodious tune.

49  Menecles, our master, had come there from Thessalonica, as I've said, for the following reason: he had promised to put on in his native city an exhibition of fighters trained for armed single combat. The men were by this time all ready for the contest, and the time for departure had arrived. So we moved off at dawn, and I carried my master wherever there was a rough stretch of the road that made it difficult for the carriages to proceed. As we arrived in Thessalonica, there was no one who didn't dash out to see the spectacle and get a glimpse of me. My reputation had preceded me well in advance, what with my acting ability and the human character of my dancing and wrestling. My master, however, showed me off only to the most eminent of his fellow citizens over drinks and presented at dinner those astounding comic tricks I had mastered.

50  My overseer found a way to make a great many drachmas out of me, for he used to lock me standing in a stall and charged a fee to open the door for those who wished to see me and my amazing tricks. They used to bring in different kinds of food, particularly the sorts they believed would be indigestible to the stomach of an ass. But I used to eat them, so that in a few days, after dining with my master and the townspeople, I had become by this time terribly big and fat.

One day a foreign woman of more than moderate means and decent looks came in to watch me eating and fell hotly in love with me,[36] not only because she saw what a beautiful ass I was, but also because the amazing nature of my talents stimulated in her a longing to sleep with me. She spoke to my custodian and promised him a large sum if he would allow her to spend the night with me. Since he didn't care whether she would succeed with me or not, he accepted the money.

When it was evening, and our master had dismissed us from the party, we returned to our quarters and found that the lady had long since settled down in my bed. Soft pillows had been brought for her, mattresses had been laid down inside, and a bed was all nicely prepared for us on the floor. Then the lady's servants laid themselves down to sleep somewhere near the room, and she inside lit a huge, flaming lamp. Then, taking off her clothes, she stood totally naked by the lamp, and, pouring out some oil from an alabaster jar, she smeared it on herself. Then she rubbed the oil on me, inserting quantities of the fragrant stuff into my nose. Then she kissed me and said all the things she would say to a beloved who was human, and, grasping me by the halter, she dragged me onto the palliasse. I needed no additional invitation for this; tipsy from large amounts of vintage wine and stimulated by the perfumed oil, I beheld a young girl beautiful in every detail. I lay down and of course felt at a great loss as to how to mount a female; for since I had become an ass, I had had no experience of even the intercourse usual for asses, and I had not had recourse to a female ass. Indeed, this fact aroused in me an excessive fear that the lady could not accommodate me and she would be torn apart and I would have a fine penalty to pay as her slayer. I didn't realize that I was needlessly frightened, for the lady emboldened me with lots of kisses, and amorous ones at that. When she saw I was losing control, lying beside me as though I were a man, she pulled me into her arms and, lifting me inside her, took the whole length. I was a coward and still frightened, so I began gently withdrawing, but she gripped my tenderloin so that it couldn't slip out, and her body came after it as it moved back. Once I was properly convinced that more was required of me for her pleasure and gratification, I serviced her after that without restraint, thinking myself no worse than Pasiphaë's seducer.[37] The woman was so ready for sex and so insatiable for the delights of intercourse that she spent the whole night with me.

51

36. The unbridled and unnatural lusts of upper-class women provide a frequent theme for ancient myths, novels, and satires. Examples similar to this may be found in Petronius, Juvenal, Apuleius, and others.

37. Pasiphaë, queen of Cnossos in Crete, fell in love with a handsome white bull. With the aid of Daedalus, she mated with him and gave birth to the Minotaur. Mythical tales of heroines mating with gods in various animal guises are of course numerous and were accepted as part of the natural order of things, unlike incest.

52    With daylight she rose and left, arranging with my guardian to pay the same price on the same conditions for that night. Since he wanted to get richer from my activities and at the same time show his master my latest performance, he locked me in with the woman, and she wore me out dreadfully. Then when the occasion arose, the custodian went to his master with the news of my performance, as though he'd trained me to it himself, and without my knowledge, he conducted him, when it was now evening, to where we lay together, and through a crack in the door he displayed me inside bedding down the girl. Exhilarated by the show, his master fancied exhibiting me with this performance in public and told him to tell nobody outside about it. "In this way," he said, "on the day of the show we may bring him into the amphitheater along with one of the condemned females, and in front of everybody's eyes he'll mount the woman." Then they brought into my presence one of the women who had been condemned to death by wild beasts, and ordered her to come near me and play around with me.

53    Then at last the big day arrived when my master was to display his generosity to the public,[38] and they decided to introduce me in the amphitheater. So I came on. There was a large couch, fashioned from Indian tortoiseshell, inlaid with gold; they laid me down on it and laid the woman there by my side. Then they put us on a mechanical conveyer, and, rolling us out into the amphitheater, they set us out in the center, and the people yelled out loudly, and there was applause for me from every hand. A table was set on one side of us, and on it were served many of the delicacies that gourmets have for dinner. Handsome young wine waiters were in attendance, serving us wine in golden chalices. Then my custodian, standing behind me, encouraged me to eat. But I was embarrassed at being exposed in the amphitheater and also scared that a bear or

54    a lion from somewhere would leap on me. At this point a man passed by carrying flowers,[39] and among the other flowers I noticed also the petals of fresh roses; with no more fear I jumped up and tumbled from the bed. The audience thought I was standing up to dance. But running through the flowers one by one, I culled the roses from them and swallowed them down. While they were still aghast at me, that bestial form fell away from me and was erased, and the old ass vanished, and Lucius himself, inside my own skin, stood there naked.

At the extraordinary and utterly unexpected spectacle everyone was stunned and raised a terrible hullabaloo, with the audience divided into two minds. Some demanded that I should be immediately burned to death in there as an expert in evil spells, an evildoer with many shapes;

---

38. For those with political ambitions games and spectacles were a frequent way of courting popularity.
39. Macleod's reading (Loeb).

other recommended delay and hearing what I had to say before pronouncing on the matter. I ran to the governor of the province, as he happened to be there at the show, and told him from below that a Thessalian woman, the slave of another Thessalian woman, had anointed me with a magic lotion and turned me into an ass, and I begged him to take me and hold me in custody until I could persuade him that I was not lying about my change of shape.

The governor said, "Tell us your name, that of your parents and any relations, if you claim to have any close kin, and your city." 55

"My father," I said, "is … [40] My name is Lucius, and my brother's name is Gaius. The other two names we have in common with our father. I am a writer of stories and other things, and he is an elegiac poet and a fine prophet. Our native town is Patras[41] in Achaea."

When the magistrate heard this, he said, "You are the son of people most dear to me, who have received me as hosts in their house and honored me with gifts, and I know that if you are their son, you would tell no lie." And jumping from his chair, he hugged me and kissed me many times and escorted me to his own home like an equal. Meanwhile my brother arrived, bringing me money and a lot of other things, and with this the governor, as everyone listened, publicly released me. We went down to the sea, sought out a ship, and loaded our baggage. I thought it 56 a very good idea to pay a visit to the lady who had been in love with me as an ass, telling myself that I would look more handsome now I was in my human shape. She welcomed me happily, titillated, I suppose, by the whole extraordinary affair, and she begged me to have dinner and stay the night with her. I accepted, thinking that I would deserve the vengeance of heaven if the adored ass, on returning to human shape, were to become fastidious and reject the woman who had loved him. I dine with her, anoint myself profusely with fragrant oil, and crown myself with roses, the dearest of flowers, that had saved me to rejoin mankind. When it is now deep night and bedtime, I get up, and as though I was doing her a great favor, I take off my clothes and stand naked, under the impression that I would be still more attractive by contrast with the ass, but when she saw that everything about me was human, spitting at me, she said: "Why don't you go to hell? Leave me and my house. Go away and sleep somewhere else, far away from here."

When I asked, "And what terrible outrage have I committed?" she said: "I was in love not with you, by God, but with your ass, and it was he I slept with, not you, and I thought that even now you would still keep trailing along that one mighty badge of the ass. But you have come

---

40. The name of Lucius's father has dropped out of the manuscripts.
41. Patras, in the Peloponnese, is situated on the Gulf of Patras and is about 75 miles from Corinth.

to me transformed from that beautiful and serviceable animal into a monkey."

She immediately summoned her servants and ordered me carried from the house stretched high on their backs. I was pushed outside in front of the house, and there, naked, elegantly wreathed, and perfumed, I clasped the naked earth for my bed partner. At the break of dawn, I ran to the ship, naked as I was, and told my brother of my amusing debacle. Then with a fair wind we sailed away from that city, and within a few days I reached my native home. There I made sacrifices and set up memorials to the gods who had preserved me, since after so long and so narrowly I had escaped home, not, by God, "from the ass of a dog," as the saying goes, but from the snooping of an ass.[42]

42. Contextually these two proverbial allusions seem to mean "I escaped the consequences, not of evildoing, but of excessive curiosity." The meaning of "the ass of a dog" (found twice in Aristophanes) may go back to the fable of the reed that pricked the dog before it could defecate on it—its moral: Keep wrongdoers at a distance. "The snooping of an ass" may be a variant on the earlier proverbial phrase, used at the end of chapter 45, or may just refer to the excessive curiosity that turned Lucius into an ass. See the Loeb edition for further details.

# LUCIAN

# A TRUE STORY

## TRANSLATED BY
## B. P. REARDON

### Introduction

The name of Lucian is well enough known, but usually one thinks of him not as a writer of romance but as a satirist. He did, however, write some works that we should characterize as not only satire but also prose fiction: *The Lover of Lies,* for instance, and, above all, *A True Story (Verae Historiae),* which has been a favorite since the Renaissance, whether for the simple Greek of its narrative or for its amusing quality as an early Baron Munchausen tale. It is an account of a fantastic journey—to the moon, the underworld, the belly of a whale, and so forth. It is not really science fiction, although it has sometimes been called that; there is no "science" in it. Above all, it is a parody of literary "liars" like Homer and Herodotus. Whatever it may now be to us, in intention the tale is a sort of literary criticism. But we are not in an ideal position to judge it as such, since many of the works the author is making fun of are not now extant, except in fragments in some cases: those of Ctesias, Iambulus, and Antonius Diogenes, for instance, all of whom wrote of wonderful journeys. Antonius Diogenes wrote on *The Wonders Beyond Thule* (included in this volume), and his work included a description of a trip to the moon. He has often been regarded as Lucian's main source and target, but this may be a mistaken view.[1] *A True Story* certainly reflects a wide range of earlier literature. And the very title is ironic: "I warn you,"

---

1. See J. R. Morgan, "Lucian's *True Histories* and the *Wonders Beyond Thule* of Antonius Diogenes," *Classical Quarterly* 35(1985): 475–90; and C. P. Jones, *Culture and Society in Lucian* (Cambridge, Mass., and London, 1986), 53–54.

says Lucian at the outset, "that I am going to tell you the biggest lies you ever heard; and this is the only true statement in the whole book."

The claim of this piece to inclusion in the present volume may be thought tenuous, but the novel, or romance—prose fiction—cannot be confined too fine, in antiquity or any other age. In his way Lucian was making use of the classical tradition rather as his novelist contemporaries (such as Achilles Tatius) were. He lived from about A.D. 120 to some time after 180, so the piece was probably written in the third quarter of the second century; and that seems to be the very heyday of the novel. Lucian himself was not a Greek, but a Syrian, from Samosata on the Euphrates; Greek was not his native language. But he had a strong regard for the heritage of Greece, and was also keenly alive to the literary and cultural movements and quarrels of his own times. The existence of this bubbling work is itself testimony to the vigorous literary life of the period. The reader will no doubt notice that the fantasy is well sustained throughout the first book, but the author evidently grows increasingly tired of it in the second. That is characteristic of Lucian.

Because of the nature of this work, full annotation could be cumbrous. Many of Lucian's targets are familiar figures or elements in classical tradition and can easily be pursued in standard reference works, such as *The Oxford Classical Dictionary*. The reader may also profitably be referred to volume 1 of the Loeb edition of Lucian, to which I am indebted for some of the material in the notes.

## Bibliography

TEXT

*Lucian.* Vol. 1. Edited by A. M. Harmon. London and Cambridge, Mass., 1913 (Loeb Classical Library).

Luciani. *Opera.* Vol. 1. Edited by M. D. Macleod. Oxford, 1972 (Oxford Classical Texts).

GENERAL

Anderson, G. *Lucian's Comic Fiction.* Leiden, 1976. See pages 1–11.

Bompaire, J. *Lucien écrivain.* Paris, 1958. See pages 658–73, in particular.

Reyhl, K. "Antonios Diogenes." Diss., Tübingen, 1969.

# A TRUE STORY

## *Book One*

ATHLETES AND PEOPLE who take an interest in the care of the body do not confine their attentions to physical exercise and attaining a good condition. They take thought also for relaxation at appropriate intervals; indeed, they consider it the most important element in training. Similarly, in my opinion, literary people should after extended reading of serious authors relax mentally, to refresh themselves against subsequent exertions. They will find this interlude agreeable if they choose as company such works as not only afford wit, charm, and distraction pure and simple, but also provoke some degree of cultured reflection.

I trust the present work will be found to inspire such reflection. My readers will be attracted not merely by the novelty of the subject, the appeal of the general design, and the conviction and verisimilitude with which I compound elaborate prevarications, but also by the humorous allusions in every part of my story to various poets, historians, and philosophers of former times who have concocted long, fantastic yarns— writers I should mention by name did I not think their identities would be obvious to you as you read. For instance, Ctesias of Cnidos, the son of Ctesiochus, wrote an account of India and its customs; he had neither himself seen nor heard from any reliable source the things he wrote about. Iambulus, too, wrote a long account of the wonders of the great ocean; anybody can see it is fictitious, but it is quite entertaining nonetheless as a theme. And there have been many others who have written with the same intention, purporting to relate their own travels abroad and writing about great beasts and savage tribes and strange ways of life. The founder of this school of literary horseplay is Homer's Odysseus, with his stories at Alcinous's court of winds enslaved and men with one eye and cannibals and wild men, of many-headed beasts and of how his crew were drugged and transformed; he spun many such fanciful stories to the Phaeacians, who knew no better.

So when I came across all these writers, I did not feel that their romancing was particularly reprehensible; evidently it was already traditional, even among professed philosophers;[1] though what did surprise me was their supposition that nobody would notice they were lying. Now, I too in my vanity was anxious to bequeath something to posterity; I did not wish to be the only one to make no use of this liberty in

---

1. An allusion to Plato's penchant for allegory (e.g., *Republic* 10).

yarn spinning—for I had no true story to relate, since nothing worth mentioning had ever happened to me; and consequently I turned to romancing myself. But I am much more sensible about it than others are, for I will say one thing that is true, and that is that I am a liar. It seems to me that to confess voluntarily to untruthfulness acquits me of the charge, should other people bring it. My subject, then, is things I have neither seen nor experienced nor heard tell of from anybody else: things, what is more, that do not in fact exist and could not ever exist at all. So my readers must not believe a word I say.

5    I set out one day from the Pillars of Hercules and sailed with a following wind into the western ocean. My voyage was prompted by an active intellect and a passionate interest in anything new; the object I proposed to myself was to discover the limits of the ocean and what men dwelt beyond it. For this reason I took a great deal of food on board, and plenty of water. I got hold of fifty men of my own age and interests, as well as quite a store of arms, hired the best navigator I could find at a considerable salary, and strengthened the ship—a light transport—for a long and trying voyage.

6    For a day and a night we sailed along gently with a following wind and with land still in sight. At dawn the next day the wind began to rise, the sea grew stormy, and the sky was overcast. Soon we could not even take in sail; so we ran before the wind and let ourselves be tossed hither and thither for seventy-nine days. On the eightieth the sun came out suddenly, and we saw a mountainous, thickly wooded island close by, with the sea murmuring gently around it—for by now the swell had almost subsided. So we put in and went ashore. There we lay on the ground for a long time, after our long ordeal; however, we did get up, and split ourselves into two parties, thirty staying to guard the ship and twenty coming with me to explore the island.

7    Going through the woods, about six hundred yards from the shore we saw a bronze pillar with a faded, worn inscription in Greek that said "Hercules and Dionysus reached this point." Nearby, on a rock, were two footprints, one a hundred feet long, the other smaller. The smaller I supposed to belong to Dionysus, the other to Hercules.[2] We made our obeisances and went on. Before we had gone very far, we found ourselves beside a river running wine very like Chian; it was of some size and depth, even being navigable in some places. We were led to put much more confidence in the inscription on the pillar when we saw this evidence of Dionysus's visit. I decided to find the source of the river. Going upstream I found, not indeed any spring from which it issued, but a great many large vines loaded with grapes. By the root of each of these

2. Herodotus (4.82) speaks of a footprint three feet long left by Hercules in Scythia.

flowed a trickle of clear wine, and it was from these that the river was formed. We could actually see a lot of fish in it. Their flesh was vinous both in color and taste; anyway, we caught some and got drunk eating them. Of course they were full of wine lees when we cut them open. Later on, though, we hit on the idea of mixing them with water-fish and thus diluting this strong wine-food.

Then we crossed the river where there was a ford, and discovered  8 some vines of a marvelous kind; they had firm, thick stems lower down, but the upper parts were female figures, complete in every detail from the flanks up. They looked just like the pictures one sees of Daphne turning into a tree just as Apollo takes hold of her. The vine shoots, loaded with grapes, grew from the tips of their fingers; the hair of their heads also was tendrils and leaves and fruit. They gave us welcome as we approached and greeted us in Lydian, Indian, and—the majority of them—Greek. They also kissed us, and anyone who was kissed became drunk immediately and began to stagger about. But they would not let us pluck the fruit, crying out in pain as we tugged at it. Some of them even evinced sexual passion; two of my comrades embraced them, only to find themselves caught by the genitals and unable to free themselves. They became one with the plants and took root beside them; their fingers at once put forth shoots, tendrils grew all over them, and they too were on the point of bearing fruit.

We left them and hastily regained the ship; there we told those who  9 had stayed behind everything that had happened, including our comrades' affair with the vines. Then we took some jars to fill with water and also with river-wine, and camped for the night on the shore near the boat.

In the morning we put to sea with a gentle wind. About midday, when the island was out of sight, a whirlwind suddenly arose, whirling our ship around and raising it some forty miles into the air. But it did not deposit us back on the sea, for when we were hanging in midair, a wind struck, billowed our sails, and carried us along. For seven days and  10 as many nights we sailed through the air, and on the eighth saw a large tract of land suspended in the atmosphere like an island; it was bright and spherical, and bathed in strong light. We put in to it, anchored, and went ashore. On exploring the land, we found it to be inhabited and cultivated. We could see nothing from it during the daytime, but when night fell many other islands became visible near to it, some larger, some smaller, the color of fire. There was also another land below us, with cities, rivers, seas, forests, and mountains; this we supposed to be our earth.

Deciding to continue the voyage, we fell in with and were appre-  11 hended by what they call Horse-vultures. These are men mounted on

great vultures, which they manage like horses. The vultures are very big,
and most of them have three heads. You may imagine their size from the
fact that every one of their feathers is longer and thicker than the mast of
a big cargo ship. The job of these Horse-vultures is to patrol the land and
bring any intruder they may come across to the king—as they did with
us.

The king inspected us and, guessing from the look of us and from our
dress that we were Greeks, asked us, when we said we were, how we
had managed to cover all that distance in the air to get where we were.
We told him the whole story; whereupon he launched into a complete
account of himself. It appeared that he too was a man, called Endymion;
he had been snatched from our earth one day while he was asleep and
conveyed to where he now was, and on his arrival had become king of
the country. The land was, he said, what appeared as the moon from
earth. He told us to be of good heart and not suspect danger, for we
would have everything we needed. "And if I am successful," he said, "in
the campaign I am now beginning against the inhabitants of the Sun, you
will have the happiest life imaginable with me."

We asked him who the enemy were and what the quarrel was about.
"Phaethon," he said, "the king of the Sun-dwellers—for the Sun is inhabited just as the Moon is—has been conducting a war against us for a
long time now. It began when one day I collected together the poorest
people in my realm, with the intention of sending a colony to the Morning Star, which is uninhabited and deserted. Phaethon was jealous of the
idea. He mounted his Horse-ants and encountered us half way there to
prevent the colonization. Well, on that occasion we were defeated, being
unequal in strength, and withdrew. But now I want to restart the war
and send out my colony. So if you would like to join my expedition, I
shall mount you all on vultures from the royal stables and provide all
your equipment. We start tomorrow." "All right," I said, "if you want
us to."

So for the time being we stayed to be entertained at his court. At
dawn we rose and took our positions, the scouts reporting that the enemy were near. The army numbered a hundred thousand, not counting
baggage trains, engineers, infantry, or allied forces from elsewhere.
Eighty thousand of these were Horse-vultures, twenty thousand were
troops mounted on Vegetable-wings—another kind of bird, also very
large, with vegetable shoots all over its body in place of plumage and
quill feathers just like lettuce leaves. Next to those were the Millet-
slingers and Garlic-fighters. Allies came to his assistance from the Great
Bear also—thirty thousand Flea-archers and fifty thousand Wind-runners. The Flea-archers ride great fleas—hence their name—and each flea
is as big as twelve elephants. The Wind-runners are infantry but travel

through the air without wings, in the following manner: they wear tunics that reach to their feet, and by so girding them as to make the wind belly them out like sails, they are blown along like ships. They are generally used as light troops in battle. There were also supposed to be seventy thousand Sparrow-acorns and five thousand Horse-cranes coming from the stars above Cappadocia. As they did not arrive, I did not see them; hence I have not presumed to describe them—report made them out wonderful creatures, too wonderful to be credible.[3]

This was Endymion's army. They were all armed the same way: the helmets were made of beans, which grow big and hard there; the breastplates were all of overlapping lupine scales, stitched together, the scales being hard as horn. The shields and swords were Greek in style. When the moment came, they were drawn up as follows. On the right were the Horse-vultures and the king, with his best troops around him; we were among these. On the left were the Vegetable-wings, and in the center the allied contingents in no particular formation. The infantry numbered about sixty million, drawn up as follows. On the Moon there grow enormous spiders, each one much bigger than the islands of the Cyclades; these were instructed to spin a web across the sky between the Moon and the Morning Star, and as soon as they had constructed a plain by this means, the infantry was drawn up on it, under the command of Bat, son of Fairweatherlord, and two others.

14

15

The enemy left wing was held by Phaethon with the Horse-ants. These are great beasts with wings, just like our ants except in size,[4] for the biggest of them was two hundred feet long. It was not only their riders who fought; they themselves were very effective with their horns. There were said to be about fifty thousand of them. On their right were drawn up the Sky-gnats, also about fifty thousand in number, all archers riding on great gnats. Next to them came the Sky-dancers, light-armed infantry but useful in battle nonetheless, for they slung great radishes from long range, and whoever was struck by them could not last even a short time but died from the foul-smelling wounds they caused; they were said to rub mallow juice on their missiles. Close by them were drawn up the Stalk-mushrooms, heavy-armed close fighters, ten thousand of them, so called because they used mushrooms as shields and asparagus stalks as spears. Near them were the Acorn-dogs, sent to Phaethon by the people of the Dog Star. There were five thousand of them, men with dogs' faces,[5] fighting from winged acorns. It was reported that some of the enemy's allies also missed the battle—the slingers he sent for from the Milky Way, and the Cloud-centaurs. The latter did

16

3. Herodotus often withholds his own belief in what he records.
4. See Herodotus 3.102 for ants bigger than foxes.
5. See Herodotus 4.191 for dog-headed men in Libya.

arrive, unfortunately, when the battle was already over; the slingers did not appear at all, for which reason it was said Phaethon afterward vented his anger on them by scorching their land.

17     This was the force with which Phaethon advanced. As soon as the standards were raised and the donkeys on each side had brayed—they used donkeys as trumpeters—they began to fight. The Sunite left fled at once without waiting for the Horse-vultures to come to close quarters, and we followed them, slaughtering as we went. Their right wing, however, overcame our left, and the Sky-gnats pressed their pursuit as far as the infantry. Then, when these came to the rescue, they turned and fled, especially when they saw their own left wing beaten. It was a splendid victory, with many prisoners taken and many casualties; a great deal of blood flowed onto the clouds, so that they appeared to be dyed red, as we see them at sunset. A deal of blood also dropped onto the earth, leading me to wonder if it was not some similar event in the heavens long ago that made Homer suppose Zeus had rained blood at the death of Sarpedon.[6]

18     Returning from the pursuit, we set up two trophies, one in celebration of the infantry battle, on the spiders' webs, the other on the clouds for the fight in midair. In the middle of this activity, scouts announced that the Cloud-centaurs, who should have reported to Phaethon before the battle, were approaching. And indeed we could see them close at hand; they were a very odd sight, a mixture of men and winged horses. The human part, from the middle up, was the size of the Colossus of Rhodes;[7] the horse part as big as a cargo vessel. I do not record the numbers of them, however, lest I be disbelieved, so many were they. Their commander was the Archer of the Zodiac. When they saw that their side had been beaten, they sent a message to Phaethon to tell him to come back and attack again, and themselves made a formation attack upon the scattered Moonites, who were in disorder all over, in pursuit and in search of plunder. They routed the whole army and pursued the king himself to the city, killing most of his birds. They also tore down the trophies and overran the cobweb plain. I and two of my comrades were taken prisoner. By now Phaethon was on the scene also, setting up his own trophies. We were taken to the Sun that day, our hands tied behind our backs with a piece of cobweb.

19     They decided not to besiege the city but turned back and built a wall through the sky between Sun and Moon, so that the Sun's rays no longer reached the Moon. The wall was made of a double thickness of clouds;

6. See *Iliad* 16.459–61.

7. A huge statue of the sun-god, Helius, at the entrance to the harbor at Rhodes; despite Shakespeare and popular belief, it did not *bestride* the entrance. It was brought down by an earthquake in 224 B.C.

the Moon was totally eclipsed and plunged into continuous night. Endymion was severely tried by these measures; he sent to beg the Sunites to tear down the wall and not make his people live their lives in darkness, promising to pay tribute, to conclude an alliance, and not to make war again, and expressing readiness to give hostages for the observance of these conditions. Phaethon's people held two assemblies. In the first they would not temper their anger in the slightest degree, but in the second they changed their minds,[8] and peace was concluded on the following terms.[9]

Terms of the peace treaty concluded between the Sunites with their allies and the Moonites with their allies.    20

1. The Sunites shall demolish the separating wall, not invade the moon again, and restore the prisoners at fixed rates of ransom.

2. The Moonites shall give autonomy to the other stars and not bear arms against the Sunites.

3. Each party shall assist the other in the event of any aggression.

4. The King of the Moonites shall pay to the King of the Sunites a yearly tribute of ten thousand jars of dew and give hostages of his own subjects to the number of ten thousand.

5. The colonization of the Morning Star shall be undertaken jointly, and anyone of any other nationality who so wishes shall take part.

6. The treaty shall be inscribed on a pillar of amber and set up in mid-air at the border.

Sworn to by Fireman, Hot, and Blazer of the Sunites, and by Nighttime, Moonday, and Flashbright of the Moonites.

These were the terms of the peace. The wall was pulled down at once,    21 and we were released from captivity. When we reached the Moon, my comrades and Endymion himself met us, weeping for joy. Endymion wanted me to stay and take part in the colonization; he promised me his own son in marriage (there not being any women on the Moon). I did not want to, however; I asked to be sent down to the sea again. When he saw that we were not to be entreated, he entertained us for a week before sending us off.

I should like to describe the novel and unusual things I noticed during    22 my stay on the Moon. First of all, they are born not of woman but of man; their marriages are of male with male, and they do not even know the word "woman" at all. Up to the age of twenty-five they all act as female partners, and thereafter as husbands. Pregnancy occurs not in the womb but in the calf of the leg, for after conception the calf grows fat. After a time they cut it open and bring out a lifeless body, which they lay

8. Like the Athenians over Mytilene; see Thucydides 3.36 and 49.
9. Cf. any Greek treaty, e.g., Thucydides 5.18.

out with its mouth open facing the wind and bring to life. I imagine that this is the origin of the Greek word "calf,"[10] inasmuch as on the Moon it is this part of the body that produces young, and not the belly. But I shall tell you about something more marvelous yet. There is on the Moon a kind of men called Treemen, and the manner of their generation is as follows. They cut off a man's right testicle and plant it in the ground; from it there grows an enormous tree of flesh, like a phallus. It has branches and foliage, and its fruit is acorns as long as the forearm. When they are ripe, they harvest them and carve men from them, adding genitals of ivory, or of wood for the poorer ones; these are what they use to consummate their male marriages.

23    When a man grows old, he does not die but dissolves into the air like smoke. They all consume the same food; they light a fire and roast frogs on the embers—on the Moon there are a great number of frogs flying in the air—and as they are roasting, they sit in circles as if around a table and suck in the vapor that arises;[11] this constitutes their meal. Such, then, is their food; their drink is air compressed into a cup to give off a moisture like dew. They do not, however, perform the functions of evacuation as we do; indeed, they do not have orifices where we have them—in their intercourse with the young they use orifices behind the knee above the calf of the leg.

To be beautiful on the Moon is to be bald and hairless; people with a thick head of hair they abominate. On comets the opposite holds good: it is people with good hair who are thought handsome, as some foreigners told me.[12] They grow beards, though, just above the knee. They do not have toenails, and they all have one toe on each foot. Over the buttocks they all have large cabbages growing, like tails; these cabbages are evergreen, and do not break off if the owner falls on his back.

24    When they blow their noses, they get a bitter honey; and after hard work or exercise the whole body sweats milk, to which they add a drop of the honey to make it congeal into cheese. They make from onions a very shiny oil, as fragrant as perfume. They also have a lot of water vines; that is, the grapes are like hail. To my mind, it is a gust of wind shaking these vines that bursts the clusters and makes hail fall on earth. The belly they use as a bag to put necessaries in; it opens and shuts, and appears to contain no intestines, only an inner lining of thick hair—their young creep inside when it is cold.

25    The clothing of the rich is of soft glass; that of the poor of woven brass;[13] their land is rich in brass, which they moisten with water and

---

10. The Greek word for "calf of the leg" is literally "belly of the leg."

11. See Herodotus 1.202.

12. Because "comet" means "hairy star."

13. Herodotus (7.65) speaks of clothing "made from wood"—i.e., of cotton; and Lucian extends this.

work like wool. I hesitate to mention the nature of their eyes; it sounds incredible; still, I will do so. Their eyes are removable. They can take them out at will and put them away until they need to see; then they insert them, and their sight returns. They often lose their own and borrow other people's to see with; some of them, the rich, have a large reserve of them. For ears they have plane leaves—except the acorn people, who have wooden ones.

And I saw another marvelous thing in the palace. There is a huge mirror there, suspended over a quite shallow well. If you go down the well, you can hear everything that is said down here on earth; and if you look in the mirror, you can see every city and nation just as if you were standing over them. I actually saw my own people and country when I was there; whether they saw me too I cannot say for sure. Anyone who does not believe this has only to go there himself someday to find out that I am telling the truth.     26

Well, anyway, we took a fond farewell of the king and his court, embarked, and set out. Endymion actually presented me with two glass tunics, five brass ones, and a complete set of lupine armor, all of which I left behind in the whale. He also sent a thousand Horse-vultures to escort us for the first sixty miles.     27

On our journey we passed various countries, and actually landed on the Morning Star to take on water; it was in the process of being colonized. Entering the Zodiac, we passed the Sun on our port bow, almost touching the land as we sailed; many of the crew were very keen to land, but the wind was against us and we did not. We could, however, see that the land was fertile and rich and well watered and full of good things of many kinds. The Cloud-centaurs, Phaethon's mercenaries, saw us and flew at the ship; learning, however, that we were covered by the treaty, they went away again. By now the Horse-vultures had left us too.     28

    29

We sailed all that night and the next day, and by evening had reached Lamptown, as it is called; we were now on the downward voyage. Lamptown lies in the air between the Pleiades and Hyades but is much lower than the Zodiac. Going ashore, we did not find any human beings but saw a lot of lamps running around and hanging about in the marketplace and around the harbor. Some of them were small, the poorer ones as it might be; a few were big and powerful—they were very bright and distinct. Each had his own dwelling, or lamphouse; they had names, like human beings, and we heard them talking. They did us no harm; in fact, they offered us entertainment; but we were apprehensive, and none of us was prepared either to eat or to go to sleep. They have a town hall in the middle of the city, where their mayor sits all night long calling each one of them by name. Any of them who does not answer to his name is condemned to death for desertion; death involves being put out. We stood and watched what happened; we heard lamps making their defense and giving their reasons for being late. I also recognized our own lamp there. I spoke to him and asked him how things were at home, and he told me all about it.

That night, then, we stayed there; the next day we set sail and were now traveling near the clouds. At this point we actually saw Cloudcuck-ooland,[14] to our surprise, but were prevented from landing on it by the wind. I gathered, however, that their king was called Hookbeak, son of Blackbird. I thought of the dramatist Aristophanes, a wise and truthful man, whose works arouse undeserved disbelief. Three days after this we could in fact see the ocean, but no land except the islands in the sky, which now appeared a bright fiery color. On the fourth day, about noon, the wind gradually slackened and fell, and we were deposited on the sea.

30     When we touched the water, we were delighted beyond belief, beside ourselves with joy, and celebrated as gaily as we could in the circumstances. The sea was quiet and the weather calm, so we dived overboard and swam about. But it seems that a change for the better is often the prelude to greater disaster, for after only two days' sailing in calm weather, as the sun rose on the third, we suddenly saw a great number of sea beasts and whales. They were of various kinds, and one of them, the biggest of all, was not far short of two hundred miles long. It came at us with its jaws wide open, disturbing the sea far in front of it, and washed about with foam; it was showing its teeth, which were much bigger than our phallic symbols, all as sharp as stakes and white as ivory. We said our last words to each other, embraced, and waited. The beast was now on us. Sucking us in, it swallowed us, ship and all, but before its teeth crushed us, the ship tumbled inside the gaps between them.

31     When we got inside, it was dark at first and we could see nothing; later on, however, when the whale opened its jaws, we saw a great cavern, broad in every direction and high, big enough to hold a large city. It had fish large and small, and fragments of many and various animals were lying in the middle of it, as well as ships' masts, anchors, human bones, and merchandise. In the middle also there was land, with hills—formed, I suppose, by the settling of the mud the creature swallowed. There were even woods with trees of all kinds; vegetables were growing, and the whole area appeared to be cultivated. The circumference of the land was thirty miles. Seabirds could be seen also, gulls and kingfishers, nesting in the trees.

32     Well, for a long time we wept, but eventually we roused the crew and had the ship underpropped. We ourselves lit a fire by rubbing sticks together and made a meal from what we could get. There was plenty of

14. Invented by Aristophanes in *Birds*.

fish of all varieties lying about, and we still had the water from the Morning Star. On getting up the next day, whenever the whale opened his jaws we saw sometimes mountains, sometimes nothing but sky, and often islands. We realized that he was moving swiftly through the sea in various directions. When eventually we grew accustomed to this state of things, I took seven of the crew and went into the wood to explore it thoroughly. Not quite a thousand yards away I came upon a shrine—to Poseidon, as the inscription showed—and shortly afterward upon a large number of graves, with gravestones, near a spring of clear water. What is more, we heard a dog bark and saw smoke in the distance. We concluded that there was some kind of habitation there. So we hurried on and found ourselves in the presence of an old man and a young one who were very carefully tending a plot of land and irrigating it with water from the spring.

We stood there in simultaneous delight and fear. They seemed to be in the same state and stood speechless. At last the old man spoke. "Who are you, strangers?" he said. "Are you spirits of the sea or unfortunate human beings like us? For we are men, brought up on land but turned sea creatures, swimming about with this beast that envelops us, not even very sure of our condition. We suppose we are dead, but we trust we are alive." I replied. "Sir," I said, "we too are men, newly arrived, swallowed with our ship just the other day. Now we have come out to see what things are like in the wood, for it seemed thick and extensive. It looks as if some spirit has guided us to the sight of you so that we may realize we are not the only people enclosed in this beast. But you tell us what happened to you. Who are you? How did you get here?" He refused to answer our questions or ask any until he had offered us what entertainment he could. Taking us with him to his house—which was quite complete, equipped with beds and other furniture—he set vegetables and fruit and fish before us and poured us wine.

When we had had all we wanted, he asked what had befallen us. I told him the whole story: all about the storm, the events on the island, the journey in the air, the war, and everything else up to the descent into the whale. He expressed great surprise and in turn told us his own story. "My friends," he said, "I am from Cyprus. I set out from home to trade, with my son, whom you see here, and many of my servants as well. I was sailing to Italy with an assorted cargo in a large vessel, which you may have seen broken up in the whale's mouth. Well, we had a good voyage as far as Sicily, but on leaving there we were seized by a strong wind and for three days driven out into the ocean. There we came upon the whale. He swallowed us, crew and all. Only we two survived; the rest were killed. We buried them and built a temple to Poseidon, and now we live like this, growing vegetables and living on fish and fruit.

"The wood is very big, as you can see. It has vines in abundance, which produce a very sweet wine. You may have noticed the spring; its water is very good and very cold. We make beds of leaves, we can light a fire whenever we want, and we snare birds that fly in. We can catch living fish by going out into the monster's gills; we also bathe there when we feel like it. And then there is a lake not far off, over two miles around, with all kinds of fish in it; we swim in it and sail a small boat I built myself. It is twenty-seven years since we were swallowed.

35    "One could perhaps put up with the rest, but the neighbors who live near us are unpleasant, offensive, unsociable savages." "Why," I said, "are there others in the whale too?" "A great many," said the old man, "and they are unfriendly and monstrous in shape. The western part of the wood, by the tail, is the land of the Saltfish, a tribe with eels' eyes and lobsters' faces; they are warlike and fierce, and they eat raw flesh. Of the sides, the starboard wall is in the possession of the Sea-satyrs,[15] who are human in their upper parts and like lizards below; they are not so lawless as the rest. The port side is held by the Crabhands and the Tunnyheads, their friends and allies. The land in the center is inhabited by the Shellbacks and the Flatfishfeet, a swift and warlike tribe. The eastern regions near the mouth are mostly desert because they are periodically flooded by the sea; still, I have this patch of ground, which I rent from the Flatfishfeet for five hundred oysters a year.

36    "Well, that is what the land is like. You must find out the best way of fighting all these tribes, and how we shall live."

I asked him how many there were of them, and how they were armed. They were more than a thousand strong, he said, but their only arms were fish bones. "Well then," I said, "since they are unarmed and we are not, the best thing to do would be to bring them to battle; if we beat them, we shall live hereafter with nothing to fear." This was agreed, and we went off to the ship to get ready. The excuse for the war was to be failure to pay the rent; this was now due, and indeed they sent to collect it. The old man made a rude answer to the collectors and chased them away. The Flatfishfeet and the Shellbacks were incensed with Scintharus (that was the old man's name) and took the offensive against him with a great deal of clamor.

37    Expecting this attack, we waited in full armor. Ahead of us we had laid an ambush of twenty-five men, with instructions to rise and attack when they saw the enemy had passed them. They did rise in their rear and began to cut them down, while we too, also twenty-five in number—Scintharus and his son were with us—joined with them from the

15. Transliterated from the Greek the name of these creatures is *Tritonomendetes*. According to Herodotus 2.46, *mendes* was Egyptian both for "goat" and for "the god Pan"; with the latter meaning, the half-man, half-animal creatures mentioned here are Sea-satyrs.

front, fighting bravely, with spirit and might. Finally we routed them and pursued them to their dens. The enemy lost a hundred and seventy men; we lost one, our navigator, who had a mullet rib driven through his back.

For that day, then, and the night following, we made our quarters on the battlefield, and we set up a trophy by driving the dry backbone of a dolphin into the ground. But the other tribes heard what had happened and appeared the next day. The Saltfish, under the command of Tunnyfish, formed their right wing, the Tunnyheads their left, and the Crabhands held the center. The Sea-satyrs kept out of the fighting, preferring to remain neutral. We did not wait for them to attack but joined with them by Poseidon's shrine, raising a great shout that echoed in the hollow space as in a cave. They were unarmed; we routed them and pursued them into the wood and thereafter were masters of the area. Shortly afterward they sent heralds, took up their dead, and made overtures for peace. We decided, however, not to come to terms and the next day set out against them and cut them down—all except the Sea-satyrs, who fled when they saw what was happening and threw themselves out into the sea from the gills. We occupied the country, which was now empty of enemies, and thereafter lived in security.

Most of the time we spent in exercise or hunting or dressing the vines or picking fruit from the trees. It was like living in a great prison where we were free to live an easy life but from which we could not escape. This was how we lived for a year and eight months. On the fifth of the next month, about the second opening of the mouth—the whale opened his mouth once an hour, you see, and that was how we told the time—about the second opening, I was saying, we suddenly heard a great shouting and uproar; it sounded like someone giving the stroke to crews rowing. In some alarm we crept right into the monster's mouth and from a position behind its teeth looked out on the strangest sight I have ever seen—giants a hundred yards high sailing great islands as one does triremes. I know this is going to sound farfetched, but I shall describe it nevertheless.

The islands were long but not very high, and each was over eleven miles in circumference. Their crews numbered about a hundred and twenty of the men I have mentioned, who, appropriately disposed along the sides of the island, were rowing with great cypresses—branches, foliage, and all—for oars. Behind them, in what was evidently the stern, a helmsman stood on a high hill at a bronze steering oar a thousand yards long. For'ard there were some forty armed men, the fighting element. They were just like men except for their hair, which was burning fire—they did not need crests. The wind caught the forest area, which was considerable on every island, as if it were sails, filled it out, and took the

38

39

40

ship wherever the helmsman wished. They had a coxswain giving them the stroke, and the islands responded vigorously to the rowing like warships.

41     At first, we saw two or three, but later on some six hundred appeared, formed up, and fought an action. Many of them crashed head-on; many were rammed and sunk. Some grappled, fought stoutly, and were very difficult to shake off, for the troops posted for'ard boarded and slew with great ferocity; no prisoners were taken. They grappled not with irons but with huge captive squids, which entwined themselves in the trees and held the island fast. As missiles—and they inflicted wounds—they used oysters, any one of which would fill a cart, and hun-

42 dred-foot sponges. Aeolocentaur commanded one side, Seadrinker the other. They were fighting over an act of piracy, it appeared; Seadrinker had driven off a good many herds of dolphins belonging to Aeolocentaur, to judge from the accusations they hurled at each other as they called out their kings' names.

    Aeolocentaur's fleet won in the end, sinking some one hundred and fifty of the enemy islands and taking three others with their crews; the rest backed water and got away. After pursuing them for some way, the victors returned to the wrecked ships when evening came on, took possession of most of them, and recovered their own, of which no fewer than eighty had been sunk. They also set up a trophy for the battle of the islands by pinning one of the enemy islands to the whale's head with a stake. That night they spent in the vicinity of the monster, attaching their hawsers to him and riding at anchor hard by; they had anchors, big, strong ones made of glass. The next day they made sacrifice on top of the beast, buried their own dead on him, and sailed off in high spirits, singing a kind of victory paean. That was what happened in the battle of the islands.[16]

## Book Two

1     Latterly I grew tired of being stuck there and could not bear to live in the whale any longer. So I looked around for some way of getting out. My first idea was to cut a tunnel in the starboard wall and get away that way. We began to hack away, but after going a thousand yards without any success we gave up digging and decided to set fire to the wood. We thought that this would kill the whale, and then we would have no difficulty getting out. We did set fire to it, then, beginning from the tail region. For a whole week he did not feel it, but on the eighth and ninth days we could see that he was not well; his jaws opened more slowly and

---

16. Lucian uses a Thucydidean turn of phrase here; cf. the famous last sentence of Book 7, which laconically concludes the tragic account of the Sicilian expedition.

shut again quickly every time. On the tenth and eleventh days mortification finally set in, and he began to stink. We realized on the twelfth day, only just in time, that unless we wedged his molars apart when he opened his jaws, to stop them from closing again, we should probably be imprisoned in his dead body and die there. So we propped his mouth open with great beams and got the ship ready, taking on board as much water as we could and other supplies. Scintharus was to navigate. The next day the whale at last died.

We dragged the ship up, then swung it from the teeth, guided it through the gaps between them, and let it down gently onto the sea. Then we climbed onto the whale's back, sacrificed to Poseidon, and since there was no wind, camped there for three days by the trophy. Getting away on the fourth day, we came across and went aground on many of the dead bodies from the sea fight; it was a startling experience to measure them. For some days we had a mild wind behind us; then there was a fierce gale from the north, which brought a very cold spell. The whole sea froze, not just at the surface but to a depth of six fathoms; we could actually get out and run on the ice. The wind continued unbearably, so we hit on the idea (it was Scintharus who suggested it) of digging an enormous cave in the water. There we stayed for thirty days, lighting fires and living on fish, which we got by digging them out of the ice. But eventually supplies began to fail, and we left the cave. The ship was frozen in; we extracted it, spread the sheet, and swept along smoothly and easily, gliding over the ice as if we were sailing. By the fifth day the temperature had risen; the ice melted, and all was water again.

We sailed for some thirty-five miles and put in at a small desert island, where we took on water (our supply having now run out) and shot two wild bulls—whose horns were not on their heads but under the eyes, as in Momus's prescription.[17] Shortly after leaving, we entered upon a sea of milk, not water, with a white island, covered in vines, standing out of it. The island was, as we later found out by eating it, a huge, very solid cheese, three miles around. The vines were loaded with grapes, but when we squeezed them to get a drink, it was not wine that came but milk. A shrine had been built in the center of the island to the Nereid Galatea,[18] according to the inscription. As long as we were there, the earth provided bread and meat, and we drank the milk from the vines. Tyro,[19] the daughter of Salmoneus, was said to be the ruler of these regions; she had been given the office by Poseidon after departing this life.

2

3

---

17. So that they could see what they were doing with them. Momus ("fault-finding") was rather a literary than a genuinely mythological figure; Lucian uses him elsewhere, as a mouthpiece for his satire.
18. *Gala* means "milk."
19. *Tyros* means "cheese."

4    We stayed five days on the island and set out on the sixth; a breeze
took us on our course, and the sea was rippling gently. On the eighth
day—we were past the milk by now and were sailing on blue salt water—we saw a large number of men running on the sea. They were like
us in anatomy and size, and in every respect except the feet, for theirs
were of cork—which is why they were called Corkfeet, I suppose. We
were surprised to see that they walked quite confidently on the waves
without going under or getting wet. They actually came up to us and
greeted us in Greek; they were in a hurry, they said, to get to their country, Cork. They accompanied us for some way, running alongside, then
turned aside and went off, wishing us bon voyage. Shortly after a number of islands came in sight; not far off on the port bow was Cork, the
city they were hurrying to, built on a great round cork. A long way off
and slightly to starboard were five enormous ones, rising high out of the
water and burning very fiercely.

5    Straight ahead there was one flat, low island, nearly sixty miles away.
We were soon close to it, and a marvelous air breathed round us, sweetly
scented, such as the historian Herodotus says issues from rich Arabia;[20] as
it came to us, it was like the scent of roses, narcissi, hyacinths, lilies, and
violets, and of myrrh and laurel and flowering vine too. Reveling in the
odor and hoping for comfort after our long labors, we drew gradually
closer to the island. Once there, we found many great harbors all around
a tideless coast, and rivers of clear water flowing gently into the sea; we
saw meadows and woods and melodious birds, some singing by the riverbanks and many in the branches of the trees. Light air breathed gently
all over the land; sweet breezes played and softly rustled the trees; the
branches as they swayed gave forth delicious unending melodies, like the
sound of flutes in a deserted place. With them were mingled human
sounds, in some numbers; not noisy, but as they might sound at a banquet, some playing the flute, others singing, and some clapping their
hands to flute or harp.

6    We were bewitched by all this and put in to land. Mooring the ship
and leaving Scintharus with two of the crew on board, we went ashore.
On our way through a flowery meadow, we fell in with the guard on
their patrol; they bound us with wreaths of roses (the strongest chains
they have) and took us before the governor, informing us as we went
that this was what was called the Island of the Blest and that the Cretan
Rhadamanthus[21] was its ruler.

    When we reached his precincts, we took our position as fourth in the
7  line of those awaiting judgment. The first case concerned Ajax, the son

20. Herodotus 3.13.
21. One of the judges of the dead in Hades.

of Telamon; the question was whether or not he was to be allowed to associate with the heroes. The prosecution argued that he had gone out of his mind and taken his own life. Finally, after a great deal of discussion, Rhadamanthus decided that for the present Ajax was to take a dose of hellebore[22] and put himself under the care of Hippocrates, the doctor from Cos, and be admitted to the banquet later, when he regained his senses. The second case called for a decision in a matter of the heart; Theseus and Menelaus were taking issue over which one of them Helen should live with.[23] Rhadamanthus decided in favor of Menelaus, on the grounds that he had gone through a great deal of toil and danger over his marriage; added to which, Theseus had other wives in the Queen of the Amazons and the daughters of Minos. Third came judgment on the issue of precedence between Alexander, son of Philip, and Hannibal the Carthaginian; it was given in favor of Alexander, who was accorded a seat next to Cyrus the Elder of Persia.

After these cases, we were taken into court. The judge asked us why we had set foot on the holy ground while still alive, and we told him the whole story as it had happened. He made us stand aside for a long time while he considered our case in conjunction with his colleagues; the latter were numerous, and included Aristides the Just, of Athens. When he had reached his decision, they announced that on the charges of inquisitiveness and traveling in foreign parts we were to give account of ourselves when we died; for the present, we were to stay on the island for a fixed period of time, as members of the company of heroes, and after that to depart. They also fixed the outside limit of our stay, namely, seven months. At this, the wreaths fell off us of their own accord; we were released and taken into the city, to the banquet of the blest.

This city is made of gold throughout and has a wall of emerald around it. There are seven gates, each a single piece of cinnamon wood. The foundation of the city, all the land within the walls, is of ivory. There are temples to all the gods, made of beryl, with great altars inside made of single blocks of amethyst; here they offer hecatombs. Around the city runs a river of fairest perfume, a hundred royal cubits broad and five deep, very convenient for swimming. There are baths also—great glass buildings with cinnamon burning inside, with warm dew instead of water in the actual troughs.

Their clothing is fine purple cobweb. The people themselves have no bodies: they are intangible, without flesh; their only attributes are shape and form.[24] Although devoid of body, they have position and move-

----

22. The name of a genus of plant that can be used medicinally; supposed in antiquity to cure madness.

23. When a child, Helen was carried off by Theseus.

24. This description appears to borrow from Plato's theory of "ideas" or "forms."

ment, they think and speak. It is, in fact, as if it were naked soul moving about, endowed with the semblance of body; without touching them one would never be convinced that what one saw was incorporeal; they are like shadows, but upright and not dark. No one grows old; each person stays the age he was when he came.

They have neither night nor bright daylight; the light that envelops the land is like the gray dawn in the early morning before the sun is up. They have only one season, moreover—it is always spring with them— and only one wind, the west wind.

13   All kinds of flowers bloom in the land, and all kinds of plants are cultivated for their shade. The vines bear fruit twelve times a year, once a month. Pomegranates, apples, and other fruit, they said, ripened thirteen times, twice in their month of Minos. Corn puts forth not grain but fully finished loaves at the ends of the stalks; thus the general appearance is that of mushrooms. There are three hundred and sixty-five springs of water around the city, as many again of money, and five hundred of perfume; these last are smaller. There are seven rivers of milk and eight of wine.

14   Their banquets take place outside the city in what is called the Elysian Fields, a beautiful meadow with all kinds of trees thick around it giving shade to the diners; cushions of flowers are strewn on the ground. It is the winds that serve everything: they are the waiters. They do not pour the wine, though; that is not necessary, since around the table are great trees of quite pellucid glass whose fruit is wineglasses of every shape and size; and on arriving at table, the diner plucks one or two of these and sets them at his place, where at once they fill with wine. That is the way they get their drink. As for garlands, nightingales and the other melodious birds pick flowers with their beaks from the meadows round about and fly overhead, singing and snowing flowers. The way they scent themselves is as follows: thick clouds draw perfume up from the springs and the river, settle over the banquet, and as the winds squeeze them gently, rain down a sort of fine dew.

15   At dinner they give themselves to music and song, Homer's poetry being very popular; Homer himself is there, and sits next to Odysseus at table. The choirs are of boys and girls, led and accompanied by Eunomus the Locrian, Arion of Lesbos, Anacreon, and Stesichorus[25] —for I saw him there too; he had managed to make his peace with Helen.[26] When they stop singing, another choir, made up of swans, swallows, and

25. Famous choric or lyric poets.
26. One of the few remaining fragments of Stesichorus is a palinode, or recantation, on Helen, in which the poet appears to deny an earlier malicious statement about Helen in his work. (All the "denial" says, in fact, is that she "did not go to Troy"!) Stesichorus was said to have been struck blind for his "malice," and to have had his sight restored upon recanting.

nightingales, takes its place; and when they sing, all the woods make music under the direction of the winds.

But the greatest inducement to happiness they have is the two springs near their table, that of Laughter and that of Pleasure. At the beginning of the banquet they all drink from both of these, and thereafter spend their hours laughing and enjoying themselves. 16

I should like also to record the famous people I saw there. All the demigods were present, and all those who took part in the expedition against Troy except Ajax the Locrian; he was the only one of them, they said, who was undergoing punishment in the abode of the wicked.[27] Of non-Greeks, I saw the two Cyruses, the Scythian Anacharsis, Zamolxis the Thracian, and Numa of Italy. There were Lycurgus the Spartan, Phocion and Tellus from Athens, and the wise men except Periander.[28] I also saw Socrates, the son of Sophroniscus, chatting with Nestor and Palamedes; around him were Hyacinthus of Sparta, Narcissus of Thespiae, Hylas, and other handsome youths. He seemed to me to be in love with Hyacinthus—at any rate, he was the one he was arguing most with. I was told that Rhadamanthus was displeased with him and had often threatened to expel him from the island for his nonsense if he didn't drop his self-deprecation and enjoy himself.[29] Plato was the only one missing. They said he was living in the republic he constructed himself, under the constitution and laws of his own devising. The people best spoken of there were Aristippus and Epicurus; they were pleasant and obliging, and convivial company. Aesop the Phrygian was there too; he acts as their jester. Diogenes of Sinope had so changed that he had married Lais the courtesan, frequently got up and danced when in his cups, and acted like any drunkard. There were no Stoics in the company—apparently they were still climbing the steep hill of virtue;[30] and about Chrysippus, we heard that he was not permitted to land on the island until he had taken the hellebore treatment a fourth time. The Academics, it was said, were ready to come but were holding back and considering the matter, since they did not yet accept the possibility of there being such an island.[31] And then I suppose they were apprehensive about the judgment of Rhadamanthus too, seeing that they themselves had denied the possibility of proper judgment. Many of them had set out, I gathered, in the tracks of people on their way to the island, but had fallen behind through laziness, without grasping their object, and turned back halfway. 17

18

27. For raping Cassandra when Troy fell and for blasphemy on his journey home.

28. The tyrant of Corinth is regarded as too cruel for heaven.

29. Socrates' famous "irony" (*eironeia*): he criticized others' "knowledge" while protesting that he himself knew nothing—except that he knew nothing.

30. Stoics commonly claimed that they aspired only to "make progress" towards virtue.

31. One development of the philosophy of the Academy was Scepticism, a doctrine which held that knowledge was impossible.

19  Well, these were the most notable of the company; the most respected members of it are Achilles and, next, Theseus. Their sexual practice is as follows. They make love openly, in the sight of all, with both women and men; this is not considered in any way shameful. Only Socrates had sworn formally that his associations with the young were pure; but everybody thought he was guilty of perjury—Hyacinthus and Narcissus kept saying so, anyway, though he himself denied it. Women are common property, and no one is jealous of his neighbor; they are very Platonic in this respect. Boys submit to anyone who wants them, without any resistance.

20  Before two or three days had gone by I approached Homer the poet, neither of us being occupied, and asked him various questions. I said his birthplace was a bone of contention on earth to this day. He replied that he was well aware that some people said he came from Chios, some from Smyrna, and many from Colophon; but the truth was, he was a Babylonian, and his name in his own country was not Homer but Tigranes—he had changed his name when he was held as a hostage[32] by Greeks. I asked him also whether the obelized lines were of his composition; he said they were, all of them. My regard for Zenodotus and Aristarchus and scholars of that sort, with all their pedantry, dropped.[33] Having got satisfactory answers to these questions, I then asked him why on earth he had started with the wrath. He said that was how it had come to him; he had no definite purpose in it. I was also very anxious to know whether he had written the *Odyssey* before the *Iliad* as most people thought; he said he hadn't. Another thing they say about him is that he was blind, but I knew at once that he wasn't; I could see that, so there was no need for me to ask him. As a matter of fact, I used to do this often afterward, go up and ask him questions, whenever I saw he was not busy. He was very ready to answer, especially after his acquittal in court—Thersites brought a libel action against him on the grounds of having been subjected to ridicule in his poetry;[34] Odysseus spoke in Homer's defense and won the case.

21  It was at this time that Pythagoras of Samos arrived; he had been through seven transmigrations and inhabited as many animals and completed his psychic peregrinations. All his right side was gold. He was admitted to the community, but there was still some doubt as to whether he should be called Pythagoras or Euphorbus. Empedocles turned up

32. The Greek word *homeros* means "hostage."
33. In the earliest editions of Homer, these Alexandrian critics obelized certain lines as spurious.
34. In *Iliad* 2.211ff.

too, well cooked and with his whole body roasted; but he was not admitted, despite much entreaty.[35]

In the course of time their athletic contest, the Games of the Dead, 22 took place. The judges were Achilles, who was holding the office for the fifth time, and Theseus, holding it for the seventh. I shall summarize the events; a full report would take a long time. The wrestling was won by Caprus[36] the Heraclid, who beat Odysseus for the title. The boxing was a draw between Areius the Egyptian, who is buried in Corinth, and Epeius. They have no pancratium, and I cannot now recall who won the race. In poetry, Homer was really much the best; Hesiod won, though. The prize for every winner was a garland of peacock feathers plaited.[37]

Just after the games were finished, news was brought that those who 23 were being punished in the abode of the wicked had broken their chains and overpowered their guard and were advancing upon the island, under Phalaris of Acragas, Busiris the Egyptian, Diomede the Thracian, and Sciron and Pityocamptes and their followers. On hearing this, Rhadamanthus marshaled the heroes on the beach, giving the command to Theseus, Achilles, and Ajax the son of Telamon (now restored to sanity). They joined battle and the heroes won, Achilles being particularly successful. Socrates also fought bravely on the right wing—much more bravely than he did at Delium,[38] when alive; he did not run away when four of the enemy advanced towards him, and his countenance showed no emotion. He actually received a special prize afterward for his conduct—a large and very lovely park in the suburbs, to which he used to invite his friends for conversation; he called it the Academy of the Dead.[39]

Seizing the vanquished, then, they bound them and sent them back 24 for yet more punishment. Homer wrote an account of this battle; when I left, he gave me the text to bring to men on earth, but we lost it afterward along with everything else. The poem began

Now tell, my Muse, of the fight of the dead heroes.

Then they boiled beans,[40] as is their habit after a successful war, and held

---

35. Empedocles was a philosopher of the fifth century B.C., who was said to have died by leaping into the crater of Mount Etna; he wanted people to think he had been translated to heaven. But the volcano cast up his shoe, thus proving that he had merely committed suicide.

36. Caprus: I have adopted a conjecture for "Caranus" here. Caprus was a historical figure, who won a double victory in 212 B.C. See C. P. Jones, *Culture and Society in Lucian* (Cambridge, Mass., and London, 1986), 55 and n.47.

37. The prize at the Olympic Games was a laurel wreath.

38. See Plato *Symposium* 220–21.

39. Plato, Socrates' disciple, founded the Academy.

40. An allusion to the Pyanepsia, a festival at which beans were eaten.

a great celebration at which they ate the victory meal. Pythagoras alone took no part in it; he would not eat, because he disapproves of bean eating, and sat well away.

25    Six months had gone by, and we were about halfway through the seventh when an incident took place. Scintharus's son Cinyras, an upstanding, handsome lad, had already long been in love with Helen, and she was evidently passionately fond of the youth; at any rate, they used to exchange glances at table and drink each other's health and get up and go off for walks in the wood by themselves. Eventually Cinyras, in love and not knowing what to do about it, conceived the notion of abducting Helen and making his escape. She was willing; the plan was to go off to one of the nearby islands, Cork or Cheeseland. They had long ago taken into their confidence three of the boldest of my crew, but Cinyras did not tell his father, knowing that he would put a stop to it. They carried out the plan as intended. When night came—I was not there; as it happened, I had fallen asleep at table—they picked up Helen without attracting atten-

26    tion and put out to sea, going as fast as they could. About midnight Menelaus woke up and realized that his wife was not in the bed. Raising a cry and getting hold of his brother, he went to King Rhadamanthus. When day dawned, the lookouts reported that they could see the ship a long way off; so Rhadamanthus put fifty of the heroes on board a ship made from a single asphodel log, with instructions to give chase. They rowed hard and caught them about noon, just as they were entering the sea of milk near Cheeseland—they were as near as that to effecting their escape. They sailed back, towing the other ship by means of a chain of roses. Helen was weeping; she was embarrassed and kept her face covered. Rhadamanthus examined Cinyras and his associates, to see if there were any others privy to the plot. They said there were not, and he had them whipped with mallow, bound by the genitals, and taken off to the abode of the wicked.

27    They decreed also that we were to leave the island before the appointed time, with only one day's grace. At this I besought their pity, weeping at the thought of all the comfort I was leaving to set out once more on my travels. They gave me some consolation, however, by saying that it would not be many years before I returned to them; they showed me in advance the chair and the couch I was to have at table—in excellent company. I approached Rhadamanthus with the earnest request that he foretell the future for me and point out my route.[41] He said I should reach my own country after much wandering and danger, but refused to add when I was to return. He did, however, point out to me the neighboring islands—there were five of them visible, and a sixth a long

41. It is standard in ancient literature for heroes to visit the afterworld and learn of the future; cf. *Odyssey* 11 and Virgil *Aeneid* 6.

way off; these, he said, were the islands of the wicked, the nearby ones, "from which," he said, "you can see great flames rising, even at this distance. The sixth one there is the city of dreams. Beyond that—you cannot see it from here—is Calypso's island. After passing these, you will come to the great continent opposite the one where you people live. There you will have many adventures, pass among various tribes, and live among inhospitable men; then at last you will reach the mainland opposite."

That was all he said. And he pulled up a mallow root[42] and handed it 28 to me, bidding me invoke it at times of greatest danger. He also enjoined me, if ever I reached this world, not to poke fires with a sword, not to eat lupines, and not to associate with boys over eighteen;[43] if I kept these things in mind, he said, I could have hopes of returning to the island.

So then I prepared for the voyage, and at dinnertime joined them at table. The next day I went to Homer the poet and asked him to compose a couplet for me to use as an inscription. He did so, and I inscribed it on a pillar of beryl, which I set up near the harbor. It ran as follows.

> Lucian, befriended by the blessed gods,
> Saw this land and returned to his own country.

I stayed that day and set out the next; the heroes came to see me off. 29 Odysseus took the opportunity to give Penelope the slip and hand me a letter for Calypso on the Island of Ogygia. Rhadamanthus sent the ferryman Nauplius with us, to save us from being seized if we were driven onto the islands and vouch for our having other destination.

As soon as we had passed beyond the scented air in our progress, a dreadful smell assailed us in its turn, a smell as of asphalt and brimstone and pitch all burning at once, and an intolerable, foul odor, as of human flesh roasting. The air was dark and murky and precipitated a dew like pitch, and we could hear the crack of whips and a multitude howling.

We put in at only one of these islands and found it precipitous and 30 sheer in every direction; it was rough with rocks and stones, had no trees, and was without water. Still, we clambered up by the cliffs and went ahead through ugly country, by a thorny path covered with sharp stakes. The first thing that struck us when we reached the punishment compound was the general character of the area; blades and sharp stakes thrust out of the ground itself like massed flowers, and there were rivers running around it, one of slime, another of blood, and a third of fire. This last was very broad—impassable, in fact. It flowed like water, heaved like the sea, and contained many fish, some like burning brands, others small ones, like blazing pieces of coal; these were called lampkins.

42. Cf. *moly*, *Odyssey* 10.281–306.
43. Mock-Pythagorean precepts; the first may be genuine.

31 One narrow way led across all three, with Timon of Athens[44] guarding the entrance to it. Nauplius took us across it, however, and we witnessed the punishment of many kings and many private citizens too, some of whom in fact we recognized; we even saw Cinyras there, wreathed in smoke and suspended by the testicles. Our guides described for us the life of each of the victims and the reason for his punishment. The people who suffered the greatest torment were those who had told lies when they were alive and written mendacious histories; among them were Ctesias of Cnidos, Herodotus, and many others. You may guess that, seeing them, I had high hopes for the next world—I knew very well I had never told a lie.

32 I soon turned back to the ship—the sight was more than I could stand—said good-bye to Nauplius, and sailed off. Soon there came into sight nearby the Island of Dreams, but it was faint and hard to make out. The island itself was like the dreams in a way, in that as we approached, it receded before us, retreated, retired farther off. At last we caught up with it and sailed into Sleep Harbor, as it is called, and landed in the late afternoon near the Ivory Gates and the Temple of the Cock. Then we went into the town and saw many dreams of various kinds. I am going to talk about the town first, because no one has ever written about it except Homer,[45] and what he says is not very accurate.

33 It is encircled by a wood of tall poppies and mandragoras, among which live a great many bats—the only winged things on the island. Near it there is a river, which they call Somnambule; beside the gates there are two springs, called Deepsleep and Allnight. Around the town runs a high wall all the colors of the rainbow. There are, however, four gates, not two as Homer says: two facing Dozy Moor, one of iron and one of earthenware—these were the gates through which frightening and murderous and grim dreams were said to leave; and two facing the harbor and the sea, one of horn and the other, the one which we had come through, of ivory. To the right as you enter the town is the Temple of Night, and the Temple of the Cock is near the harbor; these are the principal cults of the island. On the left is the Palace of Sleep; Sleep is their ruler and has under him two satraps, or governors—Nightmare, the son of Pointless, and Richman, the son of Daydream. In the middle of the market square is a spring called Idlewater, and nearby are the temples of Truth and Untruth; there too is the town shrine and oracle, whose superintendent and mouthpiece is the dream interpreter Antiphon, appointed to the office by Sleep.

34 The dreams themselves varied in character and appearance. Some

44. A misanthrope of the fifth century B.C.
45. In *Odyssey* 19.559ff.

were tall and handsome and well proportioned, others short and mis-shapen; some appeared to be made of gold, others were poor and shabby. There were winged dreams among them and monster-dreams and dreams in carnival costume—some dressed up as kings, some as gods, and so on. Many of them in fact we recognized, having seen them before at home; they came up and greeted us like old friends, took us in charge, put us to sleep, and showed us most excellent and ingenious entertainment. Their hospitality was splendid; among other things, they promised to make us kings and satraps. Some of them actually took us home and showed us our families and brought us back the same day.

Well, we stayed thirty days and nights there and enjoyed ourselves 35 immensely sleeping. Then suddenly there came a great clap of thunder; we woke up, jumped out of bed, took on some supplies, and set sail again. After three days we put in at Ogygia and landed, but first I opened Odysseus's letter. It read as follows.

Dear Calypso,

This is to let you know what happened to me. As soon as I sailed away from you in the raft I built, I was shipwrecked. Thanks to Leucothea, I just managed to get ashore in Phaeacia. The Phaeacians sent me home, and I caught a lot of men trying to win my wife and having the time of their lives in my house; but I killed them all. Later, I was murdered by Telegonus, my son by Circe; now I am on the Island of the Blest, and very sorry that I left my life with you and the immortality you offered me. So if I get a chance, I'll slip away and come to you.

Odysseus

In addition to this, the letter said that we were to be entertained. I went 36 inland a little from the sea and found the cave, just as Homer described it. Calypso was at home knitting. She took the letter and read it and wept a great deal. Then she asked us in and gave us a very good meal. She asked about Odysseus, and about Penelope—what she looked like, and whether she was as faithful as Odysseus used to boast she was. We made such answer as we thought would please her. Then we went off to 37 our ship and slept near it on the shore, and at daybreak we put to sea in a freshening breeze.

After riding a storm for two days, on the third we fell in with the Pumpkin-pirates. These are savages from the islands nearby who raid passing ships in vessels made out of great pumpkins ninety feet long; they dry them and remove the pulp, thus hollowing them, and equip them with masts made of cane, with pumpkin leaves for sails. Well, they attacked with two vessels, and during the fight inflicted many casualties with the pumpkin seeds that they used for stones. The fight went on for a long time, and the issue was doubtful; then about midday we saw the Nut-sailors coming up astern of the Pumpkin-pirates. They were their enemies, it appeared, for as soon as the Pumpkin-pirates saw them approaching they forgot about us, turned around, and engaged with them.

38 Meanwhile we hoisted sail and took to flight, leaving them to fight it out. The Nut-sailors were clearly going to win; they were superior in numbers, being five ships strong, and their vessels were stronger. These vessels were nutshells split in half and emptied; each half was ninety feet long. When we had lost sight of them, we attended to our casualties, and thereafter we were in armor almost all the time, and constantly on the lookout for attacks.

39 It was just as well, for before sunset some twenty men mounted on dolphins assailed us from a desert island. They were pirates too; the dolphins carried them safely, and as they leapt, they whinnied like horses. When they were within range, they split into two groups and attacked us from both sides, firing dried cuttlefish and crabs' eyes at us. But we were using arrows and javelins; they could not stand up to it, and most of them were wounded when they fled back to the island.

40 About midnight, in a calm sea, we accidentally ran aground on an enormous halcyon's nest, a good seven miles in circumference. The halcyon was riding on it, hatching her eggs; she was almost as big as the nest. She rose into the air and very nearly capsized us with the wind her wings made; she went off, though, uttering a mournful cry. We climbed onto the nest when day began to dawn and saw that it was like a great raft, being made of large trees laid together. There were five hundred eggs in it, each bigger than a jar of Chian wine. The chicks could already be seen inside, and they were making a croaking noise; so we hacked open one of the eggs with axes and dug out an unfledged chick fatter than twenty vultures.

41 We sailed off and were about twenty-five miles from the nest when some very startling phenomena occurred. The goose that formed our figurehead suddenly flapped its wings and cackled; our navigator, Scintharus, who was bald, grew hair; and, oddest of all, the ship's mast began to sprout, putting forth shoots and, at the top, fruit—figs and black grapes, not yet ripe.[46] We were understandably very perturbed at this sight and prayed to the gods because of the strange nature of the apparition.

42 Before we had gone sixty miles, we saw a great forest, dense with pine and cypress. We supposed it was the mainland, but in fact the sea was bottomless there, and on it there were trees growing—they had no roots but stayed upright without moving, as if they were sailing on the

---

46. Cf. *Homeric Hymn to Dionysus* 38.

sea. We approached, and when we saw the whole situation we had no idea what to do. It was impossible to sail through the wood—it was dense and continuous—and turning back presented difficulties. I climbed the highest tree to see what it was like farther on, and saw that the forest extended about six miles; beyond it was the beginning of another ocean. We decided to raise the ship onto the foliage, which was thick, and take it across, if possible, to the other sea. And that is what we did. We put a thick hawser around the ship, climbed the trees, and just managed to haul it up; then we got it onto the foliage, spread the sails, and sailed as on the sea, with the wind carrying us forward. At this point that line of Antimachus[47] came to my mind; he says somewhere,

> And as they journeyed, sailing through the wood.

Still, we made our way through the wood, with an effort, reached the 43 water, and let the ship down again the same way.

Then we sailed through clear, transparent water until we came to the edge of a great chasm in the sea, which was split, just as you often see great gaps in the earth, caused by earthquakes. We struck sail and just managed to bring the ship to a stop in time; she was very near plunging over. We looked over the edge and saw a drop of well over a hundred miles. It was very strange and very frightening: the water stood there as if cut in half. We looked around and saw, not far off to starboard, a bridge of water joining the seas at surface level, going from one side across to the other; so we struck out with our oars and went across by it. With a lot of effort we managed to get across; we never expected to.

On the other side, we entered upon a calm sea and came upon a fairly 44 small island, easy of access and inhabited. Living on it were savages, Ox-heads, with horns like the Minotaur in our myth. We landed and went inland to get water and food if possible—we had none left. The water we found close by, but nothing else was to be seen. We did, however, hear a loud lowing not far off. Thinking it was a herd of cattle, we went forward a little and came upon the men. As soon as they saw us they gave chase; three of my crew were caught, but the rest of us made our escape to the sea. There we all put on our armor, not wanting to leave our friends unavenged, and fell upon the Ox-heads as they were dividing up the flesh of their captives. They all panicked. We pursued them, killed about fifty, and took two alive. Then we returned with our captives. But still we had no food; so when everybody else was clamoring for the death of the prisoners, I refused to sanction this course but bound them instead and kept them until a deputation arrived from the Ox-heads to ransom them—that was how we interpreted their head nodding and

47. A poet of the fifth century B.C. of whose work some fragments have survived.

mournful, supplicatory lowing. The ransom was a great number of cheeses, dried fish, onions, and four deer; these last had three feet each—two behind, and the front feet joined into one. In return for this we gave back the prisoners; then, after staying there one day, we put to sea.

45     By now we could see fish, and birds flying, and various other indications of the proximity of land; and before very long we saw men sailing in a novel manner, for they were both crew and ship as well, as I shall explain. They floated on their backs in the water, erected their penises, which were very big, stretched sails from them, and then took the sheets in their hands and sailed along when the wind struck. After them appeared others sitting on corks and driving pairs of dolphins by means of reins; the dolphins pulled the corks along behind them. These people did not commit any aggression on us, nor did they avoid us; they rode past without fear or hostility and examined our ship from every side, expressing wonder at the shape of it.

46     That evening we put in at a small island, inhabited by women, as we thought, speaking Greek. They approached and received us with open arms. They were decked out like courtesans; all of them were young and lovely, and they wore garments that trailed around their ankles. The island was called Witchcraft, and the city Watertown. Well, the women paired off with us and entertained us; but I had a presentiment of something sinister and remained apart for a time.[48] On looking around more carefully, I saw the bones and skulls of a great many people lying about; but I did not want to raise the alarm, gather my men, and take arms. I took the mallow in my hand and prayed fervently to it for escape from our present troubles. Shortly afterward, as my hostess was looking after me, I saw that her legs were not those of a woman, but a donkey's with hooves.

    At this I drew my sword, seized the lady, tied her up, and questioned her about the whole business. She was very loath to answer but did so, saying that they were women of the sea, called Donkey-legs, and lived on strangers who came to the island; they made them drunk, she said, went to bed with them, and fell upon them as they were sleeping. On hearing this, I left her there tied up, climbed up onto the roof, and shouted to call my crew together. When they gathered, I told them the whole story, showed them the bones, and took them in to the woman I had tied up. At once she vanished, turning into water; still, to see what would happen, I thrust my sword into the water, and it turned into

47  blood. So we quickly returned to the ship and sailed off.

    As dawn began to break, we descried a continent that we supposed to be the one opposite to ours; so we saluted it with respect, prayed, and

48. Cf. *Odyssey* 10, the Circe episode, with this passage.

began to debate what to do next. Some thought we should merely land and turn back again right away; others wanted to leave the ship there, penetrate the interior, and see what the inhabitants were like. In the middle of this debate a fierce storm arose, caught the ship, and dashed it on the shore in wreckage. We just managed to swim to safety, each man snatching up his arms and anything else he could.

Such were my experiences as far as the other continent: on the sea, during the journey among the islands and in the sky, then in the whale; and after we left the whale, among the heroes and the dreams, and finally with the Ox-heads and the Donkey-legs. What happened on the continent I shall relate in the books to follow.[49]

49. Lucian never wrote them; this sentence, says a scholiast, is the biggest lie of all.

PSEUDO-CALLISTHENES

# THE ALEXANDER ROMANCE

## TRANSLATED BY
## KEN DOWDEN

## *Introduction*

*The Alexander Romance*, as it is usually called, was antiquity's most successful novel. Its author is unknown, its date uncertain, its literary quality doubtful; but eighty versions in twenty-four languages testify to a popularity and diffusion exceeded only by the Bible.

The author was more a compiler than a creative artist. A Greek-speaker living in Alexandria at some time between A.D. 140 and 340, he seems to have used mainly two books, merging them to form the *Life and Deeds of Alexander of Macedon*, which is often falsely ascribed in our manuscripts to Kallisthenes, Alexander's court historian. The first of the two books was a varied collection of fictions concerning Alexander. It included a sort of epistolary novel of about 100 B.C., which consisted chiefly of the correspondence of Alexander with his adversaries, notably Darius and Poros, and revealed the character of the correspondents, as ancient epistolary fictions were meant to do (examples start at 1.36). In this book was also a different sort of letter, in which Alexander sent back a description of marvels and monsters at the fringes of the world to his mother, Olympias (2.23–41), and to his tutor Aristotle (3.17, though our particular version no longer presents it as a letter). Other pieces in this collection may have included Alexander's interview with the "naked philosophers" of India (3.5–6); the romantic novelette of Alexander and Kandake, queen of Ethiopia (3.18–23—destined to become even more romantic and "courtly" in the Middle Ages); and a pamphlet—maybe even a piece of contemporary propaganda—on how Alexander died, including his last will and testament.

The other main source for the romance was a history deriving from Kleitarchos (circa 300 B.C.), who is said by Cicero to have written "rhetorically and dramatically"—not, one notes, truthfully. It comes as a shock to realize how quickly historians fictionalized Alexander: Onesikritos, who had actually accompanied Alexander, told how Alexander had met the queen of the (mythical) Amazons (cf.3.25-26). Historians could become preoccupied with character, meaningful incidents, and impact: even in this historical novel one should be guided by Plutarch's observation (at the very beginning of his own *Life of Alexander*) that a trivial action, remark, or joke can be more useful in biography than a major battle. Major battles are especially disappointing in the romance.

The author may have had other sources too—in particular, more popular Egyptian stories, available in Greek, of Nektanebos (see note 1 on 1.1) and of Sesonchosis (see note 38 on 1.33)—though scholars no longer think that oral tradition played a significant role.

It is easy to undervalue the author's product through hasty judgments about his intentions. Its style is limp and rarely rises above mediocre; chronology and geography are grossly muddled;[1] fact and inept fictions are indiscriminately combined. But the style may be deliberately humble: such is the style used by Xenophon of Ephesos and by Dares and Diktys, the authors of the fictional histories of Troy, and such is the style that Christians commended for their nonelite audiences. Correct chronology and geography were readily available to the author from his historian if he wanted them. And "factions" are a recognizable taste that it is perhaps too severe simply to dismiss with the judgment of R. Merkelbach that "mankind had become childlike again in late antiquity and the Middle Ages."[2] It should not be thought that the author or his audience was un-

---

1. I append a brief chronological table to illustrate the author's confusing disregard for chronology in Books 1 and 2.

| | |
|---|---|
| 335 B.C. | 1.27 (repeated at 1.46): Alexander destroys Thebes |
| 334 B.C. | 1.42: omens at the beginning of the expedition against Darius |
| | 1.43–44: Alexander between Macedonia and the Hellespont |
| | 1.42: Alexander at Troy |
| | 1.28: battle of the river Granikos |
| | 2.7: Darius's council of war |
| 333 B.C. | 1.41 (repeated at 2.8): Alexander healed by the doctor Philip |
| | 1.41: battle of Issos |
| | 2.17: Darius seeks the return of his family |
| 332 B.C. | 1.35: siege of Tyre |
| | 1.34: Alexander enthroned as pharaoh of Egypt |
| | 1.30: the shrine of Ammon at Siwah |
| 331 B.C. | 1.31–33: foundation of Alexandria |
| | 2.16: battle of Gaugamela (Arbela) |

It will be seen that, apart from 1.27–29 (which are peculiar to recension B), Alexander's campaigns are related in more or less inverse order.

2. R. Merkelbach, *Die Quellen des griechischen Alexanderromans* (2d. ed., Munich, 1977), 60.

able in the cold light of day to recognize fiction. His subject was not what Alexander was, but what Alexander meant, half a millennium after his death. For in this short and humble work is encapsulated, however inadequately for educated tastes, the striving of a real man, and a great man, at the limits of human nature, something more important than either fact or simple fiction. In this conception lie the grounds for the otherwise bewildering success of the romance.

It would be easier to judge the work if we knew what the author's original looked like. We have the author's manuscript of no ancient work of literature, only copies of copies of copies; but whereas in most other works scribes attempt to make exact and accurate copies, in the *Alexander Romance* the theme—Alexander's life and deeds—is so dominant over the form in which it is expressed that scribes at times alter its shape: episodes can be added, subtracted, or moved, and their expression curtailed or elaborated. The process of translation too can weaken its fixity. In short, the work proved uniquely flexible to meet the demands of different writers and audiences. On the other hand, its flexibility can be exaggerated: older versions are close enough to each other for us to come within sight of the author's original.

There are a number of recensions of the story in the Greek tradition. Recension A, though itself damaged and abbreviated, comes closest to the original. Rather more abbreviated is recension B, which includes the manuscript L on the basis of which H. van Thiel prepared the edition of the text that I use for this translation. It includes, notably, the influential letter to Olympias (2.23–41), which is missing in A; and it shows one way out of the very many in which the *Alexander Romance* could be instantiated—a way adopted by Girard of Patras, who wrote manuscript L in the early fifteenth century. On the other hand, I have adopted a less purist attitude than van Thiel: I have corrected some passages that no longer make much sense because of mistakes introduced in copying and abbreviation.[3] In so doing I have attempted to return to the author's original (usually as in A). In addition, I have corrected proper names as far as possible.

The same book and chapter numbers are used for the various ancient Greek recensions. Thus, when our manuscript omits an episode found in another ancient Greek recension, the appropriate chapter numbers are missing (e.g., 2.1–5). I have indicated briefly at these points the nature of the missing episode, though it may not always be part of the author's original text.

The letter to Olympias (2.23–41), though omitted by A, was included, at least in part, in the author's original. In the form in which we

3. For typical, but uncorrected, examples, see note 7 to 1.13 and note 91 to 3.26.

find it in L, it displays a change of register from the preceding narrative, from the historical to the fantastic. The real Alexander's restless curiosity is transfigured through the medium of myth, as he reaches through darkness for the ends of the earth and the Land of the Blest, as he probes the depths of the sea and observes from the heights of the sky the slightness of the whole world he is conquering. This mixture of fantasy and revelation at the heart of the novel has something of the spirit of Apuleius's *Cupid and Psyche* tale in *The Golden Ass,* or even of Aeneas's descent to the underworld in Vergil's *Aeneid.* Remarkably, though, the limiting of the human condition through the fantastic quest of its greatest king finds its nearest parallel in the ancient Sumerian *Epic of Gilgamesh.*

In Greek, the *Alexander Romance* has been continuously read and revised through ancient, Byzantine, and modern Greek versions from its composition to the present day (Lolos cites a film of 1980 as its latest instantiation). To the East, an Armenian translation of the fifth century was its gateway to numerous languages; it influenced the great Persian poet Firdawsi and Persian manuscript illumination; through the Arabic it even reached India and Indonesia. Among the Slavs, a Bulgarian translation of recension B began the diffusion. But for European literature it was the Latin translations that were important: as early as the fourth century, Julius Valerius Polemius, consul in 338, made a stylish translation in the manner of Apuleius, an abridged version of which was well known in the Middle Ages. But the major source for the Europeans was the *Historia de Preliis Alexandri,* an enlarged edition of a translation made by Leo, an archpresbyter at Naples around 960. Of this edition there survive more than one hundred manuscripts. In addition, the *Letter to Aristotle* (the basis of 3.17) and *Alexander and Dindimus King of the Brahmans* (cf. 3.5–6) circulated separately.

Already in Old English times such texts were known. In 781 Alcuin at York sent Charlemagne a copy of *Alexander and Dindimus.* The principal *Beowulf* manuscript (circa A.D. 1000) also contains a translation of the *Letter to Aristotle.* And a late eleventh century English manuscript contains the abridged Julius Valerius, the *Letter to Aristotle,* and *Alexander and Dindimus.* But the great importance of the *Alexander Romance* began in the late twelfth century, when French chivalrous epic became fashionable. Alexander was one of a select number of favored subjects, including Troy (as in Dares and Diktys), Arthur, and Charlemagne, "factions" all. About this time Thomas of Kent used principally the abridged Julius Valerius to produce *le roman de toute chevalerie,* as the Anglo-Norman Alexander poem is called, which was soon enlarged from the French *roman d'Alexandre* prepared by his contemporary Alexandre de Bernays (or de Paris) on the basis of the *Historia de Preliis.* During the next two centuries a number of Alexander poems circulated, more than now survive, making Alexander a household name. Thomas of Kent was the main source for the early fourteenth-century *King Alisaunder* and for an episode in John Gower's *Confessio Amantis*. The same century saw Alexander in a variety of meters, such as the alliterative blank verse of the not inconsiderable *Wars of Alexander* and the heroic couplets of Sir Gilbert Hay's *Alexander*. In the originally French *Travels of Sir John Mandeville,* the *Letter to Aristotle* provides, for instance, the marvel of the speaking trees (3.17); and in Scotland, French poetry supplied the raw material for the *Buik of Alexander* (possibly by John Barbour). Chaucer could easily sum it up:

> The storie of Alisaundre is so commune
> That every wight that hath discrecioun
> Hath herd somwhat or al of his fortune.
> (Monk's Tale, 7.2631–33).

## Bibliography

TEXT

Merkelbach, R. *Die Quellen des griechischen Alexanderromans.* 2d ed. Munich, 1977.
Van Thiel, H., ed. *Leben und Taten Alexanders von Makedonien.* Darmstadt, 1974. Reprint, 1983.

GENERAL

Hägg, Tomas. *The Novel in Antiquity.* Oxford and Berkeley, 1983. Pages 125–40 deal with *The Alexander Romance.*

# THE ALEXANDER ROMANCE

## Book One

I NO FINER OR MORE COURAGEOUS man is held to have existed than Alexander, king of Macedon. He had a special way of doing everything and found his own qualities always had Providence for a partner. In fact, his wars and battles with any one nation were over before historians had time to gather full information on its cities. The deeds of Alexander, the excellences of his body and of his soul, his success in his actions, his bravery, are our present subject. We begin with his family—and the identity of his father. People generally are under the misapprehension that he was the son of King Philip. This is quite wrong. He was not the child of Philip but rather, as the wisest Egyptians assert, the son of Nektanebos,[1] conceived after he had been driven from his throne.

This Nektanebos was an expert in the art of magic, and since his magic gave him the advantage over all nations, by the use of this power he lived in peace. If ever an enemy force attacked him, he did not start preparing armies or constructing engines of war or readying a weapon transport or bothering his officers about battle dispositions. Instead he would set down a dish and practice dish divining. He would pour springwater into the dish, form wax models of ships and men in his hands, and put them in the dish. Then, he would don the robes of a prophet, holding a staff of ebony in his hand; and, standing, he invoked the "gods"[2] of his spells—spirits of the air and demons of the earth beneath—and at his spell the model men came alive. In this way he sank the model ships in the dish, and immediately, as they were being sunk, the ships at sea belonging to the enemy attacking him were destroyed through the man's expertise in magic. So then, his kingdom remained at peace.

After some time had passed, some *exploratores* (which is what the Romans call spies) came to Nektanebos and reported to him that a great war cloud, armies of innumerable warriors, was advancing on Egypt. Nektanebos's general came to him and said: "O King, live long! Dismiss now all your ways of peace and get ready for the dispositions of war: a great cloud of barbarians is attacking us. It is not just one nation that is advancing upon us, but millions of people. Advancing on us are Indians, Nokimaians, Oxydrakai, Iberians, Kauchones, Lelapes, Bosporoi, Bastranoi, Azanoi, Chalybes, and all the other great nations of the East, armies of innumerable warriors advancing against Egypt.[3] So postpone your other business and consider your position."

1. Nektanebo(s) II was the last native Egyptian king of Egypt. Coming to the throne in 360 B.C., he repulsed the attack around 350 B.C. of Artaxerxes III Ochus, king of Persia. But in 343 Artaxerxes led a better-prepared invasion force, spearheaded by Greek mercenaries, and overwhelmed Egypt. Nektanebos lost heart early and fled—south to Ethiopia, never to return and never to become father of Alexander. This King Arthur, as it were, of Egypt figures in a papyrus fragment of the second century B.C. that has been thought to cast some light on the origins of the Greek novel. The papyrus preserves the so-called *Dream of Nektanebos,* part of an Egyptian story translated into Greek, which seems to tell how the gods turned against Nektanebos. It could have continued by making Nektanebos Alexander's father. To be legitimized as ruler of Egypt, Alexander would need to be son of Nektanebos and also son of Ammon.

2. *The Alexander Romance* appears to have been written from a pagan point of view, though the term "Providence above," which otherwise first gains favor with the early Christian fathers, is embedded in the novel. Our manuscript L extends the use of this Christian term and likes to emphasize that Nektanebos's gods are only so-called gods. In a later recension one even finds Ammon, who appears in a dream to Alexander at 2.13, replaced by the prophet Jeremiah!

3. This overwhelming list of frighteningly exotic barbarian tribes fails to mention the Persians who were actually conducting the invasion: our author is concerned more with effect than accuracy.

At these words of the general, King Nektanebos laughed long and said to him: "From the point of view of carrying out the responsibilities of your post, what you say is fine and reasonable; but it is still a cowardly and unsoldierlike statement. Power is not a matter of numbers; war is a matter of drive. After all, it only takes one lion to overpower many deer, and one wolf to ravage many flocks of sheep. So you go with the armies under your command and maintain your position! With one word I shall engulf the innumerable host of barbarians in the sea." And with that Nektanebos dismissed the general from his presence.

3    He himself, however, arose and went into the palace. When he was quite alone, he used the same invocation and looked into the dish. And there he saw the gods of Egypt steering the vessels of his foreign enemies and their armies being guided by the gods themselves. Nektanebos was a man of much experience in magic and accustomed to talking with his gods, and, learning from them that the end of the kingdom of Egypt was at hand, he put in his pocket a large quantity of gold, shaved off his hair and his beard, changed his appearance, and fled via Pelusion. After a voyage he reached Pella in Macedonia and set himself up there at a particular place as an Egyptian prophet, with a thriving business in astrology.

Meanwhile, the Egyptians were asking their "gods" whatever had become of the king of Egypt (by now the whole of Egypt had been devastated by the foreigners), and their "god" in the sanctum of the Sarapeion uttered an oracle to them in these words.

This king who has fled will come again to Egypt, not in age but in youth, and our enemy the Persians he shall subdue.[4]

They debated the meaning of what had been said to them, but finding no solution, they inscribed the oracle given to them on the pedestal of Nektanebos's statue.

4    After his arrival in Macedonia, Nektanebos became well known to everyone. His calculations were of such accuracy that even the queen, Olympias, heard of him and came to him by night while her husband Philip was away at war. And she learned from him what she had been seeking, and left. A few days later, she sent for him and told him to come to her. When he saw how beautiful she was, Nektanebos was filled with desire for her loveliness and, reaching out his hand, said, "Greetings, Queen of the Macedonians!"

4. An oracle to the effect that Nektanebos would return to rule again is apparently presented in the Egyptian "Demotic Chronicle" (third century B.C.). The implication of our oracle should be that he will return as the youthful Alexander. The Sarapeion is the shrine of the god Sarapis.

"Greetings to you also, most excellent prophet!" she replied. "Come here and sit down." She continued: "You are the Egyptian teacher whose complete reliability has been established by those who have tried you. Even I have been convinced by you. By what method can you command true predictions?"

He replied: "There is a wide choice of method, O Queen. There are horoscope casters, sign solvers, dream specialists, oracular ventriloquists, bird observers, birth-date examiners, and those called magoi, who have the gift of prophecy." And with that he looked up fiercely at Olympias.

Olympias said to him, "Prophet, has your gaze become fixed at the sight of me?"

"Yes, lady," he replied. "I was reminded of an oracle given to me by my own gods that I must be consulted by a queen, and, look, it has come true. So now tell me what you wish."

Putting his hand in his pocket, he took out a little tablet, which mere words could not describe. It was made up of gold and ivory, with seven stars and the ascendant. The sun was of crystal, the moon adamant, Jupiter aerial jasper, Mars bloodred hematite, Saturn serpentine, Venus sapphire, Mercury emerald, and the ascendant white marble. Olympias, fascinated by so precious a tablet, sat down beside Nektanebos and, dismissing all the servants, said to him: "Prophet, cast my horoscope and Philip's"; for there was a rumor concerning her that if Philip returned from the war, he would divorce her and marry another.

Nektanebos replied, "Tell me your date of birth and tell me Philip's." And what did Nektanebos do next? He put his own date of birth with that of Olympias and, having completed his calculations, said to her, "The rumor you have heard about yourself is not wrong; but, as an Egyptian prophet, I can help you avoid being divorced by Philip."

"How can you?" she asked.

He replied, "You must have intercourse with a god on earth, conceive by him, bear a son and rear him, and have him to avenge you for the wrongs Philip has done you."

"What god?" Olympias asked.

"Ammon of Libya," he told her.

"And what is this god like, then?" Olympias asked him.

"Middle-aged," he replied, "with golden hair and beard and with horns growing from his forehead—these too just like gold. So you must get yourself ready like a queen for him, because today in a dream you shall see this god have intercourse with you."

And she said to him, "If I see this dream, I shall revere you not as a magos, but as a god."

So Nektanebos left the queen and picked from the wasteland herbs he knew for bringing dreams and extracted their juices. Then he made a wax model in the shape of a woman and wrote on it the name of Olympias. He lit lamps and, sprinkling the juice from the herbs over them, invoked with oaths the demons appointed to this function so that Olympias had a vision. And she saw the god Ammon embracing her that night and as he arose from her, saying to her, "Woman, you have a male child in your womb to be your avenger!"

6    Olympias arose from her sleep in amazement and with all speed sent for Nektanebos, and when he came, said to him: "I have seen the dream and the god Ammon you told me about. I beg of you, Prophet, bring me together with him again. And do be careful about when he is going to come to me, so that I may be better prepared for my bridegroom."

He replied: "First of all, mistress, what you saw was a dream. When the god comes in person into your sight, he will see to your needs. But if Your Majesty commands, give me a room to sleep in, so that I may intercede with him on your behalf."

"Here," she said, "have a room in my quarters. And if I manage to become pregnant by this god, I shall honor you greatly, as a queen can, and treat you as though you were the child's father."

Nektanebos said to her: "There is something you must know, mistress. Before the god enters, there is this sign: when you are sitting in your room in the evening, if you see a snake gliding towards you, dismiss the servants but do not douse the lamps that I now give you, having prepared them expertly to be lit in honor of the god. Instead, go back to your royal bed and get ready: cover your face and do not look directly at the god you saw coming to you in your dreams."

So saying, Nektanebos left, and the next day Olympias gave him a bedroom immediately next to hers.

7    Nektanebos got ready for himself a very soft ram's fleece, complete with the horns on its temples, and an ebony scepter and white clothing and a cloak of the exact color of a snake, and went into the bedroom where Olympias was lying covered up on the bed. But she was looking out of the corner of her eye: she saw him coming and was not afraid, since she was expecting him to be as he had appeared in the dream. The lamps lit up, and Olympias covered her face. Nektanebos, setting down his scepter, got into her bed and lay with her. And he said to her: "Have strength, woman! You have in your womb a male child to be your avenger and king and sovereign of the whole world." Then Nektanebos took his scepter and left the bedroom and hid all the props he had.

In the morning Olympias awoke, went into the room of Nektanebos, and roused him from his sleep. He rose and said: "Greetings, Queen! What news do you bring me?"

"I am surprised, Prophet," she replied, "that you do not already know. Will this god be coming back to me? I had such pleasure from him."

"Listen to me, Queen," he said to her. "I am the prophet of this god. So, when you wish, provide me with this place to sleep undisturbed so that I may perform the purification appropriate to him. Then he will come to you."

She replied, "Have this place from now on," and gave instructions that he was to be given the keys of the bedroom.

He put his props away in a secret place and went to her as often as Olympias wanted—with her thinking he was the god Ammon.

Day by day her stomach enlarged, and Olympias asked Nektanebos, "If Philip comes home and finds me pregnant, what am I to say?"

"Have no fear, mistress," Nektanebos replied to her. "The god Ammon will help you with this by appearing to Philip in his dreams and letting him know what has happened. As a result, Philip will be unable to find fault with you."

In this way, then, Olympias was taken in by Nektanebos, thanks to his magical powers.

Presently Nektanebos took a sea hawk and enchanted it. He told it everything he wanted said to Philip in a dream, using the black arts of magic to prepare it. And the sea hawk, released by Nektanebos, flew through the night to the place where Philip was, and spoke to him in a dream. Philip, seeing the hawk speak to him, woke greatly disturbed. So without delay he sent for a dream interpreter, a distinguished Babylonian, and related the marvel to him, saying: "I saw a god in a dream. He was very handsome, with grey hair and beard, and he had horns on his temples, both like gold; and in his hand he held a scepter. It was night, and he was going to my wife, Olympias, lying down, and having intercourse with her. Then, as he rose, he said to her: 'Woman, you have conceived a male child who shall tend you and shall avenge the death of his father.' And I thought I used papyrus thread to sew her up and that I put my seal upon her. And the seal ring was of gold, containing a stone with a relief of sun, lion's head, and spear. While I was having these impressions, I seemed to see a hawk perched over me, waking me from my sleep with its wings. What does all this mean for me?"

So the dream interpreter said to him: "King Philip, live long! What you saw in your dream is true. Sealing your wife's womb is indicative of your confidence that your wife has actually conceived: people seal a full vessel, not an empty one. As for your sewing her up with papyrus, papyrus is produced nowhere else except in Egypt. So the seed is Egyptian, and not lowly, but dazzling and glorious, as the gold ring shows: what, after all, is more glorious than gold, a medium through which men worship the gods? As regards the seal with the sun, a lion's head beneath, and a spear: this child—who is going to be born will reach the rising sun, waging war with all—like a lion—and capturing cities by force—on account of the spear beneath. As for your having seen a god with ram's horns and grey hair, this is the god of Libya, Ammon." This was the interpretation of the expert, and Philip did not like what he heard.

9     Now Olympias was in distress, as she had little confidence in Nektanebos's arrangement to deal with Philip, and when Philip returned from the war, he saw his wife was upset and said to her: "Wife, why are you upset at what has happened? It is someone else's fault—that has been shown to me in a dream—so you cannot be blamed. We kings have power over all, but we do not have power over the gods. Your affair was not with one of the people, but with one of the most magnificent beings." With these words, Philip cheered Olympias, and she thanked the prophet who had let her have advance knowledge of Philip's experiences.

10     A few days later Philip was with Olympias and said to her, "You have deceived me, wife: you were made pregnant not by a god, but by someone else—and he is going to fall into my hands!" Nektanebos heard this. There was a great banquet in the palace, and everyone was feasting with King Philip to celebrate his return. King Philip alone was downcast—because Olympias, his wife, was pregnant. So, in front of everyone, Nektanebos turned himself into a serpent larger than the original one and came into the middle of the dining hall and hissed so hideously that the foundations of the palace shook. The king's guests leapt up in panic at the sight of the serpent; Olympias, however, recognized her bridegroom and reached out her right hand to him. And the serpent stirred himself to rest his head in her hand and coiled down to Olympias's knees and, putting out his forked tongue, kissed her—a token of his love for the benefit of the onlookers. And while Philip was simultaneously protesting and yet gazing insatiably in amazement, the serpent changed himself into an eagle; and where he went, it would be pointless to say.

Regaining his composure, Philip said: "Wife, I have seen the god coming to your assistance in peril, and that proves his concern for you. But I do not at present know the identity of the god: he has displayed to me the shape of the god Ammon and of Apollo and of Asklepios."

Olympias replied, "As he revealed to me in person when he came to me, he is the god of all Libya, Ammon."

Philip counted himself lucky at what he had seen: the child his wife bore was going to be known as the seed of a god.

11     Some days later, Philip was sitting in one of the royal gardens, when a mass of birds of various kinds was feeding there. Then, suddenly, one bird leapt into King Philip's lap and laid an egg; but it rolled off his lap

and broke as it fell on the ground. From it sprang a tiny serpent that coiled around the shell and then attempted to reenter where it had emerged; but, having got its head inside, it died. King Philip was disturbed at this, sent for an interpreter, and outlined to him what had happened. The interpreter, inspired by God, said: "King, you will have a son who will go round the whole world, bringing everyone under his sway. But, turning back towards his own kingdom, he will die young; for the serpent is a royal beast, and the egg from which the serpent came is like the world. So, having encircled the world and wanting to return where he had come from, he did not reach it but died instead." So then the interpreter, having resolved the problem, was duly rewarded by King Philip and left.

When the time came for Olympias to give birth, she sat on the 12 birthing stool and labored. Nektanebos stood beside her and, calculating the courses of the heavenly bodies, distracted her from delivering too quickly. Using his magical powers violently to adjust the celestial bodies, he learned what the situation was and said to her: "Woman, hold yourself back and defeat the situation nature presents. If you give birth now, you will produce a servile prisoner or a monster."

When again the woman was in distress from her labor and was no longer able to hold out against the intensity of the contractions, Nektanebos said: "Persevere a little longer, woman. If you give birth now, your offspring will be a eunuch and a failure." In addition, with encouragement and kindly words he instructed Olympias how to hold her hands over the paths of nature and himself used his magic to restrain the woman's delivery.

Now once more observing the courses in heaven of the celestial bodies, he realized that the whole cosmos was at its zenith; and he saw a brilliance shining from heaven, as from the sun at its zenith, and said to Olympias, "Now give out the birth cry!" Indeed, he himself urged on her delivery and said to her, "You are on the point of bearing a king who will rule the world." and Olympias, bellowing louder than a cow, gave birth with good fortune to a male child. As the child fell to the ground, there were continual thunderclaps and lightning flashes stirring the whole world.

In the morning, Philip saw Olympias's newborn child and said: "I had 13 wanted not to rear it, as it was not my offspring; but since I see that the seed came from a god and that the birth has been specially marked by heaven, he shall be raised in memory of my son by my previous wife, who died; and he shall be called Alexander." That was what Philip said, and the child received every attention. And garlands were worn throughout Macedonia, Pella, and Thrace.

I do not want to take long over Alexander's upbringing: he was weaned, and he grew older. When he became a man, his appearance was not like Philip's and, indeed, not even like his mother Olympias's or his real father's—he was a type all of his own. Indeed, he had the shape of a man, but he had the mane of a lion and eyes of different colors—the right eye black, the left grey—and teeth as sharp as a serpent's; he displayed the energy of a lion. And there was no doubt of how his nature would turn out.[5]

His nurse was Lanike (the sister of Kleitos the Black); his school attendant and governor, Leonidas; his primary teacher, Polyneikes; his music teacher, Leukippos of Lemnos; his teacher of geometry, Menippos from the Peloponnese; of rhetoric, Anaximenes of Lampsakos, son of Aristokles; of philosophy, Aristotle of Stageira, son of Nikomachos.[6]

Having followed the entire curriculum, even astronomy, and being released from his studies, Alexander began in turn to teach his classmates. He drilled them for war and, standing apart, set them fighting; and when he saw one side being defeated by the other, he would go over to the losing side and help them out; and it would start winning again—so it was clear that he was victory. This, then, was Alexander's upbringing.

Now, one day Philip's horse breeders brought a colt of outstanding size from his studs and presented him to King Philip, with the words: "Lord King, we have found this horse born in the royal studs of a beauty that exceeds that of Pegasus. So we bring it to you, master." Looking at its size and beauty, King Philip was amazed. It needed the strength of them all to hold it back, and the horse breeders added, "Lord King, it is a man-eater!" "This really does show," King Philip replied, "the truth of the Greek proverb 'Close to good stands evil.' But since you have already brought him, I will take him." And he instructed his attendants to make an iron cage and to lock the horse in there without a bit "and any who are disobedient to my rule and require punishment after disobeying the law or being convicted of piracy[7] shall be thrown to him." And the king's instructions were carried out.

14     Alexander grew older, and when he was twelve, he started accompanying his father on troop maneuvers: he armed himself, swept along with the armies, leapt on the horses. As a result, Philip, seeing him, said, "Alexander, my boy, I like your character and your bravery, if not your appearance—because it is not like mine."

---

5. L makes no sense of this sentence: I have substituted the version of A.

6. This list of teachers came from Favorinus's *Universal History* and provides the *terminus post quem* for the dating of the romance (circa A.D. 140).

7. A rather illogical alternative, an example of thoughtless rewriting in our manuscript; A has "so that we may throw to him those who require punishment by law, convicted of piracy or murder."

All of this was upsetting for Olympias; so she called Nektanebos to her and said to him, "Investigate what Philip intends to do with me." He set out his tablet and investigated her stars as Alexander sat by them. And Alexander said to him, "Sir, can't these stars you are talking about be seen in the sky?" "Of course they can, boy!" he replied. And Alexander said to him "Can I not know about them?" "Yes, boy," he replied, "you can when evening falls."

So in the evening Nektanebos collected Alexander and took him outside the city to a solitary spot and, looking up to the sky, showed Alexander the stars in the heavens. But Alexander took him by the hand, led him to a pit in the ground, and let him fall. Nektanebos, as he fell, took a fearful blow on the back of his head and cried: "Ah, Alexander, my boy, why did you decide to do that?"

Alexander replied, "Blame yourself, astrologer!"

"Why, boy?" he asked.

"Because," said Alexander, "you make a study of the heavens in ignorance of things on earth."

"Boy," said Nektanebos to him, "I am badly wounded. But there is no way that any mortal can overcome his fate."

"Why?" asked Alexander.

"Because I had read my own fate," said Nektanebos to him. "I was to be slain by my own child, and I have not escaped my fate: I have been slain by you."

"Am I your son then?" asked Alexander.

Then Nektanebos told him how he had been king in Egypt, had fled from Egypt, had come to live in Pella, had met Olympias and cast her horoscope, and how he had gone to her as the god Ammon and had had intercourse with her. With these words, he breathed out his spirit.

Alexander heard him say this and, being convinced that he had killed his father, was heartbroken and did not leave him in the pit for fear that he might become food for the beasts (it was night, and it was a solitary place). Moved by filial affection, he girt himself up and lifted him bravely onto his shoulders; then he took him to his mother, Olympias. At this sight Olympias said to Alexander, "What is this, my child?" And he replied, "I am another Aeneas and carry my Anchises," and proceeded to relate to her in detail everything he had heard from Nektanebos. She was astonished and blamed herself for having been deceived by him and his evil magical skills into adultery. But moved by affection, she buried him as befitted the father of Alexander, and, constructing a tomb, she had him placed there. It is one of Providence's notable marvels that Nektanebos, an Egyptian, received a funeral in the Greek style in Macedonia, but that Alexander, a Macedonian, received a funeral in the Egyptian style.

15    On his return from abroad Philip went off to Delphi to consult the oracle on who would succeed him as king. And the Pythia at Delphi tasted
the Kastalian spring and with an oracle of the earth replied as follows:[8]

*oracle*

> Philip, he shall be king over the whole world and shall subject all to
> his power, whosoever shall leap upon the horse Bucephalus and
> ride through the center of Pella.

(It was called Bucephalus because its shank was branded with the head
[*cephale*] of an ox [*bus*].) Philip, hearing the oracle, was expecting another
Hercules.

16    Alexander had Aristotle as his sole teacher. Many other children were
studying with Aristotle, among them the sons of kings, and one day
Aristotle asked one of them, "If you inherit your father's kingdom, what
will you give me, your teacher?" He replied, "You shall hold a unique
position of power as my companion, and I shall make you famous everywhere."

He asked another, "If you, boy, succeed to your father's kingdom,
how will you treat me, your teacher?" He replied, "I shall make you a
minister and consult you on all matters that require my decision."

And he also asked Alexander, "If you, Alexander, boy, succeed to the
kingdom of your father Philip, how will you treat me, your teacher?"
Alexander replied: "Are you asking me now about future matters,
though you have no certainty about tomorrow? I shall give you your reward when the time and opportunity arrive." And Aristotle said to him,
"Hail Alexander, world ruler: you shall be the greatest king."

Everyone liked Alexander, since he was intelligent and a good warrior. Only Philip had mixed feelings: it gave him pleasure to see such a
warlike spirit in the boy, but it pained him to see that the boy was unlike
him.

17    Alexander was fifteen when by chance one day he was passing the
place where the horse Bucephalus was caged. He heard a terrifying neigh
and, turning to the attendants, asked "What is this neighing?" In reply,
the general Ptolemy said, "Master, this is the horse Bucephalus that your
father caged because he was a man-eater." But the horse, hearing the
sound of Alexander's voice, neighed again, not in a terrifying manner as
on all previous occasions, but sweetly and clearly as though instructed by
God. And when Alexander went up to the cage, straightaway the horse
extended its forefeet to Alexander and licked him, indicating who its
master was. Alexander observed the striking appearance of the horse and

8. The Pythia's trance was usually attributed to the effect of fumes supposed to issue
from the ground, but here is ascribed to drinking the springwater of Kastalia. The phrase
"with an oracle of the earth" is odd and may result from rewriting of an earlier version of
this recension.

the remains of numerous slaughtered men at its feet, but elbowed aside the horse's guards and opened the cage. He grasped its mane;[9] it obeyed him, and he leapt on it without a bridle, then rode through the center of the city of Pella. One of the horse breeders ran and informed King Philip, who was outside the city of Pella, and Philip, remembering the oracle, went to meet Alexander and greeted him with the words "Hail, Alexander, world ruler." And thereafter thought of the child's future made Philip glad.

Now one day Alexander found his father at leisure and, giving him a kiss, said, "Father, please, will you let me sail to Pisa for the Olympic Games—because I would like to take part."    18

"You want to go?" asked Philip. "So what sport have you been training in?"

"I want to enter the chariot race," replied Alexander.

"My boy," he said, "I shall now see to suitable horses for you from my stables. So they will be taken care of; but you, my boy, must train yourself more seriously—it is a prestigious competition."

Alexander replied, "Father, you just let me go to the competition: I have horses that I have reared for myself since they were young."

Philip gave Alexander a kiss and, astounded at his determination, said to him, "Boy, this is what you want; so go with my blessing."

Alexander went off to the harbor and gave instructions for a brand new ship to be built and for the horses complete with their chariots to be put aboard. Alexander embarked together with his friend Hephaistion and after a voyage reached Pisa. On disembarkation, he received numerous gifts and instructed the lads to rub down the horses. Himself, he went for a walk with his friend Hephaistion, and they ran into Nikolaos, son of King Andreas of Akarnania,[10] a man proud of his wealth and good fortune—two unstable gods—and confident in his physical strength. He went up to Alexander and hailed him with the words "Greetings, young man!"

"Greetings to you too," he replied, "whoever you are and wherever you come from."

Nikolaos said to Alexander, "I am Nikolaos, king of Akarnania."

But Alexander said to him, "Do not be so proud, King Nikolaos, or preen yourself in the opinion that you are well equipped to deal with your life tomorrow: Fortune does not stay in one place, and change shows up the worthlessness of braggarts."

9. "Mane" according to A; "halter" according to the Armenian, which adds that Alexander used brute strength rather than good luck to tame the horse; "tendon" (?) according to L. In Plutarch *Life of Alexander* 6 Alexander takes the *rein* and turns Bucephalus towards the sun because he is worried by his shadow. The sense of this story has been lost by either our author or the recensions.

10. Nikolaos is invented by our author—and Akarnania was not ruled by a king!

Nikolaos replied: "What you say is right, but what you imply is not. Why are you here? As a spectator or a competitor? I understand that you are the son of Philip of Macedon."

"I may be young," Alexander replied, "but I am here to compete with you in the horse-racing."

"You should rather," said Nikolaos, "have come for the wrestling, the boxing, or the all-in fighting."[11]

Alexander replied, "I want to take part in the chariot-racing."

Then Nikolaos boiled over with rage and contempt for Alexander, observing how young he was but not having discovered the capacity of his soul, and spat in his face, saying: "May no good come to you! See what the stadium of Pisa has sunk to!"

But Alexander, taught by nature to control his feelings, wiped off the spit that insulted him and, with a smile that meant death, said, "Nikolaos, I shall defeat you forthwith, and in your homeland of Akarnania I shall take you prisoner." And they parted as enemies.

19  A few days later the time for the competition arrived. Nine men had entered for the chariot race, four of them sons of kings: Nikolaos the Akarnanian himself, Xanthias the Boeotian, Kimon the Corinthian, and Alexander the Macedonian.[12] The rest were sons of satraps and of generals. Everything for the competition was in place, including the urn, from which the lots were now drawn. Nikolaos drew first place, Xanthias second, Kimon third, Kleitomachos fourth, Aristippos of Olynthos fifth, Pieros of Phokaia sixth, Kimon of Lindos seventh, Alexander of Macedon eighth, Nikomachos of Lokroi ninth. Next they took up position for the race. The trumpet rang out the signal to begin. The starting gates on the stalls were opened up. They all leapt forward at an enormous pace— first lap, second and third and fourth. Now those at the back slackened as their horses gave out; but Alexander was driving in fourth position, and behind him was Nikolaos, not so much trying to win as to kill Alexander: Nikolaos's father had been killed by Philip in a war. Alexander had the intelligence to realize this, and when the leading drivers caused each other to fall, he let Nikolaos get past. And Nikolaos, unaware of the trap, overtook him, with his thoughts on the crown of victory. Now he was driving in first position, but, two laps further on, the right-hand

11. A contest (*pankration*) combining traits of boxing and wrestling, sometimes compared to judo. Biting and gouging were not allowed, but dislocation of limbs and bone breaking were—clearly not a sport for aristocrats. Plutarch remarks how Alexander never instituted contests in boxing or all-in fighting; he also reports an anecdote in which Alexander declines to take part in foot-racing on the grounds that he would not have kings for competitors. These are the materials out of which this episode has been invented.

12. The names of the participants other than Alexander appear to be fictional.

horse of Nikolaos stumbled against the front of the chariot, and the front horses came down together with it, and Nikolaos fell. Alexander hurtled forward, thanks to the pace of his own horses, and as he passed, seized the pole of Nikolaos's rear horses, and the whole of Nikolaos's chariot collapsed together with the charioteer, and Nikolaos was killed. Now Alexander and no one else was left, and the man who died suffered what the proverb says: "Whoever makes trouble for another, makes trouble for himself."

Now Alexander was crowned and, wearing his victory crown of wild olive, went up to the temple of Olympian Zeus. And the prophet of Zeus said to him: "Alexander, Olympian Zeus makes this prediction for you: 'Be of good cheer! As you have defeated Nikolaos, so shall you defeat many in your wars.' "[13]

Alexander, receiving this omen, returned victorious to Macedonia to find that his mother, Olympias, had been divorced by King Philip and that Philip had married the sister of Lysias, by name Kleopatra. Philip's wedding was taking place that very day, and Alexander, wearing his Olympic victory crown, entered the banquet and said to King Philip: "Father, accept the victory crown of my first exertions. And when in turn I give my mother, Olympias, to another king, I shall invite you to Olympias's wedding." So saying, Alexander reclined opposite his father, Philip, but Philip was hurt by Alexander's words.   20

Then Lysias, a joker who was reclining at table, said to Philip, "King Philip, ruler over every city, now we celebrate your wedding with Kleopatra, an honorable lady, by whom you will have legitimate children, not the product of adultery—and they will look like you." Hearing Lysias say this made Alexander angry, and he reacted instantly, hurling his goblet at Lysias; it hit him on the temple and killed him. Philip, seeing what had happened, stood up, sword in hand—pointed in fury at Alexander—and fell over, tripping against the bottom of the couch. Alexander laughed and said to Philip, "Here is the man eager to take over the whole of Asia and subjugate Europe to its very foundations—and you are not capable of taking a single step." And with these words Alexander seized the sword from Philip, his father, and left all the guests half-slaughtered. It was just like watching the story of the Centaurs: some fled under the couches; some used tables for cover; others hid in dark areas. The result was that you could see Alexander as another, latter-day, Odysseus killing the suitors of Penelope.   21

Then Alexander went off and brought his mother, Olympias, into the palace, becoming an avenger of her marriage, but Lysias's sister Kleopa-

13. It is probably relevant that Niko-laos means literally "defeat-people."

tra he drove into exile. The bodyguards took up King Philip and laid him down on the couch—in extremely bad condition.[14]

22    Ten days later, Alexander went in to Philip and, sitting down by him, said to him, "King Philip—I shall call you by your name so that you may not have the displeasure of being called Father by me—I have come to you not as your son, but as your friend to intervene in your unfair treatment of your wife."

Philip said to him, "You did a bad thing, Alexander, by killing Lysias for the improper words he uttered."

"But you," replied Alexander, "did a fine thing by standing up sword raised against your child, wanting to kill me, and by wanting to marry another though your previous wife, Olympias, had done you no wrong? So get up and pull yourself together—I know what is making your body sluggish[15]—and let us forget these errors. I shall now appeal to Olympias, my mother, to be reconciled to you: she will be persuaded by her son—even if you are not prepared to be called my father!"

With these words Alexander left and, going to his mother, Olympias, said to her: "Mother, do not be angry at what your husband has done. He does not know about your indiscretion, whereas I, the son of an Egyptian father, am the living evidence against you. So go and appeal to him to be reconciled to you: it is the decent thing for a wife to take second place to her husband." And he took his mother to King Philip, his father, and said: "Father, turn to face your wife—I shall now call you Father, as you for your part follow the advice of your child. My mother stands at your side as a result of the many appeals I have made to her to come in to you and forget what has been done. Now embrace each other: there is no shame in your doing so in front of me—I was, after all, born from you." So saying, he reconciled his parents, and all the Macedonians were amazed by him. And from then on people who were getting married avoided mentioning the name of Lysias, in case by the mention of his name[16] they should be parted.

23    The city of Methone had rebelled against Philip. So Philip sent Alexander with a large army to conduct the war. But Alexander, on his ar-

---

14. This overcolored episode of the marriage banquet rather inverts historical truth. In 337 B.C. Philip married Kleopatra, his sixth wife, who, as a native Macedonian, posed a special threat to the position of Olympias (who came from Epirus), though there was no question of divorce. At the banquet, Attalos, a Macedonian general and uncle of Kleopatra, played the role assigned here to Lysias. But Alexander did not proceed to slaughter the wedding guests: rather, he fled with Olympias to Epirus, and was only able to return after a negotiated reconciliation. In 335 B.C. Olympias murdered the baby daughter of Philip and Kleopatra and caused Kleopatra to commit suicide.

15. The fuller version of A may make this clearer: "I know why you are sluggish: it is not your body I am talking about, but you are anguished in your soul at your errors."

16. Lysias means "he who parts."

rival at Methone, persuaded them by clever argument to resume their allegiance.[17]

On his return from Methone, having gone in to his father Philip, he was standing and saw ahead of him men dressed in foreign costume. He asked about them, "Who are these people?" and was given the reply "Satraps of Darius, king of Persia."

Alexander asked them, "What are you here for?"

"To demand from your father the usual tribute," they replied to him.

"On whose behalf," Alexander asked them, "do you demand tribute?"

The satraps of Darius replied to him, "On behalf of Darius, king of the Earth."

"If the gods," said Alexander to them, "have given men the earth as a gift for their sustenance, is Darius taking a percentage of the gods' gift?" And again he said, testing them, "What would you want to take?"

"One hundred golden eggs," they told him, "made from twenty pounds of gold."

In reply Alexander said to them, "It is not right for Philip, king of the Macedonians, to pay tribute to barbarians: it is not open to anyone who so wishes to make Greeks his subjects." So Alexander told the satraps of Darius, "Go back and tell Darius, 'Alexander, son of Philip, hereby informs you, "When Philip was on his own, he used to pay you tribute. But now he has begotten a son, Alexander, he no longer pays you tribute, and, indeed, the tribute that you have taken from him I shall come in person and take back." ' " And with these words he sent away the emissaries, not even deigning to write to the king who had sent them. Philip, king of the Greeks, was pleased at this, seeing the style of Alexander's daring.[18]

The emissaries, however, took some money and gave it to a Greek friend of theirs who was a painter, and he did them a miniature portrait of Alexander, which they took to Darius in Babylon when they reported back to him everything Alexander had said to them.

Now another city in Thrace revolted from Philip, and he sent Alexander with a large number of soldiers to make war on it.

There was a man called Pausanias in Pella, a man of importance and great wealth who was the leader of all the Thessalonicans.[19] Now, this

24

17. Methone had in fact been destroyed by Philip in 354 B.C., when Alexander was two.

18. The episode of the Persian emissaries is based on a tale (Plutarch *Life of Alexander* 5) of how Alexander once entertained Persian envoys while Philip was away, asking them useful questions about their empire. Demands for tribute and haughty dismissal are fictional amplifications.

19. Thessalonike, the second city of modern Greece, was founded about 316 B.C., seven years after Alexander's death. Pausanias was in fact an aristocrat from the western fringe of Macedonia who had become a royal bodyguard. He was said by Aristotle to have killed

man had fallen in love with Olympias, Alexander's mother, and sent some people to her to persuade her to leave Philip, her husband, and marry him, sending her many gifts. But Olympias refused; so Pausanias headed for the place where Philip was, having discovered that Alexander was away at war, and arrived as a stage competition was being held. Philip was conducting proceedings in the Olympic theater when Pausanias appeared, sword in hand, in the theater with a number of other brave men, with the intention of killing Philip so that he could seize Olympias. He attacked him and struck him in the side with his sword but failed to kill him. Pandemonium resulted in the theater. And Pausanias rushed off to the palace to seize Olympias.

Now it just so happened that Alexander returned victorious from the war on the same day and saw massive uproar in the city. He asked what had happened and was told, "Pausanias is in the palace intending to seize Olympias, your mother." And immediately he went in with those of his guards he had with him and found Pausanias violently restraining Olympias as she screamed. Alexander wanted to strike him with a spear but was afraid he might hit his mother too: he was keeping hold of her with considerable force. But Alexander tore Pausanias away from his mother and used the spear he was holding to strike him. Discovering Philip was still alive, he went to him and asked, "Father, what do you want done with Pausanias?" "Bring him here to me," he replied. And when they brought him, Alexander took a dagger, put it in the hand of Philip, his father, and brought Pausanias up to him. And Philip took hold of him and cut his throat. And Philip said to Alexander: "Alexander, my boy, it is no sorrow to me that I am dying: I have had vengeance, killing my enemy like this. So Ammon the god of Libya was right when he said to Olympias, your mother, 'You shall have in your womb a male child who shall avenge the death of his father.'" So saying, Philip expired. He had a king's funeral, and the whole of Macedonia attended.

25    When calm had been restored in Pella, Alexander went up to his father Philip's statue and at the top of his voice cried out, "Sons of the Pellaians

---

Philip because of a personal grudge, but it has seemed suggestive that his homeland had originally been under the influence of Epirus, Olympias's home. His passion for Olympias is romantic fiction; and he was apprehended not by Alexander, but by three bodyguards as he tripped over a vine root.

20. The Amphiktyonic League was a loose confederation of the states of central Greece, between Macedonia and Attica (the territory of Athens). It was prompt to recognize Alexander as Philip's successor. Philip had already federated the Greeks (except the unwilling Spartans) at Corinth in 337 B.C. for a campaign against Persia and became leader of this "League of Corinth." Alexander took over his leadership and reaffirmed the intention to invade the Persian Empire, at Corinth in 335 B.C., and that is where he would have made this sort of speech—not at Pella. This event is referred to at the end of 1.27.

and Macedonians and Greeks and Amphiktyons[20] and Spartans and Corinthians, join with me, your comrade-in-arms, and pledge yourselves to me, to campaign against the barbarians and free ourselves from slavery to the Persians so that we who are Greeks may cease to be slaves to barbarians." And having made this speech, Alexander issued royal edicts in every city. Then men mustered from all the states and arrived in Macedonia—volunteers, all of them, as though summoned by a god-sent voice—to join the campaign. Alexander opened his father's armory and issued the young men with full military equipment. And in addition he brought all the guards of his father, Philip, by now old men, and said to them, "Veterans and mighty comrades-in-arms, consent to add your distinction to the Macedonian campaign and march with us to war!"

"King Alexander," they replied, "we have grown old marching with your father, King Philip, and our bodies are no longer strong enough to match our adversaries. Consequently, we seek to be excused from campaigning under you."

"But I am all the more keen," replied Alexander to them, "to march with you if you are old: age is often stronger than youth. Indeed, on many occasions youth, trusting in the effectiveness of the body, deviates into ill-advised action and finds the scales weighted against it and encounters sudden peril, whereas the old man thinks first and acts later, using judgment to avoid peril. So you, sirs, march with us; you will not be lined up against the enemy but will show your mettle by encouraging the young men. The contribution of both is necessary; so lend the support of your minds to the army: the conduct of war too needs intelligence. The fact is, if you will consider the battle, it is clear that your own security too depends on victory for the homeland: if we are defeated, the enemy will have no opposition save those unfit through age; whereas if we win, the victory reflects on the judgment of the advisers." So saying, Alexander persuaded all the veterans by his words to follow him.

So Alexander succeeded to the kingdom of Philip, his father, at the age of eighteen. And the disturbance occasioned by Philip's death was quelled by Antipatros, a clever man and a fast thinker. He took Alexander armed with a breastplate into the theater and developed a number of arguments in his appeal to the Macedonians to support Alexander. 26

Alexander was, it seems, more fortunate than his father, Philip, and immediately took upon himself great affairs. He brought together all his father's soldiers, counted them, and found there were 20,000 horsemen (including 8,000 armed with breastplates), 15,000 infantry, 5,000 Thracians, 30,000 Amphiktyons, Spartans, Corinthians, and Thessalonicans. He found the total of all those present was 70,000, and 6,590 archers.

As the Illyrians, Paionians, and Triballoi had rebelled, he marched against them, but while he was fighting these nations, Greece revolted. A 27 rumor had got about that Alexander, king of the Macedonians, had been killed in the war, and it is said that Demosthenes brought a wounded man before the Athenian assembly who claimed he had seen Alexander lying dead. When the Thebans discovered this, they cut down the garrison that Philip had put in the Kadmeia after the battle of Chaironeia.[21] According to the story, Demosthenes persuaded them to do this. Alexander in anger attacked the Thebans. And the Thebans had signs of the misfortunes that lay in store for them: a spider wove its web over the shrine of Demeter and the water of the spring "Dirke" turned bloody. The king took and demolished the whole city, sparing only the house of Pindar. And he is supposed also to have compelled the flautist Ismenias to play to the demolition of the city. So the Greeks took fright: they elected Alexander their leader and handed over to him the rule of Greece.

28    Back in Macedonia, he got everything ready for the expedition across Asia, constructing Liburnian cruisers and triremes[22] and a very large number of battleships. He embarked all his troops and wagons, together with all manner of arms. And, taking 50,000 talents of gold,[23] he gave the order and came to the region of Thrace, where he took 5,000 picked men and 500 talents of gold. And all the cities received him with garlands.

At the Hellespont, he took the ships and reached Asia from Europe. There he fixed his spear in the ground and claimed Asia by right of conquest. From there Alexander came to the river Granikos, as it is called: the satraps of Darius were defending this. After a mighty battle, Alexander was victorious. He took spoils and sent them to the Athenians and to his mother, Olympias, as a gift. He decided first to subdue the coastal areas and so took possession of Ionia and after that Caria, after which he took Lydia and the treasures at Sardis. And he captured Phrygia, Lycia, and Pamphylia—where something amazing happened: Alexander had no ships with him, but part of the sea receded to let his infantry cross.[24]

29    Pressing on, he rendezvoused with his fleet and crossed to Sicily.[25]

21. Philip decisively defeated the joint forces of Athens and Thebes at Chaironeia in 338 B.C., establishing his supremacy over Greece. Alexander destroyed Thebes in 335 B.C. L tells of the destruction twice over, here and at 1.46. The other recensions omit most of 1.27–29.

22. Liburnian ships were fast warships with two banks of oars, which became important only after Octavian (Augustus) deployed them at the battle of Actium in 31 B.C. Triremes had three banks of oars.

23. A talent was the largest weight in Greek currency, roughly the weight a man can carry, about fifty pounds.

24. By Mt. Klimax in Lydia; the coastal area was only passable when northerlies blew— as they did on Alexander's arrival.

25. Alexander never went to Sicily, Italy, or Africa, though a western expedition was alleged to be among his last plans, and "What if he had?" later became a popular debating topic. On the other hand, envoys from Europe and Africa met Alexander on his return from India to Babylon, wisely, to offer congratulations, and one witness claimed that Romans were among them, something not impossible.

Subduing some people who opposed him, he crossed to the land of Italy. And the Roman generals sent Marcus, one of their generals, with a crown of pearls and another of precious stones, saying to him, "We add to your crowns, Alexander, king of the Romans and of every land," bringing him also five hundred pounds of gold. Alexander, accepting their gifts, promised to make them great and powerful and took from them two thousand archers and four hundred talents.

From there he crossed over to Africa. And the African generals met him and begged him to keep away from their city, Carthage. But Alexander despised their weakness and said to them, "Either become stronger or pay tribute to those stronger than you." 30

Setting off from there, he crossed the whole of Libya and reached the shrine of Ammon.[26] (He put most of his troops aboard ship and instructed them to sail away to the island of Proteus and await him there, while he himself went off to sacrifice to Ammon on the supposition that he had been begotten by Ammon.) He prayed to him in these words. "Father Ammon, if she who bore me tells the truth when she says that I was begotten by you, give me an oracle!" And Alexander saw Ammon embracing his mother, Olympias, and saying to him, "Alexander, my child, you are my seed." Discovering the actual power of Ammon, Alexander renovated his shrine and gilded his idol and consecrated it with this inscription.

DEDICATION OF ALEXANDER TO HIS FATHER, THE GOD AMMON.

He also asked to receive an oracle from him on where he might found a city named after him so that it might last in perpetual memory of him. And he saw Ammon, aged, golden-haired, with ram's horns on his temples, saying to him:

> O King, you the ram-horned Phoebus addresses:
> If you wish through ages unsullied[27] to retain your youth,
> Found your city greatly famed opposite the Isle of Proteus,
> Over which presides Time, son of Wealth, himself its lord,
> Turning the boundless world on his five-peaked ridges.[28]

26. As pharaoh of Egypt, Alexander became son of Ammon and was apparently greeted as such at Ammon's shrine at the oasis Siwah (in the depths of the Egyptian desert). This chapter, which accepts the parentage by Ammon, is of course inconsistent with the tale of the trickery of Nektanebos in 1.7, which maintains continuity with pharaonic rule in a different way.

27. A has "through centuries unaging," more plausibly.

28. Phoebus here denotes the sun-god (Egyptian, Ra) with whom Ammon was identified. The city to be founded is, of course, the Egyptian Alexandria, perpetuating Alexander's name. Proteus, an elusive god who could transform his appearance, lived according to Homer (Odyssey 4.351ff.) on Pharos. "Time, son of Wealth" refers to Sarapis, the great god developed at Alexandria for the use of Greek Egypt. The final line depicts the site as the center of the universe; van Thiel refers the five peaks to five elements in Perisan lore, as there are in fact no mountains at the site.

Receiving this oracle, Alexander tried to work out what island was meant by "the Isle of Proteus" and who the god was that presided over it. And as Alexander tried to work this out, he made another sacrifice to Ammon and journeyed to a village in Libya, where he let his troops rest.

31    As Alexander was taking a walk there, an enormous deer ran by and entered some undergrowth. Alexander called out to an archer and instructed him to shoot the beast. The archer drew his bow but did not hit the deer, and Alexander said to him, "Fellow, that was a miss [*paratonon*]"; and as a result of this, that place was called Paratone on account of Alexander's exclamation. So he built a small town there, and, inviting certain local people of good class, he gave them houses there, calling the place Paratone.

Traveling on from there, he came to Taphosirion.[29] Then he questioned the locals on the reason for this name, and they told him that the shrine was the grave [*taphos*] of Osiris. So, having sacrificed there too, he reached the end of his journey and came to the land of present-day Alexandria and saw a huge area stretching as far as the eye could see, containing twelve villages. Alexander marked out the length of the city from Pandysis, as it is called, to the Herakleotic mouth; and its width from the district of Mendes up to the small Hormoupolis (it was called Hormoupolis, not Hermoupolis, because everyone coming down the Nile put in [*pros-hormein*] there).[30] So it was as far as that locality that King Alexander marked out the city, and up to the present day it is registered as the territory of the Alexandrians.

King Alexander was advised by <u>Kleomenes</u> of Naukratis and <u>Deinokrates</u> of Rhodes <u>not to found the city on so great a scale</u>, "because you will not be able to find enough people to fill it; and even if you do, the administration will be unable to supply the food it would need. In addition, the inhabitants of the city will be at war with each other because of its excessive and boundless size: it is small cities that think constructively together and form constructive plans for the good of the city; whereas if you build it on the enormous scale you have planned, there will be differences and dissension among its inhabitants, as the population will be boundless." Alexander was persuaded and commissioned the architects to lay out the city on the scale they wanted, and they, under King Alex-

29. More accurately, Taposiris, the modern Abusir, thirty miles west of Alexandria. The derivation of this native Egyptian place-name from the Greek word for "grave" is naturally false. Osiris was the Egyptian god of the underworld, with whom the dead pharaoh was identified.

30. Pandysis was to the west of Alexandria, and the Herakleotic mouth of the Nile was at Kanobos, twenty miles to the east. The lesser Hermoupolis ("city of Hermes" in Greek, referring to the Egyptian god Thoth, who was identified with Hermes) was thirty miles upstream from Kanobos; Mendes (L mistakenly talks of the "shrine of Bendis" instead) was in the northeast area of the delta. This fictional first plan of Alexander would have put New York and Greater London to shame.

ander's instructions, marked out the length of the city from the river Drakon at the spit of land with Taphosirion on it up to the river Agathodaimon at Kanobos, and the width from the district of Mendes to Eurylochion and Melanthion. And Alexander ordered those who lived in this area within thirty miles of the city to move into the districts of the city, granting them areas of land and entitling them to be called Alexandrians. The chief officials of the districts were Eurylochos and Melanthos—which is where the names came from.

Alexander consulted other master builders for the city too, including Noumenios the stonemason, Kleomenes of Naukratis the engineer, and Krateros of Olynthos. Noumenios had a brother called Hyponomos: this man advised Alexander to build the city on proper foundations and to install water channels and sewers discharging into the sea—and it is called a hyponomos because he divised it.[31]

[From the land he saw an island in the sea and asked what it was 32 called. "Pharos," the locals replied. "Proteus lived there. And we have his tomb also, which we worship, on a high mountain." They took him to what is now called the Hero's Shrine and showed him the coffin. He sacrificed to the hero Proteus and, seeing the tomb had in the course of time fallen into disrepair, gave instructions for it swiftly to be restored.]

Alexander ordered the perimeter of the city to be marked out so that he could take a look at it. So the workmen marked the city out with wheat meal, but all sorts of birds flew down, ate up the meal, and flew off. Alexander was very disturbed at what this sign might mean; so he sent for the interpreters and told them what had happened. Their reply was, "The city that you, King, have ordered to be built will nourish the whole world, and men born in it will be found everywhere: birds fly round the whole world."[32]

So he gave instructions for the building of the city. When he had laid the foundations for the most part of the city and marked it out, Alexander inscribed five letters— A B Γ Δ E—A for "Alexander," B for "King" [Basileus], Γ for "of the Race" [genos], Δ for "of Zeus" [Dios], E for "has founded [ektisen] an inimitable city."[33] Donkeys and mules were working away. But as the gateway of the shrine was being erected, an enormous and very ancient slab, covered with letters, suddenly fell, and a large

31. Another false etymology: *hyponomos* is just Greek for "something that runs underground." The bracketed paragraph that follows is omitted by L and restored by Van Thiel from A.

32. L now omits a paragraph in which a snake troubling the workmen is caught and killed, and Alexander orders a shrine to be built for it—it is the Good Spirit (in Greek, Agathos Daimon). This is the shrine referred to in the next paragraph.

33. This is a colorful explanation for the fact that Alexandria was divided into 5 districts, lettered A, B, Γ, Δ, E. One may compare divisions of modern cities for postal purposes.

number of snakes came out of it and crept into the entrances of the houses, whose foundations had by now been laid. (Alexander was still present to found the city on the new moon of the month Tybi—that is, January—including the actual shrine.)[34] And this is why doorkeepers revere these snakes as Good Spirits entering the houses (they are not poisonous); and they garland their working animals and let them rest. This is why up to the present day the Alexandrians have kept the custom of holding the festival on the twenty-fifth of Tybi.

33     Alexander found a cult statue stationed on the high hills, together with the Pillars of Helion and the Hero's Shrine.[35] In addition he looked for the Sarapeion, in accordance with the oracle given to him by Ammon. (He had spoken to him in an oracle like this.

> O king, you the ram-horned Phoebus addresses:
> If you wish through ages unsullied to retain your youth,
> Found your city greatly famed opposite the Isle of Proteus,
> Over which presides Time, son of Wealth, himself its lord,
> Turning the boundless world on his five-peaked ridges.

So Alexander was looking for him who beholds all.)[36] He constructed opposite the Hero's Shrine a great altar, now called the Altar of Alexander, at which he celebrated a costly sacrifice. And he offered this prayer. "You are the god who takes care of this land and beholds the boundless world—this is clear. Yourself now accept my sacrifice and be my helper in the wars." So saying, he put the victims on the altar. Then suddenly a huge eagle flew down and snatched the entrails of the offering, carried them off through the air and dropped them at another altar. Alexander, observing the spot, went there quickly and saw the entrails lying on the altar. The altar, he saw, had been set up by men of olden times. There was a precinct, with a wooden idol presiding inside. With its right hand it was soothing a beast of many shapes;[37] in its left hand it held a scepter. And beside the idol was a huge statue of a maiden. So he asked the people that lived there who the god of the place was. They replied that they

34. The sentence in parentheses seems to belong a few lines later.

35. The nonexistent "high hills" have been invented on the basis of the oracle. The Hero's Shrine is that of Proteus. The Pillars of Helion are puzzling: they may refer to obelisks at the Kaisareion, but they sound like Pillars of the Sun and their function here, set on high mountains, may be to mark the center of the universe as indicated in the last line of the oracle.

36. The author seems to have thought that the rare word for "turning" in the last line of the oracle meant "beholding."

37. The "beast of many shapes" is the three-headed dog, Cerberus, who guards the entrance to the underworld. In the standard iconography Sarapis, who controls the underworld, is depicted seated with scepter and with Cerberus, both of which details appear only in recension B. The "maiden" is Sarapis's consort Isis. Sarapis and Isis, when translated into traditional Greek mythology, have the status of Zeus and Hera.

did not know, but had received a tradition from their forefathers that it was a shrine of Zeus and Hera.

Here too he saw the obelisks that stand to this day in the Sarapeion, outside the present precinct. On these there were hieroglyphic letters inscribed, of the following content.[38]

[I, Sesonchosis, King of Egypt and world ruler, built and dedicated this to Sarapis, the first god revealed to this land. (Sarapis then appears in a dream to Alexander, prophesies that Alexandria will indeed perpetuate the memory of Alexander and its name will not be changed, and tells of its future prosperity. A phrase then tries to smooth over the omission in the manuscript.)] The reward of the actual city [will be]: (and the manuscript continues) ... possessed of fine temples, exceptional in the huge size of its population, superior in its healthy climate. And I shall be its champion and stop hardships, either famine or earthquake, from taking hold: instead, they shall pass swiftly through the city, like a dream. Many kings shall come to it, not to bring war, but to pay homage. And when you become a god, your body will constantly receive homage and gifts from many kings, and you shall live in the city, dead and yet not dead: for you shall have the city that you are founding as your tomb.

Receive now, Alexander, a concise proof of my identity: add twice one hundred [S][39] and one [A]; then another hundred [R] and one [A]; then four times twenty [P] and ten [I]; and, taking the first letter, put it at the end— then you will understand who has appeared to you.

Having delivered this oracle, he withdrew. Alexander, recalling the oracle, realized it was SARAPIS. The layout of the city is as Alexander arranged it, and the city was established, growing stronger day by day.

Alexander took his armies and hurried on to Egypt. When he arrived at the city of Memphis, the Egyptians enthroned him as king of Egypt

34

38. Recension B here omits about two pages, scarcely deliberately. I indicate in the text the content of what intervened. When the recension resumes, Sarapis is delivering a prophecy, but B does not notice it is in verse and, paraphrasing, destroys the meter.

There is some confusion between the names Sesonchosis and Sesostris, and the reference here is in fact to Sesostris III (1877–1839 B.C.), whose fabulous conquests, supposedly as far as Scythia and Thrace, are reported already in Herodotos and were invented, it seems, to restore the Egyptian ego by outdoing the conquests of Darius I of Persia (521–486 B.C.). In the generation after Alexander they were extended to outdo Alexander's exploits. Our author may have borrowed material from a Sesonchosis novel (of which fragments survive), and in any case he uses him here as a forerunner of Alexander.

39. Greeks, not having arabic numerals, used letters of the alphabet instead, so that 200, for instance, is S. Cf. Heliodoros 9.22.

on the throne of Hephaistos.[40] In Memphis Alexander saw a tall statue of black stone with the following inscription on its pedestal.

> THIS KING WHO HAS FLED WILL COME AGAIN TO EGYPT,
> NOT IN AGE BUT IN YOUTH, AND OUR ENEMY THE PERSIANS
> HE SHALL SUBJECT TO US.

Alexander asked whose statue this was and the prophets told him: "This statue is of the last king of Egypt, Nektanebos. When the Persians were coming to devastate Egypt, he saw by his magical powers the gods of Egypt guiding the armies of the enemy towards us and Egypt being destroyed by them. He then realized their impending betrayal and fled. But when we conducted a search for him and inquired of the gods where our king, Nektanebos, had fled to, they gave us this response.

> This king who has fled will come again to Egypt, not in age but in youth, and your enemy the Persians he shall subject to you.

When Alexander heard this, he leapt onto the statue and embraced it, saying: "This is my father—I am his son. What the oracle told you was not false. But what amazes me is that you were taken over by the barbarians even though you have invincible walls that could not be pulled down by the enemy. This must be the working of Providence above and the justice of the gods, so that you, who have a productive land and a natural river to fertilize it, are subjected to and ruled by people who do not have these advantages; otherwise, through not having them the barbarians would perish." And so saying, he demanded from them the tribute they used to pay to Darius, saying this to them, "It is not so that I may collect it for my own treasury, but rather so that I may spend it on your city, the Egyptian Alexandria, capital of the world." When he had put it this way, the Egyptians were glad to give him great quantities of money; and it was with awe and full honors that they escorted him on his departure at Pelousion.

35 He took his armies and marched for Syria. There he enlisted two thousand armored cavalry and arrived at Tyre. The Tyrians formed up against him to prevent his passing through their city, because of an ancient oracle that had been given to them, as follows.

> When a king comes against you, men of Tyre, your city shall be razed to the ground.

This is why they offered opposition to his entry into their city. So they formed up against him. having walled the entire city, and in the violent battle between them the Tyrians killed many of the Macedonians. Alex-

---

40. The Egyptian god Ptah, god of craftsmen, like the Greek Hephaistos.

ander retired, defeated, to Gaza. When he had recovered his strength, he tried to work out how to sack Tyre. Then in a dream Alexander saw someone saying to him, "Alexander, do not consider going yourself as a messenger to Tyre." So when he awoke from his sleep, he sent emissaries to Tyre with a letter of the following content.

King Alexander, son of Ammon and King Philip, I who am Greatest King of Europe and the whole of Asia, of Egypt and Libya, to the Tyrians, who no longer exist:

Journeying to the regions of Syria in peace and lawfulness, I wished to enter your land. But if you Tyrians are the first to oppose our entrance as we journey, then it is only by your example that others will learn the strength of the Macedonians in the face of your mindless action and shall cower in obedience to us. And you may rely on the oracle you have been given: I shall come through your city.

Farewell, men of sense—or, otherwise, farewell men of misfortune!

Having read the king's letter, their government ordered the messengers King Alexander had sent to be flogged, asking them, "Which of you is Alexander?" And when they replied that none of them was, they crucified them.

So Alexander was trying to work out what route to enter by and how to strike down the Tyrians—he had discounted his defeat. And he saw in his sleep a satyr, one of the attendants of Dionysos, offering him a cheese [tyros] made from milk; he took it and trampled it under his feet. On waking, Alexander related the dream to a dream interpreter, and he said to him, "You shall be king over all Tyre, and it shall be under your control, because the satyr [sa Tyros, 'your Tyre'] gave you tyros ['cheese' or 'Tyre'], and you trampled it under your feet."

Three days later, Alexander collected his troops and, together with the three neighboring villages, who had fought bravely with Alexander, in the night opened up the gates in the walls, entering and killing the guards. Alexander sacked the whole of Tyre and razed it to the ground, and the byword "The ills of Tyre" continues to the present day. As for the three villages that had fought with him, he combined them into one city and called it Tripoli ["triple city"].

Appointing a satrap of Phoenicia at Tyre, Alexander broke camp and 36 followed the coast of Syria. Emissaries of Darius came to meet him, bringing him a letter, a strap, a ball, and a money box of gold. Alexander accepted the letter of Darius, king of Persia, and, on reading it, found its contents were these.

King of Kings, kinsman of the gods, I who rise to heaven with the Sun, a god myself, I Darius to my servant Alexander give these orders:

I instruct you to return to your parents, to be my slave, and to sleep in the lap of your mother, Olympias: that is how old you are—you need to be corrected and nursed. So I have sent you a strap, a ball, and a money box of gold, and you can take whatever you like first. I sent the strap to let you know you still need correction. I sent the ball so that you can play with children your own age and not mislead so many  young men at such an arrogant age into going around with you, like a brigand chief, and disturbing the peace of the cities: not even if this whole world is brought together by a single man, will it be able to overthrow the kingdom of the Persians. I have such huge numbers of troops that, like grains of sand, no one could even count them; and I have enough gold and silver to fill the whole earth. I have also sent you a money box full of gold so that should you run out of food to give your fellow brigands, you may give them each the wherewithal to go back to their own homeland.

But if you do not obey my instructions, I shall send a force after you, and the result will be that you will be arrested by my soldiers—and you will not be educated as the son of Philip but crucified as a rebel.

37 Alexander read this out before all his troops, and they were all frightened. Alexander noticed their fright and said to them: "Men of Macedonia and comrades-in-arms, why are you upset at what Darius has written, as though his boastful letter had real power? There are some dogs too who make up for being small by barking loud, as though they could give the illusion of being powerful by their barking. That is what Darius is like: in practice he is powerless, though in what he writes he seems to be someone to reckon with, just like the dogs with their barking. But even let us admit that what he says is true: it illuminates for us who it is that we must fight courageously for victory, to help us avoid the shame of defeat."

With these words, he gave instructions for Darius's letter carriers to have their arms tied behind their backs and to be taken away to be crucified. They said: "What harm have *we* done you, King Alexander? We are messengers: why do you give instructions for us to be killed miserably?"

Alexander replied, "Blame King Darius, not me: Darius sent you with a letter like that, as though it were to a brigand chief, not to a king. So I am killing you as though you had come to a ruthless man, not a king."

"Darius," they said, "had seen nothing when he wrote you that sort of letter. But we see such an array before us and realize that the son of King Philip is a very great and intelligent king. We implore you, Greatest King and Master, grant us life!"

Alexander said to them: "Now you have shown cowardice in the face of your punishment and beg not to die, I shall—for that reason[41]—release you. I am not of a mind to kill you, but only to show the difference between a Greek king and a barbarian one. So do not expect any ill-treatment at my hands: a king does not kill a messenger."

Having spoken to them in this way, Alexander told them, as dinner was being prepared, to join him at table. The letter carriers wanted to tell Alexander how, when it came to war against Darius, he could capture Darius in an ambush; but he said to them: "Do not tell me anything: if you had not been returning to him, I would have wanted to know about this from you. But as you are making your way back to him, I am not prepared to, in case any of you should report what has been said to Darius, and I should be found to deserve punishment as much as you.[42] So be quiet and let us calmly pass over this point." The letter carriers of Darius spoke much in his praise, and the whole mass of troops cheered him.

Three days later, Alexander wrote a letter to Darius, which he also    38
read in full to his own troops in the absence of Darius's letter carriers. And its contents were as follows.

> King Alexander, son of King Philip and his mother, Olympias, to the King of Kings, enthroned with the gods, who rises to heaven with the Sun, a Great God, King of the Persians, greetings:
>
> It is a disgrace if someone priding himself on such great power and "rising with the Sun" eventually falls into base slavery to a man, Alexander. The titles of the gods, when they come into the possession of men, do not confer great power or sense upon them. For how can names of the immortal gods take up residence in destructible bodies? Note how we have condemned you for this also: you have no power over us, but usurp the title of the gods and attribute their powers on earth to yourself. I am going to wage war on you in the view that you are mortal, and which way victory goes depends on Providence above.
>
> Why did you write also to tell us that you have in your possession all this gold and silver? So that, on discovering the fact, we would fight the war more courageously so as to capture it? For my

---

41. A stresses that it is *not* for that reason (which makes more sense).

42. A adds "for allowing you to escape punishment at my hands," which reveals the author's thought.

part, I shall be famous when I have defeated you, and I shall be a great king among Greeks and barbarians because I have killed Darius, such a mighty king. But if you defeat me, you will not have achieved anything remarkable: you will have defeated a brigand—according to your letter to me; but I shall have defeated the "King of Kings, great god, Darius."

You also sent me a strap, a ball, and a money box of gold, having a joke at my expense. Well, I have received these, counting them good messages. I have taken the strap so that I may flay the barbarians with my spears and weapons and reduce them by my hands to servitude. As for the ball, you are indicating to me that I shall gain control over the whole world: the world is spherical and round. The money box of gold you sent me is an important symbol: you will be defeated by me and pay me tribute!

39 Having read this to his troops and sealed it, King Alexander gave it to Darius's letter carriers and gave them as a present the gold they had brought. Having experienced the magnanimity of Alexander, they withdrew and returned to Darius.

Darius read the letter of Alexander and realized the forcefulness in it. And he asked detailed questions about Alexander's intelligence and his preparations for war. This disturbed him, and he wrote his satraps a letter with the following contents.

> King Darius to the generals beyond the Taurus, greetings:
> I have received a report that Alexander, the son of Philip, has risen up against me. Arrest him and bring him to me, without doing him any physical harm, so that I can strip him of the purple and flog him before sending him back to his homeland, Macedonia, to his mother, Olympias, with a rattle and dice (which is how the Macedonian children play). And I shall send with him men who teach all aspects of correct behavior. And sink his ships in the depths of the sea and put the generals that accompany him in irons and send them to us. Send the remaining soldiers to the Red Sea to make their homes there. The horses and all the pack animals I give to you.
> Good health.

The satraps too wrote to Darius, in these terms.

> To the Great God, King Darius, greetings:
> So large an army is advancing on us that we are astonished that you did not know about it before now. We have sent you those of them we have found astray, but have not dared to interrogate them

before you. So come quickly with a large force so that we do not become spoils of war.

Darius received this letter at Babylon in Persia and, reading it, wrote them this reply.

King of Kings, Great God Darius, to all his satraps and generals, greetings:

Do not expect any help from me—just show your renowned bravery! What sort of beast has sprung upon you and panicked you—you who can quench lightning bolts but cannot take the roaring of a low born man?[43] What have you to say for yourselves? Has one of you fallen in battle? What policy am I to adopt with you, who hold my kingdom and make excuses for a brigand because you are not prepared to have him arrested? But now, as you said, I shall come and arrest him myself.

Learning that Alexander was nearby, Darius encamped by the river Pinaros[44] and wrote a letter to Alexander in these terms.    40

King of Kings, Great God Darius and Lord of the Nations, to Alexander, who has plundered the cities:

You are apparently unaware of the name of Darius, which the gods have honored and have decreed should share their thrones. In addition, you have not considered it happiness to escape notice as ruler of Macedonia without my authority: instead, you have passed through obscure countries and alien cities, proclaiming yourself king there and collecting desperadoes like yourself. And you fight wars against inexperienced cities, whose lordship I have always restrained from assuming and which I have considered unimportant because of their isolation; whereas you have sought tribute from them as though you were taking a collection. Are you convinced then that we are like you? But you shall not boast of your possession of the places you have taken. So you have misjudged the situation badly. In the first place you should have made amends for your foolish errors and come to me, your lord, Darius, and not continued accumulating forces of brigands. I have written to you to come and do obeisance to King Darius—and I swear to you by Zeus, the greatest god and my father, that I will not hold against you what

43. This sentence makes little sense in any recension (I present a stopgap). Clearly, in an earlier letter in the epistolary novel (see the Introduction), not, however, incorporated in our novel, the satraps had boasted they could quench lightning bolts.

44. The river at Issos, a town on the coast of Cilicia, in modern Turkey somewhat north of Iskenderun and around thirty miles from the Syrian frontier. The battle of Issos (333 B.C.) was Alexander's second major battle, after the Granikos (1.28).

you have done. But you persist in another, foolish, course; so I shall punish you[45] with an indescribable death; and those with you who have failed to instill good sense in you shall suffer worse than you.

41  When Alexander received the letter of Darius and read it, he was not incensed at Darius's haughty words.

Darius mustered a large force and came down with his children, his wife, and his mother; and around him were the ten thousand "Immortals" (they were called Immortals because their number was kept up, and new men were brought in to replace those that died).

Alexander made his way through the Cilician Taurus Mountains and came to Tarsos, the capital of Cilicia. There he saw the river Kydnos, which flows below it, and as he was pouring with sweat from the march, he took off his breastplate and took a swim in the river. But he caught a chill and became very seriously ill and was only with difficulty cured. The man who cured him was Philip, a famous doctor. Having regained his strength, he pressed on against Darius. And Darius was encamped at the place called Issos in Cilicia.[46]

Provoked, Alexander hurried to do battle in the plain and drew up his forces opposite Darius. But as Darius's officers saw Alexander bring the might of his army against them at the point where he could hear Darius, they positioned the chariots and arranged the whole battle lineup. Indeed, as both sides were standing ready to engage in battle, Alexander was not prepared to let them break through inside the phalanx or to ride through and attack his rear (the majority of the chariots, pinned down on every side, were destroyed and dispersed). Mounting his horse, Alexander gave the order for the trumpeters to play the war signal, and with a huge roar from the armies a fierce battle began.

There was a lengthy engagement with missiles at the ends of the wings, where they used their spears and, struck by each other, were driven here and there. They parted, then, with each side claiming victory. But Alexander's company pressed on that of Darius and by main force broke them, so that they were routed and stumbled over each other because of the mass of soldiers. Nothing could be seen there except horses lying dead on the ground and slain men; and it was impossible to distinguish Persian from Macedonian, allies from satraps, infantry from cavalry, for the clouds of dust; for the sky was not visible, and the earth could not be made out for all the gore. Even the sun felt sympathy at

45. A has, more sensibly, "But if you persist in another, foolish, course, I shall punish you."

46. The last two paragraphs are found only in recension B and disturb the order of the novel. Darius has already arrived at Issos at 1.40 *init.*, and the incident concerning the doctor Philip is told in full later (2.8).

what was happening and, refusing to contemplate all that pollution, clouded over. But it was the Persians, forcefully driven back, who began to flee. With them was Amyntas of Antioch,[47] who had fled to Darius, having previously been dictator of Macedon. When evening fell, Darius, afraid, got away with difficulty and kept going.[48] But the royal chariot was conspicuous; so, leaving behind his own chariot, he mounted a horse and fled. Alexander was eager to capture Darius and went after him to prevent someone killing him. After pursuing him for seven miles Alexander captured Darius's chariot, bow and arrows, his wife, daughters, and mother; but Darius himself was saved by darkness; and in addition he got a fresh horse and fled.

Alexander captured Darius's tent and used it for himself. He had defeated the enemy and made himself a great reputation, but he did nothing extravagant: he simply gave instructions for the bravest and noble Persians who had died to be buried. Darius's mother, wife, and children he took with him and treated honorably. In the same way he spoke to the other prisoners too and encouraged them. The number of the fallen Persians was enormous; the fallen Macedonians were found to number 500 infantry and 160 cavalry, with 308 wounded; of the barbarians, there were 20,000, with around 4,000 men taken as slaves.

Darius, having got away safely, began enrolling more forces. And he 42 wrote to the nations under his control to come to him with a large force. One of Alexander's spies found out that Darius was mustering armies and wrote to Alexander about the situation. On hearing this, Alexander wrote to his general Skamandros in these terms.

Alexander the King to our general Skamandros, greetings:
Take the phalanxes under your command and all your forces and come with all speed to us: the barbarians are said not to be far off.[49]

Alexander himself took the force he had and marched onward. Crossing the Taurus, he fixed a massive spear in the ground and said, "If any mighty king, Greek, barbarian, or other, lifts this spear, it will be an evil sign for him: his city shall be lifted from its foundations."[50]

47. Actually, as our author probably wrote, "Amyntas, son of Antiochos." Recension B alone preserves the detail that he had "previously been dictator," confusing him with his associate Amyntas IV, who had been child king until his regent, Philip II, deposed him. Alexander naturally had him murdered.

48. There is something amiss in this area of the text; I have improvised this sentence.

49. There was no general named Skamandros (the *river* Skamandros is mentioned a few lines later). Perhaps Kassandros is meant: he came to Alexander at Babylon in 324 B.C., shortly before Alexander's death; later (305–297 B.C.) he was king of Macedonia. In any case, this letter makes no sense in this context.

50. This is an elaboration of the authentic spear story, told in its right place at 1.28 by recension B.

He came next to the city of Pieria in Bebrykia,[51] where there was a temple and a statue of Orpheus, and also the Pierian Muses and the animals standing next to his statue. As Alexander looked at it, the idol of Orpheus sweated all over. Alexander tried to find out the meaning of this sign, and Melampous the interpreter told him: "You will have to work hard, King Alexander, with sweat and toil to bring barbarian nations and Greek cities under your control. Just as Orpheus through playing the lyre and singing won over Greeks, brought barbarians round, and tamed beasts, so you too, toiling with your spear, will subject all to your rule." Hearing this, Alexander rewarded the interpreter richly and dismissed him.

And he reached Phrygia. Coming to the river Skamandros, where Achilles had leapt in, he himself leapt in too.[52] Seeing the seven-layered shield, not very big, nor as striking as Homer had described it, he said, "Happy are you men who have found a herald such as Homer: in his poems you have become great, but from what we can see you are not worthy of what he wrote." And a poet came up to him and said, "King Alexander, we will write of your deeds better than Homer." But Alexander replied, "I would sooner be a Thersites in Homer than an Agamemnon in your writing."

43    From there he came to Pyle,[53] where he mustered the Macedonian army, together with the prisoners he had taken in the battle with Darius, and marched on to Abdera. But the inhabitants of Abdera shut the gates of their city. Alexander, enraged at this, instructed his general to burn the city. They sent him representatives, saying: "We have not closed our gates to oppose your power, but in fear of the kingdom of Persia: if Darius stays in power, he might sack our city for having received you. So come when you have defeated Darius and open the gates of the city: we will be subjects of the stronger king."

Alexander smiled at what he heard and told the representatives that had been sent to him: "You are afraid of Darius's royal power—that he will remain king and at a later date sack your city? Go back, open the gates, and live undisturbed! I am not going to enter your city until I have

51. The Bebrykes were a tribe in northern Turkey mentioned only in legend. Pieria is a region of Macedonia that includes the town Leibethra, where this episode, interpreted by the seer Aristandros, is said to have occurred before Alexander set out.

52. In the Armenian recension, and probably the author's original, Alexander does not leap in; instead, the smallness of the Skamandros is emphasized. Before this, there seems to have been a scene where Alexander makes a dedication at Achilles' tomb and connects himself with Achilles in a genealogical poem. Afterward, Olympias (!) returns home with a retinue of distinguished prisoners.

53. It is difficult to determine what place the author has in mind (Amphipolis?), especially as his account is proceeding backwards (see the chronological table in the Introduction). Abdera, on the coast, two-thirds of the way from Thessalonike to the Turkish border, had in fact been under Macedonian control since 352 B.C.

defeated Darius, the king you fear; then I will take you as my subjects."
With these words for the representatives, he marched on his way.

In two days he had reached Bottiaia and Olynthos[54] and devastated the whole land of the Chalkidians and killed those in the neighborhood. From there he came to the Black Sea and subjected all the cities next to it.[55] But the Macedonians' food supplies were running out, so that they were all about to die of starvation. Alexander devised a tremendously intelligent solution. He searched out all the horses of the cavalry, slaughtered them, flayed them, and gave instructions for them to be roasted and eaten. This filled them, and they recovered from their hunger. But some of them said: "Why has Alexander decided to kill our horses? Look, for the present we are filled with food, but we are unprepared for battle with cavalry." Alexander heard this, went into the camp, and said: "Comrades-in-arms, we have slaughtered the horses, despite the fact they are vital for war, so that we may be filled with food: when an evil is replaced by a lesser evil, it is less painful. When we come to another land, we shall easily find other horses; but if we die from starvation, we shall not presently find other Macedonians." Having calmed the soldiers, he marched on to another city. **44**

[Recension B omits 1.45, in which Alexander is associated with Hercules by an oracle—maybe that at Delphi. It also omits 1.46, but some manuscripts, including L, restore this highlight to the text.]

And from there he marched on to the Thebans. He sought men from them to join his campaign, but they closed the gates in the walls and did not even send representatives to him; instead, they lined up and armed themselves, ready to fight Alexander. And they sent 500 men to him to tell him "Either fight or keep away from our city." Alexander smiled and said to them: "Brave Thebans, why do you lock yourselves away inside your gates and bid King Alexander fight you? Indeed, I will fight, but it will not be against brave men with experience of war, but against amateurs and women brimming with cowardice: shutting yourselves away like little women inside your walls, you address those outside." **46**

So saying, he instructed 1,000 cavalry to ride across outside the walls and shoot those standing on the walls and another 1,000 to use double axes and beams to dig out the foundations of the wall, to set fire to the gates, and to use battering rams to demolish the walls (these are appliances on wheels, heaved vigorously by a team of soldiers—they are launched at the walls from a distance and demolish even the best-constructed walling). Alexander hurried across with another 1,000 slingers

54. Bottiaia was a region of Macedonia. Olynthos, in the Chalkidike, was destroyed by Philip in 348 B.C.

55. Now, in fuller versions, Alexander reaches the Sea of Azov and land so cold it is impenetrable.

and spearmen. Fire was everywhere; and stones, missiles, and spears were being cast. The Thebans fell wounded from the walls, unable to form up against Alexander.

For three days, the whole city of Thebes was besieged. The first gate to be broken through was the Kadmean, at which Alexander was standing; and without hesitation Alexander was the first to get in, inflicting wounds on them, striking panic and confusion into them. But masses of soldiers followed him in through the other gates too—the whole horde was about 4,000 men. They killed everyone and demolished the walls: it was with the utmost rapidity that the Macedonian soldiers used to carry out all Alexander's orders. Great quantities of human gore drenched the earth. Many Thebans fell to the ground with the towers. And as their city burned furiously in the fires, the Thebans were killed by Macedonian hands.

46a    Then it was that one of the Thebans, a professional flute player and a man of intelligence, saw Thebes cast to the ground and people of every age being killed. He groaned for his native city but realized that he stood out for his expertise in the flute; so he decided to fall down before Alexander and throw himself at his mercy. He came to Alexander's feet and, sinking to his knees, played a melancholy, fearful, and pitiful theme. In this way, playing a lament and entreaty by flute, he was able to placate Alexander with his many tears. And he began to speak as follows.

Great King Alexander, now learn we by experience thy godlike head to worship ...

[Recension B now omits a substantial section, replaced by 1.27. Ismenias's lament, in origin a rhetorical set piece, continues for four pages. In response, Alexander denounces Thebes and the Thebans and has the city destroyed; but (1.47) at the Isthmian Games the Theban fighter Kleitomachos so impresses him that he orders Thebes to be refounded.

Book 2 begins with Alexander at Plataia, removing its Athenian commander (!) from office. His conflict with Athens is resolved after letters and much debate among Athenian statesmen. Spartan opposition too (2.6) is ineffective, and Alexander sets off for Asia.]

## Book Two

6    Immediately Alexander took his armies and set out via Cilicia for the land of the barbarians.

7    Darius gathered together the leaders of the Persians and consulted them on the question of what they should do. Darius said: "As I can see, the war is becoming increasingly serious. I thought Alexander had a brigand's ambitions, but he is undertaking the business of kings. And we

Persians may think we are great men, but Alexander is greater because of his considerable intelligence—and we sent him a strap and a ball for his play and correction! So let us consider what would serve to put things right again, in case by dismissing Alexander as worthless (because we are elated by this great Persian kingdom), we are defeated across the whole face of the earth. My worry is that the greater may be discovered inferior to the lesser, if circumstances and Providence allow the crown to change hands. It is now in our interest to rule over our own nations of barbarians and not, by seeking to redeem Greece, to lose Persia into the bargain."

Oxyathres, Darius's brother, addressed him. "That means you are doing Alexander a great favor and providing him with the confidence to march on Persia by conceding Greece to him. You yourself should emulate Alexander—that is the way you will maintain control of your kingdom. He has not delegated the war to generals and satraps as you have: he is first to rush into battles and fights at the head of his troops and by fighting sets aside his kingship; and when he has won, he takes up his crown again."

Darius asked him, "Why should I emulate him?"

Another general replied: "By doing this, Alexander is supreme in everything, postpones nothing, does everything with resolution, because he has courage. He even looks exactly like a lion."

"How do you know that?" asked Darius.

"When I was sent by you, King, to Philip," he replied, "I saw the awe in which Alexander was held in Macedonia, and his appearance, intelligence, and character. So in your turn, King, should send for your satraps and all the nations you rule—Persians, Parthians, Medes, Elamites, and Babylonians in Mesopotamia[56] and the land of the Odynoi, not to mention the names of the Baktrians and Indians (you rule many nations)—and levy troops from them. If it is possible for you to have the gods as allies to help defeat the Greeks, then well and good; all the same, we will dumbfound our enemies with the massive size of our forces."

Darius, hearing this, said, "Your advice is good, but inappropriate: one Greek idea confounds hordes of barbarians, just as one wolf heads off a herd of sheep." And with that Darius gave orders for his hordes to be mustered.

Alexander, having made his way through Cilicia, came to the river "Ocean." The water was clear, and Alexander, as he saw it, wanted to bathe in the river. He stripped and leapt into it, but the water was very cold, and it brought him no relief. The chill gave him a headache and internal pains, and he was in a bad way. As Alexander lay there suffering,

8

56. This part of the list of tribes has been thought to be drawn from Acts of the Apostles 2.9 and to show that our author was a Christian.

the Macedonians themselves contracted illness in their souls, worrying that Darius might learn of Alexander's illness and attack them. So it was that the one soul of Alexander broke so many souls of his troops.

At this point a man called Philip, who was a doctor,[57] prescribed Alexander a medicine that would cure his illness. Alexander was keen to take it, and Philip was making up the prescription, but a letter was handed to Alexander, sent by Parmenion, a general of King Alexander's, which ran

> Darius told the doctor Philip to poison you when he had the opportunity, promising to give him his sister in marriage and to make him a partner in his kingdom; and Philip agreed to do this. So be on your guard, King, against Philip.

Alexander took the letter, but reading it did not upset him: he knew the attitude Philip had towards him. So he put the letter under his pillow. The doctor Philip came up and gave King Alexander the cup of medicine to drink, with the words "Drink, Lord King, and be rid of your illness." Alexander took the cup and said, "Look, I am drinking it," and drank it straight down. After drinking it, he then gave him the letter. Philip read the letter on his own and said, "King Alexander, you will not find this an accurate picture of me."

When he had recovered from his illness, Alexander embraced Philip and said to him: "You now know my opinion of you, Philip. I received the letter before the medicine and then proceeded to drink the medicine, entrusting myself to your name: I knew a Philip had planned no evil against Alexander."

"Lord King," Philip replied, "now you should punish the one who sent you the letter—Parmenion—as he deserves. The fact is that he himself has on many occasions tried to persuade me to poison you, the terms being that I should have Darius's sister Dadipharta in marriage. And when I refused, you can see what a dreadful situation he tried to put me in." Alexander investigated the matter, and, finding Philip to be innocent, he relieved Parmenion of his command.

9      From here Alexander took his armies and reached the land of the Medes. He was in a hurry to capture Greater Armenia.[58] Having subjugated it, he marched for quite some days into waterless territory, full of ravines, and, passing through the Aryan land, he reached the river Euphrates. This he bridged with arches and iron spokes,[59] and then he or-

57. This episode, duplicated in our recension at 1.41, belongs to 333 B.C. Philip the Akarnanian had been Alexander's personal doctor since youth. Parmenion, Alexander's elderly and expert second-in-command, in fact remained in his post until his execution in 330 B.C., following his son's involvement in a plot against Alexander.

58. Armenia was divided into Greater and Lesser 150 years after Alexander. Greater Armenia in fact lay east of the Euphrates.

59. Alexander used rafts and chains. The reader may speculate on how one might use "arches and iron spokes."

dered his troops to cross. But as he saw they were afraid to, he gave orders for the animals, the carts, and everyone's food to be taken across first, and only then the troops. But they were afraid, when they saw the current of the river, that the arches might come adrift. As they did not dare cross, Alexander took his guards with him and went over first. And so his whole army followed.

Immediately he gave orders for the bridges over the river Euphrates to be broken up. The whole army took this badly, and they were even more afraid, saying, "King Alexander, if it should happen that when we fight, we are routed by the barbarians, how are we going to get away safely and cross the river?"

Alexander, seeing their panic and hearing the mutterings among them, brought together all his troops and made a statement to them as follows. "Comrades-in-arms, you present fine hopes of victory, entertaining thoughts of defeat and retreat. It was for this reason that I ordered the bridge to be cut down—so that you would fight and win, or if you lost, not run away: war is not for those who run away but for those who pursue! Let us, after all, make our return to Macedonia together and return victorious. Engaging in battle is mere play for us!"

Following this statement of Alexander's, the troops cheered him, entered upon the war with confidence, and pitched camp.

Likewise, Darius's army was encamped above the river Tigris. They met each other in battle, and both sides fought valiantly against each other. One of the Persians came up behind Alexander—he had got Macedonian armor and looked like one of the Macedonian allies—and struck Alexander on the head, breaking his helmet. He was instantly arrested by Alexander's soldiers and presented to him in chains. Alexander, under the impression that he was a Macedonian, said to him, "My good man, what made you do this?"

"King Alexander," he replied, "do not let my Macedonian armor deceive you. I am a Persian, a satrap of Darius's. I had gone up to him and said, 'If I bring you the head of Alexander, what favor will you grant me?' And he promised me a kingdom and his daughter in marriage. So I came to you and acquired Macedonian costume, and, having failed, I stand in chains before you."

On hearing this, Alexander sent for his whole army and, with everyone watching, freed him. And he said to his own army, "Men of Macedonia, this is what soldiers should be like: daring in war."

The barbarians were now without food supplies and made a detour  10 into Baktria, but Alexander stayed on there and took control of the whole area. Another of Darius's satraps came to Alexander and said: "I am a satrap of Darius's and have brought about some great successes for him in wars, but have received no thanks from him. So give me ten thousand armed soldiers, and I shall give you my king, Darius."

Alexander replied to him, "Go and assist your king, Darius: I am not entrusting other people's men to you who are attempting to betray your own."

Now, the satraps of those regions reported on Alexander as follows.

To Darius, Great King, greetings:
We had previously informed you urgently of the assault that Alexander was making on our people. We now in turn inform you that he has arrived. He has laid siege to our territory; he has killed many of our Persians, and we ourselves are in mortal danger. So make speed with a large force to reach here before he does and do not give him the chance to advance on you: the Macedonian army is powerful and enormous and is stronger than us.
Farewell.

Darius received and read their letter and then sent a letter to Alexander along the following lines.

I call upon the great god Zeus to witness what you have done to me. My mother I consider has gone to join the gods; my wife I consider I never had; my children I deem not to have been born. Myself, I shall never cease to follow up the outrage done to me. In the letter to me, it says that your behavior to my family is just and respectful. But if you were in fact acting justly, you would have acted justly towards me. You can be merciless to my family: maltreat them and take your vengeance—they are enemy children. Being kind to them will not make me your friend, nor will being cruel to them make me your enemy.

Alexander received and read Darius's letter: he smiled and wrote him this reply.

King Alexander to Darius, greetings:
Your pointless stupidity, your gabbling and ineffectual talk, the gods utterly and completely detest. Are you not ashamed at such evil words and pointless thoughts? It is not out of fear of you that I have treated those who were formerly yours with courtesy, nor in the hope that I may come to a settlement with you, so that on my arrival you might show your gratitude to us. And do not come to us: my crown is not of the same value as yours. You will certainly not impede the respect I show everyone—I shall display even more extreme kindness to those who were once yours.
This is my last letter to you.

11    Having written this letter to Darius, Alexander prepared for war and wrote to all his satraps.

King Alexander to all the satraps under him, those of Phrygia, Cappadocia, Paphlagonia, Arabia, and to all the others, greetings:

I want you to supply tunics for a very large army and dispatch them to us at Antioch in Syria.[60] And send us the supplies of arms that you have built up. Three thousand camels have been provided between the river Euphrates and Antioch in Syria to assist in carrying out our orders so that work proceeds on schedule. So be quick to join us.

Darius's satraps also wrote.

To Darius, Great King:

We hesitate to write to you in this way but are obliged to by circumstances. Know, King, that the Macedonian leader, Alexander, has slain two of us lords and that some of the lords have gone over to Alexander together with their harems.

Learning of this, Darius wrote to the nearest generals and satraps to get ready and set up camp. He also wrote to the kings nearest him.

Darius, King of Kings, greetings.

We are to fight a miserable nation, the Macedonians, and it will be like wiping off sweat.

The Persian army too he instructed to be in readiness, and he wrote also to Poros, king of India, requesting assistance from him.[61] King Poros, on receipt of Darius's letter, read of the misfortunes that had befallen him and was distressed. He replied to him as follows.

Poros, King of India, to Darius, King of Persia, greetings:

I was greatly distressed to read what you write but am in an impossible situation, because although I want to join you and offer advice on what might help, I am prevented from so doing by the illness that has a grip on me. So keep your spirits up, just as though we were with you, unable to tolerate this outrage. Write to us for anything you want: my forces are at your disposal—even the remoter nations will follow my orders.

Learning about this,[62] Darius's mother sent to Darius, writing to him secretly like this.

60. Antioch was founded in 300 B.C.
61. The chronological order of these letters from the epistolary novel (see the Introduction) is disturbed. A letter corresponding to these stated contents is included at 2.19. Alexander came into conflict with Poros, a king in the Punjab, in 326 B.C., but there is no reason to suppose Darius was in contact with him.
62. Namely, "that Darius was preparing to fight another battle with Alexander" (from Leo's Latin translation).

To Darius, my child, greetings:

I hear you are gathering nations and wanting to engage in another battle with Alexander. Do not inflict chaos on the world, child: the future is unclear. Give up your hopes for an improvement in the situation and do not, when you are in doubt, act inflexibly and lose your life. After all, we receive the greatest respect from King Alexander: he has not treated me as the mother of an enemy, but with great courtesy, and as a result I hope that a decent agreement will be reached.

Darius read and wept, remembering his family bonds; but at the same time he was in confusion and came down on the side of war.

13     Alexander arrived with a large force in Persia. The city walls were high and could be seen by the Macedonians from far off. Now, the intelligent Alexander thought up a scheme. Taking the goats that were grazing there and chopping down branches from the trees, he tied the branches to the backs of the goats, and the goats followed behind the soldiers. As they were dragged along the ground, the branches disturbed the dust, and the cloud rose to Olympus, so that the Persians looking from the walls thought the mass of soldiers was beyond counting. When evening fell, he gave orders for torches and candles to be attached to the horns of the goats and for these to be lit and burn—the region was flat—and the whole plain looked like burning fire, and the Persians were afraid.

So they came within about five miles of the city of Persis,[63] and Alexander was looking for someone to send to Darius to declare to him when they would engage in battle. Now, Alexander was asleep that night and saw in a dream Ammon standing by him in the shape of Hermes, with his herald's wand, cloak, staff, and a Macedonian cap on his head, saying to him: "Alexander, my boy, when it is time for assistance, I am by your side. If you send a messenger to Darius, he will betray you: you yourself must become a messenger and go on your way in the dress you see me in."

"It is dangerous," Alexander replied to him, "for me, a king, to be my own messenger."

Ammon said, "But with a god to aid you, no harm shall befall you."

Alexander, having received this divine message, rose in good spirits and shared it with his satraps; but they advised him against doing this.

14     Taking with him a satrap by the name of Eumelos and collecting three

---

63. The author thinks wrongly that there is a city called Persis that is the capital of Persia. Similarly at 3.17, the land Prasiake is thought to be a capital city. Our manuscript even presents Macedonia as a city at 3.32.

horses, he set out without delay and reached the river Stranga.[64] This river freezes in icy weather to such an extent that it forms a rock-hard surface, and beasts and wagons go over it. Then, days later, it thaws and becomes deep enough to sweep away with its current those caught trying to cross. Well, Alexander found the river frozen over, and, putting on the dress he had seen Ammon wearing in his dream, he sat on his horse and crossed alone. And when Eumelos urged him to cross together with him in case he should need help, Alexander said: "Stay here with the two horses. I have the help of him who gave me the oracle to put on this dress and travel on my own." The river was about two hundred yards wide. At the other side, Alexander went on his way and came right up to the gates of Persis. The guards there, seeing him in such dress, thought he was a god, but they held him and asked him who he was. "Take me to King Darius," replied Alexander. "I will report who I am to him."

Darius was outside the city on a hill, constructing roads and training his troops in phalanx formation as though they were Macedonians.[65] Alexander turned all heads towards him because of his strange appearance, and Darius all but fell down before him, thinking him a god descended from Olympus and that he had been adorned with barbarian robes. Darius was sitting, wearing a crown of precious stones, a silken robe with Babylonian gold embroidery and the royal purple, and golden shoes with precious stones inset up to the leggings. And he had scepters on either side and thousands upon thousands of men around him.

Darius inquired of him who he might be, observing him wearing a costume he had never seen before. Alexander replied, "I am the messenger of King Alexander."

King Darius asked him, "And why have you come to us?"

Alexander replied: "I declare to you that Alexander is here and ask when you are going to engage in battle. You must realize, King Darius, that a king who is slow to join battle has already revealed to his adversary that his battle spirit is weak. So do not be careless but announce to me when you wish to engage in battle."

Darius was angered and asked Alexander: "Is it you I am joining battle with or is it Alexander? You display enough audacity to be Alexander himself, and you reply boldly as though you were a companion of mine. But I shall proceed to my usual dinner, and you shall dine with me, see-

64. In some later recensions this river possesses the fairy-tale attribute of freezing for the night and thawing for the day; the author must surely have intended this originally—that is why Alexander travels at night. The satrap Eumelos is equally fictional.

65. "As though they were Macedonians" is my guess at the author's meaning, as the various recensions are muddled. What follows in L is ungrammatical, and in other important recensions it is Alexander who thinks Darius a god.

ing that Alexander himself also gave dinner to my letter bearers." And so speaking, Darius took Alexander by the hand and went inside his palace. And this action Alexander took as a good omen, being guided by the tyrant. Entering his palace, immediately Alexander was the first to recline at Darius's banquet.

15   The Persians looked in amazement at Alexander's small stature, not realizing that in a small vessel was contained the glory of heavenly Fortune. As the drinks came round more frequently, Alexander thought up this scheme: all the cups he got, he put in his pocket. People saw him and told Darius, and Darius stood up and asked, "My good man, why are you putting these in your pocket when you are at a banquet?" Then Alexander used his ingenuity and said, "Greatest King, this is what Alexander does when he gives a dinner for his officers and guards—he makes a present of the cups—and I thought you were like him."[66] So the Persians were astonished and amazed at what Alexander said: for every story, if it carries conviction, always has its audience enthralled.

A deep silence fell, and a man called Pasarges, who was a leader in Persis, examined Alexander. In fact he knew Alexander by sight: when he had first gone to Pella in Macedonia, sent as an emissary by Darius to demand the tribute, and had been prevented by Alexander, he took note of him. And having taken a reasonably long look at Alexander, he said to himself, "This is Philip's son, even if he has changed his appearance: many men can be recognized by their voice, even though they remain in darkness." Convinced by his awareness that it was Alexander himself, he leaned over to Darius and said to him, "Greatest King Darius and lord over every land, this emissary of Alexander is Alexander himself, king of Macedon, son of the late Philip, displaying his valor."

Darius and the feasters were very drunk. So Alexander, hearing what Pasarges had said to Darius at the meal and realizing that he had been recognized, outwitted them all, jumped up with the golden cups in his pockets, and left stealthily. Mounting his horse to escape the danger and finding a Persian guard at the gate with torches in his hands, he killed him and took them, leaving the city of Persis. When Darius found out, he sent armed Persians to arrest Alexander. But Alexander urged on his horse, guiding his path: it was the depths of night, and darkness had fallen from Olympus. A very large number pursued him, but they did not catch him: he managed to keep to the road surface, but the others stumbled in the darkness over cliff edges. Alexander was like a beaming star in heaven that rises alone, and as he fled he led the Persians to destruction.

66. I have omitted here an incomprehensible clause. There was in fact such a custom among the Macedonians, though the author evidently supposes there was not and glorifies the crafty acquisitiveness of Alexander.

Darius sat on his couch in misery and in addition saw an omen. A portrait of King Xerxes of which Darius was particularly fond (because it was a very fine piece of painting) fell suddenly from the roof.

Alexander got away and, continuing through that night, came at dawn to the river Stranga. He had scarcely crossed it, with his horse reaching the bank and putting its forefeet on the land, when the river melted at the sun's rays. The horse was snatched by the water and swept away, but it threw Alexander onto the land. The Persians in their pursuit of Alexander came to the river when he had already crossed and, as they were unable to cross, turned back—no man could cross the river. So the Persians turned round and reported to Darius Alexander's good luck. Darius, dumbfounded by the unexpected omen, was greatly pained. Alexander, making his way by foot from the river, found Eumelos sitting with the two horses he had left behind, and told him everything he had done.

Returning to the camp of his troops, he immediately ordered the 16 Greek phalanxes, by their names, to arms in readiness to attack Darius. He himself stood in the midst of them, encouraging them. When he had mustered all the troops, he found the number to be 120,000. Standing at a high point, he exhorted them in these words. "Comrades-in-arms, even if our number is small, all the same we have great sense, spirit, and power—more than the Persians, our opposition. So let the thoughts of none of you admit any weakness when you see the mass of the barbarians: one of you, baring his sword, will kill thousands of the enemy. Let none of you be afraid: there are millions of flies crowding the meadow, but when wasps buzz at them, they scare them away with their wings. In just this way, massive numbers do not bear comparison with intelligence: when wasps come, flies count for nothing." So speaking, Alexander encouraged his troops, and his troops showed themselves good men and cheered Alexander.

Proceeding on his way, then, he came to the region of the river Stranga, that is, to its banks. Darius, collecting his force, came himself also to the Stranga; and as he saw it was very slight and frozen, he crossed it and pressed on, sweeping through the middle of the desert. His intention was to take Alexander's troops by surprise[67] so as to find them unprepared and rout them. And criers went into their midst and called out for the best fighters for the battle, and Darius's whole army put on its full armor. Darius was on a high chariot, and his satraps sat in chariots equipped with sickles; others brought fiendish weapons and artillery.

---

67. The motif of surprise, of which no effective use is made, is peculiar to recension B. The battle in question is the final great battle against Darius—Gaugamela (or Arbela) of 331 B.C.

The Macedonian troops were led by Alexander mounted on the horse Bucephalus—and no one could approach this horse.

Once both sides had sounded the signal for battle, some flung stones, some shot arrows like a rainstorm sweeping down from heaven, some flung spears, others again used slings with leaden shot so as to obscure the light of day. Confusion reigned as men struck and were stricken. Many, wounded by missiles, died; others lay half-dead. The air was dark and full of blood. When many Persians had met their grim end, Darius panicked and turned the reins on the sickle chariots, and as they rotated, he mowed down the vast hordes of the Persians, like farmhands shearing corn in a field.

When Darius came to the river Stranga in his flight, he himself and his companions crossed over, finding the river frozen. But the hordes of Persians and barbarians wanting to cross the river and get away came onto it in all their numbers, and it gave way and took all it found. The remaining Persians were killed by the Macedonians.

Darius came, a fugitive, to his own palace and threw himself on the floor, wailing and tearfully lamenting for himself, having lost so huge a number of soldiers and having emptied the whole of Persia. In the grip of such calamities, he mourned to himself, saying: "Darius, so great a king, with so many nations under my control and all the cities subject to me, I who shared the thrones of the gods and rose with the Sun—now I am a solitary fugitive. It is a fact that no one plans securely for the future: Fortune only needs a slight tilt, and it raises the lowly above the clouds and draws those in the heights down to Hell."

17 Darius, then, lay bereft of men, he who had been the king of so many nations. Recovering a little, standing up, and regaining his composure, he wrote a letter and sent it to Alexander. Its content was as follows.

Darius to my master Alexander, greetings:

He who showed me the light of glory, in haughtiness of mind, conceived a great passion to invade Greece, unsatisfied with the gold and other riches that we have inherited from our ancestors.[68] He died after losing much gold and silver and many tents, though he had been richer than Croesus of Lydia, and he did not escape the death that awaited him. So, Alexander, you in your turn, as you have observed luck and its nemesis, set aside grandiose thoughts. Pity us who come to you for refuge, by Zeus of Suppliants and our common descent from Perseus,[69] and give me back my wife, mother, and children, recalling to your mind the hopes a father has.

---

68. Darius refers to his ancestor Xerxes, who invaded Greece in 480 B.C.
69. "By Zeus...Perseus" is corrupted in all recensions; a papyrus of the epistolary novel preserves the original.

In return for this I undertake to give you the treasures that our ancestors deposited in the earth in the land of Minaia and at Susa and in Baktria. I also undertake that you may be lord of the lands of the Persians, Medes, and the other nations for all time.

Farewell.

Having learned the content of this letter, Alexander gathered together his whole army and his lords and ordered Darius's letter to be read out to them. And when this letter had been read out, one of the generals, by name Parmenion, said, "King Alexander, I would have taken the money and the land he has offered you; and I would have returned Darius his mother, children, and wife, after sleeping with them."

Alexander smiled and said to him: "I, Parmenion, am taking everything from him. I am amazed that Darius thought he could ransom his own family, using my money, but much more amazed that he undertakes to hand over my own land to me. Darius fails to realize that if he does not defeat me in battle, this is all mine, together with his family. However, it is a disgrace, an outright disgrace, for the man who has defeated men manfully to be miserably overcome by women. The battle we press upon him is for what is ours: I would not have come into Asia in the first place if I had not supposed it to be mine. And if he ruled it first, he should consider that his gain, in that he held someone else's land for so long and did not suffer for it."[70]

This is what Alexander said, and he told the emissaries of Darius to go back and report this themselves to Darius, without giving them a letter. Then Alexander gave instructions for the soldiers wounded in the battle to be tended with all care and for the dead to be mourned and buried. Staying there for the winter, he ordered Xerxes' palace, the finest in that land, to be burned down; but shortly after, he changed his mind and instructed them to stop.

He also saw the tombs of the Persians, decorated with great quantities 18 of gold. And he saw also the tomb of Nebuchadnezzar (who is called Nabuchodonosor in Greek) and the offerings of the Jews that were kept there and gold mixing bowls, like those of heroes to look at. Nearby he saw the tomb of Cyrus too: it was a twelve-story tower of stone, and he lay in a golden sarcophagus on the top floor, with glass round him so that his hair and whole body could be seen through the glass.

There were Greeks here, with their feet or noses or ears mutilated, bound by shackles and nailed to the tomb of Xerxes, men of Athens, and they shouted to Alexander to save them. Alexander, seeing them, wept: it was a terrible sight. So he was deeply upset at this and ordered them to be released and to be given a thousand didrachms and to be returned each

---

70. The more celebrated reply, which no recension preserves accurately, was "And so would I if I were Parmenion." See Plutarch *Alexander* 29.

of them to his own country. But they took the money and asked Alexander to grant them an area of land in that place and not to be sent off to their home countries—in their present condition they would bring embarrassment upon their relatives. So he gave instructions for an area of land to be granted to them and for a gift to be made to them of corn and seed and six oxen each and sheep and everything useful for farming among other things.

19    Darius was preparing to engage Alexander in another battle. And he wrote to Poros, king of India, as follows.

> King Darius, to Poros, King of India, greetings:
>
> A disaster has befallen my house in these days, and now I inform you of it—the Macedonian king has attacked me and, with the feelings of a wild beast, is not prepared to return me my mother, wife, and children. I have offered him treasures and much else besides, but he will not take them. So as a result, to destroy him for what he has done, I am preparing another campaign against him, until I have vengeance on him and his nation.
>
> It is only right, then, that you should be annoyed at what I have suffered and that you should march out to avenge the outrage done to me, remembering our traditional obligations to each other. So assemble as many nations as possible at the Caspian Gates and supply the mustered men with plenty of gold, corn, and fodder. And I shall grant you half of all the spoils I take from the enemy and the horse Bucephalus, together with the royal lands and his concubines.
>
> On receipt of our letter muster your hordes in great haste and send them to us.
>
> Farewell.

Alexander learned about this from one of Darius's men who had fled to him, and as soon as he had read it, he took his whole force and marched to Media. He heard that Darius was at Ekbatana at the Caspian Gates and made his pursuit intense and more audacious.

20    Darius's satraps, Bessos and Ariobarzanes, realized Alexander was near, and, with an insane change of mind, these men planned to kill Darius. They said to each other, "If we kill Darius, we shall receive much money from Alexander for having killed his enemy." So, having formed their evil plan, sword in hand they attacked Darius. And when Darius saw these men setting upon him with swords, he said to them: "Masters of mine who were my slaves before, what wrong have I done you that you should kill me with barbarian audacity? Do not do any more than the Macedonians have: leave me cast down like this in my palace to lament the inconstancy of Fortune; for if Alexander, king of Macedon, comes now and finds me slaughtered, as a king he will avenge a king's

blood." But they paid no attention to Darius's pleading and repaid him with murder. Darius used both hands: with the left he took hold of Bessos and brought his knee up into his groin; he checked Ariobarzanes with his right hand and held him in such a way that he could not bring his sword down on him. So their blows missed. And as the criminals no longer had the strength to kill him, they wrestled with him—he was a strong man.

Now, the Macedonians, finding the river Stranga frozen, crossed it, and Alexander entered Darius's palace. The criminals learned of Alexander's arrival and fled, leaving Darius behind, half-dead. And coming to King Darius, Alexander found him half-dead, the blood pouring from his wounds; over him he raised a lament to match his grief, poured tears upon him, and covered the body of Darius with his cloak. And laying his hands upon Darius's breast, he spoke over him words laden with pity.

"Arise, King Darius, and rule over your land and be master of what is yours! Take your crown as lord over the Persian people: keep the greatness of your realm. I swear to you by Providence above, I speak the truth to you, not fabrications. Who are they who struck you? Declare them to me, so that I may now give you rest."

And at these words of Alexander Darius groaned and, stretching out his hand, drew Alexander to him. Embracing him, he said: "King Alexander, never exult in your royal position. When you succeed in a project of divine scale and want to reach heaven with your hands, consider the future: Fortune knows no king, though he rule a vast people; with indiscriminate mind she comes down on any side. You see what I was and what I have become.

"When I die, Alexander, bury me with your own hands. Let Macedonians and Persians conduct my funeral. Darius and Alexander shall be of one family. I entrust my mother to you as though she were your mother; pity my wife as though she were your sister. My daughter Roxana I give to you as wife, so that you may leave children in remembrance for endless ages; and rejoicing in them, as we rejoice in our children, you yourself will perpetuate the memory of Philip and Roxana will perpetuate that of Darius, as time passes and you grow old together."[71] So spoke Darius, and, holding onto Alexander's neck, he breathed his last.[72]

Alexander wailed and wept with feeling for Darius, then gave instructions for him to be buried in the Persian manner. He ordered the Persians to lead the procession, then all the Macedonians to follow in arms. Alexander put his shoulder to the bier of Darius and carried it together with

21

71. The Roxana whom Alexander married was not the daughter of Darius but a Baktrian princess whom he met later in the campaign.
72. Arrian (*Anabasis* 3.21) says that Darius died before Alexander saw him.

the satraps. Everyone wept and keened, not so much for Darius as for Alexander, seeing him bearing the bier. Having conducted the funeral in accordance with the Persian usages, he dismissed the crowds.

Immediately an edict was published in each city, containing the following.

I, Alexander, son of King Philip and Queen Olympias, to those who inhabit the cities and lands of Persia, give these instructions.

I do not wish such vast numbers of men to come to an evil end. The goodwill of heaven makes me victorious over the Persians; so I thank Providence above. Now recognize that I intend to appoint satraps over you, whom you are obliged to obey, as under Darius. And recognize no other king but Alexander. Keep your own customs and your usual festivals, sacrifices, and carnivals, as under Darius. Each of you shall live in his own city; but if anyone leaves his own city or land and takes up residence in a foreign place, he shall be food for the dogs. Each of you shall have control over his own property except gold and silver: I instruct that the gold and silver should be brought to our cities and lands, but the coinage you have we allow you each to keep as your own property. I order all weapons of war to be brought to my armories. The satraps shall remain in their posts. No longer shall any nation approach you except for trade. And I intend to bring prosperity to your lands and to see that the roads of Persia are used for trade and business in total peace, so that people from Greece may trade with you and you with them: from the Euphrates and the crossing to the river Tigris up to Babylon I shall build roads and construct signs to indicate where the road leads.

It was not I who killed Darius; who his killers were, I do not know. I owe it to them to reward them richly and grant them extensive lands, as they killed our enemy.

At these words of Alexander, the Persians were bewildered, thinking Alexander was going to destroy Persis utterly. But Alexander, realizing the distress of the crowd, told them: "Why do you think, Persians, that I am looking for the men who killed Darius? If Darius had been alive, he would have launched a campaign against me, but, as it is, war has totally ceased. Accordingly, whether the man who killed him is a Macedonian or a Persian, let him come to me confidently and receive whatever he asks from me; for I swear by Providence above and by the life of my mother, Olympias, that I shall see they are marked out and notable before all mankind."

And at this oath of Alexander's the crowd broke into tears, but Bessos and Ariobarzanes came up to Alexander, expecting to receive large gifts from him and said, "Master, we are the men who killed Darius." And straightaway Alexander ordered them to be arrested and to be crucified at Darius's grave. They cried out and said: "Did you not swear that you would see the killers of Darius were marked out and notable? How is it that you now break your oath and order us to be crucified?" To which Alexander replied: "It is not for your sake, you miserable wretches, that I shall justify myself, but for the mass of troops. Otherwise it would not have been possible to find you so easily or bring you into the open, had I not for a short while applauded the death of Darius. This is what I was praying for: the chance to sentence his killers to the severest punishment. After all, how are men who have slain their own master going to spare me? And as far as you go, you miserable men, I have not broken my oath: I swore I would see you were marked out and notable before everyone, that is, that you would be crucified for everyone to see." At these words everyone cheered him, and the detestable murderers were crucified at Darius's grave.

Alexander, having restored the whole land to peace, said to them, "Whom would you like to be viceroy of your city?" and they replied, "Adulites, the brother of Darius." And he gave orders that he should be appointed.  22

He had left Darius's mother, wife, and daughter in a city two days' journey away and he wrote to them like this.

King Alexander to Stateira and Rodogoune and my wife, Roxana, greetings:

Though we drew our forces up against Darius, we did not take vengeance upon him. It was instead the opposite: I prayed to have him alive under my supremacy but found him mortally wounded, and in pity covered him over with my cloak. I tried to establish from him who had struck him; however, he said nothing to me except this: "I entrust to you my mother and my wife, and particularly Roxana, my daughter and your wife." He did not manage to disclose to me what had happened to him. But those responsible for his death I have punished appropriately. He instructed us to bury him by the graves of his fathers, and this has been done.

I imagine you too have heard all this. So bring an end to your grief for him: I shall restore you to your royal prerogatives. But for the time being, remain where you are, until we have arranged everything here properly. And in accordance with Darius's instructions, I intend that Roxana, my wife, shall share my throne, providing you find this acceptable. I also wish and order her to receive obeisance from now on as Alexander's wife.

Farewell.

Rodogoune and Stateira received Alexander's letter and wrote him this reply.

> To King Alexander, greetings:
> We have prayed to the heavenly gods who have laid low the name of Darius and the pride of the Persians that they appoint you eternal king of the world, so full are you of reason, wisdom, and power. We know that in your arms we have not been treated as prisoners. So we pray also to Providence above to give you, moreover, all that is best so that you may rule for immeasurable time. And your deeds show that you belong to a superior race. But now we are no longer like prisoners, and we know that Alexander is another Darius for us. We do obeisance to Alexander, who has not shamed us, and we have sent letters everwhere saying, "People of Persia, look how Darius at his death has found Alexander to succeed him as Greatest King: Fortune gives Roxana in marriage to Alexander, king of the whole world. So all of you must bring proper thanks to Alexander because the pride of the Persians has now been raised even higher. Rejoice, then, with us, proclaiming Alexander Greatest King." This, then, is what we have declared to the Persians.
> Farewell.

Alexander received their letter and wrote this reply.

> I applaud your sentiment. And I will struggle to act worthily of your affection—since even I am a mortal man.
> Farewell.

And in another letter he wrote to Roxana of his decisions.
He also wrote this letter to his mother, Olympias.

> King Alexander, to my sweetest mother, greetings:
> I am writing to you to send me the women's jewelry and clothing of Darius's mother and his wife, and the royal attire for Roxana, Darius's daughter and my wife.

On receipt of his letter, his mother sent him all her royal clothing and all the jewelry, made from gold and precious stones. When he had received these things, Alexander got preparations for the wedding in Darius's palace under way. And who could adequately describe the joy there at that time?

23     After this, Alexander wrote this letter to his mother.

> King Alexander, to my much-beloved mother and to Aristotle, my most-esteemed teacher, greetings:

I thought it necessary to write to you of the battle I had with Darius. Hearing he was at the Gulf of Issos with a mass of soldiers and other kings, I took a large number of goats and fastened torches to their horns, then set out and marched by night. They saw the torches in the distance and thought it was an innumerable army, as a result of which their thoughts turned to panic and they were defeated. This was how I gained the victory against them. At that spot I founded a city which I called Aigai;[73] and I founded another city on the Gulf of Issos, calling it Alexandria. Darius was abandoned, captured, and wounded by his own satraps, and I was extremely distressed about him: having defeated him, I did not want to murder him but to have him under my command. I came upon him still alive and took off the cloak I had on and covered him. Then, recognizing the uncertainty of Fortune, as displayed in Darius's case, I lamented him. I gave him a royal funeral and ordered the ears and noses of those guarding his tomb to be cut off, following the native custom. And I ordered the killers of Darius to be crucified at Darius's grave. Leaving there, I won control of the kingdom of Ariobarzan and Manazakes; I subjugated Media and Armenia, Iberia and the whole territory of Persia that Darius ruled over.[74]

[Recension C contains a narrative converted from a different letter, including chapters 24–32, in which Alexander shows respect for Jewish religion, captures Egypt, where he is crowned by the statue of Nektanebos, and founds Alexandria—again, but now his monotheism (!) is highlighted. Now follow giant ants, a river in which sand flows, Lilliputians, and a statue of Sesonchosis whose inscription denies the possibility of going further—Alexander covers it up!]

Picking up guides there, I wanted to go into the interior of the desert, following the Plough, but they advised me against going there because of the large number of wild animals that live in those places. All the same, I ignored what they said and began the journey. So we came to a region full of ravines, where the road was very narrow, and we traveled along it for eight days. We saw strange animals in those places, the like of which we had never known before. When we had crossed that region, we came to another, more dismal, one. We found there a great forest of trees

32

73. *Aiges* is Greek for "goats," and Aigai a common enough name for a town.
74. Manazakes is probably the Mazaios who surrendered Babylon after Gaugamela; Ariobarzanes surrendered after Darius's death (but the Ariobarzanes of chapter 20 = Satibarzanes, satrap of Areia). Alexander never visited Armenia or Iberia (a region north of Armenia in the Caucasus).

called anaphanda, with odd and peculiar fruit: they were enormous apples like the largest melons. And there were men too in that forest called Phytoi ["plantmen"], 24 cubits tall, with necks 1½ cubits long, and likewise with long feet. Their arms and hands were like saws. When they saw us, they rushed at the army. I was beside myself, seeing them. So I ordered one of them to be caught. But when we rushed at them with cries and the sound of trumpets, they ran away. We killed thirty-two of them, but they killed one hundred of our soldiers. So we stayed there, eating the fruit from the trees.

33 Setting out from there, we came to a green land where there were wild men like giants, round bodied with fiery faces, who looked like lions. There were some others with them called Ochlitai ["mobmen"] who had no hair at all, four cubits high and a spear's length across. And seeing us, they ran at us. They wore lion skins and were extremely strong and quite ready to fight without weapons. We struck them, and they struck us with staves, killing a considerable number of us. I was afraid they were going to rout us; so I gave instructions to set fire to the wood. And when they saw the fire, those fine specimens of men ran away. They killed 180 soldiers of ours. On the following day I decided to visit their caves. We found beasts like lions tethered at their entrances—and they had three eyes. And we saw fleas there leaping about like our frogs.

Moving on from there, we came to a place where an abundant spring rose. I ordered my chariot to be halted there, and we stayed there two months.

Leaving there, we came to the Melophagoi ["apple eaters"]. There we saw a man whose whole body was covered with hair, a huge man, and we were terrified. I ordered him to be taken, and when he was taken he glared savagely at us. I gave orders for a naked woman to be brought to him: he took her and started eating her. And when the soldiers rushed in to get her away, he gabbled in his language. His neighbors heard him and came at us from the marsh, maybe 10,000 men, but our army was 40,000 strong, and I ordered the marsh to be set on fire. And when they saw the fire, they fled. We chased them and caught three of them, who would not take any food and died after eight days. They did not have human intelligence but barked like dogs.

[In recension C, Alexander now comes to the Pillars of Hercules and Semiramis and meets further monsters. Then come the gymnosophists—whom we meet at 3.5ff.]

36 Setting out from there, we came to a river. So I gave orders to

pitch camp and for the soldiers to disarm in the usual way. There were trees in the river, and as the sun rose, they grew until midday; after midday, they grew smaller until they could not be seen at all. They gave off droplets like Persian oil of myrrh, with a very sweet and fine scent. I gave instructions for incisions to be made in the trees and the drops to be caught with sponges, but suddenly the collectors were whipped by an invisible divinity. We heard the sound of them being whipped and saw the weals rising on their backs, but we could not see who was striking them. And a voice came, saying not to make incisions or collect the liquid, "and if you do not stop, the army will be struck dumb!" I was afraid and forbade any of them to make incisions or collect the liquid.

There were black stones in the river; everyone who touched these stones turned the same color as the stones. There were also many snakes in the river and many types of fish—which were not boiled above a fire, but in cold spring water. One of the soldiers caught one, washed it, and dropped it in a container—and found the fish cooked. There were birds on the river, very like our birds, but if anyone touched them, fire came from it.

The following day we became lost. The guides said to me: "We 37 do not know where we are going, Lord King Alexander. Let us return so that we do not stumble into worse places." But I was not prepared to return. We came across many animals: six-footed ones, three-eyed ones, five-eyed ones ten cubits long, and many other kinds of animals. Some of them ran away; others leapt at us. We came to a sandy place, from which emerged animals like wild asses of more than twenty cubits. And they had not two eyes each but six each, but only saw with the two; they were not aggressive but tame. Many others too the soldiers shot with arrows.

Moving on from there, we came to a place where there were men without heads, though they spoke as men do in their own language; they were hairy, wore skins, ate fish. They caught sea fish and brought us them from the sea they lived next to. Others brought truffles from the land weighing twenty-five pounds each. We saw a great many large seals crawling on the land. And my friends persistently advised me to turn back, but I would not, because I wanted to see the end of the earth.

Pressing on from there, we traveled through uninhabited land to 38 the sea, no longer seeing anything—not bird nor beast—only the sky and the earth. We no longer saw the sun; the air was dark for ten days. We came to a place on the coast and pitched our tents and made camp there, staying very many days. In the middle of that sea there was an island, and I was keen to find out about the interior of it. I ordered a very large number of boats to be constructed. Around a thousand men boarded those boats, and we sailed to the island, which was not far from the land. And on it we heard the voices of men saying in Greek

> Son of Philip, seed of Egypt,
> The name you received indicates the future
> Success you shall achieve courageously:
> From the womb you have been called ALEXANDER.
> You have warded off [ALEX-] men [ANDR-] by chasing
>   them off
> And scaring kings away from their possessions.
> But you shall swiftly in any case become an ex-man
>   [EX-ANDR-]
> When you complete the second letter
> Of your name, which is called lambda [=30, i.e., 30 years old].

We heard these words but did not see who spoke them. Some soldiers risked their lives to dive in and swim from the boats to the island to find out about it; and straightaway crabs emerged, dragging them into the water and killing them. We were afraid and turned back to land.

When we had disembarked from the boats and were walking about on the seashore, we found a crab emerging from the water onto the dry land. It was the size of a breastplate and its front feet, the so-called pincers, were each six feet long. Seeing it, we took spears and killed it with a struggle, because the iron would not penetrate its shell, and it smashed our spears with its front feet. When we had killed and shelled it, we found inside its shell seven pearls of great value—no man has ever seen such pearls. Seeing them, I realized they must be formed at the bottom of the unsailed sea. So I had the idea of taking a large iron cage and putting an enormous glass demijohn inside the cage, a cubit and a half thick; and I ordered a hole to be sited in the base of the demijohn to take a man's hand, because I wanted to go down and discover what was at the bottom of this sea. My intention was to keep the hole at the base of the demijohn closed from inside, but when I got down immediately to open it up, put my hand through the hole, and pick up from the sand beside it whatever I found at the bottom of this sea, then to bring my hand back in and straightaway to seal off the hole. And that is what I did. So I ordered a chain of 308 fathoms to be made and gave instructions that I was not to be pulled back up until there was a tug on the chain. "When I have been down on the bottom, I will immediately shake the demijohn for you to bring me up."

When everything had been prepared, I entered the glass demi-john to attempt the impossible. When I had entered it, the entry was immediately sealed with a leaden cap. I had descended 120 cubits when a passing fish shook the cage with its tail, and they brought me up because the chain had been tugged. I descended again, and the same thing happened to me. Going down for the third time, around 308 cubits, I saw all sorts of fish swimming around me, when, lo and behold, the biggest fish of them all came and seized me and my cage in its mouth and took me far off to the land a mile away. Now, in the boats there were the 360 men who were managing my descent: the fish took all of them with it and the four boats as well. Having reached dry land, it crushed the cage with its teeth, then cast it aside. I was scarcely breathing and frightened to death. And I fell down and worshiped Providence above who had preserved me from the terrifying beast. And I said to myself, "Alexander, give up attempting the impossible, in case by investigating the deep you lose your life." Immediately I instructed the army to move on from there and to proceed onward.

Traveling again, we came in two days to a region where the sun does not shine. There lies the Land of the Blest. As I wanted to find out about and see that region, I attempted to take my own slaves and advance there, but my friend Kallisthenes recommended that I should advance with 40 friends, 100 slaves, and 1,200 soldiers—only the reliable ones. So, leaving behind the infantry, together with the old and the women, I took soldiers, all young and hand-picked, and marched on with them, having given orders that no old man should march with us. But one inquisitive old man, with two brave sons who were real soldiers, said to them: "Children, listen to the voice of your father and take me with you—you shall not find me useless on the march. After all, look, in time of crisis King Alexander will be looking for an old man. So if you are found to have me with you, you will be greatly rewarded."

But they replied, "Father, we fear the king's threats and do not want to be found to have contravened his orders and lose not just the chance of this expedition, but even our lives."

The old man replied, "Get up and shave my chin and alter my appearance. I will march with you in the midst of the army, and in time of need I shall be a great help to you." And they did what their father told them.

So, traveling on from there for three days, we found a misty place. We could not go further, because there were no paths or tracks, and pitched our tents there. On the following day I took a thousand armed men and went with them to investigate if the end of the earth was here. We went leftward (there was more light on that side) and journeyed through rocky ground with steep drops up to midday (this I did not work out by the sun; rather, by measuring out ropes in accordance with the science of surveying I calculated the distance and the time). After this we were afraid and returned because the route was impassable. I wanted to set out again and go to the right: it was an extremely level plain, but it was dark and murky. But I was in an impossible position because the young men all advised me not to proceed into that area, in case the horses got separated because of the darkness and the distance, and we were unable to get back. I said to them: "O brave men, all of you, in war! Now you realize that there is no such thing as great bravery without planning and intelligence. If an old man had come with us, he would have given us advice on how to advance into this murky area. But who among you is brave enough to go back to the camp and fetch me an old man? I will give a reward of ten pounds of gold." No one was found to do this because of the length of the journey and because the atmosphere was without light.

Now, the old man's sons came up to me and said, "If you will listen to us with forbearance, master, we will tell you something."

I replied, "Tell me whatever you wish—I swear by Providence above I shall do you no harm."

They straightaway explained about their father and how they had come to bring him; then they ran off and presented the old man himself. Seeing him, I embraced him and asked him to give us his advice. And the old man replied: "King Alexander, you must realize that unless you go there with horses, you will never see the light again. So pick out mares with foals and leave the foals here while you go off with the mares; then they will bring you out because of the foals." Having searched throughout the army, we only found 100 mares with foals. So I took these and another 100 select horses, as well as some other horses to carry what we needed, and went off, following the old man's plan, and left the foals behind.

The old man instructed his sons to collect anything they found lying on the ground after they set out, and drop it in their saddlebags. So 360 soldiers set out, and I gave orders for the 160 infantry to march in front. So it was that we journeyed about fifteen schoinoi [perhaps seventy-five miles]. We found a place, and in it there was a translucent spring, whose water flashed like lightning, and very many other sources of water. The air too in that place was fragrant, and it was not entirely dark. I became hungry and wanted to have some food; and I called over the cook, who was called Andreas, and said to him, "Prepare us a meal." He took salt fish and went to the translucent water of the spring to wash the food. But the moment it was doused in the water, it came to life and escaped the cook's hands. In his fear he did not report to me what had happened but took some of the water and drank it, then put some in a silver container and kept it. The whole place abounded in springs, and we all drank from them. Alas for my ill luck, that it was not ordained for me to drink from that immortal spring that brought life to the lifeless and was not denied to my cook!

After taking food, we rose and traveled on more or less 230 schoinoi [circa 1,100 miles!]. After that we traveled on and saw light, but not from sun, moon, or stars. And I saw two birds flying, and they had human faces; they were crying in Greek: "Alexander, why do you tread the land that is God's alone? Turn back, poor man, turn back; you will not be able to tread the Isles of the Blest. Turn back, human being; tread the land that is granted you and do not bring trouble upon yourself!" I shivered and swiftly obeyed the instruction the birds had given me. The other bird in turn spoke in Greek. "The East," it said, "calls you, and the kingdom of Poros shall be assigned in victory to you." So speaking, the bird flew off. I succeeded in persuading the guide to stand aside and put the mares at the front of us; then with their mothers leading us back[75] we returned in twenty-two days to the cries of the foals. 40

Now, many individual soldiers brought back what they had found. But in particular the old man's sons filled their saddlebags, following their father's instructions. And when we got back to the light, they were discovered to have collected pure gold and pearls of great value. At the sight of this there was regret—among those who had collected something that they had not collected more, and among those who had not that they had not. And we all expressed deep gratitude to the old man for giving us such excellent advice. 41

After our return, the cook told what had happened to him at the spring. Hearing this, I was overwhelmed with grief and punished him severely. All the same, I said to myself, "What good does it do you, Alexander, to have regrets over a matter that is past?" But I did not know that he had drunk the water or kept some; he had only admitted that the salt fish had come to life. But the cook approached my daughter by the concubine Ounna, Kale by name, and seduced her by promising to give her water from the immortal spring—and this he did. On learning of this—I will tell you the truth—I envied them their immortality. I summoned my daughter

75. I have emended the text of L at this point; it oddly refers to following the Great Bear simultaneously.

and told her: "Take your clothes and depart from my presence: you have, after all, evidently gained immortality and become a spirit. And you shall be called a Neraïd, since you received eternity [aïdion] from the water [neron]."⁷⁶ She departed from my presence, weeping and wailing, and went to live with the spirits in uninhabited regions. As for the cook, I ordered a millstone to be tied to his neck and that he should be cast into the sea. There he became a spirit and went off to live in a part of the sea, which was called Andreas after him. So much then about the cook and my daughter.

As a result of all this, I formed the opinion that here was the end of the earth. And I gave orders for a huge arch to be built in that place and for it to be inscribed as follows.

YOU WHO WISH TO ENTER THE LAND OF THE BLEST,
TRAVEL TO THE RIGHT AND AVOID DESTRUCTION.⁷⁷

But I had second thoughts and wondered whether the end of the earth was really here and whether the sky sloped down [i.e., to meet the earth] here. So I decided to find out the truth. So I ordered two of the birds from that place to be caught. They were huge white birds, extremely powerful and tame: they did not fly away when they saw us. Some of the soldiers mounted their necks, and they flew up, carrying them. They eat carrion, and this is why a very large number of these birds came to us—because of the horses that were dying. So I ordered two of them to be caught and not to be given food for three days. And on the third day I gave instructions for something like a yoke to be made of timber and for it to be attached to their necks. Then I made a sort of basket from oxhide and got into the basket myself, holding a spear about seven cubits long with horse liver on its tip. So straightaway the birds flew up to eat the liver, and I was carried up with them into the air, until I considered I was near the sky. I shivered all over because of the extreme cold of the air being beaten by the birds' wings. At that point a flying creature in the shape of a man met me and said to me: "Alexander, do you investigate the things of heaven when you have not grasped things on earth? So return swiftly to the earth and avoid becoming food for these birds!" And again he spoke to me, "Alexander, direct your gaze to the earth below." I did so with fear and saw there before me a large coiled snake and, in the middle of the snake, a tiny disk. And the creature that had met me said to me,

76. The author of this episode, then, explains the name Nereid—a nymph of the sea, daughter of Nereus, known since Homer—by misspelling it and deriving it from a word for "water" that no ancient Greek had ever heard.

77. Some ancient mystics thought it important that the dead man's soul should keep to the right on arrival below. Tablets with such instructions have been discovered in tombs.

"Turn your spear, then, against the disk—it is the world, because the snake is the sea that encircles the earth."

I turned back and by the wish of Providence above came down to earth seven days from the camp. I was utterly drained and half-dead. I found there a satrap under my power and, with three hundred cavalry from him, came to my camp. And I resolved never again to attempt the impossible.

Farewell.

[In recension C, chapter 42 tells of a sweet-tasting lake and a fish with a stone in its stomach that can be used as a torch. Women emerge at night from the lake, singing; and there is a battle with Centaurs. Chapter 43 contains a letter to Olympias summarizing Alexander's fantastic adventures. In chapter 44, downcast by a prophecy of his early death, Alexander is cheered by a dwarf's foolery.]

## Book Three

After all this, Alexander marched with his forces against Poros, king of 1 India. Having marched through much uninhabited land, through terrain without water and full of ravines, the army commanders said to their troops: "It is enough for us to have waged war as far as Persis and to have subjugated Darius for demanding tribute from the Greeks. Why then do we laboriously march against Indians, into the haunts of wild animals, no concern of Greece? If Alexander, with his great spirit, is a man of war and wants to subjugate nations of barbarians, why are we following him? Let him march and fight wars on his own!"[78] Hearing this, Alexander separated the Persian troops from the Macedonians and other Greeks and said to the Macedonians and Greeks: "Comrades-in-arms and allies, Macedonians and all you lords of the Greeks—these Persians are your enemies and mine—so why are you grumbling now? You have instructed me to march to war and fight the barbarians on my own. I will, however, remind you of this: I have won the previous wars on my own too; and, taking with me all the Persians I want, I shall win on my own again. A single idea of mine encouraged the souls of you all for the battle, when you were already weakening against the hordes of Darius. Was I not there with my shield at the head of the army in the battles? Did I not go as my own messenger to Darius? Did I not expose myself to danger? So take your own counsel and march to Macedonia on your own and get yourselves back safely and do not have any disputes with each

78. The author here blends the two mutinies: (a) in 326 B.C., after the defeat of Poros, the army refused to cross the river Hyphasis (Beas or Sutlej) into India and demanded to turn back; (b) in 324 B.C., at Opis (near Babylon), the Macedonians rebelled at the inclusion of Persians in privileged positions in Alexander's army, but later begged forgiveness.

other—so that you may learn that an army is powerless without the intelligence of a king." So spoke Alexander, and they pleaded with him to set aside his anger and to keep them with him right to the end.

2    When he arrived with all his forces at the border of India, letter bearers sent by Poros, king of India, met him and gave him the letter of Poros's. Alexander took it and read it out before his army. Its contents were these.

> King Poros of India, to Alexander, who plunders cities:
>     I instruct you to withdraw. What can you, a mere man, achieve against a god? Is it because you have destroyed the good fortune of others by meeting weaker men in battle that you think yourself more mighty than me?[79] But I am invincible: not only am I the king of men, but even of gods—when Dionysos (who they say is a god) came here, the Indians used their own power to drive him away. So not only do I advise you, but also I instruct you, to set off for Greece with all speed. I am not going to be frightened by your battle with Darius or by all the good fortune you had in the face of the weakness of the other nations. But you think you are more mighty. So set off for Greece. Because if we had needed Greece, we Indians would have subjected it long before Xerxes; but as it is, we have paid no attention to it, because it is a useless nation, and there is nothing among them worth the regard of a king—everyone desires what is better.

So Alexander, having read out Poros's letter in public before his soldiers, said to them: "Comrades-in-arms, do not be upset again at the letter of Poros's that I have read out. Remember what Darius wrote too. It is a fact that the only state of mind barbarians have is obtuseness. Like the animals under them—tigers, lions, elephants, which exult in their courage but are easily hunted thanks to man's nature—the kings of the barbarians too exult in the numbers of their armies but are easily defeated by the intelligence of the Greeks."

Having given this declaration to encourage his army, Alexander wrote in reply to Poros.

> King Alexander, to King Poros, greetings:
>     You have made us even more eager to be spurred on to battle against you by saying that Greece has nothing worth the regard of a king but that you Indians have everything—lands and cities. And I know that every man desires to seize what is better rather than to keep what is worse. Since, then, we Greeks do not have these

---

79. In this and the following sentence L makes insufficient sense: I have translated A with slight alterations.

things and you barbarians possess them, we desire what is better and wish to have them from you. You write to me that you are king of gods and of all men even to the extent of having more power than the god. But I am engaging in war with a loudmouthed man and an absolute barbarian, not with a god. The whole world could not stand up to a god in full armor—the rumble of thunder, the flash of lightning, or the anger of the bolt. So the nations I have defeated in war cause you no astonishment, and neither do boastful words on your part make me a coward.

Poros, receiving Alexander's letter and reading it, was very much spurred on and immediately mustered the barbarian hordes and the elephants and many other animals that used to fight beside the Indians. When the Macedonians and Persians came close, Alexander saw Poros's line and was afraid not of his numbers but of the animals. He was astonished to see the strangeness of the animals: he was accustomed to fighting men, not animals.

So once more Alexander became his own messenger and entered the city where Poros was, dressed as a soldier buying provisions. Seeing him, the Indians straightaway presented him to King Poros, and Poros asked him, "How is Alexander?"

"He is alive and well," he replied, "and keen to see such a king as Poros."

Then he went out with Alexander and showed him the number of his animals and said to Alexander, "Go to Alexander and tell him, 'I am bringing animals like you to fight with you.'"

Alexander replied, "King Poros, Alexander has heard what you have said before I return to him."

"From whom?" asked Poros.

"From Poros," said he. "Being the son of a god, he cannot fail to know what is said."

So Poros sent him away with gifts.

As Alexander left Poros, he saw the lineup of animals and exercised his mind with much hard thinking. So what did the intelligent man do next? He took all the bronze statues he had and the suits of armor won in battle and had these carefully heated until the bronze was red-hot, and ordered them to be placed at the front of the battle line, like a wall. They sounded the signal for battle. Poros immediately ordered the animals to be released. So the animals, sweeping in, sprang at the statues and clutched them; immediately they burnt their mouths, and thereafter they touched no one. So in this way clever Alexander eliminated the attack of the beasts. The Persians were overpowering the Indians and pursued them with arrowshots and battles on horseback, and great was the battle as men slew and were slain. And there fell Alexander's horse, Bucephalus, its judgment having weakened.[80] And at this event, Alexander neglected the battle; for twenty days they continued fighting with each other. And Alexander's side was beginning to surrender through fear.

4     So realizing that he was about to be forced into surrender, Alexander ordered a halt in the battle and made a declaration to King Poros, saying: "This is not royal power, if, whichever of us wins, our armies perish between us. But this is our nobility of body, if each of us stops the army and enters a single combat for the kingship." Poros was delighted and promised Alexander he would fight a single combat with him, seeing Alexander's body was no match for his own body—Poros was five cubits high, but Alexander not even three.[81] So each side took up position to watch Poros and Alexander. But suddenly there was a disturbance in the camp of King Poros. So Poros turned round, worried, to see what the noise was. But Alexander pulled the feet from under him, leapt on him, and drove his sword into his flank, instantly killing Poros, king of India.[82]

Both armies set to fighting each other, but Alexander said to the Indians, "Poor Indians, why are you fighting, when your king has been slain?"

They replied, "We are fighting to avoid being taken prisoner."

Alexander said to them: "Stop fighting; turn round and go to your city as free men. It was not you who recklessly attacked my army, but Poros." He said this, knowing that his army was not capable of fighting the Indians.

Immediately he gave instructions for King Poros to receive a royal burial. Then he took all the treasures from his palace and marched for the Brahmans, or Oxydrakai, not because they were warlike and numerous, but because they were gymnosophists who lived in huts and caves.[83]

5     The Brahmans, on learning that King Alexander was coming to see them, sent their best philosophers to meet him with a letter. Receiving and reading the letter, Alexander found its contents to be as follows.

80. In A, more sensibly, Alexander's judgment weakens, not the horse's: he saves the corpse of the horse and neglects the fighting.

81. A cubit was eighteen inches in Athens, fourteen in Macedonia. Poros was said by historians to be five cubits high, and Alexander to be too short for Darius's throne (though he was doubtless more than three feet six inches).

82. There was no single combat; and Poros, though wounded in the battle, survived to retain his kingdom under Alexander's overlordship and to hold others won by Alexander.

83. In 326 B.C. at Taxila (near Islamabad), before the battle with Poros, Alexander had Onesikritos, a pupil of the Cynic philosopher Diogenes, meet Indian ascetics, for whom Taxila seems to have been a center. Greeks, always impressed by exotic wisdoms, had a word for them: *gymnosophistai*, "naked philosophers." One, Kalanos, joined Alexander's party, but Alexander's supposed meeting with the community became a favorite part of the romantic tradition (even in a Buddhist text, the *Sayings of Milinda*).

The Gymnosophists, to the man Alexander, write this letter:

If you come to us in war, you will not profit from it: you will not have anything to take away from us. But if you want to take what we have, there is no need for war, only for a request—not to us, but to Providence above. If you want to know who we are, the answer is: naked men who have devoted their lives to philosophy, fashioned not by ourselves, but by Providence above. War is your companion, philosophy ours.

Reading this, King Alexander traveled to them in peace. And he saw many woods and many extremely beautiful trees with all sorts of fruit and a river encircling that whole land, whose water was translucent, white as milk, and countless palm trees laden with fruit, and the vine rods with a thousand bunches of grapes, gorgeous and enticing. And Alexander saw the sages with no clothes living in huts and caves. Away at a great distance from them, he saw their women and children grazing the flocks.

Alexander inquired of them, "Do you not have graves?"

They replied: "This area where we live is our grave as well: here we take our rest on the earth and bury ourselves for sleep. The earth begets us, the earth feeds us, and when we die, we lie beneath the earth in eternal sleep."

He asked another question. "Who are more numerous, the living or the dead?"

They replied, "Those who have died are more numerous, but as they no longer exist, they cannot be counted—those who can be seen are more numerous than those who cannot."

He posed another question. "Which is stronger, death or life?"

They replied, "Life, because the sun has bright rays when it rises, but is weaker to the sight when it is setting."

Again he asked, "What is greater, the land or the sea?"

They replied, "The land: even the sea itself is confined by the land."

He asked another question. "Which is the most dangerous of all animals?"

They replied, "Man."

He asked, "How?"

They replied, "Your own case will convince you: you are an animal, and look how many animals you have with you so that you alone can rob the other animals of life."

He was not angry but smiled. He asked something else. "What is kingship?"

They replied, "An immoral force for superior power, daring maintained by opportunity, a golden burden."

He asked another question. "What came first, night or day?"

They replied, "Night: creatures being born develop in the darkness of the womb and are then delivered to receive the light of day."

He posed another question. "Which side is better, the right or the left?"

They replied: "The right: the sun himself rises on the right and travels to the leftward regions of the sky. And a woman suckles first on the right breast."

Then Alexander proceeded to ask them, "Do you have a lord?"

They replied, "Yes, we have a leader."

He said, "I should like to greet him."

And they pointed out Dandames to him, who was lying on the ground, with lots of tree leaves strewn over him and with cucumbers and other produce laid out before him. Seeing him, Alexander greeted him, and he in his turn said to Alexander, "Hail," but did not rise or give him the honors due to a king.

Alexander asked him if they had property.

He replied: "Our property is the land, the trees that bear fruit, the light, sun, moon, the troupe of stars, the water. When we are hungry, we go to the leafy trees and eat the fruit that grows of its own accord. As the moon waxes, all our trees produce fruit. And we have too the great river Euphrates, and whenever we are thirsty, we go to it, drink water, and are gladdened. We have, each of us, our own wife, and, during the waxing moon, each of us goes and has intercourse with his own partner, until she bears two children. We reckon one to replace the father; the other, the mother.

Hearing this, Alexander said to them all, "Ask me for what you want, and I shall grant it to you."

And they all shouted out, "Give us immortality."

Alexander replied, "I do not have power over that: I too am mortal."

"Why, then," they asked, "if you are mortal, do you wage so many wars? To win everything and carry it off somewhere? Are you not in your turn going to leave these things behind for others?"

"That," said Alexander, "is managed by Providence above, so that we may be slaves and servants of their [the gods'] commands. The sea does not stir if no wind blows upon it, nor do trees if no wind blows. The fact is that man displays no activity but for Providence above. I too would like to stop conducting wars; only, the master of my mind does not allow me. But in fact if we were all of one mind, the world would be a dull place: the sea would not be sailed, the earth not worked, marriages not celebrated, children not born. Think how many have met misfortune in the wars I have been responsible for and have lost what they had! Yet, others have had good fortune from other people's property. Everyone takes things from everyone else and delivers them up to others: nothing belongs to anyone."

So saying, Alexander brought Dandames gold, bread, wine, and olive oil. "Take these, old man, to remember us by." But Dandames laughed and replied, "These are no use to us, but so as not to seem proud, we will take the oil from you." He made a pile of wood, set fire to it, and poured the oil into the fire before Alexander.

[Chapters 7–16: Recension A now inserts a booklet partly by Palladius (circa A.D. 364–430), *On the Tribes of India, and the Brahmans.*]

After this, Alexander left them. So he returned along the river Hypha- 17 sis, which leads to Prasiake, which is held to be the capital of India and was where Poros was king.[84] And all Poros's subjects received Alexander. He had managed all affairs along the Hyphasis, and the Indians eagerly gathered. And some of them said to Alexander, "Greatest King, you will take marvelous cities and kingdoms and mountains on which no king of the living has ever set foot." And some of the sages came to Alexander and said, "King, we have something amazing and worth your attention to show you: we will show you plants speaking with human voice." So they brought Alexander to where a shrine of the Sun and Moon was. There was an enclosure to protect them and two trees like cypresses: encircling them were trees like the myrobalanos of Egypt— their fruit too. The two trees in the middle of the garden spoke, one in a male voice, the other in a female. The name of the male one was Sun, and of the female Moon, which they called in their own language Mithras and Mao.[85] The two trees had been clothed in skins of various animals, the male one with skins of male animals, the female with female. In their vicinity there was no iron, bronze, or tin, and not even potter's clay. When Alexander asked what sort of skins were covering them, they replied by saying they were lion and leopard skins.

Alexander sought to learn more about the trees, and they told him: "In the morning when the sun rises, a voice comes from the tree, and when it is at its zenith, and a third time when it is on the point of setting. And the same thing happens in the case of the moon." And men who were clearly priests came up to Alexander and said, "Enter in purity, worship, and you will receive an oracle." But the priests said, "King

---

84. "Along the river Hyphasis" is an emendation of L, though Alexander actually returned by the river Hydaspes (Indus), of which the Hyphasis (Sutlej) is a tributary. Prasiake was in fact the land of the Prasioi (Sanskrit for "Easterners"), whose capital was Pali(m)bothra (near today's Patna, on the Ganges 150 miles west of the Bangladeshi border)—unvisited, of course, by Alexander, and far from Poros.

In other recensions 3.17 is the *Letter to Aristotle*. Recension B omits a number of marvels and monsters at the beginning and converts the rest into narrative.

85. This emendation (of "Mutheamatus") produces Iranian words for "sun" and "moon."

Alexander, no iron is allowed in the shrine." So he ordered swords to be laid down outside the precinct. A considerable number of men went in with Alexander, and he ordered them to form a ring and keep watch on the place. Then he called over some of the Indians who were attending him so that they could act as interpreters for him. And he swore to them that "if the sun sets and I do not hear the voice of the oracle, I shall burn you alive!"

But it happened as the sun set: an Indian voice came from the tree, but the Indians with him were afraid and did not want to translate. After some thought, Alexander took them aside individually. And they whispered in his ear, "King Alexander, soon you must die at the hands of your own people." All present were thunderstruck, but Alexander wanted to receive another oracle. Having heard the future, he went in and asked that he might embrace his mother, Olympias. And when the moon rose, the tree said in Greek, "King Alexander, you must die in Babylon and you will be killed by your own people and you will not be able to return to your mother, Olympias."

Alexander was amazed and wanted to put magnificent garlands on the trees, but the priests told him: "This is not permitted. But if you are going to use force, do what you will: for a king every law is canceled." Alexander was very upset, and, rising at first light, he went back into the shrine with the priests, his friends, and the Indians. After a prayer, he went up with the priest and, placing his hand on the tree, asked if the years of his life were complete—as this was what he wanted to know. And as soon as the sun began to rise and cast its rays on the top of the tree, a voice came out, explicitly declaring: "The years of your life are complete, and you will not be able to return to your mother, Olympias; instead, you must die in Babylon. And shortly afterwards your mother and your wife will die miserably at the hands of your own people. Ask no further questions about these matters: you shall not hear anything more." On hearing this, he was very upset. And on his departure from there, he broke camp and left India. And he came to Persia.

18　　He hurried to see the palace of Semiramis—it was famous.[86] There had become queen of that whole country a woman of sublime beauty in middle age. So Alexander sent her a letter with the following content.

---

86. Semiramis, a legendary queen of Babylon, so appealed to Greek imagination that she seems even to have been the heroine of the early (ca. 100 B.C.?) *Ninos Romance*. The author seems to think Semiramis's city is the same as Kandake's Meroë. Meroë, on the Nile in central Sudan, was the capital of the Nubian kingdom of Napata, and Kandake was the regular name of its queens. But for Greeks the land beyond Egypt was Ethiopia and was perceived as lying to the southeast—even up to India; hence maybe our author's confusion. It has been thought that the Kandake episode was in origin a separate novelette.

King Alexander, to Queen Kandake at Meroë and the princes under her, greetings:

On my travels to Egypt I heard from the priests there about your dwellings and graves, and that for some time you had ruled Egypt. So I have sent to you. Take advice and send what seems appropriate to you.

Farewell.

Kandake replied as follows.

Queen Kandake of Meroë and all the princes, to King Alexander, greetings:

Do not think the worse of us for the color of our skin. We are purer in soul than the whitest of your people. We are in number 80 squadrons ready to do harm to aggressors. The emissaries sent by us bring you 100 solid gold ingots, 500 Ethiopians not yet mature, 200 chimpanzees, an emerald crown of a thousand pounds of gold, 10 sealed necklaces of unpierced pearls, 80 ivory caskets, and various kinds of animals from our country: 5 elephants, 10 tame leopards, in the cages 30 man-eating hounds, 30 fighting bulls, 300 elephant tusks, 300 leopard skins, 3,000 ebony staves. So send us immediately the men you want to receive the presents. And write to us about yourself when you have become king of the whole world.

Farewell.

Receiving Queen Kandake's letter and reading it, Alexander sent 19 Kleomenes, an Egyptian,[87] to receive the presents. Kandake, on hearing how Alexander was defeating such important kings, called one of her people, a Greek painter, and gave him instructions to go and meet him and secretly to paint a likeness of Alexander. And he did so. Receiving the likeness of him, Kandake hid it away.

Some days later it happened that Kandake's son, Kandaules, in the company of some riders, was attacked by the prince of the Bebrykians;[88] and Kandaules, the son of Kandake, rode in to Alexander's tents in his flight. The guards arrested him and brought him before Ptolemy, surnamed Soter, who was second-in-command to Alexander (King Alexander was asleep). Ptolemy questioned him, "Who are you and your companions?"

87. Kleomenes of Naukratis, recognized as satrap of Egypt by Alexander, but later subordinated to Ptolemy and executed by him.

88. The names connect this story with Asia Minor: the Bebrykians are a legendary people of Bithynia; Kandaules, a king of Lydia; Amazons have several important Asia Minor connections; the real Antigonos was satrap in Asia Minor.

He replied, "I am the son of Queen Kandake."

Ptolemy asked him, "Why have you come here, then?"

He replied: "Together with my wife and a few soldiers I was on my way to celebrate the annual mystery rite among the Amazons. But the prince of the Bebrykians saw my wife and came out with a huge force; he seized my wife and killed most of my soldiers. So I am returning to collect a larger force and burn the land of the Bebrykians."

Having heard this, Ptolemy went in to Alexander, woke him, and outlined to him what Kandake's son had told him. Alexander listened and straightaway rose. He took his crown and put it on Ptolemy, put his mantle on him and said to him, "Sit on the throne as though you were Alexander and say this to the secretary, 'Call Antigonos, the principal guard.' And when I come, relate to me what you have told me and ask me, 'What policy are we to adopt here? Give me your advice.'"

So Ptolemy sat on the throne, dressed in the royal robes—and the troops, seeing him, worriedly discussed what new plan Alexander had thought up. But the son of Kandake, seeing him in the royal robes, was afraid he would order his execution—he thought it was Alexander. Then Ptolemy gave the order "Call Antigonos, my principal guard." And when Alexander came, Ptolemy said to him: "Antigonos, this is the son of Queen Kandake. His wife has been seized by the prince of the Bebrykians. What action would you advise?"

"I would advise you, King Alexander," he replied, "to arm the troops and make war on the Bebrykians so that we may free his wife and return her to him, out of respect for his mother." Kandaules, the son of Kandake, was pleased to hear this. And Ptolemy said: "If this is what you want, Antigonos, go ahead and do this as my guard. Instruct the army to prepare."

20 Ptolemy gave instructions, as though he were Alexander, to Antigonos, and this was done. Antigonos reached the region of the prince in one day together with Ptolemy. And Antigonos said to Ptolemy: "King Alexander, let us not be seen by the Bebrykians by day, in case the prince discovers and kills the woman. So let us break into the city by night and set fire to the houses: then the masses will rise and return Kandaules his wife. Our battle is not about the kingdom, but about demanding back the woman."

As Antigonos said this, Kandaules fell down before him and said: "Ah, your intelligence, Antigonos! I wish you were Alexander and not a guard of Alexander."

So then they broke into the city by night, while the people were asleep, and set fire to the suburbs. And as they woke up and asked why the city was being set on fire, Alexander had the shout raised "It is King Kandaules with a massive force, demanding you return his wife before I set your whole city on fire." They were surrounded and all advanced to the prince's palace and by force of numbers broke it open. Kandaules' wife was in bed with the prince: they dragged her away and returned her to Kandaules, and they killed the prince.

Kandaules thanked Antigonos for his advice and idea and, embracing Antigonos, said, "Put yourself in my hands so that I can take you to my mother, Kandake, and give you the royal presents you deserve." Alexander was overjoyed and said to him: "Ask King Alexander to release me. I too would like to see your country." So Alexander sent a message to Ptolemy to send him with Kandaules as his messenger. And Ptolemy said to Kandaules: "I wish to greet your mother by letter. So take my messenger Antigonos with you and bring him back safe here to me, in the same way that I restore you and your wife safe to your mother." Kandaules replied: "King, I take this man as though he were Alexander himself. And I shall send him back to you with royal gifts."

So then Kandaules set out and took with him Alexander, a consider- 21 able number of soldiers, beasts, wagons, and many presents. On the way Alexander marveled at mountains marked out with veins of quartz that reached up to the clouds of heaven and at the towering trees laden with fruit—not of the Greek sort, but a marvel in themselves: they were apple trees glinting gold with fruit the size of citrons in Greece. And there were enormous bunches of grapes and nuts with the girth of melons and full-grown apes the size of bears and other animals of various colors and strange shapes. And there were some rocky places with downward passages. And Kandaules said, "Antigonos, these here are called the dwellings of the gods." So they journeyed on and reached the palace. He was met by his mother and brothers; but when they were about to embrace him, Kandaules said, "Do not embrace me before you have greeted the man who has saved me and been so good to my wife, Antigonos, the messenger of King Alexander." And they asked him, "In what way did he save you?" Then, when Kandaules had told them about the prince of the Bebrykians seizing his wife and the assistance Alexander had given him, the brothers and their mother, Kandake, embraced him. And there was a splendid banquet in the palace.

The next day, Kandake came forward in the royal crown, displaying 22 enormous stature and having the appearance of a demigod, so much so that Alexander thought it was his own mother, Olympias. And he looked at the palace glittering with its golden ceilings and marble walls. And there were cushions of woven silk with contrasting gold embroidery on couches with legs of gold and reclining chairs with golden webbing. The tables were studded with ivory inlays, and ebony colors gleamed from the capitals of Median columns. There were countless statues of bronze and sickle-bearing chariots sculpted from porphyry complete with the horses so that you might think they were alive and running; and there were elephants sculpted from the same stone, trampling enemies underfoot and sweeping over opponents with their trunks; and there were whole temples complete with columns sculpted from a single stone. Seeing this, then, Alexander was filled with amazement. And he ate with the brothers of Kandaules. Kandaules called his mother over and asked her to give Alexander's messenger the gifts he deserved for his good sense and to release him.

The next day, Kandake took Antigonos by the right hand and showed him translucent chambers made of indescribable stone that made one think the sun was rising inside and shining through the marble. Among the rooms she showed him a dining room of imperishable timbers, and a house not built firmly on foundations on the ground, but fixed on massive square timbers and drawn on wheels by twenty elephants. And wherever the king went in order to make war on a city, he stayed in it.

Alexander said to Kandake, "This would all be astonishing if it were among the Greeks rather than in your country, where you have mountains with such varied stone."

Kandake replied angrily, "You are right, Alexander."

Addressed by the name Alexander, he turned round and said, "Lady, my name is Antigonos. I am Alexander's messenger."

"All right," replied Kandake, "your name is Antigonos—but I am not calling you that: you are King Alexander. And now I will show you the evidence." And she took him by the hand into a chamber and brought him the portrait of him. She asked, "Do you recognize your appearance?"

Alexander recognized his picture and was disconcerted and trembled.

Kandake asked him: "Alexander, why are you trembling and disconcerted? The destroyer of Persia, the destroyer of India, he who tore down the trophies of the Medes and Parthians and overthrew the whole East, now without battle and army you have fallen under the control of Kandake. So you must now realize, Alexander, that whenever a man thinks that he is brilliant, there will be another man still more brilliant than him. Kandake's mind has been more than a match for your ingenious plan, Alexander."

Alexander was furious and gnashed his teeth. Kandake said to him: "Are you gnashing your teeth? What can you do? Such an important king and you are in the power of a single woman!"

Alexander wanted to kill himself and Kandake with a sword, but Kandake said to him: "Very brave and royal! Do not agonize, Alexander, my boy. Just as you have saved my son and his wife from the Bebrykians, I in my turn shall protect you from the barbarians—by calling you

Antigonos; for if they recognize you as Alexander, they will immediately kill you, because you killed Poros, king of India. The wife of my younger son is a daughter of Poros's. So I shall call you Antigonos: I shall protect your secret."

Having said this, Kandake went out with him and said: "Kandaules, 23 my boy, and you, my daughter Marpessa, if you had not found Alexander's army at the right time, I would not have seen you again, and you would not have found your wife. So let us treat Alexander's messenger properly and give him presents." And the other son, the younger one, said to her: "Alexander saved my brother and his wife. But my wife is in sorrow because her father, Poros, was killed by Alexander, and as he is here in her power, she wants to kill Antigonos, his messenger." But Kandake said: "And what good would it do you, my boy? If you murder him, do you defeat Alexander?" And Kandaules said to his brother: "He saved me and my wife: I in my turn will save him and send him to Alexander. So are we on this man's account to join in battle here with each other?" And his brother said, "I, my brother, for my part, do not want to; but if you do, I am readier than you." With these words, they went to start a single combat with each other.

Kandake was in anguish at the prospect of her children fighting each other. She took Alexander aside and said to him, "You are an intelligent man and have dealt with so many matters—can you not use your intelligence to devise a way of stopping my children fighting each other on your account?"

"I will go," replied Alexander, "and make peace between them." And Alexander went between them and said: "Listen, Karagos, and you, Kandaules! If you kill me here, it will not matter to Alexander: messengers that people send are not very valuable compared with the battles of kings. So if you kill me here, Alexander has more messengers. But if you want through me to take your enemy Alexander prisoner, promise to give me a share of the gifts here; in this way I will be able to stay with you and get Alexander to come here on the grounds that you want to give him the gifts you have prepared for him in person. Then, having got your enemy in your power and having avenged yourselves, you will have your cure."

He convinced the brothers, and they were reconciled. Kandake admired Alexander's intelligence and said to him, "Antigonos, I wish you were my son—through you I would have controlled all nations: you would not have defeated the enemy and their cities by war, but by your sharp mind." Alexander was delighted at the respect shown him, and Kandake resolutely kept Alexander's secret. Ten days later he set off, and Kandake gave him royal presents: a precious diamond crown, a breastplate with pearls and beryls, and a cloak of purple, star-bright with gold work. And she sent him on his way with a large escort and his own soldiers.

24    Having traveled the set number of days, he came to the place where Kandaules had told him the gods dwelt. Going inside with a few soldiers, he saw a semblance of figures and a flash of fire. Alexander, caught at the front, was frightened but stayed on to see what would happen. He saw some men reclining with a sort of torchlight gleaming from their eyes, and he saw one of them say to him: "Greetings, Alexander! Do you know who I am? I am Sesonchosis, the world ruler,[89] but I did not have your luck: you have an immortal name through founding that loved city in Egypt, Alexandria."

Alexander asked him, "How many years will I live?"

He replied, "It is good for a living man not to know when he is to die: through awaiting that hour, he has died from the moment he learns. But for the living man to be in ignorance provides him with the forgetfulness of not having in his mind whether he will even die at all. But as for the city you found, famous among all mankind, many kings will step upon its ground worshiping you as a god. And you shall live in it dead and not dead: for you shall have the city you are founding as your tomb."

25    When he had said this, Alexander left. Taking his men, he marched back to his army. The satraps met him and gave him the royal clothing. From there he marched to the Amazons; and when he had reached them, he sent them a letter of the following contents.

> King Alexander, to the Amazons, greetings:
> I think you will have heard about the battle with Darius. After that I campaigned against the Indians and defeated their leaders and subjected the people, thanks to Providence above. After that we journeyed to the Brahmans, the so-called gymnosophists. Taking tribute from them, we allowed them to stay in their own regions, on their request, and left them in peace. After that we are marching to you. Meet us with joy; we do not come to do you ill, but to see your country and at the same time to do you good.
> Farewell.

Receiving Alexander's letter and reading it, they wrote Alexander this reply.

> The leading Amazons and the mightiest, to Alexander, greetings:
> We have written to you so that you may be informed before you set foot on our land and not have to withdraw ignominiously. By

89. In other recensions Sesonchosis (see note 38 on 1.33) shows to Alexander the creator and omnipresent god Sarapis, who then delivers the prophecy.

our letter we shall make clear the nature of our country and of ourselves, who have a way of life to be reckoned with.

We are on the other side of the river Amazon, but we live on an island:[90] the perimeter of our land is a river with no starting point, whose circuit takes a year to travel. There is a single road into our land. We virgins who live here are under arms and number 270,000. There is nothing male among us: our men live on the other side of the river and graze the land. Every year we keep a festival and make a horse sacrifice to Zeus, Poseidon, Hephaistos, and Ares, which lasts thirty days. All of us who wish to end our virginity stay with the men. But they send all the female children they bear across to us when they reach the age of seven. But when an enemy marches against our country, 120,000 of us ride out on horseback, while the rest guard the island. And we go to the border to meet them, with the men drawn up behind following us. And anyone who is wounded in the war receives adoration from our proud hearts, is garlanded, and is remembered forever. If anyone dies in battle fighting for their country, her next of kin receives no small sum of money. If anyone brings the body of an enemy to the island, the reward for this is gold, silver, and maintenance for life. So we compete for our individual reputations. If we defeat the enemy or they just run away, a terrible disgrace stays with them for all time; but if they defeat us, they will be in a situation of having defeated women. So, King Alexander, see that the same thing does not happen to you.

When you have reached a decision, write us a reply; you will find our camp on the border.

Alexander read their letter and with a smile wrote them this reply.  26

King Alexander, to the Amazons, greetings:

We have taken control of three-quarters of the world, and we have not stopped setting up monuments of our victories over every nation. A legacy of shame will be left to us if we fail to campaign against you. Now if you want to be killed and want your land to be uninhabited, stay at the border. But if you want to live in your own land rather than to try your luck in battle, cross your river and be seen by us. The men likewise are to remain on the plain. And if you do this, I swear by my father and my mother, Olympias, that I shall not harm you but shall take from you the amount of tribute you wish to give and shall not enter your land. Send whomever

90. I have adopted the Armenian version of this sentence, in the absence of sense from L or A. According to the historian Diodoros (3.53.4), the Amazons lived on an island in a marsh near Ethiopia.

you select on horseback to us; and we shall give each person you send an allowance of a stater of gold per month and maintenance. After a year, these will return, and you must send replacements.

When you have reached a decision, write us a reply.

Farewell.

On receiving and reading Alexander's letter, they held an assembly and after a debate wrote him this reply.

The leading Amazons and the mightiest, to King Alexander, greetings:

We give you permission to come to us and see our country. And we undertake to give you 100 talents of gold a year and have sent you the 500 mightiest of us to meet you, bringing you the money and 100 thoroughbred horses. You will have these women, then, for a year. But if any of them loses their virginity to a foreigner, she shall remain with you; you will inform us in writing how many stay with you; send the others back, and you will receive replacements. We accept allegiance to you, in your presence and in your absence—we have heard of your exceptional qualities and your bravery. We are people who dwell beside the world, but you have come to us as our master.[91] We have decided to write to you, to live in our own land, and to be subject to you as master.

Farewell.

27    After this exchange of letters, Alexander wrote his mother, Olympias, this account of his deeds.

King Alexander, to my dearest mother, Olympias, greetings:

After drawing up my army against the Amazons, I marched to the city Prasiake.[92] On my arrival in the suburbs I saw a river there, full of animals. The soldiers became very despondent. Although it was already midsummer, the rain over the land had not ceased, and many of the infantry had sore feet. There were also enormous claps of thunder and lightning flashes and bolts. As we were about to cross the river Prytanis, as it was called, it happened that many of the local inhabitants were killed by the soldiers.

Then we came to the river Thermodon, as it was called, which

---

91. This line only makes sense in a fuller recension: "We are nothing in comparison with the whole world you have traversed to make it worth your intervening in our affairs."

92. This is a muddled chapter: the Amazons occur twice over, as does a river full of animals. I have introduced "the city Prasiake" from the Armenian (L has instead the "river Prytanis," but rivers do not have suburbs). Even so, the city Prasiake fits badly with 3.17. The river Prytanis (a few lines later) is presumably a mistake for the river Hyphasis. These problems result from adding an independent (and incompatible) letter to Olympias to the narrative.

flows out into a flat and fertile land inhabited by the Amazons, women of exceptional height, much taller than other women, notable for their attractiveness and strength, wearing bright clothes. They used silver weapons and axes—they did not have iron or bronze. But they were drawn up with intelligence and ingenuity. When we reached the river where the Amazons lived—it is a large river that cannot be crossed and is full of animals—anyway, they crossed and formed up against us; but we persuaded them by our letters to become subject to us.

Taking tribute from them, we withdrew to the Red Sea and to the strait. And from there we came to the river Atlas. There it was impossible to see either earth or heaven, but there were many races of all kinds living there. We saw men with the heads of dogs and men with no heads at all who had their eyes and mouths on their chests; and further men with six hands, with the faces of bulls; troglodytes who lived in caves and wild men with straps for legs; and others again as shaggy as goats and with the faces of lions; and animals of every sort, various in appearance.                                     28

We sailed off from that river and came to a large island, 120 stades [15 miles] from land. And we found the City of the Sun there. There were twelve towers built of gold and emeralds, and the wall of that city was in the Indian style. In the middle was an altar built of gold and emerald, with sixty steps, and on top of it stood a chariot with horses, and the charioteer was of gold and emeralds, but it was not easy to see him for the mist. The priest of the Sun was an Ethiopian dressed in pure linen. He spoke to us in a barbarian language to the effect that we should leave that place. Leaving there, we walked along the road for seven days. Then we found darkness, and not even fire was to be seen in that region.

Leaving there, we came to the meadow of Nysa, and we came across a very high mountain;[93] I went to it and saw fine houses laden with gold and silver. And I saw a large precinct wall of sapphire with 108 steps leading up to a round temple with 100 sapphire columns forming a circle. Inside and out were figures carved in relief as though by demigods: bacchae, satyrs, women initiates playing the flute and dancing ecstatically. And the old man Maron was on a donkey. In the middle of the temple lay a couch with golden legs, made up with cushions, on which there was a man dressed in

93. An emendation of L here gives us Nysa, the mythical birthplace of the god Dionysos, but also a real town encountered by Alexander in Afghanistan, east of Kabul. The mountain is the world mountain of Indian mythology, Mt. Meru. The decorative figures belong to Greek Dionysian religion and art; Maron, a son or grandson of Dionysos, is confused with Silenos, the old reveler-companion of Dionysos who educated Maron.

silken cloth. I did not see what he looked like, as he was covered up, but I did see his strength and the heftiness of his body. And in the middle of the shrine there was hanging a one-hundred-pound golden chain and a golden wreath. Instead of fire, precious stone provided light that illuminated that whole place. A quail cage of gold was suspended from the ceiling, in which there was a bird the size of a dove, and as though with human voice, it cried out to me in Greek, saying, "Alexander, from now on stop matching yourself with the gods: return to your own palace and do not rush head over heels into the ascent to the paths of heaven." I wanted to take it and the chandelier down to send you, but I saw the man on the couch stirring, evidently to rise, and my friends said to me, "Don't, King—it is sacred." Going out into the precinct I saw there two mixing bowls of chased gold with a capacity of sixty firkins—we measured them out at the banquet. I gave orders for the whole camp to be there for a feast. There was a large, well-equipped building there and striking goblets to grace any level of elegance, carved from stone. As we and the troops were taking our places for the feast, suddenly there was a sort of violent thunder of countless flutes, cymbals, Pan-pipes, trumpets, drums, and lyres. And there was smoke all over the mountain, as though we had been hit by a storm of lightning bolts.

We were afraid and left that region, proceeding to Cyrus's palace. We found many cities deserted, including one noteworthy city with a large building where the king used to give audiences. They told me there was a bird there that spoke with human voice. When I went into the building I saw many amazing sights: it was entirely of gold, and in the middle of the ceiling there hung a gold quail cage like the first one, and inside was a golden bird like a dove. They told me it spoke to kings in whatever language was needed. I also saw there a large mixing bowl of chased gold—these things were inside Cyrus's palace—with a capacity of 160 firkins. And it was quite amazing in its decoration: on its rim it had statues, and on the top band a sea battle; its center had a blessing, and its outside was of chased gold. They told me this was from Egypt, from the city of Memphis, and had been brought from there when the Persians took control. The building where the king himself used to give audiences was constructed in the Greek style, and on it was a relief of Xerxes' naval battle. Also in the building was a throne decorated with gold and precious stones and a lyre that played itself. And around the throne was a goblet cabinet sixteen cubits long with eight shelves, and above it stood an eagle overshadowing the whole circle with its wings. And there was a climbing vine of gold with seven branches, and everything was worked in gold. As for the other sights, what point is there in my attempting to tell you so much? They are such that their number prevents me from expressing their outstanding quality.

Farewell.

[Chapter 29 is missing in manuscript L. Other manuscripts include at this point an account of how Alexander encountered "vile peoples" who ate human corpses; to avoid contamination he enclosed them within an area surrounded by high mountains.]

Alexander also wrote another letter to his mother, Olympias, when he was in Babylon the Great and would presently leave the life of men, as follows.[94]    30

Great they say is the foresight of the divine powers. One of the native women gave birth to a child, the upper part of whose body, as far as the flanks, was all natural and human; but from the thighs downward there were animal heads so as to make the child just like the Scylla—there were the heads of lions and of wild dogs. And the forms moved, and everyone could make them out and recognize what each was, but the child's head was stillborn. Once the woman had given birth to the baby, she put it into the cloth and, having covered it up, arrived at Alexander's palace. She told his announcer, "Inform King Alexander that I have come concerning an amazing matter—I wish to show him something." It was midday, and Alexander was taking a siesta in his bedroom, but when he woke, he was told about the woman and ordered her to be brought in. When she came, the king dismissed all present, and when they had all gone, the woman showed him the monster that had been born, adding that she herself had given birth to it.

Seeing this, Alexander was astounded and immediately gave instructions for expert interpreters and magicians to be brought. When they came, he ordered them to deliver an interpretation of this portent that had been born, threatening them with death if they failed to tell him the truth. Of the Chaldaians, there were five who had the greatest reputation and intelligence, and one of them was much superior to them all in skill, but he, so it happened, was not in the city. Those who were in fact present said that Alexander would be stronger than all others in his wars and would become master over all mankind. The animals, they said, were the mightiest nations, subject to man's body—and this was what they indicated.

After them, the other Chaldaian too came to Alexander and, seeing what the omen was like, screamed out aloud in tears and tore his cloth-

---

94. There is no further letter to Olympias: what follows is not a letter (first person) but narrative (third person). This mistake occurs also in some other versions.

ing apart from sorrow. Alexander grieved not a little to see him so distressed and told him to have confidence and tell him what he saw in the sign. He made this reply to him, "King, one can no longer count you among the living."

Alexander pressed him for the details of his interpretation of the sign, and he replied: "King, most powerful of all men, you are the human shape; the animal forms are those around you. Now if the upper part was alive and moving like the animals under it, then you would have gone on to rule over all men. But just as it has departed life, so have you, King. And those around you are just like the animals under it: they have no sense and in fact are savage to men, and those around you are disposed in just this way to you." With this the Chaldaian left. As for the baby, the Chaldaian said it should be burned forthwith. After hearing this Alexander put his affairs in order daily.

31      Antipatros rose against Olympias, Alexander's mother, and treated her as he wished.[95] Alexander's mother wrote to him about Antipatros on many occasions (as Alexander's mother, she was distressed) and wanted to go across to Epirus, but Antipatros prevented her. When Alexander received the letters of his mother, Olympias, and learned from them of the pain she was experiencing, he sent a man called Krateros to Antipatros in Macedonia to be governor of it. Antipatros realized what Alexander's plan was; he knew Krateros was coming and that the soldiers were returning from Alexander to Macedonia and Thessaly on his account. He was frightened and decided to assassinate Alexander, fearing, after his treatment of Olympias, that he might be humilatingly punished. He had, indeed, heard that Alexander had become very haughty as a result of the successes he had achieved. With this in mind, he prepared a poison, which no vessel could contain without immediately breaking—not bronze nor glass nor earthenware. So Antipatros put the poison in a lead casket, and, covering it up with another casket, of iron, he gave it to his son and sent him to Babylon to Iollas, butler of King Alexander,[96] after having told him about how terrible and lethal the poison was, so that if anything happened to him in the wars at the hands of the enemy, he might take it and end it all.

Arriving in Babylon, Antipatros's son told Iollas, Alexander's butler, secretly about the giving of the poison. Now Iollas had a grudge against

95. Antipatros, the aged former minister of Philip II, was left in charge of Macedonia and Greece while Alexander was in the East. The friction with Olympias is historical, and Krateros was indeed to replace him. In the end (316 B.C.) Antipatros's son Kassandros killed Olympias.

96. Iollas (Iolaos) was actually a son of Antipatros, thus Kassandros's brother. Alexander in fact cannot have been poisoned and probably died of malaria. Medios was a Thessalian aristocrat, a Companion of Alexander's. The plot as presented recalls the unsuccessful Conspiracy of the Pages (327 B.C.).

Alexander: a few days earlier Iollas had made a mistake, and Alexander had beaten him on the head with a staff, injuring him badly. So, as a result, Iollas, in his anger at Alexander, agreed to help Antipatros's son with the crime. Iollas took in with him a man called Medios who had been badly treated like him. And they arranged among themselves how they would give Alexander the poison to drink. Alexander was resting one day after a large dinner, and the next day Medios came to him with an invitation to come to his house. Alexander accepted Medios's invitaton and came to dinner with him. Others too dined with King Alexander. The plot to murder him by poison was unknown to Perdikkas, Ptolemy, Olkias, Lysimachos, Eumenios, and Kassandros; but all the others dining with Alexander were implicated in the criminal deed and had made an agreement with Iollas, King Alexander's butler, having sworn oaths to each other; by now they had ambitions on Alexander's powers. When Alexander had reclined with them, Iollas brought him an ordinary goblet of wine. There was a conversation to pass the time, and the drinking had by now been going on for a considerable time when Iollas gave him another goblet containing the poison. Alexander, as chance would have it, took the cup and upon drinking it suddenly screamed as though he had been struck through the liver by an arrow. He waited a short time and endured the pain, but then went to his own house, instructing those present to continue with the dinner.

But they were upset and immediately brought the dinner to a close and waited outside to see what would happen. Alexander, losing control of himself, said, "Roxana, lend me your help a little,"[97] and supported by her returned to his palace and lay down.

At daybreak he ordered Perdikkas and Ptolemy and Lysimachos to come to him and said that no one else should come in with them until he had made his will. Suddenly there was a roar from the Macedonians and a rush upon the courtyard of Alexander's palace to kill his bodyguards if they did not show them the king. Alexander asked about the noise; so Perdikkas came up to him and informed him of what was being said by the Macedonians. Alexander gave instructions for his bed to be raised to a place where the whole army could file past, see him, and go out through another door. Perdikkas carried out King Alexander's instructions, and the Macedonians alone filed in and saw him. And not one of them failed to weep at Alexander, so great a king, lying near to death on his bed. And one of them, a man not undistinguished in appearance, but an ordinary man, came close to Alexander's bed and said: "It was for the good, King Alexander, that your father, Philip, ruled and for the good

32

---

97. The unabridged version is more sensational: Roxana intercepts Alexander leaving to drown himself in the Euphrates, and Alexander complains that she is robbing him of glory for little benefit to herself.

that you too have ruled, my king. You are abandoning us; and it would be good for us in our turn to die together with you who have made the city of Macedonia free." Alexander wept and stretched out his right hand in a sign of consolation.[98]

33  He ordered his registrar to come in and told him, concerning his wife, Roxana: "If a male child is born to me by my wife, Roxana, let him be king of the Macedonians. But if a female child is born, let them choose whomever they wish as king." And he instructed him to write to his mother as follows.[99]

> King Alexander to my dearest mother, greetings:
> When you receive this, my last letter, prepare an expensive meal to thank Providence above for having given you such a son. But if you wish to do me honor, go on your own and collect together all men, great and humble, rich and poor, for the meal, saying to them: "See, the meal is prepared! Come and feast! But no one who now or in the past has experienced suffering should come, as I have prepared a meal not of suffering but of joy."
> Farewell, Mother.

Olympias did this, but no one came to the meal—neither great nor humble, not rich, not poor, could be discovered without suffering. So immediately his mother recognized his wisdom and realized that Alexander there had departed from the living and had written this to console her, on the grounds that it was nothing strange that had happened to him, but something that had happened and continued to happen to everyone.

When Alexander had said this and much more, a mist formed in the air, and a great star appeared, shooting from heaven to the sea, and together with it an eagle; and the statue in Babylon that they said was of Zeus stirred. The star returned back up to heaven, and the eagle followed it too. And when the star was lost from view in the heavens, immediately Alexander sank into the eternal sleep.

34  The Persians fought with the Macedonians to take Alexander's body back with them and to proclaim him as Mithras. The Macedonians on the other hand wanted to take him back to Macedonia. Ptolemy told them, "There is an oracle of Babylonian Zeus; so we will seek an oracle from him telling us where we are to place Alexander's body." And the oracle of Zeus gave them this response.

> I shall say what will benefit all. There is in Egypt a city called Memphis. There enthrone him.

98. The procession of soldiers is historical; Alexander by now could not speak.
99. The banquet episode appears only in L of the major manuscripts. A has Alexander's last will and testament, at great length.

After the oracle, there was no further discussion; they assented to Ptolemy's proposal that they should march and convey his embalmed body in a lead coffin to the city of Memphis. Ptolemy put him on a wagon and made the journey from Babylon to Egypt. And the people of Memphis heard of this and came to meet Alexander's body and escorted it into Memphis. But the archprophet of the temple at Memphis said: "Do not settle it here, but at the city he founded in Rhakotis. For wherever this body shall be, that city shall continuously be in turmoil from wars and battles." So immediately Ptolemy took it to Alexandria and erected a tomb in the shrine called The Body of Alexander and rested Alexander's remains there.[100]

Alexander lived thirty-two years. His life was as follows. From the age of twenty he was king; and he fought wars for twelve years—and won the wars he fought. He subdued twenty-two barbarian nations and fourteen Greek tribes. He founded twelve cities, namely, Alexandria in Egypt, Alexandria by the Horpes, Alexandria at Issos, Scythian Alexandria, Alexandria on the river Granikos, Alexandria in the Troad, Alexandria at Babylon, Alexandria in Persia, the Alexandria named after the horse Bucephalus, Alexandria named after Poros, Alexandria at the river Tigris, Alexandria by the Massagetai.[101]

Alexander was born on the new moon of the month of January, at sunrise, and died on the new moon of the month of April, at sunset. And they called the day of his death Neomaga[102] because Alexander died young. Alexander died in the year of the world 5176, at the end of the one hundred and thirteenth Olympiad [325–324 B.C.] (the Olympiad is four years, and the first Olympiad began in the 4th year of the reign of Ahaz.)[103] From the death of Alexander to the incarnation of the Divine Logos by the Virgin is three hundred and twenty four years.

100. After two years of preparations, Alexander's body was being sent to Macedonia, but Ptolemy diverted it and after displaying it in Memphis took it to Alexandria.

101 Alexander founded many more than twelve cities. The list of names is somewhat garbled, and I have restored sense where I can. Alexandria at Issos = Iskenderun in Turkey; Alexandria Bucephalus = Jalalpur in Pakistan; Alexandria by the Massagetai may be Alexandria Eschate ("remotest") = Leninabad (formerly Khojent) in Turkestan (USSR).

102. Neomaga probably represents some Egyptian word in which Greeks thought their own word *neos* ("young") was present.

103. Ahaz was king of Judah (733–718 B.C.). The first Olympiad was in 776 B.C. Alexander died on 10 June 323 B.C.

## 35

ANONYMOUS

# THE STORY OF APOLLONIUS KING OF TYRE

## TRANSLATED BY
## GERALD N. SANDY

### Introduction

Apollonius of Tyre is a suitor for the hand of the daughter of King Antiochus of Antioch. He solves a riddle by detecting that the king is committing incest with his daughter; finding himself endangered by this knowledge, he takes to flight. He is shipwrecked, and before long marries the daughter of the king of Cyrene. Later, when they are traveling by sea, she gives birth to a baby girl, but herself "dies" and is committed to the sea in a coffin. Apollonius leaves his daughter in the care of others and travels in distant parts for many years; at the end of this time he finds his daughter again, in a brothel—where, however, she has succeeded in preserving her virtue. He is also reunited with his wife; she had been carried to land in the coffin, and turned out to be not dead but in a coma. Apollonius ends up as king of Antioch and Cyrene as well as Tyre.

The story as we have it is in Latin (*Historia Apollonii Regis Tyri*), but there are strong grounds for thinking that it is an adaptation of a Greek original (the question of its inclusion in the present collection is discussed in the General Introduction). The extant version can be dated to the fifth or sixth century from the general characteristics of the language and the incorporation of Symphosius's riddles, which must postdate the fourth or fifth century; the earliest reference to the work occurs towards the end of the sixth century. But other indications, notably the value of gold specified in chapter 34, suggest a date some three centuries earlier—during the heyday, in fact, of the ideal romance, which apart from this example is an exclusively Greek form. Now a number of expressions in the text are distinctly curious as Latin, but fall into place as translations of Greek idioms. Furthermore, *Apollonius* shows a strong resemblance in

736

motifs and treatment to other romance texts, notably Xenophon's *Ephesian Tale* and the Pseudo-Clementine *Recognitions,* a Christian romance which is in Latin but was originally Greek. Although there is no way of settling definitively the question of the work's genesis, which has been much debated, the latest editor concludes, after a detailed discussion that adduces important new evidence, that "in its original form [*Apollonius*] was a typical representative of the Greek romance, ...it may be taken to have come into being at the end of the 2nd or the beginning of the 3rd century."[1]

*The Story of Apollonius King of Tyre,* like the *Ephesian Tale,* is built on a core of strong popular stories and folktales, and embodies an uncomplicated, satisfying morality and a happy ending. It also shares its manner: excited, hasty, often inconsistent, and anything but subtle. But such qualities are by no means a barrier to popularity in any age, and *Apollonius* underwent widespread and complex diffusion, through translation and adaptation, from the time of its original composition through the Middle Ages and Renaissance; it has reached as far as modern Greek fairy tale and the Iceland of recent centuries.[2] The pervasive influence of the story is exemplified in English literature by Gower's *Confessio Amantis,* the probably Shakespearean *Pericles, Prince of Tyre,* and T. S. Eliot's *Marina.* A major source for these echoes and many vernacular adaptations is the Old English translation of *Apollonius,* which dates to the early eleventh century.[3] The inclusion of the romance in the fourteenth-century Latin *Gesta Romanorum,* which was compiled in England, gave a further major impulse to both Latin and vernacular versions of the story, especially in Scandinavia and central and eastern Europe. For the fourteenth and fifteenth centuries G. A. A. Kortekaas lists numerous prose or verse translations or adaptations for France, Germany, and England; and an indication of the work's exceptional popularity can be found in the existence of over a hundred manuscripts of the Latin version of the story.

The manuscript tradition is naturally complex. It consists of several recensions, two of which, usually called A (RA) and B (RB), form the basis of most modern critical editions. Except for specified deviations I have based my translation on A. Riese's text of the A recension.[4] In spite of its apparent simplicity I have found *The Story of Apollonius King of Tyre* difficult to translate, the major problem being the abrupt stylistic

1. G. A. A. Kortekaas, ed., *Historia Apollonii Regis Tyri* (Groningen, 1984), 130.

2. Kortekaas, *Historia Apollonii,* 6; see his introduction, 5–9, to which I am indebted here, for an account of the fortunes of the tale.

3. The remains of the Old English version have been edited by P. Goolden, *The Old English Apollonius of Tyre* (Oxford, 1958).

4. Kortekaas's edition appeared after this translation was prepared. At a few textual trouble spots I have compared my translation with it and also with the edition of D. Tsitsikli and G. Schmeling's forthcoming Teubner edition, of which he very kindly allowed me

changes, the wild fluctuations from simple, almost primitive narrative to stylized and elaborate forms of expression. It has also been hard to resist the temptation to correct deficiencies such as repetition, parataxis, and the failure to subordinate one idea or event to another, or even to differentiate between distinct periods of time. I have not corrected the spelling of the name Athenagora to Athenagoras, but have adjusted the transmitted spellings of Tharsus and Tharsia to the conventional forms Tarsus and Tarsia.

## Bibliography

TEXT

Kortekaas, G. A. A., ed. *Historia Apollonii Regis Tyri*. Groningen, 1984.

Riese, A., ed. *Historia Apollonii Regis Tyri*. 2d ed. Leipzig, 1893. Reprint. Stuttgart, 1973.

Tsitsikli, D., ed. *Historia Apollonii Regis Tyri*. Königstein, 1981.

GENERAL

Goepp, P. H. "The Narrative Material of *Apollonius of Tyre*." *Journal of English Literary History* 5(1938): 150–72.

Klebs, E. *Die Erzählung von Apollonius aus Tyrus*. Berlin, 1899.

Perry, B. E. *The Ancient Romances: A Literary-Historical Account of Their Origins.* Berkeley, 1967. Pages 294–324 treat *The Story of Apollonius King of Tyre*.

# THE STORY OF APOLLONIUS KING OF TYRE

1   IN ANTIOCH there was a king named Antiochus. Indeed, from him the city derived its name. He had one daughter, a very lovely young woman in whom Nature's only mistake was making her mortal.

---

to see a typescript; I have concluded that extensive revision would pay very little dividend. Kortekaas discusses the manuscript tradition very fully. In a few places I have adopted emendations made by J. M. Hunt in a series of articles: "Apollonius Resartus: A Study in Conjectural Criticism," *Classical Philology* 75(1980): 23–27; review of *The Story of Apollonius King of Tyre*, ed. and trans. Zoja Pavlovskis, *Classical Philology* 76(1981): 340–44; "Ei and the Editors of *Apollonius of Tyre*," *Harvard Studies in Classical Philology* 85(1981): 217–19; "A Crux in *Apollonius of Tyre*," *Mnemosyne* 35(1982): 348–49; and "More on the Text of *Apollonius of Tyre*," *Rheinisches Museum* 127(1984): 351–61. In some other places I have used passages from the B recension in place of missing or obviously unsuitable parts of A; these passages are printed in parentheses. Lacunae are indicated by...

When she reached the age of marriage and was becoming more and more beautiful, many suitors started to come for her hand in marriage and to press their suit with promises of large dowries. While her father tried to decide to whom it would be most advantageous to give his daughter in marriage, the shameful flames of desire and lust compelled him to fall in love with his daughter and to have feelings towards her that a father should not have. Though he struggled against his passion and fought against his emotions, he was overcome by love. He lost all sense of propriety and, forgetting that he was a father, took on the role of husband.

One morning, after lying awake and being unable to endure the passion in his heart, he burst into his daughter's bedroom and dismissed the servants on the pretext of discussing private matters with his daughter. With the madness of lust goading him on, he severed the knot of his daughter's virginity in the face of her repeated resistance and once he had accomplished his crime slipped out of her bedroom. The girl stood dumbfounded by her wicked father's breach of faith and at first kept it hidden. But drops of blood fell to the floor.

Her nurse suddenly entered the room. When she saw the girl's tears and flushed face and the blood on the floor, she said, "Why are you so upset?" The girl said, "Dear nurse, just now, in this bedroom, two noble reputations perished." The nurse did not understand and said, "Mistress, why are you saying this?" The girl said, "You see me violated before the appointed day of my marriage by violent crime." When the nurse heard this and realized what had happened, she shuddered and said, "Who has been so bold as to violate the bed of a princess?" The girl said, "Breach of faith committed the crime." The nurse said, "Why don't you tell your father?" The girl said: "Where is my father? Dear nurse, if only you understood what has happened—the name Father has ceased to exist for me. I have decided that death is the remedy against revealing a parent's crime. I shudder at the thought that this defilement should become widely known." When the nurse realized that the girl was seeking death as a remedy, she made an effort to find soothing words that would dissuade her from her awful intention of committing suicide and urged her against her will to comply with her father's wishes.

He kept his feelings disguised and passed himself off to his subjects as a dutiful parent, but within the walls of his palace he took delight in being his daughter's husband. So that he could always enjoy the sinful fruits of her bed he would propose riddles to drive away her suitors, saying: "Whichever of you finds the solution to my riddle will have my daughter in marriage. Whoever does not will be beheaded." Anyone who was knowledgeable enough to happen to find the solution to the riddle was beheaded as if he had not answered it, and his head was hung from the top of the city gate. Still, many kings and princes from everywhere hurried to defy death because of the girl's incredible beauty.

4      While King Antiochus was perpetrating these atrocities, a very
wealthy young man of Tyrian stock, named Apollonius, arrived by ship
in Antioch. He set out to the king and saluted him thus, "Greetings, my
lord, King Antiochus." And he said: "Because you are a dutiful father, I
have hurried here to comply with your will. I am descended from a royal
family, and I seek your daughter's hand in marriage." When the king
heard these unwelcome words, he gave the young man an angry look
and said to him, "Young man, do you know the conditions of marriage?" He said, "I know them, and I saw them on the city gate." The
king said: "Listen to the riddle, then: I ride on crime; I feed on a mother's
flesh; I seek my brother, my mother's husband, my daughter's son; I do
not find them.[1]

       After hearing the riddle, the young man left the king for a short time.
By subjecting the riddle to his intelligent consideration he found the solution to it by the grace of God. He set out to the king and spoke thus.
"My lord king, you set a riddle for me; therefore, hear its solution.
When you said 'I ride on crime,' you did not lie: look to yourself. When
you said 'I feed on a mother's flesh,' you did not lie about this either:
look to your own daughter."

5      The king realized that the young man had found the solution to the riddle and spoke to him thus. "You're wrong. Nothing you've said is true.
You'll surely earn a beheading for yourself, but you have thirty days:
think some more. When you return with the solution to the riddle, you'll
have my daughter's hand in marriage." The young man was greatly disturbed. He boarded the ship that he had been keeping in readiness (and
set sail) for his native Tyre.

6      After the young man's departure, King Antiochus called for his reliable
steward Thaliarchus and said to him: "Thaliarchus, as my trusted
confidant, you know that Apollonius of Tyre has found the solution to
my riddle. Board a ship immediately and go in pursuit of the young
man. When you reach his native Tyre, you will find an enemy of his to
kill him with a sword or poison. After you return, you will have your
liberty."

       After hearing this, Thaliarchus took money and poison, boarded a
ship, and set sail for Apollonius's homeland. Apollonius, however,
reached his homeland first, unharmed. He entered his house, opened the
bookcase, and studied the riddles of all the philosophers and astrologers.
When he found nothing except what he had already discerned, he said to
himself: "What are you doing, Apollonius? You have solved the king's

       1. See G. A. A. Kortekaas ed., *Historia Apollonii Regis Tyri* (Groningen, 1984), 112–13
for discussion of a similar riddle found as an inscription at Pergamum. None of the story's
riddles is invented by the author; all are found elsewhere in antiquity (or late antiquity),
which was fond of such puzzles.

riddle; you have not won his daughter. You've been fobbed off only to be killed later."

And so he ordered that ships be loaded with grain. Apollonius himself with a few of his most trustworthy slaves accompanying him secretly boarded a ship. Taking with him a great amount of gold and silver and an abundance of clothing, he entrusted himself to the high seas during the deep silence of midnight.

The next day the citizens of his city came to greet him, but he was not to be found. The entire city resounded with the shouts of grief and wailing. So great was his subjects' love for him that for a long time the barbershops were without customers, the public entertainments were suspended, and the baths were closed.

Thaliarchus, who had been sent by King Antiochus to kill the young man, arrived in Tyre while these things were happening there. When he saw that everything was closed, he said to a boy, "Can you tell me, please, why mourning has brought the business of this city to a halt?" To him the boy said: "What a nuisance he is! He knows but still asks. Who can there be who does not know that this city is in mourning because its prince, Apollonius, suddenly disappeared after returning from Antioch?"

After hearing this news, the king's steward, Thaliarchus, joyfully returned to his ship and after a voyage of some time reached Antioch. He made his way to the king and said: "Good news, Your Highness! Young Apollonius of Tyre has suddenly disappeared because he fears the might of your kingdom." The king said, "He can go away, but he cannot get away." He immediately issued this edict.

A REWARD OF 100 TALENTS IN GOLD TO ANYONE WHO BRINGS IN ALIVE TO ME APOLLONIUS OF TYRE, WHO DOES NOT RESPECT MY RULE; 200 TALENTS TO ANYONE WHO BRINGS ME IN HIS HEAD

After the proclamation of this edict, not only Apollonius's enemies but even his friends were impelled by greed to race off on the manhunt. They hunted for Apollonius on land, mountains, and in forests, by every method of search possible, but they did not find him.

The king then ordered that a naval force be readied to go in pursuit of the young man. Apollonius put in at the city of Tarsus while the naval force was slowly being readied. As he was walking along the shore, he was spotted by one of his subjects, a man named Hellenicus, who had just arrived there. Hellenicus approached him and said, "Greetings, King Apollonius." Apollonius, however, did what dignitaries usually do when greeted: he scorned his lowly subject. The old man then became angry and again saluted him with these words. "I said, 'Greetings,' Apollonius. Return the greeting and don't despise me because of my poverty, for my character is noble. If you are being kept informed, be on guard. If not, you must be informed. Perhaps you don't know that a price has been put on your head."

To him Apollonius said, "Who could have put a price on the king of my country?" Hellenicus said, "King Antiochus." Apollonius said, "Why?" Hellenicus said, "Because you wanted to take the place of the father." Apollonius said, "What price has he put on my head?" Hellenicus answered, "A reward of one hundred talents in gold to anyone who brings you in alive; two hundred talents to anyone who cuts off your head. So I advise you to seek safety in flight." After Hellenicus had said this, he left. Apollonius then ordered that the old man be called back and he said to him, "You have done me a great favor by warning me." He ordered that a hundred talents in gold be offered to him, and said: "Take your reward. Though you are a very poor man, your character is exemplary. Imagine that you have cut off my head and brought joy to the king: look, you have the hundred talents in gold, and your hands are innocent of bloodshed!" To him Hellenicus said: "Far be it from me to take payment for this. Among men of goodwill, friendship is not bought and sold." He said good-bye and left.

9 Afterward, while Apollonius was walking about on the same part of the shore, another man, named Stranguillio, met him. To him Apollonius said, "Greetings, my good friend Stranguillio." And he said: "Greetings, my lord Apollonius. Why are you wandering around here so disturbed?" Apollonius said, "You're looking at a man with a price on his head." Stranguillio said, "Who's put a price on your head?" Apollonius said, "King Antiochus." Stranguillio said, "Why?" Apollonius said: "Because I sought the hand of his daughter, or, to tell the truth, his wife, in marriage. If it's possible, I would like to hide in your city." Stranguillio said: "Apollonius, my lord, our city is poor and cannot support a nobleman like you. Besides, we're suffering from both severe famine and harshly blighted crops. There's no hope of salvation for our citizens. Instead, the most excruciating kind of death stares us in the face."

Apollonius, however, said to Stranguillio: "Then thank God that my flight has brought me to your country. If you keep my flight a secret, I will give your city a hundred thousand baskets of grain." When Stranguillio heard this, he dropped to his knees at Apollonius's feet and said, "King Apollonius, my lord, if you help the people of our starving city, not only will they keep your flight a secret, but they will go to war to preserve your safety."

10 After he had said this, they proceeded to the city. Apollonius mounted the speakers' platform in the marketplace and addressed the citizens and elders. "Citizens of Tarsus, you are disturbed and overwhelmed by a shortage of food. For my part, I, Apollonius of Tyre, will help you, for I am confident that you will keep my flight a secret out of gratitude for

my act of kindness. Please be advised that I have been exiled by a decree of King Antiochus. But your good fortune has brought me here to you. And so I will give you a hundred thousand baskets of grain at the price at which I bought it in my own country, that is, eight copper coins per basket."

The citizens of Tarsus, who were paying a gold coin per basket, were delighted. They expressed their joy with shouts and began eagerly to take the grain. Apollonius, however, so that he would not appear to be discarding his royal status and to be playing the role of merchant instead of benefactor, gave back to the public treasury what he had received. Enriched by these great contributions, the citizens voted to have a bronze statue erected for him. They had placed in the city center a statue of him standing in a two-horse chariot, holding grain in his right hand and placing his left foot on a container of grain. On its pedestal they had this inscribed.

TARSUS PAYS TRIBUTE TO APOLLONIUS OF TYRE
FOR BRINGING AN END TO BLIGHT AND FAMINE

A few months or a few days later Apollonius consented at the urging  11
of Stranguillio and his wife, Dionysias, and in accordance with the demands of Fortune to sail to the city of Pentapolis in Cyrene so that he could go into hiding there. And so Apollonius was conducted to his ship with full honors, and he bade the people farewell as he boarded his ship. Within two hours of his departure by ship the reassuring calm of the sea changed.

Reassurance gave way to uncertainty.
A violent storm made the universe blaze red.
Aeolus occupied the plain of the sea with rain-producing
    winds and squalls.
The South Wind was darkened by pitch-black mist,
and it splintered the sides of all the ships and churned
    the eddying waters.
The North Wind blew, and the sea could no longer
    withstand the East Wind.
Sand was stirred up and swirled about in the sea.
As the waves crested and subsided,
everything was thrown into a mass of confusion. The
    sea beat against the heavenly stars.
The storm intensifies.
Clouds, hail, snow, west winds, floods, lightning, and
    thunder all occur at the same time.
Flames fly on the wind. The disturbed sea bellows.

Here the South Wind, there the North Wind, here the
bristling wind of Africa, all threaten.
Neptune scatters the sands with his trident.
Triton sounds his awesome horn over the waves.[2]

12    Then everyone held onto a piece of ship's timber and had a presentiment of his own death.[3] In that pitch-black storm all perished. Apollonius, however, thanks to a single piece of ship's timber, was driven onto the shore of the people of Pentapolis. Apollonius stood, naked, on the shore for a while and as he looked at the now calm sea, said: "Neptune, ruler of the sea and destroyer of blameless men, have you preserved me in this destitute condition so that cruel King Antiochus can pursue me more easily? Where am I to go? What corner of the earth should I seek? Who will give the necessities of life to a stranger?"

While he was exclaiming to himself he noticed an old man dressed in a filthy cloak. He fell prostrate at his feet and with tears streaming down his cheeks said: "Take pity on me, whoever you are. Come to the aid of a destitute, shipwrecked man of noble birth. So that you'll know the kind of man I'm asking you to pity, I am Apollonius of Tyre, a king in my native land. Take heed of my tragic downfall, for I have fallen prostrate at your knees and am begging for help. Grant that I may live."

And so the fisherman, when he saw that he was a man of distinguished appearance, was moved by compassion. He helped him to his feet and taking him by the hand led him to his house, where he offered the best food he could. And to comply still more with his compassionate sensibilities, he took off his threadbare little cloak, cut it in half, and gave one half to the young man, saying: "Take this cloak of mine and go to the city. Perhaps you will find someone to take pity on you. If you don't find anyone, come back here and work as a fisherman with me. The little bit that I have will be enough for us. I ask only that you remember this: that when with God's approval you recover your birthright, you remember the suffering imposed on me by my poverty." To him Apollonius said, "If I don't remember you, may I suffer shipwreck again and not find anyone like you!"

13    After saying this he made his way along the route that had been pointed out to him and went through the city gate. While he was thinking about where he should look for the necessities of life, he saw a boy running through the streets. His hair was anointed, he wore a linen cloth, and he was carrying the athletic equipment used by young people at the gymnasium. He was shouting as loudly as he could, "Townsfolk

2. The transmitted text of these seventeen lines of ponderous and lifeless verse is corrupt at a few points. The passage is in part a clumsy pastiche of lines from Virgil's *Aeneid*, Ovid's *Metamorphoses*, and other poems.
3. For the text see Hunt, "Apollonius Resartus," *Classical Philology* 75(1980): 26–28.

and visitors, freeborn citizens and slaves, hear me: the gymnasium is open." When Apollonius heard this, he took off his threadbare little cloak and entered the bathing room. He anointed his body with oil, and as he watched the others exercising individually, he looked in vain for a match for himself.

At that point Archistrates, the king of the city, suddenly entered the gymnasium with a great throng of attendants. While the king was playing ball with his household staff, Fortune smiled on Apollonius, and he was able to approach the king's attendants. Apollonius picked up the ball that the king was playing with and threw it back with well-judged speed. He did not let it drop when it was thrown back to him. Then King Archistrates, after noticing the speed with which the young man threw, not knowing who he was and having no evenly matched opponent to play ball with, faced his household staff and said: "Stand back. I believe that this young man is meant to be matched against me." When the attendants had withdrawn, Apollonius's practiced hand returned the ball with well-judged speed. Indeed, it seemed to the king and all the others, even the young boys who were there, to be a great miracle. Realizing that the townspeople were applauding him, Apollonius walked straight up to the king. Then with his practiced hand he applied a salve to the king so delicately that he transformed him from an old man into a youth. He repeated the welcome application of the anointment in the bathtub and extended a solicitous hand to the king as he stepped out. After this he left.

When the king saw that the young man had left, he turned to his friends and said, "My friends, I swear by all that is dear to me that I have never had a better bath than the one I've had today through the kindness of an unknown young man." Then he turned to one of his attendants and said, "Find out who the young man is who performed such a welcome service for me." 14

The slave promptly followed the young man, and when he saw him dressed only in a threadbare little cloak, he returned to the king and said, "Your Excellency, the young man has just suffered shipwreck." "How do you know?," said the king. The servant replied, "He said nothing, but his clothing told the story." The king said, "Go quickly and say to him, 'The king invites you to come for dinner.'"

Apollonius accepted the invitation delivered by the servant and followed him to the king's residence. The servant entered first and said to the king, "The shipwrecked man is here, but he is distressed about entering because of his shabby clothes." The king immediately ordered that he be dressed in suitable clothes and that he proceed to dinner.

As Apollonius entered the dining room, the king said to him: "Recline at the table and eat, young man. The master will give you whatever he has. Forget about what you lost in the shipwreck." Apollonius immediately reclined opposite the king at the place indicated to him. The first course was served, followed by a regal main course. He alone of all the diners did not eat but instead kept staring at the gold and silver, the table and the table service, and as he looked at them, he wept mournfully. But when one of the elders reclining next to the king saw the young man examining each item closely, he turned back to the king and said, "Good king, look, look how enviously the young man to whom you've shown your generous spirit is staring at your possessions and good fortune!" To him the king said, "My good friend, your suspicions are unfounded, for that young man is not begrudging me my possessions and good fortune but, I think, is showing the signs of having lost more." With a cheery look on his face he turned towards the young man and said, "Young man, join us in eating; rejoice and be of good cheer and hope for better things from God."

15    While the king was offering words of encouragement to the young man, his daughter suddenly arrived, a beautiful maiden glittering with gold and already grown up. She first kissed her father and then all his dining companions. As she made the rounds kissing them, she came to the shipwrecked man. She returned to her father and said: "Good king and best of fathers, who is the young man reclining opposite you in the place of honor? His appearance is mournful, and he is in a state of grief." To her the king said: "This young man has been shipwrecked, and he performed a most welcome service for me in the gymnasium. That is why I invited him to dinner. However, I don't know who he is or where he's come from. But if you wish, ask him. You're a very bright young woman, and it's right that you should know everything. Perhaps when you've learned about him, you'll have pity on him."

Encouraged by her father, the girl began very timidly to question Apollonius. As she approached Apollonius, she said: "Although your reserve shows that you are unhappy, your nobility of origin is evident in your nobility of appearance. If you don't mind, tell me your name and fortune." Apollonius said, "If you want to know my name, it's Apollonius; if you want to know my fortune, I lost it at sea." The girl said, "Explain more clearly so that I'll understand."

16    Apollonius described all that had happened to him and at the end of his account began to weep. When the king saw him weeping, he looked at his daughter and said: "My sweet child, you have made a mistake. For by inquiring too closely about the name and fortune of the young man, you have reawakened the former causes of his grief.[4] And so, my sweet and bright daughter, it is just that you should show him queenly gen-

---

4. For the text see Hunt, *Classical Philology* 75(1980): 24–26. There is an echo here of *Aeneid* 2.3, where Aeneas is about to tell Dido the story of the fall of Troy.

erosity now that you've learned the truth from him." The girl looked at Apollonius and said: "You are our friend, young man; so set aside your gloominess. Since I have my father's permission, I shall make you rich." Apollonius sighed and thanked her.

The king was delighted to see that his daughter was capable of such generosity and said to her: "Sweet daughter, bless you. Have your lyre brought and banish the young man's tears. Cheer him up for the party."

The girl ordered that her lyre be brought. When she took it up, she combined her sweet voice, the music of the stringed instrument, and the melody in perfect harmony. All the guests began to express their admiration, saying, "Nothing could be better or sweeter than what we've heard." Apollonius alone remained silent. To him the king said: "Apollonius, your behavior is disgraceful. Everybody is praising my daughter's musical accomplishments. Why do you alone insult her by remaining silent?" Apollonius said: "Your Majesty, with your permission, I'll tell you what I think. Your daughter has natural musical talent, but she has not studied music. Have the lyre brought to me, and you will soon come to appreciate what you had no inkling of before." King Archistrates said, "I know that you are a man of many talents."

He assumed the part, put a wreath on his head, took up the lyre, and entered the dining room. He did so in such a way that the guests thought that he was Apollo rather than Apollonius. Once there was silence,

he grasped the plectrum, and put his soul into his art.[5]

He modulated his voice in harmony with the strings. The guests in unison with the king began to shout their praises and say, "Nothing could be better or sweeter." He then put down the lyre and appeared dressed as a comic actor and with marvelous gestures and movements mimed the parts. He next adopted the role of a tragic actor. This was greeted with no less admiration, with the result that all the king's friends swore that they had never heard or seen anything like this performance.

Meanwhile, the king's daughter, when she saw that the young man  17 was accomplished in all arts and skills, was wounded by burning passion. She had fallen in love. At the end of the banquet she spoke thus to her father. "King and best of fathers, you said a little while ago that I should give at your expense whatever I chose to Apollonius." To her he said, "I did say so, I say so now, and that is my wish." Now that she had her father's permission to bestow whatever she chose, she turned to Apollonius and said, "Sir, accept by my father's leave two hundred gold talents, forty pounds of silver, twenty slaves, and a very large supply of clothing." Turning to the slaves whom she had given to Apollonius, she said,

5. The source of this verse quotation is not known.

"Bring out all the goods that I have promised and show them to all the guests in the dining room." They all praised the girl's generosity.

All the guests got up at the end of the party and said good-bye to the king and princess. Apollonius too spoke. "Good king, supporter of those in distress, and princess, lover of studies, good-bye." As he spoke, he looked back to the slaves whom the princess had given him and said, "Slaves, collect what the princess has given me: gold, silver, and clothing; and let us go and look for a place to stay."

In her fear that she would be tortured by not seeing the man she loved, the princess looked at her father and said: "Good king and best of fathers, are you content that after bestowing gifts on Apollonius we should let him go today to run the risk of being robbed by wicked men of what you have given him?" To her the king said: "You are right, my lady. See to it that he's provided with suitable accommodation for sleeping." Now that he had somewhere to stay, Apollonius, hospitably welcomed, went to rest, thanking God for granting him a king who was willing to provide comfort.

18 But the princess, "long wounded by love" for Apollonius, "fixed in her heart his face and words," and mindful of his singing "believed that he was of the race of the gods."[6] "Her longing did not grant rest to her limbs" or sleep to her eyes. She woke at the crack of dawn and burst into her father's bedroom. When he saw his daughter, he said, "Sweet daughter, why are you awake so much earlier than usual?" The girl said: "Yesterday's studies have left me excited. And so I beg of you, Father, to assign me to our guest Apollonius to undertake my studies."

The king was filled with joy and ordered that the young man be summoned. To him he said: "Apollonius, my daughter greatly desires to learn the happy fruit of your studies from you. I ask therefore that you comply with my daughter's wish, and I swear this by the strength of my realm: whatever you lost to the angry sea I shall restore on land."

After hearing this, Apollonius began to teach the girl what he himself had learned. Within a short time, when the girl could in no way endure the wound of love, she collapsed in great weakness, her limbs prostrate, and began to lie helpless in bed. The king became concerned about the sudden onset of her illness and summoned doctors. They took her pulse and examined all parts of her body but did not find a trace of the cause of her illness.

19 A few days later as the king was escorting Apollonius hand in hand to the marketplace, three young aristocratic students who had been seeking his daughter's hand in marriage greeted him in unison. When the king saw them, he laughed and said to them, "Why did you greet me in

6. Chapter 18 contains partial quotations from *Aeneid* 4.1–12, where Dido's star-crossed love for Aeneas is recounted.

unison?" One of them said: "We've been seeking your daughter's hand in marriage, and you've worn us out by repeatedly putting off a decision. And so we've banded together. Choose the one of us you want as your son-in-law." The king said: "You've caught me at a bad time. My daughter spends her time at her studies and because of her zeal for study is confined to bed helpless. But so that I won't appear to be putting you off any longer, write your names and the financial terms of your offers of marriage on tablets. I will send the tablets to my daughter and let her choose for herself the man she wants as her husband."

And so the three young men wrote their names and the financial terms of their offers of marriage. The king took the tablets, sealed them with his signet ring, and gave them to Apollonius, saying: "You are her teacher—if it is not a nuisance to you, take these tablets and deliver them to your pupil. It is your place to be with her."

Apollonius made his way straight to the royal palace with the tablets, 20 entered the bedroom, and handed over the tablets. The girl recognized her father's seal. To her beloved she said, "Why have you entered my bedroom alone, my teacher?" To her Apollonius replied: "Mistress, you are not yet a woman, and you take it amiss! Rather, take your father's tablets and read the names of your three suitors."

The girl opened the tablets and read them to the end, but did not read there the hoped-for name of the man she loved. Looking at Apollonius, she said, "Apollonius, my teacher, are you not sorry that I am going to be married?" Apollonius said, "Rather, now that you have mastered the full course of studies taught by me, I offer my congratulations that you are going to marry the man you desire to marry, with God's blessing." To him the girl said, "Teacher, if you loved teaching, you would regret the loss of it."

She wrote on the tablets and after sealing them with her signet ring handed them over to the young man. Apollonius took them to the marketplace and handed them over to the king. The king took the tablets, broke the seal, and opened them. On them his daughter had written

> Good king and best of fathers, since you generously and indulgently permit me to express myself, I shall. I desire as my husband the man who was robbed of his inheritance by shipwreck. If, Father, you are surprised that a modest young woman should have written so immodestly, I have entrusted my feelings to wax, which has no sense of shame.

After reading through the tablets the king did not know who the ship- 21 wrecked person was whom she had named. Looking at the three young men who had written their names and the financial terms of their offers of marriage, he said to them, "Which one of you has been shipwrecked?"

One of them, a young man named Ardalion, said, "I have." Another one said: "Be quiet, damn you! Plague take you! I know that you're the same age as I am and that you went to school with me. You've never been outside the city gates. So where were you shipwrecked?"

Since the king could not discover which one of them had been shipwrecked, he looked at Apollonius and said: "Apollonius, take these tablets and read them. Perhaps you will understand what I didn't, since you were there." Apollonius took the tablets, read them, and blushed when he realized that the princess loved him. The king held out his hand to him and withdrew a short distance from the young men and said: "What is it, Apollonius? Have you discovered who was shipwrecked?" Apollonius said, "If you'll permit me to say so, I have discovered him."

His blushes revealed to the king the meaning of what he had said, and he joyfully spoke: "My daughter wants what I have prayed for. None of this can happen without God willing it." Looking at the three young men, he dismissed them with these words. "I told you quite clearly that you had caught me at a bad time. Go away, and when the time comes, I shall send for you."

22   He entered the royal palace hand in hand with the person he now regarded as his son-in-law rather than his guest. The king left Apollonius and made his way alone to his daughter and said, "Sweet daughter, whom have you chosen to be your husband?" The girl threw herself down at her father's feet and said: "Dearest Father, since you wish to hear your daughter's desire: I want as my husband the man I love, the man robbed of his inheritance by shipwreck, my teacher, Apollonius. If you do not betroth me to him, you will soon lose your daughter."

Since the king could not bear to see his daughter cry, he pulled her to her feet and addressed her with these words. "Sweet daughter, don't give this any further thought, for you desire to wed the man I've wanted you to wed from the time I first saw him. I can understand your feelings since I became a father by being in love."

Going outside, he saw Apollonius and said: "I have questioned my daughter about what she has in mind as regards marriage. She broke into tears and implored me, and among many other declarations she said this to me: 'You promised my teacher, Apollonius, that if he complied with my wishes and agreed to teach me, you would give him whatever the angry sea had taken away. Because he has complied with your very own pleas and with my wishes in educational matters, he seeks not gold or silver or clothing or slaves or possessions but only the kingdom that he believed he had lost. In accordance with your oath and my request, restore that to him by giving me to him in marriage.' Therefore, Apollonius, I ask you not to have any compunctions about marrying my daughter."

Apollonius said, "As God wills, so be it; and if it is your wish, let it be
23   fulfilled." The king said, "I shall soon set the wedding day."

The next day his friends and the great and noble men of the neighboring cities were invited, and once they were assembled, the king said, "Friends, do you know why I have invited you together?" They replied, "We don't know." The king said: "I wish to inform you that my daughter wants to marry Apollonius of Tyre. I entreat all of you to rejoice, for she is a very intelligent girl and will be wed to a very knowledgeable man." At the same time he at once announced the wedding day and instructed them to assemble.

To make a long story short, the wedding day arrived, and all assembled happily and eagerly. The king rejoiced with his daughter, and Apollonius of Tyre rejoiced to have got the wife he deserved. The marriage rites were celebrated with pomp worthy of the royal family. The whole city rejoiced; citizens, foreigners, and visitors were overjoyed; lutes, lyres, solo songs, and choral song with organ accompaniment gave great pleasure. After the festivities the newlyweds became very fond of each other. There was between them wonderful affection, incomparable delight, and unparalleled happiness; and joined to these was everlasting love.

Some six months later, when the girl's stomach was swollen by pregnancy, her husband, King Apollonius, came to her. While walking on the shore with his beloved at his side he saw a very beautiful ship, and while they were both praising it, Apollonius recognized that it was from his native land. He turned and said to the skipper, "Tell me, please, where you've come from." The skipper said, "From Tyre." Apollonius said, "You've named my homeland." To him the skipper said, "Are you Tyrian?" Apollonius said, "I am exactly that." The skipper said, "Then can you tell me this: Did you know someone by the name of Apollonius who was king of that city?" Apollonius said, "I know him as well as I know myself." The skipper did not understand the reply and said: "If you should see him, please tell him to take heart and to rejoice, for God has struck down the very cruel king Antiochus with a thunderbolt for sleeping with his daughter. However, his wealth and kingdom are being kept for King Apollonius."

When Apollonius heard this, he turned joyfully to his wife and said: "My lady, you believed me when I was shipwrecked; now you have proof. And so I beg you, dearest wife, to allow me to set out and obtain the kingdom that has been promised to me."

When his wife heard that he wanted to leave, she burst into tears and said: "Dear husband, if you had been away somewhere on a long journey, surely you should have hurried back for my confinement. But as it is, since you are here, are you planning to leave me? Let's sail together. Whether on land or sea, wherever you are, let's live or die together."

After saying this the girl went to her father and said to him: "Dear Father, take heart and rejoice, for God has struck down the very cruel king

Antiochus for sleeping with his daughter. However, his wealth and the crown have been kept for my husband. Therefore, I request that you willingly allow me to sail with my husband.[7] So that you will be the more willing, consider that you are sending away one person but that you will get two back."

25     When the king had heard all that she had to say, he rejoiced and was overjoyed and immediately ordered that ships be drawn onto the shore and be loaded with all kinds of goods. He ordered, moreover, that her nurse Lycoris and a very experienced midwife sail with her because she was going to give birth. After providing a going-away party he accompanied them to the shore, kissed his daughter and son-in-law, and wished them a successful journey. The king returned to his palace. Apollonius and his numerous domestic staff boarded the ships with a large amount of equipment and goods and sailed directly on course ahead of the wind.

    While they were delayed at sea for some days and as many nights, the girl gave birth in the ninth month.[8] But the placenta failed to be discharged, her blood clotted, her breathing became constricted, and she suddenly died. When the slaves saw this, they shouted and screamed loudly. Apollonius came running, and when he saw his wife lying lifeless, he tore his clothing from his chest with his fingernails, pulled out his youthful, silken facial hair, threw himself onto her body, and with streaming tears began to weep bitterly, saying: "My dear wife and the king's only daughter, what has become of you? What shall I say about you and what reply shall I give to your father, who rescued me when I was a poor, destitute victim of shipwreck?"

    While he was weeping and lamenting in this fashion, the steersman came to him and said: "Master, you're showing piety, but the ship cannot continue with a corpse aboard. Order that the body be thrown into the sea so that we can escape the force of the waves." Apollonius was annoyed to hear this and said to him: "What are you saying, you scoundrel? Do you think that I should throw into the sea the body of the woman who rescued me when I was the poor victim of shipwreck?"[9]

    Some of his slaves were craftsmen. He called them together and instructed them to saw planks and to fit them together and to seal the seams and openings with pitch. He ordered that they make the coffin large and that they use sheets of lead to close the joints between the planks. After the coffin had been made, he adorned it with royal accoutrements, placed the girl in the coffin, and beside her head put twenty

7. For the text see Hunt, review, *Classical Philology* 76(1981): 343.
8. For the text see Hunt, *Classical Philology* 75(1980): 33–34.
9. For the text see Hunt, *Classical Philology* 75(1980): 29.

thousand gold sesterces. He gave a last kiss to the dead girl, wept over her corpse, and ordered that the infant be taken away and nursed carefully so that he would have some little comfort in his time of troubles and be able to show the king a grandchild in return for his daughter.

Weeping bitterly, he ordered that the coffin be thrown into the sea. 26 Three days later waves cast up the coffin. It came to rest on the shoreline of Ephesus, not far from the estate of a doctor, who on that very day was walking with his students along the shore. He saw the coffin floating on the surging waves and said to his servants, "Lift the coffin very carefully and carry it to my house."

After the servants had done so, the doctor eagerly opened it, and, seeing a very beautiful girl adorned with royal ornaments and lying in a state of apparent death, he said, "How many tears must this girl have left as a legacy to her parents!" When he suddenly caught sight of the money placed beside her head and the written tablets beneath it, he said, "Let's see what last request the bereaved are making." After breaking the seal this is what he found written.

I ask whoever finds this coffin containing twenty thousand gold sesterces to keep ten thousand for himself and to spend ten thousand on a funeral, for this dead girl has left a legacy of many tears and bitter grief. If the finder does not do what the bereaved asks, may he be the last of his family to die, and may there be no one to give his body burial.

After reading the tablet he said to his servants: "Let everything be provided for the body that the bereaved have demanded. As I hope to live, I swear that I shall spend more for this funeral than the bereaved requested."

So saying, he ordered that a pyre be constructed immediately. But while the pyre was being carefully and expertly constructed and assembled, a medical student of youthful appearance but mature judgment arrived. When he saw the corpse of the beautiful girl being placed on the pyre, he looked at his teacher and said, "What is the cause of this recent unexplained death?" The teacher said: "Your arrival is timely; the situation requires your presence. Take a jar of unguent and pour it over the body of the girl to satisfy the last rites." The young man took a jar of unguent, went to the girl's bier, pulled aside the clothing from the upper part of her body, poured out the unguent, ran his suspicious hands over all her limbs, and detected quiescent warmth in her chest cavity. The young man was astounded to realize that the girl was only apparently dead. He touched her veins to check for signs of movement and closely examined her nostrils for signs of breathing; he put his lips to her lips, and, detecting signs of life in the form of slight breathing that, as it were, was struggling against false death, he said, "Apply heat at four points." When he had had this done, he began to massage her lightly, and the blood that had coagulated began to flow because of the anointing.[10]

27     When the young man saw this, he ran to his teacher and said: "Doctor, the girl you think is dead is alive. To convince you, I will clear up her obstructed breathing." With some assistance he took the girl to his bedroom, placed her on his bed, opened her clothing, warmed oil, moistened a woolen compress with it, and placed the compress on the upper part of the girl's body. Her blood, which had congealed because of severe cold, began to flow once heat was applied, and her previously obstructed breathing began to infiltrate to her innermost organs. With the clearing up of her veins, the girl opened her eyes, recovered her breath, and said in a soft, indistinct voice, "Please, doctor, do not touch me in any way other than it is proper to touch the wife of a king and the daughter of a king."

When the young man realized that he had discovered with his skill what his teacher had failed to observe, he hurried joyfully to his teacher and said, "Come, teacher, and witness your student's skill." The teacher, on entering the bedroom, saw that the girl he thought was dead was alive and said to his student, "I commend your medical knowledge, I praise your skill, and I admire your care. But I don't want you to be deprived of the rewards of your medical expertise: take as your payment the money that accompanied the girl." And he gave him ten thousand gold sesterces and prescribed for the girl a nourishing diet and a regimen of fomentations.

A few days later, when he learned that the girl was of royal descent, he adopted her as his daughter in the presence of friends. When she tearfully pleaded that she not be touched by any man, he granted her wish and placed her within the cloistered confines of the priestesses of the goddess Diana, where all the virgins were able to preserve their chastity.

28     Meanwhile, Apollonius continued his grief-stricken voyage. With God as his pilot he put in at Tarsus, disembarked, and went looking for the house of Stranguillio and Dionysias. After greeting them he sadly described all his misfortunes and said: "I expect to take as much comfort from the preservation of my daughter as I gave tears for the loss of my wife. Faithful friends, since I do not want to take possession of the kingdom that was being kept for me, now that my wife has been lost, or return to my father-in-law, whose daughter I lost at sea, but prefer instead to become a merchant, I entrust my daughter to you. Have her nursed with your daughter, bring her up with the benefit of your good and simple hearts, and call her Tarsia after the name of this country. I also en-

10. The last few lines of chapter 26 are patently corrupt; see Hunt, "More on the Text," *Rheinisches Museum* 127(1984): 358–61.

trust to you my wife's nurse Lycoris, and my wish is that she should nurse and look after my daughter."

After saying this, he handed over his daughter along with gold, silver, and expensive clothing and vowed emphatically not to cut his beard, hair, or nails until he had betrothed his daughter. Although they were amazed by this extreme vow, they promised that they would bring up the girl faithfully. After entrusting his daughter to them Apollonius boarded his ship and made for the open sea. He put in at a distant, obscure part of Egypt.

At the age of five Tarsia was assigned to a program of education in the liberal arts and was taught along with the couple's daughter. They were instructed in the development of their natural qualities as well as in the arts of listening and speaking and in moral conduct. When Tarsia was fourteen years old, she returned from school and discovered that her nurse had fallen victim to a sudden illness. She sat beside her and questioned her about the cause of her infirmity. Her nurse raised herself and said: "Mistress Tarsia, listen to the last words of an old woman on her deathbed. Listen to them and take them to heart. Who do you think your father and mother are, and what do you think your native land is?" The girl said, "My native land is Tarsus, my father is Stranguillio, and my mother is Dionysias."

The nurse sighed and said: "Listen, Mistress Tarsia, to my account of your lineage, so that you will know what you must do after my death. Your native land is Tyre, your father is named Apollonius, and your mother is the daughter of King Archistrates. When your mother gave birth, the placenta failed to be discharged, her breathing became constricted, and she notched the final day of her allotted time. Your father provided the coffin that he had had made for her with royal accoutrements and twenty thousand gold sesterces and lowered it into the sea, so that wherever she was carried she could declare her own identity. In the face of head winds the ships brought your grief-stricken father and you in your cradle to this state. Your father entrusted you along with your royal garments to his friends Stranguillio and Dionysias and vowed that he would not cut his hair or nails until he had betrothed you. If after my death the guardians whom you call your parents should do you any harm, go to the marketplace, and you will find a statue of your father, Apollonius. Clutch the statue and proclaim, 'I am the daughter of this man whose statue this is.' The citizens are mindful of your father's favors and will come to your rescue if necessary."[11]

To her Tarsia said, "Dear nurse, as God is my witness, I would have remained forever ignorant of my lineage if some misfortune had befallen

11. For the text see Hunt, *Classical Philology* 75(1980): 28–29.

you before you had told me this."[12] While they were conversing, the nurse died in the girl's embrace. The girl committed her nurse's body to the grave and mourned her for a year. At the end of the period of mourning, she resumed her former position in the world and went back to school to study the liberal arts. She would not eat until after she had visited the grave vault with offerings of a flask of wine and wreaths of flowers.[13] There she would call upon the spirits of her parents.

31    While this was happening, Dionysias was passing through a public area one holiday with her daughter Philomusia and Tarsia. To all the citizens and people of rank who saw how beautiful Tarsia was in her finery she seemed to be something miraculous, and they all said, "Fortunate is the father whose daughter is Tarsia, but the girl clinging to her side is shamefully ugly." When Dionysias heard them praising Tarsia and denigrating her own daughter, she fell into a mad rage. While sitting alone she began to think like this. "Her father, Apollonius, set out fourteen years ago and he hasn't returned to recover his daughter or sent a letter to us. He has probably died or been lost at sea. Her nurse, however, is dead. There's no one to interfere with me. There's nothing to prevent me from eliminating her with sword or poison, and I shall dress my own daughter in her fine clothes."

While she was mulling over these things, she was informed of the arrival of her steward Theophilus. She summoned him and said, "If you want your freedom and payment into the bargain, eliminate Tarsia." The steward said, "What crime can the innocent girl have committed?" The wicked woman said: "Are you disobeying me? Just do what I command. If you don't, you will feel the wrath of your master and mistress." The steward said, "How can it be done?" The wicked woman said: "As soon as she comes home from school and before eating, she always goes to her nurse's grave vault. You must go there with a dagger and kill her when she comes and throw her body into the sea. When you come and report that you have done this, you will have your freedom and payment into the bargain."

The steward took a dagger and hid it at his side and, looking up to heaven, said, "God, have I not earned my freedom without having to shed the blood of an innocent young woman?" After saying this he went, sighing and weeping, to the grave vault of Tarsia's nurse and there concealed himself.

When the girl came home from school, she poured out from a flask her customary offering of wine and entered the vault and set out wreaths of flowers. While she was calling on the spirits of her parents, the stew-

12. For the text see Hunt, *Classical Philology* 75(1980): 32.
13. The text is uncertain at this point but can be restored with reasonable probability because of the author's habit of repeating phrases (cf. chapter 31); see Hunt, *Mnemosyne* 35(1982): 348–49.

ard made his attack, grabbing the girl by the hair from behind and throwing her to the ground. As he was about to stab her, the girl said to him: "Theophilus, what wrong have I done? Why should I, an innocent girl, die at your hands?" To her the steward said, "You have done nothing wrong, but your father, Apollonius, was wrong to entrust you, with a great sum of money and fine royal clothes, to Stranguillio and Dionysias." When she heard this, the girl tearfully implored him, "Allow me to call God as my witness; this is the last hope and comfort for me during my lifetime." To her the steward said: "Call God as your witness. God knows that I do not want to commit this crime."

While the girl was praying to God, pirates suddenly arrived and, seeing an armed man about to stab her, they shouted: "Stop, you savage, stop; don't kill her! This girl is our booty, not your victim." When the steward heard their shouts, he released her and fled into hiding behind the grave vault. The pirates brought their ship into shore, seized the girl, tied her up, and made for the high seas. 32

After a time the steward returned, and when he saw that the girl had been snatched away from death, he thanked God that he had not committed the crime. He returned to Dionysias and said: "What you ordered has been accomplished. Fulfill your promise." The wicked woman said: "You've committed murder, and do you ask for liberty? Go back to the estate and perform your duties, or you'll feel the wrath of your master and mistress."

After hearing this the steward looked towards heaven and said: "God, you know that I have not committed a crime; you be the judge." He returned to the estate.

Dionysias then took counsel with herself concerning the crime that she had plotted and how she could keep it concealed. She went directly to her husband, Stranguillio, and said: "Dear husband, your wife and daughter need your help. Malicious insults aroused strong feelings of insane jealousy in me, and I suddenly thought to myself: 'It's now fourteen years since her father entrusted Tarsia to us, and he has not once sent us a letter of greeting. He must have been lost in the storm-lashed waves of the sea. Her nurse is dead. There is no one to interfere with me. I shall eliminate Tarsia and dress our daughter in her fine clothes.' You should know that that is what has happened. To satisfy the curiosity of people for the time being, put on your mourning clothes as I am doing, and with a show of tears let's declare that she died suddenly of a stomach ailment. Let's build a large tomb on the outskirts of town and say that she has been buried there."

When Stranguillio heard this, he started to tremble and to feel faint and replied in this way. "Indeed, give me mourning clothes so that I can mourn myself for my misfortune in marrying a wicked wife. Oh, what heartache! What am I to do, how am I to act towards her father? I welcomed him and advised him to leave this state after he had rescued it from destruction and the danger of famine. For the sake of this state he suffered shipwreck, looked death in the face, lost his possessions, and endured the hardships of poverty. Restored to a better fortune by God, because he is a pious man, he did not think evil thoughts instead of good, or keep the past in the forefront of his thoughts, but assigned everything that had happened to oblivion. Furthermore, still considering us faithful people with good intentions, he rewarded us, thinking us God-fearing people, by entrusting the upbringing of his daughter to us. He felt so much pure love for us that he named his daughter after our state. Oh, how blind I have been! I must mourn an innocent girl, and myself for being married to a deceitful woman who is a wicked, poisonous snake."

Looking up to heaven, he said: "God, you know that I am innocent of shedding Tarsia's blood. May you avenge her on Dionysias!" And turning towards his wife, he said, "How, you enemy of God, will you be able to keep this disgraceful crime hidden?"

Dionysias actually dressed herself and her daughter in mourning clothes and with a show of false tears summoned the citizens and said to them: "My dearest friends, we have called you here because we have lost Tarsia, who was our shining light of hope, the object of our labors, and the fruit of our years; you know her well. She has left us a cross of bitter tears. We have given her a worthy burial."

The townsfolk then continued to where the empty tomb had been provided by Dionysias and in return for the merits and favors of Tarsia's father, Apollonius, they had erected a bronze memorial and had it inscribed with these words.

> PRESENTED BY THE CITIZENS OF TARSUS TO THE SACRED
> MEMORY OF THE GIRL TARSIA IN REMEMBRANCE OF THE
> FAVORS OF APOLLONIUS OF TYRE

33   Those who had seized Tarsia arrived at Mytilene. She was put off the ship and placed out for sale in the marketplace with the other slaves. When a most unpleasant pimp heard about this, he wanted to buy no man or woman except Tarsia and began to bid for her purchase. But when Athenagora, the king of that state, heard that an aristocratic, intelligent, and very beautiful girl had been put up for sale, he offered ten thousand gold sesterces. But the pimp was willing to pay twenty thousand. Athenagora offered thirty thousand, the pimp forty thousand; Athenagora fifty thousand, the pimp sixty thousand; Athenagora seventy thousand, the pimp eighty thousand; Athenagora ninety thousand. The pimp paid down a deposit of one hundred thousand gold sesterces and said, "If anyone offers more, I'll increase the offer by ten thousand." Athenagora said: "If I want to enter a bidding war with this pimp for the

purchase of one girl, I'll have to sell several. But suppose I allow him to be the successful bidder: when he installs her in his brothel, I'll be the first to go to her and sever the knot of her virginity at little cost to myself, and as far as I'm concerned it will be as if I had bid successfully for her."

To cut the story short, the pimp was the successful bidder for the girl. She was installed by him in the reception room, where he had a gold statue of Priapus that was decorated with jewels and gold. He said to her, "Pay homage to this powerful deity of mine." The girl said, "Are you from Lampsacus?"[14] The pimp said, "Don't you know, you miserable creature, that you've landed in the house of a greedy pimp?" When the girl heard this, she was racked by convulsions throughout her body. She prostrated herself at his feet and said: "Have pity on me, master. Help me to preserve my virginity. Please don't set up this poor little body of mine for sale in this shameful brothel." To her the pimp said: "Get up, you miserable creature. Don't you know that pimps are like executioners and that pleas and tears have no influence on them?" He summoned the assistant who looked after his girls and said to him, "See to it that a room is carefully prepared and have this notice posted in it: Whoever wants to deprive Tarsia of her virginity will have to pay a half pound of gold; thereafter, she will be available to anyone for a single gold coin each time." His assistant did what the pimp had ordered.

A crowd of people and singers was conducted to the brothel two days later. Athenagora was the first to arrive, and he walked into the brothel with his face covered. After walking in he sat down. Tarsia arrived, fell at his feet, and said: "Have pity on me. I call upon you in the name of your youth not to defile me under the terms of that disgraceful notice. Restrain your shameless lust; listen to the story of the misfortunes that I have suffered; take my lineage into account."

After she had described to him all her misfortunes, the king became confused, and with intense feelings of compassion and amazement he said to her: "Stand up. We both understand the blows of fortune; we are both subject to the human condition. I too have a virgin daughter for whom I could fear similar misfortune." As he said this, he held out forty gold coins, and, putting them into the girl's hand, he said to her: "Here, Tarsia. You have more than was demanded for your virginity. Do the same thing with all the other men who come until you have your freedom." The girl wept profusely and said, "I am greatly indebted to you for your compassion."

As he was leaving, he met a colleague, who said, "Athenagora, how

14. Priapus, a fertility god represented by phallic statues, was worshiped at Lampsacus on the Hellespont.

did you find the new girl?" Athenagora said, "She was so good that I actually wept." After saying this he followed him in and stealthily waited for the chance to witness the outcome. As the colleague entered, Athenagora stood outside the door. The girl closed the door in the usual way. The young man said to her: "Greetings! Tell me, please, how much the previous young man gave you." The girl said, "He gave me forty gold coins." The young man said: "Curse him! What difference would it make to a man that rich to give you a whole pound of gold! To prove to you that I am a better man, I am giving you a whole pound of gold!"[15] From his position outside the door Athenagora said, "The more you pay, the more you'll weep!" The girl fell at the feet of Athenagora's colleague and in the same way described her misfortunes. The young man became confused and lost his desire for sex. The young man said to her: "Stand up. We are both subject to the human condition, the victims of misfortunes." The girl said, "I am greatly indebted to you for your compassion."

35      As he left, he met Athenagora, who was laughing, and said to him: "A fine fellow you are! You had nobody to cry over!" They swore not to tell anyone and began to watch for others coming out. To make a long story short, they watched through a peephole as one after another went in, paid a gold coin each, and left in tears.

At the end of the business day the girl gave the money to the pimp, saying, "Here's the price of my virginity." He said to her: "How much better it is to have you laughing instead of crying! Keep up the good work so that you can bring in more money for me every day." She spoke to him in the same way the next day. "Here's the price of my virginity. I earned it the same way, with prayers and tears, and I still have my virginity." The pimp was angry to hear that she had preserved her virginity, and he summoned his assistant and said to him: "I see that you have been so careless that you don't know that Tarsia is a virgin. If she brings in so much money as a virgin, how much will she bring in after she's experienced sex? Summon her, and you sever the knot of her virginity."

The assistant immediately took her to his bedroom and said to her: "Tarsia, tell me the truth. Are you still a virgin?" Tarsia said, "God willing, I shall remain a virgin." The assistant said, "How have you earned so much money in the past two days?" The girl said: "By tearfully describing all my misfortunes. The men felt sorry for me and showed com-

<hr/>

15. R. Duncan-Jones, *The Economy of the Roman Empire* (Cambridge, 1974), 252 argues that the equation forty *aurei* = almost a pound of gold would be most appropriate in the monetary conditions that prevailed in the second or third quarter of the third century, before the onset of rapid devaluation of the *aureus*. See also Kortekaas, *Historia Apollonii*, 122–23 and 129–30, and my introduction.

passion for the preservation of my virginity." She threw herself at his feet and said: "Have pity on me, master. Help the captive daughter of a king." When she had described all her misfortunes to him, he was moved by compassion and said to her, "The pimp is so greedy. I don't know whether you can remain a virgin." The girl replied: "I have the resources    36 of a completely mastered liberal education. Also, I play the lyre well. Arrange to have a stage erected at a busy place tomorrow, and I will give a demonstration of my eloquence. Then I will play the lyre and by means of my skill add daily to our income."

When the assistant had carried out her instructions, so much popular approval and affection for her grew up that both men and women conferred large sums of money on her daily. Tarsia was mindful of her intact virginity and of her noble birth. King Athenagora looked after her as if she were his own daughter by giving large sums of money to the assistant and by commending her to his care.

While this was happening at Mytilene, Apollonius arrived after four-    37 teen years at the house of Stranguillio and Dionysias in Tarsus. Stranguillio saw him at a distance and ran quickly to his wife, saying: "You said that Apollonius must have perished in a shipwreck. Look: he's come to recover his daughter. What are we going to say to the father about his daughter, for whom we were acting as parents?" When the wicked woman heard this, she was seized by trembling throughout her body and said: "Show pity, husband. I confess that because of my love for our daughter I destroyed somebody else's daughter. Now, in the circumstances, you must put on mourning clothes, and, with a show of false tears let's declare that she died suddenly of a stomach ailment. When he sees us dressed like that, he'll believe us."

As this was happening, Apollonius entered Stranguillio's house and pushed back the hair from his brow and the shaggy beard from his mouth. When he saw Stranguillio and Dionysias dressed in mourning clothes, he said: "My most faithful friends—if I may still call you that—why are you weeping profusely at my arrival? I hope the tears don't concern me rather than you?" The wicked woman said tearfully: "I wish there were someone besides my husband or me to break this news to you. I must inform you that your daughter Tarsia was suddenly lost to us because of a stomach ailment." When Apollonius heard this, his whole body shuddered, and he stood pale and grieving for a long time. After recovering his breath he looked at the woman and said: "My daughter Tarsia died a few days ago. Have her money and jewelry and clothes disappeared?" As he was talking, the wicked woman fetched everything and    38 returned it to him as agreed with these words. "You must believe that if destiny had allowed, we would have restored your daughter to you just as we are returning all her possessions to you. To prove that we are not lying, we have the evidence of the townsfolk, who out of gratitude to your generosity, have had erected a bronze memorial to your daughter that you can visit to pay homage."

Apollonius believed that she had really died, and he said to his servants: "Collect all these possessions and take them to my ship. I'm going to my daughter's memorial." When he arrived there, he read this inscription.

THIS BRONZE MEMORIAL PRESENTED BY THE CITIZENS OF TARSUS TO THE SACRED MEMORY OF THE GIRL TARSIA, THE DAUGHTER OF KING APOLLONIUS OF TYRE, IN REMEMBRANCE OF HIS FAVORS

After reading the inscription he stood dumbfounded. He was amazed that he could not shed tears, and cursed his eyes. "Callous eyes, you see the memorial for my daughter but cannot shed tears. What agony! My daughter may be alive." After uttering this he returned to his ship and addressed his men: "Confine me below deck. I want to breathe out at sea the last of my life, which was not allowed to see brightness on earth."

39    After the ship weighed anchor he confined himself below deck and set sail for the high seas to return to Tyre. While he was sailing with favorable winds, the sea suddenly became untrustworthy, and they were driven through a series of crises over the seas. They all prayed to God and reached Mytilene. The festival of Neptune was being celebrated there. When Apollonius learned this, he groaned and said: "Everybody is celebrating the festival day except me. But I must not appear to be too mournful and mean. It's punishment enough for my servants that an unlucky master has fallen to their lot."

He summoned his steward and said to him: "Give ten gold coins to the crew so that they can buy what they want and celebrate the festival day. As for me, I forbid that any one of you should disturb me. If any one of you does so, I command that his legs be broken."

While Apollonius's crew members were enjoying the festivities better than the crews of the other ships, it happened that Athenagora, the king of the state, who was lavishing attention on Apollonius's daughter Tarsia, was walking along the beach and observing the sailors' revels. As he was taking note of the various ships, he saw one that stood out from the others as being better fitted. He approached Apollonius's ship and stopped and began to admire it. Apollonius's crew members and servants greeted him, "If you see fit, King, you'll get a magnificent welcome aboard." He accepted the invitation and boarded the ship with five slaves. When he saw that the crew members and servants were all reclining at tables, he reclined with them as they were eating and donated ten gold coins to them. As he placed them on the table, he said, "Here, to repay your generous invitation." They all said to him, "We are greatly indebted to you for your generosity."

When Athenagora noticed that they were all reclining casually at the tables and that there was no one in authority to oversee them, he said to them: "You're all reclining casually at the tables. Who's in command of this ship?" The helmsman said: "The commander of this ship lies grieving in darkness below deck. He's mourning his wife and daughter." Athenagora was touched with grief when he heard this, and he said to the helmsman: "I'll give you two gold coins if you go down to him and say, 'Athenagora, the king of this state, requests that you come up to him out of the darkness and into the light.'" The young man said: "If I can buy a set of limbs with the pair of coins! Could you not have found another suitable candidate for the job? Find someone else to go, for he's left orders that the legs of anyone who disturbs him are to be broken." Athenagora said: "He's set this rule for you, not for me, whom he doesn't know. I'll go down to him. Tell me what his name is." The servants said, "His name is Apollonius."

When Athenagora heard the name, he said to himself, "Tarsia said 40 that her father's name was Apollonius." He went in the direction indicated by the servants and found him. When he saw him lying in the dark with squalid beard and shaggy and dirty hair, he greeted him quietly. "Hello, Apollonius." Apollonius thought that one of his servants was being disrespectful. He glowered at him, but when he saw a dignified, well-dressed stranger, he contained his anger in silence. King Athenagora said to him: "I realize that you must be surprised that I addressed you by name. I am the king of this state." When Athenagora heard no reply from him, he spoke to him again. "I left the road to look at the ships on the shore, and among them I saw your handsomely fitted and attractive-looking ship. As I approached, I was invited aboard by your companions and crew. I boarded and gladly reclined at the table. I asked who the master of the ship was. They said that you were in a state of deep grief, and I see that you are. In return for the goodwill that I've shown in coming to you, come out of the darkness and into the light and dine with me for a short time. I hope, moreover, that God will grant you greater happiness after your period of immense grief."

Weary with grief, Apollonius raised his head and spoke thus. "Whoever you are, go, my lord, recline at the table and dine with my crew as though they were your own. As for me, I am so greatly afflicted by misfortunes that I wish not only not to dine but not even to live."

Athenagora returned in a state of confusion from below deck to topside, and as he reclined at the table, he said: "I wasn't able to persuade your master to come into the light. What shall I do to deflect him from his intention of dying? I've just had a good idea. Boy, hurry to the pimp and tell him to send Tarsia to to me."

When the boy reached the pimp, the pimp was unable to disregard what he said, and though he did so against his will, he unwillingly sent her. Athenagora saw Tarsia when she reached the ship, and he said to her: "Tarsia, come here. We need the benefit of your studies. The master of this ship and of all these men is sitting in the dark mourning his wife and daughter. You must encourage him to accept comfort and urge him to return to the light. Here is an opportunity for compassion that will enable the master to become kindly disposed towards his fellow human beings. So go to him and persuade him to come into the light. Perhaps God wants him to live through our intervention. If you can accomplish this, I'll purchase your freedom from the pimp for thirty days so that you can resolutely devote your attention to maintaining your virginity; and I'll also give you ten gold sesterces." When the girl had heard this, she immediately went below deck to Apollonius and greeted him quietly. "Hello, whoever you are, and rejoice. I am not just a slut who has come here to encourage you but an innocent virgin keeping my virginity inviolable in a place of shipwrecked chastity."

41     She began to sing this song in a melodious voice.

> I walk through corruption but remain unaware of it
> just as the rose is not touched by the points of its thorns.
> Pirates seized me and struck me with hostile sword.
> The property now of a pimp, I have never offended my chastity.
> If I were free of weeping, grief, and tears for my missing loved ones
> and if my father knew where I was, no woman would be in better
>     state than I would.
> I was born of a kingly race and royal forebears,
> but now I am despised, yet still ordered to pretend happiness.
> Put an end to tears and the cares of grief.
> Raise your eyes to heaven and your mind to the stars.
> God the creator and mover of all things will help you.
> He will crush your grief; he will not allow you to weep like this
>     forever.[16]

At the sound of this song Apollonius raised his eyes and looked at the girl. He groaned and said, "Oh, what misery! How much longer can I resist her compassion?" He sat up straight and said to her: "Thank you very much for your understanding and nobility of character. In return for your compassion, I offer these words. If ever I am allowed to be

---

16. There are echoes of *Aeneid* 4.27 and 9.637 in this song.

happy, (I'll use the resources of my kingdom to advance your cause). Since you claim to be of royal stock, perhaps I'll restore you to your parents. For now, take two hundred gold coins and rejoice as if you had brought me forth to the light. Please leave and don't call me again. You've awakened in me memories of my recent grief."[17]

She took the two hundred gold coins and left. Athenagora said to her: "Where are you going, Tarsia? Were your efforts in vain? Have we been unable to show compassion and come to the aid of a man who is going to commit suicide?" Tarsia said to him, "I did everything I could, but he gave me two hundred gold coins and asked me to leave because, he said, he was being tortured by renewed grief and pain." Athenagora said to her: "I will give you four hundred gold coins on the spot if only you will go down to him. Return his two hundred gold coins and encourage him to come into the light by saying, 'I have come for your well-being, not for your money'" Tarsia went down and said to him: "If you've decided to stay forever in this gloomy filth, allow me to exchange a few words with you here in the darkness in return for the large sum of money with which you've honored me. If you undo the knot of my riddles, I will leave; if not, I will return the money that you gave me and go away."

So as not to appear to be taking the money back and because he also wanted to hear what the clever girl had to say, he replied: "Although no concern except that of weeping and grieving suits me in the midst of my misfortunes, speak your riddle and go away and stop pestering me to be happy. Please let me give vent to my grief."

Tarsia said to him: "There is a house that resounds loudly over the earth. The house alone echoes, but the silent inhabitant makes not a sound. Both, however, make haste, the house and the inhabitant together."[18] If therefore, as you claim, you are a king in your own land, solve my riddle; for no one is wiser than a king." Apollonius nodded and said, "To prove that I didn't lie: the house that resounds over the earth is the sea; the silent inhabitant of this house is a fish, which rushes along with its house."

This marvelous explanation convinced the girl that he was really a king, and she drummed him with more difficult riddles. "The sweet friend of the bank and always close to deep waters, singing sweetly to the Muses, I am the darkened messenger of the tongue sealed by my master's hand." To her Apollonius said: "God's sweet friend, which sends its song to heaven, is the reed pipe. It is always close to the bank because it grows near water and is the darkened messenger of the tongue."

17. An echo of *Aeneid* 2.3.

18. This series of riddles is found in the *Riddle Book* of Symphosius (fourth–fifth century A.D.), which was popular in the Middle Ages.

The girl resumed the exchange. "The tall offspring of a lovely forest, I am borne along swiftly, thronged by a great crowd of companions. I race over many routes but leave no tracks." Apollonius nodded again and said to her: "If only I had the chance to rid myself of my long-lasting grief, I could show you things of which you are ignorant. However, I will solve your riddle, for I marvel that a girl as young as you are is so clever. The tall tree is a ship, the offspring of a lovely forest. It is borne along swiftly by the driving wind and is thronged by crowds. It races over many routes but leaves no tracks."

The girl was again excited by the cleverness of his (solution) and said to him:[19] "The fire spreads throughout all the buildings without doing any damage. Enclosed on all sides, it surrounds me with flames, but I do not burn. Its dwelling is bare, and the visitor who goes there is bare." To her Apollonius said: "If I could rid myself of this grief, I would go unscathed through that fire. I would be entering a bath building, where on all sides flames rise through ducts. The building is bare because there is nothing inside except benches. The visitor who enters there is bare because he wears no clothing."

The girl resumed the exchange. "I am a single piece of iron joined by two points. I struggle against the wind; I fight against the deep whirlpool. I explore the middle of the sea. I bite the land at its bottom." To her Apollonius replied: "It is an anchor, which secures the ship in which you are sitting. It is a single piece of iron joined by two points. It struggles against the wind and the deep whirlpool. It explores the middle of the sea and holds onto the land at the bottom with its bite."

The girl Tarsia resumed the exchange with him. "I am not pregnant, but I am heavy with fluids. All my inner organs are interlaced by cavities and swell. There are fluids inside me, but they do not come out of their own accord." To her Apollonius replied, "Although a sponge is light, it is interlaced by cavities and swells when impregnated by fluids that do not come out of their own accord."

43 The girl resumed the exchange. "I am not adorned with locks or tresses. There is hair inside me that no one sees. I am thrown back and forth and into the air by hands." Apollonius said: "When I was shipwrecked at Pentapolis, this guided me into friendship with the king. It's a ball, which is not covered with locks or tresses because all the hair is inside. It is thrown back and forth from hand to hand."

The girl resumed the exchange. "I have no fixed figure, and no figure is alien to me. I glitter within with radiant light that reveals nothing except what it has already seen." Apollonius replied: "A mirror has no fixed figure because its figure changes with the reflected object. No figure is alien to it because it reveals whatever stands opposite it."

The girl resumed the exchange. "Four sisters fashioned identically by

19. For the text see Hunt, *Classical Philology* 75(1980): 30.

art run as if in competition but strive for harmony. Although they are joined together, they cannot touch one another." Apollonius said: "The four sisters of identical shape and appearance are wheels, which are fashioned to run as if in competition; although they are next to one another, they cannot touch one another."

The girl resumed the exchange. "We climb to the heavens as we reach for the heights. We have been joined by unifying artistry into a single series. Anyone seeking the ethereal heights does so through us." Apollonius said: "Please don't urge me to be happy. I don't want to appear to be insulting the memory of my loved ones. The rungs of a ladder reach for the heights; they are the same length, and, joined into a single series, they remain in the same position; anyone seeking the ethereal heights does so through them."

After answering in this way Apollonius said, "Here, take another hundred gold coins and go away so that I can mourn the loss of my loved ones." The girl regretted that such a clever man should want to die. She emptied out the gold coins into his lap and tried to take him into the light by pulling at his mourning clothes. He struck her and knocked her down. The fall caused blood to flow from her nostrils. As she sat there, the girl began to weep and to lament loudly. "O hard-hearted powers of heaven, how can you allow an innocent girl like me to be harassed by such great calamities right from the time of my birth! As soon as I was born, at sea in the midst of storm-driven waves, my mother died because the placenta reverted to her womb and clotted, and she was denied a grave on land. She was adorned by my father in regal finery and placed in a coffin with twenty thousand gold sesterces and entrusted to Neptune. I was placed in a cradle by my father and along with regal finery and clothes entrusted to the wicked Stranguillio and his wife, Dionysias. Because of this finery I almost suffered treacherous death and was assigned to punishment at the hands of the ignoble servant named Theophilus. When he decided to kill me, I begged him to allow me to call God to witness. As I prayed to him, pirates intervened, carried me off by force, and brought me to this land, where I was sold to a wicked pimp."

Apollonius ran to embrace her after she had finished her tearful lamentations. He began to weep for joy and to speak.[20] "You are my daughter Tarsia, my one and only hope and the light of my eyes. I have been mourning for you and your mother for fourteen years.[21] Now I shall die happy, for my hope has been brought back to life and restored to me." (Standing and replacing his mourning clothes with his most ornate clothing, he embraced and kissed her as he wept. Athenagora saw them locked in their tearful embrace and also wept most bitterly....He threw

44

45

20. For the text see Hunt, *Harvard Studies in Classical Philology* 85(1981): 217.
21. For the text see Hunt, *Classical Philology* 76(1981): 344.

himself at Apollonius's feet and addressed him. "By the living God who has restored father to daughter, I entreat you not to give Tarsia in marriage to any other man. I am the king of this state, and it was through my influence that she has remained a virgin." Apollonius said: "How can I be opposed to such generosity and goodwill? Indeed, that is my wish, for I vowed that I would not take off my mourning clothes until I had given my daughter in marriage. It remains only to avenge my daughter on this pimp at whose hands she has suffered cruel treatment.) And Apollonius said, "Destruction to this city!" King Athenagora heard this and began shouting in the marketplace, "Come quickly, townsfolk and nobles, so that the city does not suffer destruction."

46    A large crowd formed, and so greatly were the townsfolk disturbed that not a single man or woman remained at home. Athenagora addressed the assembled people. "People of Mytilene, I wish to inform you that Apollonius of Tyre has arrived here. Look! His fleet of ships is approaching with large numbers of armed troops who will destroy this province because of the author of our misfortunes, the pimp who bought his daughter Tarsia and prostituted her. To save this state, the pimp must be surrendered to him so that he can avenge himself on this one ignoble man without endangering the lives of all of us."

The townsfolk responded by seizing the pimp by the ears, tying his hands behind his back, and leading him to the marketplace. After erecting a large platform in the marketplace, they dressed Apollonius in royal vestments, removing his squalid mourning clothes, and cut his hair and placed a crown on his head; and he and his daughter Tarsia mounted the platform. As he embraced his daughter in full view of all the townsfolk, (he was unable to speak because of weeping. Athenagora) was scarcely able to persuade the crowd by his gestures to be quiet; when they were silenced, he addressed them. "People of Mytilene, your sense of duty has brought you here together on the spur of the moment. You see that her father has recognized Tarsia, whom until this very day the greedy pimp had treated shamefully in order to rob us of our money. However, she has remained a virgin because of your goodness. So that he will be still more thankful to your generosity, see to it that he is revenged."

All shouted in unison, "The pimp must be burned alive, and his possessions given to the girl." As soon as these words were spoken, the pimp was consigned to flames. His assistant, all the prostitutes, and his possessions were handed over to Tarsia. To him Tarsia said, "I grant you your life because through your kindness (I have remained a virgin." And she made a gift to him) of two hundred gold talents and his freedom. Then, turning to the prostitutes, she said: "Whatever you have earned with your bodies for the man responsible for your misfortunes I grant to you to keep; and because you have shared slavery with me, henceforth you will enjoy freedom with me."

Apollonius of Tyre stood up and addressed the townsfolk with these 47
words: "Honorable and good citizens, I am grateful to you for your
goodness. Through your persistent faithfulness you have displayed your
goodness, provided security and...safety, and lived up to your illustrious
reputation. Thanks to you, death and grief have been shown to be false;
thanks to you, virginity has not had to struggle; thanks to you, a father's
only daughter has been restored to his embrace. In return for these very
generous gifts of yours I am presenting to your state a gift of one hundred gold talents for the repair of all its walls."

After saying this he ordered that the money be given to them immediately. The townsfolk accepted the gold and had a statue produced of him
standing (on the prow of his ship) and embracing his daughter with his
right arm while he trampled on the head of the pimp. On it they had
inscribed

TO APOLLONIUS OF TYRE FOR RESTORING THE WALLS AND
TO TARSIA FOR MOST CHASTELY PRESERVING HER VIRGIN-
ITY IN THE FACE OF THE VILEST MISFORTUNES THE ENTIRE
CITIZEN BODY OUT OF DEEP LOVE HAS PRESENTED THIS
EVERLASTING MEMORIAL TO THEIR GLORY.

To make a long story short, within a few days to the delight of all the
people he gave his daughter in marriage to King Athenagora in a state
ceremony.

With his staff, son-in-law, and daughter he immediately set sail with 48
the intention of passing through Tarsus and returning to his own country. In a dream he saw someone who looked like an angel and who said:
"Apollonius, instruct your helmsman to make for Ephesus. When you
arrive there, enter the temple of Diana with your daughter and son-in-
law and recount in sequence all the misfortunes that you have suffered
since the time you were young. Then go to Tarsus and avenge your innocent daughter."

Apollonius woke up, and aroused his daughter and son-in-law to report his disturbing dream. They said, "Do what he ordered, sir." He instructed his helmsman to make for Ephesus. The voyage was uneventful.
Apollonius disembarked and with his companions looked for the temple
of Diana, where his wife was head priestess; for she was so beautiful and
so committed to chastity that no other woman was more pleasing to Diana.

Apollonius entered the temple of Diana with his companions and
asked that the sanctuary be opened so that he could recount all his misfortunes in the presence of Diana. Word was taken to the head priestess
that a certain king bearing great gifts had arrived accompanied by his

son-in-law and daughter and that he wanted to recount certain events in the presence of Diana. In response to the news that a king had arrived she put on royal gowns, adorned her hair with jewels, and went dressed in purple and accompanied by a crowd of attendants. She entered the temple. When they saw her, Apollonius, his daughter, and son-in-law rushed to prostrate themselves at her feet, for she radiated so much glittering beauty that they thought that she was the goddess Diana.

The sanctuary was finally opened, and after offering his gifts he began to speak in the presence of Diana while weeping profusely. "From the time of my youth I was recognized as a king of noble bloodline, and after I had mastered all the skills that princes and kings practice, I solved the riddle of cruel King Antiochus in order to gain the hand of his daughter in marriage. But he associated in the most disgustingly perverse way with her whose father he was by nature and became in effect her husband through his wickedness; and he tried to kill me. While I was fleeing from him, I was shipwrecked and was hospitably received by King Architrates of Cyrene to the extent that he thought me worthy of taking his daughter's hand in marriage. She wanted to accompany me on my mission to take possession of my kingdom; and on the ship she gave birth to the baby girl whom you, great Diana, through the injunctions of an angel who appeared to me in a dream, ordered me to bring into your presence. Then she breathed her last breath. I dressed her in royal gowns suitable for a funeral and placed her in a coffin with twenty thousand gold sesterces to testify when she was found that she was worthy of proper burial. I entrusted this daughter of mine to the wicked Stranguillio and Dionysias. I spent fourteen years in Egypt deeply mourning my wife and then went to recover my daughter. I was informed that she had died. While I was caught up in grief for a second time, after the death of the mother and the daughter, and wishing for my own death, you restored me to life."

49  After Apollonius had uttered such words, his wife let out a cry and shouted, "I am your wife, the daughter of King Architrates." Throwing herself into his embrace, she began to speak. "You are my Apollonius of Tyre, the teacher who guided me with expert hand; it is you who received me in marriage from my father, Architrates; it is you whom I loved not out of lust but as my guide to wisdom. Where is my daughter?" He showed Tarsia to her and said, "Look, here she is."

Word spread throughout Ephesus that Apollonius of Tyre had recognized his wife, who was none other than their priestess. There was great joy everywhere in the city, the streets were crowned with flowers, musical instruments were brought out, a banquet was organized by the townsfolk, and all the people alike celebrated.

She appointed the priestess who was second in rank and dear to her to succeed her. To the accompaniment of the tearful joy and, because she was leaving them, the very bitter grief of all the people of Ephesus, she said farewell and with her husband, daughter, and son-in-law boarded the ship.

Apollonius appointed his son-in-law, Athenagora, in his place as king; 50 and accompanied by him, his daughter, his wife and army, he reached Tarsus by ship. Apollonius ordered that Stranguillio and Dionysias should be arrested immediately and brought before him at the tribunal in the marketplace where he was presiding. When they were brought before him, Apollonius faced the townsfolk and said, "People of the most prosperous city of Tarsus, has Apollonius of Tyre been unfair to any of you in any dealings?" They shouted in unison: "We declared you to be and affirm you to be the king and savior of this country for all time; we were willing and are still willing to die for you through whose help we overcame the threat of famine or death. The statue of you seated in a two-horsed chariot that we had erected testifies to this."

Apollonius said to them, "I entrusted my daughter to Stranguillio and his wife, Dionysias, and they refuse to return her to me." Stranguillio said, "I swear by the clemency of your kingship that the reason is that she completed her allotted destiny." Apollonius said: "You see, people of Tarsus, the murder they have committed has not been enough to satisfy their base instincts; on top of this they have taken it into their heads to commit perjury by swearing falsely by the power of my kingship. I promise that what I am going to show you will be the conclusive evidence of your eyes."

As he brought his daughter forward, Apollonius faced all the townsfolk and said, "Look, here is my daughter Tarsia." When she saw her, the evil woman trembled convulsively. The townsfolk were amazed. Tarsia ordered that the steward Theophilus be brought forth into her sight. When he had been brought forth, Tarsia said to him, "Theophilus, if you want sympathetic consideration to be given to the torture and capital punishment that you deserve, and if you want to earn my clemency, tell us clearly who told you to murder me." Theophilus said, "My mistress, Dionysias."

After obtaining this sworn evidence and the true explanation of the motive, all the townsfolk assembled, seized Stranguillio and Dionysias, and carried them outside the city walls, where they stoned them to death. They threw their bodies into a field for the "beasts of the field and the birds of the air"[22] so that their bodies were denied burial on earth. Although they wanted to kill Theophilus, he was not touched, because of Tarsia's intervention, for Tarsia said, "Good citizens, if he hadn't given me time in which to call the Lord to witness, the intervention prompted by your joy just now wouldn't have saved me." She then immediately granted Theophilus his freedom and a reward.

22. The quoted phrase is based on Old Testament expressions; cf. Hos. 4.3, Jer. 7.33, and Ezek. 29.5. Throughout the entire narrative there are echoes of the phrasing of the Vulgate, too minor for individual comment but imparting a biblical flavor to the story.

vention prompted by your joy just now wouldn't have saved me." She then immediately granted Theophilus his freedom and a reward.

51 So, as a result of this situation, to bring joy to the people, Apollonius restored everything as a gift to the people.[23] He spent fifteen days there with all his companions in restoring the public baths, the city walls, and the watchtowers. He then said farewell to the townsfolk and set sail for Pentapolis in Cyrene. He arrived safely. He went directly to his father-in-law, King Archistrates. Archistrates saw his daughter with her husband and his granddaughter Tarsia with her husband. He gave a warm welcome to his granddaughter and her husband and welcomed Apollonius and his own daughter with a kiss. He spent one complete, uninterrupted year happily in their company. Afterward, having completed the course of his life, he died in their arms. He had bequeathed half of his kingdom to Apollonius and the other half to his own daughter.

Soon after all these events Apollonius was walking along the seashore. He saw the fisherman by whom he had been taken in after being shipwrecked and who had given him half of his threadbare little cloak. Apollonius ordered his servants to seize him and to take him to the palace. When the fisherman realized that he was being dragged to the palace, he thought that he was going to be handed over for execution. As he entered the palace, however, Apollonius was sitting there with his wife. Apollonius instructed that he be brought forward and said to his wife, "Your Majesty, my virtuous wife, this is my best man, who helped me by showing the way to you." Turning to face him, Apollonius said, "My kind old man, I am Apollonius of Tyre, to whom you gave half of your threadbare little cloak." Apollonius gave him two hundred gold sesterces, all the slaves, maidservants, clothes, and silver that he desired, and made him a peer for life.

Hellenicus, who had kept Apollonius informed when King Antiochus was pursuing him but who had refused to accept anything from Apollonius, followed him and approached Apollonius as he was walking and said, "Your Highness, remember your servant Hellenicus."[24] Apollonius grasped him by the hand, raised him up, and welcomed him with a kiss. He made him a peer and gave him great wealth.

After these events, Apollonius fathered a son by his wife and established him as king in place of the boy's grandfather, Archistrates. For his part, Apollonius lived for seventy-four years with his wife and ruled over Antioch and Tyre. He lived quietly and happily with his wife. Having completed the course of their lives in the number of years that I mentioned, they died peacefully in their untroubled old age.

Here ends the story of Apollonius.

23. The transmitted text is uncertain and ambiguous; the meaning may be "To the delight of the townsfolk, Apollonius restored."
24. For the text see Hunt, *Harvard Studies in Classical Philology* 85(1981): 218.

# SUMMARIES

❖❖❖❖❖

ANTONIUS DIOGENES
*The Wonders Beyond Thule*

IAMBLICHUS
*A Babylonian Story*

*Translated by*
*Gerald N. Sandy*

# ANTONIUS DIOGENES

# THE WONDERS BEYOND THULE

## TRANSLATED BY
## GERALD N. SANDY

### Introduction

The contents of the twenty-four books of Antonius Diogenes' *The Wonders Beyond Thule,* to give the work its traditional title in English, are known from the summary provided by Photius, the ninth-century patriarch of Constantinople. Some time close to the middle of the third century A.D. the Neoplatonist Porphyry cites (Antonius) Diogenes and his work by name in his biography of Pythagoras, thereby providing one of the only two pieces of evidence for the time of composition of the romance. Antonius Diogenes' pretense that Alexander the Great played a part in transmitting the documents that served as the basis of the work provides the other chronological indicator as it points to a date later than the last third of the fourth century B.C. The Latin name Antonius suggests an imperial date, however; and if, as has been argued, Lucian's *True Story* parodies Antonius Diogenes' work, then a date of composition in the first century and a half A.D. is most likely. But this view has been challenged.[1]

Neither Porphyry's citations nor the few papyrus fragments that have tentatively been assigned to *The Wonders Beyond Thule* add anything of substance to Photius's summary. From it we learn that the title is inappropriate, since Thule (probably Iceland) serves only as the place of rest from previous travels and as the staging area for subsequent travels. We have Photius's word for it that in spite of numerous digressions Antonius

1. J. R. Morgan, "Lucian's *True Histories* and the *Wonders Beyond Thule* of Antonius Diogenes," *Classical Quarterly* 35(1985): 475–90, argues that Lucian is not parodying Antonius Diogenes.

Diogenes managed to maintain a clear, orderly narrative progression. Photius's summary, however, leaves the impression of bewildering complexity (just as would a summary of Wilkie Collins's *Moonstone,* for instance): (1) Dinias reports to Cymbas for transmission (2) to the Arcadian League his mistress Dercyllis's report (3), which includes what her dead maidservant has told her (4); her reported account also includes that of Astraeus (5), who got his version from Philotis (6); and some of Dinias's account to Cymbas includes what Azoulis has told him (7).

To these seven degrees of narrative involution are added the distancing effects of the supposed mode of ultimate transmission of the story: (1) Dinias has his account to Cymbas recorded on cypress writing tablets; (2) Antonius Diogenes writes to Faustinus that he is composing a work on the wonders beyond Thule, to be dedicated to his learned sister Isidora; (3) he adds that he has compiled the work of previous writers; (4) their sources apparently included the box of documents that Alexander the Great allegedly played a part in discovering; (5) a certain Balagrus sent a transcription of the tablets to his wife. The purpose of this elaborate charade was undoubtedly to authenticate the fantastic wonders: Alexander the Great and Balagrus's wife, Phila, are historical figures who anchor the story to reality, and Isidora's knowledge puts the stamp of authenticity on the work.

The only other work of ancient prose fiction that approximates this degree of narrative elaboration is Heliodorus's *Ethiopica.*[2] The manner in which Photius reports the story sometimes adds to the confusion, for in places it is difficult to follow the syntax of the involved indirect discourse and the action of the story. The present translation tries to smooth over some of these difficulties, although without rewriting Photius.

Like Rohde later, Photius clearly thought that Antonius Diogenes occupied an important place in the history of prose fiction. He calls him the father of the genre, although this is probably technically incorrect since both Chariton's romance and the fragmentary Ninus romance, neither of which Photius mentions, seem to have preceded *The Wonders Beyond Thule.* Photius also emphasizes the moral tone of the work, in which the evildoers pay the penalty for their crimes and the innocent are spared, and brings out clearly the high degree of suspense that Antonius Diogenes generated by frequently portraying blameless characters on the brink of disaster only moments before their last-minute, unexpected rescue. Although it may not be the first work of prose fiction, in its narrative complexity, its elaborate pretense to being historical fact, its

2. See A. Borgogno, "Sulla struttura degli *Apista* di Antonio Diogene," *Prometheus* 1(1975): 49–64. Readers may usefully be referred to E. Rohde, *Der griechische Roman und seine Vorläufer* (3d ed., Leipzig, 1914; 4th ed., Hildesheim, 1960), 269–309, for discussion of many points raised by the narrative that cannot be discussed here.

endorsement of conventional morality, and its use of cliff-hanging suspense, *The Wonders Beyond Thule* nonetheless crystallizes the essential qualities of the genre.

## Bibliography

TEXT

Photius. *Bibliotheca* 166. Edited by R. Henry. Paris, 1960. See volume 2, pages 140–149.

Porphyry. *Opuscula*. Edited by A. Nauck. 2d ed. Leipzig, 1886. See pages 21–24, 34–36, 40–41.

GENERAL

Di Gregorio, L. "Sugli Ἄπιστα ὑπὲρ Θούλην di Antonio Diogene." *Aevum* 42 (1968): 199–211.

Reyhl, K. "Antonios Diogenes: Untersuchungen zu den Roman-Fragmenten der 'Wunder jenseits von Thule' und zu den 'Wahren Geschichten' des Lukian." Diss., Tübingen, 1969.

Rohde, E. *Der griechische Roman und seine Vorläufer.* 3rd ed. Leipzig, 1914. 4th ed. Hildesheim, 1960. Pages 269–309 deal with Antonius Diogenes.

# THE WONDERS BEYOND THULE

## Photius's Summary (Bibliotheca 166)

Read: the twenty-four books of Antonius Diogenes' romance *The Wonders Beyond Thule*. Its narrative is uncluttered and so pure that there is no lack of clarity even in the digressions. It is most agreeable in the ideas that it expresses because, though verging on the mythical and the incredible, it is altogether credible in the contrivance and elaboration of its episodes.

The story, then, opens with Dinias, who along with his son Demochares has wandered from his homeland in search of information. After passing over the Black Sea and away from the Caspian, or Hyrcanian, Sea they reached what are called the Rhipaean Mountains and the source of the river Tanais.[1] There, because of the extreme cold, they turned back towards the Scythian Sea and then struck out in the direction of the east to the quarter of the rising sun, skirting the exterior sea for a long time in complicated wanderings. Carmanes, Meniscus, and Azoulis joined them in their wanderings.

109a

---

1. The Rhipaean Mountains were a fabled range whence the North Wind blew. The Tanais River is the modern Don. Between it and the Danube lay the land of the Scythians, whose sea is mentioned in the next sentence.

They reach the island of Thule and use it as a place of rest from their wandering while they are there. On that island of Thule Dinias takes as his mistress a woman named Dercyllis, a Tyrian by birth who belonged to the aristocracy of that city and who was living with her brother Mantinias. While living with her, Dinias learns of the wandering of the brother and sister and of how much harm the Egyptian priest Paapis had done.[2] After his homeland had been plundered, Paapis took up residence in Tyre and was befriended by the parents of Dercyllis and Mantinias. At first, he seemed to be well intentioned towards his benefactors and the entire household. Later, he did a lot of harm to the household, the brother and sister and their parents. After the misfortune that befell her home, Dercyllis, he learned, was taken with her brother to Rhodes. From there she wandered to Crete, then among the Tyrrhenians and the people called the Cimmerians.[3] While among these people, he learned, she saw Hades and learned much about it, making use of her personal maidservant Myrto as her informant; Myrto had died long ago and returned from the dead to instruct her mistress.

109b

And so Dinias begins the narration of these things to an Arcadian named Cymbas, whom the Arcadian League sent to Tyre to ask that Dinias return to them and his homeland. Since the weight of old age prevented him from doing so, he is represented as recounting what he himself had seen during his wandering or what eyewitness accounts he had heard from others; and what he had learned from Dercyllis's account while on Thule, that is, her already reported journey, and how, after her ascent from Hades with Ceryllus and Astraeus, after she and her brother had already been separated from each other, they arrived at the tomb of the Siren; and what she previously heard from Astraeus, that is, his account of Pythagoras and Mnesarchus[4]—which Astraeus himself heard from Philotis—and the wondrous spectacle relating to his eyes; and Dercyllis's account, when she resumed the story of her own journey, of how she came upon a city in Iberia whose inhabitants see by night but are afflicted by blindness during the day, and of what Astraeus did to their enemies there by playing his flute; and of how, released from there with good wishes, they encountered some Celts, a crude and stupid people, from whom they fled on horses; and of their adventures when the horses' skin changed color. Then they came to Aquitania, and Dinias recounts the esteem that Dercyllis and Ceryllus and above all Astraeus enjoyed

2. The Egyptians were regarded by the Greeks as a devious race.
3. That is, at the entrance to the underworld, at Lake Avernus near Naples, the sanctuary of the Sibyl of Cumae.
4. Porphyry, *Life of Pythagoras*, 10–13 (*Opuscula,* ed. A. Nauck [2d ed., Leipzig, 1886]), summarizes Antonius Diogenes in describing how Mnesarchus left his native Tyre and chanced to find the infant Astraeus, whom he brought up with his own children, one of whom was Pythagoras.

there because the change in the size of the pupils of his eyes signaled the phases of the moon and because he released the kings there from strife over the right to rule; for being two in number, they took turns ruling in accordance with the condition of the moon; for these reasons, the people there rejoiced in Astraeus and his companions.

At this point is added an account of the other things that Dercyllis has seen and suffered and how she was taken to the place inhabited by the Artabri.[5] The women there are the warriors, and the men look after the house and attend to the business of women. Then comes what happened to her and to Ceryllus while among the people known as the Astures, and what happened to Astraeus in particular. While contrary to all expectations Ceryllus and Dercyllis escaped numerous dangers among the Astures, Astraeus did not avoid the punishment that befell him upon conviction for a crime committed a long time earlier; but contrary to every expectation he escaped danger and was then butchered. 110a

After this comes what Dercyllis saw in Italy and Sicily during her wanderings and how while in the town of Eryx in Sicily she was seized and taken to Acnesidemus, who was at the time the ruler of the people of Leontini.[6]

It was at this place that she again came upon her thrice-accursed enemy Paapis while he was staying with the ruler, and she found in the person of her brother Mantinias unhoped-for consolation for the unforeseen occurrence. He had wandered much and had seen many wondrous sights concerning men and other creatures and concerning the sun itself and the moon and plants and especially islands. He explained these sights to her and provided her with countless subjects of stories for her to report later to Dinias. He compiled these stories and is represented as recounting them to the Arcadian Cymbas.

Then, as they left Leontini, Mantinias and Dercyllis took Paapis's bag, the books in it, and a small wooden box of plants. They sailed to Rhegium and from there to Metapontum, where Astraeus overtook them and warned them that Paapis was hard on their heels.[7] They sailed away to Thrace and the Massagetae, together with Astraeus, who was going to visit his friend Zamolxis. There is an account of what they saw during these travels, of how Astraeus met Zamolxis, who was already regarded as a god among the Getae, and of what Dercyllis and Mantinias asked Astraeus to say to him and ask him on their behalf.[8] There, an ora-

---

5. The Artabri and their neighbors the Astures (see text below) lived in northern Spain.

6. Aenesidemus is a historical figure, whose *floruit* near the beginning of the fifth century B.C. establishes the dramatic date of Antonius Diogenes' romance, just after the death of Pythagoras.

7. They have sailed up the east coast of the toe of Italy.

8. Antonius Diogenes (or Photius) has used the terms Massagetae and Getae indiscriminately.

cle declared that they would go to Thule and that they would see their homeland later but that first they would undergo trials and make atonement for their, albeit unintentional, irreverence towards their parents by dividing their time between life and death, by living at night but being corpses each day. After hearing such predictions, they set sail from there, leaving Astraeus, who was revered by the Getae, with Zamolxis. There is an account of all the marvelous sights and tales that they encountered in the north.

All these things Dinias heard from Dercyllis on Thule, and he is presented reporting them to the Arcadian Cymbas. Next comes how Paapis followed the route of Dercyllis and her companions, overtook them on the island, and by means of magic imposed on them that affliction of being dead during the day and coming back to life at nightfall. He imposed the affliction on them by spitting openly in the faces of the pair. A person of Thule named Thruscanus, being ardently in love with Dercyllis and grieving to see his beloved stricken down as a consequence of the affliction caused by Paapis, struck him instantly with his sword and immediately killed him, thereby managing to bring to an end the countless difficulties. And Thruscanus, since Dercyllis appeared to be lying dead, killed himself over her corpse.

110b

All these things and many more like them—their burial and return from the grave, Mantinias's love affairs and their consequences, and other similar events on the island of Thule—Dinias is presented recounting one after the other on the authority of Dercyllis for the Arcadian Cymbas. And the twenty-third book of Antonius Diogenes' *The Wonders Beyond Thule* comes to an end, without, however, hinting at anything concerning Thule except for the short notice at the beginning.

The twenty-fourth book presents Azoulis as narrator and then Dinias adding Azoulis's stories to the tales he has already told Cymbas. We learn how Azoulis discovered the method of enchantment whereby Paapis had employed his magic to cause Dercyllis and Mantinias to come to life at night but during the day to be corpses, and how he freed them from the affliction when he found the secret of the punishment inflicted, and also the antidote to it, in Paapis's bag, which Mantinias and Dercyllis had brought with them. He also discovered how Dercyllis and Mantinias should free their parents from the great curse to which they had fallen victim. On the advice of Paapis, who led them to believe that they would be acting for their parents' good, they themselves had injured their parents grievously by causing them to lie like corpses for a long time.

Then Dercyllis and Mantinias hurried home to revive and save their parents. Dinias, along with Carmanes and Meniscus—for Azoulis had separated from them—extended their journey beyond Thule. This is the journey in which he saw the wonders beyond Thule, according to the report he is now presented as making to Cymbas. He says he saw things that enthusaists of stargazing maintain, such as that it is possible for some people to live at the North Pole, and that a night there lasts a month, sometimes less, sometimes more, or six months, or in the extreme case   111a twelve months, and not only is night drawn out to such an extent, but days correspond in duration to the nights.

He recounts that he saw other similar things, and he tells marvelous stories of having seen men and other things that no one else says he has seen or heard, and that no one else has even imagined. The most wondrous thing of all is that in traveling north they came close to the moon, which was like a completely stripped land,[9] and that while there they saw things that it was natural for a man to see who had invented such an exaggerated fiction.

Then the Sibyl picked up her art of divination again, with Carmanes. After this, each person made his own prayer, and everything turned out for each of the others in accordance with his prayer, but in his case, after he woke up, he was found in Tyre in the temple of Hercules, and after he got up, he found Dercyllis and Mantinias. They were safe and had released their parents from the long sleep or, rather, death, and were prospering in other ways as well.

These things Dinias told to Cymbas and provided cypress tablets on which he asked Cymbas's companion Erasinides, since he was a skillful writer, to record the account. He also showed Dercyllis to them—it was in fact she who brought the cypress tablets. He ordered Cymbas to have the accounts written down on two sets of cypress tablets, one of which Cymbas would keep and the other of which Dercyllis was to place in a small box and set down near Dinias's grave at the time of his death.

Now, Diogenes, who is also called Antonius, presents Dinias recounting all these marvelous things to Cymbas, and at the same time he writes to Faustinus that he is composing a work about the wonders beyond Thule and that he is dedicating it to his learned sister Isidora. He says of himself that he is the author of an ancient story and that even though he is fabricating wondrous and false things, he has the authority, for his numerous stories, of older writers, from whose work he has compiled his collection, at the cost of much labor. He cites at the beginning of each book the names of the persons who treated its subject previously so that the incredible events would not seem to lack authority.

At the beginning of the work he addresses a letter to his sister Isidora. In it, he explains that he has dedicated the work to her, but he presents   111b Balagrus writing to his wife, Phila,[10] the daughter of Antipater, that after

9. This has also been understood as "a land of purest light."
10. A historical figure of the time of Alexander the Great.

Tyre had been taken by King Alexander of Macedonia, and most of it had been consumed by fire, a soldier went to Alexander and said that he would show him a strange and incredible sight outside the city. The king took with him Hephaestion and Parmenion, and they followed he soldier. They came upon stone subterranean grave vaults, one of which was inscribed, "Lysilla lived thirty-five years"; another, "Mnason the son of Mantinias lived sixty-six years of seventy-one"; another, "Aristion the son of Philocles lived forty-seven years of fifty-two"; another, "Mantinias the son of Mnason lived forty-two years and 707 nights"; another, "Dercyllis the daughter of Mnason lived thirty-nine years and 760 nights"; the sixth grave vault, "Dinias the Arcadian lived 125 years."

While still in a state of confusion caused by all these epitaphs except for the first, which was clear, they came upon a small cypress box beside a wall. On the box was written "Stranger, whoever you are, open this box to learn what will amaze you." On opening the box, Alexander and his companions found the cypress tablets that, it seems, Dercyllis had buried at Dinias's orders.

He presents Balagrus writing these things to his wife and transcribing the contents of the cypress tablets so as to communicate them to his wife. For the rest, the book moves on to the interpretation and transcription of the cypress tablets, and Dinias appears telling Cymbas what has already been reported. It is in this way and on these subjects that Antonius Diogenes has contrived his work of fiction.

It seems that he is earlier than those who have made it their business to write this kind of fiction, such as Lucian, Lucius, Iamblichus, Achilles Tatius, Heliodorus, and Damascius. In fact this romance seems to be the fount and root of Lucian's *True Story* and Lucius's *Metamorphoses*. Moreover, Dercyllis, Ceryllus, Thruscanus, and Dinias seem to have been the models for the romances about Sinonis and Rhodanes, Leucippe and Clitophon, Chariclea and Theagenes, and for their wanderings, love affairs, capture, and dangers.

112a   As for the date of Antonius Diogenes, the father of fictional stories of that time, I cannot give any clear information at present, but it is possible to infer that he belongs to a time not far removed from that of King Alexander. He mentions as an earlier writer a certain Antiphanes, who, he says, spent his time on marvelous tales of the same sort.

In this story in particular, as in fictional works of its kind, there are two especially useful things to observe: first, that he presents a wrongdoer, even if he appears to escape countless times, paying the penalty just the same; second, that he shows many guiltless people, though on the brink of great danger, being saved many times in defiance of expectations.

# IAMBLICHUS

# A BABYLONIAN STORY

## TRANSLATED BY
## GERALD N. SANDY

*Introduction*

The biographical sketch of Iamblichus contained in the margin of the principal manuscript of Photius's *Bibliotheca* records, on the authority of Iamblichus himself, that our writer was a non-hellenized Syrian born to indigenous Syrian parents. It says that he received his education from a Babylonian who was taken prisoner at the time of Trajan's military presence in Babylon in A.D. 115. "This Iamblichus, then, knew his native Syrian language and Babylonian and in addition, he says, worked at Greek and acquired familiarity with it in order to become an accomplished man of letters."

There is nothing inherently implausible in this potted biography. It must be emphasized, however, that the source is Iamblichus himself, and as in the case of Antonius Diogenes autobiographical truth may here be subordinated to the needs of fiction. The alleged Babylonian connection may be only a fabrication intended to establish the writer's authority on the subject of his "history." Taking together this biography and the further autobiographical information contained in Photius's summary (for which see chapter 10 of the story), we can infer that Iamblichus was in his late sixties or seventies when he wrote *A Babylonian Story:* if Iamblichus's Babylonian tutor began to instruct his pupil immediately after his capture and sale as a slave to a Syrian in 115, then Iamblichus must have been born about 100; the details preserved by Photius imply that Iamblichus composed *A Babylonian Story* sometime between 165 and 180. The only fundamental problem with this chronological reconstruction is that Photius reports, still on Iamblichus's authority, that our writer was in the prime of his life during the period.

The remains of *A Babylonian Story* (*Babyloniaca*) survive in Photius's summary, three manuscript extracts, and some one hundred short quotations in the *Suda* lexicon of the tenth century. Most of this last category of remains is in fact only conjecturally assigned to Iamblichus. In any case, the work, at least more of it than now survives, existed in the tenth century. In the fourth century, the medical writer Theodorus Priscianus (according to a widely accepted emendation of the text) recommended the *Babylonian Story* as a stimulant for those suffering from sexual impotence. A fragile hope that the complete *Babylonian Story* may yet come to light remains; for various early seventeenth-century humanists, most notably Isaac Vossius, refer to it in ways that suggest that a manuscript of the entire work may have survived the fire that destroyed the Escorial Library in Spain in 1671. It seems more likely, however, that these ambiguous references to the *Babylonian Story* are to the two Florentine excerpts from the work, as is certainly the case with references made by P.-D. Huet, who in the seventeenth century confused the excerpts with the complete work.

In the translation that follows I have given first Photius's summary and then the three extracts from manuscripts in Florence and the Vatican (they are assigned by E. Habrich, the editor, to specific points within Photius's narrative, but without compelling reason). I have used the vivid present in some places where the text vacillates between present and past tenses, and occasionally inserted, in parentheses, a brief phrase to supplement Photius's erratic syntax or the received text.

## Bibliography

TEXT

*Iamblichi Babyloniacorum Reliquiae.* Edited by E. Habrich. Leipzig, 1960 (Teubner).

*Photius. Bibliotheca* 94. Edited by R. Henry. Paris, 1960. See volume 2, pages 34–48.

GENERAL

Borgogno, A. "Sui *Babyloniaca* di Giamblico." *Hermes* 103(1975): 101–26.

Di Gregorio, L. "Sulla biografia di Giamblico e la fortuna del suo romanzo attraverso i secoli." *Aevum* 38(1964): 1–13.

Rohde, E. *Der griechische Roman und seine Vorläufer.* 3d ed. Leipzig, 1914. 4th ed. Hildesheim, 1960. See pages 388–409 for discussion of Iamblichus.

Schneider-Menzel, U. "Jamblichos' Babylonische Geschichten." In *Literatur und Gesellschaft im ausgehenden Altertum,* edited by F. Altheim, 1.48–92. Halle and Saale, 1948.

# A BABYLONIAN STORY

## *Photius's Summary (Bibliotheca 94)*

Read: a story by Iamblichus, with a love plot. He parades salaciousness   1
less than does Achilles Tatius but exhibits more shamelessness than does   73b
the Phoenician Heliodorus. These three writers set for themselves almost
the same goal in presenting love stories. Heliodorus does so in a more
reverent and decent way, Iamblichus less so than he, and Achilles Tatius
most disgracefully and shamelessly. His vocabulary is flowing and gentle. As for its sonorous qualities, the words have not been given rhyth-
mical force so much as titillating and, so to speak, mincing movement.
Iamblichus was justified in displaying the skill and force of his writing, as
far as the merits of his language and construction and disposition of nar-   74a
rative are concerned, and on really serious subjects, not on frivolous
fictions.

The characters in the story are the attractive Sinonis and Rhodanes,   2
who are joined by the mutual ties of love and marriage, and the Babylonian king Garmus. After the death of his wife, he falls in love with
Sinonis and is eager to marry her. Sinonis refuses and is bound in gold
chains. The king's eunuchs Damas and Sacas are given the task of putting
Rhodanes onto a cross for this reason. But through Sinonis's efforts he is
taken down, and they each avoid their fate, he of crucifixion, she of marriage. Because of this Sacas and Damas have their ears and noses cut off
and are sent in search of the pair. They split up and start to track them
down.

Rhodanes and his companion are almost captured in a field by their   3
pursuer, Damas; for there was a fisherman who gave information about
the shepherds, who when tortured finally point out the field—Rhodanes
found in it gold that had been revealed by the inscription on a leonine
stele. A goatlike specter falls in love with Sinonis. For this reason Rhodanes and his companion leave the meadow. Finding Sinonis's garland of
wild meadow flowers, Damas sends it to Garmus to console him. In
their flight Rhodanes and his companion come upon an old woman in a
hut. They hide in a cave that is dug right through for over three miles
and is blocked at the mouth by a thicket. Damas suddenly arrives, and
the old woman is questioned and faints on seeing the drawn sword. The
horses on which Rhodanes and Sinonis were riding are seized; the troop
of soldiers takes up position around the spot where Sinonis and Rhodanes are hiding; the bronze shield of one of the soldiers breaks on top of
the cave; disclosure of the fugitives is caused by the empty sound of the
echo; holes are dug around the cave, and Damas shouts all over; those

within hear and flee to the innermost parts of the cave and make their escape in the direction of its other opening. Swarms of savage bees come from the cave and attack those who are digging there, and honey drops down onto the fugitives; both the bees and the honey are poisonous because the bees have fed on snakes; attacking those who have turned towards the cave, the bees seriously injure some and kill others.

Overcome by hunger, Rhodanes and his companion lick the honey off themselves, are stricken with diarrhea, and fall as if dead at the side of the road. Worn out from fighting the bees, the soldiers flee; all the same, they pursue Rhodanes and his companion, and, seeing their quarry collapsed, they pass them by, taking them to be truly dead.

In this cave Sinonis's hair is cut so that they can draw water up it by capillary action. Damas finds the hair there and sends it to Garmus as a sign that he is close to capturing them.[1] While Rhodanes and Sinonis are lying collapsed at the side of the road, the soldiers as they are passing follow the custom of their country in throwing shrouds in the form of tunics over what they take to be corpses, and whatever they happen to have, and pieces of meat and bread. In this way the soldiers pass by. The couple made unconscious by the honey wake up with difficulty; Rhodanes is awakened by the sound of crows quarreling over the pieces of meat, and he wakes up Sinonis. They get up and travel in the direction opposite to that taken by the soldiers so as to improve their chances of not being recognized as the fugitives. Finding two asses, they mount them and load them with what they retained from the things that the soldiers who supposed that they were dead threw over their bodies. They then turn into an inn, flee from there, and take lodgings at another one around midday.

The fatal episode of the two brothers occurs, and they are charged with murder and released; the elder, who has poisoned his brother, brings the charge but by his own suicide exonerates them. Rhodanes gains possession of the poison without being seen.

They stop at the house of a robber who robs travelers and makes a meal of them. Soldiers sent by Damas capture the robber and set fire to his house. They are surrounded by flames and scarcely manage to escape destruction by killing their asses and placing the dead creatures on the flames as a pathway.

During the night they are seen by those who set the fire, and when asked who they are, they answer, "The ghosts of those killed by the rob-

---

1. A lavish description of hair quoted at two points in the *Suda* and conjecturally assigned to Iamblichus (Habrich 17) may refer to Sinonis's shorn locks: "The locks were cut. They were like the locks of a wild beast that lives in the open—abundant, sun-bleached, and thick locks, nurtured by the rain, blown by the wind."

ber." Because of their pale and emaciated appearance and their weak voices they convince the soldiers and frighten them. They flee again from there, overtake the funeral cortege of a young woman, and join the crowd to watch. An aged Chaldaean astrologer arrives and forbids the burial, saying that the young woman is still breathing. That proves to be true. He prophesies to Rhodanes that he will be a king.

6
75a

The grave of the young woman is left empty, and there are left behind several robes that were to be burned on the grave, and food and drink. Rhodanes and his companion feast on the food and drink, take some of the clothing, and lie down to sleep in the young woman's grave. As daylight comes, those who set fire to the robber's house realize that they have been tricked and follow the footprints of Rhodanes and Sinonis, supposing that they are henchmen of the robber. They follow the footprints right up to the grave and look in at the motionless, sleeping, wine-sodden bodies lying in the grave. They suppose that they are looking at corpses and leave, puzzled that the tracks led there. Rhodanes and his companion leave there and cross the sweet and translucent river that is dedicated to supplying the Babylonian king's drinking water. Sinonis sells the clothing, is arrested as a grave robber, and is sent before Soraechus, the son of the tax collector Soraechus who was called the Just. Because of her beauty he plans to send her to King Garmus; and for this reason Rhodanes and Sinonis prepare a dose of the brothers' poison, for to them death is preferable to seeing Garmus. Soraechus is informed by a maidservant of what Rhodanes and Sinonis were intending to resort to. Soraechus secretly empties the cup of the deadly poison and fills it with a sleeping potion. After they drink it and fall asleep, he takes them in a covered carriage to the king. As they draw near, Rhodanes is frightened by a dream, shouts, and arouses Sinonis. She strikes her breast with a sword. Soraechus asks them to relate all that has happened to them, which they do after securing a pledge from him. He releases them and points out the temple of Aphrodite on the small island, where Sinonis can recover from her wound.

7

In a digression he tells us of matters concerning the temple and the small island, namely, that the rivers Euphrates and Tigris form the small island by flowing around it, and that the priestess of Aphrodite there had three children—Euphrates, Tigris, and Mesopotamia, the last of whom was ugly at birth but was transformed into a beautiful woman by Aphrodite. A quarrel for her took place among three lovers, and a judicial decision was reached in their case. Bochorus was the judge, the best of the judges at that time. The three presented and argued their cases: Mesopotamia had given to one of them the cup from which she drank, had wreathed one of them with the garland of flowers that she took from

8

75b

her head, and had kissed one of them. Although the one who had been kissed was declared the winner, the quarrel grew no less bitter until they killed one another in the course of their quarrel.

9     He reports parenthetically on the temple of Aphrodite, how the women who go there must publicly recount the dreams that appear to them in the temple. At this point he explains in great detail matters concerning Pharnuchus, Pharsiris, and Tanais, from whom the river Tanais takes its name; and that the mysteries of Aphrodite for the inhabitants of that place and the region of Tanais are those of Tanais and Pharsiris.

On the small island that was mentioned earlier Tigris dies after devouring a rose, for a beetle lay hidden in its bud. The boy's mother is convinced that she has transformed her son into an immortal hero by performing magical practices.

10     Iamblichus treats in great detail various types of magic—the locust magician, the lion magician, the mouse magician. The mysteries take their name from mice, for mice have preeminent magical powers.[2] He mentions the hail magician, the snake magician, the necromancer, and the ventriloquist. Greeks, he says, call a ventriloquist Eurycles; Babylonians call him Sacchuras.

The author says of himself that he is Babylonian, that he has studied the magical arts, that he has a Greek education, and that his *floruit* belongs to the time of King Sohaemus, son of the Arsacid king Achaemenides—who ruled in the kingly line of descent on his father's side and was also a member of the Senate in Rome, a Roman consul, and then once more king of Greater Armenia. It was at the time of this man, then, he says, that he flourished. He states explicitly that Antoninus was the Roman emperor; when Antoninus sent the co-emperor Verus, his adoptive brother and son-in-law, to wage war against the Parthian Vologeses, he himself, he says, predicted the war—that it would occur and how it would end; that Vologeses fled across the Euphrates and Tigris and that Parthia became a subject of Rome.[3]

11     Tigris and Euphrates, the two sons, resemble each other, and Rho-
76a danes resembles them. As I mentioned, one of them died because of a rose. Rhodanes crosses over to the small island with Sinonis. When the mother looks at Rhodanes, she shouts that her dead son has come back to

---

2. The word *mysteria* has been derived from *mys,* "mouse."

3. All the historical details agree with a date after A.D. 165. Antoninus is not Antoninus Pius but his adopted son Marcus Aurelius, who on becoming emperor took the additional name Antoninus. Vologeses is Vologeses III, who took advantage of Antoninus Pius's death in 161 to reopen the Armenian conflict. The biography referred to in the Introduction states that Iamblichus was Syrian by birth; Photius reports the author's claim that he was Babylonian.

life and that Core has accompanied him from the underworld.[4] Rhodanes plays the part, delighting in the islanders' naïveté.

Damas is informed of Rhodanes' actions and of what Soraechus has done for them. The informer was the physician whom Soraechus sent secretly to attend to Sinonis's wound. For this reason, Soraechus is arrested and sent before Garmus. The informer is dispatched with a letter from Damas for the priest of Aphrodite, ordering him to arrest Sinonis. The physician crosses the river in the customary fashion, by clinging to a sacred camel, having first placed the letter in its right ear. The physician eventually drowns in the river, but the camel crosses the river to the island, and Rhodanes and his companion learn everything after removing Damas's letter from the ears of the camel.[5] Therefore, they flee from there and meet Soraechus as he is being taken to Garmus. They all take lodgings at the same inn. During the night Rhodanes bribes some greedy strangers, and Soraechus's guards are killed; Soraechus flees with them, thereby being rewarded for his previous kindness.     12

Damas arrests the priest of Aphrodite and questions him about Sinonis; the old man's punishment is to be made a public executioner instead of a priest.[6] The customs and regulations concerning the public executioner (are described). Euphrates is arrested because his father, the priest, thinking that he is Rhodanes, addresses him as that. His sister, Mesopotamia, flees; Euphrates is led away to Sacas and is questioned about Sinonis, for he was interrogated as though he were Rhodanes. Sacas sends word to Garmus that Rhodanes has been arrested and that Sinonis will be, for Euphrates, while being questioned as though he were Rhodanes, and being obliged to call his sister, Mesopotamia, by Sinonis's name, says that she fled when he was arrested.

Rhodanes and Sinonis flee with Soraechus and find shelter at the house     13
of a farmer. He has an attractive daughter who has just been widowed
and out of regard for the memory of her husband has cut her hair. She is     76b
sent to sell (a piece of) the gold chain that Rhodanes and his companion
brought from their bonds. The farmer's daughter goes to the goldsmith.
He, seeing the girl's attractive appearance, her cut hair, and the piece of

---

4. Core is Persephone.

5. The citations in the *Suda* that are plausibly assigned to Iamblichus at this point in the narrative (Habrich 49–52) suggest that Iamblichus, like Achilles Tatius, delighted in exotic "natural history": for instance, "the camel ate the fodder but drank water from the river unwillingly; and because it exhaled vigorously, as water passed down its throat, there was a gurgling sound in its gullet and a lot of intestinal rumbling."

6. A citation from the *Suda* plausibly assigned here (Habrich 55) suggests that Iamblichus's story involved sharp swings of fortune: "the priest prepared the accoutrements of the office of public executioner, exchanging the most revered office for the most pitiable role." At the end of the story there are "rags-to-riches" transformations of Soraechus and Rhodanes.

chain, of which he was the manufacturer, suspects that she is Sinonis; and sending word to Damas and taking with himself some guards, he secretly watches her closely on her return journey. She becomes suspicious of what is happening and flees to a deserted inn.

At this point (there is an account) of the young woman named Trophime and the slave who is her lover and murderer; of the gold jewelry; of the slave's crimes; of his slaughtering of himself over Trophime's corpse; of his spattering of the farmer's daughter with his blood as he kills himself; of the young woman's fright and flight; of the guards' surprise and flight; of the young woman's arrival at her father's house and her account of what happened; of the flight from there of Rhodanes and his companion; and of the goldsmith's letter before that to Garmus saying that Sinonis has been found. To prove it, the chain that he has bought is sent, as well as a report of other suspicious matters concerning the farmer's daughter.

14  As Rhodanes is about to flee, he kisses the farmer's daughter, and Sinonis is seized by anger because of this. At first she only suspects that there has been a kiss, but then, wiping off from Rhodanes' lips the blood with which he has become coated by kissing her, she becomes completely certain. Sinonis therefore seeks to kill the young woman. She quickly turns towards her like an insane person. Soraechus follows, since

15  he is unable to control her mad anger.[7] They take lodgings at the house of a dissolute rich man, Setapus by name, who falls in love with Sinonis and tries to seduce her. She pretends to return his love, and on the very first night of their lovemaking she kills him with a sword as he lies in a drunken stupor. Ordering the door to be opened and leaving Soraechus in ignorance of what has happened, she makes her way to the farmer's daughter.[8] Once Soraechus learns of her departure, he goes back in pursuit. He takes with him some of Setapus's slaves, whom he hired to prevent the slaughter of the farmer's daughter. Seizing her, he puts her onto

77a  a wagon (for he has provided for this) and drives back. As they are returning, Setapus's slaves, since they saw their master killed, angrily confront them. They seize Sinonis and take her in bonds to Garmus to be punished for murder. Soraechus appears with dust in his hair and torn

---

7. The preceding few lines ("Sinonis therefore seeks...her mad anger") are Photius's summary of a long passage extant, in fragmentary condition, in the third of the manuscript fragments given after Photius's text in the present translation. Comparison of the fragment and this summary of it gives some idea of the nature of Photius's summary of the story in general (cf. note 1 above).

8. The *Suda* quotes a passage that seems to belong at this point in the summary (Habrich 70): "She was already filled with jealous wrath, and she took additional courage from her action. Thus when she reached the road, she said, 'The first trial has been accomplished. Let us undertake the second. Our training has been timely.'"

clothing to announce this misfortune to Rhodanes. Rhodanes tries to kill himself, but Soraechus prevents him.

When he is informed by Sacas's letter that Rhodanes has been arrested, and by the one from the goldsmith that Sinonis is being held, Garmus rejoices, performs sacrifices, and prepares for the marriage; and he has it proclaimed everywhere that all prisoners are to be set free and released. Sinonis, who is being conducted in bonds by Setapus's slaves, is released and set free because of the general amnesty. Garmus orders that Damas be put to death, and he is handed over to the public executioner, whom he himself transformed from priest to public executioner. Garmus becomes angry with Damas because he has been led to believe that Rhodanes and Sinonis were being held by others. Damas's brother Monasus is appointed as his successor. **16**

Digression about Berenice, the daughter of the Egyptian king, and her savage and unlawful love affairs; and about how she has relations with Mesopotamia; and about how Mesopotamia is later arrested by Sacas and sent with her brother Euphrates before Garmus. Garmus receives a letter from the goldsmith saying that Sinonis has escaped, he orders that he be executed and that those who were in charge of guarding and conducting her be buried alive with their wives and children. **17**

Rhodanes' Hyrcanian dog finds in that accursed inn the body of the unfortunate young woman and that of the murderous slave, unlucky in love. It consumes first the slave's body and then, piece by piece, that of the young woman. Sinonis's father arrives; and knowing the dog to belong to Rhodanes and seeing what he believes to be Sinonis's half-eaten body, he kills the dog over Sinonis's body as a sacrifice and hangs himself, after first burying the remains of the young woman and writing with the dog's blood "Lovely Sinonis lies buried here." Soraechus and Rhodanes arrive and seeing the sacrificed dog on the grave, Sinonis's father hanging, and the epitaph, Rhodanes wounds himself for the first time and with his own blood adds to Sinonis's epitaph "And the handsome Rhodanes"; and Soraechus places his head in a noose. **18**

**77b**

At this moment, as Rhodanes is about to inflict the last blow on himself, the farmer's daughter arrives and shouts loudly, "It is not Sinonis lying there, Rhodanes." Racing up, she cuts Soraechus' noose, takes away Rhodanes' sword, and with difficulty convinces them of her account of what happened to the unfortunate young woman and of the buried treasure that she has come to recover.

Freed from her bonds, Sinonis hurries to the house of the farmer towards whose daughter she still feels such insane enmity. When she fails to find her, she questions her father. He tells her where she has gone, and she returns in pursuit, unsheathing her sword. When she catches sight of **19**

Rhodanes stretched out and that young woman sitting alone beside him (for Soraechus has gone to search for a doctor) and tending the wound on his chest, she is filled with still more anger and jealousy and rushes towards the young woman. Rhodanes, prevailing over his wound at the onset of Sinonis's violence, faces her and stops her, taking her sword from her. Driven by the force of her anger, Sinonis races out of the inn and as she runs like a mad woman, shouts out these words alone to Rhodanes, "I invite you to my wedding with Garmus today!" When Soraechus returns and learns everything, he consoles Rhodanes. After nursing the wound, they return the girl along with the money to her father.

20    Euphrates is taken as Rhodanes before Garmus, and Mesopotamia as Sinonis; and Soraechus and the real Rhodanes are taken before him too. When Garmus realizes that Mesopotamia is not Sinonis, he orders Zobaras to behead her beside the Euphrates river "so that," as he puts it, "no other woman would appropriate Sinonis's name." Zobaras, who has drunk at the fountain of love and is held in bondage by his love for Mesopotamia, spares her and takes her away with him to Berenice, who has become queen of the Egyptians after the death of her father.[9] Berenice has Mesopotamia's marriage performed, and because of Mesopotamia there is the threat of war between Garmus and Berenice.

Euphrates is handed over to his father, the public hangman, but when recognized he is spared, and he himself performs the duties of his father, who has not been defiled by human blood. Later, disguised as the public
78a  hangman's daughter, he leaves the prison and saves himself. At this point there is an account of the habits and practices of a woman who sleeps with the public executioner, and of the farmer's daughter and how she is driven into exile after Sinonis marries the king of Syria and is able to vent her anger against her; and how she condemns her [the farmer's daughter] to sleep with the public executioner; she [the farmer's daughter] enters the slaves' quarters and sleeps with Euphrates who, disguised as her, leaves the quarters, and she performs the duties of the public executioner in place of Euphrates.

21    The story advances in this way. Soraechus is condemned to be crucified. The place chosen is where Rhodanes and Sinonis spent the first night, in the meadow near the stream, where the hidden gold was discovered by Rhodanes. He points it out to Soraechus as he is being led away to be crucified. A military force of Alans, which has not been paid by Garmus and is ill disposed to him, is stationed in the area where

9. Zobaras is mentioned in the *Suda*'s entry on Iamblichus, which says that Iamblichus "is said to have been of servile origin. He wrote a work called the *Babylonian Story*. It is a work of thirty-nine books about the love of Rhodanes and Sinonis. He tells about the eunuch Zobaras, the lover of the very beautiful Mesopotamia."

Soraechus is to be crucified.[10] They drive away Soraechus's guards and release him. By finding the gold that was pointed out to him and by skillfully and cleverly extracting it from the tunnel he convinces the Alans that he has been taught this and other things by the gods. He gradually makes himself one of their number and induces them to make him their king; he wages war against Garmus's army and defeats it.

But this is later. When Soraechus was being taken to be crucified, Rhodanes was being led to and hoisted onto the cross that had been designated for him earlier by a garlanded and dancing Garmus, who was drunk and dancing round the cross with the flute players and reveling with abandon.

While this is happening, Sacas informs Garmus by letter that Sinonis     22
is marrying the youthful king of Syria. Rhodanes rejoices up high on the cross, but Garmus makes to kill himself. He checks himself, however, and brings down Rhodanes from the cross against his will (for he prefers to die); he appoints him general and sends him to command his army, as lover against rival in love, in the war that he has stirred up against the Syrian king. He makes an empty show of friendliness and writes secretly to his lieutenants that if victory should be his and if Sinonis should be taken, Rhodanes is to be killed.

Rhodanes wins and recovers Sinonis and becomes king of the Babylonians. This a swallow foretold; for when Garmus arrived to send off Rhodanes, an eagle and a hawk pursued it. It escaped the eagle, but the hawk caught it. In this way the sixteenth book (concludes).

## Extracts from the Babylonian Story

### I.   ON THE PROCESSION OF THE BABYLONIAN KING

The chariot on which the king is conveyed is made completely of ivory and is very much like the Greek four-wheeled chariot. The reins of the horses are purple strips. The king stands on it wearing a special outfit that he does not wear for hunting, for sitting in judgment, or for performing sacrifices, but only for ceremonial occasions. There is a gilded purple robe made of equal parts of gold and purple. He carries an ivory scepter on the top of which he rests his right hand. Sceptered knights, satraps, cavalry commanders, and the tribunes who have the right to do so head the procession. The infantry have silver shields, and some have silver or gold breastplates; they have their hands adorned with bracelets, and their necks with necklaces. They do not have helmets on their heads, but representations of battlements and towers crown and protect their

10. The Alans were a people of north-central Europe.

heads. These are made of silver and gold. Some of the dignitaries have representations set with precious stones, and a few of them wear gold crowns that have been presented to them by the king. Some ride on Nisaean horses, some of which are decked out in military fashion with frontlets, chestplates, and flank armor, others being trained for ceremony, all with gold-studded bridles as though they belonged to wealthy women. Belts, straps, and other equestrian gear—there is not any of this that is not of beaten gold or flaked with gold.

Tied and bound with variegated purple bands, the tails of the horses are braided like women's locks; their manes are raised in crests along both sides of their necks; some of the horses have soft manes, some upright, some crinkled, some natural, some constrained through art.

They mold their gait, their way of looking, their nods, their spirits, and the neighing and whinnying of some of them. The ceremonial horse is taught everything. It stretches out its legs of its own accord on the ground and lies down to receive its luxuriously and brilliantly dressed rider. A horse trained to be more haughty does not drop to its stomach but instead falls to its knees so as to appear to make obeisance while receiving its rider. Then it makes its back supple and maneuverable in movement, like a serpent; it learns to conduct itself rhythmically and to hold itself, and at a nod to breathe through its nostrils, direct its glance, hold its head high, and posture and prance, in every respect like an athlete showing off in the amphitheater. As a result of this the horse seems more handsome, and the rider more impressive.

2. THE MASTER OF THE HOUSE CHARGES A SLAVE WITH DEBAUCHING HIS WIFE, WHO HAS RECOUNTED HOW SHE DREAMED OF HAVING SEXUAL INTERCOURSE WITH HIM IN THE TEMPLE OF APHRODITE.

"Everyone would agree with me that no one would willingly come to such a trial and choose to submit himself to you as judge, King; for you review closely not only defendants' lives but the way of life of plaintiffs. Let this be evidence that the charge is true—that the subject is distasteful to the person who is going to make the charge—for she who loses such a case is unjust, and he who wins it is unlucky.

"I beg you to forgive me; I have not made up my mind to bring an accusation, but I cannot remain silent, not only because adultery is an insufferable crime but also because in addition to the usual outrageous behavior involved in it, there is a special feature in this case: the man involved is a slave—he is spiritually base, even if my wife thinks him handsome. Furthermore, he is not even someone else's slave; he is my own. He should have been her slave too—not her master! The act of adultery is made extreme and more disgraceful by the twin facts that the adulterous woman's good reputation is united with her paramour's bad one.

"I beg you, King, to come to my aid in this, for I have been dishonored by my wife and displaced in esteem by my slave; and to let your indignation fall on those who were able to escape detection in the act but were exposed by the gods.

"I am at a loss to know which of them I should charge with being the adviser and teacher of the other in crime. He is but a boy and as such appears to be more easily persuaded to be persuaded than to persuade, to be corrupted than to corrupt. But she is a woman, and a woman seems to be a very easily deceived thing. Thus, in his defense is the weakness of his age, in hers that of her nature.

"Well, to sum things up, I have this to say. They are an attractive pair. But who would rank a slave above a husband? He is in the bloom of youth, King, and I too think him handsome; and often did I foolishly commend him to her as attractive in appearance, with his languishing eyes. I often commended his white fingers and his tawny locks. By saying these things, then, I taught her to love. You, King, know that this is the truth; for his beauty did not desert him even when he was in fear; his cheeks shone brightly with his panic; his looks did not lose their bloom even when he was in pain. He stood in bonds before you, but even his bonds were becoming to him. The curses that are showered on your head and the risk of destruction that you run adorn you, you handsome rogue. I hesitate, my lord, to say that he is even more handsome today. Do you not pity me, King? My adulterous wife is listening as I, the husband, am praising the adulterer. I am afraid that his good looks will help him even today—so much have I been praising him.

"I was suspicious of the way his eyes strayed, of his many gestures, of the way he looked beyond the wineglass, and of the way he transgressed the limits of a wine steward. I closely observed how the two of them communicated by nods—he began, and she responded. Everything was to hand for them—youth, wine, good looks. I aided them as the instigator of their adultery, the herald of his good looks.

"I thought to chastise them by sending her away barefoot and by casting him down to be trampled on. He, it seems, was not disgraced by being trampled on, but merely won more pity thereby..."[11] in the dreams of women, the woman who loves her husband stays at home; the woman who loves children gives birth; the hired servant works; the erotic woman commits adultery. If not, let each of us remind himself of his dreams, of what he frequently dreams, and of what he sees: the archer, a bow; the horseman, a horse; the king, a throne; she, her adulterous

11. There may be a lacuna in the text here.

lover. You have been caught, you wicked woman! I have discovered you sleeping with this boy. Your lovemaking at night is the memory of its occurrence during the day. What you do while awake, you rehearse in your sleep; for a dream is the image of a person's desire. While you are sleeping beside me, your thoughts are with that slave; while your body is with me, your heart is with him. Beside me, you sleep; beside him, you do not."

3. [The following fragment comes from a damaged Vatican palimpsest. The beginning is only very partially preserved; conjectural restorations are given in brackets. The passage apparently comes at Photius chapter 14.]

...but go rather and sleep with that foreign girl...or perhaps now with her face cleaned and with that little hair of hers tidied. For why do you still want Sinonis? You have a girl with short hair like mine...When Sinonis said this, Rhodanes could not put up with it but [wailed in astonishment]...Sinonis was filled with anger...raised her hands in opposition, [uttered] many threats and, pointing to the wound that had hurt her, said, "You see this...you see that Sinonis is not reluctant to risk her life...I call you to witness, Rhodanes, you will be the cause of great trouble today...farmer's daughter...[circa 10 lines missing]...Sinonis withdrew and went running through the moonlight straight to the [farm] of the farmer [where] she had been before, intending to race in and kill the farmer's daughter...

When Rhodanes and his companion understood her intentions, Soraechus said: "Wait here, Rhodanes, and do not leave this spot, so that you will not appear to be coming to the rescue of your beloved; rather, we must watch over the girl in love and in murderous mood. I will go after that girl; I am convinced that I shall soon bring her back. Cheer up...I know...to overcome Sinonis's fits of anger. Why are you crying, Rhodanes? Stay here if you want to recover Sinonis, if you trust Soraechus, who is wandering because of you." With these words he managed to persuade Rhodanes to wait; Rhodanes was greatly afraid for Sinonis, while his own concern was for the girl in danger, for fear that she would take some serious harm as a consequence of her jealousy.

At first it did not seem possible that Soraechus could overtake Sinonis; for she was far ahead and a faster runner than Soraechus, and she was still quicker because of her anger—her rapid emotions were making her more nimble. All the same, Soraechus, exerting and straining himself, shouted to Sinonis when he caught sight of her [cloak]: "Wait, Sinonis. It is I, Soraechus, alone. Rhodanes is not with me, by Baal!"

Taking him at his word because of her respect for him, Sinonis checked her flight. As Soraechus drew closer, he first called to her to allow him to approach and then said: "Sinonis, I love you both, since I was lucky enough to be assigned to you two as a father. I took charge of you before I took charge of Rhodanes. I do not absolve Rhodanes of blame, but I do not think it proper for you to indulge your anger in all matters or to exact such punishment from a young woman who has claims on us. We may be exposed to danger by her, and in any case we shall offend Zeus, the God of Hospitality, for she provided us with hospitality and welcomed us as her guests. Perhaps she was abused; perhaps she was deceived and misled. Not to you alone, my child, does Rhodanes appear handsome."

She was incensed at this and did not wait for the rest of his plea but said: "Soraechus, I have granted you this miserable utterance, and I was wrong to do so! Sooner would I die than hear that Rhodanes appears handsome to any other woman. Do not prevent me from committing murder in my loneliness—do not even desire to do so! You know that I am not lying, for you are the witness of my courage. You see that I have a sword, and that I have a wound too. Rhodanes was only crucified; I have had a brush with death, and have proved that dying people feel no pain and that death is not unpleasant. Indeed, to lovers it is sweet. Why are you holding me back, Soraechus? I swear that you want to save Rhodanes' lover for him. Do not threaten me with danger, arrest, or punishment. I fear no one—I, who did not fear night or the cross!"[12]

12. It seems from these three fragments that Iamblichus shared the liking commonly found in these novels for elaborate description (*ecphrasis*), law-court scenes, and direct speech.

Habrich prints another fragment (101), which he attributes (with much hesitation) to the Florentine manuscript as well as to the Vatican manuscript. A. Borgogno ("Da un' autopsia del Cod. Laur. Gr. 57, 12," *Rheinisches Museum* 116[1973]: 127–28) has shown that the Florentine attribution is mistaken.

# FRAGMENTS

NINUS
A PHOENICIAN STORY
METIOCHUS AND PARTHENOPE
IOLAUS
SESONCHOSIS
HERPYLLIS
CHIONE
CALLIGONE

*Translated by*
*Gerald N. Sandy and B. P. Reardon*

# INTRODUCTION

The following fragments are the most important that have so far appeared; there are other smaller pieces already published, and more may yet see the light. For a discussion of the significance of these remains see the General Introduction. The intention here is to offer readable texts which will give a fair idea of both the content of these pieces and the uncertainties surrounding them. A good deal of work has been done on the texts, but there is little to be said for using, in a work such as this, supplements that go appreciably beyond what the surviving words imply; and there is a serious risk of misleading a reader dependent on translation. We have not, therefore, translated any supplements that would bias the issue. It would of course be hazardous to build elaborate hypotheses on what is presented. Lacunae are indicated as..., and doubtful readings or supplements are shown in parentheses, in some cases with a question mark to emphasize their uncertainty. More detailed treatment cannot be given in translation, but initial bibliographical guidance is provided for those who wish to pursue the matter further. The *Phoenician Story* is the only fragment for which we have an attested title. The other fragments printed here are usually referred to as the *Ninus Romance* or the like, but for present purposes it is more convenient to call them after their presumed main characters.

# Bibliography

The following works and serial publications are standard and are referred to in abbreviated form in the bibliographies.

## COLLECTIONS OF TEXTS

Lavagnini, B. *Eroticorum graecorum fragmenta papyracea*. Leipzig, 1922 (Teubner).

Zimmermann, F. *Griechische Romanpapyri und verwandte Texte*. Heidelberg, 1936.

## SERIAL PUBLICATIONS

*POxy. Oxyrhynchus Papyri*. Edited by B. P. Grenfell, A. S. Hunt et al. London: Egypt Exploration Society, 1898–.

*PSI Papiri greci e latini*. Pubblicazioni della Società Italiana per la ricerca dei papiri greci e latini in Egitto. Florence, 1912–.

*ZPE Zeitschrift für Papyrologie und Epigraphik*. Bonn, 1967–.

## DISCUSSION

Rattenbury, R. M. "Romance: Traces of Lost Greek Novels." In *New Chapters in the History of Greek Literature,* edited by J. U. Powell, 211–57. Oxford, 1933.

# NINUS

## TRANSLATED BY
## GERALD N. SANDY

## Introduction

"The traditional picture of no other genre in Greek literature was altered so completely by the papyri as that of the romance."[1] The anonymous romance about the Assyrian king Ninus and his beloved, Semiramis (whose name does not actually appear in the fragments), was the first of the fragmentary romances made available by papyrology to alter the accepted beliefs about the development of ancient prose fiction. A document written on the back of the papyrus containing fragments A and B is explicitly dated to the third and fourth years of Trajan's reign, that is, to A.D. 100–101. On the basis of this *terminus ante quem,* as well as on the basis of palaeography and the author's literary style, papyrologists have established that fragments A and B were written down sometime between 100 B.C. and A.D. 100. This chronology annihilated the then prevailing view of Rohde that the Greek romances were a product of the Second Sophistic, the period of renewed Greek literary activity during the second and early third centuries A.D.

The fragments give a picture of a young king involved in military operations, who is in love with his cousin, as she is with him. They protest against the conventional idea that they are too young to marry. At some point in the story they are shipwrecked and apparently separated. The legendary Ninus was associated with the foundation of Nineveh and the Assyrian Empire in about the last fifth of the third millennium B.C. The legendary Semiramis was the wife of King Shamshi-Adad (reigned

1. A. Lesky, *A History of Greek Literature,* trans. J. Willis and C. de Heer (London, 1966), 857.

803

823–810) and was queen regent during the first five years of the reign of her son Adad-Nirari III (reigned 809–782). In her own right she was credited with the construction of many monuments and with the founding of Babylon. In the hands of Greek historians and essayists, and of this novelist, a period of some fourteen hundred years has been telescoped to unite the most famous representatives of Assyria. Once brought together, they were reported in the Greek historical tradition to have behaved in the way Greeks expected Orientals to behave. Ninus seized Semiramis from her husband, Onnes. Semiramis, being the daughter of the goddess Derceto (hence the name of her mother, Dercia, in the romance), emulated her mother's consuming passion for lovers, whom she put to death when she grew tired of them. Semiramis is also supposed to have tricked Ninus into allowing her to rule for five days and during that period to have ordered him to be put to death so that she could become sole ruler. As B. E. Perry concludes, the oriental despot Ninus, who seized women whenever the desire to do so moved him, and the virago Semiramis are far removed from the idealistic and diffident teenagers of the romance.[2]

There has been considerable discussion about the relative order of the fragments in the story. I am inclined hesitantly to agree with those scholars (such as Perry) who have argued for the sequence BAC, and print the fragments in that order. The translation is based for the most part on F. Zimmermann's text.

## Bibliography

Lavagnini, 1–15; Zimmermann, 13–15; Rattenbury, 211–23.

TEXT

Gaselee, S. *The Ninus Romance.* In *Longus: Daphnis and Chloe,* edited by J. M. Edmonds, 381–99. London, 1916 (Loeb Classical Library). Fragments A and B.

Norsa M., and G. Vitelli. *PSI* 1305 = 13.1(1949): 82–86. Fragment C.

Wilcken, U. "Ein neuer griechischer Roman." *Hermes* 28(1893): 161–93. First publication of fragments A and B.

GENERAL

Levi, D. "The Novel of Ninus and Semiramis." *Proceedings of the American Philosophical Society* 87(1944): 420–28. Discussion of a mosaic pavement found at Antioch-on-the-Orontes in Syria that depicts the Ninus and Semiramis of fiction.

Perry, B. E. *The Ancient Romances: A Literary-Historical Account of Their Origins.* Berkeley, 1967. See pages 153–66.

---

2. B. E. Perry discusses the Ninus fragment at length in *The Ancient Romances: A Literary-Historical Account of Their Origins* (Berkeley, 1967), 153–66 (cf. 16–17).

# NINUS

## *Fragment B*

[B1 seems to record a meeting between Ninus and Semiramis in which she is alarmed by him, but he protests innocent intentions and asks for her trust. They meet as much as they can while he is making military preparations. Their love grows. Future separation is mentioned.]

(B2) [Ninus is seen disposing his forces against the Armenians.]

In accordance with his father's decision, Ninus took the entire Greek and Carian contingent, select Assyrian forces consisting of 70,000 infantry and 30,000 cavalry, and, in addition to these, 150 elephants, and he began the march. The ice and snow in the mountain passes were a cause of great concern. However, an unusually summerlike south wind occurred that melted the snow and provided (the marching army) with climatic conditions more suitable than they had the right to expect. Indeed, they experienced greater hardships in crossing the rivers than in passing through the high mountain passes. A small number of pack animals and attendants died, but the soldiers suffered no losses and emerged, from the very risks that they had run, all the more ready to face the enemy boldly. Having mastered impassable routes and enormous rivers, they thought that they would have little trouble conquering the insane Armenians. During his attack on the area in the river basin Ninus plundered the region and established a stronghold on flat land. He remained there for ten days in order to revive the elephants, because they in particular were worn out by the traveling. (B3) When he (heard) that the enemy were (advancing in huge numbers), he led out his forces and arranged them. He (placed) the cavalry (on) the wings, the light-armed troops and the entire (royal regiment) on the (flanks) of the cavalry. A phalanx (of infantry) was stretched out in the middle. The elephants, which were equipped with turrets and (had taken up positions) at some distance from one another, stood as a defensive wall in front (of the phalanx of infantry). However, between each of them and the companies of soldiers (some) space was left so that if one of the animals became (disturbed) it would have room in which to move back. (The soldiers were arranged among the animals) so as to be able to close ranks whenever necessary or in turn to open ranks. The opening of ranks was intended to allow the withdrawal of the animals; the closing of ranks, to thwart the rushes of the enemy.

After arranging (all) his forces in this way, Ninus (rode before them). With his (hands) stretched out as if in (prayer), he spoke. "This stands as the foundation and turning point of my hopes. From this (day) either I shall rule over (a greater empire) or I shall cease to rule over my (eastern empire). The...of the (battles) against Egypt and of the other hostile..."

## Fragment A

[The bulk of A1 probably describes Ninus's love for his cousin Semiramis, and his frustration at the convention that prevented a girl from marrying until fifteen. The lovers are each too shy to approach their own mothers, and prefer to speak to the aunts—that is, each to the other's mother; the aunts are sisters. Column 1 ends with Ninus approaching Dercia, whom he addresses as Mother, i.e., "Aunt."]

(A2) He said: "It is with my pledge honored that I come into your sight and into the embrace of my most delightful cousin. Let the gods first know this, as indeed they do know and as I shall prove by my words. I have passed through so much territory and either through the might of the spear or through my father's power have become master of so many peoples who pay court to me or fall down on their knees to me that I could have satisfied to the full my every desire. Had I done so, my passion for my cousin would perhaps have been less great. As it is, I have returned still chaste to fall victim to the god and to my age. As you know, I am in my seventeenth year and for the past year have been deemed to have entered manhood. Until now I have been but an ignorant child. If I had not experienced Aphrodite, I would count myself blessed in my firmness. But now that I have become your daughter's prisoner, not dishonorably but with the consent of you both, how long shall I deny I am her captive? Men of my age are clearly ready for marriage: for how many of them have remained chaste until their fifteenth year? I am the victim of a law not written but sanctioned by foolish convention: that (A3) among us young women usually marry at the age of fifteen. Who in his right mind would deny that natural feelings are the best sanction for this kind of union? Girls of fourteen conceive, and indeed some give birth to children. Will your daughter not even marry? We should wait two years, you will say. Suppose we do wait—will our Fortune also wait? I am a mortal man engaged to a mortal girl. I am subject not only to the common lot of mankind—to illnesses and to the destiny that often carries away even those who sit quietly at home beside the hearth; but voyages and war after war await me; and I am not without daring or one to wrap myself in a veil of cowardice to keep me from harm, but am, to put it discreetly, as you know me to be. Let my kingship, let my passion, let the insecurity and uncertainty of what awaits me—let all these hasten our marriage; and let the fact that we are the only children in our families be reason for anticipation and forethought, so that if Fortune should will some disaster on us we may leave you the pledges. Perhaps you will say that I am shameless in discussing these matters. I would have been shameless if I had (A4) seduced her secretly and surreptitiously taken advantage of her with the aid of night, drink, and the complicity of servant and nurse to satisfy our mutual passion. It

is not shameless to speak to a mother about her daughter's earnestly desired marriage and to demand what you have granted and to ask that the
wishes of our two households and of the entire kingdom not be delayed
until some occasion that will not lie within your grasp."

This is what he said to Dercia; she was receptive—in fact, if he had
waited, he would perhaps have forced her to initiate discussion of these
matters. After pretending reluctance for a short time, she promised to
champion his cause.

The girl was in an equally emotional state but did not address Thambe
with the same openness, for as an unmarried girl she (lived within) the
women's quarters and could not advance persuasive arguments on her
own behalf. After (asking for) an opportunity to speak, she wept and
wanted to say something but broke off (before she had begun). (Soon she
indicated) her intention to speak by opening her lips and looking up (as
though) she was going to say something but (in the end) uttered no
sound. Her tears rolled down and her cheeks were suffused with red in
embarrassment at the prospect of speaking. When she made another
(sudden attempt) to speak, her cheeks grew pale (A5) through anxiety.
(She was) between...and desire and...shame. Her emotion increased, but
her resolve failed as she (seethed) in great (turmoil). Thambe wiped away
her (tears) with her (hands) and told her to (take courage) and say whatever she wanted. But when the girl (uttered) nothing and remained
(overcome) in the same state of distress, (she said:) "For me (your silence) speaks more eloquently than any speech. You will not (blame) my
son, will you? He has not behaved presumptuously, nor has he come
back to us (arrogant) from successful military achievements to behave
like a (drunken) soldier towards you. If he had done any such thing, you
would probably (not) have remained silent. But convention is slow for
(people ready) for marriage. My son is eager; but there is no (need) for
you to endure his advances, (if that is why) you are crying." She smiled
and threw her arms around her and embraced her. The girl...did not
venture to speak even...but lay(ing) her throbbing heart against her
breast and (kissing her) more earnestly, because of her earlier tears and
her present joy she almost seemed talkative about what she wanted.

The sisters met therefore, and Dercia was the first to speak. "On serious matters..."

## Fragment C

[The first third of this fragment offers only a few scraps. They include]
the river Hippos [in Colchis?]...my wife...my aide...sailor and knowledgeable pilot...safe...from the north to the headland of Colchis. [From
line 18 some thirty lines of more or less continuous text are preserved, as
follows:]

...a shady grove beyond it. From the middle of the grove rose a spring as large as a stream that broke on the beach. Since the sea was not deep near the shore at the headland, the ship was driven violently onto some sandbars and was being tossed and destroyed by the incoming waves. But they crossed it in water that was swirling round their chests. They saved all the things on the ship and set them down on the beach. Faced with this desperate situation, they concentrated all their efforts on saving themselves; but after securing their safety, they began to desire death. The others bore these vicissitudes with moderation, but Ninus felt them miserably. Three days earlier (he had been) the leader of forces ready to wage war against all (Asia, but now)...in any case...shipwrecked, (his wife) carried off captured in war...

# A PHOENICIAN STORY

## TRANSLATED BY
## GERALD N. SANDY

### Introduction

The second-century papyrus containing fragments of Lollianus's *Phoeni-cica*, or *A Phoenician Story*, is arguably the most important addition to our knowledge of ancient prose fiction to appear since the publication in 1893 of the Ninus romance. The importance of the fragments resides in their documentation of the history of ancient prose fiction rather than in their intrinsic literary merits. The fragmentary *Phoenicica* provides, in the present writer's opinion, clear-cut evidence that the Greeks wrote what we would probably call picaresque romances, accounts of low life presented, in this case, in an undistinguished literary style and designed to shock moral sensibilities and conventional notions of decorum. Until the publication of the *Phoenicica* and the slightly later publication of the Iolaus romance, extended fictional prose narrative of a salaciously realistic type was believed to be peculiar to Latin writers, in particular to Petronius.

The original work comprised at least three books. The fragments come from two sets of facing pages. The verso side of what the editor calls fragment A contains the subscription of what was Book 1: "Book 1 of Lollianus's *Phoenicica*." Fragment B spans the emblematically designated ending of a book of unknown number and the beginning of the following, unspecified book.

The surviving narrative opens (A1 recto) with men and women dancing, probably on the flat roof of a house and possibly at the festival of Adonis. A woman named Persis leaves the party to join Androtimus in a secluded room, where he has his first experience of sex (A2 recto). For reasons that are not altogether clear Persis offers him her jewelry. When he refuses it, she orders her steward Glaucetes to count out two thousand drachmas, probably for Androtimus. As Persis's mother appears on the scene, the papyrus fragment breaks off; a few isolated words suggest that the pair try to justify their actions to Persis's mother. Fragment B1 portrays a band of robbers. They have a boy known to Androtimus killed, and his heart cut out, roasted, and distributed to the gang members, who swear an oath of loyalty over it. The intelligible narrative ends with the robbers departing, probably in disguises intended to aid their escape.

The translation is based on A. Henrichs's definitive edition of 1972. I have included a translation of the so-called Glaucetes-fragment, which has been known since 1915. On the basis of stylistic affinities, as well as the name Glaucetes, M. D. Reeve identified it as part of the *Phoenicica*.[1] In it Glaucetes, while traveling, meets the ghost of a murdered man.

## Bibliography

Lavagnini, 33–35; Rattenbury, 246–47.

TEXT

Grenfell, B. P., and A. S. Hunt. *POxy.* 1368 = 11(1915): 119–21. First publication of Glaucetes-fragment.

Henrichs, A. "Lollianos, Phoinikika. Fragmente eines neuen griechischen Romans." *ZPE* 4(1969): 205–15. Preliminary publication.

———. *Die Phoinikika des Lollianos.* Bonn, 1972. Definitive publication, with commentary.

GENERAL

Szepessy, T. "Zur Interpretation eines neu entdeckten griechischen Romans." *Acta Antiqua Academiae Scientiarum Hungaricae* 26(1978): 29–36. Affinities with Greek love-romances.

Winkler, J. J. "Lollianos and the Desperadoes." *Journal of Hellenic Studies* 100(1980): 155–81. Sensational popular entertainment.

# A PHOENICIAN STORY

## A1 recto

...and the name...he instructed; but when none of (them)...to overturn; and meanwhile...the young male attendants (came out)...threw from the roof...overturned; keep(ing) off...and at the same time sober. And the

---

1. See A. Henrichs, *ZPE* 6(1970): 42–43, and *Die Phoinikika des Lollianos* (Bonn, 1972), 9 n.6.

...moved. But the women again...and continued dancing...one another in the dancing...

[Only isolated words survive at the end of the fragment:] but she [Persis?]...first...then was silent...to Glaucetes...stood up...Persis...head...


## A2 recto

[The first four lines are too lacunose to be intelligible.]

...to Persis...persuading and...(took) me to a hidden (room)...serving women...and I found Persis waiting (inside for me). And then I had my first experience of sex...she took off and gave to me the golden jewelry that she was wearing...(for) loss of virginity.[1] I said that I would not take it. (She) called Gla(ucetes), however, and when he came, she gave (it) to him and ordered (the steward) to bring to her two thousand (drachmas) and to count it out...she turned towards me and did not leave off until (satiety) took us both, and day dawned...outside and both knocked at the door and...I remained on the spot, but Persis...when her mother returning from the (town) caught sight of her and immediately...and then (was silent) when both...(asked)...

[The following lines yield only isolated words, some of the significant ones being] instruction [in love?]...sister...force [of passion?]...of lovers...eye of love. [These suggest that as in Achilles Tatius 2.25 the apprehended young lovers try to justify their actions to Persis's ?mother. Not even isolated words can be recovered from the remaining eighteen scraps of fragment A.]


## B1 recto

...says to him...you wretched man...to die...say(s) to them...you...the boy...self they (said) experienced...(why) shouldn't he, since...encouraging...to (him). "What an odious creature I am!" I said, "what...you perish..." (Meanwhile), another man arrived, naked except for a purple (loincloth)...throwing the boy's body onto its back...and removed the heart and placed it over the fire. (Then)...removing (it), he cut it in half. Onto the surface he sprinkled (?barley) and drenched it with olive oil. When it was adequately cooked, (?he distributed it to the) initiates. And as they held it, (?he ordered them to swear on oath) over the blood of the heart...neither to abandon nor to betray, not even (if)...they should be carried (off) or be tortured or have (their eyes) gouged out. (They)...half of the heart, the rest...Androtimus and the...(in the middle)...drinking and...to drink...and...brought everything that one of men seemed...

[The remaining fragments yield the name Persis—probably—which suggests a connection with the events of fragment A.]

---

1. It is not clear whether it is the virginity of Persis or of the man that is meant.

## B1 verso

[Only isolated words remain of the first few lines.]

...feet...from song (?magic spell)...bring down...of the boy's heart, the very thing that...to swallow and...(what had) been vomited (on the) table. They recooked it, and (Androtimus) said: "Something awful's happened to me—my food is still uncooked...this damned (girl)...belching and farting...I have put up with this sickening smell. But pour the boy's (blood...")...into a large wine cup...they called it...on it had been carved...to him...Androtimus...and in distress since...meanwhile... the belt...with...they fastened on. And others entered (...say) nothing ...everyone had entered, and there was still no one outside...the (?windows)...they began singing and drinking and making love to the women before (Androtimus's) eyes...fell asleep, exhausted. However, the eleven men (in charge of) the corpses did not drink much but only enough to warm themselves up. (When) it was the middle of the night, they first stripped the bodies of the (dead), not even (leaving) the girl's brassiere...Then raising the (?bodies/clothes) above the windows, they dropped (them) down to the...and after this they put on tunics, some white ones, some black ones...swathing their heads like...those wearing black...smeared their faces with soot and those wearing white with white lead and...they went outside, wearing white through...black made their way through the moonlight. And Androtimus...for there was no escape from them, for (they) were (being) guarded...they thought they would give information if they went away so that (necessarily)...workshop of a goldsmith...old man...to save...

[Other fragments yield only isolated words. Androtimus seems to appear again. Fragment C includes the names of Persis and probably Glaucetes.]

## Glaucetes-fragment

"...to bury her, turning off a small distance from the road. I lie under that plane tree, and with me lies a beautiful girl. Both of us were murdered." Glaucetes, naturally astonished, did not respond but only nodded and rode on. The young man disappeared when he nodded. Glaucetes rode on vigorously, all the while turning round to try to see him again, but he caught no further sight of him. It was still night when he reached the village. There was a stream near it. He crossed this and saw an open stable and in it a small mean bed of straw. So tying up his horse by the feeding trough and throwing himself onto the bed of straw, he tried to sleep. Meanwhile a woman came down a ladder leading from the loft down to the stable...

# METIOCHUS AND PARTHENOPE

## TRANSLATED BY
## GERALD N. SANDY

### *Introduction*

This text saw the light in three separate fragments. What is here called Column 2 was first published by F. Krebs in 1895. Column 1 was edited by F. Zimmermann in 1933. In 1976 H. Maehler published a papyrus that links the earlier fragments. As reconstructed by Maehler, the setting for the events recorded in the fragments is Polycrates' palace on Samos. Present are Polycrates, his daughter Parthenope, Metiochus, and Anaximenes. Not present but mentioned is Metiochus's stepmother, Hegesipyle. The event that has brought these people together is a symposium. As *magister bibendi*, Polycrates has set Eros as the topic of conversation. "The two" referred to are the hero and heroine. They are already in love, and are embarrassed that the conversation should turn to this subject. Metiochus tries to shelter his uneasiness behind a blustering, sarcastic denunciation of traditional views of Eros; Parthenope misunderstands his preemptive claim that he never wants to experience love and replies sharply in kind. Alternatively, it may be that Metiochus is concealing his love for the purpose of some intrigue.

The greatest contribution of the new material is to establish that the romance of Metiochus and Parthenope, like the Ninus romance and that of Chariton, had a historical setting.[1] Polycrates seized power in Samos

---

1. It may be only coincidental that Ninus and Metiochus are mentioned together by Lucian (*The Mistaken Critic* 25) and that both heroes, with their heroines, are portrayed on the mosaic floors of adjoining rooms in the "House of the Man of Letters" at Antioch-on-the-Orontes; see D. Levi, "The Novel of Ninus and Semiramis," *Proceedings of the American Philosophical Society* 87(1944): 420–28.

about 540 B.C. Hegesipyle was the second wife of Miltiades, who was the father of Metiochus by his first wife. Anaximenes is the philosopher, from Miletus (his name had already occurred in the earlier material and appears again in the latest fragment); it is not clear what role he may have played in the story. The additional fragment raises other questions. Although the story has a historical setting, it cannot have conformed to strict historical accuracy. Miltiades, and even more so his son Metiochus, belong to a time at least a generation later than Polycrates and Anaximenes. And there is the question of who Parthenope is. It had been assumed that she was the Siren of Naples; this identification was based on the Byzantine scholia to the early fourth-century geographical poem of Dionysius the Periegete, where it is stated that the Parthenope named in the poem is not the Parthenope of Samos but rather the Siren Parthenope, who after withstanding many attempts on her chastity fell in love with Metiochus. It seems from the new material, however, that Parthenope is indeed from Samos, and the daughter of Polycrates.

Some light has been thrown on this story by oriental sources, as is set out in two articles by Tomas Hägg.[2] In particular, an eleventh-century Persian verse romance, *Vamiq and ᶜAdhra,* was based on *Metiochus and Parthenope,* and recently published fragments from it help reconstitute the general outline of the present story; this process is also assisted by a Coptic version of a martyrdom. Although reconstruction can only be partial and tentative, it seems clear that *Metiochus and Parthenope* did indeed follow the familiar lines of Greek novels, with the lovers undergoing separation, wandering, and tribulations before recognition, reunion, and a happy ending.

## Bibliography

Lavagnini, 21–24; Zimmermann, 52–63 (but *POxy.* 435 may be discounted); Rattenbury, 237–40.

TEXT

Krebs, F. "Metiochus und Parthenope." *Hermes* 30(1895): 144–48. First publication of Maehler's column 2.

Maehler, H. "Der Metiochus-Parthenope-Roman." *ZPE* 23(1976): 1–20.

Zimmermann, F. "Ein unveröffentlichtes Bruchstück des Metiochos-Parthenope-Romans." *Aegyptus* 13(1933): 53–61. First publication of Maehler's column 1.

GENERAL

Dihle, A. "Zur Datierung des Metiochos-Romans." *Würzburger Jahrbücher für die*

2. See Tomas Hägg, "Metiochus at Polycrates' Court," *Eranos* 83(1985): 92–102, and "The Parthenope Romance Decapitated?" *Symbolae Osloenses* 59(1984): 61–92.

*Altertumswissenschaft* N.F. 4(1978): 47–55. The language of the fragments belongs to the same non-Atticist Hellenistic linguistic stratum as Chariton's.

Hägg, Tomas. "The Parthenope Romance Decapitated?" *Symbolae Osloenses*
59(1984): 61–92.

———. "Metiochus at Polycrates' Court." *Eranos* 83(1985): 92–102.

# METIOCHUS AND PARTHENOPE

## Column 1 (content as suggested by Maehler and Hägg)

[Metiochus has arrived at the court of Polycrates of Samos, from the
Chersonese. Polycrates welcomes him, possibly as a suitor for his daughter Parthenope. Metiochus talks frankly about political troubles at home
and the machinations of his stepmother. A symposium begins, at which
the philosopher Anaximenes is present and proposes for discussion the
topic of Love.]

## Column 2 (based on Maehler's text)

By chance the two...their souls recollecting Love...Metiochus disclaim-
ing...or proper knowledge...said... "(They are) fools...uninitiated in true
understanding (who) adhere to the tales about how (Eros) is Aphrodite's
young son and has (wings) and a bow on his back and a torch (in his
hand) and with these weapons (savagely)...(wounds) the hearts of (young
people). It would be ridiculous, first of all...that a child subject to Time
since long ago...from his earliest days should not reach maturity...
whereas (creatures) born of men advance in age with time, those (endowed with divine) nature should stay at the same stage like (cripples). It
would be altogether incredible, too, if Eros is (a child), that he should
stalk about (the world) firing his arrows at anyone he wants of those
who encounter him and inflame them (so that) there arises in the souls of
lovers a kind of (?holy) inspiration as in the possessed. Those who have
experienced Love's passion (?know this), but I (have not), and may I
never experience it at all. Love (is) a disturbance of the rational faculties
caused by beauty and intensified by intimate contact." He...wanted to
finish the discussion, and Anaximenes (urged) Parthenope to take part in
the inquiry. She was angry with Metiochus because he would not admit
that he had loved any woman, and prayed that...would not either...she
said: "The stranger is talking nonsense, and (I disagree)...when we first
go to school, (writers) and poets and painters and (sculptors represent)
him..."

# IOLAUS

## TRANSLATED BY
## GERALD N. SANDY

### Introduction

As is the case with the more substantial fragments of the *Phoenicica,* the importance of the truncated remains of the romance about Iolaus is historical. The surviving scraps have no intrinsic literary merit but do suggest, like the remains of the *Phoenicica,* that the Greeks wrote fictional prose narratives about low life. More specifically, the romance about Iolaus shares two distinctive features with Petronius's picaresque romance in Latin, the *Satyricon:* the mixture of prose and verse and the blending of a slightly modified quotation of a canonical verse author (Euripides) into the prose narrative. It is entirely possible that one of the texts—but we cannot say which—has been influenced by the other. The papyrus is of the second century A.D.

The editor of the fragment, P. J. Parsons, has extracted as much sense from the narrative as its truncated condition permits.

> Some person, X, is being initiated into the mysteries of Cybele, and perfects himself in them in reliance on his friend Nicon. X then addresses Iolaus and a *cinaedus;* this speech is (appropriately) in the Sotadaean metre. X says that he has become a *gallus* in order to help Iolaus; he knows everything; Iolaus must trust him. And Iolaus accordingly undergoes instruction from him.[1]

E. R. Dodds has suggested[2] that the plot of the partially surviving episode may have been comparable to that of Terence's play *The Eunuch,* in

1. P. J. Parsons, *POxy.* 42(1974): 34.
2. See Parsons, 35 n. 1.

which the character Chaerea dresses as a eunuch slave to gain access to his beloved in the women's quarters. Accordingly, Iolaus has persuaded an unnamed friend to be initiated into the mystery rites of the goddess Cybele, under the guidance of Nicon, so that he can instruct Iolaus in the religious technicalities that would allow him to masquerade as a eunuch *gallus* and thereby gain access to his girlfriend. This hypothesis accounts for the father's lamentations and the coarse expression "screw."

The *gallus* and the *cinaedus* are probably separate characters in the plot. In real life they were theoretically distinct, the *gallus* being a self-castrated servant of Cybele, and the *cinaedus* a usually effeminate entertainer; but in practice they were often thought of as identical because of their overt effeminacy and real or imagined vices. The words spoken by the *gallus* are in the Sotadaean meter characteristically used by *galli*.

## Bibliography

TEXT

Parsons, P. J. "A Greek *Satyricon?*" *Bulletin of the Institute of Classical Studies* 18(1971): 53–68. Preliminary publication.
———. *POxy.* 3010 = 42(1974): 34–41. Definitive publication.

GENERAL

Merkelbach, R. "Fragment eines satirischen Romans: Aufforderung zur Beichte." *ZPE* 11(1973): 81–100. Interprets the fragment as a parody of initiation into mystery rites.

# IOLAUS

...things called ineffable by the gallus...he learns through whom he was going to teach so that he would neither fall short to his fellow initiates, but once he had been initiated in many ways and taught to wear female...(should be) allotted...and full of (teaching) he came and, by chance finding him, (said):

"Noble Iolaus, greetings! And you, cinaedus, silence! I have become a gallus initiated into the mysteries (and shall) exhort (you in) words (known) to initiates...Iolaus, for (your sake). Nicon...so that (you) would have (me) as a gallus...who knows everything. I know to whom you...I know everything, the familiarity...the oath...(unburied body)... of someone...the bastard...everything (has happened)...wailing...your house, mother, your bedroom, I know of (your) father's lamentations,

(Eurycleia), that (she) is aware...Nicon, (trickery), cinaedus, and the (birthday)...I know of the invitation and the cinaedus (joking)...how he joked, how he fled...solution, assertion, cutting off...that you intend to screw by deceit...Therefore conceal nothing from me...and I want your..., Iolaus...and you will know. For the interval..."

And Iolaus is taught by the initiate all that he (has learned), and he is a complete gallus, having trusted his friend Nicon. There is nothing better than a clear friend, not wealth nor gold. The mob is not to be reckoned a substitute for a genuine friend.[1]

---

1. Only a few letters remain of the last sentence, but it can be restored with confidence since it and the previous sentence are a quotation from Euripides *Orestes* 1155–1157 (except that "gold" has been substituted for Euripides' "absolute power").

# SESONCHOSIS

## TRANSLATED BY
## GERALD N. SANDY

*Introduction*

Like the Ninus romance, the fragmentary romance about Sesonchosis deals with a historical oriental monarch whose reign and exploits in faraway lands were transformed into legend by the Greeks. The Egyptian monarch Sesonchosis, whose name appears also variously as Sesostris (Herodotus 2.102–110), Sesoosis (Diodorus 1.53–58), and Sesongosis (in these fragments), is to be identified with the Twelfth Dynasty monarchs named Senwosret. The achievements of Senwosret I and III became conflated, "and hence was created the saga of Sesonchosis the world-conqueror which we find already in Herodotus on a modest scale."[1] So famous did the legendary composite pharaoh become in later times that Alexander the Great is hailed in the romance about him as a new Sesonchosis (1.34.2).

There are three fragments of the story. The first preserves no continuous text but mentions a father, his son Sesonchosis, and the boy's education and youth. In the second an Arabian army under Webelis is beaten in Egypt, but Sesonchosis is not yet king. The third begins with a conversation between Sesonchosis and Pamounis. The episode seems to be on the following lines. Sesonchosis has overcome a foreign king but lost his own power in Egypt, and is in the king's land incognito. He is also engaged to the king's daughter; she sees him unexpectedly and is emo-

1. S. R. West, *POxy.* 47(1980): 11.

tionally affected. Herodotus tells us that Sesonchosis duly regained his power in Egypt.

## Bibliography

Zimmermann, 36–40; Rattenbury, 223–34.

TEXT

Grenfell, B. P., and A. S. Hunt. *POxy.* 1826 = 15(1922): 228–29.
Rea, J. *POxy.* 2466 = 27(1967): 134–36.
West, S. R. *POxy.* 3319 = 47(1980): 11–19.

GENERAL

O'Sullivan, J. N. "The Sesonchosis Romance." *ZPE* 56(1984): 39–44. Reconstruction of the plot.

# SESONCHOSIS

### Fragment 2 (POxy. 2466)

...nobly...for a sufficient time...they fought. Many of them were killed, but they also killed many of the enemy. The Arabs, seeing themselves decreasing in number every day, and the Egyptians, growing more numerous as men came in from the other districts, were routed, so that not even a fifth of their army was saved. Some were pursued; some ran away; they were trampled on by one another, and only Webelis and a small band of his men got back to their own country. The Egyptians, after defeating their enemy, to make sure Webelis did not collect an army from the other tribes on his borders and attack them a second time when he was stronger, strengthened the cities on the Arabian frontier with enough men...all...and Sesonchosis...

### Fragment 3 (POxy. 3319)

"...I took her father as a slave. He/she entrusted to me the girl whom you see, and after I persuaded her to marry me, I hurried off to the wars. Therefore she must be informed who I am, and perhaps I shall take up my old rank." Pamounis said: "Not at all! But use the excuse that I mentioned to you before. For if the king placed...under you because he found (?me/him/himself/you) (more powerful) [The next few lines cannot be

construed. There is reference to a subordinate and to Egypt.]...by villains,...(...?forced to wander) to these (regions)...With this explanation
Sesonchosis reported his mistakes to the...a woman named (Meameris)
came...to the...where Sesonchosis was. She stood and looked down at
the flowing water. She looked towards Sesonchosis (and)...saw the man.
She became emotionally disturbed (at this point) and left. After she was
cared for, she reclined at the banquet table. She reluctantly ate the serv-
ings of food that were placed before her. She kept remembering the
handsome young man. As she (?did not) conceal...one of her fellows...

# HERPYLLIS

## TRANSLATED BY
## B. P. REARDON

### Introduction

This fragment, preserved in an early second-century papyrus, describes
the separation of a pair of lovers, the (male) narrator and Herpyllis, by a
storm; in this sense it is a "genre piece," since storms and shipwrecks,
like pirates' attacks, are a common device in these novels and sometimes
give rise to elaborate descriptive passages. (See, for instance, Achilles
Tatius 3.1–4.)

### Bibliography

Lavagnini, 16–20; Zimmermann, 68–72; Rattenbury, 34–37.

## HERPYLLIS

...welcoming (us) in inlets by the sea, they invited (us), in view of the
unfavorable atmospheric conditions—in fact among the weather signs a
small (cloud) had formed unnoticed—to wait there the (following) day
and give ourselves to merriment. An invitation from a (well-meaning
man) is a very (clear) presage for delaying a journey. And I (wanted) to
stay. But the skippers (could not agree) with each other: ours urged us to
sail, but the skipper of (the big ship) foretold a great storm, one we per-

haps could not survive. Well, we decided to sail. So embracing each other and raising the sad cry of the kingfisher,[1] we each embarked on our own ship and began to lament, gazing towards each other and (throwing) kisses. Well, the big ship was rather slow to make ready for sea, whereas we put out more quickly. The sun appeared just as we were sailing out, but at once disappeared behind dark clouds. Suddenly there was a short, echoing clap of thunder. We regretted our decision but were no longer able to turn back, because there was a strong wind from astern. Herpyllis's ship, however, put out no farther, but stayed where it was, called back from the harbor wall. We could see each other for a short time, but we were snatched away from them; a great burst of wind fell on us (from the east), right from the headland. We could not put the yard over, because the boat was not strong enough to take the sea (on its beam). With the sail... before the wind and the foresails (taut) we went off our intended course. Passing Laceter, a very dangerous headland, we were swept through the sea of Crete, and could not even see Nisurus because the sky was so overcast—we tried (at that point) to catch sight of it, but without success.[2] After that we abandoned ourselves to the destructive sea. We saw no prospect of coming out alive; we all not only expected death but actually longed for it; for (now) the sea was swelling at quite long intervals; it was not being whipped up by strong winds, but was forming immense troughs and cresting as high...; it was black from the shadow of the surrounding darkness. The winds, with sudden blasts from all directions, blew the air into a discord that was awe-inspiring rather than hostile, sometimes just blowing with hurricane force, sometimes bringing squalls of rain. The whole sky was thundering around us; lights flashed thick and fast in the sky, warring with each other, and time and again we saw fire shoot from heaven right beside us. You could not tell whether it was day or night, so uniform was the darkness. We were swamped by the onslaught of the waves and the cloudbursts; we could not see either land or sky; (everything) was covered in the encompassing night. One moment the morning (light) appeared behind us; the next a wave (broke) over us. Often flashes of fire flickered briefly at each (end) of the yard; whether they were stars, as the crew asserted, calling them the Dioscuri,[3] or starlike sparks whirled about by the wind, it was impossible to say for sure, but they all fell to their knees (and) began praying to them.

1. The female kingfisher was supposed to lament when separated from her mate.
2. They were passing between a southern promontory of Cos and a small island off its coast.
3. St. Elmo's fire.

# CHIONE

## TRANSLATED BY
## B.P. REARDON

### Introduction

An initial transcription of three fragments of this story was made by Wilcken in Egypt, but the manuscript was destroyed before he could produce a finished text; it was a parchment codex of the sixth or seventh century A.D., which also contained part of Chariton's *Chaereas and Callirhoe*. The order in which the fragments appear here is probably the right order, but this is not certain. A further fragment, from a papyrus of the second or third century, has subsequently been recognized as probably from the same text, but it is very poorly preserved, and even if it is from *Chione*, it tells us virtually nothing more about the story. The princess Chione (Snow White) is to be married, and a husband is to be chosen for her, amid much public interest and fierce competition, within thirty days. One Megamedes is chosen. But Chione loves someone else. She talks with her lover, but no solution is in sight; probably the lovers plan death.

The language of the fragment recalls that of Chariton's novel.

### Bibliography

Lavagnini, 24–27; Zimmermann, 40; Rattenbury, 230–34.
Gronewald, M. "Ein Fragment zu einem Roman." *ZPE* 35(1979): 15–20.

# CHIONE

### Fragment 1

...the royal power passes to this woman and her future husband; so we must now make a decision we can never regret. We have thirty days to think about this...(fifteen lines missing)

### Fragment 2

...while they were considering their own situation, rumor went quickly through the whole city...and no one was talking about anything but the marriage. All were distressed when they considered the arrogance of their threat, and especially all those (citizens) who were themselves capable of ruling and intended to be suitors for Chione. But none of them dared to ask for her hand after those men. When Chione heard this from her mother, she no longer...

### Fragment 3

"...Megamedes is expected, while we have so far left no stone unturned[1] but have thought of no solution; and Megamedes has given you no excuse for abandoning him. So think what we should do; I am at a loss." Chione said: "I cannot think of any solution either. But I can tell you one thing: if we cannot live together...the last thing left for us...(?is to die together). We should (?think of) nothing (?else) and see to it that it be done in a dignified way. For (?if we secretly/unwittingly)..."

---

1. Literally "moved every rope, so to speak"—a common nautical metaphor.

# CALLIGONE

## TRANSLATED BY
## B.P. REARDON

### Introduction

This papyrus of the second century A.D. preserves a scene that takes place in a military camp. Calligone, the heroine, is in distress and tries to kill herself, but a friend has removed her dagger.

### Bibliography

Zimmermann, 46–50; Rattenbury, 240–44.

## CALLIGONE

...her judgment totally shaken; coming to the tent and throwing herself on the camp bed, she uttered a loud, piercing cry; she wept profusely, and she tore her tunic. Eubiotus saw to it that no one was in the tent; he sent everyone out, saying that she had had bad news about the Sauromates.[1] She wept and wailed and cursed the day she had seen Erasinus while hunting; she cursed her own eyes too and blamed Artemis...And

---

1. In the Ukraine.

absorbed in these misfortunes, she reached out for her dagger; but Eubiotus had surreptitiously removed it from its sheath as soon as she came in. She looked at him and said: "Wickedest of men! You dared to lay your hand on my sword! I am no Amazon, no Themisto;[2] I am a Greek woman, I am Calligone—no weaker in spirit than any Amazon. Go and bring me the sword, or I will strangle you with my hands!..."

2. A child murderess.

In mythology
people do not know
what they are doing
ex. Oedipus, Iphigenia, the gods
tricking each other
- not aware of what there
actions really mean

"It's to late"
            - Mindfield